REVISED EDITION

A World History

A CULTURAL APPROACH

DANIEL ROSELLE

GINN AND COMPANY

About The Author

DR. DANIEL ROSELLE, *formerly Professor of History at the State University of New York College at Fredonia, is now Editor of* Social Education, *the official journal of the National Council for the Social Studies. He received his Bachelor of Arts from the College of the City of New York and was awarded his Master and Doctoral degrees by Columbia University. After teaching in high school he served for two years as Assistant Professor of History at Fairleigh Dickinson University. He spent a year as Fulbright Research Professor to France. His articles have been published in* Clearing House, New York State Education, Social Studies, *and* Social Education. *Of particular interest are "Monsieur Dannie's Le Petit Nicos," published by* Social Education.

Special Consultants

The End-of-Chapter Exercises are by Adeline Brengle, Bloomington (Indiana) High School.

The Workbook was prepared by Anne Young, Ph.D., Gorham State College, Gorham, Maine.

The Unit and Final Tests were prepared by Mrs. Geraldine Welbourne, West Lafayette, Indiana.

The drawings for the "Let's Meet the People" stories are by Don Sibley.

The Time Lines are by Magnuson & Vincent, Inc.

Historical maps were prepared by Edward A. Schmitz.

Relief maps were prepared by Richard Edes Harrison and Norman Adams.

An Annotated Edition is available.

Acknowledgments for copyrighted material contained herein appear on pages 809–812

CONTENTS

v

MAP LIST

CHARTS AND DOCUMENTS

CULTURAL CHARACTERISTICS

Introduction: Views and Previews

History Defined

If you wish to understand the story of man, you cannot ignore facts or their significance to people. Facts without significance are not enough; and significance without facts is hollow.

The word "history" itself can be defined by using both terms. We can say: *History is the record of the facts of man's life from the past to the present and the significance of those facts to man.*

This does not mean that all historians agree on the facts of history or on their meaning. On the contrary, scholars are still arguing over such basic questions as: Who first discovered America? What were the effects of the French Revolution? When did printing begin? And hundreds of other matters.

The Problem of Knowing the Facts

Such disagreements arise partly because not all the facts are known in some cases (as the discovery of America) and partly because each person interprets events from a particular point of view. Here is an example of such a situation.

A few years ago an Italian passenger liner collided with a Swedish ship off Nantucket Island, Massachusetts. When survivors from the Italian ship were asked to describe conditions aboard after the collision occurred, two of them gave the following replies. A university student said: "It was sheer panic." A president of a radio station replied, "There was no large-scale panic, and everybody seemed to help one another."

In other words, two individuals at the same event saw matters very differently. This may have been the result of their previous experiences, their personalities, their locations on the ship at the time of the crash, and other factors. Regardless of the reason, the two passengers arrived at completely different conclusions.

History is the record of the events of the past and their significance. Just as the description of an event depends on the individual talking about it, so the writing of history depends on the viewpoint of the historian. It is the historian's duty to examine evidence critically, to get as close as possible to the truth about the past.

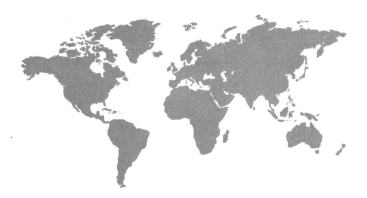

The Role of the Historian

In describing the collision of the ships, the historian faces several problems. First, he must determine what actually happened. To do this, he studies and evaluates the conflicting reports of the two witnesses as well as the accounts of other passengers. He tries to obtain as many of the facts as he can. This in itself is difficult. Then he turns to the problem of interpreting the incident. Why did it happen? What effects did it have? What is its importance or significance? His personal viewpoint will influence the way in which he answers these questions. Another historian, using the same facts, may reach different conclusions. In brief, the interpretation of history depends on the point of view of the historian himself.

Historians differ in their purposes as well as in their views. It is therefore important that you know the aims of this history book. Your textbook serves three purposes: (1) to present the facts of world history clearly and accurately, (2) to discuss the significance of events thoroughly, and (3) to aid you in understanding people in all parts of the world.

To achieve the first purpose, your book contains many excerpts from *primary source materials*. Such materials include "the direct impression or expression" of people living at the time of an event. These materials consist of diaries, letters, memoirs, constitutions, treaties, newspaper accounts, poetry, songs, and records.

You will examine the words of an ancient manuscript urging Egyptians to "Restrain appetite . . . It is a base fellow who is mastered by his belly."

You will read one of the oldest printed notices in history—a sign in Chinese that declares: "Beware of the Dog."

You will study provisions of the English Bill of Rights, the Charter of the United Nations, and many other documents.

The primary source materials in your book are useful because they are firsthand information. Since they are records written by the very people who lived at the time, they are the "life-blood" of history.

1

The Geographic Setting

Facts about the geography of the world can be fascinating because of their infinite variety. Winds, for example, travel at speeds that range from less than one mile an hour to 75 or more. A gust of wind at Mount Washington, New Hampshire, reached the speed of 231 miles an hour. Indeed, as one weather specialist, Robert Moore Fisher, points out in *How about the Weather?*

Twelve days ago, the air you are now breathing may have rushed up the slopes of Mount Fujiyama. Six days before that, it might have drifted through the halls of the Kremlin. Perhaps three and one-half weeks have elapsed since it wandered over Westminster Abbey. Or possibly it may have spent the last fortnight gliding past steaming Guiana jungles and over the waters of the Caribbean, or dodging ice-sheathed mountains in northern Canada. ... Without a doubt [the air we breathe] has a history as lengthy as a pedigree and as fascinating as an adventure story.

Statistics about our geographic world are equally impressive. Temperatures in Antarctica once went as low as 123.3° F. below zero; a single hailstone that fell in the state of Nebraska weighed 1½ pounds; the crust of the earth in some places is nearly 40 miles thick; and near the Philippine Islands, the ocean floor is almost 7 miles below the surface.

Yet unusual statistics or isolated facts are less important than the way man and his culture interact with the physical surroundings. *The significance of physical features lies in what men make of them.*

From the standpoint of world history, three fundamental geographic ideas must be kept in mind. (1) *Man lives in a physical world with many locations, landforms, soils, and climates.* It is the stage on which he enacts the events which we call history. That stage may be a fertile river valley, such as the Nile; rich grazing lands, as in the Fertile Crescent; or a strategic peninsula which juts into the sea, as does Greece. (2) This physical environment is not fixed or unchangeable. *It is constantly changing.* How a particular group of people adjust to this changing environment is one of the most important aspects of history. (3) In many cases, *the success of this adjustment depends on the culture man has developed.* For example, natural resources such as radioactive minerals may be present on the earth for a long time, but until man's culture finds a way of using them, they are not true resources. The Chinese knew of the existence of coal for centuries, but their culture did not include its use on a broad scale.

Scientific technology plays a part in determining the way a nation makes up for its lack of natural resources. Thus, one scholar speaks of "Atomic Geography" and predicts that "by 1975 Britain may be producing atomic power equivalent to 70 million tons of coal a year." Atomic power might well be the solution to shortages of coal and oil.

As with all natural resources, the key factor in the use of the earth is man himself. He can continue to pollute the lakes, rivers, and even the oceans; fill the air itself with poisons; and contribute to the decay of his society. Or he can preserve, conserve, and deserve the beauty and wealth that nature holds in store for him.

Culture Divisions. The earth can be divided into *cultural* segments, such as Western, Islamic, Oriental, African, Latin American, and others. These are based on the identification of common history, traditions, beliefs, institutions, and ways of living of people.

We must remember, however, that (a) the organization of cultural divisions is not rigidly fixed; historian-geographers can place lands and peoples in different cultural patterns depending on the criteria used; (b) cultures overlap; and (c) cultures often influence one another.

A Cultural Approach

Finally, your book will assist you to understand the lives of men by focusing on *a cultural approach* to history. This approach recognizes that (1) culture refers to "all of the ways of thinking and living" which characterize a designated group of people. (2) Culture is not part of our biological inheritance but is passed on by the actions of society; culture is learned. (3) Culture can be diffused, or spread, throughout the world. As anthropologist George Peter Murdock points out in *Culture and Society:* "It is doubtful whether there is a single culture known to history or anthropology that has not owed at least 90 per cent of its constituent elements to cultural borrowing."

Your history book will examine culture *throughout the world*: in Japan, where the people speak a language that has at least twenty words for the English "I"—in Indonesia, where a Moslem bride symbolically washes the feet of her bridegroom using water filled with rose petals—in Brazil, where children play centuries-old games on lovely mosaic sidewalks—in Africa, where Moru tribesmen craftily set their fish traps in the churning waters—and in many other areas.

In brief, a cultural approach to history takes a *world's eye view* of the lives of men. You, the reader, are in a most attractive position: you can enjoy the view at the same time that you are a part of it!

Prologue   *Prehistoric Man Moves to the*
Starting Line of History

KEYNOTE   For many years man has sought knowledge about the universe and
about his earliest ancestors. Man is so small and the universe is so
large that a writer in *The New York Times* once likened his search
to that of:

A potato-bug inside a potato inside a bag down in the hold of a
ship, seeking to know the world above through the motions of the
ship.

Despite the fact that he is a mere speck when contrasted with
giant stars and whirling planets, man has continued to challenge the
universe to reveal its secrets. He has succeeded in learning many
important facts about himself and his ancestors.

One of the key points that he has discovered is this: *The story of
man began THOUSANDS of years ago—but it is a recent story when
compared with the BILLIONS-of-years-old tale of the universe!*

Key People   *Java man · Peking man · Neanderthal man · Cro-Magnon man*

Key Events   *Paleolithic Age · Neolithic Age*

Key Terms   *solar system · prehistory · Pleistocene · glaciers · race ·
archaeologist · culture · societies · fossils · megaliths*

4

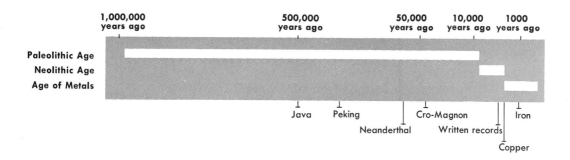

1,000,000 years ago		500,000 years ago	50,000 years ago	10,000 years ago	1000 years ago

Paleolithic Age
Neolithic Age
Age of Metals

Java Peking Neanderthal Cro-Magnon Written records Iron Copper

1. Satellites and History

At precisely 10:48 P.M., January 31, 1958, a crewman at Cape Canaveral, Florida, pressed a button. There was a tremendous thrust of flame and a rocket rose slowly from the ground. Then it picked up speed and disappeared into the darkness above. The United States had sent its first satellite, Explorer I, on its historic journey around the earth!

The American satellite was not the first to go into orbit around the earth. The Russians already had launched two successful satellites. Nevertheless, the launching of Explorer I again reminded the world that men were no longer earthbound. Since then, great progress has been rapidly made in space explorations.

The opening of the door to the Space Age was a credit to the scientists of Russia, the United States, and other nations. More important, it was a wonderful credit to man.

When we say that artificial satellites are "wonderful" or "amazing," we really mean:

"Since there had never before in history been such a feat, the launching of satellites was a remarkable achievement of man." *Note that it is history that helps us to appreciate man's present accomplishments.* History does this by giving us *perspective*—that is, by permitting us to see present-day events in relation to the whole sweep of the past.

Since history gives us perspective, how far back should we go to gain a good view of man's progress in science and other fields? As far back as possible. Back through the excitement of today's headlines, back through the drama of more distant crises, back through the tragedies and triumphs of centuries buried in time— back to the beginnings of man's adventure on this earth. Back to prehistory itself.

■ Check on Your Reading

1. What do we mean when we say artificial satellites are "amazing"?

2. How does history help us to appreciate man's present accomplishments?

5

2. The Sun, the Earth, and Man

The word *prehistory* refers to the time before there were any written records. It covers many millions of years. We can begin our study of these prehistoric times by first examining the universe itself. From there we can move to the planet Earth and then to man.

The Sun Is One in Millions

Let us start with the stars—with the more than one hundred thousand million billion stars! That is the number scientists believe exist in the universe. When they improve their methods of investigation, scientists expect to find far more than that.

Our sun is just one star. It provides the light, heat, and energy for our solar system. This solar system consists of nine planets (the origin of Pluto may have been different from the rest) and many other bodies revolving around the sun. Our earth is just one planet in our solar system.

There are millions of similar systems in the universe. Some scientists believe that in these systems there are other planets revolving around stars. It is quite possible that some of these planets support some form of life.

What all this means is that the sun is not the center of the universe. Our entire solar system is just one of many systems. As for the earth, according to astronomer Harlow Shapley, it is merely one planet "on the outer fringe of *one* galaxy [a cluster or grouping of stars] in a universe of *millions of galaxies*." And new galaxies are continually forming!

The Earth Is Like a "Restless Parent"

This earth of ours—comparatively insignificant in the tremendous universe—came into existence at least 4 to 5 billion years ago. There is no agreement among scientists on how the earth was formed. Here is one theory:

Earth was [once] a tiny piece of matter spinning through the vast envelope of gases and dust that surrounded the sun. Particles of matter [joined together] into larger masses, then attracted other materials to themselves by the force of gravity.... After 100 million years or so, earth achieved an independent existence and settled into its orbit some 93,000,000 miles from the sun.

In the beginning the earth was like a *molten* ball—that is, it was so hot that it was in a liquefied state. Then its crust cooled and hardened. If we could dig down 1800 miles, we probably would find that its outer core is still hot and flowing.

The earth is still changing. Wind, rain, snow, and ice—Nature's erasers— are slowly wearing down mountains. The

■ *The solar system is near the outer edge of the Milky Way Galaxy, which is similar in shape to the spiral nebula shown below.*

Mount Wilson and Palomar Observatories

6

■ *Archaic mammals, such as four-toed horses and Uintatherium, resembling elephants, roamed the North American continent about fifty million years ago.*

sea has long been gradually covering some coastal areas, leaving behind legends of golden cities under the water. Volcanoes are continuing to explode through the earth's surface, scattering ash particles throughout many lands. Earthquakes can destroy cities and kill thousands in a few seconds as sections of the earth's crust change position.

It is true that "Mother Earth is a restless parent, always changing her ways and doing unpredictable things."

Man Is a "Johnny-Come-Lately" to Earth

Life on earth began well over five hundred million years ago and possibly as far back as two billion years. In the beginning, life consisted of single-celled organisms living in the waters. These organisms slowly evolved into more and more complicated forms of plant and animal life.

Next, creatures from the sea moved to the land. Many types of land animals gradually developed. Some of them—like the reptiles called *dinosaurs*—reached huge sizes. Then the ancient ancestors of the horse, the elephant, and other mammals made their appearance.

Finally, man appeared on the earth, at least 500,000 years ago and possibly as far back as 1,000,000 years ago. Recent discoveries in Africa have led one authority to conclude that a manlike creature may have appeared at an even earlier time, but scholars have not yet agreed as to the validity of this theory.

In the light of the evidence to date, three prominent scientists have declared: "[Man] is a newcomer, a Johnny-come-lately, in comparison with almost all other kinds of animals." These scholars remind us that if we let the twenty-four hours in a day represent two billion years, then we can make this comparison:

At 8 P.M. the invasion of the land by plants was under way, and by 8:30 insects and the first amphibians had joined them. The Age of Reptiles began about 9:30. It ended and the Age of Mammals began at about 11 P.M. *Man appeared less than a minute before midnight. . . .*

He was a "Johnny-come-lately" indeed!

Man Shows a Unity with the Universe

The appearance of man did not mean that there was now a creature on earth who was completely different from everything in the universe. On the contrary, *man showed a certain unity with the universe in which he lived.*

For example, a number of chemical elements that are found in man's body (as well as in those of other mammals) also appear in the atmospheres of the sun and sunlike stars. The sun has oxygen, hydrogen, nitrogen, and carbon—man has these elements, too.

The sun has some elements that man has not, and the amounts of the elements in the sun and man differ. Nevertheless, astronomer Harlow Shapley was sufficiently struck by the unity of make-up of man and the universe to declare: "Obviously man is made of ordinary star-stuff and should be mighty proud of it."

Glaciers Move like Giants over the Earth

Man probably made his appearance on earth during the early part of the *Pleistocene epoch*. This period began possibly 1,500,000 or 1,000,000 years ago and extended to about 10,000 years ago.

The Pleistocene epoch (or the Ice Ages) was a time of great changes on the earth. It was during this period that enormous sheets of ice called *glaciers* started to move down from the north.

The glaciers inched their way forward for thousands of years, plowing up everything in their way. They ground immense rocks into gravel and covered the tops of mountains. Eventually they moved over

Canada, northern United States, Europe, and many other regions of the world.

Finally, after occupying a considerable portion of the earth, the glaciers slowly withdrew. Like sculptors finished with their work, they left behind them a number of valleys and lakes that they had carved out of the body of the earth. These geographic features, including the Great Lakes of North America, were formed to a great extent by the movements of the glacial ice.

The glaciers had advanced and melted away four times. However, the entire time taken up by the glaciers was probably less than 15 per cent of the Pleistocene epoch. The rest of the Pleistocene years was called *interglacial*, that is, periods between glaciers.

Some scientists think that the Ice Ages may not be over. They believe that we may be living in an interglacial period. If that is correct, it is possible that thousands of years from today glaciers may cover the very city or town in which you live. If the Antarctica icecap (the largest type of glacier) should ever melt, the oceans could rise about forty feet and flood our coastal cities.

■ Check on Your Reading

1. What is meant by the term *prehistory?*
2. Describe the universe.
3. Why is man called a "Johnny-come-lately"?
4. What were the effects of the glaciers?

3. Early Forms of Man Appear

The Pleistocene epoch was important to us for more than its glaciers. As far as we know, man first appeared on the earth during this period. Scientists believe this because they have found remains of manlike creatures who lived in Pleistocene days.

The Java Man and the Peking Man

The *Java man* and the *Peking man* (who received their names from the places where their skulls and other fragments were found) are among the oldest manlike creatures to be discovered. Their remains

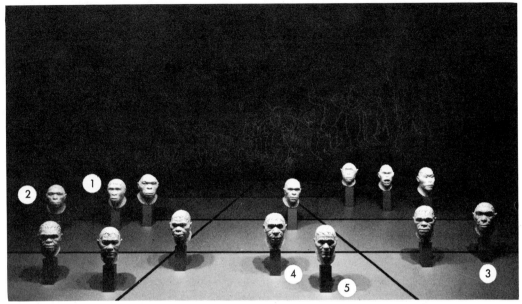

■ *Reconstructions of the heads of prehistoric men. Archaeologists have traced their beginnings to Asia, Africa, and Europe. Note the various stages in man's development. They include (1) Java, (2) Peking, (3) Rhodesian, (4) Neanderthal, and (5) Cro-Magnon man.*

date back about 500,000 and 360,000 years. Man's ancestors probably were far older than that. (Indeed, Dr. L. S. B. Leakey has dug up the remains of a creature in Africa, known as *Homo habilis*, that he describes as a manlike creature. He believes that the creature was of pygmy size, made tools, and lived about 1,820,000 years ago.)

Both the Java and the Peking man had heavy ridges above their eyes, big teeth, a large jaw, and practically no chin. Java and Peking men also had extremely low intelligence when compared with that of modern men.

The skull of the Java man was similar in many ways to that of the Peking man. Some scholars believe that both the Java and the Peking man belonged to the same group of manlike creatures. They do not consider them sharply different types of man.

The Neanderthal Man

The *Neanderthal man* appeared much later than the Java and Peking men. Neanderthal men lived in regions ranging from Asia all the way to Europe roughly from 170,000 to 45,000 years ago.

There were variations among Neanderthal men, and one group was sufficiently different to be given the name of "Progressive" Neanderthal men. In general, the Neanderthal man was short and powerfully built. He had ridges above his eyes and a retreating chin. These last two physical features were not as extreme in Neanderthal men as those of the Java and Peking men.

Contrary to popular belief, the Neanderthal man was neither "a savage animal" nor a "dim-witted brute." On the contrary, his intelligence, although still below that of modern men, was far higher than that of the Java and Peking men.

The Cro-Magnon Man

The *Cro-Magnon man* lived in Europe and adjacent regions between 50,000 and 20,000 years ago. He was tall (sometimes reaching a height of six feet and over), and he had a deep jaw and prominent chin. He could move more quickly than Neanderthal man and was very intelligent.

The Cro-Magnon man resembled modern men in many ways. One authority, Roy Chapman Andrews, has declared:

...if you saw a Cro-Magnon man on Fifth Avenue [in New York City] dressed in a sack suit and a Homburg [hat] you wouldn't give him a second glance.

The Cro-Magnon man and another variation of man that appeared at this time are classified as *Homo sapiens* (Wise or Intelligent man). They were true ancestors of modern men, who also are known as *Homo sapiens*.

Three Basic Facts about Man's Development

A number of recent discoveries have contributed to our knowledge of early men and have added to our information about the nature of man's development. These findings support the following points.

(1) In the development of man, there were no sudden changes. In fact, there is evidence that some Neanderthal men still were alive at the same time as the Cro-Magnon men. It is possible that the two groups intermingled.

(2) Various racial groups developed. A *race* is a principal division of man whose members have well-developed physical characteristics that can be passed on by heredity from generation to generation.

Scholars do not agree on how many races make up mankind. However, a number of scientists still consider the *Caucasoid*, *Mongoloid*, and *Negroid* to be the three races. Others add additional races to these three.

(3) No region in the world was the exclusive home of all early men. They lived in Europe, Africa, and Asia.

In America, man appeared at a comparatively late date. He may have come from northeastern Asia by way of a neck of land or ice connecting Siberia and Alaska.

Scholars Take Things Apart— and Put Them Together Again

How did we find out all of these things about prehistory? Since man did not begin to write until about 5000 years ago, what records provided this information?

There are no written records in prehistory. Scholars use unwritten records.

The *paleontologist* examines *fossils*. Fossils are the remains or traces of ancient animals and plants that have been preserved in many kinds of rocks.

The *physical anthropologist* studies the nature of man and the biological facts about the development of man. Such objects as skulls, bones, and teeth provide him with valuable information. He also studies the physical and mental traits of tribesmen in "primitive" cultures today.

The *archaeologist* analyzes artifacts, that is, the tools, pottery, and other objects made by ancient peoples, and the ways men lived in early times.

The *chemist* helps to determine the age of prehistoric events and materials. He uses such methods as dating by radioactive carbon and by rubidium and potassium "atomic clocks" to find the ages of prehistoric organisms.

Today scholars provide us with a picture of prehistory by putting together the findings of these and other specialists.

■ **Check on Your Reading**

1. What were the differences between Java, Neanderthal, and Cro-Magnon man?
2. What is the importance of the three basic facts about the development of man?

4. Man Develops Cultures

The picture of prehistory that has been formed for us shows many things about the life of man. One of the important facts that it makes clear is that man gradually developed abilities and skills that distinguished him from other creatures. Outstanding among these were the following: (1) the ability to think and reason at a level far above that of other creatures, and (2) the ability to make and use tools. Some animals used tools, such as sticks. However, man was the only important tool-maker. Man eventually developed organs of speech. Human beings were able to speak long before they could invent a system of writing and reading.

It was by using such assets as his mind, his hands, and later his speech that man developed cultures. The word *culture* refers to all of the ways in which a group of people deals with human beings and with its physical environment. Among these are the ways in which it gets its food, builds its houses, and protects itself. As anthropologist Robert J. Braidwood has pointed out, a culture can mean "the way the members of a group of people think and believe and live, the tools they make, and the way they do things." There were a number of cultures during prehistoric times. Each year archaeologists seem to find more.

A Word about Ages and Cultures

For a number of years it has been customary to place prehistoric cultures in one of several Ages. These have been called in order of their occurrence: Paleolithic (Old Stone Age), Mesolithic (Transitional Age), Neolithic (New Stone Age), Copper Age, Bronze Age, and Iron Age. Man was supposed to have moved up by steps from the Paleolithic to the Iron Age—somewhat like a person mounting a ladder.

■ *Paleolithic men made tools out of flint. These artifacts—the hand-ax, dagger, and scraper—were used for chipping, cutting, and scraping.*

These divisions are still useful in helping us see a general pattern of cultural development. However, we know that they can be used too rigidly. Too often such a classification fails to show three important facts: (1) that some cultures did not die out "on schedule"; (2) that there often was overlapping of cultures; and (3) that when two or more cultures existed at the same time, they sometimes intertwined.

In other words, prehistoric cultures were not neatly arranged steps. Instead of having a sharply defined beginning and ending, each one seemed to merge into the next. Prehistoric man did not know when he moved from one Age to another.

When we refer to any one of the so-called "Ages," as we shall do, we must not think of it as a division that is cut off from the rest. Rather, we must view it as a period of culture that often received a flow of ideas from other cultures.

Cultures of the Paleolithic Age

The *Paleolithic* or Old Stone Age is believed to have extended from the time of man's first cultures (possibly 1,500,000 or 1,000,000 years ago) to around 10,000 years ago. The first part of the Old Stone Age is called the Lower Paleolithic. The

11

■ *On the wall of the Lascaux cave in France is a two-color painting of a bull. Paleolithic men believed the pictures held magical power over the animals they hunted for food.*

second part, which was the shorter of the two, is known as the Upper Paleolithic.

During the Lower Paleolithic period, Neanderthal men dominated the human scene. They established cultures in Africa, Asia, and Europe. Examinations of the remains of these cultures revealed the following facts about the men of this period: (1) They were hunters and gatherers of food; that is, they did not grow their own food. (2) Sometimes these men lived in the mouths of caves to protect themselves from the weather and the animals. They also lived out-of-doors, possibly under very primitive shelters whose remains no longer exist. (3) Simple stone tools and weapons were made by these men. Common weapons were clubs and spears. (4) They used fire which they obtained from natural occurrences, such as lightning

striking a tree. (5) Their dead were buried, and some rites of magic were practiced.

During the Upper Paleolithic period Cro-Magnon men dominated the human scene. From the examinations of the remains of their cultures in Europe and other regions, many facts are known about Cro-Magnon men: (1) They were still hunters and gatherers of food. (2) Their shelters included caves, underground dugouts, and huts of sticks and brush. (3) Techniques for making tools and weapons were improved. Their methods of working with stone were precise enough to produce flint points less than half an inch in thickness. Bone and horn were used with increasing frequency to make sewing needles and other tools.

(4) They learned how to make fire themselves, using friction methods. (5) When they wished, they clothed themselves with such materials as animal skins. Even buttons have been found in the remains of some Upper Paleolithic cultures. (6) They buried their dead and had certain ideas on religion and magic. (7) They created works of art. Although they did sculpturing, they expressed themselves best in pictorial art. Some striking paintings have been found in caves and rock shelters in southern France and northwestern Spain.

What did they use for paint? The earth's clays ground into powder and mixed with the fat of animals. What did they use for brushes? Reeds or bristles. What did they use for a palette? A bone!

Generally, the Paleolithic artists depicted animals: the mammoth, the reindeer, the wild horse, the woolly rhinoceros, the bison. These animals usually were presented as they were in nature.

■ **Check on Your Reading**

1. What is a culture?
2. How did Lower Paleolithic cultures compare with Upper Paleolithic?

5. The "Food-Producing Revolution" of the Neolithic Age

About 10,000 years ago, after a period of transition, the Paleolithic Age gradually was replaced by the *Neolithic* or New Stone Age. This Age often is divided into Lower and Upper Neolithic, but we shall consider the period as a whole.

The term "New Stone Age" is not completely logical. Though men now made better stone tools by grinding and polishing, instead of chipping, man's achievements included far more.

The most important feature of the Neolithic Age was that *man began to cultivate plants and domesticate animals.* This may have occurred first in the Near East about 10,000 to 9000 years ago. One farming community, Jarmo in Iraq, has been dated as far back as approximately 7000 B.C. (*B.C.* refers to any years before the birth of Christ. *A.D.* refers to the years since Christ's birth.) Another community at Jericho, in modern Jordan, may be older.

Man's change from a gatherer of food to a producer of food eventually had such radical effects that it has been called "a revolution." The term "revolution" refers to a complete and basic change. In many ways the introduction of food production did bring about such a change. This "revolution" probably developed over a period of several hundred years.

Social and Village Organization Develop

One reason why the cultivation of plants and the domestication of animals were so important was that men then could group themselves. After food raising began, men did not wander so much in search of food. They settled down in larger and larger groups. Then villages were formed.

These villages were directed by chiefs and family heads. Rules or laws were made. Religious practices were more firmly established. Customs exercised a stronger hold on the individual. Village settlements became definite *societies*, or organized groups of people following a general way of living. Government became a reality.

■ *Early Bronze Age people built dolmens, such as the one in Stonehenge, England. This circle of upright stones is one hundred feet in diameter. It is believed that these dolmens mark burial grounds or places where religious ceremonials were held.*

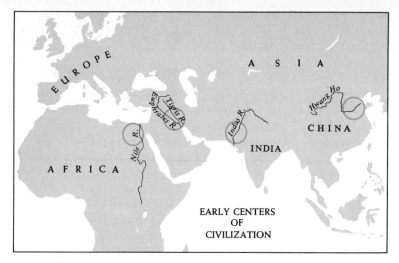

■ *Man developed cradles of civilization in the Nile, Tigris-Euphrates, Indus, and Hwang Ho valleys. In the next unit you will discover why.*

In addition, village settlements permitted men to specialize. Some men were freed from food-raising and they developed new skills. Important activities included the following: (1) the increased production of pottery, (2) the weaving of cloth, (3) the making of fishing nets and the construction of boats, (4) the increased exchange of goods, and (5) the building of better shelters.

Neolithic shelters were more developed. *Pit dwellings* were circular pits that were covered by placing brush and leaves on a framework of branches. *Pile villages* along the shores of lakes consisted of houses that were built by driving piles (wooden beams) into a muddy lake bottom. Crossbeams were bound to the top of the piles and sapling wood was placed over the beams. This "floor" was then covered with a layer of clay. Walls were made in the same way, and a thatched roof finished the house. Such Neolithic houses and weapons, like the bow and arrow, gave greater protection.

Neolithic Men Appeal to the Gods

In addition, the men of Neolithic times continued to be concerned with religion. It is believed that many villages had some local god or gods. These probably were associated with some feature of nature that

impressed men: for example, the sun or the sky. There were also shrines and religious rituals. These were used to win favor with the gods.

Some people, particularly in western Europe, also put up *megaliths*—great stones that were placed in their positions by men. Some were set up as single upright stones. Others were arranged in rows. It is believed that some megaliths were put up for religious or ceremonial reasons.

Prehistory Ends—History Begins

Starting about 5000 B.C., the so-called Age of Metals gradually replaced the Neolithic Age in the Near East. Men first began to use *copper* (4000 B.C.). Then they used *bronze*, an alloy of copper and tin (3500–3000 B.C.). Then came the use of *iron*, beginning probably in Asia Minor (1500 B.C.). Between 5000 and 3000 B.C. man began to develop civilizations (map, above). About 5000 years ago prehistory ended and history began with the appearance of the first written records.

■ Check on Your Reading

1. Define Neolithic Age.
2. What activities did villages make possible?
3. Describe Neolithic man's religion.

14

REVIEW and DISCUSSION

1. Identify the people and explain the events and terms on p. 4.

2. Name the key point of the "Prologue."

3. Give some of the estimates made by scientists on the size of the solar system and the ages of both the earth and mankind.

4. What evidence do we have that the earth is still changing?

5. Explain the statement: "Man shows a unity with the universe."

6. With which of these statements do you agree? Why? (a) Man challenges the universe to reveal its secrets. (b) Man is so small and the universe so large that he can never master it.

7. What evidence can you find to support the theory that man has changed physically?

8. What contributions have scientists made to knowledge of prehistory?

9. Name some features found in prehistoric cultures. Contrast with your culture.

10. What achievement of prehistoric man do you think was the most important in the development of man? Why?

11. Prove or disprove these statements: (a) Changes in both man and the earth occur so gradually that they are not usually noticeable to an individual in his lifetime. (b) Unwritten records can give man considerable information about his past.

ACTIVITIES

1. Write your definition of history. Use references. Better readers can use Muller, *The Uses of the Past.* Why do definitions differ?

2. Write a report on "The Objectivity of History." In preparation (a) read the subtopic, "How History Is Written," in *The World Book Encyclopedia*; (b) find out how historical research differs from scientific research; and (c) determine if historical research can be entirely objective.

3. Write a report on the estimates of the age of the earth from six different sources. Why do the answers differ?

4. Make a chart showing the key aspects of the various cultural ages.

5. Exhibit some artifacts that were found in your community. Explain them.

PAST and PRESENT

1. Can you find any geological evidence of the prehistoric period in your state?

2. Write a report on people living in the Stone Age culture today. See *Readers' Guide.*

3. Write a report on an archaeological expedition. See Ceram, *Gods, Graves, and Scholars.*

SUGGESTED READINGS

Basic books: BREASTED, JAMES H., *Ancient Times*, Chap. 1, Ginn.

CHENEY, SHELDON W., *New World History of Art*, Viking. Covers painting, sculpture, and architecture from the dawn of history to the present.

SMITH, GOLDWIN, *The Heritage of Man: A History of the World*, Chap. 1, Scribner. Useful as a reference book.

Special accounts: COON, CARLETON S. (ed.), *A Reader in General Anthropology*, Holt. Includes readings on "primitive" peoples.

FENTON, CARROLL L., *Prehistoric World: Stories of Animal Life in Past Ages*, John Day.

GAMOW, GEORGE, *Biography of the Earth*, MD 138, New American Library. A physicist shares his knowledge.

GOLDMAN, HANNAH and IRVING, *The First Men: The Story of Human Beginnings*, Abelard-Schuman. Information on primitive cultures.

LIFE, *Picture History of Western Man*, Simon and Schuster.

The Races of Mankind, Public Affairs Pamphlet No. 85. A concise explanation of the races of man.

HEYERDAHL, THOR, *Kon-Tiki*, Rand McNally. Tests the theory that Indians came to America from Polynesia.

UNIT 1 Four Centers of Ancient Civilizations

Why Should You Study Ancient Civilizations?

On September 23, 1938, a strange torpedo-shaped object was lowered fifty feet into the ground in New York. As a Chinese gong sounded, A. W. Robertson, chairman of the board of Westinghouse Electric Corporation, solemnly proclaimed:

May the Time Capsule sleep well. When it is awakened 5000 years from now, may its contents be found a suitable gift to our far-off descendants.

The object was a gift to the future, a seven-foot copper capsule filled with materials that will tell the people of the future something of how men lived during the first half of the twentieth century. It is not to be opened until *6939 A.D.*!

When archaeologists of the future open the "Time Capsule," they will learn much about this civilization. They will find inside it such varied objects as:

A clock	Books on art, music, and science
A Union Pacific timetable	A collection of coins
A pen	A cosmetic make-up kit
A set of alphabet blocks	

Consider what would happen to the contents of the "Time Capsule," if the ancient pre-Christian civilizations of Egypt, the Near East, India, and China had not existed. If the people of these civilizations had not passed on their knowledge to us, how many objects and ideas would we have today to send on to the future?

The clock and the timetable would disappear, for we learned about hours, days, months, and years from the ancients. The pen, alphabet blocks, and books would vanish, for writing was a contribution to us from the ancient world. Similarly, we could not include coins and cosmetics, for these can be traced back to pre-Christian times. The

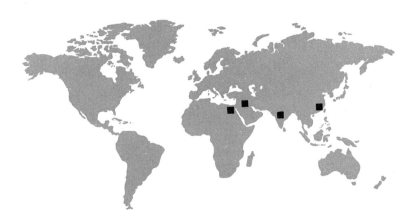

"Time Capsule" for the future would empty rapidly, if we took away from it all the materials and ideas that we have absorbed from ancient peoples.

An answer can now be given to the question: "Why should I study about ancient civilizations?" It is desirable to study about them in order *to understand many ideas and customs that are still alive today and that are important enough to pass on to the future.*

How Can You Use Information about Ancient Civilizations?

Our newspapers today carry news stories under such headings as:

CHEOPS' "GREAT PYRAMID" STILL TOURIST ATTRACTION

ANCIENT CASTE SYSTEM BLOCKS REFORM IN INDIA

CONFUCIAN SCHOLARS AND COMMUNISTS CLASH OVER FREEDOM OF SPEECH LAWS

DISCOVERIES IN DEAD SEA CAVES SHOW STRENGTH OF HEBREW MONOTHEISM

Can you completely understand these modern news stories unless you know the meaning of "Great Pyramid," Hebrew monotheism, the caste system, and Confucianism? Obviously not! Yet these are terms that date back to the time of ancient Egypt, the Near East, India, and China. An answer can now be suggested for the question: "How can I use information about ancient civilizations?" You can use such information *to provide yourself with enough background to be able to understand many events in today's news.*

Where Do You Begin?

You begin along the rivers—the Tigris-Euphrates, the Nile, the Indus, the Hwang Ho. These were the geographic starting points for history. These were the areas in which man began to develop his earliest civilizations. In Unit I you will read about that exciting story.

17

Chapter 1 — Intertwining Civilizations of the Ancient Near East

KEYNOTE There is an ancient Babylonian fable that tells of a quarrel between a proud horse and a philosophic ox. The former boasts: "Without me, neither prince nor governor nor rich nor poor could travel." The ox politely agrees, but answers: "Without me, you would not be quite so successful. Remember that man uses an ox's hide to make a horse's harness—and without a harness you could not pull many passengers!"

The fable was useful in demonstrating to the Babylonians the interdependence that existed in the animal world, even between those who seemed to be opposed to each other. In like fashion, each human being in the ancient world was dependent on other people, and the ways of life of one group were often derived from contact with others.

In the ancient Near East, many civilizations struggled for control of the land. Yet, as their warriors clashed, *their civilizations intertwined and the achievements of one people were exchanged or merged with those of other groups.*

Key People *Hammurapi · Sargon II · Assurbanipal · Nebuchadnezzar · Cyrus · Darius · Xerxes · Moses · David · Solomon*

Key Places *Tigris-Euphrates rivers · Mesopotamia · Sumer · Plain of Shinar · Ur · Babylon · Assur · Nineveh · Persepolis · Samaria · Jerusalem*

Key Events *Akkadians conquer Sumerians · Babylonian civilization develops · Hammurapi's Code · Assyrians conquer Babylon · Chaldeans rule Babylon · "Babylonian captivity" of the Hebrews · Persian Empire established : Hittites use iron · Phoenicians develop an alphabet*

Key Terms *Fertile Crescent · city-state · cuneiform · relief sculpture · ziggurat · Gilgamesh · Indo-Europeans · satrapies · Zoroastrianism · Judaism*

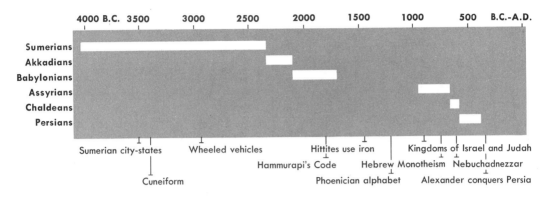

| 4000 B.C. | 3500 | 3000 | 2500 | 2000 | 1500 | 1000 | 500 | B.C.-A.D. |

Sumerians
Akkadians
Babylonians
Assyrians
Chaldeans
Persians

Sumerian city-states   Wheeled vehicles   Hittites use iron   Kingdoms of Israel and Judah

Hammurapi's Code   Hebrew Monotheism   Nebuchadnezzar

Cuneiform   Phoenician alphabet   Alexander conquers Persia

1. A Home of Civilizations: "The Land of the Two Rivers"

In western Asia, between the Tigris River to the east and the Euphrates River to the west, is a region known as Mesopotamia, or "the land between the rivers." It was in this land, today called Iraq, that the earliest civilizations of the Near East appeared. There are mountainous areas to the north and east, and desert to the west. The mountain barriers are not sufficiently rugged to prevent hostile people from attacking the valley, and the desert is not a perfect barrier against enemies. To the southeast, the Persian Gulf receives the flow of the two rivers as they move southward and empty into it. Mesopotamia forms a part of what is known as the Fertile Crescent, an arc of territory that runs northwest from the Persian Gulf and then curves southwest along the Mediterranean Sea into Syria and Palestine (map, p. 20).

Historical Importance of Mesopotamia's Location: Located between the Tigris and Euphrates rivers, this was a fertile land where many civilizations developed. Since the mountain and desert barriers did not offer enough protection, invading peoples attacked the land and some settled in it.

According to some sages of old, it was somewhere in this "land of the two rivers" that the vanished "Garden of Eden" was once to be found. Yet there were several aspects of the geography of the region that bore no resemblance to paradise.

Historical Importance of Mesopotamia's Rivers: The Tigris and Euphrates rivers did not flood at regular times. Although the land was fertile, there was not enough rainfall and constant irrigation was necessary.

Although this region had its drawbacks, it also had its advantages. For example, the waters of the two rivers could be used to irrigate the land, the soil of the valley was rich, and the region as a whole was safer than the dangerous or barren places that surrounded it. If a man planned properly, he could develop a satisfactory life in this land. (Today the term *Near East* is being replaced by *Middle East*. The lands of the Middle East include Egypt, Syria, Lebanon, Israel, Jordan, the Arabian Peninsula, Iran, Iraq, Turkey, the islands of Crete and Cyprus, and Afghanistan.)

■ **Check on Your Reading**

1. What does "Mesopotamia" mean?
2. What were some of the geographic drawbacks of the Tigris-Euphrates region that hindered its development?
3. What features of the area made it a natural center for an early civilization?

2. The Sumerians Build a Civilization

At some time before 4000 B.C. a short, stocky people called Sumerians, whose racial origin is unknown, descended from the north into "the land of the two rivers." They settled in the southern region of the Tigris-Euphrates Valley known as the Plain of Shinar. In the lower part of this plain, soon to be given the name of Sumer, they set up a number of individual city-states, separate kingdoms each consisting of a city and its surrounding districts.

As their culture developed, the methods of obtaining food, shelter, recreation, and other necessities became more complex. The word *civilization* refers to an advanced stage of cultural development. By 2500 B.C. the Sumerians had developed one of the earliest civilizations.

The Sumerian City-States

In the center of each city-state, the Sumerians built a *ziggurat*, a temple-tower that rose toward the sky in circular "wedding-cake tiers." The ziggurat was constructed to provide a dwelling place for the favorite gods of the group, for each city-state had its special deity. Governed by different ruler-priests and devoted to different gods, the city-states often clashed. Victory in war seemed a reasonable way of proving the superiority of their gods over those of the enemy.

The Sumerian cities served as centers for their civil and religious life. The famous city of Ur had beautiful temples, storehouses, and trading areas where gold (p. 42), silver jewelry, and green mascara

■ *What geographic features favored the development of civilizations in this area?*

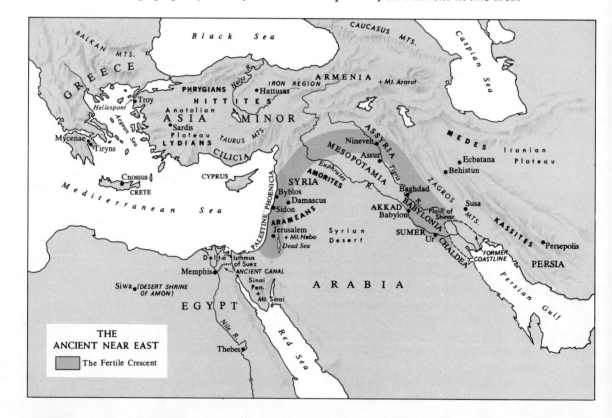

THE ANCIENT NEAR EAST

The Fertile Crescent

■ *Workers are shown excavating the ruins of the Ziggurat of Ur, which was the classic expression of religious temples in Sumer. The inset shows the probable structure. Originally the raised platform was designed to protect the sanctuary from flood.*

for the ladies could be purchased. The city was the focal point for commercial activities, and the Sumerians were one of the earliest groups to regulate business transactions formally. Contracts were arranged, bargains were made binding by using personal seals, and money was borrowed — sometimes at interest rates of 33 per cent!

The People Remain Close to the Soil

Notwithstanding their city activities, the Sumerians remained close to the soil. They dug irrigation canals to bring water to the land, carefully grew crops of barley and wheat, and domesticated cattle and goats. Their farmers probably used the first agricultural *seeder,* a plow with an attachment that carried the seed from a container through a funnel to the furrow.

Some materials were scarce; so Sumerian merchants traded with the people of Egypt and the Indus Valley for stone, copper, and gold. For their homes, peasants used reeds plastered with a mixture of sun-baked clay and straw. The life of the peasant was as simple as the house in which he lived. So long as he stayed close to the soil, he would survive.

Sumerian Scholars Develop Cuneiform

The Sumerians were one of the first peoples to develop a system of writing, and much of our knowledge of their civilization comes from deciphering their clay tablets found in Sumer. The Sumerian scholars wrote by pressing the end of a reed into moist clay tablets until wedge-shaped marks were formed; then they baked the clay. This wedge-writing is known as *cuneiform,* and the marks represented sounds. It was very important historically that other peoples near the Tigris and Euphrates rivers drew heavily on Sumerian cuneiform in patterning their languages.

The reading of cuneiform reveals that the Sumerians had developed one of the

21

■ *This is a Sumerian statue (left) of a woman in an attitude of worship. The model of a Sumerian war chariot (right) indicates the people used wheeled vehicles.*

earliest literatures in history. Their narratives, hymns, and epics sometimes contained stories comparable to accounts in the Bible about Adam and Eve, Noah, and Job.

We also know from cuneiform writing that the Sumerians recorded their legal and business transactions on clay—and even their medical prescriptions! What is probably the world's oldest medical record was recently unearthed at Nippur, Iraq. It was written in the Sumerian language, and on it an ancient physician had suggested as remedies for illness: salt; extracts of myrtle, fig, and date; and mixtures of milk, shell of turtle, and mashed snakeskin. For those who needed a more elaborate cure, he prescribed:

Grind to a powder pear-tree wood and the moon plant, then pour . . . wine over it and let [plain] oil and cedar oil be spread over it.

Ur-Nammu Establishes a Legal Code

The Sumerians used their cuneiform language to record laws as well as literature. Over two thousand years before the birth of Christ, Ur-Nammu, a Sumerian king, established a legal code that has recently been deciphered. Part of the code reads:

If [a man to a man with . . . instrument] his . . . foot has cut off, 10 silver shekels [about $50] he shall pay.

If a man to a man with a weapon his bones . . . severed, 1 silver mina [about $300] he shall pay.

If a man to a man with . . . instrument the . . . nose has cut off, ⅔ of a silver mina [about $200] he shall pay.

The Sumerian code was important because its rules were set down *in writing*. Previously, most men had only oral understandings of their responsibilities.

The Sumerians Contribute Many New Ideas

The Sumerians made important contributions to the peoples who came into the Tigris-Euphrates Valley. They introduced their neighbors to their business contracts, seed planter, cuneiform writing, narratives, medical remedies, and code of laws.

The Sumerians passed on to later civilizations their knowledge of the architectural arch and their system of measuring mathematically in units of sixty. Today we have sixty minutes in our hour and 360 degrees in the circle.

Finally, the Sumerians developed what were among the earliest wheeled vehicles in history, carts and chariots. (The exact date and place of the first wheel are still unknown.) The wheel proved to be one of the most important inventions of all time.

The Akkadians Conquer the Plain of Shinar

About 2300 B.C. a people known as Akkadians, whose kingdom was north of Sumer, attacked the Sumerians. The Akkadians were called *Semites* because of the language they spoke. It was a language that belonged to a group of Semitic tongues believed to have originated in Arabia.

Led by King Sargon, the Akkadians soon defeated the Sumerians, and later they spread their military conquests to the land north of the Plain of Shinar. In time, the victors absorbed many of the ways of the conquered. Both peoples gradually merged into a joint pattern of living.

The Akkadians adopted the Sumerian method of writing in clay, drew up codes of law that developed further several Sumerian principles of justice, and probably gave more individuals the legal right to run their economic affairs without the interference of the ruler-priest.

From time to time, Sumerian city-states temporarily overthrew the government of

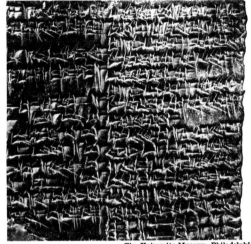

The University Museum, Philadelphia

■ *Sumerian cuneiform consisted of wedge-shaped characters. This is a segment of a tablet containing the story of the flood.*

the Akkadians. Starting about 2050 B.C., the Semitic-speaking Amorites from Syria conquered the entire region and made Babylon on the Euphrates the new capital. The Plain of Shinar took the name of Babylonia, and the civilization which next developed was known as Babylonian.

■ Check on Your Reading

1. Describe Sumerian city life.
2. What have we learned from cuneiform?
3. Evaluate these Sumerian contributions: (a) the arch, (b) irrigation, (c) measurement by sixties, and (d) wheeled vehicles.

3. The Babylonians, Assyrians, and Chaldeans

The Babylonian state soon became very prosperous. In the eighteenth century B.C., under the leadership of their ruler, Hammurapi, the Babylonians increased their territory and power. They constructed additional irrigation canals and bridges, broadened foreign trade in wool, and organized an effective system of taxation and administration for communities outside the city of Babylon. Their rulers' palaces, which featured arched doorways and decorative halls, reflected the country's prosperity.

Hammurapi's Code of Laws

Ruler Hammurapi, who claimed that he received his power directly from the chief

23

Babylonian god Marduk, is most famous for drawing up a code of laws to regulate the conduct of men. Hammurapi's Code probably appears severe by our standards today, but it may have seemed just and fair to Babylonians of the period. In addition, like the legal code of Ur-Nammu, it was important because it set down certain rules in writing. Some punishments were:

If a son strike his father, his hands shall be cut off.

If a man put out the eye of another man, his eye shall be put out.

If he break another man's bone, his bone shall be broken.

In addition, there were punishments for carelessness in farming methods:

If anyone be too lazy to keep his dam in proper condition, and does not so keep it; if then the dam break and all the fields be flooded, then shall he in whose dam the break occurred be sold for money, and the money shall replace the corn which he has caused to be ruined.

Many provisions were similar to this last rule, aiming to ensure fair dealings among members of the community and the family. On the other hand, the Code shows

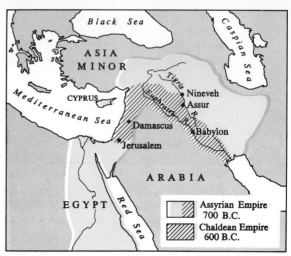

■ *The Assyrian Empire extended through the Fertile Crescent. In 612 B.C. Chaldeans conquered the Assyrians and built an empire.*

the effects of a strong caste structure in Babylonia. Punishments and fines for injuries to wealthy persons were more severe than for those to freemen or slaves.

The rulers after Hammurapi were not strong enough to ward off new invaders. By about 1650 B.C. the Babylonians had been defeated by the Kassites and other tribes, and "the land of the two rivers" was overrun by primitive peoples.

GILGAMESH	BIBLE

I caused a swallow to go forth, released it.
   The swallow went forth and returned;
   Since there was no resting place, it turned back.
 I caused a raven to go forth, released it.
   The raven went forth, saw the subsiding of the water;
   It eats, wades, croaks, and does not return.
     . . . .
   I made an incense offering on the top of the mountain
 Seven and seven . . . pots I set out,
   Poured into their bottom reeds, cedar wood, and myrtle.
 The gods smelled the savor,
   The gods smelled the sweet savor . . . .
	. . . and he sent forth a raven, and it went forth to and fro, until the waters were dried up from off the earth. And he sent forth a dove from him, to see if the waters were abated . . . but the dove found no rest for the sole of her feet, and she returned unto him to the ark. . . . And . . . again he sent forth the dove out of the ark; and the dove came in to him at eventide; and, lo, in her mouth an olive-leaf plucked off: so Noah knew that the waters were abated from off the earth.
	     . . . .
	   And Noah builded an altar unto Jehovah, and . . . offered burnt-offerings on the altar. And Jehovah smelled the sweet savor. . . .

Assyrian Warriors Sweep All Before Them

In 910 B.C. a people living to the north of the Babylonians, the Assyrians, seized the city of Babylon and continued to attack in all directions. They had perfected their tactics of war so that they soon controlled the greatest empire that the world had seen. Assur on the Tigris River was their first capital, but they later moved their government to Nineveh (map, p. 24).

Wherever they went, the mighty Assyrian armies burned and looted, as their cavalry, charioteers, and archers crushed all before them. One of their kings, Assurnasirpal II (884–860 B.C.), smashed through to the Mediterranean Sea. In the eighth century before the birth of Christ, another king, Sargon II, became master of all of the Fertile Crescent and lands almost as far north as the Black Sea. Dressed in copper or iron helmets, protected by great shields, and armed with iron-tipped arrows, maces, slings, and battering rams, the Assyrians could not be stopped.

The Assyrians also contributed to peaceful achievements. They borrowed ideas from earlier peoples and transmitted them to later civilizations. Two instances of Assyrian borrowing from other cultures were the following: (1) To construct their grand palaces, the Assyrians used the Babylonian knowledge of the arch and the Egyptian technique of glazing and decorating brick. (2) In literature, the Assyrians elaborated on Babylonian epics.

Most famous of the Assyro-Babylonian literature was the story of *Gilgamesh*, a Babylonian epic that the Assyrians made a part of their own heritage. Gilgamesh, a legendary hero, had many adventures; some probably influenced the Hebrews in the preparation of their Bible (see Chart).

The Assyrians Contribute Some New Ideas

The Assyrians were more than borrowers. Some of their activities were original,

■ *Stone reliefs, such as the Assyrian human-headed bull, decorated the entrance of Sargon II's palace. They are impressive works of art.*

as well as useful. They developed a system of administration for their empire which recognized the value of close contact between the capital and outlying provinces and subject kingdoms. Communications were improved throughout the empire by building roads and by developing possibly the first system of postal deliveries.

They also did outstanding work in the sculpturing of reliefs of animals, and Assyrian figures of winged bulls and other creatures of fiction and fact are works of art.

At least one ruler, Assurbanipal (668–626 B.C.), built up one of the first libraries in the world. It consisted of over 22,000 tablets, containing many legends and hymns.

By permission of the British School of
Archaeology in Iraq

■ *This ivory carving may be of the Syrian vegetation god, Tammuz, holding "the tree of life." It is probably of North Syrian workmanship.*

The Assyrian Empire, based on the principles of violence and brute force, could not hope to continue indefinitely. Its end came in 612 B.C., when the Chaldeans from the south and the Medes from the north joined forces and destroyed the Assyrian capital at Nineveh. The Chaldeans have been referred to as the Second Babylonians.

The Chaldeans Rebuild Babylon

With the defeat of the Assyrians, the Chaldeans soon increased their territory until they controlled nearly all of the Fertile Crescent. Their powerful king, Nebuchadnezzar (604–561 B.C.), promptly smashed any revolts against the new empire. In 586 B.C. he even destroyed Jerusalem, the capital of the Hebrews. As a lesson to other would-be rebels and to ensure against future revolts, he carried away thousands of Hebrew leaders and held them captive. This was the so-called "Babylonian captivity" of biblical fame.

Under King Nebuchadnezzar, Babylon again became a capital of color and excitement. This ruler dedicated an impressive gateway of enamelled tile to the goddess Ishtar, and a 650-foot ziggurat to the god Marduk, which may have led to the story of the "Tower of Babel." Nebuchadnezzar also built gardens on the roofs of his palace. These gardens, known as the "Hanging Gardens of Babylon," rose in a series of terraces. Around the wonders of his city, he raised a wall fifty-six miles in length, and on as many bricks as possible he ordered these words written: *I am Nebuchadnezzar, King of Babylon.*

Despite the surface splendor and the vanity of Nebuchadnezzar, the Chaldeans did not make as many contributions to civilization as the Sumerians. Primarily, they were consumers of the ideas of earlier peoples, rather than inventors of new ideas.

In a few fields the Chaldeans showed an original touch. In astrology they studied the stars to find omens of the future. Then they moved on to the scientific field of astronomy. Some of them predicted eclipses correctly, and one scholar even calculated the length of the year with considerable accuracy. The Chaldeans were known for their work in astronomy long after the palace of Nebuchadnezzar had disappeared.

■ **Check on Your Reading**

1. List the good and bad features of the Code of Hammurapi.

2. Why were the Assyrians able to build a great empire?

3. What did they contribute in literature and art? in communications?

4. Describe Nebuchadnezzar's Babylon.

5. What did the Chaldeans contribute?

■ *This is the central part of the monumental stairway to the Hall of Darius at Persepolis. On the frieze is a series of sculptures depicting the great tribute parade. This segment shows the guards of the king flanked by the Persian royal "arms"—a lion attacking a bull.*

4. The Persians

The ebb and flow of events did not permit the Chaldeans to control "the land of the two rivers" for very long. We have already seen that starting with the Sumerians, whose origins are not clear, a series of Semitic-speaking peoples had dominated the region—Akkadians, Babylonians, Assyrians, and Chaldeans. Other groups, known as *Indo-Europeans* because of the languages they spoke, were to seize control of the land.

The Great Persian Empire Rises

In the area near the Black and Caspian seas there was an Indo-European people called the Persians. Around 550 B.C. their king, Cyrus, united the various Persian tribes and defeated the Medes who had been ruling them. In 546 B.C. he conquered Lydia, an area farther to the northwest along the Aegean Sea. The Lydians were probably the first people to use a system of coinage, and their king, Croesus, was enormously wealthy. He is immortalized in the term "rich as Croesus." Cyrus made good use of the Lydian riches that he captured. Finally, he felt strong enough to attack the Chaldeans, and in 538 B.C. he conquered Babylon. Cyrus respected the religious beliefs of others and permitted the Hebrews to leave their "Babylonian captivity" and return to Jerusalem (p. 30).

Yet the conquest of "the land of the two rivers" was not sufficient expansion for the Persians. Cyrus' son, Cambyses, conquered Egypt in 525 B.C. By the time of King Darius, the Persian Empire included territory in Egypt, Asia Minor, Macedon, and east to India—the greatest empire to that time (map, p. 46).

The Persians Govern the Empire with Justice

The ancient Persian rulers have a reputation for kindliness that is not completely justified. Darius, for example, once crucified three hundred persons in an effort to force others to obey him. Nevertheless, Persian monarchs governed with far more justice than previous conquerors.

Under Darius (521–485 B.C.), Babylonia and Egypt were directly controlled from Persian headquarters in the city of Persepolis. The rest of the empire was divided into about twenty provinces or *satrapies*, each under the control of a governor, or *satrap*. So long as the conquered peoples paid their tribute to him, Darius permitted them considerable self-government and the right to worship gods of their choosing.

To unite the far-flung regions of the empire, roads were constructed. To supply the people with goods, foreign trade was encouraged. Through conquest of the

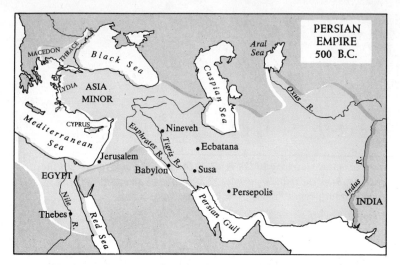

Phoenicians, the Persians became an outstanding power on sea and, although they originated few ideas themselves, they helped to spread the accomplishments of other peoples.

Zoroastrianism: Struggle of Good and Evil

Like the peoples who had preceded them, the Persians had their gods and their religious rituals. Their religion was called *Zoroastrianism*. It was based on the alleged sayings of *Zarathustra*, a semi-legendary prophet who was said to have been born by deliberate divine plan. In the *Avesta*, or the sacred books, Zarathustra's followers gathered his teachings.

To Zarathustra (Zoroaster) and the Persian believers, there was a continual struggle in the world between two great forces: Ahura-Mazda, the god of light and goodness, and Ahriman, the spirit of darkness and evil. Ahura-Mazda was the supreme god—and there Zoroastrianism came close to monotheism—but he was aided by lesser god-figures and angels. Similarly, Ahriman was supported in his Satanic designs by several evil spirits. It was believed that, after 12,000 years of struggle between the two forces, Ahura-Mazda would triumph and all good people would rise to eternal peace in heaven.

Yet not even the Persian gods could prevent the great empire from crumbling. Darius and his successor, Xerxes, attacked the Greeks unsuccessfully. Later the whole Persian Empire fell to the forces of Alexander the Great (p. 104). Persepolis was burned in 331 B.C., and gradually the great center of the Persians was buried.

■ Check on Your Reading

1. Define the term "Indo-European."
2. Who were the leaders who built the Persian Empire?
3. How was the empire administered?
4. What were the principal teachings of Zoroastrianism?

5. *The Hittites, Phoenicians, and Arameans*

From the time of the Sumerians until the downfall of the Persian Empire, "the land of the two rivers" had been the scene of clashing groups. Despite their conflicts, the various peoples had absorbed ideas from one another. Farther to the west and northwest, in Asia Minor and Syria, there were several groups who carried the ideas of these civilizations—in addition to their own—to several distant lands. The most important of these groups were the Hittites, Phoenicians, and Arameans.

Hittites: Masters of the Uses of Iron

The Hittites, an Indo-European people, were at the peak of their power in 1450 B.C. and dominated Asia Minor and Syria. At their greatest military triumph, the Battle of Kadesh in 1296 B.C., the charioteers of the Hittite king crushed the troops of the Egyptian pharaoh Ramses II.

From their center at Boghaz Keui, near modern Ankara in Turkey, the Hittites altered and transmitted these accomplishments: (1) sculpture techniques of the Assyrians; (2) cuneiform writing of the peoples of the Tigris-Euphrates; and (3) hieroglyphics showing Egyptian influence.

One idea which they did not publicize was their own method of smelting iron and using it on a large scale. This enabled them to make better weapons and made them conquerors for a brief period. When they finally lost their empire in 1200 B.C., the Hittites could no longer conceal their techniques for using iron. Knowledge of their methods spread, and the "iron age" reached several peoples about 1000 B.C.

Phoenicians: Developers of an Alphabet

The Phoenicians, who lived on a narrow one-hundred-mile strip of coastland north of Palestine, overthrew their Egyptian

■ *Phoenician colonies were established in Spain, North Africa, Sicily, and Cyprus. Why?*

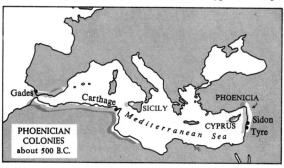

PHOENICIAN COLONIES about 500 B.C.

masters in 1200 B.C. They remained independent until about 876 B.C., when they were conquered by the Assyrians. The Phoenicians were great traders of the eastern Mediterranean who carried on commerce with western Asia, Egypt, Spain, and even Britain. From their cities of Tyre, Sidon, and Byblos their narrow ships, powered by sail and galley-slaves, carried glass, pottery, needlework, and a purple dye. They brought back ivory, tin, and silver. They also founded the colony of Carthage in North Africa (map, p. 29).

Most important, the Phoenicians contributed to the growth of written language. We are still not certain of the first people to originate the *idea* of the alphabet. Some authorities claim that the first alphabet appeared near the present Syrian port of Latakia; others that it came from Egypt. Nevertheless there is reason to believe the Phoenicians developed a true alphabet.

Using cuneiform script, or perhaps Egyptian hieroglyphics, the Phoenicians worked out an alphabet of twenty-two consonants and no vowels. The Greeks modified and used this alphabet, and the Romans based their alphabet on the Greek. Our alphabet was derived from the Roman.

Arameans: Transmitters of Language

The Arameans, whose land lay between Egypt and Babylonia, were inland traders whose caravans travelled to many areas in the Near East. Their center was at Damascus in present-day Syria. By 1000 B.C. they were using in their business transactions an alphabetic writing whose basis was probably borrowed from the Phoenicians. This Aramaic language became the commercial language of the Fertile Crescent.

■ **Check on Your Reading**

    1. What ideas did the Hittites pass on?
    2. Why are we in debt to the Phoenicians?
    3. What is our debt to the Arameans?

6. The Hebrews

The Phoenicians and the Arameans made important contributions to society. Another group small in numbers but great in influence was the Hebrews.

The Hebrews Set Up a Kingdom in Palestine

According to Biblical writings, sometime after 2000 B.C. Abraham, the father-ruler of the early Hebrews, left the Sumerian city of Ur. Between 1400 and 1200 B.C. some of the descendants of Abraham moved into Canaan, which we call Palestine, a narrow territory one hundred fifty miles long at the southwestern end of the Fertile Crescent. Other Hebrews were enslaved by the Egyptians but, under the leadership of

■ *Palestine, at the southwestern end of the Fertile Crescent, split into two kingdoms: Israel and Judah (900 B.C.).*

ANCIENT PALESTINE
about 900 B.C.

Moses, they escaped and many made their way to Palestine by 1000 B.C. (map, p. 30).

The Hebrews and the Canaanites in Palestine soon mingled; and a kingdom was established in 1025 B.C. by Saul, the first Hebrew king. Saul's successor, King David, was a sensitive ruler to whom poetry was as exciting as the clash of arms. One of his major achievements was the establishment of Jerusalem as the capital.

David's son, King Solomon, loved luxury and rich living. Yet he was attracted by the path of religion. To reconcile his two desires, he built a magnificent palace for himself and a great temple for his God.

Solomon's extravagant living was made possible by heavy taxation, and there was considerable unrest and dissatisfaction. When he died, his kingdom split. Israel became the northern kingdom with Samaria the chief city; and Judah remained the southern kingdom with Jerusalem the capital.

In 722 B.C. the Assyrians defeated the kingdom of Israel. In 586 B.C. the Chaldeans destroyed the great temple at Jerusalem. Under the Persians, the Hebrews were permitted to rebuild their temple. In 70 A.D. when they revolted against the Romans, their temple was again destroyed, and in 135 A.D. they were finally forced out of Palestine.

The Hebrew Religion: a Bond for a Scattered People

Driven out of Palestine, the Hebrews scattered throughout the earth. But during all of his wanderings, the Hebrew felt that a strong bond existed between him and his fellow Hebrews in other lands. The tie that held them all together was religion.

The Hebrews accepted monotheism. Their monotheistic faith formed the basis

30

for Christianity. Scrolls discovered in recent years near the Dead Sea contain material on the history and religious beliefs of a Hebrew sect, the Essenes.

The Hebrews were not truly monotheistic from the beginning of their history. Many of their early tribes worshiped *baals*, local gods of fertility, or believed that the Hebrew god, *Yahveh*, was merely the fiercest and the best of many deities. Even King Solomon said: "Great is our god above all gods"—not "Ours is the only god." Beginning about 750 B.C., under the guidance of such prophets as Amos, Hosea, and Isaiah, they developed a concept of a single, just, and loving God for *all* mankind. The Hebrews were the first people to accept true monotheism.

The Faith of the Jews

Today the word *Jews* refers to those people who believe in the religion of Judaism, the faith started by the ancient Hebrews. Although rituals vary, the Jews today believe in the basic ideas of the ancient Hebrews. These ideas include the following:

1. BELIEF IN ONE GOD. The Jew believes in one God, Yahveh or Jehovah, creator of all things in the world. The most important prayer of Judaism therefore is, "Hear O Israel, the Lord our God, the Lord is One."

2. BELIEF IN THE TEN COMMANDMENTS. The Ten Commandments were said to have been given to Moses by God.

3. BELIEF IN THE IMPORTANCE OF THE TORAH. The *Torah* comprises the first five books of the *Old Testament*, the sacred Scriptures of the Jews. The Torah includes the account of the creation of the world, the histories of various peoples, and the Ten Commandments.

4. BELIEF IN THE COMPASSION OF GOD. The Jew believes that if he repents of his sins, asks God's forgiveness, and then lives honorably, God will be merciful to him.

5. BELIEF IN THE BROTHERHOOD OF ALL MANKIND. The Jew believes that he must conduct himself righteously toward his fellow man, for all men are brothers.

■ Check on Your Reading

1. What did Saul, David, and Solomon contribute to the history of the Hebrews?

2. What ties held Hebrews together?

3. List five principal beliefs of Judaism.

CULTURAL CHARACTERISTICS of the Ancient Near East

The ancient Near East was a land of strong rulers. One powerful Assyrian leader, Sennacherib, thought that he was:

The wise shepherd, the favorite of the great god,
The protector of justice, the lover of righteousness,
The giver of help, the aider of the weak,
The perfect hero . . .

This "perfect hero" and "aider of the weak" destroyed 89 cities and 820 villages!

The land between the Tigris-Euphrates rivers became the setting for the earliest Near Eastern civilizations, with various warlike groups taking turns in dominating the region—Sumerians, Akkadians, Babylonians, Assyrians, Chaldeans, and Persians. Expanding their control far beyond "the land of the two rivers," several of these people established mighty empires.

Although none of these empires survived the passage of time, the useful ideas and techniques of these cultures did. "The conquered conquered the conquerors" by absorbing the victors into their ways of living.

The characteristics of the cultures of the ancient Near East were:

Governments directed by leaders involved in military conquests and the building of empires.

As in Egypt, cities that served as centers for civil and religious life, and economies based on agricultural production.

31

Concern for the relationship of man to his gods, culminating in the Hebrew belief in monotheism.

The development of effective systems of writing, and the drawing up of written legal codes.

The construction of impressive temples, palaces, and sculpture.

The diffusion of culture—that is, "the transmission of elements of one culture to another"—was not always smooth in the ancient Near East. Many individuals and groups opposed change and preferred the old, familiar ways of life. The situation in the Near East is not too different today, when dedicated defenders of ancient tradition and heritage oppose modernization and industrialization.

Yet the cultural flow of the ancient Near East could not be dammed. Even as the farmers of "the land of the two rivers" followed the time-honored ways of their fathers—their sons were having contact with other cultures and with different tools, homes, and gods. Patterns of life in the Near East became enriched by the mingling of old and new.

MAN AND HIS CULTURE

Let's Meet the People!

The following account is based on information that appeared on a clay tablet written by a Sumerian scholar over 4000 years ago! The words on the tablet can be found in "School Days 4000 Years Ago" by Samuel N. Kramer, *Parents' Magazine*, November, 1949.

A Sumerian Schoolboy

The Sumerian schoolboy awoke in the morning and almost immediately thought: "I must not be late, or the teacher will cane [beat] me." Then he hurried to his mother and asked for the lunch that he was to take with him to school. The noon-day meal that he received was by no means an elaborate affair—it consisted of two rolls!

The schoolboy failed to arrive at school punctually and he later recorded on his clay tablet: "I was afraid and my heart pounded. I entered before my teacher and greeted him most respectfully." In school, his teacher found a section of his tablet missing and caned him. During the day, three assistants of the teacher also caned the Sumerian schoolboy for such infractions of the rules as talking out of turn and standing up without permission. Then another assistant said to him: "Your handwriting is not good"—and caned him again!

The schoolboy later suggested to his father that he invite the unfriendly teacher to their home for dinner and present him with a gift. The father did as his son requested. When he arrived, the teacher was "seated in the seat of honor." Then the father "dressed him in a new garment, gave him a gift, put a ring on his hand."

Pleased by such treatment, the teacher soon changed his attitude toward the schoolboy. Looking with new favor on his young pupil, he said: "Young man, because you did not neglect my work, did not forsake it, may you reach the pinnacle of the scribal art, achieve it completely. Of your brothers may you be their leader, of your companions may you be their chief, may you rank highest of all your classmates." There is no record of whether or not the schoolboy was ever caned again after that!

CHAPTER REVIEW

REVIEW and DISCUSSION

1. Identify the people and places and explain the events and terms on p. 32.

2. Did the geographical features of the Fertile Crescent help the development of civilizations? How?

3. Why were the Sumerian interest rates so much higher than interest rates today?

4. Some Sumerian literature contained narratives that were comparable to those in the Bible. What do you conclude from this?

5. Why is the wheel "one of the most important inventions of all time"?

6. Wars among the peoples of different civilizations caused an intermingling of these civilizations. What were the results?

7. Define the word *justice*. Do you think the Code of Hammurapi was just? Why, or why not? How has the meaning of the word changed?

8. In referring to the brutality of the Assyrians the text says, "No empire based on these principles could hope to continue indefinitely." Can you give any evidence to support or refute this idea?

9. What are some of the personal characteristics common to rulers of this chapter?

10. Which contributions made by the peoples in this chapter do you think influenced mankind most? Why?

11. It has been said that ideas can outlast buildings or other material things created by man. How is this true of the peoples in this chapter?

12. What five generalizations can you make about the material in this chapter?

ACTIVITIES

1. On a map of the ancient Near East, locate Babylon, Byblos, Damascus, Egypt, Jerusalem, Lydia, Macedon, Nineveh, Palestine, Plain of Shinar, Persia, Sidon, Sumeria, Tigris-Euphrates, Tyre, and Ur.

2. Make a clay tablet of cuneiform writing similar to cuneiform tablets found in Sumeria.

3. Use the Tigris-Euphrates civilizations in analyzing "Why Great Civilizations Rise and Fall" in your notebook. Note contrasts.

4. On a map of the Persian Empire show its far-flung boundaries and the peoples ruled therein.

5. Obtain two maps of the Near East. Show the ancient Near East countries on one map and the modern Middle East countries on the other. Are there geographical reasons for the boundaries of these countries?

PAST and PRESENT

1. Find articles in *Readers' Guide* on the countries of the Fertile Crescent. Compare the contributions of these peoples today with those made in the period you have studied in this chapter. How do you explain the differences?

2. In *Readers' Guide* find articles on Israel which indicate how Biblical references are being used to develop Israel's resources.

3. Write a report to give to the class about the Dead Sea Scrolls.

SUGGESTED READINGS

Basic books: BREASTED, JAMES, *Conquest of Civilization*, Harper.

BROWNE, LEWIS, *This Believing World*, Macmillan. The world's great religions.

WELLS, H. G., *Outline of History*, Doubleday.

Special accounts: *The Bible*, Genesis 6:5–9:17, Exodus 20, I and II Samuel, I Kings 6:1–38, II Chronicles 3:1–17, Ezra, Psalms, Isaiah.

CHIERA, EDWARD, *They Wrote on Clay: The Babylonian Tablets Speak Today*, University of Chicago Press. (Paperback)

KELLER, WERNER, *The Bible as History*, Morrow. Historical explanations of the Bible, using archaeology and other sciences.

Biography and Fiction: KING, MARIAN, *Young King David*, Lippincott.

Chapter 2   Egypt and a "River of History"

KEYNOTE   Few rivers have been the setting for so much happiness and sorrow as the Nile. Think of the Nile and you may see visions of sea captains hopefully raising the sails of their vessels and sailing down the river in search of riches in the Mediterranean ... or frightened fishermen plunging their spears into the muddy waters in a desperate attempt to escape snapping crocodile jaws ... or the great Queen Cleopatra carefully rouging her face before leaning over her barge to see if the Nile would reflect her beauty in its mirror. The Nile has been a silent witness to the hopes and disappointments of men and women for thousands of years. It is, indeed, a "river of history."

Most important of all, the Nile has provided the lifeblood for *one of the first civilizations in the world, the Egyptian.* Today the desert sun and winds have erased many of the great monuments of the Egyptians and buried others in graves of sand. More may be covered with water after construction of a great new dam on the Nile. Yet the spirit of ancient Egypt still lives in the ideas of government, time, writing, and architecture passed on to us.

Key People   *Menes · Thutmose I · Hatshepsut · Thutmose III · Ramses II · Khufu · Ikhnaton · Champollion*

Key Places   *Lower Egypt · Upper Egypt · Nile Delta · Memphis · Thebes · Gizeh · Karnak*

Key Events   *New Kingdom flourishes · Persians conquer Egypt · Rosetta Stone deciphered*

Key Terms   *shadoof · irrigation · pharaoh · dynasty · artisans · pyramids · sarcophagus · polytheism · hieroglyphics · monotheism · civilization · obelisk · immortality*

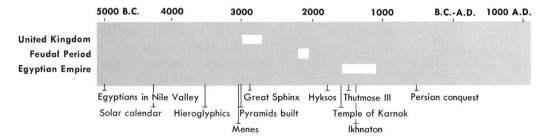

5000 B.C.   4000   3000   2000   1000   B.C.-A.D.   1000 A.D.

United Kingdom
Feudal Period
Egyptian Empire

Egyptians in Nile Valley | Great Sphinx   Hyksos | Thutmose III   Persian conquest
Solar calendar   Hieroglyphics | Pyramids built   Temple of Karnak
                             Menes   Ikhnaton

1. The Nile River Floods and Leaves Its Gifts

Rising in equatorial Africa, the Nile flows northward 3200 miles into Egypt. Here it continues for another 935 miles before emptying into the Mediterranean Sea. Where the Nile meets the sea, rich deposits of soil carried by the river form a triangular section of land known as the *delta* (map, p. 36).

Thousands of years ago—just as today—when the rains beat down on the hills to the south of Egypt and the snows melted in summer, the Nile rose and flooded both its banks. Today it is restrained by dams, but for centuries men let nature take its course. For eight to ten miles on each side the waters spread. Then the Nile slowly drew back to its channel, leaving behind its annual gifts to the people—two strips of rich soil alongside the river. These were priceless gifts, for the land had been made fertile by the deposits of river silt, and men could grow crops and prosper.

Historical Importance of Egypt's Nile: The Nile River floods its banks bringing water to Egypt's parched soil. This annual flooding permits Egypt's farmers to grow crops of wheat, barley, and cotton and to raise cattle and sheep.

There is very little rainfall in Egypt. East and west of the Nile River are empty deserts, lands of sun and sand and heat. The Egyptians depended on the annual flooding of the river for their livelihood. They dug reservoirs or basins to hold the floodwater, and they built ditches to funnel it to their fields. During the dry season they used a *shadoof*, or well sweep, that drew water from the river with buckets and hoisted it to the ditches. They thus established one of the earliest irrigation systems in history.

Historical Importance of Egypt's climate: Egypt has a warm, dry climate. It has little rainfall and many desert areas. Therefore, the majority of the people live near the Nile.

The Egyptians planted wheat, barley, and flax on the irrigated land, using a stick-hoe first and, in later years, a wooden plow to turn the soil. Beans, peas, and onions were grown in their gardens; and cattle, sheep, and goats were fed in the pastures. Grain was threshed by driving oxen over it, and grapes were raised in vineyards. So long as the waters of the Nile could be used to irrigate the land, the people could live.

Sometime after 5000 B.C., a wandering people in North Africa settled in the narrow valley formed by the two strips along

35

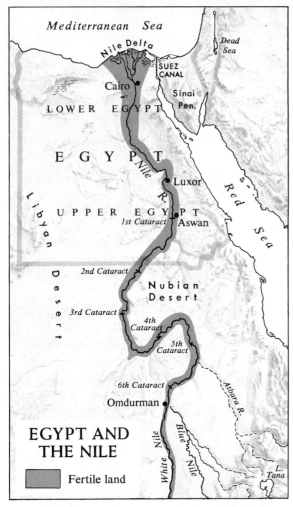

EGYPT AND THE NILE

Fertile land

■ *Egypt has built its civilization around the Nile, which is called a "river of history." Why? How has climate affected its history?*

the river. These were the Egyptians. The territory that the Egyptians controlled eventually ran from the delta to the fourth *cataract*, or great waterfall, of the Nile, a distance of about nine hundred miles. The Egyptians were grateful to the Nile River for enriching the land. Ikhnaton (c. 1375–1358 B.C.), one of their later leaders, even turned to the heavens and openly proclaimed his thanks to his god for the gift of the Nile:

> Thou has set a Nile in heaven,
> That it may fall for them,
> Making floods upon the mountains,
>   like the great seas
> And watering their fields. . . .

Even today, many Egyptians consider the sounds of their water-wheels to be the friendly "music" of their protector, Father Nile. The movement of water has always been the Egyptian rhythm of life, for it made possible the development of an important civilization in this area.

■ **Check on Your Reading**

1. How does Egypt have fertile soil in the midst of a vast desert?

2. How did the Egyptians use the Nile for irrigation?

3. What crops did the ancient Egyptians raise?

4. Explain the importance of the Nile in Egyptian life.

2. The Egyptians Build a Civilization

As we have seen, the first civilizations were developed in the Tigris-Euphrates region: Sumerian, Babylonian, Persian, and others. These civilizations influenced one another by spreading, borrowing, or exchanging their ideas. This transmission of ideas to other peoples is often called *cultural diffusion*. Effective ways of organizing society, expressing feelings,

and carrying out other life functions were advanced because of this cultural exchange.

As a result, it is now clear that some some of the features of a civilization are these: The people or their leaders (1) set up a government with some control over the individual and the group; (2) organize some forms of city life; (3) understand the concept of time—of the importance of past, present, and future; (4) have ideas on the meaning of life and death, involving their attitudes toward religion and science; and (5) express themselves in writing, the arts, and music.

The Egyptians established one of the earliest civilizations in the world, in which all five features could be found.

Government Develops in Egypt

Egyptian history is sometimes divided into periods. In the Pre-Dynastic period (before 3000 B.C.) the Egyptians were governed by chiefs who ruled various groups of families, or *clans*. In time, the clans formed two kingdoms, Lower Egypt and Upper Egypt. About 3000 B.C. Egypt was united under one king. The history of a united Egypt can be divided into the following periods:

1. PERIOD OF UNIFICATION, 3000–2700 B.C. King Menes and his successors united Lower and Upper Egypt into a single kingdom. Menes started the first Egyptian *dynasty*, a succession of rulers from the same family line. The position of the ruler of the united kingdom grew in importance.

2. OLD KINGDOM, 2700–2200 B.C. By 2700 B.C. the king was called the *pharaoh*. Pharaoh was not his name; rather, it referred to the "house" or "temple-place" of the ruler. The word was used because the Egyptians believed that the pharaohs were descendants of the gods and were not to be mentioned by name. Since the pharaohs were considered to be like gods, they were to be obeyed. The government was autocratic; that is, the ruler had absolute power.

3. FIRST INTERMEDIATE OR FEUDAL PERIOD, 2200–2050 B.C. During this period, the pharaohs' power was taken over by nobles, men of the upper class who held important government positions. The pharaohs remained in office, but the nobles really ran the country.

THE
EGYPTIAN EMPIRE
about 1450 B.C.

Scale of Miles

0   400

■ *The Egyptian Empire was built by Thutmose I, Queen Hatshepsut, Ramses II, and Thutmose III, the "Napoleon of Egypt," by conquest and diplomacy. What territories did it include?*

4. MIDDLE KINGDOM, 2050–1800 B.C. By 2050 B.C. the pharaohs regained their power from the nobles. They maintained control until 1800 B.C., keeping law in the land and encouraging work in Egyptian art, architecture, and literature.

5. SECOND INTERMEDIATE PERIOD, 1800–1580 B.C. Then about 1800 B.C. an Asian people, the *Hyksos*, defeated the Egyptians and dominated them for two hundred years. They brought the first horses.

6. EMPIRE OR NEW KINGDOM, 1580–1090 B.C. In time the pharaohs drove out the Hyksos and once again forced the nobles to obey them. From 1580 until about the end of the eleventh century B.C., the pharaohs attempted to build an *empire*—that is, they tried to spread their

■ *These four statues of Ramses II (67 feet high) form the façade of the Great Temple of Abu Simbel, built by Ramses II (1250 B.C.). The Great Temple of Abu Simbel was relocated in 1967 to preserve these structures from the flooded area of the new Aswan Dam.*

power by conquering and ruling other lands. Conquests were made by Thutmose I, Queen Hatshepsut, Thutmose III, and Ramses II. Thutmose III, the pharaoh who began his rule about 1500 B.C., was a particularly active general and conquered many cities in western Asia. Diplomacy—the practice of arranging agreements among countries—was also used in building the Egyptian Empire.

7. PERIOD OF FOREIGN DOMINATION, 1090–663 B.C. The empires that the Egyptian pharaohs sought were not destined to survive. From the tenth to the middle of the seventh century B.C., Egypt was controlled by foreign rulers who overran the country. Libyan and Ethiopian dynasties were set up to govern the Egyptians.

8. FINAL EGYPTIAN RENAISSANCE, 663–525 B.C. During this period, Egyptian rulers regained control of the government from the foreign monarchs. They tried to bring about a *renaissance*, or rebirth, of Egyptian activities. However, the Persians defeated the Egyptians in 525 B.C. and made it part of the Persian Empire.

Although we have divided Egyptian history into periods, these are not neatly packaged capsules of time but rough approximations. Actually, the story of man is continuous, and yesterday, today, and tomorrow merge without a break. Egyptian history did not halt at the end of the Period of Unification and begin anew in the Old Kingdom. On the contrary, one period flowed without interruption into the next.

What we really mean when we divide Egyptian history into periods is that the government, activities, or beliefs of the people during certain years gradually became different from those during other years.

■ **Check on Your Reading**

1. What is meant by cultural diffusion? Give examples.

2. What five features are found in Egyptian civilization?

3. What is a "period" in Egyptian history?

4. How did the pharaohs rule?

5. What did the Hyksos introduce?

6. Who finally conquered Egypt in 525 B.C. and made it part of their empire?

3. Egyptian Civilization Has Other Features

The Egyptians were one of the earliest peoples to set up governments to control the individual and the group. They also were among the first to establish some forms of city life. Memphis served as the center for the government of the pharaohs from about 2700 to 2200 B.C. Thebes was the governmental headquarters, or *capital*, after 1580 B.C.

Despite the various shifts in government, Egyptian classes remained basically the same in such cities as Memphis and in the farming areas throughout the country. At the top of the social and economic scale were the pharaohs, nobles, priests, and officials. At the bottom were most of the estimated six million Egyptians—the free peasants and the thousands of captured slaves who worked the soil. Artisans in the cities could be placed somewhat higher in the social scale than the peasants.

Artisans were the potters, tanners, carpenters, and other craftsmen. Most of them were freemen, but some were slaves. Some artisans had the special job of repairing the Egyptian boats that sailed down the Nile and along the coasts of the Mediterranean and Red seas. Trade with the Sinai Peninsula, Syria, and Asia Minor was limited, but still it brought home silver, timber, and wine.

Egyptian classes were not rigidly separated from each other. There were social and economic walls between them, but a talented individual might move from a lower class to a higher one. In addition, the status of women was quite high; and many estates were handed down from generation to generation through the female side of the family.

The Egyptians Develop Measures of Time

The Egyptians had an understanding of time. They knew the meaning of past, present, and future; and they were able to devise a workable calendar to mark the passage of the days.

While primitive peoples had judged time by changes in the moon, the Egyptians developed the first calendar based on the sun's year. This *solar* (sun) calendar had twelve months in it, each of which consisted of thirty days. At the end of each year of 360 days, the people added "five days over and above the year" for a period of feasting.

The Egyptian calendar, which went into operation in 4241 B.C., was not completely accurate. It was six hours short of the sun's cycle at the end of each year, and it should have had a "leap year" of 366 days every fourth year. Nevertheless, the Egyptian calendar was an important step toward the exact measurement of time. The calendar we use today developed from it.

The Egyptians Have Religious Beliefs

The pharaohs of Egypt were convinced that they would have a life after death. In life they had been hailed by the people as being all-powerful and unconquerable. It was unthinkable to the pharaohs that they should not continue to live after death.

They ordered that huge *pyramids* be built to house their dead bodies until the moment when their souls would be carried away into a new life. Pyramids were large tombs that had four triangular sides that met at the top. The construction of these monumental tombs required the hard labor of thousands of men working for long periods of time. The so-called Great Pyramid of Pharaoh Khufu (or Cheops) in Gizeh consisted of over two million blocks of limestone, each weighing over two tons. It took over twenty years to build, and perhaps as many as five million men worked on its construction!

■ *From relief work and painting in tombs, a picture of Egyptian life emerges. This bas-relief from the Tomb of Ti shows Egyptian artisans engaged in shipbuilding. The profile position of the head and legs and front view of the body characterize Egyptian art.*

The preservation of the ruler's body was considered to be extremely important. The body of each pharaoh was *mummified*, or preserved, by a special treatment. Then it was placed in a *sarcophagus*, a large stone coffin, in the burial chamber. Egyptians may have believed that after death some common people would be carried to the western corner of a "lower world" in clay boats. They thought that the souls of the pharaohs would travel to a heaven located in the eastern part of the sky and follow the sun god Re on his daily trips around the earth. Some of the pharaohs even had solar ships constructed to carry their souls toward Re. The Egyptians did not know the earth revolved around the sun.

The Egyptians believed in many gods (polytheism). Re, the sun god, was very important, perhaps because of geographic conditions. Osiris, for example, the son of Re, was the god of the Nile. He also came to be the king of the dead and sat in judgment on men's souls. It was necessary for the deceased to prove to Osiris and the lesser gods that he had not committed serious sins. A collection of magical sayings, known as *The Book of the Dead*, was buried with the mummified corpse so that the soul would express the proper thoughts before Osiris. Some sayings in the "First Confession" were:

I have not done injury to men.
I have not oppressed those beneath me.

. . .

I have not been a doer of mischief.

. . .

I have not caused hunger.

. . .

I have not murdered.

40

ANCIENT CULTURES

■ *An Egyptian grave stele or tombstone (2050 B.C.) depicts a middle-class couple. These figures were modeled in relief and then painted—men dark, and women light. They were drawn in the Egyptian style—heads, arms, and legs in profile, shoulders in front view.*

Courtesy of The Metropolitan Museum of Art, Rogers Fund, 1916

■ *An Egyptian pectoral, or pendant, belonging to the daughter of King S'en Wosret II (1906–1887 B.C.) excelled in beauty of design and workmanship. It was made of gold and inlaid with semi-precious stones, and it was designed in the form of two hawks.*

Courtesy of The Metropolitan Museum of Art, Rogers Fund and contribution from Henry Walters, 1916

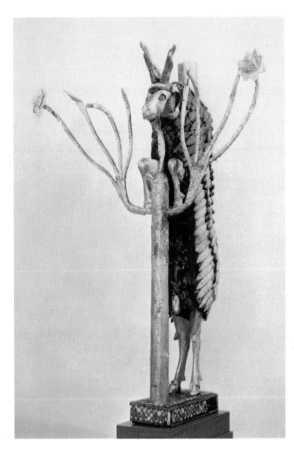

■ *A Sumerian statue, representing a Billy Goat at the Tree of Life (2500 B.C.) was found in the great death pit of the Royal Cemetery of Ur. The goat's forelegs were hobbled to the branches of a golden tree.*

Courtesy of the Trustees of the British Museum

■ *The gold ornaments of Sumerian Queen Shubad (2500 B.C.) were found at the Royal Cemetery of Ur. Among her jewels were gold earrings, a crown of gold leaves, beads from her cloak, a pin, rings, and various other ornaments.*

Courtesy of The University Museum, Philadelphia

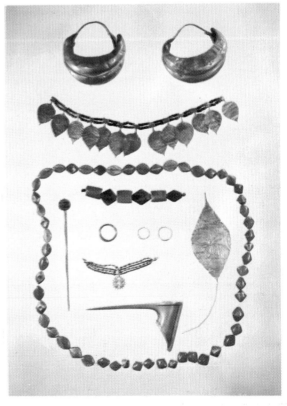

■ *During the famous Achaemenid period (550–331 B.C.) Persian art flourished. It was a royal art connected with the kings and their courts. Although influenced by Assyrian and Babylonian art, the Persians made important contributions. This is a silver drinking horn with a handle that is carved as a horned animal.*

Courtesy of the Trustees of the British Museum

■ *Skilled Persian metalworkers created outstanding decorative art, such as this model of a Persian war chariot in gold.*

Courtesy of the
Trustees of the British Museum

43

■ *One of the frescoes decorating the Minoan palace of Cnossos, Crete, is the "King of the Lilies." This painting combines modeling in relief with painting as in the athletic figure of the Prince, who is wearing plumes and a lily crown.*

■ *A Greek vase (465 B.C.) depicts scenes from the Fall of Troy, such as the Death of Priam and Cassandra at the Palladium. Attic pottery excelled in design and beauty. This is a red-figured vase in which the background was painted black and the figures were shown in the reddish color of the vase. Details could be filled in by painting lines on the clay.*

The Egyptians hoped that *The Book of the Dead* would help them to win *immortality*, or life after death.

One pharaoh, Amenhotep IV, did not believe in the powers of the various Egyptian gods. When he became ruler about 1375 B.C., he turned to a form of *monotheism*, a belief in one God. To Amenhotep IV, Aton was the one and only God in the world and the spirit of Aton was to be found in the sun. Amenhotep IV changed his own name to Ikhnaton, which means "Profitable to Aton," and praised the greatness of the "sole god, whose powers no other possesseth." Ikhnaton's idea of one God was too advanced for his time. Soon after he died, the belief in Aton died out in most of Egypt.

■ Check on Your Reading

1. What social classes were there in Egypt? What was the status of women?
2. Describe the Egyptian calendar. How accurate was it?
3. What did the Egyptians believe about life after death?
4. What was the impact on the Egyptians of Ikhnaton's monotheism?

Ashmolean Museum photo

■ *Archaeologists Carter and Callender are opening the innermost shrine containing Tutenkhamon's sarcophagus (1358 B.C.), which they discovered in 1924.*

4. *The Writing, Arts, and Science of the Egyptians*

In writing, art and architecture, and science the Egyptians made contributions to civilization. They developed a system of signs and pictures to use in their writing. Although their literature was not notable, they did write stories, histories, poems, and other works. Especially outstanding were their accomplishments in architecture. Their stone pyramids, the great Temple at Karnak, and the Great Sphinx of Gizeh are examples of their architectural achievements. Although Egyptian science often consisted of magic, the Egyptians also practiced medicine and had some knowledge of astronomy.

Writing: Methods

The Book of the Dead and other scrolls indicate that the Egyptians were able to develop the skill of writing. Writing was one of man's greatest inventions. Although the identity of the first people to write is uncertain, we know that writing was extremely important to the Egyptians. It helped them to keep a record of great events, to preserve their knowledge in various fields, to write literature, and to accomplish many other tasks of daily life and business.

In the beginning the Egyptians used pictures to represent objects. This is

■ *On the Rosetta Stone is a message in Egyptian hieroglyphics, simplified Egyptian writing, and Greek. Champollion used the Greek as a key to decipher Egyptian hieroglyphics.*

known as *hieroglyphics* or pictorial writing. These are some examples:

1. ▦ = lake   2. 🚶 = man

3. 〰️ = water

Next, they invented pictures to represent the sounds of *words*. Finally, they developed twenty-four signs to represent the sounds of *letters*.

□ = p   ⬭ = d

◗ = b

⌒ = t   ⊓ = h

The Egyptians had no vowels in their signs and they never completely used an alphabet. They mixed pictures of objects, pictures of words, and signs of letters in their writing. This writing was done by using a pointed reed for a pen. Scribes dipped the reed into an ink made by mixing water, vegetable gum, and soot from blackened pots. Then they wrote on *papyrus*, a river reed split into strips and used as "paper."

It was many centuries after the end of Egypt's great period before anyone was able to decipher Egyptian writing. Then in the early nineteenth century a Frenchman named Jean François Champollion worked out the meaning of the hieroglyphs on the so-called *Rosetta Stone*. This is a black basalt stone that was found in Egypt by some of Napoleon's soldiers. On its surface there appears the same inscription written in three different ways. At the top it is in Egyptian hieroglyphics; in the middle it is in simplified Egyptian writing; and at the bottom it is in Greek.

Champollion compared the part in the Greek language with the two sections in Egyptian. By this method he finally succeeded in deciphering the hidden meaning of many hieroglyphs and learned much about the fascinating civilization of the Egyptians.

Writing: Literature

The Egyptian literature that has been found was by no means distinguished. Nevertheless, it was important as one of the first steps in the development of written expression. The literature of Egypt included stories, histories, poetry, songs, and advice concerning moral conduct.

Some of the songs were quite simple, such as the chant that the threshers sang to their oxen:

> Thresh for yourselves. Thresh for
> yourselves.
> Straw to eat; corn for your masters;

Let not your heart be weary, your
lord is pleased.

Other poems were more elaborate, particularly where they praised a pharaoh.
Occasionally one finds in Egyptian literature a bit of advice that might well be followed today. The so-called *Prisse Papyrus*, for example, contains the following
suggestion concerning eating:

Restrain appetite; gluttony is base. . . . A cup
of water, it quenches the thirst, a mouthful
of melon, it stayeth the appetite. . . . It is a
base fellow who is mastered by his belly. . . .

Art and Architecture

Although the literature of the Egyptians
was not outstanding, their tool-making,
art, and architecture were very impressive.
It was extremely important to the development of future civilizations that the Egyptians learned how to smelt metals in closed
furnaces and how to *cast* copper, that is,
to shape it to a desired form. Axes, saws,
and other basic tools could be made of
copper and their effectiveness improved.

Egyptian paintings, which appeared in
many of the temples, had a flat "pancake"
effect (p. 41). The artists often painted
only the view from the side, did very little
color blending, and depicted objects without *perspective*, or depth. Nevertheless,
there is dignity and strength in the lines of
the painted figures, and the paintings tell
us much about the daily life of the people.

It was in the field of stone construction
and stone and wood sculpture that the
Egyptians were most impressive. Consider
the pyramids, where great blocks of granite
were fitted together precisely, like the
pieces of a gigantic jig-saw puzzle. Observe the dignity of the pointed *obelisks*,
the columns that commemorated the deeds
of the pharaohs. Or think of the great
Temple at Karnak and its magnificent
colonnaded hall.

■ *This sketch shows a clerestory in an Egyptian
temple. Egyptian architects constructed these
windows to light the interior of their temples.
Later civilizations borrowed this idea.*

Above all, there is the Great Sphinx of
Gizeh to remind us of the splendid stone
work of the Egyptians. The Sphinx, which
was carved from rock, consists of the head
of a king, Khafre, and the body of a lion.
The nose and beard of the Sphinx have
been blasted away by cannon-shot, but
there is still an odd smile on its ancient
stone face. Historian Will Durant has
called the Sphinx "a Mona Lisa in stone."

Egyptian architects did more than hand
down to us the tradition of grandeur and
size in the building of monuments. They
also passed along to later civilizations valuable ideas for the construction of clerestory
windows. A *clerestory* is the upper part of
a temple, rising above the roofs of the other
parts of the building, and its walls contain
windows for lighting the interior. Years
later, Christians borrowed from Egyptian
architecture in building the clerestories of
their churches, and today architects make

47

■ *The great Sphinx of Gizeh (right) consists of the head of a king, Khafre, and the body of a lion. The colonnaded hall of the Great Temple at Karnak (left) was the largest building in the Egyptian Empire.*

CULTURAL CHARACTERISTICS of Ancient Egypt

"In the 10 seconds it takes to read this paragraph, an average 140 tons of the United States will have been carried out to the sea by the Mississippi River and its tributaries. By this time tomorrow, we will have lost over 2 million tons to the Atlantic, Pacific, and the Gulf of Mexico!"

This striking statement from a 20th century airline brochure dramatizes the dynamic relationship between a man's country and a river. Similarly, the ancient Egyptians were aware of the close ties between their land and their river, the Nile. The main characteristics of their culture were:

The setting up of government to control the individual and the group.

The organization of forms of city life to serve as centers for political, social, and economic activities.

The acceptance of the concept of polytheism.

The development of skill in writing and mathematics.

The creation of impressive works in stone construction and stone and wood sculpture.

Yet even as the Egyptians developed these significant cultural contributions, they did so with the knowledge that the Nile River played a major role in their accomplishments. Indeed, when they wished to praise a Pharaoh to the highest, they hailed him as "a Nile which flows daily giving life to Egypt."

The culture of ancient Egypt was linked to the soil and nature, as closely as a prayer to the sun, a statue to an animal, a song to a river. "Plough the fields that thou mayest . . . receive thy bread," the Egyptians were told; and once bread had been earned, cultural activities could follow. Today Egypt is seeking to control nature by harnessing the tremendous power of the Nile River in the High Dam Project at Aswan. It will make possible cultivation of 2 million acres, improve navigation, increase electric power, and strengthen industrial production. Then as now, the aim is to seek harmony with nature.

Thus the modern Egyptians have recognized that nature, particularly the Nile, is a key to the development of their civilization. The cultural achievements of their ancestors, the ancient Egyptians, are impressive proof of that fact!

use of clerestory windows in modern houses and other buildings. Ancient Egypt thus became a reservoir of architectural ideas that were used by later peoples.

Music

Music, too, played a part in the lives of the Egyptians. Music was heard at religious ceremonies for the gods and at celebrations for military victories. Palaces had orchestras, and temples probably had choirs. The harp, flute, lute, and lyre were popular instruments. So was the *sistrum*, an instrument whose sound was produced by shaking a group of discs on wires. Even in the matter of death, there were Egyptians who thought of music. These men saw to it that instruments were buried in the vaults of the pyramids. If death was to carry the pharaohs on a long journey, music would make it more pleasant for them!

Science

The Egyptians also attempted to explain the physical facts of life by turning to science. Often Egyptian "science" consisted of superstitious efforts to drive out the dark demons of sickness which they thought had lodged themselves in a man's body. Magical sayings plus the eating of lizard's blood and tortoise's brains were considered to be "scientific cures" by some Egyptians.

On the other hand, Herodotus, a Greek historian, made mention of the great number of Egyptians who practiced medicine, not just magic. The so-called *Edwin Smith Papyrus* lists forty-eight cases in Egyptian clinical surgery. It is one of the earliest known scientific documents.

Egyptian medical men knew of the brain and called the heart the "center" of the human body. They were familiar with the anatomy of man as a result of their study of mummification. As for the care of the ordinary "black eye," they agreed with many of today's parents that the best thing to do is "bind fresh meat upon it."

The Egyptians used mathematics in many of their activities. They made careful measurements in planning their pyramids and in re-establishing the markers of their land that were washed away by the annual flood. They had knowledge of the ways to add, subtract, multiply, and divide, all of which were probably used in preparing the census lists for taxation. They were also familiar with fractions, simple geometry, and a type of decimal system.

The Egyptians had no knowledge of physics, but they knew something about astronomy. By counting the time between the moment that the star Sothis appeared in the east until it reappeared in the same place in the sky, they were able to draw up their calendar.

■ **Check on Your Reading**

1. Why was writing so important to the Egyptians?

2. How did Champollion decipher Egyptian writing?

3. What are the principal characteristics of Egyptian art?

4. Evaluate Egyptian contributions in (a) literature, (b) art and architecture, and (c) music.

5. How did Egyptian "science" differ from ours?

6. What real progress did the Egyptians make in medicine and mathematics?

MAN AND HIS CULTURE

Let's Meet the People!

This sketch of an Egyptian peasant is based on several sources: the writings of Herodotus; V. Gordon Childe, *New Light on the Most Ancient East*, 1953, Praeger; and Sir J. Gardner Wilkinson, *A Popular Account of the Ancient Egyptians*, Harper & Brothers.

An Egyptian Peasant

The Egyptian peasant was of medium height, thin, and muscular. He had dark hair, which he sometimes shaved completely; a clean-shaven face; and skin browned by the sun. In the fields, he wore a cloth around his loins; but he had no shoes. At home, he put on a linen garment. He wore a ring and colorful earrings.

The peasant lived in a simple cottage with walls of crude brick. Its flat roof was made of palm branches thrown across beams, over which mats were placed and covered with mud. Most of the year he and his family slept on the roof. The cottage had three small windows and a single door. At night, a seed-oil lamp gave light.

The peasant's food was simple: bread, vegetables, fish, and barley beer. As a treat, he would catch a bird, salt it, and eat it uncooked. As a freeman the peasant's life was not so hard as that of a slave. A freeman was not "owned" so he could not be transferred from one master to another. However, the peasant worked long hours ploughing the earth and planting wheat, barley, sorghum, vegetables, and flax. His tools were a wooden hoe with a stone blade, a wooden sickle that had flint teeth, a copper axe, a bronze saw, and a plough, made mostly of wood, which was drawn by two oxen. The land belonged to the pharaoh, and the peasant tilled it only by paying a large tax.

On feast days, the peasant, who believed that the gods were powerful, joined religious processions to the temple. There priests performed ceremonies in honor of Amon, Osiris, and other gods.

Thus the peasant lived. When he died, no stone monuments would be raised in his honor. Such glories were reserved for Pharaohs—not for simple men of the soil!

CHAPTER REVIEW

REVIEW and DISCUSSION

1. Identify the people and places and explain the events and terms on p. 18.

2. Which features of Egyptian civilization do you think were most important to the Egyptians? to our civilization? Why?

3. What features of Egyptian government do we still have in modern times? Why did some features disappear and others endure?

4. Why is the development of city life one of the first signs of civilization?

5. How was the Egyptian Empire built? Who were its rulers?

6. Do you agree or disagree with the statement: "The story of man is continuous, and yesterday, today, and tomorrow merge without a break?" Why?

7. How did the Egyptians determine dates?

8. How was the Great Pyramid constructed? What knowledge, skills, and tools were necessary?

9. How does the Egyptian belief in immortality differ from yours?

10. Why do you think the Egyptians practiced polytheism and rejected monotheism? Give reasons for your answer.

11. Arnold Toynbee, the great British historian, has stated that religion is one of the most inspiring influences in the history of man and his progress in civilization. What part did religion play in Egypt's progress?

12. What Egyptian invention do you think had the greatest value to man? Why?

ACTIVITIES

1. In your notebook section on "Why Great Civilizations Rise and Fall," analyze the causes for the rise and decline of the ancient Egyptian civilization. Consider environmental factors and significant cultural influences.

2. On a map, locate Asia Minor, the Great Pyramid (Gizeh), Karnak, Mediterranean, Memphis, the Nile River and Delta, Red Sea, Sinai Peninsula, Syria, and Thebes.

3. Write a sentence using pictures instead of words. How useful do you think picture writing was as a means of communication?

4. Find out how the Egyptians made paper.

5. Make a scroll using material from *The Book of the Dead* or other Egyptian literature.

6. Write a report on *one* of the following topics: Egyptian agriculture, architecture, art, family, government, literature, music, religion, science, costumes, or hieroglyphics.

7. Arrange to show a film, filmstrip, or slides on Egypt.

8. Invite a local speaker to present a travelogue about his trip to Egypt.

PAST and PRESENT

1. Find articles on the flooding of ancient Egyptian remains by the building of the new Aswan Dam. What problems are involved? What do you think should be done?

2. What problems of modern Egypt are similar to those of ancient Egypt?

SUGGESTED READINGS

Basic books: BROWNE, LEWIS, *The World's Great Scriptures*, Macmillan. An anthology of selected writings from sacred books of ten principal religions.

CERAM, CURT W., *Gods, Graves, and Scholars*, Knopf. Accounts on archaeology.

EVANS, MARY, *Costumes Throughout the Ages*, Chap. 1, Lippincott. Well illustrated.

GARDNER, HELEN, *Art Through the Ages*, Chap. 3, Harcourt, Brace.

MILLS, DOROTHY, *Book of the Ancient World*, Putnam.

TAYLOR, F. SHERWOOD, *An Illustrated History of Science*, Praeger.

Special accounts: BREASTED, JAMES H., *History of Egypt*, Scribner.

Fiction: McGRAW, ELOISE, *Mara: Daughter of the Nile*, Coward-McCann.

Chapter 3   Early Civilizations and Gods of India

KEYNOTE   Every time we tell children the tale of Jack and his magic beanstalk or Puss and his seven-league boots, we are touching the pulse of ancient India. Such familiar fables and legends are not of Western or European origin, but they can be traced back to Indian sources.

In similar fashion, every time we write a zero or work with equations we are dipping back into time to draw on ideas that were present in India many years ago. Little wonder that India has been called "the world's teacher" in such varied fields as fables, mathematics, grammar, philosophy, and even chess!

Yet, of all of her teachings, none are more interesting than those involving religious ideas. As the philosopher Lin Yu-t'ang has pointed out: "India is a land and people intoxicated with god." The people of India have searched for the purpose and meaning of life as strenuously as others have sought for riches. *This fascination with problems of the spirit has been the outstanding feature of Indian life from earliest times to the present.*

Key People   *Gautama Buddha*

Key Places   *India   ·   Himalaya Mountains   ·   Indus River   ·   Harappa   ·   Mohenjo-daro   ·   Punjab   ·   Ganges River*

Key Events   *Harappa destroyed   ·   Indo-Aryans invade India*

Key Terms   *Harappan civilization · caste system · Brahmans · Hinduism · Buddhism   ·   Sanskrit   ·   Arabic numerals   ·   Vedic Age   · Dravidians   ·   ahimsa   ·   Bhagavad-Gita   ·   outcastes*

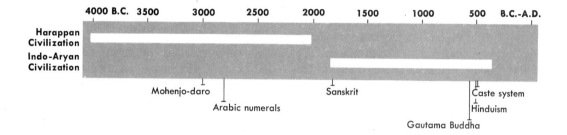

| 4000 B.C. | 3500 | 3000 | 2500 | 2000 | 1500 | 1000 | 500 | B.C.-A.D. |

Harappan
Civilization

Indo-Aryan
Civilization

Mohenjo-daro

Arabic numerals

Sanskrit

Gautama Buddha

Caste system

Hinduism

1. India Is Many "Worlds" in One

India is a vast subcontinent that projects southward from the rest of Asia like a huge triangle pointing into the Indian Ocean. It is bounded on the east by the Bay of Bengal, on the west by the Arabian Sea, and on the north by the Himalayas, the highest mountains in the world. Only in the northwest are there openings in the great Himalayan wall, and through these the Indus River flows on its way to the sea (map, p. 54).

Historical Importance of India's Geographic Barriers: India's natural barriers of seas and mountains limited the country's contact with European peoples for many years.

India's area is about half the size of the continental United States and most of it lies within the tropics. The climate ranges from the cold and fog of the Himalaya Mountains to the heat of the dry regions where, as historian Will Durant points out, "the only relief . . . is to sit still, to do nothing, to desire nothing."

Historical Importance of India's Tropical Location: Since most of India lies within the tropics, the country developed a tropical agricultural economy. This economy influenced the development of Indian society and affected political events.

India's terrain shows many variations. India has fertile river valleys in the northwest and northeast, high plateaus farther south, plains, and impenetrable jungles.

Historical Importance of the Variety of India's Terrain: Differences in the land formations helped to develop variations in the attitudes, customs, and manner of living of the people.

India is a land that changes its color with the ease of a native lizard and with more surprising results. To visit the country is to recognize that there is not one India—but many. Each region is a fascinating "world" of its own.

■ Check on Your Reading

1. What effect had India's natural geographic barriers on its history?

2. In what temperature zone does most of India fall? Name two effects of this location.

3. How do you explain the variety of attitudes, manners, and customs?

53

2. Harappa: Ancient Civilization of the Indus Valley

Antiquity, or the ancient period, is a partially opened package whose contents continually surprise us. Recent probings into antiquity have revealed that there was a third civilization in India whose age might rival that of the Egyptians and the Sumerians. Archaeologists named this early civilization *Harappa*, after a village which rests above the ruins of one ancient city.

What Was the Harappan Civilization Like?

The Harappan civilization, which possibly dates as far back as 4000 B.C., was located in northwest India in the valley of the Indus River. It was probably twice the size of the Old Kingdom of Egypt and six times the kingdom of Sumer! This civilization included over sixty towns and villages and at least two major cities, Mohenjo-daro on the Indus and Harappa on the Ravi tributary. Estimates place the total population between 70,000 and 100,000 people.

By 2500 B.C. the Harappan civilization was well organized and showed careful planning. Cities were constructed in one-mile squares, and houses were built of fired brick. Bathrooms had paved floors, drains in the house led to sewage systems, and walls contained rubbish chutes!

Outside the cities, the people grew wheat, barley, peas, and cotton; and they domesticated cattle, goats, and sheep. Craftsmen worked with bronze and precious metals, and potters used the wheel. The people seemed more concerned with peace than war. Certainly, their weapons of slings and maces were neither elaborate nor numerous.

■ *The Indian subcontinent has many variations in terrain and land formation— mountains, plateaus, valleys and jungles. Find them on the map. What early civilization developed? Name its principal cities.*

INDIA

■ *This seal-amulet of a "Urus bull" is a Harappan seal, which was probably used to stamp property.*

Museum of Fine Arts, Boston

Harappan Civilization Touches India

The Harappan civilization was noteworthy for both its careful city planning and its preference for peace over war. Three other contributions were equally important: (1) the development of a system of writing, consisting of a hieroglyphic script; (2) the establishment of a uniform method of weighing goods, making trading easier; and (3) the use of a linear measurement system, based on a foot of 13.2 inches.

In addition, the people of Mohenjo-daro were successful traders who had contact with the Tigris-Euphrates and Egypt.

Several features of Harappan life still seem to touch India today. For example, boats and carts in modern India reveal many similarities to those used in Harappa; and many Indian people still continue the Harappan customs of wearing bracelets, anklets, and nose ornaments. The existence of such remnants is proof that the past is vitally related to the present.

Harappan civilization lasted until about 2000 B.C., when it was destroyed. India, Egypt, and Sumer share the honor of being

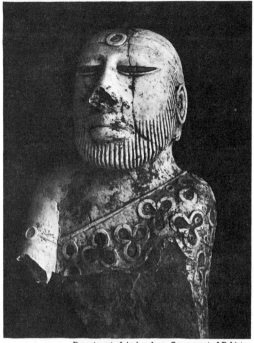

Department of Archaeology, Government of Pakistan

■ *This figure from Mohenjo-daro may represent a priest-king. Note the domineering face, receding forehead, and thick lips.*

the birthplaces of civilization. A recent discovery of an ancient civilization at Kot Diji, also in West Pakistan, may add to our knowledge of early peoples.

■ Check on Your Reading

1. When did Harappa flourish?
2. What were the major practical and intellectual achievements of Harappan civilization?

3. The Indo-Aryans Spread Through India

At least a few hundred years after the decline of the Harappan civilization, tribes speaking an early Indo-European language filtered through the northwest passages of India and spread throughout the country. These were the *Indo-Aryans*, a fair-skinned people who originally may have come from central Europe and the territory near the Caspian Sea. During the so-called "Vedic Age" (about 1800–1000 B.C.), they took control of the northwest region known as the Punjab. Then, in the "Epic Age" (1000–500 B.C.), they moved eastward to settle in the Ganges Valley (map, p. 54).

55

■ *These rock-cut Hindu temples at Mamallapuram, near Madras, India, are outstanding examples of Dravidian architecture. They were built by the Pallava king, Narasimhavarman II (680–720 A.D.). The temple pillars exemplify the distinctive Pallava style.*

The Indo-Aryans had come as strangers to a strange land, and they sought security by conquering the *Dravidians*, the short, dark-skinned natives who blocked their way farther south. Once the Indo-Aryans had demonstrated their superiority over the Dravidians in war, they felt that they had to maintain their position in peace. Therefore, they attempted to keep themselves apart from the conquered natives. Above all, they tried to prevent the intermarriage of Indo-Aryans and Dravidians. To do this they set up a *caste* system. *Caste* or *varna* (color) originally meant the rigid separation of the fair-skinned Indo-Aryans from the dark-skinned Dravidians.

In time, the word *caste* broadened to include a rigid division of the Indo-Aryans themselves into distinct groups. We cannot be certain of the reasons for the establishment of caste separations among the Indo-Aryans. Perhaps it was a result of a desire to keep members of the same occupation together. Possibly it was a device used by the priests and nobles so that they could remain above the common people. Regardless of the reason, each caste eventually became permanent.

The Caste System Divides Society

By 500 B.C. four principal castes based on occupations had developed. From the highest to the lowest these castes were (1) *Brahmans*—priests and teachers of religion, (2) *Kshatriyas*—warriors and rulers, (3) *Vaisyas*—craftsmen, merchants, and free

56

farmers, and (4) *Sudras*—servants and serfs. (Serfs are persons bound to work the soil under the will of their masters.)

Besides these four castes, there were prisoners of war, slaves, and others who had been ejected from their castes for violation of its customs or rules. These people were considered to be so low in the social scale that they were called *outcastes*. They were permitted to do only the ugliest jobs and to live in the worst quarters.

Caste regulations forbade a member of one caste to marry someone from another caste or even to eat meals with him. The life of the outcastes was even more limited. They were considered to be "untouchables," and members of other castes were not permitted to shake their hands, touch their garments, or have any contact with them. Even an outcaste's shadow was thought to be unclean.

The Faith of the Hindus

The Indo-Aryans thus developed a caste system that divided the people into separate layers of society. The descendants of these early Indo-Aryan tribes were the *Hindus*. After 500 B.C. the Hindus broadened the number of castes, until today there are over 2000 subcastes in India!

The Hindus also made many changes and additions to the religion of their Indo-Aryan ancestors, who originally had worshipped Sun, Wind, Fire, and other nature gods. Today the religion of *Hinduism* has been accepted by over three hundred eighty million people in India. Although there are many differences in individual worship, the faith of the Hindus generally includes the following beliefs:

1. BELIEF IN THE UNITY OF ALL THINGS IN THE WORLD. Imagine that there is a single string running through all of us. Each person might say that the part of the string within him belongs to him alone. On the other hand, his part is only a small piece of the whole string that unites everyone.

In like fashion, the Hindus believe that there is one spirit that runs through all humans, animals, and plants—through everything in the world. Since a part of this spirit is found in each of us, we are all spiritually united. The Hindus call this unifying spirit *Brahman*.

2. BELIEF IN AHIMSA. The Hindus believe in *ahimsa*, or the non-injury of any living creature. Since the Hindus feel that we are all united by the same spirit, or Brahman, many of them do not injure or kill animals or eat meat. The cow is especially cared for, and to kill one is considered a terrible sin.

Some Hindus today even use a broom to sweep a path before them, so that they will not accidentally step on any tiny insects hidden in the dust. Others prepare special feasts made of rice flour for ants. And Mahatma Gandhi told of his mother's refusal to kill a poisonous scorpion that she found in the house!

3. BELIEF IN MANY GODS WHO ARE DIFFERENT FORMS OF ONE GOD. The Hindus worship many gods: Brahma the Creator, Vishnu the Preserver, Siva the Destroyer, and others. Each of these gods is considered by Hindu scholars to be only a special form of the one God in the world. In a sense, the Hindu God wears many masks and plays many roles, but underneath each he remains unchanged. In the *Bhagavad-Gita*, which is part of a Hindu religious epic, a form of the one God says:

Some [people] bow to the countless gods
    that are only
My million faces.

And a warrior later proclaims: "Ah, my God, I see all gods within your body."

4. BELIEF IN TRANSMIGRATION OF SOULS. The Hindus believe that when a person dies, he will be reborn as another living

creature. This movement, or *transmigration*, of the soul from one body to the next applies to animals as well as to human beings. For example, the soul of a dead animal might *transmigrate*, or move, to the body of a child about to be born. According to the *Bhagavad-Gita*, this cycle or "wheel of rebirth and death" goes on and on: "Just as the dweller in this body passes through childhood, youth, and old age, so at death he merely passes into another kind of body."

5. BELIEF IN KARMA. Where the soul of a dead person moves depends on *Karma*. Karma is a spiritual law of the universe that has great power, even though we cannot see or touch it. It records the good and bad deeds that a man does while he is alive and determines where he will go in his next life. For example, if a person led an evil life, his soul might next move to the

body of a lowly animal as a punishment. On the other hand, if he performed many good deeds, he might be rewarded by being reborn a Hindu of the highest caste.

It is important to note that transmigration of souls and Karma are closely connected with the caste system. Members of the highest caste, the Brahmans, are said to have been born into their position as a reward for their good behavior in a previous life. Outcastes are supposed to be suffering for the evil deeds that they committed in their last life.

6. BELIEF IN WORKING WITHOUT WORRYING ABOUT RESULTS. Hindus believe that a man should do his work in the best way that he can without worrying about success or failure. They accept the idea that:

Work done with anxiety about results is far inferior to work done without such anxiety. . . . They who work selfishly for results are miserable.

Today in India these six beliefs still form the basis of the Hindu religion and affect Hindu life. Caste no longer depends on a man's occupation, but caste limits or determines occupation in many cases. The caste system is being broken down very gradually. The recent Indian constitution has outlawed the restrictions against outcastes, and the miserable lot of these "untouchables" will probably improve. The first "untouchable" to become head of an Indian state took office in 1960.

■ *A bronze statue of Siva the Destroyer shows Siva's power as a dancer performing his divine dance of creation and destruction.*

Von der Heydt collection, Rietberg Museum, Zurich

■ **Check on Your Reading**

1. What two racial groups existed in India by 500 B.C.? Which dominated the other?

2. What was the basis for the caste system? How did it divide society?

3. Identify: Brahman, Hinduism, ahimsa, *Bhagavad-Gita*, transmigration of souls, outcastes, Karma.

4. Explain the six beliefs that are basic to Hinduism.

4. Gautama and the Religion of Buddhism

By the sixth century B.C. some Hindus had come to stress the importance of religious ceremonies more than they did good behavior. They apparently thought that if they performed certain rituals their sins would be forgiven, even though they continued to live undisciplined lives. As a result of their conduct, other Hindus became dissatisfied with their faith and were ready to listen to the words of new religious leaders.

Prince Gautama and Buddhism

The man to whom they were to turn was Prince Siddhartha Gautama (about 563–483 B.C.). He was the son of a rich king who ruled a part of northeast India. While he had everything that he wanted, Gautama was disturbed by the misery of some of his people. Therefore, at the age of twenty-nine, he left his palaces and luxuries, and his wife and infant son, to search for the cause and solution for suffering.

For almost seven years Gautama wandered in a forest trying to find the reason for unhappiness in the world. He wore the clothes of a beggar and, according to legend, he sometimes lived on a single grain of rice for a day and tested his courage by lying on thorns. Finally, after sitting for forty-nine days under a tree, he felt that he was "enlightened"; that is, he knew the way to conquer suffering. Therefore, he was called the *Buddha*, or "the enlightened one," and for many years Gautama Buddha preached his message to the people of north India.

The Faith of the Buddhists

Buddhism, the religion that was started as a result of the teachings of Gautama Buddha, includes the belief in "Four Noble Truths": (1) There is suffering in the world. (2) Suffering is caused by selfish

■ *A head of the Buddha, carved from schist, is from Gandhara, India. Sculptors made Buddha images when Mahayana Buddhism was introduced in India.*

desire to have things. (3) Suffering can be removed if we will do away with our selfish desire. (4) We can do away with selfish desire by following a "Middle Path," or by never going to extremes. To keep to the "Middle Path" follow the eight principles of proper conduct. These principles, known as the "Eightfold Path," include right views, right intention, right speech, right action, right livelihood, right effort, right mindfulness, and right concentration.

The Buddhists believed that if they accepted the "Four Noble Truths," suffering would be conquered, and they would find *Nirvana*, a state of happiness and peace. Buddhists of ancient times stressed the importance of man's conduct, rather than emphasizing his performance of ceremonies. How a person acted was more important than how often he recited prayers.

59

Buddhism absorbed many teachings of Hinduism, such as its opposition to violence. Buddhists did not support the Hindu caste system. Gautama himself had told his followers:

Go into all lands and preach this [truth]. Tell them that the poor and the lowly, the rich and the high are all one, and that all castes unite in this religion as do the rivers in the sea.

Buddhism eventually lost most of its followers in India, but later it greatly influenced such countries as Thailand and Japan.

■ **Check on Your Reading**

1. How did Gautama Buddha develop his new religion?
2. Explain the basic teachings of Buddhism. What are the "Four Noble Truths"?

5. Contributions of Indian Civilization

In addition to developing the religions of Hinduism and Buddhism, the people of ancient India made at least three important contributions to future civilizations: (1) They passed on an abundance of legends, fables, and tales. (2) They advanced the knowledge of mathematics. (3) They produced a literature in *Sanskrit*.

Indian Legends, Fables, and Tales

Many stories that we tell children (including *The Adventures of Sinbad the Sailor*) can be traced to old Indian tales. From India probably came the custom of using stories to provide common sense advice. Consider these rhymes from the *Panchatantra*, a collection of Indian fables:

On Common Sense
Scholarship is less than sense
Therefore seek intelligence.

On Rascals
Caress a rascal as you will,
He was, and is a rascal still:
All salve and sweating-treatments fail
To take the kink from doggy's tail.

On Working Together
Woodpecker and sparrow
With froggy and gnat
Attacking *together* laid
The elephant flat.

Indian Knowledge of Mathematics

Many of our ideas of decimals, minus signs, and so-called "Arabic" numerals (1, 2, 3, 4, 5, 6, 7, 8, 9) can be traced back to India. So can our place-value system of numbers, in which we say 1865 is one thousand, eight hundred, sixty-five because of each number's *place* in the figure.

The zero plays a vital part in the place-value system. Some believe that the zero was of Babylonian origin, while others think that the Hindus were the first to use it. One point is certain: The zero appeared in early Indian civilization.

It is believed that the Arabs took the idea of the zero from the Indians and carried it to Europe in the eighth century A.D. The spreading of its use was of great importance to future civilizations. Man could write a complicated term such as ten thou-

SANSKRIT	GREEK	LATIN	GERMAN	ENGLISH
nama	onoma	nomen	Name	name
napat	anepsios	nepos	Neffe	nephew
bhrata	phrater	frater	Bruder	brother
tree	tria	tres	drei	three

sand, one hundred, six with only five numbers—10,106! Without the zero, we would need many additional symbols to set down large numbers.

Sanskrit Language and Literature

When the Indo-Aryans came into northern India, they brought with them and developed an Indo-European language that eventually was called *Sanskrit.* There are many similarities between Sanskrit and other Indo-European languages (see Chart). Sanskrit was a language that was used by scholars and priests; most of the people spoke a variety of dialects.

Sanskrit was an important contribution. Indian scholars worked out a system of Sanskrit grammar that later influenced the study of the grammar of other languages. Scribes also used Sanskrit to write down the *Vedas,* collections of hymns of the so-called "Vedic Age" (about 1800–1000 B.C.). The oldest and most famous of these collections, the *Rig-Veda,* adds to our knowledge of the life of the early Indo-Aryan tribes.

■ Check on Your Reading

1. Name the forms of Indian literature.
2. What great contribution did India make in mathematics? in language?

CULTURAL CHARACTERISTICS of Ancient India

The peoples of ancient India made contributions in the fields of legends and fables, mathematics, and Sanskrit grammar and literature. The characteristics of their cultures were marked by:

The development of a caste system that divided the inhabitants into separate layers of society. Economic, social, and political activities in India were greatly affected by these divisions.

The development of two major religions, Hinduism and Buddhism, and the stress placed on the spiritual aspects of life.

In the *Upanishads,* ancient Hindu scriptures, it is pointed out that one spirit runs through everything in the world. A father and son are talking:

'Place this salt in water, and then wait on me in the morning.'
The son did as he was commanded.
The father said to him: 'Bring me the salt, which you placed in the water last night.'
The son having looked for it, found it not, for, of course, it was melted.

The father said: 'Taste it from the surface of the water. How is it?' The son replied: 'It is salt.'
. . . .
Then the father said: 'Here also, in this body . . . you do not perceive the [Spirit], my son; but there indeed it is.'

This belief in an omnipresent, unifying spirit dominated many aspects of ancient Indian culture.

The passage of time has not brought real unity to India, however. Hinduism as a religion has been modified by local custom and belief, and takes a variety of forms. Cultural unity is difficult in a land where there are 179 languages—including 15 with official status—and 544 dialects.

Faced with the problems of a divided India, such modern leaders as Jawaharlal Nehru, Prime Minister of the country in 1958, did not hesitate to seek spiritual strength in the rich heritage of ancient India. He declared: "There is such a thing as a national culture, with its deep roots in the nation's soil and its history. To uproot a nation is to destroy the soul of that nation, which made it a living entity through the ages...."

MAN AND HIS CULTURE

Let's Meet the People!

This description of a wedding ceremony in the "Vedic Age" is based on primary source materials in: Margaret Cormack, *The Hindu Woman*, 1953, Bureau of Publications, Teachers College, Columbia University; and Zénaide A. Ragozin, *Vedic India*, Putnam's Sons.

An Indo-Aryan Bride and Groom

The Indo-Aryan bride and groom of the "Vedic Age" knew that the purpose of marriage was to bind them together as harmoniously as the sun and moon, "two children who wander one after the other by their wonderful power."

Contrary to the low position that women were later to hold in Indian society, the Indo-Aryan bride was considered to be on an equal footing with her husband-to-be. Although he had purchased his bride, the groom had made sure to gain her consent to marriage. She had already placed a wreath of flowers and leaves on his shoulders to show that she approved of him.

The bride and groom were now brought before a sacred fire where the priest blessed them as they joined hands. The bridegroom next took the bride's right hand and led her seven steps—called the *sapt-padi*—around the fire. As he did so, he recited the following:

I take thy hand as a pledge of our happiness; I wish thee to become my wife and to grow old with me; the gods gave thee to me to rule over our house together.... May there be happiness in our home for both humans and animals.... Come, O desired one, beautiful one with the tender heart, with the charming look, good toward thine husband, kind toward animals, destined to bring forth heroes.

After the bride and groom were thus formally united, the priest turned to those who had attended the ceremony and said: "Approach her [the bride], look at her, wish her well, and return to your own home."

When the bride arrived at her husband's house, there were additional ceremonies. As she crossed the threshold, she was told:

Here may delight be thine through wealth and children.... Live with thy husband and in old age mayest thou still rule thy household. Remain here now, never to depart; enjoy the full measure of thy years playing with sons and grandsons. Be glad of heart within thy home.

Finally, the priest accepted a gift of a cow from the bride's parents and pronounced a benediction on the newlyweds:

Remain here ... pass your lives together, happy in your home.... O generous Indra [a great Indo-Aryan god] make her [the bride] fortunate! May she have a beautiful family; may she give her husband ten children! May he himself [the husband] be like the eleventh!

The husband now rubbed vermilion, a red coloring matter, in his wife's hair parting and on her forehead. This was the sign that they were at last one.

CHAPTER REVIEW

REVIEW and DISCUSSION

1. Identify the people and places and explain the events and terms on page 52.

2. As a cradle of civilization, how did the Indus Valley compare with the Nile and Tigris-Euphrates in size, climate, floods, soil conditions, resources, and products?

3. "Variety" is a key word in the study of India. How does variety help or harm?

4. What differences or similarities can you find between Harappan civilization and the civilizations of the peoples in Chaps. 1 and 2? How do you explain them?

5. Would you agree or disagree with the statement: "The five main achievements of Harappan civilization were of equal importance"? Why?

6. Prove or disprove the statement: "Harappan preference for peace over war was surprising for the ancient [and modern] world."

7. How did the Indian caste system discourage personal ambition? with what result?

8. What part of India's ancient culture can be attributed to climate?

9. What were some factors which caused the people of India to be fascinated by the problems of the spirit?

10. Can you find any similarities between some of your beliefs and those of Hindus and Buddhists? How do you explain them?

11. Cite evidence to support the statement: "The western world does well to look eastward beyond Europe to find some of its heritage."

12. Would you agree or disagree with these generalizations? Why? (a) If a river is suitable for transportation and all other factors are equal, a civilization will develop. (b) If a higher class disapproves of intermarriage with a lower class, a caste system will develop.

13. What generalizations can you make about this chapter?

ACTIVITIES

1. On a map of India locate the Arabian Sea, Bay of Bengal, Ganges River, Harappa, Himalaya Mountains, Indian Ocean, Indus River, Pakistan, and the Punjab.

2. Pretend that you are a Hindu or a Buddhist in India. Give a talk on your religious beliefs. Consult references.

3. Write a paragraph on "The Problems of the Spirit in Ancient India."

4. Debate the statement: Resolved, that suffering can be removed if we will do away with our selfish desire.

5. Add India to your chart on the "Causes of the Rise and Fall of Civilizations."

PAST and PRESENT

1. In *Readers' Guide* find some articles on India. What similarities can you find to the ancient India described in this chapter?

2. In *Readers' Guide* find articles about the efforts that are being made to bring about new reforms which may break down old customs and beliefs in India.

SUGGESTED READINGS

Basic books: GARDNER, HELEN, *Art Through the Ages*, Chap. 8, Harcourt, Brace.

LIFE, *The World's Great Religions*, Simon and Schuster. History of the great religions.

SMITH, GOLDWIN, *The Heritage of Man*, Chap. 5, Scribner.

WELLS, H. G., *Outline of History*, Doubleday. Brief account of ancient India.

Special accounts: FITCH, FLORENCE, *Their Search for God, Ways of Worship in the Orient*, Lothrop, Lee & Shepard. Sections on Hinduism and Buddhism.

NEHRU, JAWAHARLAL, *The Discovery of India*, Doubleday. Contains Nehru's account of ancient India.

WALLBANK, T. WALTER, *Short History of India and Pakistan*, MD 224, New American Library. Information on the ancient forces which have shaped India and Pakistan.

Biography and Fiction: DOUGLAS, WILLIAM ORVILLE, *Beyond the High Himalayas*, Doubleday. A book of adventurous travel.

GAER, JOSEPH, *Adventures of Rama*, Little, Brown. A religious legend.

Chapter 4   Ancient China and a Search for Order

KEYNOTE   A newspaper reporter returning recently from Communist China reported this scene in a factory run as a commune:

On the wall of the mess hall, painted in ochre characters, there is a poem said to have been composed by a woman who was illiterate "before the liberation," and who has learned to read through the ideological education given by the Communists:

> *The machine is my husband,*
> *The factory is my family,*
> *The fruits of my labor are my children,*
> *The party* [Communist] *is my father and mother.*

This "Communist party line" continually focuses the spotlight on the activities of the Chinese Communists today. Yet there is far more to Chinese history than the fact that the Communists have lighted their Red flare over China. Certainly, the older civilizations of China have made major contributions to our lives. For example, the ancient Chinese contributed to the development of the compass, printing, ceramics, painting, and silk production. They also are believed to have invented the wheelbarrow, the crossbow, the suspension bridge, and canal-lock gates. And the orange, peach, pear, rose, camellia, azalea have all come to the West from China and its borderlands.

Above all, ancient Chinese scholars helped to develop for the world the idea that man's main purpose was to lead a happy and useful life on this earth. Man, they said, should not concern himself with questions about the nature of heaven and the after-life. Rather, he should live out his life here in accordance with his own nature.

This idea—*that man should set the standards for his conduct on this earth*—is one key to understanding the people of ancient China.

Key People   *Confucius   ·   Lao-Tse   ·   Shih Huang Ti*

Key Places   *China   ·   Canton   ·   Peiping   ·   Harbin   ·   Hwang Ho   ·   Yangtze River*

Key Events   *Shang dynasty   ·   Chou dynasty "Classical Age"   ·   First Chinese Empire established   ·   "Great Wall" built   ·   Han dynasty*

Key Terms   *pictograms   ·   ideograms   ·   feudalism   ·   Golden Rule   ·   Taoism*

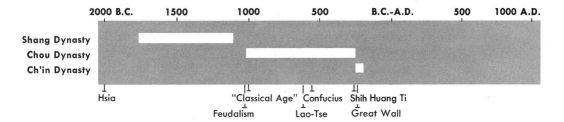

| 2000 B.C. | 1500 | 1000 | 500 | B.C.-A.D. | 500 | 1000 A.D. |

Shang Dynasty
Chou Dynasty
Ch'in Dynasty

Hsia
"Classical Age" Confucius Shih Huang Ti
Feudalism Lao-Tse Great Wall

1. China: A Land of Contrasts

China is a vast land that has been worked for centuries by the labor of men, rather than by machines. At one time it seemed as though "a million men with tea-spoons [for tools]" were trying to turn over the richness of the Chinese earth. Today over seven hundred million people live in this area. Though they are making great efforts to industrialize, manual labor is still more important than machines.

"Greater China," which includes China Proper, Tibet, Sinkiang, Inner Mongolia, and Manchuria (map, p. 66), is larger than the United States in area. Geographer George B. Cressey has calculated that if a map of all of China were placed on top of a map of North America on the same scale, China would reach from Puerto Rico to southern Hudson's Bay, and from the Atlantic to the Pacific. So extensive is "Greater China" that Canton lies in the same latitude as Havana, Cuba; Peking corresponds to Washington, D. C.; and Harbin parallels Montreal, Canada.

Historical Importance of China's Huge Size: The immensity of China has made it extremely difficult for any government in history to control all of it.

China Proper, the area we are studying in this chapter, is bounded on the east by the Pacific Ocean, on the south and west by the Himalaya Mountains, and on the northeast by mountains and plateaus. China's least protected frontier is in the

north, and a Chinese emperor in the third century B.C. built a "Great Wall" there to provide added safety against invaders.

Historical Importance of China's Geographic Barriers: China was hemmed in by a natural framework of mountain, ocean, and desert barriers. These cut the country off from extensive contact with other civilizations and peoples for many years.

All of China's great rivers, such as the Hwang Ho (Yellow River) and the Yangtze, flow eastward, but land conditions vary from north to south. North China is dry and dust-blown, and its plains are pow-dered with a fertile yellow or tan soil known as *loess*. It is a land of wheat and millet. South China is mountainous and hilly, but it is also a green humid region with many rivers and canals. It is a land of rice. An old Chinese saying points out the difference between north and south in the following way: "A Northerner to ride a horse, a Southerner to sail a boat."

Historical Importance of Geographic Differences between North and South: The differences in land conditions helped develop different histories and economies in north China and south China.

A country as large as China is naturally a land of contrasts. For example, these are some of China's geographic contrasts: (1) Rainfall varies from an inch a year in the deserts to nearly a hundred inches

65

along the coastal mountains. (2) Land formations differ. The bed of the Hwang Ho is so level with the land in certain places that it sometimes overflows its banks and is called "China's Sorrow." On the other hand, one-half of China's territory is more than a mile high. (3) China has frequent storms along the coast, averaging five typhoons a year between July and October. Yet some inland areas rarely have storms. (4) Temperatures range from intense heat in the far south to bitter cold in the far north, although much of China is in the temperate zone.

Equally important was the fact that ancient China was largely cut off from contact with Europeans. Chinese scholars thought of their land as the center of the world and called it *Chung-kuo*, or "Middle Kingdom."

■ **Check on Your Reading**

1. What kept China from contact with other civilizations for many centuries?
2. How did north and south China differ?

■ *China is a vast land of geographic contrasts. How did geography influence Chinese history?*

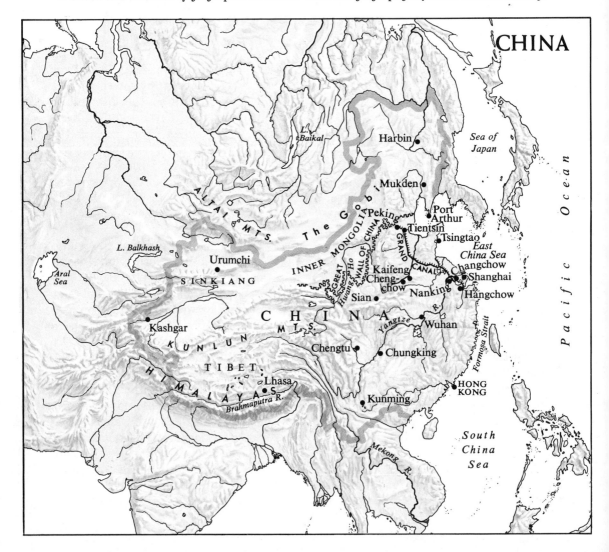

CHINA

2. Facts Replace Legends in China's History

The history of China reaches so far back in time that legend sometimes mingles with fact and colors it with fantastic figures. A Chinese legend recounts that long ago P'an Ku, the first man, made various parts of the earth using a giant chisel and mallet. P'an Ku was supposed to have grown six feet every day until he finished his work—and he worked 18,000 years. When he died, his head became the mountains, his veins the rivers, his sweat the rain, his beard the stars, and the insects that clung to his body the human beings!

Archaeologists have labelled P'an Ku as a creature invented by man's imagination. They have preferred to rely on evidence in the earth for the story of prehistoric China. Their excavations have revealed that primitive human beings lived in China in the time between 300,000 and 800,000 years ago. Remains of the type of man who lived sometime in this period near Peking, China, have been put together to form the so-called "Peking man."

The "Peking man" may have been the distant ancestor of the Chinese, although it is also possible that the Chinese migrated into China from neighboring areas. We know for certain that as early as 2000 B.C. a people who had learned how to farm and how to make and use bone tools had settled in northern China. Some people believe that their farming settlements along the Hwang Ho (Yellow River) grew into the first Chinese kingdom, ruled by a family known as the *Hsia*. But there is no conclusive proof that the Hsia ever existed.

The Shang Dynasty

"Oracle bones," on the other hand, assure us that the first real dynasty of China was the *Shang* (about 1770–1120 B.C.). With this dynasty, facts begin to replace legends. "Oracle bones" were used by

■ *Examples of Shang art are the antler (below), carved with a Shang inscription, and the bronze wine vessel (above), ornamented with stylized animal figures.*

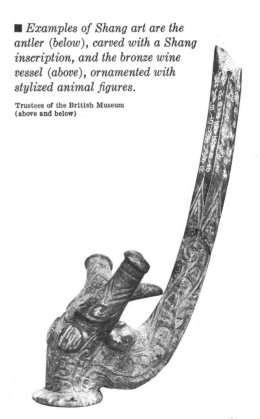

67

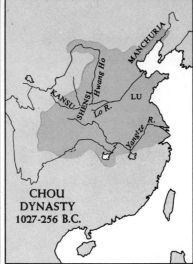
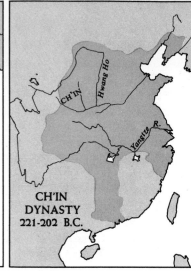

SHANG DYNASTY 1770-1120 B.C.

CHOU DYNASTY 1027-256 B.C.

CH'IN DYNASTY 221-202 B.C.

■ *Ancient China was ruled, in turn, by the Shang, Chou, and Ch'in dynasties. Each ruling dynasty extended its control over more territory. Under the Chou the Chinese enjoyed a period of great creativity in art, literature, and philosophy—a "Classical Age."*

priests of ancient times to tell the future. If someone came to him with a question about the future, a priest might scratch the question on an animal bone or tortoise shell. Next he would hold the bone or shell over a fire until it cracked. Then the priest would predict the future by "interpreting" the position of the cracks. Many of these "oracle bones" have been found, and the questions on them supply us with clues to living conditions during the Shang period.

We know that the capital of the Shang dynasty was situated on the banks of the Huan River and was less than a hundred miles north of the Hwang Ho. From here the ruler exercised some control over a group of city-states that had established themselves in the valleys. However, the leaders of these city-states often challenged the Shang monarch's political power. Soon his main function became to serve as the chief priest, rather than as a governor. He directed the people in the worship of their leading god, *Shanti*, and in their offerings to lesser gods of earth and heaven.

Economic, Social, Cultural Achievements

The people were primarily farmers. Although their tools were generally made of stone, they used them effectively enough to construct an irrigation system to help them in their farming.

In some places city life was fairly well developed. Near Anyang in modern China, evidence has been found of government palaces and temples. Men continued to dominate the field of warfare, but women had an important part in running family affairs.

Scholars of the Shang period were familiar with a form of writing. They used *pictograms*, signs representing objects—such as ☥ for man. They also wrote with *ideograms*, signs representing ideas in picture form. As historian L. Carrington Goodrich has pointed out, "to shoot" might be shown by an arrow across a bow ». Words were set down with a simple brush and ink, usually on a wood or stone surface. They were written one under the other, rather than horizontally.

During the same period, priests devised a crude calendar. Artists and craftsmen

68

were busy producing many lovely bronze vessels, woven baskets, and musical bells.

Despite these accomplishments, the Shang leaders were not able to keep the various city-states together as a single powerful military unit. In the eleventh century B.C. warriors from the region west of the Shang area attacked the country. The people defended themselves against the invaders with bows and arrows, battle axes, bronze spears, and war chariots.

However, the defenders were disunited, and each Shang city-state was cut off and destroyed. From about 1027 to 256 B.C. the victors controlled China, and the new ruling family was the *Chou* dynasty.

■ **Check on Your Reading**

1. How do historians learn about the Shang?
2. What have they learned about the economic and social life of this period?
3. What form of writing was developed?

3. The Chou Dynasty Rules China

The Chou rulers set up their capital near the location of the modern city of Sian in Shensi province. Their kingdom grew until it eventually extended from the southern part of Manchuria to the Yangtze Valley in the south, and from the seacoast all the way to eastern Kansu (map, p. 68).

The Chou leaders were grateful to those individuals who had helped them in their conquest of the Shang people. They showed their appreciation by permitting military commanders, relatives, and trusted friends to govern parts of their kingdom. A system known as *feudalism* was thus established. These were the features of feudalism: (1) All land still belonged to the Chou rulers, but they permitted important individual lords to govern parts of it. (2) In exchange for the right to control a section of the country, these individual lords were expected to be loyal to the Chou rulers and to pay them taxes in grain or cattle. (3) The lords would collect most of the taxes from the common people, who also were called upon to serve as foot soldiers in the army.

The success of feudalism depended on the loyalty of the lords to the ruler. Yet there were powerful lords whose ambitions would not permit them to take orders from the Chou king. By the ninth century B.C.

these men refused to obey their ruler's commands; and in 771 B.C. a feudal lord, aided by non-Chinese troops, attacked the capital and killed the king.

The remaining members of the Chou dynasty fled to the Lo River Valley, and from that date until their downfall in 256 B.C. the Chou rulers had little governing power. China split into a number of separate and rival states under independent rulers.

The Chinese "Classical Age"

Despite the violence during the Chou dynasty (about 1027–256 B.C.), this period was one of the most important in Chinese history. It is sometimes called China's "Classical Age" because of the many impressive achievements of the Chinese during this time. Farming continued to be the chief occupation, but iron was used in the making of farm tools. Additional irrigation systems were built and reservoirs were constructed at key points throughout the country. Economic activities also expanded. Craftsmen produced fine bronze vessels and jade decorations. Lacquer was used as a finish for furniture, and many wood carvings were designed.

Since the Chinese lords controlled most of the land, they were rich enough to have comfortable houses and enough leisure

■ *In the "Classical Age" under the Chou rulers artists produced beautiful bronzes and jade carvings. Some examples are the bronze bell (left), the jade stags (center) and the bronze statuette of a Mongolian youth holding two jade birds (right).*

Joint Administration of National Palace and Central Museums of Taichung, Taiwan (left) ; The Metropolitan Museum of Art, Rogers Fund, 1924 (center) ; Museum of Fine Arts, Boston (right)

time to spend in hunting, gambling with dice, and other amusements. But the majority of people lived in houses made of packed earth, and they did not have many rights or comforts. They lived a simple, hard life close to the soil. More and more the lives of these peasants revolved around the activities of the family, and family ties became strong and lasting.

Some Chinese writers composed lovely poetry during this period. Others collected ancient odes praising their ancestors. Still other scholars recorded the histories of the various rulers or wandered from city to city offering their wisdom.

When the Shang language that was passed on to the Chou period became too limited in vocabulary, literary leaders of the fourth century expanded it. Although the Chinese language has gone through many changes since the work of these men in the "Classical Age," the structure of the Chinese pictogram and ideogram has remained basically the same. Today, a sym-

bol continues to represent an object (pictogram) or an idea (ideogram).

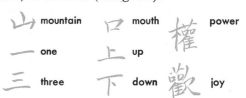

The Chinese written language is beautiful to see but very difficult to learn. It has been called "a dragon that swallows" Westerners who study it. Since it has no phonetic alphabet, there is a different symbol for every word. The language can be mastered only by memorizing as many of the 40,000 symbols as possible. Today the Chinese Communists are trying to change the structure of this language.

Yet, of all these Chinese accomplishments of the Chou period—poetry, histories, language development—none was so important as the work in philosophy. Here scholars reached a peak in achievement.

70

Confucius: a Great Teacher

Chinese philosophy is as closely bound to the name of Confucius as Chinese life is bound to the soil. Confucius (or K'ung-fu-tze, which means K'ung the Master) was born in 551 B.C. in Lu, one of the independent kingdoms during the later years of the Chou dynasty. As a child, he was not very attractive physically, and he was described in adult life in the following manner:

He has river eyes and a dragon forehead. . . . His arms are long, his back is like a tortoise. . . .

Yet, as Confucius himself pointed out, fine physical appearance no more makes a great man than a lovely rice blossom guarantees good grain.

At the age of twenty-two, Confucius established a school at his home. He was a great teacher and soon attracted a group of devoted followers. Later in life he travelled from kingdom to kingdom, "a one-man university," instructing those who sought him out and seeking rulers who would listen to his advice. When he died in Lu at the age of 72, he left behind him a heritage of wisdom.

Confucius Seeks Order and Harmony

The advice that Confucius gave to his own and to later generations was concerned with the best ways of keeping order and harmony in a troubled world. Confucius lived at a time when the Chou dynasty could no longer control the country. Independent kingdoms fought each other to gain more power, and confusion spread throughout the land. It was natural that this great scholar should try to answer the question: How can men live together in peace and happiness?

Confucius' answer can be found in six of his important principles that appear in such works as the *Analects* (an unedited collection of his sayings), and the *Liki*. These principles include the following:

1. THE IMPORTANCE OF MAN'S LIFE ON THIS EARTH. Confucius believed that man's main purpose was to lead a happy and useful life *on this earth*. Man, he said, should not concern himself with questions about the nature of heaven and an after-life. Rather, he should live out his life here in accordance with his own nature. Man should set standards for his conduct.

As Confucius said, "We don't know yet about life, how can we know about death?" Therefore, "the superior man discusses all questions of conduct on the basis of himself as the standard"—and not by thinking of punishment and reward in after-life.

2. THE GOLDEN RULE. Confucius said, "Do not do unto others what you do not want others to do unto you." This "Golden Rule," it is important to remember, is a part of every major religion.

3. THE MIDDLE WAY. Confucius believed that it is not wise to go to extremes in anything that we do. It is better to take the "middle way" and be moderate in our acts. For example, he felt that a person should be neither cowardly nor foolishly bold—rather, he should be courageous, which is the "middle way." As Confucius said: "To go a little too far is as bad as not going far enough."

4. THE FIVE RELATIONSHIPS. Confucius believed that the five most important relationships in life are between ruler and subject, father and son, husband and wife, elder brother and younger brother, and friend and friend. According to Confucius, if each of these five relationships were happy, there would be order and harmony in the world.

5 RESPECT FOR ANCESTORS. Confucius believed that we should respect our ancestors and heed their words of wisdom.

6. GOOD GOVERNMENT DEPENDS ON GOOD MEN. Confucius believed that when

the character of the rulers is good, the government will be good.

Although the words of Confucius were not listened to by many rulers in his own day, his wisdom has influenced every Chinese generation since then—including those under the domination of the Chinese Communists today.

Lao-Tse Searches for Peace

Another Chinese scholar, Lao-Tse (604–531 B.C.), also sought the answer to the question: How can men live in peace? His answer was quite different from that of Confucius. Lao-Tse believed in the following principles: (1) Man should stop striving for success or to "get ahead." He should relax completely and let Nature take its course. (2) Man should cease to worry about worldly affairs. Nothing

should disturb him. He should sit back and say to himself: "Nothing matters to a man who says nothing matters." (3) If man can forget completely about worldly problems and his personal ambitions, he may be able to lose himself in that wonderful peace and calm that runs through the universe. These principles formed the basis of a religious philosophy called *Taoism.*

■ Check on Your Reading

1. Describe feudalism in China during the Chou dynasty.

2. How did feudalism weaken the dynasty?

3. Give several reasons why the Chou period is known as China's "Classical Age."

4. What are the principal teachings of Confucius?

5. How did the teachings of Lao-Tse differ from those of Confucius?

4. The First Chinese Empire Is Established

Yet it took more than philosophy to make the rival Chinese states stop their fighting. Force finally did the job that words could not do. In the third century B.C., the leader of the northwest state of Ch'in succeeded in smashing the armies of the other states and in uniting all of the country under his command. He then took the title of First Emperor, or *Shih Huang Ti* (246–210 B.C.). It is possible that the word *China* comes from the name of the family that he represented, the Ch'in dynasty.

Shih Huang Ti Rules China

As protection against the "barbarians," Shih Huang Ti ordered that the various walls to the north be joined together in one long barrier which is called the "Great Wall." Then he increased his empire by conquering land far to the south. Soon this First Chinese Empire brought together all of the peoples under his rule behind the "Great Wall."

Shih Huang Ti unified the country by more than force. He also drew the various regions together by (1) dividing the country into military districts under the control of the Ch'in dynasty, (2) disarming his enemies, (3) building roads, (4) establishing a single style of writing, and (5) setting up one code of laws for all.

What of the fate of Confucius and other philosophers who had sought for the good life so many years before the Ch'in dynasty? Their books were considered to be dangerous to the state, for they advised moderation and respect for the opinions of the ancients—and Shih Huang Ti believed in force and in wiping out old feudal ways. The emperor ordered his men to burn the ancient Chinese books that Confucius loved so well. Only books on medicine, farming, and the history of the Ch'in family were saved.

Yet the Ch'in dynasty soon found its own foundation in flames. After the death of Shih Huang Ti, the Ch'in rulers were not strong enough to keep down revolt. Their government was overthrown, and about 202 B.C. a new dynasty, the Han, took over control of the country. The Han dynasty ruled for almost four hundred years, and the principles of Confucius were again treated with respect.

China Touches the Outside World

China was largely cut off from contact with other peoples during the period from the Shang to the end of the Ch'in dynasty. However, she was not completely isolated from outside civilizations. Wheat, for example, which was first cultivated in the Near East, reached China by 2000 B.C. Domestic fowl and rice probably came to China from the Bay of Bengal about 1000 B.C., and the ox-drawn plough of the Near East became known in China as early as 600 B.C.

Real contact with the Mediterranean area would have to wait until the opening of the "Old Silk Road" in the first century, but long before that China was lightly touching the outside world. It is difficult for any country to remain completely "closed" for any length of time. Man, apparently, was not meant to live alone.

■ Check on Your Reading

1. Describe the "Great Wall" of China.
2. How did Shih Huang Ti unify China?
3. Why did the Ch'in discard the teachings of Confucius? When were they revived?
4. How do we know China had contacts with India and the Near East before 500 B.C.?

CULTURAL CHARACTERISTICS of Ancient China

...we should subject our cultural methods to the process of discrimination and should never absorb everything unconditionally." These words of Mao Tse-tung, leader of the Chinese Communists in the twentieth century, raised serious questions concerning the fate of the ancient Chinese cultures.

The characteristics of the cultures of ancient China were:

A social structure based on family and kinship. The family was the center of social, economic, and religious activities in traditional China.

Economies based on agricultural production, in which the lives of the Chinese people were interrelated with the events of nature.

The development of a written language, which, although difficult, has survived until today.

The acceptance of philosophies of life, which stressed the importance of man's life on this earth.

As Mao Tse-tung made clear, the Chinese Communists today find it difficult or undesirable to "digest" or "absorb" these and other aspects of the cultures of ancient China. Radical changes are being made to alter the family structure, industrialize techniques of production, modernize language, and introduce a Marxist philosophy of life. Communist China wishes to "break the chains" of the past.

Yet the cultures of ancient China are not dead. Their effects linger on in many areas, especially in social structure, economics, language, and philosophy. Indeed sometimes the ancient Chinese expressed the bold, determined spirit of the modern age better than any contemporary could. Consider the maxim: "If, looking in my heart, I find I am right, I will go forward' although those opposing me number thousand and tens of thousands." Mao Tse-tung did not say that. Confucius did!

MAN AND HIS CULTURE

Let's Meet the People!

The following account is based largely on material appearing in the *Li ki*, an ancient book of rites that Confucius valued. The activities of this Chinese son can be placed in the early period of the Shang.

A Chinese Son

The Chinese son knew that one of the main purposes in life was to serve his parents. As a child, he soon found that there was much work for children to do. At the first crowing of the cock each morning, he arose, gathered up his sleeping mat, washed his hands and mouth, and dressed. Next he hurried to his parents and asked them if they were well. Then he brought them water, with which to wash, and food.

When the Chinese son married, he brought his wife home to live with him and his parents. The wife was respected by her husband. Nevertheless, each morning the wife went to the area where her mother-in-law and father-in-law slept and asked them if their dress was "too warm or too cool." If they had a pain or an itch, the wife "respectfully" pressed or rubbed the affected part with her fingers.

If her husband's parents were disagreeable, the wife would not complain. She knew her husband was forbidden to offend his father and mother—even when they were wrong—for he had been taught:

"When the parents are in error, the son with a humble spirit, pleasing [face], and gentle tone, must point it out to them ... And if the parents, irritated and displeased [by his criticism] then [punish] their son till the blood flows from him, even then he must not harbor the least resentment; but, on the contrary, should treat them with increased respect and dutifulness."

The Chinese son knew that when his parents died, he would be expected to show them as much honor as when they were alive. He had learned: "Although your father and mother are dead, if you propose to yourself any good work, only [think] how it will make their names illustrious, and your purpose will be fixed."

The Chinese son respected and honored his parents at all times. Soon his own small children would learn to respect him in this way!

CHAPTER REVIEW

REVIEW and DISCUSSION

1. Identify the people and places and explain the events and terms on p. 64.

2. Is there any difference between identifying China as a land of contrasts and India as a land of variety?

3. Do you think the Chinese legends are of any value in the study of history? Why?

4. Why does the text say that there is no conclusive proof that the Hsia ever existed?

5. Compare the approximate dates of the appearance of the first men in each of the four river valleys.

6. Why was China under the Shang unable to defend itself against invaders?

7. Would you agree or disagree with these conclusions? Why? (a) It is difficult for a government to control a country of immense size. (b) A country hemmed in by natural barriers and shut off from outside influences tends to become self-centered.

8. Is loyalty an essential feature of other governments as it is of feudalism? Why?

9. Does the fact that the Chinese used iron first for farm implements while the Hittites used it first for weapons indicate an essential difference between the two peoples?

10. Is Confucian philosophy also a religion? What are the differences between philosophy and religion?

11. Do you think it is wise to take the "middle way" and never go to extremes? Why?

12. How would a belief in Taoist teachings affect a country's civilization?

13. Do you agree or disagree with the statement: "Increasing trade among countries is a good way to keep the peace." Why?

ACTIVITIES

1. On a map of China locate the Great Wall, Himalayas, Huan River, Hwang Ho, Inner Mongolia, Lo River, Manchuria, Pacific, Peiping, Sinkiang, Tibet, and the Yangtze.

2. Write a short summary on the teachings of Confucius, using references.

3. Add China to your chart on the "Causes of the Rise and Fall of Civilizations."

4. Some paperbacks that you will enjoy owning and using are: Creel, *Chinese Thought*; Gamow, *Biography of the Earth*; Wallbank, *Short History of India and Pakistan*; Yohannan, *A Treasury of Asian Literature*.

5. Make a list of ancient civilizations you have studied and the contributions of each.

PAST and PRESENT

1. Which of the six principles of Confucius are accepted today? Where?

2. In *Readers' Guide* find articles on Communist China. Do you find any ancient Chinese influences that make Chinese communism different from Russian communism?

3. What modern ruler burned books as Shih Huang Ti did? Were the results the same?

SUGGESTED READINGS

Basic books: CHENEY, SHELDON W., *New World History of Art*, Viking.

GARDNER, HELEN, *Art Through the Ages*, Harcourt, Brace.

LATOURETTE, KENNETH SCOTT, *A Short History of the Far East*, Chap. 3, Macmillan.

LINEBARGER, PAUL M. A., CHU, DJANG, and BURKS, ARDATH W., *Far Eastern Government and Politics, China and Japan*, Chap. 1, Van Nostrand.

LINTON, RALPH, *The Tree of Culture*, Chaps. 36, 37, Knopf.

Special accounts: CREEL, HERRLEE G., *Chinese Thought from Confucius to Mao Tse-tung*, MD 269, New American Library. An interesting book about religious philosophy.

FAIRSERVIS, WALTER A., *The Origins of Oriental Civilizations*, MD 251, New American Library. Scholarly treatment of the beginnings of art, religion, ethics, and technology.

SEEGER, ELIZABETH, *The Pageant of Chinese History*, Longmans, Green.

Biography and Fiction: YOHANNAN, JOHN D., *A Treasury of Asian Literature*, MD 243, New American Library.

UNIT 2 Our Heritage
from the Greek, Roman,
and Early Christian Cultures

Why Study about the Ancient Greeks—Are You Influenced by Them?

YOU ARE—if your name is George, Anthony, Dennis, Eugene, Gregory, Homer, Myron, Nicholas, Philip, or Theodore. Or if your name is Agatha, Agnes, Catherine, Corinne, Cynthia, Doris, Rhoda, or Thelma. These names are all probably derived from the Greek language. To a degree, *your names are Greek.*

YOU ARE—if you use the words "drama" or "comedy" or "tragedy" or "democracy" in a speech, letter, or composition. They are terms developed from the Greek language, too. To a degree, *your words are Greek.*

YOU ARE—if you follow the results of the annual Boston Athletic Association Marathon Race or the Olympic Games. These athletic events can be traced back to Greece. To a degree, *your sports are Greek.*

YOU ARE—if you attend a play in an outdoor theater or see a musical that features a singing chorus. Outdoor plays and choruses date back to the ancient Greeks. To a degree, *your theater is Greek.*

YOU ARE—if you study the principles of geometry or use latitude and longitude in geography. Such information comes primarily from the Greeks—plus a considerable part of your knowledge of history, physics, philosophy, and art. To a degree, *your school subjects are Greek.*

YOU ARE—if you vote in your school elections and work for "good citizenship." The idea of responsible citizenship developed from the Greeks. To a degree, *your belief in democracy is Greek.*

In all these ways and others, YOU ARE influenced by the Greeks.

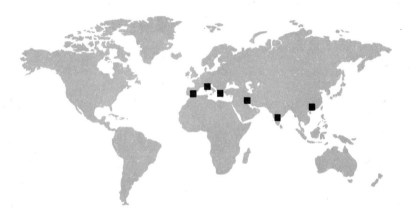

Studying about Ancient Greece Means Studying about Yourself!

Since Greek civilization is a part of you, when you learn about the Greeks you learn about yourself. Thus, when your next unit discusses the lives of the Greeks it also will be talking about you. For—in many of the things that you say and do—you are a product of Greek culture.

Four Questions for You

Four of the most important questions that face modern man are the following: (1) How can we have peace and security? (2) How can we deal with dictators and tyrants? (3) What is the role of religion in our lives? (4) How can we keep our civilization strong?

Difficult questions? Of course! Nevertheless, we can turn again to history for help in finding the answers. History will point out the wisdom or foolishness of our conclusions.

The period that we study after our survey of Greece was a time of emperors, dictators, and religious leaders. During these years, from about 500 B.C. to 500 A.D., the Roman Empire was built; Christianity was established; and Buddhism was spread throughout Asia. These were days in which the people were faced with *the same four questions that concern men today*: questions of peace, dictatorship, religion, and the future of civilization.

By studying this period, we can see how successful or unsuccessful our ancestors were in meeting their problems. Then we can use this historical information to avoid making their mistakes in solving these four problems.

Chapter 5

Ancient Greece and the Ideal of Democracy

KEYNOTE An archer sometimes aims his arrow at a target too far away for him to strike. In like fashion, a man often points his life toward ends too advanced for him to reach. We call these distant goals of man *ideals*.

Few men have been able to reach their ideals. The Greek mathematician Pythagoras was a fine scholar who aimed at the ideal of wisdom. Yet he taught his students such nonsense as: It is evil to eat beans or let swallows rest on the roof of a home. The great Greek philosopher Aristotle also had his weaknesses. He pointed toward the ideal of truth. Still he mistakenly believed that women have fewer teeth than men!

Some statesmen of ancient Greece had similar failings. Their ideal of government was *democracy*, a word of Greek origin meaning "the rule of the people." Nevertheless, they fell short of their mark. They permitted slavery to exist and gave few rights to women and foreigners.

Such failings should not blind us to the remarkable contributions of these Greek statesmen. Although they did not develop a perfectly democratic society, *they were the first to aim at the ideal of democracy.*

Key Persons *Solon · Pericles · Darius · Xerxes · Miltiades · Leonidas · Themistocles*

Key Places *Greece · Peloponnesus · Troy · Mycenae · Tiryns · Crete · Cnossus · Athens · Sparta · Delphi · Thermopylae · Salamis*

Key Events *Troy destroyed ·* Iliad *and* Odyssey *· Dorians, Ionians, and Aeolians invade Greece · Greeks achieve democracy · Pericles guides Athens · Persian Wars · Battle of Marathon*

Key Terms *Minoan civilization · Ionians · Dorians · city-state · acropolis · tyrant · democracy · monarchy · aristocracy · Olympic Games*

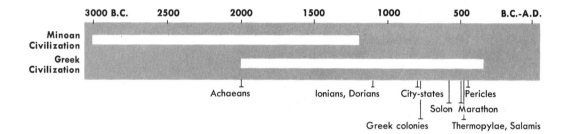

3000 B.C.	2500	2000	1500	1000	500	B.C.-A.D.

Minoan Civilization

Greek Civilization

Achaeans — Ionians, Dorians — City-states — Pericles
Solon — Marathon
Greek colonies — Thermopylae, Salamis

1. Greece: A Land Dominated by the Sea

Greece is a land dominated by the sea, and the appeal of the sea is the strongest attraction to its people. Even today Greek fishermen, pulling their shallow-bottomed boats to the safety of the shore at dusk, call to the sea in folk songs:

> Beat the billow now, O sea. . . .
> Beat the beaches now, O sea.

Such songs are a natural heritage of a people whose land touches water at many points. The Greek peninsula in southeastern Europe is rimmed by the Ionian Sea to the west, the Mediterranean Sea to the south, and the Aegean Sea to the east. The Gulf of Corinth drives a wedge of sea between the southern part of the peninsula, called the *Peloponnesus*, and the land to the north (map, p. 80).

Historical Importance of Greece's Closeness to the Sea: The sea served as an avenue through which the Greeks expanded, traded, and exchanged ideas with other peoples. The islands of Greece are lovely, the country's climate is mild, and the weather often is delightful. As the modern Greek writer George Theotokas puts it: "Nature [in Greece] is in harmony with man."

Historical Importance of Greece's Climate: The mild climate permitted the ancient Greeks to have their public art, theaters, courts, and activities outdoors. Greece's peninsula, like its islands offshore, is mountainous, and the land is split by rocky ranges. Between the ranges are narrow valleys and plains with poor to fertile soil. Here and along the hillsides the people grow crops, hoping that winter rains and dry summer sun will come on time.

Historical Importance of Greece's Mountains: The mountains were one factor that kept some ancient Greeks separated into small city-states and sometimes prevented them from uniting. Today Greece is a poor country where one-fifth of its eight and one half million people struggle against hunger. If Greece's present does not sparkle, its past does. This land once produced the most civilized men in the ancient world. Their story begins about two thousand years before the birth of Christ.

■ **Check on Your Reading**

1. How did the sea affect Greek history?
2. How did the climate affect the Greek approach to art, the theater, and public life?

79

■ *Greece is a mountainous peninsula in southeastern Europe. What aspects of its geography influenced its history?*

2. The First Greeks Reach the Aegean Sea

Who were the first Greeks? Where did they come from? What were they like? These questions have fascinated scholars in every period. From their investigations, it is known that about 2000 B.C. groups of people living near the Caspian Sea started to move westward into the lands around the Aegean Sea. These were the *Hellenes*, the earliest Greeks, and they came down from the north in several great migrations.

The first Hellenes to come were the *Achaeans*. For years it was believed that the Achaeans were a rough people who could not read or write. Then in 1954 Michael Ventris, a young English architect, deciphered some strange tablets found in the Aegean area. He discovered that the writing was Achaean, an early form of the Greek language! According to some

scholars, this meant that the Achaean Greeks were not crude invaders. They were talented enough to develop a system of writing and some skills in the arts.

Although Ventris' findings must be carefully checked, his deciphering of the mysterious tablets makes possible the study of Greek life as far back as 1800 B.C. Soon we shall know many facts about the Achaeans.

Achaeans Meet Cretans

When the Achaeans migrated from the north, they mingled with the people whom they found at Mycenae and Tiryns, cities on the Greek peninsula. Then they swept ahead to Crete, a large island southeast of the peninsula. Because Crete was strategically located, it could have contact with the cultures of Egypt and Asia Minor.

The people of Crete, whose chief city was Cnossus, already had developed a considerable civilization when the Achaeans arrived. Little is known about them, but we call their Cretan civilization *Minoan*. It dates back to 3000 B.C., when Egyptian and Sumerian civilizations flourished.

The Cretans were extremely talented in art and architecture. They built attractive palaces and theaters, made bronze by properly mixing copper and tin, and molded vases of many colors with the potter's wheel. Of particular beauty were their *frescoes*, paintings that were made upon a wall coating of wet lime (p. 44). In addition to their artistic skills, the Cretans were clever sailors who traded and exchanged ideas with people in Asia Minor, Syria, Egypt, and possibly Spain.

We cannot be sure of what happened when the Achaean Greeks met the Cretans. They may have clashed in war or merged in peace. It is clear that the Achaeans ruled the Cretans for a number of years and learned much from them.

Tales of Gods, Wars, and Heroes

In the twelfth century B.C. the Achaean Greeks attacked and defeated the people of Troy, a city on the coast of Asia Minor. About three hundred years later, a blind poet named Homer, or perhaps a number of poets to whose work Homer's name has been attached, recorded tales that were based on this war. These stories form the *Iliad* and *Odyssey*, two great epic poems. These poems are colorful mixtures of legend and fact, and they are useful in giving us a picture of the lives of the people.

According to the *Iliad* and *Odyssey*, the Achaean Greeks were farmers, herdsmen, and traders. When they exchanged goods, they used cattle instead of coined money as a standard of value. The fact that a woman slave might be bought for as little as four head of cattle, while a suit of armor cost

Museum of Candia, Heraklion, Crete

■ *"The Octopus Vase"* (1500 B.C.), an example of Cretan pottery, was decorated with marine scenes—seaweed and the arms of an octopus.

nine, indicates that the needs of war sometimes were more important than people.

In religion the Achaeans believed in many gods. These gods were said to live above the clouds on Mount Olympus, in the northern part of the Greek peninsula. They had many human traits. They laughed, boasted, and argued with each other. In the *Iliad*, for example, the goddess Hera often nags her husband Zeus, king of the gods. A self-respecting wife, she scolds him for keeping secrets and complains:

It is ever thy good pleasure to hold aloof from me and in secret meditation to give thy judgments.

To which Zeus, like any self-respecting husband, roars:

Abide thou in silence and hearken to my bidding.

The Greeks Establish Colonies

The Achaean way of life pictured in the ancient poems was jarred by new waves of Greek invaders who came down from the north. These were the *Dorians, Ionians,*

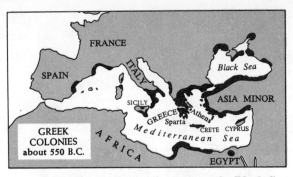

GREEK
COLONIES
about 550 B.C.

■ *There were Greek colonies near the Black Sea
and in North Africa, Sicily, southern France,
and Italy. Why were colonies established?*

and *Aeolians*, warlike Greeks who caused
much destruction as they swept through
the area about the Aegean Sea. By 1100 B.C.
they had scattered the peoples of the region
and wiped out many of their achievements.

Some historians claim that there followed three hundred years of "darkness,"
a time when civilization almost did not
exist. When we know more about the
years from 1100 B.C. to 800 B.C. we will
probably discard the term "darkness."

By 800 B.C. the various Greek invaders
had completely absorbed or assimilated the
people in the Aegean area. Life became
hard. The people barely supported themselves by farming. Some said that the
god Zeus "in the wrath of his heart" had
hidden the good things of life.

Overpopulation and meager food supplies caused a restlessness in the people.
Their elders still urged them to work "that
Famine may ever hate you," but working
the rocky soil brought little reward. In desperation the Greeks sought escape at sea.
From about 800 to 600 B.C. many Greeks
fitted out vessels and sailed the Mediterranean and Aegean seeking better conditions.

During this period the Greeks established colonies near the Black Sea and
along the coasts of North Africa, Sicily,
southern Italy, and southern France (map,
p. 82). The word *colonies* generally means
territories in which the settlers owe allegiance to the lands they left. However, the
Greek colonies soon grew so strong that
they often acted independently of their
home cities. They kept some ties with
their homelands, but they considered their
new homes more important than their old.

■ **Check on Your Reading**

1. Why can we now learn more about the
Achaeans?

2. Why can we say that the Cretans had
a highly developed civilization?

3. What can we learn about the Achaean
Greeks from the *Iliad* and *Odyssey*?

4. Why did the Greeks found colonies after
800 B.C.? Where were colonies established?

3. The City-State: a Greek's "Country"

By 600 B.C. times had improved in a
number of places in the Aegean, although
economic distress continued to plague the
peninsula of Attica. Greek colonization
had had important results, such as these:
(1) It had lessened some of the pressure of
excess population. (2) It had led to increased trade. (3) It had helped bring
about the introduction of a system of exchange by money. As a result, economic
conditions improved in various areas at

home. Many Greeks turned from despair
to optimism. They were now determined to
make their city-states excel in everything—
in commerce, politics, and the arts.

Few factors were more important in the
life of a Greek than his *polis*, or city-state.
A city-state was made up of three parts:
(1) the *acropolis*, usually a fortified area on
top of a hill, where the temples were constructed; (2) the area below the acropolis,
where the homes and the market place of

■ *On the Acropolis of Athens were many beautiful temples and buildings. The Queen of the Acropolis was the Parthenon, the chief temple of Athena. Other Greek city-states had their acropolises or "hilltops for the gods" but none could compare to that of Athens.*

the people were located; and (3) the surrounding countryside. By the end of the seventh century B.C. there were many city-states on the Greek peninsula, on the islands in the Aegean, and in Asia Minor.

The city-states were quite small by our standards today, ranging from about fifty to five hundred square miles. Populations were also small by twentieth-century figures. Some city-states had about five thousand people each, and the Athenian city-state had less than a third of a million.

Each city-state was separate from the others and completely independent. One of the reasons why they did not unite was their geographic position. The Greek mountains set up rocky barriers that cut off many city-states from the others, and poor roads made communication difficult. On the other hand, there were some city-states fairly close to each other and not separated by mountains. Yet these too failed to join together. In these cases, beliefs in different local gods, local patriotism, and the desire to keep their trade and wealth probably kept them apart.

One thing became clear: a Greek who was a citizen of a city-state owed allegiance to it and no other. In a real sense, the city-state was his country, and he was expected to sacrifice his life defending it.

The Government of the City-State

The strong attachment that a Greek citizen felt for his city-state did not depend on its form of government. This was fortunate, for the city-states had experimented with many types of rule from the eighth century to the fifth century. Although not all of the city-states followed the same pattern of development, some of them moved through five forms of government. Starting with *monarchy*, they changed to *aristocracy*, then to *plutocracy*, then to *tyranny*, and finally to *democracy* (see Chart).

It is important to remember that not all the city-states turned to democracy, for some Greeks felt that government by the citizens would be a failure. Notwithstanding this fact, the appearance of democracy by 500 B.C. in some city-states was one of the greatest events in the development of

83

civilization. The Greeks would be known in history as *the first people to discard the idea that a few men had an absolute right to rule all of the people.* Man had an ideal to work for—the ideal of political equality.

Solon Reforms Athens

This Greek ideal of democracy was a limited one. The Greeks were concerned primarily with *political* rights—that is, with giving citizens equal rights to govern. Years later, other men were to point out that the ideal of democracy also includes equal economic and social rights.

Nowhere in ancient times did men follow the Greek ideal of democracy more closely than at Athens. Athens was the center of an Ionian Greek city-state near the Aegean on the small Attic peninsula. Here democracy owed much to the intelligence and hard work of individual leaders.

An outstanding leader of the Athenian democracy was Solon. He was a nobleman who believed that the wealthy had no right to oppress the poor. In 594 B.C. he was granted special powers to make desirable changes in government and daily life.

Solon repealed most of the *Draconian Code,* a series of harsh seventh century B.C.

FIVE FORMS OF GOVERNMENT OF THE CITY—STATE

APPROXIMATE TIME	FORM OF GOVERNMENT	FEATURE OF GOVERNMENT	PRIMARY CAUSE OF CHANGE TO NEXT FORM OF GOVERNMENT
8th century B.C.	Monarchy	Rule by a king who gained his power by inheriting it and passed it on to his son.	Powerful landholding nobles desired to run the government.
7th century B.C.	Aristocracy	Rule by a small number of men belonging to important families. (In the Greek city-states, these men usually owned large areas of land.)	Wealthy merchants felt that they were more important than their aristocratic rulers.
7th century B.C.	Plutocracy	Rule by a small number of men of wealth. (In the Greek city-states, many of these men acquired their riches through commerce.)	The new rulers were often more concerned with personal gains than with the good of the city-state.
6th century B.C.	Tyranny	Rule by one man, the tyrant, who usually seized power by force. He did not rule by inheritance (as a king) or by social position (as an aristocrat) or by wealth (as a plutocrat), but by personal strength.	Several tyrants worked hard, introduced needed reforms, and gained the support of the people. However, some of them deprived men of liberty and justice.
5th century B.C.	Democracy	Rule by the citizens.	Lack of unity.

laws. Then he freed men forced into slavery because of debt, cancelled the debts of the farmers, and released persons in prison for political offenses. Other reforms covered many fields, ranging from changing the value of money to limiting women to three sets of clothes!

Most important were his governmental reforms. According to his new constitution, all citizens were to have the right to vote in a great general assembly, and they were to be permitted to appeal cases to juries made up of fellow-citizens. These provisions were major steps toward the ideal of pure democracy, or direct "rule by the people."

Pericles Guides Athenian Democracy

The reforms of Solon were followed by those of other leaders, until by the middle of the fifth century B.C. Athens had the most democratic government of its time. From 460 B.C. to 429 B.C. the government was directed by a great statesman, Pericles.

The government of Athens under Pericles gave considerable power to its citizens. Out of a population estimated at 315,000 there were only 43,000 full citizens. These were native-born males over the age of twenty-one. The 115,000 slaves, the 29,000 *metics* (Greeks from other city-states who resided in Athens), the non-Greeks, women, and some workers could not vote.

Those who were granted full citizenship were expected to take an active part in politics. Pericles himself had pointed out: "We . . . regard a man who takes no interest in public affairs not as a harmless, but as a useless, character." To keep Athenians alert, officials sometimes went to the market place and displayed a rope dipped in wet red dye to lazy citizens who did not attend public meetings. Then they threatened to place the rope around the offenders and pull them from the market place. Since a red drop on a man's clothing meant a fine, citizens hurried to their duties!

■ *Under the rule of Pericles, a great Athenian statesman, Athens became the intellectual and artistic center of Greece.*

The "Voice of the Citizens" Is Heard

In general, it did not require any urging to make Athenian citizens exercise their rights. The citizens did not rule through representatives but participated directly as a pure democracy. Except for farmers who could not reach the center at Athens easily, the citizens were willing to serve on the following organs of government:

1. GENERAL ASSEMBLY: LEGISLATURE. The *General Assembly* was the organ that gave them the best chance to express their opinions. All Athenian citizens were members of this body, which met upon a hillside anywhere from ten to fifty times a year. The General Assembly's principal duty was to vote on laws—that is, it was a *legislature*.

2. COUNCIL OF FIVE HUNDRED: EXECUTIVE. A second organ, the *Council of Five Hundred*, served as the *executive* body— that is, it *executed*, or carried out, the laws. It also proposed legislation for the General Assembly to vote on, and it controlled financial affairs. Since the city-state consisted of many parts of the peninsula of Attica, each regional government (*deme*) was rep-

resented on the Council by citizens chosen by *lot*, that is, by an impartial drawing.

3. TEN GENERALS: CHIEF EXECUTIVES. In addition, the General Assembly elected ten generals each year to help the Council of Five Hundred make day-to-day decisions. These men were more than military leaders in war. They were also directors of the government, or *chief executives*, in peace. Pericles, for example, was re-elected a general for thirty years because he was an excellent leader in peace and in war.

4. JURY SYSTEM: JUDICIARY. Citizens also held important posts on the *judiciary*—that is, on those organs concerned with giving justice to the people. The men took turns serving on juries, and they were paid so that the poor as well as the rich could be jurors. The juries usually numbered from 201 to 501 or more members in size, and in some cases 1501 members

were used. Citizens were really judge and jury. They gave their verdict and also determined the punishment that the accused was to receive. Since there were no professional public prosecutors or defense attorneys, each citizen did his own accusing and made his own defense.

■ **Check on Your Reading**

1. What were the principal results of Greek colonization?
2. Describe a Greek city-state.
3. What was the relationship among the various city-states?
4. What were five forms of government that some Greek city-states experimented with?
5. Analyze the reforms of Solon.
6. On what organs of government did Athenian citizens serve?
7. What were the functions of the legislature, executive, and judiciary?

4. Sparta Stresses Military Training

In the southern part of the Peloponnesus peninsula was another important city-state whose center was at Sparta. Its citizens were Dorians. Unlike the Athenians, the people of Sparta believed that the main purpose of government was to train good soldiers, not democratic citizens.

The Spartan government was based on a constitution said to have been prepared by Lycurgus, a law-giver who may have been a legendary figure. Although it contained some democratic features, such as the principle of citizenship, the constitution soon became an instrument to support the military training of the people.

The citizens of Sparta stressed the importance of military strength because they were few in number. By the sixth century B.C., they made up about 7 per cent of the total population of Sparta. Outnumbering them seven to one were the

helots. Helots were men who had been defeated in war and forced to farm the land under the orders of their Spartan masters. In addition to the helots, there were many *perioeci*, free Greeks from other city-states who handled commerce and handicraft work. Since there was always a danger that the helots might revolt against their masters, the Spartan citizens needed to be trained as soldiers.

The education of a future Spartan citizen was therefore a military one. It began almost at birth. If a baby were "stout and well made," it was permitted to live. If it were "puny and ill-shaped," it was left on a hillside to die. New-born children were bathed in *wine*, instead of water, to help them "acquire firmness . . . like steel."

At the age of seven, a Spartan boy was placed in a community training center along with about sixty other boys. Here his leaders tried to toughen his body by making him walk barefoot, sleep on a bed of reeds, and wear a single garment in even the coldest weather. He was taught little reading and writing and nothing about art, for such knowledge was thought to be unnecessary for a future soldier. Instead, he learned to run, wrestle, swim, sing military songs, and fight. To build up his courage, he was beaten until he bled. To develop his cunning, he was encouraged to steal. If he were caught stealing, the boy was "whipped without mercy" for not being a successful thief!

At eighteen he joined a secret police force whose job it was to kill any helot inclined to rebel. This he did quietly and secretly. Then, for the greater part of his adult life, he served as a hardened soldier of his city-state.

■ **Check on Your Reading**

1. How did the Spartan view of government differ from the Athenian one?

2. How did this view affect the life of a Spartan?

3. Describe the education that a Spartan received.

5. Common Ties Bind the City-States

There were sharp differences between Athens and Sparta, although they were not dissimilar in every respect. Both accepted the idea of rights for citizens. However, Athenians were encouraged to think, to discuss issues, and to decide by reason. Spartans were taught to obey, to vote "yes" or "no" without discussion, and to decide by physical strength. The Athenian government wanted well-rounded citizens, while the Spartans sought disciplined soldiers.

There were also differences among the other city-states. At the same time, common ties of ancestry, language, religion, oracles, and Olympic Games bound nearly all Greeks together.

Ancestry and Language

The Greeks were united by the belief that they had descended from the same male ancestor, called *Hellen*. The fact that they all spoke the same language, with various dialects, also made them feel closer.

Religion

Religion was another factor binding the people together. In the fifth century B.C., many Greeks still believed in the ancient gods described by Homer. Zeus (king of the gods), Apollo (god of music and poetry), Athena (goddess of wisdom), and other gods said to live on Mount Olympus were honored as of old.

Some Greeks preferred to pray to the local gods of their communities, rather than to the gods of Mount Olympus. Others put their trust in superstitions. Still others, although few in number, considered the actions of the Greek gods to be unreasonable and illogical. The Greeks were not completely united by religion.

Oracles

One aspect of their religion on which nearly all Greeks did agree concerned *oracles*; that is, the sacred places and sacred words through which the gods were supposed to tell men about the future. One of the most famous oracles was located at Delphi, near the center of Greece.

If a Greek brought presents to the priests of this Oracle of Apollo at Delphi, he could ask a question in writing. A priestess would then sit on a stool over an opening in the rocks, chew laurel leaves, and inhale a vapor which came from the earth. In time, she would become semi-conscious or delirious and mumble words in a strange voice. A priest would make a record of her words, usually write them in verse, and then give them to the man who asked the question. Here was his answer!

The Olympic Games

Finally, the Olympic Games played an important part in keeping the Greeks together. Every four years Greek citizens from many city-states would gather at the city of Olympia to offer prayers to Zeus. Then, for five days, outstanding Greek athletes would compete against each other in such events as the broad jump, discus heaving, javelin throwing, wrestling, boxing, and the two-hundred-yard dash. The Greek city-states stopped fighting one another during these Olympic Games.

■ **Check on Your Reading**
1. What ties helped to unite the Greeks?
2. How did religion unite the Greeks?
3. Describe the Olympic Games.

6. The Persian Wars

In the beginning of the fifth century B.C., the Greek city-states were challenged by King Darius of the Persian Empire. Darius and earlier rulers had forced Greek cities in Asia Minor to submit to their rule. In 500 B.C. these cities revolted, aided by a fleet from Athens. Darius crushed the revolt and determined to punish Athens for its interference. His first attempt ended in disaster when storms wrecked the Persian fleet.

Act 1—Battle of Marathon

In 490 B.C. Darius organized a second army to conquer Athens, Sparta, and the rest of Greece. The Persian troops advanced to the plain of Marathon, only twenty-five miles from the walls of Athens. All of Greece was in danger.

Miltiades, a great Athenian general, took command in this crisis. Although his army had received a few reinforcements from another city, it was still outnumbered at least four to one. In the great battle of Marathon that followed, the Persians fought with bows and arrows, the Greeks with spears. Miltiades cleverly let the Persians charge through the center of his line. Then he attacked them on both flanks with groups of his fiercest spearmen. Bows and arrows were useless at close quarters, and the Persians fled in terror, leaving behind six thousand dead. The Greeks had won the battle at Marathon!

Act 2—Thermopylae and Salamis

Ten years later, King Xerxes, the son of Darius, determined to avenge the defeat of his father. In 480 B.C. he led a tremendous Persian army across the *Hellespont*, a strait now called the Dardanelles, separating Asia and Europe. Then he marched around the Aegean towards Greece. Facing this Persian force were Sparta and Athens, which had joined to fight the invaders.

When the Persian troops reached the mountain pass at Thermopylae, 85 miles northwest of Athens (map, p. 89), they met serious resistance. Here Leonidas, king of Sparta, and about five thousand Greeks made a heroic attempt to check the Persians. For three days they held back the invaders. Then, betrayed by a traitor who led the Persians behind their lines, the Greek defenders were forced back to their ships. To gain time for them to embark Leonidas and three hundred picked Spartans stood their ground in the fifty-foot pass and died almost to the man.

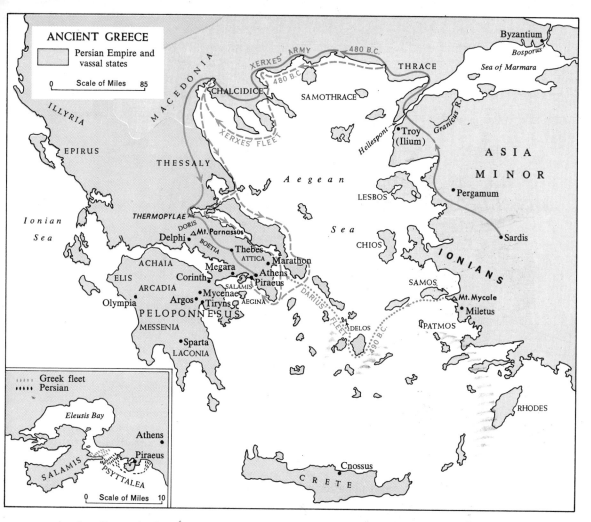

■ *Ancient Greece in the 5th century B.C. consisted of separate city-states—Athens, Sparta, Thebes, and others. Challenged by the Persian king, Darius, they fought the Persian Wars. Name the major battles and generals for each side. Which side was victorious? Why?*

Spartan heroism at Thermopylae merely delayed the Persians, and the way to Athens was clear. When the Persians reached Athens, they burned the city. Only the Greek fleet of about four hundred warships, most of them Athenian vessels, remained between the Persians and total victory. In 480 B.C., over eight hundred Persian warships attacked this Greek fleet near the island of Salamis. King Xerxes prepared to watch the final conquest of the Greeks. The strategy of the Athenian, Themistocles,

and the superior ability of the Greek seamen resulted in defeat of the Persian fleet.

His fleet defeated and his sea routes blocked, Xerxes and most of his troops returned wearily to Persia. The army that they left behind to attack the Greeks was completely routed in 479 B.C. The Persian Wars were over.

■ Check on Your Reading

1. What started the Persian Wars?
2. Name the chief victories for each side.

MAN AND HIS CULTURE

Let's Meet the People!

This sketch of an Athenian juror includes material from a play by Aristophanes (c. 448–388 B.C.); a speech by Demosthenes (4th century B.C.); *A Day in Old Athens* by William Stearns Davis, 1914, Allyn and Bacon, Inc.; and *The Wasps* trans. by Roger, G. Bell and Sons, Ltd.

An Athenian Juror

The Athenian juror (or dicast) walked to the courtrooms near the market place. He entered and sat down on a hard wooden bench covered with a mat. Surrounding him were two hundred other jurors.

The juror listened carefully to the case before him. First he heard the *plaintiff*, the accuser. Then he paid attention to the *defendant*, the accused. The statements of the witnesses had already been written down at an earlier hearing. Witnesses had little to do at the trial; they could not even be cross-examined.

Both plaintiff and defendant had finished speaking. It was time to vote. The juror had two metal discs. The one that was solid was the "not guilty" disc; the one with a hole in it was the "guilty" disc. The juror took the disc with the hole and dropped it into an urn. He was voting: *Guilty*. Most of the other jurors agreed.

The juror then watched the defendant rise before him and ask for a light sentence. Standing at their father's side, little children of the accused wept and begged the jury to show mercy. The plaintiff insisted that the accused had forced his children to weep. The result: the juror and the jury ordered the accused to pay a heavy fine.

His day's work over, the Athenian juror collected his three obols pay (about 25¢) and tossed them into his mouth between the cheeks and the gums. When he reached home, his daughter or wife might win these hidden coins away from him. As a character in a Greek play said:

> . . . with my fee . . . I come [home] . . .
> And [my daughter] washes my feet and anoints them with care,
>   and above them she stoops and a kiss lets fall,
> Till at last by the pretty Papas of her tongue
>   she angles withal my three-obol away.

CHAPTER REVIEW

REVIEW and DISCUSSION

1. Identify the people and places and explain the events and terms on p. 78.

2. Why did the colonialism of ancient Greece seem a good practice while today it is regarded as a bad policy by many people?

3. In what ways were the five forms in the development of Greek government logical steps? Compare the Greek government with that of the Persians, Egyptians, and Hebrews. Why did democracy first develop in Greece?

4. Define democracy as the Greeks practiced it. Define democracy as it exists in America today. Explain the differences.

5. The text says that the Greeks had ideals of truth, wisdom, and democracy but they did not attain them. Why is it worthwhile to have ideals even if they are not attained?

6. Do you think that it is better to choose officeholders by lot or by election? Why?

7. How did the Greek idea of justice differ from the Babylonian and Hebrew ones?

8. Why is the battle of Marathon considered one of the world's decisive battles? What was really decided there? If the Persians had won, what effects would it have had on the western world?

9. Attack or defend these statements: (a) Sparta did not achieve as great a civilization as Athens did because Spartan life and thought were too regimented. (b) People who differ to a large degree in their beliefs and practices can unite when they are faced by a common enemy.

ACTIVITIES

1. On a map of ancient Greece locate the Aegean Sea, Asia Minor, Athens, Cnossus, Corinth, Crete, Delos, Delphi, Ionian Sea, Hellespont, Marathon, Mount Olympus, Mycenae, Peloponnesus, Salamis, Sparta, and Thermopylae.

2. Make a report on archaeologist Schliemann's discoveries of ancient Troy.

3. Write a short paper on a famous ancient Greek, or on any topic or event involving ancient Greece. Consult references.

4. The Greeks left a wealth of literature. Read a selection from Greek history, the *Iliad*, or the *Odyssey*. What have you learned about Greek history from these sources?

5. Re-enact an Athenian Assembly in your class. Some members of the class may be famous Greeks while others are artisans. Debate this statement: Resolved, that in a democratic state citizens should be required to vote.

PAST and PRESENT

1. Do you agree that the four questions on p. 77 are the same ones that face modern man? Why? What other questions would you add?

2. How can we avoid the mistakes of past history? Give examples.

3. In the "Keynote" there are several examples of a paradox. Define *paradox* and give some examples of it. What paradoxes exist in American life today?

SUGGESTED READINGS

Basic books: BREASTED, JAMES, *Conquest of Civilization*, Harper.

SMITH, GOLDWIN, *The Heritage of Man*, Chap. 7, Scribner.

Special accounts: BOTSFORD, GEORGE WILLIS, and ROBINSON, CHARLES A., JR., *Hellenic History*, Macmillan.

KIERNAN, JOHN, and DALEY, ARTHUR, *Story of the Olympic Games*, Lippincott.

CERAM, C. W., *Gods, Graves and Scholars*, Chaps. 4, 5, Knopf.

MILLS, DOROTHY, *Book of the Ancient Greeks*, Putnam.

QUENNELL, C. H. B., and QUENNELL, MARJORIE, *Everyday Things in Ancient Greece*, Putnam. Gives one a good picture of Greek life.

Biography and Fiction: BULFINCH, T., *Mythology*, Crowell.

THOMPSON, STITH, and GASSNER, JOHN, (eds.), *Our Heritage of World Literature*, Holt. Contains translations of major literary works from ancient Greece to the twentieth century.

Chapter 6   *Creative Greeks Spread Their Culture through the Ancient World*

KEYNOTE   There were no great art museums in ancient Greece. The Greeks placed their beautiful marble and bronze statues out in the open for all to see.

There were no huge university buildings in ancient Greece. The Greek scholars strolled among the people in the market place and met in quiet groves to discuss what they had seen.

No high-priced indoor theaters existed in ancient Greece. Greeks of many economic levels eagerly flocked to outdoor stadiums to see the plays. Greek art, philosophy, and drama remained in touch with the people.

This does not mean that everyone in ancient Greece was an outstanding artist, philosopher, or playwright. The majority of people were probably no more talented than the majority of any other civilized group. However, the Greeks had one important advantage over most societies: They were in close contact with the best works of their cultural leaders.

The chief fame of Greece is that later civilizations were strongly influenced by its great cultural achievements. *There was "glory" too in the fact that Greek art, philosophy, and drama were alive to the people who lived in ancient Greece!*

Key People   *Phidias · Praxiteles · Socrates · Plato · Aristotle · Euripides · Aristophanes · Thucydides · Herodotus · Hippocrates · Thales · Alexander the Great · Archimedes*

Key Places   *Athens · Piraeus · Sparta · Thebes · Macedonia · Chaeronea · Alexandria · Antioch · Syria · Egypt · Persia*

Key Events   *Parthenon erected · Plato establishes the Academy · Delian League formed · Peloponnesian War · Macedonia conquers Greece · Alexander builds an empire*

Key Terms   *acropolis · Sophists · orchestra · Pythagorean theorem · Hellenistic · Epicureans · stoicism · Hades*

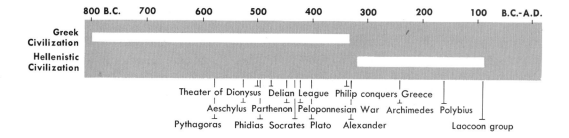

800 B.C.	700	600	500	400	300	200	100	B.C.-A.D.

Greek Civilization

Hellenistic Civilization

Theater of Dionysus Delian League Philip conquers Greece
Aeschylus Parthenon Peloponnesian War Archimedes Polybius
Pythagoras Phidias Socrates Plato Alexander Laocoon group

1. Daily Life of the Athenian Citizen

A Greek citizen would greet his neighbor in the morning with "Chaire!" meaning "Hail!" or "Rejoice!" The rest of his activities for the day were as routine and uncomplicated as this simple greeting. Few people spent their hours writing great books or carving fine statues. Most citizens were content to lead ordinary lives that did not set them off from their neighbors.

The Athenian citizen of the fifth century B.C. wore simple clothes. He dressed

■ *A Greek vase painting (c. 420 B.C.) depicts a bridal scene. Note the women's dress.*

National Museum, Athens

in a knee-length woolen tunic that was pinned at each shoulder. The tunic for a woman fell below her knees. Over the tunic a white woolen cloak was worn. Most men and women wore sandals or boots.

The citizen usually was careful about his appearance. He oiled his hair to shield it from the sun, and he visited a barber to have his beard trimmed. Women used mirrors, hairpins, tweezers, creams, and rouge. They also rubbed lampblack under their eyes. To increase their height, they placed high cork soles on the bottom of their shoes.

An Athenian Home

A citizen's home was made of sun-baked brick and was quite simple. It usually had a dirt floor and no windows. Small sleeping rooms, a dining room, a living room, and a kitchen branched off a central court. The court let sunlight in during the day. At night, olive oil lamps provided light.

The furniture consisted of a few simple, attractively designed couches, benches, stools, and chests. There was no running water or plumbing. Garbage disposal was handled by opening the door, shouting a warning, and throwing it into the street.

There were many fine painted pots and bronze vessels in the home (p. 44), but eating utensils were as scanty as furniture.

93

The Greeks did not use knives or forks. They ate with their fingers.

The Work of the Athenians

Most Athenian citizens were farmers. They raised grain, olives, and grapes. Some citizens were wealthy landowners or rich merchants who stayed in Athens and let others work for them. Others were potters, carpenters, craftsmen, and shopkeepers. Working with one's hands was thought degrading, so slaves did the heavy labor.

Athenians, young and old, were active during the day. Children played with dolls, clay soldiers, kites, and tops. Boys studied music, reading, and writing at the home of some citizen; girls received no formal education. No public schools existed.

Young men sharpened their military skills at the garrison at Piraeus, the busy port of Athens. Wealthy men strolled in the *agora*, the noisy market place, buying spun yarn, flowers, perfumes, wine. Women usually stayed at home and were spoken of by their husbands "as little as possible!"

Old men sat quietly in the sun. When death came, a coin would be placed between their teeth. A legendary boatman was supposed to collect the coin as fare and carry their bodies to *Hades*, the next world. Hades was a gloomy place, quite unappealing to a man who had lived in Athens.

■ **Check on Your Reading**

1. Describe Greek dress and homes.
2. Give examples of daily activities.

2. The Art of Greece: a Riddle Solved

On the surface, the daily life of the Athenian citizen did not appear to be filled with beauty. His home was dark and poorly ventilated, his food was not elaborate, and his market place was the scene of frequent brawls among buyers and sellers. There was little beauty in these things. Yet the Greeks created some of the loveliest art in the history of the world!

Here is a difficult riddle to solve: How could a people whose daily activities were commonplace produce so many beautiful works of art?

One possible answer is that the Greeks had contact with the Egyptians and learned some of their techniques of art. Another answer is that the Greek city-state stimulated the pride of its people. It encouraged them to surpass other city-states in art and architecture.

In addition, Greek artists were able to study the movements of the human body at public gymnasiums, athletic contests, and Olympic Games. Since Greek athletes wore a minimum of clothing, their tanned, muscular bodies furnished artists with fine living models of the human form. This helped Greek sculptors to produce excellent figures of men and gods.

Finally, Greece was fortunate in having in its population a number of outstanding individuals. It was these individual artists who produced the great art, not the majority of the people. All Greeks were given credit for the work of a few. The solution lies in a combination of all of these points.

Greek Art Is Public Art

From the standpoint of the ancient Greeks, it was not necessary to know how their great art developed. It was important that it did—and that they could see it.

They could be sure of this because Greek art was public art. Most fine statues were not sculptured for the private collections of wealthy individuals. They were ordered for the people, and figures of gods and heroes were placed in the open for all to see.

■ *The Parthenon, the most perfect example of the Doric style, represented the culmination of the Periclean period in Greek architecture. The sculptor Phidias and the architects Ictinus and Callicrates planned its design and construction.*

Beautiful columns rarely were constructed for private homes. They were used to support public temples, public meeting places at the market, and public halls. The Athenian citizen used his unattractive house merely as a place to eat and to sleep. Since the climate of Greece was mild, his real home was the outdoors. Here he could walk about and enjoy an art that has rarely been equalled.

Art treasures were always within walking distance of an Athenian's home. Many of them could be seen clearly on the acropolis. There the Athenians erected beautiful statues and temples to the gods. Other Greek city-states had their "hilltops for the gods," but none could compare with the acropolis of Athens.

The Parthenon: Queen of the Acropolis

The loveliest temple on the Athenian acropolis was the Parthenon. The great sculptor Phidias supervised its construction and designed the many beautiful

■ *Greek architectural styles included the Doric columns (left), which had a thick fluted body, or shaft, and a plain square top, or capital; Ionic (center), in which the capital was decorated with scrolls or "ram's horns"; and Corinthian (right), in which the capital was decorated with acanthus leaves.*

95

reliefs that decorated it. The architects Ictinus and Callicrates planned its design, and all the citizens of Athens owned it.

The Parthenon was rectangular in shape and made of a white marble that stood out against the blue sky. Forty-six Doric columns, each of which was six times the height of a man, surrounded the temple itself. The Greeks knew that columns that are perfectly straight sometimes give the appearance of sagging in the middle. The columns of the Parthenon therefore were gently curved so that they would appear straight from a distance.

Above the Doric columns of the inner temple was a band, or *frieze*, of sculptures. Artists carved scenes of gay musicians playing their flutes, bold warriors riding on horseback, servants carrying jugs, and old men waving sacred olive branches. Greek sculptors used their genius to bring to life on the frieze the scenes in Athens on a great festival day. Brilliant colors were used to make the scenes even more lifelike. The Parthenon frieze was a work of art.

■ *These figures of Greek horsemen on the Parthenon frieze show much movement and vitality. The frieze was designed by Phidias.*

The Appeal of Greek Art Remains Strong

The remains of the Parthenon and other temples on the acropolis have continued to inspire men. In the nineteenth century plantation owners in the American South constructed Greek columns for their mansions. The citizens of Nashville, Tennessee, even constructed their own Parthenon, a copy using the same materials that were in the original. Today Greek influence is seen in our homes and public buildings.

Why has Greek art fascinated people? The answer to this question can be found by noting the appealing features of Greek art: (1) Greek art is *simple*, avoiding unnecessary decorations that hide the simple beauty of objects. (2) Greek art is *balanced and harmonious*. Each part of a statue or building seems to fit perfectly into the next, and all blend together naturally. (3) Greek art has an air of *peace and calmness* about it. Even an athlete in the process of throwing a discus seems poised and calm in a Greek statue. (4) Greek art usually chooses for its subject-matter *figures and events in which men can take pride,* avoiding unimportant or ugly subjects. Many statues show the heroism, beauty, and strength of the Greek gods—but few point out their weaknesses. (5) Greek sculpture—particularly in the works of such artists as Phidias, Praxiteles, and Myron—shows how perfect nature could be. Sculptors eliminated the physical weaknesses of human beings and created figures of *the finest physical forms possible.*

These features combined to make the work of Greek artists appealing to men in every century.

■ Check on Your Reading

1. Why did the Greeks produce great art? How did it belong to all the people?

2. What makes the Parthenon such a great artistic achievement?

3. Why has Greek art fascinated people?

96

■ *In his Discobolus (left) Myron came close to creating a perfect human form. A 4th century B.C. statue (right) shows Demeter, goddess of the earth, as a mother sorrowing for her daughter.*

3. Greek Philosophers Search for Wisdom

Some Greek leaders found philosophy as magnetic an attraction as art. The word *philosophy* means "love of wisdom," and Greek philosophers sought the wisdom that would help people to lead happy and worthwhile lives.

The Sophists

Some of the earliest teachers of philosophy were called *Sophists*, or "wisdom-mongers." They were prepared to give courses in mathematics, grammar, astronomy, and speech to anyone who could pay —at prices ranging from $1 to $10,000! Many Sophists were good teachers, honestly seeking to impart wisdom. Unfortunately, other Sophists taught their clients tricks for winning arguments in law courts and elsewhere, rather than searched for truth. For example, here is a conversation to illustrate how a Sophist almost tricked a man into admitting that *puppies were his brothers:*

You say that you have a dog? [a Sophist]
Yes . . . [the man].
And he has puppies?
Yes . . .
And the dog is the father of them?
Yes . . .
And is he not yours?
To be sure he is.
Then he is a father, and he is yours: therefore he is your father, and the puppies are your brothers.

Because of such reasoning, the word "sophist" today denotes a tricky person. Some Sophists taught more than tricks. One of them, Protagoras, made clear that what appears beautiful and good to one person may not seem so to another. No individual should be forced to accept the ideas of others. Sophists also helped to develop grammar, logic, and speech techniques.

Socrates

More important than the Sophists was an Athenian philosopher known as Socrates (469–399 B.C.). Socrates was a stout, bald-headed man with bulbous eyes and a snub nose. He spent much of his time walking slowly about the market place asking questions, such as: What is the purpose of life? What is good? What is justice? Although his appearance was not attractive, Socrates' questions stimulated people to examine the conduct of their lives.

Socrates wrote nothing himself, but from the writings of his student Plato we know that he taught these important ideas: (1) Each person should examine his life carefully to see whether or not his conduct is desirable. (2) Each person should think for himself. (3) Each person should add to his knowledge, for knowledge helps man to be virtuous. (4) Each person should learn to understand himself. "Know Thyself" was the motto of Socrates.

These ideas of Socrates were valuable, but some leaders of Athens misinterpreted them. They accused Socrates of teaching young people dangerous ideas, and they brought him to trial. If Socrates had agreed to stop teaching, he probably would have been freed. He told his accusers:

If you say to me: Socrates, this time you shall be let off, but upon one condition, that you are not to inquire ... in this way any more ... I should reply: Men of Athens ... while I have life ... I shall never cease from the practice and teaching of philosophy. . . .

Since he refused to change his ways, Socrates was sentenced to die. At the age of seventy, he was executed in the Greek way by being given a cup of the poison hemlock.

Plato

The death of Socrates merely stirred other Greek scholars to continue their search for wisdom. Plato (about 428–347 B.C.), one of the best students of Socrates, became the leading philosopher.

Handsome, athletic, and intelligent, Plato soon attracted so many followers that he set up a school of philosophy in a grove of trees on the outskirts of Athens. This was known as the Academy.

Plato wrote many *dialogues*, books describing real and imaginary philosophical conversations among his friends. From such dialogues as the *Republic* we know that Plato believed in these important ideas: (1) Men should be guided in their lives by eternal principles, such as justice, honor, goodness, and love. They should stop thinking only of wealth, fine clothing, and rich food, for all material things disappear with time. (2) Men should do the jobs for which they are best fitted. Good laborers should work; strong warriors should fight; and men of wisdom should rule. None of these groups should do the work of the others, for:

When the cobbler ... attempts to force his way into the class of warriors, or a warrior into that of [rulers] ... for which he is unfitted ... this meddling of one with another is the ruin of the state.

(3) Only the wisest men and women should be permitted to rule the people. There should be no rule by vote of the majority. But women should have equal rights with men.

Plato has been criticized for being anti-democratic, and for not trusting the majority of people to govern themselves. On the other hand, Plato's idea that each person would be happier doing the job for which he is best fitted has been accepted by many educators.

Aristotle

Plato's fame as a scholar was equalled by that of Aristotle, one of the students who studied under him at the Academy. Aristotle (384–322 B.C.) was born in Macedonia, about two hundred miles north of Athens. He soon became so famous that he was chosen to tutor Alexander, the son and heir of Philip of Macedon. Then at the age of fifty, Aristotle set up a school (the *Lyceum*) and continued to teach there.

Aristotle was interested in many fields: astronomy, physics, mathematics, anatomy, politics, speech, art, and philosophy. He was probably the first major biologist in history, for he collected information on over five hundred kinds of living organisms.

From his writings, we know that Aristotle believed in these important ideas: (1) Men should examine, describe, and classify as many forms of life as possible, since it is important to have scientific knowledge of the world. (2) Men should use their ability at reasoning—that is, at thinking out problems—to help them lead happy lives. (3) Men should not go to extremes; they should always take the mean. By the word *mean*, Aristotle meant a middle position—"that which is neither too much nor too little for the particular individual." For example, a man should be neither rash nor cowardly. Instead, he should go between these extremes and be sensibly courageous. (4) Men should learn to live with others. According to Aristotle: "He who is unable to live in society or who has no need to do so because he is so self-sufficient must be either a beast or a god."

The books, methods, and ideas of Aristotle strongly influenced European scholars for over fifteen hundred years. Even today many students in universities study his writings. One of his wise sayings, which has a very modern ring, is that we "learn by doing."

■ **Check on Your Reading**
1. What did the Sophists contribute?
2. Why do we consider Socrates great?
3. What do you think of the ideas of Plato?
4. Explain the four precepts of Aristotle.

4. The Greeks Support "People's Theaters"

Greek dramatists were much better known to the ancient Greeks than were the philosophers. The Greeks loved to go to the theater, and they had strong opinions on the merits of their playwrights.

The Theater of Dionysus

In the fifth century B.C., the Theater of Dionysus was the most famous in Greece. This was an open-air theater on the southern hillside of the acropolis of Athens. During the March Festival in honor of the Wine God, over seventeen thousand Athenians sat jammed together on hard wooden seats to watch a series of plays. The theater, like the temples on the acropolis, belonged to the public. Admission prices were therefore low, and poor citizens were given the two obols needed to buy a ticket.

At the foot of the sloping semicircle, where the people sat, was the *orchestra*. The orchestra was a circular area of beaten earth where the actors and chorus performed. Usually only three actors, always men, were permitted to appear at the same time. Since all actors wore huge masks over their heads, the players could change masks and take many different roles. A

■ *This is a scene from a modern performance of a classical Greek drama presented in the Theater of Epidaurus, built in the 4th century B.C.*

chorus of men chanted, gestured, and danced during each play to explain the characters' actions or to help set the mood.

The Greek theater was not a quiet hall with dimmed lights, velvet curtain, and hushed audience. The people expressed their opinions. A good play or good acting brought cheers of "Authis! Authis!" (Again! Again!) A poor play or poor acting made the audience hiss and groan.

At the end of the three-day March Festival, five judges selected from the audience awarded prizes to the best playwrights and actors. The judges naturally were influenced by the comments and opinions of the audience. Greek theaters were "people's theaters." The people not only owned them but helped select the best plays.

Playwrights Examine Man and His Gods

Aeschylus (525–456 B.C.), author of *Prometheus Bound*, and Sophocles (496–406 B.C.), author of *Antigone*, were two playwrights who won fame for the excellence of their tragedies. Their plays stressed two points: (1) Men must struggle courageously against *fate*, or the will of the gods, even if they cannot change the plans that the gods have for them. (2) Men can gain wisdom through suffering.

Euripides (about 480–406 B.C.), a third major writer of Greek tragedy, took another view. He felt that the events that happened to men were the result of natural causes. They were not an expression of the will of the gods. Euripides doubted that Greek gods existed. He also condemned war in his play *The Trojan Women*. He was not popular with state and military officials.

Euripides' attacks on the Greek religion did not go unanswered. Aristophanes (about 448–388 B.C.), a writer of comedy, ridiculed some ideas of Euripides in such plays as *The Frogs*. Aristophanes was a clever playwright whose puns and coarse humor delighted audiences. He defended religion, opposed war, and tried to prevent the people from getting too much power.

His greatest contribution was in warning the Athenians against men who were frauds and rascals. Be careful, Aristophanes said, of the tricky fellows who "tickle your vanity" or praise the richness of Athens as they would "anchovies in oil"!

■ **Check on Your Reading**

1. How did the acting and the performance in the Greek theater differ from ours today?
2. What were the major ideas of Aeschylus, Sophocles, Euripides, and Aristophanes?

5. Greek Historians, Poets, and Scientists Serve Society

Greek historians and poets served society. Greek scientists and mathematicians made important contributions, too.

Greek Historians and Poets

Herodotus (about 484–425 B.C.) wrote a colorful and entertaining history of the Persian Wars. Although he was often inaccurate, Herodotus is known as the "father of history." Historians have named him their "parent" because he was probably the first to write an organized narrative of past occurrences, which can be called "history."

Thucydides (about 460–400 B.C.) is called the first *scientific* historian. In his *History of the Peloponnesian War*, he tried to check his facts carefully and to present events in an accurate chronological order. Less concerned with entertaining his readers than was Herodotus, Thucydides tried to give "exact knowledge of the past as an aid to the interpretation of the future."

While the Greek historians set down their knowledge of the past, Greek poets described their feelings about the past and present. Pindar (about 518–438 B.C.) was the greatest author of *lyric poetry*, short poems designed to be sung. He wrote many pieces honoring the victors in athletic games. Sappho (sixth century B.C.) was the first woman poet whose writings we have. Although only five per cent of her poems remain, they show that she was a sensitive writer of romantic poetry.

The writings of Greek historians and poets served society by keeping alive a record of Greek life and achievement. Sappho was therefore right in predicting:

I think there will be memory of us yet
In after days.

Contributions to Science and Mathematics

One of the reasons why the Greeks were remembered "in after days" is that their work in science affected future civilizations. The Greeks drew on the scientific knowledge of the Egyptians and Babylonians, added their own ideas, and passed on the information to others. In general these were the two features of Greek science: (1) The Greeks *reasoned* about scientific matters but did few experiments to test their beliefs. That is why their best work was in geometry, which does not require excessive experimentation, and their poorest was in physics and chemistry. (2) The Greeks discussed the structure and function of the physical world, but usually they did not put their knowledge to practical use. They would be similar to a modern scholar who works out principles of speed but does not apply them to build faster planes or rockets.

In addition to Aristotle, several scholars of Greece made scientific contributions to the ancient world. Thales (about 626–548 B.C.) was one of the first men to see the importance of establishing principles in geometry. (There is evidence that an ancient people who once lived near modern Baghdad knew how to solve geometrical problems many years before the Greeks, but their work was unknown to Thales.) Thales also was interested in astronomy. He predicted an eclipse of the sun and probably studied the effects of magnetism.

Pythagoras (about 580–500 B.C.) did important work with numbers and helped to develop several principles of geometry. He taught that (1) the interior angles of a triangle are equal to two right angles and (2) in a right triangle, the square of the hypotenuse equals the sum of the squares of the other two sides (the so-called "Pythagorean theorem"). Greek mathematics certainly is not dead—your high school geometry textbook teaches you these same two principles!

Other Greeks suggested that the world was not a fixed and rigid place. Heraclitus (540–475 B.C.) believed that everything in life changed except change. Democritus (about 460–370 B.C.) advanced the idea that the universe was composed of invisible atoms that moved about continuously.

Extremely important, too, were the contributions of Hippocrates (about 460–377 B.C.). Hippocrates is known as the "father of medical science" because he taught that diseases were the results of natural causes.

Hippocrates urged his students to be sincere and helpful to the sick, and tradition says that many of them took a pledge that they would. Modern doctors are familiar with the words of this so-called Hippocratic Oath, which includes the lines:

I will use treatment to help the sick according to my ability and judgment ... I will keep pure and holy both my life and my art.

■ **Check on Your Reading**

1. Compare Herodotus and Thucydides.
2. Who were Pindar and Sappho?
3. Contrast the Greek scientific methods with our own.
4. What real contributions did the Greeks make to science and mathematics?
5. Why is Hippocrates called the "father of medical science"?

6. The Peloponnesian War and the Conquest of Greece

Many of the splendid cultural achievements occurred during the time of Pericles. Pericles (p. 85) was the leading statesman of Athens from about 460 to 429 B.C. He was an excellent leader and encouraged the Greeks in art, philosophy, and literature. The period of thirty years covered by his administration in Athens is often called the "Golden Age of Athens."

■ *This Greek battleship, painted on a 6th century B.C. cup, was propelled mainly by oars and had an effective weapon in its ram.*

Although creative individuals had produced a "Golden Age," they were unable to solve the problems caused by the jealous rivalry of the Greek city-states. In 477 B.C., under the leadership of Athens, several Greek city-states did form the Delian League. This was a military federation for protection against future attacks by Persia. *Military federation* meant that the members were to continue to be independent, but they were to contribute money or ships for a common defensive fleet. In time, Athens changed the original purpose of the League. She used federation funds to beautify Athens, and she forced the other city-states to obey her in matters of trade. Athens soon had so much control over the others that the Greek military federation became an Athenian empire.

Wars Weaken Athens, Sparta, and Thebes

Angered by the continual interference of Athens, Sparta and other city-states fought a long war against Athens and her allies. This Peloponnesian War lasted from 431 to 404 B.C. It was a bitter war of "much banishing and bloodshedding" and ended in the defeat of the Athenians.

Athens was forced to surrender her empire and destroy the protective Long Walls that she had built from the city to her port at Piraeus. Stripped of her possessions and defensive walls, Athens was further weakened by a great plague that had carried off her leader, Pericles, and at least one-quarter of the population. The once proud Athenians had to obey the orders of Sparta.

Sparta proved to be an oppressive leader of the Greeks. As a result, troops from the city-state of Thebes overthrew Spartan rule in 371 B.C. Thebes now tried to lead the Greeks, but within ten years she too lost control.

Athens—Sparta—Thebes—had failed to bring the Greeks together. The individual ambitions and jealousies of the city-states continued to keep them apart. Without the union of all, each city-state gradually became weaker. The disorganized Greeks were a perfect target for the army of a foreign invader.

Philip of Macedonia Conquers the Greeks

The invader came from Macedonia, a country north of Greece. The Macedonians were a rough Indo-European people who lived as shepherds, hunters, and farmers. About the middle of the fourth century B.C., Philip, a Macedonian king, united many of the tribal groups and molded them into an effective fighting force. Then he moved his troops southward, determined to bring all the Greek city-states under his control by arms or bribery.

There were some Greeks who saw the danger and warned the people. The great orator Demosthenes, for example, denounced the Athenians for caring more about amusements than defense. He urged them to unite with other Greeks and prepare to meet the Macedonian attack.

The Louvre

■ *Alexander the Great conquered most of the known world. His accomplishments had considerable influence on the Hellenistic period.*

In 338 B.C. troops from Athens and Thebes finally united long enough to fight Philip's forces at the crucial battle of Chaeronea. The Greeks fought courageously, but the Macedonian cavalry drove them back until they fled from the battle. The independence of the city-states was at an end. The Macedonians controlled the future of Greek civilization.

Alexander the Great Builds a Great Empire

Philip did not long enjoy his conquests, for he was killed in 336 B.C. by one of his own officers. His son, Alexander, became the king of Macedonia and its subject territories at the age of twenty.

Alexander was a handsome, energetic young man who loved all sports except boxing and wrestling. He was physically graceful, a fine runner, and an excellent horseman and hunter. Military action always pleased him and he looked forward eagerly to the tests of battle. His greatest fear was that his father would conquer so many towns that there would be none left for him to take when he became king!

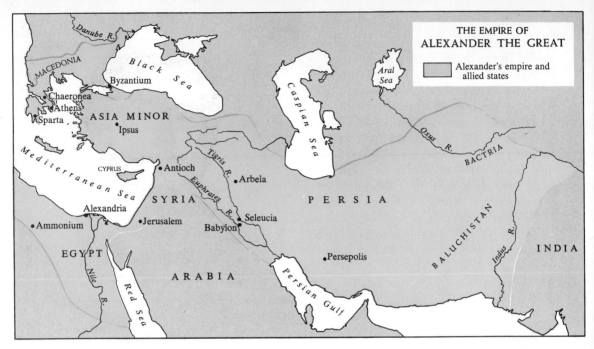

■ *Alexander's empire (327 B.C.) extended from Greece to India and from the Black Sea to Egypt —the largest empire up to that time. What countries did he conquer? How did he administer his empire? What happened to the empire after Alexander's death?*

Educated by the philosopher Aristotle, Alexander had learned to admire Greek achievements. It is said that he kept Homer's *Iliad* under his pillow at night— next to his dagger—and enjoyed reading the plays of Aeschylus, Sophocles, and Euripides. Alexander wrote to Aristotle:

... I had rather excel others in the knowledge of what is excellent, than in the extent of my power and dominion.

These words must have been pleasant for Aristotle to read, but Alexander never became a man who limited himself only to thought. He wanted "opportunities of performing great and illustrious actions."

Conquest provided the best opportunities for "glory," and Alexander spent the rest of his life trying to conquer a good part of the known world. He crushed a Greek revolt and kept all of Greece under Macedonian control. Then he took Asia Minor, Syria, and Egypt. Eventually, the whole Persian Empire and lands as far east as the Indus River fell to his forces.

By 327 B.C. Alexander's empire extended east and west from India to Greece, and north and south from the Black Sea to Egypt—the largest empire up to that date (map, p. 104). What is more, Alexander insisted that all the peoples in this empire— both his Macedonians and those whom they had conquered—should feel a sense of unity with each other. "I count all of you as my kinsmen," he told them, and prayed for "fellowship in the realm."

The Accomplishments of Alexander

Alexander the Great was cut down before his ability as an administrator of his empire could be tested. In 323 B.C. he became ill with a fever, and within two weeks he died. At the time of his death, Alexander was not quite thirty-three.

Alexander's empire eventually was divided into three major parts, each ruled by a dynasty founded by one of his generals: (1) Macedonia and Greece—controlled by the Antigonus Gonatus group, (2) Egypt—controlled by the Ptolemy group, and (3) Syria and Persia—controlled by the Seleucid group.

Alexander's military empire had split apart. However, many of his ideas and peaceful accomplishments remained. These included the following: (1) Alexander had helped to found cities—such as Alexandria in Egypt—as part of his policy to spread Greek ideas. Alexandria developed into a great center of learning. (2) He had stimulated trade among various parts of his empire. Alexandria and Antioch became the most important trading centers. (3) He had encouraged scientific investigations. The specimens of plants and animals collected by the specialists who accompanied his fighting men proved valuable to biologists of the period. (4) He had advanced the idea that all men—whether they were Macedonians, Greeks, or Persians—should feel a sense of brotherhood with each other.

As Plutarch, a Greek biographer, wrote:

[Alexander] believed that he had a mission . . . to harmonize men generally, and to be the reconciler of the world. . . . Mixing, as in a loving-cup, their ways of life and their customs . . . he bade them all consider the whole of the inhabited world as their country.

(5) Alexander's soldiers and traders had brought Greek ideas to the areas they invaded and received many new ideas in exchange. Cultures had spread and intertwined. Greek art, for example, had considerable influence on the Buddhist sculpture of India. Greek civilization came in contact with non-Greek civilizations, including those in the East. This mingling produced a new cultural era known as the *Hellenistic* period.

■ Check on Your Reading

1. Why did the Delian League fail to unite the Greeks permanently?

2. How did the Peloponnesian War end?

3. Why was Philip of Macedonia able to conquer Greece?

4. Describe Alexander's character and achievements. What happened to his empire?

7. The Hellenistic Period

The Hellenistic period lasted roughly from the death of Alexander to about the first century B.C. (about 322–90 B.C.). It introduced changes in art, literature, and philosophy. However, the greatest achievements occurred in the sciences, where Greek and non-Greek scientific ideas mingled to produce remarkable results.

The Sciences Make Important Gains

Scientists were both active and productive. For example, Euclid gathered and organized Greek knowledge of geometry. Eratosthenes calculated the circumference of the earth, and his figures came close to being right. Aristarchus suggested the *heliocentric* theory—that is, that the earth moves around the sun. At this time people believed in the *geocentric* theory that the sun moves around the earth.

Hipparchus developed the technique of finding position by latitude and longitude. He was also one of the first to use trigonometry for the study of astronomy.

No man of the period was more devoted to science than Archimedes (about 287–212 B.C.). It was said that he loved his studies so well that he even drew diagrams

Greek Sculpture and Architecture	Hellenistic Sculpture and Architecture
1. Simple.	1. Elaborate. Stressed large size and ornamentation.
2. Balanced and harmonious.	2. Often lacked balance and harmony.
3. Calm and restrained in appearance.	3. Emotional and active in appearance.
4. Interested in showing various types of gods and heroes. Not concerned with representing the faces and bodies of specific individuals.	4. In many cases, interested in representing the faces and bodies of individual men and women.
5. Considerable use of the Doric column in architecture.	5. Considerable use of the Corinthian column in architecture.

when he bathed! Archimedes did outstanding work in physics. He developed principles for floating bodies and demonstrated the many uses of levers, pulleys, and cranes. When his city of Syracuse was attacked, he used his various engines to destroy the enemy's ships.

Archimedes demonstrated in his work that he was concerned with both the principles and the practice of science. He underlined the basic difference between

■ *The highly emotional Laocoön group (1st century B.C.) is a classic example of Hellenistic art. It is the work of three sculptors of Rhodes.*

Vatican Museum

a Hellenistic and a Greek scientist: *both were interested in developing scientific theories and principles, but the Hellenistic scientist also wished to put them to practical use.* The practical inventions of Hellenistic scientists included a kind of steam engine and methods for supplying water and carrying off sewage from cities.

Greek and Hellenistic Art Compared

Just as in science, there were differences between Greek and Hellenistic art. These differences can be seen clearly when the chief characteristics of each are listed side by side (see Chart).

In general, Greek art has been considered by most critics to be superior to Hellenistic art. On the other hand, some sculpture of the Hellenistic period (such as the *Laocoön* group) was excellent. The famous *Nike* (or *Victory*) of *Samothrace* also was striking because it combined several of the best features of Greek and Hellenistic styles—styles that had some influence on the sculpture of India.

Hellenistic Writers and Philosophers

In the field of literature, several writers made important contributions during Hellenistic times. Polybius recorded history with considerable accuracy; and Theocritus introduced the *pastoral* poem, a short lyric poem dealing with life and beauty in the countryside. To house the works of Hellenistic and earlier writers, a splendid library was established at Alexandria.

Philosophers also continued to ask the question: "What is the best way for men to live?" The answers of Epicurus and Zeno were particularly important.

Epicurus (about 342–270 B.C.) and his followers, the *Epicureans,* believed that man's happiness depended on finding pleasure. Pleasure came from having a healthy body and a calm mind—not from continuous merrymaking. Epicurus wrote that man should use his intelligence to choose between trivial and truly enjoyable things in life:

By pleasure we mean the absence of pain in the body and trouble in the soul. It is not an unbroken succession of . . . revelry . . . that makes life pleasant; it is sober reasoning which searches out the ground for every choice. . . .

Zeno (336–264 B.C.) and later philosophers developed another approach to life known as *stoicism.* Men who were Stoics believed that an event became good or bad depending on how a person viewed it. For example, a fire was called "bad" by a man whose house had burned down. Yet it was called "good" by his wife who had long wanted a new house and would have one. Actually then, the Stoics said, the fire was neither good nor bad—it was an event. It was man's *attitude* that made it good or bad.

The Stoics therefore urged men to view all events with calmness and self-control and to accept success and failure without emotion. They believed that if man would use his intelligence to control his passions, he would find peace of mind.

Like Alexander the Great, Zeno and the Stoics also expressed belief in a universal spirit and in the basic brotherhood of all human beings. They urged that men should live like "one flock on a common pasture feeding together under a common law." This idea later helped to pave the way for the acceptance of Christian teachings.

Greece Is Ripe for Conquest

Writers and philosophers alone could not bring happiness to the poor. Although commerce grew and cities increased in wealth during the Hellenistic period, the poor did not benefit from these gains. A few rich people enjoyed life, while the poverty-stricken majority had to struggle still harder to survive.

Without economic or political rights, the people grew restless. The time was ripe for new rulers and different ideas.

■ Check on Your Reading

1. What were the important gains made in science in Hellenistic times?
2. Compare Hellenistic and Greek art.
3. What is Stoicism?

CULTURAL CHARACTERISTICS of Ancient Greece

The Greek mathematician Euclid delighted in stimulating love of learning for learning's sake. According to legend, a pupil once asked him what he would gain by learning geometry. Euclid answered him by saying to a slave: "Give the young man three [coins], since he must needs make a gain out of what he learns." In such ways, Euclid ridiculed the idea that knowledge must always result in personal gain.

Like Euclid, many of the ancient Greeks had the ability to enjoy life for itself alone. Among the characteristics of their culture the following are noteworthy.

The creation of many beautiful art forms constructed for the enjoyment of the Greek public.

The development of stimulating ideas in the field of philosophy.

The existence of exciting theaters well patronized by the Greek people.

Interest in the past as well as in the present, as reflected in the work of several major historians, geographers, and poets.

The exploration of the wonders of science, using intelligence as a guide.

Contributions of Greek culture to other people through cultural diffusion, such as during the Hellenistic period.

Out of the richness of Greek culture, the idea emerged that *reason* could help men to lead a good life. In government many Greeks supported the principle of "direct responsible citizenship"; that is, citizens were reasonable enough to take a direct part in their government. In art they stressed balance and harmony. In philosophy they urged men to use reason and intelligence to settle their problems. In literature they wrote plays to stimulate man to think or reason about Fate, the gods, and man himself. In science they used reason, not experimentation, to probe the problems of science. Not all Greeks had a zest for life or a love of reason, but the culture of ancient Greece was affected by both and left its mark on the modern world. In philosophy, art, and poetry we are still learning from them.

MAN AND HIS CULTURE

Let's Meet the People!
This sketch is based on the writings of Hippocrates and his students. Information was taken from Charles Singer, *A Short History of Medicine*, 1928, by permission of Clarendon Press, Oxford.

A Greek Doctor
The Greek doctor was no "specialist." He handled all cases. He treated children for coughs and earaches; adults for pneumonia and malaria; and the aged for the loss of sight and hearing. One of his most serious cases involved Thasos, a woman sick with fever. He made notes of her case history:

FIRST DAYS—*Observations:* Thasos "wrapped herself up in her bedclothes; kept silent, fumbled . . . and gathered hairs from her clothing; tears and again laughter; no sleep . . . coldness of the extremities."
   Action taken: The Greek doctor was a follower of Hippocratic methods and believed in the healing power of nature and time. He decided that he would take no extreme action. Instead, he would urge Thasos to drink a broth and to rest.

NINTH DAY—*Observations:* Thasos "talked much incoherently; and again sank into silences."

   Action taken: These were bad signs. The doctor decided that he would give the woman a drug to help fight the fever.

FOURTEENTH DAY—*Observations:* "Breathing rare, large and spaced, and again hurried."
   Action taken: This was the crisis. The doctor would remain alert, but Thasos would live or die depending on her own strength!

The Greek doctor waited for the decision. Then he hurried on to his next patient. New problems were waiting for the man who had pledged "to help the sick according to my ability."

CHAPTER REVIEW

REVIEW and DISCUSSION

1. Identify the people and places and explain the events and terms on p. 92.

2. Why didn't the Greeks use their love of beauty in building and furnishing their homes?

3. Discuss some of Socrates' questions such as: What is the purpose of life? What is good? What is true? What is beautiful?

4. Can governments keep ideas they consider unacceptable from spreading by killing the person who teaches these ideas?

5. Plato believed that only the wise should rule. Do you think this idea is democratic or anti-democratic? Why?

6. The Greeks believed that the proper study of mankind was man. What did the Greeks contribute to the knowledge of man as compared with their predecessors?

7. Do you believe man gains wisdom through suffering? Why or why not?

8. Review the important ideas of the Sophists, Stoics, Epicureans, Socrates, Plato, and Aristotle. Which ones can you accept? Why?

9. Why do you think the Greeks were more interested in the principles and theories of science than in their practical application?

10. With all the emphasis on the development of men's minds why couldn't the Athenians solve the problems caused by jealous rivalry among the city-states?

11. Do you agree or disagree with these statements? Why? (a) When two civilizations come into contact with each other, a stronger civilization will result. (b) The man who spreads ideas is as important to the world as the man who first had the idea.

ACTIVITIES

1. Write a report on the trial and death of Socrates.

2. Read a Greek play. What ideas did the author express in the play?

3. Panel discussion: Which of the people mentioned in this chapter made the greatest contribution to the world?

4. Read a selection in literature, drama, philosophy, or history written by an ancient Greek. Write a summary of your own reading.

5. Draw a diagram of a Greek theater or write a paper on Greek sculpture.

6. Become more informed on some phase of Greek life by reading several references besides an encyclopedia on your subject.

PAST and PRESENT

1. Find examples of Doric, Ionic, and Corinthian columns in your area.

2. Plato's idea on equal rights for women is still being debated in America. Women are divided on the question. Prepare for a discussion on this topic by reading Plato's dialogue on "Equal Rights and Duties for Women" and consult *Readers' Guide*.

3. In *Readers' Guide*, find some articles on modern Greece. Use them as a basis for a comparison of modern and ancient Greece.

SUGGESTED READINGS

Basic books: DURANT, WILL, *The Story of Philosophy: The Lives and Opinions of the Greater Philosophers*, Simon and Schuster.

MULLER, HERBERT J., *Uses of the Past*, New American Library.

SMITH, GOLDWIN, *The Heritage of Man*, Chap. 8, Scribner. A valuable book.

Special accounts: FREEMAN, EUGENE, and APPEL, DAVID, *The Wisdom and Ideas of Plato*, Fawcett Publications.

ROUSE, W. H. D. (trans.), *Great Dialogues of Plato*, MD 167, New American Library.

TOYNBEE, ARNOLD J., *Greek Historical Thought*, MD 164, New American Library.

Wisdom, Twentieth Issue, Wisdom Magazine, Inc. Articles on philosophy by WILL DURANT.

Biography and Fiction: THOMPSON, STITH, and GASSNER, JOHN, (eds.), *Our Heritage of World Literature*, Holt.

ROUSE, W. H. D. (trans.), *The Iliad*, MD 110; *The Odyssey*, MD 92, New American Library.

Chapter 7   *The Rise of Rome:*
From Village to Empire

KEYNOTE   The history of Rome is filled with the names of men who rose high in government and then were violently removed from office. Roman history is marked, too, by fierce wars against foreign enemies. There were land battles against Hannibal, the Carthaginian general who marched an army of men and elephants over the Alps to attack the Romans. There were rugged military campaigns against the Gauls. There were sea fights against Cleopatra, the Egyptian queen who tried to split the Roman Empire and poisoned herself when she failed.

However, the history of Rome is far more than the story of brutal conflicts at home and wars abroad. Beneath a raging surface there ran a strong, steady current of development. Rome was growing from a tiny village to the capital of the greatest empire in the world!

As Rome grew from a small republic to an empire, the Romans twisted and turned with "growing pains." They fought among themselves, they battled foreign peoples, and they moved from hero to hero in search of security. Finally, the empire was stabilized and peace and order were restored to the land.

The story of Rome demonstrates a basic point: *The growth of an empire, like the growth of an individual, is often a long, difficult process.*

Key People   *Hannibal · Cato · Tiberius and Gaius Gracchus · Sulla · Julius Caesar · Pompey · Mark Antony · Octavian (Augustus)*

Key Places   *Po and Tiber rivers · Apennines · Rome · Alps · Carthage · Zama · Gaul · Rubicon River · Actium*

Key Events   *Etruscans conquer Latins · Roman Republic established · Twelve Tables · Punic Wars · Romans conquer Mediterranean world · Caesar murdered · Augustus becomes first emperor*

Key Terms   *patricians · plebeians · Tribunes · Roman citizenship · populares · triumvirate · province · optimates · Pax Romana*

110

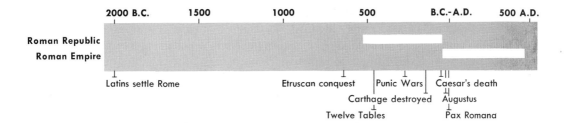

| 2000 B.C. | 1500 | 1000 | 500 | B.C.-A.D. | 500 A.D. |

Roman Republic
Roman Empire

Latins settle Rome Etruscan conquest Punic Wars Caesar's death
Carthage destroyed Augustus
Twelve Tables Pax Romana

1. Italy: "A Land That Reared a Valiant Breed of Men"

Italy is a boot-shaped peninsula in southern Europe that extends over seven hundred miles into the Mediterranean Sea. Its toe points toward the island of Sicily, and its heel curves gently into the sea. Italy has a central position in the Mediterranean area (map, p. 112).

Historical Importance of Italy's Central Position: The seas to the west, south, and east of Italy have provided avenues for expansion and trade and for the stimulation that comes from the exchange of ideas with other peoples.

Italy's surface is marked by the Apennine Mountains that run down the length of the country. In the extreme north, past the fertile Po Valley, are the Alps.

Historical Importance of the Alps: The Alps have formed barriers that often have helped to protect the people of Italy. There are passes through which these mountains can be crossed, so that Italy has always been a part of Europe.

In the western area of the country are most of the good harbors, the coastal plains, and a considerable part of the navigable Tiber River. Eastern Italy has few harbors and is handicapped by the sharp slopes of the Apennine Mountains.

Historical Importance of the Western Area: Since the western part of the country has most of the geographic advantages, the peoples of Italy have built many of their principal settlements in this area.

Italy is pleasantly warmed by the sun and gentle winds, and its climate is generally mild. It is a land where the terrain varies from hills to woodlands to fertile plains. Virgil, a Roman poet, noted the contrasts in:

stubborn lands and churlish hill-sides . . .
fields strewn wide with woodland berries . . .
soil that is rich, in moisture sweet exulting,
and the plain that teems with grasses.

The poet marvelled at such variations in its climate and terrain and hailed Italy as a fortunate land that had "reared a valiant breed of men."

■ **Check on Your Reading**

1. Did Italy's location affect its history? Explain.

2. How have the Alps affected Italy's relationship with Europe?

3. Which way does Italy "face" geographically? Explain.

111

2. The Latins Settle in the Plain of Latium

The origin of this "valiant breed of men" can be traced far back into history. Starting about 2000 B.C.—when the Egyptian civilization was already established and the earliest Greeks were migrating into the Aegean area—other groups began to move southwest into the Italian peninsula and establish settlements.

The Latins Settle Rome

These newcomers came from central Europe, and they spoke an Indo-European language. The most important of the groups, the so-called *Latins*, gradually settled on the western plain, south of the Tiber River. This region eventually was

■ *Italy is a peninsula in southern Europe. Its location and geography have influenced Italy's history. What effects have its mountains had?*

ITALY

known as Latium. One of the trading areas in Latium centered about Roma (or Rome). The name and origin of Rome are still matters for debate among historians. Some of them say that the name means "river town," while others prefer to define it as "strength."

Still other people believe that the word *Rome* was taken from the name of *Romulus*, a mythical figure who was said to have become the first Roman ruler. According to legend, Romulus and his twin brother, Remus, were sons of the war-god Mars. As babies, they were cared for by a she-wolf. When they grew to manhood, they both wished to be king of the city we call Rome. They decided to wait for a sign from the gods that would tell them which of the two should rule. Remus at last saw six vultures and declared that this meant that the gods had chosen him. But Romulus saw twelve vultures and claimed the kingship for himself. To settle the matter, Romulus killed his brother, established Rome, and made himself the first Roman ruler.

All this is legend—although the bones of a vulture recently were dug up at the very place where Romulus was believed to have been buried! As far as facts are concerned, only one point is certain: By the middle of the eighth century B.C. Rome was a permanent and growing town.

The Etruscans Conquer the Latins

Rome and the villages of Latium were sandwiched in between the Greeks to the south and the Etruscans to the north. The Greeks were the descendants of those men who had started colonies in southern Italy and Sicily. The Etruscans were a more advanced people who probably had come from Asia Minor and settled north of the Tiber River by 900 B.C.

■ *Etruscan craftsmen excelled in creating out-standing bronze sculpture. Examples of bronze artwork from the 5th century B.C. are the head of a young man (top) and the bucket (center), decorated with reliefs—one depicts Heracles strangling the Nemean lion. Other figures were carved from volcanic stone; for example, the leopard (bottom).*

Between 650 and 600 B.C., the Etruscans conquered the Latins to the south and took over the control of most of Latium, including Rome. While they occupied this territory, the Etruscans improved the sanitation system of Rome and passed on several valuable engineering ideas to the Romans. They also introduced the Romans to the architectural principles of the arch and the vault. The Etruscans probably had learned these principles from the peoples of the Near East.

However, the chief fame of the Etruscans rests on their splendid work in *metallurgy*, the extraction of metals from ores and the preparation of them for man's use. They mined copper, iron, tin, lead, and silver and exported them to countries around the Mediterranean Sea. Then they fashioned bronze into beautiful sculptures of men, gods, and animals.

Etruscan artistry in bronze was used to produce many fascinating objects—sea gods with fishlike bodies and human faces, perfume boxes shaped like birds, candle holders that twisted and turned like the smoke itself. Bronze art was the great metal legacy that the Etruscans left for the generations that came after them. Some examples of Etruscan bronze art can be seen on this page.

■ **Check on Your Reading**

1. How was Rome founded?
2. What were the chief contributions of the Etruscans?
3. Evaluate Etruscan work in bronze and stone sculpture.

113

3. The Roman Republic Is Established

Etruscan contributions to their way of life could not make the people of Rome forget that the invaders still ruled them as conquerors. In 509 B.C. the Romans joined other Latin groups and drove their Etruscan masters from the land.

The Romans were now faced with the problem of establishing a government for themselves. They had lived under a monarchy during Etruscan times. Since their town with its surrounding fields was quite small, they felt that at least some of the people could take part in running the government. The Romans therefore set up a republic—a government in which citizens elect the officials who pass and execute the laws and in which no person inherits the right to hold a political office.

The Government of the Republic

The Roman Republic lasted from 509 B.C. to 31 B.C. In the beginning its government had three main organs:

1. THE CENTURIATE ASSEMBLY. The Centuriate Assembly consisted of all citizens who performed their military duties. Its jobs were to choose two Consuls and other governmental officials and to vote on bills presented to it by the Consuls and the Senate.

■ *These are the ruins of the Roman Forum, the hub of the ancient city. In the Forum, political, commercial, and recreational activities were held. As the city grew, the Forum was adorned with magnificent arches, shaded walks, and religious temples.*

2. TWO CONSULS. Two Consuls were elected for one-year terms by the Assembly. They shared the power formerly enjoyed by the monarch. Each Consul could "veto," or prohibit, the actions of the other. Their jobs were to act as chief executives for the republic, to draw up bills for the Assembly to vote on, to interpret and carry out the laws, and to control the military forces.

3. THE SENATE. The Senate was made up of all former Consuls and any man appointed to the Senate by a Consul. Its jobs were to direct foreign affairs, to control the tax system, and to reject or accept any bill passed by the Assembly. Since the Senate also influenced the Assembly's selection of Consuls, it was the most powerful of the three organs.

Patricians Oppose Plebeians

The government of the early Roman Republic actually was in the hands of the *patricians*, men who owned considerable land or who belonged to the oldest families in Rome. The Consuls and the members of the Senate were always patricians. Many of them were experienced and mature public servants; some were concerned only with their own interests.

Opposing the patricians were the *plebeians*. The plebeians were men who owned little or no land or had newly settled in Rome. Although the majority of people were plebeians, they had little political power and were dominated by the patricians. The patricians even controlled the Centuriate Assembly, which was made up of both patricians and plebeians.

The plebeians were angered by their inferior position. They warned that they would leave Rome unless they received important rights of government. The patricians knew that the city would be helpless without the labor of the plebeians. They therefore permitted the plebeians to

Stadtisches Museum, Wiesbaden

■ *The Legionary was the foot soldier in the Roman armies that were to build the empire. The Republic's finest citizens fought its wars.*

meet in their own assembly (known as the *Tribal Assembly*) to elect their own officials called *Tribunes*. The Tribunes had the right to veto any decision by an official or by the Senate that injured the well-being of the plebeians.

The Twelve Tables

In asking for greater rights in government, the plebeians also protested that most Roman laws were unwritten. Often they had been punished for breaking ancient customs and rules that they did not know even existed. They did not have anything similar to the ancient Babylonian Code of Hammurapi to guide them. The plebeians demanded that a written record be made of their duties and privileges.

As a result, the *Twelve Tables* were drawn up (about 451–450 B.C.). This was probably the first written code of Roman law. It did not provide equal punishment to all offenders for the same type of offense.

115

Some of the provisions of the Twelve Tables included the following:

If one has broken the bone of a freeman ... let him pay a penalty of three hundred coins. If he has broken the bone of a slave, let him pay one hundred and fifty coins.

You will recall that exactly the same distinctions were used in the Code of Hammurapi (p. 38). Equality before the law was still in the future. But in spite of inequalities, the Twelve Tables helped to establish for future generations one of the first principles of law: *Laws are to be written.*

The plebeians did not stop their agitation when the Twelve Tables were written. They next won the right to marry patricians (445 B.C.). Intermarriage helped to break down distinctions between the two groups.

■ *Rome and Carthage became powerful rivals in the Mediterranean world and soon clashed in the Punic Wars. What were the results?*

EARLY ROME
AND CARTHAGE

Roman Republic in
500 B.C.

Roman power in 265 B.C.

Carthaginian power
in 265 B.C.

0   Scale of Miles   190

CISALPINE
GAUL
Rubicon R.
ETRUSCANS
ILLYRIA
CORSICA
LATIUM
Rome
SAMNITES
APPIAN WAY
Adriatic Sea
SARDINIA
Naples Mt. Vesuvius
Tyrrhenian
Sea
GREAT GREECE
Mt. Etna Strait of
SICILY Messina
Syracuse
Mediterranean
Carthage
AFRICA
Zama
Sea

The plebeians also continued to struggle against the patricians for more power in government. In the fourth century B.C., the plebeians gained the right to be elected to any office, including the positions of Consul and Senator. Finally, in 287 B.C., a law was passed that made the decisions of the plebeian Tribal Assembly binding on *all* citizens.

Roman Power Spreads

By the middle of the third century B.C., the Romans had developed a working system of *representative government*—that is, a government in which men were chosen by the citizens to represent them and to run the country. The Greek citizen had voted on laws himself (this method is known as "direct" democracy); the Roman citizen usually elected a representative to vote for him.

To defend the Roman Republic, an army of citizen-soldiers was kept in readiness. Armed with spears, daggers, short swords, javelins, bows and arrows, and battering rams the Romans proved to be powerful fighters. Both their fighting methods and their organization were effective. Discipline was strict in the army legions. A Roman soldier who fled in combat could expect the death penalty if caught; a deserter in peacetime would have a hand cut off.

Patriotism kept pace with discipline, and Roman expansion gave the people ample opportunity to demonstrate both their loyalty and courage. At first, the Romans had not deliberately planned to expand. However, threatened by jealous rivals to the north and defiant Greeks to the south, the Romans concluded that territorial expansion was their best defense. On numerous occasions other peoples asked the Romans to intervene in their defense, and Rome moved in to establish order. In later times, the Romans became even

116

■ *This is a detail from the bas-relief on Trajan's column, depicting his military campaigns. Roman soldiers are seen defending their position against the attacking Dacians.*

more ambitious. Eventually they desired to dominate all of Italy; and once they had begun to expand beyond Italy, their love of conquest grew.

The Romans first joined neighboring Latin peoples in a league for mutual military defense. When the other members of this league began to challenge her leadership, Rome defeated them and forced them to continue as her allies.

Next, Roman armies strengthened their strategic position by pushing back hostile tribes in the Apennine Mountains. Then they used diplomacy and force to check the Gauls, invaders who had come from over the Alps and plundered Rome.

Finally, the Romans conquered the Greeks who blocked their expansion through southern Italy. By 265 B.C., the one-time village of Rome controlled nearly all of the peninsula of Italy (map, p. 116).

How did Rome achieve such conquests? What were the reasons for her success throughout Italy? There are at least two answers to these questions.

(1) Roman armies succeeded because they were well trained and organized and because the soldiers believed that they were fighting for a just cause. At first, the Romans did not deliberately plan to win an empire by war. Nevertheless, when other peoples threatened to attack them, the Romans struck first and placed the conquered peoples under their control. Soldiers fought hard because they felt that they were defending their homes.

(2) The Romans succeeded because they treated conquered peoples in Italy fairly well. These peoples often were given some degree of self-government and some type of Roman citizenship in what has been called a "loosely controlled confederation." This granting of Roman citizenship, either full or partial, was one of the principal reasons for the success of the Roman administration. In addition, conquered peoples were permitted to keep their own customs. By such liberal policies, the Romans were able to prevent dangerous uprisings.

■ **Check on Your Reading**

1. How did the citizens take part in governing the Roman Republic?

2. What concessions were made to the plebeians?

3. Evaluate the Twelve Tables.

4. Why was the Roman army so significant?

5. How did Rome expand its power?

117

4. Rome and Carthage Clash

The Roman conquest of Italy brought them in contact with Carthage, a powerful city on the coast of North Africa. Carthage had been founded by the Phoenicians about one hundred years before the village of Rome was established. By the third century B.C. it had become the center of a rich and powerful commercial empire.

At first, Rome was untroubled by the power of Carthage. Later, Carthage angered the Romans by refusing to permit them to trade in the western Mediterranean area. Finally, when Carthage tried to occupy northeastern Sicily—dangerously close to the coast of Italy—the Romans turned to war in an effort to crush this new threat. The three wars fought between Rome and Carthage are called the *Punic Wars* (Punic meant Phoenician in Latin).

Rome Wins the First Punic War

In the First Punic War (264–241 B.C.) the Romans built ships, learned how to maneuver them, and finally defeated Carthage on the sea. As a result of her victory, Rome gained control of a major part of the island of Sicily. She also won additional freedom to travel on the Mediterranean Sea. The First Punic War had not settled the basic issues between Rome and Carthage. Both sides knew that the struggle would continue, and each used the period of peace to prepare for further war.

Hannibal Crosses the Alps

Carthage soon sought revenge for her defeat by Rome, and war again broke out. This Second Punic War (218–201 B.C.) was marked by the extraordinary exploits of Hannibal, a great Carthaginian general who decided to march an army over the Alps to make a surprise attack on the Romans! In 218 B.C., Hannibal led a force of 40,000 foot soldiers, 37 African elephants carrying supplies, and 8000 horsemen through Spain and southern Gaul (part of modern France) until he reached the Alps. Then, in the month of November, he started the dangerous 10,000-foot climb over the mountains.

It was a disastrous journey, but Hannibal refused to give up. "No part of the [Alps] reaches the sky," he shouted to his men and promised them that they would cross the top. And cross it they did—although only one half of them made it safely to the plain in northern Italy. Here Hannibal rested his men, drew up his military plans, and prepared to fight.

The Second Punic War Ends

The Romans sent an army to meet the Carthaginians, but Hannibal's troops crushed the Roman forces and moved forward. Lacking the equipment needed to batter down the walls of Rome, the Carthaginian leader could not take the Roman capital. Instead, he remained in Italy over fifteen years and caused much destruction.

Finally, in an effort to draw Hannibal from Italy, the Romans ordered an army under Scipio to attack Carthage directly. The Carthaginians sent a hurried call to Hannibal to return home at once to defend his people. He did—and at the Battle of Zama (202 B.C.) south of the city of Carthage, the great Carthaginian general at last was defeated. The defeat of Hannibal ended the Second Punic War. Carthage was forced to disarm and to give up most of her possessions.

■ Check on Your Reading

1. What led to the rivalry between Rome and Carthage?
2. Describe Hannibal's campaigns.
3. How was Carthage defeated?

■ *Roman galleys (biremes) were long, open warships. Slaves manned the oars of these galleys which aided the Romans in their conquest of the Mediterranean world.*

Vatican Museum

5. The Roman Empire Grows

Some Romans were not satisfied with the punishment given to Carthage. The statesman Cato, finding that Carthage was still "full of riches and all sorts of arms and ammunition," urged that the city be completely crushed. *"Delenda est Carthago!"* ("Carthage must be destroyed!") cried Cato, and soon many Romans agreed.

As a result, the Third Punic War (149–146 B.C.) was fought. The Romans were again victorious. This time they killed most of the Carthaginians, sold the rest into slavery, and burned every building. The great city of Carthage was completely "blotted out and destroyed."

Between the Second and the Third Punic War, the Romans also had conquered Macedonia, parts of Syria, and disorganized Greece. Soon Rome dominated Asia Minor and the Near East. The Roman Empire was growing. By 31 B.C. the Romans controlled the Mediterranean world.

Provinces Are Organized

Their victories over Carthage and their conquests in the East had made the Romans the rulers of a great empire. The Romans demonstrated tremendous ability as law-givers and administrators, especially in gaining the loyalty of the people of the Italian peninsula by granting them Roman citizenship, which was very valuable. It was granted only to freemen, not to slaves. A citizen's rights included these: (1) the right to vote on certain matters, (2) the right to appeal to his Assembly (and the emperor) for correction of abuses, and (3) the right to be immune from legal torture.

In exchange for these and other rights, a Roman citizen was subject to military service at call and had other duties.

To meet the problem of governing the empire, the Romans permitted several self-governing kingdoms to exist under their protection. These kingdoms were independent, except in foreign affairs. A considerable part of the empire was organized into *provinces*. Provinces were territories outside of Italy that were administered by governors sent by Rome. The governors collected taxes, and the Roman Senate made laws for the provinces. Roman law became a strong foundation for the empire.

Unfortunately, many governors considered the provinces as private treasure chests to be raided for their own profit. They taxed the people heavily, pocketed part of the money for themselves, and ignored protests. It was clear that the government of the Roman Empire could be only as strong or as weak as its officials.

Populares Oppose Optimates

The problems that the Romans faced at home were as serious as those that they encountered in foreign lands. The unsettled conditions in Italy after the Punic Wars had split the people into two clashing groups, the _Populares_ (common people) and _Optimates_ (upper groups). These replaced the old plebeian and patrician divisions.

The Populares included many farmers who had served as soldiers. During the wars they had been unable to work their land or pay taxes because they had been busy fighting. When they returned, their farms had been sold for non-payment of debt!

Other returning farmer-veterans found that their homes and farms had been destroyed by Hannibal's men, or that they faced ruin because of the importation of cheap grain from Africa. Some of them sought jobs as hired men on the great estates (_latifundia_) that were being developed by wealthy men to raise olives and fruit. They were refused even this labor because slaves would work for nothing.

Bewildered and hungry, the farmers drifted to the city, where war captives and slaves were doing the work. They joined the unemployed in Rome, ready to support men like Tiberius Gracchus who said:

The wild beasts that roam over Italy ... have their dens and lairs to shelter them. ... But the men who fight and die for Italy enjoy nothing but air and light. Homeless and footless, they wander. ... They are called masters of the world, [yet] they have no clod of earth to call their own.

Chief targets for the anger of these men were the _Optimates_, who included those wealthy individuals who had bought up the farmers' lands and combined them into large farms worked by slaves. Many traders who had become rich during the wars and most of the senators also were Optimates. The Roman Senate itself had turned into a stronghold for the upper groups. Filled with selfish aristocrats and men who had gained office by wealth, it opposed the interests of the people as a whole.

The Gracchi Fight and Die for Reforms

The struggle between the poor and the aristocrats continued from about 140 B.C. to 31 B.C., and each side had its heroes. One of the first attempts to improve the conditions of the lower groups was made by two Tribunes, the brothers Tiberius and Gaius Gracchus (the Gracchi). It was an effort that was to cost them their lives.

Tiberius tried to limit the size of farms and estates so that no one person could own great amounts of land. He hoped this would prevent the small farmer from losing his property. Tiberius angered the Senate when he used unconstitutional means to pass laws and remain in office as Tribune. In 133 B.C. the senators killed him.

Gaius, who became Tribune ten years after his brother Tiberius, suggested that the state sell grain to the poor at very low prices. He also proposed that colonies be used as places of settlement for unemployed Romans. Gaius offended the Senate by giving special powers to certain business men to win their support against the senators. One day he was trapped by his enemies, and he ordered his servant to kill him.

Civil War: Sulla Triumphs over Marius

The death of the Gracchi did not end the conflict in Rome. At a time of such confusion the people turned to a strong military hero for direction. Marius (157–

86 B.C.), a general who had been elected a Consul in 108 B.C., became the new leader.

Although he lacked skill as an administrator, Marius was supported by the lower groups and served as Consul six times. One of his important acts was to change the organization of the Roman army. Formerly, it had been made up of citizen-soldiers who were called by the state to serve in a particular campaign. Now it was to be filled with volunteers. Since many of these volunteers enlisted for terms as long as twenty years, there developed an army of permanent "professional" soldiers. To them, their general was more important than the government officials.

The senators and the upper groups did not approve of General Marius. They therefore threw their support behind Sulla, another military leader. Sulla's troops clashed with the followers of Marius, and eventually Sulla's forces won. Sulla returned political power to the Senate, and the senators again controlled the peoples' lives.

The end of the struggle between Marius and Sulla was the beginning of a new period in Roman history. In the future, *military strength—not representative government—would decide who would rule Rome and the empire.*

■ **Check on Your Reading**

1. How large was the empire by 31 B.C.?
2. In what way did the Romans show great skill in law and administration?
3. How was the Roman Empire governed?
4. Describe the causes for the rivalry between *Populares* and *Optimates.*
5. What did the Gracchi accomplish?
6. In what way was the victory of Sulla a turning point in Roman history?

6. Julius Caesar Becomes Undisputed Ruler

From 60 to 50 B.C. Rome was dominated by a partnership of three men, known as the *First Triumvirate* from the Latin words for *three* and *men.* The partners were Pompey, Caesar, and Crassus. While Pompey strengthened his position at home, Julius Caesar (100–44 B.C.) sought additional fame abroad. In 58 B.C. he became governor of Gaul (roughly, modern France). In the next eight years Caesar's troops brought Gaul under Roman control. Caesar even successfully invaded Britain, although that invasion had few permanent results, as Caesar soon withdrew to Gaul. From east to west, the Roman Empire reached from the Rhine to the Atlantic.

Caesar Becomes Roman Ruler

Caesar, ambitious for further power, wanted the people back in Rome to know of his exploits in Gaul. He therefore wrote his *Commentaries,* a history of his military accomplishments in Gaul. (This work is known as *Caesar's Gallic Wars* and is read for its clean-cut prose style and vigorous narrative.) Caesar hoped that his military fame would soon make him leader of the Roman Empire.

Back in Rome, Pompey had become disturbed at Caesar's ambitions to take over the government. Since the death of Crassus, Pompey had been the only Consul and the leading figure in Rome. Leaning more and more to the side of the aristocrats, he had won the support of the Senate. Pompey and the senators warned Caesar that he was to return to Italy without his troops!

In 49 B.C. Caesar led his army to the Rubicon, a small river that separated Gaul from Italy. Here his decision would have to be made. Should he cross the river with his soldiers and risk a war with Pompey, or return to Rome alone and give up all his political ambitions? Caesar "checked his course and ordered a halt, while he resolved with himself, and often changed his opinion one way and the other, without speaking a word." Then he shouted, "The die is cast!"—and marched his troops across the Rubicon into Italy.

Pompey, fearing Caesar's popularity with the people, fled to Greece. Here Pompey's army was defeated by Caesar's soldiers. Pompey escaped, but was finally killed in Egypt. By 45 B.C. Caesar was the undisputed Roman ruler.

Caesar: a Man of Many Traits

Julius Caesar, whom the Greek biographer Plutarch described as "a spare man

who . . . struggled with his diseases," was granted many of the important powers of government. Although the Roman Republic continued to exist, the Senate and the other governmental bodies lost most of their authority. Caesar soon was made *dictator* for life, that is, he was given great power over the government and the people for as long as he lived.

How shall we describe the character of this general who directed a great empire? If we judge him by his wild conduct as a young man, he is a selfish and self-centered person. If we judge him by the large sum of money that he paid each of his soldiers after a great victory, he is very generous.

■ *The Roman Empire (265 B.C.–167 A.D.) had expanded from the city of Rome until it included the whole land area around the Mediterranean. What leaders were responsible for its expansion?*

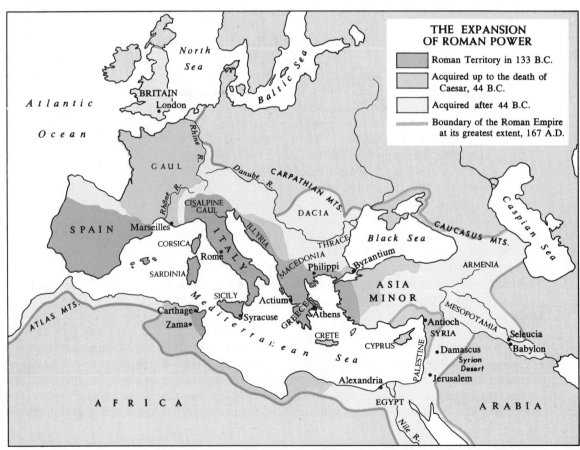

Or, to take another example, if we judge him by his plans to build time-saving canals and other waterways, he is concerned with helping others. If we judge him by the comments of the men who later killed him, he is hungry for personal power.

Which is the *true* Caesar? Obviously, none of the four judgments by itself can do him justice. Caesar—like all human beings—was a mixture of many traits. He was neither all good nor all bad, neither all angel nor all devil. Caesar was a complex Roman with a passion "to do great things," and he found the glory that he sought in many different ways.

Caesar's Program Brings Reforms

Although we cannot describe Caesar's character by a single adjective, we certainly can recognize that he was an outstanding leader whose program greatly helped many people. As leader of the Roman Empire, he was responsible for many policies and rights that benefited the people in government and economics.

In government Caesar accomplished the following: (1) He gave additional rights of self-government to towns in Italy. (2) He extended citizenship privileges to many people in the provinces. (3) He reformed the administration of the provinces; corrupt governors were removed from office.

Among Caesar's accomplishments in economics were the following: (1) He developed colonies that could serve as farming settlements for the unemployed. (2) He introduced a fairer system of taxation for the colonies. (3) He started a program of public works so that there would be additional jobs for the unemployed. (4) He tried to limit the number of slaves who could work on estates, in order to provide jobs for free farmers. (5) He distributed land to the poor. (6) He established a law of bankruptcy, that is, a law to help people who could not pay their debts.

Capitoline Museum, Rome

■ *Julius Caesar, dictator and general, ruled a great empire and instituted needed reforms. The title, Caesar, was assumed by later emperors.*

Caesar Is Struck Down!

Caesar's accomplishments, his excellent administration, and his fairness to his enemies were hailed by many Romans. However, there were others who hated him for ousting Pompey and for acting like an absolute monarch. Some senators were afraid that Caesar would abolish the Republic completely and make himself the king. These opponents of Caesar decided to destroy him.

On March 15, 44 B.C. (called the Ides of March), a group of conspirators, headed by Cassius and Brutus, surrounded Caesar in the Senate. At a sign, they pulled his robe from his neck, and "with their naked daggers in their hands" they stabbed him twenty-three times.

Thus fell Caesar—adventurer, conqueror, statesman—murdered before he had a chance to develop fully his program of reforms. Once he had said: "I have lived enough . . . for fame." Time has agreed that the tragedy of his murder in no way detracts from that fame.

■ **Check on Your Reading**
1. How did Julius Caesar gain power?
2. How did Caesar change the government?
3. What reforms did Caesar bring?
4. Why was Caesar assassinated?

7. Octavian Takes Caesar's Place

Two men challenged each other for Caesar's power—Antony and Octavian. Antony, a close friend of Caesar, was a military man. Octavian (63 B.C.–14 A.D.) was Caesar's eighteen-year-old nephew and adopted son.

At first Antony and Octavian co-operated in running the empire. Then, in the course of directing the eastern part of the empire, Antony went to Egypt where he came under the influence of their queen, Cleopatra. Although her beauty was not extraordinary, Cleopatra was a clever woman with a charming manner and a voice as pleasant as "an instrument of many strings." She used "a thousand" kinds of flattery to win Antony to her side. It was rumored that she and Antony planned to cut off the eastern part of the Roman Empire and rule it together. Octavian decided to stop them.

In 31 B.C. Octavian's fleet met and defeated the forces of Antony and Cleopatra in a great sea battle at Actium (map, p. 122). Antony and Cleopatra later committed suicide, and Octavian ruled the Roman world.

The Roman Republic Ends

During Octavian's rule, the Roman Republic came to an end. The governing bodies of the Republic gradually gave up their powers to Octavian. Soon they had granted him more rights than Caesar had. Yet, even after they had relinquished their duties, the Senate and the other bodies continued to meet.

Octavian was known as: *imperator*, commander of military forces; *pontifex maximus*, chief priest for the state; *princeps senatus*, first among all of the senators; and *Augustus*, revered ruler. Many features of the Republic seemed to exist, but actually Augustus Caesar (Octavian) had been made the first emperor—that is, the first ruler to hold *complete authority* over Rome and the Roman Empire.

This change in government from a republic to rule by an emperor did not greatly disturb the people. Tired of constant civil war and confusion, they were grateful for a man who could bring order and peace. As Tacitus, a Roman historian, pointed out:

The system by which every citizen shared in the government being thrown aside, all men regarded the orders of the emperor as the only rule of conduct and obedience; nor felt they any anxiety for the present, while [Augustus] . . . maintained the peace of the state.

Augustus Keeps Peace and Prosperity

Although Augustus conquered parts of Spain and fought to stabilize his northern

124

boundary at the Rhine and Danube rivers, he stopped his fighting and kept peace. This so-called Pax Romana, or Roman peace, was to last from 27 B.C. to 180 A.D. During this time the empire was free of any major wars.

Augustus brought more than peace to his people. Sensible in his judgments and moderate in his actions, he also introduced a program that contributed to the well-being of Rome and the empire. Among his accomplishments were the following: (1) the building of better roads and highways; (2) the protection of sea routes and the encouragement of trade; (3) the establishment of an honest administration system for the provinces; (4) the building of an effective military system for guarding the frontiers; and (5) the construction of public buildings, such as temples and theaters.

As a result of his accomplishments, Augustus helped the empire to prosper. Literature and other forms of cultural expression flourished during his time, and the period of Augustus is known as a "Golden Age."

Rome's Future in Doubt

When Augustus died in 14 A.D., the Senate paid him its highest honor by demanding that "upon their own shoulders they must bear [his] body to the pile [for burning]." Even as their emperor's body burned, worried men asked these questions: Would the next emperor be as wise as Augustus? Would he be able to keep the peace? Would the Romans trust his leadership? Would the provinces obey his orders?

The old Roman Republic had operated by a representative government. If one of its leaders died, the government could continue to rule the country safely and choose a new leader. Under the system of emperor

Museo delle Terme, Rome

■ *During the reign of Augustus Caesar, the first Roman emperor, the people enjoyed peace, prosperity, and the arts. A "Golden Age" had dawned.*

rule, the emperor *was* the government. If the man he chose to take his place were a weakling or fool, Rome and all of its empire could be destroyed.

■ Check on Your Reading

1. How did Octavian become ruler of the Roman world?
2. What was the Pax Romana?
3. Evaluate the accomplishments of Augustus, the first Roman emperor.
4. Why was the character of the ruler important under the new form of government?

MAN AND HIS CULTURE

Let's Meet the People!

This sketch of a Roman bather in the first century A.D. is based on information in two letters written by the philosopher Seneca. Seneca, Lucius A., *Ad Lucilium Epistulae Morales*, with English translation by Richard M. Gummere, 1917, G. P. Putnam's Sons.

A Roman Bather

Shortly after 2 P.M., the Roman bather paid a small admission fee and entered the public baths. He strolled about and noted that there were expensive mirrors on the walls; the vaulted ceilings were "buried in glass"; the swimming pool was marble-lined; and silver spigots poured filtered water.

The bather changed clothes in the dressing room. A well-built man, he was not embarrassed about bathing with others. He and his companions laughed at the humor in these lines by the poet Martial:

> Your legs, so like the moon at crescent,
> A bathing-tub will scarce look neat in;
> So here I send you, for a present,
> A drinking-horn to wash your feet in.

The bather now went to the exercise room. He grunted as he raised each weight and "whenever he released his imprisoned breath, [other bathers] could hear him panting in wheezy and high-pitched tones." He then moved to the massage room, where a slave rubbed his body. A sudden commotion occurred. A pick-pocket had been caught, and angry men called an attendant to arrest the scoundrel!

After the excitement, the bather walked to a "hot-air room," where artificial heat made his body perspire. He took a warm bath, washed with soap, and finished with a cold bath. This was followed by a swim in the pool. Then an attendant rubbed perfumed ointment over his body.

Clean and comfortable, he gossiped with friends, bought a snack, and tried his luck at dice. After this relaxation, he went home. He felt that he deserved a good supper after his busy day.

CHAPTER REVIEW

REVIEW and DISCUSSION

1. Identify the people and places and explain the events and terms on p. 110.

2. How did the Athenian democracy and the Roman Republic differ?

3. Compare the rights and duties of ancient Greek citizens with those of ancient Rome. Which had better living conditions?

4. Hannibal is sometimes said to be history's most glorious failure. Why?

5. Do wars usually cause disorder and unsettled conditions similar to those in Rome after the Punic Wars? Why? Check one or two other postwar periods in history.

6. Why do you think the Gracchi brothers were killed?

7. Caesar felt that it was necessary to become a dictator to accomplish his goals. Do you think a representative government would have accomplished the same things? Why?

8. Trace the development of the Roman government from a republic to an empire. Can you find any crucial points where a different decision might have changed this course?

9. What were the reasons for the success of the Pax Romana? Can we use Roman methods to bring peace to our world? Why?

10. How important is the character of a government official, especially the ruler?

11. Judging from Roman history, which brings greater wealth, cultural advancement, and unity—peace or war? Why?

12. Some people say that Augustus Caesar's reign is the supreme achievement in the history of statesmanship. Why? What determines greatness?

ACTIVITIES

1. Make a chart comparing Roman, Athenian, and Babylonian law and justice.

2. Write a biography of Julius Caesar.

3. Debate the statement: Resolved that the Golden Age of Augustus Caesar was superior to the Golden Age of Pericles.

4. On a map show the boundaries and provinces of the Roman Empire at its height.

5. Write a report on archaeological discoveries at Pompeii.

6. Draw a diagram showing the government of the Roman Republic.

PAST and PRESENT

1. Make a list of features in our government which come from (a) Greece and (b) Rome. Is it a republic, a democracy, or both?

2. What similarities are there between Rome's government of her colonies and the rule of overseas lands by modern countries, such as Great Britain, France, and Portugal?

3. It was said that during the depression of the 1930's the United States tried to aid recovery by using methods similar to those proposed by the Gracchi brothers and Caesar. Find points of similarity and difference.

SUGGESTED READINGS

Basic books: LINTON, RALPH, *The Tree of Culture*, Chap. 26, Knopf.

MULLER, HERBERT J., *Uses of the Past*, Chap. 9, Scribner.

Special accounts: DAVIS, WILLIAM S., *A Day in Old Rome*, Biblo & Tannen. Recreates life in Rome for the reader.

FRANK, TENNEY, *History of Rome*, Holt.

MILLS, DOROTHY, *Book of Ancient Romans*, Putnam. Written for youth. Invaluable.

QUENNELL, MARJORIE, and QUENNELL, CHARLES H. B., *Everyday Life in Roman Britain*, Putnam. An easy-to-read source for one of Rome's outposts.

Biography and Fiction: PLUTARCH, *Twelve Lives*, World Publishing. Biographies of famous Romans and Greeks.

SHAKESPEARE, WILLIAM, *Julius Caesar; Antony and Cleopatra*.

THOMPSON, STITH, and GASSNER, JOHN, (eds.), *Our Heritage of World Literature*, Holt. Valuable source, for it contains much literature and history of Roman period.

Chapter 8   *The Lives and Cultural Contributions of the Romans*

KEYNOTE   How many times have you been told that Roman civilization is "dead and buried"? Yet how many times has this statement been proven incorrect?

A quick look about you should be sufficient to show that Roman civilization is still very much alive. The hands of clocks on churches and public buildings often circle around Roman numerals (I, III, VI, IX, XII). Roman numerals are used for the main headings in many books. The months of July and August are named after two Roman statesmen, Julius and Augustus Caesar. January is named for Janus, the god of gates and doors and therefore of all beginnings. Indeed, the names of nearly all our months come from Roman words. The tradition of baking a wedding cake can be traced back to an old Roman custom. The cold cream that women rub on their faces as a beauty aid was probably developed by a physician of Rome. The word "salary" comes from the Roman practice of paying soldiers "salarium," or money for salt.

The daily lives of the Romans differed from our own in many ways. Nevertheless, our activities in the twentieth century are still strongly affected by our Roman heritage. The Romans adopted and passed on to us the leading achievements of Greek and Hellenistic civilization. *Particularly important to us are the original Roman contributions in the fields of government and law, engineering, architecture, and language.* Roman achievements in these areas form a fundamental part of the modern world.

Key People   *Justinian · Virgil · Horace · Juvenal · Cicero · Galen*

Key Events   *Justinian Code · Pantheon erected*

Key Terms   *toga · Forum · lares and penates · gladiators · Roman law aqueducts · arch · Romance languages · Julian calendar*

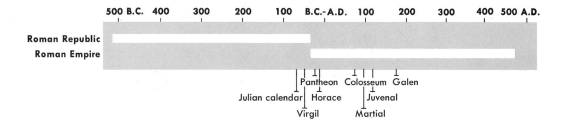

1. History and the Lives of the Romans

By the side of a dusty highway in Italy, an ancient Roman tombstone still calls to men:

This mute stone begs thee to stop, stranger, until it has . . . told thee whose shade it covers. Here lie the bones of a [Roman]. . . . It wanted thee not to be unaware of this.

Here is a simple appeal to us to remember that the lives of people are the basic materials of history. A forgotten Roman touches us from the grave to remind us that his life was once as important as our own. How did this man and other Romans live? How did they pray? How did they plan for their futures? These are questions that can be answered now.

Roman Dress and Appearance

Living in ancient Rome obviously was not the same as living in modern America. For one thing, clothing was different. A Roman gentleman wore a simple tunica and toga. A *tunica* was a short-sleeved, woolen garment that usually extended below the knees. A *toga* was a woolen robe that was close to eighteen feet in length. The Roman draped the toga around his body, over the tunica, so that only his right

arm was uncovered. Only a Roman citizen could wear a toga. In a sense, it was his cloak of membership in Roman society.

Women dressed in a *stola*, an undergarment that reached to the ground, and a *palla*, a loose wrap that was worn over the stola. Footwear for both women and men consisted of sandals (*soleae*) and high leather shoes bound with straps at the top (*calcei*).

Many people in ancient Rome were quite as vain as people today. Men covered their bald spots with false hair, and women placed a mask of rice and bean flour on their faces at night to remove their wrinkles. Although men were content to wear a single iron ring, women decorated themselves with many jewels, including brooches, rings, earrings, bracelets, pearl necklaces, and hairpins of ivory. There were no glass mirrors in those days, but squares of polished metal showed the Romans the success or failure of their efforts to make themselves attractive.

Roman Homes

The comforts of a Roman's home depended on the amount of his income. In the early days of the Republic, houses were

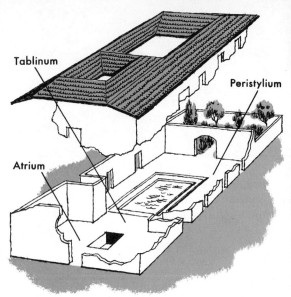

Tablinum

Peristylium

Atrium

■ *A Roman home consisted of a large room (atrium), an extension (tablinum), and a courtyard (peristylium), off which were several rooms.*

The Metropolitan Museum of Art, Rogers Fund, 1903

■ *This mural from a Roman house (1st century B.C.) shows a lady playing a cithara (similar to a lyre) and a little girl listening to the song.*

simple. They consisted of a single large room, called the *atrium*. This room had no windows, but a hole in the roof permitted some light to enter. Rain coming through this hole was caught in a hollow in the ground and used for household purposes. It was in the atrium that the Romans cooked, slept, and prayed. Here, too, the father kept his money chest—tied to the ground and in a spot where he could keep an eye on it!

In time, a narrow extension was built to one side of the main room. This was called the *tablinum*. Then the Romans borrowed an architectural idea from the Greeks and added a courtyard next to the tablinum. This courtyard (*peristylium*) was surrounded by several rooms. Eventually, three features developed in the home: (1) the atrium became the reception room; (2) the tablinum served as a combination dining room and hallway; and (3) the rooms around the courtyard were used as bedrooms, living room, and kitchen.

A wealthy Roman could construct a country home, or *villa*, that was far more complicated and expensive than the average house, but the poor people had few of the comforts of the rich. In Rome they lived in crowded brick or wooden tenements six stories high, paid high rents, and were in constant danger of losing their lives in the fires that frequently broke out. Indeed, there were so many fires in Rome that one sharp business man used them to make a fortune. He organized squads of fire fighters, who hurried to the fires. Then he charged the people large fees to put out the flames.

The home of a Roman was an important place. It was the center for many of the activities of the Roman family, and the family was the basic unit in Roman society.

The Roman Family

The Roman family usually consisted of the father, the mother, the unmarried daughters, and the married sons with their wives and children. The father held great power over the others. He was his "own master," while the rest were his "dependents." The father made all major decisions, directed the education of his sons, and served as priest by conducting services before the family altar.

The Roman mother also was treated with considerable respect. She ate her meals with her husband, helped to bring up the children, and sometimes advised her family on personal matters. In time, the power of women grew. The orator Cato once felt that Roman women influenced their men so greatly that he cried: "We Romans, who rule all men, are ruled by our women."

During the period of the Roman Empire, family ties loosened and the relationships between husbands and wives lost their closeness. Nevertheless, in the early days of the Republic the Romans demonstrated that a good family can make for a stable life.

Roman Slaves

There were many people who did not have the rights of the free citizens of the Roman family. These were the slaves, men and women seized in war or captured by slave hunters. Slaves were bought by the Romans for prices ranging from $25 to $4000 and higher per person. The purchaser had absolute power over the slave and could treat him as he wished.

Slaves held many jobs in Rome and throughout Italy. They were cleaners of public buildings, executioners, servants, stevedores, artists, musicians, businessmen, farmers, teachers, doctors, and members of other occupations. In the approximately one million population of Rome in the second century A.D., there were so many slaves that citizens rarely did any manual work.

Some Roman citizens spent their hours at the *Forum*, the public square in Rome where important political and commercial matters were discussed. Others supervised

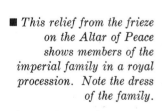

■ *This relief from the frieze on the Altar of Peace shows members of the imperial family in a royal procession. Note the dress of the family.*

131

shops or looked for excitement along the streets leading to the Forum—with time out in the afternoon for a refreshing hour at the public baths. In the countryside wealthy citizens rode about their estates to check on their slaves.

Some slaves were treated well, but others—particularly farm workers—were made to labor long and hard at heavy work. One Roman liked to "break in" his slaves "like young dogs and colts." Another treated his slaves like his sons. One master beat his slaves; another shared his food with them. As in other periods of history, the fate of the slave depended on the character of his owner.

Roman Education

The Roman citizen had to be educated to learn his relationships to his family, slaves, and other members of society. In the early days of the Republic a boy received his education from his father, while a girl was trained by her mother. Later, regular schools were set up for those boys whose parents could afford to pay the small fee. Girls continued to be taught at home to sew, spin, and cook.

The "school house" was really a shed that was open on two sides. Rough benches without backs served as seats. Discipline was as hard as the benches. Thrashing was permitted, and more than one teacher was called "a man of blows." The teacher usually was a slave or a former slave who had been freed. Many were Greek.

In a Roman elementary school of the first century B.C., the child learned reading, writing, and arithmetic. The pupil also was given instruction in proper conduct and was taught to recite such maxims as:

A scar on the conscience is the same as a wound.—Valour grows by daring, fear by holding back.—A man dies as often as he loses his friends.—Man has been lent, not given, life.

■ *A Roman father is teaching his son by listening to him recite. In the early days of the Republic a boy received his education from his father.*

After elementary school, the student could go on to a grammar school. Here he would study Greek and Latin literature. Then he might continue his training at a still higher school, where he would learn the art of public speaking. Between the ages of fourteen and seventeen the boy would remove his childhood locket (the *bulla*) from around his neck, put on the adult's white toga, and be fully accepted as a man.

Some wealthy Romans skirted this public educational system by hiring or buying Greek scholars to teach their children privately. Later they gave their sons enough money to meet all living expenses and sent them abroad to study at higher centers of learning. One Roman student in Athens was not satisfied with this generous treatment. He demanded still another favor and wrote home:

I beg you to send me a secretary at the first opportunity, if possible a Greek: for he will save me much trouble in copying out notes.

NAME OF GREEK GOD	NAME OF ROMAN GOD	DUTIES
Zeus	Jupiter	The king of all the gods.
Ares	Mars	The god of war.
Aphrodite	Venus	The goddess of beauty and of love.
Hermes	Mercury	The messenger of the gods.
Athena	Minerva	The goddess of wisdom.

Roman Religion

An important part of the education of a Roman was the training that he received from his parents in the field of religion. The practices of the Roman religion did not always remain the same. When the Romans came in contact with other people, their religious ideas changed.

In the early days of the Republic, the Romans believed that there were spirits everywhere—a fire spirit, a water spirit, a spirit that supervised the planting of seeds, a spirit that watched the baking of bread, and many others. These spirits did not have any shape or form, but they were active all the time.

To protect his home and family, the Roman father performed certain ceremonies believed to be pleasing to the spirits of the household, the *lares* and *penates*. The spirits included Janus, spirit of the doorway; and Vesta, spirit of the hearth. The Roman father felt that if he did not do this, the spirits would become angry and cause as much mischief as they could! There also were spirits that took care of affairs for the state as a whole. These spirits had to be treated well by the officials of the state.

When the Romans came in contact with the Greeks, an important change occurred. Religion became less a family matter and more a state function. The Romans accepted many Greek gods, gave them Roman names, and substituted them for the various Roman spirits. The Romans also accepted the Etruscan and Greek idea that the gods had human forms. As a result, many similarities appeared between the duties of the Greek and Roman gods. Just as the Roman father made offerings to the spirits surrounding his family, the public priests offered up sacrifices to the gods of the state.

Regardless of the changes in the number and shapes of the Roman gods, one practice remained the same: The Romans still turned to the gods for favors. One Roman asked a god to be his helper "in writing the verses which I essay to pen." Another praised a god for his willingness to give from his "store of wealth and happiness."

Most Romans did not believe that religion meant for them to lead moral lives and love the gods. Rather, they thought of religion as a bargain with the gods: "I will sacrifice to the gods—and they will reward me for these sacrifices!"

Roman Recreation

In the early period of the Roman Republic, religion was closely connected with recreation. The great public games that amused the people were presented as special tributes to the gods. Later, these spectacles lost most of their religious meaning. State officials and private individuals arranged for free public entertainments to honor a hero, to mark an important event, or to gain popularity with the masses.

■ *The great amphitheater, the* Colosseum, *was the setting for the brutal gladiatorial contests. About 50,000 people could watch them.*

The Romans were particularly fond of chariot racing and gladiatorial fights. The big chariot races in Rome were held in the *Circus Maximus,* an elliptical structure that eventually held about 175,000 people. Light chariots drawn by four horses and driven by drivers wearing white, red, blue, or green colors raced seven dangerous laps around the course to the finish line.

Far more brutal than the chariot races were the gladiatorial contests. In such amphitheaters as the *Colosseum,* which seated about 50,000 people, men who were war captives, criminals, or slaves were forced to fight each other in man-to-man combat. Their weapons were usually daggers, spears, nets, and/or swords. These *gladiators* were at the mercy of the crowd. If the spectators waved white cloths or handkerchiefs, a defeated gladiator who had fought bravely might be permitted to live. If the crowd and the emperor turned their "thumbs down," the winner would kill the loser.

■ **Check on Your Reading**

1. What was the significance of the toga?
2. What good and bad features do you see in the design of a Roman home?
3. Describe Roman education and religion.

2. Roman Contributions in Law, Engineering, and Architecture

Roman dress, religion, and recreation obviously were different from our own. Nevertheless, the Romans are still linked to us by the contributions that they made to modern civilizations. We are particularly indebted to the Romans for their achievements in government and law, engineering, and architecture.

Roman Law

We have seen that Rome grew from an unknown village to the capital of a vast empire. As it did so, the Romans had considerable success as administrators. For example, their policy of granting citizenship to the peoples of newly acquired provinces helped the Romans to gain their loyalty. As the Roman Empire grew, the structure of its government gradually changed. Side by side with changes in government went the development of Roman law, defined by the Romans as general rules "to give every man his due."

The Romans drew up laws explaining the rights and duties of the Roman citizens and of the various peoples in the Roman Empire. In doing this, they passed on to future generations such important legal principles as the following: (1) Laws are to be written wherever possible. This was not new with the Romans but they fully accepted it. (2) Citizens are to be protected by law against damage to their property. (3) Laws are to consider the rights of women. (4) An accused person is to be considered innocent until proven guilty. (5) Legal marriages can take place between citizens of different economic and social positions. (6) All men are to be considered equal before the law. No person is to receive special treatment over any other person in cases of law.

Between 528 and 534 A.D., Emperor Justinian directed that the various Roman laws should be gathered together into one complete code. This so-called *Justinian Code* made clear the legal rules involved in cases of adoption, guardianship, wills, and contracts. Most important of all, the Justinian Code showed that the Romans had tried to introduce the principle of the equality of all men before the law. Although the Romans violated this ideal of equality occasionally, other peoples later built on the Roman foundation to establish a true legal equality of all men.

Today, Roman law is still a part of our modern world. It is the basis for the legal systems of many countries in Europe and Latin America, and it is a strong influence in the state of Louisiana and elsewhere. Equality before the law is one of our basic legal principles.

Roman Engineering

Roman engineering was as impressive as Roman law. The Romans built many excellent bridges, public parks, and aqueducts. In contrast to the greatest Egyptian architectural achievement, the pyramids, the Roman aqueducts and other construction works were extremely *useful*. Even today there is an ancient aqueduct that still brings water to Rome.

Above all, the Romans excelled in the construction of roads. Roman roads were built for three purposes: (1) to make it easier to move troops, (2) to help the government in Rome to keep in touch with the peoples of the Empire, and (3) to increase trade. Aided by the spread of the Latin language, the Romans succeeded in each of these purposes. In addition, Roman roads brought improved communications that helped the spread of ideas. Rome was flooded with ideas from the East, especially philosophical and religious ideas. In time, one Eastern idea, Christianity, created vast changes in Roman life and in later history.

The rate of travel in ancient times naturally seems very slow to us. Even on such a fine Roman road as the Appian Way, a man travelling by horse-drawn cart covered no more than sixty miles in ten hours. However, to a people living long before the day of jet planes and atomic energy, this was a highly respectable rate of speed for travelling. (This rate was actually not much exceeded before the nineteenth-century railroads.)

In addition, the roads meant more to many Romans than just good routes for travel. They were also the links that bound them to their homes in Rome. However far away a native of Rome might be from the capital, there were always the roads to remind him that he was not cut off from his beloved city. He could travel home if he wished.

■ *This Roman aqueduct at Segovia, Spain, demonstrates that the Romans had impressive engineering skills. They excelled in building useful construction works such as aqueducts which brought water to the cities of the empire.*

■ *This model shows the construction of the Appian Way (312 B.C.). This highway, the chief road to Greece and the East, was 350 miles long. Its foundation was built in four layers with the stones fitted and morticed with concrete. Remains (left) prove its excellent workmanship.*

■ *The Pantheon (2nd century A.D.), the "temple of all the gods," was an impressive example of Roman architecture. It remains standing today.*

Roman Architecture

While the Romans were developing their systems of roads, they also were constructing temples, basilicas (halls originally used as banking centers and law courts), government buildings, and public baths. These structures showed six outstanding features of Roman architecture: (1) They used the arch, a curved structure capable of bearing weight. The Romans may have gained their knowledge of the arch from the Etruscans, Persians, or Babylonians. (2) They used the vault, an arched roof or ceiling. (3) They used the dome, a rounded vault that often served as the roof of a building. (4) Brick backed with a layer of cement was used in building. The Romans borrowed this method from the Syrians. (5) They frequently used Grecian columns for ornamentation, rather than for support. The Romans borrowed many architectural forms from the Greeks. (6) They placed importance on making the interiors of buildings attractive, rather than concentrating all their efforts on the outside. The *Pantheon,* the circular "temple of all the gods," contained most of the principal features of Roman architecture.

Many people insist that the Pantheon and other Roman buildings were not as beautiful as the best architecture of the Greeks. They point out that while the Greeks achieved harmony and charm in their structures, the Romans were too concerned with the size and grandeur of a building to develop its beauty. Nevertheless, the principles of Roman architecture are still important, for they were handed down and used by later generations. For example, the dome of the Capitol in Washington, D.C., shows Roman influence.

■ **Check on Your Reading**

1. Why are the legal principles passed on by the Romans so important?

2. What is "equality before the law"?

3. What practical engineering contributions were made by the Romans?

4. What were the achievements of Roman architecture? Compare them to the Greek.

137

3. Roman Literature, Language, and Science

The Romans also did important work in the field of literature and language. Some of the more interesting Roman authors were: Cicero, essayist and political writer; Lucretius, Virgil, and Horace, poets; Livy and Tacitus, historians; Juvenal, satirist; and Martial, writer of epigrams.

Roman contributions in science were not so impressive as their achievements in law and engineering. The Romans added little to the scientific knowledge that they had received from the Greeks.

Virgil

Virgil (70–19 B.C.) was the Roman poet who wrote the *Aeneid*. The *Aeneid* was written to accomplish at least two purposes: (1) to stir up the pride and patriotism of the people of Rome and (2) to encourage them to keep the peace throughout the empire. Virgil believed that the Romans had a double mission in the world:

To rule the nations as their master [and] . . . to establish firmly the law of peace.

Horace

Horace (65–8 B.C.) wrote a number of excellent *odes*. An ode was a poem designed to be sung, or to be read with a musical rhythm. In his poetry, Horace urged men to enjoy living in the present, and not to think only of the future. "Mistrust tomorrow," he said, "catch the blossom of today." Horace also told the Romans to follow "the golden mean," that is, not to go to extremes.

Juvenal

Juvenal (about 64–140 A.D.) is known for his *satires*. A satire is literature that ridicules or pokes fun at the foolishness and evils in society. The Romans are said to have been the first people to develop the satire as a literary form. Note how well Juvenal satirized the Roman practice of throwing things out of the window:

How often cracked and chipped earthenware falls from the windows! . . . You may well be accounted [careless in not protecting yourself] against unforeseen accident, if you go out to supper without having made your will. It is clear that there are just so many chances of death, as there are open windows. . . .

Martial

Martial (40–104 A.D.), who was born in Spain and lived in Rome for many years, was not a great poet. He is important because he helped to make popular the *epigram*. A Roman epigram was a short poem that usually ended with a humorous or satirical twist. Martial wrote this poem:

Silence is Golden

You're pretty, I know it; and young, that is true;
And wealthy—there's none but confesses that too;
But you trumpet your praises with so loud a tongue
That you cease to be wealthy or pretty or young!

The Latin Language

The Romans also made a great contribution in the field of language development. The Roman language, *Latin*, spread to many peoples throughout the empire. Eventually Latin became the basis for the so-called *Romance* languages (modern French, Spanish, Italian, Portuguese, Rumanian). Even the English language, which developed from other sources, was influenced by Latin. For example, the Latin, French, Spanish, Italian, and English words for color are: colore, la couleur, el color, il colore, and color, respectively.

Contributions to Science

The Romans were able to make four gains in the field of health and applied medicine: (1) They set up one of the earliest systems of medical service for the public. Government doctors gave free treatments to the poor. (2) They established a number of hospitals, the first in Europe. (3) They organized medical groups to accompany Roman troops into battle. (4) They improved the methods of public sanitation.

These four gains were a credit to the group-planning of the Romans. Indeed, few individuals were outstanding in scientific fields. One exception was the physician Galen (130–200 A.D.), who was born in Asia Minor and practiced medicine in Rome. Galen made valuable studies of the spinal cord and the nervous system, and compiled an encyclopedia of medical knowledge.

Under the direction of Julius Caesar, the Roman statesman, a more accurate calendar, the *Julian Calendar*, was drawn up. It remained unchanged until the sixteenth century A.D. Today, the number of days in each of our months can be traced back to the Julian Calendar.

■ **Check on Your Reading**

1. Why did Virgil write the *Aeneid*?
2. What is an ode? a satire? an epigram?
3. How does the study of Latin help with the study of other languages?
4. What did the Romans achieve in medicine and public health?

CULTURAL CHARACTERISTICS of Ancient Rome

In the early days of Roman civilization dining was usually a simple affair. Breakfast consisted of bread dipped in wine, or bread eaten with olives and cheese. Luncheon was made up of bread, cheese, lettuce and cress salad, and various fruits. With the increasing affluence of Roman people, dining became more complicated and one Roman feast included: sea-urchins, thrush on asparagus, loin of goat, sea-snails, head of wild boar, and other delicacies!

Like patterns of dining, many other aspects of Roman culture changed and became increasingly complicated. Nevertheless, despite variations the most significant characteristics of the culture of ancient Rome included:

Family life dominated by the father, until family ties began to deteriorate during the period of the Roman Empire.

Stress on the importance of codified law, with a listing of the rights and duties of the Roman citizens and of the various peoples in the Roman Empire.

A social system that ranged from the lowliest slave to the highest aristocratic Roman.

A belief in many gods, who were considered to be dispensers of favors rather than guides to morality.

Impressive achievements in the fields of engineering, political administration, and architecture.

The development of an extremely important language, Latin, which eventually became the basis for the modern Romance languages.

In many ways, the culture of ancient Rome was different from those of our times. Nevertheless, the practical Romans made many contributions to modern civilization. Roman law became the basis for the legal systems of many countries in Europe and Latin America. Roman engineering passed along valuable lessons in the building of roads. Roman architecture demonstrated the uses of the arch and the dome. Indeed, ancient Rome bequeathed to us a rich heritage.

MAN AND HIS CULTURE

Let's Meet the People!

The following sketch is based on information in *The Private Life of the Romans* by Harold Whetstone Johnston, Scott, Foresman. This book contains the complete inscription in honor of charioteer Crescens.

Crescens: A Charioteer of Rome

Crescens stood forward in his chariot—tense, alert, ready for the race to begin. He was a twenty-year-old slave, and he wore the garments of the charioteer: a close-fitting cap; shoulder pads; a short tunic in the blue color of the syndicate of Romans backing him; leather straps around his thighs; leather protectors on his legs.

The four horses attached to his light chariot—Circius, Acceptor, Delicatus, and Cotynus—stamped their hoofs nervously, and Crescens tightened his hold on the reins. The reins themselves were knotted together and passed around Crescens' body. That was why Crescens kept a knife in his belt. If he were thrown from the chariot, he must cut the reins quickly or else be dragged to his death.

Ready now! Go! The doors of the *carcerēs*, the chambers where the rival chariots were lined up, were thrown open and the race was on. The four chariots raced once around the sanded arena of the *Circus Maximus*. Six more laps to go to complete the distance of two and a half miles.

Crescens did everything that he could to outmaneuver the drivers who wore the white, red, or green colors. He recklessly turned his wheels into the chariot next to him and smashed against its axles until the driver bearing the white color was thrown to the ground. The crowd roared its approval. Three laps to go!

The driver of the red chariot now swung too wide around a curve, and Crescens saw his chance. Striking his horses with the reins, he raced his chariot to the inside of the track. Here he cut down the distance by staying as close as possible to the *mētae*, the pillars marking the inner line of the course. One more lap to go!

Down the straight-away came Crescens and the driver bearing the green color—horses straining every muscle—drivers shouting fiercely—chariots racing side by side. Then Crescens pulled ahead, held his lead, and crossed the final chalk line the winner. Crescens had won his first race!

There were people in Rome who never forgot that race. That was why two years later, when Crescens was a famous driver, they put up an inscription in his honor:

Crescens, a driver of the blue, . . . twenty-two years of age. He won his first victory as a driver of a four-horse chariot in the consulship of Lucius Vipstanius Messalla. . . . [After that] he was victorious *forty-seven times*. . . .

CHAPTER REVIEW

REVIEW and DISCUSSION

1. Identify the people and explain the events and terms on p. 128.

2. What achievements discussed in this chapter did Rome acquire from Greece?

3. It is generally accepted that a closely knit family life results in a stable society. What examples can you cite?

4. What evil does slavery bring?

5. Explain the changes that occurred when religion became a state function.

6. Roman amusements were extremely brutal. How do you explain this?

7. Why were the Romans such good administrators?

8. Which Roman achievements were original? Which achievements did they borrow from other peoples?

9. "Mistrust tomorrow, catch the blossom of today." Compare to "Eat, drink, and be merry, for tomorrow ye may die." Explain what these mean to individuals and nations.

10. What value does satire perform in eliminating evils in society? In what other ways can we attack the evils in society?

11. Some scholars believe that the Romans' failure to respond to all of the rising challenges contributed to the decline of Rome. What were the challenges or problems that the Romans never solved?

ACTIVITIES

1. On a map of the Roman Empire illustrate the old adage: "All roads lead to Rome."

2. Make a collection of pictures of the world's most beautiful buildings. Which ones show the influence of Greek or Roman architecture?

3. Determine why Latin is taught today.

4. A knowledge of mythology is essential to the understanding of classical literature. Read and report on several myths.

5. Draw a floor plan of a Roman house.

6. Read and report on a selection from Roman literature.

PAST and PRESENT

1. Compare the six legal principles of Roman law with the first ten amendments to our Constitution. What is missing in Roman law that we value highly?

2. Present-day fashions are often derived from costumes of past ages. Find examples of fashions based on Greek and Roman styles. Consult Evans, *Costumes Throughout the Ages.*

3. Some people say that we, like the Romans, are often boasting about the size, cost, and grandeur of buildings and other concrete objects; and that we tend to be more concerned with practicality than beauty. What do you think? Why?

SUGGESTED READINGS

Basic books: CHENEY, SHELDON W., *New World History of Art*, Viking.

SMITH, GOLDWIN, *The Heritage of Man*, Chap. 9, Scribner.

Special accounts: DAVIS, WILLIAM S., *A Day in Old Rome*, Biblo and Tannen.

FOSTER, GENEVIEVE, *Augustus Caesar's World*, Scribner. Easy. An excellent picture of the empire under Augustus.

FOWLER, WILLIAM W., *Social Life at Rome in the Age of Cicero*, Macmillan.

MILLS, DOROTHY, *Book of the Ancient Romans*, Putnam.

TREBLE, HENRY A., and KING, K. M., *Everyday Life in Rome in the Time of Caesar and Cicero*, Oxford.

Biography and Fiction: BULWER-LYTTON, EDWARD R., *The Last Days of Pompeii*, Dutton. Story of Christianity and Roman life ending with the volcanic eruption of Mt. Vesuvius.

DAVENPORT, BASIL (ed.), *The Portable Roman Reader*, Viking. Carefully translated selections from writings of leaders of Roman culture.

WALLACE, LEW, *Ben-Hur*, Dodd, Mead. A fascinating story.

Chapter 9   *Three Worlds of India, China, and Rome: Their Religions and Empires*

KEYNOTE   History can be viewed from many angles. Viewed from the West, the history of the world from about 250 B.C. to 350 A.D. appears to be dominated by the growth of Roman civilization. Viewed from the East, these same years feature the rise of great civilizations in India and China.

Actually, both of these points of view are necessary to obtain a correct picture. The Roman Empire, India, and China were all important centers of civilization during this period. Although each of the three centers developed in its own way, all of them had at least these points in common: (1) In each area a great empire was built and then was overrun by men using violence. (2) In each area a great religion was spread.

The key feature of this period was *the rise and decline of empires, and the growth and expansion of religions.*

Key People   *Chandragupta · Asoka · Kanishka · Jesus · Marcus Aurelius · Diocletian · Constantine · St. Augustine · Alaric · Attila*

Key Places   *India · Madras · China · Bactria · Roman Empire · Palestine · Rome · Constantinople · Adrianople · Châlons*

Key Events   *Maurya dynasty · Kushan Empire · Han dynasty · spread of Buddhism · Chinese trade with West · persecution of Christians · Church organization develops · Edict of Milan · German tribes invade empire · fall of Rome*

Key Terms   *non-violence · Sanskrit · Christianity · catacombs · clergy · Pope · Nicene Creed · Huns*

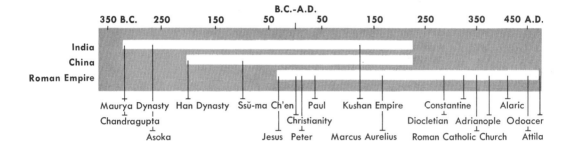

India
China
Roman Empire

Maurya Dynasty Han Dynasty Ssŭ-ma Ch'en Paul Kushan Empire Constantine Alaric
Chandragupta   Christianity   Diocletian Adrianople Odoacer
        Asoka   Jesus Peter   Marcus Aurelius   Roman Catholic Church Attila

1. The Civilization of India

In 322 B.C., a few years after the invasion of India by Alexander of Macedonia, Chandragupta Maurya fought his way to the position of ruler of northern India. He and his forces overthrew the Nanda dynasty which had ruled northern India for a short time. Chandragupta was the first in a line of rulers known as the *Maurya dynasty*.

The Maurya Dynasty is Established

Under Chandragupta, the people developed an impressive civilization. Irrigation systems were built, an excellent medical school was established, and artistic work in glass and stone was encouraged. Chandragupta's capital, near modern-day Patna, was an attractive city with fine theaters, colorful market-places, and a magnificent royal palace.

The government was organized into departments that supervised nearly every important political, economic, and social activity. Although the people had few democratic rights, they acquired a reputation for honesty. One traveler reported that "no Indian has ever been convicted of lying"—and that the homes were left unlocked and unguarded.

Chandragupta had considerable success in his military campaigns against neighboring peoples. He defeated the ruler of western Asia and won lands to the west of the Indus River. When his empire finally was handed down to his grandson, Asoka, it reached almost as far south as Madras and extended into Central Asia.

Asoka Spreads the Buddhist Principles of Peace

Asoka took control of the Maurya Empire about 270 B.C. Repelled by the horrors of war, he decided to follow the peaceful principles of the religion of Buddhism, especially the belief in non-violence to any living creature. He wanted to spread the Buddhist spirit of peace to his people.

Asoka wanted his people to know the rules that would help them to lead good lives. He therefore ordered that special *edicts*, or proclamations, be inscribed on rocks and columns. These so-called "rock

143

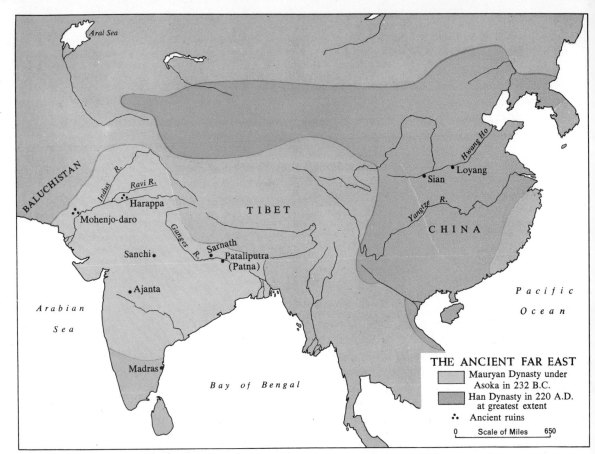

■ *In the Ancient Far East great empires were established. The Maurya dynasty in India and the Han dynasty in China extended their control over considerable land area. Under these rulers Indian and Chinese civilizations made many contributions in religion, art, and literature.*

edicts" taught the people to be peaceful, honest, and kind. Some said:

[Do] many benefits to others; [believe in] compassion; liberality; truth; purity.

. . . .

Not to injure living beings is good.

. . . .

[Let] a man watch over himself, saying: "Such . . . acts lead to corruption,—such as brutality, cruelty, anger, and pride. I will [avoid them]."

Most striking of all was Asoka's attitude toward other religions. While he remained faithful to Buddhism, he insisted that all religions should be treated with equal respect. In one edict he proclaimed:

All sects deserve reverence for one reason or another. By thus acting a man exalts his own sect and at the same time does service to the sects of other people.

Asoka respected all religions, but he also tried to spread the principles of Buddhism wherever he could. His missionaries carried the Buddhist doctrines to southern India, Ceylon, Burma, Macedonia, Egypt, and Syria.

Asoka's reign was one of the brightest periods in the history of India. Roads were built, charities were organized, and fine stone *stupas* were constructed throughout the land. Stupas were originally Buddhist burial mounds. They became shrines that served to remind the people that peace of mind came from following such principles of Buddhism as non-violence to others and elimination of selfish desires.

When Asoka died about 232 B.C., the great Maurya Empire (map, p. 144) fell apart. By 185 B.C., tribes from Central Asia had control of the country. Asoka's ideas could not be destroyed. His Buddhist belief in the value of peace and kindness spread through India and other parts of Asia.

Civilization in India Advances under Kanishka

In the second century A.D., the *Kushans*, a nomadic people from Asia, built a new empire in northwest India and Central Asia. Kanishka, a Kushan ruler who came to power about 120 A.D., was the most significant leader in India since Asoka.

Under Kanishka, Indian civilization was affected in at least two important ways: (1) The principles of Buddhism were spread to many peoples, including the Chinese. (2) Trade contacts were developed among the peoples of India, China, Central Asia, and Rome.

The Kushan Empire was marked also by the further development of the Sanskrit language. Even after the empire fell, Indian scholars continued to use Sanskrit to present their ideas. The famous poet Bhasa (about 300 A.D.) turned to Sanskrit to write lines that are known by many students in modern-day India:

When [the moon's] rays fall on its cheeks the
    cat licks them, thinking them milk;
When they are caught in the cleft of a tree
    the elephant deems them a lotus;

    . . . .

The moon in truth, proud of its brilliance,
    doth lead astray all this world.

The advances in language, religion, trade, and art during the Kushan Empire were soon threatened by marauding peoples. After 220 A.D., the Kushan Empire fell apart under the attacks of tribes from Central Asia.

■ Check on Your Reading

1. Summarize the highlights of the Maurya dynasty. Evaluate Chandragupta's military and peaceful achievements.

2. Can we call Asoka a great man and a great ruler? Why?

3. Name the principal accomplishments of Kanishka.

2. The Civilization of China

In 202 B.C.—about the time that Asoka's Indian empire was crumbling, and Hannibal's Carthaginians were facing defeat by the Romans—a great new dynasty arose in China. This was the *Han dynasty*, and its capital eventually was established at the location of modern day Sian-fu.

The Han Dynasty Is Established

The Han dynasty controlled a considerable part of China for most of the years between 202 B.C. and 220 A.D. Under the leadership of Emperor Wu-ti, Han rule spread to areas now known as Korea, Manchuria, and Indo-China (map, p. 144). When their military expeditions successfully pushed back the hostile peoples at their borders, the Han emperors turned from war to peace. An outstanding period in Chinese civilization developed, so brilliant that the Chinese since then have often been referred to as "the sons of Han."

■ *The Buddhist stupa (left) at Sanchi was built during the reign of Asoka. On the gateways and pillars were carved legends and scenes from Buddha's life. The Lion Capital (right) on Asoka's Pillar at Sarnath was one of the best examples of stone sculpture of Asoka's reign. This stone sculpture shows four lions standing over the Wheel of the Law, which Buddha set in motion.*

■ *The Old Stone Pagoda (left), near Peiping, was constructed by a 17th century emperor. Earlier wooden pagodas were sacred Buddhist towers. A Chinese wine jar (right) of the Han period was made of bronze and overlaid with gold and silver.*

Chinese Civilization Advances under the Han

Under the Han dynasty, Chinese civilization advanced in the fields of religion, commerce, science, and literature.

In the first century A.D., a Han emperor officially recognized Buddhism, that is, he approved of its right to exist. The religion began to spread throughout China. *Pagodas* appeared in important cities. In the beginning, pagodas were sacred Buddhist towers, and they were probably built in places considered to be holy ground.

Trade with the West developed under the Han emperors. In the second century B.C., the Chinese made contact with Bactria, a land near modern Afghanistan. Trade with this area soon followed, and contacts with other countries were made. By the second century A.D., Chinese silks and furs were being exchanged by traders for the products of India, western Asia, and even the Roman Empire. Rare stones, glass, and grapevines were valuable Chinese imports.

The Chinese of the Han period also made contributions in the field of practical science. These included the following: (1) the drawing up of a calendar; (2) the observation of sunspots, spots on the sun that appeared darker than the sun's regular surface; (3) the construction of a seismograph, an instrument to register earthquakes; and (4) the invention of paper.

The accomplishments of the Chinese in the field of literature were as impressive as their activities in science. One of the first major histories of China appeared about 100 B.C. It was entitled *Historical Memoirs* and was written by Ssŭ-ma Ch'ien. This author's willingness to present facts instead of improbable tales made him one of ancient China's most important historians.

Other writers worked in *lexicography*, the organization of words into a dictionary. To strengthen the government's library, scholars also gathered over 2700 volumes on philosophy and over 1300 volumes on poetry.

Some writers of the Han period wrote poetry. This is a poem written by a Han poet.

Han Poem (about 200 B.C.)

In dismal, gloomy, crumbling halls,
Betwixt moss-covered, reeking walls,
   An exiled poet lay—

On his bed of straw reclining,
Half despairing, half repining—
When athwart the window sill,
In flew a bird of omen ill,
   And seemed inclined to stay.

Some of the ideas expressed by the Han poets were similar to our own. For example, note the resemblance to *The Raven*, a poem composed by an American, Edgar Allan Poe.

The Raven (19th Century A.D.)

Once upon a midnight dreary, while I
   pondered, weak and weary,
Over many a quaint and curious volume of
   forgotten lore—
While I nodded, nearly napping, suddenly
   there came a tapping,
As of some one gently rapping, rapping at my
   chamber door. . . . .

Open here I flung the shutter, when, with
   many a flirt and flutter,
In there stepped a stately Raven of the
   saintly days of yore.

The cultural progress of the Chinese received a major setback when the Han dynasty collapsed. In 220 A.D., warring Chinese military chiefs took control of various sections, and the empire disintegrated.

■ Check on Your Reading

1. What areas outside China were controlled by the Han rulers?

2. What scientific and literary advances were made in China?

3. Christianity and the Roman Empire

We have seen that great empires were built in India and China, and that the religion of Buddhism was spread throughout Asia. At about the same time, the great Roman Empire dominated many people in the West, and the new religion of *Christianity* was spreading in the Middle East.

The Life of Jesus

The life and teachings of Jesus Christ led to the establishment of Christianity. According to the writings of early Christians, Jesus was born at Bethlehem in Palestine during the reign of Augustus Caesar. Palestine was then under the control of the Romans. It is known that Jesus was born a Jew, lived in the village of Nazareth, and was brought up in an atmosphere that stressed the monotheistic principles of Judaism. On reaching manhood, Jesus travelled among the people in Galilee and preached the doctrines of love of God, brotherhood of all men, and peace.

At about the age of thirty-three, Jesus encountered the serious opposition of Jewish religious leaders in Jerusalem. They rejected the idea of some of his followers that Jesus was the Messiah (the Saviour whose coming had been predicted by the ancient prophets). He was denounced for blasphemy and charged with wanting to become king of the Jews. He was turned over to the Roman governor, Pontius Pilate.

Jesus was accused of causing unrest and of challenging Roman authority. Condemned to death, Jesus was crucified on a great wooden cross. According to the beliefs of his disciples, Jesus rose from the dead soon after and later ascended to heaven.

The Principles of Christianity

The inspirational death of Jesus and the belief in his resurrection from the dead breathed new life into Jesus' teachings. His disciples worked hard to teach Jesus' message. A new religion known as Christianity began to spread through the western world.

Today, one out of every three persons in the world is a Christian. Although there are many different Christian churches, most of them are still based on these four principles of early Christianity: (1) There is one God, creator of all things. (2) Jesus Christ is the Divine Son of God and to most Christians a member of the *Trinity*. This refers to the belief that there are three persons in the one God—God the Father, God the Son, and God the Holy Ghost. (3) The teachings of Jesus are to be followed. Specifically, men are to love God, treat all human beings justly, and live in peace. (4) Each person is judged by God for his conduct on earth. A faithful Christian can look forward to an eternal life after death, a sinner to eternal punishment.

The heart of Christianity is found in two great commandments:

Thou shalt love the Lord thy God with all thy heart, and with all thy soul and with all thy mind.

This is the first and great commandment.

And the second is like unto it, Thou shalt love thy neighbor as thyself.

On these two commandments hang all the law. . . .

To the *Old Testament* the Christians later added the *New Testament*, which includes accounts of the life and teachings of Jesus, and the writings of early Christians.

Peter and Paul Spread the Words of Jesus

Before the crucifixion, Jesus had presented his teachings in many ways to twelve close followers. These men were known as the twelve *apostles*. Although one of them, Judas, betrayed Jesus, the other apostles carried Jesus' message to the people. The apostle Peter was particularly important. He travelled and preached as far as Rome where, it is believed, he was crucified about 65 A.D.

One man who did much to spread the principles of Christ was Saul, who was born in Asia Minor. Saul was not one of the original apostles. In the beginning he even fought against the early Christians. Then, according to Christian accounts, in 35 A.D. he heard the voice of Jesus:

... a sudden light flashed upon him from heaven, and he fell to the ground. Then he heard a voice saying to him, "Saul, Saul, why do you persecute me?" "Who are you, sir?" he asked. "I am Jesus," ... said the voice. ...

This experience so stirred Saul that he changed his name to Paul and devoted the rest of his life to spreading the gospel.

Paul travelled throughout the Roman Empire and organized churches. He spread Christian principles to people in Asia Minor, Greece, islands in the Mediterranean, and Rome. He also wrote a series of letters, his *Epistles*, in which he organized, developed, and recorded the doctrines of the new faith.

Early Christians Die for Their Faith

Christianity was not easily established in the Roman Empire. Peter, Paul, and other religious leaders have been recognized by history and praised for their heroism. Yet there were thousands of other people whose names have been forgotten. These people were early Christian *martyrs*, men and women who gave up their lives rather than renounce their religion.

For example, when Nero was emperor (54–68 A.D.), persecutions of the Christians were so extreme that on one occasion:

The victims [Christians] ... were covered with the skins of wild beasts and torn to pieces by dogs; while others were fixed to crosses and burnt to light the night when daylight had failed.

The emperors of Rome were not opposed to Christianity *as a religion*. They permitted different religions to exist in the empire, provided that the members of those religions accepted the Roman emperor as a god and did not challenge Roman rule. A number of religions and cults from Egypt and Persia had penetrated the empire before Christianity was introduced. They had existed peacefully side by side with the Roman religion and in some cases blended with Roman beliefs. Their members accepted the Roman emperor as a god.

The Christians, however, refused to offer up the customary sacrifices to the emperors or to recognize them as gods. Their religion permitted them to recognize but one God. The emperors therefore considered them to be a threat against Roman authority and a challenge to their political power. Although for almost two centuries after the death of Nero (68 A.D.) there was no concerted effort to wipe out Christianity, several rulers in the third century A.D. determined to check the Christians by force. Devout Christians were thrown into arenas to be killed by wild animals; others were beaten to death by Roman soldiers.

Under the pressure of such persecution, some Christians changed their beliefs and again worshipped the emperor's image. Most of them, however, continued to cling to their faith. Between 100 and 320 A.D. these Christians buried their dead in *catacombs*, long, twisting underground passages. The catacombs probably were used also as safe hiding places for Christians during periods of persecution. They remain as silent reminders of the days when persecuted men clung to their religion.

Church Organization Develops

Although many early Christians were united by their willingness to die for their religion, they could not agree among themselves on all religious matters. As a result,

■ *In the catacombs of Rome, inscriptions were carved on the walls of the passages by the early Christians. Carvings of olive branches (the Christian symbols of peace) and crosses were cut into the stone.*

the first Christian churches were guided by many different leaders. About a century and a half after the birth of Christ, there was still no central administration.

Nevertheless, the number of churches increased, and their officials came to be known as the *clergy*. Finally, there evolved an organization which eventually became known as the Roman Catholic Church. The *Church* was an organization through which Christians could practice their religion under a common authority. Although there were several religious groups that refused to accept its supervision, the Church extended its control over many Christians.

By the fourth century, the Church had developed certain basic features. Men known as *bishops* supervised Christian worship in various cities and territories throughout the old Roman Empire. The area administered by a bishop was called a *diocese*. Later, *archbishops* acted as overall directors of areas in the West where there were several bishops. (In the eastern

■ *Early Christian churches were called basilicas. This is the interior of the Basilica of San Lorenzo, Rome.*

part of the Roman Empire, chief bishops were known as *metropolitans* instead of archbishops. Leading metropolitans were called *patriarchs.*) *Priests* helped the bishops by administering local church areas, or *parishes*. Priests were appointed to their duties by the bishops.

The term *Pope*, which came from a Greek word meaning "father," at first referred to any bishop or even priest. It started to be used more particularly as the title of the *bishop of Rome* as early as the sixth century. The bishop of Rome eventually became the most influential leader of the Church in the West, and by the end of the eleventh century he was the only one to be called the Pope. The city of Rome, whose first bishop was said to have been the apostle Peter, was recognized by many as the most important center of Christian worship.

■ **Check on Your Reading**

1. Cite several highlights from the life of Jesus.

2. Name the principles of Christianity.

3. How was Christianity spread? Why were Christians persecuted?

4. Describe the early organization developed by the Church.

4. Strains Appear in the Roman Government

While Christianity was trying to organize, the Roman Empire was experiencing serious strains in its government. As the new religion spread, the tensions of government increased. Some of these tensions were caused by the weaknesses of the Roman rulers.

The emperors who followed the reign of Augustus Caesar (27 B.C.–14 A.D.) (p. 124) were not always qualified for their tasks. They were men who varied greatly in character and ability. Some of the emperors were brutal tyrants who delighted in ordering the deaths of innocent people; others were honest leaders who worked hard to improve the empire. Some were pleasure-mad rulers. Others were conscientious administrators who met with their officials and advisors. A few were serious men who loved philosophy and defended justice. Emperor Marcus Aurelius (161–180 A.D.), for example, was a famous Stoic philosopher, whose *Meditations* are still read.

Diocletian Reorganizes the Government

During the period from 235 to 284 A.D., the conditions of the Roman government became increasingly confused. Roman armies often used the threat of force to place their favorites at the head of the empire. The position of emperor soon became a prize to be awarded to the "highest bidder." The Roman Empire at the same time was being forced to give up some of its territories to Germanic tribes pressing over its borders (p. 154). The empire also suffered a plague lasting fifteen years in the middle of the third century. This reduced the population tremendously.

Diocletian became emperor in 284 A.D. He was a strong leader who brought order to the Roman Empire by making the government a powerful director of the people's affairs. Diocletian took several extreme actions in his attempt to stabilize economic and political conditions. He issued an edict fixing maximum prices for goods, so that high prices would no longer cause unrest. He also attacked the Christians for refusing to accept his position as a god. These actions were only partially successful. Diocletian's edict could not keep prices from rising, and his attacks on the Christians made them even more defiant.

Diocletian did succeed in his reorganization of the government. He divided the empire into two administrative parts. He supervised the eastern half from Asia Minor, and he chose a co-emperor to run the western half of the empire from Italy (map, p. 152). Each half was subdivided into prefectures, dioceses, and provinces. This reorganization permitted the central government to control many distant areas. Diocletian also reorganized the army and strengthened border defenses. By such changes, Diocletian brought order.

Christianity Wins Acceptance

During the early part of the fourth century A.D., Emperor Constantine was the ruler of the Roman Empire. Legend has it that just before an important battle, he saw a lighted cross in the sky and these words: "By this sign thou shalt conquer." Constantine did win the battle, and there were many who said that the victory had come through the aid of the cross of Christ.

Constantine now decided to help the Christians. He may have reached this decision because he was deeply moved by his victory. Or he may have realized that Christianity was spreading so widely that it would be a wise political move to recognize it. Whatever his motive, Constantine issued the *Edict of Milan* (313 A.D.), which gave full *toleration* to all religions, including Christianity. Toleration meant that

■ *The Roman Empire was reorganized by Diocletian (284–305 A.D.). He divided the empire into two parts, Eastern and Western, and subdivided each into prefectures, dioceses, and provinces.*

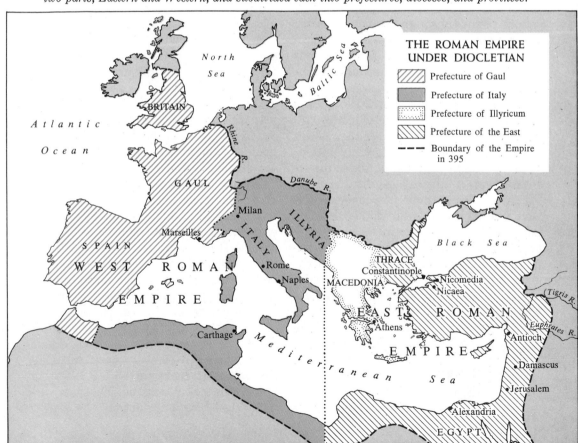

Christians could now practice their religion "freely and absolutely . . . and were not to be disturbed in any ways or molested."

In an effort to have the organization of the Christian Church fit into the pattern of his empire, Constantine also encouraged an arrangement by which the headquarters of Christian religious leaders would be set up in key cities throughout the empire— Rome, Alexandria, and Antioch.

When there were disagreements over details of the Christian beliefs among Christian leaders, Constantine called them together into a great meeting (or council) in Nicaea, Asia Minor. The Council of Nicaea (325 A.D.) attempted to put an end to arguments about Christian beliefs by preparing the *Nicene Creed,* a statement of the beliefs held by Christians. It forms the foundation of Christian ideology today.

Later, Emperor Theodosius (379–395 A.D.) made Christianity the *state religion,* that is, the official religion of the Roman Empire. He began persecuting pagans and closed the Olympic Games because they had pagan religious significance.

■ **Check on Your Reading**

1. What kind of men ruled as Roman emperors after Augustus? with what results?

2. How did Diocletian reorganize the government? with what effects?

3. How did Christianity win acceptance and become the state religion?

5. *The Empire Declines for Many Reasons*

Under Emperor Constantine (324–337 A.D.), the two parts of Diocletian's empire were governed from a single headquarters in the east. Constantine built a new capital in a strategically located city along the Bosporus, a narrow waterway that, with the Dardanelles and the Sea of Marmara, connects the Aegean with the Black Sea. This city, Byzantium to the Greeks, was renamed Constantinople for the emperor.

The efforts of Diocletian and Constantine to restore order in the land checked temporarily the deterioration of the Roman Empire. However, after the death of Constantine, the decline continued.

What caused this giant empire to decay? The Christian philosopher St. Augustine (354–430 A.D.), in his famous book *The City of God,* declared that the destruction of Rome was part of God's plan, but most historians feel that no one answer can be given. They point out that there were a number of factors that interacted on each other to produce the gradual decline of the Roman Empire after 180 A.D.

Reasons for the Decline and Fall

The following factors contributed to the decline of the Roman Empire:

(1) The empire was not always governed efficiently. There were many rulers who weakened the empire by their dishonesty, corruption, or stupidity.

(2) The people lost their rights to participate in the government. Lacking democratic rights, they soon ceased to take any serious interest in the welfare of the state.

(3) Roman armies lost their patriotic spirit and discipline. Their ranks were now filled with men from the provinces. These soldiers were more interested in loot.

(4) Economic conditions became worse. Farms were not properly operated, as people moved to the cities and left the slaves to work the land. Trade decreased. Many city workers lived in poverty.

(5) Population declined, partially as a result of epidemics and wars.

(6) Moral standards fell. Since the Romans saw scoundrels profit by dishonest

acts and go unpunished, some of them lost their confidence in the value of truth and honesty.

(7) Christianity deprived the emperors of the support of some people who formerly accepted the emperor as a god. However, the Roman religion was losing strength before Christianity developed.

It must not be supposed that all of the people were aware of the decaying condition of the empire. Few men had the foresight to prophesy the doom of an empire that had dominated the world.

Germanic Tribes Move into the Empire

Individual German tribesmen started to move across the border into the Roman Empire near the end of the second century A.D. Many of them became soldiers in the Roman armies. Mass migrations of the Germans began about two hundred years later. The origin of these German tribes is not clear. They may have come from an area near the Baltic Sea and then moved to the east and the southwest.

Physically, the Germans were described as rugged men with "eyes stern and blue; ruddy hair; large bodies, powerful in sudden exertions." These features were not found in all Germans. Although physically strong, many Germans felt that their success in battle often depended on *omens*, or signs of the future. In battle, the Germans were brave and bold. A German faced disgrace for life if he surrendered.

Romans called the Germans *barbarians*, a term which originally meant "foreigners" but which later was interpreted to mean uncivilized men. Some writers of this period pictured them as honest warriors. Others called them wildly uncivilized tribesmen interested only in looting and war. The early Germans were people who developed none of the Roman skills in literature, art, philosophy, or government. On the other hand, they developed tribal law, or-

ganized family and community life, and became familiar with some methods of agriculture.

Actually, the Germans first entered the Roman Empire in a mass to protect themselves from the attacks of warring peoples from Asia. Then they fought to increase their possessions and killed to destroy their enemies. They were far more than invaders intent on destruction for its own sake.

Visigoths Defeat the Romans

The case of the Germanic tribe known as the *Visigoths* (Western Goths) provides a good example of the way some Germans entered the Roman Empire for protection from attack—and then became attackers.

In the fourth century A.D. the Visigoths were in danger of being destroyed by the Huns, fierce warriors from Asia. The Visigoths therefore moved west until they reached the Danube River, a boundary of the Roman Empire. Here they asked the Romans for permission to cross to safety.

The Romans permitted many thousand Visigoths to enter the empire. However, Roman officials cheated them and did little to help them obtain food. The Romans further angered the Visigoths by refusing to permit the rest of their tribesmen to enter the empire. In anger the Visigoths rose in rebellion and defeated the Roman emperor and his army near Adrianople (378 A.D.).

Later, a Visigoth ruler named Alaric led his men west until they reached the city of Rome. Alaric's troops entered and sacked Rome in 410 A.D. Then the Visigoths moved on and finally settled in southern Gaul and Spain. Other Germanic groups now pushed into the empire (map, p. 155).

A number of chieftains of these Germanic groups, such as Theodoric the Ostrogoth, admired Roman achievements and tried to imitate the ways of the Romans. Roman civilization was thus increasingly absorbed by the Germans.

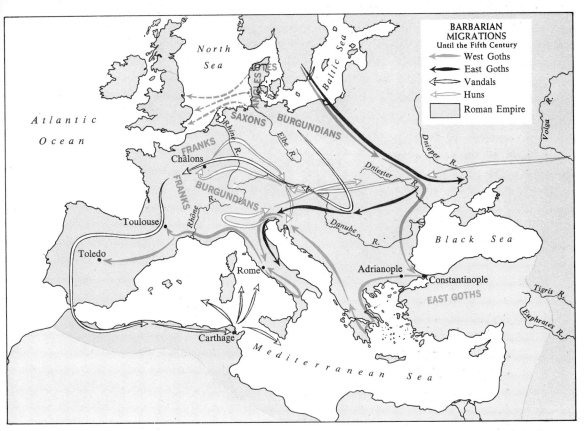

■ *The Germanic tribes—Goths, Vandals, Franks, Burgundians, etc.—began to move into the Roman Empire at the end of the 2nd century A.D. Name the tribes and the areas into which they moved.*

The Huns Spread Terror

As in the case of the Visigoths, most of the German tribes in the east probably had been forced westward by the pressure of the *Huns.* The Huns were a non-Germanic people from Asia who occupied the area of modern Hungary and Rumania. In the fifth century A.D. hard-riding Hun horsemen smashed into the Roman Empire.

The leader of the Huns was Attila, a short, broad-chested man of whom it was said: "He was the scourge of all countries and reports concerning him terrified all mankind." At the battle of Châlons in 451 A.D., Attila and his men were temporarily checked by the combined forces of the Romans and Goths. A few years later, Attila died, and the Huns withdrew.

The Western Roman Empire Deteriorates

Although the Huns had been stopped, the power of the German tribes increased. In 476 A.D. a German chieftain, Odoacer, forced the emperor of Rome to abdicate "of his own accord." Odoacer made himself king of Italy, and other German leaders seized control. *The rise of this German to the position of ruler of Italy is taken as a symbol of the final deterioration of the Roman Empire in the West.* Although the Eastern Roman Empire continued, the Western Roman Empire ceased to exist.

■ Check on Your Reading

1. Why did the Roman Empire decline?
2. Why did Germanic tribes move into the empire? with what results?

155

MAN AND HIS CULTURE

Let's Meet the People! This sketch is based on material in *A History of Rome: From Its Origins to 529 A.D. As Told by the Roman Historians*, trans. and edited by Moses Hadas. Copyright (c) 1956 by Moses Hadas; reprinted by permission of Doubleday & Co., Inc.; and Dion Cassium Cocceianus, a Roman historian—trans. in *The Universal Anthology*, R. Garnett, L. Valee, and A. Brandl (eds.), Vol. 7, Merrill and Baker.

Arminius: German Chieftain

"Roman legions are the greatest in the world," declared the Roman generals. Yet in 9 A.D. Arminius, young chieftain of the Cherusci Germans, prepared to strike against them.

Quinctilius Varus, the Roman commander in Germany, was not afraid of Arminius or the other Germans. He believed that Germans were "human only in respect to voice and limbs." He ruled them as subjects and exacted money "as from conquered foes."

Now Arminius was very respectful to the Romans. He submitted to Varus' orders. He encouraged the Germans to "trump up a series of fictitious lawsuits" and thanked the Romans for settling these disputes. He urged Varus to scatter his troops among the German tribes who needed them for hunting down robbers. Quinctilius Varus became convinced that Arminius' Germans could be trusted.

Arminius was ready to strike! First he formed a coalition with the Chatti Germans. Next he urged Varus and his troops to march against distant German tribes. Finally, Arminius gathered his own forces, overtook Varus in the Teutoberg Forest, and ambushed him.

The German warriors struck at the surprised Romans "from every direction at once." Roman soldiers, plagued by the rain that made it difficult for them to use their arrows and javelins, were massacred. Three of the finest Roman legions were annihilated.

"Roman legions are the greatest," the Roman generals had declared. But after the attack by Arminius, Emperor Augustus Caesar cried: "Quinctilius Varus, give back my legions!"

CHAPTER REVIEW

REVIEW and DISCUSSION

1. Identify the people and places and explain the events and terms on p. 142.

2. What relationships might exist between the *rise* of great empires and religions? the fall?

3. How does Asoka's attitude toward other religions compare with our own?

4. What does "peace of mind" mean?

5. What characteristics of the period of the Roman Empire's expansion were similar to those of China under the Han dynasty?

6. What is martyrdom? What effects does a martyr's death have on his fellow believers? on non-believers?

7. Does persecution make one's faith stronger or weaker? Why?

8. Why is Christianity a religion in which many sects exist, with each one believing that its creed is the true one?

9. What factors within the Roman Empire aided the growth of Christianity?

10. Compare the disintegration of the Roman Empire with that of the Han Empire.

11. As you study about Rome's decline, can you suggest anything that might have saved Rome?

12. Find examples to substantiate the factors listed in the chapter as causes for the decline of the Roman Empire.

13. It has been said that history is more often the study of the upper class of peoples. Do you agree or disagree with this statement from your study of Units I and II? Why?

ACTIVITIES

1. To your chart on the "Causes of the Rise and Fall of Civilizations," add the civilizations discussed in this chapter.

2. Write an account of a secret meeting of Christians in Rome during the persecution. Consult references.

3. Make a diagram showing the organization of the Roman Catholic Church.

4. Write a report on the mystery religions that existed in the Roman Empire and influenced Christianity in its early period.

5. Read a selection from a primary source: the four Gospels of the *New Testament* or Marcus Aurelius' *Meditations*. What do you learn about living conditions then?

6. On a map of the Empire show the movements of the Germanic tribes.

7. Continue to build your paperback library with some of these books: Livingstone, Sir Richard, *Thucydides*; Rouse, W. H. D., *The Iliad* and *The Odyssey*; *Great Dialogues of Plato*.

PAST and PRESENT

1. What might be the results if the Christian principles of "Love One Another" or the "Brotherhood of Man" were applied to the fields of economics, politics, and foreign affairs?

2. What are the implications for us in the decline and fall of Rome? Consult Muller, *Uses of the Past*, Chap. 7.

SUGGESTED READINGS

Basic books: LINTON, RALPH, *The Tree of Culture*, Knopf. See index for references to topics included in this chapter.

SMITH, GOLDWIN, *The Heritage of Man*, Chap. 10, Scribner. Challenges one's thinking on the destinies of civilization.

Special accounts: BOWIE, WALTER RUSSELL, *Story of the Church*, Abingdon Press. Story of Christianity.

FRANK, TENNEY, *A History of Rome*, Holt.

GAER, JOSEPH, *How the Great Religions Began*, Dodd, Mead. Easy-to-read account of ten major religions and their leaders.

GIBBON, EDWARD, *The Decline and Fall of the Roman Empire*, 3 vols., Modern Library. For serious students of history.

Biography and Fiction: SIENKIEWICZ, HENRYK, *Quo Vadis: A Tale of the Time of Nero*, Little, Brown.

THOMPSON, STITH, and GASSNER, JOHN (eds.), *Our Heritage of World Literature*, Holt. See Marcus Aurelius' *Meditations*.

UNIT 3 "Middle Ages" in Europe; "Golden Ages" in Asia

A Famous Puzzle Asks: When Can "Late" Be "Early"?

This is a puzzle that can be easily solved. Suppose that you were to say, "It's late—it is five minutes *before* midnight." That would seem to be a logical statement. However, from a different point of view, you also could remark, "It's early—why, it is *hardly* midnight." You are really saying the same thing—but with what a difference!

The meaning of words like "late" and "early" often depends on each man's viewpoint. "Late" can be "early" to a person who wishes to interpret it in this fashion.

Do the Historical Terms "Ancient," "Medieval," and "Modern" Ages Depend on Man?

Yes, they certainly do. Like the words "early" and "late," divisions of history into time periods depend ultimately on the views taken by historians. Remember what seems "ancient" to one historian might appear "modern" to another in a different time and place.

Here is a case in point. We who live in the twentieth century often call the period from about the end of the fifth to the fifteenth century A.D. the "Middle Ages." This seems logical to us. However, two thousand years from now, historians might call our twentieth century the "Middle Ages." They might consider everything that happened before us to be a part of "Ancient Times."

Thus it is wrong to think of the "Middle Ages" as a separate period complete for all time. Since all historical divisions are man-made, it is a mistake to believe that the "Middle Ages" began and ended on certain dates. Indeed, their influence never has ended. Some features of medieval life are still with us. Great twentieth-century universities—such as the University of Paris and Oxford University—were started in the twelfth and thirteenth centuries. Important modern cities—such as Antwerp and Venice—were developed in medieval years. Most of today's finest Gothic cathedrals

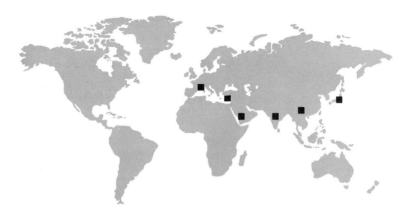

—such as the Cathedral of Notre Dame in Paris—were constructed primarily in medieval times. And twentieth-century youngsters still treasure as their own the wondrous medieval tales of King Arthur and his Knights of the Round Table. Apparently, the influence of the "Middle Ages" *never did come to an end.*

The "Middle Ages" Existed Largely in Europe

Outside Europe in the period we call the "Middle Ages" many great cultures were flourishing. This was true of the Near East and the southern coast of the Mediterranean, where the civilization of Islam was at its height. In India and China the people experienced cultural "Golden Ages" and they would not dream of referring to this great period by the drab term "Middle Ages." From another viewpoint, then, the term is a misleading one.

Can We Take a World-History Approach?

Yes, we can. Instead of using the traditional approach that studies a unit on medieval Europe and then a separate unit on Asia, let us stand off and look at *both* areas in the same unit. The significance of our unit title then becomes clear—the "Middle Ages" in Europe were "Golden Ages" in China and India.

Our study of the East in this period will prove as valuable as our study of the West. After reading about Asia, we will be able to answer such questions as: (1) How did Islam affect India? (2) What is the importance of the T'ang dynasty? (3) What is Shinto? Are these petty questions? No! Each of them involves an important aspect of the cultural history of an Asian power. We cannot neglect such questions because we do not associate them with the history of Western civilization. We must recognize that we have much to learn from the East as well as from the West.

159

Chapter 10

Christianity, Feudalism, and a Struggle for Men's Loyalty

KEYNOTE

Eugene Fitch Ware, a writer who was known as "*Ironquill*," once wrote the following lines:

> *Human hopes and human creeds*
> *Have their root in human needs.*

Many of the events in the period which followed the disintegration of the Roman Empire in Europe prove the accuracy of this view.

During this troubled time, the "medieval period," people felt need of a spiritual authority to guide their lives. What was the result? The Church became increasingly powerful. During these years, too, men had a need for protection against invaders. What was the result? People organized themselves into a protective system known as feudalism.

Men's needs were thus key factors in this period. *Need stimulated both the growth of Christianity and the development of feudalism, and need forced men to try to settle the conflicts that arose between them.*

Key People   *Alfred the Great · Clovis · Charles Martel · Pepin the Short · Charlemagne · Pope Leo III · Henry IV · Pope Gregory VII*

Key Places   *England · Gaul · Burgundy · Ravenna · Charlemagne's Empire · Spain · Holy Roman Empire · Canossa · Worms*

Key Events   *Eastern Orthodox Church established · Anglo-Saxons unite England · Carolingians rule Franks   ·   Charlemagne builds an empire · Treaty of Verdun · Vikings attack Europe · Holy Roman Empire established · Henry IV at Canossa · Concordat of Worms*

Key Terms   *Roman Catholic Church · monasticism · Benedictine Rule · feudalism · fief · vassal · manor · serf · knight · chivalry*

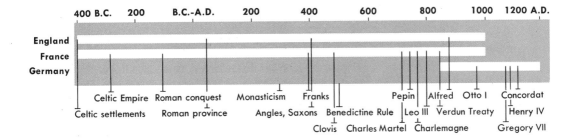

| 400 B.C. | 200 | B.C.-A.D. | 200 | 400 | 600 | 800 | 1000 | 1200 A.D. |

England
France
Germany

Celtic Empire Roman conquest   Monasticism   Franks   Pepin   Alfred Otto I   Concordat
Celtic settlements   Roman province   Angles, Saxons Benedictine Rule Leo III Verdun Treaty Henry IV
                                        Clovis   Charles Martel Charlemagne   Gregory VII

1. Popes Claim Religious Supremacy over Bishops and Kings

With the decline of the Roman Empire and the influx of German tribes, Europe entered a period of disorder and confusion. As central government disintegrated, Christian leaders grew in power.

The Popes Gain Supremacy

During the so-called "Middle Ages," from about the end of the fifth to the fifteenth century, the *Roman Catholic* Church became the dominant factor in European life. In time the organization of the Church in the West developed this pattern (see Chart).

Church Organization

Pope	Headed the Church.
Archbishops	Directed archdioceses where there were several bishops.
Bishops	Supervised worship in dioceses.
Priests	Administered local church congregations in parishes.
Laity	The ordinary members of the Christian communities.

The *Pope*, originally the bishop of Rome, had gradually proclaimed his supremacy in religious matters over bishops everywhere. Rome was recognized by many as the most important center of Christian worship, and the bishop of Rome was considered heir to the power of Peter, leader of the apostles. Under such strong Popes as Leo I (440–461 A.D.) the Church grew in power.

Since the old Roman Empire had broken up and many regions lacked a central government, the Church became a powerful influence in political as well as religious affairs. The Church owned a great amount of land, and bishops and archbishops often exercised governing power over cities and even over larger areas, bishoprics and archbishoprics. The Popes, after Rome was no longer the capital of the empire, actually ruled the city of Rome and its surroundings, called the Papal States. Some kings relied heavily on religious leaders to help them run their states, for the clergy usually had more education than most people.

The Popes took the position that the Church was not to be under the command of any civil ruler. They proclaimed that

161

in matters of religion the kings would have to obey the orders of the Church. One Pope wrote to a ruler:

Of these two powers [kings and priests] the importance of the priests is . . . much the greater. . . . Know . . . that although you rule over the human race, yet as a man of devotion in divine matters you submit your neck to the [Church].

Eastern Church Separates from the West

This position of the Church greatly disturbed the emperors in the East. The Western Roman Empire had been overrun by the Germans; the eastern half had continued to exist with its capital at Constantinople. The emperors of this eastern empire disagreed with the Pope on two main points. They wanted the state to supervise the activities of the Church, and they did not want the patriarch of Constantinople to take orders from the Pope at Rome.

When the emperors tried to dominate religion in the East, a struggle between the eastern and western sections of the Church developed. Disagreements over religious and civil issues continued, and in 1054 A.D. a final split occurred between the two sections. This division became permanent.

In the future there would be two major Christian churches: the *Roman Catholic Church* (referred to as the *Church*) in the West, and the *Eastern Orthodox Church* in the East. Both followed Christian principles. However, the Eastern Orthodox Church was more supervised by the state than was the Roman Church and did not accept the leadership of the Pope.

■ **Check on Your Reading**

1. How did the Church gain supremacy? What attitude did it develop toward kings?

2. Why did the Eastern Orthodox Church separate from the Roman Catholic Church?

2. Christian Monasticism Is Started

During the years of the development of the Roman Church, Christian *monasticism* started in both the East and the West. Monasticism referred to the practice of giving up one's worldly possessions, leaving society, and living a secluded life of prayer and meditation. Believers in monasticism felt that such a life would bring people spiritually closer to God.

Beginning as early as the third century A.D. some men left their homes to live as hermits in the deserts of Egypt and in other desolate areas. There they deliberately led lives that were stripped of all comforts. It was said that two of them ate nothing but grass; one refused to touch bread for eighty years; and one fasted for two to four days at a time. Near Antioch, one man lived thirty-six years on top of a column that was only about three feet in diameter. Such men as these hoped to gain spiritual strength by neglecting their physical well-being and by actually punishing their bodies.

Few men were able to go to the extremes of these hermits. On the other hand, there were a number of sincere Christians who wished to leave worldly society and devote their lives to spiritual meditation. Like St. Jerome, they wondered: "How long will [we] remain in the shadow of roofs and the smoky dungeons of cities?" Starting in the fourth century, these men established *monasteries*; that is, secluded religious communities where men lived their entire lives in prayer, work, and meditation. Such men were called *monks*. Religious communities for women were soon begun, too. They were called *convents*, and the women who entered them were called *nuns*.

■ *Monte Cassino monastery was founded in the 6th century A.D. by St. Benedict who devised the Benedictine Rule. This was the way it looked before its destruction in World War II. The Allies bombed the monastery because the Germans had made it a fortified stronghold.*

The Benedictine Rule Is Drawn Up

Regulations to govern life within a monastery were eventually drawn up. Rules prepared by a monk named Basil influenced the organization of monasteries in the East and West. Then, in the sixth century, St. Benedict founded the famous monastery at Monte Cassino in Italy.

For this monastery, St. Benedict devised the *Benedictine Rule,* a series of regulations to govern the lives of the monks. According to the Rule, monks were to follow these principles: (1) poverty—the giving up of worldly goods; (2) chastity—the giving up of the right to marry; and (3) obedience without delay—the readiness to obey their leader, the *abbot,* who was elected to his position for life by the monks. The Rule also provided that the monks were to say prayers at stated times and do both manual labor and reading.

St. Benedict hoped that his Rule contained "nothing severe, nothing burdensome," and that it would help monks to live together in harmony. His Benedictine Rule proved to be so effective that it became the model for many monasteries in the West. Even America was later to be affected by the Rule. Today, the United States has the second largest congregation of Benedictine monks in the world.

The Monks Make Many Contributions

Although some monasteries did not function smoothly or without corruption, the monks in general made important contributions to society. They improved the land that had been given to them by rulers and devout Christian people. Then they taught their successful agricultural methods to farmers living in the surrounding regions.

At a time when important documents and books were being destroyed by neglect, ignorance, and abuse, monks made careful and beautiful copies of old manuscripts. Although they probably destroyed some valuable manuscripts that opposed their religious views, the monks preserved an important part of ancient writings for future generations. They also recorded some of the great events of their times in "Chronicles." As a result, they furnished us with historical information about the period in which they lived.

■ *This is the initial page of the Gospel of St. Luke, copied and illuminated (decorated) in a French monastery about 1000 A.D. It exemplified Romanesque painting.*

They established schools at the monasteries. Although these schools were limited in subject matter and in the number of students, they served as places of learning at a time when there was little education in Europe.

In addition, they helped the poor, provided resting places for travellers, and gave simple hospital care to the sick.

Some monks, such as St. Patrick in Ireland and St. Augustine in England, helped to spread Christianity by doing missionary work in areas in France, England, Ireland, and Germany.

These achievements show that the monks made valuable contributions to civilization.

■ Check on Your Reading

1. What was monasticism?

2. Why did some Christians adopt a monastic life? To what extremes did some Christian monks go?

3. What were the main principles of the Benedictine Rule? How effectively did the Rule regulate monastic life?

4. Evaluate the contributions to society made by the monks.

3. The Celtic and Roman Heritage in Western Europe

There were other important developments in western Europe at this time. They can be directly traced to the Celtic and Roman heritage in western Europe.

The Celts

About 1000 B.C. an Indo-European people called the Celts had come from the European mainland and conquered the natives of England. Celtic tribes from the Danube region also built an empire in the fourth century B.C. that included the land of modern France.

The Celts were divided into clans and tribes. They lived in simple huts, ate such hearty foods as roasted meat and salt pork, and worshipped many gods. One of their religious societies, the *Druids*, followed the ritual of gathering mistletoe from oak trees during the winter solstice. When you hang mistletoe at Christmas time and eagerly await the results, you are really borrowing from an old Celtic custom!

Today, there are still remnants of Celtic culture in western Europe. Indeed, some of the old men of Britanny (France) can still use a dialect that is derived from the original Celtic tongue. "Bloavez mat d'eoc'h!" ("Happy New Year") they will shout at you in their Bretagne *patois* (speech).

The Romans and Anglo-Saxons

Starting in the second century B.C., the Romans gradually conquered the Celts and the other peoples living in the area of modern France. The Romans called the Celts *Galli* or *Gauls*, and the country became known as *Gaul*. In 54 B.C. Julius Caesar, the great Roman leader, also invaded Britain. Caesar defeated the Britons, the people formed by a fusion of the Celts and native peoples, and then returned home. About a hundred years later, the troops of another Roman ruler crossed the Channel and established a Roman province in Britain.

In the fifth century A.D., the Romans withdrew their troops from Britain because they needed them to defend Rome. *Angles*, *Saxons*, and other Germanic tribes from northern Europe now entered the country and gained control of most of England. Under an Anglo-Saxon king, Alfred the Great (871–900 A.D.) and his successors, most of the regions of England were united into a single kingdom. The Romans had also lost control of Gaul, which had been a province of the Roman Empire for five hundred years. Another Germanic tribe, the *Franks*, gained possession of a good part of this country.

Before the Germanic groups had taken over the land, the Romans had made several important contributions to the peoples of both Britain and Gaul. These included the following: (1) the establishment of greater law and order; (2) the building of military roads and bridges that aided the economic life of the people; (3) the development of cities; (4) assistance in spreading Christianity; and (5) the gradual replacement of the Celtic tongue by the Latin language, which later affected the development of French and English.

■ Check on Your Reading

1. Describe the culture of the early Celts.
2. What peoples took control of England?
3. What impact did Roman civilization have on the people of Britain and Gaul?

■ *This is a reconstruction of a Roman station in Britain behind Hadrian's wall as it was about the third century, A.D. The temples and storehouses are at the right and the military compounds at the left.*

4. Carolingian Rulers Lead the Franks

After the Roman Empire disintegrated, the Franks who had settled in Gaul played an important role in the events of western Europe. The area in which they settled included the present-day Low Countries, France, and the Rhineland area of Germany. The first Frankish ruling house, the Merovingians, established control over Gaul and the Low Countries. The outstanding Merovingian ruler was King Clovis (481–511). Clovis defeated Roman-German troops in 486 and then kept the German Alemanni from entering Gaul. (The French word for Germany, *L'Allemagne*, comes from the name of this tribe.) In 507 Clovis defeated the Visigoths and took their lands north of the Pyrenees Mountains to add to the Frankish kingdom. His sons added Burgundy.

Perhaps the most significant act of Clovis was his acceptance of Christianity. As a result, the Frankish state had the approval of Rome, and it supported the Pope.

■ *Charlemagne extended his control over much of western Europe by 800 A.D. What lands did he conquer? What happened to the empire?*

CAROLINGIAN EMPIRE
Scale of Miles 0 600
SAXONY
Mersen
Aix-la-Chapelle
Paris
Verdun
EAST
WEST
Tours
BAVARIA
Danube
Poitiers
FRANKLAND
FRANKLAND
LOMBARDY
SPANISH MARCH
KINGDOM OF ITALY
Rhone R.
Venice
Ravenna
PYRENEES MTS.
Ebro R.
Barcelona
Rome
Monte Cassino

☐ Charlemagne's original possessions
☐ Charlemagne's conquests and tributary peoples
— Division of his empire in 843 by the Treaty of Verdun

How the Carolingians Gained Power

After Clovis the Merovingian kings weakened themselves by the custom of partitioning the kingdom among all of the king's sons. They engaged in useless warfare and intrigues to gain power. By the eighth century the kings made few major decisions, and officials called "mayors of the palace" (similar to prime ministers) were the actual rulers. In this way a mayor of the palace named Charles became the real ruler of the Franks (714–741). So forceful was he in battle that he was given the honorary surname of "Martel," meaning hammer. Charles Martel was the real founder of the Carolingian dynasty ("Carolingian" comes from "Charles"). At his death, Charles' position was taken by his son, Pepin the Short (741–768).

Pepin demanded that he, rather than the weak ruler, should be recognized as king of the Franks. The Pope, the leader of the Church at Rome, agreed that Pepin should have the title as well as the power. In 751 A.D. Pepin was formally chosen king of the Franks. He and his descendants are known as the *Carolingian* rulers.

In return for the Pope's support, Pepin helped to defend the Church. He drove back the Lombards, a Germanic people in northern Italy who were threatening Rome, and forced them to surrender several cities. These cities he turned over to the Pope as a "donation of Pepin," and they formed the foundation for the *Papal States*. The Papal States, an area under the direct control of the Pope, soon ran from Rome in the west to Ravenna in the east. The Franks had helped to increase the power and strength of the Popes as temporal (civil) rulers. Of course, the Popes' spiritual role was superior to any temporal power. In 768 A.D. Pepin died and was succeeded by his son Charlemagne.

The coronation of Charlemagne by Pope Leo III at the church of St. Peter in 800 A.D. is shown in this miniature painting from The Great Chronicles of France *about 1460.*

Charlemagne Establishes an Empire

Charlemagne (768–814 A.D.) at the peak of his power controlled the greater part of western Europe. He defeated the Lombards and occupied northern Italy. Then he drove back the Saxons, a Germanic people who lived in an area east of the Rhine. Next, he conquered Bavaria and overcame a people known as the Avars. Finally, he succeeded in forming the Spanish *March*, or frontier, out of parts of northern Spain. By his campaigns, Charlemagne extended his power over the greater part of western Europe (map, p. 166).

Charlemagne was said to be "seven times the length of his own foot" in height and strongly built. His eyes were large, his nose somewhat long, and his hair very gray. Einhard, his secretary, wrote that "although Charlemagne's neck was thick and rather short, and his belly too prominent, still the good proportions of his limbs concealed these defects. His walk was firm and the whole carriage of his body was manly."

Usually Charlemagne wore a jacket of otter skin and a plain blue cloak. He always carried a sword. At great festivals he put on a magnificent jewelled sword and wore shoes studded with precious gems.

Pope Leo III Crowns Charlemagne

One of the high points in the life of Charlemagne was his coronation in 800 A.D. The year before, some subjects of Pope Leo III in Rome had accused their religious leader of misconduct and revolted. Leo fled to Charlemagne and asked for his assistance. Charlemagne went to Rome, examined the charges, and cleared the Pope of guilt. Then he helped to restore Leo to his office.

A short time later, Charlemagne attended Christmas day services for the year 800 A.D. at the church of St. Peter. As Charlemagne knelt, Pope Leo set a crown upon his head, while the people shouted:

Long life and victory to the mighty Charles, the great and pacific Emperor of the Romans, crowned of God!

167

It hardly seems likely that Charlemagne did not know that he would be crowned by the Pope, but some writers claim that he was unaware of the Pope's plan.

The coronation of Charlemagne by Pope Leo III was important for three reasons: (1) It showed that the Pope claimed a role in recognizing and crowning political rulers. (2) It was an attempt to demonstrate that Charlemagne was the successor of the rulers of the old Roman Empire. Charlemagne's possessions were later considered to mark the beginning of a new "Holy Roman Empire" which lasted until 1806. (3) It suggested that the widespread territory that Charlemagne controlled had real political unity. Actually, the coronation did not change the political or military situation in any radical way. Whatever unity there was in Charlemagne's empire continued to exist mainly because of his personal leadership.

Life under Charlemagne

Until his death in 814 A.D., Charlemagne did much to advance the well-being of his people. He tried to keep order and justice in his land by sending out *missi dominici*, men who checked on whether or not the government of Church and state was being run correctly. He strengthened Christianity by encouraging the building of churches and monasteries. He supported education by providing for the opening of schools. He even established a school at his palace, where he and his nobles studied logic and astronomy under the scholar Alcuin of Britain.

Most important of all, Charlemagne defended much of the empire against attack and prevented it from being ripped apart internally. However, commercial activity continued to decline. Cut off from foreign trade routes by *Saracens* (Arab Moslems) and other raiders, Charlemagne's empire became an inland one. Its people remained in relative isolation, making their living by working the land. Rare indeed were traders bold enough to voyage to other distant countries.

The Future Shapes of France and Germany are Molded

Charlemagne's empire crumbled soon after his death. Lothair, Louis the German, and Charles the Bald, three of his grandsons, quarrelled over who should rule the territory. In 842 A.D. Louis and Charles took the Oath of Strasbourg, in which they promised to help each other against their brother, Lothair. The oaths were taken in both early German and early French, which showed that the empire gradually was dividing into two language areas. One area, East Frankland, was eventually to develop into Germany; the other, West Frankland, was to become the nation of France.

At the Treaty of Verdun in 843 A.D., the three brothers agreed to divide the empire into three sections. Louis received the eastern part, Charles the western part, and Lothair the area between the two plus northern Italy (map, p. 166). This treaty was extremely important because it helped to mold the future shapes of France and Germany.

■ Check on Your Reading

1. What were three major achievements of Clovis?

2. How did the Carolingians gain governing powers?

3. Why was the "donation of Pepin" important historically?

4. How did Charlemagne build an empire? What territories did it include?

5. Why was the coronation of Charlemagne by Pope Leo III important?

6. Evaluate Charlemagne as a ruler.

7. How did the division of Charlemagne's empire in 843 affect the future of Europe?

5. The People of Europe Seek Safety from Invaders

The breakup of Charlemagne's empire caused considerable difficulty. Communications were cut, many roads were not kept open, and trading was limited still further. The confusion was increased by fresh attacks against Europe beginning in the ninth century. *Magyars*, known later as Hungarians, invaded parts of Italy and France. Saracen forces (Moslems from North Africa) swept into Sicily, southern Italy, and the area around the Mediterranean.

Most fearsome of all were the *Vikings* (the Northmen), who sailed down from the Scandinavian regions. The Vikings were not a primitive people without a culture. On the contrary, recent discoveries have revealed that they were skillful enough to produce fine woolen cloth, artistic wood carvings, and attractive tapestries.

Viking vessels, whose commanders never "sought refuge under a roof nor emptied their drinking-horns at a fireside," attacked the coasts of the British Isles, France, and Spain. Some moved southward to the Black Sea, and a few went as far as North America. The sight of their long vessels, whose prows often were carved into figures of powerful animals or dragons, produced fear and panic.

With the danger of attacks by invaders and marauding nobles, and with the decline of the power of central governments, the people felt isolated and wanted protection. Some of them found security by obtaining the aid of their landlords, who agreed to protect them in return for certain services. Thus *feudalism* developed.

Feudalism Develops

Feudalism, which had existed much earlier in ancient China, had appeared in fairly clear form in western Europe by 900 A.D. It had developed gradually, and in most areas it continued until about the

■ *This prow of a Viking ship of about 800 was carved into a fierce beaked head of an animal. The Vikings spread terror in many countries.*

thirteenth century. Although it varied from place to place, feudalism usually had three features: (1) loyalty of one man to another; (2) land *tenure*, or landholding, based on some type of contract (generally oral); and (3) private local government, instead of central rule by a king.

Under feudalism, loyalty of one man to another was demonstrated by the ceremonies of *homage* and *fealty*. Homage was the act by which a man who wanted to be protected by a lord—that is, to be his *vassal*—formally promised to be faithful to him. The vassal-to-be usually would kneel, place his hands between those of his future lord, and state that he would become "his man." Then the lord would kiss his new vassal, and the pledge would be considered

169

binding. After this, the vassal would take *an oath of fealty,* in which he vowed to carry out all of his duties to his lord.

Landholding by Contract

When the vassal had gone through acts of homage and fealty, he often was given a stick or a bit of earth by his lord. This showed that there was a "contract," or agreement, between them. Under the terms of this contract, the vassal received a *fief,* and in return he gave his lord loyalty and service. A fief usually was a section of land that the vassal was permitted to control and govern.

Fiefs did not have to be land. They could consist of the right to hold a castle, the right to collect bridge tolls, the right to hear court cases, and other similar rights. Sometimes a man who wanted protection would take land that he already controlled and hand it over to a lord. Then he would obtain the protection of the lord by pledging himself to be his vassal. After that, his lord would return his land to him as a fief.

Frequently, a vassal would divide the fief he had received so that he could become the lord of someone else. For example, suppose vassal Anton divided the land he had received from lord Reynard and gave part of it to a third man, Morac. In such a case, Anton still remained the vassal of his lord, Reynard; but at the same time Anton became the lord of his vassal, Morac.

Those who received fiefs under feudalism were the *holders* of the land, not the owners. In theory, nearly all of the land in a country belonged to its king. However, the king permitted his great nobles to hold much of it as his vassals. In practice, the king's powers were limited, and his powerful vassals were free to run their fiefs as they saw fit.

By the end of the tenth century, the control of the fiefs had become hereditary.

The land would pass from father to son (usually the eldest), provided that the son would perform homage to the lord. For securing this fief, the heir generally had to pay a special sum, called *relief,* to the lord.

Private Local Government

Under feudalism, the lord privately governed his vassals in his own locality, and the vassals privately governed their fiefs. There was little interference from a central government. Both lord and vassal knew what their rights and services were in the contract they had made. Some of the lord's duties to the vassals included the following: (1) to provide the vassal with enough governing powers to run his fief; (2) to protect the vassal and the fief; and (3) to see that the vassal received justice. A vassal involved in a dispute would be judged by other vassals in the lord's court.

The vassal received his fief in exchange for the loyalty and services that he gave. Some of his duties to his lord included the following: (1) to give military aid to the lord, including personal service in the army not exceeding "forty days and nights" each year; (2) to make special payments (called *aids*) to ransom the lord, to celebrate the marriage of the lord's eldest daughter, or to cover part of the expense of knighting the lord's eldest son; (3) to advise the lord, when asked, on important matters; and (4) to give hospitality to the lord in the form of food, lodging, and entertainment, when the lord and his household visited the vassal's fief. In theory, the lord had the right of *forfeiture* too, that is, the right to take back the fief from a vassal who did not fulfill his duties. In practice, the vassal usually was fined.

■ **Check on Your Reading**
1. What invaders terrorized Europe?
2. How did feudalism ensure loyalty?
3. Describe the landholding system.
4. Explain feudal government.

6. Life on a Manor

Feudalism consisted of the relationship between lords and vassals. These men were all members of the nobility, but vassals held lands under and owed allegiance to the greater lords. Their strongest bonds were with the earth and the manor.

A *manor* was an agricultural settlement, including land, buildings, tools, and farm workers. One or more manors usually were included within a fief. The vassal who received a fief became the lord of the manors. Manors existed before feudalism, but gradually they came under the feudal system.

The population of a manor usually ranged from fifty to close to five hundred persons, and the total area varied from five hundred to seven thousand acres. In many ways a manor was self-sufficient, that is, it could take care of most of its needs. Most of the people on it did not travel very far, and a peasant rarely met more than two or three hundred people in his life.

The Plan of a Manor

In the center of the manor was the village where the peasants lived. Each family had a simple one-room (rarely two-room) cottage whose walls were constructed by intertwining sticks with twigs and branches and "plastering" all of it with mud. The floor was pounded earth, the roof was thatched and attractive to rats, and the "chimney" was merely a hole in the roof. Inside, there probably would be a bench, a rough wooden table, stools, and a "bed" made by pushing straw together or filling a box with it. The whole family slept in the same "bed." If a neighbor wished to spend the night with them, there was always room for one more!

Next to the cottage, there was space for a vegetable garden and perhaps a chicken yard or a pig sty.

The peasants' clothing was very simple: coarse wool tunics, hose, and, in cold weather, cloaks. On ordinary days, they went barefoot. On special occasions, they might put on wooden clogs or leather shoes. Clothes were home-made, except in the rare village where some peasant would spend part of his time making clothing for others.

Near the cottages of the peasants was the lord's home. Perhaps it would be a walled castle or a manor house. The manor house was built on a small hill, and it was constructed of timber and clay, or of stone.

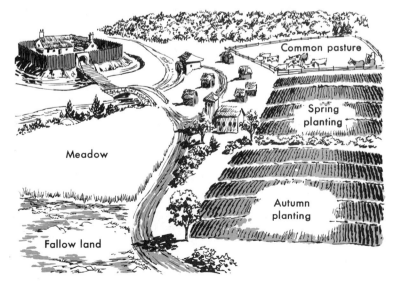

■ *This plan of a medieval manor depicts the manor house, village, fields, pasture, and woodland. Great variations developed throughout Europe in the size of manors and in their arrangement.*

Common pasture

Spring planting

Autumn planting

Meadow

Fallow land

171

It often consisted of a single great hall which served as dining room, court of justice, and bedchamber. Some manor houses had three stories and were more elaborate. Outside the manor house, there was a bakehouse, stables, cattle and poultry buildings, and a granary. The lord of the manor house might have several other manors elsewhere. He would appoint assistants called *seneschals* to run them.

The Peasants Remain Close to the Soil

Near the manor house and the cottages were the pasturelands for cattle and the fields where the peasants grew wheat, oats, rye, or barley. To add to the fertility of the soil, a "three-field system" was started in some areas. Under this system, the land was divided into three fields. Crops were rotated so that each field would remain fallow once every three years. *Fallow* meant that the field would be plowed but it would not be seeded, so that its soil could become richer by "resting." It would not have its minerals depleted by crops that year.

Within the fields each peasant had a number of strips of land, each of which was approximately an acre in size. The strips were scattered throughout the fields and separated by the strips of other peasants. This was done so that no person would have all of the best soil or all of the poorest for himself. The pieces of land were rarely next to each other. Each peasant was entitled only to what was raised on his strips. Since there was nothing except a line of unplowed earth between a strip of one man and that of another, this organization of farmland was called the "open-field system."

The peasants co-operated with each other in plowing, sowing, and harvesting. Few of them had the tools that would permit them to work individually; so men, women, and children worked together in the fields. Much of the plowing was done by using a crude plow pulled by men, women, or oxen. Around 1000 A.D., the horse collar was introduced into Europe, and horses also could be used for pulling.

The lord of the manor kept for himself about one-fifth to one-third or even more of the best land. This land was called the lord's *demesne*. It was scattered in strips among the land of the peasants or remained a separate field. The peasants would work the lord's demesne and their land.

There was also a common pasture, meadows, and woodland. The peasant could turn his cattle into the pasture and have a share of the meadow, the chief source of hay. His pigs could search for food in the woodland, and he could gather wood there to build his cottage and make his fires.

■ *This is a late medieval illustration of a reaper's cart climbing a hill. Medieval farming involved much drudgery and hard work.*

■ *Bodiam Castle in Sussex, England, was built in the medieval period. A moat surrounded the castle wall. Towers and platforms on the wall helped defenders who dropped hot oil and rocks on the enemy below.*

The Position of the Serf

Feudalism varied in different parts of Europe. However, in general there were several types of peasants living on the manors: slaves, serfs, and freemen. Slaves were people who could be bought or sold as their lords wished. Freemen sometimes were free to sell the land that they worked and move away from the manor. Most of the people on manors were *serfs*.

Serfdom, the condition of being a serf, was hereditary; a child of serfs became one himself at birth. The rights of serfs were not always the same. Usually, the lord could not sell the land that the serf worked without permitting him to continue to farm it. The serf did not own the land, but it could not be taken away from him if he did his job. Thus, usually he could not be deprived of his livelihood.

There were many restrictions and duties placed on the serf: (1) He could not leave one manor and move to another one or to a town. (2) He could not marry without the consent of his lord. Sometimes, the lord would even choose a husband or wife for a serf. (3) He had to pay taxes to the lord—in money or in animals and grain. (4) He had to work for the lord two or more days each week. (5) He had to grind his grain in the lord's mill and bake his bread in the lord's oven. For these and other privileges, he had to pay special fees.

Lord and Castle Defend the Land

The life of the serf was hard, but at least he knew that his lord would protect the land from attack. Since there were usually several manors on a fief, the lord might make his headquarters in a castle near one of them and protect his territory.

In the beginning, the castles were made of wood, but in the thirteenth century many of them were constructed of stone. The key building in the castle was the main *donjon*, a stone tower that often was a home and a fort for the lord. Around the donjon was a courtyard, and around the courtyard ran a thick wall. Outside the wall was a *moat*, a ditch that usually was filled with water. The entrance to the castle was by a *drawbridge* over the moat.

Inside the castle, there were few comforts. "Floors" of stone were covered with rushes or straw, and walls were bare except where huge tapestries were hung to keep out dampness. There were few pieces of furniture, and cooking was done over a spit in a fireplace. Food was cut with a dagger and eaten with the fingers. The windows were merely slits in the wall; and candles did not cast much light in the evening.

Life in a medieval castle was not very romantic. But there was considerable color in the system of chivalry that developed among the feudal nobility.

■ *Medieval knights engaged in jousting tournaments which provided fighting practice. The ladies of the castle watched these contests.*

Knights Train for Chivalry

Chivalry refers to the manners, customs, and ceremonies of knighthood. To be a *knight* required special training. At the age of seven, the son of a nobleman would be sent to the court of another to serve as his *page*, or special servant. He also received religious education and training in courtesy.

At fifteen he became a *squire* and was taught skills of riding, hunting, and fighting with lance and sword. He also might learn to sing or play an instrument. At twenty-one, he was ready for knighthood.

Before he was knighted, the young man "washed away" his sins by taking a ceremonial bath. Then he spent a night in front of the altar of the church. He watched his weapons and prayed to be a worthy knight. In the morning, he attended Mass. Later that day, his sword was blessed upon the altar, and he went to his lord and knelt before him. The high point of the ceremony began. The lord struck the young man on the back of the neck or shoulders with his fist or the flat of a sword. This action was known as *dubbing* a man a knight.

The new knight tried to show his strength by leaping into the saddle in one jump—without touching his foot to the stirrup! When he succeeded, he demonstrated his fighting skill by smashing the shield of a wooden dummy with his lance.

The duties of a knight were demanding. He was to fear God and defend the Church. He was to be brave and daring in battle. In all of his dealings he was to speak the truth and be honorable. He was to respect women, protect widows and orphans, and defend the weak. Not every knight followed chivalry's high code of conduct.

■ **Check on Your Reading**
1. Describe the economy of a manor.
2. What did serfdom mean?
3. How were castles planned for defense?
4. Describe the ideals of chivalry.

174

7. Feudal Lords and Church Clash

The power and prestige of the knights and other feudal lords did not go unchallenged. The Church soon clashed with feudal kings and lords over their respective rights and duties.

Actually, the Church itself had acquired considerable land, and churchmen were often a part of feudalism. A feudal fief was usually a section of land that a lord permitted his vassal to control. However, a fief did not have to be land. A fief could also be a government position, such as tax collector, or a religious position, such as the office of a bishop. Although the Church might not approve, a lord could appoint a man to a fief that gave him a Church office. In such a case, *the new Church official became a vassal of the lord and was expected to carry out his orders.*

One of his duties as vassal was to serve in the lord's army, although a churchman was not supposed to be a warrior. Instead of personally fighting for the lord, some churchmen furnished men to take their places. Others offered up prayers for their lord's soul as a substitute for military aid. Some churchmen became so concerned with military affairs that they neglected their spiritual work.

Another duty of a churchman who was a vassal was to be loyal to his lord in political matters. On the other hand, the churchman also owed allegiance to the Pope. Sometimes the political wishes of the feudal lord would conflict with those of the Pope. The clergyman then would be torn between two loyalties.

The Church gradually began to control more and more land by receiving gifts from religious people and from other sources. Soon it was the greatest landholder in Europe and a serious threat to the power of the lords. The lords, therefore, did everything that they could to have men who were favorable to them appointed to high Church offices. As a result, by the tenth century several conditions had developed that the Church felt were evil: (1) *lay investiture*, where a king or an important lord would *invest*, or appoint, one of his favorites to Church office by giving him certain symbols of power; (2) *simony*, where Church positions would be sold to the man who bid the most money—or who bribed the lord with the finest gifts; (3) marriage of the clergy; and (4) interference by rulers in the election of a new Pope.

For example, under the practice of lay investiture, a king would give a ring and a staff to a man whom he wanted to make a bishop. The ring represented the future bishop's "marriage" to the Church, and the staff showed that he was to be "a shepherd of his flock." The Church held that only a Church official should invest a man with Church office.

Some members of the Church tried to do away with these abuses. In the tenth century, a monastery was established in Cluny, France, where monks could seek "heavenly conversations" and perform "works of mercy." The Cluniac monks were determined to prevent the Church from becoming corrupted by civil rulers.

The monks of Cluny opposed lay investiture, simony, and marriage of clergymen. They were also against interference by rulers in the election of a new Pope, and they demanded a real cleansing of religious life. In the eleventh century, the Pope adopted the Cluny reform program and started a campaign to spread its principles.

Holy Roman Emperors Interfere in Church Affairs

Most of the opposition to the Church's campaign against lay investiture and other abuses first came from Germany. After

North Sea

Baltic Sea

POLAND

Elbe R.

Rhine R.

Oder R.

Aix-la-Chapelle

Worms

Paris

Strasbourg

Danube R.

FRANCE

Cluny

BURGUNDY

Rhône R.

HUNGARY

Venice

Canossa

Ravenna

Rome

PAPAL STATES

Naples

HOLY ROMAN
EMPIRE
IN 962

■ *Otto I became the first Holy Roman Emperor in 962 A.D. His territory included lands in Germany and Italy. What effects did this have later?*

Charlemagne's empire had broken into three sections, there was no ruler strong enough to reunite the territories. In the tenth century Otto I (Otto the Great), duke of Saxony, became king of East Frankland, the German section. Otto was determined to be a real king, and he brought the other German dukes under his control.

Then he and his men defeated the Magyars, pushed back the Slavs in the east, and conquered northern Italy. In 962 A.D. Otto was crowned emperor by the Pope. Historians later called his empire the Holy Roman Empire, but it was never highly centralized, and it never became as strong as the old Roman Empire. Otto's territory included much German and Italian land and ran from the North and Baltic Seas to southern Italy (map, p. 176).

The structure of the early Holy Roman Empire had a major effect on the future history of Italy and Germany. Otto and his successors had to spend so much time sending expeditions into unsettled Italy to keep order that they did not have the time or strength to unify their holdings in Germany. There were two important results: (1) Italy could not be united. (2) Germany also remained a divided country with a variety of sovereign ruling princes under the emperor for many centuries.

As Holy Roman Emperor, Otto also interfered in the elections of the Pope, for he felt that Pope John XII and his supporters could not be trusted. The successors of Otto in Germany did not hesitate to interfere in Church affairs. They appointed bishops and monastery heads and challenged the power of the Church.

Emperor Opposes Pope

The quarrel between the German kings and the Popes over the appointment of churchmen reached a dramatic peak in the eleventh century. In 1073, Gregory VII became Pope. Gregory had shown his ability by helping to put the election of the Pope in the hands of the *Cardinal Clergy*; that is, the bishops and priests in or near Rome who acted as advisers to the Pope. As head of the Church, Gregory became one of the greatest religious leaders.

Pope Gregory believed that he alone had the power to appoint and remove bishops. He went further and claimed the power to remove kings under certain conditions. Kings, he said, were descendants of men who were ignorant of God and who had gained their power by robbery and murder. He therefore would not permit any ruler to give orders to the Church.

Henry IV (1056–1106 A.D.), who was now Holy Roman Emperor, refused to accept the will of the Pope. Although Gregory had prohibited lay investiture, Henry appointed a number of bishops and abbots and invested them in office. Pope Gregory criticized him for not obeying the Church's order. Henry answered angrily that Gregory had brought to the Church "not honor but disgrace, not a blessing but a curse." Henry denounced Gregory and demanded that another become Pope!

Pope Gregory then *excommunicated* Henry (that is, he cut him off from membership in the Church and banned him from participating in the sacraments). He also announced that all of Henry's Christian subjects no longer owed allegiance to him. A number of feudal lords threatened to seize the king's power for themselves. They agreed that a new ruler would be elected for Germany unless the Pope removed the excommunication decree.

Frightened that he would lose his crown, Henry travelled to the Pope who was at Canossa, Italy, to ask his forgiveness. Gregory described what happened next:

[King Henry] stood in wretchedness, barefooted and clad in woolen, for three days before the gate of the castle, and implored with profuse weeping . . . until he had moved all who saw or heard it to . . . pity.

Gregory removed the excommunication and received Henry "into the lap of the mother Church." Gregory appeared to have won.

Henry and Gregory continued to argue after the Canossa incident. Henry led an army into Italy in 1081, took Rome in 1084, and forced the Pope to flee for safety. The struggle between Church and king over the appointment of men to Church office was not settled until after both had died.

A Compromise: the Concordat of Worms

The lay investiture issue finally was dealt with by the Concordat (or Formal Agreement) of Worms, Germany, in 1122. These were its major provisions: (1) In Germany, the Church could hold elections to choose

■ *This is a medieval painting of Pope Gregory VII. Although he was a small man, he "caressed by boxing the ears" of the Church's opponents.*

men for the positions of bishop and abbot. (2) The elections for Church offices would be held in the presence of the emperor or his representatives. This meant that the ruler still would be able to influence elections. (3) The emperor could not invest bishops and abbots with their religious or spiritual powers. This was to be done by the Pope alone. (4) The emperor could invest bishops and abbots with political powers. This would be done *before* they were consecrated by the Church.

The Concordat of Worms was a compromise. It helped to settle the dispute between Church and emperor; but it was not a permanent settlement.

■ Check on Your Reading

1. In what ways was the Church part of the feudal system?

2. On what points did the Church clash with kings and the Holy Roman Emperor?

3. Explain what the Holy Roman Empire was and how it began.

MAN AND HIS CULTURE

Let's Meet the People!

The following sketch of a day in the life of a monk in the seventh century is based on information in "St. Benedict's Monastic Rule," *Early Medieval Age*, Vol. IV, 1907, The University of Chicago.

A Benedictine Monk

It was midnight, and a solitary candle flickered in the room where the monk slept. In the same sleeping quarters were nineteen other monks. The monk rested on a separate bed, his body covered with a plain woolen blanket. He was fully clothed.

At 2 A.M. the monk arose to pray. In the chapel, he joined the other monks in reciting and singing prayers and psalms. The monk then returned to the sleeping room, where he rested. Next he arose at dawn for *matins*, early morning services. This was the first of seven services at which the monk prayed each day.

From 6 A.M. until 10 A.M. the monk labored in the monastery fields, interrupting his activities at the hours for prayer. When he worked under the sun, he wore simple work clothes. On most other occasions, he dressed in a *cowl*, a garment with a hood.

After his work in the fields, the monk read sacred writings from 10 A.M. until noon. At noon, he walked quietly to the communal dining room and ate his first meal of the day. The monk ate no more than two meals a day—and sometimes only one. He dined in silence, listening to the words of "the reader," a monk who read to the entire group about the lives of the first Christians. The monk's meal consisted of two cooked dishes and, occasionally, a vegetable or an apple.

After his noon-day meal, the monk spent the rest of the afternoon in reading, working, and praying. Whenever possible, he tried to "place a guard upon his mouth," and remain silent. With the coming of sunset, he drew his cowl over his head and went to evening prayers.

As the monk finally lay down upon his bed at night, he again expressed his love of God "with his whole heart, whole soul, and whole strength." Then the candle was lighted, and the monk slept.

CHAPTER REVIEW

REVIEW and DISCUSSION

1. Identify the people and places and explain the events and terms on p. 160.

2. Can you explain how a person may gain spiritual strength by punishing his body?

3. Why was the Benedictine Rule necessary to ensure harmony among the monks?

4. How did Charlemagne start a new age?

5. Feudalism was based upon a set of *political* conditions. Explain.

6. The manorial system was based upon *economic* conditions. Explain.

7. In medieval society every individual knew his station. Explain.

8. A peasant rarely met more than three hundred people in his life. How does the number of people a person knows affect him?

9. It has been said that the Holy Roman Empire was neither Holy, nor Roman, nor an Empire. Explain.

10. How do you explain the apparent *unity* of the Middle Ages?

ACTIVITIES

1. France and Britain are good examples of countries where several cultures interacted on each other. Write a report on one of them showing how this interaction among cultures occurred.

2. Draw a diagram of a feudal manor.

3. Draw a diagram showing the organization or class structure of medieval society.

4. There is a theory that only the Roman Empire in its political form ceased to exist, but its social, economic and religious life continued into the Middle Ages. Can you find any evidence to support this theory? Consult several references.

5. Draw a diagram of a castle and identify its parts.

PAST and PRESENT

1. Today many churches maintain retreats for purposes of meditation, discussion, and planning. What principle of medieval monks are they using?

2. Contrast or compare the contracts of indentured servants in colonial times with medieval contracts between peasants and lords.

3. What did the Middle Ages contribute to present-day society?

4. On what kind of economy was feudalism based? What kind of economy do we have today? What effects did each system have socially, economically and politically?

SUGGESTED READINGS

Basic books: LINTON, RALPH, *The Tree of Culture*, Knopf. The chapter on "Barbarians" is fine.

MULLER, HERBERT J., *Uses of the Past*, Chap. 8, New American Library.

SMITH, GOLDWIN, *The Heritage of Man*, Chaps. 15, 16, and 18, Scribner.

Special accounts: CHURCHILL, WINSTON, *A History of the English-Speaking Peoples: The Birth of Britain*, Dodd, Mead. Chapter on Roman provinces gives a good picture of what Rome contributed to her provinces. Not easy.

HAVIGHURST, ALFRED F., (ed.), *Problems in European Civilization: The Pirenne Thesis*, Heath. One of a series of pamphlets. For the better student.

MILLS, DOROTHY, *The Middle Ages*, Putnam. Excellent source of information.

PAINTER, SIDNEY, *A History of the Middle Ages*, Knopf. Has an excellent chapter on the contributions of the Middle Ages; *Medieval Society*, Cornell University Press. An essay on "The Development of Western Civilization."

Biography and Fiction: ROSS, JAMES BRUCE, and MCLAUGHLIN, MARY MARTIN, *The Portable Medieval Reader*, Viking. A voluminous collection of source material by medieval people.

THOMPSON, STITH, and GASSNER, JOHN, *Our Heritage of World Literature*, Holt. Part III contains letters, poetry, myths and sagas, songs and ballads.

Chapter 11

Islam, the Byzantine Empire, and the Crusades

KEYNOTE

A group of historians once set about to make a list of "the basic ideas of history." After they had puzzled over their problem for many months, they finally drew up their list. It had only two words on it!

These words were *change* and *continuity*. The historians meant that they could be sure of only two things in history. First, that conditions changed. Second, that some conditions developed from or continued from previous conditions.

One outstanding feature of history from the seventh to about the end of the thirteenth century was that it clearly demonstrated the presence of both change and continuity. There was change because a new religion (Islam), a productive empire (the Byzantine), and a series of military campaigns (the Crusades) altered many old ways. There was continuity because the heritage of Greek and Roman times continued to be preserved for the future.

Key People   *Mohammed · Charles Martel · Justinian · Pope Urban II · Saladin · Richard I · Pope Innocent III*

Key Places   *Mecca · Arabia · Medina · Tours · Constantinople · Byzantine Empire · Palestine · Jerusalem · Zara · Venice · Genoa*

Key Events   *Hegira · Islam spreads · Battle of Tours · Byzantine civilization develops · Council of Clermont · Crusades*

Key Terms   *Islam · Koran · Moors · Byzantine Empire · Justinian Code · Eastern Orthodox Church · Seljuk Turks · Ottoman Turks*

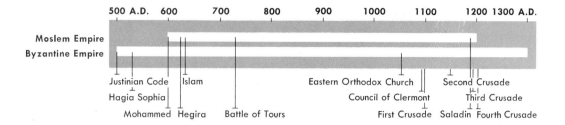

500 A.D.	600	700	800	900	1000	1100	1200	1300 A.D.

Moslem Empire

Byzantine Empire

Justinian Code   Islam   Eastern Orthodox Church   Second Crusade

Hagia Sophia   Council of Clermont   Third Crusade

Mohammed   Hegira   Battle of Tours   First Crusade   Saladin   Fourth Crusade

1. The Life of Mohammed

About 570 A.D., a child whom we know as Mohammed was born in Mecca, Arabia. His parents died before he reached the age of seven, and he was reared by an uncle.

As a boy, Mohammed mingled with Arab traders whose caravans stopped at Mecca on their way to Syria or India, and sometimes he watched them as they hurried to the square-shaped temple called the *Kaaba.* There the traders worshipped idols and looked with awe at a holy Black Stone which rested in a corner of the Kaaba. According to one legend, the archangel Gabriel had brought the Black Stone from heaven. It was said to have been originally white—and to have turned black as a result of the touches of sinful men! Some scholars today believe it to be a meteorite.

As a boy, Mohammed had almost no formal education. He probably could not write. As he grew up, he wanted to learn more about man's religious beliefs.

By his early twenties, Mohammed had grown into a sensitive young man of medium height and broad shoulders. His head was large, his black hair was long and curly, and a birthmark between his shoulders was considered to be a holy sign. At about the age of twenty-five, Mohammed married a wealthy widow and became an important merchant. When he was forty, an unusual event changed his whole life.

Mohammed Teaches a New Religion

According to his followers, one night Mohammed was meditating alone in a cave on Mount Hira when the archangel Gabriel appeared to him in a vision. "Recite!" called out Gabriel, and Mohammed recited five verses of a message sent to him by the archangel. As he continued to have other visions in the years that followed, Mohammed became convinced that he had been chosen by God to spread the words that were being told to him.

When the people of Mecca were urged by Mohammed to follow his teachings, many of them would not listen to him and some demanded that he be killed. In 622 A.D., Mohammed fled from his enemies in Mecca to the city of Yathrib (later renamed Medina) and preached his message to the people there. This flight is known as the *Hegira,* and the followers of Mohammed consider 622 A.D. to be the year One in their calendar.

In 630 A.D., Mohammed returned to Mecca. This time he and his followers were strong enough to win over the city to their cause. Mohammed threw the idols out of the Kaaba, but he blessed the Black Stone and it became an important part of the new faith. When he died at the age of sixty-two, Mohammed left behind him a powerful religion known as *Islam.*

■ *To the Moslems the Kaaba, in Mecca, is their most sacred shrine, and millions make pilgrimages to it. In a corner is the holy Black Stone.*

The Principles of Islam

Islam means "to submit" to the will of God, and the people who follow this religion are called *Moslems*. Today there are over four hundred forty-five million Moslems in the world. They believe in the following principles:

1. There is only one God, *Allah*. The idea of one God—monotheism—was already the basic principle of Judaism and Christianity.

2. Mohammed is God's greatest prophet. Mohammed is the spokesman for God, not a God himself.

3. The *Koran*, the holy book of the Moslems, contains the truths of God that were revealed to Mohammed. (Many names that are important to Judaism or Christianity appear in the *Koran*. For example, five chapters are entitled Noah, Jonah, Joseph, Abraham, and Mary. Reference also is made to Jesus and Moses.)

4. Prayers are to be said five times daily. The Moslem is to face toward Mecca when he prays.

5. Moslems are to act uprightly toward their fellow-men and are not to commit evil acts against them. Charity is to be given to the needy.

6. A fast, from sunrise to sunset every day, is to be kept during the ninth month, called *Ramadan*. Mohammed is said to have received his first message from Gabriel in that month.

7. Every Friday a Moslem is to go to his *mosque* (place of worship) for prayer and discussion of the *Koran*.

8. Each Moslem is to make a pilgrimage, or holy trip, to Mecca at least once in his lifetime. One of his duties when he reaches the holy city is to circle the Kaaba several times and touch the Black Stone.

The Moslems also believe that they will be judged after death. The *Koran* makes it clear that the good Moslem will attain paradise, but the wicked will suffer the torments of hell.

■ Check on Your Reading

1. Describe the life of Mohammed. How did he establish a new religion?

2. Identify: Kaaba, Mecca, Hegira, Islam, *Koran*, mosque, Allah.

3. What are the basic principles of Islam?

■ *This is a Moslem mosque in Tehran, Iran. Intricate mosaics cover the dome. From the two tall towers, or minarets, a crier (or muezzin), calls the faithful to prayer.*

2. The Religion of Islam Spreads

After the death of Mohammed in 632 A.D., the religion of Islam spread rapidly. Under the leadership of their *caliphs*, the men who were the political successors of Mohammed, the Moslems conquered the area of present-day Syria, Iraq, Palestine, and Egypt. By 650 A.D. they had won all of Persia, and they had pushed back the frontier of what was formerly the eastern half of the old Roman Empire to Asia Minor. Here the city of Constantinople repelled Moslem attacks for centuries.

The Moslems were successful in their campaigns because their military tactics were intelligent and because they were stirred by a desire for the spoils of war. Most important, they were not afraid to die for their religion. Mohammed had said:

I swear by God, in whose hand is my life, that . . . to fight for religion is better than the world and everything that is in it: and verily the standing of one of you in the line of battle is better than . . . prayers performed in your house for sixty years.

The Franks Check the Moslems in Western Europe

Inspired by their conquests, the Moslems moved eastward to India and westward across North Africa and into Spain (map, p. 184). The area forming modern France was next on the list. It looked as if nothing could stop the invaders.

In 732 A.D., the Moors, the Moslems of Spain, moved against the Franks. The *Moors* were descendants of Arabs who had intermarried with people of North Africa. The *Franks* were the Germanic people who had settled in Gaul (part of today's France) during the last centuries of the Roman Empire. They had been converted to Christianity at the end of the fifth century.

Charles Martel was the leader of the Franks. He led an army that included some heavily armed cavalry against a group of Moorish raiders between Tours and Poitiers. The fight was a bitter one, and the Franks finally won. This victory of the Franks at the so-called "Battle of

183

Tours" in 732 checked the Moslem advance into western Europe. However, Moslem influence continued to be strong in the territories that they had already conquered.

Moslems Bring a Love of Beauty and Learning

Wherever they went, the Moslems brought with them their love of art, beauty, and learning. From about the eighth to the eleventh century, their culture was superior in many ways to that of western Christendom.

Some of the finest centers of Moslem life were established in Spain. In Cordova, the streets were solidly paved, while at the same time in Paris people waded ankle-deep in mud after a rain. Cordovan public lamps lighted roads for as far as ten miles; yet seven hundred years later there was still not a single public lamp in London!

Some Spanish Moslems had homes with marble balconies and courts with lovely waterfalls. Bedrooms were vaulted with stained glass and speckled with gold. And metal pipes carried water into marble baths.

Nearly every mosque had a public school in which the children of the poor were taught. Many Moslem libraries were excellent; the catalogue of one caliph's library filled forty volumes. In addition, the followers of Mohammed achieved much in science, particularly in chemistry, astronomy, mathematics, and medicine (p. 285).

■ Check on Your Reading

1. Why were the Moslems so successful in spreading their religion? Where?

2. How and where were the Moslems stopped in western Europe?

3. What cultural advances were made?

■ *The Moslem and Byzantine Empires, the centers of two productive civilizations, were rivals at about 750 A.D. What territories did the Moslems conquer under their caliphs? What factors helped the Byzantine Empire to repel attacks for a long period?*

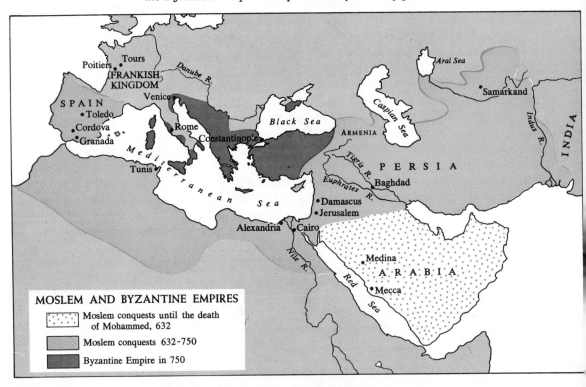

MOSLEM AND BYZANTINE EMPIRES

- Moslem conquests until the death of Mohammed, 632
- Moslem conquests 632-750
- Byzantine Empire in 750

3. Byzantine Civilization

At about the same time that Spain was the center of a productive Moslem civilization, Constantinople near the Black Sea was the focal point for the development of the so-called *Byzantine* civilization.

The Byzantine world was marked by many achievements. The period from the middle of the ninth century to the early part of the eleventh century was especially impressive. In law, art and architecture, literature, and religion Byzantine civilization made important contributions.

Constantinople: Byzantine Capital

Constantinople was strategically located between the Black Sea and the Sea of Marmara. It was at a vital point on the trade route that extended between the Mediterranean and Black seas via the Dardanelles and Bosporus straits. More than one nation was to fight to control this key city, for Constantinople could open or lock a desirable passageway between Europe and Asia.

Constantinople was particularly important during the greater part of the European "Middle Ages" because it served as the capital of the *Byzantine Empire*. The Roman Empire had once consisted of a western and an eastern half and Constantine had established Constantinople as the eastern capital in 330 A.D. When the western part disintegrated before the Germanic tribes in the fifth century A.D., the Eastern Roman Empire continued to exist and developed its own character. This Eastern Roman Empire has become known as the Byzantine Empire, and sometimes the terms are used interchangeably.

The Byzantine Empire expanded and contracted in size in different centuries. It reached its greatest geographical extent under Justinian when it included Spain, Egypt, and North Africa.

Constantinople: City of Contrasts

Constantinople was a city of contrasts, particularly in the eleventh century. Magnificent palaces where ambitious rulers praised their own glory were seen there. So were simple monasteries where monks asked forgiveness for their vanity. Busy markets where merchants of perfume, fish, and cheese hawked their wares and made their profits were everywhere. And there were "as many churches as there are days in the years," where the faithful prayed and made their peace.

In Constantinople, as the modern scholar Charles Diehl describes it, were:

Asiatics with . . . almond eyes under thick eyebrows, pointed beards, and long black hair falling over their shoulders; Bulgars with shaved heads and dirty clothes, wearing an iron chain round their waists by way of belt; fur-clad Russians with long fair moustaches; Armenian or Scandinavian adventurers, who had come to seek their fortunes in the great city . . .

There were aristocrats in silks and beggars in rags, wise men in search of knowledge and fools happy in their ignorance. Sailors, traders, money-changers, craftsmen, thieves were all there. This was a city vibrant with the lives of many different people.

Law

Justinian, a Byzantine emperor, had directed that the various Roman laws should be gathered together into one complete code, or systematic listing. This was called the *Justinian Code* (6th century A.D.).

Later, twelfth-century scholars in western Europe were able to revive man's knowledge of the principles of Roman law by examining the Justinian Code. The Byzantine civilization helped to transmit Roman law.

Art, Architecture, and Literature

In addition to preserving Roman law, Byzantine civilization made a great contribution in the field of art. Byzantine art usually was marked by the following features: (1) the powerful influence of religion; (2) the merging of Greek, Roman, and Eastern artistic styles; (3) the considerable use of *mosaics* (pictures or designs produced by cementing together small pieces of colored glass or other objects), and *frescoes* (wall paintings done on plaster or mortar that is not completely dry); and (4) the stress on luxury and splendor. The Church of Hagia Sophia in Constantinople is probably the most famous Byzantine structure.

Byzantine art and architecture are impressive, but they are also important for their influence on western Europe. For example, the Cathedral of St. Mark in Venice is a Byzantine-style building.

In literature the Byzantine civilization preserved for later generations many writings of the classical Greeks. Byzantine writers also produced histories, encyclopedias, religious poetry, and church literature.

■ *Byzantine mosaics, like this one of the nativity, decorate the interior of the Church of Hagia Sophia. Originally a Christian church, it was used as a mosque after 1453; today it is a museum.*

Religion

The rulers and religious leaders of the Eastern Empire had once disagreed with the Church of Rome over religious and civil issues. In the eleventh century a split occurred. In the future, there would be two major churches, the *Roman Catholic Church* in the West, and the *Eastern Orthodox Church* in the East.

These were the main features of the Eastern Orthodox faith: (1) The Christian principles, such as beliefs in monotheism and in the importance of the *Bible*, were followed. (2) The influence of the state was felt in some religious matters. However, contrary to a popular view, the Eastern Orthodox Church was not completely dominated by the state. (3) The leadership of the Pope at Rome was not accepted; instead, the members of the Eastern Orthodox faith followed their own religious leaders. (4) Great stress was placed on ritual in religion. (5) Religious services could be conducted in native languages rather than in Latin.

The Eastern Orthodox Church was important historically. It brought Christianity to Slavic and other groups that pressed against the Byzantine frontiers. Orthodox Christianity in Russia was one element separating that huge country from western Europe in its attitudes and traditions

■ *The Cathedral of St. Mark, in Venice, is a magnificent example of late Byzantine architecture. What Byzantine influences can you find?*

(p. 287). With religion went the many civilizing forces of the Byzantine world. As a result, *the Eastern Orthodox Church contributed to the development of civilization in Russia and the Balkan area.*

Today the Eastern Orthodox religion has several important branches and a membership of over one hundred forty million.

Trade

The Byzantine civilization also had an important influence on world trade. Commercial lines were strengthened between Constantinople and central Europe, Italy, southern Russia, Africa, and Asia.

Byzantine merchants exported embroidered silks, elaborate jewelry, and rich fabrics. They imported wheat, honey, spices, salt, fish, and other items. Although foreign traders actually transported most of the goods, the great Byzantine markets were the key centers for exchange.

Defense

The Byzantine Empire defended its civilization and Christianity by checking some of the Moslem invaders who threatened Europe. In addition, Byzantine rulers protected the great cultural heritage in Constantinople from destruction by hostile tribesmen from the north.

The Byzantine Empire was able to defend itself for over seven hundred years because it had a detailed system of government, a fine army and navy, and clever diplomats. Gradually, the empire was weakened by a combination of such factors as: (1) the struggles among leaders who wished to become emperor, (2) the ambitious efforts to expand the empire, (3) the heavy taxation, and (4) the decline of military strength. It was the Crusades that were directly responsible for the fall of Constantinople to the Ottoman Turks.

■ Check on Your Reading

1. Why was Constantinople's location advantageous? Describe life in the city.

2. What were the Byzantine contributions to law, art, and architecture?

3. How did the Eastern Orthodox Church differ from the Roman Catholic?

4. What factors weakened the empire?

4. The Crusades

The *Crusades* (1096–1291) were military campaigns and pilgrimages by European Christians to win back Palestine from the Moslems. Judaea in Palestine was considered to be the Holy Land, for it was the place where Jesus had lived and died.

In the eleventh century the Seljuk Turks, who were Moslems, captured much of Syria. In 1071 they won Jerusalem by defeating other Moslem groups. The Seljuk Turks soon began to insult and torture Christian pilgrims to Jerusalem. They threatened to take over more of the territory of the Byzantine Empire. Alexius Comnenus, the Eastern emperor, appealed to Pope Urban II at Rome for help.

Pope Urban answered his appeal. At the Council of Clermont in 1095, the Pope called upon Christians to embark on a great Crusade against the Moslem Turks to recapture the Holy Land for Christianity. He said that God willed the Crusade and would bless it:

When an armed attack is made upon the enemy, let this one cry be raised by all the soldiers of God: "It is the will of God! It is the will of God!" [*Deus vult.*]

Motives of the Crusaders

People fought in the Crusades for many different reasons. Many deeply religious people went on the Crusades because they felt that it was their duty to free the Holy Land from the Moslems. Some nobles joined the Crusades because they saw a chance to win new territory for themselves from the Moslems. Restless knights went for the love of adventure and warfare. Hardened criminals became crusaders to escape punishment at home, and scheming debtors joined the Crusades to escape their creditors.

Some men went because they felt that their country was too small to provide a living for all the people in it; they decided to seek their livelihood in the East. The Pope had endorsed this motive too. Others joined in the hope of cancelling out by their deeds the sins they had committed. The Pope had preached that those who were killed in a Crusade would be absolved from sin and assured of salvation. To medieval people, who were greatly concerned over life after death and dreaded the horrors of punishment in hell, this was a very vital reason for going on a Crusade. Some superstitious people fought in the Crusades because they heard that "the signs and omens" were favorable to the expeditions— a comet in the shape of a sword had been seen, and rumor had it that a child had been born who could talk at birth!

The crusaders came for many reasons and from many places. Kings, beggars, peasants, children—the devout, the evil, the ignorant, and curious. Sometimes it seemed as though they were bound together only by the sign of the cross they wore.

Crusaders Attempt to Win the Holy Land

Between 1096 and 1204 there were four major Crusades as well as a number of smaller ones (map, p. 189). The First Crusade started in 1096 and was led by French, Italian, and German lords. The crusaders won lands in Syria and Asia Minor and captured Jerusalem in 1099. Then they set up the Kingdom of Jerusalem.

Shortly afterward, two *orders* (or associations) of knights were established to protect Christians in the Holy Land. The Knights of the Order of St. John (the Hospitallers) and the Knights of the Order of Templars (the Templars) at first took vows of poverty, obedience, and service, and did much to help pilgrims. Later, the orders grew wealthy and selfish, and many of their members forgot their vows.

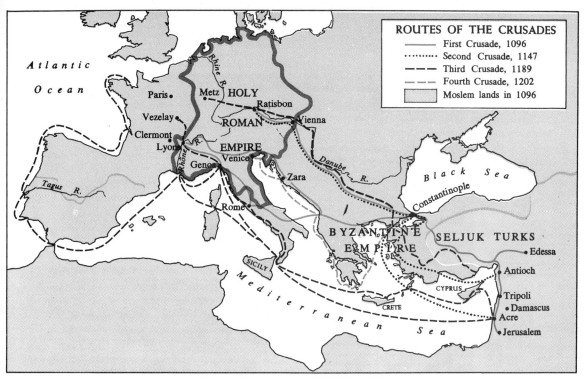

■ *The Crusades were military campaigns and pilgrimages by European Christians to win back the Holy Land from the Moslems. Between 1096 and 1204 four Crusades were organized. Who were their leaders? How successful were they? What were the results of the Crusades?*

The Kingdom of Jerusalem soon found itself again in danger from the Moslems. A Second Crusade therefore was organized in 1147, led by King Louis VII of France and King Conrad III of Germany. This Crusade ended in failure when the Christians failed to capture Damascus.

A Turkish leader, Saladin, then united most of the Moslems in Asia Minor and recaptured Jerusalem in 1187. Saladin was an extraordinary person. He was faithful, gentle, and kind to his people, and thought that money was no more important than dust. Once he told his son, "If I have become great, it is because I have won men's hearts by kindness and gentleness." Saladin was a devout Moslem who loved his religion deeply. He had no intention of letting the crusaders spread their religion or take the land he held.

A Third Crusade was started about 1189 to defeat Saladin and win back Jerusalem. Three important European rulers led this Crusade. They were Richard I (the Lionhearted) of England, Philip II of France and Frederick Barbarossa of Germany. The Third Crusade accomplished little. Frederick was drowned, and Philip went home after a quarrel with Richard. After much fighting, Richard and Saladin finally agreed on a three-year truce (1192). Unarmed pilgrims would be allowed to visit Jerusalem, and the Christians would control a strip of land along the coast.

The Fourth Crusade, started by Pope Innocent III, proved to be a black spot on the record of the crusaders. The crusaders fell in debt to the merchants of Venice, and to pay their bills they agreed to attack the *Christian* town of Zara (1202). The

CULTURAL CHARACTERISTICS of Islam

A magician who sought to destroy Christianity by magic and tricks! That is how some Latin writers of the early Middle Ages described Mohammed. Such misunderstandings and criticisms of the leader of the Moslems were also applied to Islamic culture. Indeed, as late as the nineteenth century, a popular American textbook author wrote: "No country has ever been happy or well governed where Mohammedanism prevailed."

Today such narrow and distorted views are being erased, and it is recognized that Islamic culture is one of the most important and creative in history. The basic features of Islamic culture were:

Dedicated belief of many people in the religion of Islam, a monotheistic faith that demanded a complete surrender to God.

Creativity in the fields of language and literature, art and architecture, philosophy and the sciences. Islamic cultural leaders were greatly stimulated by the rich heritage from the Greeks.

Eagerness to spread Islamic culture as widely as possible, causing conflict with other civilizations and stimulating the Crusades.

Islamic culture developed in a different setting from that of Western Christendom. As R. W. Southern points out: "For the greater part of the Middle Ages and over most of its area, the West formed a society primarily agrarian, feudal, and monastic, at a time when the strength of Islam lay in its great cities, wealthy courts, and long lines of communication." The rise of Islamic culture thus seems meteoric in comparison with the slower and more gradual growth of Western Christendom.

Today Islamic culture continues to have a major impact on the Middle East and other parts of the world, and there is a tremendous upsurge of interest in its heritage. Although serious political, economic, and social problems remain to mar the patterns of living of many people in the Middle East, the leaders of many Middle Eastern nations are convinced that the beauty and strength of Islam will prevail.

Fourth Crusade turned out to be a fight between Christian and Christian, rather than against Moslems.

The men of the Fourth Crusade did not stop with their attack on Zara. Following the advice of the Venetians, they also captured Constantinople itself (1204) and looted it. One of the crusaders, Baldwin of Flanders, became ruler of the conquered area, and this so-called "Latin Empire" lasted until 1261. Although Constantinople eventually freed itself, the Byzantine Empire never recovered its full strength. When the Ottoman Turks took Constantinople in 1453, the power and rule of the Byzantine Empire came to an end.

There were other Crusades in addition to the four described. In one Crusade, thousands of Christian children wanted the Mediterranean Sea to divide by a miracle, so that they could have a clear path to the Holy Land. This "Children's Crusade" (1212) ended as a tragic failure. Many were kidnapped and sold into slavery. In another Crusade, the Christians gained Jerusalem temporarily, not by war but by negotiation. Eventually, the Christians lost place after place until their last stronghold, Acre, fell in 1291. The great Crusades were over and the Christian armies were forced out of the Holy Land.

The Results of the Crusades

The Crusades had a considerable effect on European life in the twelfth and thirteenth centuries. We cannot say that they caused all of the changes that appeared in Europe during this period, but we can be sure that the Crusades influenced the people of Europe in many ways.

The Crusades introduced or made popular in Europe many new foods and goods: sugar, lemons, rice, melons, apricots, muslin and damask cloth, glass mirrors, and even diapers! Trade fairs all over Europe stimulated further demand for products.

New ideas as well as foods were brought back by the crusaders. Christians and Moslems were not always fighting with each other; they had many opportunities to exchange ideas. The crusaders learned the principle of the windmill and gained additional knowledge about medicine, mathematics, and astronomy.

Several Italian cities grew as a result of the Crusades. Such cities as Venice prospered by selling ships and supplies to the crusaders. Venice and Genoa became ports from which goods were shipped from the east to the west, replacing Constantinople as trade centers. This added to their wealth. Italian banking houses arose to help finance (and profit from) the crusaders. Sea power in the Mediterranean shifted from the east to the west. By the twelfth century, the Italian, French, and Spanish ports in the Mediterranean Sea were becoming more important trading centers than the Moslem ports.

The Crusades helped to break down feudalism. Many feudal lords sold their land rights in order to obtain money and supplies to go on a crusade. Other nobles who were crusaders neglected the government of their fiefs in Europe. Many peasants who left their manors to travel east did not return to their land. The presence of new products and new ideas drew others to the growing cities. Gradually, in some countries centralized control by a king took the place of local government by many feudal lords.

The Crusades introduced modern national taxation to Europe. Considerable money and supplies were needed to provide for the armies of the crusaders, which numbered from 10,000 to 25,000 men. Kings therefore began to tax their people to support the Crusades. Increased trade, which put more money in circulation, helped make such taxation possible. By 1300 national taxation was established firmly in both England and France.

As for the Church, the early Crusades probably added to the prestige and power of the Pope. The Church had taken the lead in calling for the movements against the Moslems, and it was respected for doing so. Later, some of the crusaders lost their religious spirit and became more interested in private gains. The Church often was blamed for the selfish acts of these individuals, and the Church leaders lost the respect and support of many people.

■ **Check on Your Reading**

1. Why were the Crusades begun?

2. What routes were used? What places taken?

3. Cite examples of how the Crusades were misused.

4. Evaluate the results of the Crusades.

MAN AND HIS CULTURE

Let's Meet the People!

This sketch of Michael Psellus, scholar, is based on information in *The Chronographia of Michael Psellus*, 1953, Yale University Press.

A Byzantine Scholar

Michael Psellus, a Byzantine scholar, was handsome, energetic, and intelligent. He concentrated his education on two objects: "To train my tongue by rhetoric, so as to become a fine speaker, and to refine my mind by . . . philosophy."

He also studied natural science, mathematics, music, and astronomy. In addition, Michael read books that described the ways in which the heavens affected the lives of men. However, he was a Christian and put more faith in God than in the position of the stars.

Michael loved good scholarship. He tried to be particularly careful in writing history, for he believed: "My history must be written in a methodical way: first the reference to my source, then the sifting of evidence, and finally the account of subsequent events."

Michael was fully aware of his ability. He declared:

Philosophy, when I first studied it, was [dying] as far as its professors were concerned, and I alone revived it . . . [Also] I have been told that my language is peculiarly graceful . . . Of course, I would not know this myself, had not many folk told me so in the course of conversation . . .

Soon the emperor heard of Michael's talents and ordered him to come for an interview. Michael described the results:

I told him about my family and the sort of education I had received in literature. [The emperor] was affected by a . . . feeling of pleasure, . . . to me his heart's doors were now thrown wide open, and gradually . . . he shared with me all his secrets.

Thus, Michael Psellus, Byzantine scholar, rose to a position of importance at the court. His love of scholarship had lifted him above many men—and brought him to the side of kings!

CHAPTER REVIEW

REVIEW and DISCUSSION

1. Identify the people and places and explain the events and terms on p. 180.

2. What similarities do you find among Moslem, Hebrew, and Christian faiths? What differences?

3. What are some characteristics that great religious leaders such as Moses, Buddha, Jesus, and Mohammed have in common?

4. Describe Moslem life in Spain.

5. How do you account for the rapidity of the Moslems' advance into North Africa and Europe?

6. In what ways was life in Constantinople unusual?

7. What caused the Eastern Roman Empire (Byzantine) to outlast the Western Roman Empire by about one thousand years?

8. What impressions did the Byzantine civilization make on Russia?

9. How did the Crusades help to end feudalism? with what results?

10. What unchristian acts did the crusaders commit on their way to and after their arrival in the Holy Land? How could the crusaders justify such acts?

11. How did the Crusades affect the struggle for power between Popes and kings?

12. Do you think from your study of the Crusades that it is a good thing on the whole for people to travel and see how other people live? Why?

ACTIVITIES

1. If you take a trip to Washington, D.C., visit the American Fazl Mosque and note the characteristics of its architecture.

2. If you have an opportunity, report on a visit to an Eastern Orthodox Church.

3. To your chart on the "Causes of the Rise and Fall of Civilizations" add the Byzantine civilization. What was essentially different about this civilization?

4. Write a short paper on "Our Debt to Byzantine Civilization."

5. Write a report on at least one Crusade.

6. Debate this statement: Resolved that we owe a larger debt to the Byzantine civilization than we do to the Roman civilization.

7. Write a report on the divisions within Islam. Consult Linton, *The Tree of Culture*, or an encyclopedia.

PAST and PRESENT

1. Panel discussion: The independence struggles among France's colonies in North Africa. Consider the part the Moslem religion has played in the conflicts. Panel members can represent Morocco, Algeria, Tunisia, and France.

2. Give an oral report on the Moslem features of present-day Spain.

3. In *Readers' Guide* find articles on the conflict over the possession of the Holy Land by the Jews of Israel and their Arab neighbors. What hope do you see for a settlement?

SUGGESTED READINGS

Basic books: SMITH, RUTH, (ed.), *The Tree of Life*, Viking. Legends and sacred religious writings.

VAN LOON, HENDRIK, *Story of Mankind*, Liveright.

Special accounts: FITCH, FLORENCE, *Allah, the God of Islam*, Lothrop, Lee & Shepard.

MILLS, DOROTHY, *The Middle Ages*, Putnam.

RUNCIMAN, STEVEN, *Byzantine Civilization*, Meridian Books. A detailed account of the eleven centuries of Byzantine history.

Biography and Fiction: LAMB, HAROLD, *The Crusades: Iron Men and Saints*, Doubleday.

LANG, ANDREW, (ed.), *Arabian Nights*, Longmans, Green.

ROSS, JAMES, and MCLAUGHLIN, MARY, *Portable Medieval Reader*. Viking. Contains some accounts by crusaders themselves.

SCOTT, SIR WALTER, *The Talisman*, Dodd, Mead.

THOMPSON, STITH, and GASSNER, JOHN, (eds.), *Our Heritage of World Literature*, Holt. Contains a short section on Moslem literature.

Chapter 12   *Medieval People Build Cathedrals, Towns, and Universities*

KEYNOTE   Jan Struther, a famous English writer, once declared:

> Buildings and bridges do not make a town.
> A city is greater than its bricks and mortar;
> It is greater than tower or palace, church or hall;
> A city's as great as the little people that live there. . . .

The author thus makes the point that the people—with their ideas, attitudes, and general spirit—are as important as their works. The spirit of the people can inspire and color the activities of an entire society.

In medieval times, the spirit that marked the lives of the people—both big and little—was religious. This feeling was expressed in many ways. Magnificent cathedrals were built. Town craftsmen helped their sick fellow-workers as a religious duty. Prominent university lecturers spoke on theology. And great poets stressed religious ideas.

It can be said that *a key feature of the medieval years was that buildings, town life, and scholarly activities often reflected the religious spirit of the people.* At the same time the interest in trade and business in the towns foreshadowed the coming of a new age when people would turn again to worldly matters.

Key People   *Roger Bacon · Peter Abélard · Avicenna · Thomas Aquinas · Dante · Chaucer*

Key Places   *Antwerp · Magdeburg · Paris · London · Genoa · Bruges · Hamburg · Lübeck · Oxford · Bologna*

Key Events   *Towns develop · Trade and fairs flourish · Guilds organized · Hanseatic League formed · Universities established · Bubonic plague*

Key Terms   *Romanesque · Gothic · flying buttresses · usury · bourgeoisie · craft guild · master · charter · Scholasticism · vernacular*

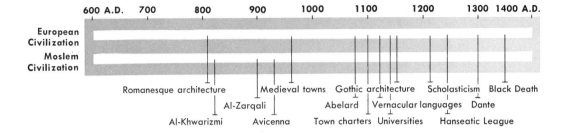

| 600 A.D. | 700 | 800 | 900 | 1000 | 1100 | 1200 | 1300 | 1400 A.D. |

European Civilization

Moslem Civilization

Romanesque architecture   Medieval towns   Gothic architecture   Scholasticism   Black Death

Al-Zarqali   Abelard   Vernacular languages   Dante

Al-Khwarizmi   Avicenna   Town charters   Universities   Hanseatic League

1. Religion Influences Medieval Architecture

Religion was such a powerful factor in medieval times that architecture was greatly affected by it. Many men and women wished to glorify the name of God, not just by prayer but by constructing houses of worship in his honor. They built many magnificent cathedrals; some took several hundred years to complete.

Lacking modern machines and power tools, no small "construction company" could handle the job of cathedral building. Instead, the task required the co-operation of the *group*—money from the rich, labor from the poor, guidance from the clergy, and moral support from all. Many members of the community willingly did their part. They felt that helping to build a cathedral was one concrete way in which they could express their feelings for God.

There were two principal styles of architecture in western Europe during the medieval period: *Romanesque* and *Gothic*. These were their principal features (see Chart, p. 197).

Some day in the future, perhaps you may be fortunate enough to walk along the Seine River in Paris, just after the sun has come up. Here you can view the Gothic Cathedral of Notre Dame and feel its strength and dignity. See how the great doorways resemble "hands joined in prayer," and how the rose window gleams in the early morning light.

Or perhaps you may voyage to Mont-Saint-Michel, the rocky islet off the coast of Normandy, France, and explore its famous medieval abbey. Here you will find such architectural sights as these: rows of columns that harmonize so well that they seem to merge into one; a room with sixty windows where sunlight forms color patterns on the floor; and a dining hall with chimneys so high and drafty that one legend says: "Toss a pancake up one chimney and the wind will carry it over into the other chimney!"

Medieval architecture was closely related to the growth of towns. Great cathedrals could be built only when men grouped themselves into centers large enough to support such projects. Of course, medieval towns were more than just builders of cathedrals. They were also the centers for many important political and economic activities.

■ Check on Your Reading

1. How did the medieval cathedrals reflect religious ideas and reveal group co-operation?

2. Compare the features of Gothic and Romanesque architecture. Give some examples of each.

■ *The Church of St. Trophime, Arles, built about 1150, is an example of Romanesque architecture. Note the rich ornamentation at the entrance and the sculptures of the apostles.*

■ *This is the interior of a Romanesque church, the Basilica of San Miniato, Florence. The columns and arches show the influence of Greco-Roman architecture, and the ornamentation has characteristics of Byzantine art.*

■ *Mont-Saint-Michel, a great medieval monastery, is located on a rocky island off the French coast. Romanesque and Gothic architectural features can be found in its buildings. Town, fortress, and monastery form a whole which seemed to Henry Adams a perfect symbol of the Middle Ages.*

A COMPARISON OF ROMANESQUE AND GOTHIC ARCHITECTURE

Romanesque	Gothic
It dominated Church architecture in the West from about 450 to 1150 A.D.	It dominated Church architecture in the West from about 1150 to 1500 A.D.
It developed in many countries in western Europe.	It developed primarily in France, and spread to England, Germany and Scandinavia.
Cathedrals had thick walls to support the ceilings.	Cathedrals had thinner walls.
	Flying buttresses, stone or wood structures built against a wall, helped to support the ceilings and walls.
Arches were usually rounded. Windows were small.	Arches were usually pointed. Windows were large and made of lovely colored glass (stained glass).
Impressive decorations were the paintings on the inner walls of the cathedrals and the sculpture at the top of columns.	Impressive decorations were the figures of men and animals carved into stone on the exteriors of the cathedrals.

■ *The Cathedral of Notre Dame, Paris, much of which was built in the thirteenth century, is a magnificent example of Gothic architecture. In its pointed arches, religious sculptures, and famous rose windows you see the elements which are outstanding characteristics of Gothic architecture.*

■ *This view of Notre Dame shows the flying buttresses which help to support the framework and thus make possible the extreme height of the vaulted interior in the Gothic cathedral.*

■ One of the best examples of the nave in French Gothic architecture is that of Amiens Cathedral. The high, ribbed vaulted ceiling and multiple piers emphasize the lightness, delicacy, and extreme height of the interior.

■ The statue of St. Theodore (left) in the south porch of Chartres Cathedral is a masterpiece of Gothic sculpture of the thirteenth century.

■ These statues of the German prince, Ekkehardt, and his wife, Uta, (right) stand in the apse of Naumburg Cathedral. They are one of the best examples of realistic medieval sculpture.

2. Medieval Towns Develop

The growth of towns was one of the most significant developments in the medieval period.

After the decline of the Roman Empire, many cities in the West lost both their prosperity and their importance. During the next several hundred years, Europeans lived in feudal communities. Gradually and without the shock that comes from sudden change, old towns revived and new towns grew up in western Europe.

When did these medieval towns appear? It is difficult to answer this question, for conditions varied from country to country. We know that Antwerp (in modern Belgium) and Bremen and Magdeburg (in modern Germany) had grown into towns as early as the tenth century. From the eleventh through the fourteenth century, other towns gained size and importance: Paris, London, and Winchester, whose histories dated back to Roman times; Genoa and Venice, whose prosperity stemmed from trade with the crusaders; Bruges, whose advantage lay in its geographic position as a natural port for trade from England and the north (map, p. 202).

There were many reasons for the growth of towns. By the late tenth century there was greater security in Europe, for the Vikings and Magyars were no longer a menace. More peaceful conditions made it possible for towns to form, and for people to leave the security of the manors to live in them. The population of Europe increased during the tenth and eleventh centuries. Some men who did not find work on overcrowded manors moved to towns.

Some towns developed from medieval castles. Since the castles were walled and protected their inhabitants, a number of people decided to live near them. Gradually towns appeared around some castles. The Crusades helped to free some men from their feudal bonds. After the wars, many men preferred to stay in the towns.

Other towns developed from the settlements that grew around monasteries and churches. These religious centers often took over the task of protecting the people, and eventually they became towns.

Trade revived in the eleventh century, and later was stimulated by contacts with the East. Demand for new products increased. Some towns were organized at key places along trade routes and were the market centers of Europe.

The population of towns in the thirteenth century varied from about four thousand to forty thousand. Many towns were surrounded by walls. Others were protected by the natural defenses of a river or ocean.

The houses of the towns were made of wood, and they were constructed in such a way that their upper stories hung over the street. The streets were narrow and twisting. Often they were filled with garbage that was thrown from the houses that lined each road.

Economic Conditions in Medieval Towns

The economic development of towns was closely linked with the activities of business men, traders at fairs, and guilds. Business men in medieval towns generally were not respected by members of the upper classes. Contrary to the situation today, it was thought unfair for men to try to make as much profit as they could. Business men therefore worked under these disadvantages: (1) Almost no important laws protected their interests. (2) No extensive system of banking existed, so that it was difficult for business men to obtain money or credit to carry on their operations. (3) The Church prohibited *usury*, or the practice of lending money at what religious leaders considered unfair rates of interest. This often made it hard for business men to obtain loans from Christians. Nevertheless, Italian banking houses developed and the Fugger family of Augsburg became the leading banking family in Europe. (4) The amount of money in circulation was limited, and the types of coinage used by people varied from town to town, hindering many business transactions. (5) The fees that business men paid to feudal lords for the right to transport merchandise by road or stream added to their expenses.

Despite these disadvantages, the activities of the business man and the merchant continued to expand. As a result, there gradually emerged a new class known as the *bourgeoisie* (meaning people of the *bourg* or town). The bourgeoisie consisted of business men, merchants, and rich townsmen. It also became known as the middle class because it was economically and socially between the poor workers and the upper clergy and landowning nobles.

The Fairs

Most men and women in the towns and surrounding countryside worked hard during the day. They did not have much time for recreation. When they did relax, the men turned to dice, wrestling, and soccer. The women preferred games such as "blind man's buff," dancing, and the gentle sport of gossip. Above all, the people looked forward to the fairs for their pleasures.

The fairs were originally connected with religious holidays. Later, they were held for several days at a time and became centers for wholesale trade, information, and entertainment. Important fairs were held in Troyes, France; Winchester, England; and other places in Europe.

The fairs served as major outlets for goods travelling over the important trade routes of the Middle Ages (map, p. 202). The fairs were always exciting. Here one

■ *These are the walls and gateways of the medieval town of Avila, Spain. The thick walls have parapets for defense against attack.*

could buy silks, satins, and spices from the East, woolen cloth from Flanders, linen from Egypt, cork from Spain, wax from Russia, and furs from Scandinavia. Here one could taste the bakers' delightful honey cakes or watch the colorful jugglers. Here one could feel that the world was larger than one's home—and that there were wonders and mysteries still waiting to be found.

Craft and Merchant Guilds

As medieval towns grew and trade at the fairs increased, craft and merchant guilds developed. *Craft guilds* were associations of men who worked at the same craft in a town, such as the shoemakers' guild and the tailors' guild. A craft guild was established (1) to control the price of the product produced by its members, (2) to regulate the quality of the product, (3) to prevent a craft from being joined by

■ *Important medieval trade routes were those from the East and return by way of (1) Baghdad, Damascus, and Alexandria, or to the lands about the Mediterranean; (2) Constantinople and Venice. A third route went from Bruges to Venice and Lübeck. Name the cities where fairs were held.*

more men than were needed, and (4) to help fellow craftsmen in distress.

In addition to regulating price, quality, and membership, each craft guild limited hours of work. Thus, the London Guild of Spur-makers forbade night work:

> . . . no man can work so neatly by night as by day. And many persons . . . , who [know] how to practice deception in their work, desire to work by night rather than by day; and then they introduce false iron. . . . And further —many of the said trade are wandering about all day without working at their trade; and then . . . they take to their work at night to the annoyance of the sick, and all their neighborhood. . . .

Craft guilds were not unions of employees to bargain with employers. They were associations directed by men who were their own employers. These men were called *masters*. If a boy wished to become a master in a certain guild, he first became an *apprentice* to a master for a number of years, lived in his master's house, and learned the skills of his craft. When his apprenticeship was completed, he became a *journeyman* (a worker for a daily wage). Now he was permitted to work for other masters, but for fixed wages set by the guild. Finally, when he was able to produce a "masterpiece," the guild might permit him to become a *master* and open his own shop.

Merchant guilds were associations of men of commerce who made their living by buying and selling goods. Merchant guilds tried to protect the interests of their members by (1) setting down rules of competition, (2) constructing warehouses to store the goods of the guilds, (3) protecting shipments of merchandise to foreign lands, (4) caring for the families of guild members, and (5) establishing definite methods for handling commercial matters. Some of the procedures used by businessmen today to make contracts can be traced back to these methods of the merchant guilds.

The merchant guilds became increasingly strong. Soon their members demanded greater political rights.

Towns Gain Governing Rights

Many medieval towns had been built on land belonging to a feudal lord or king. The people in the towns still owed allegiance to these feudal masters. However, when towns became important centers of trade and when the use of money increased, it became necessary to change this system. Many wealthy merchants felt that it would be to their advantage to run the towns themselves, without feudal restrictions. To do this, they organized themselves into groups and forced their lord or king to grant them charters.

A *charter* was a written contract whereby a town received certain rights. Some charters provided that the townspeople could pay sums of money to their feudal lord, rather than labor in his fields. In exchange for this payment, the lord agreed to permit the townspeople to govern themselves in some political and economic matters. Usually, such government was in the hands of the wealthier merchants. By the twelfth century, lords who needed money and kings who sought the support of the merchants were willing to grant these charters.

Of particular importance was the fact that the charters also gave greater freedom of movement to the merchants. In a typical charter there would be some provision similar to the following:

I [the king] concede to them . . . that wherever they shall go in their journeys as merchants . . . "by water and by strand, by wood and by land," they shall be free from toll and passage fees, and from all customs and exactions; nor are they to be troubled. . . .

Charters granting freedom of movement were to be important factors in breaking down feudalism.

The Hanseatic League

Many towns in Germany were strong enough to gain their economic independence with or without the approval of a king or lord. During the thirteenth and fourteenth centuries, these German towns formed an association known as the *Hanseatic League* (map, p. 202). This League, whose leaders were the northern towns of Hamburg and Lübeck, was organized primarily for economic reasons. It gradually took over political powers as well. These were some of the activities of the Hanseatic League: (1) It guarded and encouraged the shipping of its members on the Baltic and North seas. (2) It tried to set up a system of uniform currency. (3) It furthered the use of a system of uniform weights and measures. (4) It worked to establish a League monopoly in trading and fishing rights in the Baltic Sea. (5) It settled many disputes among its members by peaceful means.

■ **Check on Your Reading**

1. Why was the growth of towns important?
2. Under what disadvantages did medieval business men operate?
3. What was the importance of the fairs?
4. What was the importance of the craft and merchant guilds? of town charters?
5. Summarize the work of the Hanseatic League.

3. Universities Are Established in Western Europe

Towns were more than just the centers for economic and political activities. They also were the settings for the first universities in western Europe. About seventy-five universities were established in the Middle Ages. Among the most important were the universities of Bologna (Italy), Paris (France), and Oxford (England). These universities were begun as *guilds* or *corporations*. In Italy, corporations of students hired teachers. In France, England, and other countries of northern Europe, guilds of teachers formed and ran the universities on a self-governing basis.

A thirteenth-century university consisted simply of a few dingy buildings or rooms; several unreliable manuscript copies of the lecturers' remarks; students of

■ *Oxford University, England, was among the first of the western European universities. This view shows Oriel College, built in the Gothic style.*

varying degrees of enthusiasm; and, most important, the lecturers. The subjects studied varied somewhat with each university. In general, they included the same "seven liberal arts" that were taught in the lower schools. These were grammar, rhetoric (the art of expression), dialectic (the art of logical reasoning), arithmetic, geometry, music, and astronomy. To this foundation were added the three fields of professional study: law, medicine, and religious philosophy.

The fountainheads of knowledge were the lecturers. In a sense, the lecturers *were* the university. If the teachers' ideas were important and well presented, the students were stimulated. If the lectures were dull, audiences drifted away.

Students of many ages and backgrounds came to the universities. Since the Church dominated elementary education, most of these students had received their early training in Church schools. Conditions at a medieval university were far more rugged than at elementary school. Some university students fought too much and studied too little. As a result, university and town officials established regulations to keep students from getting into trouble:

... we prohibit ... the students from carrying weapons in the city, and the university from protecting those who disturb the peace and study. And those who call themselves students but do not frequent the schools, or acknowledge any master, are in no way to enjoy the liberties of the students.

Medieval universities passed on to modern men many important ideas. From them we received our titles for college degrees (such as bachelor of arts), the practice of wearing academic gowns on graduation, and—above all—the love of scholars for advanced study.

Most European Scholars Neglect Scientific Experimentation

European universities were more concerned with religious philosophy than with science. Scientific questions were considered in the light of Church dogma rather than scientific experimentation. Some medieval people thought that crocodiles wept when they ate men. Others insisted that plagues were caused by the positions of the planets. Superstitions were widespread, and "good luck" charms were cherished as guardians against sickness and death.

A few men challenged the idea of accepting Church authorities without question. One was Peter Abélard (1079–1142), known as a founder of the University of Paris. He wrote a book called *Sic et Non* (*Yes and No*) in which he cited religious authorities to prove *both* sides of a number of religious questions. His book was banned by the Church, though he was still allowed to teach.

There were a few achievements in the field of health. They included the development of systems of hospitals and the recognition that some diseases spread as a result of one person infecting another. Officials of one medieval town kept ships from docking until all passengers suspected of infection stayed off-shore for forty—or *quarantina*—days (quarantine).

Modern man also owes much to Roger Bacon, a Franciscan monk who lived in England in the thirteenth century. Bacon stressed the importance of using experimental methods in determining facts. He pointed out:

Even if a man that has never seen fire proves by good reasoning that fire burns . . . nevertheless the mind of one hearing his arguments would never be convinced. . . . But after the [listener touches fire] the mind is satisfied. . . . Hence argument is not enough, but experience is.

Unfortunately, few Europeans used the experimental method in the thirteenth century. Bacon himself sometimes ignored it. In general, experimental science continued to be neglected.

Moslem Centers Lead in Science

Most scientific knowledge during these years came from Moslem centers in Spain, Sicily, and lands to the east. Indeed, Moslem towns established places for advanced study long before Christian universities were started. The achievements of some scientists were impressive. For example, Al-Khwarizmi made valuable contributions to mathematics. Al-Zarqali made important measurements of distance in the field of astronomy. Other Moslem scientists constructed an early form of the compass.

Particularly valuable was the work of a Persian named Avicenna (980–1037), a philosopher and scientist. The *Canon* of Avicenna served as the basic medical text in the Middle East and in Europe until the end of the sixteenth century.

Some learned men in Moslem areas made Arabic translations of the writings of Aristotle. Others developed skills in chemistry. Most important of all, a number of Moslems knew and used experimental methods in their research.

Thomas Aquinas: Master of Scholasticism

When these scholars stimulated interest in the writings of Aristotle, they presented Christian philosophers in Europe with a serious problem. Aristotle had supported the use of *reason and the senses* in the search for truth. Religion maintained that *faith* would lead men to truth. Were reason and faith opposed to each other?

Some Christian philosophers tried to demonstrate that reason and faith were in harmony with each other in the doctrines of the Church. The term *Scholasticism* refers to the philosophy these men developed. Scholasticism, which tried to bring together the views of the Church and those of Aristotle, reached its height in the thirteenth century with the writings of Thomas Aquinas.

Thomas Aquinas, who later was made a saint, stressed two important points: (1) Man can prove the existence of God by reason alone, but (2) faith is necessary to give man a deep understanding of the nature of God. Thus, reason and faith were not enemies; they worked together.

Although Aquinas had great faith in God, he was willing to try to prove God's existence by reason. He might argue:

Look about you! See the way in which the world is governed. Notice how things which lack intelligence—like the sun, the rain, the trees—act in a sensible manner for certain ends. The sun rises each morning and gives man light. The rain falls and man's crops grow. Trees develop in their season and man has fruit to eat. Everywhere there is order and harmony. This order cannot be accidental. Things which lack intelligence cannot act the way they do by chance. There *must* be God who has planned it all.

Or, as Thomas Aquinas put it: "It follows that there is *someone by whose providence the world is governed.* And this we call God."

■ **Check on Your Reading**

1. Describe a medieval university.
2. How did medieval scholars differ from modern scholars in their quest for truth?
3. Describe Moslem achievements.
4. What is Scholasticism?

4. Medieval Literature is Colorful and Varied

There were important developments in the field of literature, too. At the close of the tenth century, nearly all literature was still written in Latin. During the next three hundred years, *vernacular languages* gradually emerged. They were the languages actually spoken and understood by the people. French, German, English, Spanish, and Italian were the major vernacular languages that grew at this time.

Several types of literature—oral and written—gained popularity. Among them were chansons de geste, love songs, student songs, fabliaux, and religious writings.

Chansons de Geste

At first, the popular songs that were sung in vernacular were short. Then these songs were lengthened and became ballads. Finally, the ballads were sometimes linked together around central themes. When a series of ballads revolved around the same general subject, it was known in France as a *chanson de geste.* One of the earliest was the *Song of Roland.*

In England, a famous series was *King Arthur and the Knights of the Round Table;* and in Iceland, rich *sagas*, prose narratives, related the Norsemen's adventures.

Love Songs and Student Songs

Love songs were spread in France by *troubadours*, men who composed words and music to express romantic feelings. In Germany, they were known as *minnesingers.*

During the twelfth and thirteenth centuries, the songs of students and carefree wandering scholars were heard. They often stressed the importance of enjoying physical pleasures that had nothing to do with scholarship. One such song had these lines:

When I see wine into the clear glass slip
How I long to be matched with it.
My heart sings gay at the thought of it!

Fabliaux

Fabliaux were fables in which animals poked fun at the foolishness of people. Today the fox, Reynard, still holds the reputation of being the craftiest animal because of the medieval fabliaux.

Writings on Religious Themes

"Morality" plays, presented by the Church, reappeared. The greatest writers also wrote about religious themes. Judah ha-Levi (c. 1085–1140), a Jewish poet in Moslem Spain, expressed his love of God:

> Truly the secret of my quest is in the
>   hand of the Highest
> Who formeth the mountain heights and
>   createth the wind.

The Italian poet Dante (1265–1321) explored an imaginary hell, purgatory, and paradise in his masterpiece, *The Divine Comedy*. Dante wrote in Italian and asked that God "make my tongue so powerful that it may be able to leave one single spark of Thy glory for the folk to come."

The Black Plague Tests Men's Faith

Medieval achievements in literature, architecture, and religious philosophy were forgotten in the panic that swept over Europe in 1348–1349. These were years of the Black Death—the terrible bubonic plague that terrorized people and killed over one-third of western Europe's population.

In the midst of this terror, truly religious men and women remained calm. They accepted a basic teaching of medieval life: "Trust in God, and death itself can be conquered. Those who lead good lives are to be rewarded with a life after death, in heaven at the side of God, which is far better than life on earth."

■ Check on Your Reading

1. What is a *vernacular* language? Which vernacular languages developed at this time?
2. From which types of literature can you learn much about medieval life?
3. What are *fabliaux*?
4. Describe the Black Plague. What was its cause? What were its effects?

CULTURAL CHARACTERISTICS of Europe in the "Middle Ages"

The lone generalization that it is safe to make about the "Middle Ages" is that it is unsafe to make generalizations about the "Middle Ages."

For example, historian Henri Pirenne believed that the ancient world ended and the medieval period began after Arab invasions of the seventh and eighth centuries conquered the Mediterranean area and disrupted trade. Historian Alfons Dopsch disagreed with Pirenne and was equally convinced that Roman institutions and trade continued without a break.

For example, the "three-field system" was common in northern Europe. But in Bedfordshire, England, the land sometimes was arranged into *twelve* fields! Similarly, the belief that there was a single "medieval style" of oral expression must be discarded when one remembers that rough and rugged student songs *and* delicate love songs were both heard in the "Middle Ages."

It is possible to identify the major cultural characteristics of Europe in the medieval period. They were:

The powerful effect of religion on the lives of the people.

The construction of magnificent Church architecture, first in the Romanesque style and later in the so-called Gothic.

The growth of towns, which became centers of political, economic, and social activity.

Concern of some creative individuals for the development of intellectual life, as reflected in the establishment of universities and the work of Scholastic philosophers

The emergence of vernacular languages and the writing of several types of literature.

However, it is important to remember that the culture of Europe in the "Middle Ages" was not the same everywhere. Nor was culture completely static and fixed in medieval Europe.

MAN AND
HIS CULTURE

Let's Meet the People!

This sketch is based on an account in "Memorials of London," edited by H. T. Riley, in *The Portable Medieval Reader*, David McKay Company, 1955.

John Brid: A Guild Baker

On June 4, 1327, Sheriff Roger Chauntecler and a group of aldermen gathered at a London Guildhall to hear the charges against John Brid, baker. The accusations were serious. It was charged that John "did skillfully and artfully cause a certain hole to be made upon a [baking] table of his . . . after the manner of a mouse-trap in which mice are caught. . . ." It was said further that when his neighbors brought their dough to be baked into bread, Brid placed it on the table just above the hole. Then:

. . . John had one of his household, . . . sitting in secret beneath [the hole in the table] and carefully opening it, . . . and bit by bit craftily [withdrawing] some of the dough . . . falsely, wickedly, and maliciously; to the great loss of all his neighbours.

Neighbors now testified that they had been cheated—that the hole in the baking table had robbed them of part of their bread—that the baker was a thief. The men judging the case listened carefully to the evidence. They then handed down their verdict: GUILTY!

The Saturday after John Brid's case was settled, the mayor, aldermen, and sheriffs took steps to prevent any future stealing by a baker. They issued a decree that declared:

All those of the bakers . . . , beneath whose tables with holes dough had been found, should be put upon the pillory, with a certain quantity of such dough hung from their necks; . . . and they should so remain upon the pillory [all day]."

John Brid would not cheat in the future. If he did, his guild would take away his right to bake—and the sheriff would hang around his neck the cold white dough that branded him THIEF!

CHAPTER REVIEW

REVIEW and DISCUSSION

1. Identify the people and places and explain the events and terms on p. 194.

2. How does a Gothic cathedral express man's feelings toward God? How do the architectural features aid the worshipper during a service?

3. Compare the reasons for the growth of medieval towns with those responsible for the growth of towns today.

4. Why did the Church frown on the practice of usury? Why do beliefs and practices change from one period to the next?

5. In the Middle Ages business men succeeded under many disadvantages. Do we work best when we have to overcome obstacles or when we "have it easy"? Why?

6. Is it true that groups first gain economic rights and then political power? Give reasons for your answer.

7. The Crusades helped to break down feudalism. What other conditions and events also helped to end feudalism?

8. Discuss the activities of the Hanseatic League.

9. Why did Moslem areas produce greater scientists than medieval Christian states?

10. Religion stimulated man in the Middle Ages to achieve many things. Why was this true? What stirs man's achievements today?

ACTIVITIES

1. Identify the Gothic features of the churches in your community, such as gargoyles, rood screen, reredos, vaulted ceilings, apse, rose window, and transepts.

2. Draw a floor plan of a Gothic cathedral.

3. Write a report on one of the early banking families: the Fuggers of Germany or the de'Medicis of Italy.

4. Report on the practices which modern universities have inherited from medieval ones.

5. We tend to criticize medieval people for being "superstitious." Make a list of the superstitions of today. How do you explain them?

6. Read a modern version of the *Canterbury Tales, Beowulf,* or the *Song of Roland.* Give an oral report emphasizing what you learned about medieval life from your reading.

7. Make a list of the achievements of the Middle Ages and compare them with those of Ancient Greece and Rome. Which made more progress? Give reasons for your answer.

PAST and PRESENT

1. Compare our local, state, and world fairs with medieval fairs.

2. How did a medieval craft guild differ from a modern labor union? a merchant guild from the local Chamber of Commerce?

3. What groups today operate under the authority of a charter? What does a charter say?

4. How are modern universities similar to, or different from, medieval ones?

SUGGESTED READINGS

Basic books: CHENEY, SHELDON W., *New World History of Art,* Chap. 14, Viking.

LIFE, *Picture History of Western Man,* Part IV, Simon and Schuster.

SMITH, GOLDWIN, *The Heritage of Man,* Chap. 18, Scribner.

TREVELYAN, GEORGE M., *Illustrated English Social History,* Vol. I, Chaps. 1, 2, Longmans, Green. A great British historian makes the reading of social history a rewarding experience.

Special accounts: HARTMAN, GERTRUDE, *Medieval Days and Ways,* Macmillan. Easy reading. Gives details of daily routine of living in medieval times.

PAINTER, SIDNEY, *History of the Middle Ages,* Knopf; *Medieval Society,* Cornell University Press.

Biography and Fiction: ROSS, JAMES, and MCLAUGHLIN, MARY, (eds.), *The Portable Medieval Reader,* Viking. There are two short essays by Roger Bacon.

Chapter 13   India Is Brightened by "Golden Years"

KEYNOTE   In India, after the fall harvest, it is customary for Hindus to fill saucers with oil and to light these homemade lamps in honor of a great goddess. At night the tiny lights dance with youthful gaiety, and each village takes on a golden glow rarely seen during the rest of the year.

The history of India—like the Indian year—is marked by periods of similar brightness. These periods seem to shine with the achievements of great men in the areas of religion, literature, art, and architecture. Historians call them "Golden Ages."

Under the Gupta dynasty and later the Mogul dynasty, India enjoyed some of its most creative or "golden" years. These were years of great creativity in art, architecture, and literature. These periods provide additional proof of the richness of India's civilization.

Key People   *Chandragupta II · Kalidasa · Bhartrihari · Harsha · Nanak · Tamerlane · Akbar · Tulsi Das · Aurangzeb · Shah Jahan*

Key Places   *Ajanta · Central Asia · Nalanda · Punjab · Turkestan*

Key Events   *Gupta Empire flourishes · Buddhist University at Nalanda · Moslems conquer India · Mogul dynasty rules · Taj Mahal built*

Key Terms   *Sanskrit · Ajanta Caves · White Huns · Delhi Sultanate · Sikhs · calligraphy*

210

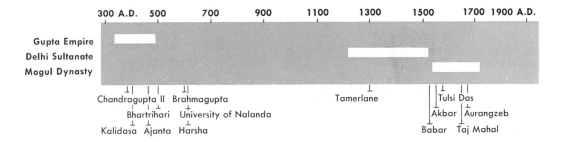

	300 A.D.	500	700	900	1100	1300	1500	1700	1900 A.D.

Gupta Empire
Delhi Sultanate
Mogul Dynasty

Chandragupta II Brahmagupta   Tamerlane   Tulsi Das
     Bhartrihari University of Nalanda   Akbar   Aurangzeb
  Kalidasa Ajanta Harsha   Babar   Taj Mahal

1. The Guptas Direct a Great Civilization

In the fourth century A.D., rulers known as the *Guptas* succeeded in uniting nearly all of northern India. While the Roman Empire was declining in the West, Indian life was brightened by a "Golden Age" under the Gupta Empire (about 320–480 A.D.) (map, p. 213). The most famous Gupta leader was Chandragupta II. Under his leadership, great contributions were made in literature, art, and science.

Literature

Most of the finest writing was done in Sanskrit. Kalidasa, who wrote in this language, was the greatest poet-dramatist of the time. Kalidasa loved nature deeply. His descriptions of the seasons of India are sensitive and charming. One can almost "feel" the heat in this selection from his poem *Summer:*

> Beneath the garland of the rays
>   That leave no corner cool,
> The water vanishes in haze
>   And leaves a muddy pool;
> The cobra does not hunt for food
>   Nor heed the frog at all
> Who finds beneath the serpent's hood
>   A sheltering parasol.

Kalidasa has been called "the Indian Shakespeare," and his famous play *Shakuntala* has been compared with Shakespeare's *As You Like It.* Critic A. V. Williams Jackson has said: "[Kalidasa's] work well merits a place in the best literature of the world."

About one hundred years later, the witty and imaginative poet Bhartrihari proved to be almost as pleasing to readers as was Kalidasa. Bhartrihari reflected with humor upon the strange ways of Fate. In the poem, *Dilemma,* he lamented his habit of being in the wrong place at the wrong time:

> I see a dog—no stone to [throw] at him;
>   Yonder a stone—no dog's in view:
> There is your dog, here stones to [throw]
>   at him—
>   The king's dog! What's a man to do?

There were other Indian writers between the fifth and seventh centuries, but Kalidasa and Bhartrihari were outstanding.

Art

The Gupta Empire excelled in religious art, as well as in literature. In sculpture,

211

National Museum of India

■ *This statue of Buddha (fifth century A.D.) from Mathura, India, was carved out of sandstone. Characteristics common to Gupta art can be seen in the calm, serene face of the Buddha and the graceful lines of the garment he wears.*

great artists carved colorful shapes representing Hindu gods or formed calm stone figures representing the Buddha.

In painting, the Ajanta Caves are treasure chests of Indian art (p. 253). These caves are rock-temples that were cut into a mountainside near modern Bombay between 100 A.D. and 700 A.D. On the walls and ceilings are magnificent frescoes. Here are pictures of wild flowers alive with rhythm, forest animals in graceful motion,

and legendary scenes from the life of the Buddha. The art of the Ajanta Caves tells us about the feelings of the people of this period. These caves are like painted books whose pictures are far more important than words.

Science

Impressive gains also were made in science in the period from 300 to 700 A.D. It has already been mentioned that the so-called "Arabic numerals" came from ancient India. Indian scholars began to devise problems in algebra.

In astronomy, Brahmagupta (7th century A.D.) came close to formulating correct ideas on gravitation long before Newton (17th century A.D.). Brahmagupta wrote:

All things fall to the earth by a law of nature, for it is the nature of the earth to attract. . . .

In medicine, free hospitals were established for the poor—three hundred years before the first hospitals were built in Europe! Although Europeans prided themselves on discovering the vaccination technique in the eighteenth century, inoculation may have been known in India as early as the sixth century.

Most important of all, the people of India were skilled in chemistry and in the application of chemical knowledge to their industrial needs. They excelled in tempering steel, dyeing cloth, making soap, and preparing glass.

■ **Check on Your Reading**

1. Name an outstanding writer of the Gupta Empire. Evaluate his work.

2. Describe the Ajanta Cave paintings. Why are they important?

3. In what areas of science and mathematics did Indian scholars make progress in this period?

212

2. Harsha Restores Orderly Government to North India

The Gupta achievements in government, industry, religion, and culture were carried to China, Burma, Indo-China, Malaya, and Java by colonists and traders. This period of growth and peace was not destined to last. White Huns, marauding nomads from central Asia, swept through the Gupta Empire, and by 480 A.D. they had crushed its rulers.

In the first half of the seventh century, an Indian leader named Harsha restored the brightness of Indian civilization in the north. Harsha, one of the great kings of Indian history, kept the peace for thirty years, permitted religious freedom, and established systems of justice and education.

Justice

Harsha kept order in the land by his honest administration of the government and by his impartiality in the dispensing of justice. Punishment for serious crimes was quickly given. Thus:

When the rules of . . . justice are [seriously] violated . . . they cut [the criminal's] nose or ears off, or his hands and feet, or expel him from the country. . . .

If an accused denied his guilt, a "trial by ordeal" took place. This worked in the following way:

When the ordeal is by water . . . the accused is placed in a sack connected with a stone vessel and thrown into deep water. They then judge of his innocence or guilt in this way—if the man sinks and the stone floats he is guilty; but if the man floats and the stone sinks then he is pronounced innocent.

■ *A scene from* Shakuntala, *by Kalidasa, is being performed by the modern Hindustani Theater, New Delhi. Acting is formal and stylized.*

■ *The Gupta Empire in India lasted from 320 to 480 A.D. Then invaders, the White Huns, crushed the Guptas. In the 7th century, another leader, Harsha, established a kingdom.*

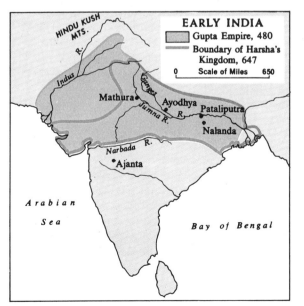

EARLY INDIA
Gupta Empire, 480
Boundary of Harsha's Kingdom, 647
0   Scale of Miles   650

HINDU KUSH MTS.
Indus R.
Ganges R.
Jumna R.
Mathura
Ayodhya
Pataliputra
Nalanda
Narbada R.
Ajanta
Arabian Sea
Bay of Bengal

■ *These are the ruins of the University of Nalanda. A student who distinguished himself in oral examination was "mounted on an elephant, covered with precious ornaments, and conducted by . . . admirers to the gate of the monastery." A failure was thrown into a ditch!*

Indian "trials by ordeal" were often similar to those of medieval Europe. In Europe, for example, there were such ordeals as having an accused person carry a red-hot iron in his hand and then examining his palm for infection, or having the accused "bound by a rope and cast into water." If he sank, he was considered innocent. If he floated, he was declared guilty; for as Bishop Hincmar of Rheims said:

The pure nature of the water recognizes as impure and therefore rejects as inconsistent with itself such human nature as has once been regenerated by the waters of baptism and is again infected by falsehood.

Although such "tests" seem harsh and unfair, they helped to keep order in a country. They frightened potential wrongdoers and prevented excessive crimes.

Education

Harsha also worked hard to stimulate education and learning. While Harsha ruled, higher education continued to grow in India. Particularly impressive were the activities of the great Buddhist University of Nalanda. Here scholars from many regions in the East studied grammar, logic, medicine, and religious philosophy. There were said to be one hundred lecture-rooms, several fine libraries, ten swimming pools, and observatories where "the upper rooms [seemed to] tower above the clouds." The course of study lasted twelve years!

■ **Check on Your Reading**

1. Why is Harsha considered a great ruler?
2. How does Harsha's system of justice compare with those you have already studied?
3. Describe Nalanda University.

214

3. The Moslems Take Control

The death of Harsha in 647 A.D. was followed by the disintegration of his empire. Southern India continued to contribute to literature, art, and engineering; but civilization in the north declined.

In time, the spark appeared that would grow to light a new era. Starting in the eighth century, Moslem Arabs from central Asia invaded northwest India. From the end of the tenth through the twelfth century, waves of Moslems continued to force back the Hindus who opposed them.

Finally, in 1206, a group of Moslems was powerful enough to establish an empire with a capital at Delhi. This so-called "Delhi Sultanate" lasted, at least in name, until the sixteenth century. Its activities laid the basis for divisions that later developed in India between Hindu and Moslem, divisions which culminated in the separation of India and Pakistan when the British granted independence in 1947.

Nanak Sees God "in All Directions"

Some men did not approve of the conflicts that arose between Hindus and Moslems over religious beliefs. Such a person was Nanak (c. 1469–1538), who was born in the Punjab. "There is no Hindu and no Moslem!" became Nanak's cry. To him, there was only man. Nanak traveled through north and west India, preaching:

I reject all sects, and know only one God, whom I recognize . . . in all directions.

Nanak opposed the caste system. He also protested against those Hindus and Moslems who performed rituals and followed religious customs without sincerely worshipping God. He declared:

Religion consisteth not in a patched coat . . . or in ashes smeared over the body;
Religion consisteth not in earrings worn, or a shaven head, or in the blowing of horns. . . .

To Nanak, religion was not formalities; it was "obeying the will of God."

Nanak became the founder of a religious group known as the *Sikhs*. Later, the Sikhs became more militant. Today there are over six million Sikhs in India.

The Mogul Dynasty Rises to Power

Delhi was sacked in the fourteenth century by Timur the Lame, known as Tamerlane, a conqueror who invaded India from central Asia. However, it was not until 1524 that Babar, a Moslem ruler from Turkestan, deposed the last leader of the "Delhi Sultanate." Babar, who could trace his ancestry back to Tamerlane, set up what is known as the *Mogul dynasty*. This dynasty lasted from 1526 to 1707, and its members helped to produce another "Golden Age" in India.

Akbar, Babar's grandson, governed from 1556 to 1605. He became a great

■ *The Mogul Empire was established by Babar in 1526. Under his grandson, Akbar, Indian civilization enjoyed another "Golden Age."*

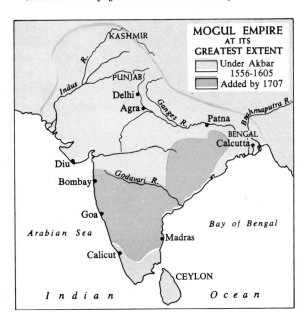

MOGUL EMPIRE
AT ITS
GREATEST EXTENT
☐ Under Akbar 1556-1605
▨ Added by 1707

KASHMIR
PUNJAB
Indus R.
Delhi
Agra
Ganges R.
Patna
Brahmaputra R.
BENGAL
Calcutta
Diu
Bombay
Godavari R.
Goa
Bay of Bengal
Arabian Sea
Madras
Calicut
CEYLON
Indian Ocean

■ *This painting of Akbar making a triumphal entry into Surat is an example of Mogul court painting. Some Chinese influence can be detected. It is taken from the daily record of the emperor's life—the Akbar-Namah.*

216

ruler of the Mogul dynasty, and one of the most famous men in the history of India. It was said that Akbar even had the mark of greatness on his face. According to his son:

On the left side of his nose [Akbar] had a fleshy mole . . . of the size of half a pea. Those skilled in the science of [appearance] considered the mole a sign of great prosperity and exceeding good fortune.

Akbar was a fine hunter, a daring rider, and a courageous leader. He was also a man of considerable originality. He even invented a lighted ball so that he could play polo in the dark!

Under the leadership of Akbar and the Mogul rulers, the government was organized into fifteen provinces. Taxes were levied more fairly. An effective system of justice was developed. Schools were established, and colleges became known as "the lights and ornaments of the empire." Indian civilization prospered.

■ **Check on Your Reading**

1. What long-range problem did the Moslem conquest of India create?
2. Explain the ideas of Nanak. What religious group believes in his teaching?
3. Summarize the accomplishments of Akbar as a ruler.

4. Akbar the Great: Religious Reformer

Akbar was an important religious reformer. His influence was felt in the areas of religious toleration, literature, and art.

Religious Toleration

Akbar urged people to respect every religion, for "if men walk in the way of God's will, interference with them would be [unfair]." He pointed out:

Miracles occur in the temples of every creed. . . .
              . . . .

Each person according to his condition gives the [same] Supreme Being a name. . . .

Later, Akbar became attached to various superstitions. It was said that he chose the color of his clothes according to the position of the planets, and that he whispered strange words at night to please the sun. Nevertheless, at a time when men were slaughtering each other for the glory of their gods, Akbar stood out for his attempt to show the oneness of God and the brotherhood of men.

Literature

A deeply religious feeling also appeared in the literature of the time. Aided by Akbar, Indian poets continued to search for the meaning of life. The outstanding writer was Tulsi Das (c. 1532–1624).

Tulsi Das's so-called *Ramayana of Tulsi Das*, written in the Hindi language, has been called "the Bible of the Hindi-speaking people of India." Mahatma Gandhi, Indian leader of the twentieth century, hailed it as "the greatest book" in all the literature of devotion. Such an opinion might have been held by the Mogul emperor himself. For Tulsi Das voiced the feelings of Akbar the Great when he wrote: "There is one God . . . creator of heaven and earth, and redeemer of mankind. . . ."

Art and Architecture

Art flourished under Akbar, who believed that artistic expression was linked with the love of God. Once he pointed out:

It appears to me [that] a painter has quite a peculiar means of recognizing God; a painter,

■ *This is the famous Taj Mahal, constructed by Shah Jahan in memory of his wife. A walk along reflecting pools and through formal gardens leads to the structure. Its fine marble, lovely minarets, and beautiful dome make it a splendid architectural achievement.*

in sketching anything that has life ... must come to feel that he cannot bestow personality upon his work, and is thus forced to think of God, the giver of life. ...

In architecture, Akbar and the Mogul rulers who followed him constructed buildings with these features: (1) the use of marble and red sandstone; (2) domes shaped like bulbs; (3) *minarets,* slender towers; (4) gateways; and (5) interlacing designs on windows.

Akbar's grandson, Shah Jahan, was responsible for building the Taj Mahal, a mausoleum (or great tomb). Constructed in memory of his wife, it is one of the most famous structures in the world. Thousands of visitors have marvelled at its fine marble, lovely minarets, and beautiful dome.

In addition to splendid architecture, there were excellent paintings of nature. *Calligraphy,* or ornamental writing, also developed as a rich decorative art.

Aurangzeb Rejects the Ideas of Akbar

Akbar had tried to cleanse religious groups of their hatred. Aurangzeb (1658–1707), another Mogul ruler, did not accept Akbar's ideas. A devout and orthodox Moslem, he refused to give equal privileges to Hindus or other religious groups. His soldiers destroyed Hindu temples, and his followers burned art treasures. Artists ceased to be stirred by the unity and brotherhood of men under Aurangzeb.

Although he conquered central and southern India, Aurangzeb could not crush the rebellions in his country. After his death, the Mogul Empire broke up.

■ Check on Your Reading

1. For what did Indian poets search?
2. What five features characterized Mogul architecture?
3. Contrast the philosophies of Akbar and Aurangzeb.

Jawaharlal Nehru, one of India's great statesmen, once pointed out:

We notice what we consider sudden changes in . . . an earthquake. Yet every geologist knows that the major changes in the earth's surface are gradual, and earthquakes are trivial in comparison with them. So, also, revolutions are merely the outward evidence of a long process of change. . . .

Nehru then urged us to keep our eyes on the growth of Indian civilization, and not on startling or dramatic events alone.

The history of India from about 300 A.D. to 1700 A.D. included the lives of rulers who overthrew their opponents by violence and revolution. At the same time men were making significant contributions to the less dramatic, but more important growth of civilization.

The tensions between Moslems and Hindus were unquestionably strong in India. Their religions and cultures conflicted on many points. Moslems had a belief in one God, while Hinduism was polytheistic. Idols were forbidden to the Moslems, but otherwise abounded in India. The eating of pork was forbidden to Moslems, while Hindus refrained from eating beef. Moslems recognized the equality of all men, but Hindus deliberately sought to erect barriers between the various castes.

Nevertheless, the impact of Islam on Indian culture was felt in several ways:

The introduction of the religion and social patterns of Islam into a country with a strong Hindu heritage. In time, Islamic culture was to become dominant in certain areas of India.

The development of administrative arrangements for the government of India.

The creation of beautiful works of architecture and literature in Islamic styles.

The stimulation of reform movements in Hindu beliefs and practices as a result of the challenges of the Moslems.

As men in India fought because of religious differences, Indian civilization continued to grow through the contributions of Hindus, Moslems, Sikhs, and peoples of other faiths. What is more, there were always individuals who recognized the basic unity of man and understood that the glories of every group were fleeting.

MAN AND HIS CULTURE

Let's Meet the People!

The following sketch is based primarily on information in the *Aín i Akbari*, a history written by Abul Fazl. Abul Fazl was an important historian and statesman during the reign of the great emperor Akbar.

An Indian Farmer of the Mogul Period

The Indian farmer lived in the northeast *subah* (or province) known as Bengal. His life was spent close to the blessed Ganges River, whose waters were said to flow from the hair on the head of Mahádeva Mountain.

The farmer and his wife were naked, except for a cloth about their loins. Their brown bodies felt the sun's rays during the summer and the heavy beat of the rain from October

to May. Their hands were calloused from labor.

The farmer felt a bond with this land and with the creatures that shared it with him: the wild elephants that trumpeted in the woods; the black, racket-tailed Drongo birds,

219

whose red eyes were always searching for a meal of lizards; the restless geese that flew in darting patterns above the trees; the shaggy goats that strayed leisurely down the paths. The farmer could understand why foreigners would become interested in this region and say: "Bengal has a hundred gates for entrance, but not one for departure!" For who, indeed, would want to leave this fascinating land?

The Indian farmer worked carefully in his rice fields. When the marshes were fairly dry, he sowed the seeds. When the rains fell, he watched the plants gradually rise by the miracle of life. He boasted that some of his long-stemmed rice could be grown in water as deep as eighteen feet.

The water rose; the rice stalks grew. The farmer sowed and reaped "three times a year on the same piece of land with little injury to the crop." The harvests were usually good, and the farmer paid his rents to the government promptly in *mohurs* and *rupees* (coins).

The farmer's home was made of bamboo, and he rarely moved away from it. He hoped that some day he might have a *Sukhásan*, "a crescent-shaped litter covered with scarlet

cloth," to transport him. Until that time, he traveled on his small river boat—or he walked.

Once, on the first day of the new moon, the farmer and his family journeyed to the seashore. It was a tragic trip. At three P.M. the following afternoon:

". . . a terrible [flood] occurred . . . which swept over the whole district. The Rajah [local ruler] held an entertainment at the time. He at once embarked on board a boat while his son . . . with some others climbed to the top of a temple. . . . For four hours and a half the sea raged amid thunder and a hurricane of wind. Houses and boats were engulfed but no damage occurred to the temple. . . . Nearly two hundred thousand living creatures perished in this flood."

There no longer seemed to be truth to the saying: "Bengal has a hundred gates for entrance, but not one for departure!" One terrible exit gate had been thrown wide open, the exit of the sea. The sea had taken away the lives of thousands of helpless people—and the Indian farmer and his family were among them.

CHAPTER REVIEW

REVIEW and DISCUSSION

1. Identify the people and places and explain the events and terms on p. 210.

2. How do you explain the fact that India was far ahead of the West in many cultural fields?

3. Compare the "Golden Age" in India with that of Pericles in Greece and Augustus Caesar in Rome.

4. During periods of great cultural achievements in India, there were also powerful rulers. Is one necessarily a corollary to the other? Why or why not?

5. Even though an ordeal was harsh and unfair, it was effective in keeping order. Do you think it was therefore justified? Why?

6. Do you think the Buddhist University of Nalanda was superior to European universities of the period? Why?

7. Compare the achievements of the Gupta and Mogul periods in literature, art, and architecture.

8. Brotherhood of man is a belief common to several religions at different periods. Why has it not eliminated wars?

9. Do you think that this line of Rudyard Kipling's poetry is true—"Oh, East is East, and West is West, and never the twain shall meet"? Give reasons for your answer.

10. It is often said that we cannot judge the East by Western values and laws. Cite two principles of Indian culture which are not a part of our Western culture.

ACTIVITIES

1. Write a report on the punishments given for crimes in the Middle Ages in Europe and India at the same time.

2. Write a special report on the Sikhs in India. Note any similarities between the religious beliefs of the Sikhs and those of other religions.

3. Study at least four rulers, such as Akbar the Great, about whom we have read. Note their characters and achievements. Write your conclusions about the reasons for the greatness of rulers.

4. Collect pictures of the Taj Mahal and write a report explaining why it is one of the most beautiful structures in the world.

PAST and PRESENT

1. Compare the difficulties between the Moslems and the Hindus in the thirteenth century with those that exist today.

2. Study India's history through the eyes of Nehru in his *The Discovery of India*. You will gain some insight into the thinking of one of India's outstanding statesmen.

3. India has been described as a culture that sets up walls between people of different groups. Undertake a study of the recent attempts to break down the caste system there.

SUGGESTED READINGS

Basic books: LATOURETTE, KENNETH SCOTT, *A Short History of the Far East*, Macmillan.
LINTON, RALPH, *The Tree of Culture*, Chap. 35, Knopf.
MULLER, HERBERT J., *Uses of the Past*, Chap. 10, New American Library.

Special accounts: MORELAND, WILLIAM HARRISON, and CHATTERJEE, ATUL CHANDRA, *A Short History of India*, Longmans, Green. For better readers. Much attention given to the pre-British period. Emphasizes culture of India and presents Indian viewpoints.
NEHRU, JAWAHARLAL, *The Discovery of India*, John Day. For the better reader.
NOSS, JOHN B., *Man's Religions*, Chap. 8, Macmillan. A brief, but useful analysis of the life, work, and teachings of Nanak.
TAYLOR, ALICE, *India*, Holiday House. Short, interesting book that shows the roots of life in India.
WALLBANK, T. WALTER, *A Short History of India and Pakistan*, MD224, New American Library. An abridged edition of *India in the New Era*.

Biography and Fiction: GAER, JOSEPH, *The Fables of India*, Little, Brown. Taken from Indian literature.

Chapter 14

Chinese Civilization Reaches New Peaks

KEYNOTE   No area in the world has a monopoly on greatness. Greece had its "Age of Pericles." India had its famous Gupta period. China had brilliant years that equalled any in man's history.

Between the seventh and the end of the thirteenth century, China was the home of many unusual individuals: a poet whose greatness was compared to "the lofty peak . . . towering above the thousand mountains"; a splendid scholar who studied day and night, and who was believed to have invented a wooden pillow to keep himself from falling asleep; a remarkable painter whose works sold for twenty thousand ounces of silver!

These and other individuals helped to produce periods of outstanding achievement in China. *These periods are important because they form peaks in the history of civilization.*

Key People   *Li Po · Tu Fu · Po Chü-i · Wu Tao-tzu · Genghis Khan · Kublai Khan · Marco Polo*

Key Places   *Manchuria · Mongolia · Annam · Persia*

Key Events   *T'ang dynasty flourishes · Sung dynasty rules · Mongols conquer China · Ming dynasty gains control*

Key Terms   *civil service · block printing · porcelain · landscape painting · Confucianism*

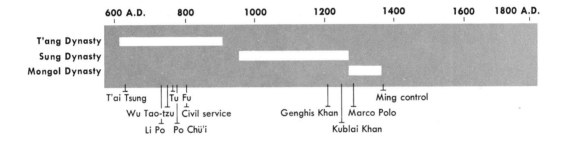

| 600 A.D. | 800 | 1000 | 1200 | 1400 | 1600 | 1800 A.D. |

T'ang Dynasty
Sung Dynasty
Mongol Dynasty

T'ai Tsung
Wu Tao-tzu
Li Po   Po Chü'i
Tu Fu
Civil service
Genghis Khan   Marco Polo
Kublai Khan
Ming control

1. The T'ang Lead a Brilliant Civilization

One of the brightest periods in Chinese history emerged from the political disorder that followed the decline of the Han dynasty in 220 A.D. For over three hundred years, China was split into rival groups. It was a period of almost constant warfare between the rival groups and against foreign invaders, who seized Chinese territory. Then, near the close of the sixth century, the country was united under the Sui dynasty. The Sui were succeeded by the T'ang dynasty (618–907 A.D.), under which Chinese civilization reached a new peak.

China under the T'ang dynasty was a land of about fifty-three million people. T'ang rulers wisely divided the huge country into fifteen provinces, built canals to link important towns, and restored order to the outlying districts. The administration of the government also improved, particularly during the reign of T'ai Tsung (627–650 A.D.). As a ruler, T'ai Tsung was an excellent leader. He defended his empire, treated all faiths fairly, and encouraged learning.

Under the effective guidance of T'ai Tsung and other T'ang rulers, China expanded in size until its southwestern border reached as far as India, and its northeast boundaries included southern Manchuria and part of Mongolia (map, p. 225). More important than this territorial growth was the fact that the T'ang (or Sui-T'ang) period produced great achievements in the fields of religion, literature, and art.

Religion

There was not always complete religious tolerance in China under the T'ang rulers. Indeed, between 842 and 845 A.D., there was a brutal campaign that checked the advances that Buddhism had made. On the other hand, several important T'ang monarchs fully respected all faiths, and

223

■ *This T'ang painting, "Two Horses and Groom," attributed to Han Kan, shows the emperor's central Asian groom with two of his famous horses—a black stallion and a grey.*

religion gained in the following ways: (1) Buddhism, which had entered China from India in the third century, expanded several of its religious principles. (2) Taoism gained new followers. (3) The Moslem faith added its influence to Chinese life. (4) Confucianism strengthened its hold on the Chinese people. To eliminate graft, civil service examinations were given to men who sought for government jobs. These examinations were based on ancient Confucian writings. As far as is known, this was the earliest use of the merit system in government.

Literature

The T'ang period can be called "the brightest age of Chinese poetry." In those years the Chinese honored their poets highly. Nearly fifty thousand poems were composed!

The finest poets were Li Po and Tu Fu, both of whom lived in the eighth century. Li Po was a particularly sensitive and lyrical writer. He wrote many poems about the beauty of nature. In these graceful lines, he expresses his envy of a friend who can live close to nature:

My friend is lodging high in the Eastern
    Range. . . .
A pine-tree wind dusts his sleeves and
    coat;
A pebbly stream cleans his heart and
    ears.
I envy you, who far from strife and talk
Are high-propped on a pillow of a blue
    cloud.

Po Chü-i was the most popular T'ang writer. Even a peasant could understand his words. In his famous poem, *The Red Cockatoo*, he protests against loss of freedom:

Sent as a present from Annam—
A red cockatoo.
Colored like the peach-tree blossom,
Speaking with the speech of men.
And they did to it what is always done
To the learned and eloquent.
They took a cage with stout bars
And shut it up inside.

The influence that literature has on society often depends on how widely it is printed and read. It was therefore extremely fortunate that block printing was invented in the general region of Korea and China about the end of the sixth century. A page of writing was cut out on a wood block, which was then inked. When paper was pressed on the block, the writing was stamped on the paper. One of the oldest printed notices was a small sign reading:

BEWARE OF THE DOG!

From such simple beginnings, Chinese printing developed to a point where Confucian classics were cut on wood blocks, printed, and distributed throughout the country. The Chinese now had access to the great wisdom of their ancestors.

Art

T'ang art has been praised as highly as T'ang literature. T'ang pottery and porcelain were exquisite, and some cups were so delicately formed that they could produce musical sounds. Above all, the Chinese excelled at painting.

The artists specialized in painting landscapes, religious scenes, and animals.

■ *The T'ang dynasty controlled China from 618 to 907 A.D., and then it declined. The Sung dynasty re-established order, ruling from about 960 to 1279 A.D.*

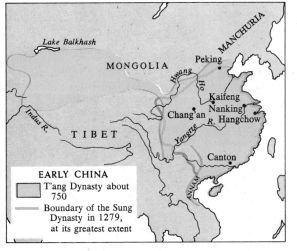

EARLY CHINA

◻ T'ang Dynasty about 750

— Boundary of the Sung Dynasty in 1279, at its greatest extent

■ *A magnificent example of T'ang sculpture is this black jade carved horse. T'ang sculpture also included religious figures, dragons, and courtiers.*

Wu Tao-tzu was the most famous painter of the period. Legend has it that Wu Tao-tzu once painted such a beautiful picture of paradise that he was able to walk into it and disappear! It is regrettable that none of his paintings remain today so that we might judge their beauty.

Although individual artists varied in their techniques, Chinese painting of the T'ang and several later periods often included the following features: (1) A painting was the artist's attempt to capture the inner spirit of the scene; it was not like a photograph of the subject nor was it completely abstract. (2) The artist did not fill every blank space with an object because space was considered to be as beautiful as lines or figures. (3) Paintings often gave the impression of being done from a mountain top. The observer had the feeling that he was "looking down" on the scene. (4) Landscapes, rather than human forms, were stressed.

■ **Check on Your Reading**

1. Describe T'ang administrative reforms.
2. How did religion gain under the T'ang?
3. Why can the T'ang period be called "the brightest age of Chinese poetry"?
4. What were the major characteristics of Chinese painting in the T'ang period?

225

意多澹染不
多皴溪景山
容自疊銀摩
詰雪江石嶂
壽展相對與
會精神
甲辰新已月
御題

Joint Administration of National Palace and Central Museums of Taichung, Taiwan

■ *This Sung landscape, "Snowy Mountains at Dusk," contains the best qualities of Sung painting—serenity, beauty, and love of nature.*

■ *In the painting, "Monkeys in a Loquat Tree" (upper right), the Sung painter portrays these lively monkeys in their natural habitat and behavior.*

■ *Emperor Hui Tsung (1082–1135) painted this scene (lower right) of ladies beating silk. It is a detail from a scroll on beating, winding, and ironing silk.*

2. The Sung Dynasty Gains Power

The T'ang period was an exciting time in China. Encouraged by the favorable reports of travellers to the East, ambitious traders from Persia and India journeyed to distant Chinese cities. Here Chinese merchants exchanged silks, spices, and porcelain for the ivory, incense, and mustard of the foreigners. When these goods were bought and sold at market, new and old ideas were also exchanged. Men learned from men and sought to learn more.

The Sung Dynasty

Despite these valuable trading contacts, the T'ang dynasty was unable to maintain stability in China. Poor administration of the government under certain leaders and dissatisfaction among the peasants finally brought about the collapse of the T'ang dynasty in 907 A.D.

Fifty years of confusion followed. Then order was established again under a new dynasty, the Sung (960–1279 A.D.). The Sung rulers controlled only a portion of China. Mongols in the north and invaders from Annam in the south were a constant threat to their reign.

The Sung Period Excels in Art

Under the Sung, Chinese life became extremely productive. New cities were built, rivers were controlled, and public and private schools were established. In the field of invention, the idea of the firecracker—which dated as far back as the sixth century A.D. in China—was used to develop simple war explosives. Most impressive of all was Sung art.

Painting was particularly distinguished. Sung artists produced some of the finest landscapes in the history of art. These were painted on silk scrolls with brush and ink or occasionally water-colors. In these landscapes, the artist expressed his deep

Joint Administration of National Palace and Central Museums of Taichung, Taiwan

Museum of Fine Arts, Boston

227

love of nature and his appreciation of the rhythms of life.

Many Sung painters were poetic and imaginative in their approach to art. They did not try to reproduce an object exactly as it was but sought the spirit of the scene. Lin Yu-t'ang, a modern philosopher, points out how the quality of imagination was treasured in Sung art:

... once the subject for a painting contest was a line: *Bamboos cover a wine-shop by the bridge.*

Many competitors tried to concentrate on the wine-shop as the center of the picture. There was one man, however, who painted only a bridge, a bamboo grove by its side, and hidden in that grove, only a shop-sign bearing the character "wine," but no wine-shop at all. This picture won because the wine-shop was hidden in the imagination.

In addition, Sung artists did excellent work with metal and jade. Porcelain making reached a peak; for example, delicate teapots and lovely flower vases were made.

Museum of Fine Arts, Boston

■ *An example of Sung pottery is this water bottle, decorated with various designs. Sung ceramic art excelled in pottery and porcelain, and it has influenced modern artists.*

■ **Check on Your Reading**

1. Why did the T'ang dynasty collapse?
2. What qualities distinguished Sung art?

3. The Mongols Conquer China

There were other cultural achievements during the Sung period. Writers produced interesting essays and histories. One of the first Chinese encyclopedias was compiled. And, while Sung poetry was not outstanding, there were still writers to remind the Chinese of the wonders of nature.

Yet soon there was no time for leisurely living. The Sung dynasty was threatened by invaders, and every man was needed for the fight. The danger came from the far north, where tribesmen known as *Mongols* lived in an area south of modern Siberia.

The Mongols were not the same people as the Moguls, who you will recall came from central Asia, but they were the same as the so-called "Huns" who swept over eastern Europe.

Led by Genghis Khan (1206–1227), Mongol forces swept through Mongolia and moved down toward the divided nomad states of northern China. Genghis Khan was a powerful military leader. His soldiers were ferocious fighters. It was reported that they could march for ten days without lighting a fire or taking a full meal. The sight of Mongol troops, dressed in

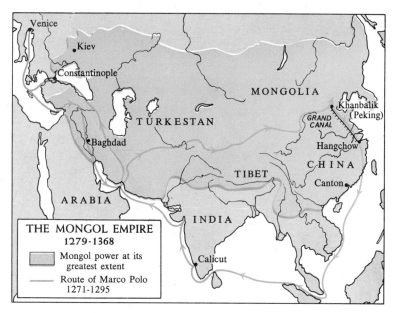

■ *The Mongol Empire, built by Genghis and Kublai Khan, controlled China from 1279 to 1368. What territories did it include? Trace Marco Polo's route.*

THE MONGOL EMPIRE
1279-1368

Mongol power at its greatest extent
Route of Marco Polo 1271-1295

tough buffalo hides and armed with bows and iron maces, was terrifying.

The Sung dynasty to the south did its best to defend itself against Genghis Khan and his successors. It was finally defeated in 1279 by Kublai Khan, grandson of Genghis. China now was ruled by the Mongol emperors (1279–1368).

The Pulse of China Quickens

The Mongol rulers fought their way to a great empire that included China, Turkestan, Persia, and lands in Russia and eastern Europe (map, p. 229). When peace was restored, trade increased between East and West, and commercial ties with India were strengthened.

Improved roads and waterways stimulated commerce, and a postal service kept centers of government informed of important news. Ideas as well as goods were exchanged. The Chinese learned from foreigners the valuable uses of cotton and sorghum; Europeans received the idea of gunpowder from the Chinese. Europeans also may have gained their knowledge of printing from the Chinese; and Chinese artistic techniques were interchanged with those of Persia. China touched the pulse of distant lands and found her own pulse quickening as a result of such contact.

Marco Polo Has Amazing Adventures

China under the great Mongol ruler Kublai Khan was a fascinating country. A young Venetian named Marco Polo, with his father and uncle, spent almost twenty years there. When they returned, dressed in tattered clothes, they told such amazing tales that they were not believed.

Later, when Marco Polo was imprisoned during a war, he related his tales to a fellow prisoner who wrote them down. These adventures make up the *Book of the Travels of Marco Polo,* a world-famous travel book about the marvels Marco Polo had seen.

What marvels they were! Marco described the forest of Kublai Khan where:

Frequently, when [the Khan] rides about this enclosed forest, he has one or more small leopards carried on horseback, behind his keepers; and when he pleases to give direction for their being released, they instantly [run and catch] a stag, goat, or fallow deer, which he gives to his hawks, and in this manner he amuses himself.

229

■ *In this scene from the Chinese opera, "The Fighting Bride," televised in Hong Kong, Princess Chao Mei-Yung is trying to persuade her son not to fight in his uncle's besieged city.*

Marco went on to describe the remarkable Grand Canal that linked distant cities together, and the Khan's private tree collection where "whenever his Majesty receives information of a handsome tree growing any place, he causes it to be dug up . . . and transported by means of elephants [to be replanted with his collection]." He described a city where "no fewer than a thousand carriages and pack-horses, loaded with raw silk, make their daily entry" and many other wonders.

Marco was so impressed by the things that he had seen that he hailed Kublai Khan as the greatest ruler in the world. There can be little doubt that Marco Polo was overly charmed by Kublai Khan. Certainly, many Chinese did not consider

China to be a paradise under the Khan's forceful rule. Nevertheless, the *Book of the Travels of Marco Polo* was a valuable record of life in Asia, and a magic carpet to transport a reader to the world of the East.

The Chinese Theater Grows

The Mongol dynasty that was visited by Marco Polo also indirectly stimulated the development of the drama and the novel. The writing of the novel probably dated back to eighth and ninth century story-tellers. Drama originated in ancient times in connection with religious dances and the rituals of ancestor worship. It was during the Mongol period that Chinese drama reached its first peak. Over five hundred plays were written at this time.

Chinese drama differed from our own in many ways. There was no scenery and few props were used. The singing, music, and, above all, the acting were the important features. The actor's gestures took the place of elaborate stage sets.

Chinese drama required great skill on the part of the actors. It called on them to express the deepest emotions by a tilt of the head, a twist of the shoulders, a movement of the hands. It believed that actions spoke louder than words.

Despite its accomplishments, the Mongol dynasty did not last very long. The Mongol rulers who followed Kublai Khan were weak, and they could not handle the difficult problems caused by floods and famines. In 1368, after a series of rebellions, the Mongol dynasty was overthrown. The Ming dynasty, whose leaders were of Chinese ancestry, took control.

■ Check on Your Reading

1. Describe the Mongol forces.
2. What ideas were exchanged with Europe and the Near East?
3. What impressed Marco Polo?
4. How did Chinese drama differ from ours?

Learn history, said the emperor T'ai Tsung, a T'ang ruler:

By using a mirror of brass you may see to adjust your cap; by using antiquity as a mirror you may learn to foresee the rise and fall of empires.

Write literature to express a love of nature, urged Su Tung p'o, a Sung author:

Isn't there a moon out every night? And aren't there bamboo and pine-trees everywhere?

Among the cultural wonders of the Mongols, observed Marco Polo, were giant golden goblets, each large enough to satisfy the thirst of eight men; paper money issued from a mint in Kanbalú at a time when other countries were still using metal currency. Other cultural attributes of this period were:

The spread of Buddhism, Taoism, and Islam to various parts of China; and the continued influence of Confucianism on the Chinese people.

Exquisite artistic creations, particularly in painting and ceramics.

The writing of sensitive poetry as well as the development of the drama and the novel.

Strengthening of commercial ties with India, and increased trade between East and West.

Today many men tend to focus on the military-political aspects of life in Communist China. The press, television, and radio give extensive and dramatic coverage to the latest strategic moves of the Communist Chinese. But international tensions have not diminished our fascination for Chinese culture.

MAN AND HIS CULTURE

Let's Meet the People! This sketch is based on information that appears in *The Travels of Marco Polo*, edited by Manuel Komroff, by permission of Liveright Publishers, N. Y. Copyright © R–1958 by Liveright Publishing Corp. Marco Polo visited China during the Mongol dynasty.

A Mongolian Postman

The Mongolian postman ran out of the *yamb*, or post-house, and leaped to his horse. The clothes he wore were designed to aid him in his fight against time. A white cloth was wrapped about his head to protect him from the sun, and a wide belt was strapped around his waist. Several shining bells were attached to the belt so that he could be seen and heard by the villagers. His jacket fitted tightly against his skin to permit his body to cut the air sharply.

In a pouch, the postman carried a message from the Great Khan and a falcon-shaped tablet that meant that this message was URGENT. The postman's destination was a post-house two hundred miles away.

As the postman urged his horse forward, a government clerk made a careful note of "the day and time at which the courier [departed]." The postman knew that his time of arrival also would be recorded. If he were slow, he might lose his excellent job and his right to be exempt from government taxes. Postal regulations were quite clear on this matter:

... officers are directed to pay monthly visits to every station, in order to examine into the management of them, and to punish those couriers [whose records of speed and efficiency show that they] have neglected to use proper diligence.

Faster and faster the postman rode, for he knew that time was slipping away. Over the hills he went, down narrow trails, across twisting brooks—always trying to keep his mount at top speed. Finally, when he had covered twenty-five miles, he arrived at a second post-house. Here:

[he] found another horse, fresh and in a state for work; [he] sprang upon it without taking any repose, and changing in the same manner at every stage, [he rode] until the day closed. . . .

Night came. Five miles from his goal it was so dark that the postman could not find the road. Suddenly, he saw a torch waving just ahead. Then he heard a voice calling to him: "Over here! Over here!" It was a runner from the post-house who had come to show the postman his way.

The runner held his torch high and ran as fast as he could in front of the horse. The rider followed him closely, the light from the torch brightening his way. At last they reached the post-house.

The Mongolian postman jumped off his horse, ran into postal headquarters, and delivered his dispatch. Then he rested quietly on the ground until strength began to return to his exhausted body.

That night the postman would have a good sleep. When dawn came, he would be ready to ride again!

CHAPTER REVIEW

REVIEW and DISCUSSION

1. Identify the people and places and explain the events and terms on p. 222.

2. "No area of the world has a monopoly on greatness." Why?

3. Is the mingling of Chinese Confucian, Taoist, and Buddhist thought a characteristic one finds among the different religions of a western country? Why?

4. How did Chinese art reflect the spirit of the people?

5. "No society has cultivated more graciously than China the art of civilized living." Explain this statement. Do you agree? Why?

6. Compare the two peaks in Chinese civilization under the T'ang and Sung dynasties. What were the main characteristics of these periods?

7. What methods of empire building were used?

8. It is said that China often absorbed the people who conquered her. How do you explain this statement?

9. What evidence is there of the interchange of ideas between the Chinese and other peoples in the world?

10. What do you think was China's opinion of herself in comparison with the rest of the world at that time? Why?

11. It is said that Confucius would have felt at home in China in any century down to the present one. Why might this be true?

12. Find out how the common people of China fared under the T'ang and Sung.

13. How important was the individual in Chinese civilization?

ACTIVITIES

1. Write a report on Genghis Khan or Kublai Khan. What do you conclude from your study?

2. Read about Marco Polo's travels in China to determine whether or not his accounts tended to exaggerate. Justify your position with specific examples in this chapter.

3. Report on a Chinese theater or dance program.

4. Arrange for a display of Chinese art in your classroom. Veterans of World War II and the Korean War, some of whom brought back Chinese art forms, may be able to help you obtain materials for your exhibition.

5. Draw a diagram showing the peaks of civilization up to this period in the countries you have studied.

6. To your chart on the "Causes of the Rise and Fall of Civilization," add the ones in this chapter.

PAST and PRESENT

1. "The problems of geography and population in modern China are not nearly so strange and new as some men think." Explain this statement.

2. At one time the Chinese had a system of checking on the efficiency and honesty of their civil servants. What systems exist today?

3. Find ten examples of Chinese influence in your community today.

SUGGESTED READINGS

Basic books: CHENEY, SHELDON W., *New World History of Art*, Viking.

LATOURETTE, KENNETH SCOTT, *A Short History of the Far East*, Macmillan.

SMITH, GOLDWIN, *The Heritage of Man*, Chap. 14, Scribner.

Special accounts: CREEL, HERRLEE, *Chinese Thought*, New American Library.

FITZGERALD, CHARLES PATRICK, *China: A Short Cultural History*, Praeger. A readable and valuable account.

LAMB, HAROLD, *Genghis Khan and the Mongol Horde*, Random House. A colorful account of the activities of Genghis Khan.

SPENCER, CORNELIA, *Made in China*, Knopf. The story of China's expression in pottery, silk, calligraphy, poetry, and other areas.

Biography and Fiction: KOMROFF, MANUEL, *Marco Polo*, Messner. Biographical.

ROSS, JAMES, and MCLAUGHLIN, MARY, (eds.), *The Portable Medieval Reader*, Viking. Contains an interesting section on the Far East.

Chapter 15 Japan Builds Its "Classical Age"

KEYNOTE For many years a number of history books stressed the military activities of the Japanese people. They left their readers with the idea that the Japanese were chiefly fierce warriors brandishing swords and charging the enemy.

Such an approach to Japanese history was not surprising since between 1895 and 1945 Japan was engaged in war and conquest much of the time. But this formed only one part of Japanese history. Actually, Japan has also contributed to the constructive work of civilization. From about the end of the eighth to the twelfth century A.D., Japan went through a period of considerable achievement in several non-military fields. This period is called Japan's "Classical Age."

Japanese history up to the fourteenth century has at least two sides: *the growth of military government, and the development of peaceful cultural activities.* Every time you think of a Japanese soldier eager to attack, think also of a Japanese poet waiting impatiently for the cherry blossoms to return in spring. Both men are a part of the history of Japan.

Key People *Lady Murasaki Shikibu · Fujiwara family · Yoritomo · Ashikaga family*

Key Places *Nara · Mount Fuji · Hokkaido · Honshu · Shikoku · Kyushu · Kyoto · Kamakura*

Key Events *Chinese civilization influences Japan · "Classical Age" · Feudal period · Shogunate established*

Key Terms *Ainus · Shinto · Mahayana Buddhism · Yamato · Shogun · Samurai · Bushido · hara-kiri · kami-kaze*

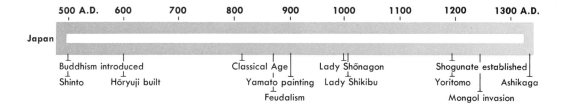

500 A.D.	600	700	800	900	1000	1100	1200	1300 A.D.

Japan

Buddhism introduced · Classical Age · Lady Shōnagon · Shogunate established

Shinto · Hōryuji built · Yamato painting · Lady Shikibu · Yoritomo · Ashikaga

Feudalism · Mongol invasion

1. Japan: A Country Binding Man to Nature

There is an old Japanese poem about a man who went to his well for water. As he was about to draw up the bucket, he noticed that the tendrils of a lovely plant had twined themselves around the rope. "Nature is showing her face to me again," he thought, and, rather than disturb the plant, he drew his water from a neighbor's well!

The closeness of the bond between Nature and man, illustrated by this tale, is an important feature of the country of Japan. This is a land marked by the many moods of Nature, and the people are respectful of those moods.

One can sense the presence of Nature everywhere: in the park at Nara, where hundreds of deer roam freely among centuries-old cedar trees; or on the snowy peak of Mt. Fuji, where the climber can see the countryside below spread out like a great quilt. Nature's presence can be seen on a boat in the blue Inland Sea, where fishermen thank the waters for their tasty breakfast of octopus eyes and tentacles; or among the cherry trees in the month of April, when spring breathes its blossoms of new life to all Japan. In every generation, the Japanese have deeply appreciated the pull and forcefulness of Nature.

The Geography of Japan Is Distinctive

Nature is important to the Japanese people because of the distinctive geographic features of their country. Japan consists of a string of islands in the north Pacific. These islands are of volcanic origin and extend in an arc for about 1300 miles off the northeastern coast of the Asian mainland. This distance would compare roughly in length with the coastal stretch between Portland, Maine, and Daytona Beach, Florida. The four principal islands are Hokkaido, Honshu, Shikoku, and Kyushu; but there are hundreds of Japanese islets scattered among them. There are excellent harbors on many islands, and no point in Japan is farther than seventy-two miles from the sea (map, p. 236).

Historical Importance of Japan's Islands: The fact that Japan consists of islands has made the Japanese heavily dependent on the sea for food and has encouraged their development as a seafaring, trading people.

235

Japan map showing the Sea of Japan, HOKKAIDO, HONSHU, SHIKOKU, KYUSHU, Pacific Ocean, and cities including Nikko, Tokyo, Yokohama, Kamakura, Nagoya, Kyoto, Kobe, Nara, Osaka, Hiroshima, Tsushima, Nagasaki, Kagoshima. Mt. Fuji and Korea Strait are labeled. JAPAN

■ *More than 3,300 islands make up the land area of Japan. The country supports a dense population. Name the four principal islands.*

The total area of Japan is almost equal to that of the state of Montana. About three-fourths of the land of Japan cannot be used for the cultivation of crops. In many places, only one acre in seven can be farmed.

Historical Importance of Japan's Limited Arable Soil: The Japanese worked every bit of available soil and even soil that was plagued with stones. They developed very careful and productive farming methods. As their population

increased, they faced a serious problem in trying to supply all of the people with sufficient food.

Japan has many lakes, but no long rivers. The country is extremely mountainous, and there is considerable timber and water power. Japan is not rich in key natural resources. She has coal, but she lacks an abundant supply of iron and petroleum.

Historical Importance of Japan's Limited Natural Resources: Japan's need for iron and other mineral resources has compelled her to develop and rely on trade with other countries. It also helped spur her to conquest in the 1930's and 1940's.

The climate varies from north to south. In many areas, the winters are fairly cold and the summers are hot and damp. There is considerable rain during June and the early part of July, and autumn and spring are the loveliest seasons of the year.

Nature often sends three violent representatives to remind the Japanese people of her power: earthquakes, typhoons, and floods. Despite such disasters, the Japanese continue to love their country for its beauty and charm.

The Japanese Are a Racial Mixture

The history of ancient Japan is so clouded by legends that it is difficult to determine the origins of the early inhabitants of the country. We know that one of the first groups to settle in Japan were the *Ainus.* They probably came from the Asian mainland, and they inhabited the islands many years before the birth of Christ. Today the descendants of these Ainus still live in Japan.

People from northern Asia—possibly of Mongolian stock—next moved down through Korea, crossed the sea to Japan, and gradually took over the lands of the Ainus. A third racial strain was added to the country when groups from either southeast China or islands in the southwest Pacific migrated to Japan.

Although the origins of the people of modern Japan are not clear, we can be certain of two important facts: (1) The modern Japanese are a mixture of several racial stocks. (2) The Japanese civilization developed at a later date than those of India, China, or the Middle East.

■ **Check on Your Reading**

1. How do the Japanese feel about Nature?
2. What has been the effect of its island position on Japan's history?
3. What have been the effects of Japan's limited soil and natural resources?
4. How does Japan's climate affect its people?
5. What two facts do we know about the Japanese?

2. Shinto, Buddhism, and China Influence Japanese Life

Japanese history comes into clearer focus in the sixth century A.D. During that time, Buddhism was introduced into Japan from China by way of Korea. When Chinese Buddhist priests arrived in Japan, they found that many people already were influenced by a native religion. This religion was *Shinto*, which means the "Way of the Gods" or the "Way of the Good Spirits."

Shinto has no holy book. Neither does it have a set of extensive rules and regulations. The Shinto faith has these features:

1. NATURE WORSHIP. The followers of Shinto respect and worship the *Kami*. The Kami are spirits of Nature, such as are found in sacred trees, mountains, and even animals; and the gods of heaven and earth, whose spirits are expressed in the forces of Nature. The Kami also may include the spirits of men who were godlike in their actions.

2. PRAYER AT SHRINES. Brief prayers are said at the shrines (*jinja*) of the Kami. These shrines are often simple wooden structures unadorned with decorations.

■ *The Shinto shrine at Nikko, the mausoleum of Ieyasu, built in the 17th century, enshrines the ashes of the first Tokugawa shogun. Compare this elaborately decorated shrine with the simple wooden ones of the Kami.*

237

3. ANCESTOR WORSHIP. It is believed that the guidance of ancestors is necessary if the living are to lead good lives. In time, there developed the idea that the emperor was entitled to obedience because his ancestry went back to the Sun-goddess.

The Japanese Turn to Mahayana Buddhism

Shinto helped the Japanese people to express their attachment to Nature, but it did not meet all of their religious needs. Thus, when Buddhism was introduced into Japan in the sixth century, it quickly won acceptance. However, Shinto was not discarded, but it merged with Buddhism in many ways.

Indian Buddhism was based on the teachings of Gautama Buddha. They can be summarized in this way: Suffering is caused by our selfish desires; we can remove suffering by doing away with our selfish desires. *Mahayana Buddhism*, the name given to the Buddhist religion in Japan, China, and Tibet, accepted this basic teaching. To this basic idea, it added these important beliefs:

1. FAITH IS AS IMPORTANT AS MONASTIC LIFE. A man need not try to subdue his desires by spending his entire life in a monastery or by avoiding the activities of daily life. If he has faith in the Buddhist religion, he can gain peace.

2. THE AMITABHA BUDDHA WILL HELP MAN. The *Amitabha Buddha* is a great god. Buddhists pray to him for protection.

3. THERE ARE MANY BUDDHAS TO GUIDE MAN. Gautama was a Buddha—that is, an "enlightened" teacher. There were other Buddhas before him, and there will be others after him. All of them will guide sincere Buddhists in their lives.

4. BODHISATTVAS WILL ANSWER MAN'S PRAYERS. *Bodhisattvas* are supernatural beings who are so worthy that they could gain peace in paradise forever. However, they love mankind so well that they will continue to remain in contact with this world. If a Buddhist prays honestly to them, they will aid him.

In brief, the Buddhism that reached Japan had turned into a religion in which various supernatural forms aided and protected man. Buddhism originally had taught that man must cast off his desires by himself. Mahayana Buddhism said that man could turn for help to powers greater than he. In honor of the compassionate beings who watched over men, the Japanese built fine temples and great statues of Buddhas.

Chinese Civilization Moves to Japan

Buddhism had a tremendous effect on Japanese life. This religion was a powerful current that carried the rich silt of Chinese civilization and deposited it on the shores of Japan. In the sixth, seventh, and eighth centuries A.D., the great knowledge and skills of China were channeled through Korea into Japan. It was on a Chinese foundation that the Japanese built a good part of their civilization.

It is difficult to overestimate the contributions of China to Japanese life. From China the Japanese learned their religion of Buddhism, their skills at working metals, their method of writing language, their techniques for raising silkworms and weaving silk cloth, and a considerable part of their arts and literature.

The Japanese were more than borrowers. Like fine craftsmen, they took Chinese materials and ideas, shaped them with graceful Japanese fingers, and gradually produced a civilization of their own. In the twentieth century they adopted the chief features of Western civilization.

■ **Check on Your Reading**
1. Explain the chief features of Shinto.
2. Describe Mahayana Buddhism.
3. How did China influence Japan?

238

3. Japan Is Productive in Its "Classical Age"

The first permanent capital of Japan was at Nara. From about 710 to 794 A.D., the emperor made his headquarters at this city, although powerful Japanese families actually ruled many parts of the country. Then the capital was moved to the site of present-day Kyoto, where it remained until 1867.

From about the end of the eighth to the twelfth century, Japan had its so-called "Classical Age." During this period, the Japanese were very productive in literature, art, and architecture. Cultural activities in these and other fields were limited chiefly to the aristocrats who lived in the capital.

Literature

Poetry was the most important literary form during the first half of the "Classical Age." Japanese poetry was usually short, concerned with Nature, and impressionistic—that is, it expressed feelings, rather than deep thoughts.

In the eleventh century, the writing of prose reached a peak. It was at this time that *The Tale of Genji* was written. This is the most famous of all Japanese novels. It was written by Lady Murasaki Shikibu, who the American author-editor Kenneth Rexroth has called "the greatest figure in Japanese literature."

A second major book was *The Pillow Book* (about 1002 A.D.). Written by the prominent Lady Shōnagon, it has a light and graceful quality. If you are an active letter writer, you should appreciate this description of a returned letter from *The Pillow Book:*

One writes a letter, taking particular trouble to get it up as prettily as possible; then waits for the answer, making sure every moment that it cannot be much longer before something comes. At last, frightfully late, is brought in—one's own note, still folded or tied exactly as one sent it, but so finger-marked and smudged that even the address is barely legible. "The family is not in residence," the messenger says, giving one back the note.... Such experiences are dismally depressing.

How similar this is to our modern postman's stamp, "MOVED AWAY—ADDRESS UNKNOWN."

Whether it was prose or poetry, Japanese writing owed a debt to Chinese civilization. In the beginning, the Japanese had a spoken language but no written language. They therefore used the characters, or written symbols, of the Chinese language to write down their own speech. By the tenth century, the Japanese had modified many Chinese characters, and a distinctive Japanese calligraphy gradually developed. Although their language was not similar to Chinese, the Japanese made considerable use of Chinese characters in their writing.

Art and Architecture

Japanese art during this period was greatly influenced by ideas coming from China. In particular, early Japanese architecture, sculpture, and painting were inspired by the religion of Buddhism, which had spread from China to Korea and then to Japan.

Many Buddhist temples and monasteries were constructed in this period. One such temple-monastery, the *Hōryūji*, built in the seventh century, has the oldest wooden buildings in the world today. Many statues of the Buddha also were made. Today the great bronze Statue of Buddha in Nara is world-famous. It is 53 feet high—and even the little finger of one of the Buddha's hands is over four feet in length!

239

■ *This 8th century bronze statue of the great "Buddha of Infinite Compassion" at Nara is the largest Buddha image in Japan. It is 53 feet high, and its little finger is almost the length of a man.*

The Japanese made considerable use of wood in their architecture. In building their wooden homes, they showed their feeling for Nature by arranging lovely gardens that were united with the house itself. Inside their homes they used little furniture. Instead, they found beauty in the artistic arrangement of a few delicate objects.

When the T'ang Dynasty of China fell at the beginning of the tenth century, Japan's official contacts with China lessened. Japanese artists found it more difficult to borrow from China. They had to depend more on themselves for ideas, and they soon began to add their own touches.

One of the most important results was the development of a distinctive style of Japanese painting. Paintings in the new style were known as *Yamato* (p. 255). These paintings stressed secular scenes, such as the life at the emperor's court, rather than concentrating only on the religious aspects of Japanese life.

Eventually, the taste for exaggerated artistic expression grew to an excess among the Japanese aristocrats. By the eleventh century, people of wealth and position were leading lives of unnecessary luxury. At the emperor's court, pompous lords and ladies spent their time admiring the shapes of leaves, composing flowery poems, or gossiping about the colors of a woman's robe. Art and literature often became the servants of vanity, instead of the masters of beauty.

■ **Check on Your Reading**

1. Describe the achievements of the Japanese during the "Classical Age."

2. What were the characteristics of Japanese poetry? of classical prose?

3. Describe Japanese writing. In what way was it influenced by Chinese?

4. In art, what did Japan borrow from China? What original contributions did the Japanese make?

5. What factors contributed to the deterioration of Japanese art and literature?

4. Feudalism Emerges in Japan

While the Japanese were developing their literature and art, an important political change was slowly being made. Between the end of the eighth and the twelfth century, *feudalism* emerged.

From our study of western Europe in the Middle Ages we know that feudalism usually had three features: (1) Lords held the land and protected the peasants who worked it. (2) Men promised to be loyal to their superiors. (3) Local governments took the place of a central government.

All three of these features appeared in the Japanese feudal system. They often came about because farmers who could not pay high taxes to the emperor turned over their lands to great lords. In return for protection, the farmers agreed to work the soil, pay rent to their lords, and be loyal to them. There were also other reasons for the gradual establishment of feudalism in Japan, such as the inability of the emperor to protect the people.

In theory, the emperor continued to govern the country. (Indeed, there never has been a break in the rule of the original Japanese dynasty. The present emperor is the 124th.) In fact, Japanese life was dominated by the will of a powerful Japanese clan, the *Fujiwara,* and by strong feudal lords throughout the country.

The Shogunate Is Established

As the feudal system grew, other ambitious *clans,* or family groups, struggled to gain control of Japan. The Fujiwara were the strongest for several centuries. Then they were succeeded by the Taira clan, and the Taira were defeated by the Minamoto clan.

In 1192 A.D., the emperor appointed Yoritomo, leader of the Minamoto clan, to be *Shogun* of the country. Shogun meant "great general" or "barbarian-subduing general." As Shogun, Yoritomo ruled Japan under a military government whose capital was at Kamakura. The emperor remained at his court in the city of Kyoto, but he had little power.

Yoritomo is extremely important in the history of Japan. When his military government took the place of civil rule, he started a system which was to last until 1868. This system of government was called the *Shogunate* (or Bakufu). It meant that the emperor reigned in theory; actually, he was merely a ceremonial head. In practice, a military chief called a Shogun ruled Japan in the name of the emperor. Later, strong military leaders often dominated the Shogun.

The Samurai Serve as Feudal Warriors

When Yoritomo took command of the country, he found that feudalism already had developed a strong military side. The *Daimyos,* the "great names" or leading families of the feudal system, had gathered warriors to protect their lands. These military men were called *Samurai.*

The Samurai were supposed to live by a code of conduct known as *Bushido,* or "the warrior-knight-way." Bushido was an unwritten code, and many rough warriors did not follow all of its informal rules. Nevertheless, it served as a guide for a military man's behavior.

According to the unwritten code of Bushido, a Samurai warrior must be brave, a man of honor, loyal to his emperor and lord, and must not show emotion. To redeem his honor, a Samurai did not hesitate to commit *seppuku (hara-kiri)*—that is, to kill himself by "ripping the belly" with a short sword. A good friend usually would cut off the honorable Samurai's head when he had completed hara-kiri.

When Yoritomo gained power as Shogun, he found that the code of the Samurai, the landholding arrangements, and other features of feudalism had become powerful factors in Japanese life. He therefore accepted feudalism and made it a part of his governmental system. Then he forced as many lords as possible to be loyal.

"Kami-Kaze" Helps Destroy Mongol Invaders

The Shogunate under Yoritomo provided Japan with an effective government. Yoritomo reorganized the administration of the provinces, strengthened the legal system, and forced some aristocratic lords to pay land taxes for the good of the state. When Yoritomo died, the actual powers of government passed to the members of another family. The Shogunate continued at Kamakura.

During this period, the religion of Buddhism became increasingly popular. Various Buddhist sects were formed. Equally important with the growth of Buddhism was the successful defense of Japan against Mongolian invaders.

In the thirteenth century, the Mongols made two sea invasions of Japan. Both times Nature came to the assistance of the Japanese. Storms hindered the movements of the enemy's first fleet, and a typhoon in 1281 saved Japan again.

During this famous typhoon, "the wind blew fiercely, the tumultuous billows surged up to heaven, the thunder rolled and the lightning dashed against the ground so that it seemed as if mountains were crumbling down and high heaven falling to the earth." The terrible wrath of the storm did not stop until the Mongol fleet had been destroyed. This typhoon is known as "kami-kaze" or "divine wind."

Although the defense of Japan had been successful, it had weakened the government by draining the treasury. Ambitious men tried to seize power, and civil war broke out. A new Shogunate family, the *Ashikaga*, finally won control.

■ **Check on Your Reading**

1. Summarize Japanese feudalism.
2. How did the Shogunate govern Japan?
3. What was the code of the Samurai?

CULTURAL CHARACTERISTICS of Japan in Its "Classical Age"

Japanese civilization developed at a much later date than the civilizations in the Middle East, India, and China. Indeed, the Japanese built a good part of their civilization on a Chinese foundation, although they shaped it to harmonize with their own ideas. The cultural characteristics of Japan in its "Classical Age" were:

A society based on feudalism, which gradually emerged in Japan between the end of the eighth and the twelfth century.

The great effect of Chinese achievements on the development of Japanese culture. The diffusion of Chinese ideas and ways of living affected Japanese religion, economics, literature, art and architecture, and other fields.

The influence of the religions of Shinto and Buddhism on the lives of the Japanese people.

Productivity in literature, art, and architecture. Cultural activities in these fields were limited chiefly to aristocrats who lived in the Japanese capital.

Some forms of Japanese culture, such as art and poetry, sometimes became excessively artificial and unnatural in the latter part of the "Classical Age." Yet despite this development the Japanese people remained close to nature.

Thus a Shinto prayer to the gods of the harvest reflects the practical importance of nature:

If the sovereign gods [of the harvest] will bestow in many-bundled ears and in luxuriant ears the late-ripening harvest which they will bestow ... then I will fulfill their praises by setting up the first fruits [that is, I will offer up a sacrifice].

The famous novel *The Tale of Genji* also makes clear that nature was always close at hand to the Japanese. A representative section reads:

There was a wattled fence over which some ivy-like creeper spread its cool green leaves, and among the leaves were white flowers with petals half unfolded like the lips of people smiling at their own thoughts.

In brief, one must not think of Japanese culture in the "Classical Age" as merely being concerned with the daintiness of a floral arrangement, the soft lilt of a line of poetry, the delicate curvature of a statue. These things were important to them, but so were the sun and the rain and the conditions of the field. The Japanese seemed to stretch one hand high toward the heavens to express their sensitive thoughts and feelings—but they rarely permitted their other hand to lose contact with the earth.

MAN AND HIS CULTURE

Let's Meet the People!

The following sketch is based on details found in "The Diary of Murasaki Shikibu," from *Diaries of Court Ladies of Old Japan*, trans. by Anne S. Omori and Kocki Doi with introduction by Amy Lowell, Houghton Mifflin Co., Boston; Constable & Co., Ltd., London. In the early part of the eleventh century, Lady Murasaki Shikibu was a member of the court of a Japanese queen.

A Woman and Child

It was a day like any other day. Japanese peasants rose early in the morning and hurried out to the fields to work. Noblemen powdered their faces, dabbed perfume on their clothes, and prepared for a ride through the countryside. Ladies of wealth rouged their cheeks, blackened their teeth, and sat down at their desks to write poetry.

The woman lay on a white bed under a canopy. Around the bed, the curtains of a screen hid her face from view. To one side, "a little lantern was hung under the canopy which chased the darkness away even from the corners."

The woman was in great pain, and "her fair complexion was pale and transparently pure." All about her there was great excitement:

243

Men cried at the top of their voices to scare away evil spirits. . . . The prayers [of priests and monks] were said to the Buddhas of the three worlds. All the soothsayers . . . were summoned. Eight million gods seemed to be listening with ears erect for their Shinto prayers.

On the west side of the woman's bed, two young girls lay on couches surrounded by folding screens. They said prayers and tried to trick the evil spirits in the woman's suffering body to come into their own bodies. Outside, the woman's friends whispered: "Tears are not suitable to this occasion"—and wept. Then they scattered rice "white as snow" on their heads to bring the woman good luck.

Now the woman's pain increased. Her breathing became more difficult. The nurses worked frantically behind the screen. Death was so close that the order was given to shave a part of the woman's head. This was done:

So that she might be ordained as a priestess and insured a good reception in the next world [if she should die].

There was stillness for a moment—then the woman screamed—and her child was born!

The woman rested all afternoon. At last, at six o'clock in the evening, the ceremony of the bath was performed. The bathing area was lighted by torches. The stand for the bathtub was covered with white cloth, and two special stands were set up for the kettles. A tiger's head was held up before the baby to chase away evil spirits, and rice was scattered about the room. Then the child was blessed and bathed.

It has been a day like any other day—with one notable exception. The Queen of Japan had given birth to a son, and the Japanese people now had another heir to the throne!

CHAPTER REVIEW

REVIEW and DISCUSSION

1. Identify the people and places and explain the events and terms on p. 234.

2. Why is the sea so significant to the Japanese? to the British?

3. Do you think the people of Japan love the beauty and charm of their country as much as we do ours? Why?

4. How do you explain the fact that the Japanese developed their civilization at a much later date than did China, India, and the Middle East?

5. It is said that "the Japanese are most skillful at adopting and adapting the ideas of others." What do you think? Why?

6. What is meant by the term "Classical Age"? Describe Japanese achievements during this period.

7. What distinctive contributions did the Japanese make in the decorative arts?

8. What is wrong when "art and literature often became the servants of vanity, instead of the masters of beauty"?

9. What deep and lasting effects did the Shoguns have on Japanese national habits and values?

10. Why did Japanese commit *hara-kiri*?

11. What other stories in history are similar to the Japanese one of the "divine wind," which defeated the Mongols? Why do such stories persist?

12. "History never begins a new chapter. Only historians do." Explain.

ACTIVITIES

1. Write a report on the Fujiwara clan and its importance in Japanese history. Consult references.

2. On a map of Japan, locate Hokkaido, Honshu, Kamakura, Kyoto, Kyushu, Mount Fuji, Nara, Shikoku, Tokyo, and Yokohama.

3. Using Linton, *The Tree of Culture*, or any other reference book, write a report on the homes, occupations, and recreations of the different groups that make up Japanese society.

4. To your paperback library add the following: Wallbank, T. Walter, *A Short History of India and Pakistan*; Creel, Herrlee, *Chinese Thought*; Ross, James S., and McLaughlin, Mary, (eds.), *The Portable Medieval Reader*; Nehru, Jawaharlal, *The Discovery of India* or *Glimpses of World History*; Berry, Gerald L., *Religions of the World*; Smith, Huston, *The Religions of Man*.

PAST and PRESENT

1. Cite examples of Japanese influences on our culture.

2. Panel discussion: Changing patterns in religion, politics, economics, and social customs in Japan today.

SUGGESTED READINGS

Basic books: BERRY, GERALD L., *Religions of the World*, Barnes & Noble. Contains a useful chapter on religions of the Far East. Very brief. Easy reading.

FITCH, FLORENCE, *Their Search for God*, Lothrop, Lee & Shepard. Valuable section on Japanese religion. Brief and easy.

LATOURETTE, KENNETH SCOTT, *A Short History of the Far East*, Macmillan.

LINTON, RALPH, *The Tree of Culture*, Chap. 39, Knopf.

SMITH, GOLDWIN, *The Heritage of Man*, Chap. 14, Scribner.

SMITH, HUSTON, *The Religions of Man*, New American Library. Extremely interesting.

Special accounts: DILTS, MARION M., *The Pageant of Japanese History*, Longmans, Green. Written for youth. Presentation of the pre-modern periods is particularly effective.

LATOURETTE, KENNETH SCOTT, *The History of Japan*, Macmillan. An excellent brief history. Several chapters have information applicable to this period.

REISCHAUER, EDWIN O., *Japan: Past and Present*, Knopf. Based on lectures delivered during World War II.

WEBB, HERSCHEL, *An Introduction to Japan*, Columbia University Press. A brief but effective discussion of political, economic, social, and cultural features of Japanese life and history.

Biography and Fiction: KEENE, DONALD, (ed.), *Anthology of Japanese Literature*, Grove. Includes literary works from the earliest era in Japan to the mid-nineteenth century.

UNIT 4 The Renaissance, Age of Exploration, and Reformation in Europe

Which Career Will You Follow?

A recent report showed that twelve thousand high-school students were planning on the following careers:

CAREER	THE CHOICE OF:
Teaching	30.0 per cent
Science research and engineering	27.4
Medicine, dentistry, and nursing	13.8
Business	7.0
Law and government	4.3
Communications	2.5
Creative arts	2.0
Ministry	1.8
Home economics	1.6
Social work	1.5
Agriculture	.8
Miscellaneous	.9
Undecided	6.4
	100.0 per cent

Where do your own interests lie? Do you hope to become an engineer—a secretary—a minister—a musician—a farmer—a lawyer—a factory worker—a teacher? Which career will you follow?

Learning about Your Life's Work

Regardless of your choice of career, you probably will want to know as much as possible about your life's work. Certainly, you will be interested in learning how the people of the past contributed to your chosen occupation. How fortunate that your next unit contains information about man's activities in many lines of work.

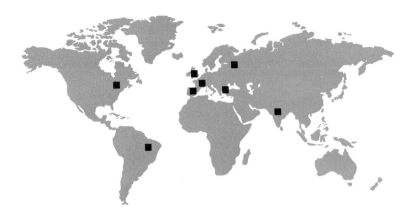

Is your career to be in teaching? In Unit 4 you can read about the ideas of Comenius, a great educator who lived many centuries ago. Do you prefer a career in art? You can study the activities of brilliant artists, such as Leonardo da Vinci and Michelangelo. Are you interested in a life of music? You can find information on the madrigal and opera. Do you intend to become a writer? You can read the words of authors like Shakespeare.

Do you aim for the profession of law? You can analyze the evolution of the jury system. Do you wish to be a national statesman? You can study the early development of modern nations.

Are you planning to be a scientist? You can become acquainted with the work of scientists like Copernicus and Newton. Will you enter the business world? You can study the development of capitalism. Will you join the ministry? You can add to your knowledge of religious reformers like Luther and Loyola.

Many of you will find material in Unit 4 that is related to your future careers. That is one excellent reason for studying the unit.

Something Special for You

Suppose that you have not made up your mind about a career. Is there something in the following pages for you? Of course, there is.

There is—if you love a good sea story or a tale of exciting exploration. There is—if you are curious about religious ideas and about your part in religion. There is—if you like to meet the people who once lived and worked in the world you now inhabit.

As you begin this unit, you can be sure that your reading will be of value to you. Here is a period of history for all—and probably something special for you!

Chapter 16   The Renaissance Brings Old and New Life to Europe

KEYNOTE   Montaigne, a great sixteenth-century writer, once used this illustration to show the folly of giving simple names to complicated matters:

What variety of herbs . . . are shuffled together in the dish, yet the whole mass is swallowed up under one name of a [salad].

To him, the word "salad" could never explain all of the ingredients in a dish—just as no single word could ever account for all of the events in history.

How disturbed Montaigne would be to find that we still use names today to describe complicated "historical dishes." For example, we attach the label *Renaissance* to an extremely complex and important period of history, the one in which Montaigne himself lived.

Actually, the word Renaissance—like all words—was invented by man. It contains no magical power to explain everything that happened at a certain time. It is merely a name that was selected for man's convenience.

If we keep this point in mind, we can find the real meaning of the Renaissance. It is this: *The Renaissance was the period of new ideas, attitudes, and creative activities that stirred and changed European life following the medieval period.*

Key People   *Petrarch · Machiavelli · Erasmus · Rabelais · Shakespeare · da Vinci · Michelangelo · El Greco · Rembrandt · Comenius*

Key Events   *Rebirth of interest in classical literature · St. Peter's constructed · Education changed*

Key Terms   *Renaissance · humanism · vernacular · Baroque · madrigal · oratorio · opera*

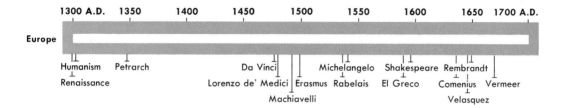

1. The Renaissance Begins Gradually

The word Renaissance means *rebirth*. It suggests that the pace of life took on fresh movement and vitality after the medieval period. When did the medieval period end and the Renaissance begin? One authority, Jefferson B. Fletcher, tells us to look to the rainbow for our answer:

Historical epochs are like the color-bands in a rainbow which, though distinct, yet merge at their boundaries. Between definitely yellow and definitely red there is a strip which has a tinge of both colors. We may call it . . . either the beginning of the red band or the ending of the yellow.

Historical periods—like the colors in a rainbow—do not end or begin suddenly. Rather, one flows into the next.

It is therefore impossible to point to the exact date that marked the "official start" or "end" of the Renaissance. All that can be said is that the Renaissance began about the fourteenth century and lasted in some lands through the sixteenth century. In some countries the Renaissance spirit did not appear until the seventeenth century. In others—such as Russia —it did not appear at all.

The Renaissance Begins in Italy

The Renaissance first developed in those Italian cities which had become centers for trade and for the exchange of ideas during the medieval period. Several of these cities were republics, at least in name, and in the fourteenth and fifteenth centuries they competed with each other in everything from trade to art. Among the most important of these cities were Venice and Florence. Venice, which was governed by a small number of dynamic individuals and families, became a key trading port and a major cultural center on the Mediterranean. Florence, under the leadership of Lorenzo de' Medici, greatly stimulated the development of commerce, literature, and art.

As the leaders in other countries received the stimulation of new ideas and acquired the wealth needed to support the arts, the Renaissance began to spread. From Italy it moved to Germany, the Netherlands, France, Spain, England, and other lands. When the Renaissance spirit died down in one country, it came to life in another.

Major Economic and Social Changes Occur

Major economic and social developments—many of them outgrowths from medieval times—were a part of Renaissance life and helped to stimulate its activity. Several important developments occurred. As the power of the princes and kings increased, feudalism gradually ended. This permitted people to travel with greater safety to other areas. More men and women met and exchanged ideas.

Merchants added to their personal riches, and cities grew in wealth. Both merchants and cities now demanded attractive buildings, beautiful paintings, and other artwork. This stimulated the work of artists.

As trade increased, trading companies were organized. Many of these companies permitted people to invest in business enterprises and to share in the profits. More people took part in commercial affairs and mingled with others.

Practical banking and money systems were established. Business and other contacts among people were strengthened.

The increase of economic and social contacts among people helped to bring about a "speeding up" of European life. So, too, did the activities of wealthy cities and rich merchants. Yet something more than social contacts, trade, and wealth was needed to produce a Renaissance. That something was creative *people*—talented individuals who could fashion with their hands and minds achievements that all the money in the world could not.

■ Check on Your Reading

1. When did the "Middle Ages" end and the Renaissance begin?
2. Where did the Renaissance begin?
3. What economic and social developments were a part of Renaissance life and helped to stimulate its activity?

2. Renaissance Humanism and Literature

Contact—trade—wealth—creative people—were factors that stimulated a Renaissance in Europe. This Renaissance had several important features.

A Rebirth of Interest in Ancient Greek and Roman Culture

The writings of the Greek Aristotle had been almost forgotten during the "Middle Ages," though copies of his works were preserved by various monks. Italian scholars revived interest in Aristotle and analyzed his works with enthusiasm. Writers also studied the style of the Roman Cicero and found the writings of other Latin authors. Almost all of the ancient Greek writings that we know today were rediscovered by Renaissance scholars searching old monasteries where such works had lain hidden during the Middle Ages.

Once discovered, these manuscripts had to be studied, catalogued, and kept in a safe place. Important libraries were established, including the great Vatican library founded by the Popes. Many other fine libraries were founded and supported in Italy by wealthy individuals.

The leaders of the Renaissance were not merely imitators of ancient civilizations. On the contrary, they added their contributions to the heritage from Greece and Rome. The Renaissance touched the hand of the past—and then raced on. It never held firmly to the grip of the ancients.

Humanism

Humanism was an attitude taken by men in which they became vitally concerned with living fully in *this* world and inspired by the civilizations of "classical"

Medici-Riccardi Palace, Florence

■ *Lorenzo de' Medici, ruler of Florence (1469–1492), worked to stimulate prosperity. He was a patron of art, literature, and education.*

Greece and Rome. The humanists disagreed with the intellectual leaders of the medieval period who thought that the major purpose of this life was to prepare for the next. They wanted to live now! This was why they went back to the writings of the worldly Greeks and Romans in preference to medieval religious works.

Humanism was particularly important in shaping the vital, energetic character of Renaissance life. The humanists examined the nature of man, not just the meaning of the Scriptures. They acted on the basis of man's present desires, not just on the prospect of future reward or punishment. They created literature, art, and music for man's pleasure, not just to satisfy God.

Differences among periods are often a matter of degree. The leaders in the medieval years also were interested in man. They preferred to place his future in a religious pattern. Similarly, the humanists could concentrate on man and still be religious. As the Renaissance writer Pico della Mirandola said, the greatness of man's powers might be taken as a gift from God:

This is the culminating gift of God, this is the supreme and marvelous [happiness] of man . . . that he can be that which he wills to be.

The humanism of the Renaissance turned the spotlight on man in this world; it did not push Christianity from the stage.

The Creation of Stimulating Literature

Another feature of the Renaissance was the creation of stimulating literature. It could be read by more people, because of the rise of *vernacular* languages in the Middle Ages. These are some, but by no means all, of the outstanding writers.

Petrarch

Petrarch (1304–1374), a lyric poet of Italian descent, was important as one of the first men to express the spirit of the Renaissance. He revived interest in the writings of the Greek Plato and the Romans Cicero and Virgil. Although he did not always take a humanist's approach to life, on many occasions he showed a humanist's concern for matters of this world. For example, he wrote, ". . . a crowd of important affairs, *though only of the world*, is waiting my attention."

Petrarch was interested in religious discussions of the world to come. He also wrote lines in praise of the beauty of Laura, a woman of the earthly world. His lovely poems to Laura are important for two reasons: (1) They were written in vernacular, that is, in Italian rather than Latin. (2) Petrarch created the Italian sonnet form, a fourteen-line poetic form much used by Shakespeare and later poets. Petrarch's description of Laura reads:

Loose to the breeze her golden tresses flowed,
Wildly in thousand mazy ringlets blown,
And from her eyes unconquered glances shone. . . .

Machiavelli

Machiavelli (1469–1527) was a polished Italian diplomat and man of letters living in Florence who described the techniques of power politics. He wrote that a ruler should not concern himself with the moral right or wrong of his actions. He should use any means to achieve success.

In a famous book called *The Prince*, Machiavelli told rulers:

...A prince should be a fox, to know the traps and snares; and a lion, to be able to frighten the wolves....

Machiavelli described political techniques that ambitious rulers have followed.

Erasmus

Erasmus (c. 1466–1536), a Dutch humanist and philosopher, has been called the "Prince of Humanists." He was an international figure; he studied and taught in many countries of Europe. He taught Greek and Latin and encouraged educated men to master them. Erasmus had faith in the dignity and worth of man. He pointed out that men were naturally good, although they often accepted foolish ideas. In his famous satire, *The Praise of Folly*, he poked fun at many of man's follies.

Erasmus was a Catholic forerunner of Martin Luther and the Protestant Reformation. He published a scholarly Greek edition of the New Testament which conflicted in some points with the accepted Vulgate. He also criticized the clergy for some corrupt practices.

Rabelais

Rabelais (c. 1494–1553), a French author, showed appreciation of the physical side of life and contempt for hypocrites. His rough satire, *The Inestimable Life of Gargantua, Father of Pantagruel*, was a seasoned stew that boiled such persons as:

brattling gabblers ... mangy rascals ... slap-sauce fellows ... ruffian rogues ... forlorn snakes ... scurvy sneakbies ... base loons ... scoffing braggards. ...

Shakespeare

Shakespeare (1564–1616) was the outstanding playwright of the Renaissance in England—and one of the greatest writers of all time. In his plays he expressed the love of the English people for their country. Even more important, he captured the thoughts and feelings of men and women everywhere. Shakespeare's works have such scope and power that they are still a vital part of literature and drama today. Splendid motion pictures and television programs have been made from his plays *Henry V, Richard III, Hamlet, The Tempest, Macbeth,* and *Julius Caesar.*

Shakespeare had extraordinary skill in using the English language. His lines excite or charm the listener (see Chart).

■ Check on Your Reading

1. Summarize the important features of the Renaissance.

2. What did Petrarch contribute?

3. What contributions were made by Machiavelli, Erasmus, Rabelais, and Shakespeare?

We Might Say:	Shakespeare Said:
"It is twelve o'clock."	"The iron tongue of midnight hath told twelve."
"Life is often boring."	"Life is as tedious as a twice-told tale, Vexing the dull ear of a drowsy man."
"People can always find good excuses for doing wrong."	"The devil can cite Scripture for his purpose."
"I don't enjoy your company."	"I do desire we may be better strangers."

FAR EASTERN, MOSLEM, and EUROPEAN CULTURES

■ *The Mogul conquest brought new influences, especially that of Persian art, to India. Painting flourished, particularly the art of portraiture. An example of Indian Mogul art is "Prince on Horseback" (18th century).*

Courtesy of the
Museum of Fine Arts, Boston

■ *This is one of the wall frescoes of the Gupta period (100–700 A.D.) that decorate the Ajanta Caves near Aurangabad, India. These paintings on Buddhist themes depict figures that are vibrant with life in glowing browns and reds.*

253

■ *Emperor Hui Tsung of the Sung dynasty (1082–1135) painted the "Five-Colored Parakeet." It is an album painting on silk, depicting a bird perched on an apricot branch with an inscription in calligraphy.*

Courtesy of the
Museum of Fine Arts, Boston

■ *During the Ming dynasty the manufacture of porcelain ceramics reached a peak. Designs in different-colored glazes and enamels were used. This Ming ceramic jar (16th century) is a fine example.*

Courtesy of the Smithsonian Institution,
Freer Gallery of Art, Washington, D.C.

254

■ *Japanese art in the late Fujiwara period (11th century) revolved around Buddhist themes. This painting on silk depicts Dai-Itoku-Myō-ō, Conqueror of Death, as a strange and terrifying figure. In his right hand he holds a sword, with which to conquer evil, but he is a benevolent deity.*

■ *In the Kamakura period (13th century), Japanese art was primarily secular, illustrating in portraits or scrolls scenes of the aristocracy and of court life. "Flight of the Court" is a detail from the "Burning of the Sanjo Palace," a scroll recording the civil war in Japan.*

■ *This is one of the costly and precious Syrian enameled mosque lamps (14th century) that hung in rows in the Moslem mosques. Their principal ornamentations were inscriptions in the beautiful Arabic script, decorations of flowers, and small figures of warriors.*

Courtesy of The Metropolitan Museum of Art, bequest of Edward C. Moore, 1891

■ *A page from an Arabic manuscript of Dioscorides (1222–23) contains a prescription for cough medicine. The illustration shows the doctor preparing it; it has the bright, flat patterning of the East.*

Courtesy of The Metropolitan Museum of Art, Rogers Fund, 1913

256

■ This magnificent stained-glass window in the Cathedral of Rouen (1235–1240) is divided into four panels depicting Biblical accounts. A copper serpent is shown by Moses, who has horns, to Jews (top left); a sacrifice is made by burning a lamb outside the city walls (top right); the Widow of Sarepta meets the prophet Elia (bottom right); and the sacrifice of Isaac is prevented by an angel (bottom left).

■ The Royal gold cup of the kings of France and England is an example of medieval secular plate at its most lavish and luxurious development. The solid gold cup is decorated with scenes, in enamels, from the legend of St. Agnes and of the evangelists. It may have been made in Paris in 1380.

257

■ *This is an illuminated page from a manuscript of the early 15th century, designed by Stefano of Zevio as a choir book for a Verona cathedral. On it he has painted in brilliant colors this initial "S" wrapped around a gentle Virgin and Child.*

Courtesy of The Metropolitan Museum of Art, Rogers Fund, 1912

■ *Sandro Botticelli's admirable work, "Adoration of the Magi," was designed for an altar in the church of Santa Maria Novella, Florence. The artist has represented the principal members of the Medici family as the key figures.*

Courtesy of the Uffizi Gallery, Florence

■ *"Young Lady Reading a Letter" by Jan Vermeer (1632–1675) exemplified Dutch genre painting. It is a simple composition showing one figure standing out clearly. The painting is filled with a cool, clear light which is reflected from the polished surfaces of household objects. Vermeer's work has the delicacy and enamel-like quality of miniature painting.*

Courtesy of the Rijksmuseum, Amsterdam

■ *"Girl at the Open Half-Door" by Rembrandt Van Rijn (1606–1669) shows the artist's skill at presenting his character's inner thoughts and feelings. Rembrandt was a master at using light and shadow.*

Courtesy of The Art Institute of Chicago

■ *Titian's "La Bella" (1536–37) is one of the artist's beautiful and significant portraits. It is noteworthy for the beauty of the face, the perfect harmony of the whole figure, and the wonderful blend of the colors of the luxurious dress with the flesh tones and hair of the subject.*

Courtesy of the Pitti Gallery, Florence

■ *In "View of Toledo" El Greco (1541–1614) painted his vision of Toledo, Spain. It was his only landscape painting. His intention was to present the city's essence or spirit, not to paint it as it actually appeared. El Greco's work had considerable influence on the development of modern art.*

Courtesy of The Metropolitan Museum of Art, bequest of Mrs. H. O. Havemeyer, 1929, the H. O. Havemeyer Collection

3. An Outpouring of Art, Architecture, and Music

One of the most impressive features of the Renaissance was its art and architecture. Many fine churches, palaces, and town halls were built throughout Europe. These structures showed the influence of the ancient Greek and Roman civilizations, particularly in the construction of columns and domes. Other characteristics of Renaissance architecture were the frequent use of windows with triangular niches for decoration; and the fine *symmetry*, that is, the harmonizing and balancing of the parts of a building.

Later Renaissance art and architecture, produced in the seventeenth century, are often *Baroque* in style. To the characteristics just described Baroque added a great deal of elaborate ornamentation and embellishment. The geometric symmetry was still there but detailed ornamentation somewhat obscured it.

St. Peter's in Rome, the largest Christian church in the world, has many features of Baroque architecture. When you enter its doors, guides sometimes point to markings on the floor and say: "Those lines will show you how much smaller other churches are in comparison with the length of St. Peter's." Yet it is not great size alone that warms the visitor to beautiful St. Peter's. Rather, it is the many little corners of peace where men and women can be seen praying to their God.

Renaissance painting and sculpture are even more famous than architecture. Technical improvements, especially the development of oil paints, helped make great achievements possible. During the Renaissance, church leaders, wealthy merchants, and rulers such as Lorenzo de' Medici of Florence competed among themselves for the services of painters and sculptors, such as Leonardo da Vinci, Michelangelo, and others.

Leonardo da Vinci

Leonardo da Vinci (1452–1519), an Italian, was one of the most versatile men of all time. He was a painter, sculptor, architect, engineer, scientist, inventor, and athlete. There are few more amazing "letters of application" than the one that Leonardo wrote to the ruler of Milan in an effort to obtain a position. He stated that some of his qualifications were:

I have plans for bridges . . . for making cannon . . . for constructing many engines most suitable for attack or defense. . . . I make covered cars. . . . I can give you as complete satisfaction as anyone else in architecture. . . . I can execute sculpture in marble, bronze, or clay, and also painting. . . .

It might be added as an obvious conclusion: P.S.—He got the job!

Leonardo was a many-sided creator whose achievements stamped him as a genius. He was also an extremely complicated human being. It was said that he had the strength to bend a horseshoe in his hands, yet he was gentle enough to buy caged birds merely to set them free. It is interesting to note that strength and gentleness also became the dominant qualities of his work in art. These qualities were particularly apparent in two of his world-famous paintings, "The Last Supper" and "Mona Lisa." The "Mona Lisa" is a beautiful portrait of a woman whose strange smile has continued to fascinate observers down to the present time.

Michelangelo

Michelangelo (1475–1564), an Italian sculptor, painter, and architect, was one of the greatest artists in history. A moody man with tremendous energy in artistic work, he created masterpieces that have rarely—if ever—been equalled. His statue

■ *Michelangelo's masterpiece was the huge fresco decorating the entire ceiling of the Sistine Chapel in the Vatican, on which he worked for four years. This is the figure of the Prophet Isaiah from the ceiling.*

■ *Italian Renaissance architecture specialized in palaces and churches. For example, the Farnese Palace, Rome (right), erected by Antonio da Sangallo and completed by Michelangelo, is noted for its round arches, graceful columns, and general symmetry of design. St. Peter's, Rome, (above) is the most famous of the Renaissance churches. Its great size and solidity are combined with extraordinary beauty of design. Michelangelo, one of its chief architects, designed the dome which dominated the building.*

■ *"Madonna of the Grand Duke" by Raphael shows the influence of da Vinci in the calm beauty of the Virgin and the soft modeling of the figures. But Raphael's Madonna paintings have their own gentle beauty and glowing colors.*

The Louvre

Pitti Gallery, Florence

■ *The "Mona Lisa" by Leonardo da Vinci is one of the most famous of paintings. With this painting the picture as a whole has become more important than its parts. The beauty and mystery of the Mona Lisa fascinate observers. Everyone wonders: "What is the Mona Lisa thinking about?"*

of David, his paintings on the ceiling of the Sistine Chapel in Rome, his sculpture on the tombs of the Medici family, and the dome that he designed for the Church of St. Peter are famous throughout the world.

Michelangelo was fascinated by the human body. His representations of human forms, more powerful and graceful than any real human being, brought the spirit of life to stone and paint. Like other Renaissance humanists, Michelangelo explored the wonders of man on this earth to find the deeper meanings of life. In one lovely poem, he exclaimed:

> My soul can find no stair
> To mount to heaven, save earth's loveliness.

Other Italian Artists

There were other outstanding artists of the Renaissance in Italy. These included Raphael (1483–1520), who painted magnificent Madonnas (p. 263); Titian (c. 1477–1576), whose canvasses were filled with rich colors (p. 260); Botticelli (1444–1510), whose people have an "other-worldly sweetness" and beauty (p. 258).

El Greco

El Greco (1541–1614), which means "The Greek," was born of Greek parents on the island of Crete. Crete then belonged to Venice. El Greco studied painting in Venice and developed his talent further in Rome. Then he went to Toledo, in

■ *"The Maids of Honor" by Velásquez shows the artist at work on a huge canvas, probably this picture. Princess Margarita with her playmates and maids of honor are in the center. The faces of the King and Queen, who have just stepped into the room, are visible in the mirror. Velásquez is noted for his splendid portraits and arrangement of light and shade.*

264

Spain, where he lived and worked for almost forty years.

El Greco loved extravagant living and physical pleasures. Yet his paintings are noted for their spiritual and religious quality. He achieved his highly emotional effects by the use of contrasts of light and dark, elongated figures, and interplay of color in his paintings.

El Greco believed that the painting "Burial of Count Orgaz" was his "sublime work," but Americans know him better for "View of Toledo" (p. 260). One of his few outstanding landscapes, "View of Toledo" captures the spiritual quality of El Greco's work. One art critic, Sarah Newmeyer, described the painting in this way:

Heavy clouds rent by flashes of light crush downward over the symbols of man's power, the proud cathedral and the massive castle. ... Then the inner eye becomes aware of movement beneath the seemingly static earth; the yellow-green meadows and the black-green trees, the motionless stream which seems just on the verge of reversing its natural flow to push upward with all the earth to meet the down-pressing heavens in a mighty ... clash that will burst open the universe.

The work of El Greco had a considerable influence on the development of modern art. His style of painting particularly interested the nineteenth-century French painter Paul Cézanne, who sometimes is called the "father of modern art."

Velásquez

Velásquez (1599–1660) was the court painter of King Philip IV of Spain. His art differed greatly from that of El Greco. Velásquez is noted for objective and realistic painting of portraits, careful use of light and shade, and excellent arrangement of objects in space.

Velásquez's portraits of the Spanish royal family are world-famous. Perhaps

Ehemals Staatliche Museen, Berlin, Museum Dahlem, Gemaldegalerie

■ *"Man with the Golden Helmet" by Rembrandt depicts man's feelings and thoughts. Despair and bitterness can be seen in this portrait.*

his most interesting painting is his "Maids of Honor." Consider the problem that Velásquez faced: On one canvas he had to place Infanta Margarita, her maids of honor, dwarfs, a dog, a painter doing Margarita's portrait, a grand marshal, and the king and queen watching the group. And the painting was not to appear to be crowded with people! Velásquez's ability to handle the problems of spacing—partly by using a mirror to show the position of the king and queen—resulted in the successful execution of this painting.

Rembrandt van Rijn

Rembrandt van Rijn (1606–1669) was a brilliant Dutch artist and one of the most creative painters in history. He is particularly famous for his portraits and for his

265

superb use of light. Art historian, Helen Gardner, explains how Rembrandt uses light in his paintings:

Light . . . is Rembrandt's basic means of expression . . . a light, usually warm, that throbs with infinite variations, entirely opposite to the cold, darting, untoned light of El Greco.

Rembrandt was far more than an excellent technician in handling light and shadow. In such works as "Man with the Golden Helmet" (p. 265), he demonstrated that he was also a genius at probing into a person's deepest feelings.

Jan Vermeer

Jan Vermeer (1632–1675), a painter of extraordinary ability, did magnificent work in the field of Dutch genre painting (p. 259).

Genre art presents everyday life in a realistic manner. It often places stress on the "story" being told in the painting or on the attitudes of the characters.

Art historian William Fleming makes clear the contrast between Rembrandt and Vermeer:

The contrast between Rembrandt's restless searching spirit and Vermeer's sober objective detachment is fully as great as that between El Greco and Velásquez. . . . With his warm personal quality, Rembrandt embraces humanity as completely as Vermeer's cool impersonality encompasses space. . . . Like a philosopher, Rembrandt lays the soul bare in his moving characterizations, while Vermeer, like a jeweler, delights the eye with his unique perception of the quality and texture of things.

■ *"Peasant Dance" by Pieter Breughel, a genre painter, is one of his famous paintings depicting the life of the peasants. This scene shows the lively gaiety and rough vitality of the peasants at a dance. An impressive feature of this picture is its composition.*

Kunsthistorisches Museum, Vienna

■ *"The Four Horsemen of the Apocalypse"—war, famine, plague, old age (death)—by Albrecht Dürer shows the horsemen deliberately riding over the people in their way. This is a woodcut; that is, the artist carved out the spaces between the lines on the surface of a wooden block, leaving a raised design.*

Pieter Breughel the Elder

Pieter Breughel (c.1525–1569) was also a genre painter, born in Brussels. In contrast to Vermeer, he painted lively scenes of peasant life. Among the most famous are "Peasant Dance" (p. 266), harvest scenes and dances, and winter scenes showing skaters on the frozen canals.

Albrecht Dürer

Albrecht Dürer (1471–1528) was an engraver, painter, and etcher who is considered one of the greatest German artists. He is particularly famous for his use of watercolor, for his excellent engravings on metal, and for his woodcuts.

"Understanding must begin to grow side by side with practice," Dürer once wrote, "so that the hands have power to do what the will and the understanding command." In such woodcuts as "The Four Horsemen of the Apocalypse," he demonstrated that he had the ability to execute magnificent works of art.

Hans Holbein the Younger

Hans Holbein the Younger (1497–1543) was born in Augsburg, Germany. Later he became a court painter under the English king Henry VIII and lived many years in England. Holbein had the ability to use line with unusual effectiveness. It is said that he once painted a picture of a fly so accurately that a fellow-artist tried to chase it out of the room!

Holbein is known for his portraits (p. 312), painted in a cool and detached manner. Art critic Joachim Fernau explains:

The language of his portraits is that of a judge or member of a jury. No glimmer of an indulgent smile or ordinary human fellow-feeling is discernible. But . . . Holbein possessed uncannily shrewd insight into human nature.

Artists of the Renaissance—A Final Word

Our brief analysis of the work of some of the great artists of Italy, Spain, the Netherlands, and Germany has demonstrated that there were various styles of art during the Renaissance. This was to be expected, for the Renaissance did not reach all countries in the same period of history or affect all men in the same way. Some of the later artists—like Rembrandt and Rubens—used the *Baroque* style. In painting, this stressed the emotional and dynamic qualities of a subject, the merging of each part into the whole, and the unending nature of space. Other artists—like Holbein—frequently avoided the emotional aspects of art and presented minute details in a coldly objective manner in their painting. Still others—like El Greco—developed highly individualized techniques of artistic expression.

In brief, when we talk of these men as artists of the Renaissance, we do not mean that they all had a similar style or approach to life. We are pointing out that *all of them made major contributions to a rebirth of creative activity—or Renaissance—when it occurred in their countries.*

Interest in Music

Another important feature of the Renaissance was the expansion of interest in music. Among the new developments were the following: (1) a greater interest in the music of instruments in addition to singing, which had dominated European tastes; (2) a growth in the popularity of the *madrigal,* generally a non-religious song for several voices usually unaccompanied by instruments; (3) the start of the *oratorio,* a musical composition for singers and instrumentalists usually based on religious themes; and (4) the beginning of *opera,* a drama in which the roles were sung rather than spoken.

Music was in the Renaissance air, too! New instruments, such as the violin, were constructed. Musical compositions were spread by printing. Italian composers were particularly active: Palestrina (c. 1524–1594) wrote magnificent masses; and Monteverdi (1567–1643) composed madrigals, masses, and such fine operas that a modern authority, Professor Martin Bernstein, calls him "the first truly great opera composer."

Orphanages were often centers for music schools. A king celebrated his wedding by sponsoring an opera. And a brilliant violinist received a gift of a small town for his skillful performances!

This enthusiasm for music was filled with the spirit of the Renaissance. More and more, music became *secular*—that is, it concerned itself with expressing man's feelings toward the world in which he lived. Religious music continued to be important, but secular music gradually was winning the affection of the people. These changes in attitudes reflected the attitude that life was worth living and to be enjoyed. A new spirit had dawned as people began to express their hopes and aspirations, their joys and sorrows in lively music.

1. What are the characteristics of Renaissance architecture? What is Baroque?

2. Why do we call Leonardo da Vinci a "universal genius"?

3. What did Michelangelo contribute?

4. Compare the work of El Greco and Velasquez; of Rembrandt and Vermeer; of Holbein and Dürer.

5. Describe developments in music.

4. Education Is Affected by the Renaissance

The Renaissance features just described had a considerable effect on the informal education of the people. In formal education, although some efforts were made to obtain training for the "common people," most schools were organized for the wealthy and upper groups. These schools were influenced by humanism. The students spent most of their time studying Greek and Latin classics.

Several men of the Renaissance advanced ideas that greatly affected the thinking of later educators. Vittorino da Feltre (1378–1446) of Italy pointed out the importance of respecting individual differences in children. Erasmus of Rotterdam proposed that women should be given an equal chance with men to obtain an education. Roger Ascham (1515–1568) of England protested against the beating of school children.

John Comenius (1592–1670), a Moravian bishop, was the most important educator of the late Renaissance period. He suggested that students should study world history. He wrote the first textbook with illustrations for children, *The Visible World*. And he tried to present knowledge in a way that would interest the child. Comenius wanted to remove all unpleasantness from the schools. For, as he put it:

It will be very well worth the [trouble]... that the scare-crows may be taken away out of Wisdom's Gardens.

The greatest effect of the Renaissance on education was the increasing secularization of the schools. Schools became interested in teaching about affairs of this world, as well as about religious matters. Religion began to lose its powerful grip on education.

■ Check on Your Reading

1. What subjects did students concentrate on in the schools?

2. What modern educational ideas were held by da Feltre? by John Comenius?

3. What ideas did Erasmus and Roger Ascham have about education?

4. State the greatest effect of the Renaissance on education.

CULTURAL CHARACTERISTICS of Europe in the Renaissance

Today crowds of visitors still hurry to the Louvre art museum in Paris to attempt to interpret the *Mona Lisa*, Leonardo da Vinci's beautiful portrait of a woman with a strange smile. Each person views her mysterious smile in terms of his own life experiences as either sad or happy.

In a sense, the same point can be made about the Renaissance in Europe. Each scholar who views the Renaissance interprets it from his own point of view, varying with his background, personality, training, and research. Who can say which man's interpretation is right?

On the other hand, the scholars' lack of agreement as to the true nature of the Renaissance provides us with one point on which we can agree: *diversity was one of the principal characteristics of the period.* The Renaissance was not a neatly organized, clearly defined, uniform period with similar features everywhere. On the contrary, it was marked by great variety. As one scholar writes: . . . this sense of diversities of Renaissance humanism is possibly the most significant feature of scholarship today. . . .

Bearing in mind that variety was the spice of Renaissance life, we can say that *in general* the cultural characteristics of Europe in the Renaissance were:

The influence of the culture of ancient Greece and Rome on the lives of the leaders of the time.

A humanistic approach to life—that is, an attitude in which men eagerly sought to live as fully as possible in this world.

Extraordinary creativity, particularly in literature, art, and architecture.

The Renaissance did not break sharply with the past. Rather, it built on man's heritage from ancient and medieval times. The creative spirit that marked many aspects of the Renaissance never completely died out. It lives on wherever individuals create beauty and then try to surpass the beauty they have created.

MAN AND HIS CULTURE

Let's Meet the People!

This sketch is based on *The Book of the Courtier* by Baldassare Castiglione, 1948, E. P. Dutton & Co., Inc., trans. by Sir Thomas Hoby, Everyman's Library; and "Galateo of Manners and Behaviors" from *Renaissance and Reformation* by Henry Lucas, 1934, Harper & Brothers.

A Renaissance Gentleman

The Renaissance gentleman was happy that he was "neither of the least, nor of the greatest size," for he did not wish to stand out in height or weight. Similarly, he rarely went to extremes. He believed that for ordinary apparel, "a black color has a better grace in garments than any other, and though not thoroughly black, yet somewhat dark." His clothes for recreation were "pompous and rich"; and his armor was decorated with "sightly and merry colors."

The Renaissance gentleman often used his fork, and he knew that it was unmannerly "to lay his nose upon the cup where another must drink; or upon the meat that another must eat, to the end to smell unto it. . . ."

The Renaissance gentleman was an excellent writer. He used "gorgeous and fine words out of every part of Italy . . . [as well as] some . . . terms both French and Spanish."

He also had some understanding of Latin and Greek. He spoke with tact and grace.

The Renaissance gentleman was a fine athlete. He rode gracefully, wrestled cleverly, swam with ease, and was efficient in "feats of arms." In addition, he could paint and play the flute fairly well.

The gentleman was a man of honor. "[He was] no babbler . . . no liar, no boaster, nor fond flatterer, but . . . keeping him always within his bounds." When he joked, he had "a respect to the time, to the persons, to his degree." When he fell in love, he did not boast about his romance. When he made friends, he tried to do so with "men of estimation that are noble and known to be good."

The Renaissance gentleman was no saint. There were many times when he did not follow proper rules of conduct. Nevertheless, he tried to lead a full life and to serve his Prince faithfully.

CHAPTER REVIEW

REVIEW and DISCUSSION

1. Identify the people and explain the events and terms on p. 248.

2. Why did the Renaissance begin in the cities that had become trading centers in the medieval period?

3. If a person believed that the principal purpose of his life on earth was to prepare for the next world, how might he live? If a person believed that the principal purpose of his life was to enjoy his earthly existence, how might he live?

4. Do you agree with the humanists or the medievalists? Why?

5. Machiavelli observed that the end justifies the means. Do you agree? Give examples to support your position.

6. Is a study of Latin and Greek necessary today to be an educated man? Why?

7. Why did art and music need to be supported by wealthy individuals during the Renaissance? What new means of support are emerging?

8. Study reproductions of da Vinci's "Mona Lisa" and "The Last Supper." What represents the qualities of strength and of gentleness?

9. Can you think of any other genius with the many interests and abilities of da Vinci? Give reasons for your choice.

10. Why did a king want a court painter or musician? Why would one accept the job?

11. Why do Renaissance painting and literature still appeal to people today?

12. It is said that the Renaissance affected the rich more than the poor. What do you think? Why?

ACTIVITIES

1. Visit an art museum to view Renaissance art. Check the pictures for the features of Renaissance art.

2. Write a short biography of a Renaissance writer, painter, architect, or musician.

3. Attend a Shakespearean play or watch one on TV. If possible, read the play first.

4. Stage an exhibit of Renaissance art in your classroom.

5. Write a summary of the new ideas in Renaissance painting, music, architecture, and literature.

6. Consult references to find out the story of why and how a famous work was painted. Suggestions: Dürer's "The Praying Hands," or da Vinci's "Mona Lisa."

7. Listen to some records of music written during the Renaissance. Identify the characteristics of this music.

PAST and PRESENT

1. What kind of work do we classify as "creative" today? Do today's creative people have talents similar to those that the cultural leaders of the Renaissance had?

2. What rulers of our own period do you think follow Machiavellian ideas? Explain why you think they are Machiavellian.

3. What evidence is there that the Renaissance is still going on today?

SUGGESTED READINGS

Basic books: CHENEY, SHELDON W., *New World History of Art*, Chaps. 16, 18, 20–23, Viking.
SMITH, GOLDWIN, *The Heritage of Man*, Chap. 19, Scribner.
TAYLOR, R. SHERWOOD, *An Illustrated History of Science*, Chap. 2, Praeger.

Special accounts: DAVIS, WILLIAM S., *Life in Elizabethan Days*, Harper.
MILLS, DOROTHY, *Renaissance and Reformation Times*, Putnam.

Biography and Fiction: CHANDLER, ANNA C., *Story-Lives of Master Artists*, Lippincott. Short biographies of great artists.
ROSS, JAMES BRUCE, and MCLAUGHLIN, MARY MARTIN, (eds.), *The Portable Renaissance Reader*, Viking. A voluminous amount of short selections of source material by Renaissance people.
THOMPSON, STITH, and GASSNER, JOHN, (eds.), *Our Heritage of World Literature*, Holt.

Chapter 17 The Rise of National States in Europe

KEYNOTE   In the fifteenth century, the French lyric poet François Villon wrote:

> Let him meet beasts that breathe out fiery rain,
>
> . . . .
>
> Who would wish ill unto the realm of France.
>
> . . . .
>
> Or sell him to the [slave buyer], to chain
> And harness like an ox, the scurvy clown!
>
> . . . .
>
> Who would wish ill unto the realm of France.

Thus, Villon dramatically expressed his loyalty to his nation, rather than to any feudal lord.

Such lines would not have been thought of in the eleventh century, when the people of Europe owed their loyalty to local feudal communities. It is clear that one of the key features of the period from 1100 to 1500 was *the rise of national states in Europe.*

Key People   *Henry II · Henry VII · Philip Augustus · Joan of Arc · Averroës · Ferdinand II · Isabella · Ivan III · Maximilian I · Suleiman the Magnificent*

Key Places   *Hastings · Runnymede · England · France · Spain · Castile · Aragon · Portugal · Muscovy · Kiev · Novgorod · Kulikovo · Holy Roman Empire · Ottoman Empire*

Key Events   *Norman conquest of England · King John accepts Magna Carta · Hundred Years' War · Wars of the Roses · Unification of Spain · Russians accept Orthodox Christianity · Muscovy extends its power · Golden Bull of 1356 · Ottoman Empire expands*

Key Terms   *nation · jury system · common law · Parliament · Estates-General · Cortes · Inquisition · Slavs · Electors*

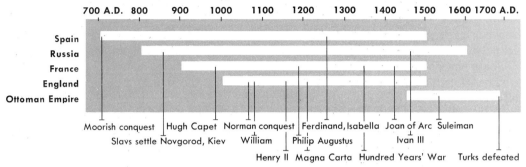

1. Introducing the Nation

The years from 1100 to 1500 saw the beginning of national states, or nations, in Europe. The term *nation* refers to a people who feel united in a common loyalty to a country that occupies a definite territory and has its own political existence.

England Grows into a Nation

For many centuries, men were loyal to families or military chiefs or religious officials or heads of dynasties or other leaders—but not to nations. It was not until late in history that the first nations began to appear in Europe. Even then, it was the kings and nobles who stood for the nation, while most of the people continued to feel that their own principal loyalty was to local regions.

Many factors helped to unite people into nations. Among these were the following:

1. GEOGRAPHY. Geographic barriers, such as mountains and large bodies of water, sometimes separated and protected one group from other groups.

2. COMMON GOVERNMENT. It was difficult to form a nation so long as the people owed their allegiance to a variety of local rulers. As feudalism disintegrated, it was possible to set up strong central governments in several countries.

3. COMMON LANGUAGE. People living in the same area often developed the same language. This common or vernacular language helped knit them into a nation. A common language also led to common cultural expressions in literature and songs.

4. COMMON CUSTOMS AND TRADITIONS. People felt close to those who respected and followed the same customs and traditions.

England was one of the first countries to grow into a nation. Its development was by no means an easy one. By the eleventh century, the Anglo-Saxon kingdom established by Alfred the Great (871–900) and his successors had lost strength. As a result, the Danes challenged and defeated the Anglo-Saxon armies. Canute, a Danish ruler, became king of England. Shortly after Canute's death, Anglo-Saxon leaders regained their power.

Celts, Romans, Danes, and Anglo-Saxons all had left their marks on England. Then came the *Normans*, a people related to the Danes. The Normans were descendants of Viking northmen who had sailed from the region of modern Scandinavia and settled in northern France. In time, they merged with the French inhabitants, and the region became known as Normandy.

The Normans Conquer England

In 1066 A.D. the Normans claimed that they had a legal right to govern England and attacked the country. The leader of the Normans was William; the king of England was Harold. The decisive engagement was the Battle of Hastings, in which the Normans were victorious. The Normans seized control of the country, and William the Conqueror became king.

The Norman conquest had four great effects on English history: (1) William greatly strengthened the position of the king and the central government by making the feudal lords of England swear allegiance to him. (2) The Normans influenced the culture of England, particularly in art, architecture, and language. The development of the English language was affected by the Norman-French tongue. However, research shows that the English borrowed the most French words in the era from 1250 to 1650—centuries after the Norman conquest. (3) Like previous invaders, the Normans gradually intermarried with the inhabitants of England. As a result, the term *Englishman* today refers to a people whose ancestry includes Romans, Britons, Normans, Anglo-Saxons, Danes, and other groups. (4) The conquest tied England to the problems of the Norman dukes in France and involved the country in French affairs until 1453.

Henry II Restores Order

After the rule of William the Conqueror and his successors, ambitious and greedy barons refused to accept the leadership of the king. England again became disorganized, and civil conflicts occurred.

About the middle of the twelfth century, Henry II became king. He was the first in a line of rulers known as the *Plantagenets*. Henry II (1154–1189), whose father was the French Count of Anjou and whose mother was related to William the Conqueror, inherited the land of England plus control of a considerable part of France. By marrying Eleanor of Aquitaine, Henry increased his French possessions to include about half of France. Henry's control of French territory had two significant results: (1) It involved him deeply in the affairs of the Continent. (2) It later formed one of the greatest obstacles to the unification of France.

Henry restored order by making the barons obey him. He required all freemen to keep arms and be ready to defend their king and country. Henry also tried to strengthen his hold on Scotland and Ireland.

Ireland, which consisted of kingdoms made up of clans, was said to be "almost a

■ *This scene from the Bayeux Tapestry, which is a pictorial narrative of the Norman invasion of England, shows part of the great Norman fleet under William's command embarking for England, 1066. William and his men defeated King Harold at the Battle of Hastings.*

■ *The towers of Durham Cathedral can be seen rising above the river. This cathedral, begun in 1093, is the finest example of Norman architecture in England. The Normans replaced the Saxon cathedrals and abbeys with their own grander buildings.*

wilderness." Although Henry claimed to be "Lord of Ireland," the English did not gain full control of the country for centuries.

The Jury System Develops

Henry II also contributed to the growth of law. He found that in England "too many people were trying to administer too many kinds of law," and that church courts and nobles courts were involved in rivalry. He therefore tried to replace the chaotic system of feudal justice, which varied from region to region, with the more orderly system of "the king's justice." This important contribution was additional evidence of Henry's broad vision.

In 1166 Henry issued the Edict of Clarendon. This provided that:

twelve of the more legal men of [each district] . . . [should investigate] whether there is . . . any man who has been accused or publicly suspected of himself being a robber, or murderer, or thief. . . .

Such a man was to be brought to trial before one or more of the judges (often called "circuit judges") whom King Henry sent throughout the country.

Henry's edict contributed to the development of the jury system. It helped to spread the idea of the *grand jury.* A grand jury came to mean a group of people who decided whether or not an accused person should be brought to trial.

During the second half of Henry's reign, so-called *petit juries* (or trial juries) had begun to take over some of the duties of the judges. A petit (or petty) jury became a group of people who decided the guilt or innocence of the accused at the trial. Today we have both grand and petit juries in the United States.

Henry II did not know that he was helping to build the foundation for a future democratic jury system. His purpose in setting up his judicial system was to tighten his control of the country, protect

■ *This scene from a medieval manuscript shows the murder of Thomas à Becket. He had "made a laughingstock" of the king.*

They therefore tried to base many of their decisions on these "common customs of the realm." As a result of their judgments and those of latter-day judges, *common law*—that is, uniform law for all of England, based on common custom—gradually took the place of a variety of laws based on local customs.

Common law, which was law made by judges, did not continue to be based only on common customs. For example, when no uniform custom could be discovered, the judges sometimes drew up new rules, which became a part of common law. The distinctive feature of English common law was the development of the so-called *case system*. This meant that cases decided by judges were considered sources of law and *precedents* for future decisions. As Professors Hall and Albion explain:

Justice B, [in deciding a case] in Devonshire, might follow the precedent established by Justice A in Yorkshire five years earlier, or, if his case seemed slightly different, might decide otherwise, whereupon his new decision would serve as a precedent for the rest of the justices. This practice has gone on continuously down through the centuries. . . .

Years later, this system of common law was introduced into the American colonies, where it was adjusted to meet conditions in the New World. Today common law plays an important role in the dispensing of justice in the United States.

A black mark against Henry was his controversy with Thomas à Becket. Henry appointed Becket, a friend, Archbishop of Canterbury, expecting that he would help weaken the system of Church or canon law that competed with the king's law. However, Becket as archbishop firmly upheld the rights of the Church and Pope in England. A serious dispute arose over whether the royal authorities or the Church had the right to punish clergymen convicted of

the royal revenue, and see that justice was done. Nevertheless, he aided the development of democratic institutions by calling on some of the people to participate in the judicial function of government. His jurors had to investigate facts and swear that these facts were true. They gained experience with the machinery of government. Such experience was necessary if people were to learn to govern themselves.

Common Law Spreads Throughout England

The judges whom Henry II sent throughout England found that customs in one part of the country often differed from those in other areas. They also observed that a similarity in customs existed throughout the land on many matters.

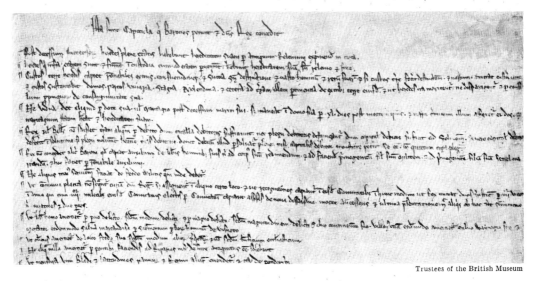

■ *These are the first few articles of the Magna Carta, as shown in an early Latin manuscript from the British Museum. The Magna Carta, granted by King John under pressure from the nobles, was a landmark in the development of democracy in England.*

crime in the bishops' courts. Finally, Henry in a fit of anger demanded to know why his subjects did not take action against Becket. Four of his nobles later murdered Becket in the Canterbury cathedral.

Henry claimed that he was innocent, but the Pope forced him to do penance, and the Church kept its right to punish its clergy. In addition, people with cases in Church courts had the right to appeal to Rome, ignoring Henry's royal courts.

King John Is Forced to Accept Magna Carta

John (1199–1216), a son of Henry II, became king of England at the end of the twelfth century. He planned to obtain more money by placing more taxes on land. To help him levy new taxes, King John permitted smaller landholders (or "knights of the shire") to attend the meetings of the *Great Council.*

The idea of the Great Council had developed during the years that followed the Norman invasion. The Council consisted of the most important men in the kingdom—nobles, religious leaders, and wealthy landowners. It met a few times each year, principally to advise the king on matters of policy and taxation. It also served as a special court of justice. The men who now were called by King John to join the Council did not rejoice at the king's "invitation." They knew that they were being asked so that the king could fill the treasury—and from taxes on their land!

In addition to levying unpopular taxes, King John interfered with the privileges of noblemen and wealthy landowners. These important men finally decided to check the king's power. In 1215 a group of barons brought their troops together on a meadow at Runnymede, west of London, and threatened to attack the king if he did not assure them of certain rights. The king finally gave in and affixed his royal seal on the famous document known as the *Magna Carta,* or Great Charter.

These were some of the provisions of the Magna Carta: (1) Earls and barons shall be fined only by their peers [that is, by their fellow earls and barons], and only in proportion to their offense. (2) No free man [most free men were nobles or religious leaders] shall be taken or imprisoned or dispossessed, or outlawed, or banished, or in any way destroyed, nor will [the king's men] go upon him . . . except by the legal judgment of his peers or by the law of the land. (3) To no one will [the king] sell, to no one will [the king] deny, or delay right or justice. (4) No taxes, except the customary feudal ones, shall be levied without the consent of the Great Council. (5) [The nobles] shall elect twenty-five barons of the kingdom . . . who ought with all their power [see that the king did not violate the Magna Carta].

Contrary to popular opinion, the Magna Carta was not concerned with giving the people democratic rights. The charter's provisions applied to barons and other noblemen, not to the "common people."

Nevertheless, the Magna Carta was a landmark in the growth of democracy because *it helped to establish the principle that the king's actions would have to be in keeping with the customs and laws of the country.*

A Two-House Parliament Evolves

In the latter part of the thirteenth century the nation grew stronger. King Edward I (1272–1307), an energetic ruler known as "Longshanks," succeeded in gaining control of North Wales. In 1295 Edward needed funds to help carry on a war, so he called together a Great Council. Some historians have named this council the "Model Parliament," the term Parliament coming from the French word *parler*, to speak. (Later, when it became so firmly established that knights of the shire [county] and representatives of boroughs could attend the Great Council, the word "Parliament" gradually replaced "Great Council.")

Edward's Model Parliament was an assembly that consisted of religious leaders, earls, barons, knights of the shire, and over one hundred seventy representatives from the towns. All of the members of the Model Parliament met in the same place. However, when they approved the king's taxes, they voted in three groups or "estates": (1) first estate—the clergy; (2) second estate—earls, barons, and knights; and (3) third estate—representatives of towns.

The three groups or "estates" in Parliament gradually—and without planning— became two. One group consisted of the nobles and higher clergymen. It resembled the old Great Council in membership and became known as the *House of Lords.* Men who went to the House of Lords were summoned as individuals; they were not elected. Later they inherited their right to be members of the House of Lords. The other group in Parliament consisted of knights of the shire and townsmen. It was called the *House of Commons.* Men who went to the House of Commons were elected from towns and boroughs, although for many years very few people had the right to vote.

The separation between the two houses was completed during the fourteenth century. Parliament had become *bicameral*; that is, it had two houses. The development of a two-house Parliament was important to the growth of democracy because it permitted the elected members to vote by themselves in their own chamber. It protected them from being overruled by the nobles and higher clergy. Had all of the members of Parliament met together, the elected members always could have been outvoted by the more numerous lords.

In the beginning, the principal job of Parliament was to approve taxes. This was an extremely important power, since Parliament sometimes could force the king to introduce reforms by refusing to grant him funds until he accepted the desired changes. After 1400, largely as a result of its authority to grant or withhold money, Parliament won the right to help in making laws.

The English Language Helps to Unite the People

The English language was as important to the growth of the nation as the activities of Parliament, for the development of a common tongue helped to unite the people. For many years, French was the language of the upper classes in England. Latin was used in scholarly works. However, most of the people did not understand either French or Latin. The ordinary speech of the people was a mixture from the tongues of the Anglo-Saxons, Danes, Normans, and other groups. This speech became known as *English*, and by the middle of the fourteenth century most men in the country spoke some form of it.

Writers like Geoffrey Chaucer (1340–1400) helped to give the language sufficient unity and order so that it could be used successfully in literature. Using the East Midland dialect of England, Chaucer wrote *The Canterbury Tales*. John Wyclif, a religious reformer, also made a major contribution by translating the Bible into English.

As the English language became widely used throughout the country, the people were drawn closer together. An Englishman now could learn more about his fellow-countrymen.

Henry VII Strengthens the Central Government

English kings had inherited lands in France. This led to rivalry between these two countries which resulted in war. This war, known as the Hundred Years' War, lasted from 1337 to 1453 (p. 281). It was interrupted by periods of truce which were followed again by periods of war. After many English victories, the French rallied under Joan of Arc to drive the English out of their country. England lost all her territory in France except Calais. Many men had lost their lives, and considerable property had been destroyed on both sides.

Soon after the Hundred Years' War ended, England was split by civil wars between two groups seeking the crown. One group was the House of Lancaster, which took a red rose as its symbol; the other was the House of York, which was represented by a white rose. The battles between these groups are known as the *Wars of the Roses* (1455–1485).

The House of Lancaster finally overcame the House of York. In 1485 Henry Tudor, one of the leaders of Lancaster, became king as Henry VII (1485–1509). The English monarchs from Henry VII to Queen Elizabeth I are known as the *Tudors*.

The nobles of England had been greatly weakened by the fighting in the Wars of the Roses. Henry VII further diminished their power by adding many of their lands to his own. Henry also enforced the collection of money owed to the central government and won the support of business men and traders by encouraging their activities. By these and other methods, Henry made the position of king one of great power.

By 1500, England had several features of a nation: (1) common government (with a king at its head and a Parliament), (2) common language, and (3) common customs and traditions.

■ **Check on Your Reading**

1. What factors helped to unite people into nations?

2. Evaluate the effects of the Norman conquest on England.

3. How were English law and justice changed by the work of Henry II?

4. Why was Magna Carta important?

5. How did a two-house Parliament arise?

2. France Develops into a Nation

France was another of the first countries to develop into a nation. In the tenth century feudal lords elected a nobleman named Hugh Capet to be the king of a small region of the former territory of Charlemagne. This region was destined to grow into the country of France. Hugh Capet (987–996) did much to establish the *Capetian dynasty* in France.

The Capetians Extend Their Power

The position of the kings of the new dynasty was strengthened by the Crusades. Many of the noblemen who were rivals of the king left their lands to fight in the East and lost power in France. In the growing cities, merchants and business men, who needed the protection of a central government, also supported the monarch against the feudal lords. As a result of these and other factors, the Capetians were able to extend their power.

The activities of the Capetian dynasty were one of the first landmarks in the development of the French nation. The Capetian rulers (1) brought a considerable part of the territory of France under their control; (2) established a system of handing down power from the king to his eldest son which lessened the danger of civil war over the question of succession; and (3) indirectly encouraged the use of the language that was to develop into French. Out of its Celtic, Latin, and Germanic past, a type of French began to appear on official documents as early as the ninth century. Then in the fourteenth and fifteenth centuries local dialects gave way to the dialect of the region around Paris. A common language helped to unite the people of France.

Philip Augustus Strengthens Government

Philip Augustus, a shrewd and vigorous man, became king in 1180 and reigned for forty-three years. He was greatly troubled because one of his most important vassals, King John of England, still controlled a considerable part of France. When John violated a feudal custom concerning marriage and then refused to come to Philip's court to explain, Philip took over John's territory in France except Aquitaine.

Philip Augustus also (1) diminished the territorial holdings and power of the feudal lords; (2) appointed men to public office who were truly the king's men (*les royaux*) and would obey him, not the feudal lords; (3) gave townsmen more influence in government affairs; (4) aided trade and changed the administration of finances; and (5) made Paris the permanent capital.

By his activities, Philip Augustus strengthened the monarchy and greatly increased the royal possessions in France. As the noted historian Albert Guérard points out: "Feudalism and monarchy were still blended, as in dissolving pictures; but *the trend was unmistakably in favor of the central power.*"

The Growth of Democracy Lags

Although France was evolving as a nation, she did not have the growth in democracy that England did. For example, under the Capetian dynasty *parlements* had developed in France. Parlements were higher *courts of law* that registered edicts of the king and could raise questions concerning those edicts that were not in keeping with the country's laws. On the surface, this seemed to be a step toward democracy. However, if the members of these courts dared to protest against the legality of an edict, the king might say: "You supply me with no remedy [to take the place of this law]"—and his edict would not be changed.

The *Estates-General* had been formed in 1302 by Philip the Fair (1285–1314), a handsome man whose contemporaries compared him with "the Great Owl, whose splendid golden eyes, by daylight, are fixed and expressionless." The Estates-General was a kind of parliament and consisted of three estates or classes: First Estate—clergy; Second Estate—nobles; Third Estate—merchants and large landowners not included in the noble class.

The Estates-General was called into session from time to time to make it easier for the king to collect taxes, but it had little power. It was reported by people of the time that "all that happens at the meetings is talking and bowing. . . ."

The point to remember is this: *While England was developing into a nation governed by democratic traditions and principles, France was emerging as a nation governed by men who sought absolute power.*

The Hundred Years' War Disrupts France

From 1337 to 1453 France was disrupted by an extended war with England. This so-called *Hundred Years' War*, which was interrupted by long periods of truce, was caused by several factors. These included the struggle for the throne of France, and the competition between England and France for land and control of trade.

King Edward III of England (1327–1377) claimed that he had inherited the right to rule France from his mother, who was sister of the last French king. The French denied this because of a very old law which prohibited the throne from being passed on through a woman heir. In 1346 Edward invaded France. In the battles that followed, French knights, clothed in their heavy and awkward armor, were defeated by versatile English troops armed with longbows and arrows.

In the 1420's, the English, aided by the Burgundians of France, controlled important parts of France. They had won many great battles and had gained territory by treaty. They threatened to sweep through all of the country.

■ *In 1328, England controlled much French territory. This led to the Hundred Years' War (1337–1453) between England and France. In 1346 Edward III invaded France, capturing much territory. Under Joan of Arc, French troops rallied, defeating the English; only Calais remained English.*

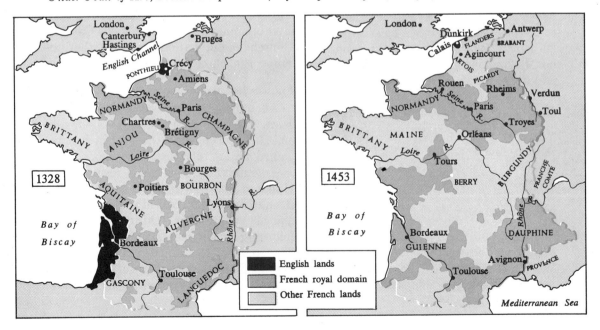

■ *A miniature painting from the* St. Albans Chronicle, *a 15th century manuscript, depicts the Battle of Agincourt. The English troops armed with longbows and arrows successfully defeated the French knights in their heavy armor.*

Joan of Arc: Symbol of a People

In this crisis, a young French girl came to rally her country's forces. She was Joan of Arc (1412–1431), a sturdy, dark-haired country girl, plain in appearance but strong in courage and determination.

Joan was a deeply religious person who claimed that she had heard "voices" from heaven. These "voices" had instructed her to help restore the French ruler to power. Although there were many who mocked her, Joan finally gained the support of several high officials. They permitted her to lead French troops against the English. Joan boldly issued a warning to the enemy:

You, men of England, have no right to be in this kingdom of France, the King of Heaven commands you through me . . . to go back where you belong; which if you fail to do, I will make such a *ha-hai* [commotion] as will be eternally remembered.

When the English refused to leave French soil, Joan and her forces attacked. What a *ha-hai* it was! So successful was she that the English troops were forced to retreat. The weak French ruler, who formerly was not certain that he could hold any part of the country, now was properly crowned Charles VII, king of France.

Joan of Arc later was captured, sold to the English, and tried for heresy and other crimes. Sentenced to be burned alive, she was put to death at nineteen. Despite her tragic end—partially because of it—Joan later became a saint of the Roman Catholic Church and a national symbol that inspired Frenchmen with a love of country.

France Becomes a Strong National State

About twenty years after the death of Joan, the Hundred Years' War finally ended. By this time the French had regained most of their territory (map, p. 281).

An important long-range result of the Hundred Years' War was that it helped to strengthen the position of the French king and his government. During the war the following developments had occurred: (1) The wealthy townsmen and traders had become financial supporters of the king because their business activities depended on having a stable and unified government. (2) Many nobles were killed; others lost control of much of their land. (3) The king had obtained an army paid by the national government, and he did not have to rely on his nobles for military assistance. All three developments aided the growth of the central government and nation.

France continued to grow as a national state. King Louis XI (1461–1483) added considerable territory, encouraged trade, organized an extensive postal system, and set up a powerful central administration.

Most important of all, Louis XI greatly increased the power of the monarchy over the feudal lords. As the fifteenth century drew to a close, France appeared well on its way to becoming strong and unified.

■ **Check on Your Reading**

1. How did the Capetian rulers help make France a nation?

2. How did Philip Augustus strengthen the monarchy and increase French possessions?

3. How democratic were the *parlements*?

4. What effects did the Hundred Years' War have on France as a nation? on England?

Archives de France, AE^{II} 447 (*inset*)

■ *This heroic statue shows Joan of Arc, who led the French forces to victory in the Hundred Years' War. The inset was drawn at her trial by a scribe, who added the sword and standard.*

3. Spain Emerges as a Nation

Another of the early nations in Europe was Spain. The history of Spain began many centuries before the birth of Christ. Among the earliest inhabitants of the country were the so-called *Iberians*. The Iberians may have come to Spain from northern Africa. Later they interbred with Celtic invaders who moved into the Iberian Peninsula from central Europe.

Important regions in the peninsula were held, in turn, by the Phoenicians, the Greeks, the Carthaginians, and the Romans. The Romans called the peninsula *Iberia* or *Hispania*. Spain (or Hispania) remained a province of the Roman Empire for over six hundred years, during which time the Romans introduced Christianity, Roman law, and the Latin language.

Beginning about the fifth century A.D., Germanic tribes swept through the Iberian Peninsula. One of these tribes, the *Visigoths*, dominated it. The Visigoths, many of whom later became Christians, ruled Spain until the early part of the eighth century. Then in 711 A.D. the *Moors* of North Africa attacked Spain. They overran the Visigoth kingdom and conquered most of the country. The defenders were forced to fall back to the mountainous regions of the northwest.

■ *The Court of the Lions in the Palace of the Alhambra, Granada, is the finest example of Moorish art and architecture. The balanced columns, harmonious arches, and decorations make the court beautiful.*

The Moors Build a Great Civilization

The Moors were descendants of those Arabs who had intermarried with the inhabitants of North Africa. They were Moslems. The Moors now proceeded to build a great civilization in Spain, a civilization that has influenced the people of Spain—and the world—to the present.

The cities that the Moors constructed in Spain were admirable settings for their many economic and cultural activities. Cordova in the tenth century ranked with Constantinople and Baghdad as a center of beauty and culture. It had attractive palaces, lovely mosques, over one hundred thousand homes, and a university.

The Moors Excel in Art, Architecture, and Literature

The Moors gained particular fame for their art and architecture. Their artistic work in pottery, metal, mosaics, and textiles was outstanding. The Moors also helped to show the beauty of these architectural features: (1) the horseshoe-shaped arch; (2) arabesque decorations (those with interlacing lines that often give the impression of flowers, leaves, and branches); (3) carved wooden doors and ceilings; and (4) graceful columns.

"The Court of the Lions" in the Palace of the Alhambra is an example of Moorish art and architecture at their best.

In addition to achievements in art and architecture, the Moslem period in Spain was marked by the production of outstanding literature. The Moslems were not the only ones to write effectively. Jewish writers also created literature of beauty in the Hebrew language. After the Romans captured Jerusalem in 70 A.D., many Jews left Palestine and settled throughout the world. A number of them eventually came to Spain. During the height of Moslem civilization in Spain, poets of the Hebrew language were as active as their Moslem neighbors in producing literature (p. 207).

Moslems and Jews Are Active in Science and Medicine

The Moslems and Jews of Spain also did valuable work in medicine and in the theory and use of science. *In medicine,* Maimonides, the brilliant Jewish philosopher and physician, encouraged the use of hygienic methods of living. Ibn Wāfid, a Moslem scholar, drew up a treatise on drugs that could be used to fight diseases. Albucasis, a Moslem court physician, compiled and added information on surgery. His writings later helped Europeans develop their practice of surgery.

In scientific knowledge, Averroës, a Spanish-Arabian philosopher, helped to modify and pass on to others the knowledge of Aristotle. Ibn-al-Awwam, a Moslem living in Seville, completed an important treatise on the properties of soil and on the nature of almost six hundred plants.

In the use of scientific knowledge, more scientific methods of farming and industry were introduced in the country. The orange tree and several other fruit trees of Asia were brought to Spain and from there to the rest of Europe. A paper manufacturing industry was established in Spain. (The manufacture of paper probably had originated in the East.) Knowledge of the techniques of paper manufacture was later passed on by the Moslems to the people of Europe. Paper combined with the knowledge of printing put books within the reach of many more people.

Moslems and Jews in Spain were active also in the study of mathematics, astronomy, optics, and other fields.

Portugal Becomes a Separate Kingdom

A Moorish government continued to exist in Spain for almost eight hundred years. During that time, the Christians who had fled to the north formed a number of small states. These Christian kingdoms made an effort to reconquer Spain. Alfonso VI, king of Castile, one of the most important Christian states, captured Toledo from the Moors in the latter part of the eleventh century.

Significant changes also were made in the land that was to become modern Portugal. A French leader, Henry of Burgundy, aided Castile in its drive south. As a reward, he was permitted to marry a princess who held territory in Portugal. Henry was recognized as Count of Portugal. His son, Alfonso Henriques, pushed back the Moors in the country and made Lisbon his capital. Alfonso Henriques became the first king of Portugal (1139–1185).

Portugal continued to be a separate kingdom until she was returned to Spain near the end of the sixteenth century. In 1640 Portugal won back her independence and has remained independent.

A Common Language Helps Link the People

Efforts to unify Spain showed important results in the thirteenth century. Alfonso X (1221–1284), king of Castile, contributed greatly to unification by working to establish the Castilian language as the national tongue. He stimulated cultural activities and supported the following measures: (1) The accepted form of the Castilian language had to be used in all legal matters in the territory that he controlled. (2) Under his sponsorship, the Old Testament was translated into the Castilian language. (3) Under his direction, *Las Siete Partidas* (*The Seven Parts*) was prepared in the Castilian language. *The Seven Parts* was a type of encyclopedia of laws, rules, and opinions. Drawing heavily on Roman law but adding to it, *The Seven Parts* later had considerable influence on jurists.

In these ways, Alfonso X helped the Castilian language to gain in popularity over other tongues and dialects in the country. In the thirteenth century this language, which became known as *Spanish,* was widely used throughout central Spain. A common tongue gradually made the people feel closer to each other and assisted in the unification of Spain.

SPAIN IN 1490

Christian lands

Moorish lands

FRANCE

K. OF NAVARRE TO CASTILE 1512

KINGDOM
Tordesillas

TO CASTILE 1479

• Salamanca

KINGDOM OF ARAGON

Barcelona

OF LEON

KINGDOM OF PORTUGAL TO SPAIN 1580-1640

• Toledo

Valencia

BALEARIC IS.

Lisbon

AND CASTILE

Cordova •

• Seville   Granada •

K. OF GRANADA
TO CASTILE 1492

Mediterranean Sea

■ *Spain, in 1490, consisted of separate Christian states and the Moorish kingdom of Granada. How did Spain become unified?*

A Marriage Unites Rulers and Kingdoms

By the fifteenth century the Moors had been driven far into southern Spain. The rest of the country remained divided into separate Christian kingdoms. The most important states were Castile and Aragon.

In 1469 Ferdinand, heir to the throne of Aragon, married Isabella, daughter of the king of Castile. Their marriage was extremely important because it resulted eventually in the union of Aragon and Castile (1479) and the formation of a single nation. Even after their union, Castile and Aragon kept parts of their governments separate.

Ferdinand and Isabella now worked hard to build their country into a great nation. They restored order to Spain, reorganized the court system, and conquered the last Moorish stronghold in Granada in 1492. Isabella also supported Christopher Columbus and other explorers. Spain built an empire that was to include lands in America, Europe, Africa, and Asia.

Ferdinand and Isabella helped to build the nation and to strengthen the powers of the central government, but they did not contribute to the development of democracy. For example, assemblies known as *Cortes* had appeared in Spain about the twelfth century. The kings had decided who would be permitted to join these assemblies, but many Cortes did have the power to vote taxes and to petition the kings for new laws or for reforms of old laws. Ferdinand and Isabella seriously checked the Cortes' growth by rarely consulting them.

Jews and Moslems Are Driven from Spain

Ferdinand and Isabella, the so-called "Catholic Kings," also felt that it was to the country's best interests if everyone accepted Catholicism. In addition, they supported the dreaded *Inquisition,* an institution designed to fight heresy. Its work revolved around ecclesiastical (church related) courts whose origin could be traced back to the thirteenth century. One of their chief duties was to try people who opposed the doctrines of the Catholic Church. Those who were found guilty were handed over to some civil authority. They could be fined, imprisoned, or burned at the stake!

The Jews and Moslems suffered greatly under the Inquisition. In 1492, a decree stated that any Jew who did not give up his beliefs and accept Catholicism would be expelled from Spain. By this and other decrees, thousands of Jews and Moslems were forced to leave. Many who went into exile were outstanding scientists, physicians, and merchants. The government of Spain had tried to add strength. All that it accomplished was to weaken the nation.

■ **Check on Your Reading**

1. What contributions did the Moors and Jews make to Spanish civilization?

2. How did Portugal become independent?

3. How did Ferdinand and Isabella build a nation?

4. Russia Moves toward Nationhood

Although it became a united nation later than England, France, and Spain, Russia also had moved in the direction of nationhood before the sixteenth century.

Early History of Russia

Our knowledge of the ancestors of today's Russians is limited, but we know that in the early centuries after the birth of Christ there were *Slavs* in the land between the Vistula River (in modern Poland) and the Dnieper River (in modern Russia). The Slavs were an Indo-European people whose origin is still in doubt. They probably migrated in several directions, and some of them moved eastward into Russia. The eastern Slavs became the ancestors of today's Russians. Other Slavs moved into Poland and the Balkan area.

On the great Russian plain, long overrun by invaders, the eastern Slavs developed such towns as Novgorod and Kiev. These towns were on the trade route between the Baltic and the Black seas. During the second half of the ninth century, a people known as Varangians (who were of Scandinavian origin) gained control of Novgorod and adjacent areas. Rurik, a Norse chief, probably became the first prince of the Novgorod region.

From here Varangians and Slavs moved to the town of Kiev, located on the Dnieper River. Kiev became the center of a Varangian-Slavic state dominated by the Slavic culture. The people and the state of Kiev gradually became known as *Russian*. The Kievan Russians built up an important culture. In time, Kiev grew to be larger in size than most west European cities.

The Russians Adopt the Eastern Orthodox Faith

The Russians of Kiev had considerable contact with the Byzantine Empire. They fought, traded, and exchanged ideas with the peoples of the Byzantine world. About 988 A.D. Vladimir, the Kievan ruler, was converted to the Christian faith of the Greek or Eastern Orthodox Church. Shortly after, he proclaimed this faith to be the religion of all his subjects.

The Russians of Kiev had believed in many gods and spirits. When they adopted Christianity, it was difficult for them to understand all of the ideas of their new religion. Nevertheless, the Eastern Orthodox Church affected them in at least four important ways: (1) It helped to make the

■ *The state of Muscovy was founded in the 13th century. Under Ivan III, Muscovy expanded, becoming the center from which Russia emerged.*

THE EXPANSION OF MUSCOVY

The Principality of Moscow in 1300
Grand Principality of Moscow in 1462
Acquisitions under Ivan III, 1462-1505

0   Scale of Miles   650

■ *The Bell Tower of Ivan III in the Kremlin, Moscow, has characteristics of Byzantine architecture. Ivan thought of himself as the heir to Byzantine greatness and of Moscow as the "third Rome."*

Russians feel closer to each other by giving them a common religion. (2) It aided the Russians to develop a literature. The language used by the Orthodox Church in Russia was known as Church Slavonic. Its alphabet had been developed in the ninth century by the missionary Cyril (hence "Cyrillic" alphabet). Translations of religious books were made in Church Slavonic and passed on to the Russians. In this way some Russians learned their first written language, and they used this language to create a religious and secular literature of their own. (3) It supported the idea of the "divine right" of the ruler; that is, the Orthodox Church defended the belief that the monarch was supreme in power and responsible only to God for his acts. (4) It contributed to the separation of Russia from Roman Catholic western Europe.

Tatars Dominate Russia

The Russians of the Kievan period accomplished much. They built lovely churches, developed trade, drew up their first code of laws, and allied themselves through marriage with the ruling families of Europe. However, they were unable to eliminate civil conflicts. In the thirteenth century the Kievan state fell before the onslaught of the "Golden Horde"—the fierce Mongols or Tatars from the east—led by the dreaded Batu Khan, grandson of Genghis Khan. This occurred shortly after the Mongols had overrun northern China. The city of Kiev was conquered in 1240.

The Tatars dominated Russia for many years. Although they were defeated by Russian princes in the great battle of Kulikovo in 1380, the Tatars continued to hold land in Russia until the latter part of the fifteenth century. During that time they permitted Russians to collect taxes for them and to help administer the country. These Russians gradually adopted for themselves the Tatar idea that a ruler should govern autocratically. The Tatar belief that a ruler should demand absolute obedience continued to exist in Russia long after the Tatars had been driven out.

The Russian Nation Emerges from Muscovy

During the Tatar period, the Russian principality of Muscovy rose to importance. Located in a region between the Volga and Oka rivers, Muscovy had access to a number of water and land routes. It was therefore strategically situated.

Under Ivan III (1462–1505)—or Ivan the Great—Muscovy developed both as a state and as an autocracy. Ivan strengthened his state by (1) extending the power of Muscovy over Novgorod and other territories in the north (within another hundred years the Muscovite state included most of the principalities in Russia); (2) encouraging expansion to the west, east, and the Baltic Sea; and (3) using tactics that helped end the remaining Tatar control.

At the same time, he strengthened his autocratic rule by (1) depriving Novgorod of the right to call assemblies; (2) weakening the power of the nobles (or *boyars*); and (3) bringing the Russian Orthodox Church more closely under his control and using it to support autocracy.

As a result of these measures, Muscovy became the center from which there gradually emerged one of the major nations of the world. That nation was Russia.

■ Check on Your Reading

1 How did conversion to Orthodox Christianity affect Russia's later history?

2. How did Tatar rule affect the development of attitudes toward government?

3. How did Ivan the Great change Russia?

5. Germany and Italy Fail to Form Nations

While England, France, Spain, and later Russia were developing into national states, two areas in Europe remained divided. These were the regions that today are the nations of Germany and Italy.

In 962 A.D. Otto the Great was crowned emperor of what historians later called the Holy Roman Empire. Otto's territory included considerable German and Italian land and ran from the North and Baltic seas to southern Italy (map, p. 176).

The structure of the early Holy Roman Empire had a major effect on the future of Germany and Italy. Otto and his successors had to spend so much time sending expeditions into unsettled Italy to keep order that they did not have the time or strength to unify their holdings in Germany. When a Holy Roman Emperor went to Italy to protect his power there, his feudal lords in Germany might rise against him. When he remained in Germany, leaders in Italy might shake off his control. The emperor faced the impossible task of balancing a geographic seesaw where either Germany or Italy rose defiantly against him. As a result, both Italy and Germany remained divided lands.

Germany

In Germany, no Holy Roman Emperor was strong enough to unite the country permanently. The feudal lords became a variety of princes, dukes, counts, and bishops who ruled many separate states. At the same time, the strong cities in the north set up independent governments.

Three developments important to the later history of the Holy Roman Empire occurred between 1273 and 1519.

(1) In 1273 Rudolf of Hapsburg became emperor. He came from a minor German noble family with most of its estates in Switzerland. He used the imperial throne to build Hapsburg power in Austria.

(2) In 1356 the Golden Bull was issued by Emperor Charles IV, making the imperial throne elective. Emperors were to be

chosen by majority vote of seven German electors—the Archbishops of Mainz, Trier, and Cologne, the Count Palatine of the Rhine, the Duke of Saxony, the Margrave of Brandenburg, and the King of Bohemia. These Electors held complete sovereignty over their own states, as did the rulers of the many large and small German states.

(3) In 1438, imperial power, though still elective, passed permanently to the house of Hapsburg. It remained with them as long as the Holy Roman Empire lasted.

Italy

In Italy, the Holy Roman Emperor lost almost all of his power by the middle of the thirteenth century. The city-states of Venice, Florence, and Milan in the north had their own governments.

The Pope claimed control of the Papal States, based on the Donation of Pepin. French and Spanish rulers dominated lands in southern Italy and Sicily, the Kingdom of the Two Sicilies.

It was not until the second half of the nineteenth century that Italy and Germany finally became nations.

■ Check on Your Reading

1. Describe the Holy Roman Empire.
2. How was Italy governed after the middle of the thirteenth century?

6. *The Ottoman Empire Penetrates Southeastern Europe*

The Ottoman Turks were Moslems who took over the lands of the Byzantine Empire. They besieged and captured Constantinople in 1453 and began to expand into the Balkan peninsula. By 1470 they controlled all of it except tiny Montenegro. They made the Crimea a vassal state and took all of Rumania.

The Ottoman Empire had an unusual approach to administering its territories. Nearly all posts in the administration up to the top, just below the Sultan, were held by *slaves*, the children of Christian subjects of the Ottomans. The sons of all Christians were taken as children, converted to Islam, and trained for posts in the government. Though they gained positions of great power, they were still slaves. Those who were less able were trained as soldiers, called *janissaries*.

The Ottoman forces twice penetrated all the way to Vienna, threatening to conquer Christian Europe. For a time, under Suleiman the Magnificent (1520–1566), the Ottoman Empire was allied with France against the Hapsburg power in Hungary

■ *Suleiman the Magnificent, recognized by the Hapsburg emperor as overlord of Hungary, appoints John Zapolya king of Hungary.*

and Spain. In time the Hapsburg emperor recognized Suleiman as ruler of Hungary.

By 1600 the Ottoman Turks' strength began to decline. In 1683 they were defeated at Vienna after a long siege of that city. In the seventeenth century the Ottoman Turks were pushed back from Hungary, though they held power in the Balkans until the nineteenth century (map, p. 548). They were frequently involved in the great power struggles of Europe, especially with Russia and the Hapsburgs.

■ **Check on Your Reading**

1. How did the Ottoman Turks administer their empire?

2. How much of Europe came under Ottoman control?

MAN AND HIS CULTURE

Let's Meet the People!

The growth of the English nation was not always smooth. In the fourteenth century, a peasants' rebellion disrupted the country. The following sketch of one of the rebels, John Ball, is based on primary source material in J. R. Green, *A Short History of the English People*, Harper and Brothers; and Edward Cheyney, *Readings in English History Drawn from the Original Sources*, Ginn and Company, 1922.

John Ball: Rebel

"Good people [shouted John Ball], things will never go well in England so long as goods be not in common. . . . By what right are they whom we call lords greater folk than we? . . . Why do they hold us in serfage? If we all came of the same father and mother, of Adam and Eve, how can they say or prove that they are better than we. . . .?"

The landlords denounced John Ball and called him "the mad priest of Kent." Yet he continued to preach to the people who gathered in the Kentish courtyard:

[The lords] are clothed in velvet and warm in their furs and their ermines, while we are covered with rags. They have wine and spices and fair bread; and we oat-cake and straw, and water to drink. They have leisure and fine houses; we have pain and labour, the rain and the wind in the fields. And yet it is of us and of our toil that these men hold their state.

Thus John Ball spoke, and it was said that "many of the [humble] people loved him . . . [and] they would murmur one with another in the fields and in the ways as they went together, affirming how John Ball said truth."

The authorities could not permit the ideas of John Ball to spread. They charged him with preaching views that were "dangerous to the liberty of ecclesiastical law and order." He was tried, convicted, and sent to prison.

Still there were other voices—voices of men like Wat Tyler— urging the peasants to demand relief from heavy taxes, freedom from oppressive duties of serfdom, and other rights. In 1381 a peasant revolt broke out and spread throughout England. There was rioting and plundering in Kent and in Norfolk and in Cambridge. John Ball, liberated from prison, moved into the front ranks of the rebels. Wat Tyler found himself at the head of thousands of men!

Young King Richard II now hastened to discuss the crisis with his advisers. Then he rode forth to meet the rebels.

"I am your king and lord, good people," he told them. "What will ye?"

"We will that you free us for ever," demanded the peasants, "us and our lands; and that we be never named nor held for serfs."

King Richard II knew the dangers he faced if he refused. He hesitated no longer, but loudly proclaimed:

"I grant it!"

Yet a king need not keep his word—and a rebel rarely lived to challenge a monarch twice. Thus it was that King Richard II later broke his promise to the peasants and deprived them of their rights. John Ball? He was "drawn and hanged, then quartered, and his quarters sent to four different places!"

CHAPTER REVIEW

REVIEW and DISCUSSION

1. Identify the people and places and explain the events and terms on p. 272.

2. Magna Carta described the wrongs which autocratic governments in any age have pursued, and its "principles of redress" have changed little through the ages. Identify the "wrongs" and the "principles of redress."

3. Sir Winston Churchill said Britain and mankind owed much more to the vices of King John than to the labors of better kings. What does this statement mean?

4. How do you explain the fact that the power of the English kings was gradually restricted while the power of the French kings became more autocratic?

5. Why do business activities benefit from a stable and unified government?

6. Why was it more difficult in Spain to change the religion of a people than to change their language and government? Give evidence to support your answer.

7. Can you explain why historians know very little about early Russia and its people?

8. List the reasons why Germany and Italy failed to become nations as soon as England, France, Spain, and Russia.

9. Which ruler—in England, France, Spain, or Russia—do you think contributed most to the development of his country as a nation? Why?

10. Does "might make right"? Use the actions of the rulers in this chapter as examples.

11. Why did the Ottoman Turks choose to have Christian slaves as their government administrators?

ACTIVITIES

1. Read T. S. Eliot's play, "Murder in the Cathedral," which is based on the death of Thomas à Becket.

2. Write a report on the Bayeux Tapestry, a masterpiece of needlework commemorating the Battle of Hastings.

3. Make a chart showing the gradual development of democratic government in England, including the dates and names of milestones.

4. Construct a time chart, similar to the one on p. 273, showing the development of European nations with key events for each country. Add events not included on p. 273.

5. Most of the elements for national unity that were found in England, France, and Spain were not present in Switzerland. Consult references to find out how Switzerland became a nation. Why did it succeed without all the elements of unity?

6. Write a report on the Black Death. What were its effects on economic and social conditions, feudalism, and emancipation of serfs?

PAST and PRESENT

1. How has loyalty to one's nation replaced local loyalties in the United States and in other countries? Give examples.

2. Explain how the petit and grand juries function in your state. What do they contribute to ensure justice?

3. It is said that Russia's actions today do not all stem from communism, and that many of them are the result of Russian principles and goals developed before the Revolution of 1917. Do you agree? Why?

4 Debate the following: Resolved, that Spain would be a much stronger power today, if she had not expelled the Jews and Moors.

SUGGESTED READINGS

Basic books: PALMER, R. R., and COLTON, JOEL, *A History of the Modern World*, Knopf.
SMITH, GOLDWIN, *The Heritage of Man*, Chap. 17, Scribner.

Special accounts: ADAMS, NICHOLSON BARNEY, *The Heritage of Spain*, Holt. From pre-Roman Spain to the present.
CARMICHAEL, JOEL, *An Illustrated History of Russia*, Viking. Presents an analysis of the background of Russian history.
CHURCHILL, WINSTON, *A History of the English-Speaking Peoples, The Birth of Britain*, Dodd, Mead. Chapters on the "Making of the Nation" and "The End of the Feudal Age."
PARES, BERNARD, *History of Russia*, Knopf. Political history by an Englishman who knew Russia well. Emphasis on early periods.
ROMIER, LUCIEN, *History of France*, St. Martin's Press. Period to 1815 is well covered.
TREVELYAN, JANET PENROSE, *A Short History of The Italian People: from the Barbarian Invasions to the Present Days*, Pitman. For better readers. Good reference for the period of the great city-states and Renaissance Popes.

Biography and Fiction: MEIGS, ELIZABETH B., *Candle in the Sky*, Dutton. An effective story of Joan of Arc.
THOMPSON, STITH, and GASSNER, JOHN, (eds.), *Our Heritage of World Literature*, Holt. Includes considerable literature that reflects the nationalistic spirit.

Chapter 18

Man Explores the Earth, the Universe, and Himself

KEYNOTE On March 14, 1493, Christopher Columbus reported his great discovery of what later turned out to be the "New World."

At about the time of Columbus' voyage, Leonardo da Vinci, the brilliant artist-scientist, was making important scientific discoveries about man's body.

Was there any connection between Columbus and da Vinci? Indeed, there was! The link was that both men were explorers. The first was an explorer of the earth; the second, an explorer in the field of science and human knowledge.

In a broad sense, it can be said that the central feature of the explorations of Renaissance Europeans was this: *Not only did some men make remarkable discoveries about the earth, but others uncovered equally important facts about the theory and use of science.*

Key People *Prince Henry the Navigator · Christopher Columbus · Vasco da Gama · Ferdinand Magellan · John Cabot · Jacques Cartier · Nicholas Copernicus · Galileo Galilei · René Descartes · Isaac Newton*

Key Places *Portugal · Cuba · West Indies · Calicut · Philippine Islands*

Key Events *Discovery of America · Da Gama reaches India · Magellan circumnavigates world · Capitalism develops · Scientific progress · Printing invented · Copernican theory · Newton explains law of gravitation*

Key Terms *capitalism · Commercial Revolution · joint-stock companies movable type · heliocentric · gravitation*

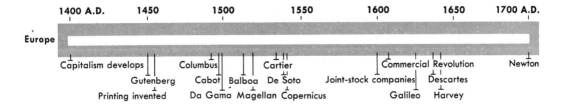

1400 A.D.	1450	1500	1550	1600	1650	1700 A.D.

Europe

Capitalism develops | Columbus | Cartier | Commercial Revolution | Newton

Gutenberg | Cabot | Balboa | De Soto | Joint-stock companies | Descartes

Printing invented | Da Gama | Magellan | Copernicus | Galileo | Harvey

1. *Economic Developments Stimulate Man's Explorations*

The latter part of the fifteenth through the sixteenth century was a period of bold overseas explorations and high adventure. It was a time when European navigators charted dangerous courses on the sea—when rugged sailors set forth to challenge the unknown—when small ships defied oceans that could swallow them with the ease of a whale devouring Jonah.

The sailing vessels of the time were about eighty feet in length and twenty at their greatest breadth. Average speed was about twelve miles an hour with a good wind. In tonnage, the fifteenth-century ships compared with our twentieth-century ocean liners as a mouse to a lion.

Captains and pilots guided their vessels by using a simple compass, an astrolabe, and by watching the position of stars. (The Chinese were using a compass for sea navigation by the early part of the twelfth century A.D. Arabs may have learned about the compass from the Chinese and later introduced it to Europe. However, some modern scholars doubt this.)

The crews of the exploring vessels consisted of about forty men. These rugged sailors fought the storms from mast or deck. They gambled and drew knives when months at sea strained their tempers.

They spread rumors of horned sea serpents and scaly monsters floating on the waves. And when the danger was greatest, they prayed to their God to bring them home safely. The "new lands" were discovered by small groups of brave men, not by the romanticized heroes of historical fiction.

What were the reasons for European explorations of foreign lands in the latter fifteenth and early sixteenth centuries? There are many answers to this question, but economic developments were one of the most important factors.

The Influence of Capitalism

Some of the methods of capitalism had been used in the ancient Greek and Roman civilizations. After the disintegration of the Roman Empire nearly all such activities stopped or were greatly limited. The earliest development of modern capitalism occurred at the end of the Middle Ages, when the restrictive economy of feudalism was crumbling. Increased trade and the growth of simple manufacturing created a greater need for money. Men began to use money to make profits, thus acquiring more. They were the earliest *capitalists*.

Capitalism is an economic system with the following characteristics: (1) The right

295

■ *These sixteenth-century Portuguese sailing vessels are anchored in Lisbon harbor. These ships were part of Portugal's commercial fleet which engaged in trade with distant lands.*

to have private property is respected. (2) Most of the production, distribution, and ownership of the goods of a country is in the hands of private individuals and companies. (3) The desire for profit is one of the principal factors stimulating men to economic activity—although it is not the only factor. (4) People are permitted to compete with each other to reach their goals.

Capitalism made it possible for some people to acquire great wealth. Some of these men sought further profit by investing their wealth in expeditions to newly discovered lands. In this way, the development of capitalism helped give impetus to the explorations by Europeans.

Italian Cities and National States Compete

The crusaders had enriched several Italian cities such as Venice, Florence, and Milan by purchasing supplies and other needs from them. The Italian cities soon became extremely important and handled much of the trade between western Europe and the East. Italian banking houses dominated

the financing of the new commerce. When the new national states appeared, serious competition arose between them and the Italian cities for foreign trade. One result was that foreign expeditions were encouraged by the national states. To take just one example, the Italian cities had dominated commerce with the East through the Mediterranean and by the overland route. When Portugal became the rival of the Italians for this trade, the Portuguese tried to find better sea routes to the East by exploration.

Competition among National States

Explorations were also stimulated by the competition among the new national states. Portugal, Spain, England, France, and the Netherlands—which declared its independence from Spain in 1581—all competed for the rich resources and markets of foreign lands.

The desire of European rulers for foreign gold and silver, and the demand of European peoples for the spices and goods of foreign countries also led to support for the voyages of exploration.

Other Reasons for Exploration

In addition to the economic factors, there were other reasons for European exploration of foreign lands. (1) The rulers of Europe desired to add to their prestige by obtaining control of territory abroad. (2) Some men wanted to bring Christianity to peoples in distant lands and "to instruct them in . . . godly knowledge and true religion." (3) Others wished to satisfy their curiosity and sense of adventure. For example, some men wanted to find a legendary ruler said to sit on a throne of rubies and pearls and to be served at dinner by seven kings. The thrill of adventure has stirred man from his first journeys on the earth to his present flights into space.

Reasons varied, but all of these factors stimulated men to explore. Stirred by these motives, men outfitted their ships, raised sails, and set out for strange lands.

■ **Check on Your Reading**

1. Describe the ships and crews used by fifteenth and sixteenth century explorers.
2. Describe the system of capitalism.
3. How did it stimulate exploration?
4. Why did rivalry and competition among national states stimulate exploration?
5. What other factors help explain the period of discovery?

2. Men Make Great Voyages and Discoveries

Portugal, a country of less than a million people, was one of the first leaders of the exploration movement. In the early part of the fifteenth century, Prince Henry of Portugal was particularly noted for encouraging the organization of voyages. Known as Prince Henry the Navigator, he gathered maps and instruments for his explorers and helped them to plan their expeditions. The rulers of Spain also supported early expeditions.

Columbus' Rediscovery of America

It seems clear that Columbus was not the first man to discover America. Almost five hundred years before Columbus made his voyage, Leif Ericson and the Vikings crossed the Atlantic in ships with thirty-two oars and single sails. Recent research makes it quite certain that the Vikings landed in North America. However, it was not until October, 1964, that the United States officially marked the first "National Leif Ericson Day." In addition, a sea chart dated 1424 suggests that some Portuguese navigators may also have preceded Columbus to the "New World."

We do not know whom to credit as the *first* discoverer of America. Nor is it too important that we name him. The significant point is this: It was Columbus' discovery or rediscovery of the "New World" that was to have the most important consequences for mankind.

Many facts about Columbus and his first voyage are known. Columbus was an Italian from Genoa who sailed across the Atlantic Ocean under the sponsorship of Queen Isabella of Spain. In October, 1492, he accidentally reached one of the islands of the Bahamas. Then he explored Cuba and the West Indies and returned to Europe with the news of his discovery of these lands and people:

All these islands are very beautiful [he wrote]. . . . [The people] show greater love for all others than for themselves; they give valuable things for trifles . . . however, I forbade that things so small and of no value should be given to them, such as pieces of plate, dishes

Christopher Columbus

■ *This portrait of Columbus by R. Ghirlandaio is said to illustrate the story that the explorer's troubles turned his hair prematurely white.*

and glass, likewise keys and shoestraps; although if they were able to obtain these, it seemed to them like getting the most beautiful jewels in the world. . . .

Columbus did not know that he had found a "New World," though he made several other voyages. He thought that he had reached the *East Indies* in Asia and the islands off Japan. America was even named after someone else—Amerigo Vespucci, who later probably sailed along the northern coast of South America. Had Columbus realized that he had discovered a new continent, our country might be called "the United States of Christopher"!

Vasco da Gama's Voyage to India

In 1497–1498, Vasco da Gama, a Portuguese explorer and administrator, led a group of vessels around the Cape of Good Hope to Calicut, India. He was trying to find a good sea route to the East that would help Portugal to break the monopoly that Italian cities had on overland trade with eastern peoples. The trip to India took ten and a half months, and only one-third of the men finally returned to Portugal. In terms of money, the goods that Vasco da Gama brought back with him were worth many times the expenses of the voyage.

Magellan's Men Journey around the World

Ferdinand Magellan was born in Portugal, but he made his great voyage for the king of Spain. In the fall of 1519, he set out with five ships and a crew of two hundred forty-three men to find a passage to the East by travelling westward.

Magellan crossed the Atlantic to Brazil, sailed down the coast of South America and through the now famous Strait of Magellan, and reached the Pacific Ocean. Then he sailed across the Pacific Ocean to the Philippine Islands. Here Magellan was killed, but his few remaining men continued the voyage home. Finally, almost three years after their departure, one ship and only eighteen men returned to Spain. The survivors included the cabin boy, a lad no older than the readers of this book.

It had been a brutal trip. Many of the crew had died of disease; others had been killed by the poisoned arrows of natives; still others had been struck down for mutiny. At one point in the voyage, the men had been starving to death. One man reported that for over three months:

. . . we only ate old biscuit reduced to powder, and full of [worms] . . . and we drank water that was yellow. . . . We also ate the sawdust of wood, and rats which cost half a crown each. . . .

Yet, out of that misery and terror, Magellan and his crew had accomplished a remarkable feat of navigation. They had circled the earth, and man's energies could now reach around the globe! For the first time men had an accurate idea of the earth's size and shape and the placement of its continents.

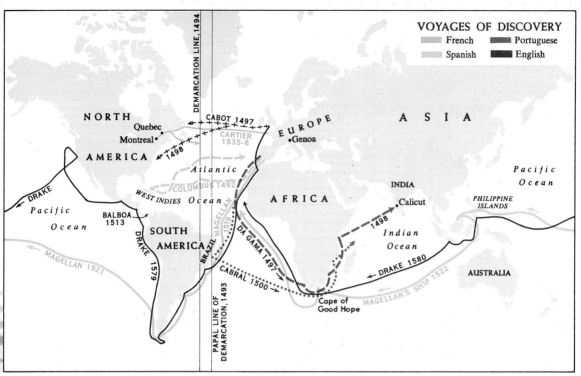

■ *In the fifteenth and sixteenth centuries, England, France, Portugal, and Spain supported voyages of exploration. Leading explorers were Balboa, Cabral, Cartier, Columbus, Drake, da Gama, and Magellan. As a result of their discoveries, European nations were able to build great overseas empires. What new lands did they discover and for which country did each sail?*

Other Explorations

Other Europeans also made important early explorations of distant lands and waters. For example, the following explorers made voyages to the New World:

1. JOHN CABOT—1497. Cabot, an Italian navigator who sailed for England, reached the North American coast somewhere in the region of Cape Breton Island, Canada.

2. PEDRO CABRAL—1500. Cabral, a Portuguese, sailed from Portugal to Brazil.

3. VASCO NÚÑEZ DE BALBOA—1513. Balboa, a Spaniard, led his men in a march from the east to the west coast of the Isthmus of Panama. He may have been the first European to see the Pacific Ocean.

4. JACQUES CARTIER—1534–1536. Cartier, a Frenchman, located the channel that led to the St. Lawrence River in Canada. Then he sailed up the river to present-day Quebec and Montreal.

5. HERNANDO DE SOTO—1539–1542. De Soto, a Spaniard, explored present northern Florida and the north coast of the Gulf of Mexico. He discovered the Mississippi River and explored west of it to present-day Oklahoma.

■ Check on Your Reading

1. What countries encouraged early expeditions and voyages? Why? What were the results of these voyages?

2. Evaluate the importance of Columbus' "rediscovery" of America in his own day.

3. What were the important achievements of Vasco da Gama, Ferdinand Magellan, John Cabot, Pedro Cabral, Vasco de Balboa, Jacques Cartier, Hernando de Soto?

3. Explorations and Discoveries Have Many Results

The expeditions by sea to America and Asia resulted in such extensive commercial expansion that it is said that they helped bring about a *Commercial Revolution.* Certainly, these explorations and discoveries had many important results.

Several European nations, especially Spain, England, France, and the Netherlands, acquired colonies. These nations began to build up overseas empires, and rivalries became more intense.

Nations that had sponsored successful expeditions added to their trade, wealth, and prestige. Such a nation was Spain.

European influence in political, economic, and cultural matters spread to many parts of the world.

Finally, writers related the exciting stories of the explorations.

Capitalism Develops Further

A significant result was that capitalism was able to develop more fully. Under this system some men accumulated enough profits to be able to invest large sums in speculative enterprises. Some of these funds had been used to support explorations, which, in turn, gave impetus to the further development of capitalism in the following ways: (1) The increased trade between East and West strengthened individuals and companies economically. (2) The gold and silver sent from the colonies provided Europeans with more *capital,* or wealth that could be used to obtain or produce additional goods. (3) The demand for funds and other economic services helped banking to grow still further. (4) The expansion of commercial activities increased the importance and power of the *bourgeoisie.* (5) The problems that arose with the expansion of trade led to the development of different types of business organizations. For example, *joint-stock companies* were organized primarily to develop commercial enterprises in overseas trade.

In a joint-stock company a number of men placed money in a common fund. In return, each man was given shares in the company. The number of shares he received depended on the amount of money invested.

The shareholders chose directors to use their money for some purpose. If the company made a profit, each man received a part in accordance with the number of his shares. Joint-stock companies had some features of later corporations.

Science Becomes Increasingly Important

The explorations, exchange of ideas, support of wealthy leaders, and other factors also encouraged the progress of science.

Science was to play a vital role in the future history of man. A modern scientist, Dr. Warren Weaver, gives one description of what science really is:

Science clearly is a way of solving problems—not all problems, but a large class of important and practical ones. The problems with which it can deal are those in which the predominant factors are subject to the basic laws of logic and are for the most part measurable.

Science is a way of organizing reproducible knowledge about such problems, of focusing and disciplining imagination, of weighing evidence, of deciding what is relevant and what is not.

[Science is a way] of impartially testing hypotheses, of ruthlessly discarding what proves to be inaccurate or inadequate, of finding, interpreting, and facing facts, and of making the facts of nature the servants of man.

■ **Check on Your Reading**

1. How did the discoveries and explorations affect relations between European nations?

2. Describe a joint-stock company.

4. *Great Progress in Science, Medicine, and Invention*

In the period from about the middle of the fifteenth to the end of the seventeenth century, most people still knew very little about science. They continued to accept nonsensical beliefs. Some of them rubbed the juice of green lizards on cuts of the skin. Others believed in witches and tortured those accused of talking to the Devil. Even professional men were not noted for their wisdom. One French playwright, Molière, had so little faith in the knowledge of doctors that he made one of the characters in a play say: "What will you do, sir, with four physicians? Is not one enough to kill any one body?"

Certainly, the majority of men and women—educated or not—were not constantly "scientific" in their attitudes. Talented individuals, rather than the mass of people, were responsible for the gains in the sciences. These individuals did outstanding work, not only in science and medicine but also in the field of invention (the *application* of scientific principles to produce something of concrete use).

Gutenberg and Others Develop Printing

Johann Gutenberg (c. 1397–1468), a German, helped to develop the idea of the printing press to a point where it had practical value. He constructed a workable press about the middle of the fifteenth century. By that date, paper and printer's ink were available for the printing process.

Gutenberg must not be called the "inventor" of the printing press. Printing developed too gradually for any one man to receive all of the credit. People living in China and Korea had movable type as early as the eleventh century A.D.; and several Europeans in the Rhineland area of Germany experimented with printing during the early fifteenth century.

The invention of printing was one of the greatest achievements in the history of civilization. Books could now be published in large numbers and sold at lower costs. Remember that in the Middle Ages each book was copied by hand on expensive parchment (made from stretched skin of a sheep or goat). A monk, illustrating and decorating the pages as he went, would take months or years on a single book. When paper was introduced to Europe, books became a little cheaper, but they were still very scarce. Movable type meant that each letter of type was a tiny engraving. The letters could be arranged in words, then sentences, then a whole page. After ink had been applied to the type and many impressions of the page made, the type

■ *This is a hand-operated printing press, 1511. Type is being set at the right while an impression of a page is made by the press.*

was disassembled and could be used over and over. Hundreds or thousands of copies of each book or newspaper or sheet could easily be printed. The reading public could now be increased tremendously.

Statistics show the importance of the printing press. In 1400, when each book was copied by hand and was very expensive, few men could afford to buy books. Yet by 1965 some 290 *million* paperback books were bought annually in North America alone! Little wonder that the printed page became a major bond of communication among people.

Copernicus Puts the Sun in Its Place

Nicholas Copernicus (1473–1543) had an "international" background. His ancestry was heavily German; his place of birth was in Poland; and a considerable part of his education was received in Italy.

Copernicus made a great contribution to astronomy. In his so-called Copernican theory, he pointed out the following: (1) The sun—not the earth—was the center of our universe. (2) The earth moved around the sun in a circular orbit, or path. (3) The other planets also circled the sun. (4) The earth made a daily spin on its axis.

Copernicus was not completely correct in all of his statements. For example, the orbits of planets are ellipses, not circles. Despite his errors, Copernicus' achievement was remarkable.

Copernicus' theory angered many theologians. Remember that up until then men had believed that the earth was the center of the universe and that the sun and planets revolved around it. It was hard to adjust to the idea that the earth was far less important. Many theologians declared that the ideas of Copernicus were opposed to statements in the Bible, and they condemned his famous book *Concerning the Revolutions of the Heavenly Bodies*. Nevertheless, Copernicus' work helped others to destroy the old Ptolemaic idea of the *geocentric*, or earth-centered, universe and to replace it with the *heliocentric*, or sun-centered, universe.

Galileo Supports the Copernican Theory

One of the most important supporters of the ideas of Copernicus was the brilliant Italian mathematician-astronomer-physicist Galileo Galilei (1564–1642). Galileo believed that man must honestly say "I know it not" about many things in Nature, and then use objective methods to "ferret out a few of [Nature's] secrets." Sir William Cecil Dampier has called him "the first of the moderns . . . [with Galileo] we know that we have reached the method of physical science which still is in use today."

Using a telescope that he had developed, Galileo examined the sun, the moon, the satellites of Jupiter, and other bodies in our solar system. His study convinced him that the Copernican theory was right. When he expressed his views, they also were condemned by religious leaders. Galileo was even imprisoned!

William Harvey Traces the Blood

As a result of his experimentation, William Harvey (1578–1657), an Englishman, was able to describe blood circulation.

The heart [he wrote] is the beginning of life . . . for it is the heart by whose virtue and pulse the blood is moved.

Several men before him had described aspects of the circulatory system, but Harvey provided proof of the way in which the blood circulated.

Descartes Shows the Way in Mathematics

René Descartes (1596–1650), a Frenchman, was a brilliant philosopher and mathematician, who made outstanding contributions in the field of analytic geometry. His method of determining the position of a point in a flat surface was one of the greatest advances in the history of mathematics.

Descartes offered a striking challenge to all mathematicians who followed him. He wrote:

... I have intentionally omitted [discussing some ideas] so as to leave to others the pleasure of discovery.

Isaac Newton Explains Gravitation

Isaac Newton (1642–1727), an Englishman, was one of the world's greatest and most devoted men of science. When he worked on a problem, he often forgot to eat, rest, or even to put on his stockings properly. He used his talents seriously to make a number of outstanding contributions to science.

Newton analyzed the nature of light, and he developed new methods in mathematics. Most important of all was his explanation of the law of gravitation:

That every particle of matter in the universe is *attracted by* or *gravitates to* every other particle of matter, with a force [that Newton then described].

Newton gave man new insight into the nature of the universe. He seemed to have discovered a basic order behind the forces that operate in the universe. His influence went far beyond science into the world of philosophy, religion, the social sciences, and the study of history. An age of rationalism began. Despite his accomplishments, Newton considered his work just a beginning. In the spirit of a true scientist, he wrote:

... to myself I seem to have been only like a boy playing on the seashore, [amusing] myself in now and then finding a smoother pebble or a prettier shell than ordinary, while the great ocean of truth lay all undiscovered before me.

© National Portrait Gallery, London

■ *This is a portrait of Isaac Newton, one of the great men of science. He had profound influence on eighteenth-century thought.*

Other Leaders Make Contributions

Other leaders in science, medicine, and invention in the sixteenth and seventeenth centuries were Vesalius, who studied the structure of the human body and the circulation of the blood; Gilbert, who studied magnetism; and Boyle, who experimented in chemistry.

New areas for investigation were opened by the gradual improvement of the telescope and microscope. New hope for the crippled and sick was provided by the development of better artificial limbs and more effective drugs. All men could appreciate these words of Newton:

We are all friends because we ... aim at the only object worthy of man, which is the knowledge of truth.

■ Check on Your Reading

1. Explain the tremendous importance of the invention of printing.

2. What were the contributions of Galileo? of Harvey? of Descartes? of Newton?

MAN AND HIS CULTURE

Let's Meet the People!

The following sketch is based on information in "Sailing by Caravel," an article by Fernando Romero in *Américas* magazine, a monthly publication of the Pan American Union.

A Seaman of the Sixteenth Century

It was daybreak, and the seaman joined the crew on the narrow deck of the ship. He wore a shirt with wide sleeves, loose-fitting breeches, and a wool cap. Inside his belt, he carried a knife.

The seaman listened quietly now as a page recited aloud the Lord's Prayer. When prayers for the safety of the ship were finished, the pages placed three platters of food in the middle part of the upper deck and called out: "Who does not come will not eat!"

The hungry seaman sat down quickly and ate his food with his hands and knife. His meal consisted of a portion of dwarf peas, a strip of dried mutton, and a biscuit that was "black, wormy, and gnawed by mice." His ration of water was very small.

All that morning the seaman worked hard. He climbed to the rigging and checked the sails. He helped to pump out the water that had seeped into the bottom of the ship. He hauled ropes to the rhythmic chant of old songs called *salomas*.

That afternoon the seaman amused himself by searching for bugs that crawled about his clothing. Then he listened with terror to the rumor that a sea serpent had been sighted. He hoped that the darkness of night would protect the ship.

In the evening, the stern lantern and the compass lamp were lighted. An altar was set up and candles were lit.

The master of the ship now stepped forward.

"Are we all here?" the master asked.

"God be with us!" answered the seaman and the crew.

Then master and crew prayed to God. They ended their religious service with the words: "Amen, and God give us a good night."

That night was good to the voyagers. A brisk wind came up and drove their ship on toward the unknown land that lay ahead.

CHAPTER REVIEW

REVIEW and DISCUSSION

1. Identify the people and places and explain the events and terms on p. 294.

2. Are the explorers of space today impelled by the same motives as the early explorers? Why or why not?

3. How did discovery of the New World upset former trade patterns and routes?

4. If you had been alive in the fifteenth century, would you have been willing to travel with Columbus on his first voyage?

5. Columbus' discovery of the New World set up a series of chain reactions. Explain.

6. Do you think the deprivations and misery encountered by Magellan's men were worth the results of the voyage? What other great advances in civilization have been made at the cost of much human misery?

7. Is historical research scientific? Can you apply scientific principles to finding the answers to historical questions? Illustrate.

8. Was the "international" education of Copernicus advantageous to him? What opportunities for an international education exist today? What are its advantages?

9. Was Isaac Newton more outstanding than his contemporary scientists and mathematicians? Justify your answer.

10. Have you, like Isaac Newton, ever been so interested in working on something that you forgot to eat or to rest? Why is it sometimes possible for one to make a great contribution during such an experience?

11. What pleasure is there in making a discovery? What part does it play in the progress of civilization?

12. Why was progress in science slower than in literature, art, music, and architecture during the late Medieval period?

ACTIVITIES

1. Write a sea-log such as an early explorer might have kept on his voyage. Read excerpts from Columbus's log as an example.

2. Write a report on the development of capitalism. Consult the *Encyclopedia of the Social Sciences* and other references.

3. Make a study of the activities of several scientists, noting their methods and habits of work. Can you make a generalization concerning the scientific process?

PAST and PRESENT

1. Name any unscientific practices, nonsensical beliefs, and superstitions that some people still accept today. Are most people really scientific today?

2. What characteristics of the exploration of space are similar to the explorations of the New World? Which are different? Why?

SUGGESTED READINGS

Basic books: GOTTSCHALK, LOUIS R., and LACH, DONALD F., *Europe and the Modern World*, Scott, Foresman. See section on science.

LIFE, *Picture History of Western Man*, Simon and Schuster. Many references to the men and events in this chapter.

PALMER, R. R., and COLTON, JOEL, *A History of the Modern World*, Knopf. See section on "Opening of the Atlantic."

SMITH, GOLDWIN, *The Heritage of Man*, Chaps. 21, 25, Scribner.

Special accounts: BUTTERFIELD, HERBERT, and others, *A Short History of Science. A Symposium*, Doubleday. Very readable. Chapters on Copernicus, Harvey, Bacon, and Newton.

Biography and Fiction: BOLTON, SARAH K., *Famous Men of Science*, Crowell. Lives of scientists presented in a brief and simple manner.

KINGSLEY, CHARLES, *Westward Ho!* Dodd, Mead. An exciting novel about Elizabethan Sea Dogs and their rivalry with Spain.

MORISON, SAMUEL ELIOT, *Christopher Columbus, Mariner*, Little, Brown. A distinguished authority writes about Columbus' life and voyages.

SOOTIN, HARRY, *Isaac Newton*, Messner. Interesting book about a remarkable scientist and an unusual man.

Chapter 19   The Reformation in Europe

KEYNOTE   The term *Reformation* refers to the great religious movements of reform and revolt that stirred Christianity in sixteenth-century Europe. When these movements resulted in a break with the Catholic Church, they were part of the *Protestant* Reformation. When they remained within the Roman Catholic Church, they were part of the *Catholic* Reformation.

The outstanding feature of the Reformation in Europe was the real desire of reformers to purify man's relationship to God. However, like a striking fabric woven into a rug of many colors, the Reformation was still a part of the complicated political, economic, and social pattern of the day.

Key People   *Martin Luther   ·   John Calvin   ·   Henry VIII   ·   Ignatius Loyola   ·   Charles V   ·   Philip II   ·   William of Orange   ·   Elizabeth I   ·   Henry IV*

Key Places   *Worms   ·   Geneva   ·   Spain   ·   Holy Roman Empire   ·   United Netherlands   ·   Belgium*

Key Events   *Luther posts 95 theses   ·   Diet of Worms   ·   Calvinism spreads   ·   Church of England established   ·   Catholic Reformation   ·   Council of Trent   ·   Dutch Revolt   ·   Spanish Armada defeated   ·   Edict of Nantes   ·   Peace of Augsburg   ·   Thirty Years' War*

Key Terms   *Reformation   ·   indulgences   ·   justification by faith   ·   Protestant   ·   predestination   ·   Anglican Church   ·   heresy   ·   Inquisition   ·   Puritans   ·   Huguenots*

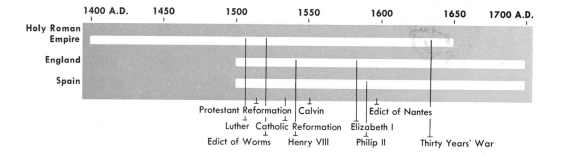

| 1400 A.D. | 1450 | 1500 | 1550 | 1600 | 1650 | 1700 A.D. |

Holy Roman Empire

England

Spain

Protestant Reformation | Calvin | Edict of Nantes
Luther | Catholic Reformation | Elizabeth I
Edict of Worms | Henry VIII | Philip II | Thirty Years' War

1. The Protestant Reformation

From its earliest beginnings as an organization, the Church had been beset by differences over *dogma*, or prescribed religious belief. Groups of churchmen had differed over the nature of the Trinity, over the nature of God and Jesus, over the powers of the Pope, and over other matters. As a result of such differences the Church had split into the Roman Catholic and Eastern Orthodox churches in 1054. Extreme differences were labelled by the Church as *heresy*, opinion or doctrine contrary to true beliefs. Those holding heretical ideas were expelled from the Church or in some cases condemned to death.

The Protestant Reformation also began as a difference of interpretation within the Church. It ended in a far greater split than the Church had ever known.

Forerunners of the Protestant Reformation

Peter Waldo—John Wyclif—John Hus —John Wessel. These names remind us that the roots of the Protestant Reformation of the sixteenth century reach back into history.

In the twelfth century Peter Waldo of Lyons, France, insisted that ordinary men and women had the right to preach. He also refused to obey any order of the Pope that he considered unjust. His view was labelled the "Waldensian heresy."

In the fourteenth century John Wyclif of England protested against the ways in which some clergymen of high position gained their wealth. He tried to bring deeper religious understanding to the people by translating the Bible from Latin into English.

At the beginning of the fifteenth century John Hus of Bohemia accused religious leaders of breaking rules of faith and conduct and was burned at the stake.

In the fifteenth century John Wessel of the Netherlands said that the Bible—not men—should be the chief authority in religious matters.

The Protestant Reformation did not originate in the sixteenth century. Rather, its foundation rested upon the protests of earlier reformers.

Several Factors Produce the Protestant Reformation

The Reformation occurred in a period that saw the spread of the Renaissance,

307

Uffizi Gallery, Florence

■ *Lucas Cranach painted several portraits of Luther, the great Protestant leader. Luther's ninety-five theses led to his split with the Church.*

Martin Luther

the rise of capitalism, and expansion of science. It was influenced by these.

Renaissance humanism stimulated many men to re-examine their religious beliefs. Most humanists loved peace and quiet too well to split violently with the Church.

Similarly, scientific discoveries excited some individuals, but most religious leaders rejected scientific findings that seemed to conflict with the Bible. For example, when Copernicus said that the sun, not the earth, was the center of our world, he was called a "fool [who] wishes to reverse the entire science of astronomy."

If humanism and science were not enough to cause the Protestant Reformation, what other factors helped to produce the movements of religious reform and revolt? Briefly stated, they were these: (1) A growth of religious feeling occurred among the people. Many men and women were disturbed by the worldliness and lack of spirituality of some clergy members.

(2) The rulers of the new national states wanted their subjects to be loyal to them and not turn to the Church for leadership.

Ambitious princes, particularly in divided Germany wished to take over the civil power and wealth of the Church.

(3) Merchants, traders, and business men—the rising bourgeoisie—resented the ways in which the Church interfered with their activities. (For example, the Church opposed *usury*—that is, the practice of lending money at high interest rates.) In many lands, these bourgeoisie were beginning to develop a feeling of patriotism, or devotion to their own country. They disliked the fact that large amounts of money from their country were being sent to Rome to support the Church.

(4) Peasants felt crushed by the financial demands of the Church. The Church levied a tax called a *tithe* on individuals, requiring them to give one-tenth of their income to support the Church.

(5) The development of the printing press made it possible to spread revolutionary religious ideas throughout Europe.

These factors could not have produced the Protestant Reformation, unless there were individuals willing to challenge the basic doctrines of the Church. The most important leader was Martin Luther.

Luther Challenges Church Practices

Martin Luther (1483–1546) was born in Germany. His father was a peasant who later became a copper miner. Luther became a monk, trained for the priesthood, and then served as a professor of religion at the University of Wittenberg. Luther has been described as sturdy, rough, and energetic. He admitted as much when he said about himself: "God uses coarse wedges for splitting coarse blocks."

Luther became disturbed by the beliefs and practices of some of the clergy, particularly about the manner of their handling *indulgences*. Indulgences were granted by the Church under certain conditions. They were supposed to remit (take away) some

308

of the penance a repentant sinner had to do on this earth and some of his punishment in purgatory. *Penance* referred to certain acts which the priest required a confessed sinner to perform before his sins could be forgiven. *Purgatory*, in the words of Dr. John A. O'Brien, is "a midway state between heaven and hell." Here souls that have not been marred by mortal (or serious) sin are "cleansed of their venial imperfections [sins that can be pardoned] and rendered suitable to enter into the august presence of their Lord and Creator in the unspeakable happiness of heaven."

Indulgences were originally gained by certain religious acts. However, in Luther's time, when the Church badly needed money, some individuals were granting indulgences in return for money contributions to the Church. Luther considered what he called the sale of indulgences by Church officials to be a serious abuse. He was indignant over such things as the campaign of a monk named Tetzel who was

■ *The clergyman is collecting money from local merchants at a market, 15th century. The bourgeoisie resented supporting the Church at Rome.*

raising money for the rebuilding of the basilica of St. Peter's in Rome. Tetzel was collecting contributions of money, and in return he was granting indulgences which he claimed had great power to remit sins.

Luther was disturbed also by other abuses connected with indulgences. The money gained from the "sale" of indulgences was often used for worthwhile purposes, such as the building of cathedrals and hospitals. However, in some places civil rulers were given part of the money. The Archbishop of Mainz even sold indulgences in order to pay back a loan that the financially powerful Fugger family had made to him.

Although indulgences were not supposed to be pardons for sins, many people began to believe that God would forgive all of their sins if they purchased enough of these documents.

In 1517 Luther placed ninety-five theses, or propositions, on the door of the Wittenberg Castle Church. Some of these theses questioned not only the abuses, but the whole theory of indulgences. Luther hoped that his statements would be discussed and debated by churchmen. Written in Latin, they included such controversial points as this:

. . . those who preach indulgences are in error when they say that a man is . . . saved from every penalty by the Pope's indulgences.

Luther had not intended to split from his Church. Nevertheless, he began to criticize other Church practices. This led him into serious conflict with the Pope.

Luther was brought to the town of Worms for trial before the Diet (an assembly of advisers) of Charles V, emperor of the Holy Roman Empire. At the trial, Luther refused to back down. He said:

I cannot and I will not [renounce] anything, for to go against conscience is neither right nor safe. God help me.

The emperor and the Diet then decreed by the Edict of Worms (1521):

Luther is to be regarded as a convicted heretic. . . . His followers also are to be condemned. His books are to be eradicated from the memory of man.

Luther was made an outlaw in the Holy Roman Empire besides being excommunicated from the Church. However, the Catholic rulers of some German states were not on friendly terms with the emperor or the Pope. They supported Luther, because his actions were in line with the rising patriotic feelings of the German princes. They resented German money going to enrich Italy and resented the power of an Italian Pope over Germans. Furthermore, Luther had written some of his most important work, notably the *Address to the Nobility of the German Nation* (1520), in vernacular German rather than Latin; and he later translated the Bible from Greek into German. His work helped to develop the modern German language. Many peasants also supported Luther. As a result, Luther's life was protected, and his ideas continued to be discussed. These ideas, which formed the basis for future Lutheranism, included the following:

1. JUSTIFICATION BY FAITH ALONE. Luther believed that each individual must justify himself before God by his deep faith in God and in the inspiration of Christ. This seemed to suggest that the performance of all sacraments (religious rites of the Church) was not the only way in which a person might gain salvation.

2. RELIGIOUS DOCTRINE SHOULD BE BASED ON SCRIPTURE. Luther felt that doctrine should depend on the Bible, not on the teachings of religious leaders.

Luther and the Peasants' Rebellion

In 1524–25, after a century of unrest in the farming areas, a series of uprisings known as the Peasants' Rebellion broke out in the German states. The peasants wanted more economic and political rights.

The Peasants' Rebellion was not *caused* by the ideas of Martin Luther. Although Luther was sympathetic to some of the peasants' views, he was afraid that the rebellion would result in the collapse of all government. He therefore urged:

If the peasant is in open rebellion, then he is outside the law of God, for rebellion is not simply murder, but it is like a great fire which attacks and lays waste a whole land.

This Peasants' Rebellion was crushed with a great loss of life to the peasants.

John Calvin: a Leader of Protestants

In time, the followers of Martin Luther broke away from the Catholic Church. Later, other leaders organized different Christian groups outside the control of the Church. Most Christians of western Europe who were not Catholics became known as *Protestants*. The word was first used to refer to those German Lutheran princes at the Diet of Speyer (1529) who issued a protest against an imperial decree that would have crushed Luther's reforms. The word "Protestant" also has a positive meaning. Protestants not only protested against certain practices; they professed or proclaimed certain beliefs. Dr. Andrew K. Rule, a twentieth-century theologian, declares, "it is only in special situations that the movement called Protestant has had the negative character which the name implies"; "positive affirmation" is a fundamental part of Protestantism.

An important Protestant leader was John Calvin (1509–1564), a man frail in body but strong in determination. Calvin was born in France and studied in several universities, seminaries, and law schools.

It was not long before Calvin's ideas angered the authorities in France. He therefore fled for safety to Switzerland, where the Protestant leader Ulrich Zwingli (1484–1531) had already boldly declared that Scriptures were always more important than Church rituals. In Switzerland, Calvin wrote his famous work, *The Institutes of the Christian Religion.*

In his writings, Calvin developed the doctrine of *predestination.* This meant that when God created mankind, He selected some people to be saved and others to be doomed. The people predestined by God to be saved, called by Calvin the *elect,* would feel a deep faith in God and a serious responsibility to live by Christian principles.

John Calvin also (1) organized religious services that were much simpler than those followed by the Catholic Church; (2) proposed that local churches be governed by laymen elected by their own congregations; and (3) commended the hard work of business men and other members of the middle class.

Calvin, who was an excellent organizer, helped to set up a Protestant-dominated government in Geneva, Switzerland. This government warned the people to avoid earthly temptations and to live by Calvinist rules of morality. The virtues approved by the Calvinists were abstinence, sobriety, frugality, and modesty. Calvin himself approved of the execution of Servetus, a man who was condemned for denying a basic doctrine.

Protestant activities in Geneva affected other religious groups in Europe, and Calvinism spread to many lands (see Chart).

As historians John B. Harrison and Richard E. Sullivan point out: "The Calvinists played a very important part in the founding of the United States, particularly the Puritans in New England, the Dutch Reformed in New York, and the Scotch-Irish Presbyterians along the frontiers of all the original states. Such well-known denominations in present-day America as the Congregationalists, the Presbyterians, and the Baptists are Calvinist *in origin.*"

A National Church in England

Protestant ideas continued to spread in Germany, Scandinavia, Switzerland, France, the Netherlands, Scotland, and Bohemia. In England, they helped to bring about the establishment of an independent, national church. King Henry VIII (1509–1547) was deeply involved in this development.

Henry VIII of England was an educated and gifted man. He was also ambitious and vain. As a young man, Henry had been considered a conscientious Roman Catholic. One foreign ambassador, Giustiniani, had observed:

[Henry VIII] is very devout. On the days on which he goes to the chase he hears mass three times, but on other days he goes as often as five times.

Country	Calvinism Was the Foundation for the Faith of:
The Netherlands	The Dutch Reformed Church
Scotland	Scottish Presbyterians (John Knox [c. 1505–1572] had a major part in establishing Presbyterianism in Scotland.)
England	Puritans
France	Huguenots

© National Portrait Gallery, London

■ *Henry VIII was a good musician, a skillful horseman, and a linguist. He was also ambitious and vain, as seen in this Holbein portrait.*

Henry in 1521 had written a reply to Luther called *The Assertion of the Seven Sacraments*. As a result, he was given the title of "Defender of the Faith" by Pope Leo X, and the monarchs of England have kept this title ever since.

However, Henry wanted to have a son to succeed him when he died. When his wife Catherine of Aragon did not give birth to a boy, he asked the Church to dissolve their marriage. The Pope refused to do this, and Henry decided to break with the Church.

There were several reasons for Henry's decision: (1) He desired to remarry. (2) He wished to seize the fine lands of Church officials. (3) He wanted to free the country from the political activities of some churchmen. (4) He hoped to increase his power over the English people.

Henry therefore split with the Pope and made himself the head of an independent national Church in England (the Anglican Church). The Act of Supremacy of 1534 stated:

Be it enacted by authority of this present parliament, that the king . . . his heirs and successors . . . shall be taken, accepted, and reputed the only supreme head in earth of the church of England. . . .

The king—not the Pope—was to be the religious leader of England.

Henry VIII did not single-handedly found the Church of England (or the Anglican Church). Before his split with Rome, there had been a long period of protest against the Pope's so-called "unwarranted usurpations of authority."

It was not until the reign of Queen Elizabeth I (1558–1603) that the Church of England was established on a permanent basis. The Church of England accepted some ideas of John Calvin, but (while not recognizing the authority of the Pope at Rome) continued to pattern its organization after that of the Catholics.

The various Episcopal churches throughout the world today are outgrowths of the movement that led to the establishment of the Church of England. In creed and religious rituals they are probably the closest to Catholicism.

Protestants Hold Common Principles

Protestant strength developed in the north of Europe. Catholic strength was in the south, particularly in Italy and Spain. In time, differences of doctrine and ritual developed among the various Protestant churches. Despite these differences, nearly all Protestants held certain basic beliefs.

Among these Protestant beliefs was the idea that the Bible provided the principal guide for the actions of men. Protestants interpreted the Bible for themselves; they did not accept the Pope as the final authority in interpreting the Scriptures.

The Protestants believed that man gained salvation by faith and trust in God. They did not think that it was also necessary to perform many rites and rituals.

According to Protestant belief, each individual was responsible for his salvation. Or, as Martin Luther put it, "We may shout into each other's ears, but each man must stand on the ramparts alone."

■ **Check on Your Reading**

1. Evaluate the background reasons for the Protestant Reformation.
2. What did Luther accomplish? with what political results?
3. Describe Calvinism.
4. Why did Henry VIII set up the Anglican Church?

2. The Catholic Reformation

Although there had been sincere Catholic reformers who wished to eliminate abuses in the Church before the Protestant Reformation, the term *Catholic Reformation* usually refers to the sixteenth-century reform movements *within the Church*. The Catholic Reformation or Counter Reformation had two major purposes: (1) to strengthen the Church, and (2) to check the spread of Protestant beliefs.

Loyola Leads the Jesuits

Ignatius Loyola (c. 1491–1556), one of the great leaders of the Catholic Reformation, established a religious order called the Society of Jesus. Members of this order were known as *Jesuits*.

The Jesuits were organized with military strictness, and Loyola was their "general." The Jesuits first disciplined themselves by rigid training. This preparation helped them to understand their weaknesses. One Jesuit, when asked if he had been shown devils in his training, answered: "They showed me worse. They showed me myself!"

Once they had learned self-discipline, the Jesuits were ready to work for the interests of the Catholic Church. They campaigned against *heretics*, people who held religious beliefs differing from the

■ *This painting by Rubens shows St. Ignatius Loyola, who came from the Basque region of Spain. He was a former soldier who founded the Society of Jesus.*

Church of San Ambrogio, Genoa

teachings of the Church. They organized schools and colleges, and they carried Roman Catholic religious ideas to the people of foreign lands. The Pope himself recognized the value of their activities.

After the death of Loyola, some criticisms were made of the Jesuit order. Nevertheless, many Jesuits worked extremely hard to combat Protestantism and to spread Catholic teachings to many areas.

The Council of Trent

The Catholic Reformation also was aided by the Council of Trent, which met in several sessions between 1545 and 1563. It defended the following principles: (1) The Pope was the earthly head of the Church. (2) No man was to interpret the Bible differently from the Church. (3) The Church dogma on the seven sacraments was correct. (4) The rites and rituals accepted by the Church were to be followed.

It also introduced the following reforms: (1) The sale of indulgences was controlled. (2) The abuses of monastery life were checked. (3) Education for the priesthood was improved. (4) Church administration was organized more efficiently.

The Council of Trent showed the gap that existed between Catholic and Protestant beliefs, and it strengthened the Church.

An Evaluation of the Reformation

The Reformation was extremely important to both Protestants and Catholics. Although reformers did not always avoid the use of violence (for example, some Catholics made use of the Inquisition (p. 286)), the Reformation had these significant results:

Protestant churches were established; Catholics eliminated several undesirable conditions in the Catholic Church; and Christianity was spread to distant lands.

■ By 1560, a number of Protestant religions— Anglican, Calvinist, Lutheran, and Zwinglian— had made inroads in predominantly Roman Catholic Europe. In what countries did Protestantism develop? Why?

THE RELIGIONS OF EUROPE IN 1560

Roman Catholics   Anglicans
Lutherans   Calvinists and Zwinglians
Eastern Orthodox

The Reformation also aided the growth of education. Schools were formed to teach reading and other skills. About 1527, Protestant universities were organized.

Vernacular literature was further stimulated. The Bible was translated, and prayer books were composed. In music, congregational singing was encouraged, and new hymns were written.

Civil rulers strengthened their powers of government as the Church lost some of its power. Many churches were *established* (tax supported) by the state.

In economics, business men were shown additional respect. More people recognized that honest merchants and traders could also be devoted Christians.

The Reformation did not cause all of these results single-handedly, but it contributed significantly to their development.

■ **Check on Your Reading**

1. What did the Jesuits accomplish?
2. Summarize the Council of Trent.
3. How did the Reformation affect religion, education, and use of language?

3. *The International Situation*

The Protestant Reformation was a key factor in several economic, political, and religious conflicts. These struggles seriously affected domestic and international developments in the new national states and in lands that were to become nations.

Charles V and Philip II Rule Catholic Spain

The Hapsburg ruler, Charles V—as Emperor of the Holy Roman Empire and King of Spain—ruled a great empire (map, p. 316). Charles's holdings were increased by inheritance, by Spanish explorations of the New World, and by military conquests. It is not surprising that Charles V was accepted as the most important ruler on the continent.

It was particularly significant that Charles V was devoted to the defense of Catholicism. Although he was not primarily interested in extending the power of the Pope or of the Catholic Church in Rome, Charles wanted the Roman Catholic faith to be the only religion in Europe. When the Protestant Reformation of the sixteenth century threatened to convert people from Catholicism, he did everything that he could to stamp out Protestantism and heresy.

■ *Philip II of Spain was an authoritarian, grave, self-possessed ruler. As archchampion of Catholicism, he tried to make it the dominant religion of Europe.*

National Maritime Museum, Greenwich

315

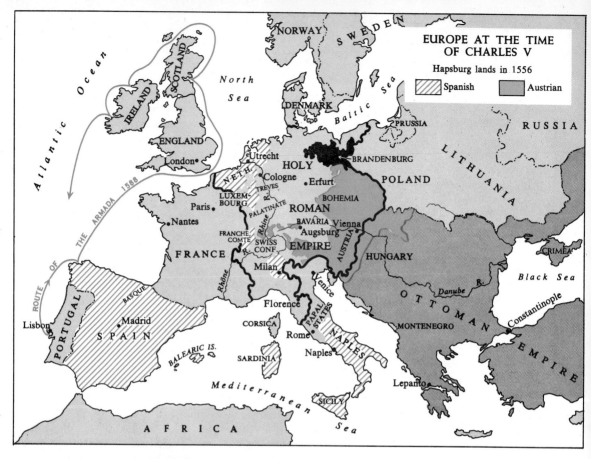

■ *Charles V as Holy Roman Emperor and King of Spain ruled a great empire—lands in Italy, Austria, Luxembourg, Germany, the Low Countries, Spain, and America. In 1556 he turned over the Holy Roman Empire to Ferdinand and his other holdings to Philip II. An international rivalry developed between Spain and England which was settled by the defeat of the Spanish Armada.*

Charles V had presided over the Diet of Worms which outlawed Luther. A series of religious wars wracked Germany from 1530 to 1555, and Charles V would have assisted the Catholic princes. However, he was engaged in fighting against France for power in Italy and he was also at war with the Ottoman Turks. In 1555 the Peace of Augsburg ended the war in Germany. By its terms, (1) the Protestant princes were allowed to hold the areas they controlled and (2) for the future each ruler in Germany was to choose his religion, whether Lutheran or Catholic, as the official religion of his state.

Near the end of his life, Charles turned over the Holy Roman Empire to his brother, Ferdinand I. He gave all his other holdings to his son, Philip II. He spent the rest of his life in a monastery.

Philip II was king of Spain during the second half of the sixteenth century (1556–1598). He was also ruler of much of the territory once held by Charles V. During Philip's reign Portugal was joined to Spain. The Philippine Islands were pacified and brought under Spanish control. In addition, Spanish colonies in America continued to ship gold, silver, and other treasure to Spain.

From his newly located capital at Madrid in Spain, Philip II directed an empire that was considered to be the most powerful in the world. Equally important, he continued to champion Catholicism against Protestantism in many countries of Europe.

The Protestant Dutch Rebel against Spain

In governing his empire, Philip II proved to be an autocratic monarch. He denied many of his subjects political rights. He placed restrictions on economic activities. Above all, he prevented freedom of religious worship.

Philip II was particularly severe in his conduct toward the Netherlands (today divided into the Netherlands and Belgium). As a powerful defender of Catholicism, he was determined to wipe out Protestantism there. However, his methods were so harsh that the people of the north—the Dutch—revolted in 1568.

Prince William of Orange (William the Silent) accepted the leadership of the rebels. Philip II hated William and promised to pay to the person "delivering him to us, alive or dead, or taking his life . . . the sum of twenty-five thousand crowns in gold." William was assassinated in 1584 but not before independence had been achieved. Today he is a national hero.

In 1579, by the Union of Utrecht, the seven northern provinces formed a confederation and agreed to fight Spain together. These were largely the Protestant provinces. The southern provinces (included in today's Belgium) were primarily Catholic and remained under Spanish rule.

Finally, in 1581 the people of the northern provinces—or the United Netherlands—declared themselves independent. The preamble to their "Dutch Declaration of Independence" shows a striking similarity to the Declaration of Independence of the American rebels of 1776 (see Chart).

In 1648, after the Thirty Years' War, Spain finally acknowledged Dutch independence. The southern provinces were added to the Dutch nation in the nineteenth century. Then in 1830 the Belgians established their own kingdom, which has remained independent.

Queen Elizabeth I Leads a Strong England

At the same time that Philip II ruled Spain, Elizabeth I was the monarch of England. Queen Elizabeth I (1558–1603) was described by a Venetian ambassador of the period as "tall and well made; her complexion fine, though rather sallow." Her hair was yellow-red, the color of autumn leaves; her face was shaped like

Preamble to the Dutch Declaration of Independence

All mankind know that a prince is appointed by God to cherish his subjects even as a shepherd to guard his sheep. When, therefore, the prince does not fulfill his duty as protector; when he oppresses his subjects, destroys their ancient liberties, and treats them as slaves . . . [the representatives] of the land may lawfully and reasonably depose him and elect another. . . .

American Declaration of Independence

. . . when a long train of abuses and usurpations . . . evinces a design to reduce [the people] under absolute Despotism, it is their right, it is their duty, to throw off such Government, and to provide new Guards for their future security.

© National Portrait Gallery, London

■ *Her biographer, Katherine Anthony, described Queen Elizabeth in this way: "Authority rather than dignity characterized her manner."*

an oval; and her eyes were deep-set. Elizabeth was a shrewd, strong-willed woman respected for her intelligence and for her ability to handle foreign languages. She became quite famous for her temper.

Queen Elizabeth ruled during one of the greatest periods in English history, and she wanted her subjects to take pride in their country. "I am the most *English* woman of the kingdom," she proclaimed. Then she worked diligently to make the people proud that they, too, were English.

Certainly, literary works written during the "Golden Age of Literature" that occurred in her reign—including Edmund Spenser's *The Faerie Queene*, Francis Bacon's *Essays*, and the plays of William Shakespeare—were reason enough for English pride. Indeed, few audiences failed

to be moved when a character in a play by Shakespeare called England: "This other Eden, demi-paradise."

England and Spain Are Bitter Rivals

Elizabeth's activities were particularly impressive in the field of foreign affairs. She strengthened the military power of her nation, increased foreign trade, and encouraged explorers to seek new lands.

As early as 1600, Elizabeth chartered the English East India Company to trade with lands in the Indian and Pacific oceans. English merchants traded with many other lands.

Two important voyages undertaken during her reign were Martin Frobisher's search for a northwest passage around America in 1576; and Sir Francis Drake's voyage to the coasts of South America, through the Straits of Magellan, and westward around the world to England. Drake's was the second ship to circumnavigate the world. Although Frobisher did not find any passage, he did locate arctic lands.

English expansion overseas had dangerous repercussions. Particularly important was that it increased the international rivalry between England and other countries, especially Spain. There were already tensions between these two nations. For one thing, Spain was Catholic and England had turned to Protestantism. In addition, Elizabeth refused to marry the Spanish ruler, Philip II. Spain became hostile to England for these additional reasons: (1) England tried to take away Spain's trade. (2) English sea captains raided Spanish vessels coming from Spain's colonies. (3) English merchants interfered with the affairs of Spain's West Indian colonies. (4) Sir Francis Drake attacked Spanish settlements in America. (5) England assisted the Dutch rebels who sought independence from Spain. Soon Spain and England would fight a great sea battle!

Elizabeth Re-establishes the Anglican Church

Even as England gained successes abroad, however, her government faced difficult problems at home. One of the most serious involved religion.

Elizabeth's predecessor as queen had been Mary, a devout Catholic who was the daughter of Henry VIII and his first wife, Catherine of Aragon. Mary (1553–1558) had restored the supremacy of Catholicism, which her father and her brother, Edward VI (1547–1553), had removed. Then she had persecuted Protestants.

When Elizabeth, the daughter of Henry VIII and Anne Boleyn, succeeded Mary as monarch, she led England into another and final break with the Roman Catholic Church. Elizabeth brought back the laws of Henry VIII, and thus established again a Church of England that was Protestant. In 1563 Parliament enacted the Thirty-Nine Articles outlining the dogma and doctrines of the Anglican Church. Elizabeth, of course, was excommunicated by the Pope; and the ambassador of Spain declared: "[England] has fallen into the hands of a woman who is the daughter of the devil!"

Tensions between religious groups continued. Roman Catholics wanted England to return to Catholicism. Protestant *Puritans* wanted England to erase every feature of the Anglican Church that still showed the influence of Catholicism—such as the robes of the clergy and the government by bishops instead of by ministers and members of the congregations. These Puritans and other *Dissenters*—that is, Protestants who refused to accept the ideas of the Anglican Church—disagreed bitterly with the government and with the Catholics.

The Catholics were eager to have Mary Stuart, Queen of Scots, replace Elizabeth. Mary Stuart was Catholic and could claim the English throne because her grandmother and Henry VIII had been sister and brother. However, uprisings in Scotland, plus a crisis that arose when Mary Stuart was accused of murdering her husband, forced her to abdicate from the Scottish throne in favor of her son, James VI. Mary Stuart fled to England for safety. Here she became entangled in an unsuccessful plot to kill Queen Elizabeth, and in 1587 she was beheaded to the cry: "So perish all enemies of the Queen!"

England Defeats the Spanish Armada

Philip II, the Catholic king of Spain, was greatly angered when Elizabeth permitted Mary Stuart to be beheaded. At last events reached a climax!

In 1588 the Spanish Armada, a powerful Spanish fleet, sailed through the English Channel. The English fleet, directed by Admiral Howard, met the enemy fleet

■ *This is a replica of Sir Francis Drake's* Golden Hind. *Queen Elizabeth knighted Drake on its deck after his voyage around the world.*

and a great sea battle began. The lightness and speed of the English ships gave them an advantage over the unwieldy Spanish ships. The weather proved to be stormy; and a number of ships in the Armada were damaged. A great North Sea storm dispersed and sank many more. The defeat of the powerful Spanish fleet was complete.

The defeat of "this invincible [Spanish] navy" was an important factor in the further disintegration of Spain as a world power. It made England supreme on the sea and added to her prestige.

France Issues the Edict of Nantes

By 1560, the Protestant *Huguenots,* or Calvinists, constituted a strong minority of the French population. A bitter struggle soon broke out between these Protestants and the Roman Catholics. The Huguenots were supported by the powerful Bourbon family of France.

The fighting, which lasted almost eight years, ended in 1570, but peaceful relations were not permanently restored. On St. Bartholomew's Day in 1572, Roman Catholics suddenly attacked and killed many Huguenots in Paris. This massacre and clashes elsewhere in France reopened the war between the Catholics and the Protestants. Philip II of Spain supported the Roman Catholic group in France that was most opposed to Protestantism.

Peace finally was restored when Henry of Navarre, of the house of Bourbon, became eligible for the throne of France. Henry was a Protestant, but he became a Roman Catholic to satisfy the Catholic majority in France. As King Henry IV, he issued the *Edict of Nantes* (1598), which granted French Huguenots the following rights: (1) freedom of religious belief; (2) the right of private worship wherever they lived; (3) the right of public worship in a number of specific towns and castles; (4) the right to hold public office; and (5) the right to control a number of walled towns and castles for their future protection.

The Thirty Years' War

In 1618 Europe was again disrupted by war. This conflict, known as the *Thirty Years' War*, was a complicated political-religious struggle that involved several countries and religious groups.

On one side were (1) Protestants, who wished to gain the right to worship as they pleased; (2) the princes of Germany, who wanted greater independence from the Holy Roman Emperor; (3) the Catholic Bourbon dynasty of France, which feared and envied the expansion of the Hapsburg rulers; and (4) the Protestant rulers of Denmark and Sweden, who desired to defend Protestantism and weaken the power of the Holy Roman Emperor.

On the other side were (1) Catholics, who wished to defend their faith and prevent Protestantism from spreading; (2) the Holy Roman Emperor, who wanted to keep control over the German princes and preserve Catholicism; and (3) the Hapsburg dynasties of Austria and Spain, which were determined to check the ambitions of the Bourbon dynasty of France.

First, the Holy Roman Emperor and his Catholic allies defeated Calvinist insurgents in Bohemia.

King Christian IV, the Lutheran ruler of Denmark, was defeated by an army directed by the great military leader Wallenstein and lost possessions in Germany.

Gustavus Adolphus of Sweden, a brilliant Protestant military leader, fought his way through Germany. After winning several victories, his army met the troops of Wallenstein in a great battle. Wallenstein was defeated, but Gustavus Adolphus was killed.

France fought against the Holy Roman Emperor and allies until the war ended.

The Treaty of Westphalia (1648) ended the Thirty Years' War. According to its provisions, Calvinism was to have the same status as Catholicism and Lutheranism in the Holy Roman Empire. Each prince could still decide on the religion for his territory, but people who belonged to none of these three sects could emigrate.

The princes in the German states were to be free to handle their diplomatic affairs and make treaties. Switzerland and the Dutch Netherlands were recognized as independent states. France received Alsace. Sweden obtained western Pomerania and Bremen. Some German princes received additional land (map, p. 321).

The Thirty Years' War greatly weakened the power of the Holy Roman Emperor in Germany, contributed to the rise of Brandenburg-Prussia (p. 343), caused terrible destruction in Germany, and played a part in the decline of Spain and in the growth of Swedish power in the Baltic.

THE TREATY OF WESTPHALIA

▒ To Sweden ▓ To France ▨ To Brandenburg
—— Boundary of the Empire in 1648

■ *The Treaty of Westphalia (1648) ended the Thirty Years' War. What countries became independent? Which ones gained territory?*

■ Check on Your Reading

1. Describe the empire of Charles V.
2. What were Philip II's relations with the Dutch? with England?

3. How did Elizabeth I strengthen England?
4. What were the causes, highlights, and results of the Thirty Years' War?

THE IMPACT of the Reformation on European Culture

The impact of the Reformation on European culture was felt in these and other ways:

The probing by people into the ideas, cultural values, and practices of their religions.

The establishment of Protestant churches, as well as reforms in some practices of the Catholic Church.

The intertwining of religious issues with political and military developments.

The influence of newer religious ideas on business practices. For example, more people recognized that a man could be both a good merchant and a good Christian.

The encouragement of a vernacular literature, particularly by the translation of the Bible.

The complexity of the Reformation—with its influences, extending to political, economic, social, and military affairs—must not conceal the fact that its impact on European culture was primarily *religious*. When the Calvinist-dominated government in Geneva gave prison sentences to "two burghers who played skittles . . . two others who played dice for a quarter-bottle of wine, [and] a man who insisted on naming his son Claude instead of Abraham," it did so for religious reasons. When the Pope praised the Jesuits for laboring "in the vineyard of the Lord," he was expressing his concern for religious values. When the question of charging interest rates on money came up, scholars turned for an answer to a religious work—*Deuteronomy*—not to business law. Religion dominated the scene.

Today serious efforts are being made to reaffirm the basic spiritual brotherhood of all those who believe in God, whether they be Catholics, Protestants, or members of other faiths. Meetings of the Ecumenical Council of the Roman Catholic Church, the conferences of the World Council of Churches, and other religious groups have all addressed themselves to the question, in the words of Pope John XXIII in the encyclical *Pacem in Terris* (Peace on Earth), of "discovering truth and paying homage to it."

In brief, some of the profound questions raised by the Reformation are still being discussed today. The sixteenth century continues to be a part of the twentieth!

MAN AND HIS CULTURE

Let's Meet the People!

The following sketch is based on information in *Social Germany in Luther's Time—Being the Memoirs of Bartholomew Sastrow.*

A German Bridegroom of the Reformation Era

Bartholomew Sastrow arrived at Greifswald near the Baltic Sea on January 1, 1551. He had come for his wedding. His sister, he later pointed out, had made most of the preliminary arrangements: "My sister, [at] Greifswald proposed to me to marry her sister-in-law. As I expected to be at Greifswald on New Year's Day, I wrote to her to arrange the wedding. . . ."

Shortly before his marriage, the bridegroom came into trouble with the law. The magistrates had been affected by the cleansing spirit of the Reformation. They "had been obliged to suppress the dances at weddings, because the manner in which the men whirled the matrons and damsels round and round had become indecent." Bartholomew, who knew nothing of this rule, later wrote:

. . . a week after our betrothal my intended and I were invited to a wedding. . . . When the wedding banquet was over, my betrothed came back to me, and, being ignorant of the [magistrates'] orders, I danced with her.

. . . an officer of the court came the next morning and summoned me to appear.

Luckily, the magistrates forgave Bartholomew his wicked deed.

His own marriage took place on February 2, 1551. At three o'clock the bridegroom stood on a square block of stone while the guests gathered near him. Then:

everybody [had] an opportunity of addressing some useful remark to the bridegroom at that critical moment. These remarks were often more forcible and outspoken than flattering. . . .

When this ceremony was over, the wedding service was held. Bartholomew's dream of peace and contentment did not come true, however. If it had, he would never have written in his memoirs: "From the moment of my marriage the devil seemed to have declared war against me."

CHAPTER REVIEW

REVIEW and DISCUSSION

1. Identify the people and places and explain the events and terms on p. 306.

2. Historical events are often caused by many factors. What factors caused the Protestant Reformation?

3. Why was the Church so vulnerable to attack in the sixteenth century?

4. Was Luther's opposition to the Peasants' Rebellion consistent with his beliefs?

5. Explain how Lutheranism differed from Catholicism.

6. During the Reformation period, were dissent and heresy considered the same? In our day?

7. Were reformers in the British Isles more concerned with the relations between Church and State than with religious dogma? Why?

8. The Puritans left England to seek freedom to worship. In Massachusetts they took strong measures to ensure religious conformity. How do you explain this apparent inconsistency?

9. Do you think the Edict of Nantes was a sensible compromise? Why?

10. How did the Thirty Years' War affect Europe?

ACTIVITIES

1. Visit a church besides your own to observe the rituals or ceremonies, sacraments, and vestments.

2. If you are a Protestant, write a historical report on the development of your own church—its origin, beliefs, ceremonies, practices, and activities. Note how its origin fits into the Reformation. If you are a Catholic, write a report on the Catholic Reformation. If you are Jewish, write a report on the emergence of Reformed and Conservative Judaism. If you hold other views on religions, show how they evolved in history. Consult encyclopedias, documents, and other references.

3. Can a man become wealthy and still be a Christian? Some theologians said "No," at one time. Calvinists said "Yes." What do you think? Why?

4. Write a report on one religious reformer. Conclude your report with your own evaluation of his activities.

5. Add the following paperbacks to your personal library: Butterfield, Herbert, and others, *A History of Science, a Symposium*; Bainton, Roland, *Here I Stand*; More, Sir Thomas, *Utopia*; Ross, James, and McLaughlin, Mary, (eds.), *The Portable Renaissance Reader*.

PAST and PRESENT

1. What features of life in the twentieth century can trace their origins back to the sixteenth and seventeenth centuries?

SUGGESTED READINGS

Basic books: CHURCHILL, WINSTON, *A History of the English-Speaking Peoples: The New World*, Dodd, Mead. Book IV discusses the period covered by this chapter.

PALMER, R. R., and COLTON, JOEL, *A History of the Modern World*, Chaps. 2, 3, Knopf.

SMITH, GOLDWIN, *The Heritage of Man*, Chaps. 20, 23, 24, Scribner.

Special accounts: HARBISON, ELMORE HARRIS, *The Age of Reformation* in "Development of Western Civilization" series, Cornell University Press. Brief and objective.

GRIMM, HAROLD J., *The Reformation Era, 1500–1650*, Macmillan. Scholarly, interesting reading.

MILLS, DOROTHY, *Renaissance and Reformation Times*, Putnam.

Biography and Fiction: BAINTON, ROLAND, *Here I Stand*, Abingdon Press. The life and times of Martin Luther.

BILL, ALFRED H., *The Ring of Danger: A Tale of Elizabethan England*, Knopf. A novel about Mary, Queen of Scots.

ROSS, JAMES, and McLAUGHLIN, MARY, (eds.), *The Portable Renaissance Reader*, Viking. Part V has excerpts from the writings of both Catholic and Protestant.

VANCE, MARGUERITE, *Elizabeth Tudor, Sovereign Lady*, Dutton.

UNIT 5 The Rise of Autocratic Powers in Europe

The Sultan of Swat—Czars— and History

How many titles can you find in history that refer to a person of great power? There is Emperor, Kaiser, Caesar, Mikado, Mogul, and many others which designate rulers who have autocratic power. Even in the modern world of sports and entertainment, power is recognized. Babe Ruth, one of the greatest hitters in baseball, was given the title "The Sultan of Swat." And Eric Johnston, as head of the Motion Picture Producers and Distributors of America, was called "The Czar of Motion Pictures."

Power, and the men and women who control it, has always played an important part in determining the course of history. Historians and other scholars are fully aware of this fact. They call certain governments autocracies. An *autocracy* is a type of government in which one person usually holds all of the power. He may permit others to use some of this power, but it still belongs to him. Since this power is not granted to the ruler by the consent of the people, he is not responsible to them for his actions.

Physician—Judge— Engineer— and You

In the coming unit you will read about "The Rise of Autocratic Powers in Europe" from about 1550 to 1770. You may ask: "Why should I study about autocratic men and the methods they used to obtain power? I don't live under an autocratic government. Why should I be concerned with this topic?"

You can find one answer to these questions by considering the following questions and answers: Q. What does a physician do who

324

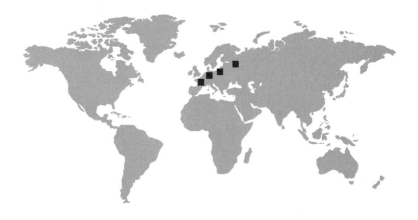

wishes to protect his patients? A. He studies the diseases that attack men. Q. What does a judge do who wishes to protect society? A. He learns about crimes that are committed against society. Q. What does an engineer do who wishes to protect the people who will use the bridge that he is constructing? A. He examines the river currents that might endanger the bridge. Q. Finally, *what does a citizen do who wishes to preserve democracy in his country?* A. He learns as much as he can about the types of men who seek dictatorial powers, and the methods they use to *undermine the democratic form of government.*

In other words, one of the principal reasons for studying the next unit is *to learn how to keep our own republic strong and prevent autocratic men from gaining power.*

Knowledge—Understanding—and the Future

Yet you do not study about autocratic countries merely through fear of them. Knowledge of the ways of men has other purposes than to protect you against tyrants. It should help you to operate more intelligently in today's world. For example, one pound of chlorine can disinfect 200,000 gallons of water. Similarly, a few sound ideas, used with intelligence and understanding, might help to clear up the relations of thousands of people.

Thus, an equally important reason for studying the history of these nations that were not democratic is *to acquire understanding and ability to deal more effectively with their leaders in international affairs today.*

Chapter 20

The Russian Nation Grows While Autocrats Block Freedom

KEYNOTE In the year 1838 a high-strung Russian student, convinced that he was being treated unjustly by his school authorities, struck the director of his medical school on the ear. This action was so shocking that it was reported to the ruler of Russia. When the Russian monarch heard about the case, he permitted the student to be beaten by the blows of five hundred men. Then he sentenced him "to spend ten years wearing chains"!

Why did the Russian czar impose such severe punishment? Certainly it was not because he was concerned about the director's ear. Rather, it was because the student had dared to challenge *authority*. This was a very serious crime in the eyes of the monarch.

The government's insistence on absolute obedience to authority—whether it be that of the ruler or an official—was a feature of Russian life. As the Russian minister for education put it: "Autocracy is the main condition of Russia's political existence."

Yet the minister of education did not stop there. He added this comment: "Equally important and equally strong [is] patriotism." A feeling of devotion to the nation was to go hand in hand with obedience to authority.

The existence of both national feeling and autocratic rule was not limited to this period in the nineteenth century. On the contrary, one of the basic facts of Russian history is this: *As the Russian nation and Russian patriotism developed through history, autocracy continually exercised a strong influence on Russian life. It does so today!*

Key People *Ivan IV · Michael Romanov · Peter the Great · Catherine II*

Key Places *Moscow · Novgorod · Siberia · Poltava · Saint Petersburg · Poland · Crimea*

Key Events *Ivan IV rules as first czar · Time of Troubles · Romanov dynasty · Peter the Great changes Russia · Catherine the Great expands the empire · Pugachev rebellion · Poland partitioned*

Key Terms *boyars · Zemsky Sobor · serfdom · Cossacks · Enlightenment*

Russia

| 1500 A.D. | 1550 | 1600 | 1650 | 1700 | 1750 | 1800 A.D. |

Ivan IV · Time of Troubles · Serfdom recognized · Pugachev rebellion

Zemsky Sobor meets · Michael Romanov · Peter the Great · Catherine II

Poltava · Partitions of Poland

1. Russian Geography and History Are Linked

The most striking geographic fact about Russia (today called the Union of Soviet Socialist Republics) is its enormous size. It is the largest country in the world and occupies about one-sixth of the land surface of the earth (map, p. 328).

Historical Importance of Russia's Size: Russia is huge because it includes lands in both Europe and Asia. Throughout its history Russia has been affected by events in both continents. One of the constant factors has been Russia's drive to the east, west, and south.

Russia's border is over 35,000 miles long. Despite her long seacoasts, Russia does not have many good ports. Her coastlines on the Pacific and Arctic oceans are frozen during much of the year.

Historical Importance of Russia's Limited Access to the Sea: History has been influenced by Russia's many efforts to gain access to the sea—particularly by her attempts to obtain the straits that lead from the Black to the Aegean Sea.

Russia is a land rich in a variety of natural resources, including petroleum, iron ore, coal, and timber. The terrain of the country also varies. There are regions of frozen earth, forest, rich black soil, desert, and semitropical land. Most of Russia consists of a huge plain extending from Poland into Siberia.

Historical Importance of Russia's Great Plain: This great plain has served as a passageway for many invaders. Its openness has made it difficult to defend.

The climate of Russia is generally colder than that of the United States. The weather in the great plain is biting cold during the winter months. But Russia has a variety of climates. The weather in some of Russia's southern cities is sometimes similar to that of Florida.

Russia has many great rivers. Among the important rivers are the Volga, flowing into the Caspian Sea; the Dnieper, flowing into the Black Sea; the Don, flowing into the Sea of Azov; and the Amur, flowing into the Pacific Ocean.

Historical Importance of Russia's Rivers: Although many do not flow in the most advantageous direction, the rivers later tied the Russian empire together.

In the light of these relationships, we can understand why one Russian geography book today states: "The lines and signs of the map [of Russia] indicate the path history has traversed!"

■ Check on Your Reading

1. Name two ways in which Russia's size has been historically important.

2. What two geographic assets has Russia historically sought to acquire?

2. Ivan IV: First "Czar of All the Russias"

In the second half of the sixteenth century, the land held by Russia was not as extensive as it is today. A most important ruler was Ivan IV (1533–1584), the grandson of Ivan III. *Ivan IV was the first ruler to take the title "Czar of All the Russias."*

After the death of Julius Caesar, the surname *Caesar* was retained by Roman emperors as a title showing authority. Some scholars believe that the term *czar* was later derived from the word Caesar; other scholars dispute this point.

In addition, since the days of Ivan III, religious leaders of the Russian Orthodox Church referred to Moscow as the *Third Rome.* This meant that they considered Moscow to be the third center to be responsible for maintaining the Christian faith in a pure state. (According to them, Rome and Constantinople had been the first and second "repositories of religious truth," but they had declined in influence.)

The use of the word czar meant that Ivan IV considered himself to be the absolute ruler of Russia. A czar, he declared, was "born into [power] by the will of God"—and was responsible only to God for his acts.

■ *Russia, or the Union of Soviet Socialist Republics, today is a federation consisting of fifteen republics. Its size is about two and one third times the United States and its 35,000-mile border touches on twelve countries. What are its principal cities, rivers, and types of terrain?*

THE SOVIET UNION
THE FIFTEEN SOVIET SOCIALIST REPUBLICS

1. RUSSIAN (includes small area north of Poland)	2. ESTONIAN	5. BYELORUSSIAN	8. GEORGIAN	11. TURKMEN	14. TADZHIK
	3. LATVIAN	6. MOLDAVIAN	9. ARMENIAN	12. UZBEK	15. KIRGHIZ
	4. LITHUANIAN	7. UKRAINIAN	10. AZERBAIJAN	13. KAZAKH	

Certainly, Ivan IV did everything possible to concentrate authority in himself. Thus, he took away the power of the *boyars,* that is, the nobles who usually held their land by inheritance. When they continued to challenge his authority, Ivan IV deprived them of many of their rights. Ivan then helped to organize a new group of nobles who would be faithful to him in exchange for land and position.

To those Russians who dared oppose him, Ivan IV showed a cruelty that has rarely been surpassed. He tortured boyars, set ferocious bears on unarmed peasants, and killed his own son with a steel-tipped staff.

Ivan also sent out officials whose task it was to destroy his enemies. These officials spread terror wherever they went. Dressed in black robes and riding black horses, they became fearful messengers of death to many Russians.

At the same time that he used terror to build his autocratic power, Ivan IV supported the expansion of the Russian nation. His activities included the following: (1) He fought with Poland and Sweden in an effort to extend Russia's borders to the Baltic Sea. (2) He encouraged the colonization of lands to the east and southeast. Just as Americans "went west," so Russians (drawn by the fur trade and other attractions) "went east." Russian expansion, however, was more thoroughly

■ *Ivan IV, known as "Ivan the Terrible" and Ivan the Dread, was the first "Czar of all the Russias." He developed autocracy.*

planned and controlled by the government. (3) He permitted the English to develop and expand their trade with Russia.

■ **Check on Your Reading**

1. Explain the significance of "czar."

2. How did Ivan IV contribute to the expansion of the Russian nation?

3. A "Time of Troubles" and the Romanov Dynasty Begins

Despite the terror produced by Ivan IV, it was in his reign that a *National Assembly,* or *Zemsky Sobor,* of Russia was first called (1550). During the next century, there were other Zemsky Sobors. These assemblies discussed such matters as war and peace, foreign affairs, and taxation. They also could give advice to the czars, *but they could not pass laws or force a ruler to take action.*

The Zemsky Sobors were not "representative assemblies." Although their membership varied, they generally consisted of government officials, church leaders, trusted nobles, and important merchants and townsmen. Two National Assemblies

■ *In this painting by Repin, Cossacks are shown writing letters of defiance to the Turkish Sultan. Gogol's novel* Taras Bulba *vividly describes the bold adventurous life of the Cossacks who frequently fought the Turks and attacked the Poles.*

probably included a few free peasants. Usually the majority of people were ignored.

A "Time of Troubles"

It was a Zemsky Sobor that helped to restore order in a time of crisis in the seventeenth century.

After Ivan IV died, the czars gradually lost their hold on the country. In the so-called "Time of Troubles" (c. 1604 to 1613), there were many conflicts among men ambitious for the throne. There were also peasant uprisings, famines, and foreign invasions. So great was the confusion that Swedish forces occupied Novgorod and Poles seized Moscow.

Then a feeling akin to nationalism seemed to surge through many Russians. They wanted Russian land to be freed from foreign troops, and Russian cities to be returned to them. They wanted Russians to be governed by Russians.

The Russians were still divided into several factions at this time, but it must be admitted that there were definite signs of national feeling. This Russian nationalism was to develop in future years.

Toward the end of the "Time of Troubles" a more representative Zemsky Sobor met. In 1613 this assembly unanimously elected Michael Romanov to be the new czar. Michael (1613–1645), the first of the *Romanov dynasty* which ruled until 1917, continued the work of pushing back foreign invaders and restoring order.

Serfdom Checks the Growth of Democracy

Despite the fact that the Zemsky Sobor had used the method of election to choose Michael Romanov to be the new czar, democracy did not grow stronger in Russia. One of the factors that seriously hindered its growth was the development of *serfdom.*

Serfdom in medieval Europe was a system in which the peasants remained on the land of a lord. In exchange for the lord's protection and a share of the crops, the serfs worked the soil and made various payments to, and performed duties for, the lord.

Serfs had few personal freedoms. They could not take an active part in government, express their opinions, or change their occupations.

Serfdom did not appear suddenly in Russia. It developed gradually and by several methods: (1) For example, a poor peasant borrowed from a noble in order to obtain tools or seed. If the peasant could not pay back his debt, he might be forced to stay on the lord's land as a serf.

(2) At times the lives and fields of many peasants were threatened by marauders. Some of these peasants became the serfs of a lord to gain protection.

(3) Since serfs usually remained in the same place, serfdom helped rulers to collect taxes from them. Some rulers, to be sure of collecting taxes, issued decrees that brought more people under a system of serfdom.

Serfdom increased in Russia during the fifteenth century. It was in this century, too, that Ivan III issued a famous law code (1497). This code had provisions that limited the peasants' right to move away from their lords. Serfdom was widespread in Russia long before it legally came into existence in the country. Under the Romanov dynasty, serfdom was *legally* recognized in 1649.

Serfdom could not wipe out every trace of democratic living—not as long as there were *Cossacks*. Cossacks were bold and adventurous men who had moved to the southern frontier of Russia. Here they developed a sturdy tradition of independence. The Cossacks established communities along the Don and Dnieper rivers and in other regions. Until about the end of the seventeenth century, Cossack communities had several democratic features.

Yet the Cossacks were only a tiny minority of the people. Most Russian peasants were not bold and independent frontiersmen. Rather, by the middle of the seventeenth century, the great majority lived under the heavy yoke of serfdom.

■ **Check on Your Reading**

1. Describe the Zemsky Sobors.
2. What was the "Time of Troubles"?
3. How did the Romanovs come to power?
4. Explain how serfdom affected social, economic, and political life.

4. Peter the Great Tries to "Modernize" Russia

The Romanov rulers legally recognized serfdom, but they did not give up any governing powers to the Zemsky Sobor. No one expected or ordered them to do so. As they grew stronger, the Romanovs used the assemblies less frequently. The Zemsky Sobor did not develop into a democratic or permanent institution. It declined and came to an end in 1682.

Autocracy remained strong while the nation continued to grow. The reign of Peter the Great (1682–1725) was particularly important in Russia's development. Peter was a giant in height (6 feet 7 inches). Dynamic, energetic, and filled with restless curiosity, he was determined to make Russia one of the great nations of the world. To achieve this goal, he felt Russia had to sweep away many of her old ways. He was convinced of the need to "modernize."

Peter Attempts to Use Western Ideas

Peter, with about two hundred Russians, made a visit to western Europe.

THE GROWTH OF RUSSIA

- Russia before 1682
- Added by Peter the Great, to 1725
- Added 1725-1762
- Added by Catherine II, to 1796

■ *Expansion of Russia's territory continued to be the policy of the czars, especially under Peter and Catherine. What territories did they add?*

One of their chief objectives was to learn western methods and techniques that could be used in Russia. Peter and his group visited Germany, Holland, England, and other countries. The Russians soon discovered that they had much to learn about western life. That was obvious from such reports as this one, by a slightly shocked German noblewoman:

... in dancing, [the Russians mistook] the whalebones of our corsets for our bones, and the Czar showed his astonishment by saying that the German ladies had ... hard bones.

Despite such mistakes, the Russians returned to their country with many valuable ideas. Peter the Great now decided to use drastic measures to make his people

give up their old ways. Peter ordered the nobles to shave off their old-fashioned beards. He told Russians to cut off the long sleeves of their robes and to dress more like the people of the West. He even arranged for the publication of a book of etiquette. This book informed the Russian nobles that gentlemen did not pick their teeth with their knives!

Peter cannot be called the first ruler to bring western ideas into Russia. Other czars already had established trading and cultural contacts with the West. Some changes introduced by Peter were superficial. They did not affect the great mass of people. Nevertheless, Peter must be given considerable recognition for his conscientious efforts to westernize Russia.

Peter the Great: Reformer and Autocrat

During his reign as czar, Peter was active in many fields. Some of his most important accomplishments were these: (1) He fought against Sweden and other countries and obtained territory along the Baltic coast. This gave Russia a "window to the West"—that is, Russia now had outlets to and contacts with European trade and culture.

(2) Peter reformed the Russian army and played an important role in building a Russian navy. The Russians were recognized as a major military power in Europe when they defeated the forces of Charles XII of Sweden at the Battle of Poltava (1709).

(3) During Peter's reign, exploration, trade, and industry were stimulated. A new city, Saint Petersburg (Leningrad), was built on the Gulf of Finland. It became the Russian capital in place of Moscow. Peter revised the structure of government, but he was unable to develop a really efficient and honest system of government.

(4) Education of the upper classes was encouraged. Peter approved the founding of the first Russian newspaper, and he

supported plans to establish a Russian Academy of Science. He simplified the forty-two letter alphabet of Church Slavonic, which made it easier to write secular literature. (5) Peter changed the Russian calendar. January first was recognized as the beginning of the Russian new year.

Despite these accomplishments, Peter the Great was neither a democrat nor a great humanitarian. He ruled as czars were expected to rule—as an autocrat. Peter was very severe with the lower groups and the clergy. The serfs were treated harshly. Wars and projects were financed with taxes that fell heavily on the poor. Uncooperative religious leaders were subdued by bringing the Russian Orthodox Church more completely under state control.

Peter hoped to raise Russia to a point where she could rival the nations of western Europe. He even discarded his title of czar and took the more westernized title of emperor. Yet no man could change Russia radically in a few years. People continued to call their leader *czar*, and Russian life continued to follow many old patterns.

Peter the Great

■ *A dynamic, energetic, inquiring ruler, Peter the Great wanted to make Russia a great nation. He instituted many reforms but he ruled as czars were expected to rule—as an autocrat.*

■ **Check on Your Reading**

1. How did Peter the Great attempt to "modernize" Russia? with what success?

2. Evaluate Peter's achievements as czar.

3. In what ways was Peter "neither a democrat nor a humanitarian"?

5. Catherine Cares More for the Empire than for the People

The reign of Catherine II (1762–1796), or Catherine the Great, was another important and colorful period in Russian history. Catherine was a vigorous woman with an alert mind and a determination to bring "glory" to herself and Russia. Eager for new plans, she would sometimes rise at 5 A.M., light a fire, and work for hours on a promising project. Little wonder that the mere men who were her ministers found it difficult to keep up with her.

Catherine was a talented person who was greatly affected by the *Enlightenment* that swept through England, France, and Germany in the eighteenth century. The Enlightenment was a movement that stressed the idea that men should assemble as much knowledge as possible and solve their problems by *reason and intelligence*. As the eighteenth-century German philosopher Immanuel Kant pointed out: "Dare to use your own understanding [was] the motto of Enlightenment."

The spirit of the Enlightenment affected men's studies of science, religion, history, and political affairs; and Catherine was not immune to it. Her pen became as active as her mind. She exchanged brilliant letters with many of the leading intellects of Europe, including the French philosopher Voltaire. She wrote plays, satires, and fairy tales; compiled books of proverbs; and wrote one of the first Russian textbooks for children. She was willing to try her hand at anything that might prove stimulating.

For a time, she was influenced by the liberal ideas of Voltaire and other philosophers. She gained considerable fame as an "enlightened" ruler. This reputation was partially deserved, for she did perform many useful acts. For example, she encouraged the education of the children of the nobility; supported the study of science and medicine; helped to increase interest in French culture; stimulated the writing of literature, the creation of works of art, and the construction of new buildings; and extended freedom of worship to several religious groups.

Yet an accurate picture of Catherine's reign cannot be drawn from these activities alone. It is equally important to examine her actions in regard to serfdom and foreign affairs.

Catherine and Serfdom

Catherine extended serfdom through many parts of Russia, including the Ukraine. She treated serfs brutally, ignored their basic needs, and made their lives more wretched than before. At the same time that she gave the nobles new privileges—such as exempting them from compulsory military service and taxation —she took away most of the remaining rights of the serfs.

Some men were considered to be no better than cattle. Newspapers like the *Moscow Gazette* ran such advertisements as:

To be sold, a barber, and in addition to that four bedsteads. . . .

To be sold, banqueting tablecloths and also two trained girls and a peasant.

It is clear that Catherine was not a democrat but an autocrat.

Certainly, she cared little for Russia's approximately thirty-four million peasants. Of these, about twenty million were now serfs on private estates. The rest were serfs of the state or monarchy, or free peasants. They were not much better off than privately owned serfs. This meant that out of a total Russian population estimated at thirty-six million, *a great majority of the people were in some condition of forced service.*

In 1773 the oppressed Russians could stand it no longer. A major revolt broke out against Catherine's regime. It was led by a Cossack named Pugachev. Pugachev's following consisted of fugitive serfs, religious dissenters, Cossacks, Tatars, and others. They swept through the Ural region and the lands around the middle and lower Volga. Their revolt was finally crushed, and Catherine continued her rule.

Poland Is Partitioned

In foreign affairs, Catherine used diplomacy and war to expand Russia's territory. The kingdom of Poland was one of Russia's chief targets. Poland had been a large and powerful kingdom in the fifteenth and sixteenth centuries. By the eighteenth century, Poland was still large, but a weak country with a feudal economy. Its king had little real authority. He was elected by an assembly of nobles, but monarchs of other European countries continually interfered in these elections. The rulers of Poland were unable to build a strong army or to settle the clashes among minority groups.

Russia, Austria, and the new state of Prussia, ambitious for territory, therefore joined in wars against Poland. Despite the efforts of Polish heroes like Thaddeus Kosciuszko, Poland was partitioned, or divided, among Russia, Austria, and Prussia three times (1772, 1793, and 1795). Russia received a considerable part, and at the end of the third partition, Poland ceased to appear on the map. It did not reappear until 1919 (map, p. 335).

Russia and the Ottoman Empire

Russia also pushed southward, fought the Ottoman Empire, and eventually conquered the Crimea. This gave the Russians a stronghold on the northern shore of the Black Sea. It increased Russia's determination to control Constantinople and the straits that linked the Black Sea with the Aegean and Mediterranean.

In the east, the vast area of Siberia continued to be settled. By 1800 Russia was larger than any state in Europe. Like a giant stretching its arms, it embraced many lands and peoples.

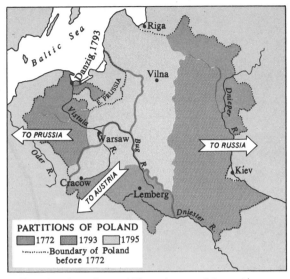

PARTITIONS OF POLAND
■ 1772 ■ 1793 □ 1795
·······Boundary of Poland
       before 1772

■ *Russia, Austria, and Prussia agreed to partition Poland among them (1772, 1793, 1795,) and Poland ceased to exist as a country.*

■ Check on Your Reading

1. Explain why Catherine the Great is called an "enlightened despot."
2. What happened to the serfs in the reign of Catherine the Great?

3. How did Catherine handle relations with (a) Poland, (b) the Ottoman Empire?
4. Explain why Poland was divided so often?

CULTURAL CHARACTERISTICS of Russia—16th through 18th Century

Life was good for the autocratic leaders of Russia from the sixteenth through the eighteenth century. Nobles with as many as 17 footmen, forty-course dinners, and gold embroidered coats worth hundreds of thousands of dollars were all part of the luxurious style of living of the Russian nobility.

Yet the rulers of Russia were hard workers too. Catherine began her day before sunrise; and Peter the Great enjoyed showing people the callouses he had earned by hard physical labor. In brief, the Russian leaders were autocratic rulers, but they were also earnest workers at the task of building a strong nation. This fact was reflected in the cultural characteristics of Russia from the sixteenth through the eighteenth century:

A society based on a powerful nobility that governed Russia autocratically.

The development of serfdom embracing the great majority of Russian peasantry by the middle of the seventeenth century.

Efforts by the ruling group to stimulate the cultural growth of Russia by borrowing from Western Europe in such fields as education, science, literature, and art and architecture. These activities were designed primarily for the intellectual elite and for people who held political, economic, and social power.

Because of the great size of Russia, stimulation of the cultural life was difficult. Today, even with the coming of jet power, size continues to be a significant factor in Russian life today. So does autocracy. So does the rulers' determination to stimulate the growth of their nation. And—as in days past—the world tensely awaits the direction of Russia's future.

335

MAN AND
HIS CULTURE

**Let's Meet
the People!**

This sketch is based primarily on the observations of William Tooke, an Englishman who spent a number of years in Russia. Extracts from his report appear in *Readings in Russian History*, edited by Warren B. Walsh, 1959, Syracuse University Press.

**A Peasant
of
Eighteenth-Century
Russia**

The Russian peasant we are considering was a heavy-set man with a long and bushy brown beard. He wore a collarless shirt, loose trousers of homespun cloth, and mat-slippers or half-boots. To protect himself from the cold, he tied wrappings around his feet and legs. During the winter months he also put on an old sheepskin coat.

The Russian peasant lived in a one-room house. Light was admitted into this house "through two or three holes in the walls furnished with shutters." Smoke found its way out "as well as it could." Sleeping places were set close to the oven.

The peasant's house was infested with vermin. It was reported: "Besides the common house-rat and mouse, [it swarmed] with . . . crickets, bugs, fleas in abundance; various kinds of very troublesome flies, gnats, moths, bullmoths, wood-lice."

The Russian peasant usually ate simple meals. They consisted of such foods as: cabbage soup, bread, fish, turnips, onions, melons, and tea. The peasant ate "very poorly" most of the time. He also was fond of *kvas* (a kind of beer), and sometimes he became quite drunk. But drink could not prevent bad weather nor keep away the famines that occasionally spread through the land.

The Russian peasant labored long. He manured the soil with wood-ash; he pushed the one-horse plough; he cut the grain with sickles and threshed it with flails; he worked the rye and the barley and the oats until his muscles ached—and then he went on working.

Thus the peasant lived. Food or famine he drew from the soil. But happiness or sorrow he drew from himself.

CHAPTER REVIEW

REVIEW and DISCUSSION

1. Identify the people and places and explain the events and terms on p. 326.

2. Explain the relationship between Russian history and geography.

3. "Our greatest enemy is space," an old Russian proverb says. When was space an enemy? a friend?

4. Compare the great westward movement of nineteenth-century Americans with Russian expansion eastward across the plains to Siberia.

5. Compare the life of the Russian serfs with that of the slaves in the United States in the 1800's.

6. Why did Peter think it was necessary to westernize Russia? Were his methods of "modernizing" Russia logical? Why?

7. Peter ruled "as czars were expected to rule—as autocrats." Why did the Russians expect their rulers to be autocrats?

8. How do you explain Catherine's lack of "enlightenment" about the conditions of the peasants?

9. What is your explanation for the ruthlessness and cruelty of the Russian rulers?

10. What territories were added to Russia by Peter and Catherine? How?

ACTIVITIES

1. Write a short paper on absolutism or autocracy. Consult the *Encyclopedia of the Social Sciences* and other references.

2. Compare the activities of Peter and Catherine with those of other autocratic rulers. What are your conclusions?

3. On a map of Russia locate the Amur River; Baltic and Black seas; Crimea; Dnieper, Don, and Lena rivers; Moscow, St. Petersburg; Siberia; and the Ural and Volga rivers.

4. Report on Peter's Grand Tour of western Europe as Peter might have told it on his arrival home.

5. Write a report on Thaddeus Kosciuszko's deeds in Poland and America.

PAST and PRESENT

1. In what ways do modern dictators resemble Peter and Catherine?

2. Debate the following: Resolved, that the Soviet Union's present expansion policy is a continuation of Russia's historic foreign policy.

3. How many similarities can you find between the methods of communism and those of previous Russian autocracies?

SUGGESTED READINGS

Basic books: PALMER, R. R., and COLTON, JOEL, *A History of the Modern World*, pp. 312–318, Knopf.

SMITH, GOLDWIN, *The Heritage of Man*, Chap. 22, Scribner. Highly recommended.

Special accounts: CHARQUES, RICHARD D., *A Short History of Russia*, Dutton. (Paperback). Reference for pre-Communist period.

LAMB, HAROLD, *The City and the Tsar: Peter the Great and the Move to the West, 1648–1762*, Doubleday. Interesting reading for high school pupils.

LAMB, HAROLD, *The March of Muscovy; Ivan the Terrible and the Growth of the Russian Empire, 1400–1648*, Doubleday. For better readers.

PAYNE, ROBERT, *The Terrorists; The Story of the Forerunners of Stalin*, Funk and Wagnalls. Describes the use of terror as a way of abolishing differences of opinion.

SEEGER, ELIZABETH, *The Pageant of Russian History*, Longmans, Green. Interesting. Easy reading. Covers the entire range of Russian history.

WALSH, WARREN B., (ed.), *Readings in Russian History*, Syracuse University Press. One of the few source books available.

Biography and Fiction: SCHERMAN, KATHERINE, *Catherine the Great*, MD 270, New American Library. Fiction that makes effective use of historical background.

SLONIM, MARC, *An Outline of Russian Literature*, Oxford. A history of Russian literature from the beginning to the revolution of 1917.

Chapter 21   *Autocratic Rulers Clash in International Wars*

KEYNOTE   King Philip III, who ruled Spain in the first part of the seventeenth century, once had an unfortunate accident. According to the historian Paul Tabori, King Philip fell asleep in a chair before the fire and was burned "because his courtiers could not find the [official] whose duty it was to move the chair away from the fireplace." The king had decreed that only one official should move the royal chair, and his subjects would not disobey that order!

Such incidents were dramatic reminders of how absolute a ruler's authority might become in Europe. This fact was demonstrated again in the reigns of "enlightened despots" like Maria Theresa, head of the Hapsburg realm, and Frederick the Great, king of Prussia. The ambitions of these and other absolute rulers led to wars that destroyed or injured many people. Nevertheless, the orders of these autocrats were obeyed. One of the key features of the seventeenth and eighteenth centuries was this: *Autocracy remained strong in Europe while countries clashed in international wars.*

Key People   *John Sobieski · Maria Theresa · Joseph II · Frederick William the Great Elector · Frederick William I · Frederick the Great · Johann Sebastian Bach · George Frederick Handel · Wolfgang Amadeus Mozart*

Key Places   *Austria · Prussia · Hungary · Bohemia · Balkans · Vienna · Silesia*

Key Events   *Turks defeated at Vienna · War of the Spanish Succession · Hohenzollerns rule Prussia · War of the Austrian Succession · Seven Years' War*

Key Terms   *absolute ruler · "enlightened despot" · Pragmatic Sanction · oratorio · symphony · chamber music*

338

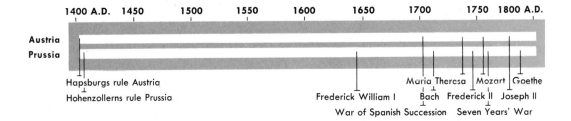

| | 1400 A.D. | 1450 | 1500 | 1550 | 1600 | 1650 | 1700 | 1750 | 1800 A.D. |

Austria

Prussia

Hapsburgs rule Austria
Hohenzollerns rule Prussia

Maria Theresa   Mozart   Goethe

Frederick William I   Bach   Frederick II   Joseph II

War of Spanish Succession   Seven Years' War

1. Austria and Prussia: Geography Influences History

The most important Germanic areas of Europe were Austria and Prussia. The history of Austria is a long one. The Prussian state came into existence in the 1700's.

Austria: Geography Affects History

The history of Austria is closely linked with this geographic fact: Austria is located in a central position in Europe.

Historical Importance of Austria's Central Position: Because of its location, Austria was a land where the north-to-south and east-to-west movements of peoples crossed. As a result, Austria was invaded by many groups from Europe and Asia during ancient and medieval times.

Another geographic factor that has contributed to the shaping of Austrian history has been the Alps Mountains.

Historical Importance of Austria's Mountains: The Alps cut across Austria so that only one half of the land was used for agriculture. Wheat, rye, oats, and grapes for wine were grown. Cattle were raised. Austria was not self-sufficient in food production and had to depend on other countries for many foodstuffs.

Prussia: Geography Influences History

Prussia was chiefly an agricultural land. On its Central Plain were large estates.

Historical Importance of Prussia's Central Plain: The Central Plain was the principal agricultural region. There the Junkers (great-landed nobles) had large estates which were worked by serfs, while many nobles served as officers in the Prussian army. These Junkers became so powerful that they greatly influenced Prussian history.

Prussia also has many mineral resources, which were essential to the development of industry and manufacturing.

Historical Importance of Prussia's Mineral Resources: Valuable mineral deposits were coal, lead, zinc, copper, and potash. When Prussia later became part of Germany, that country used the minerals to develop important manufactures.

Thus, in Prussia, as in Austria, geography helped to shape the course of history.

■ **Check on Your Reading**

1. How has location affected Austria?
2. Why was the Central Plain important?

CENTRAL EUROPE

■ *Central Europe is composed of a number of countries. The two most important German states are Austria and Prussia, which became part of modern Germany. How has geography influenced the history of Central Europe?*

2. History of the Austrian Empire

When you think of Austria today, what comes to mind? Usually it is a picture of many peaceful and charming scenes. One sees the untracked slopes of snow-covered mountains in the Tyrol province; the historic Danube River; and the "Schuhplattler" dance, in which men gaily slap their knees, thighs, and shoes. And one hears music—the music of Austrian composers like Mozart, Schubert, and Johann Strauss.

It is little wonder that men sometimes forget that Austria was not always a small country of peace and harmony. Yet a study of history will show that Austria was once not only an empire but a land in ferment.

The Hapsburgs Rise to Power

In the years before 1200 A.D. Austria was the scene of many important historical

events. In the thirteenth century the Hapsburg family became the rulers of Austria.

After the early part of the fifteenth century, the Hapsburgs of Austria were almost always chosen to serve as emperors of the Holy Roman Empire (p. 290). They spread their influence over Europe and the New World by marrying into other royal families. In this way, the kingdoms of Hungary and Bohemia were united with Austria. By a variety of means, the Hapsburgs built up a great empire which reached a peak in the sixteenth century under Charles V (p. 315).

The Hapsburgs suffered several defeats in the Thirty Years' War (p. 321). The various states in Germany were granted greater independence from the Holy Roman Emperor, an Austrian Hapsburg.

340

Nevertheless, Austria continued to be the most important power in Germany.

The Turkish Threat Is Checked

The Turks were another power that challenged Austria as well as other European countries. The Ottoman Turks came from the central tablelands of Asia and overthrew the decaying Byzantine Empire. In the middle of the sixteenth century the Ottoman Empire reached its peak. It included lands in Asia, Africa, the Middle East, and Europe, including Hungary.

Especially important for future events, the Turks controlled the *Balkans*, that is, the rugged, mountainous peninsula in southeast Europe. The peninsula is about twice the size of the state of Utah. The Balkans were—and are—in a position of great strategic importance. For many centuries the peninsula was a geographic "bridge" between Asia Minor and Europe, a bridge crossed by many peoples.

In the latter part of the sixteenth century, Turkish power began to decline. In 1683 the Turks tried to capture Vienna, the capital city of the Hapsburgs. The Turks almost succeeded in their attempt, but they were finally defeated by John Sobieski, King of Poland, who came to the aid of the Hapsburgs. According to Sobieski, the Turkish leader who attacked Vienna "barely escaped, on horseback, with nothing but the coat on his back."

By the end of the seventeenth century, as a result of the efforts of Austria, Poland, Russia, and other countries, the Turks had lost valuable land in the Balkans (such as Bosnia). Equally important, Austria had obtained control of Hungary.

Austria Gains Additional Land

Austria was soon involved in another conflict, the War of the Spanish Succession (1701–1713). This war developed from a dispute over the choice of a successor to the throne of Spain. Louis XIV of France upheld the right of a French Bourbon prince to inherit the throne from the Spanish Hapsburg king, Charles II. England, Austria, and their allies were determined to prevent such an increase in the power and territory of the Bourbon rulers of France. In the War of the Spanish Succession, Austria, England, Holland, and others fought against France, Spain, and Bavaria.

Austria and her allies were successful in the fighting (p. 361). By the Treaties of Utrecht (1713) ending the war, Austria received (1) the Spanish Netherlands (modern-day Belgium), which were renamed the Austrian Netherlands, and (2) Naples, Milan, and Sardinia, formerly held by Spain.

Maria Theresa Leads the Austrian Empire

In 1740 Maria Theresa succeeded her father, Charles VI. She became ruler of the Austrian state as well as of the many

■ *In 1740 Maria Theresa became ruler of the Austrian Empire, which included lands in Italy, Germany, Hungary, and the Netherlands.*

lands and peoples under its control. Before his death, Charles VI had tried to protect his daughter by having the rulers of Europe accept the *Pragmatic Sanction*. This was an agreement in which the European monarchs promised not to seize Maria Theresa's possessions. Although Charles VI had given them considerable territory in exchange for their acceptance of this agreement, several rulers later broke the Pragmatic Sanction. However, Maria Theresa, aided by advisers like Prince Kaunitz, soon demonstrated that she was quite capable of ruling—with or without the Sanction.

Maria Theresa (1740–1780), who was only twenty-three years old when she ascended the throne, proved to be one of the strongest Hapsburg monarchs. Her blue eyes, light hair, and graceful movements were constant reminders of her femininity.

But her orders and decisions indicated that she ruled as an absolute monarch.

Maria Theresa was an extremely complicated person. Her biographer, Constance L. Morris, says: "[Maria Theresa] was instinctively possessive." Yet, to aid her country, she pawned her precious personal jewels. She was a deeply pious person; yet she ruthlessly persecuted Protestants and Jews. She was the mother of sixteen children and enjoyed domestic life; yet she guided her country through the brutalities of war. In brief, she was a monarch as well as a woman—and many of her subjects loved her doubly for that!

Maria Theresa as an "Enlightened Despot"

Maria Theresa was ruling at the time when the Enlightenment was spreading through Europe. Maria Theresa, like

■ *Maria Theresa and her husband Emperor Francis I with eleven of their children are shown on the terrace of Schönbrunn, the magnificent royal palace in Vienna. Maria Theresa made Vienna the cultural center of her empire.*

Catherine the Great of Russia, has been called an "enlightened despot." During her reign, she accomplished the following things: (1) centralized the government and weakened the power of the nobles who were blocking the unity of the state; (2) reorganized and centralized the financial system; (3) improved the living conditions of the peasants; (4) strengthened education; and (5) introduced a new penal code.

These reforms never departed from the principle that maintained that Maria Theresa was the absolute ruler. "I flatter myself that I shall be able to prevent the ruin of the State," she had once written. It was Maria Theresa's conviction that only she—and not the people—could run the country.

Her son, Joseph II, was a more enlightened ruler than his mother. He ruled with her from 1765 to 1780 and alone from 1780 to 1790. He accomplished many genuine reforms in Austria. Among his accomplishments were the following: (1) completing the freeing of the serfs and taking away the rights of the nobles to administer justice to the peasantry; (2) establishing greater equality before the law; (3) abolishing capital punishment and the use of torture in most cases; (4) providing good elementary school books and teachers; (5) granting religious toleration to Calvinists, Lutherans, and Orthodox Christians; (6) improving the treatment of the Jews; and (7) curbing the political power of the Church.

Both Maria Theresa and Joseph faced the problem of ruling a great, widespread empire of many different nationalities. Both tried to "Germanize" this empire, but in vain. Not even a strong leader like Maria Theresa could solve all of the problems facing the Hapsburgs. How could she when her possessions were scattered over Germany, Italy, the Netherlands, and Hungary! As her biographer Constance L. Morris makes clear: "What was known as the Hapsburg realm was really little more than the ruling power of a dynasty controlling a loose aggregation of kingdoms and lands, each of which retained its own individuality and was dominated by its ancient traditions. In this mass of dynastic possessions only the lower and interior Austrian districts showed any close coherence." A serious threat to Maria Theresa's empire arose from Germany.

■ **Check on Your Reading**

1. How did the Hapsburgs build an empire?
2. How was the Turkish threat met?
3. Evaluate Maria Theresa as ruler of Austria and as an "enlightened despot."
4. Summarize Joseph II's accomplishments.

3. History of Prussia

In the tenth century A.D. Emperor Otto the Great claimed control over territory known as the Holy Roman Empire. It included considerable German and Italian lands. As the years passed, "Germany" in this empire became a land governed by many princes and other local rulers.

The Hohenzollerns Rise in Germany

In the fifteenth century, a member of the *Hohenzollern* family was chosen by the Holy Roman Emperor to be the Elector of Brandenburg, a province in northern Germany. In the future the Hohenzollerns would rule the province of Brandenburg.

The Reformation produced considerable religious, social, and political conflict among the many rulers of Germany. The Peace of Augsburg (1555) permitted each German prince to choose either the Roman Catholic or the Lutheran faith as the religion for his territory. The Hohenzollerns

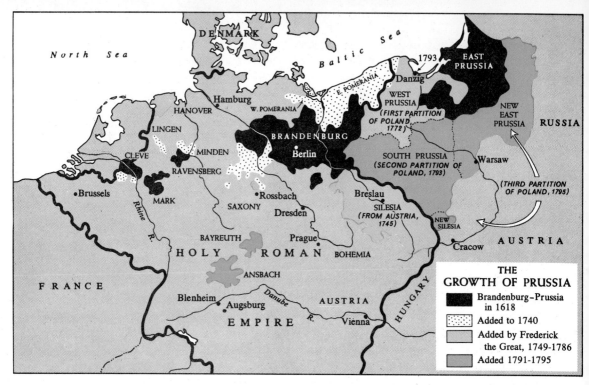

THE GROWTH OF PRUSSIA

Brandenburg–Prussia in 1618

Added to 1740

Added by Frederick the Great, 1749-1786

Added 1791-1795

■ *From the small state of Brandenburg-Prussia, Prussia increased its territory primarily through war. A ruler like Frederick the Great fought several wars to add Silesia and West Prussia. What other territories were added? How?*

chose Lutheranism for Brandenburg. In time, they inherited important territories and added them to their holdings.

During the Thirty Years' War, Frederick William became Elector of Brandenburg, and an important duchy was added to Brandenburg's territory. Frederick William (1640–1688), who was known as the *Great Elector*, provided his subjects with forceful leadership. He helped to unify the government, centralize the system of finances, stimulate business activities, and build up a powerful army.

Frederick William the Great Elector was succeeded by a ruler named Frederick. In exchange for Frederick's aid in the War of the Spanish Succession, the Holy Roman Emperor permitted him in 1701 to take the title Frederick I, "King *in Prussia*." Prussia—a new state—had officially emerged

from what was once a small province. It lay outside the Holy Roman Empire, and therefore the Elector of Brandenburg was called "King in Prussia." His entire domain soon came to be called "Brandenburg-Prussia," later just *Prussia*.

Prussia under Its "Drill-Sergeant" King

Frederick William I (1713–1740), whom the historian-philosopher Thomas Carlyle described as a short, stout man with a metallic voice and "a terrible volcanic fire in him," succeeded Frederick as ruler of Prussia. Frederick William I was a king with many eccentricities. He would order women selling apples to knit while they sat at their stalls. He would hit loungers and time-wasters with his cane and shout "Home . . . and take to some work!" And he had a "mad passion" for collecting tall soldiers and putting them in his favorite regiment of grenadiers. He once paid out twice the annual salary of a Prussian general to obtain one giant Irish soldier.

Nevertheless, Frederick William I was a hard-working and efficient king. A strict disciplinarian, he labored long and hard. He helped to improve elementary education, increase trade, establish centers for manufacturing, introduce new methods of farming, and run the government economically.

Most important, he greatly strengthened the army of Prussia. Military historian Theodore Ropp points out: "By 1740 the Prussian army of 80,000 men was the fourth in Europe, just behind the armies of France, Russia, and Austria. Though Austria had many times Prussia's population, she had less than 100,000 professional soldiers. Where France kept one soldier for every 150 inhabitants, Prussia supported one for every 25." As Thomas Carlyle says:

In a military, and also in a much deeper sense, [Frederick William I] may be defined as the great Drill-sergeant of the Prussian Nation. . . . Prussia is all a drilled phalanx, ready to the word of command; and what we see in the Army is but the . . . essence of what exists in the Nation everywhere.

Prussia was ready to challenge the authority of the Hapsburg dynasty itself!

Frederick the Great Leads Prussia into War

Frederick II (1740–1786), known as Frederick the Great and "Vater Fritz" (Father Fred), became ruler of Prussia in 1740. He was a monarch of great ability. His prominent nose, receding brow, alert gray eyes, and long head tilted to the right gave him the appearance of a bird surveying an unfamiliar piece of land. An energetic person, he exchanged ideas with philosophers like Voltaire, enjoyed the dramas of the French playwright Racine, and was

Frederick the Great

Painting by Adolph von Menzel

■ *Frederick the Great, an "enlightened despot," made Prussia a first-class power in Europe through diplomacy, wars, and hard work.*

such an animated conversationalist that Dr. Moore, a contemporary of his, declared: "[Frederick the Great] speaks a great deal, yet those who hear him, regret that he does not speak a good deal more. His observations are always lively." Like Maria Theresa and Catherine the Great, Frederick was an "enlightened despot." He provided Prussia with an efficient government, improved the system of education, encouraged trade, and issued the first proclamation in Europe guaranteeing almost unconditional religious toleration.

Frederick the Great was determined that Prussia should expand. In 1740 he invaded Silesia, a rich province to the south and east of Prussia. Although many Germans lived in Silesia, the province was under the jurisdiction of Maria Theresa. Frederick's action led to war—the War of the Austrian Succession (1740–1748).

Many countries and peoples were drawn into this conflict. Eventually Prussia was allied with France, Spain, Poland, Sardinia, Bavaria, and Saxony, who fought against the forces of Austria, Hungary,

England, and Holland. At the end of the war, Prussia still held Silesia.

The Seven Years' War Disrupts Europe

Maria Theresa, whose husband became emperor of the Holy Roman Empire as Francis I, was not content to let Frederick the Great keep Silesia. Her dispute with Frederick over this province led to another war—the Seven Years' War (1756–1763).

In the Seven Years' War, Prussia and England opposed the forces of Austria, Saxony, Russia, France, Bohemia, and Sweden. This war was fought in America and India as well as in Europe (pp. 385–386). A comparison of the opponents in the Seven Years' War and those in the War of the Austrian Succession shows that eighteenth-century monarchs did not hesitate to switch allegiance if they could profit.

Prussia faced a formidable group of enemies in the Seven Years' War, and her armies often were outnumbered. Under the brilliant military leadership of Frederick the Great, Prussia was able to win important battles. Just as it appeared that Prussia could no longer withstand the tremendous forces against her, Peter III ascended the Russian throne. This new Russian ruler, favorable to Frederick, helped prevent Prussia's military collapse by withdrawing Russia from the war.

By the Treaty of Paris of 1763, which ended the Seven Years' War in Europe, Prussia kept Silesia while European territories and boundaries remained the same.

Prussia had preserved her territorial expansion into Silesia, but she had lost many men, and considerable money and property during the war. Under the efficient administrative leadership of Frederick the Great, she rebuilt her economy.

Frederick's Kingdom Is United

A serious problem remained: Frederick's kingdom was not territorially united. The region of East Prussia was separated from the rest of Prussia by a province belonging to Poland. Frederick the Great therefore joined Russia and Austria in the First Partition of Poland (1772) which enabled him to unite his kingdom.

A great German writer like Johann Wolfgang von Goethe (1749–1832), author of the drama *Faust*, might later write:

. . . it is the privilege and duty of the philosopher and poet *to belong to no nation* and no time, but rather to be a contemporary of all times.

Yet the rise of Prussia as a united power gave impetus to events that were to lead to the formation of the German nation.

■ **Check on Your Reading**

1. How did the Hohenzollerns build their power and acquire territory up to 1701?
2. Evaluate Frederick William I as king.
3. Summarize the achievements of Frederick the Great.
4. What were the results of the Seven Years' War?

4. Music Amid the Sounds of War

It must not be thought that the Austrians and Germans were concerned only with military matters in the seventeenth and eighteenth centuries. Both peoples made major contributions to culture. This was particularly true in the field of music.

The German, Johann Sebastian Bach (1685–1750), for example, probably did more than any man in history to develop church music. Dedicating himself to the creation of "a regulated church music in the honor of God," he originated no new form

■ *This scene from a modern production of Mozart's opera* The Magic Flute *by the Marionette Theater of Salzburg, Austria, shows Pamina and Papageno. This charming opera lends itself well to such an unusual mode of presentation.*

but composed some of the finest choral music. His *Passion According to St. Matthew* and *B Minor Mass* are two of his superb compositions. Although Bach received little recognition from the composers of his day, he did have contact with Frederick the Great. He even improvised a musical composition for the "enlightened despot."

In this period George Frederick Handel (1685–1759), who was born in Germany but became an English subject, wrote the *Messiah*. This *oratorio* (that is, a musical composition for singers and instrumentalists, usually based on a religious theme) has become world-famous. Hugo Leichtentritt, twentieth-century musicologist, makes clear that the *Messiah* differs in style from much of Handel's other excellent music. He calls it "one of those mysterious marvels of great art that appear but once in a century."

Franz Joseph Haydn (1732–1809), a gifted Austrian composer, used a variety of instruments in his musical compositions. He wrote over one hundred symphonies and some eighty-three quartets. One of his best known works is *Symphony No. 101 in D Major*, the so-called *Clock Symphony*. Haydn is sometimes called the "father of the symphony."

The Austrian genius, Wolfgang Amadeus Mozart (1756–1791), gave the world some of its most delightful symphonic and operatic works. These included such famous operas as *The Marriage of Figaro*, *Don Giovanni*, and *The Magic Flute*; forty-one symphonies; many concertos; and chamber music (music for a small number of instruments, usually performed in a small concert hall). As two present-day critics, Milo Wold and Edmund Cykler, point out:

The genius of Mozart enabled him to keep his operatic works in the tradition of theatrical entertainment, while at the same time the music was cast in the finest classical mold.

Despite the musical beauty created by these geniuses, kings and countries continued to clash. For the ordinary poor person, neither war nor music played an important part. Wars were fought by professional armies and most music was played at the courts of rulers.

■ **Check on Your Reading**

1. What are the greatest works of Bach? of Handel? of Haydn? of Mozart?

2. What did each of the above contribute to music?

MAN AND HIS CULTURE

Let's Meet the People!

Frederick the Great: an "Enlightened Despot"

The following sketch is based on primary source material in Thomas Carlyle's *History of Friedrich II of Prussia.*

It was 4 A.M. and Frederick the Great, king of Prussia, was ready to begin his day. Frederick rose from his bed and quickly took off his sleeping garments: a cloth robe that covered his body, and a hat "which was . . . kneaded to softness as its first duty, and did very well [as a pillow]." Then he dressed in the following manner:

Stockings, breeches, boots, he did sitting on the bed . . . the rest in front of the fire, in standing posture. Washing followed. . . .

Finally, he put on his sky-blue velvet *casaquin* (a dressing-gown) with silver embroideries, and shouted: "Here!"

At the sound of Frederick's voice, a valet hurried into the bedchamber carrying letters received during the night. A secretary read this correspondence to Frederick. Then the king discussed important problems with his General-Adjutant.

It was 5 A.M. and Frederick the Great was ready to begin his flute playing. The king first stepped into his writing room, reread a letter from the French philosopher Voltaire discussing a new play, and drank "several glasses of water; then coffee, perhaps three cups with or without milk." Then he picked up his flute and began to play. Frederick stopped from time to time to breakfast.

Soon it was 6 A.M. and Frederick the Great was ready to begin his writing about Machiavelli's book, *The Prince.* Yet, even as he worked, Frederick looked forward impatiently to eleven o'clock. It was then that the king would:

fling off his casaquin, take his regimental coat; have his hair touched off with pomade, with powder; and be buttoned . . . ready for Parade.

For Frederick the Great—lover of philosophy, music, and literature— loved nothing better than the sight of his soldiers preparing for war!

CHAPTER REVIEW

REVIEW and DISCUSSION

1. Identify the people and places and explain the events and terms on p. 338.

2. Compare Maria Theresa with Catherine the Great of Russia. Who do you think was the more "enlightened"?

3. Evaluate either the Hapsburg or the Hohenzollern family, with emphasis on its impact on European history. Give reasons for your answer.

4. What are the possible effects of a nation's having great military strength?

5. The army was the very essence of Prussia. What does this statement mean?

6. Why have many countries aspired to expand by conquering other territory? Why have other countries not expanded like this?

7. Were all the wars described in this chapter justified conflicts? Why?

8. In the light of your study of the individuals and events of this chapter, do you believe that "history makes great men" or "great men make history" or both? Why?

9. Do you agree or disagree with Goethe's statement that poets and philosophers belong to no nation and no time? Why?

10. Why might the autocratic rulers of the eighteenth century be pleased with the ideas expressed in Machiavelli's *The Prince*?

ACTIVITIES

1. Listen to a recording of Handel's *Messiah*. Do you agree that this composition is "great [music] that appears but once in a century"?

2. Debate the following: Resolved, that women have been as successful absolute rulers as men.

3. On one map of Europe show the boundaries and names of the countries in 1648. On another map of Europe show the boundaries and names of the countries in 1763.

4. Write a short biography of one musician about whom you have read in this chapter.

5. Make a chart showing the steps in the disintegration of the Holy Roman Empire.

6. Add the Holy Roman Empire to your chart on the "Causes of the Rise and Fall of Civilizations."

PAST and PRESENT

1. Panel discussion: What problems today face the middle European countries?

2. How does Turkey's position in the world today compare with that of the Ottoman Empire in the sixteenth century?

3. What evidence can you find in this chapter of the birth of modern Germany?

SUGGESTED READINGS

Basic books: BAUER, MARION, and PEYSER, ETHEL, *Music Through the Ages*, Chap. 5, Putnam. Comprehensive history of music.

GOTTSCHALK, LOUIS, and LACH, DONALD, *Europe and the Modern World*, Chap. 9, Scott, Foresman.

PALMER, R. R., and COLTON, JOEL, *A History of the Modern World*, Chap. 5, Knopf.

SMITH, GOLDWIN, *The Heritage of Man*, Chap. 24, Scribner.

Special books: BUFFINTON, ARTHUR H., *The Second Hundred Years' War, 1689–1815* (Berkshire Studies in European History), Holt. A concise but authoritative study.

FAY, SIDNEY BRADSHAW, *The Rise of Brandenburg-Prussia to 1786* (Berkshire Studies in European History), Holt. A short, useful work by a noted scholar.

PRICE, M. PHILIPS, *History of Turkey*, Macmillan. Short, but comprehensive. Effectively presented.

SHUSTER, GEORGE, and BERGSTRAESSLER, ARNOLD, *Germany: A Short History*, Norton. A brief history that is easy to read and comprehend.

Biography and Fiction: DAVENPORT, MARCIA, *Mozart*, Scribner. Accurate for the historical period during which Mozart lived.

ERGANG, ROBERT, *The Potsdam Führer: Frederick William I, Father of Prussian Militarism*, Columbia University Press.

Chapter 22

Absolutism Reaches a Peak in France

KEYNOTE

"O kings! Ye are like gods!" declared Bishop Bossuet, a prominent religious leader of France in the seventeenth century. He went on to proclaim "Royal power is absolute." Little wonder that one of the first penmanship exercises given to the boy destined to be King Louis XIV of France was to copy the words:

> HOMAGE IS OWED TO KINGS:
> THEY DO ALL THAT IS PLEASING TO THEM.

It was this idea of the right of the monarch to be absolute ruler of his country that dominated France in the seventeenth and first half of the eighteenth centuries. It was an idea that was to enable the French kings to lead their country into remarkable cultural achievements and into wars from which it never recovered.

Key People
Henry IV · Duke of Sully · Louis XIII · Cardinal Richelieu · Cardinal Mazarin · Louis XIV · Jean Baptiste Colbert · Molière · Corneille · Racine

Key Places
Seine River · Alps · Vosges Mountains · Juras · Pyrenees · Rhine River · Lille · Spanish Netherlands · Franche-Comté · Palatinate · Blenheim

Key Events
Bourbons rule France · Fronde uprisings · Colbert's mercantilist program · Revocation of Edict of Nantes · Palace of Versailles built · War of Spanish Succession

Key Terms
autocracy · parlements · Huguenots · "Sun King" · "divine right of kings" · mercantilism

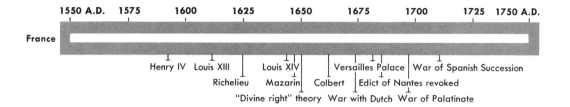

1550 A.D.	1575	1600	1625	1650	1675	1700	1725	1750 A.D.

France

Henry IV Louis XIII   Louis XIV   Versailles Palace War of Spanish Succession

Richelieu   Mazarin   Colbert   Edict of Nantes revoked

"Divine right" theory War with Dutch War of Palatinate

1. France: An Intertwining of Geography and History

Men rarely think in terms of miles, acreage, or inches of rainfall when they think of France. Instead, they often see fascinating visions of the French people: an old fisherman sunning himself along the banks of the Seine River; a balloon-shaped chef happily sniffing his steaming pot of "bouillabaisse" (fish chowder); a paint-stained artist enriching his canvas with the reds and browns of a Paris sky. Such romantic observations must not conceal these important geographic facts.

France is a country in western Europe about twice the size of Colorado. On the north, it is separated from England by the Straits of Dover and the English Channel. On the east, it is bounded by Belgium, Luxembourg, Germany, Switzerland, and Italy, and on the south, it borders on the Mediterranean and Spain (map, p. 352).

Historical Importance of France's Location: The fact that France borders on many countries has contributed to her involvement in important European movements and developments.

The Vosges Mountains lie between France and Germany; the Juras and the Alps between France and Switzerland; the Alps between France and Italy; and the Pyrenees between France and Spain.

Historical Importance of France's Mountains: In the past, the mountains have provided some protection for France against attack. Today, jet-propelled planes and high-powered missiles have lessened their importance.

The French probably love their rivers even more than their mountains. Important rivers are the Loire, Rhône, Garonne, and Seine.

Historical Importance of France's Rivers: The rivers have provided a valuable means of inland transportation and have helped to unite the country.

The soil of France is rich in many areas, particularly in the plains in the north, and at least forty-five per cent of the population is connected with agriculture.

Historical Importance of France's Fertile Soil: The fertility of the soil made agrarian life a major factor in the French economy. This, in turn, has linked the peasants and farmers to many important events in French history.

■ **Check on Your Reading**

1. What geographic factor has involved France with other countries?

2. What have her rivers and fertile soil contributed to France's economy?

351

2. The Bourbon Kings Rule France

France was one of the first countries to develop into a strong and unified state. As it did, autocracy also grew stronger. The leaders who ruled France during the late sixteenth, seventeenth, and early eighteenth centuries were sometimes kings, sometimes government ministers, sometimes religious officials, and sometimes women of unusual charm. Almost all were unconcerned about democratic rights.

Henry IV Strengthens France

Henry IV (1589–1610), the first Bourbon king of France, was willing to use persuasion to gain his objectives. But in a crisis he did not hesitate to declare, "I am the King now: as King do I speak, *and mean to be obeyed....*"

Despite the tone of these words, Henry IV was an extremely popular monarch. One reason for his popularity was that the French knew that they needed a strong ruler to prevent the anarchy that accompanied clashes between local lords, Church officials, and other rivals. A famous historian, Albert Guérard, points out that the French accepted autocracy as "a weary compromise" that would keep order, not as an abstract principle that had to be obeyed blindly.

Henry IV proved that even an autocrat could be concerned about his people. Not

■ *In France, a country in western Europe, geographic factors such as location, mountains, rivers, and fertile soil have influenced its historical development. How did geography influence French history under the rule of the Bourbon kings?*

The inset shows France as it was under Louis XIV, the "Sun King." What territories did he add?

Added during the reign of Louis XIV

only did he express the hope that every peasant should have "a chicken in the pot every Sunday," but he worked hard to bring about such a miracle. Henry IV, aided by strong ministers like the Duke of Sully, encouraged agriculture, supported industrial activities such as the famous tapestry industry of the Gobelins, built a navy, constructed fine highways, and stimulated foreign trade. Henry IV also issued the important Edict of Nantes (1598) (p. 320) which granted the Huguenots significant rights.

In international affairs, Henry IV checked Spain when she attempted to interfere in the affairs of France. He was the ruler of France when Champlain founded Quebec (1608). It is an irony of history that this king who "hated to hurt" met his death at the hand of an assassin.

Cardinal Richelieu Builds the Royal Power

King Louis XIII (1610–1643), who eventually succeeded his father, Henry IV, to the throne, was not the weakling that earlier historians believed. Certainly, he did not hesitate to order the death of his opponents; and he once warned the *parlements* (the highest law courts in France): "If you continue your schemes, I will clip your nails so close that your flesh will suffer from it." Louis XIII did turn over much of his power to Cardinal Richelieu, however. As chief minister, Richelieu dominated the government of France from 1624 until his death in 1642.

Cardinal Richelieu was a scarlet-robed official whose strong will and shrewdness contrasted sharply with his frail and sickly body. A moody and high-strung person who could weep at one moment and break into a rage the next, he devoted himself principally to one cause: *the strengthening of the power of the monarchy and central government at home and abroad.* "My first goal," he once said, "was the majesty of the King; the second was the greatness of the realm." Cardinal Richelieu's activities helped to strengthen both.

In the name of the king, he governed France autocratically. When the matter arose of giving some rights to the people, he declared:

It is absolutely needful to suppress the growth of [democratic ideas] since otherwise France will never be that which she ought to be. . . .

He weakened the power of the nobility. The nobles, he said, held fast to feudal privileges "as if they were sovereign in their offices." He therefore increased the power of the *intendants*, government officials (usually from the middle class) who were responsible directly to the crown. In this and other ways he reduced the authority of the nobles.

He broke the power of the Huguenots, the Protestants in Catholic France. Richelieu was convinced that the Huguenots challenged the royal authority by maintaining their own officials and fortifying their towns. He therefore destroyed their military and political strength, although he permitted them to have freedom of religious belief, guaranteed them by the Edict of Nantes.

High standards were established for the French language by Richelieu so that it would add to the glory of France. He created the French academy of forty men (known today as "the forty immortals") "to give certain words to our language and to render it pure."

He attempted to weaken the political power—but not the Catholicism—of Spain and Austria, lands ruled by the Hapsburgs. Even though the Hapsburgs were Catholics, they were rivals of the Bourbons of France. Richelieu therefore allied Catholic France with the Protestant rulers who opposed the Hapsburgs during the Thirty Years' War (p. 321). At the time of

Painting by Philippe de Champaigne, Musée Condé, Chantilly

■ *Cardinal Richelieu (1624–1642) governed France autocratically, broke the Huguenots' power, and tried to weaken Hapsburg power.*

Richelieu's death in 1642, the Hapsburgs had been humbled in several parts of Europe, and the boundaries of France reached the Rhine.

Mazarin Continues Richelieu's Policies

In 1643, Louis XIII died. He was succeeded by Louis XIV, but since the new king was then a child, France at first was governed by Cardinal Mazarin and his associates. Cardinal Mazarin, whose opponents ridiculed him as a clown, played a key role in the French government until his death in 1661. Mazarin continued many of Richelieu's policies.

In foreign affairs, the high point of the period was the signing of the Treaties of Westphalia (1648) (p. 321). By provisions in the treaties, the Austrian Hapsburgs received a serious setback, and France increased its power as well as its territory.

Yet Mazarin, who could be quite unscrupulous in foreign affairs, was not satisfied. The French fought Spain and, after a decade of fighting, defeated the Spaniards. By the Peace of the Pyrenees (1659), the Spanish Hapsburgs turned over territory to the French that extended the boundaries of France to the Pyrenees and arranged for the daughter (Marie Thérèse) of the Spanish monarch to marry Louis XIV of France. The position of France in foreign affairs was now the strongest in Europe.

In France, Mazarin continued Richelieu's policy of making the crown absolute. Mazarin's actions against the nobles, his insolent attitudes, and his habit of taking graft earned him the hatred of the nobility. Many nobles agreed that he was an "outcaste . . . troubler of the public peace . . . scoundrel."

Mazarin's tyrannical decisions, his restrictions on the privileges of the nobles and the courts, the dislike of the French people for "foreigners" (Mazarin was of Sicilian ancestry), and the rising price of food resulted in two uprisings called the *Frondes* (1648–1653). The first was led by magistrates of the law courts, the second by dissatisfied nobles. (The term *la Fronde* means "the sling" in French.)

During the Frondes, there was considerable confusion in the government. Finally, the uprisings were brought under control. When young King Louis XIV took over at the death of Mazarin, he found himself both an absolute monarch and the ruler of the dominant country in Europe.

■ **Check on Your Reading**

1. Why was Henry IV a very popular king?
2. What did Cardinal Richelieu achieve?
3. What did France gain under Mazarin?

3. Louis XIV, the "Sun King"

Louis XIV (1643–1715) was a solidly built man of medium height who added to his physical stature by wearing high heels. His nose was long and curved like the beak of an eagle. His hair was abundant and fell in curls about his shoulders. And his blue eyes took on whatever expression he felt was necessary for the role he played in what he called "the profession of king." He was a fine horseman, an enthusiastic hunter, a graceful dancer, a charming companion to the ladies, and an extremely polite host. Bolingbroke, an English political writer and statesman of the time, declared: "He was the best actor of majesty . . . that ever filled a throne."

Louis XIV was not a man of brilliant intellect; neither was he well educated. As his biographer W. H. Lewis makes clear, he could not even open a book "without distaste." Nevertheless, he was dignified, energetic, hard-working, and wise enough to use common sense to counteract the sweetness of flattery that he absorbed.

Above all, Louis XIV was an absolute ruler. His motto was "Nec Pluribus Impar"—"None His Equal." His emblem was the sun, for he was the "Sun King" whose rays touched every aspect of French life. Although he probably never really said, "L'état, c'est moi!" ("The State—I am the State!"), he made this statement a reality. Little wonder that the wigged and perfumed lords and ladies of his great court hurried to do his slightest wish. For, when Louis XIV shouted, "That man is a man whom I do not see," it was understood that another career had come to an end.

The Idea of "Divine Right of Kings"

Louis XIV's absolutism was based on the important idea of the *divine right of kings*—that is, that the ruler derives his powers from God and is responsible only to God. Did not the Bible state that God commanded the prophet Samuel to anoint Saul as king of Israel? And were there not other biblical sections where God gave power to kings? So argued the supporters of the divine right of kings.

This idea was best expressed in *Politics Drawn from the Words of the Holy Scripture*, a book written by Bishop Bossuet. His major statements can be arranged in this sequence:

The royal throne is not the throne of a man, but the throne of God himself.

It appears from . . . this that the person of the king is sacred, and that to attack him in any way is sacrilege.

Therefore, *the royal power is absolute.*

When Louis XIV composed his *Memoirs*, he set down the following advice for his son:

The most clever persons, in their own interest, take advice from other clever persons. . . . But in the important occasions . . . the decisive action, my son, is up to us.

Colbert Leads France in Mercantilism

Absolute power belonged to Louis XIV, and he handled as many details of government as he could. He realized, however, that even a king needed the advice and labor of others. In economics he turned to the efficient Jean Baptiste Colbert.

As France's Finance Minister, Colbert made important contributions to the country by developing several parts of its economy. Working sometimes as long as sixteen hours a day, he did the following: (1) stimulated France's trade; (2) supported the establishment of trading companies and colonies; (3) encouraged the growth of industries and subsidized factories for producing wool and silk; (4) aided

355

■ *This scene from a Gobelins tapestry shows Louis XIV and his courtiers renewing their alliance with the representatives of the Swiss cantons at Notre Dame Cathedral, Paris. Compare the dress and general appearance of the French (right) and the Swiss (left).*

the development of industrial crops, such as flax and hemp; (5) organized an effective merchant marine and formed a navy to protect France's interests; and (6) regulated the quality and quantity of goods.

Colbert followed the economic philosophy of *mercantilism*. Mercantilism was the policy that advocated that a country should export more in value than it should import, establish and use colonies to increase the wealth of the home country, keep a strong navy to protect national interests, and protect its industries by placing high tariffs on the goods of other countries. The basic aim was to attract and keep as much gold and silver (specie) as possible within the country. Colbert even went so far as to declare:

I believe . . . that it is only the abundance of money in a state which makes the difference in its greatness and power.

Colbert did his best to balance the budget of the government. He urged the king to save even pennies and declared that an expensive state dinner brought him "unbelievable pain." Louis XIV was not inclined to accept this advice to economize. Colbert's hard work could not eliminate the evils that came with senseless extravagance.

Nevertheless, many European countries followed Colbert's economic policies during the late seventeenth and a considerable part of the eighteenth century. Mercantilism became widespread. Extreme mercantilism has been termed aptly "the economic phase of royal absolutism."

The Edict of Nantes Is Revoked

An event of great religious significance also had economic repercussions in France. The Huguenots, the French Protestants who made up less than ten per cent of the population of the country, were very active and successful in industry. Many of them served as merchants, traders, and skilled artisans, and they had frequently demonstrated their loyalty to France. Since the Edict of Nantes (1598), they had been permitted freedom of religious belief.

Louis XIV, a devout Catholic despite his rather loose personal standards, determined to make the Huguenots give up their faith. The king's decision may have been motivated by a desire to aid Catholicism, to unite the country through religious conformity, to punish those who refused to accept the faith of their absolute ruler, or to please his ardent Catholic advisers.

Louis XIV first excluded the Huguenots from many privileges; then he tried to convert them by forceful tactics; and finally he revoked the Edict of Nantes. The Revocation of the Edict of Nantes (1685) meant that Protestants could not legally worship. Protestant churches were closed.

The results of Louis XIV's action proved to be disastrous to France economically. Although they were not permitted by law to leave France, thousands of Huguenots fled. Eventually, between 300,000 and 500,000 went to Prussia, Switzerland, the Dutch Netherlands, Great Britain, South Africa, and the English colonies in America. They took with them their valuable skills.

As a result of the exodus of the Huguenots, the silk industry of Tours crumbled, the province of Normandy became depopulated, and commercial transactions declined seriously. Other countries gained from France's loss. For, wherever the Huguenots went, they contributed to the economic welfare of the lands they inhabited—countries that often were bitter rivals of France. The great French historian, André Maurois, even said that the Revocation of the Edict of Nantes was "the greatest mistake of the whole reign."

Cultural "Glory" of Louis XIV's Reign

If there were economic problems, Louis XIV did not permit them to interfere with the pleasures of court life. Cultural activities in art, architecture, and literature were so impressive that the reign of Louis XIV has been called a "Golden Age."

The Palace of Versailles

It has been said by a contemporary writer, Doré Ogrizek, that "[Louis XIV's] love letters were written in freestone." The most famous building of all is the great palace of Versailles, into which Louis XIV and his court moved in 1682.

At Versailles there were decorated walls that seemed to have received the golden touch of Midas. There were seventeen arched windows and seventeen arched mirrors in an orange-scented Hall of Mirrors. There were graceful fountains with fourteen hundred jets; and formal gardens with the hedges neatly clipped. There was almost too much grandeur for beauty and too little simplicity for real charm. This was the architectural reflection of the "Sun King"—which other monarchs tried to capture.

At the palace of Versailles, cut off from contact with the people, King Louis XIV held sway over what the French historian Taine called "a nobility for ornament." The gentlemen wore embroidered coats and covered their hair with powdered wigs. The ladies dressed in jewelled robes and supported high headdresses. Living in this tinselled world, far from their neglected estates, the nobles, in time, lost their sense of independence and became human puppets.

Literature

More significant was the stimulation given to literature. Great playwrights like Corneille and Racine stirred influential men with their tragedies. Charles Perrault

■ *At the great Palace of Versailles King Louis XIV and his court developed a pattern of life that set the style for other European courts. The palace with its decorative sculptures, lovely fountains, and formal gardens probably cost over a billion dollars (in our currency) to construct, and its staff of servants was extremely large.*

set down his Mother Goose stories and made Cinderella and her fur (later glass) slipper world-famous. The satirist Molière delighted his audiences by poking fun at pompous men in scenes such as this from *The Would-Be Gentleman:*

> Mr. Jourdain: "...I am in love with a lady of quality, and I would like you to help me to write a letter to her....
> Master of Philosophy: "[Shall I write the letter in prose or in verse?]"
> Mr. Jourdain: "Neither. I wish neither prose nor verse."
> Master of Philosophy: "It *must* be one or the other."
> Mr. Jourdain: "Why?"
> Master of Philosophy: "For the reason, sir, that there is no other way to express yourself except in prose or verse."
> Mr. Jourdain: "And when I speak, what is that?"
> Master of Philosophy: "Prose."
> Mr. Jourdain: "My word! I have been speaking prose for forty years without knowing it!"

The period of Louis XIV was a time when "classical" writers—that is, men who could see lasting order and unity to life and nature—reached a peak in France. As André Maurois points out:

What makes a writer *classical*, said Valéry, is that he seeks not "to make the new" but to "make enduringly," which means fashioning a masterpiece which shall be independent of circumstance and of date.

The works of the French playwrights who were sponsored by Louis XIV are still admired and performed today.

■ **Check on Your Reading**

1. Explain "L'état, c'est moi!" and "divine right of kings."
2. How did Colbert strengthen France?
3. What were the results of the Revocation of the Edict of Nantes?
4. What did court life at Versailles do to the French nobility?
5. Why was the reign of Louis XIV called a cultural "Golden Age"?

4. Louis XIV Follows a Policy of Expansion

Despite French literary and artistic achievements, many people were still not content. There were signs that the political, social, and economic foundations of French society were decaying. The heavy burden of taxes on the peasants (the upper classes were exempt from direct taxation), the wasteful expenditures of king and court, and the ever-present danger of bankruptcy of the treasury caused unrest in the country.

Some men, angered by his extravagance and wars, mocked the king by "praying":

Our Father who art in Versailles, thy name is no longer hallowed; thy kingdom is diminished; thy will is no longer done on earth or on the waves. Give us our bread, which is lacking to us. . . .

France's Position in the World

To understand the effects of foreign affairs during the reign of Louis XIV, it is first necessary to take a general view of France's position in the world.

France was the strongest power on the continent. Its rulers, the Bourbon kings, were the rivals of the Hapsburgs, particularly of the Hapsburg Holy Roman Emperor. Overseas, France had an empire in America and the East, which brought her into serious conflict with the English.

Despite the territories that France controlled, King Louis XIV decided to follow an aggressive policy of expansion. Louis XIV had at least five objectives in his handling of foreign affairs: (1) to extend the boundaries of France to the Alps and to the Rhine and Scheldt rivers; (2) to assure the supremacy of France in Europe; (3) to increase France's overseas empire and trade; (4) to guard the security of France—although Louis XIV often confused his personal desires with the security of the state; and (5) to win glory for himself.

France Fights Four Wars

To achieve his objectives, Louis XIV prepared for war. Louvois, the French Minister of War, created the first standing army. Vauban, a talented engineer, built impregnable strongholds for French troops and developed the use of shells to destroy enemy earthworks. Turenne and Condé, military leaders, made brilliant plans to direct the French armies. Louis XIV involved France in four major wars.

The War of Devolution (1667–1668) arose over Louis XIV's claim that he was entitled to Spanish territory. In this war, France gained Lille and eleven other towns in the Spanish Netherlands, but her plans to expand were checked by the opposition of a Triple Alliance, composed of Holland, England, and Sweden.

A few years later, Louis XIV, angered that the Dutch opposed his plans to expand and jealous of their success, attacked Holland. In the War against the Dutch (1672–1678) the opponents were France and England against Holland, the Holy Roman Empire, Spain, Sweden, and Denmark. At the end of the war, France gained Franche-Comté and several fortresses from Spain, which extended her boundaries toward the Alps.

In 1686, the Palatinate, a rich country west of the Rhine, joined the Holy Roman Empire, Sweden, Spain, Bavaria, and Saxony in the so-called League of Augsburg. Later England joined. In the War of the Palatinate (1689–1697), France opposed the League. At the end of the war, France (1) lost some territory on the right bank of the Rhine but kept Strasbourg and part of Alsace; (2) granted commercial concessions to the Dutch and permitted them to garrison forts in the Spanish Netherlands; and (3) recognized William III's right to be king of England.

The War of the Palatinate was also fought in lands overseas, where the English opposed the French for colonial empire. When the conflict ended, France regained Nova Scotia in North America and gave Fort Albany, Hudson Bay, to England.

Louis XIV proceeded to lead France into its most unfortunate war, the War of the Spanish Succession (1701–1713). In this conflict, England and Austria showed their determination to prevent Louis XIV from uniting the crowns of Spain and France.

The war proved to be disastrous for France. The famous English general the Duke of Marlborough crushed the French and Bavarians at Blenheim (Germany); and the French suffered defeats elsewhere. Economic conditions in France became desperate. By the Treaties of Utrecht (1713) ending the war, Philip V, grandson of Louis XIV, was recognized as king of Spain and its possessions; and the crowns of France and Spain were never to be united. And Austria gained a solid foothold in the Italian peninsula.

The War of the Spanish Succession was also fought overseas, where the English opposed the French (p. 386). England made much progress toward driving France out of North America. The Seven Years' War (1756–1763) completed this process (p. 386). The French royal treasury was drained, and the economy seriously weakened.

■ **Check on Your Reading**

1. What factors caused unrest in France?
2. What was France's position in the world?
3. What were Louis XIV's objectives?
4. What were the results of the four wars?

LOUIS XIV'S MAJOR WARS

War of Devolution, 1667–1668
Opponents: France vs. Spain
Treaty: Aix-la-Chapelle, 1668
Terms: France acquired Lille and eleven other towns in the Spanish Netherlands.

War against the Dutch, 1672–1678
Opponents: France, England (part of war) vs. Holland, Holy Roman Empire, Spain, Sweden, Denmark
Treaty: Nimwegen, 1678
Terms: France acquired Franche-Comté and several fortresses from Spain.

War of the Palatinate, 1689–1697
Opponents: France vs. League of Augsburg: Palatinate, Holy Roman Empire, Sweden, Spain, Bavaria, Saxony, England
Treaty: Ryswick, 1697
Terms: In Europe: France lost some territory on the right bank of the Rhine but kept Strasbourg and part of Alsace. France granted commercial concessions and the right to garrison forts in the Spanish Netherlands to the Dutch, France recognized the right of William III to be king of England.

In America: France regained Nova Scotia and gave Fort Albany, Hudson Bay, to England. (The war was called King William's War.)

War of Spanish Succession, 1701–1713
Opponents: France, Spain, Bavaria, Savoy (to 1703), Portugal (to 1703) vs. Grand Alliance of 1701 (England, Austria, Prussia, German states, Holland), Denmark, Sweden
Treaties: Utrecht, 1713
Terms: In Europe: Philip V, grandson of Louis XIV, was recognized as King of Spain and its possessions, and the crowns of France and Spain were never to be united. Austria received the Spanish Netherlands (present-day Belgium), Naples, Milan, and Sardinia from Spain. Savoy was officially recognized, and acquired Sicily and Nice. England gained Minorca and Gibraltar as well as trading rights from Spain.

In America: England was given Nova Scotia by France. France recognized England's claims to Newfoundland and the Hudson Bay region. (The war was called Queen Anne's War.)

Modern writers wax poetic about France. France is "an emerald, sparkling on the finger of the Eurasian Peninsula," writes journalist David Schoenbrun. No, it is like "a ragged bearskin spread between the English Channel and the Mediterranean [Sea]," observes *Holiday* magazine. To me, it is "a huge window" facing out on the sea, declares author Helen Hill Miller.

In the late sixteenth, seventeenth, and early eighteenth centuries, an increasing number of people in France also felt the beauty and appeal of the natural features of their country.

However, not the moods of nature but the artificial controls of men began to shape this culture. Strong rulers were determined to fashion society into their favorite image. From the reign of Henry IV through the reign of Louis XIV, these aspects of French culture were noteworthy:

A society in which powerful autocrats restricted the freedom of individuals and groups.

An economy regulated and directed by the government.

Religious tensions between Huguenots and Catholics which were affected by government policies and government actions.

Extraordinary creativity in art, architecture, and literature, much of which was sponsored by the ruler. Today the plays of Corneille, Racine, and Molière are still treasured and performed by modern Frenchmen.

The eighteenth-century French *philosophe* Voltaire in his *Age of Louis XIV* termed this period the "most enlightened age the world has ever seen." Yet the buildings, plays, and dances were primarily the exclusive enjoyment of the nobles and aristocrats. It was a precious age in which gentlemen's coat buttons were the size of eggs, ladies' headdresses were over four feet high.

Most of the people of France did not prosper by this cultural feast. On the contrary, the political, economic, and social foundations of society were crumbling. Neither ornate buildings nor witty plays nor charming ballets could stop the decay.

MAN AND HIS CULTURE

Let's Meet the People!

This sketch is based on information in *Memoirs of Courts of Europe* by the Duke of Saint-Simon, The Macmillan Co.; *The Ancient Régime* by Hippolyte Adolphe Taine, Holt; and *The Natural Science of Stupidity* by Paul Tabori, copyright 1959 by the author. Reprinted with the publisher's permission, Chilton Books, Philadelphia and New York.

The Grand Master of the Wardrobe

At eight o'clock in the morning, the Chief Lackey drew the curtains that surrounded the royal bed of Louis XIV, King of France. The Chief Physician, the Chief Surgeon, and the Nurse of the King came into the room— the first to rub Louis' body, the last to give him a morning kiss. Then the Chief Lackey opened the winged doors of the bedroom and several princes entered, followed by the Grand Master of the Wardrobe and chamberlains.

The Grand Master of the Wardrobe stood close to Louis XIV as the various ceremonies of the *lever* (the rising of the monarch in the morning) continued. The Chief Lackey sprinkled a few drops of "spirits of wine" upon the King's hands. Next, the Chief Lackey presented Louis XIV with holy water from a vase, and the King crossed himself and said a prayer. Finally the King rose from his bed!

The Grand Master of the Wardrobe took the royal dressing gown from the First Chamberlain and helped the King into it. Next he accompanied Louis XIV to the royal armchair, where the King sat down and had his nightcap removed by the Court Barber. Then the Grand Master of the Wardrobe supervised the combing of the King's hair.

The doors of the bedroom were opened again, and generals, ambassadors, and magistrates entered. Various privileged nobles came forward and helped Louis XIV to don his clothing and his sword. Finally, the Grand Master of the Wardrobe brought a silver tray with three embroidered handkerchiefs, and the King selected one. Then he handed Louis XIV his hat, gloves, and stick—and waited for a smile of approval from the "Sun King."

CHAPTER REVIEW

REVIEW and DISCUSSION

1. Identify the people and places and explain the events and terms on p. 350.
2. Define "good government." Do you think Henry IV's government was good?
3. Do you agree with Richelieu's goals: first, the majesty of the King; and second, the greatness of the realm? Why?
4. Why was Richelieu an enemy of the Hapsburgs?
5. Do you think Cardinal Mazarin was as brilliant a leader as Cardinal Richelieu? Why?
6. How do you explain the religious toleration sanctioned by the two Catholic Cardinals after so much war and strife over religion?
7. Name the principles of mercantilism.
8. How did mercantilism contribute to royal absolutism?
9. What relationships do you see between court life and cultural achievements?
10. Compare the Golden Age of Louis XIV with those of Pericles and Augustus Caesar.
11. Was Louis XIV a wise ruler? Why?

ACTIVITIES

1. Debate the following: Resolved, that Louis XIV did more good than harm.
2. On a map of France, locate the Alps; Amiens; Bordeaux; Brest; Brittany; Burgundy; Calais; Garonne River; Jura Mountains; Le Havre; Loire River; Lyons; Marne River; Marseilles; Normandy; Paris; Pyrenees; Reims; Rhine, Rhône, and Seine rivers; Versailles; and Vosges Mountains.
3. Imagine that you are Louis XIV. Write a paragraph entitled "The Grand Monarch."
4. Display pictures on the bulletin board of the styles set by Louis XIV in dress, hair arrangement, furniture, and soldiers' uniforms.
5. Draw some cartoons of Louis XIV in his various roles as absolute king.
6. Compile a list of rulers whom you have studied whose ambition led to disaster. What conclusions can you draw?
7. Add France to your chart on the "Causes of the Rise and Fall of Civilizations" in your notebook.

PAST and PRESENT

1. Contrast Colbert's theory of the value of having a large amount of gold and silver in the treasury with present economic practices.

2. Our government subsidizes certain industries and businesses. Colbert did the same. Were his reasons the same as the reasons for government subsidies today?

3. Is the navy as necessary today for the protection of commercial interests as it was in Colbert's age? Give reasons for your answer.

SUGGESTED READINGS

Basic books: EVANS, MARY, *Costumes Throughout the Ages*, Chap. 6, Lippincott.

MILLS, DOROTHY, *Renaissance and Reformation Times*, Putnam.

PALMER, R. R., and COLTON, JOEL, *A History of the Modern World*, Chap. 4, Knopf.

SCHEVILL, F., *A History of Europe: From the Reformation to the Present Day*, Harcourt, Brace. Chapter on Louis XIV.

SMITH, GOLDWIN, *The Heritage of Man*, Chap. 24, Scribner.

Special accounts: CHURCH, WILLIAM F., (ed.), *The Greatness of Louis XIV, Myth or Reality?* (Problems in European Civilization Series), Heath. For the better reader. Each chapter written by a different person, many of whom lived during Louis XIV's reign.

COSTAIN, THOMAS B., *The White and the Gold, The French Regime in Canada*, Doubleday. History written in "the terms of the people who lived it." One of a series on Canada.

GUÉRARD, ALBERT, *France: A Short History*, Norton. For better readers. Good for an understanding of the French people.

LEWIS, WARREN HAMILTON, *The Splendid Century: Life in the France of Louis XIV*, Sloane. A descriptive reference.

Biography and Fiction: DUMAS, ALEXANDRE, *The Three Musketeers*. Dodd, Mead. Novel of intrigue.

UNIT 6 Revolutionary Struggles Throughout the World

Sandors of Today

On November 4, 1956, according to the eye-witness report of Italian journalist Bruno Tedeschi, a sixteen-year old Hungarian named Sandor "lifted his batch of grenades and tossed them on the platform [of an enemy tank]" in Budapest, Hungary. His mission finished, he jumped back and started to run away. Sandor thus became a part of the 1956 Hungarian revolution against the foreign power, Soviet Russia, that dominated and oppressed the Hungarian people.

Journalist Tedeschi goes on with the story :

When I turned to look at the tank again I saw that the grenades had rolled to the ground. "Sandor," I cried, "come back, come back fast!" I can still see his face. He had certainly heard me. His eyes were wet with tears. He picked up the grenades, climbed on to the tank, and threw the lot of them at the tower. There was a blinding flash, a horrible explosion. We all threw ourselves to the ground to avoid the splinters. I didn't want to look. Sandor was dead.

To Sandor, and others like him, who fought against foreign powers that dominated their countries, the word *revolution* had proved to be the crucial term in life. It is a term that Professor Edward C. Smith, a noted political scientist, defines in this way: "the overthrow of a constitution or government as a result of armed rebellion of the citizens or by peaceful extralegal means generally acquiesced in."

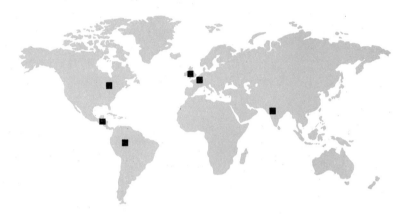

Sandors of Yesterday

There have been many other Sandors in history—men and women of all ages who have given their lives in revolts against governments they considered despotic. There were Sandors in the struggle against King Charles I of England in the seventeenth century. Sandors played an important part in the American and French Revolutions of the eighteenth century. There were Sandors in the Latin American revolutions of the nineteenth century.

Not every revolution has been fought for freedom, and not every revolutionist has had democratic aims. Many revolutionists wanted to impose their own tyranny over other men rather than destroy despotic governments. One central fact remains: In the past, as in the present, revolution has directly involved millions of people.

Sandors of Today

As the story of Sandor demonstrates, men of our own time have fought in revolutions in Indonesia, Egypt, Korea, and many other areas. There have been over eighty revolutions in Latin America since 1900; and there have been over twenty revolutions in Europe, the Middle East, Africa, and Asia in the last twenty-five years!

The importance of studying the history of earlier revolutions in the unit, "Revolutionary Struggles Throughout the World," should be clear. Since our own times are marked by revolutions, *we can learn to understand today's revolutionary movements better by studying the nature of the revolutions of the past.*

Chapter 23

Democracy Grows by Evolution and Revolution in England

KEYNOTE   Spurs and sword—golden bracelets—robe of cloth of gold—orb—sapphire and ruby ring—sceptre with cross—and finally the crown! These were the magnificent articles that were presented to Elizabeth II at her coronation as Queen of England in London in 1953.

Even as the crowds shouted "God Save the Queen," they knew that the real governing power remained in the hands of the people. Men and women hailed their new monarch and rejoiced at the greatness of their nation. At the same time, they were thankful that their democracy had freed them from the absolute power of royalty.

The people took pride in both their nation and democracy. It was a pride based on this important fact of history: *As the English nation developed, so did the democratic rights of the people.*

Key People   *James I · Charles I · Oliver Cromwell · Charles II · James II · William of Orange · John Locke · Queen Anne · George I*

Key Places   *Great Britain · England · Scotland · Wales · Ireland · Thames River · North Sea · Holland*

Key Events   *Petition of Right accepted · Charles I beheaded · Commonwealth government · Ireland conquered · Navigation Act, 1651 · Restoration of Charles II · "Glorious Revolution" · Bill of Rights · Cabinet government developed*

Key Terms   *"divine right" theory · Puritans · Roundheads · Cavaliers · "Long Parliament" · Dissenters · mercantilism · prime minister · cabinet · ministerial responsibility*

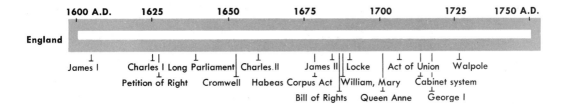

| 1600 A.D. | 1625 | 1650 | 1675 | 1700 | 1725 | 1750 A.D. |

England

James I — Charles I — Long Parliament — Charles II — James II — Locke — Act of Union — Walpole

Petition of Right — Cromwell — Habeas Corpus Act — William, Mary — Cabinet system

Bill of Rights — Queen Anne — George I

1. British Geography and History Are Closely Related

Harold Nicolson, a famous English writer, once said:

I have sought to persuade my American friends that what they resent as our [the English] patronizing manner is due almost entirely to an adenoidal infection resulting from the dampness of our soil and climate.

Mr. Nicolson was joking. Even in jest, however, he was making the important point that a person cannot understand the people of a nation without understanding the geography of their country. In our study of England, it is therefore necessary to keep in mind these geographic facts.

Great Britain is an island off the northwest coast of the European mainland. This island is separated from the mainland by the English Channel, the Straits of Dover, and the North Sea. Great Britain consists of England, Scotland, and Wales. Although people sometimes use the word *England* to mean all of Great Britain, England is only the southern part of the island.

Farther to the west is Ireland, the second important island in the British Isles. It is separated from Great Britain by St. George's Channel, the Irish Sea, and the North Channel. This island today is divided politically into two areas—Northern Ireland and the Republic of Ireland. The term *United Kingdom* (of Great Britain and Northern Ireland) refers to England, Scotland, Wales, Northern Ireland, the Isle of Man, and the Channel Islands (map, p. 368).

Historical Importance of the United Kingdom's Island Position: The United Kingdom's closeness to and dependence on the sea has helped to make her a great sea power.

The United Kingdom has many good harbors and bays. The country also has a number of rivers, including the Thames in southern England, which flows eastward through London to the North Sea. In addition, the land is rich in mineral resources, particularly coal.

BRITISH ISLES

The British Isles, located off the coast of Europe, consists of England, Ireland, Scotland, and Wales. How have its position and size affected it?

Historical Importance of the United Kingdom's Mineral Resources: Rich mineral resources helped the United Kingdom to become one of the first countries in the world to industrialize. Today nine out of ten of its people work in mining, manufacturing, and building.

The United Kingdom is quite small. It covers an area about the size of the state of Wyoming.

Historical Importance of the United Kingdom's Small Size: The small area of the country, which resulted in a lack of certain raw materials and markets for its products, has been a major reason for British expansion and trading with lands overseas.

■ **Check on Your Reading**

1. How has its island position affected the history of the United Kingdom?
2. What has been the twofold effect of the United Kingdom's wealth of mineral resources and lack of certain vital raw materials?

2. James I and Charles I Believe in the "Divine Right of Kings"

From the seventeenth through the eighteenth century, the people who lived on these British Isles were deeply involved in two important developments: (1) the growth of democratic government in England; and (2) the establishment of a British empire overseas. These two developments were intertwined. In this chapter, we shall concentrate on the rise of democracy in England, and in the next, on the evolution of the British Empire.

After the death of Elizabeth, King James VI of Scotland became the king of England as James I (1603–1625). Although James was a member of the *Stuart* royal family of Scotland, Scotland and England continued to have separate governing bodies. With the exception of brief intervals, the Stuarts ruled England for over one hundred years.

King James I believed that he ruled by divine right (p. 355). He intended to govern without the interference of Parliament, and he told its members:

I conclude ... That as to dispute what God may do is blasphemy, ... so is it sedition in subjects to dispute what a king may do in the height of his power.

James argued with Parliament over the matter of his extravagance, his methods of taxation, and his plan to establish friendly relations with England's traditional rival, Spain. He also did not please the *Puritans*, men who wanted people to lead "morally pure" lives. They continued to insist that formality and excess rituals should be eliminated from the Church of England. To anyone who criticized his actions or lack of actions, King James pointed out: "It is . . . high contempt in a subject to dispute what a king can do, or say that a king cannot do this or that."

Charles I Is Compelled to Accept the Petition of Right

Charles I, the son of James I, ruled from 1625 to 1649. Like his father, Charles quarrelled with Parliament over taxation. He also waged unsuccessful wars against Spain, the Netherlands, and France; and he imprisoned people who would not lend him money for his activities. Finally, while he was having serious trouble financing a war, Charles was forced to accept the Petition of Right drawn up by the Parliament. The *Petition of Right* (1628) was a landmark in the growth of democracy in England. These were three of its important provisions: (1) no taxation without the consent of Parliament, (2) no imprisonment of freemen without a proper trial, and (3) no military trial of civilians in time of peace.

Two of these three provisions were not new. Nevertheless, the Petition of Right made these principles a more permanent part of English life.

"Scepter and Crown . . . Tumble Down!"

Charles I was too proud a king to keep his word. He neglected the provisions of the Petition of Right. For eleven years

■ *The ill-fated King Charles I is conferring with his officers on the eve of the battle of Edgehill, 1642. The Cavaliers, in handsome dress, gallantly surround the king and Prince Rupert (seated) of the Palatine, his nephew and cavalry leader.*

Painting by C. Landseer, Walker Art Gallery, Liverpool

■ *This painting by John Pettie, called "Cromwell's Saints," satirized the condition of the soldiers in Cromwell's Puritan army.*

(1629–1640) he ruled the country without any meeting of Parliament. He raised funds by illegal methods; he tried people in special courts; and he permitted his officials to persecute members of Protestant sects.

Then an uprising occurred in Scotland. A number of Scots who insisted on following their Presbyterian faith rose against Charles. Desperate for funds to finance a campaign, the king was forced to call Parliament into session again. This Parliament, which lasted from 1640 to 1660, is known as the "Long Parliament."

A bitter struggle arose between the king's opponents (*Roundheads*, because they wore their hair short) and the king's supporters (*Cavaliers*). The Roundheads included in their ranks middle-class Englishmen, a number of Parliament members, and many Puritans. One of their leaders was Oliver Cromwell, a dedicated Puritan. The Puritans could not accept the king's claims to special God-given privileges. The Cavaliers included wealthy landowners, aristocrats, and Catholics.

Civil war broke out between Cavaliers and Roundheads in 1642, and the king's forces were defeated. Charles I was tried by a special court. This court was chosen by the so-called "Rump Parliament," which was bitterly opposed to the king. It was a dramatic moment when the court made this decision:

[The king is] a tyrant, traitor, murderer, and public enemy to the good people of this nation, [and he] shall be put to death. . . .

In 1649 the executioner's axe beheaded King Charles I. These lines by poet James Shirley had special significance:

> Death lays his icy hand on Kings,
> Scepter and crown
> Must tumble down
> And in the dust be equal made,
> With the poor crooked scythe and spade.

This successful rebellion gave a severe setback to the idea of "the divine right of kings."

■ **Check on Your Reading**

1. Explain James I's "divine right" theory.
2. What rights were won in the Petition of Right?
3. Why did the Roundheads revolt?

3. Oliver Cromwell Rules the Commonwealth

The execution of Charles I left the country without a king. England became a "Commonwealth and Free State"—that is, a country with a republican form of government—but Oliver Cromwell was the actual ruler of the state. In 1653, Cromwell dismissed the "Long Parliament" and took over supreme power. Supported by his army, he became "Lord Protector" and governed the country as a dictator.

Puritan Principles Influence Government

Oliver Cromwell was a devout Puritan and a strict ruler. As the great English poet John Milton described him, he was guided in all things "by faith and matchless fortitude." Like other Puritans, Cromwell believed in the following principles: (1) There was a close spiritual relationship between himself and God. (2) The people who truly believed in God would have common interests to bind them together. (3) Sin was real and should be strongly resisted. (4) Self-reliance and hard work were highly desirable. When carried to the New World by other Puritans, these ideas influenced American history.

Cromwell tried earnestly to restore discipline. Clad in plain black clothes, he frowned on lace-trimmed clothing, dancing, and frivolity; and he closed the theaters as unnecessary amusements. He also advocated religious toleration for all Puritan sects, including the Presbyterians and Independents, but he put down any attempt to restore Catholicism or Anglicanism.

Foreign Affairs under Cromwell

In foreign affairs, Cromwell had some degree of success. In Ireland, Irish Catholics and influential noblemen declared that Charles II, son of the beheaded English monarch, was their new ruler. They also vowed to overthrow the Commonwealth.

Cromwell and his troops therefore invaded Ireland and conquered the island. After much bloodshed, Englishmen confiscated a considerable part of the land.

Cromwell's action was one more step in the long history of antagonism between England and Ireland. In the sixteenth century, King Henry VIII had put English laws into effect in Ireland; Queen Mary had tried to colonize Ireland with Englishmen; and Queen Elizabeth I had ordered that the Roman Catholic religious services followed by most of the Irish people be stopped. In the seventeenth century, King James I had attempted to colonize north Ireland with Scottish settlers.

In Scotland, a number of Scots had announced in February, 1649, that the same

■ *Oliver Cromwell's dedicated Puritan seriousness of purpose and his lack of tolerance for weakness seem to show in this portrait.*

Painting by Robert Walker, © National Portrait Gallery, London

Charles II had agreed to become the king of Scotland and to support Presbyterianism. Charles II landed in Scotland in June, 1650. Cromwell crushed the Scots as he had the Irish rebels, and reaffirmed that he was "Lord Protector of the Commonwealth of England, Scotland, and Ireland." Then Charles II led an army into England. It was defeated and he fled to France.

When the Dutch challenged English control of the seas, England fought until the Dutch agreed to accept the terms of the Navigation Act of 1651. This act provided that only English vessels could transport to England goods from Asia, Africa, and America. The only products that Dutch ships were permitted to carry to England were those made in Holland. This act helped the English to gain commercial supremacy over the Dutch. England also battled against Spain, and an English fleet seized Jamaica in the West Indies. These wars, as well as the conflicts in Ireland and Scotland, were heavy financial drains on the treasury.

■ **Check on Your Reading**

1. What were Cromwell's religious beliefs and his code of behavior? How did these affect his approach to government?
2. What did Cromwell do about Ireland? Scotland?
3. What was the effect of the Navigation Act of 1651?

4. Charles II Is Restored to the Throne

Shortly after the death of Oliver Cromwell, the Commonwealth came to an end. The loss of "the strong man" and discontent with the rigidity of life under a military government made the English people and Parliament turn again to monarchy. The exiled Charles II erased their fears by promising to pardon those who had rebelled against his father and to permit many rights. Charles was brought back from France and made king in the so-called *Restoration.*

Charles II (1660–1685) was opposed to the further weakening of the king's power. However, he promised to respect the Magna Carta and the Petition of Right and to recognize the rights of Parliament. He exercised his royal rights so carefully that one of his nobles said in jest:

> Here [is] a great and mighty king,
>   Whose promise none rely'd on;
> He never said a foolish thing,
>   Nor ever did a wise one.

Gone were the solemn, puritanical days of Oliver Cromwell. The reopening of the theaters was symbolic of the change in spirit. The drab clothing of the Commonwealth era was replaced by frills and ruffles. Women began to wear beauty patches. Men carried muffs to protect their hands. Young dandies covered their heads with elaborately curled wigs. The pace of life speeded up, and even carriages—aided by new roads and methods of changing horses at posthouses—could travel at the unprecedented speed of fifty miles in one day!

Important events occurred during this Restoration period. Under Charles II, who personally preferred Roman Catholicism, Parliament reinstated the Anglican Church as the official Church of England. The *Dissenters*—Presbyterians, Baptists, and other Protestants who did not accept the doctrines of the Anglican faith—were permitted to worship, but only under many restrictions. The Test Act (1673) made it impossible for Catholics to take part in the government of the nation. By another act, neither Catholics nor Dissenters could participate in local government.

In foreign affairs, economic rivalry led to a renewal of the overseas war between England and Holland. In America, the English gained some islands in the West Indies, and in 1664 they took New Amsterdam and renamed it after the Duke of York (p. 382).

The Habeas Corpus Act Is Passed

Under Charles II, political parties began to develop in Parliament. The growth of parties was important to the development of democracy because it permitted individuals to unite to achieve their goals. The *Tory* party (from a Gaelic word meaning "robber") supported the policies of the king and the Church of England. The *Whig* party (from "wig") wanted to reduce the king's powers and supported toleration for other Protestant groups.

In 1679 the Whig party helped to pass the famous Habeas Corpus Act. This law was designed for "the more speedy relief of all persons imprisoned for any . . . criminal or supposed criminal matters." It gave a judge authority to grant a *writ of habeas corpus*, an order protecting an arrested person's rights: (1) to be brought before a judge and told why he was arrested; (2) if his arrest was legal, to be given a trial within a reasonable period of time; and (3) if his arrest was illegal, to be released. This law proved to be a bulwark against unfair and arbitrary arrest. Although little interest was taken in its passage at the time, the Habeas Corpus Act is a landmark in the history of democracy. The right to *habeas corpus* is one of the most basic safeguards of Americans against illegal arrest.

Mercantilism Affects the Nation

In addition to making political and legal changes, England tried to strengthen herself economically during the seventeenth century. The English followed many of the practices of mercantilism (p. 355).

Mercantilism, which became important in the late seventeenth and lasted well into the eighteenth century, was a European-wide development that affected many areas in the world. It brought a number of significant results, including the following: (1) It stimulated the development of industries at home and the exploration of overseas areas. (2) It increased the competition for empire and markets overseas. The Dutch, French, Prussians, Austrians, and Russians established trading companies and stations to compete with the English for trade. (3) It intensified the rivalries between European countries and often led to war. (4) It often created dangerous tensions between colonies and home countries. The Navigation Acts passed by the English, for example, restricted the trade of the American colonies and attempted to benefit England. Opposition to these acts was one of the principal factors that led to the American Revolution.

Mercantilism was not only an economic system of controlling trade, but also an attempt to build strong political states. The idea was to create a self-sufficient state that did not have to depend on outsiders, who could be rivals or potential enemies. Currency and foreign trade controls are a survival of the mercantilist spirit.

■ Check on Your Reading

1. Why was Charles II restored to the throne? How did life in England change in the Restoration period?

2. How did Parliament deal with religion?

3. What was the Habeas Corpus Act?

4. How did mercantilism affect relations among the European nations?

5. The "Glorious Revolution"

James II (1685–1688), the brother of Charles II, became king of England upon the death of Charles. James was a Catholic, and he tried to restore the power of the Catholic Church in his country. He also was determined to rule with a strong hand, and he dissolved a Parliament that disagreed with his activities. By 1688 he had become so unpopular that his opponents decided to oust him.

Parliament invited James' Protestant daughter, Mary, and her husband, William of Orange, to come from Holland and govern England. William and Mary accepted the offer and entered England with their Dutch soldiers. Realizing that he had lost the support of the influential men in his kingdom, James fled the country.

Parliament then offered the crown to William and Mary. They accepted and became the rulers of England in 1689, with the understanding that they were to rule with the advice and guidance of Parliament. This bloodless overthrow of James II and the crowning of William and Mary is known as the "Glorious Revolution." It was extremely important because *it made clear that Parliament—not the king—was supreme in the government of England.*

The Bill of Rights

To protect itself in the future, Parliament made William and Mary sign a Bill of Rights. This Bill of Rights (1689) was one of the most significant landmarks in the growth of democracy. It had the following provisions: (1) The king could not suspend or carry out a law without the consent of Parliament. (2) The king could not levy taxes or keep an army without the consent of Parliament. (3) Full respect would be given to "freedom of speech, and debates or proceedings in Parliament."

This English Bill of Rights also contained other points that later were included in the American Bill of Rights (see Chart).

The Philosophy of John Locke

The English Bill of Rights was to influence many people and several nations. It is important to understand the philosophy, or basic ideas, behind it. These ideas were best expressed by the Englishman John Locke (1632–1704). Locke believed:

Governments are formed to protect men's life, liberty, and property.

Government must be by the consent of those who are governed. Or, as Locke put it: "The

ENGLISH BILL OF RIGHTS	BILL OF RIGHTS IN THE U.S. CONSTITUTION
It is the right of the subjects to petition the king. . . .	Congress shall make no law . . . abridging . . . the right of the people . . . to petition the government for a redress of grievances.
The subjects which are Protestants may have arms for their defense. . . .	. . . the right of the people to keep and bear arms shall not be infringed.
Excessive bail ought not to be required, nor excessive fines imposed, nor cruel and unusual punishments inflicted.	Excessive bail shall not be required, nor excessive fines imposed, nor cruel and unusual punishments inflicted.

liberty of man, in society, is to be under no other legislative power but that established by consent in the commonwealth. . . ."

If a government interferes with men's life, liberty, or property—or rules without the consent of those who are governed—the people may take steps to change the government.

Locke completely rejected the idea of "divine right of kings." Locke insisted that government should be based on the consent of the governed. He was convinced that men were endowed with enough reason to judge whether or not a government protected their life, liberty, and property— and to change any government that denied them these rights.

Parliament Deals with Religious Problems

In addition to redefining the position of the monarchy, Parliament dealt with serious religious problems. The Anglican Church continued to hold its key position; but provisions were made for Dissenters, Catholics, and future rulers of England.

For Dissenters, the Act of Toleration was passed (1689). This act permitted them freedom of public worship, but not the right to hold government office.

For Catholics, permission was given to members of the Catholic faith to participate in private religious observances—but not to have complete religious toleration or to hold government office. By a provision that was included in the Bill of Rights, no Catholic was to be permitted to become king. Later, by the Act of Settlement (1701)—which was drawn up because the next English ruler, Queen Anne, had no Protestant heirs—Parliament provided that the crown should be passed to other Protestants, members of the German House of Hanover. (This family was related to the Stuarts through the Electress Sophia, granddaughter of James I.)

■ Check on Your Reading

1. What was the importance of the "Glorious Revolution"?
2. How did the Bill of Rights strengthen democracy in England?
3. Explain Locke's basic ideas.
4. How did Parliament increase religious freedom but ensure Protestant rule?

6. The "United Kingdom of Great Britain" Is Formed

Queen Anne (1702–1714) was the last of the Stuart monarchs to rule Great Britain. During her reign, an event of great importance occurred: Scotland was united with England to form the "United Kingdom of Great Britain."

The Act of Union

Since the time of James I (1603–1625), Scotland had been under the jurisdiction of the ruler of England, but the Scots had maintained their own separate Parliament. By the Act of Union (1707), one Parliament was established for both England and Scotland. It also was agreed that there would be a sharing of "all . . . rights, privileges, and advantages, which do or may belong to the subjects of either kingdom."

The square red cross representing England was united with the diagonal white cross representing Scotland to form a single flag for both lands. That flag was the Union Jack—the symbol of the new United Kingdom.

Leaders Become Responsible to the House of Commons

Upon the death of Queen Anne, George, Elector of Hanover (in Germany), was the nearest Protestant relative. In accordance

■ *A single flag, the Union Jack, was formed. It became the symbol of the new United Kingdom.*

with the terms of the Act of Settlement, Parliament named George to be king.

Unfortunately George I (1714–1727) could not understand English. The new king therefore turned over most of the affairs of government to a man known as the *prime minister* and his Cabinet. The Cabinet was a group of advisers tracing its origin back to the days of William and Mary. Sir Robert Walpole is recognized as the first prime minister of England.

Gradually a system developed by which the prime minister and his Cabinet directed the government of the country (see Chart). This system is still in operation. It is a system of *ministerial responsibility*. This means that the prime minister and his Cabinet are responsible to the House of Commons for their actions. The development of ministerial responsibility was very important to the growth of democracy. In time, the British leaders became fully responsible to the elected representatives, the House of Commons. Gradually the hereditary House of Lords lost almost all of its power. The prime minister, the Cabinet, and the House of Commons control the British government today.

■ **Check on Your Reading**

1. What was achieved by the Act of Union?

2. How did Cabinet government develop? How does it work?

3. Define: prime minister, Cabinet, ministerial responsibility, majority party.

THE CABINET SYSTEM

Prime Minister: The monarch invites one member of Parliament to become prime minister, that is, to direct the government. The prime minister must be the man who is the leader of the majority party in the House of Commons or who has the support of the majority of the members of the House of Commons.

Cabinet: The Cabinet is a group of advisors to the prime minister. The prime minister suggests the names of the men he wishes to have in his Cabinet, and the monarch appoints them to their offices. Most of the Cabinet members are heads of departments, such as Defense, Foreign Affairs, and Labor.

Period of Office: If a majority of the House of Commons stops supporting the policies of the prime minister, he and his entire Cabinet must resign or ask that the people be permitted to elect a new House of Commons.

Assume an election is held. If a majority in the new House of Commons supports the prime minister, he keeps his position. If the majority opposes him, he resigns and a new man is appointed prime minister.

CULTURAL CHARACTERISTICS of Seventeenth-Century England

The history of England in the seventeenth century is extremely complicated. Indeed, one scholar, Samuel Rawson Gardiner, required forty years to write the history of that country from 1603–1656!

Some seventeenth- and early eighteenth-century English writers, viewing the twists and turns in the course of events, even doubted man's ability to reason logically. Despite such criticism, the English did succeed in working out several of their political, economic, and religious problems in the seventeenth century. The cultural characteristics of England in this period were:

A society reflecting the governmental changes from "divine right" to the climax of the Glorious Revolution.

The granting of political and judicial rights to a broader number of citizens, as Parliament curbed the powers of the king.

A predominantly agricultural economy with a rising and influential class of merchants and businessmen.

Religious tensions that were gradually lessened by extending "toleration" to certain religious groups.

Yet it is possible to oversimplify in our judgment of seventeenth-century England. Did Parliament or the Stuart monarchs make the greater contribution to the welfare of the lower economic groups? How important or unimportant was the "middle class" in the cultural development of England? Were the political parties in England really "parties" in the modern sense of the word and how did they influence English culture? Or were the parties merely factions of the King's friends or enemies?

Like a man who wears a favorite jacket each day, we tend to treasure the garment of democracy without thinking about the nature of the cloth. However, it is no longer sufficient to do so or simply to state that "democracy triumphed in England during the seventeenth century." Patterns of democratic growth are highly complex, offering both problems and opportunities for cultural growth.

MAN AND HIS CULTURE

Let's Meet the People!

This sketch is based on: Edward P. Cheyney, *Readings in English History Drawn from the Original Sources*, Ginn and Company; Mary I. Curtis, *England of Song and Story*, copyright 1931 & 1945 by Allyn & Bacon, Inc.; G. M. Trevelyan, *Illustrated English Social History*, courtesy of David McKay Co., Inc.; Percy H. Boynton, *London in English Literature*, The University of Chicago Press, copyright 1931 by The University of Chicago Press; D. Yarwood, *English Costume from the Second Century B.C. to 1950*, B. T. Batsford, Ltd.

A Coffeehouse Proprietor in the Eighteenth Century

Tobacco smoke filled the large room and rose toward the beamed ceiling of the English

coffeehouse. The proprietor moved quickly about the sanded floor and past the bare-topped tables. He was dressed in a white shirt and a waistcoat, plain breeches fastened below the knees, cotton stockings, and black leather shoes. And he seemed to be everywhere! Most of his customers agreed that:

377

Though he be no great traveler, yet [the proprietor] is in continual motion, but it is only from the fire-side to the table; and his tongue goes . . . faster than his feet. . . .

The proprietor had many tasks. First, he had to see to it that the coffee was brewed properly. Since the beverage was drunk without sugar or cream, the taste had to be acceptable.

The proprietor also had to point out to his customers that coffee was good for their health. He hoped that they would agree with him that, while it cost only a penny a cup,

[Coffee] makes the heart lightsome. It is good for a cough. It is excellent to prevent and cure the dropsy, gout, and scurvy. . . . It will prevent drowsiness and make one fit for business. . . .

Most important of all, the proprietor had to be sure that the latest printed and spoken news was made available to his customers. He knew that many men who came into his coffeehouse hungered for political news, particularly those who spoke boldly of ob-taining greater freedom. Some of his customers even went so far as "to show reasons against acts of Parliament, and condemn the decrees of general councils."

"What news have you, Master?" a customer would ask him.

The proprietor would stop promptly. Then—in a whisper loud enough to be heard by almost all in the room:

He [would relate] some mysterious intrigue of state, told him last night by one that is a barber to the tailor of the servant of a great man!

The proprietor kept himself well informed by thrusting his head into groups of earnest debaters and listening with great attention "to the narratives that were made in those little circular audiences." He tried to keep his establishment a "university of information" for these men, for—above all—he wanted his customers to continue to say:

So great a University
I think there ne'er was any,
In which you may a scholar be
For spending of a penny.

CHAPTER REVIEW

REVIEW and DISCUSSION

1. Identify the people and places and explain the events and terms on p. 366.

2. John Milton, the English poet, spoke out boldly against people in any age who flee rather than fight for what they believe in. Which is better? Why?

3. Why were arguments about religion not separated from the political questions in seventeenth-century England?

4. How was the English Civil War similar to the American Civil War? In what ways was it different?

5. How did Cromwell and the Puritans contribute to the growth of democracy in England?

6. How well did Charles II perform his duties as king?

7. Why was *habeas corpus* important?

8. "Competition is the life of trade," is an old saying. Did mercantilism illustrate its truth? How?

9. Can you find the theory of the "right to revolt" against tyranny in the philosophy of John Locke? In what American document was this theory adopted by a group of people?

10. Why didn't Parliament give complete religious freedom to all people in 1689?

11. What democratic gains were made in the age of the Stuarts?

12. Is the Cabinet system more or less democratic than our own presidential system?

ACTIVITIES

1. Write a report to give to the class on how the King James Version of the Bible came into being.

2. Make a list of the steps taken toward the development of democratic government that were made by evolution; by revolution.

3. Make a chart of the great documents that contributed to the growth of democracy in England. Use different colored ink or crayon to emphasize rights for common people and restrictions on the king. Place a star next to the rights which we have today.

4. On a map of the British Isles, locate Belfast, Dublin, Edinburgh, England, English Channel, Great Britain, Irish Sea, Isle of Man, London, North Sea, Northern Ireland, Republic of Ireland, Scotland, United Kingdom and Wales.

5. Write a short essay on John Locke's philosophy and influence.

PAST and PRESENT

1. Can you find any examples of mercantilism in the world today?

2. Cite examples of "divine right" rulers in the twentieth century.

3. What nations today are strongly "democratic"? Why?

SUGGESTED READINGS

Basic books: EVANS, MARY, *Costume Throughout the Ages*, Chap. 12, Lippincott.

LIFE, *Picture History of Western Man*, Section VIII, Simon and Schuster.

PALMER, R. R., and COLTON, JOEL, *A History of the Modern World*, Chap. 4, Knopf.

SMITH, GOLDWIN, *The Heritage of Man*, Chap. 24, Scribner.

Special accounts: CHEYNEY, EDWARD, (ed.), *Readings in English History Drawn from the Original Sources*, Ginn.

CHURCHILL, WINSTON, *History of the English-Speaking Peoples, The Age of Revolution*, Chap. 1, Dodd, Mead; *History of the English-Speaking Peoples, The New World*, Chaps. 11–26, Dodd, Mead. Read the account of the execution of Charles I.

HARTLEY, DOROTHY, and ELLIOT, M. M., *Life and Work of the People of England: Seventeenth Century*, Putnam. Good illustrated reference. Easy reading.

QUENNELL, MARJORIE, and CHARLES, H. B., *A History of Everyday Things in England*. 4 Vols. Putnam.

TREVELYAN, GEORGE M., *English Social History*, Chaps. 8 and 9, Longmans, Green. An excellent reference by a well-known British historian. For better readers.

Biography and Fiction: THOMPSON, STITH, and GASSNER, JOHN, (eds.), *Our Heritage of World Literature*, Holt. The section on seventeenth-century English literature gives an account by Samuel Pepys of the Great London Fire, Milton's *Areopagitica* on freedom of press, and a description of the coronation of Charles II.

Chapter 24   England Wins an Empire and Loses Her American Colonies

KEYNOTE   James F. Green, a contemporary writer on political affairs, recently recalled the remark of an expert in international law who said:

[Empire-building] resembles opening a window. When *you* do it, it's fresh air. When the *other* fellow does it, it's a draught.

This statement is particularly meaningful when applied to the activities of the English in the eighteenth century. It was in this period that *Britain won an empire in India and America* and felt a sense of pride in that achievement. Yet it was in this same century that *the American colonies—resentful rather than pleased by Britain's control over them—revolted and established their own nation.*

Key People   *Philip II · Robert Clive · Joseph Dupleix · Jacques Cartier · Samuel de Champlain · Henry Hudson · William Pitt · John Locke · Thomas Paine*

Key Places   *New Amsterdam · Calcutta · Plassey · Jamestown · Plymouth · Nova Scotia · Newfoundland · Quebec*

Key Events   *Dutch colonize in East · English East India Company chartered · English take New Amsterdam · England wins India · France in North America · English settlements in North America · Queen Anne's War · French and Indian War · American Revolution · Declaration of Independence*

Key Terms   *empire · Sepoys · Separatists · Puritans · Quakers · Continental Congress · loyalists*

380

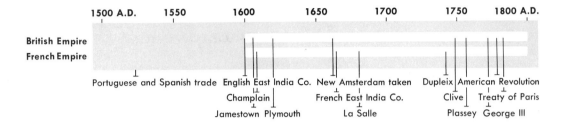

1500 A.D.	1550	1600	1650	1700	1750	1800 A.D.

British Empire

French Empire

Portuguese and Spanish trade   English East India Co.   New Amsterdam taken   Dupleix | American Revolution

Champlain   French East India Co.   Clive | Treaty of Paris

Jamestown Plymouth   La Salle   Plassey George III

1. Portuguese, Dutch, and English Clash

At the same time that democracy was developing in England, the English were building a powerful empire overseas. They were active in India and North America.

In the sixteenth century, Portugal and Spain were the leaders in establishing contacts with the East and with America. Eventually, the Portuguese set up trading posts on Ceylon; on Java, Sumatra, and the Moluccas or the Spice Islands (all of which are part of Indonesia today); and at Goa, on the west coast of India. Meanwhile the Spaniards had pacified the Philippine Islands and gained a considerable empire in America (p. 433).

The Dutch Oppose the Portuguese

Portugal was annexed to Spain in 1580 and did not regain its independence until 1640. Under Spain's control, Portuguese merchants were handicapped by the acts of the Spanish king, Philip II. For example, Philip forbade his enemies— England, France, and the United Netherlands—to trade with the chief ports of Portugal; and he weakened both Spain and Portugal by his unsuccessful struggle against England, climaxed by the defeat of the Spanish Armada in 1588.

Spain declined in power after the defeat of the Armada. Portugal faced serious problems, too. The United Netherlands had won its independence from Spain in 1581, and the Dutch became the rivals of the Portuguese for foreign trade. In 1602 the Dutch East India Company was organized to develop trade with the East. Aggressive Dutch officials and bold merchants moved into trading areas held by the Portuguese. So successful were the Dutch in their tactics that by the beginning of the eighteenth century they had taken over most of the trading posts once controlled by the Portuguese.

The English Oppose the Dutch

Just as the Dutch had moved against the Portuguese in the East, so the English were determined to drive out the Dutch. English merchants were particularly eager to trade with ports on the coast of India and with the Molucca Islands. They hoped to exchange English cloth for spices, calico, dye woods, and precious stones.

381

In 1600 Queen Elizabeth I therefore chartered the English East India Company to trade with lands in the Indian and Pacific oceans. This company obtained or assumed the right to administer the government of trading areas it controlled, protect itself against traders from other countries, and fight against native peoples who would not co-operate with English traders. The English established posts at Madras and other places in India and worked hard to take over Dutch trade in the East. During the period of the Commonwealth, the English forced the Dutch to accept the Navigation Act of 1651 (p. 372). The Navigation Act was one of a series of acts designed to ensure English control over the trade of their colonies. It did not bring peace. In the reign of Charles II (1660–1685), economic rivalry led to a renewal of the overseas war between England and Holland. The Dutch forced the English out of the Spice Islands, and the English took over Dutch islands in the West Indies. The English also attacked the Dutch colony of New Amsterdam in America. In 1664 New Amsterdam (later renamed New York) surrendered to the English, the Dutch garrison "retiring with all their arms, flying colors, and beating drums."

Relations between the English and the Dutch became more stable. In its search for empire in India, England faced an even more dangerous enemy, France.

■ Check on Your Reading

1. How did the Dutch gain control of most of the Portuguese trading posts in the East?

2. What did the English East India Company achieve in the East?

3. What did the English gain from the Dutch? How?

■ *By 1700, European nations—Spain, France, England, Portugal, and the Netherlands—had established trade contacts and colonies in the East and in America. What colonies were established by each of these nations? Where? How did colonies benefit the European nations?*

EUROPEAN COLONIZATION ABOUT 1700

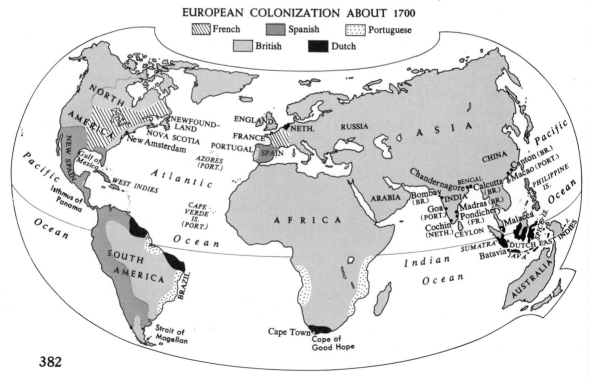

Painting by I. Sailmaker, National Maritime Museum, Greenwich

■ *Ships called "East Indiamen" were specially built and equipped for the long voyages between England and India, the East Indies, and China. These "East Indiamen" are in port about 1675. The Dutch also used "East Indiamen" in their thriving trade with the East.*

2. The English and French Clash

The setting for the struggles among the English, the French, and rulers of India had come into focus by the eighteenth century (map, p. 382). The English East India Company had established trading stations or forts at Madras, the Bengal area, Calcutta, and Bombay.

The French East India Company had been chartered in 1664. Like the English East India Company, it had authority to trade and, if necessary, to fight to establish its position in India. It had set up trading bases at Chandernagore in the northeast and Pondichéry in the southeast.

In India, shortly after the death of the ruler Aurangzeb in 1707, the Mogul Empire had disintegrated. India had split into many provinces ruled by native princes. It was not strong enough to repel foreigners.

Clive Helps Win India for the English

France had its important colonial administrators, such as Joseph François Dupleix, who in 1742 became the commander of the French possessions in India. Dupleix made alliances with native princes in southern India, trained natives to fight as soldiers for the French, and led the French in their battles against the English. A series of disagreements with the French East India Company led to his recall to France in 1754.

The English were still more fortunate. They had the services of young Robert Clive who, according to the legend, even as a boy had demonstrated his courage by sitting on the top of a church steeple. Clive started as a clerk and transferred to the military arm of the English East India

383

■ *Robert Clive is shown receiving from the Mogul emperor, the diwani, a right of collecting revenue for the English East India Company (1766). Indians collected for the Company.*

Company. He built up a strong military force that included native Indian soldiers (*sepoys*). Clive proved a brilliant, if moody, leader who loved action and who was most effective in times of danger.

In 1757 the nawab (or native ruler) of the region of Bengal, who favored the French and who was angry because the English were strengthening their defenses in Calcutta, seized the town. Then he locked up one hundred forty-six Englishmen in a small cell described by an eyewitness as "a room not twenty feet square, with only two small windows, and these obstructed by the veranda." All that night the terrified prisoners remained in this so-called "Black Hole of Calcutta"—some raving in delirium; others praying madly; still others scrambling over the heads of those who stood between them and the windows. The pressure of the bodies against one another, the terrible heat, and the lack of air suffocated most of them. In the morning, when the doors were finally opened, only twenty-three were still alive! Recent scholarship suggests that the number of people locked up in the "Black Hole" has been exaggerated, and that the event was later overdramatized.

Robert Clive determined that the nawab should be punished for this action and for challenging the rights of the English. He attacked and recaptured Calcutta. Then he crushed the nawab's army at the great battle of Plassey (in Bengal) in 1757. Clive's victory was extremely important for future history, since it made possible the control and use of Bengal as a center for further English expansion in India by the English East India Company.

Finally, during the Seven Years' War (1756–1763), which was fought in India as well as in Europe and America, Clive and other English leaders captured the important French settlements in India. By the end of the war, the prestige of France had been seriously weakened. The English permitted the French to return to their Indian posts but took away their power by prohibiting them from maintaining troops. The supremacy of the English East India Company was firmly established in India. In addition, the English and French struggled against each other in North America.

The French in North America

About seventy years after the French explorer Jacques Cartier discovered the St. Lawrence River (1535), France began to build a colonial empire in the New World. In 1604, the French established a permanent settlement at Port Royal, Acadia (Nova Scotia). A few years later, Samuel de Champlain, called the "father of New France," founded a colony at Quebec (1608). The French also established a permanent settlement at Montreal (1642) which became an important center for trade.

Father Jacques Marquette, a Jesuit missionary, and Louis Joliet, a fur trader, followed the Mississippi River from Wisconsin as far south as the Arkansas River in 1673. Another French explorer, La Salle, took an expedition down the Mississippi River to its mouth (1680–1682). He claimed for France a region which he named Louisiana in honor of King Louis XIV. Eventually, the French claimed the land between the Gulf of Mexico and the Great Lakes, and their holdings extended far to the west and northeast (map, p. 387).

The English in North America

The English settled in the New World at a later date than the French. In 1607 the London Company founded the colony of Jamestown in Virginia. This was the first permanent English settlement in America. Living conditions in Jamestown were extremely bad; during one bitter winter the starving colonists were forced to live almost like animals. Despite the hardships, the Jamestown settlement survived.

In 1609 the river we call the Hudson was discovered by Henry Hudson, an English sea captain in the employ of the Dutch. In 1620, Pilgrims seeking a place where they could worship as they wished established a second English colony at Plymouth, Massachusetts. The Pilgrims believed in Calvinistic ideas. They were *Separatists*, that is, they wanted to break away completely from the Anglican Church rather than try to reform it from within.

During the reigns of James I and Charles I, Separatists and Puritans were discriminated against or persecuted in England. Those who were not persecuted feared "contamination" by men who did not worship with their own sincerity. In addition, many who dissented from the Anglican Church were without work because of agricultural and economic problems. Between 1620 and 1640, about 70,000 people left England and came to the New World. Most of these settlers sought religious freedom for themselves, land, and work.

Additional English settlements appeared during the seventeenth century. The Puritans were active in Massachusetts. The Catholics, who sought a religious refuge, settled in Maryland. The Quakers (the Religious Society of Friends), who rejected many ideas of the Catholics, the Puritans, and the Anglican Church, migrated to what is Pennsylvania. According to church historian, Williston Walker, they believed that (1) "every man received from the Lord a measure of light, and . . . if this 'Inner Light' is followed, it leads surely . . . to spiritual truth" and (2) a professional ministry is unnecessary.

385

English military men also were active. In 1664 they forced the Dutch to give up New Amsterdam. By 1733 the English controlled the thirteen colonies along the Atlantic coast (map, p. 387).

The English Settlers Come to Stay

Unlike the French, the English settlers had come to stay. They were determined to settle permanently in America—rather than to come for trading, missionary, and similar purposes, like the French. While the English continued to think of England as the "home" country, they soon developed real pride in their American surroundings.

The English settlers wanted to have considerable self-government in local affairs—rather than to accept the nearly absolute control of the home government in Europe as the French did. In 1818 John Adams, who had served as the second President of the United States, wrote:

I have always laughed at the affectation of representing American independence . . . as a late invention. The idea of it . . . has been familiar to Americans from the first settlement of the country.

■ Check on Your Reading

1. Why were France and England able to establish trading stations in India?
2. Describe the work of Dupleix and Clive.
3. What were the results of the Seven Years' War in India?
4. Contrast the French and English settlements in North America.

3. The English Gain Supremacy in North America

The international wars occurring in the eighteenth century in Europe spread. In North America, they led to a bitter struggle between the English and the French.

Queen Anne's War

Europe was busy fighting the War of the Spanish Succession (p. 360). The struggle became so widespread that it led to fighting between the French and English in America (Queen Anne's War).

Settlers in New England waged a successful campaign against France's Port Royal in Acadia. By the Treaties of Utrecht (1713), France gave Nova Scotia to England; and France recognized England's claims to Newfoundland and the Hudson Bay region.

The French and Indian War

The Seven Years' War (1756–1763) involved most of the countries of Europe (p. 346), and again England and France were on opposite sides. In America, the war was known as the French and Indian War (1754–1763).

Under the leadership of the English statesman, William Pitt, English troops and American colonists fought successfully against the French. The climax came when the French stronghold of Quebec in Canada was captured by General Wolfe and his English forces. Then the English troops spread through Canada, capturing Montreal in 1760.

By the Peace of Paris (1763) ending the war: (1) France gave Canada, Prince Edward Island, Cape Breton Island, and most of her lands east of the Mississippi to England. She kept St. Pierre and Miquelon (two islands off the coast of Newfoundland) and her West Indian island possessions. (2) France gave New Orleans and Louisiana west of the Mississippi to Spain. (3) Spain gave the Floridas to England.

■ Check on Your Reading

1. What were the results of Queen Anne's War?
2. What were the provisions of the Peace of Paris (1763)?

CHANGE OF OWNERSHIP OF NORTH AMERICA

■ *The two maps show the territory that France lost to England as a result of the Seven Years' War. What territory did England obtain in North America by 1763?*

BEFORE 1754

AFTER 1763
- - - Proclamation Line

4. The American Revolution

From 1689 to 1763 England had struggled against France in the New World. The French finally were defeated and forced to turn over most of their holdings in America to the English. To the victors belonged the spoils. However, it was not long before American colonists arose to spoil the victory.

Complaints of the American Colonists

During the reign of King George III (1760–1820), American colonists became increasingly displeased with the home government in England. They were angry for several reasons.

(1) British officials placed oppressive economic restrictions on the colonies, such as prohibiting them from exporting articles that would compete with those produced in England. (2) They also interfered with the colonies' right to trade. For example, the Navigation Acts required American colonists selling goods to other countries to transport them in English ships and to have these vessels stop at England on their voyages; permitted colonists to sell their sugar and several other products only to

the American colonies or to England, not to foreign markets; and established other restrictions on colonial trade.

(3) Britain taxed the colonies without permitting them to send representatives to the British Parliament. For example, the Stamp Act of 1765—passed by the British Parliament, not by the colonists—required the American colonists to buy special government stamps and place them on newspapers, business documents, and other papers. This unpopular act aroused resistance and disorderly demonstrations. It was finally repealed after a Stamp Act Congress (1765) of representatives from nine colonies denied that Parliament could tax the colonies without their consent.

(4) British officials took away a number of political rights of colonial governments, stationed British soldiers in the homes of colonists, and in other ways violated the privacy of the people.

The Viewpoint of the British Government

The British government took the position that the colonies were a small part of a great empire and that (1) Parliament

■ *American colonists in Boston are burning stamps sent from England, 1765. This was one of many demonstrations against the Stamp Act.*

colonists from French domination—was about thirty-six billion dollars (by our currency standards today). (4) The protest of the colonists against "taxation without representation" was unreasonable. The British Parliament had free debate on matters involving the American colonies, and British statesmen represented *all* Englishmen and expressed *all* viewpoints—including those of the colonies. So they said.

The Colonists Have a "Tea Party"

Tensions increased during the 1770's, reaching a climax in the famous "Boston Tea Party." The Tea Act of 1773 had given the British East India Company a monopoly on the tea trade in America. No American could buy his tea legally from anyone but this company. Many colonists were angered by the establishment of this monopoly and by other regulations concerning the importation of tea. They boycotted the trade in tea, and some of them warned that if a person drank the tea of the East India Company, "the devil will immediately enter into you."

Finally, on the night of December 16, 1773, about one hundred fifty colonists, disguised as Mohawk Indians, boarded a tea ship in Boston harbor and threw its cargo of three hundred forty-two chests of tea overboard. This act led the British to close the port of Boston and to place more restrictions on the people of Massachusetts. The incident indicated clearly that the colonists were willing to defy British authority.

The Continental Congress Declares War

Ignoring the advice of English statesmen like Edmund Burke, who opposed the British use of coercion in the colonies, the British government continued to restrict the rights of the colonists. As a result, the First Continental Congress met in Philadelphia in 1774 to determine what to do.

had an obligation to pass measures, including laws that established a mercantilist relationship between Britain and her colonies, to protect the well-being of Britain. The British believed that the prosperity of the home country would stimulate the prosperity of the colonies.

(2) The Navigation Acts were designed to help Britain, not to hinder the colonies. The British had given bounties and monopolies to the colonists to develop industries that did not compete with those of Britain.

(3) According to this viewpoint the British government had the right to expect American colonists to pay taxes to help meet the costs of administering and defending the colonies. Britain needed money desperately. Its debt at the end of the Seven Years' War—a conflict in which England helped to protect the American

The First Continental Congress consisted of fifty-six representatives from twelve colonies, a group which the English writer Dr. Samuel Johnson contemptuously called "croakers of calamity." The Congress drew up plans to make the British change their policies, but it did not advocate that the colonies break away.

In 1775 violence replaced discussion. On April 19 British troops and Americans clashed at Concord and Lexington in Massachusetts, and it was too late to speak of keeping the peace, though some hoped to restore it. As the *New-York Mercury* then observed: "All that is attended to, besides plowing and planting, is making ready for fighting." The Second Continental Congress officially declared war on Britain on July 6, 1775.

The Declaration of Independence Is Drawn Up

The American Revolution did not pit class against class and, far from being a radical mass uprising, was led by moderates and members of the upper class. Some of the colonists known as *loyalists*, about one-third of the total population in the colonies, even remained loyal to the British. They distrusted what loyalist Samuel Seabury called "our sovereign Lord the Mob."

Other colonists joined the American forces directed by George Washington, the commander-in-chief. Sturdy farmers enlisted, dressed in "clothes [they were] accustomed to wear in the field." Excited fifteen-year-old boys volunteered, handling their muskets awkwardly but willing to learn. And one brave woman dressed herself in a man's clothing, said that her name was Robert Shurtleff, and enlisted!

Most of these people at first were fighting to regain their rights, not to separate from Britain. However, the king branded them "rebels," and it was not long before they were willing to play that role. Still, there were great disagreements over how far the colonists should go in defying England. Then in January, 1776 there appeared a pamphlet, *Common Sense*, by Thomas Paine. Paine was a believer in a republican form of government, and he condemned monarchy. He pointed out that it was ridiculous for America, a great continent, to be ruled by a small island, Britain. America should move toward free trade, independence, and westward expansion. It should set up a republic, remain clear of European problems, and develop its rich resources.

Common Sense was widely read and highly influential in moving public opinion toward seeking American independence. Finally, as the British refused to make major concessions, a Declaration of Independence was drawn up (adopted July 4, 1776). It announced to the world:

... these United Colonies are, and of Right ought to be, Free and Independent States; ... they are Absolved from all Allegiance to the British Crown, and ... all political connection between them and the State of Great Britain, is and ought to be totally dissolved....

Thomas Jefferson, a key figure in the writing of the Declaration of Independence, declared that he "turned to neither book nor pamphlet" in working on this document. However, there were ideas in the Declaration that were very similar to those of John Locke (p. 375), with whose writings Jefferson and other educated men of the time were quite familiar.

An Evaluation of British and American Strength

Noble as its words were, the Declaration of Independence alone could not guarantee independence. If the *United States* (the thirteen former colonies) were to be free, the Revolutionary War would have to be won. The death of patriots would be needed to give life to a new country.

Fortunately for the Americans, there were men ready to make sacrifices. Men like Tom Paine, whose pamphlets helped to fan the sparks of revolution; Benjamin Franklin, who served with distinction as American representative to France; the Frenchman Marquis de Lafayette, the German Baron von Steuben, the Pole Casimir Pulaski, who came to America from Europe to fight for liberty; and George Washington, who led the ragged and motley American troops through what Tom Paine called "times that try men's souls."

The odds for victory seemed to favor the British. They had the following advantages: (1) Their army was better trained than the American troops. (2) Their navy was far more powerful than the ships available to the Americans. (3) They had the money necessary to hire mercenary troops (paid professional soldiers, such as the Hessians) to fight for them. (4) They retained the loyalty of many colonists.

On the other hand, the Americans had these advantages: (1) The war was being fought on their home grounds, while the British were many miles from England. (2) They had the effective leadership of Washington and other men whose tactics often proved superior to those of British generals. (3) They had the eventual support of France and of Holland and Spain. (4) Their cause stirred some Americans to deeds of unusual heroism.

■ **Check on Your Reading**

1. What were the colonists' grievances? What was the British government's attitude?

2. What incidents and events led to the outbreak of the American Revolution?

3. In your opinion, which side had the greater advantages in the war? Why?

5. Americans Win Their Independence

There were bitter campaigns in New England, Canada, South Carolina, New York, and New Jersey; and the Americans had to survive some serious setbacks. Then, in 1777, American troops won an important victory at Saratoga, New York, where they defeated the forces of the British General Burgoyne.

France Supports the Americans

The victory at Saratoga, plus the convincing arguments presented by Benjamin Franklin to the French court, made France realize that Americans were capable opponents of the British. Eager to strike back at a Britain that had fought against French interests, France made an alliance with the Americans in 1778. The French recognized the independence of the new American nation and provided it with vital financial and military assistance.

Aided by the French, the revolutionists fought on. Finally, with the support of a French fleet, Washington forced the British General Cornwallis to surrender at Yorktown, Virginia (1781). Soon after this American victory, the Revolutionary War came to an end.

By the Treaty of Paris (1783): (1) The independence of the United States was recognized by Britain. (2) The Mississippi River was recognized as the western boundary of the United States, and navigation on the Mississippi was opened to both the United States and Britain. (3) The fishing rights of Americans off Newfoundland were protected.

To the south, Spain held Florida, which she had reconquered from the British in 1783. To the west, Spain controlled land west of the Mississippi. And to the north, the British remained in Canada.

■ *From thirteen colonies along the Atlantic coast in 1783, the United States gained control over more territory through annexation, purchase, and war until it extended to the Pacific Ocean. What territories were acquired? How?*

The United States Looks Forward to Becoming a United Nation

The successful American Revolution had a number of important results: (1) It brought into existence a new nation, the United States. (2) Written constitutions were devised for the newly freed states and later for the American nation. (3) Americans now could settle on the western lands that had been under the restrictive control of the British government. (4) It weakened the prestige of monarchical governments. (5) It influenced events in France, a country moving toward revolution.

The United States was still not a united nation. As a leading American historian, Merle Curti, points out, all during the Revolution and long afterward, the American leader John Adams called *both* Massachusetts and the United States "my country." Thomas Jefferson and James Madison still spoke of *both* Virginia and the United States as "my country." And the states of the new nation continued to feel considerably separate and different.

Even the language of the United States was not national in the sense of being distinct from that of England. It would take time—and patience—to fuse the former colonies into a truly united nation. By 1800, most Americans were convinced that it could be done.

■ **Check on Your Reading**
1. What was France's role?
2. What did the Americans gain in 1783?

391

MAN AND HIS CULTURE

Let's Meet the People!

During the American Revolution, the British used anchored ships as prisons. This sketch is based on William Slade's own account as it appears from: *The Spirit of 'Seventy-Six* by Henry Steele Commager and Richard B. Morris, copyright © 1958 by The Bobbs-Merrill Company, Inc., reprinted by special permission of the publishers.

William Slade, Prisoner of War

"*Fort Washington, the 16th day November, A.D. 1776.* This day I, William Slade, was taken [by the British] with 2,800 more."

William Slade, a young soldier in the forces of the American revolutionists, wrote the above notation in his diary. Then he waited for his British captors to determine his destination.

On December 2, William Slade was moved to the North River and transported to the *Grosvenor*, a British prison ship. "Their was . . . 500 men on board," he observed, "this made much confusion." In the days that followed, Slade struggled to survive in the dark and putrid hold of the prison ship. He conserved his small rations of wormy biscuits, watered broth, rice, and bits of rotting meat. He protected himself from the cold and the vermin as best he could. And he kept "hoping for good news."

On December 23, Sergeant Kieth and Job March "broke out with smallpox," and the dreaded disease spread rapidly. William Slade counted the number as the prisoners died about him. "One dies almost ever day," he wrote in his diary. Then the disease struck William Slade! A British sailor made two incisions in William's hand and let out "the impure blood." Still Slade grew weaker.

Finally, on December 28, Ensign Smith came for William Slade. The ensign's orders were to move the sick man ashore at once. When Slade heard the news, he wrote with feverish fingers: "I now feel glad." For, though his body was tormented by disease, he was leaving the prison ship at last. Leaving it—perhaps—forever.

CHAPTER REVIEW

REVIEW and DISCUSSION

1. Identify the people and places and explain the events and terms on p. 380.

2. Why did Spain enter a long period of decline after the defeat of the Spanish Armada?

3. Do you think that the native people of a country have the right to challenge a foreign invader? Why?

4. Is it better to remain within an organization of whose actions you do not approve or to resign and establish a new organization? Consider the Pilgrims, the American revolutionists, and the Confederates.

5. On what grounds do you think John Adams based his opinion that the spirit of independence had existed in the English colonies since the first settlement?

6. If you were a British citizen in the seventeenth century, how would you have justified the control of colonial possessions and at the same time accepted John Locke's philosophy of liberty and self-government at home?

7. How did the English manage to defeat the French in India and America?

8. How do you explain the fact that the chief supporters of the American Revolution included businessmen, lawyers, and landowners?

9. What did France gain by aiding the American colonies in the Revolutionary War?

10. An historian has said that "something new and portentous was injected into world affairs by the successful revolt" of the American colonists. What was it?

11. The establishment of the United States convinced many liberals in Europe that the ideas of the "Enlightenment" were practical. What events might have convinced them?

12. What makes a revolution justified?

ACTIVITIES

1. Make up and analyze several generalizations from this chapter. Sample: When a people have experienced many injustices, they will eventually rise in revolt. Questions: How many injustices? What is an injustice? Will the people always rise in revolt? Do you agree with the generalization?

2. On a map show British and French world possessions before the Peace of 1763.

3. Make a chart showing the steps leading to the outbreak of the American Revolution.

4. Write a report on the question: "Was Britain able to give her undivided attention to the war in the colonies?" What are your conclusions?

5. Write a summary contrasting a pro-British account of the Revolution with a pro-American account. What conclusions can you draw?

PAST and PRESENT

1. Compare the American Revolution of 1776 with those of the African states today. What differences and similarities are there?

2. Find out if the revolutions occurring in the world today are following the steps in the chart you worked out in No. 3, Activities.

SUGGESTED READINGS

Basic books: COMMAGER, HENRY STEELE, and NEVINS, ALLAN, *The Heritage of America*, Chaps. 6 and 7, Heath. Excerpts from original sources.

PALMER, R. R., and COLTON, JOEL, *A History of the Modern World*, Chap. 8, Knopf.

SMITH, GOLDWIN, *The Heritage of Man*, Chap. 28, Scribner.

Special accounts: AMERICAN HERITAGE, American Heritage (check Index for articles on the Revolution). Beautifully illustrated and well written.

CHURCHILL, WINSTON, *A History of the English-Speaking Peoples: The Age of Revolution*, Chaps. 10, 12, 13, 14, 17, Dodd, Mead.

Biography and Fiction: EATON, JEANETTE, *That Lively Man, Ben Franklin*, Morrow. Discusses Franklin's activities in France.

MALONE, DUMAS, *Story of the Declaration of Independence*, Oxford. Illustrated, interesting work. Includes biographies of signers.

ROBERTS, KENNETH, *Rabble in Arms*; *Oliver Wiswell*, Doubleday. Present picture of Tory side.

Chapter 25 *The French Revolution Shakes Europe's Foundations*

KEYNOTE   In 1958, when the French people were preparing the constitution of the Fifth Republic that governs their country today, they wrote the following words into the document:

> The motto of the Republic is
> "Liberty, Equality and Fraternity."

These words were not new. On the contrary! They formed the slogan of the French revolutionists who overthrew the monarchy and established the first republic in France about one hundred seventy years ago. One of the central facts of history is this: *The French Revolution in the eighteenth century brought great changes, and these have continued to affect France and the world down to the present day.*

Key People   *Louis XV · Voltaire · Montesquieu · Rousseau · Louis XVI ·*
Marie Antoinette · Robespierre · Danton

Key Places   *Paris · Varennes · Valmy*

Key Events   *Estates-General becomes National Assembly   ·   Fall of Bastille   ·*
First French Constitution   ·   National Convention meets   ·
Louis XVI executed · Reign of Terror · Directory established

Key Terms   *Old Régime · Estates-General · bourgeoisie · enlightenment ·*
philosophes · deism · separation of powers · Physiocrats ·
Jacobins · laissez-faire

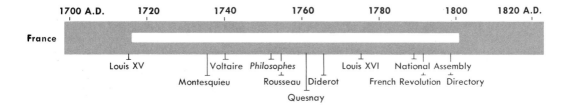

France

Louis XV   Voltaire   *Philosophes*   Louis XVI   National Assembly

Montesquieu   Rousseau │Diderot   French Revolution   Directory

Quesnay

1. Louis XV Ascends the French Throne

In 1715 the Duke of Bouillon placed a black feather on his cap and walked out to the balcony of the great palace at Versailles. He looked for a moment at the crowd below, which, according to biographer Nancy Mitford, was "curious but not sad." Then he solemnly announced: "The King is dead." The Duke returned to the palace, put on a white feather, and went out to the balcony again. This time he proclaimed: "Long live the King." With this symbolic switching of a black feather for a white, the long reign of Louis XIV had ended, and the rule of Louis XV, his great-grandson, had begun.

Louis XV (1715–1774), the new king of France, was a boy when he came to the throne. Even after he reached manhood, he refused to face his responsibilities. Historian Albert Guérard points out:

. . . untrained except to laziness, prejudiced and unprincipled, timid at heart while absurdly proud, superstitious and skeptical, he yawned his life away.

Yet there were times when Louis XV's observations proved to be uncannily right. This was the case when he declared:

"Bah! the old machine will last out my time, at any rate!" He was equally correct when he agreed with his companion Madame de Pompadour that "After us [comes] the deluge!" The "old machine" is better known as the *Old Régime*, a term that refers to the institutions and conditions of life in eighteenth-century Europe before the French Revolution.

Government

Louis XV could not provide strong leadership, and the government of France was extremely inefficient. Attempts to administer the multiplicity of laws merely added to the confusion in the country. "Repose was never known in [the] domain," later observed the French author-statesman Alexis de Tocqueville. "New rules followed each other with such bewildering rapidity that its agents never knew which to obey."

In addition, the Estates-General, or assembly, had not met since 1614, and there was little development of representative government. The *parlements*, the high courts of justice, did assume the right to

395

■ *A French pre-Revolution cartoon shows the First and Second Estates crushing the Third Estate under taxes, tithes, and feudal dues.*

refuse to register some of the decrees of the king. However, the parlements themselves were hereditary courts of justice whose magistrates were chiefly concerned with adding to their own power.

The Three Estates

There were three principal classes or "Estates" in France. The First Estate was the clergy, numbering about 100,000. They were members of the powerful Roman Catholic Church, which had many privileges. The Second Estate was the nobility, who numbered about 400,000. The Third Estate consisted of the great majority of the population of 26,000,000.

It is extremely important to remember that there were great variations in income and social position *within* each of the three estates. Some historians point to as many as seven different social groups, instead of three. Nevertheless, the three estates, or orders, were recognized by the French legal system.

The first two estates were privileged. They helped to run the government and were exempt from the land tax and other burdens. The Third Estate bore the costs of government and was denied many rights.

The *bourgeoisie* in France—that is, the businessmen, merchants, lawyers, and other members of the "middle class"— were becoming more powerful economically. They wanted freedom of competition in trade and industry and a reasonable system of taxation. As members of the Third Estate, they were denied many economic, political, and social rights.

The French Economy

Compared to other Europeans, the French people were relatively well off during the Old Régime. Commercial activities increased; Nantes and other ports prospered; and useful public works spread throughout the country. Even the peasants, who constituted nine-tenths of the population, had a better standard of living than those elsewhere on the continent.

However, the government was close to bankruptcy, as a result of the extravagance of the king and court, the policy of exempting the upper classes from direct taxation, and the chaotic system of collecting taxes. Taxes were "farmed out" to private individuals or companies who collected them for the king—and who did not hesitate to line their own pockets with the people's money. Over 60 per cent of gross revenue collected never reached the government.

As a result of the Seven Years' War, France added to her public debt and lost an empire in America and India to Britain. The French philosopher Voltaire shrugged off this loss and called Canada "a few acres of snow." But it was a disaster that was later to deprive France of many economic resources. In addition, France's participation in the American Revolution drained a large sum from the French treasury.

Remnants of Feudalism

The remnants of feudalism—such as the payment of fees for the use of a lord's mill to grind grain into flour—still existed in

■ *French rococo painting of the 18th century developed from Baroque art. It stressed color, movement, and pleasure in living. For the nobles, it was a way of pretending that life was free from worry. Watteau's "The Tune of Love" is a prime example.*

■ *François Boucher, another rococo painter, portrayed the lives of the aristocracy and bourgeoisie. "The Breakfast" depicts a family of the bourgeoisie. Note the costumes, toys, and furniture of the period.*

397

parts of the country. Feudal dues and duties did not make the peasants want to overthrow the king, but such feudal restrictions continued to annoy them.

Several outdated feudal relationships continued to exist. For example, the nobles originally had been exempt from taxation in exchange for the protection that they provided for their lands. Since then, many nobles had left their estates to live at Versailles. They no longer had to defend their lands. Nevertheless, the feudal tradition continued, and the nobles remained free from nearly all direct taxation.

■ **Check on Your Reading**

1. Under the Old Régime, what groups helped run the government?
2. Why was the government of France nearly bankrupt?
3. In what ways was the tax structure unfair to many people?

2. The Enlightenment Spreads Throughout Europe

During the Old Régime the so-called *Enlightenment* reached a peak in France and Europe. The Enlightenment was stimulated by the work of Galileo (1564–1642), Descartes (1596–1650), Newton (1642–1727), and other scientists who applied reason to the study of natural phenomena to derive the laws of nature. It was not long before "enlightened men," taking their cue from these scientists, determined also to use *reason* to find the *natural laws* of society and to solve the problems of mankind. The term *natural law* meant a law according to which society would operate if there were no formal governmental law, just as the law of gravitation naturally operated in the universe. For example, it was said that one natural law of society was that each person tries to survive for as long as he can. As historian Crane Brinton said: Reason and Nature became "the great watchwords of the Enlightenment."

Ernst Cassirer sums up the meaning of the Enlightenment extremely well:

The basic idea underlying all the tendencies of Enlightenment was the conviction that *human understanding* is capable, by its own power and without recourse to supernatural assistance, of comprehending the system of the world and that this new way of understanding the world will lead to a new way of mastering it.

The Enlightenment tried to apply this idea—of reason interpreting the world of sense experience—to all fields: science, politics, law, and even religion. Religious beliefs were to be based on reason, not on revelation, dogma, or authority.

The *Philosophes* Stimulate Men's Minds

During the Enlightenment, particularly in the period between 1750 and 1770, the sharpest critics of abuses in society and the most effective spokesmen for reform in France were men known as the *philosophes*, or the philosophers. Among the most important of the *philosophes* were Voltaire, Montesquieu, Rousseau, and Diderot. Although the ideas of these men did not single-handedly cause a revolution in France, they did stimulate people to think seriously about conditions in their country.

Voltaire and Freedom of Thought and Speech

François Marie Arouet, who was known as Voltaire (1694–1778), was a thin and sickly person whose fragile, egg-shaped head contained greater wisdom than many of his more muscular but empty-shelled contemporaries. In his life and writings he was one of the best representatives of the Enlightenment. Voltaire wrote a vast number of works—essays, histories, plays, long poems, and stories. He was the author of many letters, among them letters to enlightened rulers like Frederick the Great of Prussia and Catherine the Great of Russia. Among his best-known works are his satire *Candide* and his *Essay on the Manners and Spirit of Nations.*

Voltaire was a staunch and brilliant defender of a man's right to think and to say what he pleased, provided that he did not commit crimes against society. Voltaire made his position clear when he wrote:

Do I propose, then, that every citizen shall be free to follow his own reason, and believe whatever this enlightened or deluded reason shall dictate to him? Certainly, provided that he does not disturb the public order.

Voltaire was particularly insistent that men be permitted to follow their own thoughts about religion and to worship as they wished. As he put it:

The supposed right of intolerance [toward another's religion] is absurd and barbaric. It is the right of the tiger; nay, it is far worse, for tigers do but tear in order to have food, while we [rip] each other for paragraphs....

Voltaire, like many other eighteenth-century *philosophes* and philosophers in other countries, believed in no traditional religion but in what was called *deism.* Deists believed in God as the creator of the universe, but they held that God had merely started the universe going as a person starts a watch and never after interfered in events. This meant that God did not answer prayer or extend grace to anyone, though he judged human conduct. Deists usually attended no church, though they often claimed that God was present everywhere in nature.

Montesquieu and Separation of Powers

Baron de Montesquieu (1689–1755), whose most important book is *The Spirit*

Voltaire

Pastel by La Tour

■ *Voltaire's keen wit and intelligence, as well as his fragility, are suggested in this pastel portrait by a contemporary.*

of Laws, was a nobleman who was convinced that liberty could best be protected by placing checks on the unlimited power of government. He believed that no person or governing body should have all of the power in a country.

Montesquieu supported the idea of the *separation of powers*; that is, the executive, legislative, and judiciary branches of government would be separate. Each one would have certain responsibilities and serve as a check on the power of the other two. Montesquieu issued a warning that anticipated the rise of future tyrants:

There would be an end of everything were the same man or the same body ... to exercise those three powers, that of enacting laws, that of executing the public resolutions, and of trying the causes of individuals....

Montesquieu's ideas were to influence American leaders. The Constitution of the United States takes the separation of powers as one of its basic principles.

Rousseau and the Social Contract

Jean-Jacques Rousseau (1712–1778), who was born in Geneva, Switzerland, was a highly emotional and colorful person. He differed from most of the other French *philosophes* in that (1) he believed that instinct was more important than reason; (2) he rejected the sophisticated society of the Parisian *salons*, or private drawing rooms where distinguished guests gathered to converse; and (3) he preferred the natural goodness of primitive man to the artificial ways of civilization.

Above all, Rousseau loved nature and despised the corrupt ways of society. "Man is born free; and everywhere he is in chains," he declared with passion. To Rousseau, the "chains" were those that the rulers of society had forged to deny men their freedom.

Rousseau expressed his ideas of government in a book called *The Social Contract* (see Chart). The *Social Contract* stressed the importance of the national community and protested against rulers who violated the will of the people.

Rousseau's ideas, expressed in *The Social Contract* and *Emile* (on education), had a considerable influence on the thinking of

IDEAS OF THE SOCIAL CONTRACT

In the beginning of history, men were free.

Then men joined together in a common community for their mutual protection. Each man accepted an informal "contract" or agreement in which he placed himself and all of his power under "the supreme direction of the general will of all." Historians are not agreed on the exact meaning of the term "general will." In time, many people interpreted the term to mean that each person owed obedience to the will of the community even if his own personal will or desires differed from the community, or general, will.

No one—not even a king— had the right to go against the will of the community as a whole. If a ruler was tyrannical and ignored the will of the people, the Social Contract was broken and men had the right to demand their freedom.

many future leaders of European and American nations. The twentieth-century scholar Wilson O. Clough suggests that the "We, the people" phrase in the preamble of the Constitution of the United States "possibly owes something to [Rousseau's] emphasis on the popular will." In many of his writings Rousseau urged love of one's nation, and he thus influenced the development of modern *nationalism*, which became an important factor in the world by the late eighteenth century.

Diderot and the Encyclopedia

Denis Diderot (1713–1784) was the editor of the famous *Encyclopedia*. In preparing this work of twenty-eight volumes, published in spite of government censorship, Diderot's goal was an aim of the Enlightenment as a whole:

to assemble the knowledge scattered over the face of the earth; to explain its general plan to the men with whom we live, and to transmit it to those who will come after us ... so that our descendants, by becoming better informed, may in consequence be happier and more virtuous. ...

Voltaire, Rousseau, and other *philosophes* were among those who wrote articles for the *Encyclopedia,* and they did not hesitate to criticize slyly the existing régime. For example, in the article on "Torture," Diderot quoted these words of La Bruyère, a seventeenth-century author: "[The use of torture is] a sure means of convicting an innocent man who is physically weak and of acquitting a guilty person born with great endurance." In this way— without directly attacking the methods of justice in France—Diderot struck at a most undesirable feature, the use of torture.

François Quesnay and the Physiocrats

In the area of economics, there were men in France who tried to find the natural laws that would keep the economy strong. For example, the natural law of "supply and demand" might determine price in this way: If the demand of people for a product exceeded its supply, prices would go up; if the supply of a product exceeded the demand for it, prices would go down.

One group, known as the *Physiocrats*, led by a French physician, Francois Quesnay (1694–1774), declared that government regulation of the economy was frequently contrary to natural law. The Physiocrats also claimed that land is the only source of wealth and that agriculture increases wealth. They suggested that a single tax on the net income from land be the sole tax of a country. They favored the protection of property but few restrictions on commerce or business.

The Physiocrats, like some other Europeans of the time, believed in *laissez-faire*, a policy which included removing government restrictions on the economy and keeping to a minimum government interference in economic affairs.

The principles of *laissez-faire*, which was an abandonment of mercantilism, were best expressed by the Scottish economist, Adam Smith, in his book *The Wealth of Nations* (1776) (p. 462). The idea of *laissez-faire* also had much influence on the leaders of the American Revolution.

This was the situation in France under the Old Régime. France was a country with (1) an extravagant and inefficient government; (2) a society divided into three estates, with the Third Estate deprived of political power; (3) a bourgeoisie becoming economically powerful; (4) a nearly bankrupt government; (5) the remnants of feudalism; and (6) *philosophes* whose questions and answers stimulated the minds of men. This was the setting for one of the most important events in history—the French Revolution.

■ **Check on Your Reading**

1. What were the "watchwords" of the Enlightenment? Explain.
2. What were the principal ideas contributed by Voltaire, Montesquieu, Rousseau, and Diderot?
3. What were the economic principles of the Physiocrats?
4. Summarize the situation in France under the Old Régime.

3. The French Revolution

In 1789 the king of France was Louis XVI (1774–1792). Louis was a heavy-set and awkward man who dozed at state functions and who was quite incapable of providing France with the leadership she needed. Madame Roland, who later joined the revolt against the government, described his character with considerable accuracy: "He was neither [a] brutish blockhead . . . nor [an] honest, kind, and sensible creature." Rather, he was a man "without . . . energy of mind, or firmness of character."

Louis' wife, the beautiful Marie Antoinette, was an Austrian archduchess and the daughter of Empress Maria Theresa. Fond of luxury and extremely extravagant, Marie Antoinette was too superficial to aid her husband in affairs of state. Her brother pointed out the shallowness in her character in his reply to her question:

"How do you like my coiffure?"
"Rather flimsy to bear a crown," her brother answered.

The Revolution Begins

In 1789, neither Louis XVI nor Marie Antoinette was worrying about losing a crown. The king's chief concern was to obtain more money for his empty treasury. This became such a serious problem that in the month of May he was compelled to call a meeting of the *Estates-General* to be held at Versailles. The Estates-General was the so-called "national assembly" of France, but it had not met since 1614.

In the past, the Estates-General had voted by separate Estates. This meant that the clergy as a group (the First Estate) had one vote. The nobles as a group (the Second Estate) had one vote. The Third Estate, which included about 96 per cent of the population, also had one vote. In round figures, the Third Estate had about 600 representatives to the Estates-General of 1789, as compared with approximately 300 representatives of the clergy and approximately 300 representatives of the nobles. Nevertheless, the clergy and nobles were able to outvote the far more numerous Third Estate by two to one.

Most of the representatives of the Third Estate came from the middle class. They felt that the system of voting would have to be changed if any improvements were to be introduced into the country. They therefore proposed that the three Estates should meet together, that each man should have a single vote, and that the vote of the majority should be accepted.

King Louis XVI, supported by the clergy and nobles, rejected this proposal. When the king tried to prevent the Estates-General from meeting, the Third Estate defiantly gathered on an indoor tennis court. Here its members proclaimed themselves to be the real National Assembly of France. They also took the so-called Tennis Court Oath, by which they promised "never to separate, and to reassemble wherever circumstances require, until the constitution of the kingdom shall be established and fixed upon firm foundations."

A number of the lower clergy and liberal nobles joined the newly formed Assembly, and King Louis XVI finally changed his position. He instructed all three of the Estates to meet together and to vote as a single organization. The old Estates-General had developed into a body known as the *National Assembly*, and the drama of the French Revolution had begun!

The Bastille Falls

The uprising of the Third Estate in 1789 was primarily the work of members of the bourgeoisie. As French historian André Maurois points out, these men "had a mind to repair the house, not to tear it down." However, the king had no intention of following their wishes, and he did not realize the seriousness of the situation.

To King Louis XVI, July 14, 1789, was just another day. When it came time for him to jot down in his diary the important

■ *Queen Marie Antoinette with two of her children in the park of Trianon Palace.*

■ *On July 14, 1789, a Paris crowd stormed the Bastille—the prison which had become a symbol of the king's oppression. This drawing was made by a French artist of the early nineteenth century.*

Musée Carnavalet, Paris

events of the day, he wrote a single word—"Nothing." Yet it was on July 14 that a crowd in Paris stormed the Bastille!

The Bastille was an old fortress that had been converted into a prison. The people believed that its dungeons held many innocent men and women whose only crime was opposition to the king. Equally important, the crowd desired the arms which were stored in the Bastille. The prison became a hated symbol of the king's oppression. On July 14 a crowd of Parisians, angered by the uncooperative attitude of the king and his officials, attacked the Bastille. They cut the chains to the drawbridge, withstood the fire of the guards in the courtyard, and forced the commanding officer to surrender. When they rushed through the prison to free the prisoners, they found only seven men. Two of these prisoners were madmen, four were forgers, and one had been imprisoned for cruelty.

Despite the relative emptiness of the prison, the date of the storming of the Bastille is celebrated as national independence day in France.

Many Flames Light the Revolutionary Fires

The storming of the Bastille at last made Louis XVI aware of the crisis in Paris. When the king awakened on the morning of July 15, the Duke of Liancourt quickly told him what had happened:

"Is this a rebellion?" asked Louis XVI.
"No, Sire, it is a revolution!" was the reply.

And it was! The attack on the Bastille was followed by uprisings of the peasants in the country, new demands on the monarchy, and a general speeding up of movements for reform. The French Revolution was on in earnest.

What had caused this revolution that so greatly affected France and the world? The answer is that no single cause can account for the French Revolution. The revolution was a result of a combination of factors, including these: (1) Louis XVI and his administrators were not performing their duties of keeping justice, order, and harmony in the land. (2) The national treasury of France was facing bankruptcy, and both the collection and distribution of

403

national finances needed reorganization. Efforts of the economist Turgot and the banker Necker to introduce economies in the French government were blocked. French aid to the Americans during the American Revolution had increased the national debt further.

(3) The bourgeoisie wanted greater political rights and better management of the state's economic affairs. They also desired social equality with the upper classes. (4) The bourgeoisie and peasants were angry because the nobles and higher clergy enjoyed special privileges, such as being exempt from paying heavy taxes.

(5) A major economic depression from 1787 to 1789 added to France's economic troubles. Crops were damaged by frost, drought, and rain. City workers faced unemployment because peasants could not afford to buy manufactured goods. The peasants wanted to be free of all feudal restrictions which added to their economic hardship. Spain's tariff and England's competition interfered with the sale of French goods abroad and contributed further to the depression.

(6) The ideas of the French *philosophes* stirred a number of men to desire greater freedom. (7) The ideas of the American revolutionists, carried to France by Frenchmen who had supported the Americans, influenced the intellectuals. An English traveler, Arthur Young, wrote: "The American Revolution has laid the foundations of another in France. . . ."

The National Assembly Introduces Major Changes

The various factors listed above had interacted to produce a revolution in France. It was the responsibility of the newly formed National Assembly to introduce the changes that the country desired.

The unsettled conditions in the countryside—where peasants were setting manor houses on fire to eliminate the records of their feudal obligations and refusing to pay their taxes—made the National Assembly focus its attention on the peasant. On August 4, 1789, the National Assembly issued a series of decrees that (1) abolished feudalism in France completely; (2) did away with the tithe (a tax to support the Church or the clergy); (3) wiped out all class privileges in taxation and provided that the "collection [of taxes] shall be made from all citizens and on all property, in the same manner and in the same form"; and (4) granted all citizens, "without distinction of birth," the right to hold any public office.

These decrees were not designed to overthrow the king. It concluded:

The National Assembly solemnly proclaims King Louis XVI *Restorer of French Liberty.* . . . [and shall] bear him the homage of its most respectful gratitude. . . .

The Declaration of the Rights of Man

After doing away with all feudal privileges, the National Assembly issued a most famous document: the *Declaration of the Rights of Man* (August 26, 1789), which affected the histories of France, and other European countries. These ideas included the following:

Men are born, and always continue, free and equal in respect of their rights.

[The natural rights of Man are] liberty, property, security, and resistance of oppression.

The Nation is essentially the source of all sovereignty; nor can any Individual, or Any Body of Men be entitled to any authority which is not expressly derived from it.

The Declaration of the Rights of Man was, in the words of historian Eugen Weber, "the death certificate of the old régime."

Shortly after the Declaration of the Rights of Man, several thousand poor women of Paris—and perhaps some armed men partially disguised in women's clothes—marched out to Versailles and boldly demanded bread from the king (October, 1789). Then they made the "baker"—Louis XVI—and his family ("the baker's wife and the baker's little boy") return with them to Paris. The royal family was compelled to live in the Palace of the Tuileries in Paris, and the National Assembly also moved from Versailles to Paris. This change was similar to placing a frying pan on top of a fire, for the men directing the government were now located where the hotheads of Paris could make them sizzle.

The Civil Constitution of the Clergy

In addition to abolishing the remnants of feudalism and issuing the Declaration of the Rights of Man, the National Assembly dealt with the clergy of the Roman Catholic Church. In November, 1789, the Assembly confiscated Church property, and in December it issued *assignats*. Assignats were paper money based on the future sale of the confiscated property of the Church and the king.

On July 12, 1790, the National Assembly issued the *Civil Constitution of the Clergy*. This provided that all bishops and parish priests were to be civil servants of the state. They were to be elected by all citizens—including Protestants, Jews, and non-believers—"by the absolute majority of the votes." They also were to be paid by the state and were to take an oath of allegiance to the Constitution.

This action by the National Assembly added to the tensions and troubles of France. The Pope denounced the Civil Constitution of the Clergy, and thousands of clergymen refused to take the oath. What is more, the measure angered many French Catholics. These people now turned away from their revolutionary companions.

Louis XVI had signed the Civil Constitution of the Clergy with misgivings. As a faithful Catholic aware of the penalties for defying the Pope, he was shocked and frightened by what he had been compelled to do. This was one of the principal reasons why he decided to flee France and join the *émigrés* and his loyal troops. The *émigrés* were nobles who had left the country and who were plotting to invade France and drive out the revolutionists.

On the night of June 20–21, 1791, Louis XVI and Marie Antoinette fled in secret from their palace in Paris. They had almost reached the border—and safety— when they were caught at Varennes. The royal couple was brought back to Paris through jeering and hooting mobs. Louis XVI's flight completely discredited him in the eyes of many leaders of the National Assembly. Some extremists even spoke of the king as a "fat pig" and prophesied that he would some day have his throat slit.

The First French Constitution

The National Assembly also made changes in the administration of the government. Most important of all, it drew up a constitution for France. Its provisions were put into effect piecemeal, but the entire document was not completed until 1791 after two years of work. This constitution, which the king had to sign, was based on moderate principles and was designed to establish a constitutional monarchy. It provided the following:

1. A LEGISLATIVE ASSEMBLY. This was a one-house body to make the laws. All Frenchmen over twenty-five were citizens, but only those who paid certain direct taxes could vote for the members of the Legislative Assembly.

2. THE KING. The monarch could block the passage of a law for four years, but he could not prevent its ultimate passage. The armed forces were no longer under the control of the king.

3. DÉPARTEMENTS. Eighty-three *départements* (departments), or territorial

divisions, were set up to take the place of the provinces, which had varied in size and had been administered under different laws. These departments were arranged so that they were more uniform in size and so that their governments could be coordinated with one another. Each department was subdivided into districts (roughly comparable to the American county); and each district was subdivided further into communes (comparable to the American town).

The National Assembly had finished its task and prepared to disband. Yet, as Malouet, one of its members, declared, "There remained for us only one great mistake to make, and we did not fail to make it." This mistake was that the National Assembly decided that none of its members were to be eligible for election to the Legislative Assembly. This meant that the new government would be in the hands of inexperienced men. And experience during the French Revolution often was gained by making disastrous mistakes!

France Forms a Republic

The French Revolution soon moved from a moderate to a radical stage. The Legislative Assembly, elected under the new constitution, met in October, 1791. This body made it clear that it intended to help spread revolutionary ideas throughout the rest of Europe.

Leopold II of Austria (Holy Roman Emperor and brother of Marie Antoinette), various rulers of the German states, and other European monarchs were being stirred up by the French *émigrés*. These rulers became fearful that the uprising against royalty would be carried to their own countries. They decided to check the French Revolution, and they prepared their forces for a possible conflict with France. In April, 1792, the French Legislative Assembly took the initiative by declaring war on Austria. Prussia came to the aid of Austria, and France was involved in a major war.

In the beginning, French troops were defeated and the enemy entered France. The country became filled with disorder and panic. In the summer of 1792 a mob smashed its way into the king's palace in Paris. Its leaders accused the royal family, particularly Marie Antoinette, of plotting with foreign rulers to invade France and crush the revolution. They made the king and his family virtual prisoners, and Paris came under the sway of the radical city government known as the *Paris Commune*.

Under pressure by the radicals of Paris, the Legislative Assembly in August called for the election of a *National Convention* to establish a republic for France. In the six weeks before the National Convention met, France was torn by great internal strife. In the so-called "September Massacre" alone, hundreds of citizens accused of opposing the revolution were killed. Finally, the National Convention met and proclaimed France a republic (September 22, 1792). This was the *First French Republic* (1792–1795).

French Patriotism Is Aroused

Louis XVI was beheaded on January 21, 1793, and Marie Antoinette met a similar fate several months later. Louis' cry from the scaffold "People, I die innocent!" was a plaintive sound in the revolutionary roar.

The beheading of Louis XVI made the monarchs of Europe more fearful than ever that the ideas of the French Revolution would spread to their lands. Had not France's General Dumouriez finally stopped the allied forces at Valmy and pursued them across the Rhine and into the Austrian Netherlands? Had not the French stated that they intended to extend their borders to the Rhine? Had not the National Convention proclaimed "the Liberty and Sovereignty of all the peoples to whose Homeland [the French troops] have carried and are carrying their arms"? In 1793 England, Spain, and Holland decided to aid Austria and Prussia in the conflict with France. The French National Convention promptly declared war against all three powers.

The French people met the new threat to their country with heroism and patriotic fervor. "To arms, citizens! To arms!" was the cry. Aided by the planning of the French military expert Carnot, the French army was reorganized and strengthened. A decree of August 23, 1793, declared that "all Frenchmen are permanently requisitioned for service in the armies." This was the first national conscription in European history. Single men between the ages of 18 and 25 were conscripted, or drafted, and all Frenchmen were urged to take part in the defense of the country. "Let every one take his post," said the government:

The young will fight; the married men will forge arms . . . the women will work at the soldiers' clothing . . . and the old men [will] inflame the courage of the young warriors and propagate the hatred of the kings. . . .

The *Marseillaise* was written in 1792 by Rouget de Lisle and was heard throughout the land. Today it is the French national anthem. Altars were constructed and inscribed with the words: "The citizen is born, lives and dies for the fatherland." The welfare of *La Patrie* (the fatherland) became the chief concern of Frenchmen. Despite the patriotism of the French, the Austrians succeeded in defeating the army of Dumouriez in 1793, driving the French out of the Netherlands.

The Reign of Terror Bleeds France

At the same time that French troops were fighting their foreign enemies, the revolution at home had reached a bloody stage. Faced with a situation where France's soldiers were battling many foes abroad and where the revolutionary government itself was not secure, the National Convention created a Committee of Public Safety. This small committee became dominated by the *Jacobins*, led by Robespierre and Danton. The Jacobins were a radical group who replaced the more moderate Girondist group as leaders of the National Convention. Under the direction of Robespierre, some of these extremists started a *Reign of Terror* in France.

From 1793 to 1794 thousands of people were charged with being traitors or potential traitors and were sent to their deaths. It was said that heads fell like "roofing-slates." About twenty thousand people were beheaded by the *guillotine* (which consisted of a heavy blade that dropped between two upright grooves); and another twenty thousand were killed by other means or died in prison. Some of them were guilty; more of them were innocent; all of them were equal before the impartial blade of the guillotine.

The leaders of the Terror claimed that their aim was to save France by eliminating all those who supported foreign countries or opposed the revolution. As the fanatical Robespierre viewed matters: "It [was] wholly necessary to establish briefly the despotism of freedom in order to crush the despotism of Kings." He therefore was convinced that "Terror is nothing else than swift, severe, indomitable justice; it flows . . . from virtue."

At the same time that it supported the Terror at home, the Committee of Public Safety had approved the conscription of citizens and taken other measures to aid the army. As a result, France had over 800,000 well-trained, well-armed, and well-led troops—the most powerful army on the continent—and their morale was excellent. This army drove back France's enemies and won additional victories in the war.

By July, 1794, France was no longer in danger of being conquered.

As Albert Guérard puts it: "Robespierrism [or the Reign of Terror] died of victory." When the country was under attack, the people would accept the brutal Terror. Now that France was safe, the French leaders brought the blood bath to a close. Danton died on the guillotine. After Robespierre himself was executed in July, 1794, the Reign of Terror ended.

The Directory Is Established

At the end of the Reign of Terror many people of France yearned for a return to stability. The peasants had gained the lands of the *émigrés,* but the lot of the city workers was rather hard. When sentries demanded, "Who goes there?" many workers replied: "A hollow stomach." Inflation, a large national debt, and insufficient food supplies added to their problems.

The National Convention drew up a new constitution for the Republic (the Constitution of the Year III). It provided for a government with a two-house legislature and five "directors" chosen by the legislature. Suffrage rights were limited to those who had certain property qualifications. This government is known as the *Directory* (1795–1799).

A royalist uprising in Paris against the National Convention on October 5, 1795, was put down by troops faithful to the government. These troops were led by Napoleon Bonaparte, whose role in saving the National Convention was important, but not as decisive as historians later declared. The Directory took over the government of France on October 26, 1795.

The years of the Directory were marked by the graft, immorality, and profiteering of a small circle of government and business leaders in Paris and other cities. Equally important, the Directory was unable—and unwilling—to keep peace with other nations. Many of its members felt that victories abroad would help to keep them in power. France's military adventures provided an opportunity for Napoleon Bonaparte to take over the government. The Directory ceased to exist after 1799.

■ **Check on Your Reading**

1. Why was the Estates-General called and how did it become a National Assembly?
2. What were the causes of the French Revolution?
3. What reforms were put into effect by the National Assembly?
4. Why was a republic formed? How was patriotism aroused?
5. What caused the Reign of Terror? its end?

4. Results of the French Revolution

The French Revolution had finally run its course, and the French people had shown their contempt for royalty in many ways. They had taken the kings and queens from their decks of playing cards and substituted cards called "Liberties" and "Equalities." They had removed the word "Royal" from the signs of their shops. Some of them had even changed the names of their children from Louis to Constitution.

These were colorful but minor aspects of the revolutionary years. What were the important results of this great revolution that shook France and the world from 1789 to 1799? Some of the important results of the revolution included the following:

(1) The Revolution overthrew the auto-

cratic French monarchy and set up a republican government based on a written constitution. (2) It helped to complete the unification of France by unifying the financial and legal systems and by eliminating the variety of provinces governed by different laws. As Napoleon, the future leader of France, said:

The Revolution destroyed all these little nations [the provinces] and made out of them a new one. There was no more Normandy, Brittany, Burgundy; there was one France....

(3) The revolution deprived the clergy of special privileges, supported the idea of freedom of worship, and strengthened the idea of social equality by sweeping away the privileges of the classes. (4) It removed the last remnants of feudalism from France. The peasants were able to acquire more land by purchasing property confiscated from the *émigrés* and the Church. France now became a country of independent farmers.

(5) The revolution aided business activities by abolishing guild restrictions, setting up a single code of commercial law, and introducing a uniform system of weights and measures—the *metric system*. The metric system was particularly important, for, as historian Crane Brinton explains:

It was almost impossible under the Old Régime to manufacture and market bushel measures from a single center when the definition of a bushel varied from town to town; under the metric system, grain measures could be made on a large scale and sold all over France.

(6) The revolution introduced a system of universal military service in France. (7) It stimulated discussion of ways to establish a national and secular system of education in France.

(8) The revolution influenced the growth of democracy in many countries of the world (although its extremism strengthened the antidemocratic convictions of a number of people). For example, the ideas expressed in the *Declaration of the Rights of Man* affected the thinking of men everywhere who believed in the growth of democratic rights. (9) It stimulated the development of nationalism in France and Europe. Nationalism soon encouraged the peoples of Germany, Italy, and other divided lands to fight for the right to have their own united nations.

■ **Check on Your Reading**

1. What were the significant results of the revolution?
2. What economic effects did the revolution have?
3. How did the revolution change French government and administration? business? education?
4. What significant effects did the revolution have outside France?

THE IMPACT of the French Revolution on European Culture

The heavy steel knife of the guillotine must not be taken as the only symbol of the French Revolution. Cultural changes accompanying the revolution were far more significant than the bloody movements of the knife.

The period of the French Revolution was not a time of great creativity in architecture, literature, or music in France. How could it be when men were struggling for survival itself? Nevertheless, cultural activities and revolutionary demands soon intertwined. The field of art is a case in point. At the outbreak of the revolution only 350 pictures were exhibited in the "aristocratic" art Salon; in 1791, after the National Assembly opened the Salon to all artists, almost 800 pictures were on display. In addition, Jacques Louis David, brilliant French artist, became a secretary of the National Convention. Even during the Reign of Terror the government took time to purchase works of art and great paintings by Rubens and Rembrandt!

Most important of all, the French Revolution had a tremendous impact on European culture:

It helped eliminate political, economic, and social privileges of certain groups in France, and stimulated men in countries outside France to work for democratization of society.

It encouraged many Europeans to think of culture on a *national* basis, thereby contributing to the development of nations in Europe.

It spread the idea that cultural offerings should not be limited to a small section of society, but extended to the majority of people.

The spirit of the French Revolution is still felt throughout Europe today: in the singing of the *Marseillaise,* in the European constitutions that borrowed words or phrases from the French *Declaration of the Rights of Man,* in the widespread use of the metric system, in the joyous celebrations and street dances on July 14, Bastille Day, and in many other ways.

The historian Hippolyte A. Taine, recognizing the disruptive aspects of the revolution, wrote: "Nothing remains but individual particles, twenty-six millions of equal and disconnected atoms [Frenchmen]." Yet these "atoms" were powerful enough to generate energy that still stirs European life today!

MAN AND HIS CULTURE

Let's Meet the People!

Madame Jullien kept a diary and wrote numerous letters. The following sketch is based on these materials, and on passages from the book *Women of the French Revolution* by Winifred Stephens. Published by E. P. Dutton & Co., and reprinted with their permission.

Citizeness Jullien, Defender of the French Revolution

"The blindness of kings is the scourge of humanity!" declared Madame Jullien during the French Revolution. Citizeness Jullien, as she was called, could be recognized as a defender of the revolution by her appearance as well as by her opinions. She dressed in the white robes worn by women favorable to the revolution, and she displayed almost no jewelry. On her hat she wore the tricolor cockade of the revolution, a knot of ribbon of red, white, and blue colors. Let anyone disturb this national cockade—and she would deal with him!

Yet, although she was a loyal revolutionist, Citizeness Jullien sometimes saw events and heard stories that filled her with horror. How shocked she was to discover that innocent men were being slaughtered in prison by fanatical revolutionists!

My pity makes me weep over the fate shared alike by the guilty and the innocent [she wrote]. My God! have mercy on a people provoked to such horrible bloodshed!

Her appeal to God was in keeping with her religious nature. Yet Citizeness Jullien's love of the nation and liberty almost became a new religion for her. One summer day she visited the lovely Church of St. Germain l'Auxerrois. There in the nave she saw a stone tablet, and on this tablet was engraved the Declaration of the Rights of Man. Citizeness Jullien was so moved by this democratic symbol in a house of God that she fell to her knees and offered up a special prayer.

When she finally left the church, Citizeness Jullien could embrace more fully than ever the idea expressed in these revolutionary words: "I believe in a Supreme Being, who has made men free and equal!"

CHAPTER REVIEW

REVIEW and DISCUSSION

1. Identify the people and places and explain the events and terms on p. 394.

2. In the United States our taxes are based upon our ability to pay. On what basis were taxes collected in France under Louis XV?

3. Why do you agree or disagree with the statement: If the "Enlightenment" had not taken place, there would have been no French Revolution in 1789?

4. Is real liberty limited? What might Voltaire's reply be to this question?

5. Was it dangerous for a philosopher in France to criticize existing conditions?

6. Compare the American Declaration of Independence with the Declaration of the Rights of Man.

7. How was the French Revolution a result of the interaction of social, economic, intellectual, political, and religious factors?

8. Do you agree that the National Assembly made a great mistake in preventing its own members from being eligible for election to the Legislative Assembly? Why?

9. Evaluate Robespierre's justification for his Reign of Terror.

ACTIVITIES

1. Write a report of the influence of one American, Benjamin Franklin, on the French Revolution.

2. Enact an imaginary interview between Louis XVI and a representative of the peasants or merchants about grievances against the state.

3. Debate the statement: Resolved that the French Revolution had more significance for other peoples of the world than the American Revolution.

4. Debate the statement: Resolved that "books rule the world" (Voltaire).

5. Have four members of the class take the part of four French *philosophes*. Other class members can ask them questions about liberty, government, and revolution.

6. Have a mock trial of Robespierre. Let class members serve as judge, prosecutor, defense attorney, witnesses, and jury.

PAST and PRESENT

1. In contrast to the French who fought several wars in the 1790's, new countries today want a period of neutrality in which to establish themselves. How do you explain this difference?

2. Foreign affairs affected the course of the French Revolution. Have they also influenced the development of revolutions in Asia, the Middle East, and Africa in the twentieth century? How?

SUGGESTED READINGS

Basic books: DURANT, WILL, *The Story of Philosophy*, Chap. 5, Simon and Schuster. The sketch of Voltaire is well worth reading.

GOTTSCHALK, LOUIS, and LACH, DONALD, *Europe and the Modern World*, Chap. 14, Scott, Foresman.

PALMER, R. R., and COLTON, JOEL, *A History of the Modern World*, Chap. 9, Knopf.

SMITH, GOLDWIN, *The Heritage of Man*, Chaps. 29 and 30, Scribner.

Special accounts: BERLIN, ISAIAH, *The Age of Enlightenment* (Mentor Philosophers Series), MD 172; New American Library. For the better reader who is interested in philosophy.

LEFEBVRE, GEORGES, *The Coming of the French Revolution*, Knopf. Said to be "the best single brief account of the background" of the revolution. For better readers.

TOCQUEVILLE, DE ALEXIS, *The Old Régime and the French Revolution*, Doubleday. A "classic."

Biography and Fiction: BRINTON, CRANE, (ed.), *The Portable Age of Reason Reader*, Viking. Source material from writings of the period.

DICKENS, CHARLES, *A Tale of Two Cities*, Dodd, Mead. A novel of the French Revolution during the Reign of Terror.

VANCE, MARGUERITE, *Marie Antoinette, Daughter of an Empress*, Dutton. Gives an excellent picture of life at the French court.

Chapter 26   Napoleon Bonaparte Dominates France and Europe

KEYNOTE   When Napoleon Bonaparte, a French general, took over the command of one of his first armies, he told his troops:

Soldiers! You are naked, ill-fed. . . . I [am going] to lead you into the most fertile plains of the world. Rich provinces, great cities, will be in your power; you will find honor, glory, and riches there.

Napoleon kept that promise and others like it. However, he did it by concentrating all power in his own hands and by leading France into bitter military campaigns throughout Europe. "He was," says historian Albert Guérard, "a Louis XIV streamlined into formidable efficiency."

The key fact of the period in Europe from 1799 to 1814 was that *Napoleon obtained great power and used it to dominate France and Europe.*

Key People   *Napoleon Bonaparte · Joseph Bonaparte · Alexander I · Lord Nelson*

Key Places   *Egypt · Corsica · Marengo · Hohenlinden · Confederation of the Rhine · Cisalpine Republic · Ulm · Austerlitz · Trafalgar · Waterloo · Elba*

Key Events   *Treaty of Campoformio · Napoleon becomes First Consul · Code Napoléon · Napoleon becomes Emperor · Napoleonic Wars · Confederation of the Rhine formed · Invasion of Russia · Napoleon abdicates · The Hundred Days · Battle of Waterloo*

Key Terms   *coup d'état · départements · Continental System · Orders in Council · nationalism · "Napoleonic legend"*

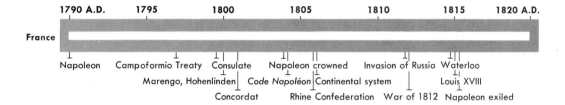

1. Napoleon Builds His Reputation as a Conqueror

"I am not like other men; the laws of convention and morality do not apply to me!" Thus spoke Napoleon Bonaparte, the military genius who dominated the affairs of Europe in the first part of the nineteenth century.

Napoleon Bonaparte was born on the island of Corsica in 1769. France had recently purchased Corsica from the Italian state of Genoa, and Napoleon's parents were of Italian ancestry. Napoleon attended a military academy in France, where his teachers noted that he was "ambitious [and] aspiring to everything." He became a second lieutenant in the artillery of the French army and rose rapidly to the position of brigadier-general.

The Directory, which involved France in wars against several European countries, gave Napoleon command of the French army in Italy. Prior to starting on his new assignment, he married Josephine de Beauharnais, a creole (a person of French or Spanish descent born in the New World) from the island of Martinique.

When the ragged French soldiers in Italy first saw Napoleon, who was extremely short, they called him "Puss-in-Boots." He soon won their admiration by leading them to victories. "Soldiers," Napoleon was able to announce, "you have in two weeks won six victories [and] taken twenty-one battle flags." Indeed, the Austrians were defeated in less than a month!

The terms of the Treaty of Campoformio with Austria (1797)—which Napoleon, not the Directory, arranged—were these: (1) A Cisalpine Republic, under the domination of France, was formed in Italy. Napoleon thus tried to show the people of Italy that he was "liberating" them from Austrian rule. (2) Austria gave the Austrian Netherlands and the Ionian Islands to France. (3) What remained of the Republic of Venice was given to Austria.

Napoleon Becomes First Consul

Napoleon next directed a campaign against Egypt (1798). He captured Alexandria and crushed the Egyptian forces at the Pyramids. However, the French fleet was defeated by the British Admiral Nelson. Cut off from France, Napoleon suffered major setbacks in Syria.

In 1799 Napoleon learned that the Directory was having serious difficulties. He

He helped establish a new government known as the *Consulate* (1799–1804). It consisted of a legislature and three executives, or Consuls. Napoleon became First Consul for a ten-year term, and most of the power was placed in his hands. In 1802 he was made First Consul for life by a vote of about $3\frac{1}{2}$ million to 8000.

Napoleon the Man

What kind of person was Napoleon? He was described by John Leslie Foster, one of his contemporaries, as a very short man "his hair a dark brown crop . . . his complexion smooth, pale, and sallow . . . his mouth and nose, fine, sharp, defined, and expressive beyond description." Madame de Rému-sat, a friend of Napoleon's wife, added, "the heart was left out [of him]" for "he was always too much engrossed by himself to be influenced by any sentiment of affection."

Mentally, Napoleon was intelligent and alert. He was also extremely hard-working and once said: "I am born and built for work. I have known the limitations of my legs, I have known the limitations of my eyes; I have never been able to know the limitations of my working capacity."

Napoleon believed that everyone should have an equal opportunity to advance. As a leader, he loved political power and had no intention of dividing it with the people. A friend, Prince Czartoryski, explained:

He would willingly have agreed that every man should be free, on the condition that he should voluntarily do only what [Napoleon] wished.

Or, as Napoleon himself said: "I must command, or be silent."

Painting by Isabey,
Chateau de la Malmaison

■ *This painting shows Napoleon as First Consul in a familiar position—staring moodily, legs apart, with his right hand in his blouse.*

left his sick, weary troops in Egypt and hurried to France. He found the Directory plagued by financial confusion, graft, inefficient administration, and the heavy expenses of war. France was ready for a "strong man," and Napoleon believed that the French would say, "This is the man!"

On November 9, 1799, he and a group of leaders overthrew the Directory. Napoleon explained this *coup d'état* (sudden overthrow of a government by a group of conspirators) by proclaiming to the people:

Frenchmen, you will doubtless recognize in this conduct the zeal of a soldier of liberty, of a citizen devoted to the Republic.

■ Check on Your Reading

1. What did Napoleon gain for France by the Treaty of Campoformio?
2. How did Napoleon become First Consul?
3. Describe the character of Napoleon.

414

2. The Napoleonic Program in France

As First Consul and later emperor, Napoleon was responsible for major changes.

The Concordat of 1801

Napoleon lessened the tensions between the Roman Catholic Church and the state by arranging the Concordat of 1801. This formal agreement re-established peaceful relations. It had the following provisions: (1) People who had purchased Church lands from the state—that is, Church lands confiscated by the state during the French Revolution—could keep them. (2) Church buildings would be returned to the Church. (3) The state would pay the salaries of the clergy. (4) Bishops would be nominated by the state, but they would be consecrated and installed in office by the Pope.

The Concordat of 1801 recognized that Catholicism was "the religion of the great majority of French citizens." However, the Church remained under the control of the government, and Napoleon even spoke of "my bishops." By other agreements, Protestants and members of other faiths were permitted to worship as they wished.

The Code Napoléon

Napoleon chose a committee of legal experts to codify and bring uniformity to the laws of France. It drew up the so-called *Code Napoléon* (or the Code of Civil Law of 1804), in which Roman law appeared as the heart of French law. Geoffrey Bruun, an American historian, points out:

In four important particulars the new code preserved the social aims of the [French] Revolution, for it affirmed:

The equality of all citizens before the law.
The right of the individual to choose his profession.
The supremacy of the lay state.
The freedom of the individual conscience.

However, other laws placed numerous restrictions on the liberty of the individual. For example, one of the first orders issued by Napoleon limited freedom of the press. Napoleon's secretary, Louis Bourrienne, declared: "Great man as he was, [Napoleon] was sorely afraid of little paragraphs." Other codes (five major ones between 1800 and 1810) placed heavy penalties on persons guilty of political offenses.

The principles of the *Code Napoléon* spread from France to Italy, the Netherlands, southern Germany, and other European countries; and the Code still affects the laws of Europe today. It also influenced the legal system of the state of Louisiana in the United States. (Louisiana once belonged to France. Napoleon sold the entire Louisiana region to the United States in 1803.)

Centralization of Government

Napoleon also centralized the government of France. The prefects (or heads) of the *départements*, and even lesser officials, were appointed by and responsible to Napoleon and his advisers. Despite the existence of a legislative body and various assemblies, Napoleon and his central government made all major decisions.

Reorganization of Education

Napoleon supported the reorganization of the educational system of France. He helped to establish an extensive system of public schools under the supervision of the central government. However, historian André Maurois states:

[Napoleon] organized education as though it were the training of an army. In all France's secondary schools, the same Latin passage was being translated at the same hour; the military drum would summon the pupils to recitations—and it was still rolling in 1900. . . .

By 1813 only one-eighth of school-age children were enrolled in primary schools.

Economic Activities

In the field of economics, Napoleon wanted to strengthen agriculture, build up manufacturing, and finally stimulate commerce "as an aid to the functioning of the other two branches." His government therefore took an active part in economic affairs. It (1) collected taxes efficiently, (2) established animal-breeding stations to improve the quality of stock, (3) sponsored exhibitions for the exchange of information about industrial inventions, (4) constructed commercial as well as military roads, (5) made efforts to increase exports, and (6) tried to balance the national budget (later by using indemnities,

or forced payments, required from countries that Napoleon conquered).

Equally important, Napoleon encouraged the founding of the Bank of France (1800), which was based primarily on private investment. The Bank of France, Napoleon declared, "does not belong exclusively to the stockholders; it belongs also to the State, for the latter gives it the privilege of [issuing] money."

■ Check on Your Reading

1. How did the Concordat of 1801 change the position of the Church in France?
2. How did the *Code Napoléon* preserve the social aims of the French Revolution?
3. How did Napoleon organize education?
4. How was the French economic system affected by Napoleon?

3. Napoleon Crowns Himself Emperor

Napoleon tried to satisfy many groups: the peasants by letting them keep the lands they had acquired; the clergy by restoring them to a position of respect; the liberals by granting all citizens equality before the law; the bourgeoisie by protecting property and encouraging economic growth; and all of the people of France by giving them a sense of security. Yet Napoleon's chief love remained the military. He was convinced that his future depended on the might of his armies.

Under the Consulate, Napoleon was as active in foreign affairs as he was in France's domestic problems. In Europe he fought successfully against the Second Coalition, an alliance whose principal members were Great Britain, Austria, and Russia. This group of countries wanted to (1) regain lands in Italy for Austria; (2) restore the independence of Switzerland, where Napoleon had set up a centralized, French-dominated republic which

wiped out many rights of the Swiss cantons; (3) release Holland from the domination of France, which had controlled it since 1795; and (4) add to the possessions of Great Britain and Russia at the expense of the French.

In 1800 Napoleon defeated the Austrians at Marengo (Italy), and another French army crushed the Austrian forces at Hohenlinden (Germany). As a result of the Treaty of Lunéville and other treaties signed with her enemies (1801–1802), France (1) gained control of lands on the west bank of the Rhine held by the Holy Roman Emperor, (2) strengthened her position in Italy, and (3) regained the Austrian Netherlands (present-day Belgium).

Napoleon ruined the plans of the Second Coalition, and in 1802 even Great Britain signed a peace treaty with France (Treaty of Amiens). "Well, well!" declared the ever-ambitious Napoleon, after signing the peace treaty with Great Britain. "What a beautiful fix we are in now. Peace has been declared."

The ambitions of Napoleon could no longer be contained. He decided to discard the position and title of First Consul for something more powerful, and the obedient French Senate promptly invited him to become "Emperor of the French." The people voted their overwhelming approval.

On December 2, 1804, a coronation service was held at the Cathedral of Notre Dame in the presence of the Pope. When it came time for the Pope to crown the new emperor, Napoleon motioned him aside. Then Napoleon took the crown and placed it on his head himself. He also crowned Josephine as Empress of France. It was a striking gesture that was not lost on the people—Napoleon was showing that he owed his position to no one but himself.

Napoleon's Armies Win an Empire

As emperor of France, Napoleon faced new challenges. In 1803 war again broke out between France and Great Britain. Two years later a Third Coalition (Great Britain, Russia, and Austria, assisted by Sweden) was formed to fight the French.

In 1805 Napoleon's Grand Army was in excellent condition. It had fine generals, veteran soldiers, and good equipment. It was directed by Napoleon, who dictated orders "bending over and sometimes

■ *In this painting, Napoleon is shown crowning Josephine Empress of France, after his coronation as emperor in 1804. Napoleon later divorced Josephine to marry Marie Louise, archduchess of Austria. The painting is by J. L. David, a famous artist of the revolutionary and Napoleonic era.*

■ *A famous painting by Francisco Goya, "The Third of May, 1808," shows the execution of Spaniards in Madrid by French forces under the command of Joachim Murat. This was painted at the same time as the series of etchings by Goya entitled "Disasters of War."*

stretched at full length upon his map where the positions of the enemy were marked." The French tactics of (1) launching rapid offensives supported by massed artillery barrages, (2) concentrating superior numbers of troops in key battle positions, and (3) living off the land in which they fought, all proved effective.

Napoleon forced an Austrian army to surrender at Ulm (Germany) in 1805. In the same year he defeated the armies of the Austrian and Russian emperors at Austerlitz. By the Treaty of Pressburg (1805), Austria gave up Venetia and other areas in Italy. These became part of the Kingdom of Italy which Napoleon had created (1805) with himself as king.

The Confederation of the Rhine

In 1806 Napoleon set up a *Confederation of the Rhine* in Germany. This was a loose confederation of sixteen large south German states (by 1808 the number was thirty-eight) with Napoleon as "Protector." The establishment of the Confederation of the Rhine brought about the dissolution of the Holy Roman Empire. It was an early step toward the unification of Germany in 1871 (p. 514). In 1806 Francis II abdicated as Holy Roman Emperor, but he remained Emperor of Austria with the title Francis I. In the same year Napoleon placed his brother Joseph on the throne of Naples and made his brother Louis ruler of Holland.

The Treaties of Tilsit

A Fourth Coalition was formed against France. Its principal members were Great Britain, Prussia, and Russia. Yet, despite the power of the new alliance, Napoleon continued to triumph. In 1806 the French defeated the Prussians at Jena and Auerstädt in Germany and occupied Berlin. In 1807 they were victorious against the Russians at Friedland in East Prussia. The chief provisions of the Treaties of Tilsit (1807) were the following: (1) Prussia lost considerable territory to France. (2) The Grand Duchy of Warsaw was set up to the east of Prussia. (3) The Kingdom of Westphalia, with Napoleon's brother Jerome as its king, was carved out of Prussian and other land. (4) Emperor Alexander I of Russia agreed to assist France to crush Great Britain by economic methods.

Napoleon Triumphant in Europe

In an effort to stop Portugal and Spain from trading with Great Britain, the French forces next occupied Portugal (1807). Then Napoleon forced the Bourbon rulers to abdicate from the throne of Spain. He made his brother Joseph the new king of Spain (1808), and appointed his brother-in-law Joachim Murât to rule Naples in place of Joseph.

In 1809 Napoleon again defeated the Austrians at Wagram in Lower Austria. By 1810 Napoleon held or controlled most of the lands in Europe (map, p. 421).

Napoleon was the most powerful ruler in Europe, the head of an empire that exceeded in size the territory once held by Charles V. After Napoleon had divorced Josephine (who had not provided him with an heir), Emperor Francis I of Austria even permitted him to marry his daughter, the Archduchess Marie Louise (1810). Little wonder that many Frenchmen proudly said:

[God] in loading our Emperor with gifts, both in peace and in war, . . . has made him the minister of His power . . . upon the earth. *To honour and to serve our Emperor is then to honour and to serve God Himself.*

■ Check on Your Reading

1. What did the Second Coalition wish to achieve? How did Napoleon defeat the Coalition by 1802?

2. Why did Napoleon crown himself?

3. What areas had Napoleon conquered by 1807? What changes had he made in the governments of Italy, the Holy Roman Empire, Poland, Prussia?

4. What was Napoleon's position in Europe by 1810?

4. The Continental System and Its Effects

One nation still remained to defy Napoleon. That was Great Britain, a country which Napoleon had hoped to invade and conquer. "Watch out or Boney'll get you!" English nurses had warned their disobedient children. Their warnings proved to be unnecessary.

In 1805 Lord Nelson and the British fleet had defeated the French fleet at the Battle of Trafalgar, off the southwest coast of Spain. This setback had made it too

difficult for France to invade Britain. Napoleon therefore had decided to try to subdue Britain by economic warfare.

In 1806, after Britain announced a blockade of the French coast, Napoleon put into effect the *Continental System* (which can be traced back to 1803). This system was to include all of the European countries under the control of Napoleon. The Continental System (1) forbade European countries to import any British products or to export goods to Britain, and (2) denied admittance to continental ports to any ship—British or neutral—that sailed from Britain or any of her colonies or stopped at a British port.

Napoleon hoped that Britain would see "her vessels laden with useless wealth wandering around the wide seas . . . seeking in vain . . . for a port to open and receive them." However, Great Britain began to issue Orders in Council (1807) declaring that all ships that traded in European ports closed to British vessels were liable to capture by the British. (Some exceptions were made later.) A blockade was placed on all ports that excluded British vessels.

The War of 1812

The French and British restrictions affected the trade of the United States and other neutral countries. However, British interference with American ships and seamen angered the United States even more than did France's Continental System. The British insisted that their Orders in Council must be obeyed by the Americans.

Disputes over these and other matters and the desire of some Americans for land in Canada led to the War of 1812 between Great Britain and the United States. The war settled very little. Neither side could win a clear-cut victory, and the conflict ended in 1814.

The Continental System Fails

Meanwhile, Napoleon tried to close the gaps in the Continental System. One of the reasons that he occupied Portugal and placed his brother on the throne of Spain was to stop the British from trading with these countries. Nevertheless, the Continental System did not achieve its goal. There were several reasons for its failure.

The Continental System deprived France of some vital raw materials, such as cotton and sugar. In addition, it could not be completely enforced. Napoleon lacked the necessary sea power, and smuggling continued. The peoples dominated by the French needed British goods. They also were stirred by growing feelings of attachment to their countries (nationalism) and wanted to be free from French control. For example, the Spanish and Portuguese peoples revolted and, aided by the British, fought heroically against the French in the Peninsular War (1808–1814).

Napoleon's brother Louis, the King of Holland, summed up the economic situation: "You might as well prevent the skin from sweating" as to stop British goods from entering Europe. (Napoleon removed him in 1810 and annexed Holland.)

■ Check on Your Reading
1. Describe the Continental System.
2. What caused the War of 1812?

5. Napoleon's Invasion of Russia Ends in Disaster

Unable to subdue Great Britain in the West, Napoleon turned toward the East. In 1812 he invaded Russia! In the beginning, Napoleon's army of about 600,000 men was successful. It defeated Russian forces in several engagements and pushed on toward Moscow. However, the Russian emperor, Alexander I, refused to risk the outcome of the war on a single battle.

His forces retreated deep into Russia until, as the French General Caulaincourt said: "We [the French] were in the heart of inhabited Russia and yet . . . we were like a vessel without a compass in the midst of a vast ocean, knowing nothing of what was happening around us."

Napoleon's army entered Moscow the middle of September and found—a deserted

■ *By 1810 Napoleon controlled most of Europe except Great Britain and Russia. Napoleon's Russian invasion ended disastrously in 1812. The European nations then rose against their conqueror and forced him to abdicate. What territories were part of the French empire?*

city! Napoleon waited for the Russian emperor to surrender. He waited while Russian peasants stole into Moscow at night and set fire to parts of the city. He waited while Russian Cossacks raided his supply routes and cut his lines of communication. He waited while the winds of Russia became colder and sharper. He waited, but Emperor Alexander I in St. Petersburg said nothing.

With the approach of winter and his supplies running dangerously low, Napoleon finally decided to move his army out of Russia. On October 19 he left Moscow.

Thus began one of the most disastrous retreats. Soldiers starved or froze to death, and horses, kept on the move for fourteen and fifteen hours a day, collapsed. The wounded fell off carts only to have the drivers of other vehicles ride over their bodies so as not to lose their place in line. The Cossacks waylaid stragglers and raided transport wagons. Brotherhood was forgotten by the French, and, according to General Caulaincourt, "every man thought of himself, and of himself alone."

Napoleon, who rarely concerned himself about the men who lost their lives, issued

■ *Napoleon's retreat from Russia, 1812, is shown in this painting, "Retreat of the Great French Army," by Russian artist V. Vereshchagin. The bitter cold Russian winter numbed the French army. A half million of Napoleon's army were prisoners, deserters, or dead!*

this bulletin: "His Majesty [Napoleon] has never been in better health." Then on December 5, he abandoned his doomed army and hurried to Paris to strengthen his position in France. About 100,000 of Napoleon's troops completed the retreat.

Napoleon Is Forced to Abdicate

The crushing setback suffered by Napoleon in Russia encouraged the countries of Europe to rise against their conqueror. Equally important, many of the actions of Napoleon—like forcing conquered countries to supply the French with soldiers and money and interfering with their governments—stimulated the growth of nationalism among the peoples of Europe. *Nationalism*, as historian Hans Kohn, an expert on the subject, puts it, is "a state of mind" in which a person feels that his supreme loyalty should be to his nation.

Many of the people of Holland, Belgium, and Italy—lands under Napoleon's domination—became increasingly nationalistic. In Germany, rebellions further threatened the French position.

Prussia had developed into a major opponent of France. Under the leadership of statesmen like Baron vom Stein, Prussia had done away with serfdom; reorganized its army, making all citizens liable for duty "to defend the state"; and modernized itself in other ways. National feelings, whose roots in Prussia reached back to before the French Revolution, also grew stronger. The philosopher Fichte demanded "the devouring flame of higher patriotism, which embraces the nation . . . for which the noble-minded man joyfully sacrifices himself."

The opportunity came after Napoleon's disastrous invasion of Russia. In October, 1813, Prussia, Russia, and Austria, aided by Great Britain and Sweden, combined their forces and defeated Napoleon in the great Battle of the Nations (near Leipzig,

Germany). The armies of the allies converged on France itself. "A year ago, all Europe was marching with us," lamented Napoleon, "today all Europe is marching against us." On March 31, 1814, the allies entered Paris. On April 11, the once invincible Napoleon abdicated.

Napoleon Takes One Last Gamble

Napoleon was sent into exile on the little island of Elba, off the coast of Italy, and the Bourbon monarchy was restored in France. Louis XVIII, the brother of the executed Louis XVI, was made the French king. Even as the allies met in Vienna and discussed a peace settlement for Europe, Napoleon decided to take one last gamble to win back his power. Near the end of February, 1815, he escaped from Elba and returned to southern France.

The French government sent troops to capture him but the soldiers joined him. Napoleon reached Paris in March. Thus began the famous "Hundred Days," the period from the arrival of Napoleon in Paris to the return of Louis XVIII in June.

Napoleon gathered an army of about 125,000 men. "The moment has come to conquer or perish," he told them. Proudly mounted on his white horse with its purple saddle blanket embroidered with the letter N and the imperial eagles, Napoleon was ready to lead his troops to victory.

The allies were equally determined to stop him, and they quickly regrouped their forces. Finally, at the Battle of Waterloo in Belgium (June 18, 1815), British, Prussian, Dutch, and Belgian soldiers under the British Duke of Wellington and the Prussian Blücher crushed Napoleon's army for the last time.

Napoleon was exiled to the isolated island of St. Helena in the South Atlantic, where he died in 1821 at the age of 52. His last words were said to have been: "France, Chief of the Army . . . Josephine!"

Napoleon in Perspective

Napoleon had said: "What will they say when I die? They will say, 'Phew! Thank Heaven!'" In a sense, he was right; but the legacy left by Napoleon continued to affect people. Important effects of Napoleon's activities included these:

(1) Napoleon consolidated some of the gains of the French Revolution—such as establishing the equality of all men before the law in his *Code Napoléon*. (2) His troops conquered other countries, and they carried to other peoples many of the ideas of the French Revolution. These ideas later helped to undermine antidemocratic societies that granted special privileges to the few and discriminated against many.

(3) Napoleon remade the map of Europe. Most of his territorial changes would be cancelled. Others, such as the erasure of the Holy Roman Empire, would remain. (4) His oppressive treatment of other countries stimulated the growth of nationalism. They, too, demanded to be nations.

(5) Napoleon left to France the memories of his past "glories." A "Napoleonic legend" grew up. After his downfall, the history of France was marked by struggles among three groups: people believing in "Bonapartism"—that is, that one "strong man" should govern France; people favoring a return to some type of monarchy; and people seeking to establish a democratic republic. André Maurois explains:

All France's history in the nineteenth century was that of [these] three [groups] in quest of a legitimacy.

■ Check on Your Reading

1. How was Napoleon defeated in Russia?
2. How had Napoleon stimulated the growth of nationalism in Europe?
3. How was Napoleon finally defeated after the Hundred Days? What was his fate?
4. What were five important effects of Napoleon's activities?

MAN AND HIS CULTURE

The following sketch of a French soldier is based on an extract from *The Narrative of Captain Coignet*, edited by Lorédan Larchey. It appears in Theodore Ropp's *War in the Modern World*, 1959, Duke University Press.

A Soldier in the French Army—1799

There was a loud knocking on the door of the house of Jean-Roch Coignet! When he opened it, two gendarmes (policemen) handed him a written order to report for military training. He was to leave at once for Fontainebleau.

When he reached Fontainebleau, Jean-Roch was given a blue jacket, leggings, and a bucket-type hat. Then every day he was trained in the use of musket and bayonet. In the evenings, he and other trainees had to gather around the liberty pole and sing "Les aristocrates à la lanterne" ("Hang the aristocrats"). On Sunday they sang "La Victoire" ("Victory").

Then—quite unexpectedly—the news was heard that General Napoleon Bonaparte had returned from Egypt and was on his way to Paris! Jean-Roch hoped that some day he would be able to serve under Napoleon. His chance came on November 9, 1799. On that day, he and his company were stationed in front of the building that housed the officials of the Directory. Suddenly Napoleon appeared. Then, according to Jean-Roch:

[Napoleon] ordered us into line of battle, and spoke to the officers . . . He went up the steps alone. Suddenly we heard cries, and Bonaparte came out, drew his sword, and went up again with a platoon [of soldiers].

Jean-Roch could see "stout gentlemen [officials of the Directory] jumping out of the windows." "Vive Bonaparte!" Jean-Roch shouted, along with the other soldiers. Then he rushed forward to help Napoleon seize the government of France!

CHAPTER REVIEW

REVIEW and DISCUSSION

1. Identify the people and places and explain the events and terms on p. 412.

2. Why do you agree or disagree with this statement: Napoleon "was a Louis XIV streamlined into formidable efficiency"?

3. What did Napoleon mean by "the laws of convention and morality" which, he said, did not apply to him?

4. Why do you agree or disagree with this statement: Hard work is the key to the success of great men; it is also the key to success of lesser men? How might Napoleon have answered this question?

5. Was Napoleon a democratic ruler? Give evidence to support your answer.

6. What contributions did Napoleon make to the cultural life of France?

7. Napoleon tried to model much of his career after that of Julius Caesar. Compare their lives.

8. Military ambition has been a major factor in the downfall of several great leaders. Prove or disprove this statement.

9. Why didn't Napoleon build up his sea power to match that of Great Britain?

10. What were the factors that contributed to Napoleon's downfall? Which were most important? Why?

11. Which of the three types of government do you think would have been best for France after Napoleon's downfall—Bonapartism, monarchy, or a democratic republic? Why?

ACTIVITIES

1. Debate the following: Resolved, that freedom is a greater asset than security.

2. Write a short report on "Nationalism." Consult the *Encyclopedia of the Social Sciences* and other references.

3. Debate the following: Resolved, that unification of Europe under Napoleon would have been very beneficial.

4. On a map of Europe, show Napoleon's empire at its greatest extent.

5. Panel discussion: Who was the greatest ruler—Napoleon, Julius Caesar, Charles V, Alexander the Great, or Charlemagne? Each panelist should prepare a three-minute talk on one of the men named.

PAST and PRESENT

1. In the light of the world's experiences with Napoleon, what do you think is the best way for men to deal with ambitious military conquerors today?

SUGGESTED READINGS

Basic books: PALMER, R. R., and COLTON, JOEL, *A History of the Modern World*, Chap. 10, Knopf.

SMITH, GOLDWIN, *The Heritage of Man*, Chap. 31, Scribner.

Special accounts: GOTTSCHALK, LOUIS, *The Era of the French Revolution, 1715–1815*, Houghton Mifflin.

WINWAR, FRANCES, *Napoleon and the Battle of Waterloo*, Random House. Brief, exciting account of Napoleon's military feats.

Biography and Fiction: COSTAIN, THOMAS B., *Ride With Me*, Doubleday. A novel about an English soldier who fought in the wars against Napoleon. Well-documented.

GUÉRARD, ALBERT, *Napoleon I*, Knopf. Well-written study of Napoleon's failures and successes.

HALE, JOHN, *Napoleon: The Story of His Life*, Roy. Short, informative, well-rounded treatment of his life. Uses primary sources.

HARDY, THOMAS, *Trumpet-Major*, St. Martin's Press. A novel about an English trumpet-major.

MARKHAM, F. M. H., *Napoleon and the Awakening of Europe*, Macmillan. Adult reading. Comprehensive and careful interpretative biography.

TOLSTOY, LEO, *War and Peace*, Modern Library. A great novel that studies the lives of individuals of several Russian families caught in the web of Napoleonic wars.

Chapter 27 Latin Americans Revolt Against Foreign Rule

KEYNOTE Wendell Phillips, an American orator and reformer of the nineteenth century, once declared: "Revolutions are not made; they come." He meant that revolutions are not manufactured artificially but are a natural outgrowth of certain historical conditions.

Such was the case in Latin America, where centuries of rule by Spain led to revolutions. In the first quarter of the nineteenth century *Latin Americans rose in revolt against foreign domination, and the roots of their revolution were embedded in the past.*

Key People *Hernando Cortés · Francisco Pizarro · Pedro Cabral · Simón Bolívar · José de San Martín · Pedro I*

Key Places *Andes Mountains · Magdalena-Cauca · Orinoco Amazon · Tenochtitlán · Tikal · Copán · Cuzco · Hispaniola · Ayacucho*

Key Events *Mayas build a civilization · Aztec civilization develops · Inca Empire organized · Cortés conquers Mexico · Pizarro conquers Peru · Jesuits convert Indians · Spain and Portugal rule colonies · Wars of Independence*

Key Terms *Latin America · Mayas · Aztecs · Incas · conquistadors · mestizos · creoles · mulattoes · Papal Line of Demarcation*

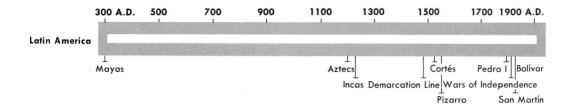

| 300 A.D. | 500 | 700 | 900 | 1100 | 1300 | 1500 | 1700 | 1900 A.D. |

Latin America

Mayas — Aztecs — Incas — Demarcation Line — Pizarro — Cortés — Wars of Independence — Pedro I — San Martín — Bolívar

1. False and True Images of Latin America

Luis Quintanilla, a prominent twentieth-century Mexican writer, once protested against the exaggerated ideas that exist about Latin Americans. Many people, he wrote, think of the Latin American as a man with a jet-black mustache who is dressed in "ball-fringed sombrero, embroidered jacket, [and] brilliant satin sash." Others picture the Latin American woman as always wearing "a huge Spanish comb, a lace mantilla, a fluttering fan, a gardenia nestled in her curls, and a red rose between her gleaming Spanish teeth." These are false images, Luis Quintanilla angrily declared. It would be better if people learned the facts. He was right. There is not *one* Latin American man or woman—there are over 230 million!

The neatly dressed businessman who calmly sips his coffee in an outdoor café is a Latin American. So is the wild-eyed dancer in the near-by hills who whirls about to frighten away evil spirits.

The tall, fashionably-dressed young lady in lace who smooths a wrinkle out of her soft white gloves is a Latin American. So is the bent Indian woman with her shawl, felt hat, and many petticoats.

The chef in Argentina who cooks whole sides of beef around glowing beds of coal is a Latin American. So is the Panamanian who prepares to eat the meat of the five-foot iguana (lizard).

The little flower girls in the cities—the old women driving their burros to market—the farmers working in the fields with their machete knives—the priests strolling quietly before their churches—the drummers beating rhythms until they fall—the serious medical students at the universities—all these are Latin Americans. The individuals of Latin America are as varied as people everywhere—and just as interesting.

What is Latin America?

The words that describe the land of Latin America are often as distorted as our picture of the people. Consider the term *Latin* America. In five of the countries, the population is heavily *Indian*. In seven others, *mestizos* (mixtures of Indians and whites) are the largest single groups. In Haiti, Negroes predominate; and in the Dominican Republic, *mulattoes* (mixtures of Negroes and whites) are the most numerous. Most of the ancestors of these

427

people did not speak Latin and had little contact with Roman civilization. Why do we call this land *Latin* America?

One reason is that the Spanish and Portuguese who settled in this area had a Latin heritage. (Latin Europe includes those countries whose language is directly descended from Latin.) Even more important, we have become accustomed to this expression and would find it difficult to replace it.

The Giant Lying Southeast of the United States

Latin America extends from the northern boundary of Mexico to Cape Horn at the southern end of South America—a distance of roughly 7,000 miles. This is about three times as long as the air route from Seattle, Washington, to New York City.

Latin America includes Mexico, Central America, several islands in the West Indies, and South America (Atlas, pp. 756–757). It is a huge territory over twice the size of the United States. Brazil is over five and a half times the size of Alaska, and Argentina is four times larger than Texas.

Historical Importance of Latin America's Huge Area: In the past, the tremendous size of Latin America has made it difficult for the Latin American countries to work closely in political, social, and economic affairs. Modern means of transportation are helping to solve this problem.

There are twenty-two independent countries in Latin America. Most of Latin America lies in tropical regions, and only about one third is in the temperate zone. The climate varies and often depends on altitude and winds. The highlands, where many Latin Americans live, are usually cool. The lowlands are generally hot.

Like the woven shawls of its Indian women, the land of Latin America presents a variety of colors and patterns. The lofty Andes Mountain chain runs through the western part of South America from the Strait of Magellan to Venezuela. It is a rugged, unsettled chain of mountains still subject to earthquakes. The older Brazilian highlands are in the east. In Central America, other highlands lift their stubby volcanic fingers. And in Mexico, two ranges—the Sierra Madre Occidental and the Sierra Madre Oriental—stand on the western and eastern sides of the plateau.

Historical Importance of Latin America's Mountains: In the past, the Andes, which run through the western part of South America, made it difficult for peoples on the west coast to have much contact with the eastern parts. This problem is being solved by modern transportation.

The four important river systems in Latin America are located in South America. These are the Magdalena-Cauca and Orinoco, which flow into the Caribbean; and the Paraná-Paraguay and the great Amazon, which empty into the Atlantic.

Then there are the jungle areas of Latin America. There are thick forests soaked by rains and steaming with heat; rotting trees with creepers that twist about them; and dangerous swamps coated with slime. These jungles contrast sharply with the deserts of South and Central America, where the sun beats down and rain seldom falls.

Historical Importance of Latin America's Jungles: The jungle regions have been major obstacles to the settlement of the interior of Latin America. In many countries, they also have interfered with efforts to unite the various peoples.

Finally, there are the plateaus, the mountain valleys, and the plains. Here people work the soil, graze cattle, and build their lives in the world of Latin America.

■ Check on Your Reading
1. How do Latin Americans differ?
2. How has Latin America's history been affected by its size, mountains, and jungles?

2. Mayas, Aztecs, and Incas

We cannot be sure when man first appeared in Latin America. However, it is believed that between 23,000 and 15,000 years ago hunters from northeast Asia entered North America by crossing the Bering Strait. Their descendants gradually moved down through Canada, the United States, and Latin America. Long before Columbus came to the New World, man had developed various societies in Mexico, Central America, and South America.

Achievements of the Mayan Civilization

One of the peoples who built an important early civilization in Latin America were the *Mayas*. They occupied a region in Mexico and Central America. Their civilization, which had two distinct periods of development, lasted from about the fourth to the seventeenth century A.D.

The Mayas grew enough corn (the basic food) to meet their needs. It was reported by a sixteenth-century Spanish bishop, Diego de Landa:

At the time of sowing, those who do not have their own people to do their work join together in groups of twenty, or more or less, and all together they do the work of all of them . . . and they do not leave it until everyone's is done.

They built cities. One American specialist on Latin American history, Hubert Herring, estimates that the Mayan cities of Tikal (in Guatemala) and Copán (in the west of Honduras) may have had populations of 200,000 or more!

The Mayas developed a system of writing. They also constructed fine pyramid temples and monuments, and they sculptured beautifully in jade and basalt. In addition, they learned much about astronomy and devised a calendar that has been called "more accurate than the one used in Europe when Columbus discovered America." They worked out methods of mathematics, including the use of the zero.

For those who believe that tastes of ancient civilizations always differed from our own, it might be added that Mayan women liked perfume and that a favorite sport of Mayan men was a type of basketball.

Weaknesses of the Mayan Civilization

The Mayan civilization was not without defects. It had many weaknesses: (1) The Mayas were organized into a society where the upper classes enjoyed more privileges than the mass of people and the slaves. (2) They did not know how to conserve the soil, and in time they lessened the fertility of land. (3) They could not put an end to civil wars or control the epidemic diseases that attacked the people.

(4) During some periods of Mayan history, the religious practices of the people were brutal by our standards. Priests sometimes sacrificed human beings on a stone altar in order to please the many Mayan gods. Sometimes, according to Bishop Landa, who kept a record of Mayan life:

they threw living victims into the well . . . believing that they would come out on the third day, although they never appeared again.

As a result of these and other factors, the Mayan civilization declined as a creative society. By the middle of the sixteenth century, the Mayas were forced to give way to other peoples.

Aztecs Gain Power in Mexico

Another people who built an early civilization in Latin America were the *Aztecs*. In 1325 they founded their capital city upon the islands in Lake Texcoco, Mexico. Then they extended their power and built an empire that eventually included several million people.

■ *These examples of Mayan architecture and sculpture show the variety of their artistic achievements and fine workmanship. They include the ruins of a Mayan pyramid temple in Yucatán, Mexico (top), the carved serpent columns from the "Temple of the Warriors" in Yucatán (lower left), and the incense burner (lower right), which was found by divers at the bottom of a lake in Guatemala. A human head with nose- and ear-plugs looks out from between the jaws of an unknown animal.*

Courtesy of Dr. Stephan F. de Borhegyi

The Aztec society was based on agriculture and depended primarily on corn. Similar to the Mayan civilization, the community rather than the individuals usually owned the farming areas. The land was then distributed among various groups.

The Aztecs produced fine pottery, massive stonework, attractive mosaics, and lovely ornaments of jade. However, they added little of value to science or mathematics, and their system of writing was very primitive. They were involved in many wars, and they did not build as creative a civilization as the Mayas did.

In war and peace, the Aztecs turned for help to their gods. They believed in gods of war, sun, rain, wind, corn, death, and many others. These deities were very real to the Aztecs, who described them in words such as these:

> He the Wind [god]
> On his neck a golden collar,
> Gleaming golden necklace wears he.
> On his back are wondrous feathers
> Fashioned like to glowing fire-flames.
> Leggings has of spotted tiger;
> Shield adorned with precious jewels.

To please the more blood-thirsty gods, the Aztecs offered up human sacrifices. To satisfy others, they danced and sang. Yet all the sacrifices and all the dances to the gods could not save the Aztec civilization. Farming problems, Spanish conquerors, and other factors brought about its decline in the sixteenth century.

Incas Organize an Empire

A third people who built an early civilization in Latin America were the *Incas*. The Incas (actually the word *Inca* referred only to their king) started to dominate the valley of Cuzco, Peru, between 1200 and 1438 A.D. From 1438 to 1530 the Incas extended their power further by conquest. Eventually, they controlled an empire that

■ *This is an Aztec sculpture of the God Xochipilli, which was carved out of basalt. It dates from the 14th or 15th century A.D.*

reached from northern Ecuador and southern Colombia through Peru and Bolivia to the Maule River in Chile. It included between 4,500,000 and 7,500,000 people.

Like other Indian groups of Latin America, the Inca society was based on agriculture. The land was owned by the community. Each individual belonged to an *ayllu*, a clan of families who shared together the land, crops, and animals.

Civilization today owes a debt to the Incas and their predecessors, and to others who later tilled the soil of the Andes and Upper Amazon regions. One recent writer, Victor W. von Hagen, believes that "more than half of what the world eats today was developed by these Andean farmers." He lists as some of the plants cultivated in

431

■ *These are the ruins of Machu Picchu, the "Lost City of the Incas," situated above the Urubamba Valley in southern Peru. The fine stonework of the Incas can be seen in the walls, stairs, and great stone terraces leading to the summit.*

this area: corn or maize (20 varieties), potatoes (which the Incas dehydrated by stamping on them with their feet), beans (many varieties), sweet potatoes, yams, squash, manioc (from which are derived tapioca and farina), peanuts, and cashews.

The religion of the Incas was related to their agricultural activities. The people believed in many gods of nature. The sun god, who cared for the crops, was the most powerful. Later, the Incas began to accept the idea of one Supreme Creator who was above all other gods.

The life of the Incas—whether it was in farming, religion, war, or other fields—was not a free one. It was strictly regulated by the Inca (the ruler) and by his assistants (some were later called "Big Ears" because they pierced their ear lobes and placed golden and jeweled disks in them).

The Inca king, who was often called "Son of the Sun," had tremendous power. It was the Inca king and his administrators who dominated the empire and its subjects.

Achievements of the Incas

Although the Incas never developed writing, they were able to use *quipus* (knots on colored strings attached to a cord) to help them remember events and to do simple mathematics. In addition, they can be credited with these important achievements: (1) They organized their empire more efficiently and successfully than any other Indian people of Latin America. (2) They constructed an excellent system of roads and bridges to bind their empire. (3) They worked well in the cutting and fitting of stone, building many stone structures throughout their empire.

Many buildings were constructed on foundations that had been made by the people who lived in the area before the Incas.

The Incas of the fifteenth and sixteenth centuries have long been gone—crushed by civil war and foreign conquerors.

Mayas, Aztecs, and Incas Are Not Democratic

In comparing these three Indian civilizations—the Mayas, the Aztecs, and the Incas—the following facts become clear: (1) The Mayas were the most scientific and artistic. (2) The Incas were the best governors of empire and the best engineers. (3) The Aztecs, who were not as creative, were productive in such arts as the working of stone and the carving of jade.

None of these societies was a political or social democracy. It is true that the land was usually owned by the community, and that the people had some economic rights and security. Tribal or clan customs sometimes affected the kings' decisions. However, in nearly every matter, the real rulers of the Mayas, Aztecs, and Incas were their kings, religious heads, and military chieftains. It was the duty of the people to obey these leaders without question.

It is not difficult to understand why these societies did not become democracies. They were still at early stages of development and had little opportunity to learn from more advanced civilizations. The peoples lived in regions that were filled with dangers. Little wonder that they turned over their lives to rulers and priests who claimed to have special influence with the gods.

By the end of the fifteenth century, there was still no important tradition of democracy in Latin America.

■ **Check on Your Reading**

1. What were the Mayan achievements in agriculture, architecture, writing, science, and mathematics?
2. Why did the Mayan civilization decline?
3. Describe the Aztec civilization.
4. What did the Incas achieve?
5. Why did democracy fail to develop?

3. Explorers and Conquerors

In 1493, shortly after the first voyage of Columbus to America, Pope Alexander VI drew on the map an imaginary line that ran through the New World. This was the so-called *Papal Line of Demarcation,* one of whose purposes was to establish regions for Christian missionary work. According to the arrangement made, Spain was permitted to have all of the land that she discovered to the west of the line. This meant that Spain could claim nearly all of the Americas. Portugal was granted territory that Portuguese explorers found to the east of the line. By the Treaty of Tordesillas, Spain (1494), the line was moved farther westward (map, p. 299). This change gave Portugal her later claim to Brazil.

The Spanish and Portuguese explorers came into the world of Latin America. The Spaniards soon established bases on the island of Hispaniola (today's Haiti and Dominican Republic) and Cuba. From here the Spanish *conquistadors* spread their power over many areas.

Cortés in Mexico

In 1519 Hernando Cortés and about six hundred men sailed from Cuba and landed in Mexico. According to his private chaplain, Cortés was "very strong, high-spirited, and skilled in the use of arms." On his shields Cortés put the motto: "The judgment of the Lord overtook them; and his strength supported my arm."

■ *An Aztec Indian drawing from the sixteenth century shows Cortés (seated, with high feathers) accepting the surrender of the Mexican ruler. Mexican dignitaries are guarded by a Spanish soldier (below).*

When Cortés invaded the lands of the Aztecs, he was not thinking primarily about religion. He was looking for riches, land, and commerce. The Aztecs' golden bowls and silver dishes were tempting bait.

The Aztecs viewed Cortés and his men with mixed emotions. Many of them were impressed by the horses that the Spaniards rode (the Aztecs had never seen a horse). Others considered Cortés to be a great god who had been expected to return to the Aztecs some day. Still others extended a hand of friendship and then turned it into a fist of war when abused.

Cortés was a rugged conqueror. He did not hesitate to use force and treachery to subdue this people who greatly outnumbered his soldiers. He had a great advantage in possessing steel swords and firearms, which the Aztecs had never seen before. Aided by reinforcements and by Indians who hated their Aztec rulers, he pushed on and finally took the Aztec capital of Tenochtitlán (Mexico City). By 1521 Spain controlled Mexico.

Pizarro in Peru

In January, 1531, Francisco Pizarro and about one hundred eighty men sailed south along the Pacific coast from Panama. They landed on the coast of Ecuador. From here they gradually marched into Peru. The people of Peru, the Incas, misunderstood many things about Pizarro. They thought that the Spaniards' horses were useless at night, their swords were poor weapons, and their guns could fire only twice. Pizarro was quite willing to use deceit and military power to conquer the Incas.

On one occasion, the Spaniards arranged for a meeting with the Inca king, Atahualpa. When Atahualpa came with an estimated five thousand unarmed troops, the Spanish soldiers remained in hiding. A friar tried to convince the Inca ruler to become a subject of the Spanish king and to accept Christianity. Atahualpa refused and is said to have replied:

I will be no man's tributary. I am greater than any prince on earth. . . . For my faith, I will not change it.

Pizarro then raised a scarf as a signal, and the Spanish soldiers rushed out and killed several thousand Indians.

Using such methods and profiting from a civil war that had disrupted the country, Pizarro and his men were able to conquer the Inca people. By 1533 Spain controlled the land of the Incas. Indian resistance continued. The Spanish conquerors also quarrelled and fought among themselves. It was not until almost four decades later that peace and order were restored.

Other Explorers and Conquerors

Other explorers and conquerors were active in spreading Spain's power. These included Pedro de Alvarado in Central America and Pedro de Valdivia in Chile.

Portugal was more concerned with obtaining the spices and riches of the East than with searching for the wealth of the New World. Even so, Pedro Alvares Cabral from Portugal is generally credited with the official discovery of Brazil in 1500.

By about 1580, as a result of the work of these and other men, many of the known regions of Latin America had been brought under Spanish and Portuguese control.

Evaluation of the Conquerors' Activities

The work of the sixteenth-century conquerors was extremely important. They opened the way for colonists to come to Latin America and to develop regions that later became nations, but they often treated the Indians unfairly and used force. They did almost nothing to help democracy grow.

When the conquerors used cruel and undemocratic methods, they were not doing anything differently from the Indian rulers. Historian Hubert Herring wrote:

Spain did not introduce cruelty and war: exploitation was an old story to the Indians. Spain did not destroy human freedom: it had never been enjoyed by Maya, Aztec, Inca. . . .

The Spanish conquerors and the Indian rulers whose power they seized *both* bore a responsibility for the checks on freedom.

■ Check on Your Reading

1. How did Spain and Portugal obtain claims to Latin America?
2. How did Cortés conquer Mexico?
3. How did Pizarro conquer Peru?
4. What were some good and bad effects of the Spanish conquests?

4. The Colonial Period

The conquerors had fought their way to power. Colonists followed the conquerors and came to settle in Latin America.

Colonists Have Little Democratic Experience

What did the colonists from Spain bring besides their worldly goods? Did they come with a knowledge of the tools of democracy, as the English settlers later did? In general, they did not. In Spain they had few opportunities to take part in democratic government.

Did they come seeking religious freedom, as the English settlers did? Again, in general, they did not. They had learned long ago that such ideas led to trial before the Inquisition.

Did they come with the idea of working the land themselves, as the English settlers did? Not if they could help it! They came to find riches or to obtain lands that could be worked for them by the Indians.

Spain's System of Colonial Government

Spain's over-all approach to her colonies was that of a master to a servant. The Spanish rulers intended to use the colonies as places from which to obtain gold, silver, and other raw materials; markets for the products of Spain; areas in which to spread Christianity; and means of increasing their prestige among other Europeans.

The government established in Spanish America reflected Spain's desire to dominate her colonies. The political institutions of government included the following:

1. THE COUNCIL OF THE INDIES. The Council members were chosen by the king of Spain and were responsible for the overall direction of the colonies.

2. VICEROY. These were appointed by the king and the Council of the Indies. The Viceroys were the personal representatives of the king of Spain in Latin America.

3. AUDIENCAS. These were law courts with administrative and legislative duties.

What about the people's role in this system of government? The people—whether they were the Spanish settlers, Indians, mestizos, Negro slaves, or mulattoes—had one principal duty. This was to obey the orders of their superiors.

In general, Spain's system of colonial government was a major obstacle to the growth of democracy. On the other hand, this system of government aided the development of future Latin-American nations by imposing governmental control on regions and areas disrupted by lack of organization.

Catholicism Spreads Throughout Latin America

The Catholic religion also played an important role in the settlement of the colonies. Most of the Spanish colonists were Catholics, and the Spanish king dominated the Church in Spanish America. He nominated Church officials, collected revenues, and approved the establishment of monasteries and churches.

Through the efforts of missionaries the Indians of Latin America were converted. The Jesuits were particularly active.

Sometimes the Jesuits challenged the authority of civil officials, landholders, and even the kings themselves. As a result, they were expelled from Spanish America in 1767.

A Small Group Holds Social and Economic Power

Although the people believed in a common religion, Catholicism, they were still kept apart by their different social and economic positions. Most of the power in society was controlled by a small group. At the top were the *peninsulares* (people born in Spain of Spanish parents). Next came the *creoles* (people usually of Spanish descent born in the New World).

The mixed groups came next. These included mestizos, mulattoes, and *zambos* (mixtures of Indian and Negro). Below these groups were the Indians. At the bottom of the scale were the Negro slaves.

The land also was concentrated in the hands of a few. Influential persons were awarded *encomiendas* by royal order—that is, they were given control of lands and entrusted with Indians to work these lands. The kings tried to protect these Indians and declared that they were to be cared for by their masters. However, the encomiendas' owners often exploited the Indians. Changes were made in the system, but the encomiendas continued to exist until the end of the eighteenth century. The concentration of social and economic power in the hands of a small group proved a major block to the development of democracy.

Spanish and Portuguese Rule Compared

Finally, some similarities existed between Spain's rule of colonies and Portugal's government of Brazil. For example, in Brazil, as in the Spanish colonies, Catholicism spread through the country; and great social and economic power was held by the large plantation owners.

On the other hand, differences existed. Although Portugal was under Spanish control for sixty years (1580–1640), Brazil succeeded in keeping clear of many Spanish restrictions. The government of Brazil was less stern and elaborate, and relations among the various racial groups were better.

As for the condition of democracy, Brazil and the Spanish colonies permitted some degree of representative government in the cities, but autocracy was the rule.

Cultural Progress in the Colonial Period

The first printing press was set up in Mexico about 1535. Despite censorship, reading material and ideas circulated among the intellectual groups.

Universities were established; and in 1580 a position was arranged for professors who distinguished themselves in medicine. Histories were written and considerable poetry was composed. In architecture, many churches with interesting features were built.

Colonial Latin America was the setting for progress in several fields. By 1800 some felt that the colonies were strong enough to stand on their own feet.

■ **Check on Your Reading**
1. How did Spain govern her colonies?
2. What role did the Church play?
3. Describe government and society in Spanish America.

5. The Wars of Independence

In 1808 Napoleon Bonaparte of France had gained control of Spain. The Spanish king was forced to turn over his power to the French. Napoleon placed his brother Joseph on the Spanish throne. However, several city councils in the Spanish colonies first refused to permit France to rule them. Then, realizing that here was an opportunity to rid themselves of Spain as well, the councils also rebelled against the Spanish authorities. In 1810, the Wars of Independence against Spain broke out in Spanish America.

At the outbreak of the revolutionary wars, the population in the colonies was roughly seventeen million. About three and one-half million of this number were whites, most of whom were creoles. Although there were Indian, mestizo, mulatto, and Negro heroes among the revolutionists, the creoles provided most of the leadership.

What were the factors that led the creole leaders and their followers to rise against Spain? Among the most important causes were these: (1) The creoles objected to the power of the Spanish officials and wanted to play a more important part themselves in the government. (2) The intellectuals were stimulated by the liberal ideas of French, English, and American authors. (3) The American and French Revolutions encouraged some colonists to believe that a rebellion might succeed.

(4) Many large landholders and Spanish officials had abused their workers. This made the workers eager to check the power of their masters. (5) Spain's restrictions on the trade of the colonies were considered unjust. (6) The heavy taxes imposed by Spain angered the colonists.

The Wars of Independence were *not* mass uprisings. Probably about one-third of the population remained loyal to Spain. Neither were the revolts always carefully planned and unified. Many who fought for independence were dedicated men.

437

Federal Palace, Caracas

■ *This portrait shows Simón Bolívar, the "Liberator," in dress uniform. Bolívar led the revolutionary forces in northern South America.*

Simón Bolívar and Other Liberators Lead the Way

There were many leaders of the independence movements. There was Miguel Hidalgo, the white-haired priest who led the Indian revolt in Mexico. There was Bernardo O'Higgins, son of a Chilean mother and an Irish father, who fought heroically to free Chile. There was José de San Martín, who directed the fight in southern South America and yet said, "I do not want military renown—I have no ambition to be the conqueror . . . I want solely to liberate the country from oppression."

Above all, there was Simón Bolívar (1783–1830), known as the "Liberator." Bolívar's physical appearance was not impressive, for he was only five feet, six inches in height. His chest was narrow, his body slender, and his skin somewhat rough. Yet there was something striking about his personality. One could sense Bolívar's con-

viction that he was doing right. One could feel that he had the energy and courage to support his ideas with action.

Some claim that Bolívar was chiefly interested in personal glory and power. Bolívar himself denied this and predicted that:

History will say [that] Bolívar took the command in order to free his fellow-citizens, and, when they were free, he permitted them to govern themselves by laws, and not by his will.

Bolívar led the revolutionary forces in northern South America. He helped to liberate the lands of present-day Venezuela, Colombia, Peru, and Ecuador. San Martín headed the attack in southern South America. At the Battle of Ayacucho, Peru, in 1824, the revolutionists delivered the final defeat to Spain.

Latin America Divides into Many Nations

The Wars of Independence against Spain (1810–1824) were the most important landmark in the development of future nations of Latin America. These wars resulted in independence for almost every Spanish colony in Latin America (map, p. 439).

The colony of Brazil had gained independence from Portugal without a major war. In 1807 when Napoleon had occupied Portugal, the Portuguese king had fled to Brazil. In 1821, six years after Napoleon's defeat, the king returned to Portugal. His son Pedro was left behind to rule Brazil.

The people of Brazil were no longer willing to have their country remain a colony. They demanded their freedom. Pedro accepted their wishes. On September 7, 1822, he proclaimed the independence of Brazil and became its king as Pedro I.

■ **Check on Your Reading**

1. What factors led to revolt in the colonies?
2. Describe the work of Bolívar.
3. What independent nations emerged?

438

■ *By 1828, almost all the Latin American countries had obtained their independence. In 1830 Venezuela and Ecuador broke away from Colombia and became separate states. After 1838 the United Provinces divided into the states of Guatemala, El Salvador, Honduras, Nicaragua, and Costa Rica. Haiti and the Dominican Republic remained united until 1844, and Panama became independent of Colombia in 1903. The inset (below) shows the areas where the early Indian civilizations—Aztec, Maya, and Inca—developed.*

CULTURAL CHARACTERISTICS of Latin America at the Beginning of the Nineteenth Century

The Incas of the fifteenth and sixteenth centuries disappeared long ago. Yet from that period one person is still with us. He is a little Inca boy who sits with his arms and legs drawn close to his body and with his head inclined to the left. Near him are his possessions: a bag of feathers and coca leaves; a tiny idol; a purse with locks of hair and other objects; and a small gold and silver figure of a llama. This little Inca boy was found in 1954 and now rests alone in the National History Museum of Chile. He has been frozen for possibly five hundred years.

Many leaders in the nineteenth century thought about the culture of Latin America as we might about the boy. They mistakenly considered it frozen into the past, rather than recognizing it as living, on-going, and constantly developing. Yet the cultural characteristics of Latin America at the beginning of the nine-teenth century were very much alive and were to have a marked effect on the future. They were:

A society with a rigid social structure clearly marked by a number of political, economic, and social divisions.

An economy in which ownership of land predominated.

A strong tradition of Catholicism, with the Church playing a major role in the lives of the people.

Valuable art, architecture, literature, engineering, and other cultural achievements, reflecting the heritage from earlier periods of Latin-American history.

Latin America of the early nineteenth century lacked political, economic, and social unity. Regionalism and

439

local peculiarities continued to produce marked differences in cultural patterns. They still do today.

During the Wars of Independence Simón Bolívar said: "[Under Spanish rule] the South Americans traversed the centuries like blind men in a world of color. They found themselves on the field of action with bandaged eyes: they could see nothing, hear nothing. Why? Because they had never been permitted to see justice, much less hear the truth." The nineteenth and twentieth centuries were to test whether the new rulers could stimulate the growth of both liberty and culture in Latin America.

MAN AND HIS CULTURE

Let's Meet the People!

The following sketch is based primarily on information from the research and field expeditions of Victor W. von Hagen, a contemporary scholar, who set down his findings in *Realm of the Incas*, Mentor: Ancient Civilizations, New American Library, 1957.

An Inca Worker

The Inca worker was about medium in height. His chest was large, his legs were well built, and his skin was the color of bronze. His long hair was drawn together with woolen strings. He wore a breech clout, a tunic that resembled a poncho, and sandals with woolen laces. When he felt the cold mountain air, he also put on a cape.

The Inca worker lived near the city of Cajamarca in Peru. His house consisted of one windowless room. It was built of unburnt brick dried in the sun. The roof was thatched with grass and there was no chimney. Inside there was almost no furniture. When he slept, he rested on a blanket or animal hide. When he ate, he squatted about the pots of food.

The Inca worker belonged to an *ayllu*, a clan of families who shared the land, crops, and animals in common. He worked long hours in the field of his ayllu. He also helped to till the lands set aside for the uses of government and religion. The Inca worker believed in many gods and appealed to them for help with the crops. If there were no rain, he and his neighbors would sacrifice a llama. If the rain still did not come, the priests would kill a human being and offer his blood to the gods.

One day the Inca worker was ordered to accompany the royal guard when it marched with the Inca ruler to Cajamarca to meet a army of strange men. As instructed, he went unarmed. His family waited for his return. So did his land and his animals and his gods. But the Inca worker did not come home. The Spaniards ambushed the unarmed Incas, and he fell in battle!

CHAPTER REVIEW

REVIEW and DISCUSSION

1. Identify the people and places and explain the events and terms on p. 426.

2. How has the geography of Latin America affected its history?

3. Why did some Indians south of the Rio Grande develop a higher degree of civilization than most North American Indians?

4. Did the Spanish conquerors completely destroy or absorb the Indian cultures they found?

5. What differences might there be between a man who had never known freedom and one who had been deprived of it?

6. What two factors dominated Latin America in the colonial days?

7. Simón Bolívar is often called "the George Washington of Latin America." In what ways does his career parallel George Washington's?

8. Was interest in the liberty of the Latin American countries the only reason for the United States and England to be concerned about Latin America?

9. How do you explain the fact that Portugal did not strongly resist Brazil's desire for independence?

10. Do you think that if an authoritarian ruler brought order to all Latin America, he could help its growth?

11. Do you agree or disagree with this statement: A supply of nourishing food and mineral resources are necessary to the development of a high culture? Why?

ACTIVITIES

1. Add the three Indian civilizations of Latin America to your chart on the "Causes of the Rise and Fall of Civilizations."

2. On a map of Latin America show the boundaries and important cities, rivers, and mountains of the Latin American countries.

3. Make an album including maps; pictures of scenery, people, rulers, buildings, industry; cartoons; and flags of Latin America.

4. Inform yourself thoroughly on the history of one Latin American country, and report your findings to the class. Consult pamphlets from the Organization of American States and other references.

5. On a map of Latin America indicate the areas where the Mayan, Aztec, and Inca civilizations were established.

6. Add the following to your paperback library: Von Hagen, *Realm of the Incas; World of the Maya;* and *The Aztec: Man and Tribe.*

PAST and PRESENT

1. Panel discussion: The major problems of Latin America today and in the past.

2. What do the United States and Latin America have in common?

3. What historical events are responsible for the similarities and differences between the United States and Latin America?

SUGGESTED READINGS

Basic books: LINTON, RALPH, *Tree of Culture,* Chap. 51, Knopf.

SMITH, GOLDWIN, *The Heritage of Man,* Chap. 33, Scribner.

Special accounts: BAITY, ELIZABETH, *Americans Before Columbus,* Viking. Early cultures of Mayas, Incas, and Aztecs.

GOETZ, DELIA, *Half a Hemisphere,* Harcourt, Brace. For young people. Good history of Latin America and useful source book.

PECK, ANNE M., *Pageant of Middle American History,* Longmans, Green. Focuses on America from earliest times.

PECK, ANNE M., *Pageant of South American History,* Longmans, Green. Easy reading, rich in information.

Biography and Fiction: LANSING, MARION F., *Liberators and Heroes of Mexico and Central America,* L. C. Page.

LANSING, MARION F., *Liberators and Heroes of South America,* L. C. Page. Biographies.

WHITRIDGE, ARNOLD, *Simón Bolívar, the Great Liberator* (Landmark book), Random House. Ably written.

UNIT 7 Inventions Revolutionize Industry and Change Society

The Frightened People

In the nineteenth century, one of the first railroads in history was being planned in England. When the people heard the news, many of them became frightened. Angry cries were heard:

> The noise will keep our hens from laying eggs!
> Our house will be burned down by the sparks!
> Our grass and trees will be ruined by smoke!
> Our friends will be killed by exploding boilers!

More than one villager agreed with the writer on the *Quarterly Review* magazine who declared: "We trust . . . that Parliament will, in all the railroads it may sanction, limit the speed to eight or nine miles an hour."

Does all this seem absurd to you? If it does, remember that you are familiar with railroads. These people of the early nineteenth century were not. They were frightened because they faced inventions that were new and unknown to them.

The Crowded People

In the latter part of the eighteenth and in the nineteenth century, new industries were developing throughout England. The rise of factory towns disturbed the lives of many people, especially those who moved to them from country districts. In some areas, families of ten or more were crowded into cellars. In others, men and women had to walk a mile for drinking water. In still others, there were official government reports of:

> filthy and crowded streets [where] you see human faces . . . sinking down to the level of . . . brute tribes. . . .

442

Do such living conditions seem strange to you? If they do, remember that you have housing laws and other protection. These did not exist in 1800. Men could exploit the new factory workers in new industries that were started without proper safeguards for the welfare of the people. Only with the passage of time did the workers find ways to improve their situation.

And You! "What has all this to do with me?" you may ask. "Why should I concern myself with the effects of invention and industry on civilization in the past? After all, I live in the twentieth century and conditions are different today."

Conditions are different, but remember that today there are more inventions than ever before, an increasing number of new industries, and many nations just beginning to industrialize. These nations have many of the same difficulties that once were encountered by countries that industrialized in the nineteenth century.

We still have the same three basic problems that were faced by men in the latter part of the eighteenth and in the nineteenth century: (1) how to adjust ourselves to the new inventions, (2) how to safeguard the welfare of those affected by new industries, and (3) how to use our experience to help non-industrialized peoples to introduce industry into their countries.

One of the principal reasons for reading this unit is to prepare yourself to meet these three problems. You can do this by learning about the errors of those who blundered in the past and by absorbing the wisdom of those of our ancestors who met the challenge of industrial change with intelligence.

Chapter 28   *An Industrial Revolution: New Inventions, Techniques, and Power*

KEYNOTE   Beginning in the second half of the eighteenth century, great industrial expansion occurred in England and several other countries. Progress in industry was sparked by a number of extremely valuable inventions and discoveries. Three of the most important of these inventions were a spinning machine, a steam engine, and an electric telegraph.

Yet the East Indians had a crude machine to spin yarn hundreds of years before Christ. Several of the ancient Greeks were acquainted with a type of steam power. And a physician in the days of Queen Elizabeth I had pointed out the importance of electricity.

Although many of man's inventions and discoveries seem to appear suddenly, they often have their roots in the past. This fact serves to underline one of the key features of history from about 1750 to 1860. It was this: *An Industrial Revolution speeded up tremendously the pace of life in England and elsewhere. However, this so-called "revolution" grew out of the past, rather than breaking sharply with it.*

Key People   *Richard Arkwright   ·   Eli Whitney   ·   James Watt   ·   Henry Bessemer   ·   John McAdam   ·   Robert Fulton   ·   Cyrus Field   · Alexander Graham Bell*

Key Events   *Textile machines invented   ·   Whitney uses interchangeable parts   · Steam engine invented   ·   Steel making improved   ·   Railroads built   ·   Steamboat invented   ·   Telegraph developed*

Key Terms   *"Industrial Revolution"   ·   enclosure movement   ·   applied science   · inventors   ·   factory system   ·   technological unemployment*

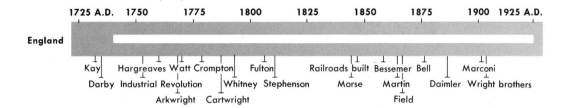

| 1725 A.D. | 1750 | 1775 | 1800 | 1825 | 1850 | 1875 | 1900 | 1925 A.D. |

England

Kay | Hargreaves Watt Crompton | Fulton | Railroads built Bessemer Bell | Marconi
Darby Industrial Revolution | Whitney Stephenson | Morse Martin Daimler Wright brothers
Arkwright Cartwright | Field

1. England and the Industrial Revolution

Between 1000 and 1750 A.D. few basic changes were made in the way men lived in England. Most of the people in 1750 were still tilling the soil, and they were doing it about the same way their ancestors had in the year 1000. Their crops, animals, and tools had not changed very much either.

England's population was small, a little over six million. Her customs were deeply rooted. Her pace of living, according to British historian G. M. Trevelyan, was that of "a slowly-moving stream."

There were some industries, but most of them were small. There was some manufacturing, but much of this work was done in private homes. There were some important business centers, but none of them had yet felt the frantic rush of modern industrial life.

England was not a rural paradise. If the villagers danced about the Maypole on days of festival, they also worked hard on other days. If they breathed free air, they also lacked some of the goods that came with the smoke of factories. If they had sufficient time to eat, they also rarely dined on rich meats and pastry. In short, life in England in 1750 was peaceful but rugged.

In the next one hundred years, vast changes took place. By the middle of the nineteenth century the English landscape was transformed in many places. There were smoky factories, roaring machinery, crowded towns, and a new way of life. Our story is concerned with the reasons for this remarkable change.

From about 1750 to 1860, new inventions, new techniques, and new sources of power helped to speed up tremendously the pace of life in England and elsewhere. The many economic and social events and changes of this period make up what has been called the "Industrial Revolution."

The term "Industrial Revolution" is far from accurate. It suggests that there was a sudden overthrowing of the past. Such was not the case. Actually, the economic and social changes of this so-called "revolution" grew out of the past and extended far into the future.

■ **Check on Your Reading**

1. How would you describe the economy of England in 1750? What did this mean in the daily life of the average person?

2. What happened to England in the next century? Is this movement accurately named?

445

2. The Industrial Revolution Develops First in England

The Industrial Revolution developed first in England. There were numerous reasons why it developed there.

England's Escape from Military Destruction

The European continent had been plagued by the French Revolution and the Napoleonic Wars. England had escaped military destruction. She also had gained valuable markets by selling to war-torn countries.

England's Wealth and Natural Resources

England had a number of people wealthy enough to invest money in new industries. Many of them had gained their riches through England's trade with her colonies and other overseas areas. The demands of the overseas markets for goods also encouraged manufacturers to search for ways to increase their production. England also had many of the natural resources necessary for industrial development. These included coal, iron ore, and water power.

Labor Supply

England had the supply of labor that was necessary to develop new industries. Part of this manpower came from an increase in population. England's population increased by over 50 per cent from 1750 to 1801. Other laborers came to England from Ireland and Scotland.

Changes in Agriculture

For many years English farmers had owned (or worked as permanent tenants) small strips of land in open fields. A farmer's holdings were not united but were scattered in different parts of the field. There were also special areas that were set aside for the use of all. These "common lands" could be used for grazing cattle, gathering firewood, and other purposes.

In the sixteenth, seventeenth, and the first half of the eighteenth century, this system of farming was gradually eliminated by the *enclosure* movement. By the enclosure movement, the farmers' scattered strips of land were combined and fenced in, and the "common lands" were brought under the control of private individuals.

Many small farmers sold their strips to large landowners and became tenant-farmers or farm laborers. In the eighteenth century many of them left the farms and migrated to the towns. They made up a considerable proportion of the workers in the factories.

Despite this shift in farm population, people in the growing towns could still be fed, for there were many changes in agriculture after 1700. Important improvements came with better methods of planting seed, rotating crops, and breeding cattle. The result was an increase in production of crops and meat animals. Machinery developed in the Industrial Revolution further improved agricultural production.

Creative Men, the Special Factor

A land free from destruction, plus wealth, natural resources, and labor supply—all these were important factors in helping England to become the center for the Industrial Revolution. But they were not enough. Something else was needed to spark the industrial process. That "something special" was *men*—creative individuals who could invent machines, find new sources of power, and establish business organizations to reshape society.

The men who created the machines of the Industrial Revolution came from many backgrounds and many occupations. Many of them were more *inventors* than *scientists*. A man who is a pure scientist is primarily interested in doing his research accurately. He is not necessarily working so that his findings can be used.

An inventor or one interested in *applied* science is usually trying to make something that has a concrete use. He may try to solve a problem by using the theories of science or by experimenting through trial and error. Regardless of his method, he is working to obtain a specific result: the construction of a harvesting machine, the burning of a light bulb, or one of countless other objectives.

Most of the men who developed the machines of the Industrial Revolution were inventors, not trained scientists. A few were both scientists and inventors. Even those who had little or no training in science might not have made their inventions if a groundwork had not been laid by scientists years before.

■ **Check on Your Reading**

1. Why did the Industrial Revolution begin in England?
2. What is the difference between a scientist and an inventor?
3. Why were inventors essential to the Industrial Revolution?

3. Inventors Set the Textile Industry Spinning

In England the textile industry, especially the production of cotton goods, was the first to expand as a result of new machines. John Kay's invention of the "flying shuttle" in the 1730's may be used as a starting point for this exciting story of industrial growth. Kay's "flying shuttle" lessened the amount of labor necessary for weaving cloth. It was followed by a number of equally important inventions.

James Hargreaves and the "Spinning Jenny"

In the 1760's James Hargreaves invented the "spinning jenny." Previously, there had been a simple, one-thread spinning wheel. Hargreaves' machine made it possible for one wheel to operate eight spindles. (Spindles were revolving rods which twisted fibers into yarn.) The "spinning jenny" produced far more yarn than the old spinning wheel.

A number of textile workers were afraid of what we call *technological unemployment*, that is, unemployment that results from technical progress in the use of machinery. They feared that the sweetly-named "jenny" would be cruel enough to deprive them of their work as spinners. James Hargreaves was rewarded for his efforts by having a mob break into his house, threaten his life, and drive him from town! In some places rioting workers destroyed the new machinery.

Richard Arkwright, the Water Frame, and the Rise of Factories

About 1769 Richard Arkwright showed the value of the water frame, although he probably did not invent this machine. The water frame had sets of revolving rollers that pulled out and stretched the cotton fibers. As a result, it turned out a tighter yarn than that produced by the "spinning jenny."

The fact that the water frame was a large machine driven by water power and requiring considerable space made the use of factories necessary. Workers had to come to the machine instead of operating small machines in their homes. Arkwright, who set up water frames in a number of mills in England, is therefore credited with being one of the founders of the "factory system." Richard Arkwright was also a clever businessman.

■ *James Hargreaves' "spinning jenny"*
(a replica)

■ *Richard Arkwright's carding engine (1775)*

■ *Eli Whitney's cotton gin (a model)*

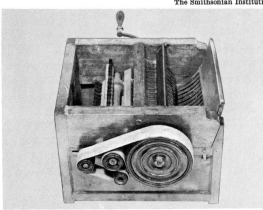

Samuel Crompton and the "Spinning Mule"

Samuel Crompton in 1778 combined some of the points of the water frame with others of the "spinning jenny." The result was a machine called the "spinning mule." The "mule" was easier to run than Arkwright's water frame. It also produced better results. What was equally remarkable, the "mule" could spin a thread 300,000 yards long from a single pound of cotton.

Edmund Cartwright and the Power Loom

In 1787 Edmund Cartwright completed a rather clumsy power loom to weave cloth from the thread produced by the spinning machines. In the 1820's a more efficient power loom was marketed. After 1830 a considerable amount of hand weaving was replaced by the work of power looms.

Eli Whitney, the Cotton Gin, and Interchangeable Parts

About 1793 Eli Whitney, who once was the only person in the United States making ladies' hat-pins, invented the cotton gin. Whitney's cotton gin made it possible to separate the seeds from cotton fibers by machine. It could work as rapidly as fifty men laboring by hand. Abundant and cheaper supplies of raw cotton could now be sent to the factories. The American South and the whole textile industry were radically affected.

Perhaps an even more important contribution to the Industrial Revolution was Eli Whitney's development of the technique of using uniform and interchangeable parts in the manufacture of rifles. This

■ *These inventions aided the development of the textile industry in England. With the cotton gin, abundant supplies of raw cotton could be sent to the textile factories. With the "spinning jenny" and the carding engine, raw cotton could be manufactured into yarn at a much faster rate.*

448

made it possible to assemble and turn out guns in large numbers. Today Eli Whitney is recognized as one of the founders of *mass production*, the true basis of our modern factory system.

"Flying shuttle"—"spinning jenny"—"mule"—these and other early machines of the Industrial Revolution increased tremendously the export value of England's cotton manufactures. (In 1835 England produced over 60 per cent of the cotton cloth manufactured in the world.) These machines eventually led to the gradual movement of people from the home to the factory.

Watt's Invention Sends Industries "Full Steam Ahead"

The Industrial Revolution made it obvious that if the hand were quicker than the eye, the machine was more powerful than the hand. Few machines demonstrated this more clearly than the steam engine.

In the early part of the eighteenth century Thomas Newcomen had invented a type of engine run by steam. However, it was neither very efficient nor economical. It remained for James Watt to develop by 1769 a really workable steam engine.

Watt had gone through moments of discouragement and despair. At one point he wrote: "Of all things in life, there is nothing more foolish than inventing." But the spark within him drove him. When his steam engine was marketed in 1776, its fourteen strokes per minute became the pulse beat for new industrial growth.

Crown copyright, Science Museum, London

■ *This is a model of James Watt's steam engine. The steam-driven piston at left causes rotation of the wheel through the movement of the beam, connecting rod, and crank shaft.*

Watt's steam engine was important for several reasons: (1) It made it possible to establish mills anywhere. Previously mills had to be built near streams to obtain water power. (2) It helped industries to expand tremendously. (3) It contributed to development of new means of transportation. A monument was erected to Watt's memory in Westminster Abbey hailing him as one of the "real benefactors of the world."

■ Check on Your Reading

1. What changes did the new machines bring to the textile industry? to workers?

2. How did the new textile machines affect the economy of England?

3. Why was the steam engine important?

4. Iron—the Backbone of the Industrial Revolution

Steam was the heart, and iron was the backbone of the Industrial Revolution.

Abraham Darby Uses Coke in the Making of Iron

For many years charcoal had been used as a fuel for the smelting of iron. A serious lack of the woods that served as the basis for making charcoal threatened the future of the iron industry in England. It was therefore fortunate that about 1735 Abraham Darby worked out a method of using coke to make iron. The substitution of coal for charcoal stimulated coal mining, increased iron production, and aided industries requiring iron.

Henry Cort Improves Iron Production

Henry Cort was next to contribute to the growth of the iron industry. In 1784 Cort developed a method of using "puddling furnaces" to change pig iron into wrought iron. Pig iron was iron cast in molds as it first came from the ore. Wrought iron was iron that was ready to shape. Cort's process made it possible to produce more and better iron than before.

Sir Henry Bessemer Makes Steel

Henry Cort's puddled iron was very useful in industry. However, after the middle of the nineteenth century, the demand increased for a metal that could withstand tension and strain better than iron. That metal was steel.

In those days it was difficult to produce good steel inexpensively. What was to be done? Sir Henry Bessemer in England, William Kelly in America, and others set about answering this question. Bessemer was convinced that he could make steel from iron by using blasts of air to clear molten pig iron of most of its impurities. "The whole scheme [is] the dream of a wild enthusiast," wrote one newspaper. Many others refused to take Bessemer seriously.

Nevertheless, in 1856 Bessemer succeeded in his efforts. His "Bessemer converter" blew air through molten pig iron at a tremendous pressure, and the oxygen in this air burned out most of the impurities from the iron. The "Bessemer converter" made steel from pig iron in twenty to thirty minutes. It also lowered the cost of producing steel from two hundred dollars to about four dollars a ton. Eight years later, another method of making steel was invented by Pierre Martin (French)—the Siemens-Martin "open-hearth process."

■ Check on Your Reading

1. Why was the substitution of coal for charcoal in smelting iron so important?

2. Why is steel superior to iron? Explain the Bessemer process of making steel.

5. Transportation and Communication

The growth of industry required that people and places be linked together. Unfortunately, the conditions of the roads during the early part of the eighteenth century blocked rather than encouraged the movement of people and goods.

Improvements in Road Building

English roads were narrow, poorly maintained, and often both impassable and impossible. According to the English writer Daniel Defoe, after a heavy rain the water remained on the roads "as in a dish," and horses sank in it "up to their bellies." Roads were so dangerous that men sometimes wrote their wills before starting on a journey. And coach travel was so slow that a print of the time showed a sailor with a wooden leg refusing a ride on a coach "because he was in a hurry."

In the seventeenth and eighteenth centuries England made some efforts to improve conditions. Individuals and private companies ("Turnpike Trusts") were encouraged by Parliament to construct and improve roads. As a reward for their efforts, they were permitted to charge tolls. Although the "Turnpike Trusts" did not develop an orderly or properly supervised system of highways, at least they made some contribution to the building of English roads.

■ *This diorama illustrates the problems of transportation in the nineteenth century. The roads were narrow and often impassable. The horses of the stagecoach were frightened by steam-operated vehicles (right). Other means of transportation included railroad trains and bicycles.*

Even more important were the attempts made to improve the surface of the roads. Pioneers were "Blind Jack" Metcalfe, who had the wisdom to see that highways must have well-drained foundations; Thomas Telford, who built roads in two layers; and John L. McAdam, whose "macadamized" (crushed stone) roads are well known throughout the world.

As a result of the work of these and other men, problems of road travel gradually began to be solved. In 1692 an advertisement declared:

There is an admirable [convenience] . . . to travel from London, the like of which has not been known in the world; and that is, by stage-coaches . . . the stage-coaches called "Flying Coaches" make forty or fifty miles a day.

By 1775, "Flying Coaches" were covering the then amazing distance of one hundred miles a day. The better road surfaces helped account for the improvement.

Like the improvement in roads, the increased construction of canals in England after 1760 was a major stimulus to industrial growth. Since they provided routes for the inexpensive shipment of coal and iron ore, canals were in many ways even more important than roads. Nevertheless, roads and canals could not meet all of the needs of the Industrial Revolution. Faster means of transportation had to be developed.

The Railroad Links Men by Land

The railroad with its steam locomotives proved to be the principal answer to the problem of developing faster transportation. The early experiments with locomotives merely stirred up the fear and ridicule of many people. "Good gracious," cried a woman, when she saw one of the first engines, "What will be done next? I can't compare [that engine] to anything but a walking puffing devil!"

Inventor George Stephenson was called "mad" and "out of his senses" when he

451

■ *This railroad excavation was cut through Mount Oliva on the Liverpool and Manchester Railway, the first all-steam railroad (1830).*

tried to construct a successful locomotive. Stephenson answered his critics with the words, "One locomotive is worth fifty horses"—and went on with his work.

In 1814 he built an engine that could pull thirty tons uphill at the speed of four miles an hour. Then, in a trial run in 1829, one of his steam locomotives reached the then extraordinary speed of twenty-nine miles an hour. Stephenson named this engine the *Rocket*.

By about 1850 Great Britain had over six thousand miles of railroad track. Goods could be shipped to and from industrial centers. Men could move more rapidly throughout the country. Distant regions could be linked. And all because of those remarkable "walking puffing devils."

The Steamboat Links Men by Water

Steam power could be used on water as well as on land. This fact had been demonstrated even before the coming of the railroad. A Frenchman, an Englishman, a Swiss, and a Russian all had done important work on the development of the steamboat. Then Robert Fulton, an American, proved that the steamboat could be of commercial value.

In 1807 Fulton's famous *Clermont* steamed up the Hudson River. An observer reported the amazement of the people who watched this steamboat from the banks or who heard about its journeys:

Some imagined it to be a sea monster, whilst others did not hesitate to express their belief that it was a sign of the approaching judgment. . . . the whole country talked of nothing but the sea monster, belching forth fire and smoke.

The black smoke, the fearful fire, the rushing fury of the paddle wheels—these heralded the coming of great days in water travel. In 1838 the *Great Western*, a steamship, crossed the Atlantic in a little over two weeks. After about 1860 steamboats gradually began to replace sailing ships in sea transportation.

The Telegraph and Cable Help Men Communicate

As men came into closer touch by land and sea, they also were joined together by electricity. Carl Steinheil, Sir Charles Wheatstone, and Samuel F. B. Morse helped to develop the electric telegraph. This made it possible to send messages by making and breaking the current in an electric circuit. Morse's first telegraph line, between Washington and Baltimore, was opened in 1844. The first message on the line was: "What hath God wrought!"

In 1866 Cyrus W. Field was successful in laying a cable under the Atlantic Ocean.

■ *The Britannia, a wooden paddle-wheel steamship built in 1840, was a pioneer in the Cunard Line's transatlantic mail service.*

This permitted the sending of telegraphic messages across the ocean. A cable between Europe and the United States was of tremendous value. As one American President, James Buchanan, said:

[Laying an Atlantic cable] is a triumph ... far more useful to mankind than was ever won by a conqueror on the field of battle.

The Stream of Invention Flows On

When would the stream of inventions and discoveries stop? In 1876 Alexander Graham Bell excited men with his successful demonstration of the telephone. Three years later, Thomas Edison made blazing news with his electric incandescent light. The *New York Herald* hailed it as:

a light that produces no [harmful] gases, no smoke, no offensive odors—a light without flame, without danger, requiring no matches to ignite ... free from all flickering ... a little globe of sunshine, a veritable Aladdin's lamp.

Outside the United States, many similar discoveries were being made. In Russia, for example, Lodigin and others did pioneer work in developing the electric light.

Still the inventions kept coming! In 1887 Gottlieb Daimler built probably the first automobile in history. In 1901 Guglielmo Marconi perfected wireless telegraphy to a point where it could send trans-Atlantic messages.

Then in 1903 the Wright brothers answered the old question "The birds can fly an' why can't I?" by making a successful flight with the airplane. (We have already seen that different men can be doing about the same work in different parts of the world. Perhaps that is one reason why the Russians today claim that A. F. Mozhaisky was the man "who built the world's first airplane.")

When did the inventions and discoveries stop? The answer is: They never did! Neither did their effects on the Industrial Revolution as it spread to other parts of the world. That is why it is impossible to say that the Industrial Revolution came to an end about 1860. Some writers even speak of a "Second" and a "Third Industrial Revolution" after that date.

As we turn to a study of the effects of inventions and discoveries on society, it would be well to recall this: There are no breaks in the story of man. There are only different rates of speed in a history that flows from past to present to future.

■ **Check on Your Reading**

1. How was road travel improved?
2. When did railroads become important? What economic effects did they have?
3. Explain the importance of the steamboat, the telegraph, the telephone, the transoceanic cable, the automobile, and plane in changing transportation and communication.

MAN AND HIS CULTURE

Let's Meet the People!

The following sketch is based on primary source materials in an article, "The Man Who Invented Just About Everything" by David A. Weiss, reprinted from *Coronet*, August 1956, and on extracts from Howe V. Underwood, "12 Federal Cases," © 1956 by Esquire, Inc., as they appear in Roger Burlingame, *March of The Iron Men*, 1949, Charles Scribner's Sons.

Walter Hunt, Inventor

In 1827 Walter Hunt invented a gong to warn pedestrians of the approach of stagecoaches. In 1833 he invented a stove to give off heat equally in all directions. In 1847 he invented the fountain pen. In 1848 he invented suction shoes to enable people to walk upside down on ceilings. In 1849 he invented the safety pin. Yet, while other people benefited from his ideas, Hunt was forced to sell many of his inventions for small sums in order to pay off his debts. Those that he kept brought him little profit.

Finally, Hunt had one last chance. Between 1832 and 1834 he had invented the first workable model of a sewing machine that could sew a lock stitch. However, it had never been patented.

In 1846 Elias Howe patented a sewing machine similar in principle to that of Walter Hunt's machine. Isaac M. Singer also manufactured the same type of sewing machine and became involved in a law suit with Howe over patent rights. Hunt believed that when the suit came to trial, he himself would surely receive reward as the first inventor of the lock-stitch sewing machine. Hunt was wrong again. The judge ruled that he was not entitled to legal rights to the machine.

It seemed that Walter Hunt would never make a fortune. However, in 1858, Isaac M. Singer called him to his office and said: "We'll give you $50,000 [in installments] for all [of your] claims against our sewing machine." Hunt accepted the offer at once. At last he would be rich. Then—shortly before the first payment was to be made— Walter Hunt died!

CHAPTER REVIEW

REVIEW and DISCUSSION

1. Identify the people and explain the events and terms on p. 444.

2. Explain how enclosures could be a disaster to one group, but profitable to another.

3. Why did the first inventions occur in the textile industry?

4. Why should Eli Whitney be held in esteem by most giant industries?

5. Are all inventors "benefactors of the world"? Why or why not?

6. Are inventions as likely to develop under a dictatorial government as they are in a democracy? Give reasons for your answer.

7. Is the adage, "Necessity is the mother of invention," really true? Apply it to each invention mentioned in this chapter.

8. Do you agree or disagree with President Buchanan that the laying of the Atlantic cable "is a triumph . . . far more useful to mankind than was ever won by a conqueror on the field of battle"? Why?

9. "The fate of man has always depended upon courage as well as brains." How does this chapter give meaning to this statement?

ACTIVITIES

1. Debate the statement: Resolved that the leisurely life of the pre-Industrial Revolution era was more desirable than the fast-moving, hectic pace of living after the Industrial Revolution.

2. If you are interested in farming, make a report on stock-breeding in England in the 1700's. Many of our breeds of hogs, horses, cattle, and sheep were developed at that time.

3. Make a chart of inventions, inventors, and the countries in which the inventions were made for the period 1750 to 1860. What are your conclusions?

PAST and PRESENT

1. When the Industrial Revolution began, men moved from the farms to the cities. Is the movement of population in the United States today still from agricultural areas to urban centers? Why?

2. What is the chief difference between the Industrial Revolution of the eighteenth century and the great industrial changes of the twentieth century?

SUGGESTED READINGS

Basic books: PALMER, R. R., and COLTON, JOEL, *A History of the Modern World*, Chap. 11, Knopf.
SMITH, GOLDWIN, *The Heritage of Man*, Chap. 26, Scribner.

Special accounts: DIETZ, FREDERICK C., *The Industrial Revolution* ("The Berkshire Studies in European History"), Holt. A brief, clearly written, and valuable account.
FORBES, ROBERT J., *Man the Maker, A History of Technology and Engineering*, Abelard-Schuman. For better readers. Chronological approach from "The Dawn of History" to the days of steel and electricity.
HARTMANN, GERTRUDE, *Machines and the Men Who Made the World of Industry*, Macmillan. Development of industry traced in this well illustrated book.
TUNIS, EDWIN, *Oars, Sails and Stream*, World Publishing. Drawings and explanations of boats from the earliest type to the "Queen Mary"; *Wheels: A Pictorial History*, World Publishing. Drawings and descriptions of wheels from the earliest types to automobiles.
VAN LOON, HENDRIK W., *Story of Inventions: Man the Miracle-Maker*, World Publishing. Easy reading. Stories of great inventions.

Biography and Fiction: MIRSKY, JEANETTE, and NEVINS, ALLAN, *The World of Eli Whitney*, Macmillan. Stresses importance of Whitney in American industry.
MONTGOMERY, ELIZABETH R., *The Story Behind Great Inventions*, Dodd, Mead. Easy to read. Biographical sketch of inventors and description of each invention.

Chapter 29   *Machines and Ideas Alter the Lives of Men*

KEYNOTE

George M. Trevelyan, a famous British historian, made this observation in the twentieth century:

Up to the Industrial Revolution, economic and social change, though continuous, has the pace of a slowly-moving stream; but in the days of Watt and Stephenson it has acquired the momentum of water over a mill-dam. . . . Nor . . . does it ever reach any pool at the bottom and resume its former leisurely advance. It is a cataract still. . . . the Industrial Revolution may yet continue [for a long time], creating and [erasing] one form of economic and social life after another.

In these words the author dramatically states two important points about the Industrial Revolution: (1) It was continuous. (2) It greatly affected and will continue to affect the people.

The first point has already been discussed in our preceding chapter. The second will be examined in the present chapter. It will then become clear that *one of the outstanding features of the Industrial Revolution was that it affected the lives of people in many ways and over a long period of time.*

Key People   *Adam Smith · Claude Henri de Saint-Simon · François Fourier ·
Robert Owen · Karl Marx · Friedrich Engels*

Key Events   *Social effects of the factory system   ·   Corporations developed   ·
Industrial Revolution spreads   ·   Trusts and cartels formed   ·
Wealth of Nations written · Factory Act of 1833 · Education
Act of 1870 · Labor unions organized · Co-operative movement ·
Socialist experiments · * Communist Manifesto *written*

Key Terms   *domestic system · mass production · capitalism · corporation ·
cartel · division of labor · laissez faire · socialism ·
communism · proletariat*

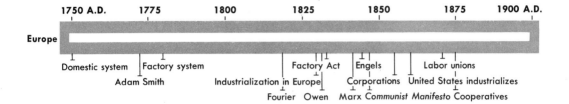

1750 A.D.	1775	1800	1825	1850	1875	1900 A.D.

Europe

Domestic system | Factory system | Factory Act | Engels | Labor unions
Adam Smith | Industrialization in Europe | Corporations | United States industrializes
Fourier Owen | Marx Communist Manifesto Cooperatives

1. Machines Change Their Masters' Lives

Dr. Erasmus Darwin made this prophecy in 1791:

Soon shall thy arm, unconquered steam, afar
Drag the slow barge, or drive the rapid car.

In many ways it came true during the Industrial Revolution. Machines sped through the land, overcame the resistance of the sea, and prepared to meet the challenge of the air. The machines of the Industrial Revolution had been designed to be the servants of man. Too often, however, they changed the lives of their masters.

The Domestic System

In 1750 most of the people in England grew their own food and made their own clothing. There was some organized manufacturing, but it was usually on a small scale. In several areas the *domestic system* (or *putting-out system*) was used to manufacture goods. It had been introduced to the textile industry of England as early as the sixteenth century. This is how the domestic system worked.

An employer, sometimes called a "merchant capitalist" or a "factor," provided the raw materials to the worker, who labored in his own home and made the finished product. His machinery was hand-operated and often was owned by the

worker. The employer paid the worker for his labor, collected the finished product, and sold it for profit.

Men, women, and children labored in their own homes. Some of them farmed the land in addition to turning out goods. Many others spent nearly all of their time in their cottages spinning, weaving, or making things by hand.

The Factory System Replaces the Domestic System

The Industrial Revolution gradually brought an end to the domestic system. New inventions and sources of power—particularly the development of large, power-driven machinery—made it necessary for the factory to take the place of the home in industry. They also created a need for a division of labor in the factory, in place of the situation where one person might do all the work himself.

The change was not a sudden break with the past. Workers under the old domestic system were already familiar with industrial labor. It was not too difficult for them to transfer their work to the new factory system. In some countries, a simple factory system had existed in some industries at the same time that the domestic system flourished. Workers went to a factory or

457

■ *Young children are shown performing heavy labor in an English coal mine about 1840. Conditions in the coal mines were wretched.*

a large workshop where a great many of them worked for the owner, each doing some work by hand or using a simple hand-operated machine. The silk industry of France, the Low Countries, and Prussia was operated this way. Cannon foundries and shipbuilding yards were also run under this system.

In time, the beginnings of the modern factory system replaced both the domestic system and the earlier factory system. Under the modern factory system, as it first developed, the factory, tools, and materials were generally owned by *capitalists*, who hired the workers. (*Capital* is wealth used to produce additional wealth. Men who used their factories, tools, and materials [or wealth] to turn out more goods are called capitalists.) Work was done in factories, rather than in homes. The workers labored in the same establishment, rather than separately in different places. A division of labor appeared in factories.

After about 1780, an increasing number of men, women, and children left their homes to seek work in factories and mines. They came for many reasons: (1) Some had lost their farms by the enclosure movement and wanted jobs. (2) Some were part of the labor surplus that resulted from the rapid increase in population. (3) Others were immigrants from Ireland who sought jobs in industry. (4) Still others, particularly children, were paupers who were assembled by unfair tactics. The factory towns developed into important industrial centers in England, France, Belgium, the Netherlands, and Prussia.

The Factory System: Good or Evil?

When the workers moved to the factories and mines, their ways of living came to depend on the treatment they received in the new industrial centers. How were they treated in the factories and mines during the Industrial Revolution? At one time the answer generally given to this question was: "With unbelievable harshness!"

There was considerable evidence to support this view. Factory discipline was very strict, and a worker could even be fined for "leaving his oil can out of place." Wages were low for most workers, and some women and children labored for as little as two dollars a week—or less. Factories had few safety devices, and little attention was paid to preserving the health of workers. Housing for workers was usually wretched. In famous "Frying-pan Alley" (London), houses were built over sewers. According to the British government's *Report on the State of Large Towns and Populous Districts*, one tenant told an investigator:

That hole [in this room] is over a common sewer and the rats come up, sometimes twenty at a time, and if we did not watch for them they would eat the baby up.

Women and children worked in the coal mines from twelve to sixteen hours a day. If they fell asleep at their work, they could be beaten with the "billy roller," a heavy rod. Some of the children were only four and five years old.

On the other hand, recent scholarship indicates that conditions may not have been as bad in English factories and mines as once was believed. Certainly, only the worst abuses received publicity, and there were a number of laborers who had satisfactory working conditions. One can conclude that the factory system in England was accompanied by many abuses in factories and mines, but that living and working conditions were not evil everywhere.

They varied with the time, the place, and the employer.

■ Check on Your Reading

1. Explain the domestic system.
2. What were the features of the factory system?
3. Describe early working conditions.

2. The Industrial Revolution and the World

In time, the Industrial Revolution spread to other countries from England. The industrialization of countries developed at different times and at different rates of speed.

Europe Becomes Industrialized

Belgium was one of the first countries to use new machines and techniques to develop industry. It had natural resources, such as coal and iron, and skilled workers necessary for industrialization. A leading industry was the making of cloth.

After 1825, France slowly made progress in industry. It had skilled workers and natural resources, which favored industrial growth. French factories were small and usually owned by individuals. French luxury goods, such as silks, linens, perfumes, and gloves, were well known. The rate of industrial growth increased after 1855, with major industrial expansion after 1890.

Germany made headway in developing her industries between 1850 and 1860. Textile and steel industries developed after 1850. After Germany became a united nation in 1871, industrialization occurred rapidly. The Germans were skilled in applying science to industry, and by 1910 Germany was Britain's chief competitor.

Spain and Italy remained agricultural countries even though they did have some mineral resources to develop industry. Northern Italy developed some industries after Italy became a united nation in 1861.

Russia, a European and Asian country, had its principal development in industry after 1890. It had many mineral resources but it lacked capital, a supply of free labor, and the skills for early industrial growth.

United States: A Great Industrial Nation

Industry became important in the United States after 1860 as textile, steel, and shoe industries developed. Why did the United States become a great industrial nation? (1) It had a wealth of natural resources, including coal, oil, and iron. (2) Immigrants from many countries were a ready source of labor for the growing industries. (3) Some Americans had inventive skills and the ability to apply science to industry. For example, Charles Goodyear experimented with rubber, and Charles Hall discovered an inexpensive process for making aluminum. (4) Some Americans had excellent business skills. Men like Andrew Carnegie and John D. Rockefeller built great empires in steel and oil.

(5) In the twentieth century, methods of mass production were perfected. By these methods, parts of a product were turned out in large numbers in standard forms and quickly assembled into finished articles. Henry Ford was a pioneer in using mass production for automobile manufacturing. By 1918 the United States had become the leading industrial nation in the world, producing great quantities and varieties of goods.

■ *This is a hand-powered moving assembly line at the Ford Motor Company plant in Highland Park, Michigan, in 1913. An engine is being placed on one of the cars' chassis which are moving along the assembly line.*

Industry in Latin America, Asia, Africa, and the Middle East

Modern methods of industrialization were introduced to the Latin American countries in the nineteenth century. However, it required World War I and World War II to provide real stimulation to industrial growth. Many countries in Latin America remain underdeveloped today.

As late as 1939 only one major nation in Asia was highly industrialized. That nation was Japan. Japan had adopted modern industrial methods in the latter part of the nineteenth century. Today she is an important competitor among the leading industrial countries.

India was active in the cotton and jute industries, but by 1939 she was still primarily an agricultural country. And China's lack of sufficient industrialization was one of the most serious problems faced by the Communists when they took control of the country in 1949 (p. 696).

Countries in Africa and the Middle East did not seriously attempt to industrialize until comparatively recent times. In some regions, the functions of machines are still not clearly understood today. One of the great problems of the many newly independent African states is how to modernize their economies.

Results of the Industrial Revolution

The industrialization of countries took place at different times and at different rates of speed. Great areas are still not industrialized, and the drive of nations to "catch up" in industrialization is an important factor in modern international relations.

In countries where the Industrial Revolution did occur, the results were important: (1) It increased greatly the production of goods. (2) It strengthened the importance of urban centers, and supported the growth of commerce. (3) It made more workers dependent for their income on wages paid by employers, while the wealth and political influence of industrial capitalists increased. (4) It brought new problems of housing, urban development, health, and the use of leisure time.

(5) The Industrial Revolution also stimulated countries to obtain overseas territories as sources of raw materials and as markets. (6) And it broke down many of the old customs and traditions of the people.

■ Check on Your Reading

1. What countries experienced the Industrial Revolution before 1900? after 1900? What countries are still underdeveloped?

2. Which do you consider the most important results of the Industrial Revolution?

3. The Industrial Revolution and Business Organization

The Industrial Revolution not only affected the daily lives of the people. It also produced important changes in the way businesses were organized. The following sketch will help you understand these changes.

Earliest Forms of Business Organization

Private business was at first generally owned and operated by individuals or partners, who shared equally in the risks and rewards of an enterprise. Some merchants and businessmen were efficient. Others were careless and lacked skills of good business practices. Robert L. Heilbroner, an American economic historian, describes a fourteenth-century French fair:

... inside the tents we meet with a strange sight. Books of business, open on the table, are barely more than notebooks of transactions; a sample extract from one merchant reads: "Owed ten gulden by a man ... I forgot his name." Calculations are made largely in Roman numerals and sums are often wrong; long division is reckoned as something of a mystery and the use of zero is not clearly understood.

After the fourteenth century, however, there was an increasing number of influential capitalists in Europe.

The explorations and overseas expansion of the fifteenth and sixteenth centuries stimulated economic growth. The great increase in trade and commerce made it possible for capitalism to develop more fully. The growth of capitalism and the increase in foreign trade brought demands for more money and resources than individuals had. Therefore about 1600 joint-stock companies were organized (p. 300).

Corporations

The ownership of business enterprises remained largely with individuals or partners until about 1855. Then an organization known as the *corporation* became increasingly important.

In a modern corporation the public buys shares of *stock* in a company. "Buying shares of stock" means that a person is purchasing a part of the ownership of the company. The company generally is run for the stockholders by directors who receive payment for their services. If there are profits, they are divided among the stockholders according to the number of shares each holds. If there are debts, each stockholder generally is responsible only for his share of them—and not for all of the debts. This feature, called "limited liability," was introduced in England in 1844.

The development of *investment banks* about the middle of the nineteenth century supported the growth of corporations. These banks, particularly in France and Germany, helped to raise funds that could be invested in new enterprises.

The rise of corporations produced many significant results. Huge sums of money could be accumulated to support the growth of business, and the corporation eventually separated the people who owned a company from those who operated it. Many stockholders of large-scale corporations never even saw the factories of their companies. It was enough for such people to collect their dividends.

Combinations of Corporations

Beginning in the late nineteenth century, some corporations producing or selling the same or related products merged their interests. They formed organizations that are popularly known as *trusts*. These organizations were designed primarily to (1) permit several corporations to operate under one policy; (2) cut down costs by controlling the production or distribution of a product; (3) eliminate the competition from rival corporations; and (4) regulate the price of the goods produced.

Cartels also developed in Europe. A cartel has been defined by John W. McConnell as "a relatively loose association of businessmen in similar industries in the same or different countries who agree to control the amount and method of production and sale of their product or services." Although the terms "cartel" and "trust" often were used interchangeably in Europe, they were not technically the same. One of the principal differences is that a cartel is an association of independent business firms, while a trust is an organization that brings a number of business firms under one management.

Trusts and cartels frequently disregarded the rights of smaller companies or took advantage of the public. Laws eventually were passed to regulate or break them up. On the other hand, many large-scale corporations dealt fairly with smaller organizations. They also provided the public with necessary goods at reasonable prices.

■ **Check on Your Reading**

1. What advantages are there in corporate organization?
2. Why did some corporations combine?

4. The Industrial Revolution and Reform

The Industrial Revolution also stimulated serious discussion of the *attitudes* that men should take toward their economic system. One of the most important questions raised was this: To what extent should a government regulate the economic activities of its people?

A man named Adam Smith proposed an answer even before the factory system had grown to any extent. Smith died before many of the great changes of the Industrial Revolution. Nevertheless, his writing influenced the thinking of every generation.

The Philosophy of Adam Smith

Adam Smith (1723–1790) was a Scottish scholar who for a number of years served as a professor at the University of Glasgow. He presented many of his ideas in a book known as *The Wealth of Nations*. Adam Smith supported the idea of "laissez faire":

Every man, as long as he does not violate the laws of justice, [should be] left perfectly free to pursue his own interest his own way, and to bring both his industry and capital into competition with those of any other man, or order of men.

"Laissez faire," he believed, would promote the economic well-being of a nation by promoting the economic well-being of individuals through free competition.

Adam Smith also pointed out that "the man whose whole life is spent performing a few simple operations [under division of labor], of which the effects are perhaps always the same, or very nearly the same . . . generally becomes as stupid and ignorant as it is possible for a human creature to become." Smith declared that this would occur unless the government "takes some pains to prevent it."

In other words, Adam Smith was not opposed to all government action. Rather, he wanted to keep government interference in private affairs to a minimum.

Reformers Remove the "Keep Out" Sign

There were other men in Britain who wanted the government to take a more active part in the economic activities of the people. They were disturbed by evils in the factory system, and they wanted the government to correct many abuses. If the state refused to take action, they were determined to remove the "Keep Out" sign from economic affairs and bring about reforms themselves.

These reformers tried various methods. Some sought to pass laws to help workingmen. Others tried to establish unions, organize co-operatives, introduce socialism, or uproot the economic system.

Legislation Improves Working Conditions

The British Parliament did not blind itself to the evils that accompanied the factory system. It established parliamentary committees to investigate conditions in factories. These committees interviewed workers, supervisors, and others. Their reports stimulated some members of Parliament to work for reform. Other representatives were motivated by more practical political reasons. (After 1832, as more and more people obtained the right to vote, a politician who wished to be re-elected had to pay increasing attention to the voters!)

For these reasons, laws were passed to improve living and working conditions. These laws were approved only after a hard fight. Many members of Parliament continued to resist change.

The Factory Act of 1833 was a landmark in labor legislation. This act (1) prohibited the employment of children under the age of nine in silk mills; (2) limited children under thirteen to nine hours of work a day; and (3) set a maximum workday of twelve hours for those between the ages of thirteen and eighteen. Factory inspectors were to enforce its provisions.

Equally important, this act pointed the way to further reform. In 1847, a law was passed that limited women and children to ten hours of work a day in factories. Other significant labor laws were passed later.

In the twentieth century, legislation was approved that provided compensation to the injured worker, pensions to the old, and insurance to the unemployed and sick.

Educational Reform

The Industrial Revolution stimulated the education of adults in Scotland and England. For example, after 1823 industrial engineers and mechanics who wished to add to their education could attend Mechanics' Institutes.

Legislation was needed to strengthen education. Not until 1833 did Parliament make its first grant for public education. Even in the middle of the nineteenth century, one half of English children received no regular school training!

The Education Act of 1870 (the Forster Act) was therefore an important step forward. It provided for the establishment of secular schools where church schools were insufficient to educate all of the students. It permitted local school boards—if they wished—to establish compulsory school attendance for those between the ages of six and thirteen. In 1876, elementary education was made compulsory by law.

Labor Unions Are Organized

Some people in England believed that the establishment of *labor unions* was one of the best ways of improving the conditions of workers. Unions often strive for higher wages, shorter hours, and better working conditions for their members. They carry on much of their work by *collective bargaining*. This means that the members of the union, usually through their leaders, act as a group in bargaining with an employer. In unions there is strength. When unions do not gain their objectives by collective bargaining, they sometimes *strike*.

At the beginning of the nineteenth century labor unions were illegal in England. The wealthy tailor Francis Place, the physician Joseph Hume, and others led the fight to win recognition for unions. In 1824 Parliament finally made labor unions legal. However, there were so many labor

■ *This is a London slum area, located beneath railroad viaducts, about 1871. The houses and backyards are cramped and congested and the atmosphere is thick with train smoke.*

Drawing by Gustave Doré

disturbances that a law in 1825 practically prohibited unions from striking and from forming into permanent organizations.

Workers made some gains in the next half century, but labor unions often were checked in their efforts to organize properly and perform their functions. In 1871, the right of unions to exist was again declared by law.

In the first decade of the twentieth century, the position of labor unions finally became secure in England. The right of unions to strike peacefully also became firmly established. Today unions are of great importance in England and in many countries of the world.

Co-operatives Are Tried

Some reformers tried to improve living conditions not by legislation or labor unions but by *co-operatives*. There were several types of co-operatives. A *producers' co-operative* was generally an organization of workers to control the production and sale of the goods they turned out. The members of producers' co-operatives hoped to produce and sell their goods more advantageously than they could separately.

Far more successful were *consumers' co-operatives*. A consumers' co-operative was generally an organization of people who participated in the purchase of goods and the resale of such goods to members of the co-operative (and often nonmembers). The members of a consumers' co-operative hoped to obtain good merchandise at less expense than if they bought separately.

Efforts to establish co-operatives won the support of important men in Great Britain. Co-operatives also became quite successful among farmers' organizations in Denmark, Sweden, Norway, and Finland. In 1950, five years after the end of World War II, co-operatives of all types had a total membership of about seventy-five million people in thirty-six countries.

■ **Check on Your Reading**

1. Explain the ideas of Adam Smith.
2. Why were laws enacted?
3. How did labor unions and co-operatives try to help workers and consumers?

464

5. Socialism and Communism Offer Different Solutions

The gains made by workers through legislation, labor unions, and co-operatives did not satisfy some reformers. They believed that several basic features of capitalism—such as continual competition among men—were evil. They wanted to eliminate abuses of the capitalist system.

Many of these people were *socialists*, and the system they favored is known as *socialism*. Although they differed, the socialists in general: (1) protested against excessive competition among men for private profit; (2) believed that private property had resulted in evils; (3) wanted the public to own many of the means of production (such as factories and mines), and the means of distribution (such as railways and ships); (4) wanted consumer goods (such as homes and clothing) to continue to be owned privately; (5) wanted each person to work according to his ability and receive according to his work; and (6) believed in attaining their goals by peaceful, gradual, and constitutional means.

Utopian Socialists

Some of the more idealistic socialists are known as the *Utopian Socialists*. There were many different groups of Utopian Socialists, and they did not agree on all of their aims. In general, they wanted to establish ideal and self-sufficient societies, or *Utopias*. (The word "Utopia" comes from the title of a sixteenth-century book by an English statesman, Sir Thomas More. It refers to a place or situation of ideal perfection, usually impossible to attain.) The Utopias of the nineteenth century wanted to eliminate poverty, unhappiness, and conflict. The members of these societies were to (1) use reason to free themselves from all greed, selfishness, and desire for private gains; (2) own or control together many of the means of producing and distributing goods; (3) live and labor together as a harmonious community; or, in the words of the French Utopian Saint-Simon, "behave as brothers to each other"; and (4) share together the fruits of their labor. The Utopian Socialists believed that the success of such communities would encourage capitalists to turn over their holdings to similar communal societies.

The dream of a perfect community was not a new one. In ancient times, the Greek philosopher Plato had suggested that property should be communally owned. Between 1600 and 1700, there were nine important books about Utopias.

In the first half of the nineteenth century the Frenchmen, Claude Henri de Saint-Simon (1760–1825) and François Fourier (1772–1837), and the British industrialist Robert Owen (1771–1858) were outstanding Utopian Socialists. However, the several Utopian communities that were set up in Europe and America were not permanently successful. They would last for a time, then break up as the members disputed over various problems.

Despite the ultimate failure of their communities, the Utopian Socialists stirred up considerable debate over the need for changing society. They prepared the ground for the more revolutionary seeds.

Some Men Seek to Uproot the Economic System

The word "radical" has meant different things to different people. Actually, it comes from the Latin "radix"—meaning "root." A radical, therefore, is a person who wishes to solve a problem by going to its roots. He wants immediate, fundamental, and extreme changes made in government and society. Two of the most important radicals of the nineteenth century were Karl Marx and Friedrich Engels.

Karl Marx Searches for Ways to Slay the "Monsters"

Karl Marx (1818–1883) was a thick-set, broad-shouldered, heavily bearded man who was dedicated to his work. He would study even when his body was tormented by carbuncles, boils, and a lung tumor.

Karl Marx worked hard to do something about the evils in the world. He protested against people who "make-believe that there are no monsters." To Marx, the abuses of society were monsters.

Born in the Rhine province of Prussia, Marx spent time in several countries. Wherever he went, he searched for the answer to the world's problems. He read the writings of Locke and Voltaire. He studied at German universities. And he discussed his ideas with other men, sometimes in a rather dogmatic manner.

Marx exchanged ideas especially with Friedrich Engels (1820–1895), who also was born in the Rhine province. Engels vividly described many of the shocking conditions of workers in the *Condition of the Working Class in England in 1844*. Then Marx and Engels wrote the revolutionary *Communist Manifesto* (1848). Marx later wrote the first volume of his famous book, *Capital* (1867). Engels, working from Marx's manuscript but contributing ideas, edited two more volumes of *Capital*. These and other writings by Marx and Engels, with additions made by the Russian Vladimir Lenin (1870–1924), form the basis for the present-day economic-social-political philosophy known as *communism*.

The Philosophy of Karl Marx

The major ideas of Karl Marx and his disciples, with the objections raised by scholarly critics, are discussed below.

1. ECONOMIC INTERPRETATION OF HISTORY. Marxists took the view that the events and institutions of society and history are basically determined by *economic* forces. Thus the method by which man produces and exchanges goods is said to be the foundation for his political, social, religious, and cultural activities.

Objections: The economic interpretation oversimplifies history. Certainly, there have been major events that were *not* based primarily on economics. The growth of the Christian Church is one example.

2. SURPLUS VALUE THEORY. The Marxists took the view that the value of the goods produced rests on the "human labor" that goes into their production. Despite the fact that workers produce the goods, they receive only low wages. Most of the profit that comes from the sale of the goods is taken by the *capitalists*, the men who own the factories and the other means of production. Thus, the capitalists grow richer and the workers poorer.

Objections: Economists point out that there are *many* people who give value to goods by providing buildings, tools, materials, and ideas to help produce goods. "Capitalists," too, are entitled to reward.

Moreover, despite some areas of poverty that have necessitated anti-poverty legislation, the poor are not growing poorer in the United States or in most industrialized countries of Europe. With the growth of unions, collective bargaining, and labor legislation, American workers generally are given a substantial part of the value of the goods they produce.

It is true that there is still great poverty in Asia, the Middle East, Africa, and in other places. But these areas are mainly agricultural, not industrial. Indeed, as Milovan Djilas, a once prominent Communist leader who broke with the Communist party of Yugoslavia, has pointed out, "Marx's theories about the increasing impoverishment of the working class were not borne out by developments in those countries [industrialized Europe] from which his theories [were] derived."

466

3. CLASS STRUGGLE. The Marxists took the view that inevitably there is a continuous struggle between the *proletariat* (the wage workers) and the *bourgeoisie* (those who own or control the means of production and exchange). This class struggle is a bitter and hateful one.

Thus, Marx and Engels wrote in the *Communist Manifesto*, "The history of all hitherto existing society is the history of class struggles. Freeman and slave, patrician and plebeian, lord and serf . . . in a word, oppressor and oppressed."

Objections: Marxists completely overlooked the rise of the vast *middle class*, including industrial workers receiving good wages, salaried workers engaged in basically nonmanual jobs, professional people, and many others. A recent survey conducted by *Fortune* magazine showed that 80 per cent of Americans list themselves as members of the middle class. This middle class has served as a balancing factor to prevent great extremes which Marx counted upon to bring about the class struggle.

4. USE OF FORCE. The Marxists took the view that the proletariat have the right to use force to overthrow the bourgeoisie and seize control of a country. Karl Marx admitted that in certain countries (like the United States and England) the proletariat might attain their objectives without violence. However, Marx believed in the general necessity for the use of force.

Objections: Violence destroys men physically. It degrades the role that reason can play in the settlement of problems. It fails to see that major changes can be made peacefully in democratic societies.

5. DICTATORSHIP OF THE PROLETARIAT. The Marxists took the view that after the proletariat overthrow the bourgeoisie by force there will be a temporary period in which the proletariat dictates to the bourgeoisie until all opposition is wiped out.

Class distinctions will be abolished and a classless society will emerge.

Objections: What has resulted has been the dictatorship of a small group of men in the Communist party over the proletariat and over everyone else in the country. Instead of being temporary, the Russian dictatorship has already lasted five decades. Indeed a "new class" of Communist bureaucrats has arisen. Such dictatorship has led to frantic efforts to escape on the part of millions of people.

6. THE ESTABLISHMENT OF COMMUNISM. Marxists took the view that during the period of dictatorship of the proletariat, the state "withers away" and communism eventually is established. Under communism: (1) There would be only public ownership of the means of production, distribution, and consumption. This would eliminate competition among men for profit. Since there would be no classes there would be no class struggle. (2) Each person would work according to his ability and receive according to his need, as directed by the people for the good of all.

Objections: Communism in practice has seen a constant strengthening of the power and size of governments rather than a withering away. The result has been more regulation and an increasing bureaucracy rather than less. The ideal of "from each according to his ability, to each according to his need" still lies in the distant future rather than in the regimented present. It is ironical that the ideas of Marx, to whom the all-powerful state was abhorrent, should have contributed to statism.

■ **Check on Your Reading**

1. What are the basic ideas of socialism?
2. What did the various Utopian Socialists have in common?
3. What are the major ideas of Karl Marx and his followers? Discuss objections.

MAN AND HIS CULTURE

Let's Meet the People!

This sketch is based on some of William Henden's statements, which appear in *Readings in English History Drawn from the Original Sources* by Edward P. Cheyney, 1922, Ginn and Company.

William Henden, An English Factory Worker

At nineteen William Henden's face and body bore the marks of a life of hard work. William Henden of Leeds, England, had begun to work at the age of six in John Good's woolen mill. At ten he was an experienced factory worker in Mr. Hammond's flax mill at Leeds.

William started his work at Mr. Hammond's mill at 5:30 A.M. and labored until 8 P.M. Forty minutes a day were allowed for "breakfast and dinner and drinking [of water]." William worked continually at the mill, and he never forgot what happened to him when he fell asleep at his job. As he described it, "The overlooker used to come with a strap and give us a rap or two, or if they caught us asleep they would give us a pinch of snuff till we sneezed. . . ."

William was "pretty fair in health" when he started to work at the age of six. Still, as he told a parliamentary committee investigating conditions in factories, the long hours had twisted his limbs. "State . . . the effect upon your health and limbs of those long hours of labor" the committee had asked him. "It produced a weakness in my knees," William had answered, "I was made crooked with standing the long hours." The clerk had dutifully recorded: "The witness exhibited to the committee his limbs, which appeared exceedingly crooked."

William Henden never went to day school or night school. He labored even at night, though the flickering gas lights might torture his eyes.

Little wonder that William Henden at the age of nineteen looked like an old man. He was only four feet nine inches tall, his limbs were deformed, his eyesight was failing. What work could he do?

The parliamentary committee had asked him: "What do you do now?" William Henden's answer was simple: "I sell potatoes."

CHAPTER REVIEW

REVIEW and DISCUSSION

1. Identify the people and explain the events and terms on p. 456.

2. What motives, in addition to the profit motive, stimulate economic activities?

3. How do you explain the fact that Belgium was one of the first countries in Europe to advance technologically?

4. How did mass production help the United States become one of the greatest industrial nations in the world?

5. Europe and the United States have had a long period of time to develop industrially. What problems face a country trying to industrialize rapidly?

6. Do you agree or disagree with the philosophy of Adam Smith? Why?

7. Should labor groups be active in political life? Why?

8. How can education aid a worker to improve his economic status?

9. What methods are available to labor today to achieve its goals?

10. Why were co-operatives formed in some European countries?

11. Give examples to show the differences between the following: each person working according to his ability and receiving according to his work; and each person working according to his ability and receiving according to his need.

12. Why have some men through the centuries dreamed of establishing a perfect community? Why has this goal never been attained?

13. Sometimes people confuse the terms socialism and communism. What are the essential differences?

ACTIVITIES

1. Try to find an example of single ownership, a partnership, a corporation, or a co-operative in your community.

2. Write a report on the activities of Robert Owen or Francois Fourier.

3. Re-enact a hearing that might be held by a nineteenth-century parliamentary committee investigating factory abuses.

4. Make parallel lists of the good and bad effects which resulted from the Industrial Revolution. What conclusions can you make from your study?

PAST and PRESENT

1. Write a report on any socialized industry found in Norway, Denmark, or Sweden. Consult *National Geographic Magazine, Readers' Guide*, and other references.

2. What examples of government ownership do we have on the local, state, and national levels in the United States? In your opinion, what areas of our economy should remain in private hands? Over what economic areas should the government have some control?

SUGGESTED READINGS

Basic books: CHEYNEY, EDWARD P., *Readings in English History Drawn from the Original Sources*, Nos. 370–374, Ginn.

CHEYNEY, EDWARD P., *A Short History of England*, Chap. 18, Ginn.

PALMER, R. R., and COLTON, JOEL, *A History of the Modern World*, Chap. 11, Knopf.

SMITH, GOLDWIN, *The Heritage of Man*, Chap. 26, Scribner.

Special accounts: QUENNELL, MARJORIE and CHARLES, H. B., *Everyday Things in England from 1733–1851*. Putnam. Uses source material. Makes clear the undesirable impacts of Industrial Revolution upon people.

SMITH, ADAM, *The Wealth of Nations*, Modern Library.

TREVELYAN, GEORGE M., *English Social History*, Chaps. 15 and 16, Longmans, Green.

Biography and Fiction: DICKENS, CHARLES, *Hard Times*, Dutton. Points out the unfair treatment of laborers in England; *Oliver Twist*, Dodd, Mead. Novel that presents a picture of life of people in early industrial England.

Chapter 30

The Industrial Revolution Has a Powerful Impact on Culture

KEYNOTE   During the nineteenth century, when a number of reform groups were formed in England to improve the living and working conditions of people, an organization appeared with the initials S.P.A.B. This was the Society for the Protection of Ancient Buildings.

The S.P.A.B. dedicated itself to protecting beautiful old buildings from destruction or disfigurement at the hands of men interested chiefly in industrializing England. It proclaimed its determination to save ancient architecture from "the civilized world of the nineteenth century [that] has no style of its own."

The existence of the Society for the Protection of Ancient Buildings was but one indication of the effect that the Industrial Revolution had on cultural affairs. There were many more. *One of the key features of the second half of the eighteenth and most of the nineteenth century was the impact of the Industrial Revolution on culture.*

Key People   *Thomas Malthus · Percy Bysshe Shelley · Victor Hugo · Charles Dickens · Honoré de Balzac · John Constable · Francisco Goya · Claude Monet · Pierre Auguste Renoir · Paul Cézanne · Ludwig van Beethoven · Edward Jenner · Charles Darwin*

Key Events   *Romantic movement in literature · Industrialization's impact on art · Realistic movement in literature · Impressionism in art · Pre-Raphaelite movement · Scientific discoveries · Medical advances ·* The Origin of the Species *published*

Key Terms   *"iron law of wages" · romanticism · realism · naturalism · impressionism · evolution · natural selection · Social Darwinism*

470

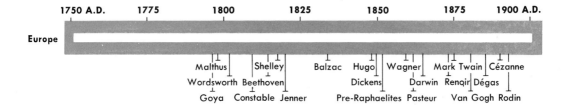

1750 A.D.	1775	1800	1825	1850	1875	1900 A.D.

Europe

Malthus | Shelley | Balzac | Hugo | Wagner | Mark Twain | Cézanne
Wordsworth Beethoven | Dickens | Darwin Renoir | Dégas
Goya Constable Jenner | Pre-Raphaelites Pasteur | Van Gogh Rodin

1. The Industrial Revolution Affects Literature

The effects of the Industrial Revolution were not limited to economic affairs. Industrial changes also influenced—and were influenced by—literature, art and architecture, music, science, and philosophy.

The Writings of Malthus and Ricardo

Some writers at the end of the eighteenth and the first part of the nineteenth century viewed with considerable pessimism the maladjustments that came with the Industrial Revolution. The English sociologist Thomas Malthus (1766–1834), for example, in his *Essay on Population* declared that poverty could not be avoided because population was increasing at a faster rate than the food supply. The British economist David Ricardo (1772–1823), in his *Principles of Political Economy and Taxation*, stated that an "iron law of wages" made it practically impossible for workers' wages to rise above the barest subsistence level. Other men took equally pessimistic views of conditions.

Romantic Writers

Other authors, known as Romantic writers, sought escape from the dreariness of daily existence by (1) revolting against artistic convention, (2) giving freedom to their emotions, and (3) fully expressing their personal feelings. The last part of the eighteenth and the first half of the nineteenth century often is called the "Romantic Period" of English Literature. In England, William Blake (1757–1827), an artist and poet, wrote poetry that expressed his misty visions of a highly imaginative world. This was particularly true of his poems in *Songs of Innocence*. The famous Scottish poet and novelist, Sir Walter Scott (1771–1832), filled his historical novels—*Ivanhoe*, *Kenilworth*, and others—with romantic adventures drawn from legend. Samuel Taylor Coleridge (1772–1834) wrote poems—such as the well-known *The Rime of the Ancient Mariner*—that were marked by a supernatural and eerie quality.

Other writers rejected life's artificialities and turned to nature. William Wordsworth (1770–1850), one of the most noted poets, and Samuel Taylor Coleridge wrote *Lyrical Ballads*. In this work, Wordsworth urged men to turn to "humble and rustic life" because "in that condition the essential passions of the heart find a better soil in which they can attain their maturity." The brilliant English poet Lord Byron (1788–1824), in *Childe Harold, Don Juan,* and other works, not only described nature

471

beautifully, but also attacked the hypocrisy of society. John Keats (1795–1821) lived only a short life, but he produced romantic poetry of great beauty. His command of language and his love of beauty dominate his famous "Ode on a Grecian Urn." In his long poem *Endymion* he wrote the famous line: "A thing of beauty is a joy forever. . . ."

In France, the poet-dramatist-novelist, Victor Hugo (1802–1885), was the leading figure of French romantic literature. Hugo's ability to analyze human behavior and to depict a variety of characters was outstanding. *Notre Dame de Paris* (*The Hunchback of Notre Dame*) and *Les Misérables* are two of his famous novels. Alexander Dumas (1802–1870) wrote historical novels of intrigue and adventure. Two of his novels, *The Three Musketeers* and *The Count of Monte Cristo*, are familiar to many readers.

In Germany, poet-dramatist-novelist Johann Wolfgang von Goethe (1749–1832) wrote several outstanding works. One of his most famous is the superb poetic drama, *Faust*. "I am ever the new-born child," Goethe said; and he wrote like a person who discovers something fresh and fascinating in the world each day.

Romanticism in American literature developed later. Washington Irving (1783–1859), sometimes called the "father of American literature," wrote such popular romantic stories as "The Legend of Sleepy Hollow" and "Rip Van Winkle." Nathaniel Hawthorne (1804–1864) wrote about the inner conflicts of men and women in his novels, *The Scarlet Letter* and *The House of the Seven Gables*. Edgar Allan Poe (1809–1849), who played a major role in the development of the short story, is famous for his tales and poetry of mystery and suspense. The poem, "The Raven," and his tales, "The Purloined Letter" and "The Pit and the Pendulum," are familiar.

A great American essayist and poet, Ralph Waldo Emerson (1803–1882), was strongly influenced by European romantic writers and mystics. Walt Whitman (1819–1892) was a product of American democracy. He glorified the plain people and their work in his poetry. He is best known for his volume of poetry, *Leaves of Grass*. In the preface he wrote: "The United States themselves are essentially the greatest poem. . . . Here at last is something in the doings of man that corresponds with the broadest doings of the day and night. Here is action untied from strings. . . ."

Voices of Protest in Britain

Some British writers used their pens as swords to fight for social and economic reforms. They described the deplorable working conditions and the effects of misery.

Percy Bysshe Shelley (1792–1822) was a magnificent romantic lyric poet who raised his voice against injustice. He was concerned with the inequalities among men. He told the working people:

> The seed ye sow, another reaps;
> The wealth ye find, another keeps;
> The robes ye weave, another wears;
> The arms ye forge, another bears.

Shelley urged people to free themselves from selfish and tyrannical masters. He wrote:

> Shake your chains to earth, like dew!
> Ye are many, they are few!

Thomas Carlyle (1795–1881) pointed out the ugly aspects of industrialization. In his book *Sartor Resartus* (*The Tailor Retailored*), he attacked these evils:

Call you that a Society [asks Professor Teufelsdröckh] where . . . each [person] . . . regardless of his neighbor, turns against his neighbor, clutches what he can get and cries, "Mine!" and calls it Peace, because in the cut-purse and cut-throat Scramble no steel knives . . . can be employed?

Charles Dickens (1812–1870), the most famous realistic English novelist of his day, had personally experienced the hardships of poverty. In his books, particularly *Hard Times*, *Oliver Twist*, and *David Copperfield*, he vividly pictured wretched living and working conditions. In *Oliver Twist*, he showed the ill treatment that children received in poorhouses and how slums bred crime and delinquency.

John Ruskin (1819 1900) was an art critic and writer as well as a social reformer. It was he who declared:

Even a laborer serves his country with his spade and shovel as the statesman does with his pen, or the soldier with his sword.

Ruskin protested against any society that robbed men of spiritual and ethical values. "The high ethical training of the nation," he warned, ". . . is . . . inconsistent with filthy or mechanical employment."

Realistic Literature in Europe and America

Realistic writers of the nineteenth century, such as Charles Dickens, tried to (1) describe the lives of people as honestly as possible, (2) give attention to the ordinary activities of men and women, and (3) stay close to the facts and details of human existence, rather than color them with romantic imagination.

French realistic literature was dominated for many years by Honoré de Balzac (1799–1850). In a series of ninety-four novels, novelettes, and short stories, called *The Human Comedy*, Balzac depicts contemporary French society. His characters show the effects of greed, misery, and self-satisfaction on their lives. Gustave Flaubert (1821–1880) helped to perfect the realistic novel. His famous work, *Madame Bovary*, is a portrait of a weak, romantic woman.

More naturalistic in his writing was Émile Zola (1840–1902). The naturalistic writers (1) attempted to be completely

Percy Bysshe Shelley

Painting by Amelia Curran.
© National Portrait Gallery, London

■ *Percy Bysshe Shelley was a magnificent romantic lyric poet. He also used his pen to fight injustice and inequalities among men.*

objective in depicting life, even if this meant showing all the ugliness in people; (2) stressed the grim, sordid, and animalistic aspects of human existence; and (3) showed how man's physical and social environment affected his life. Zola wrote twenty novels in a series known as *The Rougon-Macquart* ("The Social and Natural History of a Family under the Second Empire"), as well as other novels.

The American writer, Mark Twain (1835–1910), was a great humorist who also commented on what he considered to be evil in society. Mark Twain, who could write imaginative and romantic tales as well as realistic accounts, disliked undemocratic distinctions between people. He believed that, like certain vegetables, the differences among men were often a result of their rearing. "Cauliflower," he declared, "is nothing but cabbage with a college education." Mark Twain is well known for his novels *The Adventures of Tom Sawyer* and *The Adventures of Huckleberry Finn*. Another American author, Stephen Crane (1871–1900), wrote realistic

473

and naturalistic novels. His most famous novel is *The Red Badge of Courage.*

Henrik Ibsen (1828–1906), a Norwegian dramatist, wrote a number of realistic plays. He stirred up considerable controversy with his plays *A Doll's House* and *An Enemy of the People.* In them, he exposed the hypocrisy and false values and ideals in the society of his day.

■ **Check on Your Reading**

1. Why are Malthus and Ricardo called pessimists?
2. What qualities characterized the Romantic writers? the Realistic writers?
3. Identify: Dickens, Shelley, Hugo, Goethe, Hawthorne, Coleridge, Balzac, Flaubert, and Ibsen.
4. What was naturalistic writing? Name some naturalistic authors.

2. Art and Architecture in the Industrial Age

The growth of industry also affected the attitudes of men toward art and architecture. Most artists found little that was beautiful in industrial life. Like many romantic writers, they turned to nature and emotional events for their themes.

Romanticism in Art

In England John Constable (1776–1837) painted lovely scenes of the countryside at Suffolk and Brighton. Using unmixed colors and placing paint on the canvas in tiny strokes or dots of color, he created works that gave the *impression* of light playing over a surface. Constable's art had a considerable effect on the French Romantic artist Delacroix and later on the Impressionists.

J. M. W. Turner (1775–1851) was another superb interpreter of nature. He painted poetic landscapes in which objects seem to dissolve mysteriously into the limitless space of light (p. 486). Turner demonstrated that there can also be beauty in the relationships of mechanical objects to nature.

The leader of the French Romantic movement in painting was Eugène Delacroix (c. 1798–1863). Delacroix brought an exciting note of Romanticism to French art, choosing his subjects from literature and history (p. 498). Another French painter, Camille Corot (1796–1875), was noted for his landscape paintings into which he infused an aura of mystery and romance.

Realism in Art

Many artists turned from Romanticism to Realism. One of the earliest painters to include some realistic themes in his art was Francisco Goya (1746–1828). As the official painter of the Spanish king, he did many portraits. However, he is more famous for his etchings depicting the struggles of the Spaniards against Napoleon's army. The horror and suffering inflicted by war is pictured in many of his paintings, such as *The Third of May, 1808* (p. 418). Goya has been called a Romantic, a Realist, and other terms. However, as art historian Sarah Newmeyer points out, "he cannot be circumscribed within any or even all of those labels.... The great Spanish artist was above all an individualist...."

In France, Jean Francois Millet (1814–1875) painted scenes showing the everyday life of the peasants. For example, *The Gleaners* shows three women gleaning (gathering) grain. Gustave Courbet (1819–1877) also painted the life of the workers and peasants. Courbet's *The Stone Breakers* shows peasants removing stones from fields.

Honoré Daumier (1808–1879) kept his art close to the people. Daumier was a brilliant newspaper illustrator for many years. In his satirical drawings, he at-

474

■ *The works of art presented on the next few pages were executed between the late eighteenth and the early twentieth century. Note the changes in content and style. "The Morning Walk" (right) is by Thomas Gainsborough, the famous portrait painter of eighteenth-century England.*

■ *"The Hay Wain" (below) by John Constable (1776–1837) shows oxen drawing a wagon across a stream in a lovely English country setting. Constable depicted the changing moods of nature in a Romantic vein.*

■ *"The Bridge of Narni" by Camille Corot contains many features common to early nineteenth century Romantic painting. For example, the Roman ruins, the mysterious landscape, and the simple peasants with their animals are Romantic subjects.*

■ *Gustave Courbet's "Village Girls" shows the artist's three sisters in the country with a simple young peasant girl. Courbet was a Realist who portrayed the life of the workers and peasants as it really existed.*

476

tacked dishonesty, hypocrisy, poverty, and social injustice. He showed the strength of character of ordinary men and women.

In the United States, Winslow Homer (1836–1910), a realistic artist, painted seascapes and fishermen at work. His paintings, *The Maine Coast* and *The Herring Net*, are two of his well-known works. Another American, James McNeill Whistler (1834–1903) is famous for his oil portrait of his mother. He was particularly good at using color in his paintings.

Impressionism in Art

The movement in art known as *Impressionism* began during the 1870's. According to art historian Sarah Newmeyer, impressionism is art in which the painters "attempted to record on canvas not what they knew was form but what they saw as light." The term "Impressionists" came from a reference to a painting by the French artist Claude Monet (1840–1926) entitled *Impression, Rising Sun*. The French artist Édouard Manet (1832–1883) was the chief precursor of Impressionism. The French painters—Claude Monet, Camille Pissarro (1830–1903), and Pierre Auguste Renoir (1841–1919)—and the English artist, Alfred Sisley (1839–1899) were among the leading Impressionists (pp. 486–487).

The Phillips Collection, Washington

■ *In some of his satirical paintings and drawings Honoré Daumier sharply criticized lawyers and judges of the French courts. The satirical drawing of "Three Lawyers" is an example. To Daumier, people, not riches, were the chief possessions of society.*

The Art Institute of Chicago

■ *This well-known painting, "The Herring Net," is one of many paintings done by Winslow Homer depicting the sea and fishermen along the Atlantic coast of the United States.*

477

Impressionist art had these features. It (1) showed the momentary play of light on objects, particularly outdoor light; (2) paid more attention to primary colors than to line; (3) tried to create an impression of an action that could be gone in a moment (such as that of a woman about to take off her gloves); (4) stressed spontaneity; (5) viewed objects from unusual angles; and (6) used "undisguised" brush strokes.

Claude Monet captured the Impressionists' spirit when he said "he wished that he had been born blind and then had suddenly gained his sight so that he would have begun to paint without knowing what the objects were that he saw before him."

Some French artists who were affected by Impressionism added their distinctive

■ *In the sculpture, "The Thinker," Auguste Rodin conveys the human feelings of the subject. It stands before the Pantheon in Paris.*

features to art. Edgar Degas (1834–1917) was famous for his paintings of ballet dancers; and Toulouse-Lautrec (1864–1901) was well known for his impressions of café life.

Other artists, *post-Impressionists*, tried to correct what they considered to be deficiencies in Impressionist art. The post-Impressionists included the French artists Paul Cézanne (1839–1906) and Paul Gauguin (1848–1903), and the Dutch artist Vincent Van Gogh (1853–1890). Paul Gauguin spent the later years of his life in Tahiti. In his paintings he captured the bright colors of the tropics and obtained striking results with pure colors and design. Vincent Van Gogh poured his own feelings into his work. Flaming colors and twisting forms dominate his painting.

Paul Cézanne was to have an extremely important effect on twentieth-century art. He influenced the development of Cubism, Expressionism, and other styles; and he is often called the "father of modern art." In his paintings—which included landscapes, still life (p. 487), and figure compositions—Cézanne tried to go beyond the fleeting quality of Impressionist art and to present his impressions of objects in a more permanent manner. He used form and space with greater control than the Impressionists. He gave the light in his paintings an appearance of permanence, painted with unusually rich and full colors, and attempted to show that nature could be reduced in art to certain basic forms: the cube, cone, and cylinder. He said: "I wanted to make Impressionism into something as solid and durable as the art of the museums."

Sculpture

An outstanding sculptor was the Frenchman, Auguste Rodin (1840–1917). His figures of marble or bronze, such as *The Thinker*, are superb art works. An American, Augustus Saint-Gaudens (1848–1907),

■ *One of many paintings of ballet dancers in action and repose by Edgar Degas is the "Foyer de la Danse at the Rue de Peletier Opera." Degas showed motion by the interplay of light on the human form. Note the realistic details in this scene.*

was also a great sculptor. His marble statues of Abraham Lincoln and the Adams Memorial in Washington, D.C., are among his best works.

Industrialization Affects Society

Industrialization affected society far more than it did the work of individual artists. Two effects on society were:

Industrialization contributed to the cheapening of the tastes of many people by lessening the importance of beauty and originality in art. The cold and commonplace products of the machine often were substituted for the beautiful handmade articles of the craftsman. It also led some men to care more about the number of buildings constructed than about the gracefulness of the new structures. Most architects borrowed freely from earlier civilizations and created few new ideas. A favorite model was the medieval Gothic style.

Industrialization also contributed to the separation of art from daily life. Art was no longer an integral part of the lives of the people, but something special, to be "looked at" on occasion and guarded in museums rather than freely exposed in the homes and market places of the people. The people of the industrial countries, with the exception of men of wealth who desired and could afford art forms, were cut off

479

from regular contact with artistic beauty. Their daily surroundings were marked by ugliness.

The Pre-Raphaelite Brotherhood

The ugliness of industrial life did not go unchallenged in Britain. It stimulated some artists to join together to try to raise the standards of art. About the middle of the nineteenth century, several of these men formed the Pre-Raphaelite Brotherhood, under the leadership of poet-painter Dante Gabriel Rossetti (1828–1882). The name "Pre-Raphaelite" came from the group's belief that the standards of art could be raised by returning to the spirit and artistry of medieval painters before Raphael.

The Brotherhood's chief purpose was to improve craftsmanship, examine nature with honesty, and replace superficial work with creative activity. Its members were active in literature, too. In a sense, they were the "conscience" of the times.

■ Check on Your Reading

1. What were the principal characteristics of Romanticism, Realism, and Impressionism in art?
2. Identify: Delacroix, Constable, Daumier, Monet, Van Gogh, Goya, and Rodin.
3. What contribution did Paul Cézanne make to modern art?
4. In what way did industrialization affect art?
5. What were the aims of the Pre-Raphaelite Brotherhood?

3. Music in the Industrial Age

Music flourished in the last half of the eighteenth and in the nineteenth century, and it was also affected by industrialism.

Romanticism in Music

Romanticism in music—that is, music that was subjective and stressed the deep emotional feelings of the composer—was a powerful factor in the nineteenth century.

Ludwig van Beethoven (1770–1827), a German composer, was a genius whose works cannot all be fitted into a single type of music. As music historian Helen L. Kaufmann states: "In his improvements on the formal side, Beethoven belongs with the classical school. But his strides toward greater freedom and more individual expressiveness take him straight into the camp of the romantic composers of the nineteenth century. . . . It is best to think of Beethoven in large general terms."

Beethoven brought a strong note of Romanticism to music. He demonstrated that music could superbly express deep emotions and intense and idealistic feelings.

Beethoven composed nine symphonies, many piano sonatas, several concertos, and other musical works. Among his symphonies are the Third, or *Eroica*, and his magnificent Ninth, or *Choral*.

A German composer, Felix Mendelssohn (1809–1847), created many musical works that expressed great romantic feeling. One of his best compositions is *Overture to a Midsummer Night's Dream*. Another important work on a religious theme was *Elijah*. Hector Berlioz (1903–1869), a French composer, wrote considerable *program music*, that is, music that relates a story, depicts a character, or describes an event. His *Requiem* and *Fantastic Symphony* are well known.

Frederic Chopin (c. 1810–1849), a Polish-French composer, wrote many piano compositions. In his music he often used the rhythms of Polish peasant dances. The Hungarian Franz Liszt (1811–1886) was a superb pianist. He also composed the *Hungarian Rhapsodies.*

Richard Wagner (1813–1883), a German, was a great operatic composer. Among his famous operas are *Tristan and Isolde, Tannhäuser,* and *Lohengrin.* Wagner stressed the dramatic qualities of opera, and skillfully fused words, music, and actions into a powerful whole that reflected philosophic ideas.

Johannes Brahms (1833–1897), another German, continued the musical tradition of Beethoven. Music historian Helen L. Kaufmann declares "[Brahms] may be labelled neoclassic, but trailing scarlet robes of romanticism cling about him." Among the well-known works by Brahms are the *Lullaby, Hungarian Dances,* and *Symphony No. 4 in E Minor.*

Impressionism in Music

Impressionism became as important in music as in art. Musicologist Paul Grabbe has defined Impressionism as "a musical style which [forsakes] the bold statement of dramatic emotion in music in favor of the suggested emotion, the subtle nuance, the elusive but evocative mood."

A Frenchman, Claude Debussy (1862–1918), was stimulated by the paintings of Renoir and other Impressionists. He was determined "to free [music] from the barren traditions that stifle it." Debussy's Impressionist compositions include *Nocturnes for Orchestra* and the orchestral suite *The Sea.* One of his loveliest compositions is the tone poem *Prelude to the Afternoon of a Faun.*

■ **Check on Your Reading**

1. What characteristics did Romantic music have? Impressionist music?

2. Identify: Beethoven, Mendelssohn, Berlioz, Chopin, Wagner, Brahms, and Debussy.

4. Science Advances Rapidly

Scientists in Denmark, England, and France had done significant work on magnetism and electricity. Then in 1831 Michael Faraday (1791–1867) in England and Joseph Henry (1797–1878) in the United States discovered that electricity could be generated from magnetism.

This extremely important discovery led imaginative men to devise valuable inventions: the dynamo, the telegraph, and the telephone. It also contributed indirectly to the development of the electric light, the radio, and other inventions.

Science also contributed greatly to the protection and saving of human lives.

For example, smallpox had spread terror, tragedy, and death. Men had given up the hope of ever conquering this dread disease. Then Edward Jenner (1749–1823), an English physician, developed a method of vaccination against smallpox. The disease at last could be checked.

Edward Jenner was just one of many scientists and physicians who added to knowledge. There were many more: for example, Lavoisier in the field of quantitative chemistry and Pasteur and Koch in the area of bacteriology. Antoine Lavoisier (1743–1794) is often called the "father of modern chemistry." He proved that burning was a result of a chemical combination in which the burning substance unites with the gas oxygen. This process is called oxidation. He also presented evidence to prove the law of conservation of matter—this is, matter can neither be created nor destroyed but can only be changed from one form into another.

Louis Pasteur (1822–1895), a French bacteriologist, disproved the theory of "spontaneous generation"—that is, living things can be produced from inanimate matter—which was held by scientists of his day. He discovered that certain tiny living organisms, called bacteria, visible under a microscope, could cause disease. He developed a vaccination to prevent rabies (hydrophobia) in man and animals. The German physician Robert Koch (1843–1910) discovered the germs that cause the diseases tuberculosis and Asiatic cholera.

Charles Darwin's Theory of Evolution

The man who raised the greatest scientific and intellectual controversy was the English scientist Charles Darwin (1809–1882). He was a great *naturalist*, that is, one who carefully observes nature and the ways of plants and animals.

In 1859 Darwin startled the scholars of the world with his book *The Origin of Species*. In 1871 another of Darwin's major works, *The Descent of Man*, was published. The impact was sensational.

Darwin's writings stimulated much discussion about the theory of evolution (see Chart), and possible changes in the relationship between religion and science.

Alfred Russel Wallace, an English naturalist, developed a similar theory independently about the same time.

Some people accepted the theory of evolution. Others considered it basically correct but insisted that several points had not been proved. Still others rejected Darwin's theory because it contradicted certain aspects of the story of creation in the Bible.

The ideas of Charles Darwin had a great impact. They helped to destroy the idea that life was fixed, rigid, and without change.

THE THEORY OF EVOLUTION

All forms of life are descended from previous forms. The ancestry of each living thing of today reaches far back in time.

More individuals of each species of life are born than can possibly survive. The result is that each individual struggles against others to survive. Darwin called this the struggle for existence.

Individuals, even of the same species, are not all alike. They vary (in build, color, muscle formation, or some other feature). An individual may have a variation that gives him a better chance to survive.

If the favorable variation can be inherited, it may be passed on to the offspring. Darwin called this process Natural Selection. Individuals favored by natural selection usually survive while the less fortunate members of a species usually die out. Through this process and by other means, life slowly and gradually evolves through the ages. Some species gradually change; others die out completely.

Man is descended from some earlier "less highly-organized" form of life.

The Philosophy of Social Darwinism

Other men carried the ideas of Charles Darwin to the social world. One result was the development of the philosophy known as *Social Darwinism*. The English economist and historian Walter Bagehot (1826–1877), in *Physics and Politics*, wrote of the application of the laws of natural selection to men and races as follows:

The strongest nation has always been conquering the weaker. . . . [It is by these means that] the best qualities wanted in elementary civilization are propagated and preserved [since] the most warlike qualities tend principally to the good.

■ Check on Your Reading

1. Name several scientific discoveries.
2. Explain the theory of evolution. Why were Darwin's ideas rejected by some?
3. Explain Social Darwinism.

Today's machines perform incredible feats. Almost nothing seems beyond their ability. Jacques Ellul in *The Technological Society* predicts an even more awe-inspiring future for the machine in our society. "Knowledge will be accumulated in 'electronic banks' and transmitted directly to the human nervous system by means of coded electronic messages. There will no longer be any need of reading or learning mountains of useless information; everything will be received and registered according to the needs of the moment. . . ."

However much twentieth-century machines startle our imagination, we must not underestimate the importance of the far simpler machines of centuries ago. Certainly, the Industrial Revolution in the period from about 1750 to 1860 left its mark on European culture:

It broke down many of the customs and traditions of the people, and fathered many new ideas.

It heightened the importance of cities and contributed to the rise of urban life.

It fostered the organization of individuals into groups—for example, corporations, unions, and co-operatives—as a means of increasing their effectiveness.

It stimulated the formulation of communal theories of society, such as those of socialism and communism.

It produced conditions of society that brought forth a variety of reactions and expressions from writers, artists, and composers.

It is true that in some areas the Industrial Revolution brought misery. "In the year 1836," wrote one medical officer, reporting on the overcrowded housing conditions, "I attended a family of thirteen—twelve of whom had typhus fever, without a bed in the *cellar. . . .* They lay on the floor, and so crowded that I could scarcely pass between them." According to another report, in one cotton factory fines were given to any spinner "found with window open [or] washing himself [or] whistling [or] being sick and cannot find another spinner to give satisfaction."

Yet it is necessary to keep in mind that living and working conditions varied with the time, the place, and the employer.

MAN AND HIS CULTURE

Let's Meet the People!

The following sketch about William Morris is based on primary source material in J. W. Mackail, *The Life of William Morris*, Vol. I, 1901; and Philip Henderson, *William Morris*, 1952 (*Writers and Their Work* Series No. 32, Longmans for the British Council).

William Morris, Pre-Raphaelite

William Morris viewed with pleasure the meadow where his new home, Red House, would soon stand. It was close to the little village of Upton and not far from London. Here, surrounded by apple and cherry trees and away from the ugliness of industrial life, William Morris would build his house.

William Morris—writer, painter, architect, printer, interior decorator, and social reformer—was a heavily bearded man with a

mop of curly hair. He was a short, muscular man who spoke in a loud voice and dressed carelessly. Despite his rugged appearance, William Morris was sensitive. He expressed "a deep love of the earth and the life on it, and a passion for the history of the past of mankind." He read romantic poetry "rocking from one foot to the other like an elephant." And he loved to walk alone through the fields.

Above all, William Morris disliked what he called "the dull squalor of [industrial] civilization." He was convinced that "art cannot have a real life and growth under the present system of commercialism." So William launched "a crusade and holy war against the age"—and went to build a house in the green countryside where beauty could be found.

William Morris built his house carefully and well: an L-shaped two-storied house with a plain, red-brick exterior, Goth porches, a steep red-tiled roof, and a well-house of brickwork and oak timber. He planned the garden with its wattled fences covered with roses. Then, when the structure was completed, William Morris and his friends set about to make the furniture and decorations to be placed in the house. "Have nothing in [the] home, which is not *both* beautiful and useful," William declared, and they all tried to follow this rule.

William and his friends now designed and made a fine oak dining table, sturdy chairs, delicate copper candlesticks, and lovely table glass. They painted pictures that depicted scenes from ancient Greek wars and from medieval romances. They placed on the walls designs in tempera (painting on a prepared wooden panel with pigment mixed with egg)

that blended with the furniture of the house. They even arranged the window ledges so that apples would fall gently through the open windows in autumn. "[William] thrives," observed Burne-Jones, William Morris' friend, "and is slowly making Red House the beautifullest place on earth."

Finally, the house and all of its furnishings were completed. In 1860 William Morris and his wife at last moved into Red House. How pleasant were the next five years! William and his friends smelled "the sweet air" of the apple and cherry orchards; they took "swinging rides" through the countryside in a carriage with leather curtains; and they cast away from them the ugliness of the new industrialization and "laughed because we were happy."

In 1861, William Morris helped to found the firm of Morris, Marshall, Faulkner, and Co., Fine Art Workmen in Painting, Carving, Furniture and Metals, with an office in London. By 1865 the firm's business had grown so large that William knew that the time had come for him to return to the city. Thus, five years after Red House had been built, William Morris sold his lovely home and went back to live in the increasingly industrial city of London.

William never tried to see Red House again. As he himself said: "The sight of it would be more than I could bear!"

FAR EASTERN and CONTEMPORARY CULTURES

■ *"Pea Fowl and Flowers" by Masuyama Sessai (1755–1820) belongs to the Japanese Nagasaki School. The artist has painted magnificent peafowls against a colorful background of flowers and forest scenery.*

Courtesy of the Museum of Fine Arts, Boston

■ *"Ladies in a Garden" is an Indian painting of the Rajput School (late 17th century). It is a folk art. The figures are shown in profile, and their hands express significant gestures. They are symbols rather than real people. Splendid designs and bold color schemes characterize these works.*

Courtesy of the Museum of Fine Arts, Boston

■ *In his work, "Venice: Dogana and San Giorgio Maggiore," Joseph Mallord William Turner (1775–1851) paints a romantic scene of graceful boats with dashing gondoliers carrying treasures of the East. The artist has created an impression of radiant light.*

■ *"Vétheuil: Sunshine and Snow" (1881) is one of several winter landscapes by Claude Monet. The artist depicts the rays of the winter sun on the countryside, creating a vibrant, colorful, Impressionist painting.*

■ "On the Terrace" (1881) by Pierre Auguste Renoir is one of the artist's paintings emphasizing the grace and beauty of youth. The shimmering colors and dominant eye-catching hats are found in many of Renoir's works.

Courtesy of The Art Institute of Chicago

■ The "Still Life with Apples" by Paul Cézanne (1839–1906) is one of the artist's many still-life paintings. This work combines solidity and form with a balanced design and subtle color harmony.

Collection, The Museum of Modern Art, New York; Lillie P. Bliss Collection

487

■ *"Interior with Egyptian Curtain"*
is an Expressionist painting by Henri
Matisse (1869–1954). Note the highly
decorative pattern and intense colors
in this work.

Courtesy of The Phillips Collection, Washington

■ *"Three Musicians" (1921)*
by Pablo Picasso represented
the high point of Cubism.
The colors are rich and
decorative and the "cut"
shapes are fitted together
with meaning so that the
image of the three seated
musicians emerges.

Collection, The Museum of Modern Art,
New York; Mrs. Simon Guggenheim Fund

488

CHAPTER REVIEW

REVIEW and DISCUSSION

1. Identify the people and explain the events and terms on p. 470.

2. It is often said that art and literature reflect the life of the people of the period. Do you think this statement is true of life during the Industrial Revolution? Why?

3. Why did most nineteenth-century artists find little that was beautiful to paint in industrial life?

4. Do you agree with Daumier that people, rather than riches, were the chief possessions of society? Why?

5. How did industrialization "cheapen" the artistic tastes of many people? How do you feel about the importance of beauty and originality in art?

6. Why would industrialization contribute to "the separation of art from daily life"? Is our daily life separated from art today in the United States?

7. What movements developed in art, literature, and music as a reaction against the Industrial Revolution?

8. Do you agree with Walter Bagehot that "the most warlike qualities tend principally to the good"? Why or why not?

9. What is the essential difference between revolution and evolution? Why do people fear change?

ACTIVITIES

1. Have each member of the class pick one man mentioned in this chapter who he thinks contributed most to change. Write a report on the man you selected and give reasons for your choice.

2. Write a short biography of a nineteenth-century writer, artist, or musician. Use several references.

3. Have an art exhibit in your classroom illustrating the art movements discussed in this chapter.

PAST and PRESENT

1. Panel discussion: "The population explosion—past and present."

2. Describe how some modern writers use their pens to fight for social and economic reforms.

3. Which historic buildings in the United States have been preserved for our benefit?

SUGGESTED READINGS

Basic books: PALMER, R. R., and COLTON, JOEL, *A History of the Modern World*, Chap. 11, Knopf.

SMITH, GOLDWIN, *The Heritage of Man*, Chap. 38, Scribner.

THOMPSON, STITH, and GASSNER, JOHN, (eds.), *Our Heritage of World Literature*, Holt. Section on the writers mentioned in this chapter.

Special accounts: BUTTERFIELD, HERBERT, and others, *Short History of Science*, Free Press. Chaps. 9, 11, 12, 13, 14. Highly recommended.

GOMBRICH, E. H., *The Story of Art*, Doubleday.

TAYLOR, F. SHERWOOD, *An Illustrated History of Science*, Praeger. Check index for pages dealing with major scientists of the period.

TAYLOR, FRANCIS H., *Fifty Centuries of Art*, Harper.

TREVELYAN, G. M., *English Social History*, Longmans, Green. Use index for topics covered by this chapter.

Biography and Fiction: BENZ, FRANCIS E., *Pasteur, Knight of the Laboratory*, Dodd, Mead.

GOSS, MADELINE, *Beethoven, Master Musician*, Holt. A well-written biography.

HUGO, VICTOR, *Les Misérables*, Dodd, Mead. France in 1800's, shows harshness of life among the people.

MONTGOMERY, ELIZABETH R., *The Story Behind Great Medical Discoveries*, Dodd, Mead. Short biographies from Harvey to present leaders.

MOORE, RUTH, *Charles Darwin* (Great Lives in Brief Series), Knopf.

SOOTIN, HARRY, *Michael Faraday: From Errand Boy to Master Physicist*, Messner.

489

UNIT 8 National Loyalties, Wars, and Imperialism

How Much Does a War Cost?

Can you guess what was the cost of the first world-wide conflict of our century, World War I (1914–1918)? According to historian Louis Snyder, who examined the findings of the Carnegie Endowment for International Peace, the money spent on World War I was enough to do the following: (1) provide every family in England, Ireland, Scotland, Belgium, Russia, the United States, Germany, Canada, and Australia with $4000 to improve their housing; (2) provide a five-million-dollar library and a ten-million-dollar university for every community possessing a population of 20,000 or over in those countries; (3) create a fund which, at 5 per cent interest, would yield enough to pay an additional $1000 a year to 125,000 teachers and 125,000 nurses; and (4) leave a surplus big enough to purchase every piece of property and all the wealth in both France and England.

How Many Casualties in a War?

How great would you estimate the casualties to be when an army captures one square mile of land against heavy opposition? Statistics vary depending on the war and the situation. Using World War I as an example, Major General J. F. C. Fuller of the British army presents figures that show:

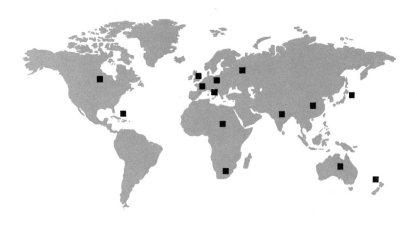

In the five months July to November, 1916, the British army lost approximately 475,000 men . . . and occupied some 90 square miles of enemy territory.

475,000 ÷ 90 square miles = 5277 casualties per square mile. More men were killed in this one war than all the people who live in Belgium, Sweden, Norway, Denmark, and Finland.

What Have Military Statistics to Do with You?

Or, to be more exact, what has war to do with you? Here is one question that you should be able to answer. For it is you, and millions in your generation, who may bear the weight of any future war. You may pay the costs. You may suffer by the casualties. You may sacrifice your life.

It is essential, therefore, that you understand why men have gone to war: that some people fought to defend liberty—some to establish a nation—some to unify a country—some to gain wealth—some to build an empire—and some because they feared or hated or hoped. The unit that you are about to read will help you to understand these "Whys" of war. In so doing, it will aid you to see the things that can be done to avoid future conflicts.

Unit 8 may be one of the most valuable for you. For, unless you and others of your generation concern yourselves with ideas discussed in this unit, you yourself may become a military statistic!

Chapter 31

Revolutions Challenge Reactionary Rule

KEYNOTE Koppel S. Pinson, a contemporary historian, recalls a story that is told about Prince Metternich, the Austrian chancellor in the post-Napoleonic period:

One day in the garden of his castle on the Rhine, [Metternich] watched an eclipse of the sun. A great sense of relief came over him when the moon finally completed its path across the sun and the temporary darkness was dispelled. There was *order* again in the world.

In a sense, this story illustrates a key feature of the years from 1815 to 1848: *It was a period in which Metternich and other leaders worked hard to keep the old order unchanged in Europe, while liberals and nationalists struggled to change the existing political system.*

Key People *Prince Metternich · Alexander I · Louis XVIII · Charles X · Louis-Philippe · Napoleon III · Louis Blanc · Louis Kossuth*

Key Places *Vienna · Paris · Belgium · Prussia · Austrian Empire · Berlin · Frankfurt · Bohemia · Hungary · Rome · Sedan*

Key Events *Congress of Vienna · Quadruple Alliance formed · Revolutions of 1820, 1821 · Monroe Doctrine · Revolutions of 1830 and 1848 · Napoleon III becomes emperor of France · Austria-Hungary becomes "dual monarchy" · Frankfurt Assembly*

Key Terms *nationalism · balance of power · reactionary · Concert of Europe · "Bourgeois Monarchy" · National Workshops*

492

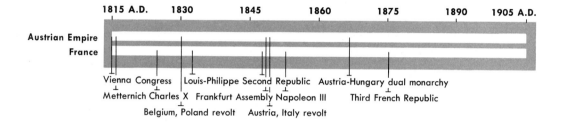

| 1815 A.D. | 1830 | 1845 | 1860 | 1875 | 1890 | 1905 A.D. |

Austrian Empire

France

Vienna Congress | Louis-Philippe Second Republic Austria-Hungary dual monarchy
Metternich Charles X Frankfurt Assembly Napoleon III   Third French Republic
Belgium, Poland revolt   Austria, Italy revolt

1. The Congress of Vienna Rearranges the Map of Europe

If necessity is the mother of invention, as the Greek philosopher Plato claimed, it is equally true that invention creates new necessities. Similarly, if the problems of peace end in war, war ends in peace and new problems. This becomes clear when we turn from the Industrial Revolution and return to our story of other developments in Europe.

Napoleon had been defeated for the second time and had been exiled to the tiny island of St. Helena. Meanwhile the Congress of Vienna (1814–1815) had gathered to work out a peace settlement after the Napoleonic Wars. It was an exciting affair. The colorful uniformed military leaders, the famous statesmen and their ladies riding in horse-drawn carriages, the noisy coffee-houses crowded with visitors, the banquets of roasted doves and gilded suckling-pigs, the sounds of dance music— all gave the impression of a holiday season in Vienna. Yet the representatives of the Congress of Vienna had come to try to solve a number of problems involving the boundaries, governments, and possessions of the countries of Europe.

The Congress was dominated by Austria, Russia, Britain, and Prussia. Later,

as a result of the clever maneuvering of the French diplomat, Prince Talleyrand, defeated France was admitted to this select circle. Most of the representatives wanted to establish a *balance of power*—that is, they wished to prevent any one nation from becoming powerful enough to threaten the security and independence of the others. The leaders of the Congress also followed the principles of *legitimacy* (restoring rulers to the thrones they held before the French Revolution and Napoleon) and *compensation* (giving territory to countries as compensation for the loss of lands held before 1789).

The members of the Congress of Vienna failed to take two factors into consideration. One was the force of *nationalism*. Nationalism grew in strength during the early nineteenth century, and as a result some settlements made at Vienna were doomed to survive for only a brief period. Nor was the Congress of Vienna concerned with *liberalism*, or the aspirations of the people for greater political rights. Prince Metternich, Austrian Chancellor and dominant figure of the conference, expressed the opinion of many of the representatives when he later wrote, "The first need of society is to be

493

maintained by strong authority . . . and not to govern itself."

The Congress therefore restored to power those so-called legitimate monarchs who had lost their positions during the Napoleonic period. Louis XVIII, a Bourbon, became king of France. Other Bourbons were returned to the thrones of the Two Sicilies and Spain. Hapsburg monarchs were re-established in Modena, Parma, and Tuscany—north Italian states.

The Congress of Vienna compensated the countries which had lost lands held before 1789 with other territory (see Chart).

The Congress of Vienna made many settlements which were changed or undone in the decades between 1815 and 1871. Yet the Congress should not be dismissed as a failure. It inaugurated a period of *relative* peace in Europe despite numerous small wars and revolutions.

■ **Check on Your Reading**

1. Why did the Congress of Vienna meet? What powers dominated it?

2. How did the Congress change the map?

3. What principles did the Congress follow? What factors did it ignore?

CONGRESS OF VIENNA

Members	Leaders	Territorial Changes
Austria	Chancellor Metternich Emperor Francis I	Gained Lombardy, Venetia, and the Duchy of Milan in Italy. Regained most of Galicia, principally inhabited by Poles.
Britain	Viscount Castlereagh Duke of Wellington	Received Ceylon and the Cape of Good Hope (South Africa) from Holland plus other overseas areas from France and Spain.
Germany		A loose union of thirty-nine states, including Austria and Prussia, was set up as the German Confederation. Each state was ruled by its own sovereign, and Austria acted as head of the confederation.
France	Talleyrand	Returned to frontiers of 1790.
Holland		Belgium was joined to Holland to form the Kingdom of the Netherlands. This compensated Holland for losing several colonies to Britain and established a stronger state to check future French aggression.
Italy		Italy remained divided into many states, dominated by the Austrian Hapsburgs. The king of Sardinia regained some territory.
Prussia	King Frederick William III Prince Hardenberg	Gained Swedish Pomerania, about two fifths of Saxony, and important lands on the Rhine.
Russia	Tsar Alexander I Count Nesselrode	Received the Duchy of Warsaw and the part of Poland that Prussia had once taken from Poland.
Sweden		Norway was taken from Denmark and joined to Sweden.
Switzerland		Swiss Confederation was granted its independence, and its neutrality was guaranteed.

494

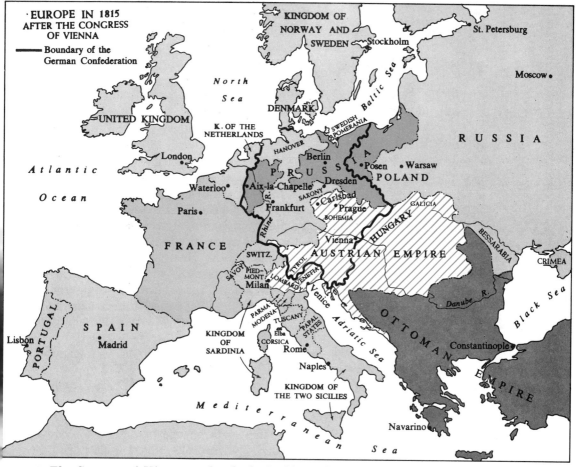

■ *The Congress of Vienna, under the leadership of Prince Metternich, restored the legitimate monarchs to their thrones and compensated the countries that had lost lands with other territories. What settlements were made regarding Austria, France, Italy, Prussia, and Russia?*

2. The Metternich System Attempts to Hold Europe in a Vise

Under the leadership of Metternich, a *reactionary* period began. Rulers tried to (1) erase all remnants of the revolutionary spirit, (2) restore political and social conditions as they were before the French Revolution, and (3) retain the *status quo*. From 1815 to 1848 this approach to affairs, the *Metternich System*, dominated Europe.

Metternich Fights Freedom

Metternich led the attack on freedom of the press, constitutional rights, and nationalism. In Austria and her possessions, he established censorship of books and newspapers, and he set up an extensive spy system. In Germany, he pressured the German Confederation to issue the Carlsbad Decrees (1819) censoring the press and suppressing liberal activities. Everywhere Metternich fought those who "deny... the value of the past and declare themselves the masters of the future."

To achieve their objectives, Metternich and the other leaders of Europe decided to

Painting by Sir Thomas Lawrence

■ *Under Prince Metternich, the leader of reaction, the Metternich System dominated Europe. It collapsed under revolutionary uprisings.*

band together. Russia, Austria, and Prussia joined the so-called *Holy Alliance.* Under this alliance the monarchs of these three countries agreed to be guided in domestic and international affairs by rules of justice, Christian charity, and peace. Most of the other rulers of Europe eventually signed this resolution, but they rarely followed its high-sounding principles.

A far more important agreement was the *Quadruple Alliance* between Great Britain, Russia, Austria, and Prussia. France joined in 1818 and the alliance became known as the *Concert of Europe.* The powers agreed to meet regularly:

for the purpose of consulting upon their common interests, and for the consideration of measures . . . most salutary for the repose and prosperity of nations, and for the maintenance of the peace of Europe.

Liberals Rise against Oppression

The Concert of Europe worked hard to check liberalism. *Liberals* were people who did not accept the sacredness of the past and who did not fear change. They were reformers who demanded such things as these: national rights, or freedom of their countries from foreign control; constitutions and governments more representative of the people; civil liberties, like freedom of speech and press; and political rights, like the right to vote. The liberals were active in many countries.

In Naples the liberals forced the king to grant the country a constitution in 1820. Metternich, with the approval of Russia and Prussia, used Austrian troops to help the king cancel this constitution. However, there were other uprisings in Piedmont and in other regions of Italy.

In Spain, in 1820, the liberals forced the autocratic King Ferdinand VII to promise to restore the constitution of 1812, which he had annulled. French troops helped the king to put down this uprising.

In Greece the people revolted against the Turks in 1821, and a year later declared their independence (p. 548).

In Latin America the countries gained their independence from Spain and Portugal between 1810 and 1824 (p. 437). When members of the Concert of Europe discussed helping the Spanish king, Ferdinand VII, to regain these lands, Great Britain and the United States opposed the plan. The leaders of both countries knew that their nations would be deprived of trading rights if Spain regained her possessions. In addition, they recognized that most British and Americans favored the independence of Latin America.

The Monroe Doctrine (1823)

George Canning, the British foreign minister, suggested that Great Britain and the United States issue a statement jointly opposing any attempt to crush the new Latin American republics. However, John Quincy Adams, the American Secretary of State, preferred that the United States make its own declaration. Why, he asked, should the United States always be a "[small boat] in the wake of the British man-of-war"? The United States could count on the support of the British fleet, so why not make a policy statement of our own? On December 2, 1823, President James Monroe sent a message to Congress, known as the *Monroe Doctrine*. The major points in the Doctrine were the following: (1) The Western Hemisphere was no longer to be an area for future colonization by European countries. (2) The United States would consider any attempt by European countries to extend their system of government to the Western Hemisphere as "dangerous to our peace and safety." (3) It would be "unfriendly" to the United States for any European country to try to regain areas in the Western Hemisphere that had declared themselves independent. (4) The United States would not interfere with the way in which European countries ran their own affairs in Europe.

The Monroe Doctrine was designed to discourage European countries from helping Spain regain her former colonies and prevent the Russians in Alaska from expanding southward.

■ **Check on Your Reading**

1. Identify: reactionary, Metternich System, Holy Alliance, Quadruple Alliance, Concert of Europe, liberals, Monroe Doctrine.

2. How did Metternich and his allies try to maintain the status quo?

3. The Revolutionary Years (1830-1848) in France

The Congress of Vienna in 1815 restored the so-called legitimate dynasty to the throne of France. Louis XVIII became the new monarch. He was a stout and gouty man with sufficient common sense to avoid the mistakes that had led to the execution of his brother, Louis XVI. Louis XVIII followed a moderate course and governed within the terms of the Charter granted to the people in 1814. This Charter provided that the king was to co-operate with the national legislature in making the laws. It also guaranteed religious freedom.

Rebellion under Charles X

Louis XVIII died in 1824, and his brother (the Count of Artois) became the new king as Charles X. Charles X (1824–1830) was an autocratic person who believed that "Louis XVI was lost through concessions. I have but one choice, to drive or be driven." He attempted to restore the absolute power of the monarchy. He curtailed religious freedom, strengthened the position of the Catholic Church, gave the nobles large sums of money to compensate for their loss of property during the French Revolution, and interfered with the activities of businessmen. He also issued royal decrees, the July Ordinances of 1830, that suspended freedom of the press, dissolved the Chamber of Deputies (national legislature), and gave the king powers to crush liberty.

As a result of these acts, a rebellion broke out against Charles X in July, 1830. Republicans, journalists, businessmen, dissatisfied government deputies, university students, and workers joined in the uprising. The rebels obtained control of Paris, and Charles X was forced to abdicate.

■ *In the famous romantic painting "Liberty Guiding the People," Eugène Delacroix depicts the Revolution of 1830 with dramatic power.*

The monarchy was not abolished, but the national legislature chose Louis-Philippe of the House of Orléans to be the new king. "Take him," advised Lafayette, the French general. "He will prove the best of republics." The white flag of the Bourbons was replaced with the tricolor of the French Revolution, and the Revolution of 1830 was deemed a success.

From Monarchy to Second Republic

Louis-Philippe (1830–1848) was a hard-working ruler who at first played the role of a "Citizen-King" whose powers were limited by the constitution.

Representatives of the middle class or bourgeoisie dominated the government. As historian Albert Guérard points out, "the divine right of property was officially beyond question." Louis-Philippe's reign was so favorable to businessmen, merchants, and the middle class that it is known as the "Bourgeois Monarchy." Even the right to vote was limited to wealthy people who paid heavy taxes. "If you want a vote, get rich!" advised François Guizot, Louis-Philippe's chief minister.

It was a period of great cultural creativity in France, particularly in literature. It was also a time in which the drive for business gains led some men to ignore the importance of cultural achievements. The novelist, Honoré de Balzac, compared that business world with "a basket of live crabs seeking to devour one another."

Some of the most serious problems of Louis-Philippe's reign resulted from the change from the domestic system of production to the factory system. Many workers who formerly worked at home now labored long hours at low wages in factories that were not safe. Reforms in working and living conditions were badly needed. However, when socialists openly and secretly demanded such reforms, the government placed a ban on all writings and actions critical of the regime.

The "Bourgeois Monarchy" could not last. The government's failure to grant more people the right to vote, its censorship of the press, its timidity in foreign affairs, and its financial difficulties all led to serious dissension. In February, 1848, when Guizot attempted to prevent opponents of

498

the government from holding a meeting, street riots broke out. Louis-Philippe was overthrown, the monarchy was abolished, and the Second French Republic was proclaimed on February 27, 1848.

Rebellion in the Second Republic

The first months of the Second Republic formed a difficult period of transition. A provisional government was established, and the city workers, who had played a major part in the February revolution, demanded immediate reforms. The provisional government, which contained a number of middle-class leaders, reluctantly established *national workshops*, which were government work projects to provide jobs.

The workshop plan, whose chief supporter was the socialist Louis Blanc (1811–1882), was not administered properly and did not prove effective. Louis Blanc protested that he had wanted the workshops "to consist of workmen belonging to the same trade . . . [who] were to pursue their business, the State lending them capital, to be repaid according to certain stipulations." Instead, the state had set up workshops that were "utterly unproductive and absurd" and did little more than feed "a rabble of paupers." The number of unemployed still continued to increase. They were supported by unemployment relief payments from the government.

A new National Assembly was elected. Dominated by the bourgeoisie and unsympathetic to the workers, the new government abolished relief payments to the unemployed. This action led to bloodshed. In June, 1848, Paris was filled with fierce battles between government troops and the unemployed, directed by socialists. According to Alexis de Tocqueville, a French author and statesman of the time, "the insurgents fought . . . without leaders, without flags, and yet with a marvelous harmony." *Du pain ou du plomb*—bread or

Painting by Jacquand, Musée de Versailles

■ *Louis Philippe, the "Citizen-King," is shown with his ministers. It is said he looked like a French middle-class businessman.*

lead—was the cry! Many Frenchmen, frightened by the chaos in Paris, became convinced that only a strong leader could save the country. When elections for national office were held in December, 1848, Louis Napoleon, nephew of Napoleon Bonaparte, was elected president of the new republic.

From the Second Republic to Empire

Louis Napoleon believed in "Bonapartism"—that is, he wanted all power to be placed in the hands of a strong ruler, himself. Then, as "strong man" of France, he would have the responsibility of ruling in the interests of the people. The "Napoleonic legend" and the Bonaparte name helped to elect Louis Napoleon.

When Louis Napoleon was campaigning for the presidency of the Second French Republic, he promised to protect the republic. A few years after he was elected, he tried to persuade the people to do away with the republic and make him emperor.

President Louis Napoleon failed to persuade the National Assembly to amend the 1848 Constitution to allow him a second term as president. Therefore, on December 2, 1851, he seized power by a *coup d'état*. He re-established universal male suffrage (the right of all men to vote) and called for a plebiscite, or popular vote, to "give me means to assure your prosperity, or choose another in my place." The people accepted his rule by a vote of 7,500,000 in favor to 640,000 opposed. This gave him the right to draw up a new constitution in place of that of 1848.

A year later, after weakening the power of opposition political leaders and newspapers, he made himself emperor of France as Napoleon III. The Second French Republic had lasted only four years, from 1848 to 1852. The period of the Second Empire began, and Napoleon III remained emperor for nearly two decades.

■ **Check on Your Reading**

1. Why did the French accept the rule of Louis XVIII but revolt against Charles X?

2. Describe the "Bourgeois Monarchy." What problems were immediately faced by the Second Republic?

3. Describe Louis Napoleon's career.

4. Revolutionary Fires Spread Throughout Europe

Revolutionary forces were at work throughout Europe in the years 1830 to 1848. The liberals in many countries were inspired by the example of France; and revolutionary uprisings broke out in Belgium, Poland, the Austrian Empire, Germany, and Italy. Most of these revolutions were unsuccessful.

Belgium Becomes a Nation

When the diplomats at the Congress of Vienna joined Belgium and Holland together in 1815, they ignored the fact that there were seeds of conflict in both countries.

Belgium and Holland differed in religion and language. The Belgians were principally Roman Catholic; the Dutch were chiefly Protestants. The two peoples clashed over religious affairs. They also did not speak the same language. The Belgians spoke French and Flemish. They were therefore disturbed when Dutch was made the official language in government documents.

The Belgians were proud of their past. They recalled the fifteenth and sixteenth centuries, when Antwerp was a great center. They spoke with admiration of their brilliant artists, and they hailed the work of their ancient craftsmen. Similarly, the Dutch were proud of their own history, particularly of their "Golden Age" in the seventeenth century. Pride of each group in the superiority of its own history was sometimes a cause of tension.

The Belgians felt that under the union with Holland they did not receive equal treatment with the Dutch in government, education, military service, or economic well-being. The union between Belgium and Holland lasted until 1830 when the Belgians revolted. One significant reason for the uprising was that many Belgians earnestly desired to have their own nation. The nationalistic feelings of the people of Belgium were too strong to be held in check. Their revolt was successful, and the new nation of Belgium was born in 1830.

500

The Polish Revolt Fails

In 1830, the Poles revolted against the Russian rulers who dominated them, but their revolt was crushed. Poland was deprived of all constitutional privileges and was placed under rigid military control.

One-tenth of the Polish land was seized by the Russians; Polish universities were closed; and thousands of Poles were killed or imprisoned. The Polish poet Krasinski described Poland after 1831 as:

The land of graves and crosses. Thou mayest know it by the silence of its men and the melancholy of its children.

Although other revolutionary efforts were made, particularly in 1863, Poland did not obtain its independence until 1919. By then Poland had been out of existence as a nation for almost 125 years. Yet its people preserved their language, traditions, literature, and strong feeling of nationality. The history of Poland provides an outstanding example of the power of nationalism, a force overlooked by the Congress of Vienna.

The Austrian Empire

Meanwhile, the Austrian Empire continued to be filled with dissension. Many of the tensions resulted from the rising nationalism among various groups. These nationalistic feelings had grown out of the past, for Austria's geographic location and history had filled it with many different and rival peoples. These included Germans; Magyars; Italians; and Slavs— Czechs, Poles, Slovenes, Slovaks, and Croats. The problem that faced the Hapsburgs in ruling these peoples has been aptly described by historian Hans Kohn:

In the 19th century—the age of nationalism— this multinational [Austrian] empire faced the problem of establishing an order which could give its various nationalities freedom of development and a feeling of equality.

Austria did not solve this problem, and a spirit of rebellion grew. In 1848 the Magyars and other peoples sympathetic to their cause revolted against the Austrian emperor. The Magyars had moved west through central Europe. In the tenth century they had settled along the Danube. This land, known as Hungary, eventually had become a part of the Austrian Empire.

Louis Kossuth (1802–1894), leader of the Magyars, first demanded constitutional government in Hungary—then independence. Many of the rebels had strong nationalistic feelings. They fought, they said, "to save ourselves from being struck off the earth as a nation." And Louis Kossuth later shouted at the Austrian emperor: "Thou beardless young Nero! Thou darest to say Hungary shall exist no more! We, the people, answer, we do and will exist. . . ." Liberals in Bohemia, part of the Austrian Empire, also demanded that they be granted an independent constitution.

On March 13, 1848, the Liberal party in Vienna, excited by the February revolution in France, rose against the Austrian government. The rebels became so strong that Prince Metternich—the "coachman of Europe"—was forced to resign. He went into exile in England, where he insisted that the things he had done were right. "My mind has never entertained error," he declared.

By the end of March, the Austrian emperor had been compelled to grant both Hungary and Bohemia the right to have new constitutions and more freedom. However, conflict between the Germans and Czechs in Bohemia, tensions between the Magyars in Hungary and the minority groups whom they sought to dominate, and other problems prevented these lands from consolidating their gains. As a result, by the end of August, 1848, Austrian and Russian troops had crushed the revolutionary movements. Bohemia and Hungary again fell under the control of Austria.

501

■ *A poster in Vienna in 1848 demands the ouster of Metternich and a constitutional government for Austria. The rebels were successful in forcing Metternich to resign, but their revolution was crushed.*

In 1867, shortly after Austria was defeated in a war with Prussia, the Austrian Empire was changed into a "dual monarchy" known as Austria-Hungary. Under this organization, Austria and Hungary had a common ruler, defense organization, budget, and foreign policy. The problems of governing people belonging to different nationality groups remained.

Italians Revolt against Austrian Control

The Annual Register, a British publication, noted that the news of the February revolution in France (p. 498) acted "like an electric shock upon Italy." Then in March, 1848, when word of the fall of Metternich reached the Italians, the people of Milan boldly rose against their Austrian rulers. Milanese rebels built barricades out of pianos, sofas, and chicken coops. Women pulled up rows of paving stones from the streets to obstruct the Austrian troops.

A part of Lombardy broke away from Austrian control, and the people of Venetia set up an independent republic. In Rome, Italian rebels forced the Pope to flee the city, and Giuseppe Mazzini and his followers established a Roman Republic. In Naples, Tuscany, and Piedmont, the rulers granted their people constitutions.

Despite their heroic efforts, the rebels were crushed. Austrian troops put down the revolt in Milan; French troops captured Rome and returned control of the city to the Pope. The Kingdom of Sardinia, ruled by the Italian House of Savoy, had gone to war against Austria. The Sardinians were defeated by the Austrians, and the Sardinian ruler Charles Albert abdicated. He was succeeded by his son, Victor Emmanuel II. By the end of 1849, Austria had regained its hold on Italy. Italian efforts to gain freedom had been checked.

German Liberals Revolt

News of the February revolution in France also provided the stimulus needed to stir the liberals of Germany to action. In March, 1848, German liberals led a series of militant demonstrations throughout Germany, and events reached a climax in an insurrection in Berlin. The frightened king of Prussia, Frederick William IV (1840–1861), agreed to call for the meeting of an assembly to write a constitution satisfactory to the liberals and to work to free the German Confederation from Austrian control. This assembly met at Frankfurt in 1848. It consisted of representatives of all of the states in the German Confederation. Austria also attended the conference.

The Frankfurt Assembly did not achieve its objectives. Its members did not cooperate sufficiently with each other, and they were not strong enough to force Austria out of Germany. When a constitution was drawn up, King Frederick William IV of Prussia rejected the invitation to become emperor of the new government. He refused because he did not want to risk a war with Austria and because he believed a crown came from God, not from an assembly of men. The Frankfurt Assembly failed and was disbanded. The old diet (assembly) of the German Confederation continued to exist in a divided Germany. German liberals had suffered a serious defeat. After the failure of 1848, many of them left Germany. These included a number of liberals who emigrated to the United States.

In 1850 the king of Prussia did grant his own country a constitution. However, it established a government whose leaders were responsible to the monarch—not to the people.

Results of the Revolutions

On the whole the revolutionary uprisings during the years 1830 to 1848 were failures. The revolutions in Poland, the Austrian Empire, Italy, and Germany were crushed. Only Belgium obtained its independence. Autocracy was weakened but it still retained a strong hold on most European countries. Efforts to win constitutions failed, except in Prussia and Sardinia. The liberals learned that they would have to use other methods.

Why did the revolutions fail? The revolutionaries were united in their efforts to drive out the rulers, but they could not agree on the kind of government—monarchy, democratic republic, or other form— to institute. They also failed to agree on the extent and type of political privileges to be granted to different classes. Religious differences and national loyalties further divided them. Reactionary monarchs had to make some concessions in the beginning; but their forces soon crushed the revolutionaries, who disagreed among themselves. The era of revolutionary activities seemed to be at an end.

■ **Check on Your Reading**

1. Why did the Belgians revolt against the Dutch in 1830? What was the result?

2. Describe the uprisings in Poland, the Austrian Empire, Italy, and Germany. What were the results?

5. The Second Empire in France

By 1852, Louis Napoleon had become emperor of France as Napoleon III. He granted a constitution that provided for a Legislative Assembly to be elected by universal manhood suffrage. While maintaining the semblance of a democratic government, Napoleon III kept the real governing power in his hands. He imposed strict censorship and controlled the elections so that candidates who supported the government were elected. Newspapers critical of the government were suppressed, and the government's opponents were either jailed or exiled.

Domestic Affairs

As emperor, Napoleon III appealed to all groups. To Catholics, he pledged defense of the Church; to businessmen, prosperity; to workers, public works projects.

Painting by H. Flandren, Musée de Versailles

■ *Louis Napoleon became emperor of France as Napoleon III in 1852. He married Eugénie de Montijo, a Spanish noblewoman.*

At first, conditions favored him. It was a time of business prosperity. Napoleon III supported the building of factories, banks, and railroads. A program of public works, under the direction of Baron Haussmann, created new jobs. Magnificent public buildings, monuments, and theaters were built throughout Paris; and long, broad avenues were constructed. Historian René Sedillot reported, "Paris grew, sprawled, and swelled." The city again became the cultural and intellectual capital of Europe.

Napoleon III also tried to win the support of the Church. He permitted Church leaders to control a number of areas of education in the schools and universities. In addition, he stationed French troops in Rome to protect the Pope.

Yet, despite all his efforts to please all groups, opposition to Napoleon III increased. Republicans were displeased because he had destroyed the Second French Republic and had taken away many of the people's rights. Catholics were angry because he had encouraged the unification of Italy. Conservatives were opposed to many of his policies. To divert people from their opposition, Napoleon III focused attention on foreign affairs.

Foreign Policy Leads to Disaster

Napoleon III had once pledged: "The Empire stands for peace." Yet, in 1854, France joined Britain against Russia in the Crimean War (p. 549). A victory in this war enabled France to regain some of the prestige and power she had lost. A few years later, Napoleon III supported the Italians against the Austrians (p. 511).

In Mexico, Benito Juárez, an Indian, led a revolt against the Mexican dictator and overthrew the regime. He declared that his government could not repay the foreign debts of the previous dictatorship, including money borrowed from European financiers. As a result of Juárez's actions and for other reasons, France joined Great Britain and Spain in sending armed forces to Mexico in 1862. Their troops occupied Veracruz.

Spain and Britain soon reached an agreement with Juárez and withdrew their troops, but French troops remained. Napoleon III thought that he could establish a French colony in Mexico as a "grand design" of his reign. His troops overthrew Juárez, and Napoleon III persuaded Archduke Maximilian, brother of the emperor of Austria, to become emperor of Mexico. Maximilian declared that he would "place the interests of [the Mexican] people above all other"; but Juárez and his men continued to fight.

The United States protested this violation of the Monroe Doctrine, but it could not take immediate action because it was involved in the War Between the States, which ended in 1865. Then the United States sent an army to the Mexican border to force Napoleon III to withdraw his troops. Juárez and his forces captured

Maximilian and executed him in 1867. Napoleon III lost considerable money, troops, and prestige.

Meanwhile, conditions at home were becoming worse. Napoleon III had to grant concessions. Workers were again permitted to strike, and the press could criticize the government. The Legislative Assembly was permitted to initiate legislation, vote on the budget, and require ministers to be responsible to it. However, these concessions did not satisfy the opposition.

Meanwhile, Prussia had become a strong power in Europe. In 1870, France fought against Prussia in the Franco-Prussian War (p. 516). In six weeks, the French armies were defeated, and Napoleon III and a large army surrendered at Sedan, near the Belgian border. When the news reached Paris, the Legislative Assembly deposed the emperor and proclaimed France a republic. Napoleon III had lost his empire on the battlefield.

■ **Check on Your Reading**

1. How did Napoleon III maintain control and try to satisfy opposition groups?
2. Describe the Mexican intervention.
3. What was a major result of the Franco-Prussian War for France?

6. The Third French Republic

A provisional republic was established. A difficult period of transition followed, during which a National Assembly governed France (1871–1875). The government had to sign a peace treaty ending the Franco-Prussian War. By the Treaty of Frankfurt, France lost Alsace and a part of Lorraine and had to pay an indemnity of one billion dollars.

Another crisis followed. A revolutionary city government—known as the Paris Commune—was established. Its forces were finally crushed by the National Assembly, which tried to restore order to France. In 1872, a system of obligatory five-year military service was started.

In 1875, the National Assembly drew up laws that established a Third French Republic. This government consisted of a two-house legislature (a Chamber of Deputies and a Senate), a president chosen by both houses, and a premier responsible to the Chamber of Deputies. A number of small political parties developed.

France's efforts to rebuild were hindered by the struggle between Church and Republican leaders. These men argued over the Church's desire to control education and the government's policy to keep the clergy out of secular affairs. About 1880 a national system of public education was established. Under this system, primary education was to be free, compulsory, and in the hands of lay teachers. Religious instruction was not permitted. In 1905 legislation was passed separating Church and State. This meant that the clergy would not be paid by the government, and bishops would no longer be nominated by government officials.

France passed an important tariff in 1892 to aid both industry and agriculture. France also expanded overseas in Tunis, Indo-China, and Northwest Africa.

Between 1871 and 1914 the French made conscientious efforts, both at home and abroad, to surpass the other countries of Europe. National pride—and hostility to Germany—stimulated these efforts.

■ **Check on Your Reading**

1. What problems did the Third French Republic face?
2. How was the Republic governed?

MAN AND HIS CULTURE

Let's Meet the People!

The following account is based on primary materials in *The Quest for a Principle of Authority in Europe, 1715 to the Present* by Thomas C. Mendenhall and others, 1948, Holt.

Lieutenant-Colonel Courant and Rifleman Henri

It was the evening of February 23, 1848, and Paris was filled with excitement. Around the Ministry of Foreign Affairs—official residence of Louis-Philippe's unpopular minister, Guizot—there was "a heavy force of military, of troops of the line, dragoons [mounted infantrymen], and municipal guard."

Lieutenant-Colonel Courant, commander of the Fourteenth Regiment, and his troops were stationed near Guizot's residence. It was the lieutenant-colonel's assignment to protect the building against demonstrators. Rifleman [Private] Henri was a soldier in the first squad of the regiment. It was his job to do as he was told.

Lieutenant-Colonel Courant now ordered his first squad to block the boulevard. Rifleman Henri made the move with the others. They were not a moment too soon, for a mob of Parisians, including some national guardsmen, was rapidly approaching. The demonstrators shouted "Long live reform! Down with Guizot!"

Then, suddenly, someone fired a shot! It may have been an overly excited soldier, or perhaps one of the mob aiming at the lieutenant-colonel. Only one thing was certain: The bullet missed its intended target—and struck Rifleman Henri in the face. The rifleman fell to the ground dead. The mob was now out of hand, and it took great effort to restore order.

In March, a few weeks after this uprising, Lieutenant-Colonel Courant made an official report of what had happened: "I believe that this event has been exaggerated [he declared, calmly] . . . only one man from my squad was killed."

The late rifleman Henri was not in a position to argue whether the event was exaggerated or not.

CHAPTER REVIEW

REVIEW and DISCUSSION

1. Identify the people and places and explain the events and terms on p. 492.

2. What did the victorious countries gain by trading territories at the Congress of Vienna?

3. What was the fate of each settlement made at the Congress of Vienna?

4. Why did the Congress of Vienna fail to check the growth of nationalism?

5. What role was played by the Concert of Europe, 1820–1848?

6. Make a chart of the revolutions of 1830 with causes and results of each.

7. How could Poland keep the spirit of nationalism alive?

8. Why did the first revolt in 1830 and 1848 break out in France rather than in another country?

9. Make a chart of the revolutions of 1848. List the countries, leaders, causes, and results.

10. A historian has said that Metternich's policy in enforcing the decisions of the Congress of Vienna was like a fire department putting out the fires of liberty. What do you think? Why?

11. What difficulties did Austria-Hungary encounter in governing the many nationalities in her empire? How did she attempt to solve them?

12. What were the major achievements of Napoleon III? What events caused the downfall of the Second Empire?

13. What changes in French government, education, church-state relations, and economic life were made under the Third French Republic?

ACTIVITIES

1. In parallel columns list the principal actions of Louis Napoleon and Napoleon Bonaparte. To what extent did Louis Napoleon imitate his uncle?

2. On a map of Europe, indicate the boundaries and territorial changes of the European countries as a result of the Congress of Vienna.

PAST and PRESENT

1. What groups, if any, today hold ideas comparable to those of Metternich?

2. Compare the views of "liberals" of the nineteenth century with those held by "liberals" today.

3. Compare or contrast Metternich's "sense of mission" with that of the leaders of the Soviet Union today.

SUGGESTED READINGS

Basic books: CHURCHILL, WINSTON, *A History of the English-Speaking Peoples, The Age of Revolution*, Chap. 25, Dodd, Mead.

MAY, ARTHUR, *The Age of Metternich, 1814–1848* (Berkshire Studies in European History), Holt. A short but very useful book.

PALMER, R. R., and COLTON, JOEL, *A History of the Modern World*, Chaps. 10, 11, 12, and 13, Knopf.

SMITH, GOLDWIN, *The Heritage of Man*, Chap. 32, Scribner.

Special accounts: KOHN, HANS, *Nationalism —Its Meaning and History*, Van Nostrand (paperback). A brief but useful study of nationalism.

NICOLSON, HAROLD, *The Congress of Vienna, A Study of Allied Unity, 1812–1822*, Peter Smith. A fascinating book suitable for better readers.

STEARNS, RAYMOND, (ed.), *Pageant of Europe—Sources and Selections from the Renaissance to the Present Day*, Chaps. 25, 28, and 30, Harcourt, Brace. Contains excellent source materials on the challenges to reactionary rule.

Biography and Fiction: GUÉRARD, ALBERT, *Napoleon III* ("Great Lives in Brief" series), Knopf. A very well-written biography.

MACK SMITH, DENIS, *Garibaldi* ("Great Lives in Brief" series), Knopf. A brief account that holds the attention of the reader.

Chapter 32   *Italy and Germany Form Nations*

KEYNOTE   Many of us have become accustomed to thinking of Italy and Germany as old nations. We order Italian pizza in a restaurant and wonder if it is as good as in "old Italy." We compare our Wagnerian opera singers with those who sang in "the old days in Germany." And when we give children names like Marguerita or Otto, we sometimes say that we are naming them after relatives in "the old country."

Yet actually both Italy and Germany are comparatively young nations, younger than our own. One of the important facts of history is this: *Italy and Germany did not become nations until the second half of the nineteenth century.*

Key People   *Giuseppe Verdi · Giuseppe Mazzini · Camillo Cavour · Victor Emmanuel II · Giuseppe Garibaldi · Otto von Bismarck · Napoleon III · William I*

Key Places   *Rome · Piedmont-Sardinia · Sicily · Naples · Lombardy · Venetia · Tuscany · Papal States · Prussia · Schleswig-Holstein · German Empire · Alsace-Lorraine*

Key Events   *Cavour helps strengthen Sardinia · North and Central Italy are joined · Garibaldi conquers Sicily · Kingdom of Italy proclaimed · Law of Papal Guarantees · Schleswig-Holstein question · Austro-Prussian War · North German Confederation established · Franco-Prussian War · German Empire created*

Key Terms   *"Risorgimento" · "Red Shirts" · "prisoner of the Vatican" · Zollverein · Ems Dispatch · Chancellor · Reichstag · Bundesrat · Kulturkampf*

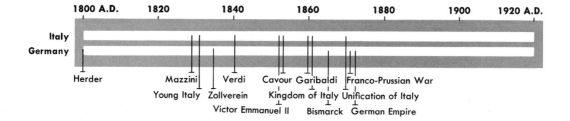

| 1800 A.D. | 1820 | 1840 | 1860 | 1880 | 1900 | 1920 A.D. |

Italy

Germany

Herder — Mazzini — Verdi — Cavour — Garibaldi — Franco-Prussian War

Young Italy — Zollverein — Kingdom of Italy — Unification of Italy

Victor Emmanuel II — Bismarck — German Empire

1. Italy Is Unified

Italy as a nation is comparatively new. Italy? The word itself had largely a geographic meaning until well after the first half of the nineteenth century. Prior to that time, Italy consisted of a number of separate states (map, p. 511). These included the Kingdoms of Piedmont-Sardinia and the Two Sicilies; Lombardy-Venetia; the Papal States; and the Duchies of Parma, Modena, Lucca, and Tuscany. Most of these lands were dominated by rulers from Austria and other foreign countries.

Giuseppe Mazzini, leader of "Risorgimento"

Napoleon's domination of Italy had helped to spread the ideas of the French Revolution. It also had stimulated Italian nationalism and caused many people in Italy to demand freedom from their foreign masters. The Carbonari ("Charcoal Burners"), a secret society, began to work to rid the country of foreign rulers.

The awakening of Italian nationalism in the early nineteenth century became known as the "Risorgimento" (the "Revival" or "Reawakening"). Giuseppe Mazzini (1805–1872) was one of the important leaders of the "Risorgimento." A sensitive

man, Mazzini was said to have shown his sympathy for persecuted people by usually wearing black clothing as a sign of his mourning for them. In 1831, he was so disturbed by the condition of his countrymen that he founded Young Italy.

Members of Young Italy attempted to "educate" the people to the need for insurrection against the foreign rulers of Italy. It was Mazzini's hope that an Italian republic could then be established. Young Italy dedicated itself

to the great aim of reconstituting Italy as one independent sovereign nation of free men and equals. . . .

Although the groundwork for rebellion had been laid by Mazzini and other Italians, the revolution of 1848 failed (p. 502).

Other Factors Unite Italians

Other factors helped to unite the Italian people, too. (1) Common customs, religion, and traditions existed in Italy. (2) Most of the people of Italy spoke a common language, though local dialects existed. (3) Members of the growing commercial and agricultural middle class believed that

509

■ *The three leaders of Italian unification:*
Victor Emmanuel (left), Cavour (center), and
Garibaldi (right) meet to discuss problems.

they would benefit by having a united country. A united Italy could remove tariff barriers that existed between separate states, eliminate the confusion that resulted from the variety of coinage systems, build roads and railways to aid commerce, and stimulate foreign trade. It could eliminate Austria's interference in their economic activities.

(4) Music also served to unite the Italian people. Giuseppe Verdi (1813–1901), an outstanding composer, is famous for such operas as *Rigoletto*, *La Traviata*, and *Aïda*. Choruses from Verdi's *I Lombardi*, *Ernani*, and *Attila* often produced patriotic anti-Austrian demonstrations. As Francis Toye, an English music critic, points out: "Verdi's music became especially identified with the national cause."

(5) Writers, such as Count Giacomo Leopardi and Alessandro Manzoni, helped to create a national Italian literature. Manzoni (1785–1873) is particularly famous for his novel *I promessi sposi* (*The Betrothed*). According to Denis Mack Smith, a specialist in Italian history, this novel helped to make the Tuscan dialect "the classic prose style for Italian literature." It strengthened national consciousness by helping to establish a common language for Italian literature. The story dealt with a local tyrant in seventeenth-century Lombardy and with the oppression of Italians by foreigners (the Spaniards). It thus indirectly preached anti-Austrian nationalism.

Cavour Strengthens the Position of Sardinia

In the 1850's there were many Italians who were ready to make another attempt to expel foreign rulers. Their principal need was for energetic and imaginative leaders to direct their actions. Such leaders appeared in the Kingdom of Sardinia (Piedmont-Sardinia), which was ruled by the Italian House of Savoy.

Under King Charles Albert, the Sardinians had previously fought against the Austrians. Although defeated, Charles Albert had granted his people a constitution. Many people looked to the new king of Sardinia, Victor Emmanuel II, for the same courageous leadership provided by his father.

In 1852 Victor Emmanuel appointed Count Camillo Cavour as his prime minister. Cavour was a short, stout man whose eyeglasses made him appear a solemn scholar. Yet he was one of the best diplomats. As Maurice Paléologue, a French writer, states: " [He had] . . . daring with prudence . . . impetuous driving power with charming persuasiveness . . . vivid imagination with cold reason." As prime minister of Piedmont-Sardinia from 1852 to

■ *The Kingdom of Sardinia, under the leadership of Cavour, led in efforts to unify Italy. In 1861, the Kingdom of Italy was formed. What territories did it comprise? How were Venetia and Rome acquired?*

THE UNIFICATION OF ITALY
1859-1870
▓ Kingdom of Sardinia, 1859
☐ United with Kingdom of Sardinia to form Kingdom of Italy, 1859-1860
▨ Added 1866
⠿ Added 1870

1859 and 1860 to 1861, Cavour proved to be a liberal statesman who stood for "Independence, Union, Moderation, and Reform." He was determined to make the dream of a united Italy come true.

Cavour first helped to strengthen the economy of the Kingdom of Sardinia by supporting public works, aiding agriculture, and stimulating the development of industry. Then he joined with England, France, and Turkey in a war against Russia, the Crimean War of 1854–1856 (p. 549). He used the peace conference after the war as a place to denounce Austria's domination of Italy.

Northern and Central Italy Are United

Cavour realized clearly that to achieve his goal of driving out the Austrians and uniting the country, he would need the help of other countries. Using shrewd diplomacy, he obtained the assistance of Emperor Napoleon III of France. Napoleon III promised to aid the Kingdom of Sardinia in a war against Austria provided that Austria could be made to attack the Kingdom of Sardinia first and thus justify France's entry into the war to defend Sardinia. For this France would receive Nice and Savoy.

Cavour then succeeded in maneuvering Austria into a position where she declared war on the Kingdom of Sardinia, and in 1859 Sardinia and France allied themselves in the conflict against the Austrians. Austrian armies were defeated in bloody battles. However, in a few months—and without consulting Cavour—Napoleon III made a separate peace with Austria. This peace agreement had the following provisions: (1) Lombardy was ceded to the Kingdom of Sardinia; and (2) Venetia continued to be a province of Austria. The war also aided the unification of Italy in another way, for Tuscany (which included Lucca), Modena, Parma, and Romagna (a part of the Papal States) deposed their Austrian rulers. Then these regions agreed to unite with the Kingdom of Sardinia. Northern and Central Italy at last were joined together.

Garibaldi Conquers the Kingdom of the Two Sicilies

The first parliament of Italy met in 1860 at Turin, capital of the Kingdom of Sardinia. However, Sicily and the southern part of the Italian peninsula (known as the Kingdom of the Two Sicilies) still remained outside the nation. So did Savoy and Nice, which had been given to France "for the services she [had] rendered."

Giuseppe Garibaldi (1807–1882), who went to sea at sixteen and was a sea captain at twenty-four, was the military hero who did much to free Sicily and Southern Italy from foreign rulers. Heavily bearded and dressed in his famous red shirt, grey flannels, and old grey cloak, Garibaldi was a dramatic and colorful figure.

Garibaldi assembled about a thousand volunteers and prepared to invade the island of Sicily, which was under the rule of an autocratic Bourbon king. "Our war-cry will be Italy and Victor Emmanuel!" proclaimed Garibaldi. "I trust that . . . the Italian flag will not be dishonored." In 1860, when the people of Sicily revolted, Garibaldi saw his chance to attack.

Garibaldi's troops, known as the "Red Shirts" because of their red woolen shirts, were small in number. Nevertheless, with Garibaldi as their leader, the "Thousand" successfully invaded Sicily and took the island. They crossed over to the mainland and freed the rest of the Kingdom of the Two Sicilies.

The New Kingdom of Italy Is Proclaimed

Garibaldi turned over his conquests in Sicily and Southern Italy to Victor Emmanuel II. Italy's territory had been greatly extended, and the new Kingdom of Italy was proclaimed in 1861. Victor Emmanuel II became king and Cavour prime minister.

In 1866 Italy joined Prussia in a war against Austria. As a result, Venetia was added to Italy. In 1870 the city of Rome was taken from the Pope when French troops who were defending it had to be withdrawn. Rome became the capital of Italy, and the unification of Italy had been achieved.

■ Check on Your Reading

1. What factors inspired Italian nationalism in the 1850's?

2. What did each of these men contribute to Italian unification: Mazzini, Verdi, Cavour, Napoleon III, Victor Emmanuel II, Garibaldi?

3. Explain how northern and central Italy were united and how the Kingdom of the Two Sicilies was acquired.

2. Independent Italy from 1870 to 1914

The leaders of the newly unified Italy made a number of changes in the organization of the country. A limited monarchy was established with (1) a two-house parliament made up of an elected Chamber of Deputies and a Senate consisting primarily of members appointed by the monarch; (2) a prime minister responsible to the Chamber of Deputies; and (3) suffrage limited to those who were property owners and who paid certain taxes. Universal manhood suffrage did not come until 1919.

The Pope's Position in a United Italy

The Pope had lost Rome as well as considerable land and civil power as a result of the unification of Italy. *The New York Sun* had even predicted: "Should the temporal power of the Pope be wrested from him, it is not unlikely that he may find a home in our happy republic." The Pope was very angry at the seizure of the lands he had ruled. Nevertheless, efforts were made to reconcile him to the Italian government's occupation of Rome.

The Law of Papal Guarantees, passed by the Italian government in 1871, provided the following: (1) The Pope was to be sovereign, but only within the Vatican. (2) An annual payment of over $600,000 was to be made to the Pope by the Italian government to replace the income he previously had received from the Papal States. (3) The government was to give up its right to appoint bishops. (4) Many monasteries were to be closed. (5) Ecclesiastical courts were to cease to function.

Pope Pius IX and later Popes refused to accept either the money or the other terms of the Law of Papal Guarantees. To show their opposition, they refused to leave the Vatican. From 1871 to 1929 each Pope was known as the "prisoner of the Vatican." A settlement between Church and State was at last reached in 1929 under dictator Benito Mussolini.

Economics and Social Welfare

The government built railroads and canals, helped subsidize shipping, and tried to stimulate the development of industries. Laws were passed between 1886 and 1914 to regulate the conditions of child labor and to provide workers with compensation in case of industrial accident, sickness, and old age.

International Affairs

As a new nation, Italy was eager to equal the achievements of other nations in securing non-European territories. The temptations of imperialism, so powerful after 1870, caused Italy to seek colonies in North Africa and to attack Abyssinia, or Ethiopia, in 1896 (p. 564). Italy also joined Austria-Hungary and Germany to form one of the great European alliances, the Triple Alliance.

Italy Has Other Problems

A number of serious problems continued to plague Italy from 1870 to 1914. These included the following: the Italians' lack of experience in self-government; the tensions between the Italian government and the Papacy; class distinctions that separated group from group; and the large national debt and high taxes. The taxes, many of which were levied to obtain money for armaments, were a heavy burden on the poor.

In addition, many people of the industrialized north were hostile to those in the relatively underdeveloped south of Italy. The people in many parts of the country had a low standard of living.

In 1860, between 70 and 75 per cent of the people were illiterate. A system of compulsory education was declared to be established in 1877, but it was not enforced.

All these problems remained to be solved. As a result, more than eight million people emigrated between 1876 and 1905. About one half went to the United States and South America, particularly Argentina. Others resettled throughout Europe. This exodus relieved some of the economic pressures. It also made Italian leaders more aware that serious work had to be done if Italy was to become a politically stable and economically sound country.

■ Check on Your Reading

1. Describe the Italian government's relations with the Pope from 1871 to 1929.
2. What problems did the new government of Italy solve? Which remained unsolved?
3. Where did Italy wish to expand? Why?

3. Germany Is Unified

Germany, like Italy, did not exist as a nation until the second half of the nineteenth century. "Germany" in the 1840's consisted of a loose confederation of thirty-nine large and small states, the most important of which was Prussia. Each of these states had its own sovereign ruler, military forces, and diplomats for foreign affairs. The German Confederation did have a diet or parliament. However, it was made up of representatives of the rulers, not of the people or country as a whole. Austria dominated this German Confederation, and the revolutionary uprisings of 1848 (p. 502) failed to drive the Austrians out of Germany.

Many Factors Unite the Germans

As in Italy, there were a number of factors that inspired the nationalism of many Germans and helped bring them closer together. These included a common language, though there were local dialects; common traditions and customs; and pride of the people in the great cultural achievements of the Germans. Napoleon's domination of Germany had stimulated the growth of German nationalism. After Napoleon's defeat, Prussia had taken the lead in efforts to unify the country.

Prussia helped to establish the Zollverein, a customs union among certain states in the German Confederation. The Zollverein made it possible for goods to pass more freely among its member states. By 1834, nearly all of the states in the German Confederation belonged, but Austria was excluded from membership. The co-operation developed by the Zollverein in the exchange of economic goods was an important step in the direction of future political union.

Literature was also directly connected with nationalism, particularly in the work of Johann Gottfried von Herder (1744–1803). He wrote that every nation has its own individual spirit, which can be felt in its literature. Early literature became of great interest to the Germans, who investigated the medieval German tales. The brothers Jakob and Wilhelm Grimm published their famous collection of *Fairy Tales*, stories going back to early German legends.

The failure of the Frankfurt Assembly of 1848 (p. 502) made the German leaders realize that it would take far more than words to unite the German people. The man who saw this most clearly was Otto von Bismarck.

Otto von Bismarck

Otto von Bismarck (1815–1898) became chief minister of Prussia in 1862. He was a strong, bulbous-faced, broad-shouldered man about six feet two inches tall. Bismarck was a conservative who supported monarchy and had little patience with parliamentary democracy. He said, however, that "absolutism primarily demands impartiality, honesty, devotion to duty, energy, and inward humility in the ruler." Bismarck believed in the importance of strength and power in dealing with men of other countries. In one of his best-known statements, he declared:

Not through fine speeches and majority votes are the great questions of the day decided . . . but by blood and iron.

This great diplomat, a man who knew when it was necessary to use force and when it was wiser to act with moderation, played the leading role in the building of the German nation.

Three Wars Lead to German Unification

Bismarck gradually became interested in the idea of unification and, as chief minister of Prussia, he determined to do everything possible to unite Germany. His plan of action was (1) to have Prussia provide the necessary leadership to unite Germany; (2) to center national loyalty around the Prussian ruler; (3) to isolate Austria and drive her out of Germany; and (4) to use military power to accomplish his objective of unifying Germany.

The War Against Denmark

In 1864 both Prussia and Austria fought against Denmark over Schleswig and Holstein. Although both these territories were the personal possessions of the King of Denmark, Holstein was in the German Confederation and there were many Germans living in southern Schleswig and throughout Holstein. Denmark was defeated in the war, and by the terms of the peace settlement, (1) Prussia gained the right to administer Schleswig and to establish a naval base at Kiel; and (2) Austria gained the right to administer Holstein.

The Austro-Prussian War

Bismarck next worked carefully on Napoleon III to gain France's neutrality in case of a war involving Prussia. He also obtained Italy's promise of aid if a conflict broke out between Prussia and Austria. He had made friends with Russia, partly by supporting Russia against the Poles when they revolted in 1863. Then Bismarck used arguments over the future of Schleswig-Holstein—disagreements which he deliberately encouraged or created—as one of several excuses for stirring up a war between Prussia and Austria. The Austro-Prussian War came in 1866.

"So the die is cast!" wrote the Prussian king, as hostilities started. "Either we conquer or we will bear with honor what Heaven decrees for Prussia!" Prussia conquered! Led by the astute General von Moltke and using improved weapons, the

Painting by Franz von Lenbach, Pinakothek, Munich

■ *Otto von Bismarck was physically powerful, strong in will and determination, and conservative. He played a key role in unification.*

Prussians defeated Austria in seven weeks. The terms of the peace settlement, which were not too harsh on Austria, provided that Austria give Holstein to Prussia and agree to the dissolution of the German Confederation and to the formation of a new confederation of North German states under the leadership of Prussia. This North German Confederation (1867) had a total population of thirty million people, twenty-five million of whom were governed directly by Prussia. Austria was excluded from membership. However, the South German states—where Catholicism, rather than Protestantism, was the principal religion—remained outside the confederation.

The Franco-Prussian War

Bismarck felt that one more war was necessary. He wanted to find an enemy against whom *all* Germans—the Catholic

515

South Germans as well as the Protestant North Germans—would fight. He hoped that such a war against a common enemy would stir up the nationalism of the South German states, especially the three largest, Bavaria, Württemberg, and Baden, and make them want to join the North German Confederation in a united German nation.

Bismarck considered France to be the enemy. He therefore used a dispute over who should inherit the throne of Spain to help cause a war between France and Prussia. The issue was whether a Hohenzollern prince, related to the king of Prussia, should seek the Spanish throne. Under French pressure, King William I of Prussia had the Hohenzollern candidate withdraw. It seemed as if the matter was settled, but Bismarck used the incident to incite a war with France. One of the ways in which he did this was by deliberately reducing the words in a diplomatic dispatch (the Ems Dispatch describing William I's interview with the French ambassador). He made it appear that the French and German governments had insulted each other. This helped spread a war fever in both countries. Inept French diplomacy and emotional reporting by

■ *Prussia, under the leadership of Otto von Bismarck, led the movement for German unification. Bismarck fought three wars against Denmark, Austria, and France in his drive to unite Germany. How did he succeed in uniting the South German states with the North German Confederation?*

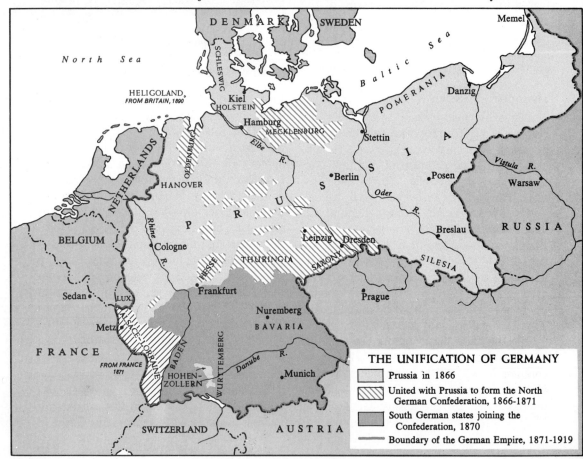

THE UNIFICATION OF GERMANY

[ ] Prussia in 1866

[ ] United with Prussia to form the North German Confederation, 1866-1871

[ ] South German states joining the Confederation, 1870

— Boundary of the German Empire, 1871-1919

■ *A German painting entitled "Count Moltke before Paris" shows the victorious German army, which besieged Paris for many weeks and received its surrender early in 1871. A German victory in the Franco-Prussian War helped to complete the unification of Germany.*

French newspapers led France to declare war on Prussia.

The war proved to be disastrous for France. Not only was she defeated, but her emperor, Napoleon III, was captured with his army. By the terms of the Treaty of Frankfurt (1871), France turned over to Germany all of the region of Alsace and the eastern part of Lorraine, and France had to pay Germany a war indemnity of one billion dollars.

The Franco-Prussian War helped to complete the unification of Germany. The South German states had joined with the North German states in the fight against France. They now agreed to form a single Germany. The new German Empire was officially proclaimed in a ceremony at Versailles on January 18, 1871. William I, king of Prussia, became the first emperor; and Bismarck was made the first chancellor. Emperor William wrote to Bismarck: "The most distant generations will never forget that the elevation of the Fatherland to new power ... [is] essentially due to your penetration, your energy, and skill."

Italian and German Unification: A Comparison

Looking back at the unification movements in Italy and Germany, we can see that there were differences as well as similarities in the ways these countries became nations.

The role of the liberals in the unification movements differed. In Italy, the liberals played a more important part in uniting the country, and tried to establish a democratic government. In Germany, the liberals failed to unite the country by 1848. Unification was primarily imposed

517

from above—that is, it came about principally through the actions and military triumphs of the autocratic leaders of Prussia. Nationalism became so strong in Germany that many Germans were willing to deny themselves liberty if it would help to unify the country. The political correspondent of a German journal, *Preussische Jahrbücher*, expressed this point of view in 1867:

... if Germany is faced with the choice between unity or liberty, it must, in accordance with its history and its position, unconditionally choose the former ... the realization of the national idea dare not be frustrated by the liberal idea.

The religious problems also differed. In Italy, the people were not divided by their religious beliefs; Roman Catholicism was the religion of the great majority. But the position of the Pope in Rome and the existence of the Papal States presented a unique problem. In Germany, religious tensions between the Catholic south and the Protestant north posed an obstacle.

The unification movements in Italy and Germany were alike in that war was used to unite the countries; Austria had to be driven out; and the growth of nationalism and patriotism was a key factor.

■ **Check on Your Reading**

1. How did Bismarck plan to unite Germany? Show the step-by-step development of his plan.

2. What group was chiefly responsible for uniting Italy? Germany? How did this difference affect the kind of government in each?

3. How were the unification movements in Germany and Italy alike? different?

4. Independent Germany from 1871 to 1914

The leaders of newly united Germany set about reorganizing the country, and there were many important developments from 1871 to 1914. The government, established for the German Empire, was organized as follows: (1) The emperor chose the chancellor, controlled the military forces, and provided over-all direction of foreign affairs. (2) The chancellor was the most powerful government official in the country. (3) The two-house legislature consisted of a lower house (the Reichstag) elected by universal manhood suffrage and an upper house (the Bundesrat) chosen by the rulers of the various states in the Empire. Neither house had power to control the actions of the chancellor.

Religious Affairs

Bismarck was chancellor from 1871 to 1890. In the beginning, he directed a struggle against the Catholic Church and its political ally, the Catholic Center party in Germany. This is known as *Kulturkampf* (literally: "struggle for civilization"). Bismarck tried to undermine the position of the Church because he felt that the Church's political influence weakened the power of the state and that the Church would never co-operate fully with a Protestant government. Most of the Poles in Germany were Catholic and joined with the Center party to oppose Bismarck.

Laws were passed requiring civil marriage; Catholic clergy were fined heavily for criticizing the government; religious organizations were forbidden to instruct in the schools; and the Jesuits were expelled. Nevertheless, the Catholic Center party remained strong. After 1880, when he needed Catholic support against the socialists, Bismarck finally stopped the government's anti-Catholic policies. Most laws restricting Catholics were repealed.

Economic Affairs

One of the outstanding developments in Germany from 1871 to 1914 was the transformation of the nation from a predominantly agrarian economy to a highly industrialized country. Between 1871 and 1900 there was an Industrial Revolution. This revolution was given impetus by the progress in science and technology, the unification of the country, and the annexation of Alsace and part of Lorraine—areas which had important textile factories and iron-ore deposits. Economist John Maynard Keynes concluded: "The German Empire was built more truly on coal and iron than on blood and iron."

Germany constructed railroads, strengthened its merchant marine, and built up its armaments. By 1913 it was the rival of Great Britain in many economic fields.

Social Welfare

The industrialization of Germany brought many problems, such as wretched working conditions and the employment of women and children. In 1881 Chancellor Bismarck declared that "the state is not only an institution of necessity but also one of welfare"; and the government took steps to deal with social welfare.

Bismarck and the German government took action in this area for these reasons: (1) To prevent the socialist party in Germany from growing stronger, they passed some of the legislation it advocated, while at the same time they dissolved socialist organizations and suppressed their publications. Emperor William I said:

the healing of the social ills is not to be carried out by the repression of the [socialists'] excesses but is at the same time to be sought in the positive furthering of the welfare of the workers.

(2) By providing for the needs of the people they felt that they could strengthen the nation and keep the loyalty of its citizens. (3) They believed that better living and working conditions would raise the physical ability and morale of the men recruited into the army. (4) They were influenced by the activities of the Conservative party in Britain, a political party that helped bring about social reforms.

The German government passed important social legislation that included the following: (1) a Sickness Insurance Act (1883), financed by employers and employees; (2) an Accident Insurance Act (1884), financed by employers; and (3) an Old Age and Incapacity Act (1889), financed by employers, employees, and the German government. Other laws regulated working conditions in factories; Germany became a pioneer in setting up government systems of social welfare.

Foreign Relations

Germany under Bismarck played a major role in European international relations. Bismarck had great skill in diplomacy and he used it to preserve the balance of power and prevent any alliance of great powers against Germany. He allied Germany with Austria-Hungary and Italy while working to maintain satisfactory relations with Russia and Britain. He prevented an alliance of France and Russia, which he felt was highly dangerous to German security. Bismarck tried not to antagonize European nations. He wanted Germany to concentrate on building up its strength in Europe rather than seek a colonial empire.

■ **Check on Your Reading**

1. Describe the German government.
2. What was the *Kulturkampf*?
3. Describe the important economic and social-welfare changes in Germany between 1871 and 1914.
4. What was Bismarck's foreign policy?

MAN AND HIS CULTURE

Let's Meet the People!

This sketch is based on primary materials in G. M. Trevelyan, *Garibaldi and the Making of Italy*, Longmans, Green, 1912; *Passages from the French and Italian Notebooks of Nathaniel Hawthorne*; *Readings in European History*, compiled and edited by Bernard and Hodges, Macmillan, 1958; and *Fifty Major Documents of the Nineteenth Century*, edited by L. L. Snyder, Van Nostrand, 1955.

A Soldier in Garibaldi's Army

The soldier in Garibaldi's army was dressed in a long-sleeved woolen shirt, trousers tucked in below the knees, leggings, and old shoes. He wore a "wide-awake," a soft-brimmed felt hat, or a cap held to his head by a chin strap. He was armed with a rifle and bayonet.

The soldier rarely had enough to eat, and his pay was very low. Yet he learned not to complain. Had not Garibaldi himself said: "What do you want with pay? . . . when the affairs of the country are going well, what more can any one want?"

Yet there were times when the soldier was shocked by the horrors of war. Certainly, he would find it difficult to forget Palermo, Sicily, where he saw the ruins of shelled houses and where:

you stumble over the remains of a human body, a leg sticking out here, an arm there. . . . You look round and see half a dozen gorged rats scampering off in all directions. . . .

Little wonder that there came a day when the soldier wanted to stop fighting. Later he told why he had not:

I was in despair myself, and thought of giving up the whole thing. I was sitting on a hillock. . . . Garibaldi came by. . . . Well, he laid his hand on my shoulder and simply said . . . "Courage; courage! We are going to fight for our country." Do you think I could ever turn back after that?

The soldier did not turn back. Stirred by nationalistic feelings he continued to fight for himself, for Garibaldi, and for a free Italy!

CHAPTER REVIEW

REVIEW and DISCUSSION

1. Identify the people and places and explain the terms and events on p. 508.

2. Make a generalization supported by historical facts about the growth of national consciousness that would apply to Italy, Germany, and other countries that you have studied.

3. How did Italy become a unified country?

4. Why did so many Italians emigrate in the late 1800's and early 1900's?

5. Which country do you think was more democratic from 1871 to 1914—Italy or Germany? Why?

6. Since Austria had the same language as the other German states, why was she not included in the growth of German national consciousness?

7. How was Germany unified?

8. Evaluate Bismarck's contributions to the unification of Germany.

9. Who do you think was right—Keynes, who said that the German Empire was built on iron and coal, or Bismarck, who believed it was built on blood and iron? Why?

10. Why were advanced social-welfare programs put into effect in the German Empire?

11. What idea was the most turbulent in the minds and actions of many people in the nineteenth century? Why?

ACTIVITIES

1. Make two parallel columns listing the steps taken by Cavour and Bismarck in the unification of their respective countries. What are your conclusions?

2. In a source book find a copy of the Ems Dispatch. Show the class how Bismarck changed the original.

3. Panel discussion: In building a nation, are any means justified to achieve worthwhile ends?

4. Draw a cartoon illustrating an important event in Bismarck's career. Cavour's.

PAST and PRESENT

1. In what ways were Italy's efforts to "catch up" with the more developed countries similar to the efforts of the new African nations today?

2. Compare the welfare legislation in Germany between 1871 and 1914 with that of the United States in the 1930's.

SUGGESTED READINGS

Basic books: MARRIOTT, SIR J. A. R., *The Makers of Modern Italy, Napoleon-Mussolini,* Oxford. Easily read. This book portrays effectively the leaders of unification.

PALMER, R. R., and COLTON, JOEL, *A History of the Modern World,* Chap 13, Knopf.

PINSON, KOPPEL S., *Modern Germany, Its History and Civilization,* Macmillan. A well written and logically organized history.

SMITH, GOLDWIN, *The Heritage of Man,* Chap. 36, Scribner.

Special accounts: BRINKLEY, ROBERT, *Realism and Nationalism 1852–1871* ("The Rise of Modern Europe" series), Harper. A scholarly analysis suitable for better students.

EYCK, ERICH, *Bismarck and the German Empire,* Macmillan. For better readers. Gives credit to Bismarck for his achievements without expressing undue admiration.

GLADSTONE, ERSKINE WILLIAM, ST. AUBYN, E. R., and REES, BRIAN, *The Unification of Italy,* Macmillan. Brief, interesting, clear. By English authors.

SNYDER, LOUIS L., *Fifty Major Documents of the Nineteenth Century,* Van Nostrand. Includes important documents.

Biography and Fiction: DAVENPORT, MARCIA, *Garibaldi; Father of Modern Italy,* Random House. Simple, concise, colorful.

HUMPHREYS, DENA, *Verdi: Force of Destiny,* Holt. Verdi was involved in many of the events of Italian unification.

Chapter 33

Britain Strengthens Itself at Home and Expands Overseas

KEYNOTE   Professor Goldwin Smith concludes his book, *A History of England*, with the words of the philosopher who said: "History never begins a new chapter. Only historians do." This point was particularly apparent in nineteenth-century Britain.

It was then that the British people strengthened their democracy at home and expanded their power abroad. In doing so, they were not starting new chapters in British history; they were continuing the pattern of domestic and foreign developments that reached back to the seventeenth century—and beyond.

Key People   *Lord John Russell · Queen Victoria · William Gladstone · Benjamin Disraeli · David Lloyd George*

Key Places   *Irish Free State · Northern Ireland · Canada · Ontario · Quebec · Australia · South Africa · Cape Town · Transvaal · Orange Free State · India*

Key Events   *Reform Bill of 1832 · Corn Laws repealed · Chartists press for reforms · Reform Act of 1867 · House of Lords loses power · Irish Free State formed · British North America Act · Boer War · Sepoy Mutiny*

Key Terms   *"rotten boroughs" · "pocket boroughs" · Liberal (Whig) party · Conservative (Tory) party · People's Charter · Australian ballot · Labor party · home rule · Lord Durham's report*

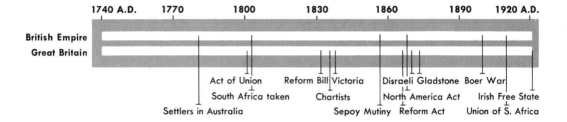

British Empire
Great Britain

1740 A.D.   1770   1800   1830   1860   1890   1920 A.D.

Act of Union   Reform Bill | Victoria   Disraeli Gladstone   Boer War

South Africa taken   Chartists   North America Act   Irish Free State

Settlers in Australia   Sepoy Mutiny   Reform Act   Union of S. Africa

1. The Growth of Democracy in Britain

"Swans seem whiter if black crows are by" observed the Frenchman Guillaume de Salluste in the sixteenth century. This statement, repeated by British reformers of the nineteenth century, seemed true in 1815. Certainly, the many political, economic, and social evils that blackened the continent of Europe made life in England appear unusually bright. England was governed primarily by Parliament, the power of the king was limited, the press had considerable freedom to express its opinions, and the wealth of England exceeded that of any European country.

Political Abuses in Britain

On the other hand, while England seemed progressive, she still was plagued by a number of evils, particularly in the area of political rights. For example, the right to vote for members of Parliament was limited to wealthy property owners. Some 96 per cent of the male adults in England and Ireland could not vote, and only one in every five hundred persons in Scotland had suffrage rights. No women could vote in Great Britain, or in most other countries. Only men who belonged to the

Church of England were legally eligible for government offices. Roman Catholics and Dissenters were denied political equality, but they had to contribute to the support of the Church of England.

Election contests were often corrupt and costly. For example, Lord John Russell, a statesman of the period, pointed out that in Liverpool "bribery [was] employed to the greatest extent ... every voter receiving a number of guineas [coins] in a box, as the price of his corruption."

Certain old districts, called "rotten boroughs," continued to send representatives to Parliament even though their populations had declined to a point where they had few or no voters. Dunwich, a town that was sinking under the North Sea, still had representation in Parliament.

In some areas, called "pocket boroughs," the voters were controlled by landlords who practically named the representatives to be sent to Parliament. In 1831 the Duke of Buckingham appointed the representatives from Buckingham (population 13), and Lord Monson chose the representatives from Gatton — population 5!

New cities that had grown up as industrial centers (Manchester and Birmingham) were permitted no representation in Parliament at all.

Lord John Russell, describing the situation in 1831, asked the members of the House of Commons to imagine what "a stranger from some distant country" would see if he visited England:

What then would be his surprise, if he were taken by his guide, . . . to see a green mound and told that this green mound sent two Members to Parliament—or, to be taken to a stone wall . . . and told that [three niches in it] sent two Members to Parliament. . . .

The visitor's astonishment would increase, Lord Russell went on:

if he were carried into the North of England, where he would see large flourishing towns, full of trade and activity, . . . and were told that these places had no Representatives in the Assembly which was said to represent the people.

The time was ripe for political reform, and there were men like Lord Russell ready to introduce the necessary changes.

Demands for Political Reform

The demand for political reform became even stronger because the wealth of England was the possession of the few. As Cobbett's *Weekly Political Register*, a popular newspaper, pointed out: "Elegant dresses, superb furniture, stately buildings, fine roads and canals, fleet horses and carriages, numerous and stout ships, warehouses teeming with goods—all these . . . are so many marks of national wealth and resources. But all these spring from labor." Thousands of laborers, declared the *Register*, were living in poverty and misery. Indeed, in 1801 one out of every seven persons had to receive financial aid (poor relief) from the government.

Workers in Britain were burdened by many things: long hours and low pay, lack of permanent employment, poor housing, high taxes, and depressions. They had to pay high prices for food, largely as a result of the *Corn Laws*, which protected British gentlemen farmers by imposing duties on grain coming from other countries. An increasing number of British reformers became convinced that the best way to change such economic conditions was to give political power to more people.

The Pressure for Reform Grows Stronger

The pressure for reform became stronger. In 1812 there were "bread riots" in Sheffield, where mobs of women rushed through the markets emptying stalls of their wares. In 1819 there was a clash between agitators for reform and troops of the government in Manchester, where cavalrymen drove back the people. In 1828 laws discriminating against Dissenters were repealed; and in 1829 the Catholic Emancipation Act finally granted Roman Catholics equal political rights.

In 1830 the Tory party, which had blocked efforts to make basic changes in the country, lost some of its power in Parliament to the more reform-minded Whig party. The Whigs promptly presented a major reform bill to Parliament. This bill met with great opposition but, after Parliament was dissolved and a new election held for the House of Commons, it was passed by the lower house. The largely hereditary House of Lords still refused to pass the bill, and there were angry demonstrations and riots in the country. Finally, Lord Charles Grey, the Whig leader who was prime minister, made it clear that, if necessary, the king would appoint new members to the House of Lords to assure the passage of the bill. The Lords then gave ground, and the Reform Bill of 1832 was passed.

Keep back Johnny — keep back — leave 'em to me. I'll clear them out. I warrant ye!

Touch me if you dare — Murder, fire, Thieves!

To Windsor & Reform

REFORM

Old Sarum

■ *This is an English cartoon on behalf of the Reform Bill of 1832. Earl Grey, a strong backer of the bill, is sweeping out the rotten boroughs.*

The Reform Bill of 1832

The Reform Bill of 1832 was a high point in the political development of Britain. Its principal provisions were the following: (1) It lowered the property requirements necessary for suffrage, giving the right to vote to many members of the middle class (merchants, businessmen, industrialists and others). (2) It eliminated many "rotten" and "pocket" boroughs and redistributed the seats of Parliament. Large towns and counties which formerly had no or little representation could send more representatives to Parliament. (3) It increased Scotland's representation to Parliament by eight new members and Ireland's representation by five. (4) It provided for the more careful registration of voters.

The extension of suffrage was extremely important. Historian James E. Gillespie points out that: "the grip of the aristocracy on the political system was broken. In 1688 power had been transferred from the sovereign to the nobility; now it was divided between the landlords and some of the bourgeoisie."

The Reform Bill of 1832 did not give the ballot to workers in industry, farmers with little property, women, or many others. Even after its passage, twenty-one out of every twenty-two adult males in Britain could not vote. Nevertheless, the Reform Bill opened the way to later legislation that would establish suffrage on a broad and democratic basis in Britain.

A Cluster of Reforms

The Reform Bill of 1832 was followed by other laws improving living conditions in Britain. The Emancipation Act of 1833 provided for "freeing under certain conditions all slaves owned by British subjects or in British dominions." It also prohibited slavery on British soil in the future. The Factory Act of 1833 (p. 463) tried to improve working conditions in the factories.

The New Poor Law of 1834 was designed to make employers and workers depend on themselves instead of on financial aid from the government. It had these provisions: (1) Paupers could receive relief only if they were willing to live in the poorhouse or were too old and sick to leave their homes. (2) Paupers who were physically well were to be sent to workhouses to labor. (3) Paupers could move wherever they wished to obtain work.

■ *The wretched conditions existing in English prisons can be seen in William Hogarth's painting, "The Prison." Prison reform began in the 1830's and continued for thirty years.*

The New Poor Law of 1834 could be called a reform only in that it provided more freedom of movement for members of the working class. The system of poorhouses and workhouses which it set up was unsatisfactory. In them children and adults suffered both physically, from bad and scanty food, and psychologically, from loss of self-respect and actual mistreatment.

The history of English justice had been filled with cases of unjust and inhumane treatment of offenders. In the nineteenth century, the death penalty could be given for over two hundred crimes, including shoplifting or "injuring Westminster Bridge." Many juries refused to declare a person guilty—even when he had committed a crime—because they felt that it was unfair to sentence him to death.

In 1835, a law was passed eliminating many cruel and inhumane methods of treating people in prison. As a result of reforms introduced during the next three decades, the use of the death penalty for petty offenses was discontinued. Capital punishment was reserved for only the most serious crimes.

The Liberal and Conservative Parties Develop

Changes also were made in the political parties. The Whig party became the *Liberal* party, and included manufacturers, merchants, some landlords, nonconformists, and some radicals. The Tory party became the *Conservative* party and included landed gentry, some shopkeepers, wealthy industrialists, and military officers.

There was considerable overlapping in party membership. Neither party could claim the support of all of the members of a class. For example, workers who had not yet been given the right to vote could be found supporting both parties. Neither party had a monopoly on reform legislation. Both the Liberals and Conservatives made contributions to the important changes introduced into the country.

■ **Check on Your Reading**

1. What conditions in England made political and economic reforms necessary?

2. Summarize the Reform Bill of 1832.

3. Summarize the provisions of the New Poor Law of 1834.

2. The "Victorian Age" in Britain

In 1837 eighteen-year-old Victoria became Queen of the United Kingdom of Great Britain and Ireland; she was to reign for sixty-three years. This young and inexperienced queen proved to be one of the most highly respected and popular monarchs in English history. Biographer Lytton Strachey sums up her character in this way: "Vitality, conscientiousness, pride, and simplicity were hers to the latest hour." During Queen Victoria's reign, Britain developed at home and expanded abroad. In tribute to her, this period is known as the "Victorian Age."

The Corn Laws Are Repealed

Shortly after Victoria ascended the throne, there was bitter agitation over the Corn Laws, the tariff or tax placed on grains imported from foreign countries. These laws were designed primarily to protect the sale of foodstuffs produced by the British themselves. However, opponents of the Corn Laws protested that they resulted in high prices for bread and other foods and caused many hardships.

More and more people demanded that the Corn Laws be abolished. Merchants and manufacturers joined in the Anti-Corn-Law League to fight for repeal of the Corn Laws so that food would be cheaper for the growing numbers of industrial workers. They also wanted to encourage the exchange of their industrial products for the food of other countries. They thus had good practical reasons for seeking freer trade. A crop failure in England and a potato famine in Ireland increased the cries for economic reform. In 1846 the Corn Laws were repealed.

During the next two decades, the protective tariffs on other imported articles were removed. This was done because it was believed that other countries would be able to obtain funds to buy British products if they could sell their own goods in Britain. As early as 1852 Parliament passed a resolution declaring that:

[Free trade] will best enable the industry of the country to bear its burdens, and will thereby most surely promote the welfare and contentment of the people.

England became one of the leading exponents of the philosophy of free trade.

The Chartists Demand Reform

In the middle of the nineteenth century the demands for reform grew stronger. Reformers known as the Chartists had organized in 1836. In 1848 they marched angrily through London demanding these reforms in their "People's Charter": universal manhood suffrage, secret ballot, annual election of members of the House of Commons, abolition of property qualifications for members of the House of Commons, salaries for members of the House of Commons, and equal election districts.

The year was 1848, and revolutions were sweeping through Europe. The British government, fearful that the revolutionary fever might cross the Channel, took sharp measures against the Chartists, arresting several of their leaders. The leadership of the Chartists was not strong enough in this crisis, and the movement collapsed. Even in failure the Chartists provided later reformers with many goals and rallying cries. By 1918 all of their program, except the annual election of members of the House of Commons, had been put into effect.

William Gladstone and Benjamin Disraeli

The two men who now dominated the political scene of Britain were Benjamin Disraeli of the Conservative party and William Gladstone of the Liberal party.

Between 1868 and 1894, except for six years, these two outstanding statesmen alternated as prime minister of Britain.

William Gladstone was a leader of great physical vitality. John Morley, his biographer, claims that "he was born with a frame of steel"; and Sir James Graham, a contemporary of Gladstone, believed that "Gladstone could do in four hours what it took any other man sixteen to do, and he worked sixteen hours a day."

Benjamin Disraeli was a colorful and romantic figure who followed his political star until he became prime minister—or, as he put it, until he "climbed to the top of the greasy pole." Clever, witty, and often brilliant in his approach to problems, Disraeli was a worthy rival of Gladstone in Parliament.

Disraeli was fortunate in winning the friendship and support of Queen Victoria; but as a realist, he knew that it was Parliament, not the queen, who held the governing power. He worked energetically to gain parliamentary support. Nevertheless, he continued to rely primarily on his own judgment in making decisions.

Suffrage Rights Are Extended

Under the leadership of men like Gladstone and Disraeli, the British government continued to introduce gradual changes. New laws extended suffrage rights.

The Reform Act of 1867 was passed under a Conservative ministry. It gave the vote to townsmen who paid taxes or rented lodgings at an annual rent of at least $50; granted suffrage rights to more people in rural areas by lowering the property and rental requirements necessary to vote; and provided for four industrial cities (Manchester, Birmingham, Liverpool, and Leeds) to send additional representatives to Parliament. *This act gave the vote to urban workers and nearly doubled the electorate.* Some legislators warned that this would lead to disaster. However, instead of fomenting revolution, the Reform Act of 1867 stimulated additional reforms.

Other acts granted Jews the right to be elected to Parliament. Later atheists were also officially permitted to serve in the House of Commons. In 1872 the secret ballot (or the Australian ballot) was adopted for use in elections. The Reform

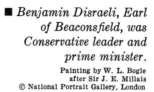

■ *William E. Gladstone, Liberal leader, served as prime minister of Britain for fifteen years between 1868 and 1894.*
Painting by George F. Watts,
National Portrait Gallery, London

■ *Benjamin Disraeli, Earl of Beaconsfield, was Conservative leader and prime minister.*
Painting by W. L. Bogle
after Sir J. E. Millais
© National Portrait Gallery, London

Act of 1884, passed primarily through the efforts of Gladstone, extended the franchise to many agricultural laborers and other men living in rural areas. The electorate was increased by about two million new voters. The Redistribution of Seats Act of 1885 took steps to establish equal election districts throughout the country.

The suffrage laws of the nineteenth century were a landmark in the growth of democracy in Britain because they extended the right to vote to most men. It was not until 1928 that all men and women over the age of twenty-one could vote.

The House of Lords Is Stripped of Power

Despite the major reforms passed by the House of Commons, the House of Lords continued to stand in the way of change. The House of Lords consisted of a body of men who held their positions principally by inheritance.

In 1909 the Lords' battlements were challenged! The Liberals were in power and the Chancellor of the Exchequer, David Lloyd George, submitted a budget that hit hard at the upper classes. This budget provided for taxes on large incomes and estates and on lands whose value had increased without their owners contributing to their improvement. The House of Commons passed this budget, but the House of Lords refused to accept it. A

bitter struggle followed. After a newly elected House of Commons exerted pressure on it, the House of Lords passed the budget.

The actions of the House of Lords had infuriated the Liberals. They were determined that the Lords should never again block important legislation. In 1911, the Parliament Act stripped the Lords of most of their power. It provided that: (1) The House of Lords could no longer prevent the passage of any money bill passed by the House of Commons. (2) Any other bill passed by the House of Commons in three successive sessions would become a law—even if the House of Lords did not accept it. Two years had to elapse between the first presentation of the bill and its final passage. (3) The House of Commons would be elected every five instead of every seven years.

In the beginning of the twentieth century a group of moderate socialists united with members of labor unions to form the Labor party. After World War I, the Liberal party declined and the Labor party spearheaded the reform movement.

■ Check on Your Reading

1. Why did people oppose the Corn Laws?
2. Summarize the political reforms of the Reform Act of 1867, the Reform Act of 1884, and the Parliament Act of 1911.

529

3. Britain and Ireland

The relatively peaceful growth of democracy in Britain contrasted sharply with developments in Ireland. In Ireland it was a story of bitter—and often bloody—clashes between the English and the Irish.

The English Dominate Ireland

The history of Ireland has been marked by the efforts of the Irish to win their freedom from their English rulers. By the Act of Union of 1801: (1) The Irish Parliament at Dublin was abolished. (2) Ireland was given some representation in the British Parliament. (3) Great Britain and Ireland were to be governed by the same body, the British Parliament. The British Isles were to form a single state known as the United Kingdom of Great Britain and Ireland.

Reasons for Irish-English Tensions

Throughout history, English rulers had deprived Irish farmers of their land and had turned it over to English noblemen. As a result, most of the Irish did not own the land they worked. Much of the land was owned by absentee landlords who lived in England and rarely came to Ireland. The Irish had to pay rent and taxes that were heavy burdens on them.

Most of the Irish were Roman Catholics. (The most numerous exceptions were the Scotch Presbyterians, who lived primarily in Northern Ireland.) Like everyone else, the Irish Catholics had to pay tithes to support the Anglican Church, to whose religious principles they did not subscribe. The Irish showed their opposition to this situation by trying to prevent the collection of tithes.

The Irish felt that they were not sufficiently represented in the British Parliament. They also were convinced that the British government did not take enough interest in the welfare of Ireland. Some Irish leaders, stirred by nationalistic feelings, wanted to build an Irish nation that would be free from foreign domination.

Gladstone Works for Reform

In the late 1840's a terrible potato crop failure in Ireland brought great famine.

■ At this midnight meeting, the Fenians, a secret organization dedicated to overthrowing British rule in Ireland, are protesting against the Perpetual Coercion Act passed by a Conservative Parliament in 1887. This act was passed after a Home Rule Bill for Ireland, sponsored by the Liberals, had been defeated.

Thousands of Irish left their country and emigrated to America and other lands.

During the latter part of the nineteenth century the Liberal prime minister of Britain, Gladstone, worked to improve conditions in Ireland. Specifically, Gladstone helped to bring about the separation of Church and state in Ireland. This meant that the Irish people no longer had to pay taxes to support the Anglican Church. He introduced land reforms in Ireland, which provided for the following: (1) The tenant's rent would be fair to him. (2) The tenant would have "fixity of tenure" (for example, he could not suddenly be forced off the land by a landlord who demanded a rent that he could not pay). (3) The tenant could sell his own property and receive compensation for the improvements that he made.

The Irish demands for *home rule*, or self-government, continued to grow. "Ireland stands at your bar expectant, hopeful, almost suppliant. Her words are the words of truth . . . ," Gladstone told Parliament. His efforts to have Parliament pass a Home Rule Bill were not successful.

The Irish Free State Is Formed

The *Sinn Fein* ("We Ourselves") movement developed during the beginning of the twentieth century. The supporters of the *Sinn Fein* were very nationalistic. They insisted that Ireland should be governed only by the Irish.

In 1916, while Britain was deeply involved in war with Germany, the Irish revolted. This so-called "Easter Rebellion" was crushed, but there was bitter fighting between the Irish and English from 1919 to 1921. In 1921 the self-governing *Irish Free State* was formed. It would have a Parliament with the authority to make laws and an executive responsible to that Parliament.

Northern Ireland contained people of Scottish descent and was largely Protestant. It did not join the Irish Free State but remained a part of Great Britain.

■ Check on Your Reading

1. What were the basic reasons for tensions between the Irish and English?
2. What did Gladstone try to do for Ireland? What success did he have?

4. Britain and Canada

England had acquired Canada from France in 1763 as a result of the Seven Years' War (p. 386). At this time there were about 70,000 people, mostly French, living in Canada. Then a number of Englishmen migrated to Canada. Differences in origin, language, customs, and education produced conflicts between the English and the French. Another area of conflict was religion. Most of the English were Protestant and most of the French were Catholic, which tended to keep them apart. In 1774, Parliament passed the important *Quebec Act*. This act granted to the French Canadians the right to have their own civil laws, language, customs, religion, and system of land tenure.

The English population in Canada continued to grow. It increased primarily as a result of the influx of *Loyalists* (American colonists loyal to England) who fled to Canada during the American Revolution.

In 1791, Parliament passed an act that divided Canada into two provinces— Lower Canada, inhabited principally by the French; and Upper Canada, inhabited chiefly by the English. Each province was permitted to have its own assembly, and both the Anglican and Roman Catholic Churches were permitted to exist.

Lord Durham's Report

Basic political and religious problems still remained, and a newly born political press fanned the fires of discontent. Some publications demanded that the language, religion, and culture of the English dominate Canada. Others, like *Le Canadien*, defended the interests of the French people and chose as a motto: "Our [French] language, our institutions, and our laws." When the disagreements were not settled, rebellions broke out in both provinces (1837–1838) against the government of Britain. These rebellions were put down.

In 1839, after studying conditions in Canada, Lord Durham presented a report to the British Parliament. He recommended that Lower and Upper Canada be reunited, and the people of Canada be given self-government in their internal or domestic affairs. By the Union Act of 1840, these and other reforms were carried out.

Lord Durham's report proved to be very important. In his report Lord Durham had declared that "vigor" in the administration of Canada would come:

not by weakening, but strengthening the influence of the people [of Canada] on its government. . . .

Such comments helped to advance the idea that the colonies should be given self-government when they were ready for it.

The British North America Act

The British North America Act was passed in 1867. This act, which Professor George W. Brown of the University of Toronto has called "the most important single law in Canadian history," provided for the formation of a Canadian confederation to consist of Ontario (Upper Canada), Quebec (Lower Canada), Nova Scotia, and New Brunswick. Provision was made to

■ *By 1914, Great Britain had built a vast empire, including lands in Australia, Canada, India, New Zealand, South Africa, and other areas. What problems did Britain encounter in ruling these varied and divergent areas? How did she solve them?*

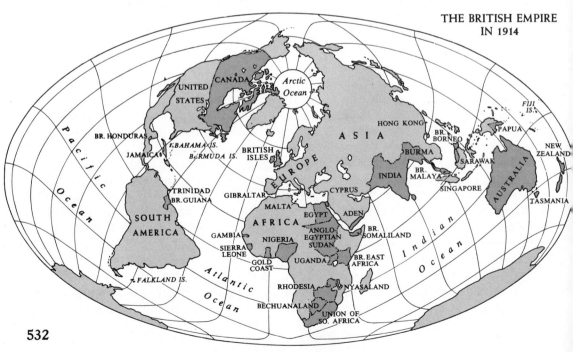

THE BRITISH EMPIRE
IN 1914

admit additional provinces and the confederation was called the Dominion of Canada. The British North America Act also provided that there were to be separate governments in each province to deal with provincial matters, such as education; and a common government at Ottawa to deal with matters involving all of Canada, such as the defense of the country. Canadian union had been achieved.

The idea of Dominion status within the British Empire was considered a sound one. This status was later extended to other areas, including Australia, India, and the Union of South Africa (p. 536). They became self-governing countries with ties of economic interests, traditions, and loyalty holding them to Britain.

■ Check on Your Reading

1. What problems complicated Britain's government of Canada after 1763?

2. Summarize Lord Durham's report.

3. Why was the British North America Act called "the most important single law in Canadian history"?

5. Britain and Australia

In the seventeenth century a Dutch mariner named Abel Tasman discovered lands which are known as Tasmania, New Zealand, and Australia. The Dutch never took possession of these islands. Captain James Cook of the British navy also explored the coasts of Australia and New Zealand during 1769–1770. The report of Cook's expedition helped to stimulate the settlement of Australia, a land about the size of the United States not including Alaska and Hawaii. Englishmen became interested in this faraway country with its rugged coasts battered by the surf, its waving grasses and drifting desert sands, its brilliantly colored wild flowers, and its fascinating and strangely named birds.

Australia Is Settled

After 1776 the British began to use Australia as a penal colony. A number of the criminals sent to Australia were guilty of only petty offenses, such as poaching. Some parts, such as South and Western Australia, were first settled by free men. Much of Australia later was colonized by free settlers and by some liberated prisoners. After 1840, prisoners were not sent to most of the regions of Australia.

In 1851 gold was discovered in New South Wales and Victoria, and thousands of adventurers and settlers came to Australia. However, sheep-raising and the production of wool proved to be far more important to the Australians than the mining of gold. Although much of the land was desert or heavily forested, there were fertile plains and the raising of wheat also became a major occupation.

Australian Union Is Achieved

Men now came to Australia, in the words of Sir Keith Hancock, "not in despair but in hope." In time, six colonies developed in Australia and the island of Tasmania. These colonies gradually gained rights of self-government from Great Britain.

Then in 1901, with the approval of the British Parliament, a constitution permitting a federal union of all of the colonies (or states) went into effect. Included in the Commonwealth of Australia were New South Wales, Victoria, South Australia including Northern Territory, Western Australia, Queensland, and Tasmania.

■ Check on Your Reading

1. How did Britain acquire Australia?

2. How was Australian union achieved?

6. Britain and New Zealand

In 1642 Abel Tasman discovered a group of islands lying to the southeast of Australia. The *Maoris*, the Polynesian people who were natives of these islands, called their land *Ao-tea-roa* (Long White Cloud); but the Dutch renamed it *Nieuw Zeeland* (New Zealand) after the province of Zeeland in Holland. In 1769 Captain James Cook of the British navy explored the coasts of New Zealand and wrote of the Maoris: "All their actions and behaviour towards us tended to prove that they are a brave, open, warlike people and void of treachery."

Britain Gains Sovereignty over New Zealand

In 1840 Great Britain signed the Treaty of Waitangi with the Maoris' chiefs, each of whom received a blanket and some tobacco as a special gift. According to Professor I. L. G. Sutherland, an authority on Maori culture, this treaty had the following provisions: (1) The Maoris ceded to the British Crown the sovereignty of New Zealand. (2) The Queen guaranteed the Maoris the full, exclusive, and undisputed possession of their lands, except as the Crown might wish to purchase them. (3) The Queen gave to all Maoris the rights and privileges of British subjects.

Settlers from England, Scotland, Wales, and Ireland began to move into the country. The Maoris became angry at the ways in which the settlers were acquiring land, and fighting broke out. These clashes eventually were ended.

As in Canada and Australia, the people of New Zealand were able to obtain additional governing privileges. In 1852 a federation of settlements was formed, and the provinces of New Zealand were given self-government. Thirteen years later a central government for all of New Zealand was established.

New Zealand Introduces Advanced Legislation

New Zealand has a total area that is slightly smaller than the state of Nevada, and even today its population is about two and one half million. Nevertheless, the New Zealand government cared for its people so well that the country became known as a leader in political, economic, and social laws. For example, in the last decade of the nineteenth century the following things were done by the government: (1) Large estates were broken up to provide land that could be sold to small farmers. (2) Suffrage was extended to women in 1893, making New Zealand the first country to permit women to have the same voting rights as men. (3) Boards were established to settle labor disputes by arbitration. (4) A program of accident insurance was set up for workers. (5) A system of old-age pensions was developed so that "veterans of industry shall have pensions as well as veterans of war. . . ."

In 1904 an American observer was so impressed with the accomplishments of New Zealand that he called its inhabitants: "an earnest, open-minded, common-sense, true-hearted people . . . [with] laws and institutions based on principles that accord with the public good." In 1907 Great Britain formally granted New Zealand the right to develop as a nation, and it became a British Dominion.

■ Check on Your Reading

1. How did Britain gain control of New Zealand?

2. Why did clashes occur between the white settlers and the Maoris?

3. What form of government was gradually established there?

4. Give examples of New Zealand's advanced social legislation.

7. Britain and South Africa

The British also were active in the area known today as South Africa, although they were not the first settlers there. In 1486 Bartholomew Diaz, a Portuguese explorer, discovered the Cape of Storms, or the Cape of Good Hope. In 1652 the Dutch East India Company, which had taken control of Portuguese trading areas, established a "refreshment station" at Cape Town. It was used by the crews of ships as a place to take on fresh supplies of green vegetables, to care for the sick, and to leave mail to be carried back to Europe.

The native inhabitants of Cape Town were the Bushmen and Hottentots. Both of these groups were small in number and had developed rather simple cultures. The Bushmen, for example, still wandered from waterhole to waterhole in search of game; lighted fire with firesticks; dined on locusts, ants, and scorpions when meat was not available; and followed many *soxas*, or taboos—such as the rule that animals killed with bow and arrow could not be eaten until tasted by the chief. On the other hand, the rock paintings found in caves demonstrated that some Bushmen had unusual artistic ability.

The Hottentots were in many ways more advanced than the Bushmen, but they were also a pastoral people. Eventually, some of them became a part of the European settlements. Today in South Africa the term *Colored* (or Mixed Ones) is given to those who are considered descendants of Hottentots, slaves, and some Asians and Europeans.

The Dutch East India Company's station in South Africa gradually developed into a Dutch colony on the Cape of Good Hope. As late as 1710, there were only seventeen hundred white settlers. About 50 per cent of these were Dutch; the rest were Germans or French Huguenots. In South Africa today those considered descendants of these Dutch, German, and French settlers are called *Afrikaners*.

About 1775 these European settlers of South Africa came in contact with the *Bantu*, native Africans who are believed to have migrated southward from the central part of the continent. The Bantu were struck by the strange color of the Europeans and called them "men whose ears reflect the sunlight" and "men having the color of a yellowish clay pot." Bantu groups eventually made many contributions to the development of South Africa, such as working the farms, constructing roads, building towns, and enriching language. However, the Europeans and Bantus did not live in peace but fought fiercely on many occasions. Today the tensions between the groups form the basis of a serious racial problem in South Africa (p. 720).

When the Dutch opposed Great Britain in the Napoleonic Wars, the British seized and kept possession of the colony at the Cape. Today in South Africa the term *English* naturally is given to descendants of the Englishmen who settled in South Africa after the Napoleonic Wars, as well as to those who later migrated there.

The "Great Trek"

When the British took control of the colony at the Cape, they came in close contact with the *Boers*. The Boers (word for farmers) were a hardy people of primarily Dutch descent who had settled in South Africa. The Boers disliked the British, for they felt that the British did not give them sufficient political or social power. They also were angered when the British freed the slaves in Cape Colony, because the Boers needed slaves to work their farms.

Many Boers therefore made a long move—called the "Great Trek"—north to

535

the interior, starting about 1836. It was a dangerous journey, but in the words of the South African writer Alan Paton: "Like the thorn tree, [the Boer] put his roots down into the rock and stone, and in the face of all calamity survived." The Boers were able to establish two new states in the interior, the Orange Free State and the Transvaal. Here they hoped "to govern ourselves without [British] interference."

The British recognized the independence of the Orange Free State and the Transvaal in 1852. However, disputes continued. The British quarrelled with the leaders of the Orange Free State over a section of land that both claimed. Then the British government annexed the Transvaal in 1877 and denied its people self-government for about four years.

The Anglo-Boer War

About 1885–1886 gold was discovered in the Transvaal. Attracted by the riches in the gold and diamond mines, many British as well as people of other nationalities hurried into the Transvaal.

The Boers resented the coming of these *Uitlanders*, or "foreigners," most of whom were British. Eventually they taxed the Uitlanders heavily, made it difficult for them to become citizens, and refused to give them voting rights. These acts served to increase the hostility between the Boers and the Uitlanders. The actions of British empire builders like Cecil Rhodes, the prime minister of Cape Colony who was believed to have encouraged a conspiracy against the Boers, added to the tension.

Finally, the allied Boer states of the Transvaal Republic and the Orange Free State declared war on Great Britain (Anglo-Boer War, 1899–1902). After a determined struggle, the Boers were defeated. In 1902 the British annexed these Boer states.

Formation of the Union of South Africa

The victorious British did not deprive the Boer states of all governing powers. In 1906–1907 the right of self-government was returned to the Transvaal and Orange Free State. In 1910, the *Union of South Africa* was officially formed, and South Africa was permitted to develop as a nation. The new union consisted of Cape Colony, Natal, Orange Free State, and the Transvaal.

■ **Check on Your Reading**

1. Describe the principal native and white groups living in South Africa. What tensions developed after 1852?

2. What events led up to the Anglo-Boer War? What were the results of the war?

8. Britain and India

England's claims on India were first established by the English East India Company. The Company was far more than an organization for trade. In many regions of India, it ruled people, collected taxes, handled justice, and backed up its decisions with military force. Soon there was evidence that a number of Company officials were accepting graft and administering their areas dishonestly. The English historian Thomas Macaulay, for example, reported that "Enormous fortunes were ... rapidly accumulated at Calcutta, while thirty millions of human beings were reduced to the last extremity of wretchedness."

The British Parliament passed the Regulating Act in 1773 to supervise the actions of the East India Company. This act was designed to keep the Company's trading practices separate from its policies of government. Warren Hastings was appointed the first Governor-General of the British lands in India and was expected to help supervise the over-all situation.

The British Expand Their Control of India

In the nineteenth century the British expanded throughout India. The British forces defeated marauding tribesmen in northern India and gained control of their land. In western and central India, they crushed a group of native princes, known as the Mahratta Confederation, and annexed much of their territory. The British also added the Sind, an important region in northwestern India, to their possessions.

The British forces fought two wars against the Sikhs and took over the Punjab region. They also pushed back Burmese invaders, taking possession of Burma in 1884–1885. Eventually, British control extended to the borders of Afghanistan, Nepal, China, and Indo-China.

The Sepoy Mutiny

British annexations in India continued to be challenged. Differences between the practices of Europeans and the beliefs of the peoples of India were major causes of tension. In 1857 a number of Indian troops (the *Sepoys*) became angry because they believed that the rifle cartridges given to them by British officers were coated with cow and pig grease. The Hindus considered the cow to be a holy animal, and the Moslems considered the pig to be too unclean to touch. This grievance combined with other factors to produce the *Sepoy Mutiny* (1857). During this uprising many Sepoys mutinied and massacred the British in Delhi and other cities. After a number of atrocities by both sides, the mutiny was brought under control.

After the Sepoy Mutiny, the British government took away the political power of the East India Company. By the Act for the Better Government of India (1858) the Crown took over direct control of India. Parliament appointed a viceroy as the chief administrative official in India, and the British Queen Victoria and her council asked the Indian people:

to be faithful, and to bear true allegiance to us, our heirs and successors, and to submit . . . to the authority of those whom we may . . . see fit to appoint to administer the government.

On January 1, 1877, Victoria was proclaimed "Empress of India." This title remained with the British royal family until the middle of the twentieth century.

■ Check on Your Reading

1. How did the English East India Company govern India?
2. Describe the Act for the Better Government of India (1858).

CULTURAL CHARACTERISTICS of the "Victorian Age"

In 1837 Victoria became Queen of the United Kingdom of Great Britain and Ireland. A mere eighteen upon ascending the throne, she did not even know what to do with the orb (a sphere surmounted by a cross as a symbol of royal power) at her coronation.

This young girl, so bewildered by the pomp of the coronation ceremony, was to be Queen for sixty-three years; and her reign was to leave its imprint on one of the most significant periods in British history, often styled the "Victorian Age."

Society in a state of transition in which, as Disraeli put it, "the very principles of our political and social systems are called in question."

Relations between people become more democratic, but John Stuart Mill's dream that "human beings are no longer born to their place in life" was not realized until the twentieth century.

Industrialization of the economy. As a result, the pace of economic life speeded up greatly. A dramatic illustration was the fivefold increase in the speed of ships since the days of Columbus.

Literary and cultural activities that portrayed the special problems of an imperial power.

Tradition has always played an important role in English history. (Even today the wings of the ravens in the Tower of London are clipped to keep them from flying away, because it is believed that the departure of these birds will cause the fall of the Tower and other disasters!) Yet one of the strongest traditions of all is that of change. Certainly, the "Victorian Age" stimulated changes that were to engage the British people in new cultural adventures.

MAN AND HIS CULTURE

Let's Meet the People!
The following sketch of a schoolmaster at the close of the nineteenth century is based on an eye-witness account in Clifton Johnson, *The Isle of the Shamrock*, 1901, the Macmillan Company.

A Schoolmaster of Ireland
The schoolmaster was a tall, thin man with a ragged brown beard and hair that tumbled over his eyes. He wore "[a coat] that hung limply from his sloping shoulders. There was a great square patch on one knee; his collar had long been a stranger to water and starch."

The pupils sat on backless benches. They were "nearly all barefoot, and their clothing was ragged and much patched." The schoolmaster declared: "Now, then, we will read!"

A red-headed boy stepped forward and opened the *First Book of Lessons*. The aim of the book was to make a child "recognize the differences between [words] that resembled each other closely," and many of its paragraphs were deliberately jumbled. The boy read:

Can a worm walk? No, it has no feet; but it can creep. The child is sick; tell her not to cry; let her stay in bed and sleep. This cliff is steep, and I feel my head light as I look down. Did you meet Fred in the street? Weep no more. My boot is too tight; it hurts my foot.

The boy read slowly, stumbling over many words.

"Scoundrel, try that again!" declared the schoolmaster, angrily.

The boy started to read, only to be interrupted again.

"Say it out!" shouted the schoolmaster. "Or I'll put your face on the other side of your head! I'll throw you out of the door. ..." And he knocked the book out of the boy's hand.

"Now, pick that up and give it to me!" was his next command.

The boy obeyed, tears trickling down his face. The schoolmaster looked at him for a moment; then he sent him back to his seat.

"I have been harsh with him again," thought the schoolmaster, "but he must learn. He must be educated so that he can raise himself above this poverty. He must do this—for he is my son."

CHAPTER REVIEW

REVIEW and DISCUSSION

1. Identify the people and places and explain the events and terms on p. 522.

2. Why was Britain one of the first nations to develop into a democracy?

3. Did the fact that Britain had a limited monarchy make it easier or more difficult to gain needed reforms? Why?

4. How much of the success of nineteenth-century reforms in Britain was a result of freedom of the press?

5. What political reforms were achieved, 1832 to 1911?

6. What humanitarian reforms were carried out in the same period?

7. Britain had religious toleration but not complete freedom of religion. What is the difference?

8. What economic reforms were achieved, 1832 to 1911?

9. How might an increase in the political power given to the people help bring about economic reforms?

10. With what other political documents in English history would you rank the Reform Bill of 1832? Why?

11. How do you explain the support which the British Conservative party gave to reform legislation?

12. Why would the payment of salaries to members of Parliament be important?

13. Which of the Chartists' goals were eventually achieved?

ACTIVITIES

1. Panel discussion: Is free trade or high tariffs the better policy for international trade?

2. On a map of the British Isles locate England, Northern Ireland, the Republic of Ireland, Scotland, and Wales. Then designate the principal cities and bodies of water.

3. On a map of the world show all the possessions of the British Empire in the nineteenth century. Indicate which of these possessions became dominions, and the dates on which they secured dominion status.

PAST and PRESENT

1. What nations of the "free world" were once under British control?

2. Why was dominion status considered sound? What have been its results in this century?

SUGGESTED READINGS

Basic books: CHURCHILL, WINSTON, *A History of the English-Speaking Peoples: The Great Democracies*, Chaps. 3, 6, 7, 16, 19, 21, Dodd, Mead.

HALL, WALTER PHELPS, and ALBION, ROBERT GREENHALGH, *A History of England and the British Empire*, Ginn. A reference high school pupils can read with enjoyment.

SMITH, GOLDWIN, *The Heritage of Man*, Chap. 33, Scribner.

Special accounts: CHEYNEY, EDWARD, *Readings in English History Drawn from the Original Sources*, Ginn.

PATON, ALAN, *The Land and the People of South Africa*, Lippincott. Easy to read, interesting. Geographical and political backgrounds are accurately presented.

TREVELYAN, G. M., *English Social History*, Chaps. 17 and 18, Longmans, Green.

WALLBANK, WALTER, *India in the New Era*, Chap. 4, Scott, Foresman. A clear analysis of "The Structure and Spirit of British Rule."

Biography and Fiction: DICKENS, CHARLES, *Oliver Twist*, Macmillan. Novel that describes the system of workhouses and the effects of the New Poor Law.

MAUROIS, ANDRÉ, *Cecil Rhodes* ("Brief Lives" series), Macmillan. Brief, speedily read by most pupils.

MAUROIS, ANDRÉ, *Disraeli: A Picture of the Victorian Age* ("Appleton Modern Literature" series), Appleton-Century-Crofts. Interesting, lively reading for high school students.

Chapter 34

Autocratic Russia: a Culturally Creative International Power

KEYNOTE   Leo Tolstoy, one of the great Russian novelists of the nineteenth century, once wrote:

> In every hurtful thing there is something useful. [When a house is burning down], we may sit and warm ourselves, and light our pipes with one of the firebrands; but should we therefore say that a conflagration is beneficial?

Tolstoy's question had symbolic significance in the nineteenth century. In this period the Russian people suffered severely under the harsh rule of autocratic czars. Yet in this same century Russian culture was brightened by the literature, art, science, and music of some of the most talented men in history.

Should historians therefore say that the nineteenth century in Russia was a period of repression and destruction or of creation? Perhaps the most logical answer is to recognize that both existed. *A key feature of nineteenth-century Russia was the appearance of superb cultural achievements at the same time that the government acted autocratically at home and abroad.*

Key People   *Nicholas I · Alexander II · Alexander III · Alexander Pushkin · Nikolai Gogol · Ivan Turgenev · Fyodor Dostoyevsky · Leo Tolstoy · Peter Ilich Tchaikovsky*

Key Places   *Moscow · St. Petersburg · Ukraine · Siberia · Black Sea · Balkan peninsula · Ottoman Empire · Crimea · Bosnia · Herzegovina*

Key Events   *Decembrist Revolt · Reign of Nicholas I · Reign of Alexander II · Polish Revolt (1830) · Serfs are freed · Alexander II assassinated · Greek Revolt · Crimean War · Russo-Turkish War · Congress of Berlin*

Key Terms   *serfdom · emancipation · "Russification" · mir · pogroms · Slavophiles · Westernizers · "The Sick Man of Europe"*

1. Autocracy in Nineteenth-Century Russia

In 1837 two Russians were condemned to death for attempting to escape from Russia. Czar Nicholas I (1825–1855) commuted the death penalty and decreed: "The convicts are to [be clubbed by] a thousand men—twelve times." This brutal decree was in keeping with the character of Nicholas I, which had been deeply affected by the events of Russian history.

Nicholas I, a Czar of Repression

Nicholas I had become czar of Russia in 1825, after the death of his brother Alexander I, but opposition to his rule arose immediately. On December 26, 1825, two thousand persons rose in rebellion. Among them were members of the Northern Society, an organization that wanted a constitutional monarchy for Russia; the Moscow Guards Regiment; some young nobles and officers; and some workers.

The rebels demanded a government by "Constantine [the brother of Nicholas I] and [a] Constitution," but this Decembrist Revolt was crushed by Nicholas' troops. The revolt remained a symbol of the efforts of Russian intellectuals and others to oppose autocracy. As historian Sidney Harcave points out: "Nicholas was convinced that he had crushed a revolution, not a mere revolt; and he lived under the shadow of the events of December 26 ... for the rest of his life."

The Rule of Czar Nicholas I

Nicholas I attempted to develop an effective government for Russia; for example, he encouraged the codification of law. However, he was equally determined that the people should obey his orders without question. He ruled as an autocrat in many ways. Men who dared to challenge his authority were punished by his political police. Publications were censored by government agencies. Education was controlled by the state, and all "dangerous ideas" were eliminated. Religious sects that refused to accept the principles of the Russian Orthodox Church were persecuted.

Equally important, non-Russian nationality groups under Russian control were forced to accept the almost complete domination of Russia and to undergo forcible "Russification." ("Russification" was a program to eliminate cultural differences in the Russian empire and to establish uniform language, institutions, and loyalty.)

Alexander I had transformed the Grand Duchy of Warsaw into the Kingdom of Poland. He had granted Poland a liberal constitution and the right to exist as an autonomous state. Then in 1830 the Poles

541

revolted and demanded an independent Poland. When the revolt spread to the Russian-controlled province of Lithuania, Nicholas I crushed it with great cruelty. The former "Kingdom of Poland" was made a province of Russia, and a program of "Russification" was imposed on the Polish people.

The Serfs Are Freed

Czar Alexander II (1855–1881), the successor of Nicholas I, was keenly aware that the domestic conditions of the Russian masses needed reform. Alexander II felt that it was better to introduce reform "from above" than to "have it happen from below." It was he who brought about one of the greatest reforms in Russian history—the freeing of the serfs.

The Act on the Emancipation of the Peasants from Serfdom, March 1861, and later decrees had the following provisions: (1) About twenty-two million serfs were declared to be free. (2) These newly freed peasants were permitted to buy from their landlords some of the land they had worked as serfs. (3) Under certain circumstances the state agreed to pay the landlords for the lands that they sold to the former serfs. These peasants were to repay the state in installments spread over a number of years. A law of 1866 also made it possible for the almost twenty-five million peasants who worked for the state to obtain land. By 1881 about 85 per cent of the landlords had given up part of their lands.

The land was not sold outright to the peasants but was transferred to village communes. These communes—called *mirs*—supervised the redistribution of the land among the peasant families living in them and collected payments and taxes owed to the state. They also directed farming activities and kept order.

The emancipation of the serfs was an extremely important reform. The serfs of Russia not only were freed but also were assisted in buying land.

On the other hand, Alexander II's freeing of the serfs did not greatly improve the conditions of the peasants. There were too many weaknesses in the system of emancipation to make possible a strong and balanced economy. The peasants often could not buy enough good land to provide themselves with a decent living. The lands that the peasants bought on installment were usually overvalued, which made their payments to the state a heavy burden. Most peasants were still not completely independent farmers, for the mirs regulated many of their activities. "What is decided by the mir must come to pass," became a popular Russian proverb. As the population of a mir grew, the land was continually redivided. This made for a smaller share of land for each family.

The life of the peasant remained a difficult one, and protests continued throughout Russia. From 1855 to 1861 there had been 474 cases listed where groups of serfs on private estates had challenged the authority of their lords. Within several months *after* the Emancipation Decree of 1861, there were over three hundred peasant outbreaks that had to be put down!

Alexander II's reforms were not limited to the emancipation of the serfs. In addition, he (1) developed a system of local self-government; (2) re-established town councils; (3) reformed the court system and introduced trial by jury; and (4) established universal military conscription in place of a less democratic system of army service. Despite these reforms, an attempt was made to assassinate Alexander II in 1866. This and other events caused him to draw back from reform and to become more autocratic. Despite increased activity by groups demanding reform, the government of Russia remained firmly in the hands of the czar and his officials. After several unsuccessful attempts were made on his life, Alexander II was assassinated in 1881 by members of a revolutionary group. His successors ruled Russia as autocrats.

Alexander III Suppresses Freedom

Alexander III (1881–1894) and his officials did everything that they could to wipe out liberal movements. In the latter part of the reign of Alexander II, thousands of people had been exiled for their political views. Alexander III continued this policy with real determination.

The police of Alexander III were everywhere—spying on the people, beating those who complained, exiling to Siberia anyone listed as "dangerous" to the government. The czar's police did not need evidence before they acted.

The press also was censored. George Kennan, an American writer who was visiting Russia, reported that one Russian newspaperman had been arrested, kept two days in prison without food, flogged, and sent home in weather that was thirty-five degrees below zero. His crime was "furnishing his paper with news."

Innocent men and women were attacked for their religious beliefs. The Jews were singled out. They were called "monsters" and subjected to *pogroms*, or organized massacres. In desperation, thousands of Jews left Russia to seek asylum in the United States and other countries.

At the close of the nineteenth century autocracy was still the dominant factor. When Nicholas II succeeded Alexander III in 1894, the new czar left no doubt that he would continue in the autocratic tradition. Nicholas II made this declaration:

Let it be known by all that I shall devote my whole power to the best service of the people, but that the principle of autocracy will be maintained by me as firmly and unswervingly as by my lamented father.

■ **Check on Your Reading**

1. Why did the Decembrist Revolt occur?
2. How did Nicholas I rule Russia? What did he do about non-Russian nationalities?
3. Describe the emancipation of the serfs. What problems remained?
4. How did Alexander III and Nicholas II rule?

2. Russians Create Great Literature

No country, however autocratic, has ever been without its defenders of freedom. No leader, however repressive, has ever been without his critics urging reform.

In Russia many who cried out for liberty, reform, or the regeneration of man were writers. They included Pushkin, Gogol, Turgenev, Dostoyevsky, Tolstoy, Chekhov, and others. They helped to create the so-called "Golden Age of Russian Literature."

Alexander Pushkin

Alexander Pushkin (1799–1837) is recognized as one of Russia's greatest poets.

He wrote superb lyrics and contributed heavily to the development of the Russian language. At times he also used literature to defend man against oppression. In his poem "Message to Siberia," he urged Russia's exiles to "keep your patience proud" and predicted:

> The heavy-hanging chains will fall,
> The walls will crumble at a word;
> And Freedom greet you in the light,
> And brothers give you back the sword.

It was Pushkin's belief that Russia would someday "rouse from her long sleep" and break the hold of autocracy.

Nikolai Gogol

Nikolai Gogol (1809–1852), a Ukrainian, is a most important writer in the development of Russian literature. Professor Ivar Spector declares: "In the history of Russian literature, 1842 should be hailed as a red-letter year. For the appearance of *Dead Souls* [a satirical novel by Gogol that dealt with the problems of serfdom and government bureaucracy] in that year marked the birth of the genuinely realistic Russian novel, thereby inaugurating the age of prose in Russian literature. Gogol was the father of the Russian novel...."

Gogol is also famous for his short story "The Cloak" or "The Overcoat," in which he examines the pitiful condition of the poor Russian clerk. His play *The Inspector-General*, in which he ridicules corrupt and inefficient bureaucrats, is well known.

Gogol's humor and satire have delighted thousands of readers. Yet it must be remembered that his wit was directed against the tragic evils in Russian society. As he wrote in *An Author's Confession*:

But if we must laugh, why not laugh at what really deserves to be laughed at by us all. In my *The Inspector-General* I decided to bring together and to deride all that is bad in Russia....

Ivan Turgenev

Ivan Turgenev (1818–1883) was a leading *Westernizer*. He urged Russians to study the ideas and methods of Western countries. He wanted Russia to discard her outmoded ways of doing things and to "modernize" herself. He believed that Russia could be reformed if men acted by their reason, rather than by their emotions.

In his famous novel *Fathers and Sons*, Turgenev popularized the word *nihilist*. Turgenev defined a nihilist in this way:

[He] is a man who does not bow before any authority whatever, who does not accept a single principle on faith....

Turgenev seemed to be saying: Unless Russia reforms herself, some men will become nihilists. They will challenge the authority of everyone, and the result will be destruction.

Fyodor Dostoyevsky

Fyodor Dostoyevsky (1821–1881) was Russia's leading literary *Slavophile*. In contrast to the Westernizers, the Slavophiles believed Russia should develop her own unique Slavic qualities and not try to imitate the West. Dostoyevsky urged Russians to find strength in the heritage of their country, rather than in the ways of Western nations. He believed that it was dangerous for men to be guided by reason alone, and he was convinced that it was better for Russians to "listen to their hearts" than to their minds. He wanted people to follow their natural emotions.

Crime and Punishment is one of Dostoyevsky's and the world's great novels. Its plot revolves around this problem: A young student wishes to continue his education so that someday he can serve mankind. Yet he is too poor to go on with his studies or even to help his family. Does he have the right to rob a useless and corrupt old pawnbroker to obtain money for his education and other worthwhile purposes?

Dostoyevsky puts the question this way:

[Should he] take her money and with the help of it devote [himself] to the service of humanity? Would not one tiny crime be wiped out by thousands of good deeds?

Dostoyevsky's answer in this book is a resounding NO! The crime is committed, and it involves the murder of the pawnbroker by the student. Dostoyevsky then shows how the crime "drives the murderer through the tortuous blind alleys of attempted escape and suffering conscience to a confession of his crime and an expiation of it [atonement] in the frozen wastes of

Siberia. From this . . . comes redemption for the man. . . . Seldom have the incalculable implications of a crime been explored with such meticulous detail."

In a sense, Dostoyevsky was the conscience of Russia, calling the Russian people back to the basic values of life. He was also concerned with the welfare of mankind. In a famous speech he declared, "To become a true Russian is to become the brother of all men, a universal man."

Leo Tolstoy

Leo Tolstoy (1828–1910) is generally recognized as Russia's greatest writer of prose, and his book *War and Peace* is considered "the national novel of Russia." In his writings and life Tolstoy showed his hatred for war, his love for the peasants, and his understanding of human beings.

In *War and Peace*, which covered the Napoleonic period, Tolstoy denounced war:

War is . . . the most horrible thing in life. . . . [Armies] kill and maim tens of thousands, and then have thanksgiving services for having killed so many people. . . . How does God above look at them and hear them?

In the same novel, Tolstoy demonstrated his understanding of human beings. For example, here is a scene in which a father has just said good-by to his son who is leaving for war. The father is in the study. He loves his son deeply and finds it difficult to hold back his tears. Nevertheless, he is too much of a man to admit his grief. Tolstoy captured both the sorrow and the strength of the father:

[The son] walked quickly out of the room. . . . From the study came, like pistol shots, the repeated and angry sounds of the old [father] blowing his nose. Then suddenly the door of the study was flung open, and the old man in his white dressing-gown peeped out.

"Gone? Well, and a good thing too!" he said. . . . He shook his head and slammed the door.

Fyodor Dostoyevsky

■ *Dostoyevsky's great novels introduce you to nineteenth-century Russians of many classes and probe deeply into their minds and emotions.*

Anton Chekhov

Anton Chekhov (1860–1904) is noted for his superb short stories and for such plays as *Uncle Vanya, Three Sisters,* and *The Cherry Orchard.*

The dominant theme in many of Chekhov's works is the inability of people to face reality or to check the disintegration of their lives. This theme he presented with a realism found in everyday life. As Chekhov said:

No literature can surpass actual life in its irony. . . . Artistic literature is called so just because it depicts life as it really is. Its aim is truth—unconditional and honest. . . .

Chekhov described life as truthfully and objectively as he could.

■ **Check on Your Reading**

1. How did Gogol criticize Russian government and society?

2. What did Turgenev try to teach?

3. Why is Dostoyevsky called a Slavophile and "the conscience of Russia"?

4. What were the contributions of Tolstoy and Chekhov?

3. Russian Art, Science, and Music

The creative activities of the Russians in the nineteenth century were not limited to literature. Progress also was made in art and architecture, science, and music.

Art and Architecture

Russian art and architecture from about the middle of the tenth to the eighteenth century had been marked by (1) the influence of Byzantine art, (2) the deep religious feelings of the Russians, and (3) contact with the art of Persia, Italy, India, and other areas.

Peter the Great had stimulated secular art and had encouraged the study of the artistic styles of the West. In the nineteenth century several artists tried to depict events more realistically and to put more "Russian" feeling into art. The historical scenes painted by two of these artists, Vereshchagin (p. 422) and Repin (p. 330), are still famous.

Mathematics, Science, Invention, and Medicine

In mathematics, science, invention, and medicine, the Russians accomplished many things. Some of their outstanding achievements included the following: (1) Lobachevsky developed principles of non-Euclidean geometry. (2) Mendeleyev aided modern chemistry by drawing up his Periodic Law for the elements. (3) Metchnikov described the action of the white corpuscles in the blood. (4) Pirogov advanced the methods of surgery used during war.

In addition, Lodigin may have developed an electric light before Edison, and Popov sent radio signals before Marconi.

Music

In the field of music, Russian nationalism gained strength. More composers

■ *St. Basil's Cathedral, Moscow, shows strong Byzantine influence in its architecture.*

turned away from the influence of foreign countries and sought to write music that evolved from Russian life. These composers were inspired by Russian history, including the Oriental heritage; folklore and legend; folk-songs; and patriotism.

Mikhail Glinka was one of the founders of "national Russian music." Other important composers belonged to a group known as "The Mighty Five," which comprised Balakirev, César Cui, Borodin, Mussorgsky, and Rimsky-Korsakov.

"The Mighty Five" were interested in capturing in music the national flavor of Russia. Borodin composed a great opera, *Prince Igor*, that was based on a Russian epic. Mussorgsky went to the lives of the Russian people for many of his themes. Rimsky-Korsakov drew heavily on Russian folklore and folk-songs.

Perhaps the most famous of all Russian composers was Peter Ilich Tchaikovsky (1840–1893). He wrote operas, symphonies, ballets, and other compositions. (Examples: *Eugene Onegin, The Fourth Symphony, Swan Lake, The Sleeping Beauty, The Nutcracker,* and *Capriccio italien*.) Although Tchaikovsky was an individualist, he too showed his nationalistic feeling in such works as his *1812 Overture.*

■ Check on Your Reading

1. What influences made Russian art and architecture quite different?
2. Describe the chief Russian contributions to mathematics, science, medicine, and music.

4. Russia and the Ottoman Empire in World Affairs

In the nineteenth century Russia also played a role in world affairs. She extended her empire by adding lands in the Caucasus, Central Asia, the Far East, and other regions. As Professor Warren Walsh points out: "The Russian counterpart of overseas expansion was overland expansion into adjacent territories. . . ." Equally important, Russia became involved in events in Turkey and southeastern Europe.

Turkey Becomes "The Sick Man of Europe"

The Ottoman (or Turkish) Empire, of which modern-day Turkey is an important remnant, had a very complicated history. We have already traced its history briefly to 1700 (p. 290).

The Turks early extended their control over the Balkans. In 1683 the Turks were defeated in their attempt to capture Vienna. After this setback, the Ottoman Empire continued to decline. In the eighteenth century, the Russians defeated the Turks and forced them to give up land near the Black Sea. Russia's determination to control Constantinople and the straits that linked the Black Sea with the Aegean and Mediterranean seas became stronger.

In the nineteenth century the Ottoman Empire was called "The Sick Man of Europe." Czar Nicholas I of Russia, assuming the attitude of a physician, declared: I repeat to you that the sick man is dying; and we must never allow such an event to take us by surprise.

There were many factors that contributed to the "sickness" of the Ottoman Empire. These included the following: (1) The Turkish government and the governors (*pashas*) sent to rule its possessions were inefficient and frequently corrupt. (2) Some of the Moslem Turks clashed with the Christian subjects of the Ottoman Empire. (3) Jealousies and rivalries developed among the different peoples living under the control of the Turks. (4) Nationalism grew stronger among the various Balkan groups and led to demands for the establishment of new nations.

Russian leaders felt that they had a responsibility to protect their fellow-Slavs in the Ottoman Empire. Austria, France, Russia, and Great Britain had conflicting interests in Turkish territories. Great Britain was determined to check Russian expansion into the Mediterranean.

The Greeks Revolt

In 1804–1805 the Serbs in the Balkans had rebelled against the Turkish rulers. Then in 1821 the Greeks revolted. Nationalism played an important part in the Greek revolt. The Turks recognized Greece as an independent nation in 1829–1830.

■ *The Ottoman Empire, which had reached a peak in the 16th century, gradually declined. By the 19th century, it was called "The Sick Man of Europe." In the Balkans, nationality groups demanded their own nations. By 1913, the Ottoman Empire had lost much of its former territory.*

The Great Powers Go to War

After Greece gained its independence, tensions continued in the Ottoman Empire. Great Britain was particularly worried that Russia might seize the city of Constantinople and other Turkish areas. If that happened, Britain's interests in the Middle East might be threatened.

A religious dispute developed. The czar demanded that Russia be given a protectorate over all the Sultan's Orthodox Christian subjects in European Turkey

and their holy places. Emperor Napoleon III claimed that the French already had the right to guard the Christian holy places on behalf of the Roman Catholics because of a French agreement with Suleiman. Great Britain, fearful that Russia would use the argument as an excuse to take over Turkish lands, supported France.

This religious dispute, the Russian army's occupation of certain Turkish regions, Britain's fear of Russian expansion into the Mediterranean, and other factors led to the outbreak of the Crimean War (1854–1856). Great Britain, France, Sardinia, and Turkey fought against Russia.

The Crimean War

The war, fought on the Crimean peninsula, was marked by disastrous errors. One such tactical error was "the charge of the Light Brigade," when about six hundred British cavalrymen attacked and were slaughtered by a Russian army "30,000 strong." "I am an old man and I have seen many battles, but this is the worst of all!" declared one French general.

Hurrying to scenes of desolation and misery came a courageous Englishwoman, Florence Nightingale, and a small group of volunteers. They established hospitals at Scutari and Balaclava; and here they struggled to keep sanitary quarters, nursed the wounded, and fought cholera.

After many soldiers on both sides lost their lives, Russia was defeated. Some important provisions of the peace treaty included the following: (1) All the signers agreed to guarantee the independence of the Ottoman Empire and promised not to interfere in Turkish internal matters. The Sultan was to treat his subjects fairly. (2) The Black Sea was to be neutralized— no ships of war were to be permitted to enter the Black Sea, and the shores of the sea were not to be fortified. Ships of commerce were to be free to travel on the Black Sea. (3) Russia had to give up control of important territories.

The Congress of Berlin

The Crimean War did not put an end to the territorial ambitions of Russia or to the national hopes of the Balkan peoples. In 1876 the Bulgarians revolted against Turkish rule. Then the peoples of the Balkan regions of Serbia and Montenegro went to war against the Turks. Finally, in 1877 Russia declared war on Turkey.

The Russo-Turkish War (1877–1878) ended in a victory for Russia and her Balkan allies. When the peace treaty gave Russia great control over the Balkans, Great Britain and Austria refused to accept it. They supported the call for a general conference of major powers to decide the future of Turkish territories.

Russia finally agreed. The delegates met in Berlin, where Bismarck tried to influence the negotiations. Some important results of the Congress of Berlin (1878) were the following: (1) Austria was granted the right to occupy and administer Bosnia and Herzegovina in the Balkans. (2) Great Britain received Cyprus, a large island in the Mediterranean. (3) Macedonia remained a part of Turkey. (4) Russia was given some territories near the Black Sea. (5) The Congress of Berlin recognized the independence of the nations of Serbia, Rumania, and Montenegro, and made Bulgaria into a self-governing principality.

■ Check on Your Reading

1. How did Turkey become "the sick man of Europe"?
2. Describe the Crimean War.

CULTURAL CHARACTERISTICS of Nineteenth-Century Russia

In dealing with Russian culture there is always a danger of seeing in the past a picture of the present— as if the past were the photographic negative and the present the developed print. Thus nineteenth-century Russian writers such as Nikolai Gogol, Fyodor Dostoyevsky, Ivan Turgenev, and others felt the repressive hand of the government; and in our own times Boris Pasternak, Ilya Ehrenburg, and Yevgeni Yevtushenko have also encountered censorship or bitter criticism. Significant parallels can be drawn between the two situations. However, it is even more important to view the cultural characteristics of Russia in the nineteenth century *within the framework of its own period of history.* These characteristics included:

A society generally dominated by an autocratic government that restricted the civil liberties of the people.

An economy in which the village commune as part of a paternalistic government played a key role in shaping the agricultural life of Russia.

A flowering of creative activity in literature, art, science, and music.

Autocratic Russia fascinated many of the cultural leaders of the time. Gogol wrote in one of his novels:

Ah, Russia, from my beautiful home in a strange land

I still can see you! In you everything is poor and disordered and homely. . . . Yet what secret, what invisible force draws me to you? . . .

Gogol went on to ask: "Whither are you speeding, Russia of mine? Whither? Answer me! But no answer comes. . . ."

The answer to Gogol's question was to come in the twentieth century, in the revolutionary year of 1917 in which the Russian monarchy was overturned by war-weary Russians and revolutionaries.

Today the same question—"Whither are you speeding, Russia?"—continues to challenge the interpretive skills of the most astute analysts and scholars. The answer is yet to come.

MAN AND HIS CULTURE

Let's Meet the People!
The following sketch is based on an eyewitness account in Donald M. Wallace, *Russia*, 1877, London; selections from this book can be found in *Readings in Russian History*, compiled and edited by Warren B. Walsh, 1959, Syracuse University Press.

A Russian Landowner in 1860
Ivan Ivanovitch, a well-to-do Russian landowner of the nineteenth century, sat in his comfortable armchair by the window. At nine A.M. he had tea. After tea Ivan Ivanovitch began his labors of the day "by resuming his seat at the open window and having his Turkish pipe filled and lighted by a boy whose special function [was] to keep his master's pipes in order." Here Ivan sat "till the sun [had] so far moved round that the veranda at the back of the house was completely in the shade." Then he ordered a servant to move his armchair to the veranda, and he sat there until dinner.

Ivan ate an excellent dinner at one o'clock. Then "a deathlike stillness [fell] upon the house." It was the time for the after-dinner nap. Ivan Ivanovitch retired to his room, from which the flies had been chased by a servant, and slept for two hours.

In the afternoon Ivan Ivanovitch rode about in the fields for an hour. He returned to the house long before it was time for supper and rested himself in his chair by the window.

That evening, after supper, a group of serfs came to see him.

"Well, children, what do you want?" Ivan demanded.

"Little father! Grant us [more grain for our families]. Please, little father, please," the serfs begged.

"Now enough—enough!" declared Ivan Ivanovitch. "You are blockheads! There's no use talking; it can't be done."

With these words Ivan Ivanovitch re-entered the house. He had had a tiring day, and he did not intend to let his serfs keep him from a well-earned night of rest.

CHAPTER REVIEW

REVIEW and DISCUSSION

1. Identify the people and places and explain the events and terms on p. 540.

2. What ideas were considered dangerous to the state under Nicholas I?

3. Why was there a long period of unsuccessful revolts against autocracy in Russia?

4. Some historians say that serfdom in Russia and slavery in the United States came to an end at this time because they both were becoming unprofitable to the landowners. Evaluate this statement and compare the way in which serfs and slaves were freed.

5. What relationship can you find between a people's type of government and their cultural achievements?

6. Do the art, music, and literature of nineteenth-century Russia have anything in common? Justify your answer.

7. Some historians state that the intelligentsia of Russia who believed in and wrote about liberal reforms did not reach the common people because they themselves did not belong to the lower groups or fully understand the people's problems. What evidence can you find to support or refute this statement?

8. Why didn't Russia undertake extensive overseas expansion as did England, France, Spain, Holland, and Portugal?

9. The term, "Turbulent Balkans," has often been used to describe southeastern Europe. What does it mean? Is it true? Why?

10. What causes for future wars can you find in the results of the Congress of Berlin?

ACTIVITIES

1. Have a concert in class. Play records of music by Tchaikovsky and other well-known Russian composers.

2. Tolstoy frequently used in his writings the very old theme that "happiness consists in living for others." Have a round-table discussion on the status of this theme today.

3. Make a chart of nineteenth-century scientists and mathematicians, indicating their country of origin and their discoveries or work. Consult Smith; Palmer; and Carmichael.

4. Make a chart of nineteenth-century writers, indicating their country of origin and their important works.

5. What differences can you find between the autocracy or absolutism of the Romanovs, Bourbons, Hapsburgs, and Hohenzollerns? Consult Palmer, encyclopedias, or source books.

PAST and PRESENT

1. What similarities and differences are there between the *mirs* in the nineteenth century and the collective farms in Russia today?

2. During the reigns of Nicholas I, Alexander II, and Alexander III, were any practices and principles of the government similar to those of the Russian government today? Justify your answer.

SUGGESTED READINGS

Basic books: CARMICHAEL, JOEL, *An Illustrated History of Russia*, Viking. Several sections on the nineteenth century.

CHARQUES, RICHARD D., *A Short History of Russia*, Dutton.

PALMER, R. R., and COLTON, JOEL, *A History of the Modern World*, Chap. 13, Knopf.

PARES, BERNARD, *History of Russia*, Knopf. Detailed political history.

SEEGER, ELIZABETH, *The Pageant of Russian History*, Longmans, Green.

SMITH, GOLDWIN, *The Heritage of Man*, Scribner. Use index to find references to this chapter's contents.

Special accounts: NAZAROFF, ALEXANDER, *The Land of the Russian People*, Lippincott. Greater stress on geography than history.

PAYNE, ROBERT, *The Terrorists: The Story of the Forerunners of Stalin*, Funk and Wagnalls.

WALSH, WARREN B., (ed.), *Readings in Russian History*, Syracuse University Press. Contains excellent primary source material.

Biography and Fiction: SLONIM, MARC, *An Outline of Russian Literature*, MD 270, New American Library. Biographical sketches and literary appraisals.

Chapter 35   *Imperialism and World Tensions*

KEYNOTE   At the close of the nineteenth century Mr. Dooley, a fictitious character created by author Finley Peter Dunne, commented on current affairs in a newspaper column. When the United States had just occupied the Philippine Islands after a war with Spain, Mr. Dooley turned to his friend Mr. Hennessey and said:

I've been r-readin' about th' counthry [the Philippines]. 'Tis over beyant ye'er left shoulder whin ye're facin' east. Jus' throw ye'er thumb back, an' ye have it as ac'rate as anny man in town. 'Tis farther thin Boohlgahrya an' not so far as Blewchoochoo. It's near Chiny, an' it's not so near; an', if a man was to bore a well through fr'm Goshen, Indianny, he might sthrike it, an' thin again he might not. It's a poverty-sthricken counthry, full iv goold an' precious stones, where th' people can pick dinner off th' threes an' ar-re starvin' because they have no stepladders.... An' yet, Hinnissy, I dinnaw what to do about th' Ph'lippeens . . . I don't know.

To which Mr. Hennessey answered: "Hang on to thim. What we've got we must hold."

Thus Finley Peter Dunne described, in comic terms, *one of the most important developments of the late nineteenth century: imperialism.*

Key People   *John Hay   ·   Hideyoshi   ·   Matthew Perry   ·   David Livingstone   ·   Henry Stanley   ·   Leopold II   ·   Theodore Roosevelt*

Key Places   *China   ·   Korea   ·   Philippines   ·   Japan   ·   Congo Free State   ·   Algeria   ·   Morocco   ·   Egypt   ·   Suez Canal   ·   Fashoda   ·   Cuba   ·   Panama*

Key Events   *Sino-Japanese War   ·   Boxer Rebellion   ·   Tokugawa Shogunate   ·   Perry's expedition to Japan   ·   Meiji period   ·   Russo-Japanese War   ·   Imperialism in Africa   ·   Suez Canal   ·   Spanish-American War*

Key Terms   *imperialism   ·   extraterritoriality   ·   sphere of influence   ·   colony   ·   protectorate   ·   "Open Door" policy   ·   shogun*

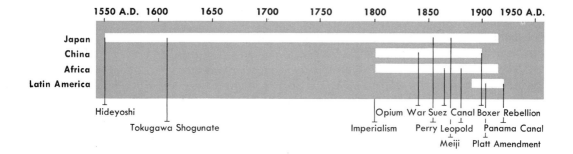

Japan
China
Africa
Latin America

1550 A.D. 1600   1650   1700   1750   1800   1850   1900 1950 A.D.

Hideyoshi

Tokugawa Shogunate

Opium War Suez Canal Boxer Rebellion

Imperialism   Perry Leopold Panama Canal

Meiji   Platt Amendment

1. A Brief Sketch of the History of Imperialism

Imperialism has been defined by Professor Norman Hill, a specialist on international politics, as "the political domination of a state over an alien people, usually for an indefinite period of time but conceivably with a promise of eventual independence." A country may gain a strong influence over a foreign area by economic, military, or cultural activities. However, imperialism is not complete until the country achieves political domination.

Imperialism has had a long history. In ancient times imperialist governments built great empires—the Egyptian Empire, the Empire of Alexander the Great, and the Roman Empire. Imperialism in the "modern world" began in the fifteenth and sixteenth centuries. In time, Portugal, Spain, England, the Netherlands, and France built empires.

During the latter part of the eighteenth and most of the nineteenth century, imperialism lost favor. There were several reasons for this: (1) England's loss of her American colonies; (2) Spain's and Portugal's loss of their Latin American colonies; and (3) the increasing popularity of the idea of free trade. Prime Minister Benjamin Disraeli even said: "These wretched colonies . . . are a millstone around our necks!"

In the 1870's, efforts to gain colonial possessions increased tremendously. The next few decades were filled with some of the most intense imperialism.

Reasons for Nineteenth-Century Imperialism

There were many reasons for the revival of imperialism and the race for empires in the latter part of the nineteenth century. These included the following: (1) The Industrial Revolution had greatly improved the means of transportation and communication among peoples. It also had increased the demand for raw materials and markets where finished articles could be sold. (2) Government leaders thought that by obtaining colonies they could increase their nation's power abroad, add to its military security, and strengthen it in case of war.

(3) The nationalistic feelings of the people during the nineteenth century stirred them to want their nation to excel others in the size of its empire. They felt that imperialism was a symbol of success.

(4) Government leaders believed that colonies would become lands to which their surplus populations would migrate. Ambitious businessmen, investors, banks, and corporations were convinced that colonies would help them to make great profits.

And some ambitious statesmen believed that they could add to their own popularity by imperialistic efforts.

(5) Some people felt that their country had the duty to educate and "civilize" the inhabitants of other lands. (6) Other groups wished to spread Christianity to the other peoples of the world.

These factors stimulated imperialist activities in the Far East, Africa, Latin America, and other parts of the world.

■ **Check on Your Reading**
1. What is imperialism?
2. Why was there a revival of imperialism?
3. Analyze the motives behind imperialism.

2. Imperialism in the Far East

When European leaders became convinced that imperialism was a good policy, they worked hard to spread their nations' influence in the Far East. China was one of the lands most affected by imperialism.

China and the Opium War

Serious tensions developed between China and Great Britain in the early nineteenth century. These tensions were caused by a number of factors, including Britain's desire for three things: more trading rights in China, greater recognition of British diplomats, and better treatment of British citizens in China. Britain's initial interest in China was in developing trade, rather than in building an empire.

Finally a bitter argument arose over the opium trade. British merchants were making considerable profit supplying the people of China with opium, a narcotic drug from India. The Chinese government insisted that this undesirable trade be stopped. The Special Commissioner Lin also demanded that the British give up all supplies of opium "by virtue of that reason which Heaven hath implanted in all of us." When the British refused, the so-called Opium War broke out.

China was defeated in the Opium War (1839–1842), and a treaty of peace was signed at Nanking in 1842. These are the key provisions of this treaty: (1) Canton, Shanghai, and three other ports were to be open to British trade. (2) The island of Hong Kong was ceded to Great Britain. (3) British trade with China was made easier in several ways.

The Treaty of Nanking was important because it gave Great Britain a commercial hold in China and excited the ambitions of other countries. In 1843 the British also were granted the right of *extraterritoriality*. This meant, in part, that a British citizen who committed a crime in China could be tried by British judges or British officials under British law.

Foreign Nations Move into China

Other countries were quick to follow the British in acquiring rights in China. Several European countries and the United States soon won the right of extraterritoriality. As a result of the Anglo-Chinese War (1856–1860), more ports and regions were opened to foreign trade. Great Britain, France, Russia, and the United States gained additional commercial privileges. In 1858 China also ceded territory to Russia that permitted the Russians to expand eastward.

Meanwhile China was disrupted by an internal conflict known as the T'ai P'ing Rebellion (c. 1850–1864). Its principal leader was Hung Hsiu-ch'üan, a village teacher who had been influenced by the Christian faith and several Western ideas. Hung tried to overthrow the Manchus and establish a new dynasty to be called "T'ai P'ing" or "Great Peace." However, the Chinese government, aided by an army organized and led by foreign officers, finally suppressed the rebellion.

Foreigners continued to exploit China. Gradually European countries established *spheres of influence* in China. A sphere of influence was an area in which a foreign nation claimed practically exclusive rights to develop economic enterprises, build railroads, and profit from commercial exchange. It differed from a *colony* (a foreign area that belonged to and was completely subject to some nation); and from a *protectorate* (a foreign area that still maintained its sovereignty but was controlled by some nation). By the twentieth century, Great Britain, France, Russia, and Germany all had established economic or political domination over sections of China.

Reasons for China's Weakness

Why was a huge country like China unable to defend itself in the nineteenth century? Some of the factors that helped foreign nations to gain power in China were the inefficiency of Manchu officials, the lack of industry, the absence of modernization, a low standard of living, and a disorganized Chinese army and fleet.

The Sino-Japanese War

Despite warnings of imminent destruction issued to the Chinese by patriotic societies, China continued to be a target for imperialistic powers. In 1894 friction over Korea led to the outbreak of war between Japan and China. This Sino-Japanese War (1894–1895) resulted in a victory for the Japanese. The Treaty of Shimonoseki, which ended the war, deprived China of more territory. By the treaty terms, China gave Japan the Liaotung peninsula, Formosa, and other territories; and China recognized the independence of Korea,

■ *A Chinese painting portrays the Mongol Empress of Yung Chêng (1723–1735). Chinese officials considered Europeans "barbarians."*

which was annexed by Japan in 1910. Although several European nations forced Japan to return the Liaotung peninsula to China, the Japanese still controlled important areas.

The United States in Asia

Meanwhile the United States had not been immune to the fever of imperialism. After winning the Spanish-American War (1898), the Americans had taken possession of the Philippine Islands, Puerto Rico, and other areas from Spain. Senator

555

Albert J. Beveridge had even dramatically proclaimed:

We will not abandon our opportunity in the Orient. We will not renounce our part in the mission of our race, trustee, under God, of the civilization of the world.

The United States' early experiences in the Philippines showed that occupying a land in Asia brought problems. William Howard Taft, the president of the commission to govern the Philippines, called the Filipinos "our little brown brothers." However, Philippine patriots hiding in the jungles fought American troops with such fervor that American soldiers sang:

He may be a brother of Big Bill Taft
But he ain't no brother of mine!

The United States determined to end such hostility by introducing a program of reform. It built schools, roads, and hospitals; and in many other ways it helped to build up the country. It also gradually gave the Filipinos experience in governing themselves. On July 4, 1946, with the approval of the United States, the Philippines became independent.

The "Open-Door" Policy

In China, American merchants had tried to increase their trade. William McKinley, President of the United States from 1897 to 1901, described American policy in China: "[Our policy] is to . . . preserve Chinese territorial and administrative entity, protect all rights guaranteed to friendly powers by treaty and international law, and safeguard for the world the principle of equal and impartial trade with all parts of the Chinese Empire."

■ *By 1910 European nations, Japan, and the United States had established economic or political domination over the Far East. What areas did they control? The inset shows the results of the Russo-Japanese War (1904–1905). Over what territory did Japan gain control?*

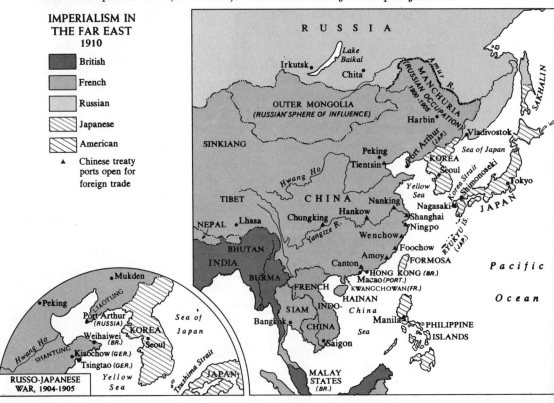

IMPERIALISM IN
THE FAR EAST
1910

■ British
■ French
■ Russian
▨ Japanese
▨ American
▲ Chinese treaty ports open for foreign trade

RUSSO-JAPANESE
WAR, 1904-1905

In the last decade of the nineteenth century, the United States became increasingly alarmed over China. American officials and businessmen feared that if China were partitioned among the powers, American commercial interests would be seriously endangered. The American Secretary of State, John Hay, therefore sent notes to the nations in China, suggesting that an "Open Door" policy be established.

Hay proposed that the "Open Door" policy (1899) include these features: (1) The commercial rights of all nations should be respected in China, including the spheres of influence. (2) The nations holding spheres of influence should not discriminate against the rights of other nations. Hay also pointed out that there would be "undoubted benefits" if there could be "perfect equality of treatment for . . . commerce and navigation [of all nations] within such 'spheres' . . . ."

The proposed "Open Door" policy did not radically change the actions of most of the powers. It was too idealistic. Spheres of influence continued to exist in China. In addition, when in 1898 the young Chinese Emperor tried to reform the government and armed forces of China, he was blocked by the Empress Dowager (widow of a former emperor) who seized control of the state and abolished his decrees.

The Boxer Rebellion

During the summer of 1900 a Chinese organization known as the *Boxers,* or the "Righteous Harmonious Fists," rose against the foreigners in China. "Though these foreigners ride in sedans unbefitting their rank, China yet regards them as barbarians, of whom God disapproves and is sending down spirits and genii for their destruction!" the Boxers proclaimed. Then they rioted in Peking and other cities, killing a number of Europeans and destroying their property.

The Boxer Rebellion, which had the approval of the Empress Dowager, finally was put down by a joint army that included troops from Japan, Britain, Russia, France, Germany, and the United States. The Chinese government was ordered to pay an indemnity for the damages the Boxers had caused. The United States returned most of its share of this indemnity. The money was used as a scholarship fund to send Chinese students to American colleges.

■ Check on Your Reading

1. What was the importance of the Opium War and the Treaty of Nanking?
2. Why was China weak? What did it lose in the war with Japan (1894–1895)?
3. What was the "Open Door" policy?

3. Japan Becomes a Modern Nation and an Empire Builder

Unlike China, Japan was able to stop itself from being exploited by foreign powers. One way in which it did this was by adopting some methods of the foreigners. This meant making changes in living patterns that had roots in history.

Hideyoshi and the Tokugawa Shogunate

Japan was not unified until the sixteenth century. Three leaders helped to unify Japan; the most important of these was Hideyoshi.

Hideyoshi (1536–1598) was a man of many names. His soldiers called him "Cotton" because he was a warrior whose talents could be put to many uses. His advisers called him "Taiko" ("Supreme Official"). And his biographers have since called him the "Napoleon of Japan," for he was a great conqueror.

In the latter part of the sixteenth century, Hideyoshi and his troops completed the unification of Japan. As dictator, Hideyoshi spread his influence over the entire country. Hideyoshi also tried to extend his power abroad. He failed "to bring the whole of China under my sway."

After the death of Hideyoshi, Tokugawa Ieyasu fought his way to leadership. The descendants of Ieyasu became Shoguns (military chiefs) of Japan. The Tokugawa Shogunate gave Japan a period of rigidly controlled peace from 1603 to 1867.

Commodore Perry's Expedition to Japan

From about 1640 to the middle of the nineteenth century, Japan deliberately avoided contact with Europeans. The Japanese were prohibited from traveling to other lands, and foreigners were told that they were not wanted. The only European settlement in Japan was the Dutch trading post at Nagasaki. Japan continued to be a non-westernized land with a feudal structure and rigid social system.

In 1853 four ships under the command of Commodore Matthew Perry of the United States arrived in the harbor of Yedo (Tokyo), Japan. Commodore Perry, on instructions from his government, asked the Japanese to grant Americans rights of "friendship, commerce, [supplies] of coal and provisions, and protection for our shipwrecked people." Perry and his ships then left for China to await the Japanese answer.

The Japanese were still hostile to foreigners. However, they knew what had happened to China, and they did not wish their country to become involved in wars with the foreigners. Therefore, when Perry returned several months later with warships, the Japanese made a treaty with the Americans. According to this treaty, Americans could trade, under Japanese regulations, at a few ports, which could

also be used as refueling stations by American vessels; and sailors shipwrecked off the Japanese coast would receive better treatment from the Japanese people.

Townsend Harris Establishes Official Relations

The "opening" of Japan by Commodore Perry was a dramatic achievement. Equally important was the less publicized work of Townsend Harris, the first American Consul to Japan. It was an important moment in history when Harris came before the Shogun on December 7, 1857, to present his credentials.

In his *Journal*, Harris recalls that the Shogun was seated in a chair placed on a platform raised about two feet from the floor. His dress was made of silk, and his crown was a black lacquered cap shaped like an inverted bell. He wore neither rich jewels nor gold ornaments.

"My earnest wishes are to unite [our] two countries more closely in the ties of enduring friendship. . . ." declared Consul Harris.

The Shogun stamped his right foot. Then he answered: "I am pleased with [Consul Harris'] discourse. . . ."

Thus were established official relations between the United States and Japan.

Harris proved to be an excellent diplomat. In 1858, as a result of his activities, five more ports were opened for American trade, and Americans were granted the right of extraterritoriality in Japan. The Netherlands, Russia, and Great Britain soon gained similar rights.

Japan Remakes Herself During the Meiji Period

In 1867–1868 the Shogunate government fell as a result of (1) dissatisfaction of many Japanese with the outmoded methods of government; (2) the inability of weak Shoguns to keep the support of

■ *In these paintings Japanese women of different classes are portrayed. The painting by Hokusai(1760–1849) depicts an aristocratic lady arranging her hair (left). In "Salt Maidens of Suma" (right), by Shonman (1757–1820), two peasant girls are collecting salt crystals along the shore.*

Museum of Fine Arts, Boston

the nobles; (3) the opposition that arose to the granting of concessions to foreigners; (4) the anger of military leaders at the military weakness of the country; and (5) the revival of support for the emperor, much of whose power had been taken over by the Shogun. After 1868 Japan was no longer ruled by a Shogun, or military chief. The new emperor—the first of the Meiji (meaning "enlightened rule")—became the head of the government.

During the Meiji reign (1867–1912) Japan went through changes that transformed the country. These changes were introduced "from the top"—that is, they came from the ruling groups, rather than from the people. A new constitution was put into effect in 1889. Although there was a House of Representatives elected by the people, great power rested in the hands of the leaders of the armed forces. A national army was organized, and a new navy was built. Feudal divisions were eliminated.

Railroads were constructed; modern industries were established; and foreign trade was stimulated. Education was encouraged, and Japanese students were permitted to do advanced study at universities in foreign countries. Japan made herself into a modern nation.

"Western" methods were used in the remaking of Japan. However, as Professor Kenneth Scott Latourette points out, the ideas and techniques borrowed from Western countries were "fitted into existing Japanese patterns." This was done so successfully that Japan gradually became a strong nation. Foreigners were unable to exploit Japan. The foreign powers eventually gave up their extraterritorial rights.

At the same time that the Japanese leaders were reorganizing their country, efforts were made to stimulate the nationalism of the people. Love of country was linked with loyalty to the emperor.

Pride of nation grew. The desire to add to national power combined with other factors stirred the Japanese leaders to show a strong interest in expansion. An already weakened China seemed to be a logical place for Japanese imperialism.

Japan Defeats China and Russia

Japan defeated China in 1895 in the Sino-Japanese War (p. 555). In 1904, two years after Britain had agreed to support Japan if any nation joined Russia in a war against Japan, the Japanese attacked the Russians at Port Arthur without warning. In the Russo-Japanese War (1904–1905), stakes were high. Professor K. Asakawa,

who lived during the war, states that the goal of both Russia and Japan was "the immensely rich and yet undeveloped North China, of which Manchuria is a part, and to which Korea is an appendix." The Japanese soon demonstrated their superiority over the Russians, and by 1905 Japan had won the war.

By the Treaty of Portsmouth, New Hampshire, Japan was given a protectorate over Korea; was permitted to lease the Liaotung peninsula, including Port Arthur; received control of the southern half of Sakhalin Island; and was awarded valuable fishing rights in the Pacific Ocean. China was permitted to keep control of Manchuria. After the Russo-Japanese War, Japan was recognized as the leading power in the Far East.

■ **Check on Your Reading**

1. What was accomplished by Hideyoshi? by Tokugawa Ieyasu?

2. What was gained by Perry's expedition to Japan? by Townsend Harris?

3. What changes did Japan make in its government and economy in the Meiji period?

4. How did the Russo-Japanese War make Japan the leading power in the Far East?

4. Imperialism in Africa

Africa was another target for imperialism. It was the second largest continent in the world, with an area over three times the size of the United States today, including Alaska and Hawaii. It was a land with the longest river system (the Nile), the greatest desert (the Sahara), and some of the most magnificent scenery on earth.

In this fascinating continent there were rich diamond deposits, gold and copper, and unlimited trading opportunities. And there were black- and brown-skinned peoples who seemed to be an easy prey for Europeans bent on rule, riches, or reform.

The Peoples and Cultures of Africa

Most of Africa lies in the tropics and consists of a succession of plateaus. Large inland water basins feed into the rivers. The most important of these basins are those of the upper Niger, Congo, East African Lakes, upper Nile, Chad in central Sudan, and Northern Kalahari in south central Africa. When the Europeans came to Africa in the nineteenth century, many Africans were living on the inland plateaus. On the plateaus the soil was fertile, the climate was suitable, and the danger of coastal raids was eliminated.

In the nineteenth century there were people of three major physical types in Africa. (1) The Negroid lived primarily in the Sudan, the Guinea Coast, Central Africa, East Africa, Southeastern Africa, and Madagascar. (2) The Caucasoid lived primarily in North Africa. (3) The Bushman-Hottentot lived primarily in Southwest Africa. These three major types included a variety of peoples who spoke many different languages.

From a cultural standpoint there was not one Africa, but two. Africa *north* of the Sahara Desert had been influenced by the ancient civilizations in the Mediterranean area, and by the Moslems who carried the Islamic faith to North Africa in the seventh century A.D. Africa *south* of the Sahara had been isolated for centuries from extensive contact with the outside world.

Most Africans of the nineteenth century lived without modern industries, modern means of transportation, and benefits of modern science. They survived by staying close to the soil and working at occupations that reached far back into history.

They farmed the land, planting crops of maize, rice, sorghum, and many other foods. As anthropologist George Peter Murdock points out, today Africans grow "approximately nine-tenths of all the cultivated plant varieties known to man. . . ."

Goats, sheep, camels, and cattle were raised. Africans hunted animals in the forests and fished in the streams. They collected locust beans, kola nuts, and fruits.

The peoples of Africa lived in a variety of social organizations that ranged in size from the small family group to the large tribal state. They were affected by *kin* relationships—that is, they were closely tied to persons who were members of their "blood family" or descended from their ancestors. Into this African world came Europeans with imperialist ambitions.

Prelude to Modern Imperialism in Africa

Portuguese explorers established a trade in slaves and spices with Africa in the fifteenth century. Later the Spaniards, Dutch, English, and French came and set up trading stations along the coasts. From the middle of the sixteenth century to the early part of the nineteenth century, some Europeans expanded the trade in African slaves.

During the first half of the nineteenth century, British, French, and German explorers made important journeys into the African interior. Europeans crossed the Sahara Desert, traced the course of a major river in the west, and examined the Sudan region.

One of the most dramatic events in the history of African explorations involved the finding of Dr. David Livingstone, a Scottish explorer and missionary, by Henry Morton Stanley, a newspaperman turned explorer. In the 1850's Dr. Livingstone had made a remarkable east-to-west journey across Africa. He also had discovered Victoria Falls and Lake Nyasa. In 1866, he disappeared while traveling through East Africa. The *New York Herald* later sent Stanley to find Dr. Livingstone. The story of his success is famous.

But Dr. Livingstone refused to return home! He stayed in Africa and continued his valuable explorations. Stanley never lost his own interest in Africa. He, too, made African journeys that were of considerable importance, including one in which he followed the Congo River from its source to the Atlantic Ocean.

Beads, Treaties, and Land

Several factors now combined to excite Europeans' interest in Africa. These included the fascinating reports by the early explorers of Africa; the geographic information accumulated by various expeditions; Stanley's account of his adventures;

■ *In the 1870's Africa became the major target for European imperialism. Over what African areas did Belgium, France, Germany, and Great Britain gain control? What problems did imperialism create in Africa? Which African states became independent in the twentieth century (map, p. 717)?*

the news of trading opportunities in Africa; and the increased determination of Christian missionaries to spread their faith.

The powers of Europe competed with each other to seize portions of Africa. From the 1870's through the early years of the twentieth century, Africa was divided among the European nations. This period was appropriately named "the time of the Great African Hunt."

There was no single method by which a foreign nation gained control of African territory. Methods varied according to the situation and the individuals involved.

For example, a popular method was for a European nation to send one of its explorers into Africa. It would be his job to persuade an African chief to sign a "treaty." This treaty amounted to the chief's surrender of his land to the European nation. If the chief would agree to sign the treaty, he would be given such gifts as beads, cloth, or perhaps liquor. One chief was told that he would receive a steamboat!

Some chiefs were so pleased with the gifts that they readily "splodged" their crosses on the strange pieces of paper—treaties that they did not understand.

King Leopold II, the Congo, and the White Man's Face

One of the most important acquisitions was made by Leopold II, King of Belgium. Using Henry Stanley as his representative in Africa, Leopold was able to gain control over a huge area in the Congo (1879–1880). This territory, the Congo Free State, was eighty times the size of Belgium. It became the possession of King Leopold.

Leopold developed rubber and other natural resources in the Congo. Private companies were allowed to use native labor. There was a forced labor system with work camps, and native workers often were beaten and tortured. The native population often was treated so harshly that Professor Starr, an American writer who returned from the region, declared:

... after my visit ... I see the cruelty and fierceness of the white man's face. ... For the first time I can appreciate fully the feelings of the natives. The white man's face is a dreadful prediction; where the white man goes, he devastates, destroys, depopulates.

In the early years of the twentieth century, several nations and various missionary groups were so disturbed by abuses in the Congo that they demanded that investigations and changes be made. Leopold finally was compelled to turn over his territory to the Belgian government itself in 1908. It was felt that the government would treat the people of the Belgian Congo, as the land was renamed, more fairly.

The French Expand in Africa

The French also were active in building an empire in Africa. In Algeria, the Arab ruler of Algiers in North Africa struck a French envoy in the face with a fan in 1827. Three years later Charles X, the Bourbon king of France, and his government decided that the time was ripe to "avenge this insult." Charles' chief objective was to restore the prestige and power of the Bourbons by acquiring land abroad. In 1830 France sent troops to Algiers and captured the city. By 1871 the French finally were able to subdue most of the tribesmen and control the rest of Algeria.

Tunis lay adjacent to Algeria. It belonged to the Ottoman Empire, but it was governed by the Moslem *Bey*, or governor. The Bey borrowed heavily from foreigners—at an average interest rate of 13 per cent. When he could not repay his debts, he was compelled to give the French, British, and Italians financial concessions in Tunis. In 1881, after military incidents on the border between Algeria and Tunis, the French made Tunis a colony.

France gained control of a considerable part of Morocco in North Africa by making it possible for other European nations to expand elsewhere. France permitted Italy to try to take Tripolitania and Cyrenaica, two Turkish provinces in North Africa. After a war with Turkey (1911–1912), Italy obtained these provinces, combined them, and renamed the area Libya. France allowed Great Britain to be the dominant power in Egypt.

In return for this French support, Italy and Britain gave France a free hand in

Morocco; and in 1904 France and Spain secretly divided the land between them. Germany objected to France's actions in North Africa, and the French did not gain full control of Morocco until 1912.

In West Africa, the French set up colonies along the coastal regions of Senegal, Dahomey, French Guinea, and the Ivory Coast. Then they moved into the Sahara area. Eventually they built a great empire in French West Africa.

The Germans and British Gain Colonies in Africa

Germany, which had not been unified until 1871, sought African lands later than most European nations. Between 1884 and 1891 she acquired Togoland, German Southwest Africa, and the Cameroons. Great Britain, whom many Germans considered their greatest rival, established the important colony of Nigeria and smaller colonies on the west coast of Africa.

Both the Germans and British also competed for control of East Africa. Finally, in 1886, an arrangement was worked out. It had the following provisions: (1) The northern part of the region became British East Africa. (2) The southern part of the region became German East Africa. (3) The ruler of Zanzibar kept a strip of land along the coast. (4) France became the dominant power on Madagascar.

The Italians Clash with the Abyssinians

European nations also struggled for power in the Eastern Sudan (a region that controlled the Nile Valley) and in Abyssinia (Ethiopia). Great Britain, France, and Italy were the chief competitors.

The leaders of Italy were particularly eager to seize Abyssinia, which they called an escape from "[Italy's] imprisonment in the Mediterranean." In 1896 Italy therefore went to war against the Abyssinians. This time a European nation did not win.

The Abyssinians, whose army had been trained by the French, crushed the Italians at Adowa, killing or wounding six thousand Italian soldiers. Abyssinia was able to keep its independence until 1936, when it was conquered by Italy (p. 638).

Marquis di Rudini, the Premier of Italy after the 1896 war with Abyssinia, wanted to prevent Italy from setting out on other imperialist adventures. Nevertheless, the ambitions of other Italian leaders could not be checked.

The British Occupy Egypt

Meanwhile the Frenchman Ferdinand de Lesseps and a French-organized company had obtained permission from the Pasha (or governor) of Egypt to build the Suez Canal. Egypt, although theoretically linked to the Turkish Empire, was virtually independent of Turkey's control. The Pasha, subordinate to the Turkish sultan, considered himself to be the actual ruler. He therefore felt authorized to grant permission for the construction of the canal.

French investors bought over half of the shares of stock in the canal company. The Pasha also purchased a considerable part of the stock. Construction work began in 1859, and the canal was completed in 1869. The Suez Canal was extremely important because it linked the Mediterranean and Red seas and provided a shorter route to India and beyond.

When the Khedive of Egypt (Khedive was a title later given to the Pasha) became involved in financial difficulties, he offered to sell his shares in the Suez Canal company. The Suez Canal was vital to the British because it was part of the water route to their possessions in India. Disraeli, Prime Minister of Great Britain, therefore boldly arranged for the purchase of the Khedive's shares in 1875. He thus gained for his country a strong voice in the company that controlled the canal.

■ *These are some examples of African art.*
An ivory mask (right), inlaid with iron,
from Nigeria was carved about 1520. It was
probably worn as an ornament by the king.
The statue (lower right), carved about 1810,
is from the Congo. It is a figure of
Kata Mbula, 109th king of the Kuba tribe
(Kasai region). A twentieth-century
wooden dance headdress in the form of
antelopes (lower left) is from the Bambara
tribe in the western Sudan.

565

Drawing by John Tenniel

■ *A* Punch *cartoon, 1875, showed the Suez Canal as the key to India. Disraeli* (holding key) *purchased the controlling shares for his government from the Khedive of Egypt.*

After the British purchase of the Khedive's shares in the Suez Canal company, financial difficulties continued to plague the Egyptian government. Egypt was filled with unrest and tension. There was talk that the Egyptians might refuse to pay their debts to foreign bondholders. British and French bondholders who had investments in Egypt demanded that their countries protect their interests. British and French leaders insisted that the Suez Canal be kept safe from any internal disturbances in Egypt.

From about 1879 to 1882 Great Britain and France together dominated the financial affairs of Egypt and exercised considerable influence in other matters. This further strained the relations between Egyptian nationalists and the foreigners.

British statesmen continued to demand that full respect be shown to:

all established rights . . . whether they be those of the Sultan [the head of the Turkish Empire], those of the Khedive, those of the people of England, or those of the foreign bondholders.

In 1882, after several incidents, the British landed troops in Egypt and occupied it.

In 1888 Great Britain joined France, Turkey, and six other nations in signing the Constantinople Convention, in which it was agreed:

The Suez Maritime Canal shall always be free and open, in time of war as in time of peace, to every vessel of commerce or of war, without distinction of flag. . . .

In 1914 Egypt became a protectorate of Great Britain.

The French and British Struggle over the Sudan

The British also were active in the Sudan, where, according to an Arab saying, "the soil is like fire and the wind like a flame." Near the close of the nineteenth century the British General Kitchener marched his troops south from Egypt into the Sudan. He defeated a large army of *dervishes*, followers of a leader called the *Mahdi* (Guide) who claimed that he was divinely inspired to revive the Moslem faith and drive out the Europeans. General Kitchener also recaptured Khartoum, where the dervishes had once annihilated a British garrison led by General Gordon. Then he continued south.

Meanwhile France sent an expedition headed by Captain Marchand north from the French Congo into the Sudan. After a long and difficult journey, Captain Marchand reached the village of Fashoda on the Nile on July 10, 1898. There he raised the French flag on an old fort.

566

A few months later General Kitchener and his British troops also arrived at Fashoda, and Kitchener and Marchand each claimed the Sudan for his own nation! Historian Parker T. Moon describes the situation when the men met:

Kitchener congratulated Marchand on his remarkable journey and announced that he would hoist the British and Egyptian flags in token of Anglo-Egyptian sovereignty, whereat Marchand pointed out that the tricolor was already floating over Fashoda. Kitchener courteously called attention to the numerical superiority of his own troops; Marchand retorted that he would be buried in the ruins of his fort rather than lower the tricolor without orders from Paris.

Then Kitchener politely presented Marchand with a gift of wine, Marchand graciously presented Kitchener with a gift of fresh vegetables, and both men prepared to fight if necessary.

War seemed inevitable. The French began to look for allies; and the British Chancellor of the Exchequer assured the British people that "there are worse evils than war, and we shall not shrink from anything that may come." This "Fashoda Incident" was settled. In 1899 it was agreed that Great Britain would be given the Egyptian Sudan. France's Congo Colony would be granted free commercial access through the Sudan to the Nile, and France would be permitted to strengthen her position in Central and Western Sudan.

■ **Check on Your Reading**

1. Why was Africa a target of imperialism?
2. How did European powers acquire land and governing control in Africa?
3. In what ways did the Belgian Congo typify the worst aspects of imperialism?
4. Into what African areas did France, Germany, and Britain expand? with what results?

5. Imperialism in Latin America

At the same time that the European powers were engaged in Asia and Africa, considerable tension existed in the Western Hemisphere between the United States and Spain. This was caused by Spain's harsh treatment of the people of Cuba, a Spanish colony and the largest island in the Caribbean Sea; by the desire of American businessmen to have their investments protected from the disorders in Cuba; and by the dramatic and often exaggerated stories in the American press about events in Cuba.

In February, 1898, the United States battleship *Maine* was blown up in Havana harbor and the Spanish-American War broke out. The United States quickly defeated Spain. By the terms of the peace treaty, the Spanish ceded the Philippine Islands, Guam, and Puerto Rico to the United States.

Cuba and the Platt Amendment

As a result of the Spanish-American War, Spain also gave up its control of Cuba. In 1898 the United States had pledged that after Cuba's "pacification" the Americans would "leave the government and control of the island to its people."

With the guidance of the United States, the Cubans met in convention and prepared a constitution. However, Cuba was required to add the so-called *Platt Amendment* (1901) to its constitution. By this amendment, the United States was permitted to buy or lease Cuban land for naval or coaling stations, and the United States obtained the right to intervene:

for the protection of Cuban independence, the maintenance of a government adequate for the protection of life, property and individual liberty, and for discharging [other] obligations.

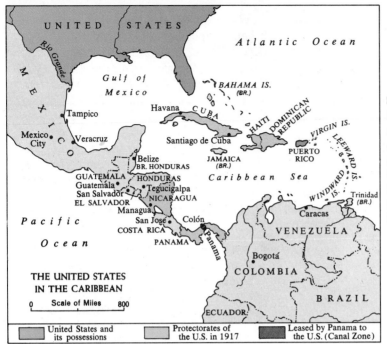

THE UNITED STATES
IN THE CARIBBEAN

0   Scale of Miles   800

| United States and its possessions | Protectorates of the U.S. in 1917 | Leased by Panama to the U.S. (Canal Zone) |

■ As a result of the Spanish-American War (1898) the United States acquired Puerto Rico and considerable influence in Cuba. How did the United States acquire the right to construct the Panama Canal?

Commercial agreements soon tied Cuba more closely to the United States. The United States was able to exercise economic as well as political influence over Cuba.

Panama and the Canal

The American government wished to construct a canal linking the Atlantic and Pacific oceans. The narrow Isthmus of Panama seemed to be a good place to build such a canal. Since Panama was under the jurisdiction of Colombia, Colombia's consent would first have to be obtained. However, when terms were offered to Colombia, the Colombian Senate refused to accept them without changes. The Colombian Senators made clear that unless their country was given greater financial compensation and additional rights, the United States would not be permitted to construct the canal.

In 1903 a revolution broke out in Panama City. The revolutionists declared their independence from Colombia and proclaimed the establishment of the new Republic of Panama. Three days after the revolution, the United States recognized the independence of the new republic. Less than two weeks later, the Republic of Panama—which now had possession of the canal area—signed a treaty with the United States permitting the United States to build the canal. In return, the Republic of Panama was to receive a sum of money that was less than that asked by Colombia.

It is generally accepted that the American president, Theodore Roosevelt, and others in the United States government, in an effort to obtain the right to build the canal, aided the establishment of the new Republic of Panama. For example, when Colombian troops were sent to put down the revolt, ships of the United States prevented them from landing in Panama. Such acts prompted the Colombian government to protest:

[the] right of Colombia has been injured by the United States by an incredible transgression of the limits set by equity and justice. . . .

And several years later Theodore Roosevelt admitted:

If I had followed conventional, conservative methods, I should have submitted a dignified state paper of approximately two hundred pages to the Congress and the debate would have been going on yet, but I took the canal zone and let Congress debate. . . .

In April, 1921, two years after Roosevelt died, the United States Senate ratified a treaty that gave Colombia an additional $25,000,000. It was hoped that this treaty would result in "amity and commerce" between the United States and Colombia. Certainly the Panama Canal, which was opened officially on July 12, 1920, proved to be of great value to Latin America as well as to other parts of the world.

■ **Check on Your Reading**

1. What were the causes and results of the Spanish-American War?
2. Describe American relations with Cuba after 1900 and explain the Platt Amendment to the Cuban constitution.
3. Describe how the United States acquired rights to build the Panama Canal.

6. The Results of Imperialism

There were other cases of imperialist activities in the world. The Dutch were active in Indonesia, the French in Indo-China, and other nations in the Middle East. Our examination of imperialism in the Far East, Africa, and Latin America is sufficient to determine many of the effects of imperialism. The most important results of imperialism were these:

(1) European nations (including Russia), Japan, and the United States extended economic and often political control over many regions in the world. (2) In colonial regions, trade with foreign countries was increased and natural resources were developed. Foreign investors helped by investing capital in colonial lands. From these and other economic activities, individuals and corporations of the foreign nations received most of the profit. (3) Some progress was made in improving the health, education, and social welfare of colonial peoples, depending on the foreign nation, colonial region, the time, and the individuals.

(4) Asia and Africa were brought into closer contact with, and were affected by, the cultures of foreign nations. For example, the lives of colonial peoples were influenced by the systems of transportation and communication established by the imperialist powers. Europe, in turn, was affected by the cultures of the African and Asian lands.

(5) The exploration of new lands added to man's knowledge of geography and other sciences. (6) Increased contact permitted people who believed in Christianity, Buddhism, Hinduism, and other faiths to learn more about each other's religion.

Imperialism also created a number of problems. The competition for colonies produced tensions among nations building empires. These tensions were one of the causes of future wars. Eventually, domination by foreign powers helped to stimulate the nationalism of colonial peoples. In time, these peoples wanted their own nations. In the mid-twentieth century many new nations were established in place of former colonies. Some had few difficulties; others had major problems as a result of their colonial status.

■ **Check on Your Reading**

1. Which do you think are the most important results of imperialism?
2. Does imperialism exist today?

MAN AND HIS CULTURE

Let's Meet the People!

The following sketch is based on primary source material in *With Perry in Japan, The Diary of Edward Yorke McCauley*, edited by Allan B. Coles, copyright © 1942 by Princeton University Press.

The American Midshipmen and the Japanese Spy

There was no doubt about it. American Midshipmen Edward Yorke McCauley and K. Randolph Breese, both members of Commodore Perry's second expedition to Japan, were being watched. The man watching them was a Spy from the Japanese government.

McCauley did not wish "to get [the Spy] into trouble by forcing him to leave us, which would have entailed punishment on him, it being a duty assigned by higher authority, and we having no particular objection to his company, excepting as a Spy." McCauley and his companion therefore began to walk away. However, they kept at a slow pace that enabled the people of the Japanese village of Shimoda to see that the Spy was doing a good job of following them.

Once out in the country, away from the eyes of the villagers, the American Midshipmen increased their speed. Four more fast miles and the weary Spy began to drop behind. "Na! Ney! No! American! Noah!" shouted the Spy, slipping and stumbling in the gullies.

The Midshipmen paid no attention to his cries. They walked faster until they came to a high hill. Then they started to dash up the hill. This act threw the exhausted Spy into "a paroxysm of anguish."

The Spy now hurried up to them. "Wait, please," he said, "while I cool myself." When the two Americans promised that they would not walk away, the Spy arranged for a peasant to rub his body, removed his clothes, and enjoyed a good massage. Then the Midshipmen and the Spy returned to the village.

When Midshipmen McCauley and Breese continued on their way, they were followed by a new agent. The first Spy left them. He went directly to a tea house, "threw himself on the floor," closed his eyes, and rested for his next assignment as a Spy.

CHAPTER REVIEW

REVIEW and DISCUSSION

1. Identify the people and places and explain the events and terms on p. 552.

2. Do you think imperialism is ever justified? Why?

3. If you had lived in China in the 1800's, what would you think about the right of extraterritoriality? Why?

4. Some historians now look upon Hay's "Open Door" policy as more proposal than policy. What was its purpose?

5. Do you think Commodore Perry's expedition to Japan was an interference in the internal affairs of that country? Why?

6. Japan made reforms during the Meiji reign with what results? Which ones aided the common people?

7. Evaluate the activities of the European powers in Africa at the end of the nineteenth century.

8. Do people living today in lands that were once colonies have a sense of urgency to "catch up" with the rest of the world? Give evidence to support your answer.

9. Evaluate the effects of imperialism in the nineteenth century.

ACTIVITIES

1. On a map of Africa, show the colonial possessions of nations in 1914.

2. On a map of the world, indicate the possessions of the United States in 1914.

3. Write a short paper on "Imperialism: Its Nature and Causes." Consult Palmer; *Encyclopedia of the Social Sciences*; and *Syntopicon* of Great Books of the Western World.

4. Continue to build your paperback library by adding these books: Latourette, *A History of Modern China*; and Tiedemann, *Modern Japan*.

PAST and PRESENT

1. Many historians point out that while most of the colonies once belonging to Britain and France have gained independence, the Soviet Union has developed a "new imperialism" dominating millions of people. Do you agree? Justify your answer.

2. What may happen to an individual of an underdeveloped country when he comes into contact with a culture more advanced in science and technology than his own?

SUGGESTED READINGS

Basic books: LATOURETTE, KENNETH SCOTT, *A History of Modern China*, Penguin. Contains a good chapter on pre-revolutionary China. *The History of Japan*, Macmillan. Short and excellent. Covers entire history of Japan.

LINTON, RALPH, *The Tree of Culture*, Chaps. 13 and 31, Knopf. Discusses African people and civilizations.

PALMER, R. R., and COLTON, JOEL, *A History of the Modern World*, Chap. 15, Knopf.

SMITH, GOLDWIN, *The Heritage of Man*, Chap. 39, Scribner.

Special accounts: LAMPREY, LOUISE, *Building an Empire*, Lippincott. Growth of the British Empire.

MOON, PARKER T., *Imperialism and World Politics*, Macmillan. Readable and interesting story of the acquisition of colonies and empires. A pioneer study of the significance of imperialism.

TIEDEMANN, ARTHUR, *Modern Japan: A Brief History* (An Anvil Original), Van Nostrand. Very brief account of modern period. Source readings in Part II.

Biography and Fiction: LOCKHART, JOHN G., and WOODHOUSE, C. M., *Cecil Rhodes: The Colossus of Southern Africa*, Macmillan. A major work on Rhodes.

STERLING, THOMAS, *Stanley's Way: A Sentimental Journey through Central Africa*, Atheneum. Dramatizes Stanley's great contribution to the opening up of an unknown continent.

UNIT 9 Revolutions, Dictators, and Two World Wars

The Sphinx Speaks

Mankind has always had a desire to learn the secrets of the past. An editorial in the *Buffalo Evening News* of June 18, 1961, indicates the extremes to which this desire can lead men:

... the giant Sphinx of Giza is no longer mute. The old boy who has held his tongue since the Fourth Dynasty is now wired for sound—literally. Through tape recordings in four languages (Arabic, English, French, and German), he lectures at times—when there is a gaggle of tourists—on Egyptian history in the days of the Pharaohs.

The Television Set Reveals

Knowledge cannot be limited to distant periods of history. Today a history book is expected to be more than a silent Sphinx when it reaches the modern period; it too must speak. Men must be informed about events in their own century, regardless of how shocking these events may be.

In 1961 the West German Television Network presented a fourteen-part program on "The Third Reich." It showed over ten million viewers the brutality and horror of Nazi Germany under dictator Adolf Hitler between 1933 and 1945. A review in *Variety* magazine noted that: "The dreadful death tablets at the end [of the television film] revealed that the Nazi era had taken a terrible toll of nearly fifty million lives as it changed the entire existence of the world."

Why did the West German Television Network recall such bitter times to the German people? It did not do it to inflict new pain. As the American *TV Guide* suggests, the answer can be found in the statement of the German citizen who said, "The war has been over for sixteen years and our most recent past is still obscured in misinformation and a desire to ignore and forget." The television program was presented to combat this tendency to "ignore and forget."

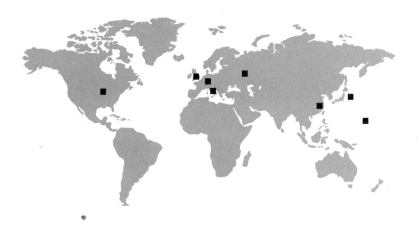

The History Book Informs and Protects

You may ask, "What has all this to do with me, a student of history?" It is a question that can be answered promptly. Certainly, if it is important for nations that once lived under dictators to remember years of brutality and war, it is equally important for democracies to learn about these periods. *If you want to protect democracy and keep it strong, you must know something about the people who oppose or have opposed freedom.*

You must know not just the names of men, but the beliefs held by the leaders of nations that challenged democracy. Not just the opinions of Nazis, but the views of Fascists, Communists, militarists, and other anti-democrats. Not just the theories of totalitarianism, but the realities of war.

Your next unit will help you to obtain such knowledge. It will be indispensable to you both as a student of history and as a citizen in a democracy.

As you study this unit these are some questions that may occur to you. Do wars always bring revolutions and depressions as their aftermath? Why may similar economic problems lead to the rise of fascism in some countries and to communism in others? What dangers may arise when democratic nations avoid planning ahead? When the horrors of war are well known to all men, why is it so difficult to make and enforce disarmament agreements? Trying to find answers to such questions will be of value to you, too.

Chapter 36　*A World War and Plans for Peace*

KEYNOTE　World War I (1914–1918) was not a glamorous war. On the contrary, it was a war where soldiers "diced with death" each time they crossed a trench—where homes were smashed into heaps of jagged stones—where scavenger rats scurried through No Man's Land at the sound and flare of a bursting shell—where barbed wire trapped the limbs of men in webs of steel. It was a war of mud and disease and loneliness.

　　This tragic conflict played a great part in history. *World War I and the treaties that ended it were key features of the world in the second decade of the twentieth century.*

Key People　*William II　·　General Pétain　·　Marshal Foch　·　Thomas Masaryk　·　Archduke Francis Ferdinand　·　Woodrow Wilson　·　General Pershing　·　David Lloyd George　· Mustapha Kemal　·　General Ludendorff　·　Georges Clemenceau*

Key Places　*Bosnia-Herzegovina　·　Sarajevo　·　Marne　·　Jutland　· Verdun　·　Galicia　·　Tannenberg　·　Dardanelles　· Gallipoli peninsula　·　Yugoslavia　·　Poland　·　Czecho-slovakia　·　Rumania　·　Ruhr*

Key Events　*Triple Alliance　·　Triple Entente　·　Balkan Wars　· World War I　·　United States enters the war　·　Treaty of Versailles　·　League of Nations established　·　United States rejects the Treaty of Versailles　·　Turkey becomes a republic　· France occupies Ruhr　·　Dawes and Young Plans*

Key Terms　*alliances　·　armaments　·　trench warfare　·　submarines　· "Fourteen Points"　·　self-determination　·　mandates　· reparations　·　war debts*

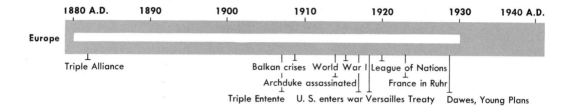

| 1880 A.D. | 1890 | 1900 | 1910 | 1920 | 1930 | 1940 A.D. |

Europe

Triple Alliance

Balkan crises   World War I   League of Nations

Archduke assassinated   France in Ruhr

Triple Entente   U. S. enters war   Versailles Treaty   Dawes, Young Plans

1. A Vital Question: What Caused World War I?

In 1914 Europe and a considerable part of the world were disrupted by the outbreak of a great war—World War I. So great was the destruction that men everywhere have asked themselves: What caused this war? Who was responsible? Which nation bears the guilt for the war? These are difficult questions to answer, but scholars point to certain facts that help explain the outbreak of World War I.

Many authorities agree that in 1914 none of the powers wanted a European war. Today it also seems clear that World War I grew out of tensions caused by a number of factors. As a result of the studies of Professor Sidney B. Fay and others, we know some of these factors.

Alliances

In the years that preceded World War I, the major nations of Europe formed alliances that divided them roughly into two opposing groups: the Triple Alliance and the Triple Entente.

The Triple Alliance was engineered by Bismarck, who tried to isolate France after the Franco-Prussian War and to prevent other nations from overpowering Germany in a future war. Bismarck particularly wanted to protect Germany from any

French attempt at revenge and recovery of the province of Alsace and part of Lorraine from Germany. In 1879, an alliance between Germany and Austria-Hungary was formed. In 1882, Italy joined to form the *Triple Alliance*. One of the key articles in the treaty establishing this alliance provided that Germany, Austria-Hungary, and Italy would come to each other's assistance if any one or two of them were unjustifiably attacked by two or more of the other Great Powers.

Six years later William II, whose grandfather was William I, became ruler of the German Empire. William II (1888–1918) was a forceful and arrogant ruler. He dismissed Bismarck from his post as chancellor and surrounded himself with men who would obey his orders without question. In his conduct of foreign affairs from 1890 to 1914, William II differed sharply from Bismarck. For example, William II wanted Germany to expand overseas and obtain as many colonial possessions as possible. He deliberately strengthened the German navy, despite the fact that his actions might result in a coalition of Britain and other powers. Germany became increasingly demanding in her relations with other countries.

575

As a defense against Germany's ambitions, the *Triple Entente* was formed by Great Britain, France, and Russia. This alliance was primarily a result of William II's abandonment of Bismarck's policies. In 1894, France aided Russia by giving her a large loan of money, paving the way for these nations to form a Franco-Russian alliance. In 1904 Great Britain and France settled their arguments over territory in North Africa and came to a cordial understanding—*entente cordiale*—over these and other disagreements. Three years later Great Britain and Russia settled their disputes over Persia: Russia was to have a sphere of influence in northern Persia, Britain was to have one in southern Persia, with a buffer zone between the two.

These settlements enabled Great Britain, France, and Russia to form a "diplomatic group" which constituted the Triple Entente (1907). Although there was not yet an official treaty binding them together, Great Britain, France, and Russia agreed to support each other in time of crisis.

The Triple Alliance and Triple Entente were not rigid alliances. No nation could be absolutely sure that it would receive the support of the other nations in its group. Nevertheless, the two alliances increased the possibility that a war in one part of Europe would spread. That is why Arthur Zimmermann, a German undersecretary of state in 1914, called this system of alliances "the curse of modern times."

Nationalism Creates Tensions

Nationalism had become a strong force in the countries of Europe during the nineteenth century. It had played an important role in the creation of the new nations of Germany and Italy. However, long-established nations did not want any other nations to gain at their expense. For example, the national pride of the French people had been given a sharp blow by the defeat of France in the Franco-Prussian War. The French people became increasingly hostile to the Germans and were determined that Germany should not surpass France as a nation in war or peace.

In Austria-Hungary, nationalism was also a powerful and disruptive factor. Austria-Hungary had become a "dual monarchy" in 1867 (p. 502). This arrangement gave rights to the Magyars, who dominated Hungary, and to the peoples of Germanic descent, who dominated Austria. However, it did not satisfy the demands of other national groups. From 1867 until the dissolution of Austria-Hungary in 1918, a number of Slavic groups struggled fiercely to obtain equal rights. They included Poles, Czechs, Serbs, Croats, and Slovenes. As a result, some of the most dangerous tensions in Europe arose in Austria-Hungary. For example, the nationalist movement of the Serbs in Bosnia almost led to World War I in 1908 and did ignite it in 1914.

In the Balkans, too, there were many peoples who demanded the right to belong to their own nations. The rulers of these peoples (in the Turkish Empire and the Austro-Hungarian monarchy) were equally determined to keep them as subjects. As a result there were clashes between rulers and nationality groups.

Nationalism, which had been a constructive factor aiding the unification of Germany and Italy, became destructive of good relations among European nations.

Armaments

Another factor increasing the threat of war was the existence of growing military forces in many European nations. This created a feeling of distrust among Europe's leaders. It also produced a military seesaw. When the heaviness of one nation's armaments placed another nation in a dangerous position, the second nation hurried to increase its own military strength. In time, the military see-saw became so heavy that it threatened to crack!

Imperialism

Imperialism often contributed to strained relations. In the Near East, for example, Russia, France, Great Britain, and Germany all had conflicting interests.

In other colonial areas, the efforts of nations to obtain economic or political control also led to arguments among imperialist powers. In North Africa, for example, France and Germany had bitter disputes over Morocco. A compromise between Germany and France ended the threat of war. France received a free hand in Morocco and Germany was given an area of 100,000 square miles in the French Congo. Imperialism was one of many factors that contributed to the tensions that preceded the great conflict.

Diplomatic Errors and Propaganda

The diplomats of the period before World War I varied in ability. Some were talented, level-headed men who worked conscientiously for peace. Others were reckless, emotional men whose errors of judgment produced dangerous results. On several occasions diplomatic errors increased tensions among nations.

Propaganda in speeches and the press also helped to make citizens of one nation hate or fear those of other nations. When it seemed that war had finally come, most people did not cry out against the conflict. On the contrary! Russians cheered; Germans marched in the streets singing war ballads; and Frenchmen wept with emotion when they were told by a Parisian mayor: "The hour of revenge for which we have prayed unceasingly for forty-four years has at last struck."

■ *In this* Punch *cartoon, "The Boiling Point" (1912), Russia, Germany, and Austria-Hungary are trying to hold the lid on the Balkan crisis.*

The Balkan Crises

The outbreak of World War I was preceded by several crises in the Balkans. In 1908 Austria-Hungary annexed the provinces of Bosnia and Herzegovina, which in theory were part of the Turkish Empire. Actually they had been administered by Austria-Hungary for about thirty years. The provinces were inhabited by many Serbian-speaking people who did not wish to join Austria-Hungary. The annexation of Bosnia-Herzegovina angered Serbia and Russia. However, Germany supported Austria-Hungary; and Russia, poorly prepared for war, was in no position to aid Serbia. Although a crisis developed, war was avoided.

The Balkan Wars erupted in 1912 and 1913. In the First Balkan War (1912) Serbia, Bulgaria, Montenegro, and Greece

EUROPE IN 1914

Central Powers
Allied Powers
Neutral Countries

■ *When World War I erupted in 1914, the European nations divided into two armed camps. What countries opposed each other?*

fought against Turkey for several reasons, including their desire to free their fellow Slavs under Moslem rule. In the Second Balkan War (1913) Serbia, Montenegro, Greece, Rumania, and Turkey fought against Bulgaria over territory taken from Turkey in the First Balkan War. As a result of these events, tensions increased between Turkey and the Balkan States, between Austria-Hungary and Serbia, and between Germany and Russia.

The climax to the Balkan crises occurred on June 28, 1914, when the Austrian Archduke Francis Ferdinand and his wife were assassinated at Sarajevo, capital of Bosnia. Their assassin was a young Bosnian who belonged to a secret terrorist society whose purpose was to "free" all Serbs living outside its borders and to create a great South Slav kingdom of all the Serbs.

The archduke was the nephew of the emperor of Austria-Hungary and heir to the Hapsburg throne. Austria charged that his assassination had been planned in Serbia and had been assisted by "Serbian officers and functionaries." Actually some

members of the Serbian government had heard about the plot before the archduke's visit, but the complicity of the Serbian government in the assassination is still uncertain. Nevertheless, the Austrians decided to take drastic steps against Serbia and to use this opportunity to crush Serbian national ambitions.

In this new crisis, Germany indicated that she would back up Austria-Hungary. In the so-called "blank check," Germany declared that she would "faithfully stand by Austria-Hungary, as is required by the obligations of . . . alliance. . . ." Germany did not expect a world war to result.

Austria sent an ultimatum to Serbia. It included the demands that the Serbian government take immediate steps to suppress the anti-Austrian movement, and that Austro-Hungarian officials be permitted to participate in the trial of persons involved in the assassination of the archduke. In her reply, Serbia suggested that the dispute be submitted to international arbitration. Not satisfied with the Serbian response, Austria-Hungary declared war on Serbia on July 28, 1914.

The system of alliances helped to spread the war. Russia, fearful that the Austrians would annex Serbia, mobilized. Russian mobilization stirred Germany to declare war on Russia. France as an ally of Russia was drawn in. After the Germans had invaded Belgium to attack France, Great Britain entered the conflict on the side of France and Russia. One nation pulled another into the center of war.

■ **Check on Your Reading**

1. What factors helped to cause World War I?

2. Explain how the Triple Alliance and the Triple Entente were formed.

3. How did problems of nationalism in Austria-Hungary and the Balkan states lead to the outbreak of World War I?

2. World War I Becomes a Bitter Struggle

World War I was a bitter struggle. On August 3, 1914, German troops violated a treaty of 1839 guaranteeing the neutrality of Belgium and invaded it. Britain entered the war at once. The Belgian army fought courageously, but by August 20 German troops had entered Brussels.

The Allies had almost twice as many mobilized troops as the Central Powers, and the British had the most powerful navy. However, the German army was the largest and strongest of all the combatants. The Germans planned to sweep through to Paris quickly and force France out of the war before the British could send help. The necessity of keeping many troops on the eastern front prevented the Germans from employing all their forces in this attack.

The War on the Western Front

The German war machine, which had invaded Belgium as the best route to

■ *World War I was fought on two fronts. On the western front the German army tried to smash through to Paris but was checked by the Allied forces. The war was carried on in the trenches. On the eastern front, the German army drove the Russians back. Name the major battles of the war.*

British soldiers are shown in the trenches. The London Times *described the trenches as "five feet deep . . . with the earth thrown up another two and a half feet as a bank on top. These trenches . . . curl and twist about in a maddening manner to make them safer from shell-fire. Little caves are scooped in the walls of the trenches, where the men live about four to a hole. . . ."*

France, moved towards Paris. Its advance units reached a point only fifteen miles from the French capital, and the Germans were confident of victory in a short time. In September, 1914, a crucial battle was fought at the Marne River. The Allies, under the leadership of the French General Joseph Joffre, finally checked the Germans and drove them back to the Aisne River. Paris was saved, and the German plan for a quick victory failed.

Fighting on the western front became stabilized. Both sides dug in and protected their positions by a network of trenches. In the trenches thousands of soldiers fought and waited and fought again from 1915 to 1917. And it was here—from the trenches—that they launched their drives for a major break-through.

In the winter of 1916 the Germans tried to smash the French line at Verdun. The French General Pétain was equally determined that the enemy "shall not pass." Both sides suffered heavy casualties in the battles that followed. Finally the French —aided by British attacks on enemy troops along the Somme, which prevented the Germans from sending reinforcements —stopped the German drive at Verdun.

An Allied counter-offensive began along the Somme River in July, 1916. Although the Allies introduced the tank as a new machine of war, their forces too failed to advance more than a few miles. In the great battles of 1914 to 1916 along the western front, there was an enormous number of casualties. France alone lost over 600,000 men in the first sixteen months of the war. The growing number of casualties and the sky-rocketing costs of war horrified the European nations involved and shocked the rest of the world.

The War on the Eastern Front

In the east, Russia faced many serious difficulties during the war. These resulted from inefficiency and dissension in the government, poor training of troops, lack of military supplies and equipment, and food shortages. Nevertheless, in the first year of the war the Russians were able to invade Germany and Austria-Hungary.

In the summer of 1914, a Russian army seized the province of Galicia and other territories. In East Prussia, poorly organized Russian armies were defeated at Tannenberg by the forces of the German General Paul von Hindenburg. Russian

■ *American-manned tanks are going forward into action in the Argonne during the great drive of September, 1918, against the German lines. Tanks were introduced in warfare by the British in 1916.*

forces suffered between 300,000 and 325,-000 casualties. In 1915 the Russians were driven back from most of Galicia and Poland.

In October, 1914, Turkey entered the war on the side of the Central Powers, closing the Dardanelles to the Allies. The Turks thus blocked one of the major supply routes between the western Allies and Russia. Fearful of Turkey's expansion and the Turkish threat to the Suez Canal, Britain declared Egypt to be independent of Turkey and a British protectorate.

Allied efforts to open the Dardanelles by seizing the Gallipoli Peninsula failed (1915). This setback helped influence Bulgaria to join the Central Powers. However, British and other Allied forces defeated the Turks threatening the Suez Canal area, stirred Arabs of the Middle East to revolt against Turkish rule, and occupied Palestine.

In May, 1915, Italy, eager to obtain land in Europe and Africa, entered the war against Austria-Hungary. Italy helped the Allies to control the Mediterranean.

In 1917 revolution in Russia led to the overthrow of the czarist government and eventually to the withdrawal of Russia

from the war in December, 1917 (p. 598) The loss of Russia was counterbalanced by the entry of the United States.

The War at Sea

In the spring of 1916 the great naval battle of Jutland was fought off the coast of Denmark between the British and German fleets. Although Germany destroyed many British ships at Jutland, the German fleet did not venture from its base again.

German submarines continued a menace. U-boats, silent marauders whose periscopes became eyes of death for hundreds of seamen, torpedoed Allied military and merchant vessels without warning. On February 1, 1917, the Germans began unrestricted submarine warfare. Ships of any nation—including the United States and other neutrals—that entered waters defined as "war zones" by the Germans were in danger of being destroyed. Many neutral vessels were torpedoed and sunk.

The United States Enters the War

In the beginning Americans had seemed grateful that the United States was not at war. President Woodrow Wilson proposed to follow a course of neutrality. Nevertheless, on April 6, 1917, the United States declared war on Germany for several reasons: (1) Germany's unrestricted submarine warfare cost the lives of a number of Americans, including those who were on the torpedoed British liner *Lusitania*. (2) Anti-German feelings resulted from Germany's efforts to win Mexico's support by promising to return to her the territory lost to the United States in 1848. (3) Anti-German articles and news stories printed in the American press produced incendiary effects. (4) Many Americans viewed the war as a basic struggle between democracy and autocracy. They were determined to help make the world "safe for democracy" by defeating what they considered to be the undemocratic Central Powers. For these and other reasons, the United States entered the war.

The War Ends

In 1918 the Germans faced a critical situation. The Allied blockade of Germany threatened the German people with starvation. The "Fourteen Points" of President Woodrow Wilson encouraged a number of Germans to desire peace instead of a continuance of the war. The increasing number of American troops arriving in Europe continued to strengthen the Allied forces. The German General Staff and General Ludendorff therefore decided to gamble everything on one final major offensive to end the war.

In March, 1918, General Ludendorff's forces, bolstered by troops freed from the east by Russia's withdrawal, launched a tremendous attack. They smashed through the British lines and moved forward rapidly. The Allies responded by placing their separate armies under the over-all command of Marshal Ferdinand Foch of France. A desperate struggle followed. Finally, the German offensive was stopped at the second battle of the Marne in the summer of 1918. Then, aided by American materials and troops under the command of General John Pershing, the Allies broke through the fortified German positions known as the Hindenburg Line.

On other fronts, the Central Powers were suffering other serious setbacks, and an Austrian offensive against the Italians ended in failure. Crushed by military defeats and disrupted by dissension within their countries, the Central Powers surrendered one after the other—Bulgaria, Turkey, Austria. Finally, Emperor William II of Germany fled to Holland, and on November 11, 1918, an armistice was signed with Germany. The great war was over, and the Allies were victorious!

■ **Check on Your Reading**

1. How did the Germans plan to achieve a quick victory?

2. Why did Russia leave the war and the United States enter it in 1917?

3. Why did the Central Powers surrender?

3. *Woodrow Wilson and the Peace*

Leading statesmen gathered at Versailles, near Paris, to draw up a treaty of peace for Germany, although the Germans were not permitted to attend. Many people hoped that the diplomats would be guided in their work by the "Fourteen Points" of President Woodrow Wilson.

Wilson, on January 8, 1918, had presented the "Fourteen Points" as a statement of "War Aims and Peace Terms of the United States" (see Chart). Germany was eager to see them used as a basis for the peace treaty. The Allies accepted most of the points, although with reluctance.

Later President Wilson also suggested that every settlement be based on *self-determination*. This meant that the desires and interests of national groups should be taken into consideration when territorial and other changes were made.

Many people wanted the diplomats to write a treaty of peace based on the ideas of Woodrow Wilson. The defeated Germans were particularly hopeful that the conciliatory nature of the "Fourteen Points" would help the statesmen to draw up a treaty that would not be too harsh.

The Treaty of Versailles

The delegates of the Allied countries who gathered to draw up a peace treaty for Germany were a varied and colorful group. The three statesmen, or "Big Three," who dominated the conference were Woodrow Wilson, President of the United States; Georges Clemenceau, Premier of France; and David Lloyd George,

Prime Minister of Great Britain. With Premier Vittorio Orlando of Italy, they constituted the "Big Four."

The delegates finally completed the treaty of peace, which was signed by Germany near the end of June, 1919. These were some of the provisions of this extremely important Treaty of Versailles: (1) Germany was to give up a considerable part of her land and all of her overseas colonies. If these areas were "not yet able to stand by themselves," they were to become *mandates* of the League of Nations, that is, be placed under the administrative "tutelage" of various "advanced nations." (2) Germany's army and navy were to be limited in size. Her air force was to cease to exist. (3) The Saar Basin, an important coal area, was to be placed under the jurisdiction of the League of Nations for a fifteen-year period. During that time, France could exploit the coal mines in the region. (4) The Rhineland area was to be demilitarized. (5) Germany

THE "FOURTEEN POINTS"

● "Open covenants of peace, openly arrived at. . . ."

● Absolute freedom of navigation upon the seas.

● Removal of economic barriers "so far as possible."

● Reduction of national armaments.

● A free, open-minded, and absolutely impartial adjustment of all colonial claims.

● Evacuation of all Russian territory. Opportunity for Russia to determine "her own political development and national policy. . . ."

● Evacuation and restoration of Belgium.

● Evacuation of France and restoration of invaded portions. Alsace-Lorraine to be returned to France.

● Italy's frontiers to be readjusted "along clearly recognizable lines of nationality."

● Peoples of Austria-Hungary to have the opportunity for autonomous development.

● Evacuation of Rumania, Serbia, and Montenegro. Occupied territories to be restored. Serbia to have free and secure access to the sea.

● Subject nationalities in Turkey to have the opportunity for autonomous development. The Dardanelles to be permanently open to all nations "under international guarantees."

● Establishment of an independent Poland with free and secure access to the sea.

● Formation of "a general association of nations" (a League of Nations) "for the purpose of affording mutual guarantees of political independence and territorial integrity" to all states.

Woodrow Wilson

Georges Clemenceau

David Lloyd George

■ *The "Big Three" dominated the Paris Peace Conference. President Woodrow Wilson of the United States wanted the conference to be guided by the Fourteen Points. He put his hopes principally into the establishment of a League of Nations. Georges Clemenceau, the Premier of France, was determined to avenge the injuries done to France by Germany in 1870–1871 and 1914–1918 and to weaken Germany. Lloyd George, Prime Minister of England, had won an election on the promise to impose a punitive peace on Germany. Therefore, he opposed a number of Wilson's ideas.*

was to give back the provinces of Alsace and Lorraine to France; she was also to recognize the independence of Czechoslovakia and Poland. (6) Japan was to receive Germany's rights in a valuable territory in China. (7) Article 231 of the treaty declared that Germany and her allies were responsible for causing the war. Therefore a commission was to be set up to decide the amount of *reparations* that Germany was to pay. (Reparations were payments in money and material that defeated nations made to victors for war damages.) (8) A League of Nations was to be established.

Other peace treaties later were completed with the other defeated nations.

The Treaty of Versailles Brings Varied Reactions

The Treaty of Versailles has been blamed for many of the ills of the post-1920 world. It has even been used by demagogues as an excuse for starting new wars. Why did it stir up such bitterness?

One of the reasons for the criticism of the treaty was that many of the decisions made by the treaty-makers were *not* based on the "Fourteen Points." Clemenceau was even reported to have said:

God gave us the ten commandments and we broke them. Wilson gave us the Fourteen Points—we shall see.

On the other hand, the delegates at Versailles had an extremely difficult job which was further complicated by the existence of secret treaties. Recent scholarship also makes it clear that not everything in the treaty was unfortunate or unfair. For example, the Treaty of Versailles and the other treaties helped to release several minority groups from the domination of foreign powers. The treaties also put into effect several of the "Fourteen Points," such as the League of Nations.

The Treaty of Versailles had been completed and representatives of Germany had signed it. Each of the governments of the Allied nations had to decide whether or

584

■ *The peace treaties that ended World War I changed many boundaries in Europe and created a number of independent countries. What territories did Germany, Austria-Hungary, Russia, and the Turkish Empire lose? What countries gained their independence after the war?*

not to *ratify* the treaty, that is, to accept it officially. Ratification was particularly important for the future of the League of Nations. The articles establishing the League were part of the treaty. If a nation rejected the treaty as a whole, it would be rejecting the League at the same time.

The United States Rejects the Treaty of Versailles

By January, 1920, the Treaty of Versailles had been ratified by nearly every major Allied power. However, one of the leading nations at the peace conference had not yet accepted it. On January 10, 1920, the League of Nations began its existence with twenty-four members. Again, one nation whose support had been counted on was not among the members. In both cases the country that refused to join was the United States.

The Senate, which in the United States is responsible for the ratification of treaties, voted against the Treaty of Versailles. Many of the objections of the senators revolved around the fact that the Covenant of the League was part of the treaty. Some senators were afraid the League

585

would drag the United States into foreign entanglements and wars. Some felt that they would be giving up American sovereignty to a foreign organization. Other senators believed that the United States should concentrate on domestic problems.

Many senators declared that they would accept the treaty and the League Covenant if *reservations* (modifications) were made in it to protect United States' interests. However, the senators could not agree, and the Treaty of Versailles with and without reservations was rejected by them.

In 1921 the United States finally made separate peace treaties with Germany, Austria, and Hungary. However, the United States never became a member of the League of Nations. Nor did it join the World Court, although Elihu Root, an American, assisted in its organization and American justices served on the Court.

The League of Nations

The Covenant (or compact) of the League of Nations was written in Part I of the Treaty of Versailles. It provided for a League whose activities were to be carried on principally by an Assembly, a Council, and a permanent Secretariat. This League, whose headquarters were in Geneva, Switzerland, was to be organized in the following way.

The *Assembly* was to consist of representatives of all the member nations of the League. It could deal with any matter affecting the peace of the world, but its decisions on important matters required a unanimous vote of the Assembly. The *Council* was to consist of representatives of the principal powers plus representatives of four other member nations. It, too, could deal with any matter involving world peace, and its decisions on important matters required a unanimous vote of the Council. The permanent *Secretariat* was to register treaties, gather information,

handle secretarial duties, and do the everyday work of the League. At the head of the Secretariat was to be the *Secretary-General*.

Plans were to be drawn up for the establishment of a *Permanent Court of International Justice*. The World Court, as it was called, was to "hear and determine any dispute of an international character which the parties thereto submit to it."

If a serious dispute arose between nations, the case was to be submitted to arbitration, to the Court, or to the Council. If any nation disregarded the League Covenant and resorted to war, the League members could stop their trade, financial, and other economic relations with the offender—that is, apply *economic sanctions*. The Council also could *recommend* that "the Members of the League shall severally contribute to the armed forces to be used to protect the covenants of the League."

Provision also was made for the supervision of mandates, the improvement of working conditions, and the raising of living standards throughout the world.

It is important to know what the League of Nations could and could not do. It *could* discuss any matter affecting the world's peace, make recommendations, warn an aggressor to stop its military activities, and serve as a forum where nations could exchange ideas. It *could not* take action on important matters without the unanimous consent of the Council or Assembly, pass laws that were compulsory for all member nations, back up its decisions with military force unless the member nations were willing to supply troops and weapons, or act as an authority superior to those nations.

■ Check on Your Reading

1. Summarize Wilson's "Fourteen Points."
2. Name the provisions of the Treaty of Versailles.

4. Nations in Transition: Legacy of World War I

A troubled world emerged from World War I. Latin American countries continued to be plagued by domestic unrest. The Middle East was unsettled. Asia was agitated by the effects of the Chinese Revolution and other events (p. 617).

The Austro-Hungarian and Turkish empires had fallen apart. Germany had lost its empire. The Russian monarchy had been overthrown. Old nations of western Europe and new nations of eastern Europe faced serious political and economic problems. A number of countries, created or recreated by the Treaty of Versailles, went through difficult periods of transition. They included Poland, Rumania, Yugoslavia, Czechoslovakia, Hungary, the Baltic states, Greece, and Turkey.

Poland, Rumania, and Yugoslavia

After World War I Poland became an independent nation. It was created out of Polish areas taken from Germany and Austria, and Poland gained access to the Baltic Sea by the "Polish Corridor," which separated East Prussia from the rest of Germany. The Poles were dissatisfied at their failure to regain territory to the east and fought against the Russians. By the Treaty of Riga (1921), Poland regained part of the eastern lands it had held before the eighteenth century partitions.

Although Poland became a republic in 1921, it did not develop into a democracy. More and more power was turned over to General Joseph Pilsudski, who by 1926 became virtual dictator of Poland. Meanwhile the country continued to be plagued by tensions between Poles and such minorities as the Ukrainians, Germans, Lithuanians, and Jews.

Post-war Rumania also had to deal with the demands of minorities. The government—a monarchy—also tried to improve economic conditions by taking the estates of large landowners (*boyars*), dividing them, and selling the land to small farmers. However, the world-wide depression of 1929 brought economic misery to Rumania. The monarchy was threatened by men seeking to establish a dictatorship.

Yugoslavia—which consisted of Serbia, Montenegro, Croatia, and other areas—was proclaimed a kingdom in 1918. Two problems that caused trouble involved religion and government. The Serbs, who were Greek Orthodox, argued bitterly with the Croats, who were Roman Catholic. In addition, various groups in Yugoslavia, particularly the Croats, protested against being dominated by the Serbs. Several minority groups demanded more rights of self-government.

New Nations Emerge from Austria-Hungary

The new nation of Czechoslavakia, formed out of lands once controlled by Austria-Hungary, was established as a republic. Thomas Masaryk, a university professor who had become leader of the Czech nationalists before independence, was chosen the first president (1918–1935).

Most of the people of Czechoslovakia were Slavs. They were bitterly opposed by the German and Magyar minorities there. President Masaryk believed in what historian James T. Shotwell called "a system of friendly neighborhoods under a régime of freedom." Under Masaryk's effective leadership, minorities eventually were given more rights of self-government.

Hungary became a republic in 1918. Then, in 1919, a revolution led to the establishment of a Communist dictatorship under Béla Kun. After five months, this Communist regime, weakened by internal strife and conflict with Rumania, was overthrown.

A monarchy was proclaimed, but the throne remained empty. Hungary was actually governed by a regent, Admiral Nicholas Horthy.

By the Treaty of Trianon, signed with the Allies in 1920, Hungary lost more than two-thirds of its land and was left without seaports. Economic conditions in Hungary grew steadily worse.

The Baltic States

The new Baltic states of Finland, Estonia, Latvia, and Lithuania—all of which were formerly part of the Russian Empire —became republics. They made progress in solving their domestic problems but faced the threat of Russian expansion.

Greece and Turkey

Greece, which had entered World War I in 1917 on the side of the Allies, fought Turkey from 1919 to 1922 for control of the Turkish city of Smyrna. By the Treaty of Lausanne (1923) the Greeks gave up claims to Turkish territory.

Greece did away with its monarchy, and in 1924 became a republic. Struggles continued between supporters of the republic and those of the monarchy. In 1929 Premier Venizelos began negotiations that led to settlement of many of Greece's disputes with Italy and the Balkan countries.

After World War I, the Turks fought against an Allied plan to divide their country. Then they drove back a Greek army that tried to seize part of their land.

Finally Turkish nationalists signed the Treaty of Lausanne with the Allies (1923). (1) The Dardanelles were to remain under the control of Turkey but were to be open to the vessels of all countries. (2) Italy was authorized to keep the Dodecanese Islands, and Britain to keep Cyprus. (3) Syria, Palestine, and Mesopotamia were to be mandates of Britain and France.

In 1923 Turkey became a republic. Mustapha Kemal (Kemal Atatürk or "Chief Turk") served as president of Turkey from 1923 until 1938. Under his strong and often dictatorial leadership, the Turks tried to modernize. They developed industries, started a system of compulsory education, introduced the Roman alphabet for the Turkish language, and extended more rights to women. Ernest Jackh, a professor of international relations, once said to Mustapha Kemal: "Your dictatorship frees an enslaved people while Hitler's tyranny enslaves a free people."

Nearly all countries faced problems of political and economic readjustment. Several factors that helped cause World War I still remained. These included tensions caused by nationalistic feelings, desires of countries to expand, and rivalries.

■ **Check on Your Reading**

1. What nations emerged from Austria-Hungary? What were some of their problems?

2. Identify and cite the achievements of Pilsudski, Masaryk, Venizelos, and Mustapha Kemal.

5. The Allies Seek Reparations for World War I

President Woodrow Wilson declared: "There is a great wind of *moral* force moving through the world, and every man who opposes himself to that wind will go down in disgrace." Then the victorious Allies placed *moral responsibility* on Germany

and her allies for causing the war. In April, 1921, *moral guilt was linked with severe economic retribution*, for Germany was ordered to pay about thirty-five billion dollars in reparations to the Allies. Payments were divided in the following proportion: France was to receive 52 per cent, the British Empire 22, Italy 10, Belgium 8, and others were to share 8 per cent.

France Occupies the Ruhr

Some of the statesmen of Germany made a concentrated effort to meet the crushing reparation payments. Many other German leaders considered the reparations payments so high that they refused to try to make them.

An unfavorable balance of trade, a shortage of capital, a decline in credit, and other economic factors made it difficult for Germany to meet her payments. When Germany failed to make her promised deliveries of coal and wood, an angry French government decided to create "a will to pay." In January, 1923, France, aided by Belgian troops, occupied the Ruhr.

The Ruhr was the "heartland" of German industry, producing over 80 per cent of its coal and steel, and its loss was a crippling blow. The Germans in the Ruhr resisted passively, but the French remained. Economic conditions became increasingly bad, and inflation disrupted Germany. By 1923 it required 2,500,-000,000,000 marks to equal one American dollar.

The Dawes and Young Plans

Germany's failure to meet her economic obligations resulted in Allied revisions of their reparations program. In 1924 the Dawes Plan went into effect. Germany was to make yearly payments on a sliding scale (from $250,000,000 in 1924–25 to $625,000,000, in 1928–29). After 1929 future payments would depend on economic conditions. Despite a large loan to help Germany, this plan failed because it left the country under too many foreign controls and failed to specify total reparations.

In 1929 the Young Plan set total reparations at eight billion dollars, to be paid in about sixty installments. The International Bank in Switzerland was to administer the program. Payment of reparations was to be closely related to payment of *war debts*, or debts that the Allies had incurred by borrowing from each other.

Reparations and War Debts

After World War I the Allies owed the United States about eleven billion dollars in war debts. The Allies took the position that (1) Allied war debts to the United States should be cancelled because the Allies had used the money to fight a war defending American interests, too. (2) The Allies intended to use the money received in reparations to pay their war debts. Therefore, if the Germans did not pay their reparations, the Allies were not responsible for paying their war debts.

The United States disagreed. For one thing, the United States was lending Germany the money to pay its reparations, which, in turn, were being used by the European powers to pay their war debts. Nevertheless, the *Hoover Moratorium* of 1931 permitted a one-year moratorium— or postponement of payment—on both reparations and war debts.

In 1932 the Lausanne Conference proposed to cut Germany's total reparations to about three-quarters of a billion dollars. It also suggested that the United States cancel all war debts. The United States refused, but with the depression of the 1930's Germany stopped payment of reparations. Except for Finland, the Allies then ceased all but token payment of war debts.

■ **Check on Your Reading**

1. Why did Germany have to pay reparations? Describe the Dawes and Young Plans.

2. How were the war debts and reparations linked together?

MAN AND HIS CULTURE

Let's Meet the People!

The following sketch is based on information in James Norman Hall, *High Adventure*, 1918, Houghton Mifflin Company.

An American Flyer in World War I

His name was Drew, and he had come from Massachusetts to join the American volunteers flying for the French. Drew had "never been farther from the ground than the top of the Woolworth building," but he soon learned to fly.

Then one day Drew had his greatest test. It was dusk and his Spad plane had strayed from formation. Drew saw a plane that seemed to belong to his squadron and guided his Spad towards it. He had made a terrible mistake. It was an enemy plane—and the pilot fired at him!

Drew recalled what happened next: "I realized my awful mistake. . . . The enemy's tracer bullets were going by on the left side, but he corrected his aim, and my motor seemed to be eating them up. I banked to the right, and was about to cut my motor and dive, when I felt a smashing blow in the left shoulder." The bullet that hit Drew in the shoulder made his left arm useless.

The plane could no longer be controlled. Down and down it fell. Finally, when the plane was about 500 feet from the earth, Drew managed to bring it level with the ground. A few seconds later the Spad crashed into a trench.

Drew opened his eyes. Where had he landed—on German or French territory? Drew wiped the blood away from his eyes and looked again. The man who stood over him was—French!

Months later, Drew made this promise, "If ever I live long enough in one place . . . on one wall of my living-room I will have a bust-length portrait, rear view, of a French ambulance-man, mud-covered back and battered tin hat." For it was a French ambulance man who carried Drew to safety that day, and the American flyer would never forget him!

CHAPTER REVIEW

REVIEW and DISCUSSION

1. Identify the people and places and explain the events and terms on p. 574.

2. How did Bismarck's policies differ from those of William II?

3. Which of the contributing factors do you think were most important in causing World War I? Why?

4. What difficulties did the Allies encounter in fighting the war?

5. What circumstances and events do you think contributed to Germany's defeat?

6. Would full acceptance of Wilson's "Fourteen Points" have helped to remove the causes of war? Why?

7. Compare the Congress of Vienna in 1815 with the Versailles Conference.

8. Do you think the Treaty of Versailles was a peace of justice, of compromise, or of vengeance? Why?

9. Can you find any provisions in the treaty which paved the way for another war?

10. What powers did the League of Nations have? What powers did it lack?

11. Explain how the principle of self-determination was put into practice in the nations that emerged after World War I.

12. Why did the Allies place moral responsibility on Germany for causing the war and expect her to pay reparations?

13. Why did the policies of reparations and war debts fail?

ACTIVITIES

1. Debate this statement: Resolved, that a balance of power does more to provoke war than to keep the peace.

2. On a map of Europe, locate the nationality groups that were discontented in Germany, Austria-Hungary, Russia, and Turkey; then show the new nations that emerged after World War I.

3. Make a study of the crises leading to the outbreak of World War I. Why was the war averted in each case? Why was war not averted in the last crisis?

PAST and PRESENT

1. Do you think such an action as the West German telecast on "The Third Reich" is a good practice? Why?

2. In the present world situation, can you find any of the causes of World War I existing?

SUGGESTED READINGS

Basic books: BENNS, F. LEE, *Europe Since 1914 in its World Setting*, Appleton-Century-Crofts. Contains a full account of the causes, events, and peoples involved in World War I. For better readers.

PALMER, R. R., and COLTON, JOEL, *A History of the Modern World*, Chap. 16, Knopf.

SMITH, GOLDWIN, *The Heritage of Man*, Chap. 43, Scribner. An excellent commentary on the causes of the war as well as a valuable account of the war itself and the Versailles Treaty.

VERNADSKY, GEORGE, *A History of Russia*, Chap. 13, Yale University Press.

Special accounts: FAY, SIDNEY B., *The Origins of the World War*, Macmillan. An important reference by a recognized authority on this period. Very useful for tracing responsibility for the war.

SCHMITT, BERNADOTTE E., *Triple Alliance and Triple Entente* (Berkshire Studies in European History), Holt. Short, clear, and well organized.

SEYMOUR, CHARLES, *Woodrow Wilson and the World War* (Chronicles of America series) Yale University Press. Interesting history of Wilson's part in World War I.

Biography and Fiction: COBB, HUMPHREY, *Paths of Glory*, Viking. Novel which shows how even human life can be sacrificed in war to satisfy ambition.

REMARQUE, ERICH MARIA, *All Quiet on the Western Front*, Fawcett (paperback). A classic story of World War I from inside German lines. Dramatic in its indictment of war.

591

Chapter 37

The Rise of Communist Power in Russia

KEYNOTE For many years the figure of the imperial eagle was a symbol of the authority of the Russian monarchy. Then, on March 16, 1917, Russians in the city of Petrograd destroyed every sign, decoration, or statue with an imperial eagle on it. It was said that the only eagle to survive that day was the American eagle on top of the Singer Sewing Machine Building. The Singer Company saved it by wrapping it in an American flag.

The widespread destruction of the imperial eagle was symbolic of the great change that had come to Russia. The czar had been forced to abdicate, ending the Russian monarchy. A new era was about to begin.

In the years that followed, democracy did not become a permanent part of Russian life. Instead, *the period in Russian history from 1917 to 1939 was marked by the rise of Communist power in Russia.* The imperial eagle had been destroyed; but the hammer and sickle, symbol of the new Soviet authority, took its place!

Key People *Nicholas II · Alexandra · Rasputin · Vladimir Lenin · Alexander Kerensky · Leon Trotsky · Joseph Stalin*

Key Places *Petrograd · Siberia · Moscow · Ukraine · Murmansk · Archangel · Vladivostok*

Key Events *Russian Marxists organize · Revolution of 1905 · First Russian Revolution · Provisional Government established · Nicholas II abdicates · Second Russian Revolution · Treaty of Brest-Litovsk · Civil war breaks out*

Key Terms *Mensheviks · Bolsheviks · Duma · Communist party · New Economic Policy · Comintern · Five-Year Plans · Supreme Soviet · party dictatorship · kolkhozy · sovkhozy · kulaks*

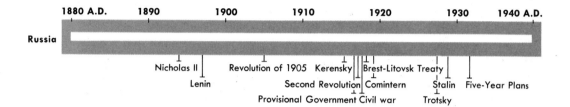

| 1880 A.D. | 1890 | 1900 | 1910 | 1920 | 1930 | 1940 A.D. |

Russia

Nicholas II
Lenin
Revolution of 1905 Kerensky
Second Revolution Comintern
Provisional Government Civil war
Brest-Litovsk Treaty
Stalin Five-Year Plans
Trotsky

1. The Fall of the Russian Monarchy

Nicholas II had become czar of Russia in 1894. A man who lacked intellectual brilliance, imagination, and self-confidence, he nevertheless felt that he had the right to rule Russia as he wished. He was dedicated to the principle of autocracy.

Alexandra, Nicholas' wife, was equally determined that the czar should enjoy absolute authority. She tried to "prop up" her husband when his actions lacked firmness. "My Angel," she wrote, ". . . The Czar rules and not the Duma."

Both Alexandra and Nicholas II were deeply attached to their only son, Alexei. Twice when it seemed that the boy was about to bleed to death, a pseudo-religious charlatan called Rasputin was said to have saved his life. The grateful Alexandra, a highly mystical woman, permitted Rasputin to influence her and her family in many decisions and helped him to gain considerable power in the Russian government.

Rasputin—described by Pierre Gilliard, a member of the imperial household, as a tall man with long hair, long beard, and "piercing grey-blue eyes under thick bushy eyebrows"—thus became a powerful figure. Rasputin proved to be a wastrel, a heavy drinker, and a man of low moral standards. He contributed to the corruption and weakness of the Russian government until he finally was assassinated.

Russian Marxists Organize

"In the pages [of Russia's history] we find only floggings, beatings, hangings, and the systematic exploitation of the people on behalf of the czar's treasury!" declared the Russian George Plekhanov. Then in 1883 he founded the "Liberation of Labor," the first Russian group that advocated the ideas of Karl Marx (p. 466). Later, in 1898, the Russian Marxists formed the Russian Social Democratic Workers' party —known as the *Social Democrats.*

There had been other Russian protest groups before the Social Democrats. The *Decembrists* had boldly demanded constitutional government and unsuccessfully rebelled against the czar in 1825. The *Narodniki,* who advocated a peasant revolution and the establishment of an agrarian form of socialism, had supported "a movement to the people" in the 1870's and later. The *Anarchists* had attacked all governments and private property as evil and unnecessary. There were others. The *Social Revolutionaries,* agrarian reformers in the tradition of the Narodniki, included a number of terrorists. The

593

Social Revolutionaries were the most numerous party in Russia by 1917, but the Russian Social Democrats proved to be the most important group of all.

In 1903 the Russian Social Democrats held a crucial conference in Brussels and London. A split occurred between two groups: the *Mensheviks* (meaning minority) and the *Bolsheviks* (meaning majority). Despite their name, the Bolsheviks at first had a much smaller following in the Russian Social Democratic party than the Mensheviks, who were actually the majority group. Both groups accepted the basic ideas of Marx and wanted to overthrow the czar. However, they differed on how to reach their goal.

The Mensheviks wanted the party to be open to as many people as possible. The Bolsheviks wanted to limit it to a small core of professional revolutionaries. As historian Ivar Spector makes clear, the Mensheviks believed that a revolution could succeed only after "a careful and intensive preparatory campaign of education had trained the masses for a democratic regime." The Bolsheviks did not want to wait. They favored "an abrupt overthrow of the existing social and political order by a resort to force."

Lenin: Leader of the Bolsheviks

The Bolsheviks, led by Vladimir Lenin (1870–1924), finally won out at the congress, although by a narrow margin. Lenin, whose real name was Vladimir Ilich Ulyanov, continued to work with the Bolsheviks for the revolutionary cause.

Lenin was a short, stocky man. One observer, Rene Fülöp-Miller, declared that his appearance was "completely that of any everyday man of the mass . . . the high, somewhat conical shape of the skull, the Asiatic cheek-bones, and the Mongolian eyebrows, are all quite ordinary in Russia. . . ." But Lenin was no ordinary man. He was an intelligent, shrewd, and ruthless leader who had dedicated his life to the cause of the proletarian revolution. Flexible in his tactics, he was still convinced that the bourgeoisie could be overthrown only by force.

Since Lenin was to play such an important role in the future events in Russia, it is essential that we understand his ideas. Here are some of his key statements:

There is no middle way [between capitalism and communism].

[We are dedicated to] overthrowing the Czar, overthrowing the capitalists, destroying the capitalist class. . . . We subordinate our Communist morality to this task.

We must [if necessary] . . . resort to all sorts of stratagems, manoeuvres, illegal methods, evasions and subterfuges. . . .

To Lenin it was a fight to the finish between capitalism and communism!

The Revolution of 1905 Breaks Out

The Russo-Japanese War (1904–05) had important effects on Russia. The defeats suffered by Russian troops, the inefficiency of the Russian government, the oppressive treatment by Czar Nicholas II's officials, the hunger of the people, and other factors contributed to unrest and discontent.

Then on Sunday, January 22, 1905, thousands of working men and women, accompanied by children, marched to the czar's Winter Palace in St. Petersburg (today Leningrad). The processions were led by a Russian Orthodox priest, Father George Gapon, who apparently was in the service of the Russian secret police. These people assembled to present a petition to the czar, asking him to improve labor conditions and grant a more liberal government. The czar was not in residence at the palace. When the people approached, the czar's soldiers fired. Many were killed or wounded that day, and even a seasoned reporter for the French press was shocked at the "streams of blood on the snow." The day became known as "Bloody Sunday."

The horror of "Bloody Sunday" set off uprisings of peasants and strikes of workers throughout the country. A Soviet [Council] of Workers' Deputies also was organized. This *Soviet* consisted of representatives of many socialist groups. It declared that it would protect the rights of the people.

The Russian government, faced with these dangerous uprisings, decided to grant concessions. In October, 1905, it issued a manifesto that promised reforms, including freedom of speech, the right of all Russians to vote, and the calling of a *Duma* (a representative assembly).

However, when the war with Japan ended, the czar used the loyal Russian troops now at his disposal to check new uprisings and to help him re-establish his authority. The czar's government also issued new laws, such as legislation to help end the evils of land distribution that followed the freeing of the serfs. The government hoped that these reforms, under which many peasant families acquired their own land between 1907 and 1915, would lessen the hostility of the peasants. Gradually, order was restored in the country.

Four Dumas were called between 1906 and 1917, and they did try to bring about some changes. However, they did not have sufficient power to alter the basic character of the czar's regime. The czar had regained most of his power in Russia.

The Pre-War Lives of the Russian People

What were the living conditions of the Russian people under the czars? Most of the Russians still gained their living from the land. In 1914, the cities of Russia included only about 15 per cent of the total population of roughly 180,000,000. Between the Revolution of 1905 and the year 1914, crops generally were good. Some improvements were made in methods of agriculture, increasing production. Steps were taken to abolish peasant communes (or *mirs*) and to establish more ownership of land by individuals. A number of peasant farms came into existence.

There was expansion in industry. The purchasing power of Russian miners and factory workers was increased, and the length of their working day was reduced.

Other developments were less encouraging. The living standards of the Russian peasants and workers were still below those of the people of Great Britain, Germany, France, and the United States. Taxes were heavy. Strikes were numerous. The government was politically unstable, inefficient, and often corrupt.

In the period before World War I, most Russian people continued to lead their lives largely as their fathers had done. They worked hard. They ate foods that included black bread and cabbage dishes. They sipped tea through a lump of sugar gripped in the teeth and drank vodka in gulps. And they remembered the old Russian saying:

> Koli khud knyaz
> Tak y gryaz—

("If the [ruler] is bad, into the mud with him.")

The day was fast approaching when these words would take on a special meaning!

■ Check on Your Reading

1. How did Czar Nicholas II rule?
2. How did the Mensheviks differ from the Bolsheviks? How were they similar?
3. Describe Lenin's principal ideas about capitalism.
4. How did life in Russia change between 1905 and 1914?

2. The First and Second Russian Revolutions

When Russia entered World War I in 1914, the Russian people at first responded with enthusiasm. The defense of Russia was at stake, and they showed their loyalty to their country. However, the situation changed. Russia soon was filled with discontent. This was the result of many factors: Russia's losses in the war, the discouraged attitude of the troops, inadequate shipments of ammunition and equipment, graft of certain high officials, arguments between the fourth Duma and the czar and czarina, and lack of food.

In 1917 there were strikes and hunger demonstrations. In March of 1917 (February by the old Russian calendar) crowds marched through the city of Petrograd (formerly St. Petersburg). They denounced Alexandra and demanded food and reforms.

The Duma asked the czar to remove the unpopular and inefficient men in his government and to take other steps. The

■ *Czar Nicholas II and his family are shown in this portrait before the Russian Revolution. All were shot by the Bolsheviks.*

czar refused and ordered the Duma dissolved. The Duma in turn refused to obey the czar's order. Instead, on March 14, it helped to establish a *Provisional Government*. This was more than a gesture of protest—it was an act of defiance.

The Provisional Government and a number of generals demanded that the czar abdicate. Lacking popular support and the loyal troops necessary to maintain his authority, Nicholas II gave up his throne on March 15. It is probably nearer the truth to say that his regime had *collapsed* rather than that it had been overthrown. The rule of the last Romanov czar was over!

The Provisional Government

This first Russian Revolution was not planned or directed by the Communists. Most of the Communist leaders were not even in Russia at the time. The men who became leaders of the first revolution were liberals, middle-class reformers, agrarian socialists, and others. These men wanted a more democratic government for Russia, not a dictatorship. They advocated freedom of speech, trial by jury, equal rights for women, self-government for local areas, and universal suffrage. The Provisional Government attempted to achieve these objectives.

Alexander Kerensky became the head of the Provisional Government in August, 1917. He worked hard to re-establish order. However, his government gradually lost the support of many Russians for the following reasons: (1) Its authority was weakened by the opposition tactics of the Petrograd Soviet, a group that demanded more radical changes for Russia. (2) It lost prestige as a result of an incident in which the troops of a Russian general attacked the Provisional Government.

(3) It could not keep order in the provinces, where the peasants were killing landlords and seizing land.

It was particularly in its conduct of foreign affairs that the Kerensky government lost support. Despite the turbulent conditions within Russia, the Provisional Government decided to fulfill its obligations to its Allies and remain in World War I. This decision alienated many Russians, particularly when the Bolsheviks had come out for "Peace! Land! Bread!"

The Second Russian Revolution Brings the Bolsheviks to Power

The first Russian Revolution was followed by a second. At about the same time that the Provisional Government was established, a Soviet of Workers' and Soldiers' Deputies also was organized in Petrograd. This Soviet demanded more radical changes than those promised by the Provisional Government. Thus there were two competing governments: The Provisional Government and the Soviet of Workers' and Soldiers' Deputies.

The exiled leaders of the Bolsheviks hurried to Petrograd. Lenin's return from Switzerland was aided by the Germans, who hoped that he would stir up further dissension and revolution and thus weaken Russia's war effort. Leon Trotsky, who was to become the organizer of the Bolshevik military forces, came from the United States. Joseph Stalin, who was later to be dictator of Russia, came from Siberia. The Bolsheviks hoped that this was their great opportunity.

The Bolsheviks did everything possible to strengthen their own position. Although they did not originally form a majority of the Petrograd Soviet, they eventually gained control of it. Lenin felt that the time had come to use violence. "Everything now hangs by a thread . . . ," he wrote. "We must not wait!"

On November 7, 1917 (October 25 by the old Russian calendar), the Bolsheviks overthrew the Provisional Government by force. When Kerensky failed to rally enough troops to his support, the Provisional Government lost all authority. The Bolsheviks controlled the government of Russia, and posters proclaimed: Long Live the Revolution of the Workers, the Soldiers, and the Peasants!

The Second Revolution: an Analysis

This second Russian Revolution is celebrated each year by the Russians. However, one fact is ignored by the celebrants. It is this: When the Bolsheviks seized power, they did not have the support of the majority of the Russians. For example, before the Provisional Government was overthrown by the Bolsheviks, it had arranged for free elections to be held for a Constituent Assembly. This Constituent Assembly was to draw up "the fundamental laws, guaranteeing to the country the inalienable rights of justice, equality, and liberty." When the elections were held on November 25, 1917, about two weeks *after* the Bolsheviks had seized power, the majority of the voters did not vote for the Bolsheviks. The Bolsheviks received only about one-fourth of the thirty-six million votes.

This did not upset the Bolsheviks' plans. They simply arrested the important representatives of opposition parties and dissolved the Assembly. As Kerensky later put it: "Lenin [succeeded] in torpedoing the democracy and fighting his way to a dictatorship."

■ **Check on Your Reading**

1. What difficulties did the Provisional Government face?
2. What was the Petrograd Soviet?
3. What were some of the reasons for the success of the second Russian Revolution?

3. The Soviet Union under Lenin

After the Bolsheviks obtained control of the Russian government, they changed their name to the *Communist* party and moved the capital from Petrograd to Moscow. The Communists continued to work under the over-all direction of Lenin. They faced the serious problems of reorganizing the economic system, wiping out opposition to their new government, and establishing satisfactory relations with minority groups. To remove some of the pressures on them, they withdrew from World War I by signing the harsh Treaty of Brest-Litovsk (March, 1918). This treaty provided that Russia would recognize the independence of Georgia and the Ukraine; accept the independence of Finland; and permit Germany and Austria-Hungary to decide the future of Poland, Lithuania, Latvia, and Estonia. This treaty later was abrogated after the defeat of the Central Powers.

Civil War and Allied Intervention

Shortly after the revolution, the Communist leaders (1) declared that title to all land belonged to the state, and that use of property and livestock would be transferred to the peasants; (2) gave workers considerable responsibility for the management of factories; (3) nationalized railroads, banks, and church property; (4) deprived the Orthodox Church of its privileges and forbade religious instruction in the schools; (5) set up new courts; (6) developed the system of local councils (Soviets) but kept all power in the hands of a small group of Communist leaders; (7) proclaimed equality of all nationalities in Russia but tried to discourage them from seceding from the country; and (8) formed a special police (later known as the *Cheka*), whose principal job was to combat counter-revolution and sabotage.

These and other actions angered a number of people: Russian generals who had supported the czar; aristocrats who had been deprived of their estates; liberals who had hoped for a democratic government; religious leaders and devout peasants who resented the anti-church decrees of the Communists.

Early in 1918 civil war broke out in Russia between the Reds (Bolsheviks) and the Whites (Russians opposed to the Bolsheviks). From 1918 through 1919 military units of several Allied powers—France, Great Britain, Japan, Italy, and the United States—came to the aid of the Whites. The British landed troops at Murmansk. The British and French sent forces to Archangel. The Americans, British, and French dispatched men to north Russia. The Americans and Japanese moved units into Vladivostok. In October, 1918, the Bolsheviks angrily denounced these "Anglo-French, American and Japanese imperialist robbers."

Historians have advanced the following reasons for Allied intervention: The Allies wanted to (1) aid Czechoslovakian troops in Russia who were successfully defying the Red Army; (2) protect the economic investments and loans that nationals of the Allies had made in Russia; (3) punish Russia for making a separate peace and withdrawing from World War I; (4) weaken the position of the Bolshevik government in Russia; and (5) check the spread of Bolshevik power, which seemed to threaten Western governments.

Under the direction of Leon Trotsky, the Soviet Commissar of War, an efficient Red Army was organized. This army, aided by the failure of the Whites to coordinate their attacks, withstood the challenge of the Whites. By 1920 most of the White forces had been defeated.

The Comintern

Allied intervention in the civil war had important results. The Bolsheviks had always intended that communism should spread throughout Europe. Now, however, as Edward Hallett Carr, a British authority on Russian history, points out, "The action of the allies *confirmed and intensified* the ideological aspect of Soviet foreign policy and made international revolution once more its principal plank. . . ."

In March, 1919, representatives of the Russian Communist party and of nineteen foreign parties and groups met in Moscow and formed the Third Communist International or *Comintern*. (The First International was founded in 1864, the Second in 1889).

The Comintern called for the support of "the working masses of all countries." Its leaders declared: "The task of the International Communist Party is now to overthrow this order [the bourgeois world order] and to erect in its place the structure of the Socialist world order." National interests were to be subordinated to "the interests of the international revolution." Despite its international membership, the Comintern was controlled by the Russian government.

The expansion of communism would be difficult. In Hungary, for example, a Soviet Republic had collapsed (p. 587). Then, in 1920, the Poles and Ukrainians fought against the Red Army. By the Treaty of Riga (1921), Russia had to turn over part of its land to Poland.

The New Economic Policy

Lenin realized in the period from 1918 to 1920 that it was difficult and dangerous to try to establish complete public ownership at once in a country economically prostrate as a result of war and revolution. In 1921 Lenin therefore introduced the *New Economic Policy* (NEP).

Lenin

■ *Lenin was a powerful and shrewd leader, always willing to shift his tactics in order to establish communism firmly in Russia.*

The NEP, which lasted seven years, temporarily restored some degree of capitalism to Russia. It permitted some private enterprise, brought freedom of trade to various areas, and encouraged some foreign capital to come into Russia. Then in 1924, in the middle of the NEP period, Lenin died.

A political crisis occurred in Russia after the death of Lenin. Instead of permitting the Russian people to elect a new leader, as the people in a democracy would, important Communists became involved in a struggle for power. After considerable intrigue and political manipulation, Joseph Stalin emerged as the new leader, as a result of actions and decisions made *within the Communist party*.

■ Check on Your Reading

1. What policies did the Communists introduce in Russia?
2. Why did the Allies intervene in the Russian civil war?
3. What were the chief purposes of the Comintern?
4. What was the New Economic Policy?

4. The Soviet Union under Stalin

Joseph Stalin (1879–1953), whose real name was Joseph Vissarionovich Dzhugashvili, emerged as the new dictator. Stalin means "steel" and, in many ways, the new dictator *was* a "man of steel."

A short man with bushy hair and a mustache, Stalin had a habit of puffing calmly on his pipe and remaining silent. From such mannerisms of Stalin, one might conclude incorrectly that he was a man of little drive. As late as 1917 Sukhanov, one of his contemporaries, said: "Stalin . . . produced—and not on me alone—the impression of a grey blur, floating dimly across the scene and leaving no trace."

Stalin was a shrewd, practical, determined, and ruthless person. Thus, in 1922 he had risen to the highest post in the Communist party, that of General Secretary.

Stalin soon faced a crisis in his career, for he lost the support of Lenin. Disturbed by Stalin's "rude" character and ambitions, Lenin recommended that Stalin should be dropped from his position as General Secretary. Lenin warned the Communists:

Comrade Stalin . . . has concentrated enormous power in his hands, and I am not sure that he always knows how to use that power with sufficient caution.

Nevertheless, Stalin clung to his power and, after the death of Lenin, he emerged as the leader of Russia.

Under Stalin's rule, all of his rivals eventually were either killed, imprisoned, or exiled. Some of these men had once been Stalin's friends. Others had been key figures in the party long before Stalin had any influence. Nearly all had devoted their lives to the Communist cause.

During the "Great Purges" of the 1930's *thousands* of people who were considered dangerous to Stalin's regime were wiped out. With his opponents out of the way, Stalin ruled as virtual dictator until his death in 1953. From his rise to power until the outbreak of World War II (1939), Stalin helped to develop a number of important policies and programs.

The Stalin-Trotsky Split

Joseph Stalin split with Leon Trotsky in a dispute that had repercussions for the whole Communist party. Trotsky had played a key role in the Bolshevik Revolution of November, 1917. He had served as the first Soviet Commissar of Foreign Affairs, had become Commissar of War, and had organized the Red Army into a powerful force. He had written with insight on the theories of Marxism. Many Communists had expected Trotsky to succeed Lenin, but Stalin had cleverly maneuvered himself to the top post.

Trotsky and his supporters thought that the Communist Revolution should be carried throughout the world at once. They advocated "world revolution." Stalin wanted to build "socialism in one country [Russia]" first. He wanted to reconstruct Russia first before concerning himself with other countries. Once Russia was strong enough, Stalin was quite willing to help spread communism throughout the world. He later supported Communist revolutionary action in many countries.

After a bitter struggle for power within the Communist party, Trotsky was expelled from the party in 1927. In 1940, while living in Mexico, he was brutally assassinated.

The Five-Year Plans

In 1928 Stalin started the extremely important Five-Year Plans in Russia. The objectives of the First Five-Year Plan were to eliminate the "capitalist elements" that

■ *One of the achievements of Russia's First Five-Year Plan was the great dam and hydroelectric station on the Dnieper River in the Ukraine. Completed in 1932, it was the world's largest hydroelectric station at that time.*

existed during the NEP and expand nationalized industry; increase industrialization and agricultural production; and advance the "socialization" of agriculture by increasing the number of peasants working on collective farms.

The First Five-Year Plan resulted in several achievements. It stimulated industrial growth and greatly increased the production of machinery and electrical power. It also greatly extended the state control of industry and agriculture.

Ruthless and brutal techniques often were used by the Russian leaders to achieve their objectives. Dictatorial methods violated freedom of speech and other democratic rights. Freedom was trampled on by men racing to reach statistical goals.

The Second Five-Year Plan (1933–1937) and the Third Five-Year Plan (1938–1941, when it was interrupted by the Nazi invasion) also concentrated on increasing industrial production and collectivizing the land. By 1938 about 93 per cent of peasant families lived on collective farms, and transportation facilities were improved and natural resources were developed.

Meanwhile, in 1936 Stalin had approved a new constitution for Russia. This constitution, with certain changes introduced in 1953, is still in existence today. Stalin continued to try to build up the national pride of the Russians.

Foreign Affairs

In foreign affairs Russia signed non-aggression pacts with a number of nations. Many of these agreements she later broke. These included the Turkish-Soviet Nonaggression Pact of 1925 (Russia denounced this pact in 1945); the Afghanistan-Soviet Nonaggression Pact of 1926 (Russia forced Afghanistan to cede frontier areas to the Russians in 1940); and the Lithuanian-Soviet Nonaggression Pact of 1926 (Russia annexed Lithuania in 1940).

In 1928 Russia signed the Kellogg-Briand Pact (p. 633). In 1929, she violated it by invading Manchuria to regain possession of the Chinese Eastern Railway.

■ Check on Your Reading

1. Analyze Joseph Stalin's method of ruling.
2. What role did Leon Trotsky have in the Communist party? How did his ideas differ from those of Stalin?
3. What were the results of the three Five-Year Plans?

5. A Picture of Russia in 1939

At the outbreak of World War II (1939), the Communists had been in control of Russia for about twenty years. This is a picture of the society that they had helped to create.

The Political Scene

In 1939 Russia consisted of a number of so-called "republics" (really regional areas). It was called the Union of Soviet Socialist Republics (U.S.S.R.) and was generally known as the Soviet Union.

The Soviet Union had a constitution, and a two-house "Congress" called the Supreme Soviet, which met occasionally. The Supreme Soviet was to represent both the people and the various "republics" that made up the Soviet Union.

Elections for the Supreme Soviet were meaningless, because all opposition political parties had been abolished. Only the Communist party remained, and it was far more than a political party. Thus, the name of only *one* candidate appeared on the ballot for each position in the Supreme Soviet, the candidate approved by the Communist party.

Those elected to the Supreme Soviet had no significant power. Indeed as Lin Yu-t'ang, a famous modern philosopher, put it, the chief job of the Supreme Soviet seemed to be "to approve unanimously what [had] already been decided."

The *real* power of government was in the hands of the leaders of the Communist party, particularly of Stalin. Stalin was both the chairman of the powerful government body called the Council of Ministers and the Secretary of the Communist party. And as he himself said: "Here in the Soviet Union . . . not a single important political or organizational question is decided by our Soviet and other mass organizations without directions from

the Party . . . . "! The government of the Soviet Union in 1939 was actually a *party dictatorship*.

Economic Scene

Practically all of the land in Russia was owned by the state. However, most agricultural property was held by *kolkhozy*, or collective farms. The peasants on a collective farm did not *own* this land, but they cultivated it together. Farm machinery was obtained from state-owned Machine and Tractor Stations.

When the crops were marketed, each person on a collective farm was given a share of the return. He was rewarded not according to his need, but according to the amount of work he had done. Everyone did not receive the same reward on the collective farm. The hard-working and efficient farmer obtained greater rewards than the slow and inefficient one.

The people on collective farms were permitted to own the small cottages in which they lived and their household goods. Each family also might have a few animals and a small garden that was generally used for raising vegetables. The family could cultivate its garden for its own private gain.

In addition there were *sovkhozy*, or state farms. Economist Harry Schwartz defined a sovkhoz as "entirely the property of the Soviet government, which operates it with hired labor directed by managers responsible to the government ministry having control of the particular farm." The sovkhozy usually were large in size.

Soviet agriculture has encountered many serious problems in the period from the First Five-Year Plan to the present day. In the beginning there were shortages of farm machinery. In addition, many peasants preferred to spend their time working their private garden plots rather than the collective lands. In 1929–1930, persecuted *kulaks* (peasants who had more land, cattle, or wealth than their neighbors or who were charged with not cooperating with the government) killed their cattle and destroyed farm implements rather than turn them over to collectives. In the early 1930's there were crop failures. Peasants who deliberately violated Soviet regulations on collective farms were treated harshly, and the kulaks were wiped out. Millions of Russians died of starvation or were killed by government troops.

Total acreage under cultivation in the Soviet Union increased. More farm machinery was produced and food shortages gradually declined. However, as recently as 1964, Soviet leaders again warned the Russian people of the same problem that had faced Stalin: Food production was lagging behind industrial growth. One explanation is that in this period Russian heavy industry increased tremendously as resources were poured into it rather than into agriculture.

Practically all Soviet industries were owned by the state. Workers in factories were assigned quotas of work and were expected to meet them. Workers usually received wages and were permitted to own the consumer goods that they bought.

Everyone did not receive the same reward in industry. Workers who exceeded their quotas were given bonuses and better housing. *Stakhanovites* (the name given to workers with outstanding production records) received special rewards. Workers who fell below their quotas, or were late to work, or were careless in their jobs were punished—sometimes quite severely.

Thus, in industry and agriculture, there developed differences in the economic status of Russians. For example, there was a considerable difference between the wages of factory managers or top workers and those of ordinary workers. Similarly, the planners and agricultural experts for collective farms received higher rewards and lived far better than most peasants. In a country where classes were to disappear, a new class system was developing!

A Party Dictatorship with a Socialistic Economy

The economy of the Soviet Union in 1939 was *socialistic,* not communistic. It had not moved past the so-called "stage" of socialism, for men still received rewards according to their *work* (under communism they were supposed to receive a share of what was available according to their *need*). There were economic differences between groups, and classes existed. Consumer goods were owned privately. That is why the Russians in 1939 (and today) did not call their country communistic. That is why the 1936 constitution of the Soviet Union declared: The principle applied in the U.S.S.R. is that of *socialism*: "From each according to his ability, to each according to his work."

There was another feature to the kind of socialism that had developed in Russia. This was the dictatorial power of the *state*. The Soviet state—in reality, the Communist party—dominated every aspect of the economy. It interfered continually with the freedom of the individual. For example, a state decree of November 15, 1932, ordered that "workers absent for one day without an acceptable excuse be fired and deprived of their housing." In addition, the state herded all its opponents into brutal slave labor camps, permitted its secret police to violate basic human rights, and used terror to achieve its objectives.

In brief, Russia in 1939 was a hybrid nation. *It was a party dictatorship with a socialistic economy.*

Social and Cultural Scene

Stalin and the Communist party dominated social and cultural activities as completely as they did political and economic affairs. It is important to understand their attitude toward religion and education.

The Communist party was opposed to religion. Most of its members believed with Karl Marx that religion was "the opiate of the people."

In 1925 the League of Militant Atheists, or the Godless League, was organized. It tried to drive out religion. Some of its more extreme members burned churches. A tactical shift occurred in 1936 when the new Soviet constitution promised the Russian people freedom of religious worship as well as freedom of anti-religious propaganda. Despite the shifts in the *policies* of the Communist party toward religious groups from 1918 to 1939, the Communists remained anti-religious.

Nevertheless, there were people in Russia—particularly those of the older generations—who continued to believe in their religions. Despite the fact that more and more young people turned away from religion, the Russian Orthodox Church and other faiths managed to survive.

The Communist party also devoted a considerable part of its energies to educating the Russian people. More schools were built. More people were trained as teachers. There was a tremendous increase in the number of children receiving some formal education.

In addition to educating the students, the Russian school had the job of *indoctrinating* them—instructing them in the doctrines and beliefs of communism. Lenin himself had said that the principal purpose of the school was "the cultivation of communist morality in the pupils." *All* educational media—teachers, textbooks, newspapers, and others—were expected to be propagandists for the Communist cause.

Russian adults and children were indoctrinated with certain ideas. One of these was that Stalin was a great man. Another idea was that the Soviet Union was progressive and "capitalist" nations were not. A first-grade reader used in the middle 1930's included the section at the top of the next page.

THE SOVIET UNION (1918–1939): A BALANCE SHEET

Credits	Debits
1. More modern methods and machines were introduced in agriculture and industry.	1. Democracy was made into a mockery, and all power was placed in the hands of a few.
2. Industrialization was increased to a great extent.	2. The people were deprived of basic liberties, and the secret police used terror methods and violated human rights.
3. The systems of transportation (railroads, highways, canals) and communication were expanded.	3. Consumer needs and agriculture were neglected so that industry could be built.
4. Huge hydro-electric projects were built and electrification was extended to many parts of the country.	4. Often brutal methods were used to achieve aims, such as building roads or canals with slave labor.
5. The people were educated, and illiteracy greatly reduced.	5. Truth was ignored or distorted in schools and other educational media.
6. Standards of public health and sanitation were raised.	6. People who opposed Stalin or the Communist party were destroyed.

604

There goes the lunch bell. . . . How good the hot soup smells! . . . We get hot lunches every day. All children in America do not get hot lunches. All children in England do not get hot lunches. Only the children in the Soviet Union get hot lunches in school every day.

A third idea that was stressed was that there was great waste in "capitalist" nations. A textbook explaining the First Five-Year Plan (1928–1932) declared:

We have a plan.
In America they work without a plan.

. . . .

We make what is essential.
In America hundreds of factories consume raw materials and energy in order to make what is altogether unnecessary.

Similarly, the ideas of *patriotism, national pride,* and *the need for hard work and sacrifice* were instilled in the people.

Even in the fields of music, literature, and art the importance of propaganda was not forgotten. Composers were expected to write music that would inspire the people with love of Russia and communism. Authors were expected to write books in praise of Communist ideas. Artists were expected to paint pictures favorable to the Communist cause. Thus propaganda influenced and molded the ideas and lives of the Russians.

■ Check on Your Reading

1. How was the Soviet Union governed under Stalin?

2. Describe the life of a peasant on a collective farm.

3. What problems did the Russians encounter in agriculture?

4. Why was Russia called "a party dictatorship with a socialistic economy"?

5. What were the functions of Soviet schools?

CULTURAL CHARACTERISTICS of the Soviet Union, 1918–1939

Pravda, one of the most important newspapers in the Soviet Union, included this poem in one of its issues for 1936:

O great Stalin, O leader of the peoples,
Thou who broughtest man to birth,

• • • •

Thou who restoreth the centuries,
Thou who makest bloom this spring,

• • • •

Thou, splendor of my spring, O Thou
Sun reflected by millions of hearts . . . .

These lines invoking an almost mystical quality dramatically point up the "hero worship" shown the dictator of the Soviet Union at that time. Such adoration and obedience to the dictator's will made it possible for the government to drive ahead ruthlessly toward its goals. Among the earmarks of Soviet culture from 1918 to 1939 were:

Governmental ownership, direction, and, above all, planning that penetrated nearly every aspect of life—political, economic, and social.

A society which aimed to wipe out "class differences," but failed to produce complete political, social, and economic equality among Russians.

A tremendous upsurge of effort to modernize conditions of Russian life, especially in education, health, and related fields.

Dictatorial methods, including the use of force, to make cultural activities conform to Communist ideas and values.

Clement Attlee, a former British prime minister, once called a Russian election "a race with one horse," for there was no real opposition to the nominated candidate. This political dictatorship clamped its iron hand over the cultural activities of the Russian people. Conformity, not freedom, became the goal in literature, art, music, and even science. Yet, even in this period from 1918 to 1939, there were indications that Russian culture would not remain in a rigid governmental mold indefinitely.

The death of Stalin brought a lessening in control of artistic expression. However, the thaw did not last long, as cultural freedom was checked in the late 1960's.

MAN AND HIS CULTURE

Let's Meet the People!

The following account is based on information in *I Chose Freedom* by Victor Kravchenko, 1946, Scribner.

Comrade Dukhovtsev and the Purge Trial

The three-man Purge Commission, headed by Comrade Galembo, sat behind a table on a platform decorated with portraits of Communist leaders. They called Comrade Dukhovtsev before them.

"Comrade Dukhovtsev, are you married?" they asked.

"Yes, I am."

"Tell me," continued Comrade Galembo, "did you register your marriage or not? In other words, how was your marriage consecrated?" (The Communist party believed that registering with the state was all that was necessary for marriage. It was violently opposed to church marriages.)

Dukhovtsev fidgeted. Then, in a low voice, he told the truth: "I was married in church!" The audience in the hall laughed.

"I know, comrades, that it sounds funny," Dukhovtsev continued quickly. "It's ridiculous and I admit it. A church ceremony means nothing to me, believe me. But I was in love with my wife and her parents just wouldn't let her marry me unless I agreed to a church comedy. They're backward people."

The laughter of the audience became louder.

"We are not believers, I can assure you," shouted Dukhovtsev. "... I beg you, comrades, to forgive my mistake. I confess that I'm guilty for having hidden this crime from the Party."

Dukhovtsev's words of defense were useless now. Comrade Galembo rose stiffly and solemnly proclaimed, "Comrade Dukhovtsev, you are expelled from the Communist Party!"

Dukhovtsev looked about him in bewilderment. Then he left the hall. It would be of little comfort to him to remember that the suicide of an expelled Party member was never unexpected.

CHAPTER REVIEW

REVIEW and DISCUSSION

1. Identify the people and places and explain the events and terms on p. 592.

2. What underlying causes can you find in pre-revolutionary Russia that explain the First and Second Revolutions?

3. What methods did the Bolsheviks use to gain control of the government?

4. Can you find any evidence in this chapter to support this statement: A militant minority can easily gain control of a country in which the people are not trained to govern themselves democratically?

5. Why did the Communists in 1918 sign the humiliating treaty of Brest-Litovsk?

6. Evaluate Stalin's policy of establishing communism first in Russia before attempting to spread it throughout the world.

7. How valuable is the practice of establishing a set of goals to be achieved within a specified time, such as the Five-Year Plans? How successful were the Five-Year Plans?

8. Why was the membership of the Communist party limited to a small number?

9. What is the purpose of having an *elected*, powerless Supreme Soviet?

10. How does education in Russia differ from that in the United States?

11. Why did the Communists oppose religion in Russia?

12. Evaluate the contributions of the Communist government to the development of the Soviet Union.

ACTIVITIES

1. Consult references to find an account of the Soviet Constitutions of 1936 and 1953. Can you find any provisions guaranteeing the rights of individuals such as the first ten amendments to the U. S. Constitution?

2. Panel discussion: Choose one of these topics: agriculture, conditions of the working man, foreign policy, music, sports, theater. Compare Communist with czarist Russia.

3. Draw a diagram showing the government of Russia in 1939. What conclusions can you make?

PAST and PRESENT

1. Compare the careers of Stalin and Khrushchev.

2. Has the condition of the Russian peasant changed since 1917? Consult *Readers' Guide* and other references.

3. In what other countries today have leaders maneuvered their way to leadership as Stalin did, that is, without benefit of election?

SUGGESTED READINGS

Basic books: BRUUN, GEOFFREY, and MAMATEY, VICTOR S., *The World in the Twentieth Century*, Part V, D. C. Heath.

CARMICHAEL, JOEL, *Illustrated History of Russia*, Viking.

HARCAVE, SIDNEY SAMUEL, *Russia, A History*, Lippincott. Has more emphasis on post-1917 period.

PARES, BERNARD, *A History of Russia*, Chaps. 24, 25, and 26, Knopf. Covers the pre-revolutionary period to World War II.

SEEGER, ELIZABETH, *The Pageant of Russian History*, Longmans, Green. To 1945.

VERNADSKY, GEORGE, *A History of Russia*, Chaps. 13–16, Yale University Press. Many details on the political, economic, and social aspects of the Revolution and post-1917 period.

Special accounts: DALLIN, DAVID, *The Changing World of Soviet Russia*, Yale University Press. Emphasizes class structure, role of Communist party, and foreign policy.

KENNAN, GEORGE F., *Russia and the West under Lenin and Stalin*, Little, Brown. Based on lectures on Russia's policy toward the West.

Biography and Fiction: BAKER, NINA, *Lenin*, Vanguard. A biography written for high-school readers.

ORWELL, GEORGE, *Animal Farm*, Harcourt, Brace. Contains satire on the Revolution and on the Trotsky-Stalin quarrel.

PASTERNAK, BORIS, *Doctor Zhivago*, New American Library.

Chapter 38

Fascism and Revolution in Europe and the Far East

KEYNOTE   At the town of Dachau, fifteen miles from Munich, Germany, there stands a gas chamber where certain Germans called *Nazis* once killed thousands of innocent people. Scratched into one of the chamber's walls are words asking that the Nazis be pardoned for their horrible acts: FORGIVE THEM

Just below someone has written in pencil the word: NEVER

These words on the wall of the death house are sharp reminders of the not-too-distant past. They recall the days when the brutal and inhumane actions of the German Nazis shocked the world. Many insist that the Nazis knew what they were doing and should be held fully responsible for their acts.

An outstanding feature of the time was the *rise to power of men who preferred violence to reason, and tyranny to justice.* Such leaders appeared in Italy, Germany, and Japan.

Key People   *Benito Mussolini · Victor Emmanuel III · Adolf Hitler · Paul von Hindenburg · Joseph Goebbels · Dr. Sun Yat-sen · Yüan Shi-k'ai · Chiang Kai-shek*

Key Places   *Rome · Vatican City · Munich · Peking · Canton · Hankow · Nanking*

Key Events   *Fascists' "March" on Rome · Mussolini becomes dictator · Lateran Treaty · Weimar Constitution · Hitler becomes dictator · Militarists control Japan · China becomes a republic*

Key Terms   *Fascists · martial law · syndicates · totalitarianism · corporate state · Reichstag · Nazism · Putsch · Fuehrer · anti-semitism · "Aryan race" · Gestapo · militarists · Kuomintang*

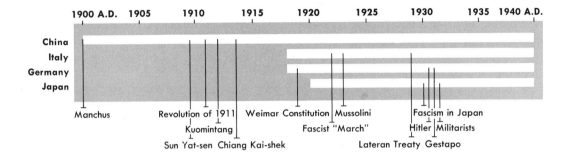

	1900 A.D.	1905	1910	1915	1920	1925	1930	1935	1940 A.D.
China									
Italy									
Germany									
Japan									

Manchus   Revolution of 1911   Weimar Constitution | Mussolini   Fascism in Japan
                     Kuomintang   Fascist "March"   Hitler | Militarists
           Sun Yat-sen Chiang Kai-shek   Lateran Treaty Gestapo

1. Fascism Becomes a Powerful Force in Italy

Italy after World War I was a troubled land. Although she had fought on the side of the victorious Allies, the war had cost her about twelve billion dollars and the lives of over 600,000 soldiers. Italian military leaders and members of the Foreign Office were convinced that the Treaty of Versailles had not rewarded Italy sufficiently, as she had not received all of the territory she demanded.

Economic conditions were bad. Many industrial workers and thousands of demobilized troops looked in vain for jobs. The value of Italian money dropped, and prices rose to many times their prewar level. Food supplies were inadequate. Strikes upset the country. And peasants burned houses and confiscated land. Conditions improved toward the end of 1921 and the beginning of 1922. However, the Italian government, a constitutional monarchy, did not demonstrate enough leadership or unity to satisfy many Italians.

Dangerous tensions resulted from a widespread fear of communism. Men known as *Fascists* sent groups of armed ruffians to attack anyone they considered "radical," to beat up left-wing leaders, and to stop labor strikes. These conflicts added to the unrest in Italy.

The Fascists "March" on Rome

A number of groups demanded that reforms or radical changes be made in the Italian government and economy. Among the more violent agitators were the Fascists. A Fascist group known as the *Fasci di Combattimento* had been organized in March, 1919. It was led by Benito Mussolini (1883–1945). The Fascist groups did not then have a clear political doctrine for the nation. However, they (1) fought against those who advocated communism; (2) used the fear of communism to gain support; (3) tried to weaken the Socialist party, which had adopted an extremely radical program; and (4) demanded that Italy be developed into a world power.

In 1921 the Fascists made up only a small part of the Italian population of forty-five million. Nevertheless, their influence and power were growing stronger, particularly among the intellectuals, young people, and the lower-middle economic group.

609

Near the end of October, 1922, the Fascists "marched" on Rome. This so-called "March" was carried out by poorly coordinated and ill-disciplined groups. According to historian Gaetano Salvemini, they were armed with "a few machine guns, rifles, revolvers and a small amount of ammunition, bludgeons, table legs and branches of trees." The Fascist marchers probably could have been dispersed if the government had acted with strength.

Mussolini, the leader of the Fascists, was not even in Rome during the "March"; he remained in his barricaded newspaper office in Milan—four hundred miles from Rome. "We must defend our fort at all costs," declared this leader, bravely. Then he waited for the results of the "March."

Despite these unheroic aspects of the undertaking, the "March" on Rome was a success. The weak Italian parliamentary government was unable to take strong action against the Fascists. King Victor Emmanuel III, for various reasons, refused to establish martial law (government by military authorities over civilians during a time when civil government is ineffective). Military forces were not ordered to stop the Fascists. Finally, Mussolini was called by the king to become premier.

Why did the Fascist "March" on Rome succeed? Actually, many factors helped Mussolini to power. These included the following: (1) the weakness of the Italian government; (2) the support given to the Fascists by certain military chiefs, industrialists, and even the king's cousin; (3) the king's refusal to establish martial law; (4) confused and unsettled economic conditions; (5) low morale among the people; and (6) the fear of communism.

Benito Mussolini: Leader of the Fascists

In 1928 the billboards of Italy were plastered with signs that stated: "Il Duce ha sempre ragione," which means "The Leader [Benito Mussolini] is always right." The same year Richard Washburn Child, a former American ambassador to Italy, declared: "The Duce is now the greatest figure of this . . . time." And Mussolini himself modestly admitted: "I feel that all Italians . . . love me."

Seventeen years later Benito Mussolini was shot by a group of his own people. His body then was hung on a lamppost where men could shout insults at it as they passed! From billboard to lamppost in a few years. This is the story of the rise and fall of Mussolini.

Benito Mussolini was a rugged man who liked to stand with his fists pressed against his hips, his head tilted back, his jaw jutting forward. He nodded his head quickly when he spoke and he gestured with short-fingered hands. He was willing to use any means to achieve his ends. As he said, "Sometimes I must act like a surgeon, because operations are at times indispensable, but when the patient recovers he clasps the surgeon's hand and kisses the instruments that have restored him to health." Often Mussolini "operated," and the patient did not recover.

Basic Ideas of Italian Fascism

Benito Mussolini had once declared, "I want to be feared and hated." Once in power he seemed likely to accomplish these goals. In a few years he crushed most of his opponents and placed Fascists in key positions in the country by using methods that included terror and bribery. Although Victor Emmanuel III remained king, Mussolini eliminated the democratic features of the Italian government and made himself dictator of Italy. Meanwhile, he built a government based on political, economic, and social ideas that became a part of Fascism.

What is Fascism? Many scholars doubt that the word can be exactly defined.

■ *Benito Mussolini is shown at the height of his power (June, 1939). Surrounded by his black-uniformed bodyguard with their daggers raised, he gives the Fascist salute as he reviews detachments of the Italian military police.*

Nevertheless, *in time* Italian Fascism came to be based on these ideas:

(1) The state was all-important. To most political scientists, the term *state* refers to a politically organized society, occupying a definite territory, and having a government with power to handle its affairs independently of the control of other governments.

The Italian Fascists believed that the individual must serve the state and sacrifice his own well-being for the good of the state. Mussolini declared: "Nothing outside of the state, nothing against the state, nothing above the state."

(2) According to Fascism, the majority of the people was not fit to rule. Under Fascism a small group of men (the so-called elite), directed by Mussolini, was to govern the country. The rest of the people were to take orders.

This does *not* mean that the Fascists did not seek the support of the masses. On the contrary, Fascism depended on mass support; but it repudiated the democratic principle of majority rule.

(3) The Italian Fascists believed in using force to achieve their goals in domestic and foreign affairs. They were convinced that war was good, not evil.

(4) The Italian Fascists opposed freedom of speech, freedom of press, freedom of elections, the existence of anti-Fascist parties, and other features of democracy.

(5) The Italian Fascists believed that the economy should be organized into a "corporate" economic system. This meant that the economy was dominated by the state—and in reality the "state" was the Fascist government.

In addition, the Italian Fascists believed in intense nationalism, imperialism, and totalitarianism—that is, the Fascists should have unlimited power to control every aspect of life in Italy.

Fascist Italy under Mussolini

Italy remained a monarchy in name under Mussolini. However, between 1925 and 1928, Mussolini obtained full dictatorial powers. His decrees were considered law, and all political parties except his

Fascists were outlawed. Freedom of speech was suppressed. The words "Mussolini is always right" appeared under the dictator's picture in all classrooms!

The Italian economy was reorganized to form a *corporate state*. According to political scientist William Ebenstein, "The economy was divided into *syndicates* [associations] of workers, employers, and the professions. Only one syndicate was recognized in each branch of business or industry. ... the fascist government established *corporations*, which were administrative agencies in a given industry designed to unite and control the associations of *workers* and *employers* in that industry." The corporations controlled the Italian economy. They, in turn, obeyed Mussolini's decrees on economic matters. Strikes and lockouts were forbidden.

In religious affairs, Mussolini, although not religious, tried to lessen tensions between his government and the Papacy by settling the "Roman Question." The "Roman Question" referred to problems that had existed between the Italian government and the Papacy since the final territorial unification of Italy in 1870 (p. 512). The Popes had refused to accept this loss.

In February, 1929, the Lateran Treaty and accompanying Concordat were concluded between Mussolini and a representative of the Papacy. This agreement had the following provisions: (1) The Pope was recognized as sovereign with "exclusive and absolute dominion" over the Vatican City. (2) The Papacy recognized Rome as the capital of Italy. (3) The Roman Catholic Apostolic religion was recognized as "the only religion of the State," and the marriage sacrament was recognized as "legal for civil purposes, when administered according to Canon Law." (4) Catholic religious education was to continue in public elementary schools and be extended to secondary schools. (5) Italy agreed to pay the Papacy compensation for territorial and other losses.

The Lateran Treaty was popular with many Italians. It increased Mussolini's prestige at home and abroad.

■ **Check on Your Reading**
1. What problems faced postwar Italy?
2. How did the Fascists rise to power?
3. What are the basic ideas of Fascism?
4. What were the important provisions of the Lateran Treaty and the accompanying Concordat?

2. The Growth of Nazism in Germany

After the defeat of the Germans in World War I, a republic with many democratic features was established under the Weimar Constitution (1919). This constitution provided for universal suffrage for all citizens over the age of twenty, a two-house legislature, a chancellor appointed by the president but responsible to the *Reichstag* (the principal body of the legislature, elected by the people), and freedom of the individual. It also included Article 48, which provided that in an emergency the president could suspend important rights and freedoms of citizens.

Despite the Weimar Constitution there was great unrest. Germany was suffering from heavy losses of men and material in the war. Many Germans felt humiliated by defeat. There was dissatisfaction, both real and manufactured, with the Treaty of Versailles. Many Germans believed that the treaty was harsh and unfair.

Economic conditions in Germany were bad from 1919 to 1923. There was much unemployment, and demobilized troops looked in vain for work. The value of German money dropped and inflation spread throughout the country. The food supply was not adequate to meet the needs of the nation. Huge reparations provided an additional burden. The German economy recovered greatly between 1923 and 1929. However, after 1929 the world-wide depression and other factors seriously weakened German economic life.

Dangerous tensions resulted from a widespread fear of communism. Immediately after World War I there were a series of uprisings in Europe. Not only did Russian Communists take over Russia, but Hungarian Communists established a government in Hungary. In 1918 and 1919 there were two Communist revolts in Germany itself. As in Italy, counter-revolutionary forces in Germany used the almost hysterical fear of communism among the middle class and business leaders to promote fascism.

The Nazis Rise to Power

Several groups—Communists, monarchists, and others—demanded that reforms or changes be made in the government and economy of Germany. Although the German Republic achieved some reforms, the Reichstag became too divided to permit strong leadership by the government. Among the agitators who used force were the National Socialists or *Nazis*.

The future Nazis had organized themselves as early as 1919–20. In 1923 in Munich the Nazis joined some army men in the so-called Beer-Hall *Putsch*, an effort to overthrow the German Republic by an armed rising. This attempt failed and one of its leaders, Adolf Hitler, was put in jail. Here he wrote his famous autobiography, *Mein Kampf*, in which he expressed many of his ideas. However, the growth of the Nazi movement was very slow *before* the postwar depression in Germany. Some scholars believe that a rapid economic recovery might have erased Nazism as a political factor. The severe depression contributed heavily to the rise of the Nazis, who promised the people food and work for all. Eventually, the Nazi ranks included many different people: veterans; ardent nationalists; workers; small shopkeepers; intellectuals; men who hated Jews, democrats, and Communists; industrialists; and dissatisfied young people.

In April, 1932, the Nazi leader, Adolf Hitler, received 36.8 per cent of the votes cast in the election for president of the German Republic. Paul von Hindenburg, with 53 per cent, was elected president. On January 30, 1933, after a complicated series of political maneuvers, Adolf Hitler was appointed chancellor by President von Hindenburg.

In the next few months, by the use of Article 48 of the Constitution and by the Enabling Act of March, 1933, Hitler took over most of the powers of government. In a short time he abolished all parties except his National Socialists (or Nazis). Adolf Hitler became the dictator of Germany. Thus, while Benito Mussolini came to power in Italy through the impetus of his "March," Hitler assumed dictatorial control primarily through constitutional channels.

Adolf Hitler: Leader of the Nazis

In 1922 a German citizen was convinced that Adolf Hitler was "the man of destiny, the vitalizing force in the future of Germany. . . . I had given him my soul."

In 1934 a German writer Konrad Heiden declared: "As a mob-leader Hitler is certainly unrivalled today and almost unequalled in history. . . . Nothing like him has been seen in modern Europe."

And Hitler himself, with typical modesty, admitted, "I am indispensable."

Yet, on April 30, 1945, in a bunker below the German Chancellery in Berlin, a bitter and defeated Adolf Hitler placed a gun to his head and pulled the trigger! The story of his rise and fall is indeed a striking one.

Adolf Hitler (1889–1945) claimed that Germany would be saved by "those who direct universal hatred to themselves." Few men in history have been so universally and deeply hated as he. Conscientious about keeping his brushlike mustache in healthy condition and careful to see that his unruly stomach received the kindest of treatment, Hitler decreed the death of millions of people. As he said in 1922, his motto was: "If you will not be a German, I will bash your skull in."

Hitler distorted the facts to sell Nazism. Always he presented only one side of an argument—*his* side. After all, he wrote in *Mein Kampf* (My Struggle), "What would one think of a soap ad which also recognized the value of other soaps?"

How did Hitler win the support of so many people? Historians are still debating this question, but these are some of the reasons. He was a remarkable orator. When he spoke there was an emotional fire in his voice, a dramatic forcefulness, at times almost an hysteria that swept his audience along with him. "His words were like a scourge," wrote one of his listeners. "When he spoke of the disgrace of Germany, I felt ready to spring on any enemy . . . glancing round, I saw that his magnetism was holding these thousands as one . . . ."

In addition, Hitler had drive, cunning, ability to glamorize his program, understanding of the methods of propaganda and, of course, strong-armed men to convince the doubters. Finally, conditions in Germany and the world made some people believe that only a man like Hitler could "save" the German people.

The Rise of Hitler and Mussolini Compared

Viewed in perspective, a number of facts become clear about the rise of Hitler and Mussolini. Both developments had important roots in history. Although severe economic conditions were not the only reason for the growth of Nazism and Fascism, depressions helped make it possible for the Nazis and Fascists to obtain power. Other important factors contributing to the rise of Nazism and Fascism included the following: (1) the psychological effects of World War I, which unsettled the lives of many people; (2) the inability of postwar governments in Germany and Italy to keep the respect of their citizens; (3) the emotional appeal of Nazism and Fascism; (4) the nationalistic feelings of the people; (5) the propaganda that was circulated about the injustice of the Treaty of Versailles; (6) the terror that was spread by the violence of the Nazis and Fascists; and (7) the fear of communism.

Basic Ideas of German Nazism

(1) The Nazis believed that they belonged to a so-called "pure Aryan race," that "Aryan blood" was superior to that of all other people, and that they were destined to rule the world. These Nazi ideas were completely unscientific.

(2) The Nazis were anti-Semitic—that is, they were bitterly opposed to the Jews. They believed that people of the Jewish religion or those descended from Jews should be denied all rights, driven from Germany, or executed.

(3) Nazi leaders opposed the principles of Christianity and tried to substitute devotion to Germany for devotion to God.

(4) The state was all-important and was to have supreme power over individuals.

(5) A dictator, Hitler, would rule with the aid of a Nazi "elite," or chosen few.

(6) The economy would be based on a system of private ownership of the means

614

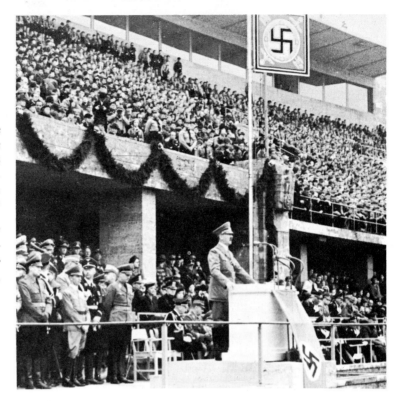

■ *Adolf Hitler is addressing 132,000 members of the Hitler Youth in Berlin on May 1, 1939. A magnetic orator, Hitler frequently spoke before such huge crowds, which roared "Heil, Hitler" as a sign of their allegiance to* Der Fuehrer *(The Leader).*

of production, distribution, and consumption under *strict state control.*

In addition, the Nazis approved of the use of force and war, rejected democratic rights, and supported the principles of intense nationalism, imperialism, and totalitarianism. Many Nazi ideas resembled those of the Italian Fascists. Indeed, Nazism was a German form of Fascism.

Nazi Germany under Adolf Hitler

Adolf Hitler—aware of his words "To be a leader means to be able to move masses"—ruled as dictator. Every region and local area had to obey the orders of the central government. All political groups except the Nazis were banned. The *Gestapo,* or secret police, viciously eliminated any opposition to the Nazi regime.

The German economy was dominated by the state. Strikes were prohibited and unions were abolished. The interests of the state came first. In 1935 Hitler increased the number of German troops in violation of the Treaty of Versailles, and Germany concentrated on massive rearmament.

Hitler believed that the masses "more easily fall a victim to a big lie than to a little one." Schools indoctrinated students with bitter Nazi propaganda. Orators screamed Hitler's name at mass meetings. Censors, directed by Joseph Paul Goebbels, minister of propaganda, burned books considered dangerous. Nazi axes destroyed publications that criticized.

Under the Nazis, religious groups were ridiculed, persecuted, and attacked. Jews were hounded, deprived of rights, branded with the Star of David, and sent to torture and death in concentration camps.

■ Check on Your Reading

1. What were the principal provisions of the Weimar Constitution? Why did it fail?

2. How did Adolf Hitler become dictator?

3. Describe life in Germany under Hitler.

3. Fascism Influences Japan

While Fascism and Nazism were growing in Italy and Germany, important changes were occurring in Japan. The Japanese were working to add to the power of their own nation. In the 1920's there was a liberal trend. Although Japan's constitution was fairly conservative and respect for authority remained strong, steps were taken toward representative democracy. For example, efforts were made to increase the powers of the lower house of the Parliament (or Diet); and the right to vote was granted to all adult men. Out of a total population of about fifty-five million, fourteen million people now could vote. At the same time, the power of military leaders was held in check, although army and navy officials still were very important. Various students and intellectuals tried to encourage a freer exchange of ideas.

In addition, many businessmen favored a friendly policy in trading and other relations with foreign countries. They hoped for economic expansion and prosperity through a growing export trade.

Fascist Ideas Gain Strength

The liberal trend of the 1920's did not last. During the 1930's the government again became authoritarian. It is sometimes said that Japan followed a system of Fascism similar to that of Italy or Germany. Actually, there were many differences. The ideas of Fascism *did* become strong in Japan during the 1930's. However, *these Fascist ideas developed within the framework of Japanese society and took on a distinctive Japanese coloration.* These are some Fascist ideas that influenced Japanese life in the 1930's:

(1) Force was accepted by many Japanese leaders, although not by all, as a means of achieving goals. War and preparation for war were glorified.

(2) Super-patriotic societies stirred up a nationalistic fever. They urged the people to believe that Japan was a great nation whose "destiny" was to dominate others. Government leaders also stimulated national pride as a means of winning approval for imperialistic adventures. For example, the Japanese foreign minister told Japan's Parliament in 1938, ". . . the Chinese must be made to realize that they are inferior to the Japanese in culture and arms and must follow in the footsteps of the Japanese. . . ."

(3) The Japanese government wanted the economic system to be organized in such a way that it could support Japan's military adventures and wars. In an effort to do this, it passed the National General Mobilization Law in 1938, which permitted the government or state to regulate closely or administer industries.

(4) The Japanese promoted the idea of pride in "race." Some Japanese felt that they were racially superior to other peoples. They pointed to such "evidence" as Japan's successes in the Russo-Japanese War (1904–05) to support their position.

Other Fascist ideas that influenced Japan in the 1930's were the state's dominant role, rule by an elite, rejection of democratic rights, and totalitarianism.

The Militarists Control Japan

When Japan came under the domination of militarists, its domestic and foreign policies were affected. As Professor Edwin O. Reischauer, later ambassador to Japan, pointed out, the Japanese were influenced by "the raising of protective tariffs throughout the world as an aftermath of the 1929 depression. This seemed to spell ultimate disaster for Japan's foreign trade. The businessman's program of continued economic expansion and prosperity through a growing export trade was suddenly revealed to be no more than a vain dream. . . . Japan, which depended on other lands for much of its raw materials, and . . . for a vital part of its consuming market, was entirely at the mercy of the tariff policies of other nations."

Japanese military leaders and certain bankers and big business men supported a program of increased armaments to strengthen Japan's position and prestige as a great military power. They favored overseas expansion to advance Japanese trade by obtaining the sources of raw materials and markets. In addition, they advocated extension of Japanese control over areas in the Far East to be used as outlets for Japan's increasing population; and they urged military action against China to obtain Manchuria and other territory.

■ **Check on Your Reading**

1. Can you find any evidence of the existence of a liberal trend in the 1920's in Japan?

2. What Fascist ideas became popular in Japan in the 1930's?

3. What policies did Japan's militarists and some bankers and big business men support?

4. Revolution in China

While Fascism increased in strength in Japan, many important changes were occurring in China. There was a revolution, a new republic, and civil conflict.

The Manchus, who had come from the region known as Manchuria, had ruled China since the middle of the seventeenth century. The Ch'ing, the ruling family line of the Manchus, eventually governed a vast, populous, and wealthy area. During the Manchu period, the Chinese made significant contributions in historical studies and other cultural areas.

In time the power of the Manchus declined. The Manchu government became weak, inefficient, and corrupt. Living conditions cried out for reform. Human beings did the work of machines; millions lived in huts; and the spiritual life of the people was seriously undermined.

During the first years of the twentieth century, the Manchus did permit some reforms. One of the most important of these involved efforts to modernize the educational system. However, these changes came too late to save the regime.

Chinese reformers and revolutionists, under the leadership of Dr. Sun Yat-sen and others, continued to agitate for an end to abuses. In 1911 a revolution overthrew the Manchus. After centuries of being ruled by dynasties, the Chinese established a republic.

China Fails to Unite

On January 1, 1912, Dr. Sun Yat-sen was inaugurated as Provisional President of the Republic. The Chinese had no real experience in running a republican form of government. As a result, the years that followed the establishment of the republic were filled with considerable confusion. In February, 1912, in an effort to avoid civil war, Dr. Sun resigned as president in favor of Yüan Shi-k'ai. Yüan was a powerful general whose army might have challenged the republic if he had not been made president. Later in 1912 a number of men who had supported the revolt against the Manchus organized the *Kuomintang*, or National People's Party, which became the most important group in the Chinese national parliament.

Yüan, the new president, was an ambitious man. In 1913 he dismissed the Kuomintang from the national parliament. He also tried to make himself emperor. Although Yüan failed in his attempt and died in 1916, China remained a divided and disrupted country.

When China entered World War I in 1917, it was still a land filled with internal dissension. After the war, the armies of rival war lords continued to clash with each other. Despite a supposed central government at Peking, China was disunited.

Dr. Sun Yat-sen: National Hero

Members of the Kuomintang refused to be discouraged. They had established a government at Canton, and in 1921 they elected Dr. Sun Yat-sen as its head. Thus, there was one government at Canton, another at Peking, and several lesser ones in regions run by war lords. Dr. Sun and the Kuomintang determined to eliminate the rival governments and to unite China.

Dr. Sun (1866–1925) was a graduate of the medical school in Hong Kong. A patriotic and visionary man, he became more interested in overthrowing the Manchus than in attacking the diseases of individual men. As leader of the government at Canton, Dr. Sun did not prove to be an efficient administrator; but he inspired his associates with his patriotism, sincerity, and hard work.

Dr. Sun became one of the national heroes of the Chinese. Since Dr. Sun had such influence on the Chinese people, it is essential to know what he believed. An important part of his philosophy can be found in his famous *Three Principles*. Dr. Sun proposed these principles as guides by which to organize China. The Three Principles were *nationalism*, the idea of freedom from the control of foreigners; *democracy*, a limited democratic government; and *livelihood*, a decent standard of living and economic justice for all.

Dr. Sun hoped that the Chinese could build a strong, united nation. He was willing to accept outside help to achieve this goal. In 1923 he accepted advice and assistance of Communists from Russia. However, Dr. Sun was not a Communist. On the other hand, a number of members of the Kuomintang were Communists or favorable to communism. Some of these men were to play important roles in the future history of China.

Chiang Kai-shek: Leader of the Kuomintang

After Dr. Sun died in 1925, the Kuomintang continued his work. In 1926, under the command of Chiang Kai-shek, Kuomintang armies left Canton and moved northward. They were determined to unite the country.

Town after town fell to the advancing Kuomintang forces, or welcomed them as the men who could restore order. Then, in 1927, a struggle for power occurred *within* the Kuomintang between the Communist members and those who opposed them.

Chiang Kai-shek sided with the opponents of the Communists. He set up his headquarters in Nanking while the Communists and their supporters established themselves at Hankow. By the end of 1927 the Communist government in Hankow lost public support and fell.

Chiang's armies continued northward. In 1928 they took Peking. By 1931 the Kuomintang controlled considerable territory in China, although the Communists and war lords still dominated some regions.

Chiang Kai-shek (1886–   ) had led an active life before becoming leader of the Kuomintang. He had received Chinese military training, entered the Imperial Military College in Japan, joined the Chinese revolutionary movement, spent several months in Moscow, and had become the first head of the Whampoa Military Academy in Canton.

Chiang was a wiry man, about five feet nine inches tall, with dark eyes, and an angular face. He generally wore a plain khaki uniform and a black cloak. Chiang did not smoke and he drank only water or tea. He went to bed early, awoke early, and worked hard during the day. In the 1930's he became a Christian, and it was his custom to start each day with an hour of prayer and meditation.

Chiang's character is still the subject of heated dispute. Although his name meant "Firm Rock," Chiang has been called "ruffian," "resourceful leader," "corrupt reactionary," "spiritual person," "peanut," and "hero." Despite other differences of opinion concerning his character, most scholars agree that Chiang was shrewd, stubborn, and determined in working toward his goals.

Chiang did not establish a democratic government for China. Even if he had seriously tried to do so, it would have been difficult to introduce democracy. The state of the country, the lack of democratic experience of the people, the weaknesses within the Kuomintang, and the invasion of the Japanese all interfered with democratic growth. Chiang became the "strong man" of China rather than head of a democratic government.

China Struggles Between the Old and New

Chinese life was greatly affected by events from 1911 to 1931. In addition to the upheavals in political affairs, there were significant occurrences and changes in other fields. In education modern methods were introduced. To broaden their learning many Chinese went to Japan, the United States, and other countries to study. Educational changes helped Chinese women and girls obtain more rights in everyday life.

In literature, some authors began to write in the vernacular of the Chinese, rather than in the classical style. In religion Confucianism declined in importance, although it continued to be a significant factor in the lives of many Chinese. In foreign affairs China was freed from a number of foreign controls and concessions.

Despite the real and superficial changes that occurred during this period, many of the old ways of living continued. Most family ties remained strong. Numerous ancient customs were followed. Thus, the Chinese struggled between old and new ways of life. Before the Chinese could readjust themselves, Japanese invaders disrupted their country again.

■ **Check on Your Reading**

1. Describe the living conditions of the Chinese people under the Manchus.
2. Why did Dr. Sun Yat-sen fail to unite China?
3. How did Chiang Kai-shek extend his control over China?
4. What changes occurred in Chinese life from 1911 to 1931?

CULTURAL CHARACTERISTICS of Nazi Germany

Some actions of the Nazis reached extreme heights of absurdity. For example, in 1935 the Nazis did not want to lose foreign exchange by importing foreign lemons. They therefore tried to force the people to eat German rhubarb instead of lemons *by claiming that rhubarb created German blood.* In a tragic distortion of reality a pro-Nazi newspaper declared:

Only the fruits of the German earth . . . can create German blood. Through them only are transmitted to the blood, and hence to the body and the soul, those delicate vibrations which determine the German type. . . . Farewell lemon, we need thee not! Our German rhubarb will take thy place fully and entirely.

Nearly every aspect of German culture reflected similar ideological distortions for the Nazis' fanatical purposes.

A society in which the Nazi state apparatus dominated every aspect of the cultural, political, economic, and social life of the people.

Emphasis on a doctrine of racial superiority that led to brutal anti-Semitic and anti-Christian actions.

Power and authority given to highly nationalistic groups in many fields of German life. Hitler even proposed a new commandment: "Thou Shalt Have No Other God But Germany."

Under the Nazis culture became a handmaiden of destruction. Even *music* played its part. William L. Shirer described the Nazi gas chambers in this way:

The gas chambers themselves and the adjoining cremazoria, viewed from a short distance, were not sinister-looking places at all . . . . Over them were well-kept lawns with flower borders; the signs at the entrances merely said BATHS. The unsuspecting [victims] thought they were simply being taken to the baths. . . . And taken to the accompaniment of sweet music!

For there was light music. An orchestra of "young and pretty girls all dressed in white blouses and navy-blue skirts," . . . had been formed from among the inmates. While the selection was being made for the gas chambers, this unique musical ensemble played gay tunes from The Merry Widow and The Tales of Hoffmann.

The "showers" consisted of crystals of hydrogen cyanide that were dropped into the chambers and brought death to the helpless victims.

There was no time for the music—or art or literature or science—of peace in Germany in this period. The revival of a German culture worthy of its brilliant past awaited the obliteration of the Nazi regime.

MAN AND HIS CULTURE

Let's Meet the People!

The information in the following sketch was drawn from a diary of one of the prisoners and appears in *From Day to Day* by Odd Nansen, translated by Katherine John, 1949, G. P. Putnam's Sons.

A Boy in a Nazi Concentration Camp

Tommy Bürgenthal, age ten, had been in Nazi concentration camps for two and a half years. He had been sent there because he was guilty of the "crime" of being born a Jew.

Tommy's grayish-brown eyes still had a calm expression, but his delicate hands revealed his nervousness. Tommy could not keep his hands still. Tommy's nervousness developed from his life in the concentration camp at Auschwitz. It was to Auschwitz that thousands of innocent men and women were sent to die in the gas chamber. Tommy was forced to work as an errand boy at the crematory where their dead bodies were burned.

Tommy could not read or write, but he soon became familiar with numbers. He knew that the gas chamber could hold two

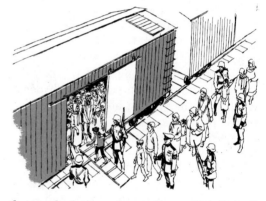

thousand victims at one time—that it took ten minutes to kill a human being by gas—and that two boxes of gas containers were sufficient to exterminate all of the people packed in the chamber.

"But how do you know that?" someone asked him.

"Because I got the boxes," he answered.

Later Tommy was moved to another concentration camp. Here—where each day men were starved, beaten, and hanged—Tommy continued to live. To live and to hope for the day when he would be reunited with his parents. No one ever told Tommy that his parents had been burned in the very type of crematory where he once had worked.

CHAPTER REVIEW

REVIEW and DISCUSSION

1. Identify the people and places and explain the events and terms on p. 608.

2. Do you agree or disagree with this statement: "No dictator who wants to stay in power can shrink from violence." Why?

3. What similarities are there between Fascism and communism? What differences?

4. In Germany and Italy, democracy made a beginning but was overpowered by dictators, who established totalitarian governments. Why were dictators able to overthrow the struggling democracies?

5. How did Mussolini's government in Italy differ from Hitler's in Germany? How were they similar?

6. What were the similarities and differences between European and Japanese Fascism of the 1930's?

7. What was Sun Yat-sen's guiding philosophy? What changes did he advocate?

8. Why did China fail to develop into a strong democracy?

9. How was the desire for economic expansion related to the rise of Fascism in Japan?

10. What underlying causes can you find that help explain why the Communists were later able to control China?

ACTIVITIES

1. Compare the dictators in this chapter in regard to their lives before becoming dictators; time in office; methods; conditions contributing to their rise; and causes of their fall.

2. Write an essay on "Totalitarianism." Consult *Encyclopedia of the Social Sciences, Syntopicon of Great Books,* and other references.

3. Write a biographical report on Dr. Sun Yat-sen or Chiang Kai-shek.

PAST and PRESENT

1. Read newspaper and magazine articles about China and Japan to find examples of the people's struggle between the old and the new.

2. Compare the dictators discussed in this chapter with Franco in Spain, Castro in Cuba, or Tito in Yugoslavia.

3. How can you explain the existence of concentration camps in the twentieth century after several thousand years of civilization?

SUGGESTED READINGS

Basic books: BENNS, F. LEE, *Europe Since 1914 in Its World Setting,* Chaps. 14, 15, and 24, Appleton-Century-Crofts.

BRUUN, GEOFFREY, and MAMATEY, VICTOR S., *The World in the Twentieth Century,* Chaps. 24, 25, 34, Heath.

LATOURETTE, KENNETH SCOTT, *A Short History of the Far East,* Chaps. 14, 15, Macmillan.

SMITH, GOLDWIN, *The Heritage of Man,* Chap. 45, Scribner.

TIEDEMANN, ARTHUR, *Modern Japan, A Brief History,* Van Nostrand. Part II contains brief but valuable readings from Japanese writings.

Special accounts: EBENSTEIN, WILLIAM, (ed.), *Man and the State,* Chaps. 7 and 8, Holt. Includes selections from the writings of Hitler, Mussolini, and Rocco, who served as Fascist minister of justice.

MARRIOTT, SIR J. A. R., *Makers of Modern Italy; Napoleon—Mussolini,* Oxford University Press. Easily read. Biographical.

SANSOM, SIR GEORGE BAILEY, *The Western World and Japan; A Study in the Interaction of European and Asiatic Cultures,* Knopf. For better readers. Gives an excellent account of the impact of one civilization on another.

SHIRER, WILLIAM L., *The Rise and Fall of the Third Reich,* Fawcett (paperback). A history of Nazi Germany.

Biography and Fiction: WALN, NORA, *The House of Exile,* Little, Brown. An extremely interesting picture of life of a Chinese family. Written by a woman who lived for a number of years in China.

Chapter 39

The Democracies and International Peace Efforts

KEYNOTE   Lucia Ames Mead, an analyst of international affairs, tells the following true story:

"Four years after the League of Nations was established, a prominent civic worker in New York had heard so little of it that he remarked to someone going to the headquarters of the League, 'I suppose that by this time you have a regular secretary who remains the year around.' At that time there were 300 men and women from 34 countries working at the Secretariat of the League!"

The civic worker and others like him often overlooked one of the key features of the period in which they lived. *During the 1920's and 1930's the democracies—Britain, France, the United States—occupied themselves with serious domestic problems, but they also devoted considerable energy to international efforts to strengthen their security and protect the peace.*

Key People   *Raymond Poincaré · Léon Blum · Lloyd George · Ramsay MacDonald · Stanley Baldwin · Edward VIII · George VI · Franklin Roosevelt*

Key Places   *Syria · Lebanon · Palestine · Trans-Jordan · Ruhr · Egypt · Alsace-Lorraine · Iraq · Suez Canal*

Key Events   *Syria and Lebanon become French mandates · First Labor Ministry · Iraq and Palestine become British mandates · Edward VIII abdicates · Statute of Westminster passed · stock market collapses · "New Deal" introduced · Briand-Kellogg Treaty signed · Washington Conference*

Key Terms   *coalition · Bloc National · Left Bloc · National Union · depression · tariff · Popular Front · Maginot Line · suffrage · National Coalition · dominions · Little Entente · disarmament*

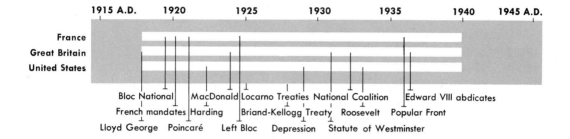

| 1915 A.D. | 1920 | 1925 | 1930 | 1935 | 1940 | 1945 A.D. |

France
Great Britain
United States

Bloc National | MacDonald | Locarno Treaties | National Coalition | Edward VIII abdicates
French mandates | Harding | Briand-Kellogg Treaty | Roosevelt | Popular Front
Lloyd George | Poincaré | Left Bloc | Depression | Statute of Westminster

1. *France Rebuilds after World War I*

"Germany will pay!" declared the French Finance Minister, as he bitterly surveyed the battered condition of France after World War I. Yet efforts to rebuild the economic health of France by draining away the strength of Germany through reparations were not enough. Many serious problems remained to be solved in postwar France.

World War I had ravaged France. According to the figures of economic historian Shepard B. Clough: "In the devastated regions . . . 900,000 buildings, 200 coal mines, and 34 iron mines had been damaged or destroyed, 85 per cent of the arable land had been devastated, and 94 per cent of the cattle had disappeared. . . . French foreign commerce had shrunk to the point where exports were only 25 per cent and imports 87 per cent of the weight of those in 1913. . . . The franc had lost about 72 per cent of its purchasing power."

France faced other postwar problems. The loss of manpower as a result of the war, combined with a low birth rate, weakened France's labor force. According to Professor Clough, France's population decreased from about 39 million in 1911 to 37 million in 1921, with a loss of 11 per cent in the number of males between the ages of 15 and 50.

Commerce declined within France. Between 1913 and 1921 the volume of railway transportation declined by over 40 per cent. France lost many foreign markets.

Other problems included France's increased indebtedness, which amounted to almost seven billion gold francs owed to foreign nations; an ineffective tax system; and tensions caused by the French search for security against German revenge.

Many Frenchmen looked to the government to save France, but the French legislature was splintered into many conflicting groups. It required a coalition (or bloc) of several political parties to obtain a majority in the Chamber of Deputies. "A civilization is as fragile as a life," the French poet Paul Valéry had warned in 1919. It was a warning that French statesmen began to take seriously.

Various Coalitions Govern France

From 1919 to 1924 the *Bloc National*— a coalition of parties supported by the middle classes—worked to rebuild damaged regions in France and tried to force Germany to meet its treaty obligations.

623

In the Near East France had obtained mandates over Syria and Lebanon following World War I. Problems of governing these mandates led to tensions that culminated in a Syrian rebellion in 1925–27.

Meanwhile, to solve France's serious financial problems the government needed funds. When Germany defaulted on its reparations, Premier Raymond Poincaré sent French troops into the Ruhr in an effort to force payment (p. 589). The Germans passively resisted the French occupation but it seriously weakened the German financial structure and increased international tensions. England and the United States disapproved of this action. Poincaré's Ruhr policies and his failure to maintain the value of the franc contributed to the fall of the Bloc National.

Under the *Left Bloc*, a coalition of Socialists and other left-wing parties governed from 1924 to 1926. There were continued efforts to stabilize the franc; French troops were pulled out of the Ruhr; and Alsace and Lorraine (ceded to France by the Treaty of Versailles) were incorporated as parts of France in 1925. The Left Bloc fell when the decline in the value of the franc continued as people invested their funds in England and the United States rather than in unstable France.

France was governed from 1926 to 1929 by the *National Union*—a coalition of right-center parties dominated by Poincaré. It strengthened the franc, improved the tax system, and raised the general economic position of France. By 1926 industrial production had been raised to twice the level of 1919. The years 1928 and 1929 were prosperous ones. France had made an extraordinary recovery.

The Great Depression

On October 24, 1929, "Black Thursday," the *New York Times* carried a feature story of the "worst stock crash" in the United States and "the most disastrous decline in the biggest and broadest stock market of history." The story was a dramatic prelude to the terrible depression that swept the world. Paul Reynaud, French statesman of the time, described this world depression in these words: "oceans . . . deserted, the ships laid up in the silent ports, the factory smoke-stacks dead, long files of workless in the towns, poverty throughout the countryside. . . . Then came the stage when wealth was destroyed [for example, Canadians burned corn in railway engines to keep up the price of corn]. Just as a man, leaving a house at a moment's notice, burns his papers, civilization seemed to destroy, before disappearing, the wealth it had created."

There were many reasons for this worldwide depression: (1) World War I caused dislocation of industry and it was difficult to return the economy to a sound peacetime basis after 1918. (2) Overproduction of goods in many countries made it hard to sell excess products on the world market. (3) Trade barriers in the form of high protective tariffs were erected between nations. As a result the amount and value of American and European exports declined.

(4) Income was unequally distributed among groups in various countries, and consumers throughout the world lacked sufficient income to buy the great quantities of goods being produced. (5) Speculation increased. Many people, hoping to make their fortunes quickly, invested in stocks without knowing the production or earning power of the company selling the stock.

The great depression began to make itself felt in France about 1931. The volume of France's foreign trade dropped sharply, industrial activity declined by one-fourth from 1931 to 1935, prices of

■ *In the late 1930's the French felt a false sense of security behind their defensive Maginot Line. Here rails embedded in the ground to stop tanks and barbed wire to slow down troops lie outside the concrete fortifications and tunnels. The Germans by-passed the line.*

agricultural products fell to disastrous levels, and unemployment became a serious problem. The situation clearly demanded immediate action.

The Popular Front Battles the Depression

In the elections of 1936 the *Popular Front*—a coalition of Radical Socialists, Socialists, Communists, and others—gained control of the French government. The Socialist leader Léon Blum became premier. Blum was an intelligent, scholarly, and cultivated man of whom journalist John Gunther wrote in 1938: "In an age of violence and unreason, with Fascism spreading like eczema beyond Germany and Italy, he represents something like a breath of the past, the spirit of scholarship, intellectual detachment, humanism." Blum was determined to settle problems by peaceful means, not war.

Under the leadership of Blum, the Popular Front tried to check the growth of Fascist groups in France and to pull the country out of its economic depression. The government representing the Popular Front helped workers by setting up a forty-hour work week, took steps to raise the prices for farm products, and began to bring the armament industries under government control. It also raised taxes, devalued the franc in an effort to improve foreign trade, and weakened the tremendous power of the handful of men who dominated the Bank of France.

The Popular Front governed France from 1936 to 1938. Then several factors, including Blum's demands for increased authority to control finances, led to its downfall. France soon went off the gold standard and the value of the franc dropped again. In the spring of 1938 Édouard Daladier formed a ministry and became the new premier of France.

As the danger of war grew, the French continued to build up their economy. Meanwhile, they felt secure behind their *Maginot Line*, a 350-mile line of concrete and underground fortifications that they had constructed along the German and Luxembourg frontiers for protection against foreign attack.

■ Check on Your Reading

1. What postwar problems did France have?
2. What factors helped to cause the great depression?
3. What steps did the Popular Front take to improve economic conditions?

2. Developments in Great Britain after World War I

Like France, postwar Britain faced many serious problems, and Prime Minister Lloyd George complained of a "restlessness" everywhere. It was a restlessness that was evident in many areas of British life in the 1920's: In the bold activities of the "flappers," independent young women who took jobs in the business world of men and who dared to smoke—in public; in the rise and fall of "dance crazes," like the "Charleston"; and in the divorce rate, which zoomed from an average annual number of 823 in 1910–1912 to 3619 in 1920–1922.

The economy also reflected the unsettled conditions of the country. After enjoying a brief boom, the people of Britain faced major economic crises. There were many reasons for Britain's postwar economic problems: (1) Foreign trade declined partially as a result of the competition provided by the United States and Japan. A number of nations placed high tariffs on goods coming from Britain.

(2) There was a heavy national debt; Britain had spent about nine and a half billion pounds to finance her part in World War I, and over 70 per cent of this sum had been borrowed. (3) Unemployment increased. In 1920 2.2 per cent of the employable population of Britain was unemployed; in 1924 this figure was 10.3 per cent. (4) High costs of production often resulted from the use of antiquated machinery.

(5) Economic inequalities existed. As late as 1938, 2 per cent of the property owners of England owned 64 per cent of the national wealth. (6) A heavy loss of ships and talent had resulted from the war. Over 2000 British vessels had been destroyed and between 700,000 and 750,000 British young men had lost their lives. In Britain, as in France, many people looked to the government to stimulate economic recovery.

Lloyd George Coalition

From 1916 to 1922 a coalition of Conservatives and Liberals ran the British government. Lloyd George served as prime minister. This government passed the Fisher Education Act of 1918, providing for a system of free, compulsory, elementary education to the age of 14; the Unemployment Insurance Act of 1920, increasing benefits to the unemployed; and the Safeguarding of Industries Act, placing a 33⅓ per cent duty on certain commodities, other than goods from the dominions.

MacDonald Becomes Prime Minister

The Conservative party controlled the government from 1922 to 1924 and tried to aid the economy by raising tariffs still higher. Then, in January, 1924, a coalition of Liberals and Laborites came into office. Although the Labor party needed the support of the Liberals to form a majority in the House of Commons, James Ramsay MacDonald, leader of the Laborites, became prime minister. MacDonald's ministry lasted only until November, 1924, but it was historically important because MacDonald was the *first* Labor prime minister in the history of Britain.

The Labor Ministry officially recognized the Soviet Union in 1924, but it did not enact radical or experimental legislation in Britain. MacDonald himself was not an extremist. When he was prime minister, he wrote that a Socialist (most Labor party members believed in a form of socialism) was "an evolutionist" who "rejects everything of the nature of violent breaks and brand-new systems."

Stanley Baldwin Heads a Conservative Ministry

A Conservative Ministry regained control of the government in 1924, and Stanley

Ramsay
MacDonald

■ *MacDonald was Britain's first Labor prime minister. He was forced out of the Labor party when he organized the National Coalition.*

Baldwin became prime minister. The Baldwin ministry was active in foreign affairs. It signed the Locarno Pact (p. 633), and it broke off diplomatic relations with the Soviet Union in protest against Communist efforts to expand into British territory.

In domestic affairs, the Conservative government had to deal with the General Strike of 1926. This strike started in the coal industry as a protest against longer hours and less pay for coal miners; then it spread throughout the country. The strikers did not achieve their objectives, and Parliament soon passed legislation declaring a general strike to be illegal.

Progress was made in the extension of suffrage. All during the first part of the twentieth century, British suffragettes had fought for rights for women—indeed, some of them had cut telephone lines, filled opponents' mailboxes with tar, and set off bombs. In 1928, all women over the age of twenty-one were given the right to vote.

A second Labor Ministry took office in 1929 with Ramsay MacDonald again prime minister. This government tried to strengthen Britain's position among other nations and re-established relations with Russia. However, the storm of the worldwide depression broke upon Britain. Faced with a decline in national income, unemployment, and other problems, the ministry fell in 1931.

A National Coalition Governs during the Depression

A financial crisis and other economic conditions brought demands for a strong ministry. Many British agreed with *The (London) Times* when it wrote: "Every hour which passes without some check upon the flood of national expenditure, and without some decision in national policy ... delays, by a period which may be disastrous, the return of confidence at home and abroad in this country's will and power to set its financial house in order." The king asked Ramsay MacDonald to organize a ministry. He responded by forming a *National Coalition* ministry, representing individuals of all parties. Laborites bitterly charged MacDonald with deserting them and their principles. Eventually, he was driven out of the Labor party but continued to be the British prime minister.

The National Coalition (1931–1935) took important steps to stop the decline of British overseas trade and to stimulate the economic recovery of Britain. It took Britain off the gold standard to lower the costs of production and help the British compete with other nations for world markets. It strengthened the national budget by greatly limiting the payment of Britain's war debts. It also passed an Import Duties Bill designed to protect British goods, and it increased the benefits paid under the system of unemployment insurance. A World Economic Conference was held in London in 1933 to discuss plans for combating the world-wide depression. Though unsuccessful, it was a forerunner of future, more successful conferences.

Edward VIII Abdicates

The British economy began to improve. Then the British were startled by events involving the royal family. In January, 1936, King George V died, and the Prince of Wales succeeded to the throne as Edward VIII. A crisis soon developed. Edward desired to marry Mrs. Wallis Simpson, an American divorcée, but encountered the serious opposition of Prime Minister Baldwin, other members of the government, and leaders of the Church of England. Finally, on December 11, 1936, Edward VIII abdicated. On May 12, 1937, Edward's brother became King George VI.

The abdication of Edward VIII did not seriously upset the processes of government in Britain. The Prime Minister, the Cabinet, and the Parliament continued to govern the country, as they had done for many years. The new king accepted his responsibilities as (1) titular head of the state, (2) guardian of British customs and traditions, and (3) symbol of unity.

■ *Britons learned the dramatic news of the abdication of King Edward VIII from newspapers and a personal radio broadcast by the king.*

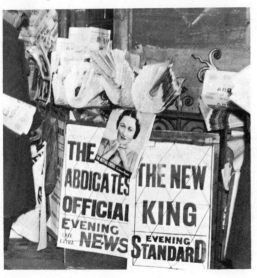

Great Britain and the Dominions

During the postwar period, Britain also clarified her relations with her *dominions*— Canada, Australia, New Zealand, Union of South Africa, Ireland, and India. The relationships between Britain and the dominions were defined by a declaration of the *Imperial Conference of 1926*:

They [Britain and the dominions] are autonomous Communities . . . *equal in status*, in no way subordinate one to another in any aspect of their domestic or [foreign] affairs . . . and freely associated as members of the . . . Commonwealth of Nations.

The important *Statute of Westminster of 1931* made it clear that even if the parliament of a dominion passed a law that conflicted with British laws, that law could not be voided by Britain; and even if the British Parliament wanted to do so, it could not pass a law that applied to a dominion without the dominion's consent.

Dominions were recognized as equal in rights with Great Britain. The term *British Empire*, implying domination by Britain, had been replaced by *British Commonwealth of Nations*, implying partnership with Britain. The governments of the various dominions could direct their countries' affairs as they wished.

Dominion status also meant that Britain and the dominions would have special associations with one another. They would all accept the British monarch as the symbolic head of the Commonwealth, voluntarily cooperate in matters of trade and defense, discuss at conferences questions of common interest, and plan for the solution of common problems.

Great Britain in the Middle East

The relationships between Britain and lands in the Middle East were different from her associations with the dominions. For example, Egypt was made a British

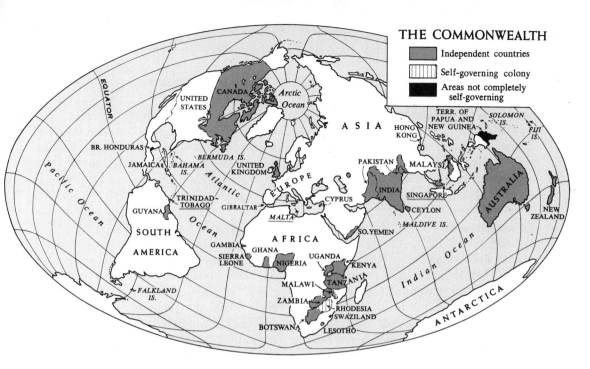

THE COMMONWEALTH

- Independent countries
- Self-governing colony
- Areas not completely self-governing

■ *The Commonwealth of Nations today includes dominions, federated countries, and areas still governed by Britain. The Commonwealth had gradually replaced the British Empire. Which countries are dominions? What is dominion status? Which areas are not completely self-governing?*

protectorate at the outbreak of World War I, a conflict in which the Turks fought against the Allies. A proclamation of 1914 ended Turkey's nominal control over Egypt, and declared that Britain would "adopt all measures necessary for the defense of Egypt, and protect its inhabitants and interests." In 1922, Britain recognized Egyptian independence, but the British kept special military and administrative rights in Egypt, particularly in the Suez Canal zone.

Palestine and Iraq also were separated from the Ottoman Empire. Palestine became a mandate of Britain under the League of Nations in 1922. Jews and Moslems continued to clash over the desire of Zionists to establish an independent state in Palestine. British power remained an important factor in the country. Iraq (once Mesopotamia) became

another British mandate. In 1932 it was recognized as an independent nation, but the British continued to exert considerable influence in Iraq.

British diplomats and administrators in Egypt, Palestine, and Iraq faced many problems: rising nationalism of native populations, demands for independence, agitation for economic reforms, and religious conflicts.

■ **Check on Your Reading**

1. Describe Britain's postwar problems.
2. Why was Ramsay MacDonald's ministry important?
3. How did the National Coalition deal with the depression?
4. How did Edward VIII's abdication affect the British government?
5. Describe Britain's relations with her dominions.

3. Developments In The United States

The postwar years in the United States were marked by domestic disorders stemming from the readjustment problems left by World War I. In 1919 there were strikes of harbor workers, dress and waist makers, cigar makers, subway workers, and steel workers for higher wages, better working conditions, or recognition of unions.

In 1919 and 1920 prices continued to rise. Shoes, for example, which before the war could be bought for $3 a pair, now sold for $10 and higher. The *Buffalo News* declared ironically: "How cheerful it is to see a $4 pair of shoes marked down from $20 to $17.98."

There were other signs of dissatisfaction and unrest: race riots, bomb scares, the wild-eyed pursuit of anyone labelled "radical," and the efforts of isolationists to "keep foreigners out" of America by means of immigration quotas. It was, as social historian Mark Sullivan pointed out, "a time of extraordinary public irritation."

"Return to Normalcy"

The man who had the responsibility for guiding the United States through these troubled times was President Warren G. Harding. In May, 1920, Harding described his task: "America's present need is not heroics, but healing; not nostrums but normalcy; not revolution but restoration . . . not surgery but serenity."

The Harding Administration (1921–1923) tried to hasten a "return to normalcy" by passing the Fordney-McCumber Act (1922), providing for the highest tariffs in American history. Efforts also were made to lessen tensions in international affairs. At the Washington Naval Armaments Conference (p. 633), plans were drawn up to limit armaments. The Harding Administration was blackened by scandals involving high officials.

The United States Enjoys an Economic "Boom"

Vice-President Calvin Coolidge succeeded to the presidency on the death of Warren Harding in 1923, and he was returned to office in the election of 1924. The United States moved into a period of rising prosperity, a time when the national debt was reduced and the personal income of many people rose rapidly.

"How the money rolls in!" was the cheerful line of one popular song of the day, and a boom was indeed on. More and more the pace of American living quickened, while the jingle of "smart money" and the blast of jazz bands covered the less pleasant side of life. However, beneath the glittering surface were indications that America was moving toward economic disaster. The farmer had never recovered from the postwar collapse of agricultural prices, while installment buying and rash stock speculation had reached fantastic volumes.

The Stock Market Collapses

The crash came during the administration of President Herbert Hoover. Near the end of October, 1929, the stock market collapsed, and the *New York Times* reported: "crowds about the ticker tape, like friends around the bedside of a stricken friend. . . ."

Soon the United States was deep in a depression that spread throughout the world. The effects of the depression were felt everywhere in America. In Ohio, the total amount paid to wage earners dropped nearly 60 per cent between 1929 and 1932. In New York City, unemployed men sold apples on street corners or tried to earn a living shining shoes. In Chicago, several hundred homeless unemployed women slept nightly in the parks. Such examples could be multiplied many times. In 1932 the average number of unemployed people in the United States was about thirteen million; and in 1935, 9 per cent of all farmers were receiving relief or rehabilitation grants from the government.

The Great Depression in the United States produced repercussions throughout the world. The depression had these world-wide effects:

(1) A sharp drop occurred in the income of American families. As a result, American consumers had far less money to spend on foreign or American goods.

(2) The depression decreased American trade with foreign countries and thus seriously weakened world commerce. In 1929 United States' imports and exports had a value of about ten billion dollars. In 1933 the value of American imports and exports had declined to about three billion dollars. The decline in the American market contributed to the closing of factories and the rise in unemployment abroad.

(3) Foreign investments by Americans declined, and American long-term loans to foreign countries were practically ended. Indeed, the depression resulted in the calling in of many American loans.

The value of many nations' currencies dropped sharply. A feeling of panic spread among many people in Europe.

Meanwhile, President Herbert Hoover and his advisers were trying earnestly to bring about an economic recovery in the United States. Their measures were not enough to stimulate an economic recovery, and the American people turned to a new president for leadership.

Roosevelt Introduces the "New Deal"

Franklin Delano Roosevelt, a Democrat who was president from 1933 to 1945, proved to be one of the most dynamic and controversial leaders in American history.

He broke precedents by being re-elected for a third and fourth term.

President Roosevelt in his first inaugural address introduced the policies and programs known as the "New Deal." Under the "New Deal," the Federal government played an extremely important part in the lives of the American people. It carried out many programs to help restore the economic health of the country. Most important for world economic conditions was the Reciprocal Trade Agreements Program. Three objectives of this program were to reduce tariffs, revive trade, and lessen international frictions by the freer movement of goods among countries.

The Reciprocal Trade Agreements Act (1934) authorized the President of the United States to negotiate trade agreements with other countries. He could lower American tariff rates by as much as 50 per cent for a three-year period, depending on the degree of cooperation of other nations. By 1940 the United States had over twenty reciprocity agreements. They helped to increase American trade with Canada and with countries in Latin America and Europe. However, the agreements were not sufficient to bring about a general major reduction of tariffs throughout the world.

Gradually, as Roosevelt continued what he called his "persistent experimentation," the United States emerged from the depression. A recession between August, 1937, and June, 1938, spurred the government to renewed efforts. The outbreak of World War II in September, 1939, ended the depression as war and defense production created new jobs.

■ Check on Your Reading

1. What economic problems were evident in the United States in the postwar years?

2. How did the depression affect the United States and the economies of other countries?

4. International Peace Efforts

At the same time that the democracies struggled with domestic problems, they and many other nations searched for peace and security in international affairs. Unfortunately, as historian Raymond P. Stearns makes clear, "national views as to what constituted *security* differed so sharply as to jeopardize *peace*." To France, security meant a weak Germany. To Great Britain, security meant a revival of British overseas trade and power. To the United States, security meant insulating the country from situations that might drag it into foreign wars. To many nations, security meant protection from Communist expansion.

The League of Nations Works for Peace

Meanwhile, the League of Nations continued to work for peace. Operating with an extremely small budget, the League helped settle a number of disputes that might have ended in conflict. The League of Nations was aided in its work of settling disputes by the Permanent Court of International Justice, known as the World Court, which handed down judgments on cases within its jurisdiction. However, the nations were free to accept or reject these decisions voluntarily.

Between 1920 and 1928 the League of Nations sponsored numerous international conferences dealing with a variety of important matters, such as the stabilization of international finance and the suppression of the trade in narcotics. It also assisted in the financial reconstruction of Austria and Hungary.

The League helped in the resettlement of war refugees, including thousands of starving refugee soldiers from Russia. In addition, it aided in the *repatriation* (the return to one's own country) of Greeks and Turks. Commissions were established by the League to examine ways to improve the health of the peoples of the world. For example, a world-wide service to warn peoples in advance of the spread of epidemics was worked out.

By association with the International Labor Organization, an independent body whose membership eventually included the United States, the League worked "to secure and maintain fair and humane conditions of labor for men, women, and children. . . ." It also published a number of scientific and technical journals to spread important information throughout the world. Further, it supervised the administration of mandates.

In the long run, the League of Nations was unable to keep the peace indefinitely because it did not have real authority to control the actions of its members. Each nation was still sovereign in domestic and foreign affairs and could do as it wished.

Alliances

One result of the search for security was the formation of alliances for protection. Between 1920 and 1921 Czechoslovakia, Yugoslavia, and Rumania—all of which had obtained land once belonging to Hungary—signed treaties forming themselves into an alliance known as the *Little Entente*. Its principal purposes were to protect the three nations against "an unprovoked attack on the part of Hungary"; and to guard against future efforts of the Hapsburgs to restore their former power.

Between 1921 and 1927 France allied herself with the Little Entente by making alliances with Czechoslovakia, Yugoslavia, and Rumania. She also completed an alliance with Poland. The French now felt more secure against Germany.

In 1922 Germany and Russia, countries which had experienced periods of upheaval, signed the Treaty of Rapallo. By this treaty Germany officially recognized the Soviet Union; and Germany and Russia cancelled their prewar debts.

Peace Pacts

In 1925, Great Britain, France, Germany, Italy, Poland, Belgium, and Czechoslovakia met in the Swiss town of Locarno to work out security pacts. Treaties were drawn up. Germany, Belgium, France, Great Britain, and Italy agreed to respect and guarantee "the frontiers between Germany and Belgium and between Germany and France" that were established by the Treaty of Versailles. However, the Locarno Treaties did not guarantee the *eastern* borders of Poland and Czechoslovakia nor the security of East Central Europe. Gustav Stresemann, the German representative, admitted: "This obligation [for guaranteeing boundaries] we undertook in the West, but we refused it in the East." The signers also agreed to settle all future disputes by arbitration and not by war.

After the Locarno Treaties were signed, Germany joined the League of Nations (1926) and took a more active part in international affairs.

In 1928 representatives of fifteen nations—including the United States, France, Great Britain, Germany, Italy, and Japan—met and drew up the Pact of Paris or the Briand-Kellogg Treaty. The Briand-Kellogg Treaty declared that its signers "condemn recourse to war for the solution of international controversies, and renounce it as an instrument of national policy in their relations with one another." It eventually was accepted by over sixty nations.

In 1933 Great Britain, France, Germany, and Italy signed a Four-Power Pact agreeing to respect the Covenant of the League of Nations, the Locarno Treaties, and the Briand-Kellogg Pact.

Disarmament Conferences

Several nations made efforts to encourage the reduction of national armaments. In 1921–22 the representatives of nine nations met in conference in Washington, D.C. The following agreements were reached: (1) The United States, Great Britain, Japan, Italy, and France set ratios (or relative sizes) for their capital ships (battleships, cruisers, and aircraft carriers). However, no limit was placed on the building of destroyers and other warships. (2) The United States, Great Britain, France, and Japan agreed to respect the rights of the others in regard to island possessions in the Pacific for ten years. (3) Nine powers agreed to respect the independence and integrity of China.

At the London Naval Conference of 1930 earlier naval reduction agreements were extended. The conference also limited the tonnage of cruisers, destroyers, and submarines. (The United States, Great Britain, and Japan accepted this; France and Italy did not.) An "escalator clause" permitted the United States, Great Britain, and Japan to exceed their limits if their national security was threatened.

The disarmament and peace pacts did not keep the peace. There were several reasons for their failure: (1) Diplomats placed national interests above treaty obligations. (2) The pacts did not have the machinery to compel nations to abide by their agreements. (3) Japan and Germany withdrew from the League of Nations in 1933, and both nations continued to build up their arms. In 1935 Germany repudiated the armament limitations of the Treaty of Versailles. Fear of attack caused other nations to prepare for war.

■ Check on Your Reading

1. What contributions did the League of Nations make to keeping peace in the world?

2. What pacts and agreements were made?

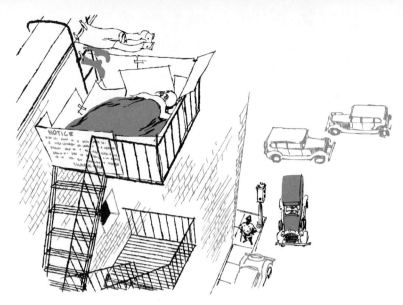

MAN AND HIS CULTURE

Let's Meet the People!

The following sketch is based on a factual account in the *New York Times* of July 9, 1932, and reprinted in *The Great Depression*, edited by David A. Shannon, Prentice-Hall.

Louis Bringmann: Unemployed

On July 8, 1932, Louis Bringmann, age 60, lay sound asleep at his "home" on the top landing of the fire escape of the Atlantic Theatre in New York City. His thin body and part of his snow-white head rested quietly beneath worn but clean-looking blankets, while above him his "socks and spotless shirt fluttered in the breeze." Around the landing, walls of corrugated cardboard that Bringmann had put up protected him from falling into the street below.

At 8 A.M. Patrolman Richard Palmay climbed the fire-escape with orders to "remove the fire hazard." He waited for an hour patiently until Bringmann awoke and came down from his perch to clean himself in a rain barrel under the copper leader. Then the patrolman said to Bringmann: "You'll have to move, old man."

"I can't stay? I'm not bothering any one. I—"

Bringmann, who once had been head chef at a Manhattan hotel, did not argue long. He put on his old blue jacket, rolled his blankets, placed his few belongings in an old sea chest, and started down the street. Patrolman Palmay hesitated a moment. Then he hurried over to Bringmann and pressed something metallic into his hand.

Bringmann headed slowly toward Tin Mountain, a village of tin huts and makeshift dugouts at the foot of Henry Street. Late in the afternoon, as he sat on the chest that contained all that he owned, he said, "The past is a turned-over page. When I read it, I read alone. They tell me now that I'm even too old for dishwashing—that's the whole story. I have no friends and my money is gone."

Then he remembered the fifty-cent piece that Patrolman Palmay had pressed into his hand, and he prepared to live in his new home in Tin Mountain.

CHAPTER REVIEW

REVIEW and DISCUSSION

1. Identify the people and places and explain the events and terms on p. 622.

2. What reasons can you find to explain the fact that war often brings an economic boom?

3. Why does the end of a great war often bring on a depression?

4. It has been said that war often contributes to creating restlessness among people, laxity of morals, and even crime. Do you agree or disagree? Why?

5. What evidence can you find of an increase in scientific progress during a war?

6. How did the depression affect France, Great Britain, and the United States? How did conditions in these countries differ?

7. Can you find any developments in the period after World War I which later helped cause the outbreak of World War II?

8. What advantages do dominions have as part of the Commonwealth of Nations?

9. Why did anti-foreign feelings develop in the United States after the war?

10. International security meant different things to different countries after World War I. Do you think it could have been achieved at that time?

11. How did the League help in paving the way for later plans for keeping the peace?

12. In your opinion, was the fact that the United States did not join the League a major reason for the League's failure? Why?

ACTIVITIES

1. Panel discussion: Is each nation more or less able than an international organization to decide how to keep world peace?

2. Debate this statement: Resolved that disarmament is necessary to world peace.

PAST and PRESENT

1. Compare the 1920's with the period from 1945 to 1955 as to economic conditions and efforts to secure world peace.

2. Compare the health commissions of the League of Nations with the World Health Organization of the United Nations.

3. Are major obstacles to world peace today the same as in the 1920's and 1930's?

SUGGESTED READINGS

Basic books: BENNS, F. LEE, *Europe Since 1914 in Its World Setting*, Appleton-Century-Crofts.

BRUUN, GEOFFREY, and MAMATEY, VICTOR, *The World in the Twentieth Century*, Chaps. 20, 21, 22, 23, and 35, Heath. A comprehensive section on postwar political and economic conditions in the democracies.

GOTTSCHALK, LOUIS, and LACH, DONALD, *The Transformation of Modern Europe* (Vol. 2 of *Europe and the Modern World*), Chaps. 11 and 12, Scott, Foresman.

LANGSAM, WALTER C., *The World Since 1919*, Macmillan. A good reference on European political history.

Special accounts: FAULKNER, HAROLD U., *From Versailles to the New Deal; a Chronicle of the Harding-Coolidge-Hoover Era* ("Chronicles of America" series), Yale University Press.

GALT, THOMAS F., *The Story of Peace and War*, Crowell. Discusses a basic problem of the twentieth century.

NEVINS, ALLAN, *The United States in a Chaotic World; a Chronicle of International Affairs, 1918–1933* (Vol. 55 in "Chronicles of America" series), Yale University Press. A distinguished historian views the postwar world.

SCHLESINGER, ARTHUR MEIER, JR., *The Crisis of the Old Order, 1919–1933*, Houghton Mifflin. Volume I of a series entitled *The Age of Roosevelt*.

Biography and Fiction: GUNTHER, JOHN, *Roosevelt in Retrospect, a Profile in History*, Harper. Covers professional and political as well as personal life.

WHITE, WILLIAM, *A Puritan in Babylon*, Macmillan. A biography of Coolidge.

Chapter 40

World War II:
"The War for Survival"

KEYNOTE On September 12, 1945, in a hall bedecked with flags, an announcer stepped to the microphone and said:

Ladies and gentlemen, from the Exhibition Hall of the [United States] National Archives in our Nation's Capital is brought to you a special ceremony during which the original Japanese surrender documents will be placed on public display.

The documents that brought World War II to a close were then officially opened to public inspection. There they were—in a case in the center of the hall with military guards of honor.

There were speeches that day, praising the heroism of men. There were also silences as meaningful as words. Perhaps the most significant observation of all came from President Harry S. Truman. In a special message he declared, "[These documents] are only sheets of paper, some of them written in a language most of us cannot read, but they are an eternal reminder of that indomitable courage of our fighting forces and of the home front that led us . . . to final victory."

Most individuals already have forgotten those words. But millions of people in nations throughout the world will never forget that war. *An outstanding feature of history from 1931 to 1945 was the events leading to World War II and the terrible conflict itself.*

Key People *Winston Churchill · General Erwin Rommel · Franklin Roosevelt · General George C. Marshall · General Dwight D. Eisenhower · General Douglas MacArthur*

Key Places *Manchuria · Ethiopia · Spain · Rhineland · Austria · Sudetenland · Poland · Finland · Dunkirk · Philippines · Burma · Guam · Normandy · Okinawa*

Key Events *Fall of France · Pearl Harbor attacked · Invasion of North Africa · "D-Day" · Potsdam Conference · V-J Day*

Key Terms *blitzkrieg · collective security · Yalta Agreements · atomic bomb*

1. The League of Nations Is Defied

On September 19, 1931, Toshikazu Kase, a Japanese delegate to the League of Nations, walked into the dining room of the Hotel Metropole in Geneva, Switzerland, for his morning coffee. He sipped his coffee contentedly as he turned to his morning newspaper. On the very last page was a news report that shattered Kase's peaceful world. It declared that on September 18 Japanese and Chinese forces had clashed in Manchuria, a region that legally belonged to China. Fighting had broken out again in the Far East!

According to Kase, the news of the fighting came as a surprise to him. That was to be expected, for the Japanese Kwantung army had attacked the Chinese in Manchuria. The commanders of that army were not in the habit of notifying diplomats and statesmen of their plans.

Despite the headstrong and independent action of the Kwantung army, not all Japanese leaders approved of a program of war and conquest. Japanese leadership in the post-World War I period was divided in matters of policy. There were many disagreements between militarists and civilian statesmen.

In 1931, however, militarists and men ambitious for empire had increased influence in Japan. Thus, after the Kwantung army had conquered many miles of territory, the Japanese set up the so-called "independent" state of *Manchukuo* in Manchuria (1932). Actually, Manchukuo was under the domination of Japan.

The affair in Manchuria was of worldwide importance, because it tested the strength of the League of Nations. The League made an investigation and issued the Lytton Commission Report, which recommended that the state of Manchukuo as set up by the Japanese should not continue. It suggested the establishment of a different type of government.

Japan refused to accept the report. In 1933 she withdrew from the League of Nations. Japan *defied* the League. And almost nothing was done to punish her!

Japan's successful defiance of the League of Nations greatly weakened the prestige of that international organization. It made dictators in other nations feel that they too could break international rules and get away with it.

Japan Seizes Chinese Territory

From about 1933 to the middle of 1937 there was comparative quiet in the struggle between Japan and China. However, the Japanese people continued to be filled with propaganda for war.

637

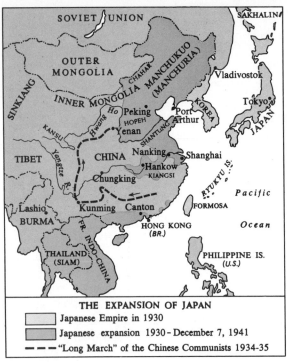

THE EXPANSION OF JAPAN

Japanese Empire in 1930

Japanese expansion 1930 - December 7, 1941

— — — "Long March" of the Chinese Communists 1934-35

■ *Between 1931 and 1941 Japan built up an empire in the Pacific through armed conquest. What territories did she gain control over?*

Then, in July, 1937, Japan used an incident near Peking to fight an undeclared war on China. This time Japan gained control of a considerable part of China (map, p. 638). The Japanese attempted to integrate the economic life of Japan, Manchukuo, and Occupied China into a so-called "Co-prosperity Sphere." Some Japanese military leaders dreamed of *Hakko Ichiyu*—"the four corners of the earth under one [Japanese] roof." Chinese patriots were determined to see that this did not come true.

Italy Conquers Ethiopia

At about the same time that Japan was expanding in the Far East, the Fascist government of Italy became hungry for empire in Africa. In 1935 dictator Benito Mussolini sent Italian troops into Africa to conquer Ethiopia (map, p. 640).

Italy's invasion of Ethiopia was a clear case of aggresstion. Haile Selassie, the emperor of Ethiopia, called on the League of Nations to check the Italian aggressor. Several important member nations of the League hesitated to stop Italy. Some feared that strong action against the Fascists would lead to a major war. Others were more concerned with their own welfare than with the future of Ethiopia.

The League of Nations eventually placed some economic sanctions against Italy. However, all of the members of the League did not apply these sanctions. In addition, the oil that was necessary for war continued to be shipped to Italy. As a result, Italy defeated Ethiopia.

Spain Is Torn by a Civil War

About a year after the Italians invaded Ethiopia, a civil war broke out in Spain and its colonies. The Spanish Civil War (1936–39) was not the result of a foreign plot but was *Spanish* in origin.

Spain had become a republic in 1931, but the new government had not been able to solve the country's many problems. There was still great poverty, injustice in land ownership, and lack of stable government. There was also hatred between monarchists and republicans, Church and anti-Church groups, and army and civilian leaders. As a result of these and other factors, army leaders rebelled against the Spanish Republic in July, 1936.

The *Rebels* eventually were led by General Francisco Franco. Those who opposed the Rebels where known as the *Loyalists*. In time Spain became an "international battleground." Italy and Germany supported Franco with men and material. The Soviet Union later aided the Loyalists, and volunteers from several countries came to fight against Franco.

Franco and many of the Rebels were Fascists, and some of the Loyalists were

Communists. However, the Spanish Civil War was *not* simply a war between Fascism and communism. Certainly, many of the men who fought and died for the Loyalists did so because they hoped to save democracy in Spain and not because they wanted a communist state. There were men on both sides fighting for reasons that had little to do with a love for either fascism or communism. The struggle in Spain was a bitter one filled with the drama and tragedy that comes from civil bloodshed. Supported by most of the army, Franco finally defeated the Loyalists.

Franco proceeded to establish a Fascist dictatorship in Spain. One of the early decrees of the Spanish Fascists declared, ". . . the leader [Franco] assumes absolute authority. He is responsible only to God and to history."

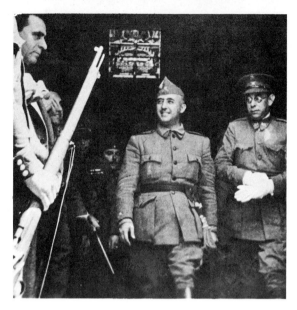

■ *General Francisco Franco, Rebel Commander-in-Chief in Spain, and one of his generals are leaving for a tour of inspection.*

German Power Spreads through Europe

Of all the aggressor nations of the 1930's none had a worse record than the Nazis. "The German Government . . . will scrupulously observe every treaty voluntarily signed by them, even if it was drawn up before they took over the Government and power," Hitler said in 1935. Yet in the same year Hitler announced that Germany would increase the size of the German army in violation of the Treaty of Versailles. A year later Germany again broke the Versailles Treaty by reoccupying the Rhineland (map, p. 640).

In 1935 Hitler said: "Germany has neither the intention nor the will to interfere in domestic Austrian affairs, to annex Austria, or to unite Austria with the Reich [Germany]." Yet in 1938 Hitler sent troops into Austria and annexed the country. Such annexation had been forbidden by the treaties ending World War I.

In 1938 Hitler demanded that the Sudetenland be ceded to Germany. This was an area in Czechoslovakia occupied by about three and a half million Sudeten Germans. The Czechs, who were the allies of France, Russia, and other nations, refused to submit to the Nazi demands. The threat of a major European war was serious.

In this time of crisis an important meeting was held in Munich, Germany, to decide the fate of Czechoslovakia. Great Britain, France, Germany, and Italy attended the meeting; but the Soviet Union and Czechoslovakia were not even invited. As a result of the pact drawn up at Munich (1938), the four powers agreed to cede the Sudetenland to Germany (map, p. 640). War was temporarily avoided by *appeasement*—that is, by giving in to Hitler.

Many people rejoiced that the Munich Pact seemed to have kept the peace. Prime Minister Neville Chamberlain, the British representative at Munich, declared that he had brought home "peace with honor." A writer for an important French newspaper, *Paris-Soir*, proclaimed: "Peace! Peace! Peace! The world can breathe again; we

GERMAN AND ITALIAN
AGGRESSION 1935-1939

■ *Germany violated the Versailles Treaty, and both Italy and Germany defied the League of Nations by the following acts of aggression: Italy conquered (1) Ethiopia, 1935; and occupied (7) Albania, 1939; Germany seized (2) the Rhineland, 1936; (3) Austria, 1938; (4) the Sudetenland, 1938; (5) the rest of Czechoslovakia, 1939; (6) Memel and Danzig, 1939; and (8) Poland, 1939.*

still can live!" And Adolf Hitler, even before the Munich conference, promised that the Sudetenland was "the last territorial demand I have to make in Europe." Then, on March 15, 1939, Adolf Hitler broke the Munich Pact and took possession of the rest of Czechoslovakia!

By 1939 Europe was on the brink of war. The plan to keep peace by *collective security*—that is, by having the countries of the world work together through the League of Nations to check aggressors—

had deteriorated. In the 1930's a number of vital questions were decided by pacts outside of the League or by appeasement.

It soon became clear that the principal aggressor nations were banding into a bloc. In 1936 Germany and Italy reached an agreement to support each other in international affairs. Mussolini called this alliance an *Axis* between Rome and Berlin.

In the same year Germany and Japan signed the Anti-Comintern Pact, agreeing to cooperate to check the activities of the

Comintern. In 1937 Italy joined the pact. Events showed that the members of the Anti-Comintern Pact were as much opposed to democracy as they were to communism. The *Rome-Berlin-Tokyo Axis*, as the Italian-German-Japanese bloc eventually was called, endangered both the democracies and the peace of the world.

■ **Check on Your Reading**

1. How did the League of Nations deal with Japanese aggression in Manchuria?

2. Why did Italy succeed in its conquest of Ethiopia?

3. Why did civil war erupt in Spain? Which group finally obtained power?

4. How did Nazi Germany increase its territory? What areas did it occupy?

2. World War II Erupts in Europe

On August 23, 1939, a startling event occurred. Germany and the Soviet Union, bitter enemies for years, signed a non-aggression pact! In it they agreed:

... to refrain from any act of force, any aggressive action and any attack on one another, both singly and also jointly with other Powers; and ... [not to] participate in any grouping of Powers which is directed directly or indirectly against [Germany or Russia]. ...

There was also a secret protocol which included a provision that Germany and Russia would each obtain control of territory in Poland "in the event of a territorial and political rearrangement of the areas belonging to the Polish state. . . ."

To Adolf Hitler, the Russo-German Nonaggression Pact was a green light for Nazi aggression. On September 1, 1939, German troops invaded Poland. Great Britain and France had promised to support Poland in case of attack. This time they did *not* back down. On September 3, 1939, both nations declared war on Germany. World War II had come to Europe!

Poland and Finland Fall

The powerful German war machine struck quickly at Poland. German tanks cut through the Polish forces like scissors through paper. German planes dropped deadly loads of bombs on soldiers and on civilians alike. German motorized infantry gained their objectives with the precision of men following a time-table. About two weeks after Germany attacked the Poles, the Soviet Union invaded Poland from the east. Sandwiched between the advancing steel of two strong armies, the Polish defense collapsed. Poland was conquered in one month, and Germany and Russia divided the country. This was indeed a *blitzkrieg*, a conquest of lightning speed.

In November, 1939, the Soviet Union deliberately invaded Finland. After meeting surprisingly fierce resistance, the Russians finally defeated the Finns.

By November, 1940, through force or the threat of force, the Soviet Union had gained considerable territory. This included (in addition to land in Finland and Eastern Poland) Estonia, Latvia, Lithuania, and Bessarabia.

The Germans Smash Their Way to the Channel

Meanwhile there was a period of calm on the western front. The French remained stationed in their defensive positions in the Maginot Line (p. 625). Many of their generals still were thinking in terms of the trench warfare of World War I and of armies slowly inching forward. They did not understand the nature of blitzkrieg war.

In April, 1940, the Germans invaded Norway and Denmark. King Christian X of Denmark protested bitterly. However, to prevent the useless loss of lives, he accepted Nazi occupation of his country. In Norway there was rugged fighting. German military strength and effective use of air power, plus subversive activities of a group of pro-Nazi Norwegians (later known as "Quislings"), forced the Norwegian armies to surrender on June 9, 1940. King Haakon VII of Norway and his governmental leaders defiantly set up a government-in-exile in London. The conquest of Denmark and Norway was important because it provided Germany with harbors for her ships, bases for her submarines and planes, and food supplies.

Meanwhile in May, without giving warning, German troops invaded the Netherlands, Belgium, and Luxembourg. The lightning movements of German motorized infantry, planes, and paratroopers quickly defeated the Netherlands.

In Belgium, King Leopold III called for the aid of the Allies, and French and British armies moved into the country to meet the German offensive. The Germans could not be stopped. They attacked powerfully and, by clever strategy, split the Allied armies. To the anger and dismay of many Belgians, King Leopold surrendered to the Germans on May 28, 1940.

The fall of Belgium left the Allied forces unprotected on one side, and a large part of the Allied troops were driven back to the city of Dunkirk, along the English Channel. With the sea in front of them and the Germans pressing in on all sides— "like a sharp scythe" the British Prime Minister Winston Churchill described it— it seemed that they were doomed.

The thousands of Allied troops who were on the beaches at Dunkirk were fiercely attacked for several days. They were bombed by hostile aircraft, which came over with one hundred planes in each formation. They were machine-gunned in the sand dunes where they lay. They were blasted by artillery fire that jeopardized the single pier that still stood. And yet the British navy and hundreds of small private craft, aided by the Royal Air Force, were able to evacuate over 335,000 men across the Channel to England.

The voice of Prime Minister Winston Churchill took on new determination as he told the world of the events at Dunkirk and concluded, ". . . we shall defend our Island . . . we shall never surrender. . . . "

France Falls

In June, 1940, a new German blitzkrieg cut around the French stationary positions, and the plan of defense by the Maginot Line proved useless. At the same time Italy, eager to be in on the prizes of victory, entered the war on the side of Germany. Then, on June 22, 1940, a defeated France signed an armistice with Germany. The fall of France was a heavy blow to liberty-loving people in Europe. A British doctor wrote: "I weep for France, and weep with Europe's eyes."

France was divided into two zones. One was occupied and governed by the Germans. The other was not occupied by the victors; it was in southern France with its government at Vichy (map, p. 646). Although this Vichy government was headed by a Frenchman, Marshal Pétain, it collaborated with the Germans.

Some Frenchmen refused to surrender or to live under Vichy rule. They escaped from France and continued to work against the Germans. General Charles de Gaulle became leader of these men. His resistance group was known as "Free France."

Britain Has Its "Finest Hour"

German forces controlled a considerable part of Europe. Great Britain was the only major Allied power that stood between Germany and complete victory.

The British government remained defiant. The Germans sent their bombers over England day after day. Then night after night. Bombs destroyed buildings that had stood for centuries—fires gutted homes once warmed by hearths—men and women died with mounds of rubble as their only monuments. Everywhere the wail of the air-raid siren turned busy cities into ghost towns as people hurried for underground shelters. Yet the more bombs that fell, the more stubbornly the people of Britain refused to surrender.

The British faced a deadlier peril. Since nearly all food and munitions supplies from Europe were cut off, supplies had to be imported from across the Atlantic. German submarines patrolled the seas, attacked merchant ships, and seriously interfered with the shipment of goods. The British faced the threat of starvation, but again they would not give in. Instead they used their ships and planes and improved their antisubmarine mines and other devices to cope with the threat.

In June, 1940, Winston Churchill had declared:

Let us therefore brace ourselves to our duties, and so bear ourselves that . . . men will say, "This was their finest hour."

In the terrible months of bombing that started in July, 1940, and continued into 1941 the British people did everything possible to make this "their finest hour." Hitler, who overestimated the actual military strength of the British defenses, decided to postpone the invasion of England!

Germany Invades the Soviet Union

The year 1941 brought additional dramatic and important events. Germany helped Italy to take Greece and crushed Yugoslavia. In Africa, a German army

■ *London air-raid wardens and firemen are putting out fires and assessing bomb damage after a German air raid in May, 1941.*

under General Erwin Rommel, the "Desert Fox," attacked the British in Libya and made its way into Egypt. Then, on June 22, 1941—though Germany and Russia had signed a nonaggression pact—the Germans invaded Russia.

The conquest of Russia had long been a dream of Hitler. However, he had misjudged the strength, courage, and determination of the Russians. His armies killed many Soviet soldiers. They captured considerable Soviet territory. They came close to Moscow itself. Yet they could not force the Russians to surrender.

Russian armies and civilians continued to defend their country through days of merciless bombings, through months of German shell fire, through periods of near starvation. Losses were terrible but still the Russians would not surrender. By 1943, after heroic defenses at Stalingrad and other cities, the Russian armies were preparing counter-offensives to force the Germans to surrender.

The United States Passes the Lend-Lease Act

While the Russians and the British were fighting desperately to hold back the Axis in Europe, the United States remained officially neutral. Nevertheless, Americans were becoming increasingly sympathetic to those nations opposing Nazism and Fascism. Thus, in March of 1941, the United States passed the Lend-Lease Act. This act made it possible for the President of the United States, Franklin Roosevelt, to lend or lease military supplies and ships to the anti-Axis powers.

■ **Check on Your Reading**

1. Describe the "blitzkrieg" warfare of the Germans.
2. How was France divided after its defeat by the Germans?
3. What happened when the Germans invaded the Soviet Union?

3. World War II Becomes Global

It took a sudden Japanese attack to bring the United States into World War II. This attack came at the end of a decade of tension between the American and Japanese governments. The Japanese were angered by the United States' opposition to Japanese expansion in the Far East and Southeast Asia. The United States criticized Japanese aggression in China, particularly the bombings of civilians. The Americans refused to recognize Manchukuo; permitted aid to be sent to Chiang Kai-shek's government in China; and eventually restricted the export to Japan of war materials, such as steel scrap and oil. One reason the Japanese wanted to conquer the Netherlands East Indies was to replenish their supply of oil.

Although some Japanese leaders did not want war with the United States, many people in Japan were convinced that Japan was right in taking actions that other countries called imperialistic.

Japan Attacks Pearl Harbor

Thus, on the morning of December 7, 1941, over 250 Japanese planes took off from their aircraft carriers and attacked Pearl Harbor, the American naval base in the Hawaiian Islands. This sudden attack came *before* Japan had formally declared war on the United States.

Unalerted American battleships were sunk or damaged by bombs and torpedo strikes. Unprepared American destroyers and cruisers were ripped apart in the harbor. Unwarned American pilots had little chance to get their planes in the air and saw most of them burn on the ground. As a result of the attack at Pearl Harbor and nearby areas, most of the American Pacific Fleet was destroyed or damaged.

On December 8, 1941, a solemn but determined President Roosevelt asked Congress to declare that "a state of war [now exists] between the United States and the Japanese Empire." The next evening, in a special radio address, he told the nation:

[The attack on Pearl Harbor] was a thoroughly dishonorable deed, but we must face the fact that modern warfare as conducted in the Nazi manner is a dirty business. We don't like it—we didn't want to get in it—but we are in it, and we're going to fight it with everything we've got.

■ *This shows a section of Pearl Harbor, Hawaii, shortly after the Japanese surprise attack, December 7, 1941. Most of the American Pacific Fleet was destroyed or damaged as a result of the Japanese surprise attack, which was the official beginning of World War II in the Pacific.*

On December 8, the United States and Great Britain declared war on Japan. Shortly after, Germany and Italy declared war on the United States, and the United States issued its own declaration of war against these two nations. The war soon became global.

The War in Asia

In the year that followed the United States' entry into the war, the military situation remained critical in Asia. Japan had launched attacks on the Philippines and other areas at about the same time that she had bombed Pearl Harbor. She quickly extended her control over Guam, Wake Island, and the Philippines. When General Douglas MacArthur, commander of all United States Armed Forces in the Far East, was forced to leave the Philippine Islands, he made the vow: "I shall return!" Burma, Thailand, Malaya, including British controlled Singapore, the Netherlands East Indies, and Indo-China also came under the control of the Japanese. Japan had gained power over lands rich in tin, rubber, oil, and other resources important for war.

The Chinese declared war on Germany, Italy, and Japan on December 8, 1941, and the conflict in China was still indecisive. Here the Chinese Nationalists under Chiang Kai-shek and the Chinese Communists agreed—at least, on the surface—to forget their differences during the war and to join in a common fight against the Japanese aggressor.

■ **Check on Your Reading**

1. What factors caused hostility between Japan and the United States?

2. Describe the Japanese attack on Pearl Harbor.

3. Over which territories did Japan quickly extend her control?

4. Describe the situation in China.

4. The Allies Turn the Tide to Victory

General George C. Marshall, chief of staff of the United States Army in World War II, and others worked hard to take the offensive. Despite the success of the Japanese, the United States decided to drive back the Axis in Europe before embarking on widespread operations against Japan. North Africa was chosen for an Allied attack.

The invasion of North Africa was considered important for several reasons: (1) This attack might relieve some of the pressure on the Russians by drawing German troops into Africa. (2) The Suez Canal needed additional protection. (3) African bases could be used for future attacks on the Axis in Europe.

■ *Germany's powerful war machine quickly conquered all of western Europe except Britain. What territories did the Axis nations control at the height of their power? To combat the Axis, the Allies launched an invasion in North Africa and then in Sicily and southern Italy. Finally, Allied forces invaded France. What factors aided the Allies to achieve victory?*

THE WAR IN EUROPE
AND NORTH AFRICA

■ Axis Powers ⬚ Neutral states
■ Greatest extent of Axis expansion
■ Allied Powers and occupied areas
⇨ Main Allied advances

■ *General Dwight D. Eisenhower talks to paratroopers, who are ready to board planes to cross the English Channel as part of the invasion of Europe in June, 1944. Land, sea, and air forces all collaborated in the great invasion.*

Thus in November, 1942, after the British Eighth Army under General Bernard Montgomery had driven Rommel's *Afrika Korps* out of Egypt, Allied forces invaded North Africa. This invasion army, which included Americans and British, was under the command of General Dwight D. Eisenhower. The fighting soon became bitter as Eisenhower's troops met determined German opposition. Bloody battles were fought on sandy ridges whipped by the wind, on desert flats baked by the hot sun, on dark roads lighted by nightly artillery barrages. By May, 1943, Eisenhower's forces controlled all of North Africa.

From North Africa the United Nations' troops invaded Sicily and southern Italy. Mussolini was denounced by a number of Italian leaders. General Emilio de Bono, one of his generals, even called him "a rascal, a roadside juggler, a clown . . . [a] coward." Mussolini was stripped of all power, his Fascist régime fell, and a new Italian government was established. In northern Italy the Germans continued to block the Allied advance.

"D-Day"!

At last—after weeks in which Allied planes had dropped many bombs on Nazi airports, ammunition depots, and supply centers—the time had come for the invasion of France itself. On June 6, 1944 ("D-Day"), Allied forces under the supreme command of General Eisenhower sailed from the British Isles and landed on the French beaches at Normandy. The American troops were directed by General Omar Bradley, and the British and Canadian were led by General Montgomery.

The Allies came with much equipment and men: with ships and planes and landing craft—with jeeps and trucks and half-trucks—with M-1 rifles and mortars and machine guns—and, most important of all, with men who knew they were expendable. The invasion was a bloody one, but the Allied troops held on. Then they slowly pushed inland. Behind them, on the beaches, the soldiers left vivid evidence of the world they once had known. War correspondent Ernie Pyle reported: "[Strewn on the beach] there were socks and shoe polish, sewing kits, diaries, Bibles . . . the latest letters from home . . . toothbrushes and razors, and snapshots of families back home . . . [and] a tennis racket that some soldier had brought along. It lay lonesomely on the sand, clamped in its press, not a string broken." Behind them, too,

647

the Allies left the men who had given up their lives to clear a way for those who were to follow.

Allied Victories Force Germany to Surrender

The fighting broadened out. Eisenhower's troops smashed through the German lines and moved eastward. Another Allied army successfully invaded southern France on August 15, 1944. Paris was liberated on August 25, and General de Gaulle was hailed for his wartime leadership. Then a desperate German counteroffensive in the Ardennes region in winter was checked at the so-called "Battle of the Bulge." Meanwhile the Russians pushed back the Germans in the east.

The Allied forces rolled forward rapidly. Eisenhower's troops crossed the Rhine. General Mark Clark, the American commander of all Allied forces in Italy, accepted the surrender of a million German and Italian soldiers. And the Russians, under Marshal Zhukov, pushed on toward Berlin.

In April, 1945, as Eisenhower's forces from the west and the Russians from the east drew ever closer to each other, a desperate Hitler shouted: "Nothing now remains! Nothing is spared me!" On April 30 he committed suicide. Germany surrendered unconditionally on May 7–8, 1945. The war in Europe was ended!

The Allies Attack in the Pacific

While the war in Europe was being fought, the conflict in the Pacific was increasing in tempo. Here American strategy was directed by General Marshall, General MacArthur, Admiral Ernest J. King, commander-in-chief of the United States Fleet in World War II, and Admiral Chester W. Nimitz, chief of the United States Pacific Fleet. These are some of the highlights of the fighting in the Pacific area.

There were great sea and air battles. A Japanese drive toward Australia was stopped at the battle of the Coral Sea (May, 1942). A Japanese invasion fleet attempted to take Midway Island (June, 1942) as a stepping stone to Hawaii and failed. American planes sank four Japanese aircraft carriers and seriously weakened Japanese naval air power.

American, Australian, and other Allied troops began an "island hopping" campaign to by-pass Japanese garrisons and recapture strategic islands from the Japanese. These islands then were used for new Allied attacks. One of the most dramatic events was the liberation of the Philippines in October, 1944.

In 1945, the Japanese stronghold at Okinawa was taken by the Allied forces. This island gave the Allies air bases close to Japan. Thus the Allies defeated or by-passed Japanese military units. Allied leaders now faced the task of carrying out a final offensive against Japan.

The War in China

Meanwhile, conditions in China were becoming increasingly complicated. The Allies tried in many ways to help the Chinese in their fight against the Japanese. Thus, General Joseph W. ("Vinegar Joe") Stilwell, who commanded the United States forces in the China-Burma-India area during World War II, served as chief of staff to Chiang Kai-shek beginning in March, 1942. (The two men later disagreed on policies, and General Stilwell was reassigned to Washington, D. C.)

The Western powers also tried to aid the Chinese by sending supplies into China by way of the 800-mile Burma Road. When the Japanese conquered Burma (1942), this supply route was closed. Some war materials were flown over the Himalayan Mountains (the "Hump") from India by unarmed C-47 transport planes. According to

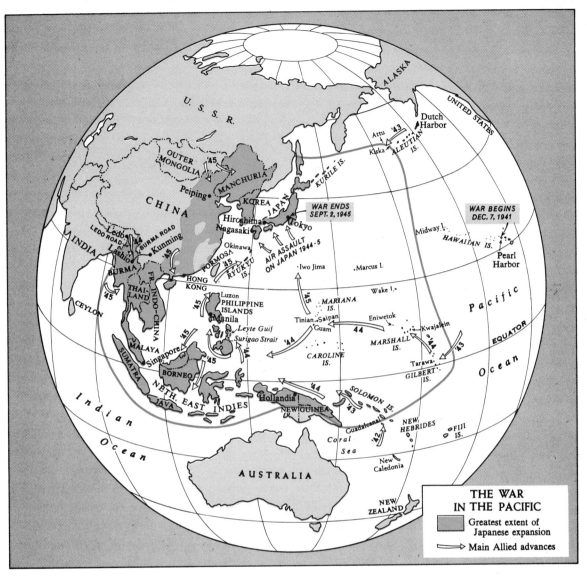

■ *In the Pacific, Japanese forces quickly seized Guam, Wake Island, and the Philippines. Burma, Thailand, Malaya, Singapore, and other areas fell to the Japanese onslaught, too. How far did the Japanese advance before they were stopped? Describe conditions in China in World War II.*

historian Louis L. Snyder, in May, 1942, only 80 tons of supplies were delivered in this way; by February, 1943, some 3,200 tons were flown across the "Hump." Work also was started on building and defending a new road west of the Burma Road. This was known as the Stilwell or Ledo Road.

At the same time that Chiang Kai-shek and his troops were fighting the Japanese, Chiang continued to work to strengthen his position against the Chinese Communists. There were indications that both Chiang's Chinese Nationalists and the Chinese Communists often were more concerned with building up their power against each other

649

■ *Chiang Kai-shek's Chinese troops in 1944 turned temporarily from fighting Chinese Communists to concentrate on Japanese aggressors.*

than in working as a team against the Japanese forces.

In 1943 Roosevelt, Churchill, and Chiang Kai-shek met in Cairo and reached several agreements. This *Cairo Conference* proved to be particularly important in the postwar struggle between the Nationalists and the Communists. One of its decisions was that Japan must return to China all territory—including the island of Formosa —that she had seized from the Chinese.

Finally, at the end of January, 1945, the Allies stopped a Japanese drive to India and regained control of Burma. The Ledo Road was joined with the Burma Road, and the Japanese position in China was greatly weakened.

The Yalta Agreements Are Signed

In February, 1945, the month after the Allies regained Burma from the Japanese, President Roosevelt, Prime Minister Churchill, and Joseph Stalin of the Soviet Union held an important conference at Yalta in the Crimea. One of the results of this meeting was that Russia agreed to enter the war against Japan. In return, Russia was to be given (1) the southern part of Sakhalin and the islands adjacent to it, and the Kurile Islands, (2) certain rights in Manchuria, and (3) other territorial privileges in the Far East.

There is considerable controversy over these provisions of the Yalta Agreements and over the decisions concerning Europe that were reached at Yalta. Some people claim that these agreements were undesirable and dangerous for several reasons: (1) They weakened the position of Chiang Kai-shek's anti-Communist government in China by strengthening Russia's power in the Far East. For example, Russian troops took northeast China from Japan in the closing days of World War II. Then, when the Russians pulled their troops out of the area in 1946, they made it possible for the Chinese Communists to take over cities in the region. (2) They permitted Communist power to expand in Manchuria and Korea.

Other people declare that, under the circumstances, the Yalta Agreements concerning the Far East were as good as could be expected. They point to the following: (1) It was the official opinion of American and British military chiefs (an opinion not shared by several American admirals) that it would take about eighteen months after the completion of the war in Europe to defeat Japan—even · with Russia's aid. The Allied leaders wanted to end the Pacific conflict as quickly and with as little loss of life as possible. It was therefore logical for them to give territory to Russia in exchange for military support that would help defeat Japan.

(2) The fact that Russia later broke her word on certain provisions of the Yalta

Agreements was no reason to condemn the agreements themselves. For example, the Soviet Union agreed at Yalta that "China shall retain full sovereignty in Manchuria." Yet later Russia supported aggressive actions in Manchuria. Russia—not Yalta—was at fault. The Yalta Agreements will remain a controversial subject.

Atomic Bombs—and Peace at Last!

In keeping with the Yalta Agreements, the Soviet Union later entered the war against Japan. Events showed that Russia's aid was not needed to end the conflict.

In the summer of 1945 the Japanese faced almost certain defeat. Nevertheless, they refused to stop fighting. The Allied leaders decided to take drastic action. At the Potsdam Conference in July, 1945, President Harry S. Truman (who had become chief executive of the United States on the death of Roosevelt), Prime Minister Clement Attlee of Great Britain, and Joseph Stalin of Russia agreed to send an ultimatum to the Japanese government. This ultimatum demanded that the Japanese surrender unconditionally or face terrible destruction to their country. And still Japan would not surrender!

It was decided to force the Japanese into a quick surrender by using the *atomic bomb*, recently brought to a successful operational point by American scientists. Thus, on the morning of August 6, 1945, one atomic bomb was dropped on the city of Hiroshima. According to a report edited by Ashley W. Oughterson, Clinical Professor of Surgery at Yale University School of Medicine, and Shields Warren, Professor of Pathology at Harvard Medical School, the bomb equalled in energy 20,000 tons of TNT, "more than 1800 times the weight of the largest high-explosive bomb used in World War II."

The atomic bomb exploded above the heart of Hiroshima. According to the Oughterson-Warren report, there was a bluish-white glare like "a prolonged lightning flash," a burst of radiant heat from the bomb's "fireball," and a terrible blast. Then "the sun was obscured, the [city was] shrouded in a pall of yellow, white, and brown smoke for about twenty minutes."

Months later, after scientists had investigated the effects of the bomb at Hiroshima, the following results became known: Approximately 64,000 of the city's total population of about 255,000 were dead by the middle of November, and thousands of people were injured by blast, heat, and ionizing radiation. Approximately 60,000 of 90,000 buildings within 9.5 square miles were destroyed or badly damaged, and most of Hiroshima was destroyed. All of this was the work of *one* atomic bomb.

Events moved rapidly. A few days after the bomb was dropped on Hiroshima, Russia entered the war against Japan and invaded Manchuria. President Harry S. Truman again demanded that Japan surrender. When she did not, a second atomic bomb was dropped, this time on the city of Nagasaki (August 9, 1945). Five days later, Japan surrendered.

In September the Japanese representative, Mamoru Shigemitsu, signed the instrument of formal surrender. Then he stopped, checked the wrist watch of another Japanese delegate, and carefully wrote down the time. It was 9:04 A.M., September 2, 1945, almost exactly six years from the Nazi attack on Poland in September, 1939.

■ **Check on Your Reading**

1. Why did the Allies launch an attack on North Africa?

2. How did the Allies defeat Germany?

3. What tactics did the Allies use in the Pacific?

4. What problems did China face?

5. Describe the results of the atomic bomb.

MAN AND HIS CULTURE

Sergeant Frank "Buck" Eversole Sergeant Frank "Buck" Eversole of Idaho was a platoon sergeant in a line company of the 34th Infantry Division. As such, he was non-commissioned officer in charge of about forty combat soldiers.

"Buck" did a good job as platoon sergeant. Several times he almost lost his life. Once a shell hit the room in which he was sitting—but did not go off. Another time he advanced through a mine field that killed everyone in his squad—but no mine exploded beneath him.

For more than a year "Buck" did everything that he could to see that the new men, and the handful of veterans, survived. Then one day it was his turn to leave the platoon and go to the rear for a five day rest. "Buck" should have been pleased, but he wasn't. He knew that his outfit was going to attack that night and he wanted to be with it. "Buck" therefore hurried over to Lieutenant Sheehy, his commanding officer.

"Lieutenant," he said, "I'll stay if you need me."

"Of course I need you, 'Buck'," answered his lieutenant, "I always need you. But it's your turn and I want you to go. In fact, you're ordered to go."

That evening, against his will, "Buck" left his platoon for a few days of rest. He kept his eyes down as he slowly walked towards the truck that was to take him away. Then he quietly said: "This is the first battle I've ever missed that this battalion has been in. . . . *I feel like a deserter.*"

Sergeant Frank "Buck" Eversole—the man who felt like a "deserter"—already had been awarded one Purple Heart and two Silver Star medals for bravery in action!

CHAPTER REVIEW

REVIEW and DISCUSSION

1. Identify the people and places and explain the events and terms on p. 636.

2. What action do you think the League of Nations should have taken against Japan in the Manchurian affair and against Italy in Ethiopia? Why?

3. Can you explain why leaders of nations at first accepted Hitler's word that he would not take any more territories?

4. Do you think appeasement was a successful policy from 1935 to 1939? Why or why not?

5. Compare the immediate cause of World War II with the immediate cause of World War I.

6. Why do the British people speak of the Battle of Britain in 1940 as their "finest hour"?

7. Compare Hitler's invasion of Russia in 1941 with Napoleon's invasion in 1812.

8. Do you think the United States was remaining neutral when it passed the Lend-Lease Act? Why?

9. Review German military strategy and decide where you think Hitler made mistakes which led to his downfall. Give evidence to support your answer.

10. Do you think the Yalta Agreements aided or harmed the Allied cause? Why?

11. What questions of moral judgment and expediency were involved in the decision to drop the atomic bomb on Japan?

12. Compare and contrast Hitler, Franco, and Mussolini as dictators. What generalizations can you make?

ACTIVITIES

1. Compile a list of the underlying causes of World War II and compare them with the causes of World War I.

2. Write a report on Adolf Hitler. Try to find the reasons for his successful rise to power.

3. Write a report on Winston Churchill. Try to find the reasons for his strength as a war-time leader.

4. Add the following to your paperback library: Latourette, *History of the Far East*; Tiedemann, *Modern Japan, A Brief History*; Rothberg and others, *Eyewitness History of World War II: Blitzkrieg*.

PAST and PRESENT

1. Compare the efforts to keep peace before World War II with efforts to keep the peace today.

2. If nuclear bombs had been as powerful in 1945 as they are today, would it have been justifiable to use them against the Axis nations? Justify your answer.

SUGGESTED READINGS

Basic books: BRUUN, GEOFFREY, and MAMATEY, VICTOR S., *The World in the Twentieth Century*, Chaps. 38–45, Heath.

GOTTSCHALK, LOUIS, and LACH, DONALD, *The Transformation of Modern Europe* (Vol. 2 of Europe and the Modern World), Chaps. 13, 14, Scott, Foresman.

SMITH, GOLDWIN, *The Heritage of Man*, Chap. 46, Scribner.

Special accounts: BLIVEN, BRUCE, JR., *The Story of D-Day: June 6, 1944*, Random House. Simple and effective account.

CHURCHILL, SIR WINSTON, *The Second World War*, 6 vols., Houghton Mifflin. A series concerning battles, diplomacy, strategy, and personalities.

HERSEY, JOHN, *Hiroshima*, Knopf. A reporter's account of what happened to six persons who survived the atom bomb.

Biography and Fiction: PYLE, ERNIE, *Brave Men*, Henry Holt. Valuable for getting the feeling of what it was like to be a soldier in World War II.

REYNOLDS, QUENTIN, *The Battle for Britain*, Random House. A vivid report from various fighting units in Britain during an 84-day period. *The Curtain Rises*, Doubleday. A war correspondent writes of his experiences in Russia, Italy, and Africa.

UNIT 10 Our Contemporary World: Threshold to a Boundless Future

Progress in Science

You may have read about Sherwood (Woody) Fuehrer in the newspapers. A fourteen-year-old student, Woody finished wiring his great "Gismo" for sound in 1955. "Gismo," a monster six-foot robot with a crew haircut, at last was able to talk. "My body is made of iron and steel. My veins are electric wires. My blood is electricity," "Gismo" announced. Then he picked up a weight to demonstrate his fine coordination. Built almost completely from parts found in the cellar and garage, "Gismo" cost Woody about five dollars to construct.

The new mechanical man with the oil-can head was not a startling invention for the period from 1945 to 1968. Woody had added merely one more piece of evidence to demonstrate that applied science was expanding at a tremendous rate. The contemporary world soon had turbo-jet planes that travelled at supersonic speed, atomic submarines that could travel beneath the polar icecaps, life-saving vaccines to check dreaded viruses, and space ships to rocket astronauts toward the moon. Mankind was successfully challenging the barriers of sound, the boundaries of space, and the intricacies of the atom.

Political, Economic, and Social Problems

You know about man's progress in science. Have you also kept informed about the economic and social conditions in the post-World War II period? In Asia the average life expectancy was only forty-five years, as compared to seventy in the United States. In the Middle East the income in most countries was $100 or less per person

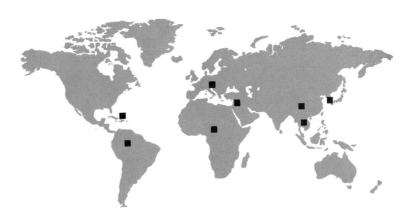

per year. In Africa nine out of ten Africans were illiterate. In Latin America in the year 1961 only 200 of the 780 children who wanted to enroll in primary school in Cali, Colombia, could meet a requirement for admission—ownership of a pair of shoes.

Such conditions not only made for economic and social insecurity, but contributed to political problems in the world. Ideological differences also set one man against the other. Tensions among nations increased to a point where the world was threatened by a nuclear war that might end civilization itself.

You and Your World In brief, the world in which you live is one of great progress in science and equally impressive problems in human relations. You will read about both in the next unit and learn two important reasons for studying world history: *to increase your understanding of desirable and undesirable conditions in the contemporary world; and if you wish to do so, to prepare yourself to make the world a better place in which to live.*

You may ask, "Can I—one individual—really contribute to the improvement of conditions in the world?" Albert Schweitzer, world-famous philosopher, physician, musician, and humanitarian, provided one answer to that question. He wrote: ". . . however much concerned I was at the problem of the misery in the world, I never let myself get lost in broodings over it; I always held firmly to the thought that each one of us can do a little to bring some portion of it to an end."

655

Chapter 41

The United Nations and Regional Organizations

KEYNOTE
The cost of World War II was 22 million dead, 34 million wounded, and billions of dollars in destruction. To avoid a repetition of such a disaster the nations of the postwar world established another international organization—the United Nations. Then they attempted to strengthen cooperation in economic and other matters by forming regional organizations.

There were some people who said that it was too late for the nations to learn world-wide or regional cooperation. Supporters of the United Nations and the regional organizations answered these critics by recalling the response of the eighty-year-old Roman, Cato, when he was asked: "Why are you beginning to learn Greek at the age of 80?" Cato had replied: "At what other age can I begin?" They too demanded: What better time was there than the present for the nations to learn to live together in peace?

The establishment and functioning of the United Nations Organization and the regional organizations became key features of the post-World War II period.

Key People
Trygve Lie · Dag Hammarskjöld · U Thant · Jean Monnet · Robert Schuman · John F. Kennedy

Key Places
New York · The Hague · France · Italy · West Germany · Benelux nations · Strasbourg · Britain · Warsaw · Brussels

Key Events
United Nations established · Brussels Treaty signed · NATO established · European Coal and Steel Community organized · European Common Market set up · Warsaw Pact signed

Key Terms
United Nations · Atlantic Charter · General Assembly · Security Council · substantive · veto · Economic and Social Council · Specialized Agencies · International Court of Justice · Secretariat · "Troika" plan · Council of Europe · European Atomic Energy Community · European Free Trade Association

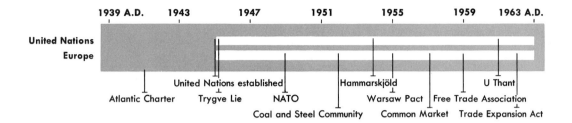

Timeline:

| 1939 A.D. | 1943 | 1947 | 1951 | 1955 | 1959 | 1963 A.D. |

United Nations
Europe

United Nations established
Atlantic Charter   Trygve Lie   NATO   Hammarskjöld   U Thant
Coal and Steel Community   Warsaw Pact   Free Trade Association
Common Market   Trade Expansion Act

1. How the United Nations Was Organized

On Manhattan Island in New York City is a tiny piece of land that *The Unesco Courier* has called "the world's most unusual independent territory." This area of only eighteen acres along the East River is the site of the permanent headquarters of the United Nations Organization.

The United Nations permanent headquarters is a fascinating and busy place. Here research scholars from many lands prepare detailed statistical studies. Secretaries turn out reports on typewriters whose keyboards are arranged in fifteen different languages. Telephone operators of many nationalities manage the UN switchboard and provide service 24 hours a day, 365 days in the year. And language specialists examine and route the 4000 or more letters received by the UN each day.

As Eleanor Roosevelt, who served as a representative to the United Nations, pointed out: "[The United Nations] is the only place in history where the whole world has hung its hat and gone to work on the common problems of mankind."

Preliminary Conferences Establish the United Nations

The United Nations was founded as a result of a series of conferences during and immediately after World War II.

In August, 1941, while World War II was raging, President Franklin D. Roosevelt of the United States and Prime Minister Winston Churchill of Britain met on the U.S. cruiser *Augusta* off the Newfoundland coast. Here, in a joint declaration known as the Atlantic Charter, the two leaders agreed on certain principles that they wished to see followed in the peace settlements (see Chart). Sigrid Arne calls this meeting "the birth of the United Nations."

On January 1–2, 1942, twenty-six nations signed the "Declaration by United Nations." The signers "subscribed to a common program of purposes and principles embodied in . . . the Atlantic Charter."

Additional progress was made at the conference held at the Dumbarton Oaks mansion in Washington, D. C., in 1944. Here the United States, the United Kingdom, the Soviet Union, and China drew up proposals that could serve as the foundation for the future Charter of the United Nations. Then, at the Yalta Conference of February, 1945, a system of voting that was to be used in the Security Council of the planned United Nations Organization was worked out.

Finally, in the spring of 1945, the delegates of fifty nations met at San Francisco

657

and drew up the Charter of the United Nations. It had to be approved by the legislatures of the nations; it was not until October 24, 1945, that the Charter of the United Nations officially went into effect.

Purposes of the United Nations

The United Nations is neither a world government nor a super-state. It is *an association of countries based on the principles of "the sovereign equality of all its members."* Its major purposes are these: (1) to maintain international peace and security, (2) to develop friendly relations among nations based on the principle of equal rights and self-determination of peoples, and (3) to achieve international cooperation in solving international problems.

■ **Check on Your Reading**

1. What were the principal provisions of the Atlantic Charter?

2. Why was the United Nations set up?

2. Principal Organs of the United Nations

There are six principal organs of the United Nations. These are the General Assembly, Security Council, Economic and Social Council, International Court of Justice, Trusteeship Council, and Secretariat (see Chart, p. 660).

The General Assembly

The General Assembly consists of representatives from all (122 in 1968) of the member nations of the United Nations. Each country can appoint five delegates, but it is permitted only one vote. Decisions in the General Assembly are made by either a majority or two-thirds of those members present and voting.

The General Assembly is a forum where the delegates of all member nations can express their country's position on many issues and make recommendations. In addition, the General Assembly can consider the general principles of cooperation in the maintenance of international peace and security, and it can initiate studies and make recommendations to promote international cooperation in political, economic, social, cultural, educational, and health fields.

When the United Nations began to operate, the General Assembly was secondary in power to the Security Council. Today, as Professor Hans J. Morgenthau points out, the General Assembly often may be considered "the main United Nations agency for the preservation of peace and security."

The Security Council

The Security Council consists of fifteen member nations of the United Nations.

These are the United Nations Permanent Headquarters in New York. Behind the curving roof of the General Assembly building rises the thirty-nine story Secretariat.

Five of these—the United States, the Soviet Union, the United Kingdom, France, and China (Nationalist)—are the so-called "Big Five." They are permanent members of the Security Council. The remaining ten are elected by the General Assembly for two-year terms.

The functions and powers given to the Security Council by the Charter include the following: (1) primary responsibility for keeping international peace and security and for drawing up plans for the regulation of armaments; (2) encouraging countries to settle their disputes by peaceful means; and (3) taking action against aggressor countries by calling on UN member nations to stop their economic relations with the aggressors or to "take such action by air, sea, or land forces as may be necessary to maintain or restore international peace and security."

The United Nations does not have a permanent army, navy, or air force of its own. If an aggressor is to be checked by force, the Security Council and the General Assembly must depend on the willingness of the member nations to send troops.

Although the Security Council was given "primary responsibility" for keeping international peace and security, the General Assembly gradually has taken over this important function of the United Nations. This was done because many actions in the Security Council were being blocked by the so-called *veto.* Article 27 makes it possible for a veto to operate in the Security Council by providing that, on procedural matters, decisions of the Security Council shall be made by an affirmative vote of any nine of its fifteen members. On all other matters—that is, on substantive (or important) matters—decisions shall be made by the affirmative vote of nine members of the Council *including the permanent members.* If any one of the five permanent members votes "No" on a substantive question, its vote is the same as a veto because it prevents the Security Council from taking action on the case.

When is a matter considered to be *procedural* and when is it *substantive?* This is a vital question to answer because *the veto cannot be used in procedural cases.* The General Assembly has drawn up a long list

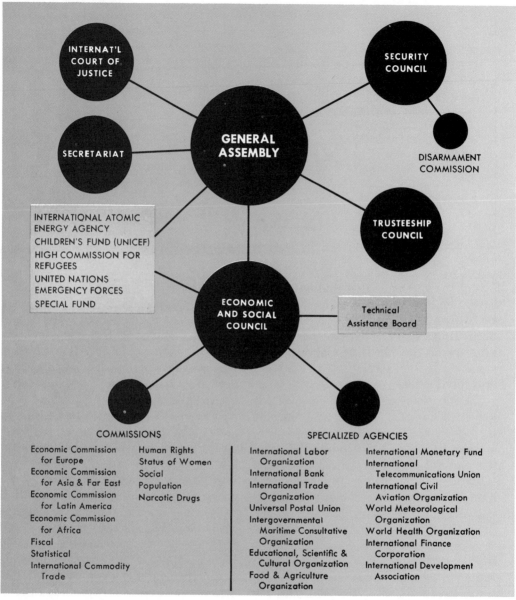

INTERNAT'L COURT OF JUSTICE

SECURITY COUNCIL

SECRETARIAT

GENERAL ASSEMBLY

DISARMAMENT COMMISSION

INTERNATIONAL ATOMIC ENERGY AGENCY
CHILDREN'S FUND (UNICEF)
HIGH COMMISSION FOR REFUGEES
UNITED NATIONS EMERGENCY FORCES
SPECIAL FUND

TRUSTEESHIP COUNCIL

ECONOMIC AND SOCIAL COUNCIL

Technical Assistance Board

COMMISSIONS

Economic Commission for Europe
Economic Commission for Asia & Far East
Economic Commission for Latin America
Economic Commission for Africa
Fiscal
Statistical
International Commodity Trade

Human Rights
Status of Women
Social
Population
Narcotic Drugs

SPECIALIZED AGENCIES

International Labor Organization
International Bank
International Trade Organization
Universal Postal Union
Intergovernmental Maritime Consultative Organization
Educational, Scientific & Cultural Organization
Food & Agriculture Organization

International Monetary Fund
International Telecommunications Union
International Civil Aviation Organization
World Meteorological Organization
World Health Organization
International Finance Corporation
International Development Association

of procedural matters. It also has urged the Security Council to decide many matters, whether they are procedural or not, without the use of the veto. The General Assembly wants to limit the number of cases classified as substantive because these are cases in which the veto can be used.

Notwithstanding the efforts of the General Assembly, by January, 1965, the veto had been used in the Security Council 111 times: 103 times by the Soviet Union; 4 by France; 3 by the United Kingdom; and 1 by China. The Security Council has the authority to decide whether some matters are procedural or substantive. As a result, it is possible for any one of the "Big Five" to have a case brought before the Security Council as a substantive matter—and then to veto action on it!

When it became clear that the veto was being used to block necessary action, the General Assembly itself decided to take a major responsibility for keeping the peace. Thus in November, 1950, the General Assembly adopted the *Uniting for Peace* Resolution. By this resolution, the General Assembly assumed the right to act

if the Security Council, due to a lack of unanimity of [the "Big Five"], fails to exercise its primary responsibility in any case where there appears to be a threat to the peace, breach of the peace, or act of aggression.

If a veto prevents the Security Council from acting during a time of crisis, the General Assembly can meet in emergency session and make recommendations to remedy the dangerous situation.

Economic and Social Council

A third important organ of the United Nations is the Economic and Social Council. It consists of 27 member nations (until August 31, 1965, the number was 18), elected by the General Assembly for a three-year term. Decisions in the Economic and Social Council are made by a majority of members present and voting.

Two of the most important functions of the Economic and Social Council are to make or initiate studies and reports with respect to international economic, social, cultural, educational, health, and related matters; and to make recommendations to the General Assembly, member nations, and to the *Specialized Agencies* concerned.

The Specialized Agencies

The Specialized Agencies are established by intergovernmental agreements and are

■ *A UN agricultural expert on sheep and wool production examines sheep in Libya, where the UN is helping improve livestock breeding.*

not an integral part of the United Nations. However, they are brought into a close relationship with the United Nations through the work of the Economic and Social Council, which coordinates their activities, and the General Assembly.

The *Food and Agriculture Organization* (FAO) is a Specialized Agency which tries to help countries raise their standards of living and to improve the nutrition of peoples everywhere.

Another Specialized Agency is the *World Health Organization* (WHO), which works for "the attainment by all peoples of the highest possible level of health."

The *United Nations Educational, Scientific and Cultural Organization* (UNESCO) is a very important Specialized Agency. It attempts "to contribute to peace and security by promoting collaboration among the nations through education, science and culture." For example, UNESCO advised Turkey on ways to establish educational radio stations. It set up the first public library in India; and it helped train teachers in Afghanistan, Bolivia, Cambodia, Laos, Libya, and other countries.

Other Specialized Agencies are the *International Labor Organization* (ILO), the *International Monetary Fund,* and many others.

Trusteeship Council

The Trusteeship Council supervises territories known as *trusts* and tries to help them to develop toward self-government or independence. Trusts can be former League mandates, areas detached from the defeated Axis powers as a result of World War II, or territories voluntarily placed under the trusteeship system by countries responsible for their administration.

International Court of Justice

The International Court of Justice is a fifth important body of the United Nations. It consists of fifteen judges elected for nine-year terms by the Security Council and the General Assembly. The Court, which meets at The Hague in the Netherlands, is the principal judicial organ of the United Nations. It can be used to judge legal disputes between countries and to give advisory opinions on legal matters that may be referred to it by various organs of the United Nations.

Thus, in 1949 the Court helped to settle a dispute between the United Kingdom and Albania over the damage done to British destroyers and crews by mines in the channel between Albania and the island of Corfu. By 1968 the Court had considered a number of other significant cases.

Secretariat

The Secretariat consists of over 6100 employees appointed by the Secretary-General under regulations established by the General Assembly. It performs the day-to-day administrative functions of the United Nations.

Although employees of the Secretariat continue to be citizens of their own countries, they also take an oath or declaration in which they promise not to be influenced by the desires of their nations.

The head of the Secretariat is the Secretary-General, who is appointed by the General Assembly upon the recommendation of the Security Council. The first Secretary-General was Trygve Lie, a Norwegian statesman, who held the post for seven years. Lie believed that "it was clearly not the intention of the Charter that the limited concept of the office of Secretary-General which . . . evolved in the League [of Nations] should be perpetuated in the United Nations." Although his activities were sometimes unpopular with the Soviet Union, Nationalist China, and some groups in the United States, Lie helped to define and develop many of the functions and powers of his office.

Dag Hammarskjöld, a former Swedish professor and statesman, was Secretary-General of the United Nations from 1953 until his death in a plane accident in 1961. The Charter states that the Secretary-General shall be "the chief administrative officer of the [United Nations] Organization." However, Article 99 declares that "the Secretary-General may bring to the attention of the Security Council any matter which in his opinion may threaten the maintenance of international peace and security." The Secretary-General gradually acquired important political duties. Mr. Hammarskjöld himself said: "This is a political job. I am a political servant. Administration is just a tool put at my command." He felt that he had a political responsibility to keep peace in the world by helping nations to settle their disputes peacefully.

Thus, Secretary-General Hammarskjöld played a part in obtaining the release of American airmen and others detained by the Chinese Communists in 1955. In 1956–1957 he drew up plans to restore order in the Middle East during a time of crisis. At other times and in other parts of the world, he was active in easing tensions that might have led to war. And he died while on a mission to mediate between opposing factions in the Congo (p. 722).

When Hammarskjöld was alive, the Soviet Union had declared, "We do not trust Mr. Hammarskjöld and cannot trust him." After his death, the Russians tried to reduce the power of the position of Secretary-General by putting forth a "Troika" plan. By this plan, the Russians proposed that *three* men serve as Secretary-General—one from the West; one from the Communist bloc; and one from the neutral nations. Each of the three men would

have a veto over the actions of the others. The plan was rejected because it would weaken the United Nations.

In November, 1961, after much discussion, U Thant of Burma was named acting Secretary-General. In 1962 he was elected to a full term. U Thant and his staff encountered such serious problems as the conflict in Vietnam and the Arab-Israeli War of 1967.

■ **Check on Your Reading**

1. What are the chief purposes of the General Assembly?

2. Describe the "veto" system in the Security Council.

3. What functions do the Specialized Agencies serve?

4. Describe the Secretary-General's duties

3. The United Nations: an Evaluation

Major changes have developed in the functioning of the United Nations since the Charter went into effect in 1945. One authority, Jacob Robinson, has found that over *twenty* articles of the Charter have been modified, become obsolete, or remained inactive since the formation of the United Nations. Three significant results of these changes were: the rise in the importance of the General Assembly; the increase in the duties and responsibilities of the Secretary-General; and the development of a tendency on the part of many countries in the United Nations to vote by *blocs*. This means that a nation often votes the same way as the members of a group of nations with common interests. Many new African and Asian nations have been admitted to the United Nations. Since every nation has one vote in the General Assembly, these new nations have as much voting power as the larger nations. They have tried to get the United Nations to concentrate on African and

Asian problems, and to condemn what they call the "colonialism" of European powers.

The United Nations has experienced both failures and successes. It has succeeded in helping stop some wars (such as one between India and Pakistan over Kashmir), and has prevented other conflicts from spreading. It has provided a forum where the United States and the Soviet Union, as well as other nations, can release their tensions peacefully by debating before a world audience; and it has helped settle several dangerous disputes—such as the clash between the Indonesians and the Dutch. It has also provided facilities for useful discussion about disarmament and control of nuclear weapons. Important gains in economic, social, and educational fields have been made by the UN. For example, it has helped inoculate over eighteen million people against tuberculosis; it has provided food for millions of needy children; and it has established centers to teach illiterates.

However, the UN has failed to prevent wars from breaking out and it has not brought about a permanent settlement of a number of disputes. It has been unable to achieve disarmament. In 1964–1965 an irreconcilable difference between the United States and Russia virtually paralyzed the UN. The United States demanded that Russia and other states pay their share of the cost of UN forces sent to the Congo and Middle East, or lose their General Assembly vote as the Charter provided. The Soviets refused, and after a voteless short session the General Assembly adjourned. Having survived its financial crisis, the the United Nations rose to new challenges during the crises in 1966–1968.

■ Check on Your Reading

1. What major changes have developed in the functioning of the UN since 1945?

2. What has the United Nations accomplished? What has it failed to accomplish?

4. Regional Organizations

During the postwar period, when tensions between nations continued to plague Europe, Jean Monnet, a prominent French economist and statesman, declared:

Wouldn't it be absurd if Texas was forever preparing for war against Mississippi, if California and New York each had its own currency, if there were tariff barriers between Pennsylvania and Ohio, and if citizens of North Carolina needed a passport to go to Georgia? Yet, that is precisely the type of thing Europeans have to contend with every day.

Monnet was expressing what an increasing number of European leaders were beginning to believe: Namely, that unless the nations of Europe joined together into organizations in which they cooperated with each other, Europe was destined to by weakened by tensions, rivalries, and wars. Or, as Giuseppe Pella, one-time premier of Italy, said: "For Europe, it's integration or disintegration."

The result was a growth of interest in *regional organizations*. Usually, a region consisted of an extensive geographic area and a number of peoples or countries drawn together by common cultural background, economic and social matters, or military needs. The Charter of the United Nations recognized the existence of regions and permitted the formation of regional organizations.

Regional organizations often were formed as a response to the developments in the "Cold War" between the United States and its allies and the Soviet Union and its allies. For example, hostility between the Soviet Union and the Western Allies (United States, Great Britain, and France) during the occupation of Germany led ultimately to the division of Germany and Berlin into two parts. When the Russians blockaded land traffic to West Berlin, the Allies set up an "airlift" to supply West Berlin with food and other necessities (p. 681). They also turned to regional agreements for mutual defense against future actions of the Soviet Union.

However, while many regional pacts stemmed from military considerations, regional organizations soon concerned themselves with matters far broader than the military. *It is therefore important to view these organizations not simply as tactical developments in the "Cold War," but as basic steps toward international cooperation.*

Benelux Customs Union and Western European Union

One of the first postwar regional agreements was the *Benelux Customs Union,* which went into effect on January 1, 1948. Under this arrangement, the Benelux nations (Belgium, the Netherlands, and Luxembourg) remained politically independent. However, they were able to take united action on tariff schedules, customs duties, and other economic matters of importance.

On March 17, 1948, the Benelux nations, Britain, and France signed the Brussels Treaty, agreeing to organize a collective defense and to cooperate in economic, social, and cultural affairs. Italy and West Germany later became members of this so-called *Western European Union,* an organization that is considered to be the forerunner of the North Atlantic Treaty Organization.

The North Atlantic Treaty Organization

In April, 1949, after the Communists had shown their aggressiveness by continuing the Berlin blockade and by seizing power in Czechoslovakia, twelve nations met in Washington, D.C., and signed a treaty to establish the *North Atlantic Treaty Organization* (NATO). The original signers were Belgium, Canada, Denmark, France, Iceland, Italy, Luxembourg, the Netherlands, Norway, Portugal, the United Kingdom, and the United States. Greece, Turkey, and West Germany later came into the organization. NATO was a military alliance in which the member nations agreed to organize a common defense and to take collective action against possible Communist or other aggression in the North Atlantic area (map, p. 666). Its members declared that an attack on one would be considered an attack on all.

When the United States joined NATO, it marked the first time that this country had entered a peacetime agreement to aid the defense of countries outside of the Western Hemisphere. By 1960 the United States had signed treaties to help defend over forty countries in the world!

In 1966 President Charles de Gaulle announced that France would withdraw all its military forces from the unified command of the North Atlantic Treaty Organization. France also asked that the military headquarters and installations of NATO be removed from France by the first of April, 1967. The military headquarters were transferred to Belgium.

Although France would continue to support programs for the mutual defense of Europe, President de Gaulle made clear that its actions were partly motivated by a desire to free itself from "subordination" to United States foreign policies. ". . . As a result of the internal and external evolution of the countries of the East," declared de Gaulle, "the Western world is no longer threatened as it was at the time when the American protectorate was organized in Europe under the cover of NATO."

The Council of Europe

In 1949 the *Council of Europe* was established, with headquarters at Strasbourg, France. In the beginning, ten nations—Belgium, Denmark, France, Ireland, Italy, Luxembourg, the Netherlands, Norway, Sweden, and the United Kingdom—belonged to the Council (map, p. 666). Later Turkey, Greece, Iceland, West Germany, and Austria joined.

In 1959 the Council of Europe had a Committee of Ministers "to provide for the development of cooperation between governments." There was also a Consultative Assembly, made up of representatives of the parliaments of the participating nations, to express "the aspirations of the European peoples." The Council of Europe was only an advisory organization.

European Coal and Steel Community

In 1950 Robert Schuman, a prominent French statesman, suggested that the coal and steel resources of France, West Germany, and other European countries be pooled. This so-called Schuman Plan was put into effect in 1952. In accordance with a treaty signed by France, West Germany, Italy, and the Benelux countries, the *European Coal and Steel Community* (ECSC) was established (map, p. 666). Under the European Coal and Steel Community the coal and steel resources of the six nations were merged into a single producing and market area, which was customs-free in the handling of coal and steel. A nine-man executive body, called the High Authority, was given power to plan and direct the coal and steel

production of the six nations, to borrow and lend money, and to perform other functions. The High Authority was *supranational* in matters dealing with coal and steel—that is, it was beyond or independent of the national governments of the six nations. A Common Assembly, consisting of representatives of the parliaments of the six participating nations, could review the work of the High Authority. The Common Assembly also had the power to dissolve the High Authority by a two-thirds vote of censure.

The European Coal and Steel Community had considerable success. It helped create a free European market in coal and steel; broke monopolies that were strangling the production of coal and steel; and aided companies in need of financial

■ *In the post-World War II period, nations formed regional organizations, such as the European Common Market, Euratom, European Free Trade Association, Warsaw Pact, and North Atlantic Treaty Organization. Name their members and principal purposes.*

assistance. It also lessened the tensions that existed between the French and the Germans; and, in five years' time, increased the coal and steel trade among the six Community nations by 93 per cent!

Equally significant, the success of ECSC inspired statesmen to make plans for other international organizations designed to develop European unity.

European Common Market and Atomic Energy Community

In 1957 the six nations belonging to ECSC (France, Italy, West Germany, and the Benelux countries) signed treaties establishing the *European Common Market* and the *European Atomic Energy Community* (Euratom).

Under the European Common Market, the six nations—the so-called Inner Six—agreed that over a period of twelve to fifteen years they would (1) lower and gradually do away with import quotas and customs duties that existed among them; (2) form a common market area and establish a single tariff on goods coming into this area; and (3) set up a bank whose funds could be used to help all six members.

The European Common Market (or EEC—European Economic Community) produced many results. The lowering of customs duties helped increase the volume of trade among the six nations by more than 40 per cent in three years. It also led to the establishment of new business agreements, such as those between Italian, German, and French automobile companies. Other economic activities stimulated economic growth and added to the wealth of countries belonging to the Common Market.

The Common Market created many new industrial jobs and encouraged the freer movement of workers from one member nation to another one. In 1962 a *Time* correspondent reported: "Of the Common Market's total labor force of 72.5 million . . . more than one million are foreign workers from partner nations lured from home by the promise of higher wages and learning new skills. About 60 per cent of the Belgian coal-mining industry is composed of Italians."

Consumers were benefiting from lower prices. Administrators of the Common Market claimed that between 1958 and 1962 the prices of many goods fell an average of 40 per cent as a result of tariff reductions among the six nations.

Little wonder that Belgium's distinguished statesman, Paul-Henri Spaak, enthusiastically called the forming of the European Common Market "the most important event in the history of Europe since the French Revolution."

The six member nations of the European Common Market also formed the European Atomic Energy Community (Euratom), which provided for a pool of nuclear resources and research. Journalist Eldon Griffiths considered Euratom to be "aimed at ending Europe's dependency on dwindling coal and uncertain Mideastern oil."

By treaty, it was agreed to merge the executive bodies of the European Coal and Steel Community, the Common Market, and the European Atomic Energy Community, effective January 1, 1966. This move was designed to strengthen regional cooperation. Euratom would develop atomic energy as a source of power.

European Parliament

In 1958 a body known as the *European Parliamentary Assembly* was established to supervise the European Coal and Steel Community, the European Common Market, and Euratom. It was planned that future representatives to this parliament would be elected by European peoples, rather than by their national governments.

European Free Trade Association

The formation of the European Common Market by the countries known as the Inner Six worried Great Britain. The British feared that the Common Market would cut seriously into their foreign trade. In November, 1959, Britain, Austria, Denmark, Norway, Portugal, Sweden, and Switzerland therefore organized the European Free Trade Association (EFTA). These countries were known as the Outer Seven. Their organization planned to lower and gradually abolish customs barriers between the members and to cooperate on other economic matters. In one year, the EFTA cut tariffs among its members by 30 per cent and increased trade among the Outer Seven members by 15 per cent.

The Common Market and the European Free Trade Association competed with each other for control of European trade. They differed in these ways: The Common Market planned to establish identical custom tariffs for goods coming from nonmembers. The European Free Trade Association planned to permit each member to set its own tariffs for goods coming from nonmembers. In addition, as Ernest S. Pisko of the *Christian Science Monitor* pointed out, the Common Market had "an unmistakable supranational tendency, something which the EFTA shuns."

At first a number of British leaders were opposed to the suggestion that Britain too join the Common Market, because they feared Britain would be flooded with duty-free goods from the Continent and would have to go along with the Common Market in setting up tariff barriers against nonmembers, including countries in its own Commonwealth. New Zealand, for example, sold almost 60 per cent of its exports to Britain under the "Imperial Preference" system, which did not levy heavy duties on goods coming from the Commonwealth members. New Zealand, Canada, and Australia would be hurt economically if the British now imposed Common Market tariffs on their goods.

Other British leaders urged Britain to join the Common Market on the grounds that it would increase British trade and increase economic and political cooperation among the powers. Britain finally applied for membership, but in 1963 France blocked her entry. President Charles de Gaulle warned that admitting Britain and other EFTA nations would result in a Community "under American domination." In 1966 and 1967 Prime Minister Harold Wilson attempted to negotiate Britain's entry into the European Common Market, but de Gaulle continued to oppose British membership.

Regional Organizations of the Soviet Union

The Soviet Union also established regional organizations, such as the Council for Mutual Economic Aid (COMECON) in 1949. This was formed with the Eastern European nations under Russian domination. It linked the economies of these countries in such a way that it was possible for the Soviet Union to control their agricultural and industrial activities.

The Warsaw Pact, designed to counteract NATO, was signed in 1955. By its terms, the Soviet Union formed a 20-year military defense agreement with Albania, Bulgaria, Czechoslovakia, East Germany, Hungary, Poland, and Rumania. Article 4 declared that "in case of armed aggression in Europe against one or several States party to the pact," the other members of the Warsaw Pact would send aid—including "the use of armed force"—to those under attack. Article 5 provided for the setting up of a "joint command of [the] armed forces" of the members of the Warsaw Pact. Satellite armies were promptly integrated with the Russian military forces.

The Warsaw Pact, called a "Treaty of Friendship, Cooperation and Mutual Aid," did not really establish a cooperative international body. The organization was directed and dominated by the Soviet Union. During the Hungarian revolt of 1956 the rebels demanded that Hungary withdraw from it.

The United States and European Regional Organizations

In the early 1960's the United States was hopeful that regional organizations would help protect the peace. Americans also gave increasing attention to the economic effects of regional organizations, particularly in Europe. The General Agreement on Tariffs and Trade (GATT) provided in 1947 for equal tariff treatment for all member nations. For that reason the United States tried to bring European trade discussions within the framework of that organization.

Many Americans saw a potential threat to the American economy in the regional organizations. The development of the Common Market could create a tariff barrier to American goods. By setting lower tariffs for the six member nations, the Common Market could effectively squeeze out the $6 billion annual American export trade in Western Europe. Economic rivalry with the United States could also weaken the Western alliance.

Faced with this economic threat, Congress, at the request of President Kennedy, passed the Trade Expansion Act in 1962. This act gave the President the power to cut tariffs up to 50 per cent on certain categories of goods in reciprocal agreements and (2) to eliminate altogether tariffs on groups of products in which the United States and the Common Market together account for over 80 per cent of world trade.

In May, 1967, the Sixth Round of Tariff Negotiations under the General Agreement on Tariffs and Trade (Kennedy Round) was concluded at Geneva. Representatives from fifty-three nations, including the United States, drew up agreements to: (a) lower substantially tariffs on many industrial goods; (b) reduce duties on chemicals; (c) include certain agricultural products in tariff negotiations, arrangements, and reductions; (d) provide food aid to the economically less developed countries in the world; (e) take steps against nontariff barriers to trade.

Since the Kennedy Round negotiations involved an estimated 60,000 items, it would require several years to determine fully the effects of the conference on world trade. Although there were serious criticisms of some of the agreements, one significant business journal declared: "The Kennedy Round agreement . . . preserves the main lines of President Kennedy's Grand Design, even though blurred and delayed. Without agreement in Geneva, there would have been danger of the same tariff escalations that strangled world trade in the 1930's."

■ **Check on Your Reading**

1. Why did regional organizations develop?
2. Why was the European Coal and Steel Community organized?
3. Compare the European Common Market and European Free Trade Association.
4. How did the Warsaw Pact operate?
5. What were the results of the Kennedy Round negotiations?

MAN AND HIS CULTURE

Let's Meet the People!

This sketch is based on information in an article by Jean Manevy. Reprinted from *The Unesco Courier*, May, 1958.

Dr. Malaria of WHO

The doctor's real name was Luigi Mara. However in Iraq, where he combatted the disease of malaria, he was known as "Doctor Malaria." A dark-haired man whose fuzzy beard was already sprinkled with grey, Dr. Malaria was an Italian citizen born in North Africa.

Dr. Malaria, a technical expert of the World Health Organization, was on a hunt for a tribe of Kurds, a nomadic mountain people who wandered with their cattle and stock between Iraq and northern Iran. The doctor's objective was to take blood tests of the Kurds and to spray their tents with DDT to kill the malaria-carrying mosquitoes.

Dr. Malaria's search for the Kurds lasted nearly two weeks. Driving a jeep and followed by a truck carrying a group of ten assistants, the doctor led his men on a dangerous journey of over 1400 miles. Up the rugged mountains they travelled, over ridges concealing deadly scorpions, across narrow bridges that threatened to collapse, through snake-infested goat-paths. Finally, in the wilderness of the Gorges of Prince Ali, on the boundaries of Iraq, Iran, and Turkey, Dr. Malaria and his men located the tribe of Kurds.

That night, as the leader of the Kurds, Sheik Salim, squatted around the samovar smoking his long pipe, Dr. Malaria told him why he had tracked down the Kurds. Would the Sheik permit him, he asked, to fight the malaria of his tribesmen?

The Sheik had seen two of his own children die of the terrible disease. He himself suffered from malarial fevers that shook him with "ferocious fits of shivering." He was more than ready to say "yes" to Dr. Malaria's request. And so:

"For the first time DDT, which kills mosquitoes, fleas, lice, and other verminous insects, was sprayed onto the insides of the tents. . . . For the first time in their history, a doctor was looking after the wild Kurd nomads."

CHAPTER REVIEW

REVIEW and DISCUSSION

1. Identify the people and places and explain the events and terms on p. 656.

2. Compare the eight principles of the Atlantic Charter with Wilson's "Fourteen Points." Explain differences or similarities.

3. What would be necessary to make the UN a world government?

4. What have the Specialized Agencies contributed to the peoples of the world?

5. What changes have been made in the functioning of the United Nations since its establishment? Have they strengthened or weakened the UN?

6. Do you think any country should be ousted from the UN? What advantages and disadvantages are there to such action?

7. What did Dag Hammerskjöld contribute to the position of Secretary-General?

8. Why did Russia oppose the political power of the Secretary-General?

9. Can you find any similarities or differences between regional organizations like NATO and the Warsaw Pact and the balance-of-power system of the nineteenth and early twentieth centuries?

10. What has the European Common Market contributed to Europe's economy? What problems has it created?

11. Do regional organizations preserve peace or promote war? Give evidence to support your answer.

12. Why has the Soviet Union established regional organizations?

ACTIVITIES

1. Have a model General Assembly meeting in your class.

2. Have a mock Security Council meeting in your class. Choose a resolution for discussion and debate; do research to find out how each nation would react; and have the class members act as representatives from different countries.

3. Panel discussion: "The European Common Market will eventually revolutionize the political structure of western Europe."

4. Find as much information as you can about one of the six principal organs of the UN and its record of success and failure. Write a report on your findings.

5. Write a 500-word biography of the person who you think has contributed most to international peace in the twentieth century.

PAST and PRESENT

1. From current magazines, newspapers, books, and United Nations publications assess how well the United Nations is carrying out its three principal purposes.

2. Compare the structure and functioning of the League of Nations with those of the United Nations.

SUGGESTED READINGS

Basic books: BRUUN, GEOFFREY, and MAMATEY, VICTOR S., *The World in the Twentieth Century*, Chaps. 46, 57, Heath.

LANGSAM, WALTER, *The World Since 1919*, Chap. 26, Macmillan.

Special accounts: ARNE, SIGRID, *United Nations Primer*, Rinehart. Conferences leading to organization of UN and its actual formation. Good basic reference.

BECKEL, GRAHAM, and LEE, FELICE, *Workshops for the World*, Abelard-Schuman. Description of work of the Specialized Agencies.

STREIT, CLARENCE, *Union Now*, Harper. Contains a proposal for an Atlantic Federal union.

WHITE, THEODORE, *Fire in the Ashes; Europe in Mid-Century*, Sloane. Many interesting facts about NATO and Europe's trade policies.

Biography and Fiction: KUGELMASS, J. ALVIN, *Ralph J. Bunche: Fighter for Peace*, Messner. An easy-to-read biography.

LIE, TRYGVE, and others, *Peace on Earth*, Hermitage House. Contains the first Secretary-General's ideas on world peace.

MILLER, RICHARD, *Dag Hammerskjöld, A Study in Crisis Diplomacy*, Oceana (also paperback). Case studies.

Chapter 42

The Struggle Between East and West in Europe

KEYNOTE

In 1947, eighteen Communist leaders drew up the following statement, "... two camps [have formed]—the camp of imperialism and anti-democratic forces [headed by the United States]... and an anti-imperialistic democratic camp [headed by the Soviet Union]. ... The battle of the two opposite camps ... is waged."

After World War II the Communists continued to drive relentlessly against those who opposed them. By distorting facts and twisting words like a corkscrew, the Communists labeled their opponents "imperialists," "anti-democrats," and other unsavory terms.

The result was a "Cold War," a great struggle between the Soviet Union and its supporters on one side and the United States and its allies on the other. Selwyn Lloyd, British Secretary of State for Foreign Affairs, called this a "strange war," for there were no formal declarations of war and "there is no advancing or retreating line of little flags pinned up where all can see; no scoreboard to tell just where we stand at any given moment."

Yet it was a real clash, a life-and-death battle between the two most powerful nations to strengthen their positions and to promote their ideologies throughout the world. *This struggle between the East and West was one of the key features of European life in the postwar period.*

Key People   *Marshal Tito · Nikita Khrushchev · Wladislaw Gomulka · Konrad Adenauer · Clement Attlee · Charles de Gaulle*

Key Places   *Greece · Turkey · Albania · Bulgaria · Poland · Rumania · Czechoslovakia · Hungary · Nürnberg · West Germany · East Germany · Berlin · Saar · Trieste*

Key Events   *Peace treaties · Russia expands into Eastern Europe · Yugoslavia breaks with Russia · Rebellion in Poland and Hungary · European Recovery Program · Berlin crisis · Fifth French Republic*

Key Terms   *Truman Doctrine · satellites · "Cold War" · Cominform "de-Stalinization" · Freedom Fighters · Marshall Plan · Technical Assistance · "de-Nazification" · nationalization · coalition · colons*

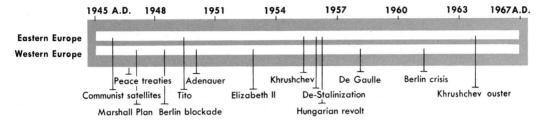

| 1945 A.D. | 1948 | 1951 | 1954 | 1957 | 1960 | 1963 | 1967 A.D. |

Eastern Europe
Western Europe

Peace treaties | Adenauer | Khrushchev | De Gaulle | Berlin crisis
Communist satellites | Tito | Elizabeth II | De-Stalinization | Khrushchev ouster
Marshall Plan | Berlin blockade | Hungarian revolt

1. The Soviet Union and Eastern Europe

In 1945, as World War II drew to a close, the leaders of the Allied Powers held conferences at Yalta and Potsdam to make plans for postwar settlements. Agreement was reached on several territorial changes: (1) The U.S.S.R. was to be ceded part of Eastern Poland and part of East Prussia. (2) The rest of East Prussia and German land east of the Oder and Neisse rivers were to be ceded to Poland.

The "Big Four"—the U.S.S.R., United States, United Kingdom, and France—drew up peace treaties for Italy, Hungary, Rumania, Bulgaria, and Finland in February, 1947 (map, p. 674). (No peace treaty was yet drawn up for Germany or Austria.) Important results of the peace treaties were the following: (1) The Soviet Union received northern Bukovina and Bessarabia from Rumania; Ruthenia from Hungary; and a lease on the Porkkala Peninsula in Finland. (2) Italy was deprived of her colonial lands in Africa and lost islands in the Aegean and Adriatic seas. Territory in northwest and northeast Italy was ceded to France and Yugoslavia. (3) Certain African lands, such as Libya, were placed under the United Nations Trusteeship Council, and Trieste was made a Free City under the administrative control of the United Nations. (4) The defeated countries had to pay reparations which were not excessively heavy.

The Truman Doctrine Aids Greece and Turkey

Shortly after the close of World War II, the Soviet Union extended its control over most of eastern Europe. Greece was one of the few nations that did not fall under Soviet domination. However, the war had left it in an extremely dangerous condition. President Harry S. Truman of the United States reported that: "More than a thousand villages had been burned. Eighty-five per cent of the children were tubercular.... Inflation had wiped out practically all savings."

As a result, an active minority of Greeks became increasingly favorable to communism, and civil war broke out. The British, who had helped to drive the Germans out of Greece, felt that they could no longer supply the country with the men and funds needed to keep order. The United States therefore decided to step in.

On March 12, 1947, after the Greek government had sent the Americans an appeal for economic aid, President Truman proposed the so-called *Truman Doctrine*. It stressed that "it must be the policy of the United States to support free peoples who are resisting attempted subjugation by armed minorities or by outside pressures." Congress approved his plan and voted the $400,000,000 that he asked to assist the rehabilitation of both Greece

673

TERRITORIAL CHANGES AFTER WORLD WAR II

- Axis countries that signed peace treaties
- Areas ceded as a result of treaties

■ *As a result of the peace treaties,* Italy *(1) ceded Alpine areas to France; lost Trieste, which became a free territory; and (2) ceded most of Venezia Giulia to Yugoslavia and (3) Dodecanesia to Greece.* Rumania *confirmed the cession of (4) southern Dobruja to Bulgaria and (5) northern Bukovina and Bessarabia to Russia.* Hungary *ceded (6) parts of Slovakia to Czechoslovakia, (7) Ruthenia to Russia, and returned (8) northern Transylvania to Rumania.* Finland *(9) ceded Petsamo and (10) leased the Porkkala Peninsula to Russia.*

and Turkey and to check the expansion of communism into the Middle East.

Greece received most of the funds under the Truman Doctrine. They were used to strengthen its financial structure, economy, and military forces.

Turkey also was sent economic aid to effect what President Truman called "that modernization necessary for the maintenance of its national integrity." In addition, Turkey received equipment to build up its armed forces. An American commission aided the Turks to organize their defenses against possible Russian aggression.

Soviet Power Extends over Eastern Europe

Although the Truman Doctrine helped to strengthen Greece and Turkey, it did not prevent the spread of Communist influence throughout eastern Europe (map, p. 675). From 1946 to 1949 Communists took over the government of the following: Albania and Bulgaria (1946), Poland and Rumania (1947), Czechoslovakia (1948), and Hungary and East Germany (1949).

The Soviet Union did not directly govern these countries. However, aided by the Russian forces and advisers that occupied eastern Europe during the war, Communists in these nations came into power. The countries became *satellites* of the Soviet Union; that is, they became dominated by Russia and dependent economically.

The satellite states had little freedom. Their governments were designed to further the interests of the Soviet Union. Russian troops could be stationed in satellite countries, and Russian officers could hold important posts in satellite armies.

The Soviet Union drained the satellites of economic goods and made them manufacture arms for Russian troops. The Council for Mutual Economic Aid (1949) linked the economies of these eastern European countries so that the Soviet Union could control their agricultural and industrial activities.

The Soviet Union led the satellites into an organization known as the *Cominform,* the Communist Information Bureau (1947). This Bureau consisted of representatives from the Communist parties of the Soviet Union, Yugoslavia, Bulgaria, Rumania, Hungary, Poland, Czechoslovakia,

Italy, and France. It declared that its tasks consisted of "the organization of an exchange of experience between [Communist] parties, and, in case of necessity, [of] coordination of their activity on the basis of mutual agreement." Yet the Cominform really was designed principally to further the interests of the Soviet Union.

The Russians then covered the satellite countries with a cloak of secrecy and the remark of the British statesman Winston Churchill seemed to describe the situation perfectly: "From Stettin in the Baltic to Trieste in the Adriatic, *an iron curtain* has descended across the Continent."

Tito Breaks with the Russians

One nation in eastern Europe refused to remain a satellite of the Soviet Union. That country was Yugoslavia, which was under the control of Communist leader Joseph Broz, known as Marshal Tito (1892–   ).

During World War II, Tito had grown into a national hero by leading his followers (the Partisans) in a rugged guerrilla war against the Nazi troops. After the war, Tito won out over groups in Yugoslavia who opposed him. He helped abolish the monarchy and became head of the new Yugoslavian government.

Tito and Yugoslavia remained in the Russian camp until 1948. In June, 1948, the Cominform denounced Tito, and he responded by making clear that he would not take orders from Moscow. Tito ardently supported the development of communism in Yugoslavia. However, he refused to accept the Russian idea that Yugolsav Communists had to obey Soviet leaders, and he would not permit his military forces, secret police, or the Yugoslav Communist party to be placed under the direct supervision of the Russians. He would not subordinate Yugoslavia's national interests to advance the welfare and development of the Soviet Union.

COMMUNISM DIVIDES·EUROPE
▨ Marshall Plan countries
▧ East European satellites of the Soviet Union

■ *After World War II, Communists gained control of eastern Europe. In western Europe the Marshall Plan aided recovery. Name the satellite countries and members of the Marshall Plan.*

Tito was interested in organizing a federation of Balkan states. The Russians were angered by this plan because such a federation would have excluded the Soviet Union and thus weakened Russian power in eastern Europe.

Tito insisted that the Soviet Union under Stalin had distorted several of the ideas of Lenin, the leader who had directed the Communists during the establishment of the Soviet state in Russia. Tito continued to believe in communism, but he was one Communist leader who would not bow down before Stalin.

■ **Check on Your Reading**

1. What were the key provisions of the peace treaties ending World War II?
2. How did the Truman Doctrine aid Greece and Turkey?
3. How did the Soviet Union extend its influence over eastern Europe?
4. What differences in theory caused Marshal Tito to break with the Soviet Union?

2. Soviet Leadership after Stalin

On March 5, 1953, at 9:50 p.m. Joseph Stalin died. The following morning the Soviet radio issued a call to the people to keep "the steel-like unity . . . of the ranks of the [Communist] Party . . . to guard the unity of the Party as the apple of the eye. . . ." The Party leaders warned against "any kind of disorder and panic."

The leadership of the Soviet Union passed to three men: Georgi Malenkov, who had been a member of Stalin's personal staff; Vyacheslav Molotov, an important figure in Russian foreign affairs; and Lavrenti Beria, head of the secret police. Malenkov was elected Chairman of the Council of Ministers, the top position in the Russian government.

The Soviet leaders declared that Russia would be directed by "collective leadership," that is, by a group of high officials rather than by one man. However, a struggle for power was going on among them, and one after another lost his authority. Beria even lost his life. Finally, on March 28, 1958, Nikita Khrushchev, who had become "First Secretary" (or leader) of the Communist party in 1953, was named Chairman of the Council of Ministers. Khrushchev was at last both head of the Russian government and leader of the ruling Communist party. In the five years that had elapsed since the death of Stalin, he had become the most powerful man in the Soviet Union.

Nikita Khrushchev: Leader of the Soviet Union

Nikita Sergeyevich Khrushchev was born in 1894 in Kalinovka, a village in southern Russia near the Ukrainian border. As a boy, he received little formal education. Instead, he went to work and became a shepherd. Then he labored for a time as an apprentice to a pipe-fitter and later as a mechanic in the coal mines of the Ukraine.

In 1918 he joined the Communist party and was sent to a workers' school, where he was indoctrinated with the ideas of communism. Starting as an official in the Ukraine, Khrushchev rose until he became head of the Party and leader of the Soviet government.

As head of the powerful Soviet Union, Khrushchev became a familiar figure in world affairs. He could be blunt, boastful, earthy, humorous, belligerent, shrewd, evasive—on the same occasion and at different times. Indeed, when he smiled and followed the Russian custom of applauding an audience that had applauded him, one could never be sure whether *inside* he was honoring the people or ridiculing them. One thing was certain: Khrushchev never lost his confidence that communism would some day spread throughout the entire world. In a program televised to the United States, he said, "I can prophesy that your grandchildren in America will live under socialism. And please do not be afraid of that. Your grandchildren . . . will not understand how their grandparents did not understand the progressive nature of a socialist society."

De-Stalinization Affects Soviet Life

Three years after the death of Stalin, Khrushchev played the chief role in an attack on the former leader of the Soviet Union. This denunciation of Stalin and the changes that resulted from it is called *de-Stalinization*. Although a de-emphasis on Stalin had started shortly after his death, de-Stalinization reached its dramatic climax at the Twentieth Congress of the Communist Party of the Soviet Union in February, 1956. At a secret meeting of this Congress, Khrushchev denounced Stalin. He said:

The cult of the individual [that is, the idolization of Stalin as the ever-wise leader who is always right] acquired such monstrous size chiefly because Stalin himself, using all conceivable methods, supported the glorification of his own person. . . . We must abolish the cult of the individual . . . and . . . [return to] . . . the main principle of collective leadership.

Khrushchev also denounced Stalin for his suspicious character, inefficiency as a military leader, unwise conduct toward Yugoslavia, and dictatorial methods by which he permitted "mass arrests and deportations of many thousands of people, [and] execution without trial and without normal investigation."

During the Twenty-second Congress of the Communist Party in 1961, it was voted to remove Stalin's embalmed body from the mausoleum on Red Square where it had rested in a place of honor next to Lenin. Stalin's body was buried in a plain grave under a simple inscription, "J. V. Stalin, 1879–1953." Communist China and Albania, whose leaders believed in many of Stalin's ideas, did not approve of de-Stalinization.

De-Stalinization affected life in the Soviet Union in many ways. Thousands of people were released from slave-labor camps. Workers were granted permission to change their jobs under certain circumstances. The number of hours in the work day was reduced in various regions. Writers and artists were given greater freedom to express themselves. The Stalin prizes for cultural achievements were changed to the Lenin prizes. Textbook statements praising Stalin were altered. (For instance, the phrase "the heroic heart of the great Stalin has ceased to beat" was changed to "J. V. Stalin died.")

At the same time, the Soviet leaders made a real effort to win Yugoslavia back

■ *Nikita Khrushchev, leader of the Soviet Union before being compelled to retire, addresses the 22nd Congress of the Communist Party.*

into the Russian camp. The Russians also tried to reassure other nations of their peaceful intentions by repeating these ideas expressed by Khrushchev at the Twentieth Party Congress:

The Leninist principle of peaceful co-existence of states with different social systems [such as the Soviet Union and the United States] has always been and remains the general line of our country's foreign policy.

War [between countries favoring communism and capitalism] is not fatalistically inevitable.

■ *This Soviet painting, "In the Mountains" (1957), was the work of Sabur Mambeyev. Compare it with the art of the Stalin period (p. 603). Notice that this painting is less realistic in style and not about a political theme.*

What were the reasons for de-Stalinization? The new leaders of the Soviet Union wanted to dissociate themselves from the past mistakes and the hated features of Stalin's regime. They also wished to stimulate further the industrial and agricultural productivity of the Russian people. They felt that it was necessary "to restore the quality of initiative that had withered in Stalin's iron grip." Many of the new rulers of the Soviet Union had secretly feared and hated Stalin for years. They expressed their hostility to him by supporting de-Stalinization.

The new chiefs of the Russian state also believed that they could strengthen their position in foreign affairs by denouncing the belligerent acts of Stalin and declaring their support for "peaceful co-existence."

Rebellion Breaks Out in Poland

De-Stalinization also encouraged some satellites to seek greater freedom from the Soviet Union. In June, 1953, a major disturbance in East Berlin had to be suppressed, and just three years later a Polish revolt began with demonstrations by auto workers in Poznan. Joined by other workers and students, they marched and shouted, "Chleba [Bread]!" Soon the peaceful demonstration became a bloody riot. People were killed as the marchers fought the Polish secret police and security troops, who restored order.

As a result of the Poznan riots and negotiations through the summer of 1956, the Polish Communist party declared that workers would receive a wage increase. The Party went through a major shakeup and pro-Stalinist members were forced out of high positions. The Polish Communist leaders, under Wladislaw Gomulka, exerted pressure on the Soviet Union for greater Polish independence. As a result, by October, 1956, high Russian officers were withdrawn from Poland, and the Soviet Union promised greater "noninterference in [Poland's] internal affairs." Poland continued to accept Russian leadership in foreign affairs while obtaining the right to have its own national existence.

The Hungarian Revolution

Four months after the Poznan riots in Poland, Hungary also was rocked by a revolutionary storm. On October 23, 1956, students demonstrated in Budapest and demanded that Hungary be given greater independence from Russian control. The demands of the students included the removal of Russian troops from Hungarian soil, withdrawal of Hungary from the Warsaw Pact of 1955, and free elections in Hungary.

The students soon were joined by workers and other demonstrators. Later, a clash between the students and the Hungarian security police ended in bloodshed, and the rebellion was on in earnest. As the rebels armed themselves with guns and ammunition supplied by workers in munition plants, the Communist government of Hungary declared martial law and issued a call to the Russians for help.

On October 23 and 24 there was fighting between Russian troops and the Hungarian people. Events moved rapidly, and Imre Nagy was appointed prime minister of Hungary. Nagy was a "national Communist"—that is, a Communist who felt a deeper concern for his own country of Hungary than for the Soviet Union.

On October 29, Nagy succeeded in obtaining the withdrawal of Russian troops from Budapest. On October 30, Cardinal Mindszenty, a religious leader whose imprisonment by the Communists had angered people throughout the world, was freed. The same day Prime Minister Nagy declared that the one-party system whereby the Communist party had dominated Hungary would be abolished. Then, on November 1, Nagy announced Hungary's withdrawal from the Warsaw Pact and asked the United Nations to consider the entire Hungarian situation.

The rebels had made it clear that they intended to go beyond the scope of the Polish revolt and end the power of Russia in Hungary. This caused Nagy's downfall. On November 4, Russian troops and tanks attacked the city in force and crushed the Hungarian Freedom Fighters.

A new government, headed by János Kadar and supported by the Soviet Union, was established in Hungary. The Freedom Fighters continued to resist for as long as they could, but the Russians finally brought the rebellion to a close. Many of the rebels fled to the West. Imre Nagy gained temporary safety in the Yugoslav legation, but later he was captured and executed. Russian military intervention in Hungary brought world-wide condemnation, and many countries provided refuge for those who escaped from Hungary.

Changes in Soviet Leadership

In October, 1964 Nikita Khrushchev was forced to retire as head of the Soviet Union. Leonid Brezhnev succeeded him as First Secretary (chief) of the Communist Party. Alexei Kosygin replaced Khrushchev as Chairman of the Council of Ministers. By the end of 1968, the problem of Soviet relations with Communist China continued to be extremely serious.

■ Check on Your Reading

1. How did de-Stalinization affect the Soviet government and people?
2. Compare the Polish and Hungarian rebellions.
3. What changes took place in Soviet leadership?

3. The European Recovery Program

World War II left western Europe with many serious problems of reconstruction. Cities had been smashed into ugly patterns of jagged rubble; factories had been burned to the ground or stood as gutted ghosts of the past; farmlands had been ripped apart by shells; and the currents of trade had been blocked. The economy of western Europe was falling apart.

In June, 1947, the United States Secretary of State, General George C. Marshall, presented the so-called *Marshall Plan* in an address delivered at Harvard University. The Marshall Plan proposed that the

United States give extensive financial assistance to the nations of Europe, provided that "there . . . be some agreement among the countries as to the requirements of the situation and the part these countries themselves will take." Funds were to be used to help the European nations to help themselves to rebuild their economies.

All European countries were invited to join the Marshall Plan, but the Soviet Union and its satellites refused. Sixteen other nations met in Paris and formed a committee to draw up plans to participate in the Marshall Plan. In April, 1948, the United States Congress supported the Marshall Plan by adopting the Foreign Assistance Act. This act made available a fund of several billion dollars and set up an administration for what was called the *European Recovery Program* (ERP).

ERP, which extended from April, 1948, through December, 1951, was a *cooperative* program between the United States and countries accepting the Marshall Plan. The participating European nations formed the *Organization for European Economic Cooperation* (OEEC) to carry out their responsibilities under ERP and to continue their efforts to establish a sound economy for Europe. The 270,000,000 people of these nations were to provide the funds to match the dollars credited to their governments by the United States. The

American financial contribution proved to be about 25 per cent of the total cost of European recovery; 75 per cent of the burden was carried by the European taxpayers themselves.

ERP contributed greatly to the recovery of western Europe. During the first two years of cooperative efforts under ERP, western Europe doubled its production of electric power. Agricultural yields increased considerably. Industrial production in Marshall Plan countries as a whole rose to 20 per cent above prewar levels.

In addition, the Marshall Plan stimulated the activity known as *Technical Assistance* (TA). The Technical Assistance program made it possible for American and European experts in industry, agriculture, and other fields to visit each other's countries, study each other's methods, and exchange creative ideas on the best ways to work.

Yet the countries in western Europe still faced many complicated political, economic, and social problems. How they met these problems can be determined by an examination of postwar developments in each of the major countries.

■ **Check on Your Reading**
1. What was the Marshall Plan?
2. Evaluate the ERP.
3. What was Technical Assistance?

4. Germany in the Postwar World

At the Potsdam Conference in the summer of 1945, President Truman, Joseph Stalin, and Prime Minister Attlee agreed to the following about Germany: (1) The Soviet Union and Poland were to receive or administer lands in Eastern Germany. (2) Germany was to pay reparations for war damages. (3) Nazi organizations, beliefs, and attitudes were to be erased—and

Nazis accused of war crimes were to be brought to trial. (4) Germany was to be divided into four occupation zones. The United States, Soviet Union, Great Britain, and France were each to occupy one of these zones. An Allied Control Commission, consisting of representatives of the four powers, was to be the supreme authority for Germany as a whole (map, p. 681).

At previous meetings it had also been agreed that Berlin, in the Russian zone, was to be divided into four sectors and occupied by the four powers and administered jointly by their representatives.

Attempts to Erase Nazism

The United States, the Soviet Union, Great Britain, and France set up an International Tribunal at Nürnberg, Germany, to try Nazi "war criminals." The Nürnberg Trials lasted from November, 1945, to October, 1946. Hermann Goering, Joachim von Ribbentrop, and other Nazi leaders were indicted for "conspiracy to commit crimes against peace, war crimes, and crimes against humanity." Of the twenty-one persons tried, three were acquitted; seven were given prison terms; and the rest were sentenced to be hanged. Verdicts of guilty also were handed down against the leadership corps of the Nazi party and other Nazi groups. Many Nazis in the lower ranks were tried and condemned in special courts, too.

The efforts to "de-Nazify" Germany thoroughly continued to be difficult to carry out. In West Germany, the Americans, the British, and the French tried to cleanse the West German systems of education, press, and radio of all Nazi influence. In East Germany, the Russians carried out their own de-Nazification program by forcing people to accept the ideology of communism in place of Nazism. Despite all efforts, de-Nazification was not immediately successful everywhere.

Tensions Lead to a Blockade and an Airlift

In the months that followed the division of Germany into four occupation zones, the Russians demonstrated that they had no intention of working with the other powers to achieve Germany's unification.

Primarily because of Russia's hostility, Americans, British, and French cooperated

■ *After World War II, Austria and Germany were both divided into four occupation zones. What problems did this create for the four occupying powers?*

more closely. In 1947 the United States and Great Britain merged their two zones into one, and later France added its zone to theirs. The single area thus formed was known as *West Germany* to distinguish it from the Soviet-controlled *East Germany*. The United States, Great Britain, and France also fused their sectors of West Berlin into one, and a new common currency was issued for all of West Germany.

The Russians angrily retaliated for these acts of the Allies by *blockading* all land traffic to West Berlin—that is, they prevented food and other supplies from passing through the Russian zone and reaching the people of West Berlin. The United States, Great Britain, and France refused to be forced out of Berlin by this blockade. They loaded airplanes with provisions, flew as many as 8000 tons of materials a day over the Russian zone, and supplied West Berlin by air. After nearly eleven months of this Berlin "airlift" (1948–1949), the Russians ended their blockade.

681

Two German Republics Are Established

In 1949, with the approval of the United States, Great Britain, and France, the people of West Germany proclaimed a new German constitution (called the Basic Law), which established the *German Federal Republic* for West Germany. In 1955, after the Allies ended their occupation of West Germany, the German Federal Republic became a sovereign state, with its capital at Bonn.

Meanwhile, the Soviet Union had encountered considerable difficulty in East Germany. Domestic conditions became so unbearable that between December 1, 1949, and May 31, 1950, more than 117,000 persons fled from East Germany to West Germany. (This flood of refugees continued until 1961, when the East German government closed the border between East and West Berlin, p. 684.) In June, 1953, a serious uprising broke out in East Berlin, and Soviet troops and tanks crushed it.

In 1954, the Soviet Union made East Germany an "independent" state. The following year the Russians recognized it as a "sovereign state." However, the so-called *German Democratic Republic* (capital in Pankow, East Berlin) continued to be dominated by the Soviet Union.

Chancellor Adenauer Leads West Germany

West Germany soon grew into a strong and respected nation. One of the most remarkable features of the postwar period was its amazing recovery.

The German Federal Republic in West Germany was led by its aged but energetic chancellor, Konrad Adenauer (1876–1967). Adenauer was a shrewd, capable, and often unbending leader who preferred to make most of the major decisions himself.

Chancellor Adenauer left no doubt that he was a friend of the West and an enemy of communism. He and his supporters were determined to destroy the remnants of Nazism and prevent the growth of communism. They also wanted to rebuild the economy and prestige of West Germany.

Assisted by large-scale American financial aid, West Germany became the economic leader on the continent. As early as 1954 West Germany's economic boom reached an all-time high. Production was 260 per cent above that of 1948; steel plants produced almost twice as much as they did in 1949; employment went up from 13.5 to 16.7 million; and exports showed a tremendous increase. Consumption of food also rose.

On January 1, 1957, the Saar territory, a heavily industrialized coal region that had been occupied by the French, became politically a part of West Germany. France received certain economic concessions from West Germany. By 1960, West German industrial production reached new highs. However, in 1967 a recession presented fresh challenges to the West German economy.

East Germany Strives to Rebuild its Economy

At the same time, the Russians were working to turn East Germany, the so-called German Democratic Republic, into a powerful satellite under the leadership of German Communists like Walter Ulbricht. The United States and other Western powers refused to recognize or deal with this republic.

The German Democratic Republic occupied an area roughly the size of the state of Mississippi. Its seventeen million people did not experience the great economic recovery of West Germany. However, there were several indications that the rate of economic growth in East Germany was speeding up. Chemical, electrical, optical, and mechanical engineering industries grew. Shipbuilding activities

■ *Konrad Adenauer, West German Chancellor during the Berlin crisis of August, 1961, speaks to the German* Bundestag. *The elderly statesman strongly condemned East Germany for closing off East Berlin from the West.*

increased. And by 1960 the production of crude steel, pig-iron, and rolled steel had risen considerably over what it was in 1958. On the other hand, there continued to be serious shortages of consumer goods.

The Berlin Crisis

Germany continued to be a focal point in the "Cold War." The United States and its allies refused to recognize the East German government because that would be accepting a permanent division of Germany. They demanded free elections throughout *all* of Germany to establish democratically a single all-German government for a united Germany.

The Russians feared a revival of a militarily strong and united Germany. They were primarily interested in having the nations recognize the East German Communist government and treat it as an independent state.

The Russians were eager to drive the Allies out of West Berlin for several reasons. West Berlin had become an avenue of escape for millions of dissatisfied people living in East Berlin. In addition, West Berlin had far outstripped East Berlin in its living standards and thus was visual evidence of the weakness of the Russian argument that a free, non-Communist government could not build a sound economy.

In November, 1958, the Russians denounced the agreements that had divided Germany and Berlin into occupation zones and proposed the following: (1) All Western troops should be withdrawn from West Berlin. (2) West Berlin should become a "free city," independent of both West and East Germany. (3) If the Western powers agreed to the first two points, the Soviet Union would "honor West Berlin's independence and secure for it 'unhampered communications' with the East and the West." In return, West Berlin was to promise not to permit "subversive activities" against communism. (4) The Soviet Union announced that it would soon turn over its occupation functions in East Berlin to the East German government.

In 1961 the Soviet leader Khrushchev declared that if Russia could not reach a satisfactory agreement with the Allies concerning Berlin, the Russians would sign a

683

separate peace treaty with East Germany and turn over their authority in East Berlin to the East German government.

These Russians proposals and statements were considered to be extremely dangerous. The leaders of the Western powers pointed out that if Western troops were withdrawn from West Berlin, and if the Soviet Union made a peace treaty with East Germany, West Berlin would be a defenseless city completely surrounded by a hostile Russian-dominated East Germany. If East Germany then cut off West Berlin's routes to the West, the city might fall to the German Communists and be made a part of East Germany. If the Allied powers tried to reach West Berlin by moving through the routes that East Germany had cut, this action might lead to a world-wide war, or force the Allies to recognize the government of East Germany in order to negotiate with it—and thus to accept a permanent division of Germany. The United States and its Allies were determined, therefore, not to withdraw their forces from Berlin.

In a dramatic action on August 13, 1961, the Communist East German government closed the border between East and West Berlin. The Communists then constructed a concrete and barbed-wire wall between the two areas. Escape from East to West Berlin at last became almost impossible. President John F. Kennedy responded by reinforcing the United States'

garrison in Berlin and stepping up the American military training program.

Then on August 31, 1961, the Soviet Union announced the resumption of its nuclear tests, thereby ending a voluntary moratorium (or postponement) since 1958.

After the Russians broke the moratorium by exploding over thirty nuclear bombs, the United States resumed its own testing to prevent Russians from moving ahead in military preparedness. Finally, on August 5, 1963, a Nuclear Test Ban Treaty banned nuclear testing in the atmosphere, in outer space, or under water (p. 756).

In October, 1963, Konrad Adenauer, who had reached the age of 87, retired from his position as Chancellor of the German Federal Republic. In departing from office, he declared: "We Germans can carry our heads high again ... [but] Germany has become more than ever a focus of world tensions." Ludwig Erhard, also a Christian Democrat, became the new Chancellor.

In late 1966 Kurt Georg Kiesinger became Chancellor. He declared: "The German Government advocates a ... peace policy aimed at removing political tension and checking the arms race."

■ **Check on Your Reading**

1. Describe de-Nazification.
2. How did Germany come to be divided?
3. Discuss U.S. and U.S.S.R. positions on the dispute over West Berlin.
4. What programs did Kiesinger offer?

5. Great Britain Adopts Nationalization and Welfare Legislation

Like Germany, Britain was left with many serious postwar problems. For example, three and a half million houses had been destroyed or damaged. Half of the merchant marine had been sunk. Exports had declined by almost a third.

In the first postwar general elections in July, 1945, the British people voted the La-

bor party into power. For the first time, a Labor government, headed by Prime Minister Clement Attlee, was organized with a majority in the House of Commons.

Key Industries Are Nationalized

The Labor party immediately went ahead with its plans for the *nationalization* of key industries, or placing them under the ownership and control of the national government. The Labor government nationalized the Bank of England, coal mining, transportation, civil aviation, international telecommunications, electricity, gas, and iron and steel. Eventually, about 20 per cent of the national assets were brought under government ownership.

Although the Labor party put through this nationalization program, the Conservatives, headed by Winston Churchill, accepted many features of it. They were opposed, however, to the nationalization of iron and steel.

National Insurance and National Health Service Are Established

The Labor government also passed important social legislation, much of it supported by the Conservatives as well. Five acts of Parliament established a system of National Insurance and Assistance and a National Health Service. As a result of these acts, every citizen was protected against what journalist-author William L. Shirer called "major disasters or disabilities which economic ill fortune or mortality could inflict," and was provided with insured medical, dental, and hospital care.

Both employees and employers contributed to the National Insurance and Assistance. Benefits covered situations involving sickness, unemployment, injury, maternity, widowhood, guardian's allowance, retirement pensions, and death.

6. France Survives Many Crises

While postwar problems in Britain were being handled by a stable and orderly government, France was going through one crisis after another because of the political instability of its government. "France is the sick man of Europe," declared the French statesman Paul Reynaud.

The National Health Service was financed primarily by taxes, and cost the people of Britain in taxes about $5\frac{1}{2}$ per cent of their national income.

A New Government and a New Monarch

In the elections for Parliament held in 1951 the Conservative party was voted back into power. Although the leaders of the new Conservative government *denationalized* the steel industry—that is, they returned it to private ownership and management—they kept many other acts of the prior Labor government.

Then, on February 6, 1952, King George VI died. The traditional coronation of the new ruler, Elizabeth II, took place on June 2, 1953. However, the real government continued in the hands of the Prime Minister and the Parliament.

The Conservatives remained in power to 1964. Harold Macmillan served as prime minister, followed by Sir Alec Douglas-Home in 1963. The Labor Party won the 1964 election, and Harold Wilson became prime minister. Thereafter, the British government concerned itself with the problems of developing ways (a) to strengthen the economy at home, and (b) to gain admission to the Common Market.

■ Check on Your Reading

1. Describe the nationalization program and the social legislation.

2. What were the problems of the Labor government after 1964?

The Government Is Plagued by Instability

Under the postwar Fourth French Republic, which was proclaimed officially on December 24, 1946, the National Assembly was the most important organ of government. The members of the National Assembly were elected by *proportional representation*, a system by which the various parties received representation in the National Assembly in proportion to the number of votes each polled. One result was that the French legislature was filled with representatives of many parties. The National Assembly became a highly unstable body, for rarely did a single party have a majority of its members.

The large number of conflicting parties made it difficult for the premier (prime minister) of France to direct the government—or even to remain in office very long. The premier, who was appointed by the president of France, needed the support of a majority of the members in the National Assembly to obtain his appointment and to stay in power. Since no single party had a majority in the National Assembly, the premier had to depend on the backing of several parties (or a *coalition*) to make up his majority. If he lost the support of any of these parties, he often lost his majority and had to resign from office.

The result was that the premiers of France frequently found it hard to stay in office long enough to put through legislation vital to the country.

France Faces Serious Economic Problems

France also was faced with serious economic problems. These included a need for greater industrialization, a shortage of housing, inflation, and an inefficient system of taxation. In addition, there was a low rate of increase in agricultural output—despite the fact that France was, in the words of Edgar Ansel Mowrer, a news commentator, "the finest piece of farmland in Europe."

France attacked these problems. She increased her coal production, rebuilt many of her war-damaged buildings, added to the tractors and other machinery used on farms, strengthened her system of social security, and raised the standard of living.

The Fifth French Republic Is Established

France was faced also with rebellions and crises in her empire in North Africa and Indo-China. An uprising in Algeria, North Africa, finally set off a string of events that led to the fall of the Fourth French Republic.

In May, 1958, while France was going through another change of premiers, reports circulated that the new premier intended to "abandon" Algeria to the Moslem Arabs and Berbers. These reports infuriated the *colons* (people primarily of French extraction in Algeria). On May 13, 1958, thirty thousand *colons* rioted in the streets and stormed the government offices in Algiers. French army leaders in Algeria, who supported the *colons*, issued a call for General Charles de Gaulle (1890–   ) to take charge of the French government. Only De Gaulle, they said, could "save" France. On May 15 he came out of retirement to meet the crisis and announced that he was "ready to assume the powers of the Republic."

Although he became a national hero and a world figure, General de Gaulle was disliked and distrusted by some Frenchmen and by some leaders of other countries. Nevertheless, few of them would have disagreed with the *Time* correspondent who wrote: "De Gaulle is a dedicated man whose entire strength, passion and intelligence have been devoted to his conception of France as a nation that 'is not really herself unless in the front rank.'" In May, 1958, many Frenchmen were convinced that De Gaulle was the man who could restore order.

De Gaulle demanded and was granted special emergency powers to meet the crisis. Next he directed that a new constitution be drawn up. This constitution, approved on September 28, 1958, by a referendum held in France and her territories, set up the Fifth French Republic.

The new constitution introduced changes designed to provide a stable two-house legislature and a strong executive. These changes included a system of voting for the National Assembly, which provided one representative for each electoral district.

Charles de Gaulle was elected the first President of the Fifth French Republic. He stressed his ardent nationalism in many ways. He blocked British entrance into the Common Market, made a treaty of friendship with Germany, and in 1964 established diplomatic relations with Communist China. In 1966 he withdrew all French military forces from the unified command of NATO. In 1967 he ordered the removal of its bases.

■ **Check on Your Reading**

1. Why was the Fourth French Republic an unstable government?
2. What economic problems faced France?
3. What changes did the Fifth French Republic introduce?

7. *Italy and Austria*

Italy and Austria also faced serious political and economic problems after World War II.

Italy Becomes a Republic

In 1943 Italy had joined the Allies in the war against Germany. Many Italians therefore felt that the treaty of peace that Italy signed with the Allies in 1947 was unnecessarily humiliating. Italy was required to give up Libya; Ethiopia; other overseas possessions; and the city of Trieste and the Istrian peninsula, which were constituted as the Free Territory of Trieste. The administration of the northern part of the Territory of Trieste was transferred to Italy in 1954. The remainder was placed under the administration of Yugoslavia.

In June, 1946, the Italian people rejected a monarchy and voted to establish a republic. Alcide de Gasperi, leader of the Christian Democratic party, served as prime minister for most of the period from 1946 to 1953. Aided financially by the Marshall Plan, De Gasperi and his associates worked to solve Italy's problems of (1) overpopulation in proportion to available farmland and (2) unemployment.

Despite political clashes between the Christian Democratic party and the Communist party of Italy, Italy gradually began to recover. Some farmers obtained more arable land, and industrial production increased greatly. In November, 1966, the worst flood in the history of Italy swept through Florence, Venice, and other cities, damaging priceless art treasures.

Austria Regains its Independence

By the Moscow Declaration of 1943, the annexation of Austria by Germany was declared null and void. Austria was to be established as an independent state. At the conclusion of the war, Austria was therefore treated as a "liberated" country.

Like Germany, postwar Austria was divided into four occupation zones (map, p. 681). Vienna was also occupied.

In 1945, while the country was under Allied occupation, the Second Austrian Republic was established. In 1955 the Austrian Republic regained its full independence. Surrounded on three sides by Communist-dominated countries, it worked to build a democratic government.

■ **Check on Your Reading**

1. What progress did Italy make toward solving her problems in the postwar world?
2. What happened to Austria after the war?

MAN AND
HIS CULTURE

Let's Meet the People!

The following sketch is based on information in Leslie B. Bain's *The Reluctant Satellites*, 1960, Macmillan.

Agatha: Hungarian Patriot

Russian troops were stationed in Budapest. A strict curfew was in effect: "No one was permitted outside except the military. Civilians were shot on sight. For one hour a day people were permitted to move around and draw food from the rapidly dwindling supply. . . ."

One afternoon a truck loaded with 1,600 loaves of bread drove into the square. It arrived after the hour for obtaining food, and the Russian soldiers fired around the truck to keep the Hungarians inside their houses. Agatha, a very old, bent, white-haired woman, stood in her doorway, watching the truckload of bread.

Slowly, old Agatha walked across to the truck. She lifted two of the five-pound loaves, turned, and carried them back to the Hungarians in the houses. Then she started back to the truck again. A Russian soldier fired a warning shot at her, but Agatha kept walking. She lifted two more loaves and returned with the bread to the houses.

Shots were fired over Agatha's head, and a Russian officer hurried over to her. "You must stop defying the curfew!" he ordered.

Agatha answered: ". . . pray to God for forgiveness for your sins."

Then Agatha went back to distributing the bread. What was it that kept the Russians from shooting her: shame, admiration, or fear of arousing the Hungarians to new fury? All through the afternoon and evening Agatha distributed the bread. Finally at about 9 P.M., when there were only a few hundred loaves still on the truck, she collapsed. "From a nearby Soviet tank a soldier ran toward Agatha . . . the Russian gently lifted the frail old woman into his arms."

The Russian soldier carried Agatha to the doorway from which she had started. He banged on the door and handed the old woman to the people within. Then he raced back to his tank—and prepared to fire on anyone foolish enough to break the curfew!

CHAPTER REVIEW

REVIEW and DISCUSSION

1. Identify the people and places and explain the events and terms on p. 672.

2. Why did not Russia trust her satellites to govern themselves without interference?

3. Should non-Communist countries be friendlier to Yugoslavia than to Russia's satellites because of Tito's refusal to take orders from Moscow? Why?

4. What does the term *co-existence* mean?

5. How do you explain the fact that Poland was able to secure greater release from Russian domination than Hungary could attain?

6. Do you think the de-Stalinization movement can erase Stalinist ideas from the minds of the Russian people? Why?

7. Was the Marshall Plan a great humanitarian movement, or a plan to aid the American economy, or a program devised for some other purpose? Defend your answer.

8. How do you explain the fact that a defeated country was aided to achieve prosperity by one of the victors? Do you think it would have been better to let the defeated country slowly struggle back to prosperity by its own efforts?

9. Compare the post-World War II problems faced by France and Britain, and analyze the ways in which each country tried to solve its problems.

10. Why was Austrian re-unification achieved by the four occupying powers without all the difficulties that arose over German re-unification?

ACTIVITIES

1. Make a comparative study of Lenin and Stalin as to their ideas about the communist state, how best to maintain it, and how to encourage its further growth. Decide whether the leaders of de-Stalinization were justified in claiming that Stalin had violated Lenin's principles.

2. Debate this statement: Resolved, that peaceful co-existence between the United States and the Soviet Union is impossible for any long period of time.

3. Panel discussion: What is the best way to punish war criminals? Review the Nürnberg Trials.

PAST and PRESENT

1. Do Russian policies toward neighboring countries of eastern Europe today differ from earlier policies of the czars? Justify your answer.

2. Compare Khrushchev and Stalin as to their policies and methods at home and abroad.

3. In the light of subsequent difficulties over Berlin, what do you think should have been decided at the Potsdam Conference, 1945?

SUGGESTED READINGS

Basic books: BRUUN, GEOFFREY, and MAMATEY, VICTOR S., *The World in the Twentieth Century*, Chaps. 47–48, 52–54, 60–61, Heath.

HARCAVE, SIDNEY, *Russia, a History*, Lippincott. Includes useful information on postwar Russia.

WALSH, WARREN B., *Russia and the Soviet Union*, Chap. 28, University of Michigan Press. Good material on co-existence, Berlin blockade, Korean crisis, and war.

WISH, HARVEY, *Contemporary America*, Chap. 22, Harper. Deals effectively with the "Era of the Cold War."

Special accounts: BAILEY, THOMAS A., *A Diplomatic History of the American People*, Chaps. 48, 49, 50, 51, Appleton-Century-Crofts. America in the postwar era.

FITZSIMMONS, THOMAS, MALOF, PETER, and FISKE, JOHN C., *USSR, Its People, Its Society, Its Culture*, Taplinger.

SALISBURY, HARRISON, *To Moscow and Beyond*, Harper. Excellent account of modern Russia by a *New York Times* reporter.

Biography and Fiction: UNTERMEYER, LOUIS, *Makers of the Modern World*, Simon and Schuster. Brief biographies of Marx, Lenin, and Stalin help us understand contemporary Russia.

Chapter 43 *New Nations of Asia on the March*

<table>
<tr>
<td>KEYNOTE</td>
<td>

In the summer of 1958 the most popular song in Communist China was a number entitled "Catch Up with Britain." It contained the lines:

> Leap forward, leap forward,
> Outstrip Britain in fifteen years.
> Gallop onward, gallop onward,
> China fears not sweat nor tears!

There was a chorus of "Hey! Hey! Hey!" at the end of each line, and the song reached a climax with the words "We can catch up with Britain if we try—by 1962."

This song and others like it—such as the tune "East Wind Prevails Over West Wind"—symbolized the fact that the peoples of Asia were on the march. Many Asian lands, long dominated by Western powers, were determined to "leap forward" into the present and in time *surpass* the West! *One of the key features of the period after World War II was the emergence of new nations in Asia and the rise of Asia to a position of great importance in world affairs.*
</td>
</tr>
<tr>
<td>Key People</td>
<td>Douglas MacArthur · Mao Tse-tung · George C. Marshall · Syngman Rhee · Mahatma Gandhi · Jawaharlal Nehru · U Nu · Ramón Magsaysay · Sukarno · Ho Chi Minh</td>
</tr>
<tr>
<td>Key Places</td>
<td>Japan · China · Formosa · Tibet · Korea · India · Pakistan · Kashmir · Burma · Ceylon · Federation of Malaya · Singapore · Philippines · Indonesia · Vietnam · Laos · Cambodia</td>
</tr>
<tr>
<td>Key Events</td>
<td>New constitution for Japan · Peace treaty with Japan · China falls to the Communists · Korean War · India becomes a republic · Philippines become independent · Republic of Indonesia formed · War in Indo-China · Geneva Conference · Civil strife in Laos</td>
</tr>
<tr>
<td>Key Terms</td>
<td>neutralism · Chinese Nationalists · commune · plebiscite · Colombo Plan · ANZUS Treaty · SEATO</td>
</tr>
</table>

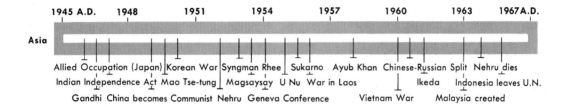

Asia

| 1945 A.D. | 1948 | 1951 | 1954 | 1957 | 1960 | 1963 | 1967 A.D. |

Allied Occupation (Japan) | Korean War | Syngman Rhee | Sukarno | Ayub Khan | Chinese-Russian Split | Nehru dies

Indian Independence Act | Mao Tse-tung | Magsaysay | U Nu | War in Laos | Ikeda | Indonesia leaves U.N.

Gandhi | China becomes Communist | Nehru | Geneva Conference | Vietnam War | Malaysia created

1. Asia Faces Many Problems

Asia consists of almost one-third of the earth's land surface, and its population of approximately 1.8 billion is more than half of the world's total. After World War II there was a "population explosion" —a tremendous growth of population—in Asia, as well as in Latin America and in other areas. This growth was due to the lowering of the death rate, the improvement in medical knowledge and care, and other factors. The population of Asia increased so rapidly that it threatened to outstrip the available food supply. Karl Sax, professor of botany at Harvard University, commented: "The recent explosive growth of the world's population could be a greater threat to world peace and prosperity than the atomic bomb."

After World War II Asian leaders were faced with other serious political, economic, and social problems. As late as 1961, three-fifths of Asians could not read or write. Average life expectancy was only 45 years as compared to 70 in the United States. Millions struggled against starvation.

There were many differences in the postwar developments in the countries of Asia. However, most Asians aspired to these things: (1) the right to form their own nations; (2) a higher standard of living and economic security; (3) better education and medical care; and (4) an end to the colonial empires of the European powers.

There were clashes in Asia between Asian peoples and white Europeans, between Hindus and Moslems, and between other groups. Events in Asia were greatly affected by the spread of communism. The Communists made gains in Asian countries—particularly in China—while democratic nations increased their efforts to stop Communist expansion.

Many nations in Asia, the Middle East, and Africa tried to maintain a position of *neutralism*, that is, not to join one side or the other in the struggle between the Soviet bloc and the United States and its allies. In October, 1961, 48 of the 103 nations in the General Assembly of the United Nations were neutrals. The neutrals, the so-called Third Force, were numerous enough to swing the "balance of voting power" to one side or the other. The major powers sought to win their support through gifts, loans, technical assistance, and surplus food shipments.

■ **Check on Your Reading**

1. Define the term *population explosion*.
2. What factors influenced postwar Asia?

691

2. Efforts Are Made to Democratize Japan

After the Japanese surrender in World War II, American troops occupied Japan. General Douglas MacArthur was appointed Supreme Commander of Allied Occupation Forces. The United States and its allies tried to develop democracy in Japan.

The Allied Occupation Forces disarmed the Japanese and tried to break up powerful monopolies that had controlled Japan's wartime industries. Japanese war criminals, like those in Germany, were tried for their acts (1946–1948). Then Japan's educational system was reorganized to help democratize the Japanese people. Under the old system, obedience to the emperor and the state was considered the chief duty of the citizen. Under the new system, respect for the individual was stressed.

A most important event was the introduction of a new constitution for Japan in 1947. This extremely democratic constitution included the following provisions: (1) The emperor was no longer to be recognized as a descendant of the gods. (2) Legislative power was placed in a two-house body (the Diet). The prime minister and his cabinet were responsible to the Diet. (3) Freedom of speech and press was guaranteed. (4) Women were given the right to vote. Determined that Japan should never go to war again, the United States also insisted that Article 9 be included in the new constitution. It stated:

... the Japanese people forever renounce war as a sovereign right of the nation. . . . land, sea, and air forces, as well as other war potential, will never be maintained.

A Peace Treaty Is Signed

The economy of Japan revived rapidly. Assisted by American financial aid, the Japanese increased their foreign trade, strengthened their textile industries, and initiated plans for economic expansion.

Political conditions also became more stable. The United States, eager to have Japan become a bulwark against communism, soon felt that the Japanese were strong enough to stand on their own feet.

In September, 1951, the United States and forty-seven other nations signed a treaty of peace with Japan (the Soviet Union ended its state of war in 1956). Its terms were these: (1) Japan agreed to conform to the principles of the United Nations Charter; to give up Korea, Formosa, the Pescadores, the Kurile Islands, and southern Sakhalin; and to renounce all special rights in China. (2) Arrangements were to be made for Japan to pay reasonable reparations. (3) Allied Occupation Forces were to be withdrawn ninety days after the treaty went into effect. "Stationing and retention" of foreign troops in Japan was to be permitted if foreign nations and Japan negotiated an agreement.

Japan permitted American military bases, and Japan and the United States signed a Mutual Defense Assistance Treaty in 1954 for protection against the spread of communism. Faced with the danger of aggressive Russian and Chinese Communist actions, the United States now encouraged Japan to rearm as an ally against communism.

Japan Seeks to Find Its Way

In time, a number of Japanese reacted to the "Cold War" by turning to Japanese nationalism. They demanded that Japan be independent from all foreign domination. Ichiro Hatoyama, who served as prime minister in 1955, spoke for them: "I would like to awaken the people to a deeper . . . sense of their independence."

Near the close of President Eisenhower's administration, riots erupted in Japan to prevent ratification of a new Japanese-

■ *These are examples of the old and new in Japan. This performance (above) with its costumes and style of acting at the Kabuki-za Theater in Tokyo is dictated by years of tradition. Yet the streets of Tokyo (below) resemble those of most cities of the West, and Western dress predominates.*

American defense treaty. The Communists, although a minority in Japan, also tried to stir up trouble. Conditions became so inflammatory that President Eisenhower cancelled his planned visit to Japan. However, the treaty was ratified.

Japan continued to prosper in the postwar period. Foreign trade expanded and new industries were built.

By 1967 Edwin O. Reischauer, who had served as United States Ambassador to Japan, was able to report: "More than ever before, Japan is the economic giant of Asia. Her society is healthy, confident and vibrant with energy."

Check on Your Reading

1. How did the Allies try to democratize Japan?
2. Describe U.S.-Japan relations after 1954.

3. China Becomes a Communist Power

"Historical experience is written in blood and iron!" declared Mao Tse-tung, leader of the Chinese Communists. In the post-World War II period, Mao and the Chinese Communist armies fought against the Chinese Nationalists of Chiang Kai-shek. China was torn by civil war.

The Chinese Communists differed sharply from the Nationalists in their principles and policies. The Chinese Communists wanted the Communist party to have absolute rule, demanded seizure of private property of persons labelled "landlords" and redistribution of their lands, and were favorable to the Soviet Union. The Nationalists wanted a period of "tutelage" (training of the people to govern themselves). Chiang Kai-shek and his associates would dominate the government until they thought the people were ready for self-government. The Nationalists also demanded the protection of private property and were favorable to the United States.

For years there had been charges of corruption, dictatorial behavior, and inefficiency levelled against the Nationalists. Then there were reports that the Chinese Communists were holding mass trials and executing all those who opposed them. In the midst of accusations and counter-accusations the struggle for control of China continued.

The Communists Gain Control

General George C. Marshall was sent to China by the United States to try to end the civil conflict. A truce was signed in 1946; it established a government that included Communist and Nationalist representatives. This peace did not last. Communist troops took Manchuria, and Mao Tse-tung started a major drive in 1947. Aided by arms sent by the Russians, the Chinese Communists eventually conquered the entire Chinese mainland.

Why were the Chinese Communists successful? Some of the reasons are these: (1) Russian military aid strengthened the Chinese Communist armies. (2) The government of Chiang Kai-shek was unpopular with millions of Chinese, while the Chinese Communists' promise of food, land, and justice appealed to many. (3) The democratic nations failed to recognize the seriousness of the Chinese Communist threat. Some leaders thought of the Chinese Communists as "democratic agrarian reformers," rather than as dedicated Communists. (4) Military supplies from the United States did not reach the Nationalists quickly enough.

In 1949 the Communists drove the Nationalists to Formosa (Taiwan). On October 1, 1949, the Communists proclaimed the establishment of the People's Republic of China with Mao Tse-tung (1893–) as chairman of the government and Chou En-lai as premier.

The Soviet Union promptly extended diplomatic recognition to Communist China, and the two countries signed a treaty of alliance and mutual assistance in 1950. In 1950–1951 the Chinese Communists seized control of Tibet.

Two Chinas Present a Problem

Thus there were two Chinas and two Chinese governments, one on China proper and the other on Formosa. The Soviet Union, Great Britain, France, and many other nations extended diplomatic recognition to Communist China. The United States refused to do so and gave its support to Chiang Kai-shek's government on Formosa.

The problem arose: Which China should be in the United Nations? The Nationalist

government, which already had a permanent seat on the Security Council, declared
that it was the legal government and
should continue to represent China in the
United Nations. The Communist government insisted that, since it controlled
China, it should be given the Nationalists'
seat in the United Nations.

Those who agreed that the Chinese Communists should be admitted to the United
Nations pointed out that the Communists
controlled all of the Chinese mainland with
its dense population, and it was senseless
not to recognize this fact. They said that
it was illogical to deny the Communists
a voice at the United Nations and permit
the tiny Nationalist minority to speak for
all of China. And they maintained that
admission of Communist China to the
United Nations would make it easier to
negotiate with the Chinese Communists by
providing an international forum for discussions of problems.

Those who agreed that Communist
China should not be admitted to the
United Nations pointed out that the Chinese Communists had seized control of
China by military conquests and other
illegal means. Article 4 of the UN Charter
declared: "Membership in the United
Nations is open to all ... peace-loving
states." Since Communist China was not
peace-loving, it should not be admitted. In
addition, admission of Communist China
would seriously weaken the position of the
Nationalists on Formosa (Taiwan).

Tensions continued between the two
Chinas, and the Communists shelled—and
threatened to invade—the Nationalist-held
islands of Quemoy and Matsu in the Formosa Strait. Some nations suggested that
both Chinas be represented in the United
Nations. The Nationalists and the Communists opposed this plan, and the United
States continued to try to keep Communist China out of the United Nations.

The Communists Reconstruct China

In China itself, the Communists worked
hard to reconstruct the political, economic,
social, and cultural structure of society.
They wanted to build a Communist society, but one that was consistent with
Chinese "national form," as Mao Tse-tung
put it.

A dictatorial government was established, sometimes called a "people's democratic dictatorship." This government was
under the complete control of the Chinese
Communist party (CCP), which as late as
1961 numbered only eight million people.
The Communists used violence to eliminate any individual who dared oppose their
dictatorship.

By the Agrarian Reform Act of 1950,
the Chinese Communists redistributed
land but at first permitted considerable
private ownership. Soon more private
property was confiscated. By 1957 individual peasant farm cultivation had been
almost completely wiped out. Then in
1958 a program of forced "communaliza-
tion" was started. According to the Chinese Communists, there were 80,000 *communes* in existence in 1960.

In the communes, farms were merged
and private property was practically eliminated. The peasants were moved into dor-
mitories where they owned almost nothing
but their clothes. Members of the communes farmed the land together in "production brigades" or worked together in
small industries. The peasants ate in communal dining rooms, and their children
were cared for in communal schools. The
communes were supposed to provide the
members with food, housing, medicine,
education, recreation, and other basic
needs. One commune even promised each
member twelve free haircuts a year and
twenty free bath tickets.

The Chinese Communists also were ac-

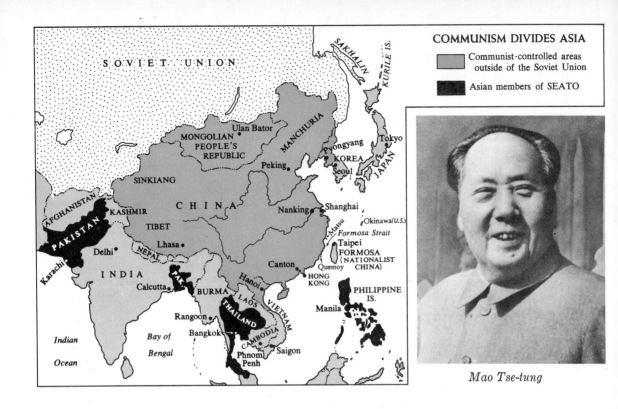

COMMUNISM DIVIDES ASIA

Communist-controlled areas outside of the Soviet Union

Asian members of SEATO

Mao Tse-tung

tive in developing industry, and they introduced a policy of forced industrialization. Great stress was placed on building up heavy industries and on increasing military production. Industries producing consumer goods generally were neglected. However, by 1962 serious food shortages and other economic complications caused Chinese leaders to give up trying to achieve the industrial level they had expected to reach in five years.

The Communist police, who were controlled by the Chinese Communist party, watched every facet of life in China. Censorship, terror, and public executions were employed to weaken or destroy anyone who dared to think differently from the Communists. The press and the schools were rigidly controlled. Literature and art were filled with propaganda.

Statesmen watched with interest as tensions appeared between Communist China and the Soviet Union. Many Chinese leaders did not support de-Stalinization and other policies of Soviet leader Khrushchev and his successors. Albania supported the position of Communist China and a rift grew between the Albanians and the Soviet Union. Communist China was openly competing with the Soviet Union for leadership of the Communist world by the 1960's.

"Great Proletarian Cultural Revolution"

In 1966 and 1967, China was disrupted by what was called the "Great Proletarian Cultural Revolution." Originally a purge against those accused of advocating "bourgeois" or "revisionist" ideas, the "Great Proletarian Cultural Revolution" developed into a fierce struggle between supporters of Mao Tse-tung and anti-Maoists.

Mao urged that China continue to develop as a radical society. He denounced

696

anti-Maoists for unnecessary moderation and deviation from the revolutionary doctrines of communism.

The struggle brought turmoil to the Communist Party, the government, the army, the schools, the peasantry, the industries—indeed, to nearly every aspect of Chinese life. Mao's opponents were called "fierce dogs," "wounded tigers," and "poisonous snakes"; and the "little red book," *Quotations from Chairman Mao Tse-tung*, became a guide for the actions of Mao's supporters. In this book were the words Mao had said in 1949: "Fight, fail, fight again, fail again, fight again . . . till . . .

victory." Both sides continued to struggle for victory.

■ **Check on Your Reading**

1. How did Chinese Communists differ from the Nationalists in principles and policies?
2. What arguments were advanced pro and con on the issue of admitting Communist China to the United Nations?
3. Describe life in a commune.
4. Describe how the Great Proletarian Cultural Revolution began.
5. What did Mao Tse-tung advocate in the revolution?
6. What was its effect on Chinese life?

4. Korea Becomes a Divided Nation

Korea has a long history. In 1910 it was annexed by Japan, which held it until World War II. At the Potsdam Conference (1945), the Allied leaders agreed that Korea would be given its independence after the war. At the conclusion of the conflict, Russian troops occupied Korea north of the 38th parallel and supervised the surrender of Japanese troops in that area, while American forces occupied Korea south of the 38th parallel and supervised the surrender there.

Korea was supposed to be given its independence, but the Soviet Union blocked every effort to unite the country. Even when the United Nations ordered that elections for a national government should be held throughout Korea, the Russians refused to cooperate. Elections were held in South Korea, and the Republic of Korea was established for this region in 1948. However, North Korea remained under Russian domination.

The Korean War

On June 25, 1950, Russian-trained North Korean troops invaded South Korea.

The United Nations Security Council immediately met in emergency session. (The Soviet Union was not present, because the Russian delegate had "walked out" earlier as a protest against the Security Council's refusal to permit Communist China to join the United Nations.) The Security Council condemned North Korea as an aggressor, called for the "immediate cessation of hostilities," and demanded that North Korean troops withdraw from South Korea.

The North Koreans refused to obey. The Security Council therefore called upon all members of the United Nations to take collective action. President Truman immediately ordered United States air, naval, and land forces to aid the South Koreans. Eventually over fifty nations sent troops, ships, or equipment for the United Nations forces. In July, 1950, General Douglas MacArthur was made commander of the United Nations troops in Korea. On September 26 Seoul, capital of South Korea, was recaptured by the United Nations; and on October 7 United Nations soldiers crossed the 38th parallel. North

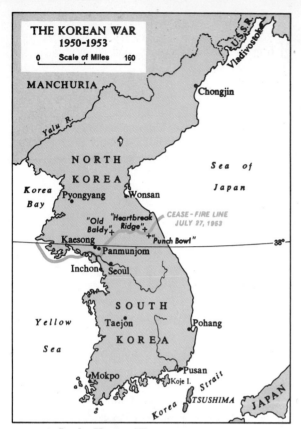

THE KOREAN WAR
1950-1953

0   Scale of Miles   160

MANCHURIA

Chongjin

Yalu R.

NORTH
KOREA

Sea of
Japan

Korea
Bay

Pyongyang   Wonsan

"Old   "Heartbreak
Baldy"+   Ridge"+

CEASE - FIRE LINE
JULY 27, 1953

Kaesong   +"Punch Bowl"   38°
Panmunjom

Inchon   Seoul

SOUTH

Yellow   Taejon   Pohang

Sea   KOREA

Mokpo   Pusan
Koje I.   Strait

Korea   TSUSHIMA   JAPAN

■ *In the Korean War (1950–1953) United Nations troops fought against North Koreans and Chinese Communists. What were the results?*

Korean troops were forced to retreat to the Yalu River on the border of Manchuria.

On November 26, some 200,000 Chinese Communist troops—calling themselves "volunteers"—poured across the Yalu, joined the North Koreans, and fought against the United Nations troops. On February 1, 1951, the General Assembly declared the Chinese Communists to be the aggressors.

General MacArthur wanted to strike at Chinese bases in Manchuria. Many statesmen were afraid that this would lead to a world war. When General MacArthur continued to oppose the decision to limit military action to Korea, President Truman dismissed him from his command in Korea (April, 1951).

By May, 1951, the United Nations troops had definitely regained the offensive. Two months later truce negotiations were started. On July 27, 1953, an armistice was signed, ending a war that had cost the United Nations 400,000 casualties. Korea remained divided into two parts: the Democratic People's Republic in North Korea under the domination of the Communists; and the Republic of Korea in South Korea supported by the United States and other nations (map, p. 698).

Syngman Rhee Is Toppled from Power

Dr. Syngman Rhee, the leader of the independence movement in Korea and later president of the Republic of Korea, hated communism. As president, he was criticized for undemocratic acts, such as prohibiting freedom of speech, allowing corruption in government, introducing police-state measures. Moreover, after massive foreign aid, the economy was faltering. After Rhee's reelection in 1960, in which election fraud was charged, student riots forced Rhee's resignation when he was unable to keep the support of the armed forces. In 1961 a new administration under General Park Chung-hee took over.

In December, 1966, the General Assembly of the United Nations passed a resolution on Korea reaffirming the United Nations' objectives of bringing about "by peaceful means the establishment of a unified, independent, and democratic Korea under a representative form of government, and the full restoration of international peace and security in that area."

■ **Check on Your Reading**

1. How did Korea become a divided nation?

2. Why did the United Nations send troops to Korea? What was the outcome?

3. Describe the political changes in Korea and United Nations aims there.

698

5. British-controlled Lands Win Their Independence

In Asia a number of countries still remained under British control. Independence movements developed slowly, but in time these countries became independent.

India Struggles for Independence

India's struggle to gain independence from Great Britain was a long one. Many obstacles blocked the way to a united and independent India, including the following: (1) the existence of Indian states ruled by princes who did not wish to surrender their power; (2) the clash between Hindus and Moslems over religious and other matters; (3) the variety of languages and dialects; (4) the lack of experience of the Indian people in governing themselves; (5) the great poverty of the country; (6) the caste barriers among the people; and (7) the desire of a number of British leaders to continue Britain's control over India.

In 1919 the British Parliament passed the Government of India Act. According to this act, the British would continue to control the military forces, the system of justice, and several key areas of government in India. Indian provincial councils would have authority over a number of local matters, such as farming. Indian nationalists continued to demand more self-government. The struggle for independence increased in intensity during the period between the two world wars.

Mahatma Gandhi: Leader of Indian Nationalists

One of the most important leaders of the Indian nationalists was Mahatma (or Great Soul) Gandhi (1869–1948). Gandhi studied law in London; then he lived in South Africa for twenty years, working to eliminate discrimination against Indians. He returned to India in 1914, and soon became the leader of millions of Indians seeking independence from Britain.

Gandhi was a gentle, compassionate person who dressed simply in a loincloth and sandals and preferred spiritual meditation to the acquisition of goods. He advocated an independent and united India.

He believed in using non-violent resistance to gain India's independence, and he thought there should be peace and goodwill between people of all races and religions. Although Gandhi was a Hindu, he said: "All religions are almost as dear to me as my Hinduism. My veneration for other faiths is the same as for my own faith." He also advocated the abolition of untouchability.

India Becomes a Republic

As a result of the efforts of Gandhi and other Indian leaders, the Government of India Act of 1935 was enacted. It organized India as a federation of governors' provinces and Indian states governed by their own princes, and established a two-house federal legislature, representing both the governors' provinces and the Indian states. The act also provided that a viceroy, appointed by the British monarch, would serve as head of the country; and it permitted the Indian people in the governors' provinces to help elect the members of provincial legislatures.

Hostility between the Hindus and Moslems continued during World War II. Mohammed Ali Jinnah, a Moslem leader, demanded that the Moslems be permitted to establish a separate state in India. Most of the Hindus opposed this plan. On August 15, 1947, the Indian Independence Act ended Britain's control of India. Two dominions were established: India, dominated by the Hindus; and Pakistan, dominated by the Moslems (map, p. 702).

■ *This portrait shows Pandit Jawaharlal Nehru, prime minister of the Republic of India from 1950 until his death in 1964. The western-educated leader tried to keep India neutral in the "Cold War" while fighting poverty and other domestic problems.*

On January 26, 1950, India was proclaimed a sovereign democratic republic, but it remained in the Commonwealth of Nations. Pandit Jawaharlal Nehru became the first prime minister.

Pakistan Emerges as a Republic

Pakistan had been set up to include the largest possible number of Moslems. As a result, the country consisted of two geographic areas—East and West Pakistan— separated by a thousand miles of territory lying in India. Faced with hostility, millions of Moslems fled for safety from India to Pakistan, and millions of Hindus moved from Pakistan to India.

Bitter clashes broke out between the two groups. Even Gandhi's call for peace did not succeed. On January 30, 1948, a Hindu fanatic named Godse "bowed to [the Mahatma] in reverence," and fired three shots that killed Gandhi instantly.

A new constitution changed Pakistan's status from that of dominion to a republic on March 23, 1956. Like India, Pakistan remained a member of the Commonwealth of Nations. In 1958 General Ayub Khan took control of Pakistan and assumed most of the powers of government. He became president, and his authority was confirmed in elections in 1960 and 1965.

Kashmir Is a Source of Tension

The state of Kashmir continued to be a focal point for clashes between India and Pakistan. Its ruling Hindu maharaja wanted to turn it over to India in 1947. However, Pakistan claimed the right to possess Kashmir on the ground that 85 per cent of the people living there were Moslems. Forces from both India and Pakistan invaded Kashmir and occupied parts of it.

In April, 1948, the Security Council proposed the holding of a *plebiscite* for the region—that is, a vote to permit the people of Kashmir to decide which country they wished to join. The plebiscite was never held. In 1957 India formally took possession of the part of Kashmir that Indian forces had occupied. Since this was two-thirds of Kashmir, tensions between India and Pakistan increased.

The Nehru Government Attacks India's Problems

Meanwhile the government of India, under the leadership of Prime Minister Jawaharlal Nehru, attacked its numerous political, economic, and social problems. It needed to raise the standard of living of millions of people in India. Acute poverty and hunger were widespread. In the early 1950's the average amount earned by nonagricultural workers was about $4 a week; and newspapers reported that over 150,000 people were sleeping on Bombay sidewalks. The rapid expansion of India's population made it extremely difficult to provide the people with sufficient food, decent housing, or other needs.

Nehru and other leaders of the government of India tried to solve these and other problems in the following ways. They established a socialistic economy in areas where it might help raise the standards of living, and they took steps to develop industry and modern technology. They also strengthened the system of education, and supported international efforts at political, economic, and social cooperation. Nehru continued to speak of the need for peace. Nevertheless, in December, 1961, India's armed forces invaded and took the Portuguese-held territories of Goa, Daman, and Diu along the western borders of India.

In the fall of 1962, Communist China invaded India. The Indians, aided by Britain, the United States, and the Soviet Union, mobilized for a "life and death struggle." In November, China ordered a cease-fire, with no settlement on the territory involved. In May, 1964, Nehru died of a heart attack. Lal Bahadur Shastri succeeded him. Upon Shastri's death, Indira Gandhi became prime minister.

Burma

Burma, a land about the size of Texas, borders on India, Thailand, and China (map, p. 702). It had been part of the British colony of India since 1886. In 1937 Burma was separated from British India and given some powers of self-government. On January 4, 1948, the Union of Burma became a fully independent country. Chief responsibility for directing the new republic was assigned to a prime minister and a two-house legislature. U Nu (1907–   ) became Burma's first prime minister. He held this position between 1948 and 1958.

During his long period in office, U Nu worked to establish peace and stability. He put down the revolts of the Karens, a minority group seeking to set up a separate state, and he introduced a reform program by which land was given to poor farmers. He also tried to check the influence of the Burmese Communists and supported the development of Burma as a welfare state. U Nu followed a policy of neutralism in the "Cold War."

In 1958 a political dispute and other factors caused serious tensions and instability. Many Burmese leaders feared that the Communists would soon seize the government. To block such a move, General Ne Win, with the approval of U Nu, formed a new military government to restore order. He checked inflation, lowered living costs, and crushed groups challenging the government. Then he and his military officials returned the government to civilian control. When new elections were held in 1960, U Nu and his associates were returned to office. In 1961 Buddhism was made the state religion. General Ne Win returned to power in 1962, following a military coup. He pursued a socialist program, nationalizing industries.

Ceylon

Ceylon, an island off the southeastern tip of India, had been a colonial possession of Britain. It was the world's principal exporter of cinnamon and fourth largest exporter of rubber. On February 4, 1948, Ceylon became a dominion (map, p. 702).

Ceylon, a member of both the Commonwealth and the United Nations, faced

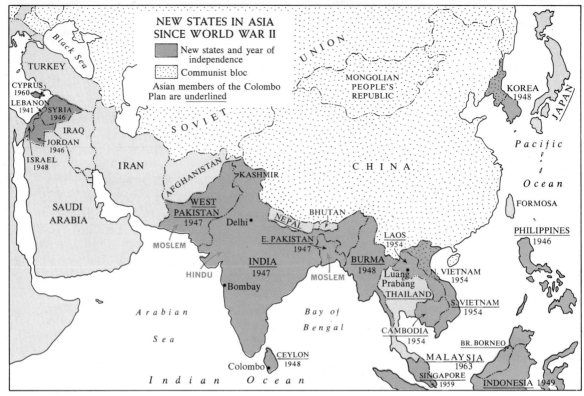

NEW STATES IN ASIA SINCE WORLD WAR II

- New states and year of independence
- Communist bloc
- Asian members of the Colombo Plan are <u>underlined</u>

TURKEY

CYPRUS 1960
LEBANON 1941
SYRIA 1946
IRAQ
JORDAN 1946
ISRAEL 1948
SAUDI ARABIA
IRAN

Black Sea

SOVIET

UNION

MONGOLIAN PEOPLE'S REPUBLIC

CHINA

KOREA 1948

JAPAN

Pacific

Ocean

FORMOSA

PHILIPPINES 1946

AFGHANISTAN
KASHMIR
WEST PAKISTAN 1947
Delhi
NEPAL
BHUTAN
E. PAKISTAN 1947
MOSLEM
HINDU
INDIA 1947
Bombay
MOSLEM
BURMA 1948
LAOS 1954
Luang Prabang
THAILAND
N. VIETNAM 1954
S. VIETNAM 1954
CAMBODIA 1954

Arabian Sea

Bay of Bengal

BR. BORNEO
MALAYSIA 1963
SINGAPORE 1959
INDONESIA 1949

CEYLON 1948
Colombo

Indian Ocean

■ *Many nations in Asia obtained their independence from foreign domination after World War II. What problems did these independent countries face? How did the "Cold War" affect them?*

many domestic problems from 1950 to 1967. There were clashes between the Sinhalese and Tamils, two ethnic-religious groups. The population of about 9.3 million was too large for the country's size, and Ceylon needed to diversify its economy.

Federation of Malaysia

On August 31, 1967, the Federation of Malaysia became a dominion. This strategically important country faced many problems, domestic and foreign. Among the domestic problems was the hostility between Malays and Chinese. The latter suffered much discrimination.

In 1959 Singapore, the British Crown Colony, became independent. In 1963 it joined the new Federation of Malaysia, which consisted of the states of Malaya, Singapore, and Sarawak and Sabah on the island of Borneo. President Sukarno considered Malaysia a threat to his nation. Britain had to defend Malaysia against guerrilla attacks.

Singapore withdrew from the Malaysian Federation and became an independent nation in 1965. Sukarno was removed from the presidency of Indonesia in 1967, and relations between Malaysia and Indonesia improved. They signed a treaty on "joint security arrangements in the border regions."

■ Check on Your Reading

1. What obstacles blocked the road to India's independence?
2. Why was India divided?
3. What problems faced Burma, Ceylon, and the Federation of Malaysia?

702

6. Other Nations of Asia Obtain Independence

Many of the other nations in Asia obtained independent status, too, and faced many difficulties. We will look at each of these countries to find out how they dealt with their problems.

The Republic of the Philippines

In 1934, by the Tydings-McDuffie Act, the United States had promised the Philippines independence in 1946. On July 4, 1946, the Republic of the Philippines was established. Manuel Roxas became the first president.

The Republic of the Philippines consisted of over twenty million people inhabiting about seven thousand islands whose total area was about equal to that of Arizona. The Americans provided the Filipino government with considerable economic assistance and signed a pact of mutual aid in case of military attack.

The Filipinos faced many problems of postwar adjustment after 1946. Ramón Magsaysay, who was president of the new republic (1953–1957), worked hard to introduce necessary reforms. He instituted a type of face-to-face democracy by always being willing to meet the people and discuss their problems. Magsaysay also distributed land to poor farmers, checked the Philippine Communists (or Huks), and tried to eliminate graft.

After the death of Magsaysay there was a gradual slowing down in the carrying out of his policies. The Philippine government tried to strengthen its economy by establishing closer trading ties with Japan. Some of the Filipino leaders also wanted to revise agreements by which the United States held a 99-year lease on military bases in the Philippines. Despite certain disagreements, the United States and the Republic of the Philippines continued to maintain friendly relations.

Indonesia Wins Its Independence

During World War II, Japan had occupied the Dutch East Indies, which had been ruled by the Netherlands for four and one half centuries. After the war, the people of Indonesia demanded freedom from Dutch rule. Although the Dutch government promised eventual self-government, Indonesian patriots such as Sukarno insisted on immediate independence. Fighting broke out, and the United Nations intervened.

In 1949 the Dutch and Indonesians agreed to form a Netherlands-Indonesian Union. The Republic of the United States of Indonesia came into existence, with Sukarno (1901–   ) as its first president.

On August 15, 1950, the new republic merged with other Indonesian territory, and the country took the name of the Republic of Indonesia. On August 11, 1954, a protocol was signed in The Hague dissolving the Netherlands-Indonesian Union.

Indonesian Leaders Face Many Problems

Indonesia had a population of over ninety-five million people, mostly Moslems. With such raw materials as oil, bauxite ores, copra, rubber, and tin, it was potentially a rich nation. The new Indonesian government declared that it would be guided by the *Pantjasila*, or five principles. These were belief in God, humanitarianism, nationalism, democracy, and social justice for all.

The new nation had many problems. It was difficult to unite a country that consisted of 3000 islands scattered between Asia and Australia. The Indonesians also struggled with the Dutch for possession of West Irian (the western half of New Guinea). In 1960–1961 the Dutch permitted western New Guinea limited self-government.

HO CHI MINH TRAIL

CHINA

Hanoi
Haiphong
Gulf of Tonkin

NORTH VIETNAM

HAINAN

Vientiane

Mu Gia Pass

Dong Hoi
17th Parallel
(Demilitarized Zone)
Hue
Ke Sanh
A Shau
Da Nang

THAILAND

Mekong R.

VIETNAM
0   100   200
Scale of Miles

Pleiku
Qui Nhon
SOUTH VIETNAM

CAMBODIA
Mekong
Phnom-Penh
Cam Ranh Bay

Saigon-Cholon

Gulf
of
Siam

MEKONG DELTA

There were serious weaknesses in the Indonesian economy. Peasant farmers could not produce enough to eat, and many parts of the country lacked basic industries. When Indonesia achieved its independence, less than 5 per cent of the people could read and write; and there was only one doctor for every 65,000 persons. Indonesia also had to maintain a position of neutrality in the "Cold War."

In 1957 Sukarno introduced "guided democracy." This was a policy by which majority rule was set aside, a coalition government of Communist and non-Communist representatives was formed, and Sukarno and a national advisory council made all decisions. In January, 1965,

Indonesia withdrew from the UN, in protest against the election of Malaysia to the Security Council. Nineteen months later Indonesia rejoined the United Nations. Indonesia also moved closer to Red China and seized American private business property as well as U.S. Information Service libraries.

In September, 1965, Indonesia was disrupted by a revolt led by Communists. It was charged by powerful Indonesian leaders that Sukarno approved of this uprising as a means of eliminating military officers who opposed Communist influence and programs. When the uprising was put down by the military, most of Sukarno's authority was taken away from him. Thousands of Communists were killed in the following months.

All governmental powers of Sukarno were withdrawn in 1967, and General Suharto was appointed as Acting President of Indonesia. A new Congress was to be elected in 1968.

War in Vietnam

The war in Vietnam became a crucible testing the beliefs, determination, and power of the men and nations involved. Although the United States and South Vietnamese forces carried the principal burden for the defense of Vietnam, military support or bases also came from South Korea, Australia, New Zealand, Thailand, and the Philippines. Thirty-two other countries provided technical and economic aid.

Civilians on both sides were the tragic victims of the war; and terror, disease, and hunger spread throughout the land. Over one million refugees, including thousands of homeless children, wandered hopelessly about the countryside. The tense faces of soldiers fighting desperately in a jungle thicket merged with the gaunt expressions of old women clawing wildly for a handful of rice. War stopped being a matter of statistics and became a daily vision of brutality and death.

The United States itself was the scene of a "great debate" over American activities in the war in Vietnam. There were those who said: (a) the war was an attempt by Communist forces to seize control of Vietnam, and the United States was justified in taking steps to check them; (b) the military actions of the United States were necessary to defend the independence of South Vietnam; (c) the entry of the United States into the Vietnam conflict was legal on the basis of American defensive agreements with South Vietnam and American membership in the Southeast Asia Treaty Organization; (d) the Vietnam war was part of an international struggle; if Vietnam fell to the Communists, other countries of Southeast Asia would be menaced; (e) peace should be the goal, but any act of appeasement towards the enemy, comparable to that of the Munich Pact of 1938, was dangerous.

On the other hand, there were those who said: (a) the war was a civil conflict between the people of Vietnam; the United States had no right to intervene in it; (b) the military actions of the United States, especially the bombings of North Vietnam, were undesirable and responsible for the deaths of thousands of innocent people; (c) the entry of the United States into the Vietnam conflict was illegal because the Charter of the United Nations barred its members from any unilateral use of force without UN authorization; (d) the Vietnam war was a national conflict; it should not be viewed as part of an international conspiracy; (e) peace should be restored by compromise and negotiation with the enemy.

In addition to these two positions, there was a variety of other opinions concerning the actions of the United States in the war. As 1968 drew near, fears increased that the war would spread to other countries. Serious efforts were made to end the fighting in Vietnam.

Meanwhile, the leaders of the Vietcong and North Vietnam introduced significant economic and social changes in the area they controlled. Programs against undesirable economic and social conditions also were started in South Vietnam. Here dedicated men and women from South Vietnam, the United States, and their allies immunized millions of Vietnamese against cholera and smallpox, sprayed homes against malaria, built new classrooms, irrigated land, constructed dams, and fought the daily problems facing the people. President Johnson called this "the other war . . . the quiet war," but its success depended ultimately on finding a solution to the sound and fury of the military conflict.

Regionalism and Problems of Diversity

One of the difficulties in forming regional organizations in Asia is the great diversity of the area. As one scholar-diplomat pointed out:

—Population density per square mile is 680 in Japan, 730 in South Korea, 900 in Taiwan, but only 30 in Laos.

—Life expectancy ranges from 69 to 30 years, and the literacy rate from over 95 to 15 percent.

—The per capita gross national product ranges from $50 in Japan to less than $100 in Korea, Indonesia, and Laos.

■ Check on Your Reading

1. Discuss the causes and results of the internal troubles in Indonesia.

2. Evaluate opposing positions in the "great debate" on the war in Vietnam.

3. What social and economic changes were introduced in Vietnam?

4. What problems does the great diversity of the Far East present to regional leaders?

MAN AND HIS CULTURE

Let's Meet the People!

The following sketch is based on information in an article in the *Shansi Jih Pao* (*Shansi Daily News*), excerpts of which appeared in *The New York Times Magazine*, June 8, 1958.

Yu-Lan and Chang: A Romance in Communist China

"In looking for a marriage prospect, true feelings should be built on mutual labor." These words were told to Yu-lan when she came from the city to work on a co-operative farm in Communist China.

Yu-lan remembered those words whenever she looked at the peasant Chang. He was good-natured, frank, outspoken, and a member of the Young Communist League. Most important of all, Chang loved to work hard. Yu-lan believed that this was the reason why she was "drawn by some unknown emotional force closer and closer to Chang." Her dictatorial rulers had led her to believe this.

Later, when Yu-lan "appeared lost in handling harvesting work," Chang showed her how to do her farm work properly. He also helped her to do the heavy manual labor that was expected of all women on the co-operative farm. They labored together on the land.

Yu-lan now thought more and more about her feelings for Chang. "These feelings have been built up through mutual labor," she told herself. Then one night Chang said to Yu-lan:

"Do you have any opinions about me, Yu-lan?"

"I'm very much satisfied with you. I have made up my mind," answered Yu-lan.

"Since you have no bad opinion, let us get married," said Chang.

Yu-lan smiled and nodded her head.

Thus it was that in early December Yu-lan and Chang were married. Immediately after the wedding, a friend of Yu-lan approached her and asked: "Why did you fall in love with Chang?"

"I am in love with *the land*," answered Yu-lan, blushing.

Her friend laughed for a moment; then she said:

"You have not said it fully. Not only have you been in love with the village land—but also with *a man* in the village!"

CHAPTER REVIEW

REVIEW and DISCUSSION

1. Identify the people and places and explain the events and terms on p. 690.

2. What problems were faced by Asia in the post-World War II period?

3. What problems may be encountered in trying to impose democracy suddenly upon a country? Use postwar Japan as a case study.

4. What factors can you find that favored the spread of Communist power in Asia? What factors can you find that opposed the spread of communism?

5. Why might Chinese leaders prefer the policies of Stalin to those of Khrushchev?

6. What problems faced the "two Chinas"?

7. Did the new nations in which the colonial power had earlier granted some degree of self-government meet their problems more or less effectively than those countries which gained their independence without advance preparation for it?

8. How can a country like Pakistan successfully govern a divided territory? Support your answer with proof.

9. Why did some leaders of new countries in Asia feel that some degree of socialism was desirable?

10. What was the attitude of the United States government toward France's actions in Indo-China?

11. What role did religion play in the reaction of Asian peoples to their political and economic problems?

ACTIVITIES

1. Panel discussion: Should the United States recognize Communist China?

2. Debate: Resolved, that a new country unprepared for independence has to have a period of dictatorship before it can become a democracy.

3. On a map of Asia show the new nations, their dates of independence, and principal geographical features.

4. Draw a diagram showing U. S. commitments in regional organizations and treaties in the Pacific area.

PAST and PRESENT

1. Contrast the world of the eighteenth century in which the United States was born with the world in which new Asian nations have recently been born.

2. Compare United States actions in Asian affairs after World War I with its actions after World War II.

SUGGESTED READINGS

Basic books: BRUUN, GEOFFREY, and MAMATEY, VICTOR S., *The World in the Twentieth Century*, Chaps. 49, 62–64, Heath.

LANGSAM, WALTER, *The World Since 1919*, Macmillan. Contains a valuable chapter on Asian developments since 1945.

LATOURETTE, KENNETH SCOTT, *A Short History of the Far East*, Chap. XVII, Macmillan. The aftermath of war in Asia.

Special accounts: LINEBARGER, PAUL M. A., CHU, DJANG, and BURKS, ARDATH W., *Far Eastern Governments and Politics*, Van Nostrand. Very useful detailed treatment of governments in China and Japan, including period after the war. For better readers.

MORELAND, W. H., and CHATTERJEE, ATUL CHANDRA, *A Short History of India*. Chap. 47, Longmans, Green. The division and transfer of power.

REISCHAUER, EDWIN O., *Japan Past and Present*, Chaps. 13, 14, Knopf. Reliable information on Japan after the war.

Biography and Fiction: EATON, JEANETTE, *Gandhi: Fighter without a Sword*, Morrow. An easy-to-read biography.

GUNTHER, JOHN, *The Riddle of MacArthur; Japan, Korea, and the Far East*, Harper. Easy reading. Attempts to explain MacArthur's role in the Far East.

ROMULO, CARLOS P., *I Walked with Heroes*, Holt. An autobiography.

Chapter 44   "Wind of Change" in the Middle East and Africa

KEYNOTE   John Scott, in recounting the events of a day spent in Africa with a well-educated African official, wrote recently:

> I noticed a small boy with fingernail-size amulets on his arm and asked [the African official, who had a university education] what they were.
> "They are *gris-gris*," he said. "They protect the boy from evil."
> "Do you believe in *gris-gris*?" I asked.
> He shrugged. "As an educated man, I cannot believe in such superstitions. On the other hand, as a man of sense, I cannot ignore them," he said.
> Here was Black Africa in a sentence. One foot in the tribal past, one in the swiftly moving twentieth century.

Harold Macmillan, who served as prime minister of Britain, and other statesmen felt optimistic about the future of this continent that lived in both the past and the present. "The wind of change is blowing through [Africa]," Macmillan declared.

"The wind of change" was blowing in other underdeveloped regions too, particularly in the Middle East. Leaders in this area also were working diligently to move their countries out of the past into the present. As a result, *one of the key features of contemporary times was the great political, economic, and social changes that occurred in the Middle East and Africa.*

Key People   *David Ben-Gurion · Gamal Abdel Nasser · Hendrik Verwoerd · Kwame Nkrumah · Joseph Kasavubu · Ian Smith · Leopold Senghor*

Key Places   *Israel · Egypt · Syria · Iran · Lebanon · Tunisia · Morocco · Ghana · Algeria · The Congo*

Key Events   *Balfour Declaration · Arab League formed · Arab-Israeli War · Suez Canal nationalized · Iran nationalizes oil fields · Baghdad Pact · Bandung Conference*

Key Terms   *Pan-Arabism · Zionists · Eisenhower Doctrine*

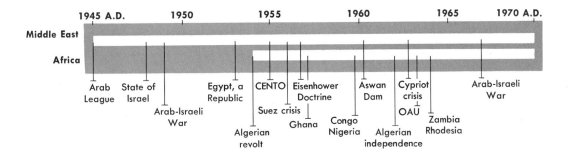

Middle East

Africa

1945 A.D.	1950	1955	1960	1965	1970 A.D.

Arab League
State of Israel
Arab-Israeli War
Egypt, a Republic
Algerian revolt
CENTO
Suez crisis
Eisenhower Doctrine
Ghana
Congo Nigeria
Aswan Dam
Algerian independence
Cypriot crisis
OAU
Zambia Rhodesia
Arab-Israeli War

1. The Middle East Is Plagued by Many Problems

The Middle East consists of the following lands: Egypt (United Arab Republic): Syria; Lebanon; Israel; Jordan; Iran; Iraq; Turkey; Crete; Cyprus; and Afghanistan (map, p. 710). Linking the continents of Europe, Africa, and Asia, the Middle East is a key geographic area. Dwight D. Eisenhower declared: "There is no more strategically important area in the world." The Middle East has about 65 per cent of the world's proved oil reserves. Before the Arab-Israel War of 1967, it provided about two-thirds of the oil used by Europe and about 60 per cent of the oil used by Japan.

About 130 million people live in the Middle East. Most of them are Arabs who practice the religion of Islam. Iran and Turkey are also predominantly Moslem, but they are not Arab. Over 2.7 million people inhabit Israel; 87 per cent of them are Jews. Roughly 80 per cent of the population of the Middle East are farmers, 15 per cent are urban dwellers, and 5 per cent are nomads.

The peoples of the Middle East faced many serious problems after World War II. These included the following:

(1) As late as 1958, a considerable part of the Middle East land mass was not being cultivated. With the exception of Egypt, less than 50 per cent of the arable land was being farmed. A United Nations survey in the 1960's showed that nearly 99 per cent of the people made their living from about one-fifth of the area, the rest being desert.

(2) A few Arab leaders were multi-millionaires from oil royalties, but the majority of people had an extremely low standard of living. The income in most countries of the Middle East was $100 or less per person per year. Even when the per capita income began to rise, the structure of society prevented many people from improving their standard of living.

(3) In some countries of the Middle East, the population was growing so rapidly that it was difficult to provide a bare living for all the people. For example, in Egypt the population rose from ten million in 1900 to almost twenty million in 1950. By the late 1960's it was over twenty-seven million.

(4) Most countries in the Middle East, with the exception of Israel, had unsatisfactory systems of education. The majority of people had little formal education.

(5) Rising nationalism increased tensions in the Middle East. Nationalistic feelings contributed to the struggles between nationalists in the Middle East and foreign nations holding interests in this area.

(6) Conflicting feelings developed between the desire of the Arab leaders to support Pan-Arabism and their deter-

709

mination not to surrender their power to other Arab leaders. Some steps were taken toward *Pan-Arabism*—that is, toward drawing together the millions of Arabs "from the Atlantic to the Persian Gulf" who wrote in a common language, Arabic, and accepted a common religion, Islam. In 1945 the Arab League was formed by Egypt, Saudi Arabia, Syria, Iraq, Yemen, Lebanon, and Jordan (map, p. 710). Later, Libya, Tunisia, Morocco, and Sudan joined the Arab League.

The Arab League, with headquarters at Cairo, was set up to enable its members to form joint policies and take joint action in matters concerning all of them. How-ever, rivalries and struggles for power among Arab leaders in the League added to the tensions in the Middle East.

Other problems in the Middle East involved the lack of industrialization, an insufficient water supply, clashes between Jews and Arabs, and the "Cold War" as it affected the Middle East.

■ **Check on Your Reading**

1. What are the chief characteristics of the lands and peoples of the Middle East?

2. What serious problems did the peoples of the Middle East have?

3. What is Pan-Arabism? What difficulties has Pan-Arabism encountered?

2. The Republic of Israel Is Established

Palestine had been a part of the Ottoman Empire from the sixteenth century until World War I. During that war, British forces defeated the Turks and captured Jerusalem. On November 2, 1917, the British government issued the *Balfour Declaration*, which stated:

His Majesty's Government view with favour the establishment in Palestine of a national home for the Jewish people . . . nothing shall

■ *In the Middle East and North Africa are many Arab and Moslem states and the Jewish state of Israel. Name the members of the Arab League and the Baghdad Pact. What are the principal purposes of these organizations?*

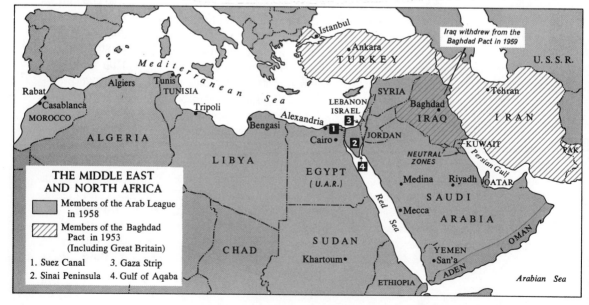

be done which may prejudice the civil and religious rights of existing non-Jewish communities in Palestine. . . .

Many Jews said that the Balfour Declaration meant that the British government promised Palestine to them as a national homeland. However, the Arabs claimed that Palestine belonged to them and they were determined that it should never come into the possession of the Jews.

The Jews declared that they had a right to a homeland in Palestine because their ancestors had inhabited the land in ancient times, and because there was a need for a land where Jews could assemble, live without persecution, and preserve their culture. The Jews in the Middle East were supported in their demands by Zionists throughout the world. *Zionists* were people of Jewish and other faiths who, according to the first Zionist Congress, "strive to create for the Jewish people a home in Palestine secured by public law." The Zionist movement began as early as 1897, and it was spearheaded by Theodor Herzl, a Viennese journalist.

The Arabs bitterly opposed Zionism and protested that Palestine had been artificially separated from Syria. They pointed out that Arabs had occupied Palestine for hundreds of years and made up the overwhelming majority of its population. They claimed that the establishment of a Jewish state would deprive Arabs of their land and interfere with the geographic and cultural unity of the Arab world.

The State of Israel Is Created

In 1923 the League of Nations made Palestine a mandate of Britain, but hostility between Arabs and Jews continued. The situation was further complicated by a great rise in Jewish immigration into Palestine, particularly during the period

■ *David Ben-Gurion became prime minister of Israel in 1948. He faced economic problems as well as the hostility of Israel's Arab neighbors.*

when Nazi Germany was persecuting the Jews. Between 1919 and 1948, over 450,-000 Jews emigrated to Palestine, and the Arabs protested that the newcomers were gradually taking over their country.

After World War II, the British turned over the problem of Palestine to the United Nations. In November, 1947, the General Assembly recommended that Palestine be partitioned into an Arab state and a Jewish state, which were to be politically independent but were to work together in economic matters. The city of Jerusalem was to be internationalized.

Jewish leaders accepted this recommendation, and in May, 1948, the British ended their mandate and the Jews proclaimed the establishment of the state of Israel.

Chaim Weizmann became the first president of Israel. David Ben-Gurion (1886–), a stocky, dynamic leader, was chosen prime minister of the new state. Ben-

Gurion believed that "the greatest contribution [Israel] can make is to build a model society that will lift humanity to greater heights, if copied in other countries."

Arab-Israeli War

The Arabs refused to recognize the existence of the state of Israel. Arab forces from Egypt, Lebanon, Syria, and Jordan attacked the Israelis. They were led by the British-trained Arab Legion.

The invading Arab troops were defeated in the Arab-Israeli War, and the United Nations worked to bring about a truce. A final cease-fire went into effect on January 7, 1949. As a result of the Arab-Israeli War and various agreements: (1) Israel increased its territory by about 50 per cent. (2) A new state of Jordan was formed out of Transjordan (the part of Palestine lying east of the Jordan River) and the Judean hills territories that were occupied by the Arab Legion during the war. Hussein, a relative of the king of Iraq, became king of the state of Jordan. (3) Jerusalem remained divided into two parts: The New City was in Israel and the Old City was in Jordan. (4) The United Nations turned over the Gaza Strip, an area 25 miles long and 5 miles wide along the Mediterranean Sea, to the Egyptian army to administer.

Arab Refugees Create a Serious Problem

Many problems remained to mar the relations between Israel and the Arab states. One of the most serious involved the future of the 900,000 Arab refugees who had fled from Palestine. These refugees were living in temporary quarters in the Gaza Strip, Jordan, Lebanon, Syria, and Iraq.

The Arab leaders claimed that the Arab refugees had the right to return to their homes in Palestine. The Israelis disagreed and declared that the Arab refugees should be resettled in Iraq and Syria.

The United Nations Relief and Works Agency for Palestine Refugees (UNRWA) attempted to provide housing and food for the Arab refugees. By 1961 UNRWA was running 58 refugee camps and had spent $360 million on the refugees. Meanwhile, there continued what novelist Martha Gellhorn called the "non-peace, non-war exercise" between Arabs and Israelis.

■ **Check on Your Reading**

1. Why did the Jews want to establish a homeland in Palestine? Why did the Arabs oppose this plan?

2. What were the results of the Arab-Israeli War?

3. What was done about the Arab refugee problem?

3. *Egypt Becomes a Republic*

Egypt in the post-World War II period was a troubled land. More Egyptians became dissatisfied with the corruption and inefficiency of King Farouk's government. They were disturbed by the social and economic inequalities in the country, and by the influence of the British in Egypt's affairs. As one Egyptian reformer, Gamal Abdel Nasser, said, "The problem was to restore human dignity in Egypt."

In the summer of 1952, Major General Mohammed Naguib and a group of army officers revolted against King Farouk and forced him to abdicate. On June 18, 1953, Egypt was proclaimed a republic. Lieutenant Colonel Gamal Abdel Nasser, one of the rebel leaders, soon became the spokesman for the Egyptian nationalists. On April 18, 1954, he replaced Naguib as prime minister of the government. Later

■ *Gamal Abdel Nasser in December, 1955, announced that further Israeli attacks on Egypt would be met by armed force. A year later Israel overwhelmed the Egyptian army in two days, but was forced by the UN to withdraw.*

Nasser was also chosen president and became the real power in the new state.

Egypt Seizes the Suez Canal

Although King Farouk had been overthrown, British soldiers remained in Egypt in control of the Suez Canal. Nasser was determined to force them out, and in October, 1954, Great Britain agreed to remove her troops from the Suez Canal zone. The last British troops withdrew in June, 1956. Great Britain reserved the right to reoccupy the base at Suez if Egypt, Turkey, or any of the Arab states were attacked. However, Egypt was free at last from foreign control.

Meanwhile, Nasser attempted to build up the military and economic strength of Egypt. In 1955, when he failed to persuade the nations of the West to provide him with arms, he made a deal with Czechoslovakia to exchange Egyptian cotton for Communist planes, tanks, and artillery. Nasser had earlier received an offer of $200 million in financial assistance from the United States and Great Britain to help Egypt build the High Dam at Aswan. It was hoped that the construction of this dam would increase Egypt's agricultural output by 50 per cent, help the irrigation and reclamation of two million acres, provide the electricity necessary for industrialization, and supply water for the permanent rice plantation of 700,000 acres.

The United States and Great Britain were disturbed by Egypt's cotton-for-arms deal with Czechoslovakia and by the anti-Western attitude of the Egyptian government. Therefore, on July 19–20, 1956, the United States and Great Britain withdrew their offer to help finance the Aswan Dam. On July 26, 1956, Nasser retaliated by proclaiming the Egyptian seizure and nationalization of the Suez Canal.

The Suez Canal had been under the control of the Suez Canal Company, most of whose stockholders were French and British. Nasser declared that the Canal was now Egypt's property. He said that he would use the toll revenues from the Canal to help finance the Aswan project. Egypt's action led to an international crisis.

Egypt promptly barred Israeli ships from the Canal and interfered with other vessels bound to and from Israel. At the same time, the British and French were concerned that Nasser might cut off the oil supplies coming through the Canal.

On October 29, 1956, three months after Egypt nationalized the Suez Canal, Israeli troops invaded Egypt's Sinai Desert. It is believed that Israel attacked in order (1) to crush Egypt's military strength before it became powerful enough to conquer Israel, and (2) to destroy Egyptian bases that were used as "jumping-off" places for border raids against Israel.

Great Britain and France issued an ultimatum ordering Egypt and Israel to cease fighting. Israel indicated a willingness to do so, but Egypt ignored the ultimatum. Two days after Israel invaded Egypt, British and French forces, based on Cyprus, also attacked Egypt. Great Britain and France may have invaded Egypt to safeguard the Suez Canal or to regain sufficient power to make Nasser place the Canal again under international control. The Egyptians sank ships in the Suez Canal to block passage of vessels.

The United Nations met in emergency session. The United States, the Soviet Union, and other countries voted to demand that Great Britain, France, and Israel withdraw from Egypt. The three nations withdrew, and a United Nations Emergency Force was sent to patrol the borders between Israel and Egypt.

The Aswan Dam project was then financed and engineered by the Soviet Union. Construction was begun in 1960 and the dam was expected to add 2 million acres of arable land. Anticipated gains were threatened, however, by increases in population and expenditures for armaments.

Egypt and Syria Unite—and Separate Again

In 1958 Egypt and Syria merged to form the United Arab Republic (UAR). Later Yemen also joined the federation.

Nasser, whom the people of Cairo cheered as "the destroyer of imperialism," became president of the United Arab Republic. Although Egypt and Syria were separated by 150 miles of Israeli and Jordanian territory, the Syrian premier declared that the UAR was "the first step on the path to achieve entire Arab unity." Egypt continued to be called officially the United Arab Republic after Syria withdrew in 1961.

■ Check on Your Reading

1. How did Nasser gain power in Egypt?
2. Why did Egypt seize the Suez Canal? What followed?
3. How was the United Arab Republic formed and dissolved?

4. Tensions and Changes in Other Middle East Lands

Other Middle East countries were faced with problems. Tensions and changes affected Iran, Lebanon, Iraq, and Jordan.

Iran Nationalizes Its Oil Fields

Iran, once known as Persia, is a Middle East country where most of the people are Moslems, but not Arabs. Iran is important in international affairs because it is a major producer of oil and because its lands border on the Soviet Union. In 1925 General Riza Pahlavi was elected

hereditary Shah, or ruler. He helped to modernize and strengthen the country by introducing modern codes of law, establishing a system of compulsory education, building roads, and abolishing the extraterritorial rights of foreigners.

After World War II, nationalism became an increasingly powerful factor in Iranian affairs. In 1951 nationalists and some Communists started strikes in the important oil fields of the Anglo-Iranian Oil Company. The largest stockholder in

■ *The Shah of Iran distributes deeds to parcels of land to Iranian peasants as part of his land reform program.*

the company was the British government, and the strikers claimed that foreigners were making great profits from oil that really belonged to the Iranians.

In March, 1951, the prime minister of Iran was shot. Dr. Mohammed Mossadegh, a nationalist leader, became the new prime minister of the country. His government seized and *nationalized* the Anglo-Iranian Oil Company's properties and the British administrators were ordered to leave the country.

After nationalization, Iran had difficulty selling its oil, and political conditions were very unsettled. The oil situation was stabilized on August 5, 1954, when Iran and eight oil companies (British, Dutch, French, American) signed a new contract. For twenty-five years plus fifteen optional years, the companies could work the oil fields that formerly were operated by the Anglo-Iranian Oil Company. In return, they would pay Iran royalties equal to 50 per cent of their earnings. The Anglo-Iranian Oil Company was to receive $70 million as compensation.

Tensions Increase in Lebanon, Iraq, and Jordan

Lebanon became a mandate of France after World War I. In 1941 the country gained its independence.

In May, 1958, President Chamoun of the Republic of Lebanon proposed a change in the constitution that would enable him to run for a second term. This proposal served as the spark for a revolt. Most of Chamoun's supporters were Christians; and most rebels were Moslems. (About 54 per cent of the population was Christian and about 44 per cent Moslem.) Chamoun declared that the rebels were receiving arms from the United Arab Republic.

The situation was complicated by events in Iraq. In July, 1958, there was an army *coup d'état*. Abdul Karim Kassem became the real ruler of the country, and established a military regime that was both nationalistic and anti-Western. The Communists in Iraq threw their support behind Kassem's government, and the United Arab Republic denounced Kassem for allowing Communist influence to remain in Iraq.

President Chamoun considered Kassem's *coup d'état* and other events in Iraq as indications of a general plan by nationalists to overthrow pro-Western governments in the Middle East. He asked the United States for help, and American marines landed in Beirut on July 14, 1958. President Eisenhower declared that the troops were sent "to encourage the Lebanese Government in defense of Lebanese sovereignty and integrity." King Hussein of Jordan also requested assistance, and British troops were sent.

The United Nations intervened to restore order in the Middle East. It succeeded in easing tensions among the Arab states. In August, 1958, an election was held in Lebanon. The newly elected president was able to gain support of most people. American troops withdrew from Lebanon, and British troops left Jordan.

■ **Check on Your Reading**
1. Why did the Iranian government nationalize the oil fields? What problems arose?
2. What caused the revolt in Lebanon?

5. *The Middle East Searches for Security*

Meanwhile, in 1955 Iran, Iraq, Turkey, Pakistan, and Great Britain signed the *Baghdad Pact* for their mutual "security and defense." They also agreed to work together to improve economic conditions in the member nations. Iraq withdrew in 1959.

Today the Baghdad Pact is known as the Central Treaty Organization (CENTO). The United States supported the purposes of CENTO, and gave military and economic assistance to several of its members.

Eisenhower Doctrine

In January, 1957, President Dwight D. Eisenhower of the United States proposed the so-called *Eisenhower Doctrine*. This proposal urged that the United States (1) assist the Middle Eastern countries in developing the economic strength needed for the maintenance of national independence; (2) authorize the Executive Branch of the government to undertake "military assistance programs" with any Middle Eastern country desiring such aid; and (3) permit the use of the armed forces of the United States "to secure and protect

the territorial integrity and political independence [of such nations] requesting such aid against overt armed aggression from any nation controlled by international Communism. . . ." The Eisenhower Doctrine was a factor in the decision to send American troops into Lebanon in 1958.

Changes in Turkey

In May, 1960, an army coup in Turkey overthrew the Menderes government. Menderes was charged with being corrupt and autocratic. In 1961 a new Turkish constitution went into effect. It contained provisions to guard against one-man rule.

In late 1963 Turkey became involved in a dispute with Greece over the rights of the Turkish minority on the Greek-dominated independent island of Cyprus. In March, 1964, the United Nations sent a peacekeeping force to stop fighting between Greek and Turkish factions. A cease-fire agreement was reached in August, 1964.

■ **Check on Your Reading**
1. What organizations developed among Middle Eastern countries to achieve security?
2. What was the Eisenhower Doctrine?

6. War in the Middle East: 1967

The Middle East continued to remain "like a cocked pistol, like a bomb with a dozen detonators." War broke out again in 1967.

In May, 1967, Gamal Abdel Nasser of Egypt demanded that the United Nations withdraw "the UN Emergency Force in Egypt and the Gaza Strip." United Nations troops had been stationed in the Gaza Strip, where they acted as a buffer between Israelis and Egyptians; and in Sharm el Sheikh, where they saw to it that the Gulf of Aqaba was kept open for all ships, including those carrying oil and other vital supplies to the Israeli port of Elath. United Nations Secretary-General U Thant, accepting the point that UN forces had entered Egyptian territory with the consent of Egypt, complied with Nasser's demand. Then, on May 23, the Egyptians announced a blockade of the Gulf of Aqaba "to vessels flying the Israeli flag and to the ships of any other country carrying strategic goods to Elath." (See map on this page.)

War broke out on June 5, 1967, each side charging the other with responsibility for starting hostilities. Vowing to crush the 19-year old nation, Egypt, Jordan, Syria, Iraq, Kuwait, Sudan, Tunisia, Morocco, Lebanon, Saudi Arabia, Algeria, and Yemen joined the conflict against Israel. Arab radio stations spoke of a "Holy War," and Israel's 2.7 million people faced over 100 million hostile Arabs surrounding them.

It was a short war, lasting but a few days, but filled with much of the drama and tragedy of longer conflicts. "On to Tel Aviv!" the Arabs shouted in the streets of Cairo. "Soldiers of the Israel Defense Forces, on this day our hopes and security are with you!" answered the Israeli Defense Minister, Moshe Dayan. Emotion took the place of reason, and men on both sides gave up their lives.

Israeli forces could not be stopped. By sudden, coordinated attacks its well-trained air force destroyed a major part of the air power of the Arab states. One military authority declared: "Israel would seem to have won the most outstanding air battle in history." In six days the "blitz" of Israeli planes, tanks, and infantry crushed their opponents and won the war.

■ *What problems does the acquisition of new territory present for the Israelis? for the Arab refugees?*

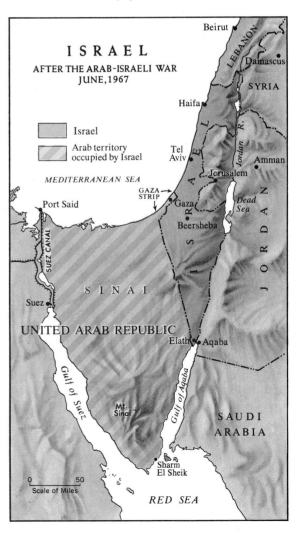

ISRAEL

AFTER THE ARAB-ISRAELI WAR
JUNE, 1967

Israel

Arab territory occupied by Israel

MEDITERRANEAN SEA

Beirut
Damascus
SYRIA
Haifa
Tel Aviv
Amman
Jerusalem
Jordan R.
Dead Sea
GAZA STRIP
Port Said
Gaza
Beersheba
JORDAN
SUEZ CANAL
S I N A I
Suez
UNITED ARAB REPUBLIC
Elath
Aqaba
Gulf of Suez
Gulf of Aqaba
Mt. Sinai
SAUDI ARABIA
Sharm El Sheik
0   50
Scale of Miles
RED SEA

In the old city of Jerusalem, which the Israelis had taken after bitter fighting, Israeli General Moshe Dayan wrote a prayer on a piece of paper and inserted it into the Wailing Wall. It read: "May Peace be upon all Israel." However, Arab leaders denounced Israel as an "aggressor," and many were already talking of vengeance against her.

The end of the Arab-Israeli War of 1967 left many serious questions and problems. These included:

1. What would be the future relations between Israel and the Arab states?

Specifically, would the Arabs accept the existence of Israel as an independent state in the Middle East or continue to try to destroy it?
2. What role could the United Nations play in helping establish permanent peace in the Middle East?
3. How do United States and Soviet policies conflict in the Middle East?
4. What could be done to bring satisfaction and security to the Arab refugees?
5. How could economic and social conditions in the post-war Middle East be improved?

7. Economic, Social, and Cultural Trends for the 1970's

Despite the conflict between Arabs and Israelis, many changes were underway in the Middle East.

One scholar, William R. Polk, director of the Center for Middle Eastern Studies at the University of Chicago, pictured a social transformation in the Middle East. Its key aspects would include: (a) "A shift in the nature of power . . . toward the creation of a modern industrial society." (b) A change in leadership that will see the increased importance of *new men*. "The 'new men' are those who possess the skill, the discipline, the orientation, and the motivation to modernize society. However much they may differ among themselves in terms of income, education, and ability, they are even more sharply differentiated, in politically more significant ways, from the traditional elements of society." (c) A continued breakdown of the cultural and educational barriers between the Middle East and the rest of the world.

Education was considered to be one of the keys to the future constructive growth of the Middle East. Between 1945 and 1960 school attendance of Egyptian children had increased nearly threefold. By 1970 it could be nearly 6 million.

Relations with the rest of the world would partly determine the social, economic, and cultural development of Middle Eastern lands in the 1970's. In the past, financial assistance from some nations had been considerable. In a ten-year period, 1957–1967, economic aid to the Middle East in loans and grants, including a Food for Peace program, was $675 million to Israel and $3.4 billion to the Arab nations.

Yet, in the long run, the future depended on the efforts of the people of the Middle East themselves. The evidence indicated that more and more individuals and groups were willing to work to achieve their objectives.

■ Check on Your Reading
1. What are the prospects for change in the Middle East?
2. Why is education the great hope of the Middle East?
3. How has financial assistance from foreign countries aided in the development of Middle East countries?

Africa in the Twentieth Century

With a land area of over 11½ million square miles, the continent of Africa is divided into three main geographic areas: North Africa; Equatorial Africa, which begins south of the Sahara; and South Africa (Atlas, p. 758). Africa produces 50 per cent of the world's gold and 95 per cent of its diamonds, and it has rich deposits of copper, manganese, cobalt, tin, and uranium.

In the early 1960's Africa had a population of nearly 275 million. About 70 per cent of the inhabitants were of Negroid stock; about 22 per cent were Arabs; and only about 29 per cent were Europeans. Most of the people in Africa were engaged in agriculture.

In the second half of the twentieth century many old ways of life continued in Africa. Yet Africa was changing rapidly. Students were studying at the University of Ghana. Farmers were beginning to use scientific methods to plant cotton in the Sudan. Africans were learning that a serum was more effective than a magic mask in guarding against disease. Yet many problems remained in Africa in the post-World War II period. In the 1960's the people were still fighting poverty (average yearly income per person ranged between $89 and $132), illiteracy (about nine out of ten Africans were illiterate), and disease (average life expectancy was 40 years). They also had to establish new relationships with foreign powers.

One of the most important factors in Africa was *nationalism*. At the end of World War II, Egypt, Ethiopia, Liberia, and the Union of South Africa were the only independent nations. Britain, France, Belgium, Spain, and Portugal controlled 90 per cent of Africa. Constant demands for political independence from the European colonial powers were heard.

HIGHLIGHTS of the African Heritage

A succession of kingdoms (Ghana, Mali, Songhai, and Kanem) existed from the end of the first Christian century to the end of the 15th century. The cultural achievements of the kingdom of Ghana, the most famous West African empire, easily equaled those of the Holy Roman Empire in Europe. About 977 Ibn Haukal wrote: "The King of Ghana is the richest king on earth."

The people of the kingdom of Mali were noted for their sense of justice. Ibn Battutah, an Arab geographer, commented: "Of all peoples, the Negroes are those who most abhor injustice. Next to the Mongol Empire, Mali was the largest imperial system of its day.

Under Askia Mohammed Touré known as Askia the Great (reign 1493–1528), Timbukto and Jenné became famous as centers of learning in the kingdom of Songhai. Negro and Moslem scholars studied law and surgery at the renowned University of Sankore. According to a report of Leo Africanus in the sixteenth century, books sold so well in Timbukto "that it was possible to make more profit from their sale than from any other article . . ."

Kanem-Bornu (800–1846), in the vicinity of Lake Chad, had a thousand years of independent existence as a government. It had a thriving trade with the Arabic world. One of the rulers created a home for students.

The kingdom of Mwanamutapa (a designation meaning "the lord of the mines") owed its existence to intensive industrial activity and the promotion of mine products which resulted in an extensive commercial trade reaching to Asia, Arabia, Persia, and even China. The imposing ruins of the capital at Great Zimbabwe gives an impression of the majesty of the empire of Mwanamutapa.

The Benin kingdom in the 12–13th centuries is linked to the Yoruba tradition. The most important contribution of the Benin kingdom are its bronze reliefs and its sculpture, which represent a high point in African art.

The Congo kingdom was founded at the beginning of the 15th century, probably by administrators of the Luba and Lunda system of states. The people were smiths, bold hunters, and warriors.

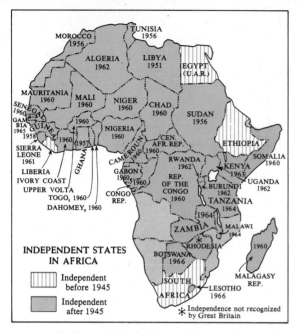

INDEPENDENT STATES
IN AFRICA

| | Independent before 1945 |
| | Independent after 1945 |

* Independence not recognized by Great Britain

■ *In the post-World War II period, many African countries gained their independence. What new African states were formed after 1945?*

Ghana, led by Kwame Nkrumah, gained its independence from Britain in 1957 and became a republic in 1960. Guinea, led by Sékou Touré, voted to break away from the French in 1958. Populous Nigeria became independent of Britain on October 1, 1960.

By October, 1961, four-fifths of the peoples of Africa were free of foreign control. Others, such as the natives of Angola who protested against Portuguese rule, demanded a change. Tanganyika, Burundi, Rwanda, Algeria, and Zanzibar achieved independence. The first and last of these joined together as Tanzania. Kenya won "Uhuru" (freedom) in 1963, Jomo Kenyatta becoming prime minister. Zambia gained "Kwacha" (freedom) in 1964. By 1967 there were thirty-nine independent African states, and only a few still under colonial status.

Between 1950 and 1960 twenty-five African countries gained their independence! For example, Tunisia and Morocco won their independence from France in 1956.

■ **Check on Your Reading**

1. What are the major features of resources and population in Africa?

2. Describe living conditions in Africa.

3. How did nationalism affect Africa?

8. African Nations Face Severe Crises

In the twentieth century, several African nations faced severe crises. War broke out in Algeria and the Congo; and tensions developed in South Africa.

Rebellion in Algeria

Algeria had been made an integral part of France. In 1947, a statute gave French citizenship to the country's eight million Moslems and assigned thirty seats in the French National Assembly to elected deputies representing Algeria's French and Moslem populations.

Moslem Algerians continued to be dominated by French officials and by the *colons*

(people of primarily French extraction who settled in Algeria). The French, who eventually owned one-third of the arable land, were a minority in Algeria. In 1954, out of a population of nine and a half million, 86 per cent were native Moslems (Arab and Berber) and 12 per cent French.

Tensions increased in Algeria after World War II, particularly between the Algerian Moslems and the colons. The Algerian Moslems became increasingly nationalistic and protested that they did not have equal status with the French. They wanted more political, economic, and social rights, or complete independence.

The colons declared that they would not be ruled or dominated by the Algerian Moslems. They demanded that the French government in Paris protect their interests. To complicate matters further, the people and political parties in France disagreed sharply on the action that the French government should take in Algeria.

A revolt by Moslem Algerian nationalists against French authority broke out in 1954. Eventually, it was directed by the rebel F.L.N. (National Liberation Front). This rebellion continued to drain strength from France for several years. Then in May, 1958, reports circulated that the new premier intended to "abandon" Algeria to the Moslems. These reports further infuriated the colons in Algeria.

On May 13, 1958, thirty thousand colons rioted in Algiers. The French army leaders in Algeria did not attempt to stop this insurrection. Instead, the French military chiefs took over the control and direction of the uprising. The insurrection spread to the island of Corsica and threatened to cause a civil war in France itself.

The French army leaders and demonstrators in Algeria issued a call for General Charles de Gaulle to take charge of the French government. On May 15 General de Gaulle came out of retirement to meet the crisis (p. 686).

De Gaulle took the position that the people of Algeria should have the right of self-determination—that is, the right to choose their own form of government—provided that peace was first established. He added that any changes in the relationship between France and Algeria should be brought about in an orderly fashion; and that there should be safeguards for the rights of both the Moslem majority and the French minority.

Some French military and others leaders in Algeria did not want France to give up Algeria under any circumstances. They formed the Secret Army Organization (OAS), which used violence and terror in an effort to keep Algeria under French control. At the same time, nationalistic Algerian rebels used similar methods in an effort to achieve immediate independence.

Between the establishment of the Fifth French Republic (October, 1958) and November, 1961, there were two rebellions among French army units in Algeria. De Gaulle's government put down these attempts to gain control of Algeria. In the same period, a referendum was held in which most of the French people showed their support for De Gaulle.

Meanwhile, Algerian Moslems continued to demand independence. They also insisted that the Sahara (with its valuable deposits of petroleum and natural gas) be given the right of self-determination.

On March 19, 1962, a cease-fire ended the war in Algeria. However, some fighting continued between the Moslems and the Europeans, and the OAS committed new acts of terror. In a referendum held on July 1, 1962, over 99 per cent of the Algerians voted for independence. On July 3, a proclamation of President Charles de Gaulle declared: "France recognizes solemnly the independence of Algeria."

After seven years of war and sixteen months of terrorism, Algeria at last was independent. The new nation found, however, that independence brought new and complex problems. Within the first months of its existence, rival factions were struggling for control of the government in Algeria.

The Belgian Congo Gains Its Independence

From 1908 until its independence, the Belgian Congo was administered by the Belgian government. By 1958, the population had reached about thirteen million. However, the minority of 125,000 whites dominated the political, economic, and

■ *Joseph Kasavubu is taking his oath of office as first president of the newly independent Republic of the Congo (June, 1960).*

social life of the country. On June 30, 1960, the Belgian government granted the Congo full independence.

Unprepared to exercise the responsibilities of independence, the Congo with a long oppressed population was immediately plunged into violence. Discord flared among those who wanted a highly centralized government, those who wanted considerable self-government for the provinces, and those who wanted primarily to protect Belgian economic interests. Congolese troops revolted against their Belgian officers. Rioting and looting broke out and whites were attacked. Thousands of Belgians prepared to flee. Then, eleven days after independence, Katanga Province seceded and formed its own government. It was a rich mining area, the wealthiest province of the Congo, and a stronghold of Belgian influence. It called on Belgium for assistance and Belgium ordered its troops in the Congo to protect Katanga, the Kasai Province, and Belgian citizens.

At the request of the Congo premier, Patrice Lumumba, Secretary-General Dag Hammarskjöld sent UN troops to the Congo to help restore order. When the UN refused to help Lumumba gain control of outlying areas of the Congo, he accepted the support of Russian arms and technicians. Forces supported by the Congo's president, Joseph Kasavubu, ordered the Russians to leave the country in September, 1960. Lumumba was dismissed (and later lost his life after capture by Katangese forces).

By the fall of 1961 progress seemed to have been made toward restoring order in the Congo. However, rich Katanga Province had not been restored to the Congo, and this meant serious economic difficulties. Premier Cyrille Adoula made clear that he would send troops to take Katanga by force. Secretary-General Dag Hammarskjöld and other United Nations officials feared that such an action would lead to further civil war. They believed that United Nations troops should move into Katanga and bring about a reunion of that province with the rest of the Congo *before* Adoula dispatched his troops.

Thus, on September 13, 1961, United Nations forces made a surprise attempt to take control of Elisabethville, the capital of Katanga. They hoped to end Katanga's secession by this display of force. The United Nations forces attacked unsuccessfully and their troops suffered a humiliating setback. The Congo was plunged into another crisis. Dag Hammarskjöld, en route to meet with Katanga's leader, Moise Tshombe, was killed in a plane crash on September 18. U Thant of Burma succeeded him as UN Secretary-General.

The Katanga secession was finally ended. On June 30, 1964, UN troops at last left the reunited Congo. Conditions again became chaotic. Premier Moise Tshombe faced a new rebellion, seemingly backed by Communist China. He used mercenary troops recruited in South Africa to put it down.

The Union of South Africa

Africa was marked by many racial conflicts. Among these were the anti-white, anti-European attacks of the Mau Mau, a secret society in Kenya.

Racial tensions became particularly severe in the Union of South Africa. After World War II, the Afrikaners (white descendants of the original Dutch families), a small minority of the total population, wanted to limit the privileges of the Negro majority and the Indians. Prime Minister Daniel F. Malan, leader of the Afrikaners, tried to hold down the non-whites through *apartheid* ("separateness"). Apartheid was a system of segregating non-whites. Each racial group was supposed to develop separately on the basis of its own culture and traditions.

In 1960, out of a total population of 14½ million, 9½ million were Bantu (blacks), almost 2 million were Indians or Colored (mulattoes), and only 3 million were whites in the Union of South Africa. Nevertheless, the Nationalist party, under the direction of Prime Minister Hendrik Verwoerd, continued the apartheid system, prevented non-whites from voting, limited the places where non-whites could own property, and restricted the freedom of movement of non-whites.

The Union of South Africa belonged to the Commonwealth of Nations until 1961.

However, several members of the Commonwealth—such as Ghana and India—denounced the apartheid policies of the South African government, and the British prime minister also criticized them.

On March 15, 1961, Dr. Verwoerd declared that he was "shocked by the spirit of hostility and vindictiveness." South Africa declared itself a republic and withdrew from the British Commonwealth.

On September 6, 1966, Dr. Verwoerd was stabbed to death. A South African court declared his white assassin to be mentally sick, disturbed, and irresponsible. Balthazar Johannes Vorster became the new Prime Minister.

By the end of 1967 the gap between whites and non-whites in South Africa remained wide. Infant mortality for whites was estimated at 29 per 1000 births; for non-whites 200+ per 1000 births. Life expectancy for whites was 67–72 years; for non-whites, 37–42. Average yearly wage for whites was $3800; for non-whites $210. The whites dominated political, economic, and social activities.

■ Check on Your Reading

1. What were the causes of the Algerian rebellion? How did De Gaulle deal with it?
2. What happened in the Congo after independence was granted?
3. How did the UN handle the Congo crisis?
4. What is the policy of apartheid? What effects has it had on non-whites?

9. African-Asian States Hold Regional Conferences

As the countries of Africa struggled towards independence, they took renewed interest in both their past and their future. Viewing their past, they were excited by new archaeological discoveries that indicated the existence of flourishing African civilizations long before the arrival of the Europeans. Viewing their future, they looked forward to the time when African states would be united in a great Pan-African union. Several important planning meetings were held.

■ *Joseph Mobutu, President of the Congo, addresses the Fourth African Summit Conference in 1967. The conferences are designed to promote solidarity among the emerging African nations.*

Twenty-nine Asian and African nations sent representatives to an Asian-African Conference at Bandung, Indonesia, in 1955. Its report urged the promotion of economic progress, self-determination of peoples, and independence for all peoples under alien domination. It declared colonialism an evil which should be speedily ended.

In January, 1961, heads of five African states met at Casablanca, Morocco, and adopted an "African Charter." It promised an attempt at "identity of views" in policy-making, neutralism in the "Cold War," and backing for liberation of African territories still under foreign domination. Plans were made to set up an African Consultative Assembly and an African High Command.

In May, 1961, representatives of nineteen African countries met at Monrovia, Liberia. At the end of the conference their five-point declaration called for: (1) equal sovereignty of African states, regardless of size or population; (2) respect for each state's right to exist and no annexation of one state by another; (3) freedom of African states to unite with one another; (4) non-intervention in affairs of other nations; (5) respect for the territorial integrity of all.

Some African states did not approve of other decisions reached at the Monrovia Conference, and rivalry seemed to be developing among the leaders of Africa.

The Organization of African Unity

The Organization of African Unity (OAU) was founded at Addis Ababa, Ethiopia, in May 1963, by the leaders of thirty-two African governments. (See map on p. 720.) The charter of the OAU described its purposes as:

(a) the promotion of the unity and solidarity of the African states;
(b) the coordination of their cooperative efforts to achieve a better life for the peoples of Africa;
(c) the defense of their sovereignty, their territorial integrity, and independence;
(d) the elimination of all forms of colonialism from Africa;
(e) the promotion of international cooperation, with due regard for the Charter of the United Nations and the Universal Declaration of Human Rights.

At the Addis Ababa Conference President Léopold Senghor of Senegal declared that "we consolidated what united us and excluded what divided us. This is a step forward toward African unity. . . ."

Having pledged itself to both the defense of national sovereignty and the promotion of African unity, OAU waited to see how the organization would resolve differences arising between national desires and all-African interests. Specific issues, such as crises in the Congo, soon tested the OAU.

■ **Check on Your Reading**

1. What major attempts were made at achieving African unity?
2. What major proposals were made during the conferences on African unity? at the Monrovian Conference? at the Addis Ababa Conference?

10. Major Problems in Contemporary Africa

The new African states made progress in some areas. Yet Africa as a whole continued to face serious problems. These included: (1) tensions and conflicts between whites and non-whites, (2) domestic instability, and (3) the need for economic development.

Conflict between Whites and Non-whites: Rhodesia

Rhodesia provided a clear-cut illustration of the racial problem in Africa. (Northern Rhodesia became the independent republic of Zambia in 1964; Southern Rhodesia became known as Rhodesia.)

In 1965 Rhodesia was a self-governing British colony, with the non-whites (about 4 million) outnumbering the whites (about 220,000) by 19 to 1. The white minority was determined to maintain white rule. Britain insisted upon increased political participation for the non-white majority. Many African countries demanded that the British refuse independence to Rhodesia as long as the white minority was allowed by the constitution to dominate the non-whites.

On November 11, 1965, despite British warnings against extreme measures, Ian Smith, Rhodesian Prime Minister, announced his Government's Declaration of Independence from British control. The new constitution specifically "repudiated the Crown's power."

The beginning of the Rhodesian Declaration of Independence bore a striking resemblance to the opening lines of the American Declaration of Independence. However, the basic issue that led to the Rhodesian declaration—the desire of the white minority to control the country and prevent the non-white majority from gaining power—was quite different. The words "all men are created equal" do not appear in the Rhodesian Declaration of Independence.

Great Britain promptly denounced the Rhodesian declaration as "an illegal act." On November 12, 1965, the Security Council of the United Nations adopted a resolution which condemned "the unilateral declaration of independence made by the racist minority in Southern Rhodesia." It called upon all nations not to recognize the new government or to give any assistance to it.

The action of the Rhodesian government stirred bitter feelings throughout the Commonwealth and Africa. In December, 1966, economic restrictions on Rhodesian trade were imposed by the United Nations. An effort was made to force Rhodesia to alter its position by weakening its economy.

About a year after Rhodesia's declaration, Albert J. Meyers, a trained observer, described the situation in Africa in this way:

At the top of the gorge on the Rhodesian side of the Zambesi River that divides Zambia from Rhodesia, there is a hotel which overlooks the vast expanse of Kariba Lake. At the entrance to the hotel is a sign that reads:

"This Hotel Is Not Multiracial"

The traveler who leaves Zambia and drives southward across the top of the Kariba Dam into Rhodesia is thus warned that he is passing from one world into another. He is crossing the boundary that divides the continent of Africa into two completely different sections.

To the north, as far as the Sahara Desert, virtually all of the continent is ruled by black Africans. . . .

To the south lies the "white redoubt" of Africa. These are lands also inhabited by millions of Africans. But it is white men, not the Africans, who are firmly in charge.

Domestic Instability: Nigeria

"In the past two months military forces have taken over the governments of five newly independent African countries. The trend is expected to continue." This report from Africa in January, 1966, was typical of domestic conditions in Africa in the latter part of the 1960's. There was instability in Nigeria, the Congo, Upper Volta, Dahomey, the Central African Republic, and others of the thirty-five nations that had emerged in fifteen years. (See map on p. 720.) Even Kwame Nkrumah of Ghana was overthrown in 1966.

Nigeria initially showed promise of sound development. Since gaining its independence in 1960, Nigeria has been a classic example of African unrest. Three factors contributing to the instability in Nigeria were:

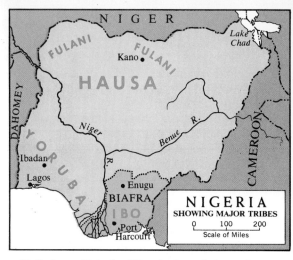

■ *Tribal conflicts in Nigeria have led to violence and a secessionist movement among the Ibos, who proclaimed the state of Biafra.*

1. TRIBAL FEARS AND DISTRUST. There were tensions and conflict between Yoruba, Fulani, Hausa, and Ibo tribes. In one series of tribal clashes between Hausas and Ibos, an estimated 2000 persons lost their lives.

2. STRUGGLES FOR POWER BETWEEN CIVILIAN LEADERS AND MILITARY OFFICERS. Attacks by the military or civilian leaders were quite frequent in Africa. The most dramatic example was the murder of Federal Prime Minister Balewa of Nigeria. The period from 1966 to early 1967 was marked by the rise of the colonels who took over the government in ten African countries.

3. WIDE VARIATIONS IN STANDARDS OF LIVING. For example, in 1966 the average income per capita in Nigeria was about $80 a month. Yet each Nigerian minister received a free house valued up to $80,000, an auto allowance of over $200 a month, and other privileges.

By the end of 1966 some persons believed that "a description of Nigeria as a nation was an exaggeration."

Domestic instability in Nigeria and other African countries led some observers to conclude that "Instant Democracy" had not worked, and could not work, in Africa. Others felt that, with sufficient time, some African countries could develop stable governments without relying on dictatorial leaders.

Need for Economic Development

As 1970 drew near, African nations continued to work hard to solve their economic problems. These included: (a) increase in population at a time when most African nations could not meet the economic needs of all their people, (b) unemployment in certain key regions of Africa, (c) insufficient application of scientific knowledge to farming, (d) lack of skilled individuals who could modernize the African economy, and (e) inexperience in industrial activities.

Some economic progress was made. Copper production increased in Zambia, and oil production rose in Algeria and Libya. Exports also increased; and foreign aid from about 1962 to 1966— estimated at almost 8 billion dollars—contributed to economic development.

Lines of communication between African nations were strengthened. Plans were made for new roads and railroads. The Ivory Coast cut a canal to the sea, opening a deep-water port. Small transistor radios, "crackling from village hut and nomad tent," were said to provide "a unifying influence across western Africa's awesome reaches."

The Tikar tribesmen of Cameroon continued to predict the future by consulting giant spiders, but more and more African statesmen turned to modern knowledge for answers to their economic problems.

■ **Check on Your Reading**

1. What is the source of the conflict in Rhodesia? Describe the moves of the British and Rhodesian governments. What is the present status of the dispute?

2. What factors explain the instability in Nigeria?

3. What are the most pressing economic problems of Africa? What attempts are being made to solve them? How does the African record compare with ours under the Confederation?

11. The "Rediscovery" of Cultural Africa

In the second half of the twentieth century the glorious past and the promise of Africa were "rediscovered" twice: once by the outside world, and once by the African people themselves.

After reading Basil Davidson's book, *African Kingdoms*, an astute editorial writer of a small-town American newspaper wrote in July, 1967:

Among the surprises that Davidson springs are his avowals that prehistoric Africans:

. . .

—Created what is called "the world's greatest gallery of prehistoric art"—15,000 rock paintings in the central plateaus of the

Sahara which reflect Africa's cultural beginnings thousands of years ago.

. . .

—Were superb sculptors.

. . .

—Developed medieval cities such as Timbuktu into centers of learning and gracious living.

. . .

Does all this fit in with the concept many of us have had of "darkest" Africa? Hardly.

Other men in other foreign lands were similarly excited by their discovery or rediscovery of African culture in the past and present. At the First World Festival of

Negro Arts, held at Dakar in 1966, over ten thousand visitors were entertained by African plays, dances, and poetry.

Differences between African cultures and those of other lands continued to fascinate foreign visitors. For example, African names like Emeanulu (Rejoicing-does-not-precede-doing), Eba Okomendan (One-who-surpasses-in-catching-little-fishes-in-a-scoop-net), and Ugbana (Fair-as-a-waterfowl) seemed to contrast sharply with names common to Western lands. On the other hand, striking similarities were noted between proverbs in countries throughout the world and African proverbs (such as these African sayings: "A roaring lion kills no game"; "It is the water that doesn't fill the pot that makes the most noise"; and "Ashes fly back in the face of him that throws them."). Greater familiarity gave promise of leading to greater understanding among peoples.

Africans also were rediscovering their culture during the decades following World War II. Joseph Palmer, United States Assistant Secretary of State for Foreign Affairs, declared in November 1966: "One of the most striking elements of the new Africa . . . is the rediscovery by Africans of themselves. . . . the African has found a new dignity in his freedom, in his history, and in his color." Literacy, which increased threefold between 1951 and 1966, helped more Africans to appreciate their cultural achievements.

African Poetry

There were important African writers of the short story, sketch, and, to a much lesser degree, the novel in the twentieth century. However, poetry was the principal means of expression in many parts of Africa. Paulin Joachim, the Dahomean editor of an influential periodical, explained the preference of many Africans for poetry in this way:

The novel is like a difficult, affected woman who must be equipped with the proper shade of make-up, words precisely suited to the occasion, and a carefully studied manner of behavior before she can present herself to the public. Poetry, by contrast, flows forth with unaffected spontaneity. It is thus the perfect medium for the African, who has his emotions on the tip of his tongue. . . .

Senegal's Léopold Sédar-Senghor, widely acclaimed poet of French-speaking Africa, captured the moods of African life with lines like these:

The tall palm trees swinging in the night wind
Hardly rustle. Not even cradle songs.
The rhythmic silence rocks us.
Listen to its song, listen to the beating of our dark blood, listen
To the beating of the dark pulse of Africa in the midst of lost villages.

Gabriel Okara, an important Nigerian poet, depicted an African drawn by two appeals—and perhaps by two worlds—in his famous poem *Piano and Drums*. Okara wrote that his "blood ripples"

When at break of day at a riverside
I hear jungle drums telegraphing
the mystic rhythm, urgent, raw
like bleeding flesh, speaking of
primal youth and the beginning

Almost at the same time he hears

. . . a wailing piano
solo speaking of complex ways
in a tear-furrowed concerto;
of faraway lands
and new horizons. . . .

Moved by both the raw power of the first and the intricacies of the second, he concludes:

And I . . .
[keep] wandering in the mystic rhythm
of jungle drums and the concerto.

These and other creative writers presented striking images, ideas, and patterns as they viewed the changing world of Africa.

African Music

There are many misconceptions about African music. The anthropologist Alan P. Merriam points out three false assumptions about African music: (1) It is "savage"; (2) It is old, comparable to Western music thousands of years ago; (3) It always relies heavily on drums.

Actually, African music can be quite subtle. Many African songs are new in origin. While drums play a very important part in African music, other instruments also are significant. These include: flutes, flageolets, zithers, lutes, lyres, and harps. Handclapping is another exciting feature.

The essential points to remember about African music are these:

1. There is a variety of musical styles in Africa. To the north of the Sahara, the music is affected by an Islamic background. To the south, the music reflects a variety of tribal cultures.

2. There is considerable public participation in African music and dance. As Professor Alan Merriam explains: "The distinctions between 'the artist' and his 'audience,' which are so sharply drawn in our society, do not seem to be of particular importance in Africa. Almost everyone sings, handclaps, and participates in group performance. . . .

3. African music can express with great effectiveness the various moods expressed by music of the West—excitement, melancholy, joy, fantasy, beauty, and many more.

4. African music is integrated into the daily lives of the people. In political, economic, and social activities, music provides the emotional tone, expresses the spectrum of feelings, and reflects both the memories and aspirations of the Africans.

In Africa, music is more than "the food of love." It is a food of life!

African Art

Art continues to be a significant part of African culture. Features of artistic activity and expression in Africa today are: (See photographs on page 730.)

First, there is a deep interest in African art of the past, and a determination to increase the people's appreciation of their artistic heritage.

Second, a variety of tribal styles exist. However, some elements, such as a fondness for sculpturing in wood, are found in art throughout most of Africa.

Third, there is impressive evidence of the skill and imagination of African artists; for example, in their cylindrical statuary and in the creation of dance masks.

Fourth, Western influences are having an impact on African artists. The opposite is also true. As early as the beginning of the twentieth century, painters in the West such as Matisse and Derain had been influenced by African sculpture.

Fifth, African art continues to be linked with the activities of the people themselves, such as religious ceremonial observances.

Throughout the world the distorted idea that African art is "childlike" or "simple" is being replaced by a view that recognizes its originality and respects its quality.

■ Check on Your Reading

1. Describe the major cultural achievements of African civilization in the past.

2. What are some of the major differences and similarities between African culture and those of other lands?

3. What is an outstanding characteristic of African poetry?

4. What are the characteristics of African music? of African art?

■ *These scenes in the door panels of the National Hall in Lagos, Nigeria, were carved by Felix Idubor. They depict traditional ways of living and aspects of African trade, agriculture, and education.*

CHAPTER REVIEW

REVIEW and DISCUSSION

1. What cultural features characterize the lands and people of the Middle East?

2. What major problems do the people and governments of the Middle East face?

3. Trace the course of Jewish-Arab tensions in the Middle East. Describe the present status of relations of these groups with the Western and Soviet blocs.

4. Prepare case-study reports on the liquidation of colonial interests in Algiers or the Congo.

5. What particular policies and problems characterize the emerging nations of Africa?

6. Account for the racial attitudes of the government in South Africa and Rhodesia. How do you think the problem will be ultimately resolved in each of those countries?

7. Are cultural development and nationalist expression related? Discuss this point of view with reference to the new African nations.

ACTIVITIES

1. Debate the following proposition: Resolved, Nasser's Arab socialism is a fine example of the useful economic policies for underdeveloped nations of the Middle East.

2. On a map of the Middle East locate (1) Arab nations; (2) members of the Arab League; (3) disputed areas near Israel.

3. Summarize the tendencies toward unity among the new black nations of Africa.

4. Hold a panel discussion on the topic: The diplomatic efforts of the United States in the Middle East have contributed to the current crisis and difficulties in the area.

5. Plan a week-long continuing program on African culture. Plan lectures, illustrated talks, and musical programs on the African heritage, citing their achievements.

PAST and PRESENT

1. Compare the map of Africa in 1945 with the map of Africa today. What factors explain the emergence of the many new nations? How would you evaluate the results up to this time?

2. The Communist and democratic countries of the West both woo the new African nations. What successes and failures have been achieved by both blocs? Is neutralism a fixed characteristic of the nations of the area? Explain your answer.

3. Prepare case-study reports on the current status of (1) one African country; (2) one Arab country; (3) one Moslem, but non-Arab country.

SUGGESTED READINGS

Basic books: HAPGOOD, DAVID, *Africa*, Ginn.
OLIVER, ROLAND, and FAGE, J. D., *Short History of Africa*, Penguin.
*WALLBANK, T. WALTER, *Contemporary Africa: Continent in Transition*, Anvil.

Special accounts: *CANTWELL-SMITH, WILFRED, *Islam in Modern History*, Mentor.
CHU, DANIEL, and SKINNER, ELIOT, *Glorious Age in Africa: The Story of Three Great African Empires*, Zenith.
*DAVIDSON, BASIL, *Africa on Slave Trade: Pre-colonial History, 1450-1850*, Atlantic-Little Brown.
DE GRAFT-JOHNSON, J. C., *African Glory. The Story of Vanished Negro Civilizations*, Walker.
*MICHENER, JAMES A., *The Source*, Fawcett.
PERETZ, D., *Middle East Today*, Holt.
WALZ, JAY, *Middle East*, Atheneum.

Biography and Fiction: DAYAN, YAEL, *Israel Journal: June, 1967*. McGraw-Hill.

*Paperback

Chapter 45   Latin America in Transition

A foreign correspondent in Latin America recently sent in this story:

[A reporter] asked his cab driver one evening in a Central American city why so many people slept in doorways. The driver looked around, shrugged his shoulder and replied: "Because it is night, señor."

About the same time, another correspondent-photographer dispatched this report:

A new luxury hotel, due to open next year, [will fold] around the flank of one of Rio de Janeiro's loaf-shaped mountains. Guests will shoot up the 370-foot shaft . . . in high-speed elevators. With its panoramic view of Rio, the hotel will be one more showplace for travelers to South America.

Which view correctly describes conditions in Latin America today —poverty or wealth? The answer is both. *One of the key features of life in Latin America in the quarter century after World War II was the existence of great problems in the present at the same time as there was great promise for the future.*

Key People

Juan Perón · Aramburu · Arturo Frondizi · João Goulart · Humberto Branco · Fidel Castro · Fulgencio Batista · Jorge Borges · David Siqueiros

Key Places

Rio de Janeiro · Brasília · Bay of Pigs · Punta del Este

Key Events

overthrow of Perón · amending Brazilian constitution · Castro in Cuba · Cuban missile crisis · treaty revision with Panama · (OAS) revolt in Dominican Republic · Organization of American States

Key Terms

land reform · caudillo · descamisados · quarantine · Alliance for Progress

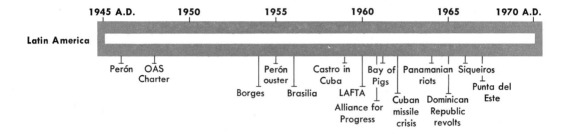

Latin America

1945 A.D. — 1950 — 1955 — 1960 — 1965 — 1970 A.D.

Perón   OAS
         Charter

Borges   Brasilia

Perón
ouster

Castro in
Cuba

LAFTA

Alliance for
Progress

Bay of
Pigs

Cuban
missile
crisis

Panamanian
riots

Dominican
Republic
revolts

Siqueiros

Punta del
Este

1. Latin America in the Modern World

"Is there a Latin America?" "Is Latin America one or many?" These were some of the questions that scholars were asking in the second half of the twentieth century. Such doubts about the nature of Latin America were due to the considerable diversity of life and cultures in Latin America. Nevertheless, we can give a general picture of conditions in this great area.

Population Growth

In April, 1967, a North American magazine author dramatized the extraordinary rise in population in Latin America by writing:

When you opened this magazine there were about 230 million people in the nations to the south of us. . . . By the time your next issue arrives, a week from now, there will be another 130,000—more than the total population of . . . Lexington, Kentucky.

Latin America had the highest rate of population growth of any of the principal areas of the world. With an annual birth rate higher than that of either China or India, Latin America could have a pop-

ulation of more than 600 million in 2000 A.D.

Of course, not all parts of Latin America were overcrowded in the 1960's. Some areas were sparsely populated. However, the increased population added to the already serious problems facing urban centers, such as lack of housing, insufficient food, and need for slum clearance. Meanwhile, life in the countryside continued to be as harsh for most people as it was in the crowded settlements around the cities.

As 1970 neared, Latin America was bristling with a variety of projects to improve its economic and social life. The gigantic Guri Dam to supply industrial power in Venezuela and startling increases in Chilean steel production were striking examples of progress in Latin America. Elsewhere road-building, irrigation, and health projects were underway. Dedicated statesmen were seeking ways to raise the standard of living.

On the other hand, many serious economic and social problems remained in Latin America. These included:

(a) *Low Standard of Living for Many People.* In the 1960's a small minority possessed great wealth, having nearly one-

733

■ *Slum conditions in this Colombian city testify to the crying need for new housing in Latin America. Housing lags in the Alliance for Progress program.*

Statistics and percentages are cold and lifeless. Far more can be learned from the human story itself. In 1967 one observer reported a conversation with a Latin American director of development:

[The director] pointed to a woman sitting outside the door of a hut, the skin on her face like a crumpled sheet of yellowed parchment, her legs shapeless as sea-swollen driftwood. "She is only 28," he said. "You can always tell a poor country by the women."

(b) *Uneven Land Distribution.* Despite legislation in some nations for land reform, land was still unevenly distributed in 1968. Millions of peasants owned no land or worked parcels of land too small to provide a decent livelihood. John F. Kennedy had called the distribution of land "one of the gravest social problems in many Latin-American countries."

(c) *Lack of Diversity.* For years many countries had lacked diversity in their economies. The economies of a number of Latin-American nations depended on a "single crop" or product. For example, from 1955 to 1958, coffee made up 78 per cent of exports from Colombia and 77 per cent of exports from El Salvador; petroleum accounted for 92 per cent of exports from Venezuela; and sugar for 79 per cent of exports from Cuba. A bad crop or a slump in the market produced economic crises.

(d) *Need for Industrialization.* Except for coal, many natural resources are found in Latin America. However, industries were slow to develop in most countries. In 1961, about 60 per cent of the population was still engaged in agriculture.

Between 1957 and 1968 several countries tried to expand industrially. For example, Brazil established a promising automobile industry. Much more remained to be done.

(e) *Relationships between Groups.* As in the past, certain individuals and groups had

third of all income in Latin America. At the same time millions lived at a bare subsistence level. The average annual income of a Latin American was estimated at between $275 and $325, a figure considerably higher than that of the people in most African and Asian countries. Average life expectancy in Latin America was only 46 years. In Haiti, there was one doctor to care for every 10,000 people. (The ratio was one to 650 in the United States.) In Brazil, one out of every five children did not live long enough to have its first birthday. (The ratio was one to 40 in the United States.)

Despite the construction of thousands of housing units between 1961 and 1966, housing remained a major problem. In 1961 almost 40 per cent of the population of Rio de Janeiro, Brazil, and 14 per cent of the entire population of Chile lived in slums— often without water, sanitation, or medical facilities.

■ *Diversification of industry is a major need in Latin America. This automobile assembly plant in Brazil is financed partly by the International Finance Corporation, an agency allied with the United Nations.*

considerable influence on economic and social developments. Among these groups were military leaders, large landowners, new industrialists, the Church, technical experts, and intellectuals.

Yet it is an oversimplification to explain present-day Latin-American life as a clear-cut struggle between "democrats and dictators" or between "liberals and reactionaries." Groups were not completely uniform in their attitudes, interests, and actions. Moreover, there were shifts in the power held by various groups. These changes had considerable impact on economic and social developments in Latin America.

Educational Activities

Some progress was made in the field of education. For example, in South America, between 1950 and 1959, enrollment in higher education (such as universities and technical institutes) increased by 80 per cent in the period from 1961 to 1966. Special programs in Latin America constructed about 30,000 additional classrooms.

However, in 1967 only one out of every two Latin-American children of school age attended any educational institution. About 85 per cent of Latin Americans of high-school age did not go to school.

In Bolivia, 70 per cent of the population could not read or write. In Haiti, the peasantry, who made up 90 per cent of the population, were largely illiterate. Conditions comparable to these existed elsewhere in Latin America.

Yet education of youth would play an important part in determining the future of Latin America since 40 per cent of the population of Latin America was less than fifteen years old.

■ Check on Your Reading

1. Indicate the nature and scope of each of the following problems in Latin America: (a) standard of living, (b) land distribution, (c) economic diversity, (d) industrialization, (e) relationship between groups. What attempts are being made to solve these problems?

2. Describe the problems of educational improvement in Latin America. What progress has been made since 1950?

2. Tensions and Changes in Latin-American Countries

Political instability was common in Latin America. Rival groups often contended for power and resorted to the use of violence. Immediately following World War II, dictatorships dominated several countries.

From 1950 to 1968, many significant changes took place in Latin America. Case studies of five of these countries—Argentina, Brazil, Cuba, Panama, and the Dominican Republic—provide a spectrum of highlights of the period.

Case Study 1: Argentina

Juan Perón had been the president and dictator of Argentina since 1946. As military *caudillo* (chieftain), he controlled the country by keeping the support of the army, the *descamisados* ("the shirtless ones"—that is, the workers), and other groups. Perón denied people freedom of speech and press. For example, he confiscated the independent newspaper *La Prensa*, of Buenos Aires, in March, 1951. He determined the curriculum in the schools and arbitrarily controlled the economy.

In time, Perón feared that the Roman Catholics in Argentina might establish an opposition political party. To counter this threat, he began to interfere with the rights and privileges of the Church. The Vatican excommunicated him on June 16, 1955, after he had expelled two Argentine prelates.

Perón's anti-Church activities proved to be the spark that ignited the opposition to his rule. Opponents of his dictatorship, Church leaders, dissatisfied military officers, university students, and others demanded changes in the government. After a revolt in a provincial garrison on September 14, 1955, the military forces in other cities rose against Perón. Then the entire navy rebelled! Perón fled the country in a Paraguayan gunboat. His dictatorship over Argentina had ended.

Under the presidency of General Aramburu (1955–1958), Perón's dictatorial rules were discarded and the Constitution of 1853 restored. In the first free election in many years, Arturo Frondizi succeeded Aramburu to the presidency in 1958. In 1962 a political crisis and military revolts forced Frondizi from office.

In June, 1966, Frondizi's duly elected successor, Dr. Arturo Illia, was ousted by the military. General Juan Carlos Onganía became the new head of Argentina.

Argentina is more industrialized than most Latin-American nations, but it is still unable to solve its economic problems. It remains the classic example of the dominant position of military leaders in Latin America.

Case Study 2: Brazil

Brazil, the largest country in Latin America and the fifth largest in the world, faced the problem of strengthening its economy. Because of the danger of having an economic system too heavily dependent on a single crop, coffee, Brazilian leaders made efforts to diversify its economy. Brazil seeks to develop new industries from its rich resources of iron ore, bauxite, and water power.

As a symbol of the future, Brasilia, a modern capital city, was constructed in the interior of the country. However, Brazil continued to be plagued by unsatisfactory housing for millions of people, inadequate medical facilities, illiteracy, and poverty (the average annual income per person in 1961 was about $250).

In 1961, after a political crisis, the constitution of Brazil was amended. The amendments provided: (1) The position of President of Brazil lost much of its power.

(The first President under the new system was João Goulart). (2) The position of Prime Minister, who was to be selected by the President and approved by the Congress, was introduced. (3) The Prime Minister and the Congress had most of the duties and responsibilities of government.

Military leaders with the support of some middle-income groups overthrew Goulart in 1964. To complete his term of office, the Brazilian Congress elected General Humberto Castelo Branco. From 1964 to 1966, President Castelo Branco's policies were opposed by some army leaders, clergymen, and university students. Marshal Artur da Costa e Silva became the 25th President of Brazil in 1967.

During these years of political changes Brazilians tried to check inflation and handle other economic problems. Political tensions and efforts at modernization often conflicted. Economic diversification was difficult to promote democratically.

Case Study 3: Cuba

In January, 1959, Fidel Castro (1926–) and his revolutionary armed forces finally overthrew the dictatorship of Fulgencio Batista in Cuba. A few days after the fall of Batista, the government of the United States expressed "the sincere goodwill of the Government and people of the United States toward the new Government and the people of Cuba."

The actions of Castro and his associates soon antagonized the United States. Great "show" trials, without full legal processes, resulted in the execution of persons accused of having aided Batista. The seizure of American-owned plantations without compensation to the owners further displeased the United States. In anti-American speeches Castro accused our government of economic aggression and denied our right to maintain a naval base at Guantanamo.

Cuba developed close ties with the Soviet Union, and Communist arms began to arrive in Cuba. Several leading officials of the Castro government adopted Communist ideology. The United States feared that Cuba, only ninety miles off the coast of Florida, might fall within the orbit of the Soviet Union. In addition, Castro expressed the hope that his revolution would spread throughout Latin America.

The United States retaliated against Cuba's actions. (1) It cut the import quotas for Cuban sugar. (2) It placed an embargo on certain exports to Cuba. (3) It sent American ships to the Caribbean to ward off any Cuban attempt to spread its revolution. On January 3, 1961, the United States broke diplomatic relations with Cuba.

In March, 1961, the Cuban National Revolutionary Council, consisting largely of exiles, set up headquarters in the United States. The president of the Council, the first prime minister in Castro's government, denounced Castro as "the tyrant who betrayed a whole nation" and as the leader who turned Cuba into "a Soviet colony." The Council called for the overthrow of Castro and establishment of "a democratic regime based on liberty and social justice."

On April 17, 1961, a force of about 1300 armed anti-Castro Cubans, mostly Cuban exiles, landed at the Bay of Pigs on the south coast of Cuba. Unofficially aided by the United States with arms and training, the anti-Castro invaders fought to overthrow the Castro government. They were easily defeated after a short battle.

The unsuccessful attack on Cuba had far-reaching effects. The United States was denounced by Cuba, the Soviet Union, and a number of other nations for supporting "an act of aggression." Cuba drew closer to the Soviet Union. Castro used the invasion to intensify the anti-American feelings of the people of Cuba.

■ *A Soviet freighter carrying a dismantled rocket launcher is shown leaving Cuban waters after the missile crisis of 1962.*

On December 2, 1961, Castro made clear that he planned to establish many features of a Communist state in Cuba. He declared that he was a "Marxist-Leninist and would be one until the day I die." In January, 1962, at the Punta del Este conference of foreign ministers of the Organization of American States, Cuba was excluded from participation in the inter-American state system.

In the fall of 1962, President Kennedy announced that the Russians were building nuclear missile sites in Cuba. Declaring a "quarantine" (a form of blockade) against all ships carrying military supplies to Cuba, he demanded the immediate removal of all ships carrying military supplies to Cuba. He demanded the immediate removal of all missile sites. Kennedy threatened instant retaliation on the Soviet Union if any missile were launched from Cuba against the United States or any Latin-American state. The Soviet Union agreed to remove its missiles from Cuba.

By 1965, Castro concentrated on internal problems. Cuba had not met its sugar export quotas to the Soviet Union, which was providing it with wheat and petroleum. Cuba struggled to increase sugar output.

At the end of 1967, Cuba still provided the most striking case study of the effect of Communist ideology on a Latin-American country.

Case Study 4: The Republic of Panama

The Republic of Panama became involved in a dispute with the United States over the Panama Canal and the role of the United States in Panama. Panamanian nationalists demanded that Panama receive a far greater share of the income from the operation of the Canal. They demanded improvements in the wages and the living conditions of Panamanian workers in the Canal Zone. They also insisted upon an end to unfair competition to Panamanian merchants from United States stores in the Canal Zone. In 1960, the United States started a program to raise the standard of living of the Panamanians who worked in the Canal Zone. After serious riots in 1964, new talks were begun to discuss revision of the treaty under which the Canal Zone was administered by the United States.

In the summer of 1967, President Marco A. Robles of Panama and President Lyndon B. Johnson of the United States announced agreement on three new and important treaties. If ratified, these treaties would (a) recognize Panama's sovereignty over the Canal Zone; (b) give Panama new rights over the canal; and (c) increase Panama's share of revenues.

Construction of a new sea-level canal in Panama or Colombia or along the Nicaragua-Costa Rica border was also discussed. Panama continued to provide an interesting example of diplomatic relations with a strategically important Latin-American country.

Case Study 5: The Dominican Republic

On May 30, 1961, Generalissimo Rafael Trujillo, who had been dictator of the Dominican Republic for over 30 years, was assassinated. The first freely elected President of the Republic in 38 years, Juan Bosch, was ousted by a military coup in 1963.

In 1965 a revolt broke out in the Dominican Republic. The United States sent in American troops to protect American citizens there and to prevent a Communist takeover. This move angered a number of Latin Americans who felt the United States had exaggerated the Communist threat and intervened unilaterally.

An Inter-American Peace Force, which was to include troops from Latin-American countries as well as the United States, was established by the Organization of American States for duty in the Dominican Republic. Chile, Ecuador, Mexico, Peru, and Uruguay voted against the resolution that created this force; and Venezuela abstained from voting.

Civilian rule finally was restored in the Dominican Republic. Joaquín Balaguer became the new president. The last contingents of the Inter-American Peace Force left the country in September, 1966.

The Dominican Republic revolt had led the United States for the first time in 30 years to enter and occupy temporarily a Latin-American country. As a result, the Dominican Republic provided an important case study of the feelings, reactions, and actions of Latin Americans who feared intervention by the United States.

■ Check on Your Reading

1. Describe the rise and fall of Perón in Argentina. What changes have taken place since 1955?
2. What social and economic problems does Brazil face? What political changes were proposed in the new Constitution of Brazil?
3. What difficulties does militarism pose for the solution of Brazil's economic problems?
4. Describe the course of the Cuban revolutionary movement.
5. What sanctions did the United States impose on Castro's Cuba?
6. Describe the influence of Marxist ideology on Cuba.
7. What were the prime causes of the conflict between Panama and the United States? What settlement was proposed?·
8. What were the attitudes toward, and the results of, U. S. intervention in the Dominican Republic?

3. Organizations for Regional Cooperation

In an effort to solve major economic, social, and political problems facing the countries in the Western Hemisphere, the United States and Latin America turned to the idea of regional organization.

The Organization of American States

In 1910 the Pan-American Union had come into being. Then, in 1948, the charter for an *Organization of American States* (OAS) was drawn up. This charter went into full legal effect in 1951.

The Organization of American States was made up of representatives from each of the twenty-one republics of the Western Hemisphere. Its major purposes were to (1) strengthen the peace and security of the Western Hemisphere; (2) eliminate possible causes of difficulties and ensure peaceful settlement of disputes; (3) provide for

■ *Central and Latin American nations are attempting to lower trade barriers by forming free-trade associations. In 1968 President Johnson visited with the presidents of five Central-American republics: El Salvador, Costa Rica, Honduras, Nicaragua, and Guatemala.*

Members of the Central-American Common Market (CACM)

Members of the Latin-American Free Trade Association (LAFTA)

common action in the event of aggression; and (4) promote, by cooperative action, the economic, social, and cultural development of the member states.

The Organization of American States suffered several setbacks, but it also had a record of accomplishments. It helped to settle disputes; sponsored research into the best ways of growing coffee, cacao, and other tropical crops; and contributed to the improvement of systems of education. It worked conscientiously to control disease and epidemics. It played a role in restoring peace to areas in turmoil; for example, the Inter-American Peace Force performed this task in the crisis in the Dominican Republic.

Criticism of the OAS continued to be heard, and there were those who doubted its effectiveness as an instrument for peace and security in the Western Hemisphere. Nevertheless, leaders of the organization went about their tasks with a determination

to succeed. In 1967 amendments to the OAS Charter designed to give new strength and energy to the organization were drawn up, and Trinidad–Tobago was admitted as the twenty-second member.

As officials of the OAS declared, "After 65 years of steady growth and expansion, the original purposes of inter-American cooperation—*Peace, Friendship, and Commerce*—[were] still the keystones of the Organization of American States."

Central American Common Market

In 1960, the Central American Common Market (CACM) was organized as a free-trade association. It aimed to unify the economies of Central America and to raise living standards by joint economic development. Its members were Guatemala, El Salvador, Honduras, and Nicaragua; Costa Rica joined later. In the 1960's their combined population was

■ *The construction of a new school takes priority in the Alliance for Progress efforts to raise Latin American living standards. The school is being built in El Salvador.*

about 12 million, and their annual per capita income was below $200. (See map on p. 740.)

To increase regional trade and strengthen the economies of Central American countries is no small problem. Much progress has been made in eliminating trade barriers. Since 1960 interregional trade has doubled, and 92.5 per cent of all trade is free of restriction in the member countries.

Latin American Free Trade Association

In February 1960, by the Treaty of Montevideo, the Latin-American Free Trade Association (LAFTA) was organized by Argentina, Brazil, Chile, Mexico, Paraguay, Peru, and Uruguay. The treaty went into effect in 1961. Eventually, LAFTA included Mexico and all the South American nations except Guyana.

The aims of LAFTA were to integrate the economies of the area by gradually lowering tariffs and eliminating trade barriers.

Several thousand tariff concessions were made, but high tariffs for industrial products remained and trading among member nations did not increase at the expected rate.

Alliance for Progress

On March 13, 1961, President John F. Kennedy proposed an *Alliance for Progress* in the Western Hemisphere. In August representatives of the United States and nineteen Latin-American nations (Cuba was not among them) signed the charter of the alliance. Its key provisions were these: (1) "The United States will provide a major part of the minimum of twenty billion dollars . . . which Latin America will require over the next ten years [for its economic and social development]." (2) "The countries of Latin America agree to devote a rapidly increasing share of their own resources to economic and social development. . . ." (3) "[The Latin-American nations agree] to make the reforms necessary to assure that all share fully in the fruits of the Alliance . . ."

The goals of the Alliance for Progress included these: to raise per capita income; to increase agricultural production; to diversify economies; to improve education; and to encourage economic and social reforms in Latin America. Estimated cost was $100 billion, with the United States providing $20 billion in loans and grants from public and private sources.

By 1965 the Alliance had helped to build schools, print textbooks, organize food projects, construct water systems, and provide farming aid in Latin America.

In 1967, however, a number of authorities expressed disappointment with the Alliance for Progress. Although recognizing its accomplishments, they pointed out that it had not achieved many of its objectives: the strengthening of democracy in Latin America; the stimulation of economic and social reforms; and the personal involvement and participation of the people in the program. Statesmen of Latin America and the United States discussed new plans to strengthen the Alliance for Progress.

Punta del Este Conference

In the spring of 1967, the Chiefs of State of twenty members of the Organization of American States, including the United States, held an important conference at Punta del Este, Uruguay. At this meeting the member states agreed to create a common market; establish "the physical foundations for Latin-American economic integration"; to increase foreign trade; modernize living conditions for rural pop-

ulations and increase food production; expand educational opportunities; employ science and technology for the benefit of the people; expand health programs; and eliminate unnecessary military expenditures. (In 1967, after nearly four years of work, the countries of Latin America, with the exception of Cuba, also completed drawing up a Treaty for the Banning of Nuclear Arms in Latin America.)

One Latin-American leader summed up the work of the conference in terms familiar to any sports fan: "The declaration of Punta del Este is only the score. Success will depend on how we play it."

■ Check on Your Reading

1. What aims does the Organization of American States have?

2. What were the major achievements of the Organization of American States?

3. Describe the purposes, membership, and achievements of the Central American Common Market and the Latin American Free Trade Association.

4. What are some accomplishments of the Alliance for Progress?

5. What agreements were made at the Punta del Este Conference?

4. Cultural Developments in Latin America

Cultural activities in Latin America in the 1960's were varied and important. Promising works appeared in the fields of literature, art, and music.

Literature

Jorge Luis Borges, Argentine poet, essayist, and story writer, was one example of the creative authors in modern Latin America. One observer of world cultures compared his style to that of Edgar Allan Poe and Joseph Conrad. In one poem Borges wrote:

What can I hold you with?
I offer you lean streets.
I offer you the bitterness of a man who has looked long at the lonely moon.
I offer you my ancestors.
I can give you my loneliness, my darkness, the hunger of my heart; I am trying to bribe you with uncertainty, with danger, with defeat.

These lines and other works of Jorge Luis Borges gradually brought him worldwide recognition.

In 1967 the Second Congress of Latin-American writers, which met in Mexico, took steps to promote the distribution of Latin-American books and other publications throughout Latin America. Plans for a "common market" for Latin-American literature were being developed.

Art

Young Latin-American artists struggled to develop their artistic styles, but the spotlight also focused on David Alfaro Siqueiros, the veteran Mexican painter. Siqueiros worked by day and well into the night on what was to be the largest mural painting in the world. Its theme was "The History of Humanity." To Siqueiros, "mural painting must express the conscience of man, his drama and tragedy." A number of younger Latin-American artists departed from the traditional Latin-American framework to develop international styles. Some continued to stress Latin-American life and heritage.

Music

There were several promising features of Latin-American music in the 1960's. These included: (a) the formation of symphony orchestras in many countries; (b) impressive opera seasons in Argentina and Mexico; and (c) new styles of musical works by young Latin-American composers.

In addition, the Inter-American Music Council (CIDEM) was founded to stimulate the development of music throughout the Western Hemisphere.

■ *Siqueiros, the Mexican painter, is shown at work on his mural "The March of Humanity," which portrays Mexican history from its beginnings to the Mexican Revolution of 1911.*

Inter-American cooperation in musical activities was strengthened in the 1960's, and music continued to be an important part of the lives of many Latin Americans.

■ Check on Your Reading

Describe cultural developments in Latin America in the fields of literature, art, and music.

MAN AND
HIS CULTURE

Let's Meet the People!

The following sketch is based on information in "The Two Worlds of Jorge Luis Borges" by Armando Alonso Pineiro in *Americas*, March, 1965, pp. 11–15; "A Visit with Argentina's Borges" by John Gunther,* pp. 96–98; and "The Writings of Jorge Luis Borges" by Keith Botsford, both in *The Atlantic*, January, 1967, pp. 99–104. Jorge Luis Borges died in 1967.

An Argentine Writer

The Argentine writer was almost sixty-five years old, but his face still had a whimsical quality. He was a tall, vigorous man who loved to take long walks. Each morning, carrying a heavy cane over a hundred years old, he walked slowly along Florida street in Buenos Aires, "his eyes fixed on the distance." As he did so, he would often say lines of old sonnets in a low voice.

In his private library there were almost three thousand volumes. His favorite authors included Robert Louis Stevenson and Rudyard Kipling. He also enjoyed motion pictures, and said: "Movies, you see, are more visible than reality." Television he disliked because "it does nothing but lavish foolish images of ephemeral events."

Images were important to the Argentine writer, and he held distinctive opinions on various sights. He disliked the color green and called the Argentine National Library the "Turkish bath school of architecture." At the Argentine Writer's Club, he liked to point out portraits that had special meaning to him.

The Argentine writer was author of several unusual volumes, and sometimes he was asked to judge the writings of others. In one contest he had to evaluate 150 works. "All bad," he said of them. "It's terrible to have to read bad works."

He loved fine literature and felt that "the writer should live for the pleasures of the intellect." As for the experiences of life, he wrote:

Fate makes no deals and no one holds that against it.

The Argentine writer knew well the meaning of those lines. For, although he could show others the visions of life, he himself was almost blind!

CHAPTER REVIEW

REVIEW and DISCUSSION

1. Latin America is suffering from a host of social, economic, and political problems. Outline the main features of the major problems. Discuss the proposed solutions and obstacles to be overcome.

2. Analyze the current difficulties in Argentina, Brazil, Cuba, Panama, and the Dominican Republic. Show how they stemmed from unresolved historical problems.

3. What have been the purposes and achievements of the major organizations for regional cooperation? What problems remain to be solved?

4. Delineate the major trends in literature, arts, and music in Latin America in recent years.

5. Draw a brief word sketch of each of the following Latin-American leaders: Perón, Trujillo, Goulart, Balaguer, Borges, Batista, Castro.

6. What factors tend to prevent political stability in Latin America?

ACTIVITIES

1. Prepare charts (bar graphs) to show progress in housing, schoolroom construction, and jobs since the establishment of the Alliance for Progress in 1961.

2. Prepare a poster display of Latin-American art. What particular appeals does it have to offer? What characteristics make it easily identifiable as Latin-American art? Is this true of the most recent offerings?

3. How would you analyze Latin-American music as to its main features and its characteristic style?

PAST and PRESENT

1. Panel Discussion: "Despite military upheavals Latin-American nations are making good progress toward the establishment of healthy democratic institutions."

2. Compare the attitudes of Latin-American countries toward the United States in the 1930's and the 1960's.

3. From an analysis of the political history of Latin-American countries, what factors predisposed them to dictatorial rule? How can greater democratization be achieved?

4. Compare revolutionary art of Mexico and the style of current works of art.

SUGGESTED READINGS

Basic books: GUNTHER, JOHN. *Inside South America.* Harper.
*HANKE, LEWIS. *Mexico and the Caribbean. Modern Latin America,* Vol. I. Anvil.
————*South America: Modern Latin America,* Vol. II, 2nd ed. Anvil.
PENDLE, GEORGE. *History of Latin America.* Penguin.

Special accounts: ALEXANDER, ROBERT J., *Today's Latin America.* Anchor.
FUENTES, CARLOS. *Whither Latin America?* Monthly Review Press.
KEEN, BENJAMIN, *Readings in Latin-American Civilization,* 2nd ed. Houghton Mifflin.
LOCKWOOD, L., *Castro's Cuba, Cuba's Fidel.* Macmillan.

Biography and Fiction: ESPAILLAT, ARTURO, *Trujillo: The Last Caesar.* Regnery.

Chapter 46

New Frontiers in Contemporary Culture

KEYNOTE

In 1961, *Changing Times, the Kiplinger Magazine* pointed out many developments and products that had affected American life since 1945. These included:

Jet planes . . . antibiotics . . . air-conditioned houses . . . Dacron and Arnel and Orlon . . . frozen, dehydrated, precooked and enriched [foods] . . . laundry [machines that] washed and dried by pushbuttons . . . computers that could almost think . . . rockets that probed the moon . . . transistors that put radios in your pocket. . . .

Many items on this list were evidence of the extraordinary progress made in science and technology. Contemporary man also developed new and exciting ideas in art, music, and literature.

On the other hand, in 1961 Norman Cousins, editor of the *Saturday Review*, warned that modern weapons had grown so deadly that he imagined another world war would kill or disable 1,400,200,000 human beings, or three out of every five persons now living!

One key feature of our times was *the tremendous progress being made in science and the equally impressive dangers that existed for the destruction of civilization.* Contemporary man was living in one of the crucial periods in history.

Key People   *Albert Einstein   ·   Wilhelm Roentgen   ·   Jonas Salk   ·   John Glenn   ·   Pablo Picasso   ·   Igor Stravinsky   ·   Leonard Bernstein   ·   T. S. Eliot   ·   Ernest Hemingway   ·   James Joyce*

Key Events   *splitting the atom   ·   anti-polio vaccine   ·   first earth satellite   ·   first man in space   ·   mass literature published*

Key Terms   *Special Theory of Relativity   ·   electronics   ·   International Geophysical Year   ·   astronautics   ·   Cubism   ·   Neo-classicism   ·   stream of consciousness*

746

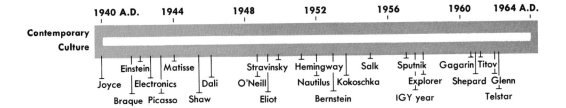

Contemporary Culture

Einstein | Matisse | Stravinsky | Hemingway | Salk | Sputnik | Gagarin | Titov

Joyce | Electronics | Dali | O'Neill | Nautilus | Kokoschka | Explorer | Shepard | Glenn

Braque | Picasso | Shaw | Eliot | Bernstein | IGY year | Telstar

1. Science: An "Outstanding Phenomenon of Modern Life"

"The outstanding phenomenon of modern life, especially in the Western World, is the impact of the acquisition, and application, of scientific knowledge." Words such as these by Dr. Clifford C. Furnas, internationally known chemist and educator, were echoed in the twentieth century.

Nuclear Energy

Albert Einstein (1879–1955), born in Germany, later became an American citizen. He was one of the scientists chiefly responsible for ushering in the Atomic Age. In 1905, at the age of twenty-six, Einstein published a paper which set forth his Special Theory of Relativity. Twelve years later, he presented his General Theory of Relativity. Einstein found that there is an equivalence of mass and energy. This means that matter and energy are exchangeable and not separate. According to his equation, $E = MC^2$, energy equals mass times the velocity of light squared.

The findings of Einstein and other scientists provided the foundation for splitting the atom. The United States achieved nuclear fission in 1942, and the development of the atomic bomb in 1945. As a result of the work of Igor Kurchatov and his associates, the Russians produced an atomic bomb in 1949.

Work with nuclear *fission* (breakdown or division of the nucleus of the atom) and nuclear *fusion* (rearranging and uniting of elements to form heavier nuclei) opened the way to *nuclear power*. Nuclear power can be used for many purposes. For example, in 1952 the United States started work on its first atomic-powered submarine, the *Nautilus*. Since then, several atomic submarines have been constructed.

In addition, *radioisotopes* (unstable forms of the ordinary atoms) have become extremely useful. Radioisotopes are used by industry to measure thickness, density, and moisture content; and, in high concentration, they give off intense radiation that can help destroy cancerous tissues and kill bacteria. Tracer radioiodine can help control thyroid tumors.

Electronics

Electronics is the science that studies the movements and actions of electrons as they flow through tubes filled with gases, vacuum tubes, and other forms. Electrons are negative charges of electricity. The discovery of X-rays by the German physicist Wilhelm Konrad Roentgen in 1895 was one of the earliest findings related to the field of electronics. Two years later, Sir Joseph Thomson, a British physicist, revealed that electrons carry electrical current. Then, in the twentieth century, electronics helped to make possible the development of radio, television, radar, and electronic computers.

747

Another remarkable achievement was the development of machines that could translate one language into another.

Medicine

A number of important advances were made in medicine. These included production of vitamin and hormone concentrates from natural and synthetic sources. In addition, there was the discovery and use of antibiotics (such as sulfa drugs; and penicillin, which was discovered by the British bacteriologist Sir Alexander Fleming) for specific diseases.

Successful anti-polio vaccines were developed, first by Dr. Jonas E. Salk and later by Dr. Albert E. Sabin. New techniques in surgery included seemingly miraculous "open-heart" operations and transplanting vital organs such as the kidney. Use of tranquilizers and other drugs revolutionized the treatment of mental illness. Fluoridation of water dramatically reduced tooth decay.

Chemical Technology

Chemical technology also made numerous contributions to the welfare and comfort of man. For example, synthetic gasolines were produced for use in the high-compression engines of modern cars. Nylon also was developed. For example, nylon clothing, pleasant to wear and inexpensive to purchase, consists of two chemical compounds: hexamethylenediamine and adipic acid!

About 1828 French chemists discovered the first heat-softening plastics. By 1959 plastics had a range of physical properties that made them competitive with metals, wood, and glass.

Synthetic resins and fibers were used. Synthetic rubber was manufactured. In addition, nylon soon was challenged by Dacron and other synthetic fibers used in clothing and home furnishings.

Transportation

Revolutionary changes were made in transportation. Henry Ford's assembly line and other mass-production techniques were adopted by automobile manufacturers. By 1966 there were approximately 90 million motor vehicles registered in America.

Meanwhile, Diesel-powered locomotives were introduced to the railroad systems of several nations. Ocean-going ships were constructed that could cross the Atlantic in less than a week. Commercial aircraft began to be used by an increasing number of people.

In 1939 Ernst Heinkel of Germany proved that jet-propelled planes could fly. In 1951 the Douglas *Skyrocket* flew faster than the speed of sound (above 738 miles per hour). By the 1960's jet planes were being used for a high percentage of commercial flights. In 1961 a new airliner capable of flying at Mach 3, or better than 2000 miles an hour, and of carrying 200 or more passengers from New York to London in less than two hours, was on the drawing boards. By the end of 1967, supersonic transport planes were being constructed in several nations.

Exploration of the Sea

Some 70 per cent of our planet lies beneath the sea, and the depths of the sea hold a strange and fascinating world. In the twentieth century, explorations of the sea revealed the following important facts:

The sea holds rich sources of mineral wealth: petroleum, phosphates, nickel, copper, cobalt, and "grapefruit-sized nuggets" of nearly pure manganese. Bromine and even a minute amount of gold have been extracted from sea water.

Plankton, tiny sea animals, may be able to supply man with an additional source of food. Vice-Admiral C. B. Momsen of the United States predicted that the day would come when fish farms in the ocean depths would supply most of the world's food.

The force of ocean tides, currents, and waves could be converted into electricity in underwater power plants. Sea water could be converted into fresh water and used to transform desert regions into fertile lands.

International Geophysical Year

As advances in pure and applied science multiplied, world leaders became increasingly aware of the need for international cooperation in scientific investigations. One result was the *International Geophysical Year* (I.G.Y.). The I.G.Y. (July 1, 1957 to December 31, 1958) involved world-wide cooperation among scientists. Thirty thousand scientists and technicians from sixty-six nations worked to make an intensive study of the environment of man.

The scientists studied the nature of the earth's atmosphere, earthquakes, weather, cosmic rays, oceans, and many other fields. One of the key principles of I.G.Y. was *simultaneous observations* of the same or related geophysical phenomena at all points on the world network. Some of the most significant results of the I.G.Y. were these:

Artificial satellites were successfully launched. These carried instruments and relayed information about the solar system to man. The Van Allen Radiation surrounding the earth was discovered.

Knowledge of the world's weather increased as a result of international projects at Antarctica. Three major countercurrents were located in the oceans. A vast mineral region was found in the Pacific.

Exposition 1967 in Canada demonstrated aspects of the scientific and technical progress of man.

■ Check on Your Reading

1. What did Albert Einstein contribute?
2. What is the science of electronics?
3. What contributions were made in modern medicine?
4. What synthetics were developed?
5. What contributions to knowledge were made in the International Geophysical Year?

2. Man Explores Space

For centuries men had been fascinated by the sun, moon, stars, and the world of space that lay beyond. In 1687 Sir Isaac Newton's laws of motion were published. When a modern rocket engine shoots a jet of gas out of its tail cone, it operates in accordance with Newton's third law: For every action there is an equal and opposite action. The gas shooting downward produces a powerful force acting in the opposite direction. This force lifts the rocket into the air.

In the nineteenth century, Konstantin Tsiolkovsky, a Russian, pointed out the importance of using liquid fuel to propel rockets. In 1926 Robert Hutchings Goddard, an American professor, made flight tests of the world's first liquid-fueled rocket. The German Hermann Oberth, "the father of practical *astronautics*" (the field of designing, building, and operating space vehicles), also did pioneer work in space rocketry.

Earth Satellites and an Artificial Planet

On October 4, 1957, the Soviet Union launched the first man-made earth satellite. Named Sputnik I ("Fellow-traveler"), this 184-pound sphere attained a maximum altitude of 560 miles and orbited the earth every 96.2 minutes. On November 3, 1957, the Russians sent up a second satellite, Sputnik II, with a dog named "Laika" aboard.

The United States launched its first satellite on January 31, 1958. It was called *Explorer I* and orbited the earth every 114 minutes. *Explorer I* was soon followed by two other successful American satellites, *Vanguard I* and *Explorer III*.

On January 2, 1959, the Russians launched a multi-stage rocket, *Lunik*, toward the moon. *Lunik* went into orbit around the sun and became the first artificial planet.

The instruments carried by the various man-made projectiles sent into space conveyed important information to scientists. The stage was now set for sub-orbital and orbital flight by man himself. (*Sub-orbital* refers to a flight into space but not around the earth; *orbital* refers to a flight into space that then circles the earth.)

Men and Instruments in Space

Man now intensified his thrusts into space. He concentrated on: (1) scientific exploration, (2) development of communications systems, (3) manned space flight.

Space vehicles became "reporters," relaying to earth scientific news from millions of miles away. *Mariner II*, launched in 1962, passed close to Venus and sent back more data about that planet than man had learned in 5000 years. In 1965 *Mariner IV* set off for Mars. In 1964–1965 the American spacecraft *Ranger VII* and *VIII* transmitted to earth thousands of close-up pictures of the moon. Other spacecraft and man-made satellites reported on the composition of space, radiation belts, and magnetic fields. *Tiros* satellites analyzed the weather.

Achievements in space communications were equally impressive. In July, 1962, *Telstar*, a communications satellite, sent live television across the Atlantic Ocean for the first time. *Syncom II* travelled at the same relative speed as earth to transmit radio and voice. In 1964 the United States and ten other countries agreed to establish the first international commercial communications satellite system.

Man himself was travelling into space. On April 12, 1961, the Russian Yuri Gagarin became the first man in space by orbiting earth in a capsule. Other achievements by Russians and Americans included simultaneous orbiting by manned space capsules and flights by two or more men in the same craft. In the latter part of 1966, one publication announced that "more than 1000 man-made objects now orbit the earth," and *Project Apollo* of the United States expected to carry man himself to the moon by 1970. Both an American and a Russian took a "space walk" from a space capsule in 1965.

■ **Check on Your Reading**
1. What contributions were made by the men who did pioneer work in space rocketry?
2. Describe the major space achievements of our day.

3. Art, Music, and Literature in the Twentieth Century

There were important developments in art, music, and literature, as well as in science, in the twentieth century.

Art in the Twentieth Century

France continued to be one of the principal centers for the development of art.

In 1906 a group known as the *Fauves* (or "wild beasts") became active. The Fauves concentrated on using color as a means of building form.

Prominent French Fauve artists included Henri Matisse (1869–1954), Raoul Dufy (1877–1953), Maurice de Vlaminck

■ *The painting entitled "Still Life: Le Jour," by a master of still-life compositions, Georges Braque, exemplified the style of art known as Cubism. Cubist artists re-created an object so as to capture its essence.*

National Gallery of Art, Washington, D.C. (Chester Dale Collection)

Collection of Carnegie Institute, Pittsburgh

■ *"Portrait of Thomas Garrick Masaryk" by Oskar Kokoschka is painted in the expressionistic style. Expressionist artists expressed intense emotions and tried to create a mood rather than present an object in their paintings.*

Room of Contemporary Art Collection, Albright-Knox Art Gallery, Buffalo, New York

■ *In his painting, "Carnival of Harlequin," Joan Miró presents a lively and colorful miniature stage, which is full of magic tricks. It is a fantasy of the artist's creation and is characteristic of Surrealist art.*

■ *Modern sculpture often expresses the abstract and symbolic rather than the realistic. An example is "Family Group" by Henry Moore.*

(1876–1958), and André Derain (1880–1954). The Fauve artists never formed a distinct "school," and many of them developed their own unique styles.

The painters Pablo Picasso (born in Spain, 1881–) and Georges Braque (French, 1882–) are credited with founding *Cubism*. Juan Gris (Spanish, 1887–1927) was another Cubist artist. According to art dealer D. H. Kahnweiler, Cubist painters wanted to show the essence, and not the appearance, of an object. They mentally broke down an object into its elements or parts; selected those parts that they wished to use in their painting; and re-created the object in a way that they hoped would capture its *essence*. They wanted their paintings to give a

"truer" sense of the fundamental nature of an object than the original object.

Picasso experimented with many forms and styles of art and became one of the great artists of the twentieth century.

Surrealist art, which attracted attention after 1924, was marked by fantasy, symbolism, dreamlike qualities, and presentation of objects that do not exist in the real world. Sigmund Freud (1856–1939), the Austrian physician who founded psychoanalysis, took the position that man's mind was affected by the subconscious—that is, by experiences and instinctual drives of which man was not aware. Freudian concepts influenced the development of surrealist art. Artists who did important surrealist paintings (although they also did other types) were Salvador Dali (born in Spain; 1904–), Giorgio de Chirico (Italian, 1888–), Joan Miró (Spanish, 1893–), and Max Ernst (German, 1891–).

Expressionism refers to art that expresses emotion as intensely, poetically, and spiritually as the artist wishes. Expressionist artists did not hesitate to express emotions by distorting figures or substituting abstract forms for the figures found in nature. Expressionists included Oskar Kokoschka (born in Austria; 1886–) and Wassily Kandinsky (Russian, 1866–1944). Kandinsky spoke for the abstract expressionists when he said:

The observer must learn to look at the picture as a graphic representation of a *mood* and not as a representation of *objects*.

The art of the twentieth century must not be considered to be exclusively of European derivation. One of the greatest painters of murals in the twentieth century was a Mexican, José Clemente Orozco (1883–1949); and the United States produced John Sloan (1871–1951) and other distinguished artists.

752

One of the chief features of twentieth century art was that it became universal. It was difficult to speak of *national* art. One referred to the Cubists, the Surrealists, the Expressionists, and used other terms that included artists from many lands.

Equally significant was the fact that *abstract* and *nonobjective* art became increasingly important in the twentieth century. Art historian Helen Gardner makes this distinction between the two:

An abstract work has been "abstracted" from nature, and vestiges of figures or objects may sometimes still be detected in it (as in Cubist paintings). A nonobjective work has no reference, in conception or execution, to natural appearances. . . .

Abstract and nonobjective art had at least one thing in common: neither was concerned with depicting objects with "photographic" exactness.

Music in the Twentieth Century

Music in the twentieth century reflected the search of composers for new, original, and striking ways to express their musical ideas. Yet, twentieth-century music was not cut off from the past. Some composers were influenced by the impressionist works of Claude Debussy (p. 481). They included Paul Dukas (French, 1865–1935); Frederick Delius (English, 1862–1934); and Ottorino Respighi (Italian, 1879–1936).

In the twentieth century a style of music known as *Neo-romanticism* developed. Neo-romantic composers tried to recapture the spirit of romanticism that dominated music in the preceding century. Neo-romanticists included Sergei Rachmaninoff (Russian, 1873–1943), and Richard Strauss (German, 1864–1949). Strauss' tone poems (such as *Till Eulenspiegel's Merry Pranks*) and operas (such as *Der Rosenkavalier*) were marked by exciting rhythms, powerful melodies, and romantic fervor.

Neo-classicism was a twentieth century movement which reacted against the emotionalism of Romanticism. Neo-classicist composers tried to write music that had order, objectivity, and detachment. They sought guidance from the works of eighteenth century classical composers.

Composers of the twentieth century who were affected by Neo-classicism were Sergei Prokofiev (Russian, 1891–1953) in his *Classical Symphony*; Igor Stravinsky (born in Russia; 1882–   ) in his *Octet for Wind Instruments*; Béla Bartók (Hungarian, 1881–1945); Paul Hindemith (born in Germany; 1895–   ); Walter Piston (American, 1894–   ); and others. Stravinsky expressed some of the ideas of the Neo-classicists when he said: "I evoke neither human joy nor human sadness. I move towards a greater abstraction." And "[Music] is given to us with the sole purpose of establishing an order among things."

Professors Willi Apel and Ralph T. Daniel define *atonality* or *atonal* music as "terms used frequently to denote certain practices in twentieth-century music in which a definite tonal center or 'key' is purposely avoided. . . . The discarding of tonal centers or other references of a traditional character (triads, scales, etc.) means that some principles recognizable in tonal music are abandoned, and are replaced by others of a much more intangible nature."

Arnold Schönberg (Austrian, 1874–1951) was one of the leading composers of atonal music. He developed what is known as "12-tone technique." Schönberg's *Three Piano Pieces* (op. 11) is a good example of an atonal composition.

Twentieth-century music had other features, too. Nationalism in music was a major factor in the nineteenth century, and some composers of the twentieth century continued to use native folk songs, dances, and legends in their work. These composers included Hector Villa-Lobos

(c. 1881–1959), who incorporated Brazilian folk melodies into his fourteen *Chôros* (Serenades); Manuel de Falla (Spanish, (1876–1946), famous for his orchestral works; Ralph Vaughan Williams (English, 1872–1958), who composed *A London Symphony*; Aram Khachaturian (Armenian-Soviet, 1904–   ), who was inspired by the folklore of Armenia; and Aaron Copland (American, 1900–   ), composer of *Appalachian Spring*.

Symphonic jazz developed. It was represented by *The Creation of the World* by Darius Milhaud (French, 1892–   ), and *Rhapsody in Blue* by George Gershwin (American, 1898–1937). Gershwin called jazz "an American folk-music."

The symphony orchestra gained in prestige and importance. Formerly, opera dominated the musical scene.

Transcribed music was widely used. The magnetic tape as a medium for recording was developed in 1947. The long-playing record appeared in 1948. Then came "high fidelity" and stereophonic sound. The annual sales of records in the United States was over $400 million in the early 1960's; and in 1966 and 1967 record fans boosted sales still higher.

Experimentation with *electronic music* began in the 1950's. Sounds that existed in nature and sounds that were produced by electronic means were recorded on magnetic tape and used by the composer.

Increased efforts were made to strengthen the people's understanding and appreciation of music. Leonard Bernstein (1918–   ), composer, pianist, and conductor, was particularly active in educational activities. Hector Villa-Lobos also contributed to the strengthening of music education in Brazil.

Special rhythms were developed for popular dancing—the music of the "Charleston," "Lindy," "Twist," and a variety of "go-go" dances at discotheques.

Literature

Literature of the twentieth century included a variety of ideas, styles, and approaches. Many authors had one point in common: *they were deeply concerned with analyzing what was happening to twentieth-century society.*

In Europe, George Bernard Shaw (born in Ireland; 1856–1950), sharp-tongued and witty playwright, dissected the foibles and fables of his time in *Man and Superman* and *Major Barbara*. In Japan, Toson Shimazaki (1872–1943), "father of modern Japanese poetry," examined the changing character of Japanese youth. In the United States, Eugene O'Neill (1888–1953) explored the problems of individuals in relation to society in *The Great God Brown* and *Long Day's Journey into Night*; and Arthur Miller (1915–   ) raised questions about America's scale of values in his play *The Death of a Salesman*. In Latin America, the Nicaraguan poet Rubén Darío (1867–1916) urged the spirit of Don Quixote to protect our earth "from detractors, malefactors, smooth and bland and evil actors." In India, Sir Rabindranath Tagore (1861–1941), poet, dramatist, philosopher, and artist, observed the restlessness of modern man and concluded:

Our restlessness and weaknesses are in reality merely stirring on the surface. That is why we must daily retire in silence far into the quiet depths of our spirits, and experience the real life within us. If we do this, our words and actions will come to be real also.

Much literature expressed *anxiety* about the future of man. The poet T. S. Eliot (1888–1965) reflected the chaos of many aspects of life in his works. In his poem *The Hollow Men*, he pointed out the emptiness of the modern world:

We are the hollow men
We are the stuffed men
Leaning together
Headpiece filled with straw. Alas!

W. H. Auden (1907–   ), a distinguished poet born in England, entitled one work of poetry *The Age of Anxiety*.

Authors also became more concerned about *time*. Literary historian J. Isaacs notes:

In this twentieth century . . . we are obsessed with time. Philosophers analyse it, scientists abolish it, mathematicians transform it, and men of letters have it on the brain.

Novelist Aldous Huxley (1894–1963), who wrote *Brave New World*, an imaginary picture of the world of the future, was concerned about time. So was the French philosopher Henri Bergson (1859–1941). He pointed out that the quality of time can be more significant than its quantity— that is, one hour filled with rich experience is worth more than one week of monotony. Above all, Marcel Proust (1871–1922), the brilliant French author of *Remembrance of Things Past*, was fascinated by time.

Some writers refused to be overwhelmed by the problems of the contemporary world. Such a man was Albert Camus (1913–1960), French novelist, essayist, and playwright who wrote *The Stranger*, *The Plague*, and other novels. Camus stressed the point that man's life may be "absurd," but man must live his life with dignity and courage. He declared: "The problem is to serve human dignity by means which remain honorable in the midst of a history which is not honorable."

There were other important developments in twentieth century literature, too. The novel rose to a dominant position in literature. There were many excellent dramatists, and some great poets, including William Butler Yeats (Irish, 1865–1939), one of the greatest lyricists, and Carl Sandburg (American, 1878–1967), who described everyday people and events. However, the novel dominated the literary scene.

In the United States Ernest Hemingway (1898–1961), author of *The Old Man and the Sea*; William Faulkner (1897–1962), *The Sound and the Fury*; and John Steinbeck (1902–   ), *The Grapes of Wrath*, were leading writers. In Great Britain there was Virginia Woolf (1882–1941), author of *Mrs. Dalloway*; and in France François Mauriac (1885–   ), *The Kiss to the Leper*, did distinguished writing. The Soviet Union's leading novelist was Mikhail Sholokov (1905–   ), author of *And Quiet Flows the Don*. In Germany Thomas Mann (1875–1955), author of *The Magic Mountain*; in Austria Franz Kafka (1883–1924), *The Trial*; and in Sweden Pär Lagerkvist (1891–   ), *Barabbas*, all contributed important works to twentieth-century literature.

Some writers experimented with "stream of consciousness" techniques. These techniques presented the free-flowing thoughts of a character without an author inhibiting them or rearranging them into an artificial pattern. James Joyce (Irish, 1882–1941) —author of *Ulysses*, a novel describing eighteen hours in the lives of a group of people living in Dublin—used "stream of consciousness" with striking results.

Literature was made available to many people. Beginning about 1940, there soon was widespread publication of inexpensive paperbacks in the United States and several other countries. The annual sale of paperbacks is more than 300 million copies. In 1967 paperback books in the United States numbered over 42,000 titles.

■ **Check on Your Reading**

1. What new movements developed in art?
2. What new movements developed in music? Name some of the leading composers.
3. Describe the major developments in twentieth-century literature.
4. What is the impact of paperback books on American life?

4. Contemporary Problems, Changes, and Crises

As man moved towards new frontiers in contemporary culture, he continued to encounter new problems, changes, and crises.

Man Seeks to Control Weapons of War

In the minds of most leaders of the 1960's was the fact that man possessed weapons that could destroy most of civilization. This point became clear in 1961 when the Soviet Union test-exploded an estimated 57-megaton nuclear bomb. It contained *three thousand* times the destructive power of the bomb that destroyed the city of Hiroshima, Japan, in 1945.

According to editor Norman Cousins, advances in other weapons of war were almost as striking. Intercontinental ballistic missiles (ICBM) could carry nuclear explosives for distances of over 5000 miles. Bacteria; nerve gas (GB), odorless, invisible, and easy to disseminate; and psychochemicals, also odorless and invisible, could bring death to millions.

Leaders of many faiths discussed ways of keeping peace, and at the Vatican Council II Pope John XXIII declared: ". . . experience has taught men that violence . . . and political domination are of no help at all in finding a happy solution to the grave problems that afflict them."

Many statesmen worked for peace. Finally, on August 5, 1963, the United States, the Soviet Union, and the United Kingdom signed a limited Nuclear Test Ban Treaty. It banned "any nuclear weapon test explosion, or any other nuclear explosion" in the atmosphere, in outer space, or under water. Over 100 countries quickly signed this treaty, but France and Communist China did not.

France, which had achieved its first atomic explosion in February, 1960, declared its determination to be free from "American domination" and worked to develop its own thermonuclear force.

On November 22, 1963, the world was shocked by the assassination of President John F. Kennedy. President Lyndon B. Johnson, who took over leadership of the American government, pledged to continue the late President's efforts for world peace. When Communist China successfully exploded its first atomic bomb on October 16, 1964, President Johnson warned: "Nuclear spread is dangerous to all mankind. . . . We call on the world—especially Red China—to join the nations which have signed the Test Ban Treaty."

In December, 1966, agreement was reached on an international treaty on the exploration and use of outer space. The Treaty (a) prohibited countries from using outer space, the moon, and other celestial bodies for military purposes; (b) declared outer space as not subject to territorial claims and (c) set down the principle of "cooperation and mutual assistance" in exploring or using outer space.

What of the Future?

Recently the editors of *Changing Times* magazine took a survey of the views of scientists, educators, businessmen, and government officials, and made these predictions of what life would be like in 1975:

In 1975 the population of the United States will top 235,000,000. . . .

The housewife will be able to use a stove that can be turned on and off by dialing "instructions" from a phone booth, a vacuum cleaner that runs itself, and ultrasonic sound waves that wash her dishes. She will dress her children in disposable paper clothing, and keep an eye on the baby by closed-circuit T.V.

By 1975 the roofs of cars may be made of indestructible glasslike materials, and bodies will be of lightweight steel, aluminum, or plastic so tough it can compete with metals. [The] electronic highways will enable drivers to sit back and enjoy the scenery while electronic devices guide and operate their cars.

Bat-shaped commercial planes will fly at Mach 3—three times the speed of sound—and it will be a mere hour and a half to Paris from New York. Hydrofoil ships for both passengers and cargo will be commonplace, skimming over the water at 80 or 100 knots.

By 1975 a preventive vaccine may be available for tuberculosis, and plastic glue will be used to replace old teeth with new. There may even be a cure for the common cold! Isotopes will be used to create new fuels from coal and oil, new kinds of synthetic fibers, new disease-resistant strains of foods and flowers, and stronger metals.

Space travel? By 1975 man will have already made a landing on the moon and established space stations. . . .

As in all ages, man stood at the crossroads. Man had to choose between the road to war and the road to peace. And, as in all ages, man went forward.

■ Check on Your Reading

1. What new weapons increased the danger that most of civilization might be destroyed?

2. Describe the predictions about life in 1975.

CULTURAL CHARACTERISTICS of Our Times

These are wondrous times to be alive. There is now a machine that can translate Russian into English at a rate soon to exceed 2400 words and idioms a minute. Composers now create new sounds for music by smashing bottles on stone, recording the noise on tape, and playing the tape upside down. Hundreds of man-made objects, including one lost glove and one lost camera, are now orbiting the earth. Wondrous times, indeed!

The cultural characteristics of our period reflect the dynamic quality of the world in which we live. They are:

An extraordinary growth of population throughout the earth—about 8000 births every hour in 1966—and the growing demand of peoples everywhere for a better life.

Science and technology shaping the lives of the people in unforeseen ways.

Experimentation in art, literature, dance, and music, as a result of the shattering of permanent absolute standards in the creation of culture.

A search—and sometimes a desperate one—for values that will enable men to find meaning in a world in constant ferment and accelerating social change.

If the rate of change in the contemporary world continues, the culture of the future may be far more startling. As one national report points out: "One profile of the scope and speed of change can be found in March's *Thesaurus*, which lists and defines 1800 words and phrases that came into use during this century. Under the letter "A," for example, the entries include A-bomb, accelerator, aircraft, allergy, amino acids, anti-acids, anti-freeze, anti-histamine, and automation. . . . At least half of today's occupations have come into existence within the past 40 years."

Yet whether we view culture from the past or the present or the future, the key factor in the development of civilization continues to be man himself. The machine may replace men, but it can never replace man.

MAN AND HIS CULTURE

Let's Meet the People!

The following sketch is based on *Orbital Flight of John H. Glenn, Jr.*; and *Astronaut John H. Glenn Orbits the Earth for America, February 20, 1962*, Senate Committee on Aeronautical and Space Sciences.

Lieutenant Colonel John H. Glenn, Jr.: Astronaut

John H. Glenn, Jr., a 40-year-old lieutenant colonel in the United States Marine Corps, awoke at Cape Canaveral at 2:20 A.M. on February 20, 1962. He breakfasted on orange juice, scrambled eggs, filet of beef, toast with jelly, and Postum. At 3 A.M. he reported for his pre-departure medical examination. The doctor checked Colonel Glenn carefully. Then he reached his decision: "Go!"

At 4:30 A.M. Colonel Glenn moved to the suiting room. Electrocardiograph sensors (to show changes in electric potential produced by the contractions of his heart) were glued to his chest, and a respirometer (to measure his breathing) was taped to his neck. After other instruments were connected, Colonel Glenn "wiggled" into his tight-fitting space suit.

A transfer van took Colonel Glenn to the launching pad. At 6 A.M. he left the van; then he stepped into the gantry elevator that carried him to the "eleventh deck" or the top of the 109D Atlas missile in its take-off position. At 6:03 A.M. he slowly eased his way into the space capsule—feet first. Technicians strapped him onto the contour couch, and at 6:59 A.M. the hatch was closed.

Now began a long wait—almost three hours—while the launching crew delayed the countdown because of technical troubles. At last, the rocket was ready for lift-off. Final countdown began: 10 seconds, 9, 8, 7, 6, 5, 4, 3, 2, 1, 0. Lift-off! A jet of yellow-white flame lifted the slender rocket off its pad.

"Lift-off!" came the voice of Colonel Glenn. ". . . We are underway."

It was 9:47 A.M., and John H. Glenn, Jr., had started on the first space flight of an American around the earth!

CHAPTER REVIEW

REVIEW and DISCUSSION

1. Identify the people and explain the events and terms on p. 728.

2. Which scientific discoveries contributed to man's welfare? Which discoveries were used for destructive purposes?

3. Discoveries in one field of knowledge can lead to important accomplishments in other fields. Find examples to prove this statement.

4. Identify some important features of art, literature, and music in the twentieth century.

5. How can the standards of mass literature be improved?

6. Your text states that man is living in one of the crucial periods in history. Do you agree? Why or why not?

7. If the social scientists were to conduct an "International Geophysical Year" to make an intensive study of man rather than of his environment, what are some of the things they might investigate?

8. The editors of *Changing Times* predict that men who live in 1975 will have more leisure time. How should they use it?

ACTIVITIES

1. Have an art exhibit in your classroom illustrating the artistic movements mentioned in this chapter.

PAST and PRESENT

1. Why do many artists, writers, and composers of the twentieth century refuse to follow the styles, techniques, and ideas of creative men of earlier generations?

2. Compare the present exploration of space with the exploration of the Western Hemisphere in the fifteenth and sixteenth centuries. Discuss such problems as financing, physical obstacles, and state of knowledge.

SUGGESTED READINGS

Basic books: BRUUN, GEOFFREY, and MAMATEY, VICTOR S., *The World in the Twentieth Century*, Part XI, Heath.

BUTTERFIELD, HERBERT, and others, *A Short History of Science*, Chaps. 15, 16, Anchor Books.

SMITH, GOLDWIN, *The Heritage of Man*, Chap. 48, Scribner.

Special accounts: BARR, ALFRED H., JR. (ed.), *Masters of Modern Art*, The Museum of Modern Art.

CLOUGH, SHEPARD B., *The Rise and Fall of Civilizations*, Chap. VII, Columbia University Press (paperback). Twentieth century.

McKINNEY, HOWARD, *Music and Man*, Chaps. 10 and 20, American Book.

RILEY, OLIVE L., *Your Art Heritage*, Harper.

Acknowledgments for Photographs

The photographs on the pages listed below are from the following sources:

ATLAS
of
OUR WORLD
TODAY

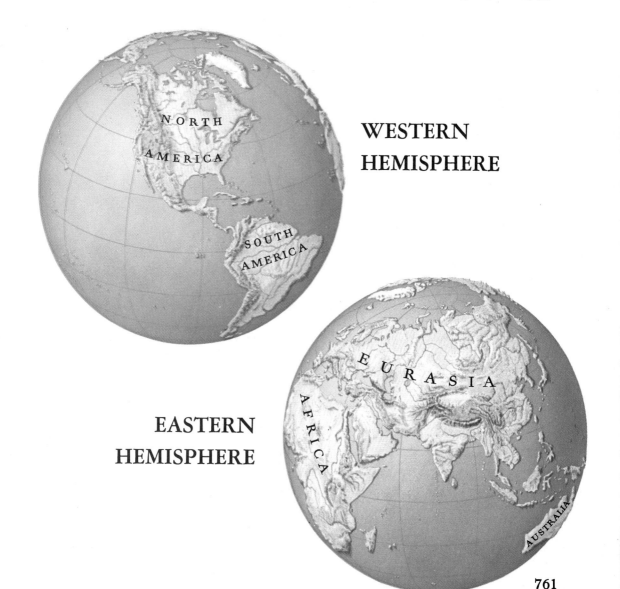

WESTERN
HEMISPHERE

EASTERN
HEMISPHERE

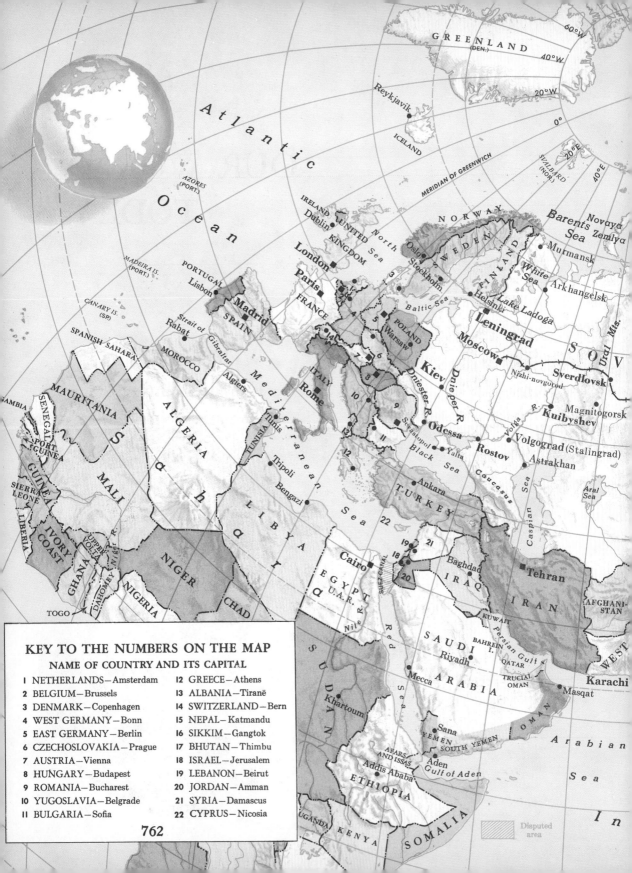

KEY TO THE NUMBERS ON THE MAP
NAME OF COUNTRY AND ITS CAPITAL

1 NETHERLANDS—Amsterdam
2 BELGIUM—Brussels
3 DENMARK—Copenhagen
4 WEST GERMANY—Bonn
5 EAST GERMANY—Berlin
6 CZECHOSLOVAKIA—Prague
7 AUSTRIA—Vienna
8 HUNGARY—Budapest
9 ROMANIA—Bucharest
10 YUGOSLAVIA—Belgrade
11 BULGARIA—Sofia

12 GREECE—Athens
13 ALBANIA—Tiranë
14 SWITZERLAND—Bern
15 NEPAL—Katmandu
16 SIKKIM—Gangtok
17 BHUTAN—Thimbu
18 ISRAEL—Jerusalem
19 LEBANON—Beirut
20 JORDAN—Amman
21 SYRIA—Damascus
22 CYPRUS—Nicosia

762

EURASIA
POLITICAL-PHYSICAL

0   400   800   1200   1600

AVERAGE SCALE OF MILES

Size of place name indicates relative size of population

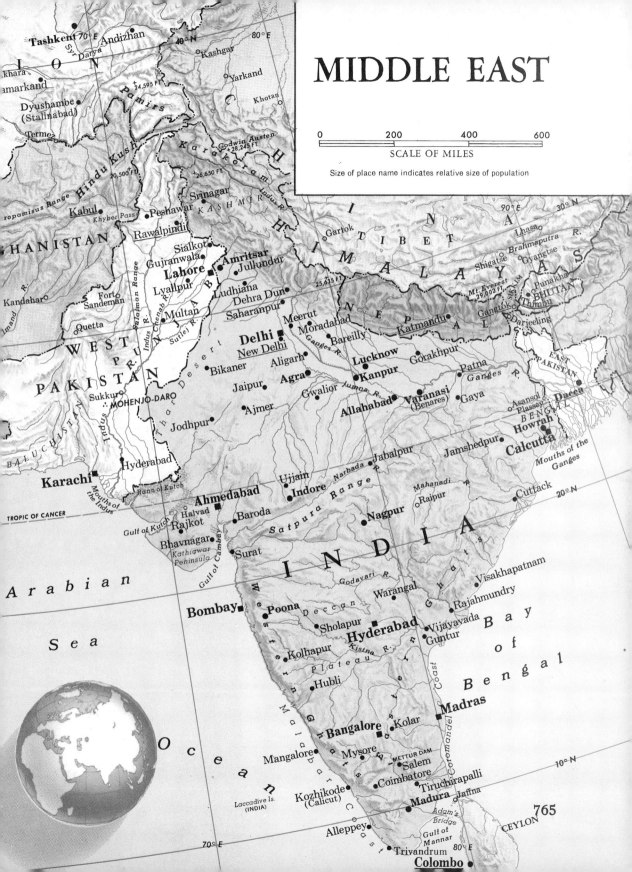

MIDDLE EAST

0   200   400   600
SCALE OF MILES

Size of place name indicates relative size of population

Tashkent 70° E Andizhan 40° N 80° E

khara
amarkand
Dyushambe
(Stalinabad)
Termez

ION

Kashgar
Yarkand
Khotan

+24,595 FT.

Pamirs

Godwin Austen
+28,245 FT.

Karakoram

20,500 FT.

+26,630 FT.

Indus R.

HI

opamisus Range Hindu Kush

Kabul
Khyber Pass
HANISTAN
Peshawar
Rawalpindi

Srinagar
KASHMIR

H

Gartok

TIBET

90° E 30° N

Lhasa

Shigatse Brahmaputra R. Gyangtse

Kandahar

Sialkot
Gujranwala
Amritsar
Lahore Jullundur
Lyallpur
Multan
Ludhiana
Dehra Dun
Saharanpur

Sialkot
Sutlej R.

Mt. Everest
29,002 FT.
Gangtok SIKKIM BHUTAN
Thimbu Punakha

Katmandu

Darjeeling

Meerut
Moradabad
Bareilly

NEPAL

A

L

Fort
Sandeman
Quetta

Kandahar

WEST

PUNJAB

PAKISTAN

Chenab R.

Taiman Range

Indus R.

Sukkur
MOHENJO-DARO

Thar Desert

25,635 FT.

Delhi
New Delhi
Bikaner
Aligarh
Jaipur Agra
Ajmer
Jodhpur
Ganges R.

Lucknow
Kanpur
Gwalior
Jumna R.
Allahabad Varanasi
(Benares)

Gorakhpur
Patna Ganges

Gaya

EAST
PAKISTAN

Asansol
Plassey Dacca
BENGAL
Howrah
Jamshedpur Calcutta

Mouths of the
Ganges

Karachi

BALUCHISTAN

Hyderabad

Mouths of
the Indus

TROPIC OF CANCER

Halvad
Rann of Kutch Rajkot
Gulf of Kutch
Bhavnagar
Kathiawar
Peninsula

Ahmedabad
Baroda
Surat

Ujjain
Indore
Gulf of Cambay

Jabalpur
Narbada R.
Satpura Range

Nagpur

INDIA

Mahanadi
Rajpur

Cuttack

20° N

Arabian

Sea

Godavari R.

Deccan

Warangal

Bombay Poona
Sholapur
Kolhapur
Hubli

Western Ghats

Plateau
Kistna R.
Hyderabad
Vijayavada
Guntur

Visakhapatnam

Rajahmundry

Bay

of

Bengal

Eastern Ghats

Coromandel Coast

O c e a n

Mangalore
Laccadive Is.
(INDIA)
Kozhikode
(Calicut)

Alleppey

Malabar Coast

Bangalore
Mysore
METTUR DAM
Salem
Coimbatore
Tiruchirapalli
Madura Jaffna
Adam's
Bridge
Gulf of
Mannar
Trivandrum 80° E

Kolar
Madras

10° N

765

CEYLON

70° E

Colombo

Helsinki
Hango Pen.
Gulf of Finland
Tallinn
Leningrad
30°E
35°E

Riga
Duna R.
S O V I E T
55°N
Smolensk
Volga R.

Neman R. Kaunas
Vilnius
Minsk
U N I O N

Kaliningrad
Masurian Lakes
Dnieper R.
Plain

Vistula R. Warsaw
P L A I N
Russian
MARSHES
Kiev
50°N

P O L A N D
OF THE
Lvov
PRIPET

Kraków
Carpathian Mts.
Dniester R.

V A K I A
ROMANIA
Odessa

Budapest
HUNGARY
Hungarian Plain
Tisza R.

Belgrade
Bucharest
Walachian Plain
Danube R.

YUGOSLAVIA
R.
45°N

Balkan Mts.
Black Sea

Sofia
30°E

BULGARIA
Bosporus

Tirane
BALKAN PENINSULA
Istanbul
TURKEY

ALBANIA
Salonika
ASIA MINOR
40°N

Granicus R.

Izmir

GREECE
Aegean Sea
Dardanelles

Ionian Sea
Athens
Dodecanese Is.

Morea Pen.
RHODES

CRETE (GREECE)
20°E
25°E

EUROPE
PHYSICAL

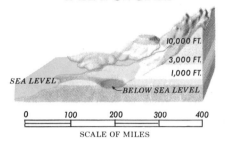

10,000 FT.
3,000 FT.
1,000 FT.
SEA LEVEL
BELOW SEA LEVEL

0   100   200   300   400
SCALE OF MILES

Size of place name indicates relative size of population

Geography Influences History in Many Ways · *Mountains*, such as the Alps and Pyrenees, are natural defenses against invasions. *Plains*, such as those of northern France, Germany, Poland, and Russia, however, are natural routes for invading armies. *Rivers*, such as the Rhine and Danube, may be barriers, or invasion routes, or highways of commerce. Can you see how?

Note the influence of the *seas* and *oceans* upon such seafaring peoples as the Phoenicians, Greeks, Norsemen, Italians, English, Dutch, and Portuguese. Consider too the power which goes to nations which control *strategic corridors*, such as mountain passes (Thermopylae and Brenner), man-made canals (Suez and Kiel), and narrow straits (the Bosporus, the Dardanelles, and Gibraltar).

Possession of *natural resources*, such as iron, copper, precious metals, coal, petroleum, fertile land, and fresh water, has likewise had great influence on the course of human events.

Geography was a key factor in the *growth of cities*. How do you think it influenced Athens? Rome? Istanbul? Venice? Paris? London? Antwerp? Cologne? Vienna? Budapest? Stockholm?

As for *climate*, the great powers of modern history are located in the middle latitudes where more temperate conditions stimulate human endeavor.

767

EUROPE
POLITICAL

Geography Affects Political Decisions · The lure of *warm water ports* brought Russian invasions of Poland, Lithuania, Latvia, and Finland on the Baltic; of Rumania, Bulgaria, and Turkey on the Black Sea; and constant pressure upon the straits which barred Russia's outlet from the Black Sea to the Mediterranean.

Poland's *lack of defensible frontiers* encouraged partitions by Russia, Prussia, and Austria. The strategic geographic position of Belgium in the very "cockpit of Europe" led to her official neutralization by England, France, and Germany.

The control of the *headwaters* of the Rhine, Rhone, and Danube rivers, and of the *vital passes and tunnels* through the Alps, resulted in the guarantee of Swiss neutrality by France, Germany, and Italy.

After repeated conflict, political control of the Danube River, which is the *vital transportation artery* for Austria, Hungary, Yugoslavia, Rumania, and Bulgaria, has been "internationalized" under a Danubian Commission, representing these nations.

England's *island position* has greatly influenced many of her political decisions regarding the "balance of power" on the continent of Europe, her "lifeline to India" (via Gibraltar, Malta, Suez, and Aden), her basic reliance upon seapower, and her concern with conditions of international trade.

769

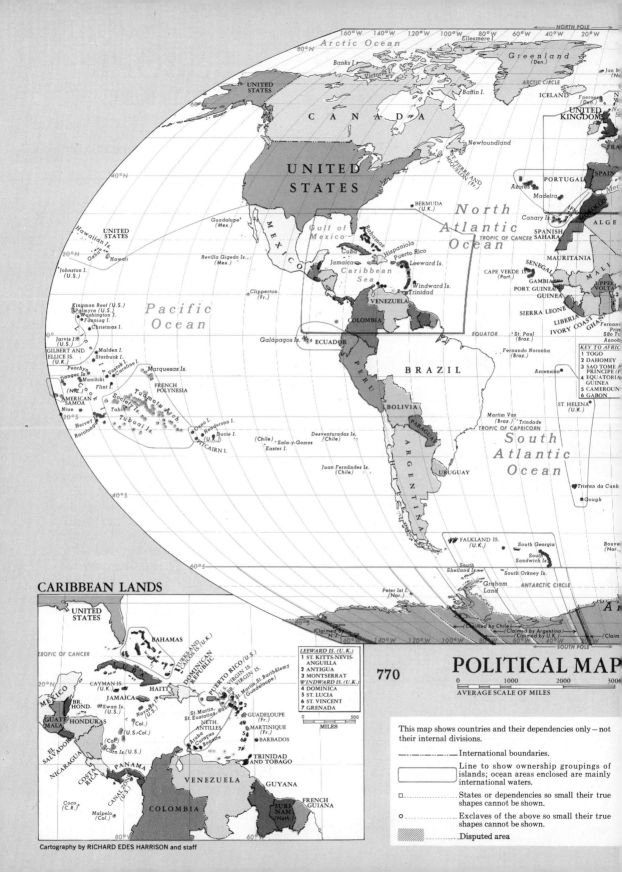

POLITICAL MAP

CARIBBEAN LANDS

This map shows countries and their dependencies only — not their internal divisions.

—————————— International boundaries.

Line to show ownership groupings of islands; ocean areas enclosed are mainly international waters.

□··········· States or dependencies so small their true shapes cannot be shown.

○··········· Exclaves of the above so small their true shapes cannot be shown.

░░░░░ ····· Disputed area

770

0 ···· 1000 ···· 2000 ···· 3000
AVERAGE SCALE OF MILES

Cartography by RICHARD EDES HARRISON and staff

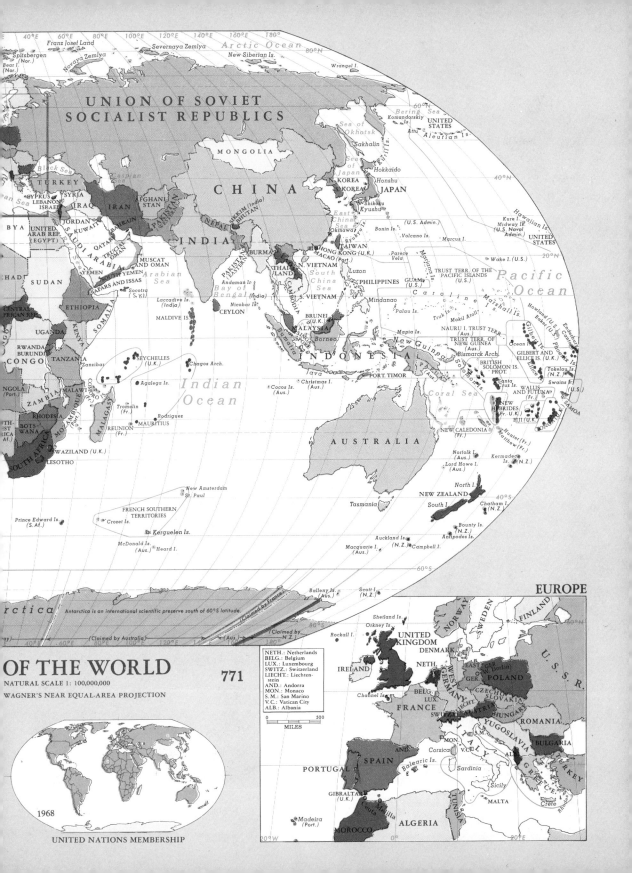

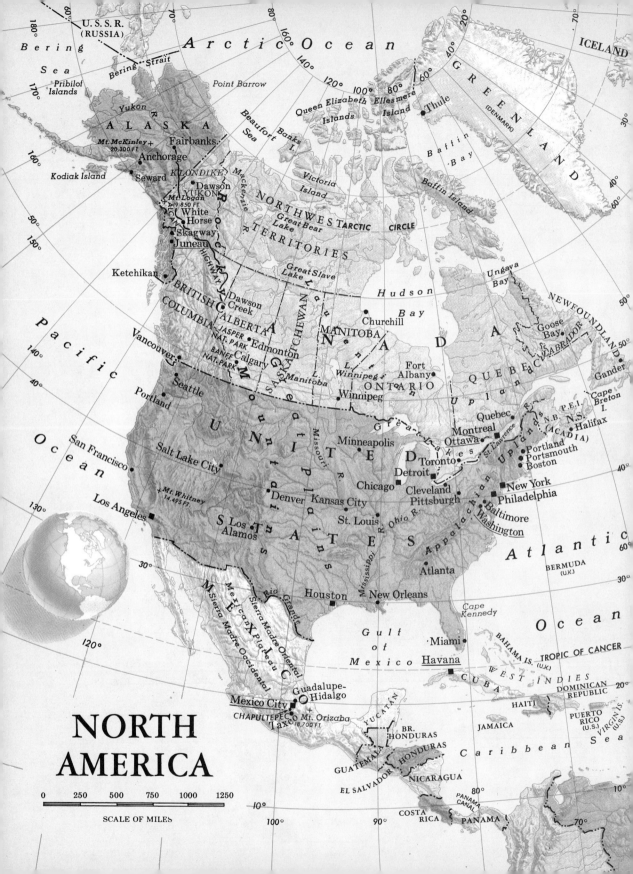

NORTH AMERICA

SCALE OF MILES

0   250   500   750   1000   1250

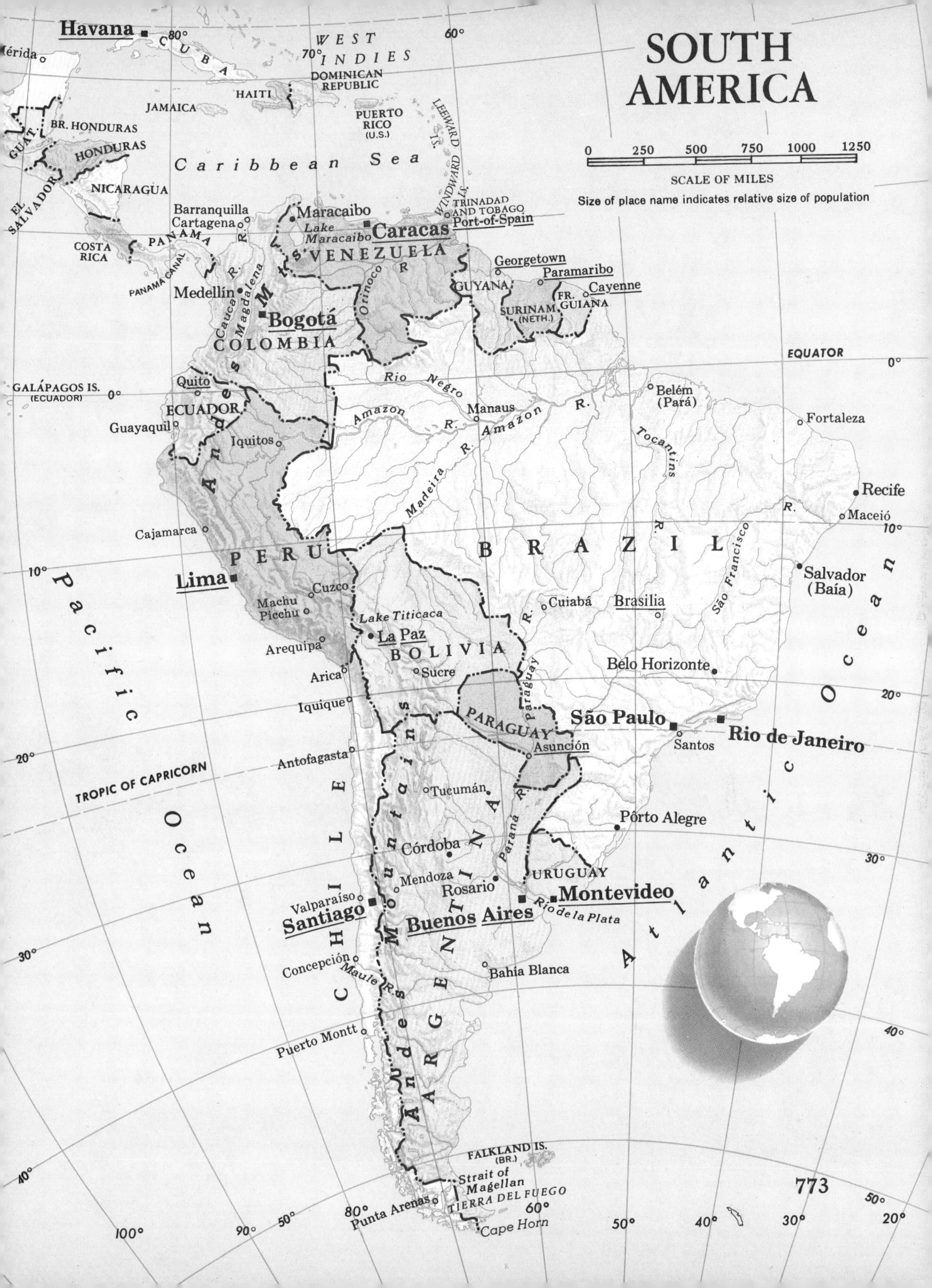

SOUTH AMERICA

Havana

MÉRIDA 80°   *W E S T*   60°
CUBA   70°   *I N D I E S*
JAMAICA   DOMINICAN REPUBLIC
HAITI
BR. HONDURAS   PUERTO RICO (U.S.)
GUAT.
EL SALVADOR   HONDURAS
COSTA RICA   NICARAGUA
PANAMA

SCALE OF MILES

0   250   500   750   1000   1250

Size of place name indicates relative size of population

C a r i b b e a n   S e a

Barranquilla   TRINIDAD AND TOBAGO
Cartagena   Maracaibo   Port-of-Spain
Lake Maracaibo   **Caracas**
PANAMA CANAL   VENEZUELA
Georgetown   Paramaribo
Medellín   GUYANA   Cayenne
FR. GUIANA
Bogotá   SURINAM (NETH.)
COLOMBIA   Orinoco R.

EQUATOR   0°

Quito   Belém (Pará)
GALÁPAGOS IS. (ECUADOR)   Rio Negro   Fortaleza
ECUADOR   Amazon   Manaus
Guayaquil   Amazon R.
Iquitos   Madeira R.   Tocantins R.

Cajamarca   B R A Z I L   Recife
10°   Maceió

Lima   P E R U   Cuzco   Cuiabá   Brasília   Salvador (Baía)
Machu Picchu   Lake Titicaca   R.   São Francisco
La Paz   Belo Horizonte
Arequipa   BOLIVIA   Paraguay R.
Arica   Sucre
Iquique   São Paulo   **Rio de Janeiro**
PARAGUAY   Santos
Antofagasta   Asunción
TROPIC OF CAPRICORN   Paraná R.   Pôrto Alegre
Tucumán
Córdoba   URUGUAY
Mendoza   **Montevideo**
Valparaíso   Rosario   Río de la Plata
Santiago   **Buenos Aires**
Concepción   Maule R.   Bahía Blanca
ARGENTINA

P a c i f i c   O c e a n

A t l a n t i c   O c e a n

Puerto Montt

Andes Mountains   CHILE

FALKLAND IS. (BR.)
Strait of Magellan
Punta Arenas   TIERRA DEL FUEGO
Cape Horn

773

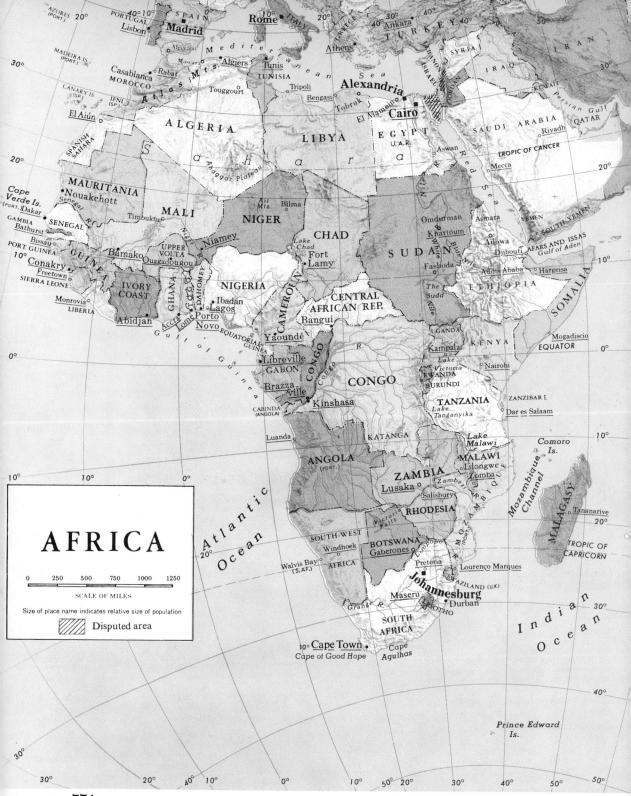

AFRICA

0 250 500 750 1000 1250

SCALE OF MILES

Size of place name indicates relative size of population

Disputed area

774

AUSTRALASIA
POLITICAL-PHYSICAL

Scale of Miles

0   300   600   900   1200

Size of place name and symbol indicates relative size of population

Cartography by NORMAN C. ADAMS and staff

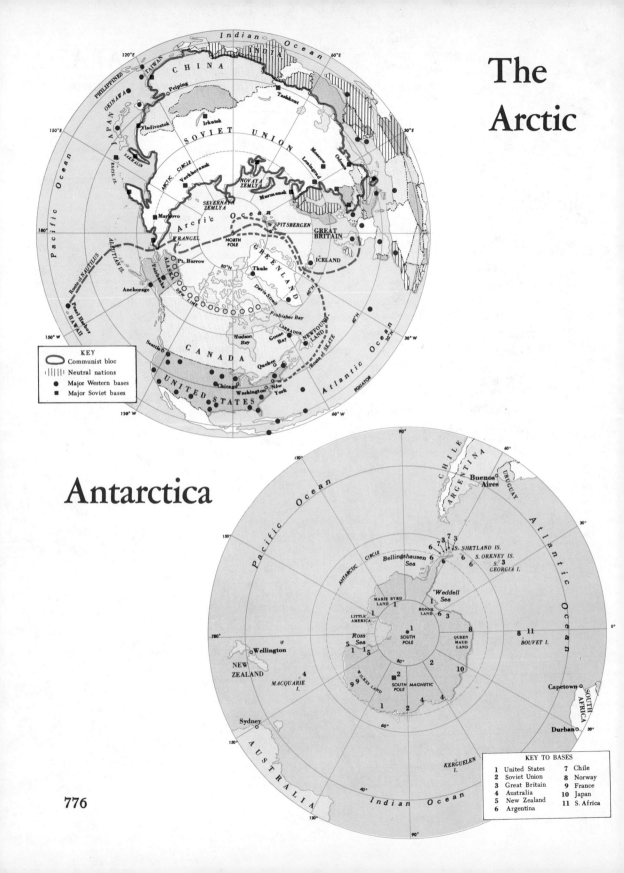

The Arctic

Antarctica

KEY
◯ Communist bloc
||||| Neutral nations
● Major Western bases
■ Major Soviet bases

KEY TO BASES

1	United States	7	Chile
2	Soviet Union	8	Norway
3	Great Britain	9	France
4	Australia	10	Japan
5	New Zealand	11	S. Africa
6	Argentina		

776

INDEX

Bhartrihari, 210, 211

Bhasa, 145

Bible, 24, 148, 186; Erasmus publishes, 252; in Reformation, 307, 310, 313, 315; Wycliffe translates, 279

Bicameral legislature, 278

Bill of Rights, 374, *chart*, 374

Biremes (bī′rēmz), *illus.*, 119

Bishop of Rome, 151. *See also* Popes

Bishops, 150, 161; and investiture struggle, 176–177

Bismarck, Otto von, 514–519; and Congress of Berlin, 549; foreign policy of, 575; as German Chancellor, 518–519; and German unification, 514–517; *illus.*, 515

Black Death, 207

Black Sea, 153, 185; in nineteenth-century diplomacy, 547, 548

Black Stone, 181

Blake, William, 471

Blanc, Louis, 499

Blenheim (blĕn′ĭm), battle of, 360

Blitzkrieg (blĭtz′krēк), 641, 642

Bloc National, 623–624

Blood, circulation of, 302, 303

"Bloody Sunday" (1905), 595

Blum, Léon, 625

Bodhisattvas (bō′dĭ săt′wás), 238

Boer (bōōr) War, 536

Boers, 535–536

Bohemia, 290, 311, 321; in 1848 revolution, 501; united with Austria, 340

Boleyn (bŏō lĭn′), Anne, 319

Bolingbroke (bŏl′ĭng brŏŏk), 1st Viscount, 355

Bolivia, 735; education in, 735

Bolívar (bŏ lē′vär), Simón, 438–439, 440, *portrait*, 438

Bologna (bŏ lō′nyä), University of, 204

Bolsheviks (bŏl′shĕ vĭks): conduct October Revolution, 597; defeat Whites, 598; split Social Democratic party, 594. *See also* Communist party

Bombay, India, 212, 383

Bonaparte family: Jerome, 419; Joseph, 418, 419, 437; Louis, 418, 420; Louis Napoleon, *see* Napoleon III; Napoleon, *see* Napoleon I

Bonapartism, 423, 499. *See also* Napoleonic legend

Bonn, West Germany, 682

Book of the Courtier, The, 270

Book of the Dead, The, 40, 45

Book of the Travels of Marco Polo, 229, 231–232

Books: paperbacks, 755; printing and publishing, 301–302

Borges, Jorge Luis, 742

Borodin (bŭ rŭ dyēn′), Aleksandr, 546

Bosch, Juan, 739

Bosnia, 549, 576, 577–578

Bosporus (bŏs′pŏ rŭs), 153, 185

Bossuet (bô′sü ĕ′), Bishop, 355

Boston Tea Party, 388

Botticelli (bŏt tĕ chĕl′lē), Sandro, 264, *painting by*, 258

Boucher (bōō shā′), François, 397

Bourbon (bōōr bon′) dynasty, 320, 321; Congress of Vienna restores, 494; rule France, 352–360, 423; Spanish, and Napoleon, 419; and War of Spanish Succession, 341

"Bourgeois (bōōr′zhwá) Monarchy," 498–499

Bourgeois Nobleman, The, quoted, 358

Bourgeoisie (bōōr zhwá zē′): and French Revolution, 396, 402, 404, 409; in Marxist theory, 467; and Reformation, 308; rise of, 201, 300. *See also* Third Estate

Boxer Rebellion, 557

Boyars (bŏ yärs′), 329

Boyle, Robert, 303

Bradley, General Omar, 647

Brahma (brä′má), 57

Brahmagupta (brä mä gōōp′tá), 212

Brahman (brä′măn), in Hinduism, 57

Brahman caste, 56, 58

Brahms, Johannes, 481

Branco, General Humberto Castelo, 737

Brandenburg: margrave of, 290; origins, 343–344, *map*, 344. *See also* Prussia

Brandenburg-Prussia, 321. *See also* Prussia

Braque, Georges, 752; *painting by*, 751

Brasilia, *illus.*, 736

Brazil, 298, 428; constitution of, 736–737; coup in 1964, 737; economic development of, 736; gains independence, 438; in 1960's, 734; housing, 736; Portugal claims, 433, 435; under Portuguese rule, 437

Bremen (brä′mĕn), Germany, 200

Brest-Litovsk (lĭ tôfsk′), Treaty of, 598

Breughel (brŭ′gĕl), Pieter, 266, 267

Brezhnev (brĕsh′nyĕf), Leonid, 756

Briand (brē än′), Aristide, 633

Briand-Kellogg Treaty, 633

Brinton, Crane, 398, 409

Britain: Anglo-Saxon period, 165; invaded by Caesar, 121; Romans in, 165; Viking attacks, 169. *See also* England, Great Britain

British Commonwealth of Nations, 628, *map*, 629; and European Common Market, 668; South Africa withdraws, 723. *See also* dominions by name

British Isles: geography, 367–368; *map*, 368

British North America Act, 532–533

Bronze: age, 11; in Etruscan art, 113

Broz, Joseph, *see* Tito, Marshal

Bruges (brōōzh), Belgium, 200

Brutus, 124

Bruun, Geoffrey, quoted, 415

Bubonic plague, 207

Buchanan, James, U. S. President, 453

Buddha (bōōd′á) (Gautama Buddha), Prince Siddhartha: Japanese, 238, 240; life of, 59–60; statues, *illus.*, 212, 240

Buddhism (bōōd′ĭz′m): Asoka spreads, 143–145; beliefs of, 59–60; in Burma, 701; in China, 147, 223–224; in India, 231; in Japan, 237, 238, 239, 240, 242; shrines, *illus.*, 146; spread of, 60; University of Nalanda, 214

Bulgaria: gains independence, 549; goes Communist, 674; peace treaty with (1947), 673, *map*, 674; in Warsaw Pact, 668; in World War I, 581

"Bulge," battle of the (1944), 648

Bundesrat, in German Empire, 518

Burgoyne, General John, 390

Burgundy (bûr′gŭn dĭ), 166

Burke, Edmund, 388

Burma, 144, 213; British conquer, 537; as independent state, 701; in World War II, 645, 648, 650, *map*, 649

Burma Road, 648, 649, 650

Burundi, 720

Bushido (bōō′shĕ dō), 241

Bushmen-Hottentots, 561

Bushmen, in South Africa, 535

Business: capitalism develops, 295–296, 300; and French Revolution, 409–410; in French Second Empire, 504; and Industrial Revolution, 457–459, 461–462; and Italian unification, 509–510, 511;

and eastern Europe, 547–549; and Egyptian crisis (1956), 713–714; empire of, 532–538, *map*, 532; frees Asian dependencies, 699–702; geography of, 367–368, *map*, 368; and Germany since World War II, 681–682, 684; Glorious Revolution in, 374–375; government reforms (19th century), 523–529; imperial wars with France (18th century), 383–386, *map*, 387; Industrial Revolution in, 442, 444–454, 456–459; intervenes in Russia (1918), 598; and Japan, 558, 560; literature of (19th century), 471–474; and Louis XIV's wars, 360; and Monroe Doctrine, 496–497; and Napoleon, 416–423; opposes revolutionary France, 407; and Palestine, 710–711; and peace efforts of 1920's, 633; in post-World War I era, 626–629; and regional organizations since 1945, 665–669; Restoration era in, 372–374; and Russia, 329, 332; and Seven Years' War, 346; since 1945, 684–685; under Stuarts, 368–370, 372–374; in UN Security Council, 659; and Versailles Treaty, 583–584; and War of Austrian Succession, 346; and War of Spanish Succession, 341; and World War I, 576–582; in World War II, 641–643, 645–651. *See also* England

Great Charter, *see* Magna Carta
Great Council, English, 277, 288
Great Elector, of Brandenburg, 344
"Great Proletarian Cultural Revolution," 696
Great Pyramid, 39, *illus.*, 48
"Great Trek," of Boers, 535–536, *illus.*, 536
Great Wall of China, 65, 72; *illus.*, 73
Great Western, steamship, 45 2
Great Zimbabwe, 719
"Greater East Asia Co-prosperity Sphere," 638
Greece, ancient: art, 92, 94–97, *illus.*, 44, 95–97; city-states of, 87–88; colonies of, 81–82, *map*, 82; cultural characteristics of, 107–108; culture, 92–102; early history, 80–89; geography and climate, 79, *maps*, 80, 89; government, 82–86, *table*, 84; in Hellenistic period, 105–107; influence of, 76–77, 104, 133, 137, 250–251; and Peloponnesian War, 102–103;

in Persian Wars, 88–89; religion, 87–88; revolts (1821), 496; Rome conquers, 117, 119
Greece, modern: in Balkan Wars, 577–578; in NATO, 665; revolts against Ottoman Turks, 496; Truman Doctrine aids, 673–674; after World War I, 588; in World War II, 643
Gregory VII, Pope, 176–177
Grey, Earl Charles, 524, *illus.*, 525
Grimm, Jacob and Wilhelm, 514
Gris, Juan, 752
Gris-gris, 708
Guam (gwŏm), 567, 645
Guantanamo (gwän tä'nä mō) Bay, 725, 737
Guatemala (gwä tě mä'lả): gains independence, 439; Mayan culture in, 429, 430
Guérard, Albert, 280, 352, 395, 408, 412, 498
Guilds: medieval, 201–203, 208; universities as, 204
Guillotine (gǐl'ō tēn), 407
Guinea (gǐn'ǐ), 720
Guizot (gē'zō'), Francois, 498–499
Gunpowder, 229
Gupta (gōōp'tả) dynasty, 210, 211–214, 215, 253; *map*, 213
Guri Dam, 733
Gustavus (gŭs tä'vŭs) III, king of Sweden, *illus.*, 334
Gustavus Adolphus (gŭs tä'vŭs ả-dŏl'fŭs), king of Sweden, 320
Gutenberg (gōō'těm běrk), Johann, 301
Guyana, 741

Haakon (hô'kŏn) VII, king of Norway, 642
Habeas Corpus Act, 373
Hades, 94
Hadrian's (hā'drǐ ăn) Wall, *illus.*, 165
Hagen, Victor W. von, 431–432, 440
Hagia Sophia, Church of, 186
Haile Selassie (hī'lě sě läs'ǐ), emperor of Ethiopia, 638
Haiti (hā'tǐ), 427; literacy in, 735; medical care in, 734
Hall, Charles, 459
Hall of Mirrors (Versailles), 357
Hamburg, Germany, 203
Hamlet, 252
Hammarskjöld (häm'är shŭld), Dag, 662–663, 722; *illus.*, 663
Hammurapi (häm ŏŏ rä'pě), Babylonian king, 37–38
Han (hän) dynasty, 73, 145–147; *map*, 144

Handel, George Frederick, 347
Hanging Gardens of Babylon, 40
Hannibal (hăn'ǐ bǎl), 110, 118
Hanover family, 375
Hanseatic (hăn sě ăt'ǐk) League, 203, *map*, 202
Hapsburgs: and Bourbons, 359–360; and Congress of Vienna, 494; in eighteenth century, 341–343; and Richelieu, 353–354; rise to power, 289–290, 291, 340; in Thirty Years' War, 320–321
Hara-kiri (hăr'ả kǐr'ǐ), 241
Harappa (hả răp'ả), 54–55
Harbin, China, 65
Hardenberg (här'děn běrк), Prince Karl von, 494
Harding, Warren G., U.S. President, 630
Hargreaves, James, 447, 448
Harold, Saxon king, 274
Harris, Townsend, 558
Harsha (här'shả), 213–215; *map*, 213
Harvey, William, 302
Hastings, battle of, 274
Hastings, Warren, 537
Hatshepsut (hăt shěp'sōōt), Queen of Egypt, 38
Haussmann, Baron, 504
Hawaii, 644; *illus.*, 645
Hawthorne, Nathaniel, 472
Hay, John, 557
Haydn (hī'd'n), Franz Joseph, 347
Hebrews: "Babylonian captivity" of, 26, 27; early history, 30–31; religion, 30–31. *See also* Jews, Judaism
Hegira (hě jǐ'rả), 181
Heiden (hī'd'n), Konrad, 613
Heilbroner, Robert, quoted, 461
Heinkel, Ernst, 730
Heliocentric theory, 105, 302
Hellen, 87
Hellenes, 80
Hellenistic period, 105–108
Hellespont, 88. *See also* Dardanelles
Helots (hěl'ŏts), 86
Hemingway, Ernest, 737
Henry II, king of England, 274–277
Henry V, by Shakespeare, 252
Henry VII, king of England, 279
Henry VIII, king of England, 311–312, 319, 371
Henry IV, king of France, 320, 352–353
Henry IV, Holy Roman Emperor, 176
Henry of Burgundy, 285
Henry the Navigator, Prince of Portugal, 297

Hera (hē′rȧ), 81
Heraclitus (hĕr′ȧ klī′tŭs), 102
Herder, Johann Gottfried von, 514
Heresy, 307, 313
Herodotus (hē rŏd′ŏ tŭs), 101
Herring, Hubert, 429, 435
Herzegovina (hûr′tsĕ gŏ vē′nȧ), 549
Herzl (hûr′ts'l), Theodor, 711
Hidalgo (hĭ dăl′gō), Miguel, 438
Hideyoshi, "Taiko," 557
Hieroglyphics   (hī′ēr ŏ glĭf′ĭks),
    Egyptian, 46; Indian, 55
Himalaya (hĭ mä′lȧ yȧ) Mountains,
    53; map, 54
Hincmar, Bishop of Rheims, 214
Hindemith, Paul, 753
Hindenburg, General Paul von,
    581, 613
Hinduism (hĭn′dōō ĭz′m), 57–58,
    219; influences Buddhism, 59–61
Hindus (hĭn′dōōz), 57–58, 210; and
    Moslems, 215, 699–700; and
    Sepoy Mutiny, 537
Hipparchus (hĭ pär′kŭs), 105
Hippocrates (hĭ pŏk′rȧ tēz), 102, 108
Hippocratic Oath, 102, 108
Hiroshima   (hē rŏ shē′mȧ), atomic
    bombing of, 651
Hispaniola, 433. See also Domini-
    can Republic, Haiti
Historians: define "Middle Ages,"
    158–159; Greek, 101; Hellenistic,
    106; and writing of history, 1–2
History: begins, 14; Chinese writ-
    ing of, 147; defined, viii, 1;
    epochs of, 249; Greek writers of,
    101; in Hellenistic era, 106;
    Marxian interpretation of, 466–
    467; in medieval chronicles, 163;
    value of, 5; views of, 142; writing
    of, 1–2, 180
History of the Peloponnesian War,
    101
Hitler, Adolph, 572; becomes dic-
    tator, 613; directs German ag-
    gression, 639–640; ideas of, 613–
    615; rules Germany, 615, illus.,
    615, 619; suicide of, 648; and
    World War II, 641–648
Hittites (hĭt′īts), 29
Ho Chi Minh (hō chē mĭn), 704
Hohenlinden (hō′ĕn lĭn′dĕn), battle
    of, 416
Hohenzollerns (hō′ĕn tsŏl′ĕrns): rise
    of, 343–344; and Spanish throne
    (1870), 516
Hokkaido (hŏ kī′dō), 235
Holbein (hŏl′bīn), Hans, 267–268
Holland: and Congress of Vienna,
    494, map, 495; and Louis XIV's
    wars, 360. See also Netherlands

Holy Alliance, 496
Holy Land: and Crimean War, 549;
    and Crusades, 188–191
Holy Roman Empire: under Charles
    V, 315–316; early history, 289–
    290, 343; Hapsburgs and, 340;
    and Louis XIV's wars, 360; Na-
    poleon ends, 416, 418; origins,
    168, 175–176, map, 176; and
    Reformation,   308–310,   311;
    struggle with Church, 176–177;
    in Thirty Years' War, 320–321
Homage, 169
Home Rule, for Ireland, 531
Homer, 81, 104
Homer, Winslow, 477
Homo sapiens (hō′mō sā′pĭ ĕnz), 10
Honduras   (hŏn dōōr′ȧs):   in
    C.A.C.M., 740; Mayas in, 429
Hong Kong, 554
Honshu (hŏn′shōō), 235
Hoover, Herbert, U.S. President,
    630, 631
Hoover moratorium, 589
Horace, 138
Horn, Cape, 428
Horthy (hôr′tĭ), Admiral N., 588
Hōryūji (hō ryōō jĕ) temple-mon-
    astery, 239
Hospitallers, 188
Hospitals: in Crimean War, 549;
    Roman origins, 139
Hottentots, in South Africa, 535
Houses: Egyptian, 30; Greek, 93–
    94; of medieval Europe, 171–174,
    200; Neolithic, 14; Roman, 129–
    130, illus., 130; Sumerian, 21
Housing: in early factory towns,
    442–443; and Industrial Revolu-
    tion, 458; in Latin America, 734
Howard, Admiral, 319
Howe, Elias, 454
Huan River, 68
Hudson, Henry, 385
Hudson River, 385
Hudson's Bay, 360, 361, 386
Hugo, Victor, 472
Huguenots (hū′gĕ nŏts), 320, 361;
    and Louis XIV, 356–357; and
    Richelieu, 353
Hui Tsung, Chinese emperor, 226
Human Comedy, The (Balzac), 473
Humanism, 250–251; of Michel-
    angelo, 264; and Reformation,
    308; in Renaissance, 270
Hume, Joseph, 463
"Hundred Days," of Napoleon,
    423
Hundred Years' War, 279, 281–283,
    map, 281
Hung Hsiu-ch'üan, 554–555

Hungary: under Austrian Haps-
    burgs, 340, 341; as Communist
    satellite, 674; in Dual Monarchy,
    502; under Ottomans, 169, 290,
    291; and peace treaty (1947),
    673, map, 674; revolts (1848),
    501; uprising (1956), 669, 678–
    679, 688; and War of Austrian
    Succession, 345; in Warsaw Pact,
    668, 669; after World War I,
    587–588
Huns, 154, 155, 213, 228
Hunt, Walter, 454
Hus, John, 307
Hussein (hōō sīn′), king of Jordan,
    712, 716
Huxley, Aldous, 755
Hwang Ho (hwäng′ hō′) River, 65,
    66, 67
Hyksos (hĭk′sōs), 21

I promessi sposi, 510
Iberian (ī bēr′ĭ ăn) Peninsula, 283.
    See also Portugal, Spain
Ibn-al-Awwam, 285
Ibn Wafid, 285
Ibsen, Henrik, 474
Ice Ages, 8
Iceland, 206, 665
Icons, Russian, illus., 546
Ictinus (ĭk tī′nŭs), 95
Ideograms (ĭd′ĕ ŏ grăms), Chinese,
    68, 70
Ieyasu   (ē yĕ yä′sōō),   Tokugawa,
    558; mausoleum of, illus., 237
Ikhnaton (ĭk nä′t'n), 45
Il Duce, see Mussolini, Benito
Iliad (ĭl′ĭ ăd), 81, 104
Illia, Dr. Arturo, 736
Imperial Conference of 1926, 628
Imperialism: in Africa, 560–564,
    566–567; British, 380–388; Dutch,
    381–382; in Far East, 554–557,
    570, map, 556; French, 505; his-
    tory of, 553–554; Italian, 513;
    Japanese,   557–560;   in   Latin
    America, 567–569; of nineteenth
    century, 552–570; results of,
    569; and World War I, 577
Impressionism: in art, 477–478; in
    music, 481
Incas: civilization of, 431–433, 439,
    440; Pizarro conquers, 434–435
India: and Alexander the Great,
    104, 105; British take control,
    537; China attacks, 701; cultural
    characteristics of, 61; early civ-
    ilization, 52–62; English-French
    struggle for, 383–385; and Euro-
    pean imperialism, 381–385; gains
    independence, 699; geography

and climate, 53, *map*, 54; "Golden Ages," 210, 211–214; Gupta art, *illus.*, 253; and Industrial Revolution, 460; and Islam, 231; languages in, 61; Maurya dynasty, 143–145; Mogul art, *illus.*, 253; under Nehru, 700–701; Rajput art, *illus.*, 485; visited by Da Gama, 298; in World War II, 648

Indian Independence Act (1947), 699

Indians of the Americas: Aztecs, 429–431, 433; conquered by Spain, 433–435; converted to Catholicism, 436–437; Incas, 431–432, 433, 440; of Latin America, 427–428; Mayas, 429, 433; social status, 437

Indo-Aryans, 55–56, 61–62

Indo-China, 144, 145, 213; as French possession, 569; gains independence, 704; in World War II, 645, *map*, 649

Indo-European languages, 112

Indo-Europeans, 45, 287

Indonesia: Dutch in, 569; as independent republic, 702; "guided democracy" in, 703–704

Indulgences, 308–309, 314

Indus River, 53, 104, 143; *map*, 54

Indus Valley, 54

Industrial Revolution: in Germany, 519; impact of, 442–443, 470–484; political effects, 462–464; and reformers, 462–467; social and economic effects, 456–462, 468, 480; spread of, 459; spurs imperialism, 553; technological changes, 444–454, 459

Industrialism, in Latin America, 734

Industry: in Communist China, 695–696; rise in Industrial Revolution, 442–460; in Soviet Union, 603–604

Inestimable Life of Gargantua, Father of Pantagruel, 252

Inflation, in Germany (1920's), 589, 613

Inner Six (of European Common Market), 667, 668

Innocent III, Pope, 189

Inquisition, 286, 314

"Instant Democracy," in Nigeria, 726

Institutes of the Christian Religion, The, 311

Intendants, 353

Inter-American Music Council (CIDEM), 413, 743

Inter-American Peace Force, 739

Intercontinental ballistic missiles, 738

Interglacial period, 8

International Court of Justice, 662

International Geophysical Year, 749

International Labor Organization, 632, 662

International Monetary Fund, 662

International peace efforts, 632–633, 756. *See also* League of Nations, United Nations Organization

Inventions: of Archimedes, 105–106; Hellenistic, 106; of Industrial Revolution, 444–454, 459; of twentieth century, 746–750, 757

Investiture struggle, 176–177

Ionian Sea, 79; *map*, 80

Ionians, 81–82, 84

Ionic column, *illus.*, 95

Iran (ĕ rän'), 709, 714–715

Iraq (ĕ räk'), 183; in Arab League, 709, 712, 715, 716; gains independence, 629; under Kassem, 715

Ireland: converted to Christianity, 164; in Council of Europe, 665; Cromwell conquers, 371; and England, 530–531; gains independence, 531, 537; geography, 367, *map*, 368; Henry II and, 274–275

Irish Free State, 531

Iron: Hittites' use of, 29; and Industrial Revolution, 449–450

Iron Age, 11, 29

Iron Curtain, 675

"Iron law of wages," 471

Irving, Washington, 472

Isabella, queen of Spain, 286, 297

Isaiah (ī zā'yà), 31

Islam (ĭs'lảm): in Africa, 561; as Arab bond, 709–710; art of, *illus.*, 256; and Crusades, 188–191; cultural characteristics of, 190; impact on Hindus, 219, 231; origin, 181; in Ottoman Empire, 290; principles, 182; as a religion, 190, 709; spread, 183–184; *map*, 184

Israel (ĭz'rà ĕl): early formation of, 30; fights Egypt, 713–714; population of, 709; republic formed, 709–710

Italian language, 138

Italy: acquires Libya, 563; attacks Abyssinia, 564; in Axis, 640–641; and Congress of Vienna, 494,

map, 495; conquers Ethiopia, 638; early settlement of, 112–113; effects of Crusades, 190–191; under Fascism, 609–611; geography and climate, 111, *map*, 112; Hannibal in, 118; and Holy Roman Empire, 289; and Industrial Revolution, 459; keeps Dodecanese, 588; Kingdom of (1870–1914), 512–513, 519; medieval, 176; and Napoleon I, 413, 416, 418; and peace efforts of 1920's, 633; peace treaty with (1947), 673, *map*, 674; and regional organizations since World War II, 665–669; Renaissance in, 249, 250–252, 269, 296; Renaissance art of, *illus.*, 258, 260, 262–263, 264; revolutions of 1820–1821, 496; revolutions of 1848, 502, 503; Rome conquers, 116–117; since 1945, 687; supports Franco, 638; in Triple Alliance, 575; unification of, 508–512, 517–518, 520, *map*, 511; in World War I, 581, 582; in World War II, 642–643, 647–648

Ivan III (ĭ vàn'), czar of Russia, 287, 289, 328; law code of, 331

Ivan IV, czar of Russia, 328–330

Ivanhoe, 471

Ivory Coast, 564, 727

Jacobins (jăk'ṓ bĭnz), 407–408

Jahan (jȧ hän'), Shah of India, 218

Jamaica, West Indies, 372

James I, king of England, 368–369, 371

James II, king of England, 374

James VI, king of Scotland, 319, 368. *See also* James I

Jamestown, settlement of, 385

Janissaries (jăn'ĭ sĕr ĭs), 290

Janus (jā'nŭs), 128, 133

Japan: art, *color illus.*, 255, 485; attacks China, 637–638, *map*, 638; attacks Pearl Harbor, 644; in Axis, 640–641; and China, 555, 557; Chinese influences on, 242; civilization of, 237–238; Classical Age, 239–242; under Fascism and militarism, 616–617; geography and climate, 235–236, *map*, 236; in Imperial Age, 242–243; industrializes, 460; intervenes in Russia (1918), 598; leaves League, 637; in nineteenth century, 558–559; and peace efforts of 1920's, 633; people of, 236–237; Russo-Japanese War, 560, 594, 595, *map*, 596;

Ming dynasty, 230; art, *illus.*, 254
Ministerial responsibility, 376
Minnesingers (mĭn′ĕ sĭng ĕrz), 206
Minoan (mĭ nō′ăn) civilization, 81
Minorca (mĭ nôr′kà), 360
Minority problems, 587–588
Miquelon (mĭk′ĕ lŏn) Island, 386
Miró, Joan, 752; *painting by*, 751
Mirs, 542, 595
Missi dominici, 168
Mississippi River, 299, 370, 385
Moat, 174
"Model Parliament," 278
Modena, Duchy of, 509, 512
Mogul (mō gŭl′) Empire, 210, 215–
    218, 383; art of, *illus.*, 253
Mohammed (mō hăm′ĕd): life, 181;
    quoted, 183, 190; teachings, 182
Mohammed Ali Jinnah, 699
Mohammed Reza Pahlavi, Shah of
    Iran, *illus.*, 714
Mohenjo-daro (mō hĕn′jō dä′rō),
    54, 55
Molière (mō lyâr′), 303, 358, 361
Molotov (mô′lŭ tôf), Vyacheslav,
    676
Moltke (môlt′kĕ), General Hel-
    muth von, 515, *illus.*, 517
Moluccas (mō lŭk′àz), 381
"Mona Lisa," 261, *illus.*, 263, 269
Monarchy: absolute, 350, 352–357;
    English, 366; French (1815–
    1848), 497–499; French ends,
    405–410; in Greece (ancient), 83,
    84; role in modern England, 628.
    See also Despotism, "Enlight-
    ened despots"
Monasteries, 162–164
Monasticism: early Christian, 162–
    164; in medieval Europe, 178.
    See also Benedictine Rule
Monet (mô nĕ′), Claude, 477, 478;
    painting by, 486
Money: and American Revolution,
    388; and early capitalism, 295–
    296, 300; in Europe after Cru-
    sades, 190–191; and French
    Revolution, 403–404; and Great
    Depression (1929–1939), 624–
    625; and Industrial Revolution,
    446; inflation of, in Germany,
    612–613; of Lydians, 27; in medi-
    eval Europe, 200–201; in mercan-
    tilist theory, 356; in Renaissance,
    250
Mongol Empire, 228–230, *map*, 229
Mongolia, 65, 228
Mongoloid race, 10
Mongols: conquer Russia, 288; in-
    vade Japan, 242; rule China,
    228–231, *map*, 229

Monks, 162–164, 178, 301
Monnet, Jean, 664
Monotheism (mŏn′ō thē ĭz′m): in
    Egypt, 45; of Hebrews, 30–31;
    of Incas, 432; in Islam, 182;
    Zoroastrianism, 28. *See also*
    Christianity
Monroe, James, 497
Monroe Doctrine, 496–497, 504
Monrovia (Liberia) Conference, 724
Montaigne (mŏn tān′), Michel de,
    quoted, 248
Monte Cassino (mŏn′tà käs sē′nō)
    monastery, *illus.*, 163
Montenegro (mŏn tĕ nē′grō), 290,
    549; in Balkan Wars, 578
Montesquieu (mŏn′tĕs kyû′), Baron
    Charles de, 399
Monteverdi (mŏn′tĕ vâr′dĕ), Clau-
    dio, 269
Montevideo (mŏn′tĕ vĭ dā′ō), Treaty
    of (1960), 739–740
Montgomery, General Bernard, 647
Montreal, 299, 385, 386
Mont-Saint-Michel (môN săN mē-
    shĕl′), 195, *illus.*, 197
Moon, rocket research on, 750
Moore, Henry, sculpture by, 752
Moors, 183–184; civilization of,
    284–285; expelled from Spain,
    286; invade Spain, 283
Morality plays, 207
More, Sir Thomas, 465
Morocco: in Arab League, 710,
    717; France controls, 563–564;
    French-German disputes over,
    577; gains independence, 720
Morris, William, 483–484
Morse, Samuel F. B., 452
Mosaics, Byzantine, 186
Moscow, 330; becomes Soviet capi-
    tal, 598; Napoleon takes, 420–
    421; as third Rome, 328
Moses, 30, 31; in *Koran*, 182
Moslems (mŏz′lĕms), 182, 183, 184,
    187; in Algeria, 720; and Cru-
    sades, 188–191; empire of, *map*,
    184; invade India, 215–218, 219;
    medieval science of, 205; and
    Sepoy Mutiny, 537; struggle
    with Hindus in India, 699–700.
    See also Islam, Moors
Mosques (mŏskz), 182, 183, 284
Mossadegh, Mohammed, 714, 715
Mother Goose stories, 358
Mozart (mō′tsärt), Wolfgang Ama-
    deus, 347
Mozhaisky, A. F., 453
Muezzin (mŭ ĕz′ĭn), *illus.*, 183
Mulattoes, 427, 437
Mummies, Egyptian, 40

Munich, 613
Munich Pact (1938), 639, 640
Murasaki Shikibu (mōō rä sä′kĕ
    shĕ kĕ′bōō), Lady, 239, 243–244
Murat (mü rà′), Joachim, 419
Murmansk, 598
Muscovy: founded, 289, *map*, 287
Music: African, 729; ancient Egyp-
    tian, 49; Latin-American, 743; of
    nineteenth-century Europe, 480–
    481; Renaissance, 268; Russian,
    546–547; of seventeenth- and
    eighteenth-century Europe, 346–
    347; secular, 268; Soviet, 605; of
    today, 753–754
Musical instruments, 268
Mussolini (mōōs sō lē′nē), Benito:
    compared to Hitler, 614; and
    Lateran Treaty, 513; leads Fas-
    cists, 609–611; ousted, 647; rules
    Italy, 611–612, *illus.*, 611
Mussorgsky (mōō sôrg′skĭ), Mo-
    deste, 546
Mwanamutapa, 719
Mycenae (mī sē′nĕ), 80
Myron, Greek sculptor, 96

Nagasaki (nä gà sä′kĕ), atomic
    bombing of, 651
Naguib, General Mohammed, 712
Nagy, Imre, 679
Nalanda University, 214, *illus.*,
    214
Nanak (nä′nàk), 215
Nanda (nŭn′dä) dynasty, 143
Nanking, Treaty of (1842), 554
Naples, 341, 360; under Joseph
    Bonaparte, 418; under Murat,
    419; revolts, 496, 502
Napoleon I: career, 408, 413–423;
    character, 412, 414; domestic
    program, 415–416; exiled, 423,
    493; on French Revolution, 408–
    410; and German nationalism,
    514; *illus.*, 414, 417; and Italian
    nationalism, 509; legacy, 423;
    and Portugal, 439; and Spain,
    437; wars, 413, 416–419
Napoleon III, 499; becomes em-
    peror, 500; and Crimean War,
    549; and Franco-Prussian War,
    515–517; and Italian unification,
    511–512; rules Second Empire,
    503–505, *illus.*, 504
Napoleonic legend, 423, 499
Nara, Japan, 239
Narodniki, 593
Nashville, Tennessee, 96
Nasser, Gamal Abdel, 691, 710,
    712–713, *illus.*, 717
Natal, 536

National Assembly: in French Fourth Republic, 685–686; in French Revolution, 402–406, 409; rules France (1871–1875), 505

National Coalition ministry, 627

National Convention, French, 406; and Reign of Terror, 407–408

National General Mobilization Law, Japan (1938), 616

National Health Service (England), 685

National Insurance and Assistance (England), 685

National Liberation Front (F.L.N.), 721

National People's Party (China), see Kuomintang

National Socialism, see Nazism

National states: defined, 273; and overseas exploration, 296–300; and Reformation, 308; rise of, 272–291. See also states by name

National Union coalition, 624

National workshops, 499

Nationalism: in Africa today, 719–720; in Balkans, 548–549; as cause of World War I, 576; and French Revolution, 409–410; and German unification, 514, 518; growth in nineteenth century, 493; influence of Rousseau on, 400; and Italian unification, 509–510; Japanese, 692–693; in music, 753–754; and Napoleon, 422, 423; in nineteenth-century revolutions, 500–503; in Russia, 330; spurs imperialism, 553

Nationalists, in China, 695

Nationality problem: in Austrian Empire, 343, 501; in Austria-Hungary, 576

Nationalization of industries, in postwar England, 684–685

Nations, see National states

Natural law, in Enlightenment, 398

Naturalism, 473

Nave, Gothic, 199

Navigation, 295

Navigation Acts, 372, 373, 382; and American Revolution, 387, 388

Nazareth, 148

Nazism: atrocities of, 608, 620; de-Nazification programs, 680–681; Germany under, 612–615, 619–620; ideas of, 614–615; in World War II, 641–648

Neanderthal (nĕ ăn′dĕr täl) man, 9

Near East: ancient, 18–32; Islam in, 181–184; Rome dominates, 119. See also Middle East, countries by name

Nebuchadnezzar (nĕb ŭ kăd nĕz′-ĕr), Chaldean king, 26

Necker (nĕ kâr′), Jacques, 404

Negroes: of Africa, 561, 719; in Latin America, 438; in Union of South Africa, 723

Negroid race, 10

Nehru, Jawaharlal, 61, 219, 691, 700–701; illus., 700

Nelson, Admiral Horatio, 413; at Trafalgar, 419

Neo-classicism, in music, 753

Neolithic Age (nē′ŏ lĭth′ĭk), 11, 13–14

Neo-romanticism, in music, 753

NEP, see New Economic Policy

Nero, Roman emperor, 149

Nesselrode (nĕs″l rōd), Count, 494

Netherlands: and Asian trading posts, 381–382, map, 382; and Belgian revolt (1830), 500; colonies founded, 300; and Congress of Vienna, 494, map, 495; and England, 372, 382, 386; frees Indonesia, 703; Germans conquer (1940), 642; and Japan, 588; and Louis XIV's wars, 359–360; and Napoleon I, 418; opposes revolutionary France, 407; in post-World War II regional organizations, 664–669; and Reformation, 311; Renaissance art of, 265–266; and Spain, 317

Netherlands East Indies, in World War II, 645, map, 649

Netherlands-Indonesian Union, 703

Neutralist nations, in Cold War, 691

New Amsterdam, 373, 382

New Economic Policy, 599

New Guinea, 703

New Kingdom, Egyptian, 37–38

New Netherlands, 382

New Orleans, 386

New Poor Law (England), 525–526

New Stone Age, 13–14

New Testament, 148; Erasmus edition, 252. See also Bible

"New World," discovery of, 297–298

New York, 373, 382

New Zealand: discovered, 533, 534; history, 534

Newcomen, Thomas, 449

Newfoundland, 361, 386, 390

Newton, Isaac, 303; and Enlightenment, 398

Ngo Dinh Diem, 704

Niagara Falls, viii

Nicaea (nī sē′à), Council of, 153

Nicaragua (nĭk à rä′gwà), 439, 740

Nice (nēs), 511, 512

Nicene (nī sēn′) Creed, 153

Nicholas I, czar of Russia, 541–542, 547

Nicholas II, czar of Russia, 543, 593, 594, 596, illus., 596

Nicolson, Harold, quoted, 367

Nigeria, 564, 720, 726

Nightingale, Florence, 549

Nihilism, 544

"Nike (nē′kā) of Samothrace," sculpture, 106

Nile River: delta of, 39; in Egyptian history, 34–50; map, 40

Nimitz, Admiral Chester W., 648

Ninety-five Theses, 309

Nineveh (nĭn′ĕ vĕ), 25

Nirvana (nĭr vä′nà), 59

Nkrumah, Kwame, 720, 726

Nobility: in ancient Egypt, 37; and Church, 175; and Crusades, 190–191; English, and Magna Carta, 277–278; in feudal Europe, 169–174; French, of Old Régime, 280, 283, 353, 357, 362, 398; in Holy Roman Empire, 289; in nineteenth-century Russia, 549–550

Normandy: Allied invasion of, 647; described, 273; and England, 274; Huguenots leave, 357

Normans, conquer England, 273–274

North Africa: Allied invasion of, 646–647, map, 646. See also Imperialism

North America: Atlas map, 772; exploration and settlement, 385; French-English clash, eighteenth century, 385–386, map, 387; Vikings visit, 169

North Atlantic Treaty Organization (NATO), 665, 687

North German Confederation, 515

North Korea, Democratic People's Republic of, 697–698

North Sea, 320, 367

Northern Ireland, 531

Northern Rhodesia, 725

Northmen, see Vikings

Norway: and Congress of Vienna, 494, map, 495; co-operatives in, 464; Germany conquers (1940), 642; in NATO, 665

Notre Dame, Cathedral of, 159, 195, illus., 198

Nova Scotia, 360

Novels: Russian, 544–545; of twentieth century, 755. See also Literature

Novgorod (nŏv′gŏ rŏd), Russia, 287, 289

Peasants, in ancient Egypt, 50; in Austria, 343; in Communist China, 696; and Crusades, 191; French, under Old Régime, 396; and French Revolution, 408–410; in medieval Europe, 171–173, *illus.*, 172; in pre-revolutionary Russia, 335, 336, 595; and Reformation, 308, 310; Russian emancipation of, 542–543; Sumerian, 21; in Wat Tyler's Rebellion, 291–292. *See also* Serfs

Peasants' Rebellion, 310

Pedro (pā'drō) I, ruler of Brazil, 439–440

Peiping (bā'pĭng), China, 65, 146

Peking (pē kĭng') man, 8–9, 67; *illus.*, 9

Pella, Giuseppe, 664

Peloponnesian (pĕl'ô pŏ nē'shän) War, 102–103

Peloponnesus (pĕl'ô pŏ nē'sŭs), 79, 86, *map*, 80

Penance, 309

Penates (pē nā'tēz), 133

Peninsulares, 436

Pennsylvania, 385

People's Charter, 527

People's Republic of China, *see* China, Communist

Pepin (pĕp'ĭn) the Short, 166

Pepys (pēps), Samuel, *illus.*, 373

Pericles (pĕr'ĭ klēz), 85–86, 102–103

Perioeci (pĕr ĭ ōs'ī), 86

Peristylium (pĕr ĭ stĭl'ĭ ŭm), 130

Permanent Court of International Justice, 586, 632

Perón (på rôn'), Juan, 736

Perrault (pĕ rō'), Charles, 357–359

Perry, Commodore Matthew C., 558

Persepolis (pĕr sĕp'ô lĭs), 28; *illus.*, 27

Pershing, General John, 582

Persia, 149, 229; art of, *color illus.*, 43; Moslem conquest, 183. *See also* Iran, Persian Empire, Persian Wars, Persians

Persian Empire, 27–28; Alexander conquers, 104; *map*, 28; under Seleucids, 105

Persian Gulf, 19, 20

Persian Wars, 88–89, *map*, 89

Persians: defeat Egypt, 38; empire of, 27–28, *map*, 28; government of, 27; and Greeks, 88–89; and Hebrews, 30

Peru: gains independence, 438; Incas in, 431–433; in LAFTA, 741; Pizarro conquers, 434–435

Pétain (pā tăN'), Marshal Henri, 580; heads Vichy government, 642

Peter, apostle of Christ, 149, 161

Peter I (the Great), czar of Russia, 331–333, *illus.*, 333

Peter III, czar of Russia, 346

Petit jury, 275

Petition of Right, 369

Petrarch (pē'trärk), 251

Petrograd, 592, 596, 597

Petrograd Soviet, 596, 597

Pharoahs (fā'rōz), 37–45

Phidias (fĭd'ĭ ăs), Greek sculptor, 95–96

Philip Augustus, king of France, 280

Philip the Fair, king of France, 280–281

Philip II, king of France, 189, *illus.*, 190

Philip, king of Macedonia, 99, 103

Philip II, king of Spain, 316–317, 318, 319–320, *illus.*, 315, 381

Philip III, king of Spain, 338

Philip IV, king of Spain, 265

Philip V, king of Spain, 360

Philippine Islands, 316; as independent republic, 703–704; and U.S., 552, 555–556, 567; in World War II, 645, 648, *map*, 649

Phillips, Wendell, quoted, 426

Philosophes, 398–401, 404

Philosophy: of Confucius, 71–72; of Enlightenment, 398–401, 404; Epicurean, 107; Greek, 97–99; of Lao-Tse, 72; rationalism, 303; Stoic, 107, 151

Phoenicians (fē nĭsh'änz), 28; and alphabet, 29; found Carthage, 118

Physiocrats (fĭz'ĭ ô krăts), 400–401

Picasso, Pablo, 752, *painting by*, 488

Pico della Mirandola (pē'kô dăl lä mĕ rän'dô lä), 251

Pictograms, Chinese, 68, 70

Piedmont: 1848 revolution in, 502. *See also* Sardinia

Piedmont-Sardinia, Kingdom of, *see* Sardinia

Pile villages, 14

Pilgrims, 385

Pillow Book, The, 239

Pindar (pĭn'dĕr), 101

Pinson, Koppel S., 492

Piraeus (pī rē'ŭs), 94, 103

Pirenne, Henri, 207

Pissaro (pē'så'rō'), Camille, 477

Piston, Walter, 753

Pit dwellings, 14

Pitt, William, 386

Pius IX, Pope, 513

Pizarro (pĭ zär'rô), Francisco, 434–435

Place, Francis, 463

Plagues: in Athens, 103; Black Death, 207; in Roman Empire, 151

Planets, 6

Plankton, 748

Plantagenet (plăn tăj'ĕ nĕt) family, 274

Plassey (plăs'ĭ), battle of, 384

Plastics, 748

Plato (plā'tō), 98–99; and Renaissance thought, 251

Platt Amendment, 567

Plebeians (plĕ bē'yäns), 115, 116, 120. *See also* Populares

Pleistocene (plīs'tô sēn) epoch, 8–10

Plekhanov (plyĕ ка́'nôf), George, 593

Plow, in medieval Europe, 172

Plutarch (plōō'tärk): on Alexander the Great, 105; on Caesar, 122

Plutocracy (plōō tŏk'rå sĭ), 83, 84

Plymouth, Massachusetts, 385

Po Chü-i, 224

Po Valley, 111

"Pocket boroughs," 523, 525

Poe, Edgar Allan, 147

Poetry: Chinese, 147, 224; Greek, 101; Hebrew, 284; Japanese, 239; medieval, 206–207; of nineteenth-century Europe and America, 471–473; of Pushkin, 543; Renaissance, 251–252; Roman, 138; of twentieth century, 754–755

Pogroms (pŏ grŏms'), 543

Poincaré (pwăN kå rā'), Raymond, 624

Poitiers (pwå'tyā'), 183

Poland, 287; under Alexander I, 541; early history, 335; gains Russian land (921), 599; Germany attacks, 641, *map*, 640; goes Communist, 674; and Locarno pacts, 633; and Napoleon, 419; nationalism of Poles, 501; partitioned, 335, 346, *map*, 335; recreated (1919), 584, 587; revolts of Poles (1830, 1956), 541–542, 678; and Russia, 329, 330, 335; and Turks, 341; and War of Austrian Succession, 345; in Warsaw Pact, 668; after World War II, 673

Polio vaccines, 748

Polish Corridor, 587

Political parties: English, 373, 524, 526; in French Third Republic, 505. *See also* parties by name

Reaction, in Metternich era, 492–497

Realism: in art, 474, *illus.*, 476–477; in literature, 473–474

Rebels in Spain, 638–639

Reciprocal Trade Agreements Act, 631

Red Badge of Courage, The, 474

Red Cockatoo, The, 224

"Red Shirts," of Garibaldi, 512

Redistribution of Seats Act, 1885 (England), 529

Reeve's Tale, The, 207

Reform Act, 1867 (England), 528

Reform Act, 1884 (England), 528–529

Reform Bill of 1832, 524–525

Reformation, 306–315; effects in Germany, 343–344; impact of, on Europe, 321

Reforms: of Alexander II in Russia, 542; of Catherine the Great, 334; caused by Industrial Revolution, 462–467; of Colbert, 355–356; of Frederick the Great, 345; of Gladstone, in Ireland, 531; of Joseph II, 343; of Maria Theresa, 343; in nineteenth-century England, 523–529; of Peter the Great, 332–333

Refugees: Arabs in Gaza Strip, 712; from Castro's Cuba, 737–738; from East Germany, 682; émigrés in French Revolution, 405–406; Huguenots as, 357; from Hungary (1956), 679; regionalism, in Latin America, 439

Regional organizations: in Asia, 705; European, 664–669, *chart*, 666; OAS, 752

Reich, German Third, 572

Reichstag, German, 518

Reign of Terror (France), 408–410

Reischauer, Edwin O., 616, 693

Relativity, Einstein's Theory of, 729

Relief, feudal, 170

Religion: Akbar's reforms, 216; of ancient Egypt, 39–40; Aztec, 431; Buddhism, 59–60, 143–145, 147; Christianity, 148–155, 161–164; divides Holland and Belgium, 500; Druids, 164; Eastern Orthodox Church, 186–187; Greek, 87–88; Hindu, 57–58; and imperialism, 554–569; Inca, 432; Islam, 181–184; of Jews, 30–31; and *Kulturkampf*, 518; Mayan, 429; and medieval architecture, 195; medieval writing on, 207; in modern China, 619; in Nazi

Germany, 615; Roman, 133; Sikhs, 215; in Soviet Union, 604; in Stone Ages, 14; in unification of Germany and Italy, 518; Zoroastrianism, 28

Religious Society of Friends, 385

Rembrandt (rĕm′brănt), 265–266; *painting by*, 259

Remus (rē′mŭs), legend of, 112

Rémusat, Madame de, 414

Renaissance (rĕn ĕ säns′), 248–270; art of, 261–268, *color illus.*, 258–260; education in, 269; explorations in, 294–300; influence on Reformation, 307–308; literature of, 250–252; music of, 268–269; science, 300–303; social life, 270

Renoir (rē nwàr′), Pierre Auguste, 477; *painting by*, 487

Reparations: problem of (1920's), 588–589; in Versailles Treaty, 584

Repin, Ilya, 546; *painting by*, 330

Republic, Roman, 114–124

Republic, The, of Plato, 98–99

Republic of China, *see* China

Republic of Korea, 697

Respighi, Ottorino, 753

Restoration, in England, 372–374

Revolutions: American, 374, 387–390, 392; Boxer Rebellion, 557; Chinese (1911), 617; Decembrist, 541; of 1820–1821, 496; of 1830, 500–501; of 1848, 501–503, 506; French (1789–1799), 394–410; French (1830 and 1848), 497–499; "Glorious," 374; Hungarian (1956), 364–365; Latin American, 437–438, 496; meaning of term, 364–365; Russian (1905), 594–595; Russian (1917), 596–597

Reynaud (rā nō′), Paul, 624

Rhee, Syngman, 698

Rhine River, 167, 354

Rhineland, 166; Germany occupies, 639, *map*, 640

Rhodes, Cecil, 536

Rhodesia, racial problem in, 725

Rhodesian Declaration of Independence, 725

Ribbentrop (rĭb′ĕn trôp), Joachim von, 681

Ricardo (rĭ kär′dō), David, 471

Richard I, king of England, 189

Richard II, king of England, 292

Richard III, 252

Richelieu (rē shĕ lyû′), Cardinal, 353–354, *portrait*, 354

Riga, Treaty of (1921), 587, 599

Rig-Veda (rĭg vä′dà), 61

Rime of the Ancient Mariner, The, 471

Rimsky-Korsakov (rĭm′skĭ kôr′sá-kŏf), Nikolai, 546

Rio de Janeiro, 732

"Risorgimento" (rē sôr jĕ mĕn′tō), 509

Riza Pahlavi (rĭ zä′ pä′là vē), Shah of Iran, 714

Roads: improved in England, 450–451; in India, 144–145; Roman, 135, *illus.*, 136

Robespierre (rô′bĕs′pyàr′), Maximilien François de, 407–408

Robles, Marco A., 738

Rock edicts, 143–144

Rockefeller, John D., 459

Rockets, 749–750

Rococo (rō kō′kō) art, *illus.*, 397

Rodin (rô dăN′), Auguste, 478

Roentgen (rûnt′gĕn), Wilhelm Konrad, 747

Roland, Madame, 401

Romagna, 512

Roman Catholic Church: Charles V defends, 315–316; dispute with Henry II, 276–277; early history, 150–154; in England, 319, 361, 372, 374, 375, 523, 524; in French Revolution, 405; in Ireland, 530; and Joan of Arc, 282; and *Kulturkampf*, 518; in Latin America, 436–437; and Maryland, 385; and monasticism, 162–164; and Mussolini, 612; and Napoleon I, 415; and Napoleon III, 504; organization, 161–162; and Perón, 723; and Reformation, 306–315, *map*, 314; and religious wars, 316–322; splits with Eastern Orthodox Church, 186

Roman Empire: and Christianity, 151–153; decline and fall, 151–155; division of, 152, *map*, 152; expansion of, 121; government, 123, 124–125; history, 121–125; *map*, 122; trade of, 125

Roman law, 139

Roman numerals, 128

Roman Question, 513, 612

Roman Republic, 114–117, 118–124

Romance languages, 138, 139

Romanesque architecture, 195, 197; *illus.*, 196

Romanov (rŭ mà′nŭf) dynasty: ends, 596; established, 330

Romanticism: in art, 474, *illus.*, 475, 476; in literature, 471–473; in music, 481

Romans: and Carthage, 118, 119; and Christianity, 148–153; contributions, 128, 134–139; daily life, 129–134; in Gaul and Britain, 165; and Hebrews, 30; and Renaissance, 250, 251; social classes, 115, 116, 120; in Spain, 283

Rome: becomes Italian capital, 512; captured (1084), 177; Christian capital, 151, 153, 161–162; civilization of, 128–140; cultural characteristics of, ancient, 139; early history, 110–125, 148–155; 1848 revolt in, 502; Fascist march on, 610; sacked, 154; trade with East, 145, 147

Rome-Berlin-Tokyo Axis, 640–641
Rommel, General Erwin, 643, 647
Romulus (rŏm′ŭ lŭs), legend of, 112
Roosevelt, Eleanor, 657
Roosevelt, Franklin D., U.S. President: and Atlantic Charter, 657; and New Deal, 631; and World War II, 644, 650
Roosevelt, Theodore, U.S. President, 568–569
Root, Elihu, 586
Rosetta Stone, 46
Rossetti (rŏ sĕt′ĭ), Dante Gabriel, 480
"Rotten boroughs," 523, 524, 525
Rougon Macquarts, The, 473
Round Table, Knights of the, 159
Roundheads, 370
Rousseau (rōō sō′), Jean-Jacques, 399–400
Rubens (rōō′bĕnz), Peter Paul, 268
Rubicon (rōō′bĭ kŏn) River, 121
Rudini, Marquis di, 564
Rudolf of Hapsburg, 289
Ruhr (rōōr) Valley, 589, 624
Rumania, 290; in Balkan Wars, 578; gains independence, 549; goes Communist, 674; joins Little Entente, 632; and peace treaty (1947), 673, *map,* 674; in Warsaw Pact, 668; after World War I, 587
Rumanian language, 138
"Rump Parliament," 370
Rupert, Prince of Palatine, 369, *illus.,* 373
Ruskin, John, 473
Russell, Lord John, 523, 524
Russia: art and architecture of, 546; autocracy in, 326, 328–335; and Bismarck, 515, 519; under Catherine the Great, 333–335; and China, 554, 555, 557; Communist rule established, 592, 596–597; and Congress of Vienna, 493–495; converted to Christian-

ity, 186–187, 287–288; cultural characteristics of 19th century, 549; cultural characteristics, of 16th through 18th century, 335; early history, 229, 287–289, *map,* 287; and Europe, 331–332, 335; geography and climate, 327, *map,* 328; and Industrial Revolution, 459; under Ivan IV, 328–329; and Japan, 556, 558, 560; literature of, 543–545; in Metternich era, 496; music of, 546–547; and Napoleon I, 416–419, 420–422, *illus.,* 422; under Nicholas II, 593–596; in nineteenth century, 540–543, 547–549; and Ottoman Empire, 547–549; under Peter the Great, 331–333; and the Poles, 501; revolution of 1905, 594–595; revolution of 1917, 581, 596–597; science and mathematics, 546; in Seven Years' War, 346; serfdom in, 330–331, 333–334, 542–543; in "Time of Troubles," 330; and World War I, 576–578, 580–581, 596. *See also* Union of Soviet Socialist Republics

Russian language, 288
Russian Orthodox Church, 186–187, 287–288, 289, 328; in Communist era, 598, 604; under Nicholas I, 541; under Peter the Great, 333
Russian Social Democratic Workers' Party, *see* Social Democratic party (Russia)
"Russification," program of Nicholas I, 541, 542
Russo-German Non-aggression Pact (1939), 641
Russo-Japanese War, 560, 594, 595; *map,* 556
Russo-Turkish War, 549
Rwanda, 720

Saar (zär), 583, 682
Sabah, 702
Sabin, Dr. Albert E., 748
Sacraments (of the Church), 310
Safeguarding of Industries Act, England, 626
Sagas, 206
Sahara, 561, 721, 729
St. Albans Chronicle, 282
St. Augustine, 153, 164
St. Bartholomew's Day Massacre, 320
St. Basil, 163
St. Benedict, 163
St. Helena (hĕ lē′nȧ), 423
St. Jerome, 162

St. Lawrence River, 299
St. Luke, 164
St. Patrick, 164
St. Peter's Church, Rome, 261, *illus.,* 262
St. Petersburg, Russia, 332, 594, 596
St. Pierre (săN′pyâr′) Island, 386
Saint-Simon (săN′sē′môN′), Claude Henri de, 465
Saint-Simon, Louis, Duke of, 361
St. Trophime, Church of, *illus.,* 196
Sakhalin (săk′ȧ lēn) Island, 560, 650
Saladin (săl′ȧ dĭn), 189
Salamis (săl′ȧ mĭs), battle of, 89
Salk, Dr. Jonas E., 748
Salvemini, Gaetano, 610
Samothrace (săm′ō thrās), Nike of, 106
Samurai (săm′ōō rī), 241–243
San Francisco Conference, 658
San Martín (sän′ mär tēn′), José de, 438
San Miniato, Basilica of, *illus.,* 196
Sanchi stupa, *illus.,* 146
Sandburg, Carl, 755
Sangallo (säng gäl′lō), Antonio da, 262
Sankore, University of, 719
Sanskrit, 60–61, 145, 211
Sappho (săf′ō), 101
Saracens (săr′ȧ sĕns), 168, 169
Sarajevo (sä′rä yĕ vō), 578
Saratoga, battle of, 390
Sarawak, 702
Sarcophagus (sär kŏf′ȧ gŭs), Egyptian, 40
Sardinia, 341, 345, 361; and Austria (1848), 502; and Congress of Vienna, 494, *map,* 495; in Crimean War, 549; and Italian unification, 510–512
Sargon (sär′gŏn) I, Akkadian king, 23
Sargon II, Assyrian king, 25
Satellite states, of Soviet Union, 674–675, *map,* 675; East Germany as, 682–684. *See also other states by name*
Satellites, *see* Earth satellites
Satires of Juvenal, 138
Satrapies (sā′trȧ pĭz), 27
Satraps (sā′trăps), 27
Saudi (sä ōō′dĭ), Arabia, kingdom of, 710
Saul, Christian teacher, 149
Saul, Hebrew king, 30
Savoy, 360, 511, 512
Savoy, House of, rules Sardinia, 502, 510

Smith, Adam, 401, 462

Smith, Ian, 725

Smyrna, Turkey, 588

Snyder, Louis, 490

Sobieski (sǒ byěs'kě), John, king of Poland, 341

Social classes: effects of French Revolution on, 409; in Latin America, 437. *See also* Social organization

Social Contract, The, 400

Social Darwinism, 483

Social Democratic party (Russian), 593, 594

Social organization: among African peoples, 561; in ancient Egypt, 39; caste system, 56–57; under feudalism, 169–174; in Neolithic Age, 13; in Soviet Union, 604–605; Sumerian, 20, 22

Social problems: of Latin America, 733–735; in pre-Revolutionary Russia, 595

Social Revolutionaries (Russian), 593–594

Social welfare legislation: in Germany, 519; in New Zealand, 534; in postwar England, 685

Socialism: and communism, 466–467; in France, 498, 499; in Germany, 519; in Soviet Union, 604; theories of, 465; Utopian experiments in, 465. *See also* Communism, Marxism

Society of Jesus, 313–314. *See also* Jesuits

Society for the Protection of Ancient Buildings, 470

Socrates (sǒk'rȧ tēz), 98

Solar system, 6

Solomon, Hebrew king, 30, 31

Solon (sō'lǒn), 84–85

Songhai, 719

Songs of Innocence, 471

Sonnet form, 251

Sophists (sǒf'ĭsts), 97–98

Sophocles (sǒf'ȯ klēz), 100, 104

Sources, historical, 2

South Africa: in British Commonwealth, 628; British-Dutch clash over, 535–536; leaves Commonwealth, 723; population, racial tensions in, 723; Union of South Africa formed, 536, 719

South America, 298; geography, 428, *map,* 773. *See also* Latin America

South German states, 515, 516, 517

South Korea (Republic of Korea), 697–698, 705

South Vietnam, 704, 705

Southeast Asia, *see* Asia

Southeast Asia Collective Defense Treaty Organization, 705

Southern Rhodesia, 725; sanctions on, 725; UN resolution on, 725

Soviet of Workers' Deputies (1905), 595

Soviet of Workers' and Soldiers' Deputies (Petrograd), 596, 597

Soviet Union, *see* Union of Soviet Socialist Republics

Sovkhozy, 602

Spaak, Paul-Henri, 667

Space exploration, 5, 749–750, 757

Spain, 118; becomes nation, 283–286, *map,* 286; under Charles V, 315–316; civil war in, 638–639; and Congress of Vienna, 494; and England, 318–320, 372; explorations and discoveries, 297–298, 299, 300; gains Louisiana, 386; in Goya's art, 474; and Industrial Revolution, 459; and Latin America, 428, 433–438; and Louis XIV's wars, 360, 361; Moslem conquest, 183, 184; and Napoleon I, 419, 420, *illus.,* 418; in North Africa, 564; opposes revolutionary France, 406, 407; under Philip II, 316–317; and Portugal, 285, 381; Renaissance art of, 264–265; revolution of 1820, 496; Spanish-American War, 567; in Thirty Years' War, 320–321; trade with Crete, 81; and Treaty of Paris (1783), 390; Viking attacks, 169; and War of Austrian Succession, 345; and War of Spanish Succession, 341

Spanish-American War, 567

Spanish Armada (1588), 319–320

Spanish language, 138, 285

Spanish March, 167

Sparta: compared to Athens, 87; government, 86; in Peloponnesian War, 102–103; in Persian Wars, 88–89; social system, 86–87

Specialized Agencies, of UN, 661–662

Spencer, Herbert, quoted, viii

Spenser, Edmund, 318

Speyer (shpī'ĕr), Diet of, 310

Spheres of influence, of European powers in China, 555, 557

Sphinx (sfĭngks), of Gizeh, 45, 47; *illus.,* 48, 49

Spice Islands, 381, 382

"Spinning jenny," 447, *illus.,* 448

"Spinning mule," 448

Spirit of the Laws, The, 399

Sports, Greek, 76, 88, 94

Sputniks, 749–750

Squires, 174

Ssŭ-ma Ch'ien, Chinese historian, 147

Stagecoaches, 450, 451

Stakhanovite system, 603

Stalin, Joseph: death, 676; Khrushchev denounces, 676–677; in October Revolution, 597; at Potsdam Conference, 651; rules Soviet Union, 599–605, *illus.,* 603; at Yalta Conference, 650

Stalingrad, siege of (1943), 644

Stamp Act, 387, 388

Stamp Act Congress, 387

Standardized parts: in auto manufacturing, 459, *illus.,* 460; Whitney uses, 448–449

Stanley, Henry M., 561, 563

Stars, 6

Statute of Westminster (1931), 628

Steam engine: invented, 449; in rail transportation, 451–452; in ships, 452, *illus.,* 453

Steamships, invention of, 452, *illus.,* 453

Steel, and Industrial Revolution, 449–450

Steinbeck, John, 755

Steinheil, Carl, 452

Stephenson, George, 451–452

Steuben (stū'běn), Baron von, 390

Stilwell, General Joseph W., 648

Stock, in corporations, 461

Stockholders, in corporations, 461

Stock-market crash (U.S.), 630

Stoicism (stō'ĭ sĭz'm), 107; of Marcus Aurelius, 151

Stoics (stō'ĭks), 107

Stola (stōl'ȧ), 129

Stone Ages, 11–14

Strachey, Lytton, 527

Straits of Dover, 351

Strasbourg (străs'bûrg), 359, 360

Strasbourg (străs'bûrg) Oath, 168

Strauss, Richard, 753

Stravinsky, Igor, 753

Stresemann, Gustav, 633

Strikes, 463

Stuart, Mary, Queen of Scots, 319

Stuart rulers of England, 368–370, 372–374, 377

Stupas (stōō'pȧz), Indian, 145; *illus.,* 146

Su Tung p'o, 231

Submarine warfare: in World War I, 581; in World War II, 643

Sudan, 566–567, 717, 719

Sudetenland, 639, *map,* 640

Ulbricht, Walter, 682
Ulyanov, Vladimir Ilich, *see* Lenin, Vladimir
Unemployment Insurance Act, England (1920), 626
Union Jack, *illus.*, 376
Union of South Africa: formed, 536; leaves British Commonwealth, 723; racial problems in, 723
Union of Soviet Socialist Republics, 327; and Castro's Cuba, 725; and Cold War, 672, 673–679; cultural characteristics of, 605; gains satellites, 674–675, *map*, 675; and Germany after World War II, 680–684; and Hungarian Revolution (1956), 678–679; invades Finland, 641; under Khrushchev, 676–679; and Korea, 697–698; under Lenin, 598–599; organizes Communist regional organizations, 668–669; and Polish revolt, 679; relations with Communist China, 694, 697; signs non-aggression pact with Germany, 641; under Stalin, 599–605; supports Spanish Loyalists, 638; territorial settlements (1945–1947), 673, *map*, 674; and Treaty of Rapallo, 632–633; and UN Secretary-General, 663; in UN Security Council, 659; in World War II, 643–644, 646–648, 650–651. *See also* Russia
Union of Utrecht, 317
Unions, *see* Labor, Trade unions
United Arab Republic, 714
United Kingdom of Great Britain and Ireland: formed, 376, 530; geography, 367–368, *map*, 368. *See also* England, Great Britain
United Nations Educational, Scientific and Cultural Organization (UNESCO), 661–662
United Nations Emergency Force, 714, 717
United Nations Organization: and Arab-Israeli war, 712; Charter of, 695, 705; Chinese membership issue, 694–695; in Congo crisis, 721–722; and Egyptian crisis (1956), 714; established, 657–658; evaluated, 663–664; headquarters, 657, *illus.*, 659; and Korean War, 697–698; organs of, 658–663, *chart*, 660; and partition of Palestine, 711; resolution on Korea, 698; Security Council, 697. *See also branches and agencies by name*

United States: in Asian regional organizations, 705; and China, 554, 556–557, 694–695; and Cold War, 672, 673–674; and Cuba, 567–568, 737–738; and Egypt (1956), 713–714; established, 389–391; and European Recovery Program, 679–680; and French in Mexico, 504–505; and Germany since World War II, 680–684; and great depression, 624–625; industrializes, 459; intervenes in Russia (1918), 598; issues Monroe Doctrine, 496–497; and Japan, 558, 692, 693; and Korea, 697–698; and Middle East, 715, 716; and NATO, 665; from 1920 to 1939, 630–631, 633; nineteenth-century literature of, 472, 473–474; and Panama, 568–569; and Philippines, 555–556; and post-World War II regional organizations, 669; rejects Versailles Treaty, 585–586; and reparations question, 589; and Spanish-American War, 567, *map*, 568; territorial growth, *map*, 391; in UN Security Council, 659; and Vietnam, 704; in World War I, 581–582; in World War II, 644–651.
Universal Declaration of Human Rights, 724
Universe, 6; Copernican theory, 302; Greek theories, 105
Universities: African, 719; Bologna, 204; in Latin America, 437; medieval, 204–206; Nalanda, 214; Oxford, 158, 204; Paris, 158, 204, 205
UNRWA, 712
Untouchables, in caste system, 57, 58
Upanishads, 61
Upper Volta, 726
Ur (ûr), Sumerian city, 20–21
Ur-Nammu, Sumerian king, 22
Urban II, Pope, 188
Uruguay, 741
Usury, 200–201, 308
Utopian Socialists, 465
Utrecht (ü′trĕKt), Treaties of (1713), 341, 359, *chart*, 360

Vaccination, 212, 482
Vaisya (vī′syä), caste, 56–57
Valdivia (väl dē′vyä), Pedro de, 435
Van Allen, James A., 749
Van Gogh (vän gŏK′), Vincent, 478
Van Rijn, Rembrandt (vän rīn,

rĕm′brănt), 265–266, *painting by*, 259, 265
Varangians (va răn′jĭ ănz), 287
Varennes (vä rĕn′), France, 405
Vassals, 169–170, 171, 175
Vatican: Popes retreat to, 513; Vatican Library founded, 250
Vatican Council II, 756
Vauban (vō′bäN′), Marquis Sebastien de, 359
Vault, in Roman architecture, 137
Vedas (vä′dĕz), 61
Vedic Age, 55
Velásquez (vä läs′kâth), Diego R. de Silvay, 264, 265
Venetia, 494, 502, 511, 512
Venezuela (vĕn ĕ zwē′lä), 438; Guri Dam, 733
Venice (vĕn′ĭs), 158, 187, 191, 200, 249, 290, 296, 413, 687
Venizelos (vâ nyĕ zâ′lôs), Eleutherios, 508
Veracruz, Mexico, 504
Verdi, Giuseppe, 510
Verdun: besieged (1916), 580; Treaty of (843), 168
Vereshchagin, V., 546; *painting by*, 422
Vermeer (vĕr mär′), Jan, 266; *painting by*, 259
Vernacular languages, 206, 251, 273, 315, 321
Versailles (vĕr sä′y′), 404, 405; Palace of, 357, *illus.*, 358
Versailles, Treaty of (1919), 583–586; Germany violates, 639; U.S. rejects, 585–586, *map*, 585
Verwoerd, Hendrik, 723
Vesalius (vĕ säl′yŭs), Andreas, 303
Vespucci (vĕs pōō′chĕ), Amerigo, 298
Vesta, 133
Veto, in UN, 659–661
Viceroys, Spanish, in Latin America, 436
Vichy government, 642
Victor Emmanuel II: becomes king of Sardinia, 502; and Italian unification, 510–512, *illus.*, 510
Victor Emmanuel III, king of Italy, 610
Victoria, queen of England, 527–528, *illus.*, 528; becomes Empress of India, 537
Victorian Age, 527–529, 537–538
Vienna (vĕ ĕn′ä): Congress of, 493–494, *map*, 495; Ottoman siege, 290–291; revolution of 1848 in, 501, *illus.*, 502; Turkish siege (1683), 341
Vietcong, 704, 705

Vietminh, 704
Vietnam, 704–705
"View of Toledo," 265, *illus.*, 260
Vikings, 169, 273, 297
Villa, 130
Villages: earliest, 13–14; on medieval manor, 171, 172, 173
Villa-Lobos, Hector, 753–754
Villon (vē yôN'), Francois, 272
Vinci (vēn'chē), Leonardo da: art of, 261, 263; as scientist, 294
Virgil, 138; quoted, 111
Vishnu (vĭsh'nōō), 57
Visible World, The, 269
Visigoths (vĭz'ĭ gŏths), 154, 155, 166, 283
Vladimir (vlăd'ĭ mĭr), king of Kiev, 287
Vladivostok, 598
Vlaminck, Maurice de, 750
Volga River, 289, 327
Voltaire (vôl târ'): and Catherine the Great, 333–334; and Frederick the Great, 345; ideas and works, 361, 398–399; *portrait*, 399
Vorster, Balthazar Johannes, 723
Vosges (vōzh) Mountains, 351
Voting, in nineteenth-century England, 523–526, 528–529
Vulgate, 252

Wagner (väg'nĕr), Richard, 481
Wagram (vä'gräm᷄), battle of, 419
Waitangi, Treaty of, 534
Wake Island, 645
"Waldensian (wŏl dĕn'shăn) heresy," 307
Waldo (wŏl'dō), Peter, 307
Wales: geography, 367; *map*, 368
Wallace, Alfred Russel, 482
Wallenstein (väl'ĕn shtīn), Albrecht von, 321
Walpole, Sir Robert, 376
War of the Austrian Succession, 345–346
War crimes: German, 680–681; Japanese, 692
War of Devolution, 360, *chart*, 361
War of 1812, 420
War of the Palatinate, 360, *chart*, 361
War and Peace, 545
War of the Spanish Succession, 341; effects on France, 360, *chart*, 361; effects on Prussia, 344
War between the States, 504
Wars: of Alexander the Great, 104–105; Anglo-Boer, 536; Anglo-Chinese, 554; Arab-Israeli, 712;
of Austrian Succession, 345–346; Austro-Prussian, 512, 515; Balkan Wars (1912–1913), 577–578; causes of, 491; Crusades, 188–191; effects of, 490–491; of 1812, 420; Franco-Prussian, 505, 515–517; French and Indian, 386; of French revolutionary governments, 406–407; Hundred Years' War, 279, 281–283; of Latin-American independence, 437–438; of Louis XIV, 360, *chart*, 360; Macedonian-Greek, 103; Napoleonic, 413, 416–423; Opium War, 554; Peloponnesian, 102–103; Peninsular War, 420; Persian, 88–89; Punic, 118, 119; Queen Anne's, 388; of the Roses, 279; Russo-Japanese, 560, 594, 595; Seven Years' War, 346, 359, 385, 396; Sino-Japanese, 555, 560; Spanish-American, 567; Spanish Civil War, 638–639; Thirty Years' War, 317, 320–321, 353; World War I, 574–582, 596, 597, 598; World War II, 641–651. *See also* Revolutions
Warsaw, Duchy of, 494
Warsaw, Grand Duchy of, 419
Warsaw Pact, 668–669
Warships, *see* Ships
Washington, D.C., 137
Washington, George, 389, 390
Washington Naval Armaments Conference, 630, 633
Water frame, 447
Waterloo, battle of, 423
Watt, James, 449
Watteau (vä'tō'), Jean Antoine, 397
Wealth: under capitalism, 296; and explorations, 296–297, 300
Wealth of Nations, 401, 462
Weapons: Neolithic, 14; of war today, 756
Weaver, Warren, 300
Weimar (vī'mär) Constitution, 612
Weizmann (vīts'män), Chaim, 711
Wellington, Duke of, 423, 494
Wessel, John, 307
West Berlin, 682, 683–684
Western Front, in World War I, 579–580, 582, *map*, 579
Western Hemisphere, *globe-map of*, 761
Westernizers (Russia), 544
West European Union, 665
West Germany, Federal Republic of: and post-World War II regional organization, 665; since World War II, 681–684
West Indies, 297, 382
Westphalia (wĕst fā'lĭa), Kingdom of, 419
Westphalia, Treaty of, 321, 354
Wheatstone, Sir Charles, 452
Wheel, early use of, 23
Wheel of the Law, *illus.*, 146
Whig Party (England): becomes Liberal party, 526; and nineteenth-century reforms, 524, 526; origins, 373
Whistler, James McNeill, 477
White Russian forces, 598
Whitman, Walt, 472
Whitney, Eli, and factory system, 448–449
William the Conqueror, 274
William the Silent of Orange, 317
William I (of Orange), king of England, 374
William III, king of England, 359, 360
William I: king of Prussia, 516; emperor of Germany, 517
William II, emperor of Germany, 575–576; abdicates, 582
Williams, Ralph Vaughan, 754
Wilson, Harold, 685
Wilson, Woodrow, U.S. President, 581, 582–584; quoted, 588
Winchester, England, 201
Wittenberg, University of, 308
Wittenberg Castle Church, 309
Woodcuts, 267
Woolf, Virginia, 755
Wordsworth, William, 471
Workers, *see* Labor
World, *political map of*, 770–771
World Council of Churches, 322
World Court, *see* Permanent Court of International Justice
World Economic Conference (1933), 627
World Health Organization, 661, 670
World War I, 490–491; battles and campaigns, 579–582; *map*, 579; origins, 575–578; Palestine in, 710; peace treaty, 582–586; Russia in, 596, 597; Russia withdraws from, 598; territorial changes following, 587–588, *map*, 585
World War II: battles and campaigns, 641–651, *maps*, 640, 646, 649; causes, 637–641; costs, 656; recovery programs after, 679–680; results, 636; treaties and settlements following, 673, *map*, 674
Worms (vôrms), Concordat of (1122), 177

Worms, Diet of, 309–310, 316
Wright, Wilbur and Orville, 453
Writing: Achaean, 80; ancient Egyptian, 45, 46; Chinese, 68, 70, 239; Japanese, 239; of Phoenicians, 29; Sumerian, 21–22
Wu Tao-tzu (wōō' dou'dzŭ'), 225
Wu-ti (wōō dē'), Han emperor, 145
Württemberg (vür'tĕm bĕrк), 516
Wyclif (wĭk'lĭf), John, 279, 307

Xerxes (zŭrk'sēz), Persian king, 28 88–89

Yahveh (yä'vĕ), 39
Yalta Agreements, 650–651, 657
Yamato (yä mä'tō), paintings, 240
Yangtze (yăng'[t]sē) River, 65
Yeats, William Butler, 755

Yellow River, 65, 66, 67
Yemen, 710, 714
Yevtushenko, Yevgeni, 549
Yoritomo (yŏ rĕ tō'mŏ), Shogun of Japan, 241–242
York House of, 279
Yorktown, Virginia, 390
Yoruba, 719
Young, Arthur, 404
Young Italy, 509
Young Plan, 589
Yüan Shi-k'ai, 617–618
Yucatán (yōō kả tăn'), Mex., 430
Yugoslavia: created (1918), 587; joins Little Entente, 632; under Tito, 675; in World War II, 643

Zama (zā'mả), battle of, 118
Zambia, 727

Zambos, 437
Zanzibar, 564, 717, 720
Zapolya (zä pô'lyă), John, 290
Zara, 190
Zarathustra (zăr'ả thōōs'trả), 28
Zemsky Sobor (zĕm'skē sŏ bŏr'), 329–330, 331
Zeno (zē'nō), 107
Zero, origin of, 60–61
Zeus (zūs), 81, 82, 87, 88
Zhukov (zhōō'kŭf), Marshal Georgi, 648
Ziggurats (zĭg'ŏŏ răt), 20
Zionism, 711
Zola, Émile, 473
Zollverein (tsŏl'fĕr ĭn), 514
Zoroaster (zō'rŏ ăs'tĕr), 28
Zoroastrianism, 28
Zwingli (tsvĭng'lĕ), Ulrich, 311

ACKNOWLEDGMENTS

We would like to thank the following publishers and copyright holders for permission to reproduce copyrighted material in this edition.

Keith Botsford: "The Writings of Jorge Luis Borges," *Atlantic Monthly*, Jan. 1967.

Tillman Durdin: "The Communist Record," *Atlantic Monthly*, Dec. 1959.

Mrs. Fine: "Dilemma" in *A Little Treasury of World Poetry*, ed. by Hubert Creekmore.

Crerar Harris: "Britons: A Self Portrait," *New York Times Magazine*, Sept. 1951.

Manuel Komroff: *War and Peace* by Leo Tolstoy.

George Soloveytchik: *Russia in Perspective.*

Bernard Ullman: "China's Grim Winter," *New York Times Magazine*, Feb. 1961.

Abelard-Schuman, Ltd.: Reprinted from *Main Currents of Scientific Thought* by S. F. Mason. By permission of Abelard-Schuman, Ltd. All rights reserved. Copyright year, 1953.

The Abingdon Press: *Here I Stand, A Life of Martin Luther* by Roland H. Bainton.

George Allen & Unwin, Ltd: *Bismarck, The Story of a Fighter* by Emil Ludwig, tr. by Eden and Cedar Paul; *History of Western Philosophy* by Bertrand Russell.

Allyn & Bacon, Inc.: *England of Song and Story* by Mary I. Curtis. Copyright 1931 and 1945 by Allyn and Bacon, Inc.; *A Day in Old Athens* by William Stearns Davis.

American Book Company: *Great Inventors and Their Inventions* by Frank P. Bachman. Copyright 1918, 1941, and 1946 by permission of American Book Company, publisher. *A Source Book of Medieval History* by Frederick A. Ogg; *Seven Plays of the Modern Theater* ed. by Vincent Wall and James R. McCormick (C) 1950.

Américas: "The Two Worlds of Jorge Luis Borges," by Armando Alonso Piñeiro, March 1965.

Antioch Press: "Hymn to the Wind God" from *Song of Quetzalcoatl* tr. by John H. Cornyn.

Appleton-Century-Crofts, Inc.: *The Middle Ages, 395–1500* by Joseph R. Strayer and Dana D. Munro, (C) 1959.

The *Atlantic Monthly*: "The Atlantic Report on the World Today—Berlin," Jan. 1958. "A Visit with Argentina's Borges," by John Gunther, January, 1967. Copyright (C) 1966 by The Atlantic Monthly Company, Boston, Mass. Reprinted with permission.

The Atlantic Monthly Press, Inc.: *Social Backgrounds of English Literature* by Ralph P. Boas and Barbara M. Hahn.

Bank of Venezuela: *Selected Writings of Bolivar*, Vol. I, compiled by Vincente Lecuna.

Bantam Books, Inc.: *Fifty Great Artists* ed. by Bernard Myers.

Barnes & Noble, Inc.: *Readings in Latin American Civilization* ed. by Edward C. Smith and Arnold J. Zurcher; *Dictionary of American Politics* ed. by A. Curtis Wilgus.

Beacon Press: *Six Keys to the Soviet System.* Reprinted by permission of the Beacon Press, copyright (c) 1956 by Bertram Wolfe.

G. Bell & Sons, Ltd.: *The Wasps* trans. by Roger.

The Bobbs-Merrill Company, Inc.: *The Four Hundred Million: A Short History of The Chinese* by Mary A. Nourse. Copyright (C) 1935, 1938, 1942 by The Bobbs-Merrill Company, Inc. Reprinted by special permission of the publishers.

Boni & Gaer, Inc.: *The Scientists Speak* ed. by Warren B. Weaver.

William C. Brown Company: *An Introduction to Music and Art in the Western World* ed. by M. Wold and E. Cykler.

Cambridge University Press: *The Cambridge Medieval History*, Vol. V, by Charles Diehl; *Le Bourgeois Gentilhomme* by Molière.

The Caxton Printers, Ltd.: *The Golden Age of Russian Literature* by Ivar Spector.

The Christian Century: "U.N.—Snare or Shield?" Copyright 1953 by Christian Century Foundation. Reprinted by permission from *The Christian Century.*

Collier's: "France Needs a New Revolution" by Edgar A. Mowrer, Jan. 1954.

Columbia Broadcasting System, Inc.: Excerpt from *Face the Nation* broadcast.

Columbia University Press: *The Hindu Women* by M. Cormarck, Bureau of Publications, Teachers College, Columbia University; *The Mind of Napoleon* ed. and trans. by J. Christopher Herold. "The Wisdom of the East," Vol. I, "The Voice of Italy," Vol. 5, "Ballad Against Those Who Missay of France," Vol. 6 from *Columbia University Course in Literature.*

F. E. Compton & Co.: *Compton's Picture Encyclopedia* (1962 ed.), "American Folklore and Its Old-World Backgrounds" by C. Cramer.

Cowles Magazine, Inc.: "The Insane World of Adolph Hitler," *Look*, Jan. 6, 1959.

Thomas Y. Crowell Company: *Famous Men of Science* by Sarah Bolton. Copyright 1960 by Thomas Y. Crowell Company, New York. Used by permission of the publishers; *Social-Economic Movements* by Harry W. Laidler.

Current History, Inc.: Remarks by Truman, April 1946; by Churchill, May 1947 issues of *Current History.*

The John Day Company, Inc.: From *The Discovery of India* by Jawaharlal Nehru, by permission of The John Day Company, Inc., publisher.

Dodd, Mead & Co.: *The Bolshevik Theory* by R. W. Postgate, copyright 1920; *The International Cyclopedia of Music and Musicians* by Oscar Thompson, copyright 1938, 1943, 1946, 1949, 1952, 1956, 1958 by Dodd, Mead & Co., Inc. Reprinted by permission of Dodd, Mead & Co.

Doubleday & Company, Inc.: *Main Street, U.S.S.R.* by Irving R. Levine. Copyright (C) 1959 by Irving R. Levine; *Lenin, A Biography* by David Shub. Copyright (C) 1948 by David Shub; *Living Biographies of Great Philosophers* by Henry

Thomas and Dana L. Thomas. Copyright (C) 1950 by Henry Thomas and Dana L. Thomas. Reprinted by permission of Doubleday & Company, Inc. *Saint Joan of Arc* by Victoria Sackville-West, Doubleday, Doran and Company, 1936. Copyright 1936 by Victoria Sackville-West; reprinted by permission of the author's Estate.

Duke University Press: *War in the Modern World* by Theodore Ropp.

E. P. Dutton & Co., Inc.: *The Book of the Courtier* by Baldassare Castiglione tr. by Sir Thomas Hoby (Everyman's Library); *Mussolini the Man* by Vitorrio E. DeFiori; *Two Treatises of Civil Government* by John Locke (Everyman's Library).

Encyclopaedia Britannica Inc.: "Gargantua and Pantagruel" tr. by Sir T. Urquhart and P. Nulbeaux, 1952 edition; *Great Books of the Western World* Vol. 14, "Alexander" by Plutarch tr. by John Dryden, revised by A. H. Clough, 1952. Reprinted with permission from *Encyclopaedia Britannica.*

Farrar, Straus & Cudahy, Inc.: *Five Gentlemen of Japan* by Frank Gibney; *A History of France* by André Maurois tr. by H. L. Binsse and G. Hopkins; *Mid-century Journey* by William Shirer.

Foreign Affairs: "The Egyptian Revolution" by Gamal Nasser, Jan. 1955.

Foreign Policy Association: *Headline Series* No. 112 by Hans Kohn; *Headline Series* No. 97 by Saul K. Padover and L. Larry Leonard; *Headline Series* No. 120 by Karl Sax.

Ginn and Company: *A History of England and the British Empire* by Robert G. Albion and Walter P. Hall; *Readings in English History Drawn from the Original Sources* by Edward Cheyney; *Readings in Modern European History*, Vol. II, James Robinson and Charles Beard.

Grosset & Dunlap, Inc.: *The Story of Orchestral Music and Its Times* by Paul Grabbe; *How Music Grew* by Helen L. Kaufmann.

Grove Press and George Allen & Unwin, Ltd.: "The Pillow Book of Sei Shonagon" tr. by Arthur Waley in *An Anthology of Japanese Literature.*

Harcourt, Brace & World, Inc.: *Fountainheads of Freedom* by Irwin Edman; *Collected Poems of T. S. Eliot* by T. S. Eliot; *Art Through the Ages* by Helen Gardner; *Europe in Perspective, 1815 to the Present* by James E. Gillespie; *Theodore Roosevelt; A Biography* by Henry F. Pringle; *Democracy Is Not Enough* by John Scott; *Life—An Introduction to Biology* ed. by George G. Simpson; *Pageant of Europe, Sources and Selections from the Renaissance to Present Day* by Raymond P. Stearns; *Queen Victoria* by Lytton Strachey.

Harper & Row, Publishers, Inc.: *Reaction and Revolution, 1814–1832* ("Rise of Modern Europe Series") by Frederick Artz; *A Decade of Revolution, 1789–1799* by Crane Brinton; *Europe and the French Imperium* by Geoffrey Bruun; *In Place of Folly* by Nornam Cousins; *How About the*

810

Scott, Foresman and Company: Warnock and Anderson, *The World in Literature.* Chicago: Scott, Foresman and Company, 1951, Volume IV, page 423. Quoted on p. 544 of this text.

Charles Scribner's Sons: *Economic History of France* by Shepard B. Clough; *My Autobiography* by Benito Mussolini, foreword by Richard W. Child; *Over There,* Vol. V, Mark Sullivan; *A History of the Christian Church* by Williston Walker.

Secker & Warburg, Ltd.: *An Assessment of Twentieth-Century Literature* by J. Isaacs.

Simon and Schuster, Inc.: *Caesar and Christ,* copyright 1944 by Will Durant; *Our Oriental Heritage,* copyright 1942 by Will Durant; *The Renaissance,* copyright 1953 by Will Durant; *The Worldly Philosophers,* copyright 1953, 1961 by Robert L. Heilbroner; *The World of Mathematics,* copyright 1956 by James Newman; *In the Thick of the Fight* by Paul Reynaud, trans. by James Lambert, copyright 1955; *History of Western Philosophy,* copyright 1945 by Bertrand Russell; *A Treasury of the World's Great Letters* ed. by M. Lincoln Schuster, copyright 1940; *The Rise and Fall of the Third Reich,* copyright 1960 by William L. Shirer. Reprinted by permission of Simon and Schuster, Inc.

State Department: Department of State "Bulletin" Vol. XXXIII, July, 1955.

Syracuse University Press: *Readings in Russian History,* 3rd ed., by Warren B. Walsh, 1959.

Time, Inc.: Courtesy *Time;* copyright Time, Inc., April, 1955; May, 1958; March, 1962.

Charles E. Tuttle Co., Inc.: *The Complete Journal of Townsend Harris* by Townsend Harris, ed. by Mario E. Cosenza. 1959 revised ed.

University of California Press: *New Zealand* ed. by Horace Belshaw.

University of Chicago Press: *The Real Conflict between China and Japan* by Harley F. MacNair, copyright 1938; *Britain Between the Wars* by Charles L. Mowat, copyright 1955; *The Panchatantra* trans. by Arthur W. Ryder, Chicago: The University of Chicago Press, 1956; *The Wisdom of China and India* ed. by Lin Yut'ang, copyright 1955; all copyrighted by The University of Chicago Press.

The University of Michigan Press: Reprinted from *France, A Modern History* ("The University of Michigan History of the Modern World Series") by Albert Guérard, by permission of The University of Michigan Press. Copyright by The University of Michigan 1959. *Italy, A Modern History* ("The University of Michigan History of the Modern World Series"), by Denis Mack Smith, ed. by Alan Nevins and Howard M. Ehrmann, by permission of The University of Michigan Press. Copyright by The University of Michigan 1959.

UNESCO Courier: Reprinted from *The UNESCO Courier,* Dec. 1955.

United Nations World: "The Nile Valley" by Pearl M. Steinhaus, March 1951.

United Press International: News release by James Baaer, Feb. 18, 1955.

United States Atomic Energy Commission: *Medical Effects of Atomic Bomb in Japan* ed. by Ashley W. Oughterson and Shields Warren.

U.S. News & World Report: "South of the Zambesi: White Man's Africa," by Albert J. Meyers. Copyright (C) December 19, 1966 by *U.S. News & World Report.*

D. Van Nostrand Company, Inc.: *Russian Writers, Their Lives and Literature* by Janko Lavrin, (C) 1954; *Fifty Major Documents of the Nineteenth Century* ed. by Louis L. Snyder, (C) 1955; *The World in the Twentieth Century* ed. by Louis L. Snyder, (C) 1955; *An Introduction to Russian History and Culture* by Ivar Spector, (C) 1961.

The Viking Press, Inc.: *Meet Your Ancestors* by Roy C. Andrews; *Poets of English Language,* Vol. II, ed. by W. H. Auden and N. H. Pearson. Copyright 1951 by The Viking Press and reprinted by their permission. *The Portable Medieval Reader* ed. and introduction by James B. Ross and Mary M. McLaughlin.

Wadsworth Publishing Co., Inc.: *Africa, Continent of Change* by Peter R. Gould, copyright 1961.

Yale University Press: From *The Chronicles of America.* Copyright Yale University Press.

ABCDEFGHIJK 0698

PRINTED IN THE UNITED STATES OF AMERICA